Railway Passenger Stations

in Great Britain

in Great Britain

A CHRONOLOGY

Michael Quick

Previously published as
Railway Passenger Stations in England, Scotland and Wales: a Chronology

First edition published 2001
Second revised edition 2003
Third revised edition 2005
Fourth edition, revised, enlarged, reset and with additional illustrations 2009

All published by the Railway & Canal Historical Society

www.rchs.org.uk

The Railway & Canal Historical Society was founded in 1954 and incorporated in 1967.
It is a company (No.922300) limited by guarantee and registered in England as a charity (No.256047)
Registered office: 3 West Court, West Street, Oxford OX2 0NP

ISBN 978 0 901461 57 5

Designed and typeset by
Malcolm Preskett
Maps by Richard Dean

Printed in Great Britain by the MPG Books Group,
Bodmin and King's Lynn

Contents

Section 1:   Acknowledgments   5
              Notes for the fourth edition   7
              Introduction   9

Section 2:   Outline History of Passenger Services   11

Section 3:   Sources and Information   17
                              – contemporary sources   17
                              – secondary sources   24
                              – combined list of sources   24
                              – atlases   35
              The information obtained   36

Section 4:   The Stations   – explanation   43
                              – general abbreviations   46
                              – abbreviations of Railway Companies' names   47
                              – glossary   49
              STATIONS A – Z   51

Section 5:   Line notes in chronological order   425

Section 6:   Metro lines   481

Section 7:   Some marginal items   483

Section 8:   Route diagrams and sketch maps   493

Section 9:   Appendix: lists of items significantly altered
              since the 3rd edition   537

              List of Subscribers   543

Please note:

Preserved lines, cliff railways and pier railways are NOT included. No reference is made to railways in Ireland, the Channel Islands and the Isle of Man. Please see 'Notes for the Fourth Edition' for treatment of temporary closures.

This edition includes changes to the start of the 17 May 2009 timetable, including stations expected to open or that might perhaps be opened during its currency.

SECTION 1

Acknowledgments

This book has developed out of one privately published in 1996, covering only opening dates. The result of going public then was that contact was made with a large number of people who have helped to make the present work much more accurate than it would otherwise be; very many additions and corrections have been made. Needless to say, the responsibility for any remaining errors and shortcomings lies with the compiler.

Pride of place has to go here to Bryan Wilson, who maintained a regular and most informative correspondence with me from 1996 until shortly before his death in 2007. Not only did he provide much original material from his own researches and point out many secondary sources with which I was unfamiliar, but he also acted as a modern-day information clearing house, passing on items from others. Even more, his encouragement was the major factor in keeping me going on a project that several times was nearly abandoned as impossible.

Major thanks must also go, in historical order, to:

The late C.R. Clinker, who published much along the lines of this work. Although this book sometimes follows a different approach from his, nevertheless a great debt remains. The original of this work was begun by adding his list of closed stations to those still in the timetable and without that as a basis it is unlikely that this would have had any existence.

The Railway Studies Library at Newton Abbot and its staff, particularly Don Steggles, who was librarian at the time most use was made of it. Its collection of *Bradshaws* provided a roughly yearly base for development.

The staff at the library of the National Railway Museum at York, especially Philip Atkins, who also answered by post a number of queries about items that had slipped through my net.

Mr M. Bell of the Bodleian Library kindly provided direct access to the Library's almost complete collection of *Bradshaws* and enabled a more exact picture to be built up than could possibly have been done in any other way. My thanks are also due to J. Slatter for his assistance at the stack.

A Brackenbury was kind enough to look at the earliest version and make many helpful suggestions and has made many later contributions, especially relating to excursions after stations had been closed for normal services.

The staff of the Somerset Local Studies Library at Taunton and the Reference Library at Bridgwater, whose facilities have been most frequently used.

The staffs of: the Public Record Office at Kew (now the National Archives); the House of Lords Record Office, the British Library, the British Library's Newspaper Reading Room at Colindale; the local studies libraries at Barnstaple, Cardiff, Cheltenham, Dorchester, Exeter, Gloucester, Hereford, Newport, Oxford, Plymouth, Portsmouth, Reading, Redruth, Stroud, Trowbridge, Weston-super-Mare, and Winchester; Somerset County Record Office, Obridge, Taunton; Bristol Central and Poole Reference Libraries; Cirencester Town, Stratford-upon-Avon Town and Tiverton Community School Libraries, Cupar Library for photocopies of *Fifeshire Journal, 1887*. Some of these have files of cuttings available for readers' use, though their contents are often mostly items from the 1960s and later.

Whilst all secondary sources are listed in Section 3, or mentioned at appropriate places in the text, it is only fair to mention briefly here also number of works that have substantially contributed: the Chronologies of the London area (H.V. Borley) and the Midland Railway (Dr J.V. Gough); the GNS Society and Highland Railway Society station lists (compiled by K. Fenwick, who has also given me information about some later findings, and others); the company histories of the Great Western (E.T. MacDermot), Great Northern (J. Wrottesley), Great Central (G. Dow), Lancashire & Yorkshire (J. Marshall), South Eastern & Chatham and its constituents (A. Gray), London Brighton & South Coast (J.T. Howard Turner) and London & South Western (R.A. Marshall).

Col. M. Cobb and Dr J.V. Gough have kindly answered postal queries. O. Smart of the RCHS has supplied photocopies of many useful articles from the earlier issues of the Society's publications.

D. Geldard provided much material from his own researches, and a massive amount about names on tickets from the collection of the late J. Britton.

R.A. Cooke provided a great deal of information for later editions from his own researches, particularly on the general workings of the Great Western, together with many references for station name-changes from RCH records for all areas.

R. Maund sent much information about post-war excursions and the like, gleaned from working timetables and publicity.

The following individuals offered information and suggestions as a result of seeing earlier versions of the book or provided it via Bryan Wilson and their help is much appreciated: M. Back, D. Banks, R. Bond (especially northern Lancashire), G. Borthwick (especially Motherwell area and Scottish working timetables), G. Boyes, Dr S. Bragg (North Eastern Railway), E. Bredee (Stockport area), Dr R. Brettle, C. Chapman, T. Cooper (especially Isle of Wight), L. Crowther, J. Edgington, R. Forsythe, J. Gilmour (much about Lancashire from local newspapers and company records), J. Glover, R. Green, M. Hale (especially on lesser South Wales companies), Dr R. Hellyer, P. Howat, C. Holden, M.H. Jack (Scottish matters), P. Jeffries, P. Kay, G. Kenworthy, Tony Kirby, A. Lauder, D.M.E. Lindsay (Scottish matters), M. Lloyd, A. Maclean, J. Mear, D.R. Pedley, P. Reynolds, J.W.P. Rowledge, A. Rush, J. Savage, P.G. Scott, W. Smith, D. Stirling (much from Scottish Record Office about North British), Dr J. Tolson, Dr D. Tunnicliffe, I. Umpleby (post-passenger use), E. Vaughan, Glyn Williams, A. Young and D. Yuill.

Various points have come from the Newsletters of the Chronology Group of the Railway & Canal Historical Society, available at Newton Abbot edited by Don Steggles and, latterly, by Ted Cheers.

Finally – and here we are back to historical order – my thanks go to the Railway & Canal Historical Society for agreeing to publish this work; to Grahame Boyes and John Gough for their initial help and encouragement; and to Stephen Bragg for much detailed sub-editorial work in removing errors, clarifying entries and achieving greater consistency of presentation, as well as providing preliminary help with the maps. Grahame Boyes has spent much time over publication and marketing.

For handling the design, typesetting and production my thanks must go to Malcolm Preskett; and for the excellent redrawn maps I must thank Richard Dean.

The illustrations now added are taken from collections of drawings from *Punch* published in Victorian and Edwardian times.

My apologies go to any who have been inadvertently omitted. This is especially likely in the case of those whose works were read long before I had any intention of publishing one of my own. The notes I made then were not related to their sources in the way that more recent ones have been.

M.E. Quick

289 Staplegrove Road, Taunton TA2 6AL

2009

Notes for the fourth edition

Temporary closures. Until fairly recently it was normal practice to keep lines and stations open as far as possible during engineering work and to resume services as soon as practicable after accidents. In those circumstances the few exceptions where there were closures of any duration seem to deserve a mention in the record. However, it has now become the practice to close lines completely for engineering work and for lengthy periods following accidents – in the latter case sometimes including stations far removed from the accident. The result is that the continued inclusion of such cases would occupy an unjustifiably large proportion of the space available. The logical cut-off date for this change of approach would seem to be 1994, with the privatisation of Railtrack; though the London Underground was not then directly affected, the approach used there seems to owe much to the example set by the main system. Thus, from then on, only particularly lengthy closures for engineering work, and closures for such reasons as conversion to metro-type services, or destruction by fire of individual stations are now included. This has involved some deletion of information included in earlier editions; a list of stations affected is included in an Appendix, which also lists entries where significant changes have been made since the Third Edition: it does not include items where the only change has been to the source cited. This would also be an appropriate place to point out that short closures on the Great Western for conversion to standard gauge were never included; for details of these see the tables at the back of MacDermot's history of the Great Western. As with much else, complete consistency is unattainable.

Revised sources. What used to be the Public Record Office has now become the National Archives. In the interests of greater accuracy, the source previously shown as *PRO* on its own has been altered to *RCG* – short for Railway Clearing (House) Goods – please see list of sources for full explanation. Where previously the source was *PRO RAIL, PRO MT* or the like, '*PRO*' has simply been eliminated and the entries for *RAIL, MT* and so on in the source list show that these are to be found at the National Archives. This has been done to make life simpler the next time a member of the Compulsive Meddlers' Society decides to give it yet another new name.

Treatment of names. Much fuller information is now given on this topic. For a full explanation please see the appropriate heading in Sections 3 and 4. Suffice it here to emphasise that the information given represents what the compiler has seen; **it does not claim to be an attempt at laying down the law on what the 'official' name of a station was at a particular time** – indeed the compiler believes that the search for a complete record of all members of this elusive species is about as likely to be as successful as the proverbial search for the crock of gold at the end of the rainbow.

Other additions. Much more has been included on excursions after regular passenger closure, thanks mainly to a vast amount of carefully-sourced material from correspondents listed in the Acknowledgements; the sheer length of the Appendix bears tribute to the help the compiler has received from elsewhere. Stations built but not used are now listed, in the interests of greater consistency with various doubtful items that have crept in over the years.

Maps. Renumbered.

The future. The present compiler feels he has now got as far as he can, given present resources. There are still many gaps but the answers, if they exist, are buried amogst a vast multitude of files at Kew or in the pages of local newspapers presently only available scattered in local studies libraries across the length and breadth of the country – one seriously limiting factor has been the considerable number of the copies held at the British Libary Newspaper collection at Colindale which are no longer available to the public because of their decrepit condition. One day it may well be that all records will be available nationally by electronic means, but that day, even if it comes, is likely to be well into the future. Please see 'Corrections' for the approach to these now adopted.

"READING BETWEEN THE LINES"

Introduction

The object is to show the outline history of all stations in England, Scotland and Wales, and to do so as accurately as the limitations of the evidence allow. The aim is to see matters as far as possible from the point of view of the traveller in times past, not, as so many railway histories do, from the companies' standpoint. Thus the information given is what did happen, not what 'officially' happened. Therefore details are given not only for stations which appeared in the public timetable but also for those provided on the main system for e.g. the private use of a landowner, workmen only, or sporting events only. Inevitably, information about this second group is far more patchy. Those stations built but not opened (and mythical ones) are included because they sometimes appear in railway books and local histories as though they did exist and anyone looking in this book might otherwise be puzzled by their non-inclusion. Some non-timetable services that operated detached from the main system are included in outline in Section 7, the object of which is to give a general idea of usage of railways and, where possible, to list books containing more about the topic. Sites visited only by railway enthusiasts' specials are not included.

At many points arbitrary decisions have had to be taken over what should be included and what not. No definitions can be constructed that allow watertight distinctions to be made: some stations do not fit neatly into the categories of 'public' and 'private' mentioned in the first paragraph. Even the term 'railway' is impossible to define exactly. Generally, for the purpose of this work, a railway is a form of transport running on rails that has exclusive use of its route, as opposed to a tramway operating along public streets with other traffic. However, mongrel lines, such as that to Weymouth Quay or the earlier part of the modern Manchester Metrolink did and do make some use of public roads whilst mostly operating on dedicated track; they are included. As far as these mongrel lines are concerned, stops on street tramway sections are generally ignored unless at some stage they were termini. Systems such as that in Sheffield are in Section 6. Section 7 contains various lines that are sometimes included in railway books but are not railways in the sense described here. In addition, operating practices have altered very much in the two centuries involved. As a result there are bound to be what some will regard as inconsistencies. Furthermore, the information has been compiled over many years and the author would be foolhardy if he were to claim that his judgement has remained consistent for all of this time.

It is hoped that this compilation will be of use and interest to a wide spectrum of readers, from those who just want the answers to those with a serious interest in railway history who might want to use it as a help for their own research. It is mainly for the latter that very full reference is made in Section 3 to the sources used; others will probably find the summary form of the explanation given at the start of Section 4 adequate for their needs. Whilst reasonably reliable dates for closures have been available for many years, the same cannot be said about opening dates. For these much contradictory evidence is in print, including many errors copied from book to book down the years. Great difficulty was often found in compiling the present work because many writers do not give the source of their information and it was impossible to tell which of two (or more) rival dates was more likely to be correct. Whilst it cannot be claimed that this work has traced everything back to its source, at least it can be reasonably claimed that much has been done to eradicate errors and that the approach used has been designed to make it as easy as possible for others to see where further work is most likely to be needed. The basic rule for those setting out on their own researches must be: check as much as you can for yourself, including material presented here. Sources have been included in the body of the text rather than as footnotes, because the numbering involved in the latter method would in itself have added substantially to the acreage of the book and driven both the compiler and those wanting to use them to distraction.

Ideally, all dates should have been derived from contemporary sources such as railway company records and local newspapers: these reduce the likelihood of error to a minimum, though they do not eliminate it completely. In practice, this is impossible, given the huge volume and geographical spread of the material that would need to be consulted. Thus secondary sources have had to be used for many items. Much has been derived, though, from primary sources, especially local newspapers, and these have generally been used in preference to secondary sources of even the most reliable kind. The obvious West Country bias that will be noted here arises because the compiler lives in Taunton.

Much has also been derived from *The Times*. This is not a perfect source, since some of its items, especially those concerned with matters well away from London, look to be second-hand. However, it is an accessible source, albeit one that has been much under-used by railway historians (the traditional letters to the Editor have the makings of an interesting book on their own).

The organisation is designed to enable extra material and corrections to be fitted into any later edition that might be published. The type of material presented here is notoriously liable to misprints and copying errors. Each time it is rewritten, further errors are likely to creep in and old ones come back. The aim is to create a basic text that can be adapted rather than one that would need rewriting.

Finally, it should be stressed that the information presented here relates only to passenger use. Whilst some stations did open and close for goods on the same dates as they did for passengers, these were a rarity. Parcels traffic, which deserves more attention than it generally receives from railway historians for the role it played in e.g. enabling village shops to offer a much wider range of goods, was generally handled by passenger stations (but not halts) since it was carried in passenger trains. Otherwise, the history of goods traffic can be a complicated matter. Some stations opened for goods long before, others long after, they opened for passengers; some only ever handled one or the other. It could happen that the first consignments of coal, general goods and livestock arrived at widely separated times. Closure could similarly occur by instalments. A further complication is that the Railway Clearing House, especially in the early years, tended to list in its Hand-books, and even show on its maps, separate passenger and goods stations in the same town as though they were a single, combined station, even though they were on clearly different sites. Goods traffic is an aspect of railway history where much further research is needed. *Clinker's Register of Closed Passenger Stations and Goods Depots* at least provides a start for those wishing to deal with this aspect for themselves.

CORRECTIONS

Since the present work is intended as a reliable and comprehensive work of reference, it would be of the greatest help to all researchers if anyone spotting an error, or able to provide better information from an alternative source, would be kind enough to let the author know. Although he does not intend to compile any further supplements or editions, he hopes that in due course someone else will and any information received will be passed on to the RCHS for this purpose.

SECTION 2

Outline History of Passenger Services

The railway system needs to be seen as something that evolved in response to the country's needs, not as something that suddenly appeared, working in roughly the same ways as the present system. However, there are also many constants of railway travel: there is a sameness about passengers' complaints down the years, whether made against early private enterprise, later nationalised or modern privatised railways. In the 1840s, letters to *The Times* repeatedly complained about, amongst other things, lack of punctuality, safety matters, overcrowding, lack of co-operation between companies, booking clerks' ignorance of their line's services, the reluctance of officials to take any notice of complaints and the tendency to put profit before other considerations. Floods disrupted railway services in the autumn of 1841; floods disrupted railway services in the autumn of 2000.

The earliest railways, often called 'tramways' or 'tramroads', were short lengths of line designed to complement existing forms of traffic, particularly river- or canal-borne. A line would be laid, for example, from a coal-mine to a canal where the gradient made a direct canal link impracticable; full trucks would go down by gravity and horses would haul the empties back up. As time went on, lines became longer and, in the early nineteenth century experiments were made with moving steam-engines, though it took a quarter of a century of trial and error before fairly effective machines were developed. Whilst these early lines were intended for the carriage of minerals, in some cases, where the route was of use to others, the practice developed of allowing 'passengers' to travel on top of the loads or in empty trucks. Needless to say, little exact information about this practice exists; it was informal (perhaps depending on a small tip to the 'driver'?) and these early lines were mostly in areas remote from the fashionable society of the time and thus resulted in little written evidence, though H. Williams, in *Railways in Wales*, refers to the '70 heroes who clambered aboard without knowing if they were going to live to tell the tale' in his description of the trial of Trevithick's engine between Merthyr and Abercynon on 21 February 1804. Perhaps even those who rode on Trevithick's circular railway near Euston in 1808 also have some remote claim to be regarded as early passengers.

As the carriage of passengers became more organised, special accommodation was provided, either in cleaner carriages attached to goods trains or in special trains restricted to passengers. They still copied established practices, such as those used on toll roads. The design of early railway carriages is itself a clear piece of evidence of the evolution from road to railway transport. Some companies allowed private individuals to put their own carriages on the line in return for payment of toll, others sold leases to private contractors, allowing them to run services: modern privatised franchises represent something of a return to a system abandoned in the 1830s and 1840s. Such services, usually still horse-drawn, were able to pick up and set down at any convenient point.

Even with the advent of company-provided and steam-hauled services, initial practice was somewhat informal. Several companies at first still set down and picked up virtually anywhere, even on some lines where 'stations' were listed. Stations as we know them were initially provided only at the main centres, perhaps even just at the termini; level crossings were favourite places for early stops. R.G.H. Thomas's description of practice on the early Liverpool & Manchester Railway would have been typical of that on many early lines: 'Passengers wishing to alight told the guard when joining the train, and if any were to be taken up, the policeman [signalman and often level crossing keeper as well] signalled the driver to stop ... There were no platforms or buildings apart from the gatekeeper's cottage, and this served as a waiting room for passengers in cold or wet weather and at night'. There was much experiment as companies sought to find the best (and most profitable) way of serving the traveller. Many early stations were cheaply built and easily abandoned if not profitable. The Lancaster & Preston Junction re-sited some of its 'sentry-boxes' very soon after opening. The Edinburgh & Glasgow classified some of its first stations as 'temporary' while it waited to see if enough people would use them to make them worth keeping. Whishaw, writing about 1840, classified stations as 'first-class' (only the faster trains stopped at these), 'second-class' and 'stopping-places', a practice followed by many railway companies. Timetables referred to some of their least important stops as 'Road', 'Gate' and 'Gatehouse' stations. 'Lodge', 'request stop', 'signal stop' and 'halting place' are also to be found in early timetables and the local press. Some companies, especially in Scotland, called their main stations 'depots' and their minor stops 'offsets'.

Initially, following the practices of road travel, fares were quoted for 'inside' and 'outside' passengers. Soon this was replaced by numbered classes, 'First', 'Second' and so on – the number of classes provided varied from company to company. Other terms were also used. The Glasgow to Greenock service advertised fares for 'stand-up' carriages. After Gladstone's Act of 1844, Parliamentary fares were introduced. These were designed to provide third-class passengers with a minimum standard of frequency, comfort and speed of travel, but they did not prervent companies from providing even cheaper services as well; excursions frequently still ran in open waggons, not always provided with seats. Gradually market forces took over and companies improved standards beyond the legal minimum as they realised that the cheapest seats provided the bulk of their revenue and the biggest potential for expansion.

Some passengers were carried by 'mixed' trains that included both passenger and goods wagons. Some companies advertised that passengers were carried by goods trains, especially overnight ones; presumably these were even cheaper and slower, perhaps not even including proper passenger carriages. The complication caused by these last is that evidence, e.g. from the Birmingham & Gloucester and the North British, shows that some places received their only passenger service in this way; since these services often only show up in vague footnote references or by the accidental survival of handbills, almost certainly some locations not listed in this book did have a passenger service of sorts by this means.

Some places were only served, at least for part of their existence, by trains (perhaps only one each way) on one or two days a week. These services were designed to take people to and from the nearest principal town on its market day(s). Many of them simply involved extra stops on passenger lines, and market-day trains were given extra time to cope with this. Others, however, ran on lines that normally only carried goods trains. In these cases the timetable only often quoted the terminus, leaving one to guess what happened in between. Since times allowed were generous and the interruption to other traffic would not have been as serious as on passenger lines it may be that in some cases the 'stop anywhere' principle applied, particularly on the homeward journey. The most surprising thing, though, is that such services ever appeared in a national timetable – they could not have been much use to travellers from outside the area. The probable explanation is that the company's clerk copied the timetable without thinking about it and sent it off to the

publishers who did likewise. One oddity is that these services show an opposite characteristic to routine ones: several are shown for lines in the North East, normally sparing with detail, while those provided by the Great Western have only been detected from the local press and company records. This suggests that some of these services have not yet come to light; it may well also be that those quoted had a longer life than the timetables suggest.

Casual ways were tolerable on short lines operating in isolation but would not do for trunk lines designed to link major centres with a fast and reliable service. Thus the Liverpool & Manchester listed 17 intermediate stops in 1831; the Great Western had 23 in nearly four times the distance when it opened throughout to Bristol in 1841. There were also great differences in the publicity given to services and stations. The Great Western gave full details of regular stops in national public timetables from the start, while many companies in the North East gave only an outline of their services, even in their own timetables and local handouts. Thus stations unrecorded so far almost certainly existed on the latter if not on the former. However, some unorthodox arrangements existed, even on major routes much later (see Pollicott, Section 4).

One option open to early travellers was to hire their own train. This happened quite frequently until the motor-car gave freedom to travel at any time. From July to September 1842 the London & Greenwich table in *Bradshaw* carried a note saying that anyone wanting to return from Greenwich after the last train had left at 10p.m. could engage a special on application to the inspectors on duty; the price of the train was fifty shillings plus one shilling (then the first-class fare to London) per passenger above fifty. Common usages included parties of the well-to do who wanted to go to race meetings and to cope with family crises. One actual case was revealed in *The Times (16, 18 January 1851)* and an accident report; on the 8th a Mr Haviland urgently wished to go to Cambridge several hours before normal service began to attend his father's death-bed (his train hit a stray goods wagon at Ponders End, killing a railwayman). The report mentioned other examples of specials, including ones to Newmarket. In March 1868 the Stockton & Darlington was faced with a request from a Mr Hildyard that additional trains should be run to and from Stanhope. Since an earlier concession to his request had resulted in trains running with an average of 1½ passengers they declined but did offer to provide a special train on reasonable terms whenever he wanted one *(RAIL 667/68)*.

A variant on this was provided by an advertisement put in *The Times* of 5 April 1852 by the Vale of Neath. They had provided covered first-class and open excursion carriages specially adapted for viewing 'the justly celebrated scenery of this valley and its tributaries' (principal waterfalls were listed). Parties taking at least twelve tickets could have an excursion carriage attached to an ordinary train or, on giving notice, a special train. Latter could be stopped at passengers' option. It is not clear whether the stop was just for a longer look at the scenery from the carriage or whether it would have been long enough for a ramble – ordinary traffic would then have been infrequent.

The Kyle of Lochalsh line included 'ladder stops' between stations, so called because a ladder was put down to help passengers from the lineside; a photograph shows one such, 'of LMS vintage, between Achnashellac and Achnasheen' on page 15 of D. Jenkinson's *The Highland in LMS Days*, Pendragon Partnership, 2004.

The system grew naturally in the sense that those lines most needed and most likely to be profitable were built first and fairly rapidly linked together in a system that joined the main centres of population. Long-distance travelling often involved the use of several companies' lines but many of these were planned from the outset to complement one another – e.g. the London & Birmingham and the Grand Junction linked London to the Liverpool & Manchester, thus joining four of England's major centres. Parliament did not seek to lay down a strategic network, as happened in some continental countries (and even to some extent in the United States, with its generous land-grants to transcontinental lines) but the basic laws of economics meant that what initially developed was not far removed from what a planned network might have looked like. Indeed, leaving the job to individual companies got lines built faster, since it resulted in development from many points at once, though much effort was also wasted on promoting lines that were never built. Here it should be noted that the 'manias' bulking large in some accounts were upsurges in the promotion of lines; the actual building and opening of new ones proceeded at a steadier pace. However, Parliament did intervene extensively over the operation of lines: an endless stream of laws was passed on such matters as safety and fares as it sought to protect the individual against possible monopoly abuse.

Private enterprise did not always benefit the traveller. When Hudson gained control of two routes to Leeds, he closed one and sent all traffic by the longer route. The hapless shareholders of the Exeter & Crediton and would-be travellers in that neighbourhood stood helplessly by whilst their completed line lay unused owing to inter-company wrangling. When the opening date was at last announced, *Trewman's* had this to say: 'Two or three haymaking seasons have passed away, the crops of grass on the line were abundant and people began to speculate upon the probability of shareholders receiving a dividend by the sale of hay'. Railway officials concerned to boost 'their' company could be deliberately obstructive of the interests of the travelling public at stations served by more than one company or at junctions. There was an odd mixture of co-operation between companies at some points and virtual warfare at others.

Once the main outline had been laid down, further lines were added: as branches, as cross-country routes, and as lines competing for existing routes (e.g. between London and Birmingham) though it needs to be remembered that the competitive element often only affected the termini, intermediate places being served by only one of the lines as they took different routes between main cities. Whilst some of these provided much needed services, it has also to be said that some, particularly in the latter part of the nineteenth century, owed more to the Napoleonic aims of certain company chairmen than to the real needs of travellers and shareholders. Examples were lines such as the Great Central's route to London, the competitive lines of the North British and Caledonian in Central Scotland and those of the South Eastern and the London, Chatham & Dover in the south-east. Whilst closure has wiped out most of the first two cited, the last mostly survive as vital commuter services; this is the result of later residential development which could not have been foreseen by those who built the lines.

There was a clear logic to the amalgamation of lines that contributed to a single route, and this happened almost from the start: in 1844 a group of lines centred on Derby united to form the Midland Railway, and in 1846 the London & North Western was formed by combining the Grand Junction (which had already absorbed the Liverpool & Manchester and several smaller lines), the Manchester & Birmingham, and the London & Birmingham. It could also provide a way of ending inter-company arguments: the South Eastern and London, Chatham & Dover Companies buried their differences by creating the South Eastern and Chatham Railway Companies Managing Committee, which effectively made one company of them, though legally they remained separate. Amalgamations were to continue right through to 1922. However, for a long time the number of companies in existence grew because new ones were being formed faster than old ones were being lost to amalgamation. Typically, a branch line would be locally promoted by those who expected to gain from it. While legally it was an independent company, usually the understanding from the outset was that it would be operated by whichever main company it joined. Occasionally such lines were independently run, but these were rarities. At a later stage such lines were usually absorbed, at a discount (most railways cost a lot more to build and were less profitable than their optimistic supporters estimated), by their big brothers. By the end of the century new openings were tailing off, so that amalgamations now tended to outweigh new creations. In Section 4, stations are generally attributed to the companies owning or operating them in 1922 or at their closure if this was earlier; reference is rarely made to the companies which had opened them.

Almost from the outset there were also closures. At that stage, companies were in full charge of their affairs and could apply a swift axe to any line or station if they felt it was not paying its way. These were comparative rarities, though a few lines were so financially insecure that they were closed and re-opened several times or lurched on precariously in the hands of a receiver.

Another early development was the creation of special arrangements for workmen, who were provided with cheap travel on early morning and evening trains. Sometimes this was an obligation placed on railways by Parliament as a condition of allowing the demolition of housing in town and city centres; in other cases, the initiative seems to have come from employers. The facility could be provided at ordinary stations, or by means of special workmen-only stations which did not appear in the public timetable. Railway historians have probably made more of a distinction between 'ordinary' and 'workmen's' stations than their users did. The most common workers' stations were those provided for coal miners and, during the two World Wars, for munitions workers – many of whom were women. In both cases, there was a need to bring workers some distance to their pits and factories and no other means of transport was available. It should be noted that many miners' stops, including those which preceded public stations, would have been on sidings off the running lines; in some cases they would have alighted directly onto the ground. A wide variety of other industries was also served. Workers were sometimes carried as 'passengers' to and from stations not used by the general public in such cases as herdsmen accompanying cattle and pigs or grooms with racehorses.

During the First World War all railways were taken temporarily into government management. This period also saw the first major batch of closures, mostly designed to free workers for the army. These were meant to be temporary but some of the stations involved never reopened. The benefits found from working the system as a whole were clear and logic might well have prevailed to maintain the railways as a single system. However, that change was too great for many to accept and the outcome was a compromise of sorts. The railways were reorganised into four big companies: Great Western, Southern, London & North Eastern, and London Midland & Scottish. This left an element of competition in services between major centres. Already the railways, which had had an effective monopoly of inland passenger traffic for much of the nineteenth century, had started to face competition over short distance inner-city routes from electric street-tramways; now they were also faced with petrol-driven bus competition in rural areas at a time when the major 'Industrial Revolution' industries such as coal and steel were in difficulties, so that the cross-subsidisation between profitable goods and some unprofitable passenger services, which had previously occurred, now became more difficult. The outcome

was that the new companies embarked on a wave of closures in the early 1930s, especially in cases where a big new company had inherited two lines which were to a large extent duplicates. There were still some new openings, but these were mostly designed to foster commuter traffic, particularly in the London area. The Great Western continued to open 'Halts' to try to beat off the competition but its example was only copied to a limited extent by others.

The Second World War again saw the network taken under government control. During this war the system was heavily worked and some parts were damaged by enemy action but the needs of the time meant that investment was minimal and that the system was simply patched to keep it going. According to *The Railway Magazine* of September & October 1942 (p.311): 'For war workers more than 200 new halts and stations have been opened, but these cannot, of course be specified'. This both illustrates the scale of the operation and helps to explain why information about these stations is hard to find – clearly, not all of them have been included in this book. The railway companies' history of their war contribution states that at one stage nearly 6,500 additional passenger trains per week were run for government factories; one factory at Chorley required 426 of these. This – plus the need to move large numbers of troops to training camps, for leave, and to the ports for embarkation – meant that civilian traffic was severely curtailed. Afterwards there was no possibility of private investment making good the damage of the war years, especially given the post-war levels of taxation Thus some form of continued government participation was inevitable, though the details might have been different. Nationalisation followed, effective from the start of 1948. It was still in some ways a partial measure: initially, an element of competition between the Regions into which the railways were divided remained and no serious attempt was made to integrate bus services, nationalised at the same time, with the railways. Although the theory was that politicians would not interfere in the detailed running of the railways, in practice the increasing losses incurred meant that they often did so; in any case, politicians tend, by a process of natural selection, to be compulsive meddlers. The result was re-organisation, re-re-organisation, and so on.

Immediately after this war, railways still had a near monopoly of travel over longer distances. This was eroded as private car ownership and long-distance coach services grew. Thus the railways faced mounting losses. A fuel crisis in 1947 led to another batch of 'temporary closures' some of which became permanent. A coal shortage early in 1951 resulted in another similar but smaller batch. Some attempt was made to fight the competition, e.g. by the electrification of some main line services, but many services were felt to be beyond redemption and from 1950 there was an accelerating number of closures. By now an elaborate system of public enquiry plus final ministerial approval had to be followed before closure could legally occur. Dr Beeching was brought in from industry to try to stem the losses; his Report, published in 1963, recommended further large-scale closures and tried to set out criteria for the future running of a profitable network. In practice, closures continued, but not according to a plan: lines were considered individually and survival or closure depended ultimately not only on the lack of profitability of a line but on such matters as who was Minister of Transport and how many marginal constituencies would be affected. The closures tailed off in the mid-1970s (the Alston branch, closed in 1976, being the last). The 'system' that has been left clearly lacks logic in some areas: the Exeter to Barnstaple line has more stations, some admittedly very poorly served, than the entire county of Somerset.

Since then, the picture has been one of mild expansion. A number of stations and short stretches of line, closed in the 1950s and 1960s, have reopened; a few new ones have been added. Much has depended on political considerations and the degree of local initiative applied; Scotland has been particularly favoured in this respect. The main developments have been the continued expansion of the London Underground and provision of 'metro' lines giving frequent services to closely-set stations in major urban areas.

Most recently, the railways were privatised in 1994. This represented the sharpest break in the railways' history: evolution was abandoned, replaced by undiluted and contrived theory. It is as yet too early to form a proper judgement on what the long-term effects will be; it may be that in years to come the problems of the first few years will be looked back on as the sort of teething problems faced by the early nineteenth century pioneers. However, the present writer felt, and still feels, that the vast sums spent on the legal and other non-productive aspects of this process, including the expenses incurred when franchises are renewed or revised, would have been far better spent on direct investment in the railways themselves. It would surely not have been beyond human ingenuity to have found a way of making private investment available by way of something akin to the debentures issued by public companies, whilst keeping the basic structure intact. No attempt is made here to follow the labyrinthine complications of the privatised system.

Fuller details on many general questions are provided by:

P. Bagwell & P. Lyth, *1750–2000: Transport in Britain from Canal Lock to Gridlock*, Hambledon & Lindon, 2002. (Deals will all forms of transport; little narrative detail but strong on analysis and explanation of changes.)

B. Baxter, *Stone Blocks & Iron Rails*, David & Charles, 1966.

R. Bell, *History of the British Railways during the War 1939–45*, Railway Gazette, 1946.

G. Biddle, *Great Railway Stations of Britain*, David & Charles, 1986.

G. Body, *Great Railway Battles*, Silver Link, 1994. [Inter-company quarrels].

M.R. Bonavia, *Historic Railway Sites in Britain*, Robert Hale, 1987.

J. Glover, *Privatised Railways*, Ian Allan, 1998.

T.R. Gourvish, *British Railways 1948–73, A Business History*, Cambridge University Press, 2002, and *British Rail, 1974–97, from Integration to Privatisation*, Oxford University Press, 2002.

A. & E. Jordan, *Away for the Day: the railway excursion in Britain 1830 to the present day*, Silver Link, 1991.

M.J.T. Lewis, *Early Wooden Railways*, Routledge & Kegan Paul, 1974 edition, paperback.

H. Pollins, *Britain's Railways: An Industrial History*, David & Charles 1971. [Economic aspects].

P.J.G. Ransom, *The Archaeology of Railways*, Worlds Work Ltd, 1981.

L.T.C. Rolt, *Red for Danger*, David & Charles, fourth edition, 1982 [accidents and safety].

J. Simmons:
The Railway in England & Wales, 1830–1914, The System and its Working, Leicester University Press, 1978.
The Railway in Town & Country, 1834–1914, David & Charles, 1986;
The Victorian Railway, Thames & Hudson, 1991.

J. Simmons and G. Biddle (editors), *The Oxford Companion to British Railway History*, OUP, 1997.

A.W. Warren, *Register of British Railway and Tramroad Companies incorporated before 1948 (also Joint Lines)*, published by the RCHS in 2005, after the compiler's death.

What's Happening to Brunel's railway ..., The findings of the Investigation into the provision of the Great Western service. Rail Passengers Committee, April 2002. [An early analysis of effects of privatisation].

Comings and goings
– some statistical comments

No exact statistical survey is worthwhile because of the difficulties of definition. Some stops listed in timetables were weekly-only market ones, perhaps just pick-up and drop-off points beside level crossings, and, over the years, many obvious stations were re-sited or replaced by others so what constituted a 'new station' is open to debate; for the second reason alone anyone seeking to balance the rough figures of openings and closures that follow is doomed to failure. Suffice it to say that at one time or another well over 9,000 clearly existed in their own right. In approximate terms 500 were open by the end of 1840. Thereafter **additions** by decades were, in the years ending:

1850	1,650
1860	1,200
1870	1,600
1880	1,000
1890	800
1900	600.

- By the outbreak of war in 1914 another 1,000 had been added;

- From then until Grouping less than 100 completely new stations were provided;

- From 1923 to the start of the Second World War about 500 more were opened;

- Less than 50 joined them between 1939 and Nationalisation in 1948;

- From 1948 to the end of 1976 only 70 or so were added;

- Since then over 400 have been opened, some on or near sites previously abandoned appearently for ever.

Closures represent even more of a problem because most of the early ones related to stations replaced by others or whose services were diverted to others nearby. Ignoring those types, half-a-dozen places had completely lost their services already by 1840. From then until 1880 50 or so were closed each decade. The last twenty years of the 19th century only saw about 30 closures but there was some acceleration in the next 14 years with about 70 going. The First World War resulted in the 'temporary' closure of about 400, half of which did not reopen afterwards. Another 60 went before the end of 1923 but then losses accelerated. By 1939 more than another 900 had gone (400 in 1930–1 alone); the Second World War accounted for 250. By the end of 1960 (before Dr Beeching's time, please note) 1,800 more had gone. The next ten years saw the end of another 2,000 (more than three-quarters in the period 1962–6). Since then the position has been much more stable: 70 were lost in the early 1970s and only 30 since.

In addition details are given of when stations were closed and reopened or moved from one site to another.

There are now about 3,000, including those on the London and Glasgow underground systems, the Docklands Light and main stops on the various 'metro' systems.

This book also includes about 800 sites used by trains but were not shown in the public timetables. Some of these were for workers and would have dealt with more passengers in their lifetimes than many orthodox stations did; others were private, for the use of a particular family, or were only used for a single day to serve a special event.

In addition, brief coverage is given of more than 130 lines that provided various services of less orthodox natures.

SECTION 3

Sources and Information

This section lists and describes the sources used, in order to aid understanding of the main text, to show the likely limits of accuracy, and to assist those who might wish follow certain items more fully for themselves. The arrangement is that the primary sources used are first discussed, and then the information derived from them is described in more detail than is given at the beginning of Section 4. Finally, all sources are listed.

Ideally, everything should have been derived from, or checked against, primary sources but there is a limit to what one person, even given the help listed in the acknowledgements, can do with such a vast topic as this. Strictly, at least two first-hand sources known to be completely independent of each other should be used for each item but the nature and availability of the evidence is such that one is often lucky to find one fairly believable source, let alone two unimpeachable ones, so that in practice a mixture of primary and secondary sources has to be used. The sources quoted are the best available to the compiler at the time of writing. A basic underlying principle of the work has been that better sources were substituted as they became available.

CONTEMPORARY SOURCES

Railway Companies

Railway companies' records, such as Board Minutes, should be the best starting point, but, remarkably, they often do not readily provide the answers, especially in the case of stations that were opened after the line on which they were situated: either the Minutes do not give the information at all or it is buried in the detailed records of some sub-committee and the volume of the records of some companies deposited at Kew is such that it would take months of research to find (or not find) one date. Even where the information is given, it should, if possible, be verified against another source, though some have tended to use railway material uncritically. The clerks and other officials who kept the records were as capable as other human beings of making copying and other errors, and of making up records to satisfy superiors interested only in seeing that spaces on the forms had been filled. Anyone thinking otherwise should remember that these employees were the ones whose carefree operating methods led to so many mishaps, fortunately mostly minor, in early railway operation. That said, it is obvious that the further one moves from the original time, the greater the possibility that some intermediary has created an error.

Official sources could be inaccurate. In 1926 a record of the *Routes, Statutes, Opening Dates & Other Particulars* of the Great Western Railway was prepared within that company as a sort of stocktaking exercise after the changes of 1922 and 1923, when a number of smaller companies were added to the GW; a reprint was published by Avon-Anglia in 1986. According to C.R. Clinker, the original was produced in a hurry; it certainly contained many errors.

Returns to Parliament

Parliament's concern for the public interest meant railway companies were called upon to provide various pieces of information which were collated and published as 'Returns', which provided much information of use in compiling this work. An early example was a Select Committee of the House of Commons, which collected information about fares, passenger numbers and the like for a period from the start of 1838 to mid-1839. In 1840 the Board of Trade was given various regulatory and inquisitive powers; its publications were initially grandly entitled *Report of the Officers of the Railway Department to the Lords of the Committee of Privy Council for Trade*, but were much more prosaically titled as time went on. In 1846, owing to the amount of work resulting from new projects, this work was transferred to a new body of Railway Commissioners (whose reports were thus ascribed) but this did not result in any gains so in 1851 the Board of Trade took over again. In 1919 the relevant responsibilities were transferred to the Minister of Transport, whose reports were published under the heading of *The Ministry of Transport*. Here their returns are all treated as though they were part of the continuous sequence of records that they were in practice. They included such matters as the reports of inspections of new lines before opening, accidents, and statistical details of the companies' operations. The last of these has provided most information for this book. The continuous sequence began with one for the second half of 1840. Initially, the returns covered half-yearly periods but in the 1860s the Board standardised on issues of figures for the complete calendar year, though some companies continued to provide information based on their own accounting years. At Kew, the returns are to be found in the series *RAIL 1053/...* The first few bound volumes contain some of all of the types of return mentioned earlier; the later ones used in connection with this book contain only statistical material. The return for the first half of 1841 is available in much less detail (in *1053/2*) than for the other half-years thereabouts. That for the half-years between July 1845 and June 1847 has only so far been found at the House of Lords Record Office.

When a company opened its first stretch of line, the date of opening was often directly quoted; in other cases, this was done indirectly – a note would say 'Return from [date X]'. Given the official nature of these returns, it should be possible to rely on this information as accurate. In the vast majority of cases where it has been possible to check against company minutes, press reports and the like, the dates do coincide. However, there are a few cases where the balance of the evidence suggests that the dates in the returns might be wrong. Perhaps a company's clerk misunderstood what was wanted or sent the wrong date (perhaps for formal rather than public opening); perhaps copying or printing errors occurred at the receiving end. Where a modern source gives one date, the return another, and no means has been found for determining which is more likely to be right, the modern source has been used for the date given in the body of the work and a note added in Section 5. It should be said that the further checking against other contemporary sources has been taken, the more frequently it has been found that the dates provided in these reports were the correct ones.

The Press

The local press is an obvious source for verification and generally a useful selection of papers is available on microfilm in the Local Studies or Reference sections of major libraries. However, there are inevitably gaps and new openings did not always make the news, especially once railways had lost some of their novelty value. Sometimes companies did what one might think would have been standard practice for commercial organisations seeking extra custom and inserted advertisements for their new line or station but this happened more rarely over time.

One trap is that sometimes one has to rest content with a statement like: 'On Monday next the line from X to Y will open'. Confirmation that it did open is not always given and there were sometimes last-minute delays owing to failed inspections and the like; since the date of the source is always quoted here, it will be evident which statements were before and which after the event. Even where it is said that a line <u>did</u> open on a specific date, it is not a guarantee of accuracy: especially with short items it is impossible to be sure that the news was first-hand. The Great Western advertised the opening of its extension to Wootton Bassett Road for 16 December 1840 but actually opened it on the 17th. At least two local papers duly announced that it had opened on the 16th. Papers sometimes referred to partly built or intended stations as if they already existed. There are also problems in interpreting 'Wednesday last' (if a Friday publication, did they mean two days ago or nine? – news was collected and published in a more leisurely fashion then). Similarly, does 'yesterday' relate to the day the item was written or to the newspaper's publishing day?

Papers also varied in their 'locality'. At one stage, some claimed to cover large areas: one such was *The Hampshire Chronicle, Southampton Courier and General Advertiser for the South & West of England, circulating throughout the Isle of Wight and the Counties of Hampshire, Sussex, Surrey, Sussex, Berkshire, Wiltshire, Dorset and Somerset*. Over time, papers became more localised in their coverage and many new ones came into existence. The Hampshire paper quoted above increasingly concentrated on events in and around Winchester; Andover was an example of a town gaining a paper of its own later.

Much has come from *The Times*, which is an accessible national source containing much relevant information. However, it was not infallible. Indeed, there is more possibility of error than with local papers when it dealt with events far from London. Prior to 1914 three sorts of information have been derived from it:

Firstly: Notices of opening placed by the railway companies in the form of advertisements. These have been treated as a first-class source though even here it needs to be remembered that there were sometimes last-minute hitches. There were also very occasional instances of a service beginning before the advertised date.

Secondly: Items concerning companies' half-yearly meetings, which usually came in series. The first would mention the dividend likely to be paid (of prime interest to the shareholders of the day but of no use for this book). A few days later would come a summary of the half-yearly report; many at one time gave information about new openings in the previous six months. Finally would come an item on the shareholders' meeting. At first the report was repeated (and in at least one case a different opening date quoted) but soon the policy was to refer readers back to what had already appeared in the paper and to concentrate on the meeting. This rarely included anything used here, though a new opening fixed for a date soon after the meeting might be mentioned by the Chairman. Dates given in these reports and at these meetings have been accepted unless there is very clear evidence to the contrary.

Thirdly: News items, at one time appearing in a regular column of 'Railway Intelligence'. These were a mixed bunch. Some appear to have been produced by the paper's own journalists, some by 'Special Correspondents', some copied from regional papers. Others look as if they were contributed by locals sending in material on their own area or by railway companies anxious to publicise their services. The remarkable thing is that the last were sporadic rather than routine offerings; whether this should be put down simply to poor public relations or regarded as the result of the arrogance of monopolists is an arguable question; it might be added that little concerning this has changed since. The compiler suspects that many of these items were provided, in outline at least, by outsiders and then handed to a journalist to put into final form. Thus there was the possibility that they could have become garbled in transmission since, even with items apparently reliably dated, some peculiar geography was included. The policy adopted has been to quote *The Times* alone where secondary sources agree with it: few authors seem to have used it when writing their books and thus it usually provides an independent check on what is in print, though there is always the possibility of common, and inaccurate, ancestry of information. However, discrepancies have been found. Where it has been possible to resolve these by reference to e.g. local press items, the unhelpful conclusion is that sometimes *The Times* is right and the 'accepted' sources wrong, but in other cases the reverse. Items from *The Times* known from other sources to be wrong have been ignored. Some give the impression of being clearly authentic and have been preferred. That leaves those where it is simply the word of a possibly second-hand item in *The Times* against that of a historian who claims to have written his book wholly or partly from primary sources. Here, if there is some possibility that *The Times* is right, the date given in Section 4 is taken from the secondary source and a note of the *Times* version added.

In all cases the most fertile early period for information from *The Times* was from the late 1840s to the early 1860s. Thereafter diminishing amounts of information were available. Understandably, the London area and the major trunk lines received the fullest coverage. However, as with the local press, what was included and what overlooked is often beyond logical explanation – what impelled those concerned to put an opening notice for the Dornoch Light Railway in *The Times*?

After 1918 there was a marked revival of interest. Items were now essentially of two types. One sort consisted of very brief items to the effect that station or line 'x' would open or close on date 'y'; these appear to have been based on company handouts (still erratically provided). The other was made up of reports, nearly all covering events in the London area, apparently provided by the paper's own journalists. Both types have been accepted as reliable.

Railway Guides

As lines opened, the fashion rapidly developed of publishing guides for travellers on the new lines; often the phrase 'Iron Road Book' or something similar was worked into the title. These normally gave a brief history of the undertaking, not usually very exactly dated, plus a description of the line, scenery and places of interest to be seen along the way. Time- and fare-tables were also included. They help to establish which stations existed at the start but they are not a foolproof source. The authors generally claimed to be writing from personal inspection but this was not always true (see the entry on *1839 June 10* in Section 5). Revised versions were commonly issued without exact dating or any mechanism for showing what changes had been made, so that the stations listed in the description no longer tallied with those in the timetable.

The disadvantage for the traveller was that these guides mostly only covered one route (though often the London, Birmingham, Manchester and Liverpool services provided by complementary companies were bound together). Also, he would not want to buy a complete new book whenever times were revised. *Freeling's Guide* (early 1841 version) to the London & Birmingham and related lines did include a wide variety of tables but they are so clearly of different dates that some must have been out of date before publication and there was an obvious need for specialist timetable publications.

Timetables

Timetables are the fall-back source. It must be emphasised that there is an element of approximation about dates found from them.

In theory the most useful timetables should be those issued by the companies themselves. However, at first these were issued in flimsy single-sheet form so that few have survived, at any rate in the continuous runs needed to establish first and last dates accurately. *The Railway Times* of 18 September 1847 reported that the LNW had outgrown the usual form and was now issued as a pamphlet, which gave a better chance of survival. Other large companies increasingly used this form but many small ones never justified more than a single sheet, often a small one. Also the large number of companies in existence meant that the evidence was produced in very scattered form. Even company timetables could err: the Liverpool & Manchester

timetable for March 1831 included a railway service to
Bolton while the local press makes it clear that this
service had not yet begun. Only later, with the larger
amalgamated companies, are these tables commonly
available at Kew, and even then there are gaps;
furthermore, to achieve the national coverage
attempted in this book, impossibly large numbers
would have had to be consulted. Regional timetables
such as *Murray's* for Scotland or *Reid's* for the north
east were issued from an early stage, but these are
difficult to track down. Thus national timetables have
to be the main source.

These seem to have developed naturally from the Guides
once the opening of the London & Birmingham in
September 1838 made this a worthwhile undertaking.
Needless to say, at first they only covered some of the
lines then operating and concentrated on those that
were connected with one another. The earliest known
were produced by James Drake of Birmingham in
about August 1838 and Joseph Bridgen in February
1839. They were soon eclipsed by George Bradshaw of
Manchester. (See letter by Canon Fellows in *The
Sunday Mercury*, 25 September 1938 and G. Royde
Smith, *The History of Bradshaw ...*', Blacklock, 1939.)

Bradshaw's early dominance in this field was kept until
1961, when economics rather than competition caused
publication to be handed over to British Rail. His first
timetable was probably a local one for Manchester
published in 1838 but the earliest timetable of which
copies are known today was issued 19 October 1839, in
a form that soon became entitled *Bradshaw's Companion*.
From the start of 1840, the theory was that a timetable,
then hard-covered, about 5 inches by 3¼ inches, would
be bought at the start of the year. Soon after Bradshaw
began the practice of issuing a monthly penny sheet
of tables which could be bought, cut up and the
relevant pieces pasted in as corrections or additions.
The publisher also sold versions with the corrections
made in the text as the year went by, but just left the
year date at the front. Needless to say, these present all
sorts of problems with dating; thus until December
1841 dates from these are usually quoted as e.g. 'about
June 1840'. The monthly sheets were dated but only
one of these from before 1842 is available at Kew.
The books also included maps of parts of the system
(rarely accurately revised), gradient diagrams (to help
the traveller understand the slow speed at some points?)
and information about cab fares in the main cities.

Starting in December 1841 Bradshaw issued his
monthly *Guide*, paper covered, clearly priced and
designed to be thrown away once out of date. The page
size was twice that of the *Companion*. Only one map
was included, a large fold-out at the front. To begin
with, the various parts of the country were shown in
turn, but he soon standardised on a national map
(of very limited use for historical purposes). For a while,
the *Companion* continued to be published as well;

double pages from it made up single pages in the *Guide*.
However, there was no real need now for the *Companion*
and this faded out after a few years. The *Guide* became
the accepted standard national timetable. Dates derived
from *Bradshaw* are ascribed to '*Brad*'. Others are
indicated as 'company's tt', 'press tt', etc. Where the
date has been derived from a seconary source, it will be
shown as in that work: this will usually be 'tt'. In most
cases *Bradshaw* is likely to have been the timetable used.

Users should be warned that for a long time a cheaper,
abridged, version of the *Guide* was issued alongside the
main one. Scotland was particularly roughly treated in
this, as indeed it had been in the early years of the other
time-tables mentioned.

There were competitors. *Robinson* and *Tuck* produced
works along the lines of *Bradshaw's Companion*, though
they retained some of the features of the earliest road-
books mentioned – diagrams showing places of interest
along the route were sometimes included. Not enough
of these rivals have been seen to make any judgements
on relative reliability possible. There were differences,
but these seem mainly to have consisted in the amounts
of detail provided: one would list all the stations on one
line but not another while a rival would provide the
reverse. The likeliest explanation for Bradshaw's victory
over his rivals lies in the convenience provided by the
monthly throw-away format. Other factors might have
been his greater coverage of steamer services and
inclusion of revenue-earning advertisements (in
themselves sometimes providing interesting insights
into Victorian life); he also omitted the irrelevant
material that others included.

Rivals continued to appear, often with a layout designed
to make their tables easier to interpret. One such was
Topham's Patented Railway Timetables. The full range
of its issues is not known but it certainly appeared at
least from May 1848 to March 1850 inclusive.
Its approach was to list stations just once, on the left-hand
side of the page; the times of down trains had to be read
down the page and the up ones up; at first one set were
printed in red to help distinguish them but later the
distinction had to be made from bold and normal type.
Topham was not the inventor of such an arrangement:
the Grand Junction used a form of it in its opening
notice and Tuck included such a table. Their form was
much easier to follow since the names were printed in
the middle of the page, with up trains on one side and
down on the other. Initially Topham looked a promising
competitor since his standards of printing were higher
and full detail was given for a number of lines that
Bradshaw only covered in outline. By 1850, however,
Topham had clearly lost the battle: many lines were not
included, others were not up to date and organisation
had become chaotic. In fairness, it should be pointed
out that this was relatively the most hectic period in
British railway history, at least as far as the numbers of
new stations are concerned. There were considerable

differences between the two, even before Topham had clearly lost the plot. As far as opening dates are concerned, Topham's tables are used if they provide earlier evidence. The differences (often random in nature) can be illustrated from the Chester & Holyhead line:

Chester – Bangor opened 1 May 1848. Both included the line in the May volume, with the same intermediate stations: Queen's Ferry; Flint; Holywell; Mostyn; Prestatyn; Rhyl; Abergele; Conway; Aber. These agree with the tt included in Parry's 1848 *Guide* to the line.

Llanfair – Holyhead opened 1 August 1848; both included this in August, without any intermediate stations.

Additions ('never' = not by March 1850); May/June = not in April tt, May tt not seen, present in June tt:

	Bradshaw	Topham
Bagillt	January 49	May/June 49
Colwyn	October 49	never
Penmaenmawr	November 49	never
Gaerwen	January 49	May/June 49
Bodorgan	October 49	May/June 49
Ty Croes	November 49	December 49
Valley	October 49	May/June 49

As far as closures are concerned (there were few anyway), the earlier is again used. The assumption has been made that where a line continued to be shown, as the Morningside line was in *Topham's* for several months after *Bradshaw* had declared 'service suspended', it was the result of failure to keep the tables up to date.

A later rival was *The Intelligible Railway Guide*, certainly in existence in 1858 and 1859. It divided tables into many small sections. It looked tidier and easier to read but also resulted in a bulkier volume. Occasional reference is also made to the *ABC Timetable* and a few local ones, but these are of very limited use for the purpose in hand.

To begin with, there was much variation in the way information was presented. This was because the companies themselves had their own ways and publishers seem to have copied their presentations, which is clear evidence that for the most part, give or take a misprint here and there, the companies must take most of the blame for any shortcomings in the timetables. It was, after all, in publishers' commercial interest to be as accurate as possible. For some lines full details were given, complete with all intermediate stops and train times at them. Others only had an outline showing times at the termini and major points in between, with other stations listed in fare tables or in notes. When these were put in a continuous line, separated just with commas, this could present difficulties of interpretation since a station with a double name might look like two (Holytown & Bellshill

was shown as Holytown, Bellshill). Yet others provided no information whatsoever about intermediate stops. Some companies' tables appeared very late (the Blyth & Tyne not until 1852).

From about 1850 until Grouping, timetables were normally issued as effective from the first day of the month. *Bradshaw* normally just put the month on the cover. However, increasingly there were exceptions. The LNW's own company timetable for May 1875 has a note on its cover that the services would not come into effect until Monday 3rd. *Bradshaw* June 1890 carried a warning that services would not start until Monday 2nd, though that did not stop the LSW from opening its independent line to Plymouth on Sunday 1st. Increasingly, especially in summer, changes might be deferred or brought forward a day or two, in order to coincide with a Monday, but this happened erratically and was not always done by all companies in the month concerned. The July 1914 issue of *Bradshaw* was a traveller's nightmare: the cover warned that not all services would start on the 1st. The marginal notes inside show that the GW, LNW and North Staffs started their new services on Sunday 12th and the Great Central and Cheshire Lines from Monday 13th (except for services noted to start on the 1st, 4th or 5th). The rest were presumed to start on the 1st.

After Grouping, practice remained mixed. Some new timetables were still introduced on the first of the month, regardless of the day of the week. Summer timetables normally ran from about the beginning of the second week in July to the end of the third week in September. These tts are dated in Section 4 by their starting date and tt is added afterwards to emphasise that, although exact dates are given, they are timetable dates and that a station given as opening e.g. 9 July 1934 tt would not necessarily have opened on that date. There were other variations: in 1938, the sixth month's issue was just 'June', though it is clear that services in it commenced on 30 May. Some short periods apparently went missing: one issue in 1944 is dated May 1–21, the next June.

Whilst there was an increasing tendency for timetables to run from Monday to Sunday, inclusive, the Southern Railway, which had few contacts with the other companies and was geographically compact, ran its new services from the Sunday preceding; there had been some tendency for its constituent companies to do this before Grouping. Thus Sunnymeads opened 10 July 1927 with the new SR tt, whilst the appropriate *Bradshaw* is dated 11 July 1927. A note on the cover of *ABC* tt July 1927 says: 'This Timetable operates from Monday July 11th, except Sunday services on the Southern Railway, which commence July 10th'. This practice even occurred at other times: the January 1930 *ABC* tt (mostly effective from the 1st) included a note on the opening from South Merton to Sutton to the effect that it started on the 5th.

In their last years all except the Great Western handed the job of timetable production over to *Bradshaw*; their own names appeared on the cover but *Bradshaw's* part was indicated inside. This practice continued after Nationalisation, except that the Scottish Region used *Murray*. Soon the various Regions published their own (some from 1950, others from 1955), using a larger format (5⅞ inches by 9 inches), which was also used by *Bradshaw* from June 1955.

From 1961 to 2007, the timetables of British Rail and its component regions have been treated as the standard. At first issues were regional, all starting on a Monday. In 1974 the first comprehensive British Rail timetable was issued. Generally, issues have been made twice a year, starting May/June and September/October. The 29 May 1994 tt saw a switch to starting new timetables on Sundays. That starting 11 December 2005 was the first to follow EU orders. The issue of Sunday 20 May 2007 to Saturday 8 December 2007 (inclusive) was the last official issue. The Middleton Press has stepped in with its *Rail Times*, first issue from 9 December 2007; with no known prior publicity H.M. Stationery Office also provided a replacement. Two versions now exist although the official one ceased because it was claimed there was inadequate demand for it.

Railway Clearing House

The Clearing House was established to deal with the consequences of a 'system' run by many companies. It helped make it possible for passengers to book for a journey that involved travel over several companies' lines (e.g. Plymouth to Edinburgh) and be issued with one ticket for the whole trip. It allocated the revenues from such journeys between the companies concerned. To help railwaymen, it issued various publications. For fuller details of its workings, see P. Bagwell, *The Railway Clearing House in the British Economy, 1842–1922*, Allen & Unwin, 1968.

Its publications evolved from private enterprise to official status. At first staff members issued their own. The start was provided in 1851 by Zachary Macaulay, one of its clerks, who published a *Station Map of the Railways in Great Britain* and a *List of all Stations on the Railways of Great Britain alphabetically arranged*. Later came the best known, John Airey: D. Garnett, in the Brunel publication listed below, wrote: 'It has never been explained how Airey ran a flourishing private enterprise, using official information, from his employers' address and in their time'. Gradually publication was taken over by the Clearing House itself. Whilst its works were aimed at railwaymen, most were also sold to the general public.

One series of publications was of national maps, with lines coloured according to companies, all stations supposedly listed. Later, Airey added more detailed maps of separate areas, showing distances between stations and junctions. He also continued the Junction Diagrams – very detailed plans of locations where two or more companies came together: the originator of these is not known.

Revised versions of all were issued from time to time; annual supplements to the Junction Diagrams were issued between full revisions. Although it was claimed in advertisements and on the published maps that they were based on information derived from the companies and were regularly revised, there were many inaccuracies, especially in the early issues, and revision sometimes failed by a wide margin to keep pace with the changes that were occurring. All ceased with Nationalisation, except for a map of Scotland published in 1960.

Only a few examples of these maps are available in modern reprints. The only ones in the original format are the 1918 Map of the West of England, published by David & Charles, the only one of a promised 'series' to be produced; the 1914 Junction Diagrams (Ian Allan) and 1915 Junction Diagrams (David & Charles). For other versions see the section on Atlases at the end of the Sources section. Needless to say, there are few differences between the two Junction Diagrams reprints. For more information, see *Railway Maps and the Railway Clearing House*, a series of articles published by Brunel University in 1986.

Another series came to be known as the *Station Handbooks* (hyphen not always included). Originally published by Airey, they became 'Official' when the Clearing House took over. The earliest give no indication of whether the names listed belonged to a passenger station, goods station, siding, physical junction or whatever. From 1877 this was remedied and a series of columns showed what sorts of traffic were handled. These books were revised from time to time; between editions cumulative supplements were issued annually. Despite the claims about the books being kept up to date, outworn information could remain for years – Seven Stones went out of use during the First War but was still shown as a passenger station in 1938.

Both these books and the Junction Diagrams provide dating traps. Between major revisions, bound copies were sold which included the last edition plus later revisions. In the Diagrams book, revised diagrams usually replaced the out-of-date ones in the appropriate place but the date at the front was not altered: the 1888 book at Kew actually dates from 1892. However, in the Hand-books the supplement was bound in at the back and the date given at the front is that of the latest information included: the Hand-book at Kew dated 1879 is actually an 1877 issue with a cumulative appendix for 1878 and 1879 bound in at the back; what has been described as the 1900 edition was in fact 1895 plus appendices. After about 1900 the Clearing House seems to have abandoned this practice, keeping appendices separate (but still cumulative). The 1904 Hand-book was reprinted in 1970 by David & Charles, with an introduction by C.R. Clinker, the dating in which needs to be corrected in accordance with what has been said above. Note that the 1938 book was the first to include Halts; even then some were omitted, to be included in later appendices. The one exception so far seen was Balgreen Halt, included in the appendix for 1936. However, earlier books had continued to include stops which had been reduced to Halt status without including 'Halt' in their names. Thus only the 1938 and 1956 books are of any use in determining which stops were Halts. 'Platforms' were always included.

Some use has been made of another series of Clearing House publications, the *Distance Books*, particularly the supplements, which listed (and usually dated) new stations, closures, and replacements. The latter were issued to staff in pamphlet form so their survival has been a matter of rather erratic chance. In this respect, the compiler has been particularly fortunate in the amount of help received from Tony Cooke.

Shareholders' Manuals

Tuck from 1841 and Bradshaw from 1848 published information aimed at shareholders. As with timetables, the latter publisher soon monopolised the field. These books gave some idea of the companies' legal powers and financial standing, listed their directors and so on. Sometimes a line's opening date was given amongst all this. In addition, a list of the previous year's openings was included at the back, though these lists were far from complete. Unfortunately, the same date did not always appear in both places. These have been used by many works in print and some are quoted here. However, they are not the most reliable source in existence and many errors in print seem to have originated there, so their dates are only used if nothing else is available. Modern reprints exist of Tuck, 8th edition, 1847 (Dragonwheel, 2003) and Bradshaw's Manuals of 1869 (David & Charles, 1969), complete with sections on European and Imperial railways and 1923 (Peter Kay, Teignmouth, 1999), British data only, canals included.

Magazines

Use has been made of a number of publications devoted to railway matters. These have been treated as being somewhere between primary and secondary sources. They have a claim to be regarded as primary sources in that they deal with events as they occur. However, much that they include seems to have been provided by readers sending in what they regard as interesting information, rather than from the investigations of their own staff, and this material has tended to be printed uncritically. It has also to be said that those designed for a wide audience have been less likely to correct errors than the more specialised works produced by enthusiasts' groups and societies.

SECONDARY SOURCES

Much has had, of necessity, to be taken from works already in print. As far as possible, those used are works limited to a particular company, line or area; Clinker's *Register* is the chief exception. A few items have come from local histories which include a little about railways among the general history of the area involved.

References are generally limited to one, though more than one is available for many stations. Where a book is cited, the choice usually depends on the order in which secondary sources were consulted for the purpose of checking this book, rather than any preference for one over another. '(Corr)' after a source, means that the date was corrected by the author (or reviser) of the book quoted e.g. in an appendix, supplement, or notes provided in a later volume. Those listed under 'Acknowledgements' provided some of the material; if this was from a newspaper, their names appear in brackets following the paper's name.

Although all books listed below were used in the compilation of the list, duplication of information means that not all will be quoted; in many instances, a book in this list was originally taken as the source but a primary source has since been substituted. It should be recognised that it is much easier to find a date in a primary source if someone has already told you where to look – even if the original information was a few days adrift. Where a book was only used to provide one or two references it has often been quoted in full in the appropriate place and is thus not listed here as well.

COMBINED LIST OF SOURCES

The alphabetical order of the abbreviations is used, following the 'nothing before something principle'; '&' is treated as 'and', with assumed gaps either side of it. Thus the A & B type of entry will appear at or near the beginning of the appropriate letter.

Some of the newspapers quoted altered their names over time; variations are generally mentioned only briefly or are ignored completely.

Names shown bold: e.g. **Barnstaple**, mean that the newspaper quoted is available, usually on microfilm, at the Local Studies Library or Reference Library in the town or city quoted. Newspapers not otherwise ascribed or only cited in the body of the book should be assumed to have been seen at the Newspaper Library at Colindale.

AB = information on excursions and other uses of closed stations provided by A. Brackenbury from his own records and personal experience. Also see his articles on Manchester Ramblers' Excursions (RCHS *Journal*, November 1979) and Race Stations (RCHS *Journal*, November 2007).

Aber = C. Chapman, *The Aber Branch*, Welsh Railways Research Circle, 2002.

Aberdare = E.R. Mountford & RW Kidner, *The Aberdare Railway*, Oakwood, 1995.

Aberdeenshire = G. Stansfield, *Aberdeenshire's Lost Railways*, Stenlake (Ochiltree), 2000.

ANSW = J. Hutton, *Newport Docks & Railway Co.*, Silver Link Publishing, 1996.

Ashover = K.P. Plant, *The Ashover Light Railway*, Oakwood, 1987.

Avon = M. Oakley, *Railways in Avon*, Avon-Anglia, 1986.

Away = A. & E. Jordan, *Away for the Day …*, Silver Link, 1991 [excursions].

Ax Jt = C.W. Judge, *The Axholme Joint Railway*, Oakwood, 1994.

AZ = A. Bevan (editor), *A–Z of Rail Reopenings*, Railway Development Society, 1998. This lists new as well as reopened stations during the last forty or so years. However, it does not distinguish between ceremonial and public dates.

Back Track. Monthly magazine of articles on railway history.

Balerno = D. Shaw, *Balerno Branch and The Caley in Edinburgh*, Oakwood, 1989.

Barry = D.S. Barrie, *The Barry Railway*, Oakwood, 1962. Also see *Glam*.

Basingstoke = D. Robertson & J. Simmons, *The Basingstoke & Alton Light Railway*, Crusader Press, 1988.

Bath & Chelt = *The Bath and Cheltenham Gazette*; **Taunton**.

Bath Chron = The Bath Chronicle; later …. *& Herald;* **Taunton.**

Bell = J.T.W. Bell's series of maps of the great northern coalfield at 2½ inches to the mile (1850s and 1860s); Cambridge University Library, maps 3 to 8; 36; 84 (S. Bragg).

Berkshire = The Berkshire Chronicle; **Reading.**

Berrow's = Berrow's Worcester Journal; **Worcester** (B. Wilson).

BG = P.J. Long & Revd W.V. Awdry, *The Birmingham & Gloucester Railway,* Alan Sutton, 1987.

Bham NS = R. Foster, *Birmingham New Street,* vol.1, Wild Swan, 1990.

Bideford = The Bideford Weekly Gazette, later *Bideford & North Devon Gazette;* **Barnstaple.**

Birkenhead = T.B. Maund, *The Birkenhead Railway,* RCTS, 2001.

Bishops Stortford = P. Paye, *The Bishops Stortford, Dunmow and Braintree Branch,* OPC 1981.

Blackburn = The Blackburn Times (J. Gilmour).

BLN = Branch Line News, issued twice-monthly by the Branch Line Society.

BM = D.S.M. Barrie (revised by R.W. Kidner), *The Brecon & Merthyr Railway,* Oakwood, 1991.

Bolton = J.R. Bardsley, *The Railways of Bolton, 1824–1959,* privately pub, 1960.

Boston = Boston, Stamford & Lincolnshire Herald (part B. Wilson).

BoT = Board of Trade. Still used for some purposes but items previously referenced thus are now '*Rtn*'. See Section 3: Returns to Parliament.

Bourn = J. Rhodes, *Bourn to Essendine,* Boston, 1986.

BR = British Railways
   AR = Anglia Region;
   ER = Eastern Region;
   LMR = London Midland Region;
   NER = North Eastern Region;
   ScR = Scottish Region;
   SR = Scottish Region;
   WR = Western Region.

BR doc = various items (e.g. letters) provided by R. Maund, considerations of space demanding abbreviation.

Brad = Bradshaw's Timetable. For fuller details see under 'Timetables', earlier in this section. Use has been made of those at Newton Abbot, York, the Bodleian Library, Kew and the British Library (especially 1843 and 1844). Some modern reprints are available, all in enlarged form, easier to read. D&C reprinted August 1887, April 1910, July 1922 and July 1938. Peter Kay of Teignmouth has reprinted c October 1841 (*Guide*), July 1845, March 1850 and February 1863 (confined to railway information only).

Brad Sh = Bradshaw's Shareholders' Guide / Railway Manual (title changed in 1860s).

Brad Sh Eng = Engineers' reports from *Brad Sh,* LNW material from J. Gough.

Bragg = S. Bragg, article on *Railway Stations in County Durham,* RCHS Journal, 1981.

Bridport = B.L. Jackson & M.J. Tattershall, *The Bridport Railway,* Oakwood, 1998 edition.

Bridgwater Merc = The Bridgwater Mercury; **Taunton.**

Bridgwater T = The Bridgwater Times; **Taunton.**

Brierley = The Brierley Hill Advertiser (M. Hale).

Brightlingsea = P. Paye, *The Brightlingsea Branch,* John Masters, 1997.

Brill = B. Simpson, *The Brill Tramway,* OPC, 1985.

Bristol E P = The Bristol Evening Post; **Bristol.**

Bristol Merc = The Bristol Mercury; **Bristol.**

Bristol NWR = Bristol New Works Register (R.A. Cooke).

Bristol Stand = The Bristol Standard; **Bristol.**

Bristol T = The Bristol Times & Bath Advocate / Daily Bristol Times / Bristol Times & Mirror; **Bristol.**

Brixham = C.R. Potts, *The Brixham Branch,* Oakwood, 2000.

BT = J.A. Wells, *The Blyth & Tyne Railway,* 3 vols, Northumberland Library, 1989, 1990, 1991.

Bury = J. Wells, *Illustrated History of Railways in and around Bury,* Challenger Robbins, 1995.

Bury & Norwich Post (B. Wilson).

Butlins = P. Scott, *A History of Butlin's Railways,* author, 2001.

By GW = Bob Yate, *By Great Western to Crewe: The Story of the Wellington to Nantwich and Crewe Line,* Oakwood, 2005.

Byles = A. Byles, *History of Monmouthshire Railway & Canal Company,* Village Press, 1982.

C to C = B. Reed, *Crewe to Carlisle,* Ian Allan, 1969.

C/W = correspondence of Col. M. Cobb and G. Webb, transcribed by D.R. Steggles (copy at Newton Abbot), and corrections to Clinker's Register that were in course of assembly by G. Webb at the time of his death. Don Steggles transcribed the latter from very rough notes so only those items that look fairly secure have been used.
In some cases entry is *C/W- another source;* this is where notes give source not presently available to compiler. Where a source given in the notes is available and has been checked, it is used as a direct reference. Some amendments have been made after following up items in e.g. timetables.

Cal = A. Brand, *Caledonian Railway: Index of Lines,* R. Millar (General Manager, Caledonian), 1902. Also available as a reprint (Caledonian Railway Association, 2004), including additional material to 1922.

Cal Cent = Caledonian Railway Centenary, Stephenson Locomotive Society, 1947.

Callander = C.E.J. Fryer, *The Callander & Oban Railway,* Oakwood, 1989.

Cam = R. Christiansen & R.W. Miller, *The Cambrian Railway,* D&C, 2 vols, 1967, undated.

Cam Coast = L. Green, *The Coast Lines of the Cambrian Railway, vol.1,* Wild Swan, 1993.

Camb Ag = J. Carter, article *Cambridge & the Royal Show,* GE Journal 1989, GE Railway Society.

Cambridge = Cambridge Independent.

Camp = N.S.C Macmillan, *The Campbeltown &
Machrihanish Light Railway*, Plateway Press, second
edn, 1993.

Caradon = M. Messenger, *Caradon & Looe: The Canal,
Railway and Mines*, Twelveheads, 1978.

Cardiff = E.R. Mountford, *The Cardiff Railway*,
Oakwood, 1987.

Cardiff & M G = *Cardiff & Merthyr Guardian* (J. Mear).

Cardiff T = *The Cardiff Times* (R.A. Cooke).

Carmarthen = *The Carmarthen Journal* (B. Wilson).

Carnarvon = *The Carnarvonshire & Denbigh Herald*
(M. Lloyd; B. Wilson).

Catterick = A.J. Ludlam, *The Catterick Camp Military
Railway and Richmond Branch*, Oakwood, 1993.

Cawood = K.E. Hartley, *The Cawood, Wistow & Selby
Light Railway*, Turntable 1973.

Chard = *The Chard & Ilminster News*; **Taunton**.

Chelt Chron = *The Cheltenham Chronicle*; **Cheltenham**.

Chelt Exam = *The Cheltenham Examiner*; **Cheltenham**.

Chelt Exp = *The Cheltenham Express*; **Cheltenham**.

Chepstow = *Chepstow Weekly Advertiser*; **Newport**
(B. Wilson, part).

Chron = item from *The Newsletter* of the RCHS
Chronology Group.

Churnet = B. Jeuda, *The Churnet Valley Railway*,
Lightmoor, 1999.

Cl = C.R. Clinker, *Clinker's Register of Closed Passenger
Stations*, Avon-Anglia, 1988 edition.

Cl 29 = list of opening dates, 1929 to mid 1960s,
compiled by C.R. Clinker; original at Brunel
University. Photocopy at Railway Studies Library,
Newton Abbot; also see '*GW H*', below.

Cl corr = manuscript corrections made by Clinker to his
various works, now at Brunel University (R.A. Cooke).

Clay = A.A. Jackson & D.F. Croome, *Rails Through the
Clay*, Allen & Unwin, 1962, [London tube lines].

CLC = P. Bolger, *Illustrated History of The Cheshire Lines
Committee*, Heyday Publishing, 1984.

CLC Portrait = N. Dyckhoff, *Portrait of the Cheshire Lines
Committee*, Ian Allan, 1999.

CMDP = M.R.C. Price, *The Cleobury Mortimer &
Ditton Priors Light Railway*, Oakwood, 1995 edtion.

Co ½ = company's half year report or meeting, mostly
from *The Times* (*co ½ T*).

Co ½ 1110/… = company half-year reports at Kew.

Co n = notice issued by the company owning or
operating the line.

Co tt = company timetable. Company timetables in the
public domain: all *PRO RAIL 981/xxx* –
Liverpool & Manchester *226* et seq.; Newcastle &
Carlisle *364*; Preston & Wyre *410*; Stockton &
Darlington *477* et seq.; Taff Vale *491*. Also South
Devon 1 November 1848 at **Plymouth**.

Cockermouth = R. Western, *The Cockermouth, Keswick &
Penrith Railway*, Oakwood, 2007 (revised edition).

Coghlan = F. Coghlan, *The Iron Book and Railway
Companion to The London & Birmingham*, 'Sixth
Thousand' – probably start of 1839 – quotes Post
Office information for January 1839.

Colliery = *The Colliery Guardian* (R.A. Cooke).

Companies = C. Awdry, *Encyclopaedia of British Railway
Companies*, Patrick Stephens, 1990.

Coniston = R. Western, *The Coniston Railway*, Oakwood,
2007.

Consett = G. Whittle, *The Railways of Consett and
North-West Durham*, D&C 1971.

Cornish & D P = *The Cornish & Devon Post*; **Redruth**.

Cornish Gaz = *The Cornish Gazette*; **Redruth**.

Cornish Guard = *The Cornish Guardian*; **Redruth**.

Cornish T = *The Cornish Times*; **Redruth**.

Cornish Tel = *The Cornish Telegraph*; **Redruth**.

Cornwall = CR Clinker, *The Railways of Cornwall, 1809
– 1963*, D&C, 1963.

Corris = appropriate section of J.I.C. Boyd, *Narrow
Gauge Railways in Mid-Wales*, Oakwood, 1952.

Corris GW = G. Brynant Jones, *Great Western Corris*,
Gomer, 2001 impression.

County Obs = *The County Observer* (Usk); **Newport**.

Course = E. Course, *The Railways of Southern England*,
3 vols, Batsford: *The Main Lines*, 1973; *Secondary and
Branch Lines*, 1974; *Independent and Light Railways*,
1976. [They cover the geographical area from
Southampton to Dover.]

Cowbridge = C. Chapman, *The Cowbridge Railway*,
Oxford Publishing Company, 1984.

Culm V = C.G. Maggs, *The Culm Valley Light Railway…*,
Oakwood, 2006. (Material quoted from *Tiverton*,
1st June)

Cumbria = P.W. Robinson, *Cumbia's Lost Railways*,
Stenlake, 2002.

D&C = David & Charles, publishers, of Newton Abbot.
Some of their books continue to be published by
Atlantic Transport Publishers. If only a number
follows, reference is to a volume in their Regional
Railway History Series:

D&C 1 = D. Thomas, *The West Country*, 1988 edition.

D&C 2 = H.P. White, *Southern England*, 1982 edition.

D&C 3 = H.P. White, *Greater London*, 1987 edition.

D&C 4 = K. Hoole, *The North East*, K Hoole, 1986
edition.

D&C 5 = D.I. Gordon, *The Eastern Counties*, 1990 ed.

D&C 6 = J. Thomas & A.J.S. Patterson,
Scotland: The Lowlands & Borders, 1984 edition.

D&C 7 = R. Christiansen, *The West Midlands*, 1991
edition.

D&C 8 = D. Joy, *South & West Yorkshire*, 1984 edition.

D&C 9 = R. Leleux, *The East Midlands*, 1984 edition.

D&C 10 = G.O. Holt, *The North West*, 1986 edition.

D&C 11 = P.E. Baughan, *North & Mid Wales*, 1991
edition.

D&C 12 = D.S.M. Barrie, *South Wales*, 1980 edition.

D&C 13 = R. Christiansen, *Thames & Severn*, 1981
edition.

D&C 14 = D. Joy, *The Lake Counties*, 1983 edition.

D&C 15 = J. Thomas & D. Turnock, *The North of
Scotland*, 1989 edition.

D&D = G. Daniels & L. Dench, *Passengers No More*,
Ian Allan, 1980 edition.

Darlington = Darlington & Stockton Times (B.Wilson).

Devizes = The Devizes &Wiltshire Gazette; **Trowbridge**.

Dist t supp = supplements to Distance Tables, issued by RCH (mostly R.A. Cooke).

Dock = Docklands Light Railway, Official Hand-book, Capital Transport, 1988.

Dorset = J.H. Lucking, *The Railways of Dorset*, Railway Correspondence &Travel Society, 1968.

Dorset Chron = The Dorset County Chronicle; **Dorchester**.

Drake = J. Drake, *Drake's Road Book of the Grand Junction Railway* (Introduction dated 1 September 1838), reprinted 1974 by Moorland Publishing.

Dudley = NedWilliams, *The Railways of Dudley*, Uralia Press, 1994.

Dumfries = The Dumfries & Galloway Standard (B.Wilson).

Dundee = P. Marshall, *The Railways of Dundee*, Oakwood, 1996. Also see *Newtyle*.

Dunston = E. Manns, *Carrying Coals to Dunston*, Oakwood, 2000.

Durham = A. Maitland, *Durham City and the Railway Age*, University of Durham, 1997 (2nd edition).

E Cos Her = Eastern Counties Herald [Hull].

E D Press = Eastern Daily Press (B.Wilson).

E Lincs = A.J. Ludlam, *The East Lincolnshire Railway*, Oakwood, 1991.

East of T J = J.K. Corstorphine (also publisher), *East of Thornton Junction*, 1995.

EC = Chronology of the Eastern Counties Railway, compiled by B.D.J.Walsh, GE Railway Society, undated.

Ed & Dalk = E.S. Lomax, *A brief historical outline of The Edinburgh & Dalkeith Railway*, typescript, Edinburgh City Library, undated.

Ed Sub = A.A. Maclean, *The Edinburgh Suburban & South Side Railway*, Oakwood, 2006.

Eddowes = Eddowe's Shrewsbury Journal.

EdenV = R.Western, *The Eden Valley Railway*, Oakwood, 1997.

Edin =W.A.C. Smith & P. Anderson, *An Illustrated History of Edinburgh's Railways*, Irwell, 1995.

EG = D. Martin & A.A. Maclean, *Guidebook to the Edinburgh & Glasgow Railway*, Strathkelvin District Library, 1992.

EK = M. Beddall, *The East Kent Light Railway*, author, 1998.

EK- F&G = M. Lawson Finch & S. Garrett, *The East Kent Railway*, two volumes (pages 1–232 in I, 233–472 in II), Oakwood, 2003.

ElyV = C. Chapman, *The Ely Valley Railway*, Oakwood, 2000.

Ewart = item at The Ewart Library, Dumfries (B.Wilson).

Ex to NA = P. Kay, *Exeter to Newton Abbot, a Railway History*, Platform 5, 1993.

Exeter = The Exeter Flying Post – later *Trewman's*; **Exeter** (card index available).

Express & E = The Express & Echo [evening paper]; **Exeter**.

Falkirk Herald (D. Stirling).

Fawley = J.R. Fairman, *The Fawley Branch*, Oakwood, 2002.

Festiniog = J.I.C Boyd, *The Festiniog Railway*, volume 1, Oakwood, 2002 reprint.

Fife =W.S. Bruce, *The Railways of Fife*, Melven Press (Perth), 1980.

Findhorn = I.K. Dawson, *The Findhorn Railway*, Oakwood, 1983.

First = G. Dow, *The First Railway Across the Border*, LNER, 1946.

Foxell = C. Foxell, *The Story of the Metropolitan and Great Central Joint Line*, author, 2001.

Freeling = A. Freeling, author of a number of Guides on early railways published by Whitaker & Co. These consisted of descriptions of lines concerned plus timetables. They are difficult to date since the books were frequently reissued with minor revisions of contents but not of date on title page.

Fur = Furness Railway 150, Cumbrian Railways Association, 1996.

Furness Rise =W. McGowan Gradon, *The Furness Railway, Its Rise and Development, 1846–1923*, J. Collins (Altrincham), 1946.

FYN = A. Blackburn & J. Mackett, *The Freshwater, Yarmouth & Newport Railway*, Forge Books, 1988 edn.

FYN Oakwood = R.J. Maycock & R Silsbury, *The Freshwater,Yarmouth & Newport Railway*, Oakwood, 2003.

G&I = B. Pask, *The Tickets of the Grimsby & Immingham Electric Railway*, Transport Ticket Society, 1999 (includes map and details of stops on street tramway section at Grimsby).

G&S = M.D. Greville & J. Spence, *Closed Passenger Lines of Great Britain 1827–1947*, RCHS, 1974 edition.

Galloway = The Galloway News (B.Wilson).

Garnkirk = The Garnkirk & Glasgow Railway, D. Martin, Strathkelvin District Libraries & Museums, 1981.

Garstang = R.W. Rush & M.R.C. Price, *The Garstang & Knott End Railway*, Oakwood, 1985 edition.

GC = G. Dow, *Great Central*, 3 volumes, Locomotive Publishing Co / Ian Allan, 1959, 1962, 1965.

GC dates = RAIL 1005/273. This contains two lists of GC openings, including ancestors and joint lines. One is a printed chronology dated January 1909; second a typescript version, somewhat expanded and continued to 1915. They appear to have been compiled within the company but no sources are cited; very few discrepancies have been noted where contemporary items are available for checking. Closure dates appear to have been quoted last day of use; they have been accepted as verifying those given in the book in the 'official' style. **In addition to individual stations given this reference, 'GC dates- line' could have been added to many items presently sourced to GC.**

GE = Great Eastern Railway Society *Information Sheet M185, Historical Calendar*, compiled 1985. Also see *EC*, used for lines to 1860.

GJ = N.W. Webster, *Britain's First Trunk Line* [Grand Junction], Adams & Dart, 1972.

Glam = C. Chapman, *The Vale of Glamorgan Railway*, Oakwood, 1998.

Glasgow = W.A.C. Smith & P. Anderson, *An Illustrated History of Glasgow's Railways*, Irwell, 1993.

Glos Chron = *The Gloucestershire Chronicle*; **Gloucester**.

Gloucester J = *The Gloucester Journal*; **Gloucester**.

Glyn = D.L. Davies, revised R.W. Kidner, *The Glyn Valley Tramway*, Oakwood, 1991.

GM's report = General Manager's Report (all GW, from R.A. Cooke).

GN = J. Wrottesley, *The Great Northern Railway*, 3 vols, Batsford 1979/81.

GN Soc = Newsletters and Magazines of the Great Northern Railway Society.

GN/GE = *Great Northern & Great Eastern Joint Railway*, GE Railway Society Journal, Special Issue, October 1982.

GN/LNW = D.L. Franks, *The Great Northern and London & North Western Joint Railway*, Turntable Enterprises, 1974.

GNS = K. Fenwick and others, *Great North of Scotland Railway Stations*, Great North of Scotland Railway Association, 2nd edition, 1997 plus later information supplied by K. Fenwick.

Grev Temp = M.D. Greville, article *Temporary Stations*, RCHS Journal vol.4, no.6, November 1958.

GU = D.L. Thomson & D.E. Sinclair *The Glasgow Subway*, Scottish Tramway Museum Society, 1964.

GSW = *Chronology of The Glasgow & South Western Railway*, Stephenson Locomotive Society, 1950.

GW = E.T. MacDermot, revised C.R. Clinker, *History of The Great Western Railway*, Ian Allan, 2 vols, 1989 reprint. This mostly provides only line dates.

GW ac = circulars issued from GW accountant's office (information supplied by D. Geldard).

GW book = G. Perry (editor), *The Book of the Great Western*, *Sunday Times Magazine*, 1970.

GW Ency = C. Awdry et al, *Encyclopaedia of the Great Western Railway*, Patrick Stephens, 1993.

GW H = C.R. Clinker, *Great Western Railway: A Register of Halts and Platforms, 1903–1979*; Avon-Anglia, 1979. Since this is the more recent work, dates from this list have usually been preferred to those from *Cl-29* (above) in the few cases where there are discrepancies.

GW Mag = *Great Western Railway Magazine*, fair number of copies at Newton Abbot.

Haddington = A.M. Hajducki, *Haddington, Macmerry and Gifford Branch Lines*, Oakwood, 1994.

Hadleigh = P. Paye, *The Hadleigh Branch*, Oakwood, 2006.

Hamilton = *The Hamilton Advertiser* (B. Wilson).

Hants Adv = *The Hampshire Advertiser*; **Winchester**.

Hants Chron = *The Hampshire Chronicle*; **Winchester**.

Hants Teleg = *The Hampshire Telegraph*; **Portsmouth** (partial card index available).

Harrogate = J. Rogers, *The Railways of Harrogate & District*, North Eastern Railway Association, 2000.

Harrow = P.G. Scott, *The London & Birmingham Railway Through Harrow*, London Borough of Harrow, 1983.

Hart = B. Hart, *The Canterbury & Whitstable Railway*, Wild Swan, 1991.

Hartlepool = S. Bragg, article, *The Railways of Hartlepool*, RCHS Journal, vol.27, November 1983.

Hasenson = A. Hasenson, *The History of Dover Harbour*, Aurum Special Editions, 1980.

Hatfield = S. & G. Woodward, *The Hatfield, Luton & Dunstable Railway*, Oakwood, 1994.

Hayling Island Railway, R.G. Harman, Branch Line Hand-books No.18, undated – about 1964?

hb = *(Official) Hand-book of Stations…* (varying additions over the years); published by Airey, and later by the Railway Clearing House (see paragraphs on RCH, earlier in this Section); 1862–1956 editions used.

hba = Appendix to *hb*. The main hand-books and these amendments were often issued at some mid-year point. The dates should only be regarded as a very general guide. There were many late additions and some items were left in for years after they should have been deleted. 1863 on seen, but many gaps in set at Kew.

hbl = amendment leaflet to *hb*, with date or number (mostly from R.A. Cooke). Numbering normally began again at '1' after issue of revised book. These were issued far more frequently than the amendment books, their contents being consolidated into the (usually) roughly yearly amendment books.

Heathfield to Exeter = L.W. Pomeroy, *The Heathfield to Exeter Railway*, Ark, 1995.

Henshaw = A. Henshaw, *GNR in the East Midlands, volume 4*, RCTS.

Herapath = *Railway & Commercial Journal* (LNW half-yearly material from J. Gough); *ZPER* series 3 at Kew; 1836–38 at Newton Abbot; (title varied over the years).

Hereford J = *The Hereford Journal*; **Hereford**.

Hereford T = *Hereford Times* (M. Lloyd).

Hertford = *The Hertford Mercury* (B. Wilson).

High = K. Fenwick, *Highland Railway Station Locations and Dates*, Highland Railway Society, revised edition, 1995.

High Maps = R.A. Cook, *Great North of Scotland and Highland Railway Historical Maps*, RCHS, 1977.

High Pamph = *Chronology of the Highland Railway*, Stephenson Locomotive Society, 1955.

High Val = H.A. Vallance, *The Highland Railway*, House of Lochan (originally published by D&C), 1996 edn.

HMRS = *Journal* of Historical Model Railway Society.

Hosp = D. Voice, *Hospital Tramways and Railways*, 2nd edition, Adam Gordon, 2006; includes maps of all sites described.

Huddersfield = *The Huddersfield Chronicle* (B. Wilson).

Huish List = list of LNW passenger stations and their passenger revenues prepared by Captain Mark Huish at the orders of the Road and Traffic Committees, April 1850. It gives totals for each half-year, the earliest being that ending 30 June 1846. (Copy from H. Jack, from original at the Science Museum).

Hull = The Hull Advertiser (B. Wilson).

Hurst = G. Hurst, *Register of Closed Railways, 1948–1991*, Milepost Publications, Worksop, 1992.

IA = Pregrouping Atlas & Gazetteer, Ian Allan, 1976 (fifth edition).

ILN = A.J. Lambert, *Nineteenth Century Railway History through The Illustrated London News*, D&C, 1984.

Immingham = A.J. Ludlam, *Railways to New Holland*, Oakwood, 1996.

Insp rpt = Inspection Report – usually MT series at Kew.

Intell tt = Intelligible Railway Timetable – some issues for 1858 and 1859 seen.

IoW = O. Smith, *Illustrated History of Isle of Wight Railways, Cowes to Newport*, Irwell Press, 1993.

IoW 1923 = R.J. Maycock & R. Silsbury, *The Isle of Wight Railways From 1923 Onwards*, Oakwood, 2006.

IoW CP = Isle of Wight County Press (T. Cooper).

IoW Obs = Isle of Wight Observer (T. Cooper).

IoW-M&S = R.J. Maycock & R. Silsbury, *The Isle of Wight Railway*, Oakwood, 1999.

Ironmasters = W. McGowan Gradon, *The Track of the Ironmasters: a History of the Cleator & Workington Junction Railway*, original 1952, reissued with extra material by P Robinson by the Cumbrian Railways Association, 2004.

IU = Ian Umpleby – mostly information on excursions and other special uses.

IWC = R.J. Maycock and R. Silsbury, *The Isle of Wight Central*, Oakwood, 2001.

James = L. James, *A Chronology of the Construction of Britain's Railways 1778–1885*, Ian Allan, 1983.

JB = information from ticket collection of late John Britton, photocopies seen by compiler; reference to this means that at least one ticket showed this form of name; other tickets might have shown different forms.

JP Morris = J.P. Morris, *The North Pembroke & Fishguard Railway*, Oakwood, 1969.

JS = Jeoffrey Spence, articles, *Alterations to names of passenger stations*, RCHS Journals, vols 11 on.

KC = items by M. Perrins and D. Anderson in GNR Society's *Great Northern News*, September/October 2002.

Kelvedon = N.J. Stapleton, *The Kelvedon & Tollesbury Light Railway*, Town & Country, 1968 edition.

Kendal Mercury (B. Wilson).

KES = S. Garrett, *The Kent & East Sussex Light Railway*, Oakwood, 1999 edition.

Kingsbridge = K. Williams & D. Reynolds, *The Kingsbridge Branch*, Oakwood, 1997 edition.

Kinross – Kinross-shire Advertiser.

Kirkcud = The Kirkcudbright Advertiser (B. Wilson).

Kittridge = A. Kittridge, *Plymouth, Ocean Liner Port of Call*, Twelveheads, 1993.

L = H.V. Borley, *Chronology of London's Railways*, RCHS, 1982.

Lakeland = H. Bowtell, *Rails Through Lakeland*, Silver Link, 1991 reprint.

Lampeter = M.R.C. Price, *Lampeter, Aberayron & New Quay Light Railway*, Oakwood, 1995.

Lancaster = Lancaster Guardian (R. Bond; C. Holden); **Lancaster**.

Lancaster Gaz = Lancaster Gazette (R. Bond); **Lancaster**.

Lancaster Obs = Lancaster Observer & Morecambe Chronicle (R. Bond); **Lancaster**.

Lancs Chesh = M.D. Greville, *Chronology of the Railways of Lancashire & Cheshire*, RCHS, 1981 edition.

Langport = Langport & Somerton Herald; **Taunton**.

LBSC = J. Howard Turner, *The London, Brighton & South Coast Railway*, 3 vols, Batsford, 1977/8/9.

LCD = A. Gray, *The London Chatham & Dover Railway*, Meresborough Books, 1984.

Lee = C.E. Lee, *Centenary of Bradshaw*, Railway Gazette, 1940; this includes an appendix with some company timetables predating *Bradshaw*.

Lee A/S = C.E. Lee, article, *Anglo-Scottish Railway Centenary*, Railway Magazine, March/April 1948.

Leeds = Leeds Intelligencer.

Leek = B. Jeuda, *The Leek, Caldon & Waterhouses Railway*, N. Staffs Railway Co (1978), 1980.

Leic = A. Moore, *Leicestershire Stations, An Historical Perspective*, Laurel House, 1998.

Leicester Mercury = Leicester Daily Mercury and weekly version of same paper (J. Gough).

Lewin = H.G. Lewin, *Early British Railways, 1801–1844*, Locomotive Publishing Co, undated, and *The Railway Mania & Its Aftermath*, Railway Gazette, 1936.

Linc R & S Merc = The Lincoln, Rutland & Stamford Mercury (B. Wilson).

Little SW Scot = D.L. Smith, *The Little Railways of South-West Scotland*, D&C, 1969.

Liverpool = The Liverpool Mercury (J. Gilmour).

Llantrisant = C. Chapman, *The Llantrisant Branches of the Taff Vale Railway*, Oakwood, 1996.

LM = R.G.H. Thomas, *The Liverpool & Manchester Railway*, Batsford, 1980.

LMS List = Alphabetical List of Passenger and Goods Stations, October 1933, for internal use of staff of LMS; facsimile published by Dragonwheel Books, 2007. [Possible that some entries were for goods use only.]

LMS S Wales = G.B. Jones & D. Dunstone, *The Origins of the LMS in South Wales*, Gomer, 1999.

LNW = M.C. Reed, *The London & North Western Railway*, Atlantic Transport Publications, 1996.

LNW Cl = C.R. Clinker, *LNW Chronology, 1900–1960*, D&C, 1961.

LNW dates = London & North Western Railway: Opening dates of sections and lines, with authority for the same (RAIL 1005/260). This was compiled, retrospectively, by/for the company's audit office. Many entries have abbreviations alongside which show sources (contemporary LNW records), but others, especially before about 1860, do not. It is clear that many early stations were given the line date and distinctions between goods/passenger and formal/public openings were not always made. Consequently this has only been used where a source is cited or where nothing better is available; in the latter case 'no

authority' is added. Where *PCC* is added it refers to
an extract from a Passenger Commercial Circular
added to the book.

LNW Officers = books containing minutes of LNW
Officers' Committee *(RAIL 410/585 and following)*.
At one time these also contained information about
other companies' activities likely to affect LNW.
Where two minute numbers are given, reason is
usually that first gave timetable, including this station,
ready for when line should open, and second gave
opening date, without station detail. Some of
references used are of 'will open first of next month'
variety; since there were also plenty of references to
delays owing to inspection problems and the like, it
seems safe to use these where there was no later
contradiction.

LNW Record = *Record of Opening and Closing Dates;
L&NW Railway (last entry 1915); continued by
London, Midland & Scottish Railway from 1931
(RAIL 1005/289)*. 'Book re-written from Old Book
(collapsed) 1938'. The original started in 1869, with
events originally entered as they occurred, sourced to
company documents. Entries were continued into
the 1950s. A few incongruous items, such as the
closure of the WCP, were included, clearly from
official information. Some pre-1869 items were later
added (none used here). A few do not agree with,
for example, company notices in *The Times*; these
discrepancies were probably the result of copying
errors and no reference is made to them here.

LO = C.E. Box, revised A. Jarvis, *The Liverpool
Overhead Railway*, Ian Allan, 1984.

Lochalsh = D. McConnell, *Rails to the Kyle of Lochalsh*,
Oakwood, 1997.

London Local = A.A. Jackson, *London Local Railways*,
D&C, 1978.

London's Termini = A.A. Jackson, *London's Termini*,
D&C, 1985 edition.

Looe = J.M. Tolson, G.F. Rouse & C.F.D. Whetmath,
The Railways of Looe & Caradon, Forge Publishing,
1974.

Loop = A.J. Ludlam, *The Lincolnshire Loop Line*,
Oakwood, 1995.

Lost Railways of East Yorkshire = P.G. Mason,
Lost Railways of East Yorkshire, Driffield, Wolds
Publications, second edition 1992.

Louth = A.J. Ludlam, *The Louth, Mablethorpe &
Willoughby Loop*, Oakwood, 1997.

LPJ = M.D. Greville & G.O. Holt, *The Lancaster &
Preston Junction Railway*, D&C, 1961.

LSW = R.A. Williams, *The London & South Western
Railway*, D&C vol.I 1968, vol.II 1973, vol.III (with
J.N. Faulkner) 1988.

LT = G.D. Beecroft et al, *London Transport Railways
Hand-book*, Foxley Press, 1983.

LTS = P. Kay, *The London, Tilbury & Southend* Railway,
author, 2 vols 1996, 1997.

LY = J. Marshall, *The Lancashire & Yorkshire Railway*,
vols I and II, D&C, 1969, 1970.

Lynton = G.A. Brown, J.D.C. Prideaux & H.G. Radcliffe,
The Lynton & Barnstaple Railway, D&C, 1971.

Macclesfield = *Macclesfield Courier & Herald*;
Macclesfield Library (E. Bredee).

Maenclochog = J. Gale, *The Maenclochog Railway*,
author, 1992.

Maesteg = C. Smith, *Maesteg Railway Tunnel (The
Explosion of 1876)*, Port Talbot Historical Society, 1998.

Manch G = *The Manchester Guardian* (E. Bredee unless
otherwise attributed)

Manchester = *The Manchester Courier* (J. Gilmour;
E. Bredee).

Manifold = (many authors), *North Staffordshire Railway*,
Henstock of Ashbourne, 1992.

Market Drayton = C.R. Lester, *The Stoke to Market
Drayton Line*, Oakwood, 2001.

Marlborough = *The Marlborough Times* (various
additions to name); **Trowbridge**.

Marx = Klaus Marx, *The Wainwright P Tanks*, Runpast,
1990.

Mawddwy Railway = L. Cozens, R.W. Kidner & B. Poole,
The Mawddwy Van & Kerry Branches, Oakwood, 2004.

MC = H. & M. Jackson, *The Maryport & Carlisle
Railway*, Hirst-Jackson, 1979.

Melbourne = A. Cooper, P. Leggett & C. Sprenger,
The Melbourne Military Railway, Oakwood, 1990.

Merioneth = *Merionethshire Herald* [later *Standard*];
Colindale.

Merlin = *The Monmouthshire Merlin*; **Newport**
(part B. Wilson).

Metro = *Manchester Metro News* (E. Bredee).

MGN = J. Wrottesley, *The Midland and Great Northern
Railway*, D&C, second edition, 1981.

MGN Circ Bulltn = Bulletin of the Group set up to
research into MGN history.

Mid = J.V. Gough, *The Midland Railway – A Chronology*,
RCHS, 1989. Items sourced to *(Mid)* are ones that
Dr Gough, who has kindly provided the compiler
with his sources, has validated from the local press
and company documents, including timetables and
working timetables and supplements which explicitly
state that station X will be opened/closed/renamed
on such a date. Where the information has been
inferred from a timetable, it is 'co tt/wtt *(Mid)*';
after Grouping this will refer to LMS timetables.
After Nationalisation the reference will simply be 'tt
(Mid)', unless *Bradshaw* is involved. *Mid* is also used
for material not in the published book but supplied
directly to the compiler by Dr Gough.

Milford = J.S. Holden, *The Manchester & Milford
Railway*, Oakwood, 2007 – second edition.

Millwall = articles by R. Green, *Millwall Junction* and
Millwall Extension Railway, GE Journals, April 2003
and October 2005.

Mining = *The Mining Journal* (R.A. Cooke).

Minor = R.W. Kidner, *Minor Standard Gauge Railways*,
Oakwood, 1981.

MK = D. Martin, *The Monkland & Kirkintilloch
Railway*, Strathkelvin District Library, 1995.

Moffat = H. Moffat, *East Anglia's First Railways*,
  T. Dalton (Lavenham), 1987.
Morecambe = D Binns, *Midland Lines Around
  Morecambe*, Trackside, 1995.
Mountford = C.E. Mountford, *The Private Railways of
  County Durham*, Industrial Railway Society, 2004.
  Very detailed survey, with generous provision of
  sketch-maps, of the many private railways built
  mostly to serve coal mines; emphasis obviously on
  industrial matters but information is given about
  known passenger services.
MSJA = F. Dixon, *The Manchester, South Junction &
  Altrincham Railway*, Oakwood, 1994 edition.
MSWJ = C.G. Maggs, *The Midland & South Western
  Junction Railway*, D&C, 1980 edition.
MT references will be from the report of an inspecting
  officer prior to opening or from an accident report,
  at Kew.
Murray = *Murray's Scottish Timetables*, Glasgow –
  scattering of issues seen.
Murray 1948 = British Rail Scottish timetable printed
  by Murray.
N Berwick = A. Hajducki, *The North Berwick & Gullane
  Branch Lines*, Oakwood, 1992.
N Devon = *The North Devon Journal*; **Barnstaple**.
N Wilts = *The North Wiltshire Herald*; **Trowbridge**.
NA = National Archives, previously Public Record Office.
N&B Gomer = G. Brynant Jones, D. Dunstone &
  T. Watkins, *The Neath & Brecon Railway: a History*,
  Gomer, 2005.
NB = J. Thomas, *The North British Railway*, D&C,
  2 volumes, 1969 and 1975.
NC = G. Whittle, *The Newcastle & Carlisle Railway*,
  D&C, 1979.
NC Fawcett = Bill Fawcett, *A History of the Newcastle &
  Carlisle Railway*, North Eastern Railway Association,
  2008.
NC MacLean = J.S. MacLean, *The Newcastle & Carlisle
  Railway*, Robinson, 1948.
NE = W.W. Tomlinson, *The North Eastern Railway*,
  D&C, 1987 reprint.
NE Express = *North Eastern Express*, Journal of the
  North Eastern Railway Association.
NE Hoole = K. Hoole, *Railway Stations of the North East*,
  D&C, 1985.
NE maps = R.A. Cook and K. Hoole, *North Eastern
  Railway Historical Maps*, RCHS, 1991, revised edn.
Neele = G.P. Neele (LNW Superintendent), *Railway
  Reminiscences*, McCorquodale, 1904.
Nelson = C. Chapman, *The Nelson and Ynysybwl
  Branches of The Taff Vale Railway*, Oakwood, 1997.
Nene = J. Rhodes, *The Nene Valley Railway*, Turntable,
  1983, 2nd edition.
NER I = C. Fraser (editor), *North Eastern Record*,
  volume I, The Historical Model Railway Society, 1988.
New Holland = A.J. Ludlam, *Railways to New Holland
  and the Humber Ferries*, Oakwood, 1996.
Newark = M.A. Vanns, *The Railways of Newark-on-Trent*,
  Oakwood, 1999.

Newcastle = J. Addiman & B. Fawcett, *The High Level
  Bridge and Newcastle Central Station*, 150th
  Anniversary Committtee, 1999.
Newmarket = *Newmarket Journal* (B. Wilson).
Newport = *The Newport Gazette*; **Newport, S Wales**.
Newquay = *The Newquay Express*; **Redruth**.
Newtyle = N. Ferguson, *The Dundee & Newtyle Railway*,
  Oakwood, 1995. Also see *Dundee*.
NGMW = J.C. Boyd, *The Narrow Gauge Railways of
  Mid-Wales*, Oakwood, 1952.
NGNC = J.C. Boyd, *The Narrow Gauge Railways of
  North Caernarvonshire*, Oakwood, 2 vols, 1972, 1994.
NGSC = J.C. Boyd, *Narrow Gauge Railways of South
  Caernarvonshire*, Oakwood, single volume edn 1972.
NGSC 2 = volume 2 of enlarged version of the above,
  Oakwood, 2000.
Nhumb = J.A. Wells, *The Railways of Northumberland &
  Newcastle-on-Tyne*, Powdene Publicity, 1998.
Nhumb Young = A. Young, *Railways in Northumberland*,
  Martin Bairstow, 2003.
Nidd = D.J. Croft, *The Nidd Valley Light Railway*,
  Oakwood, 1987 edition.
NL = *The North London Railway, a Pictorial Record*,
  National Railway Museum York / HMSO, 1979.
NLRHS = North London Railway Historical Society.
Norfolk = G. Dow, *The First Railway in Norfolk*, LNER,
  1947 (2nd edition).
Norfolk & S = R.S. Joby, *The Norfolk & Suffolk Joint
  Railways Committee*, Klafron (Norwich), undated
  (1975?).
NS = R. Christiansen & R.W. Miller, *The North
  Staffordshire Railway*, D&C, 1971.
NS-K = B. Jeuda, *The Knotty* [Illustrated History of the
  NS], Lightmoor, 1996.
Oldham E P = *The Oldham Evening Post* (J. Gilmour).
Oldham E Stand = *The Oldham Evening Standard*
  (J. Gilmour).
Ormskirk = *The Ormskirk Advertiser* (J. Gilmour).
Oswestry = *The Oswestry Advertiser* (B. Wilson).
Ox & Camb = B Simpson, *Oxford to Cambridge
  Railway*, 2 vols, OPC, 1981, 1983.
Oxford Chron = *The Oxford Chronicle*; **Oxford**.
Oxford Mail = *The Oxford Mail*; **Oxford**.
Parry = *Parry's Railway Companion from Chester to
  Holyhead*, 1848.
Peebles = P. Marshall, *Peebles Railways*, Oakwood, 2005
Pembroke = M.R.C. Price, *The Pembroke & Tenby
  Railway*, Oakwood, 1986.
Penzance = *The Penzance Gazette*; **Redruth**.
Pigeon = R. Pigeon, article in *The True Line*, January
  2004.
Plymouth = *Plymouth & Devonport Weekly Journal*
  [various additions to title]; **Plymouth**.
Poole = paper that was at various times *Poole &
  Dorsetshire Herald* / *& South West Herald* / *&
  Bournemouth Herald* / *& East Dorset Herald*; **Poole**.
Pontypool = *Pontypool Free Press*; **Newport**.
Portfolio = E.W. Fenton, *A Portfolio of Railway Notices*,
  Holland Press, 1964.

Portland = M. Smith, *The Railways of the Isle of Portland*, Irwell, 1997.

Potter = G.W.J. Potter, *History of The Whitby & Pickering Railway*, Locomotive Publishing, 1906.

PP = Parliamentary Papers (House of Lords Record Office). Mostly found via references in *Robertson*. For this book simplified references are used:

PP 1 = (222) X, Select Committee to inquire into State of Communications by Railway, Appendices 20–26 (1839). This includes a fairly comprehensive set of returns for period January 1838 to April 1839, inclusive.

PP 2 = (151) XXX, Returns of Amount of Duty paid by Railway Companies 1832–42 (1843). All figures relate to year ending 5 January; years quoted here are preceding ones – i.e. 1842 for year ending 5 January 1843.

PP 3 = (687) XIV Select Committee on Insertion of Conditions in Railway Acts to promote Interests of Public, Second Report, Appendices 13, 14 (1846).

Pratt = Derek Pratt, notes on Alan Godfrey Corwen and Dolgellau OS reprints.

Preston G = *The Preston Guardian* (J. Gilmour).

Preston P = *The Preston Pilot* (J. Gilmour).

PRO = Public Record Office (now the National Archives). Items previously given this reference are now shown as *RCG; RAIL …; MT …. See individual entries in this list.*

PSUL = *Passenger Train Services over Unusual Lines*, Branch Line Society, various years.

R Cornwall Gaz = *The Royal Cornwall Gazette*; **Redruth**.

RAC = R.A. Cooke: *Atlas of the Great Western Railway*, revised edition, Wild Swan, 1997 or items directly from his research.

Race = items provided by J. Tolson from his unpublished study on the influence of railways on the racing industry.

RAIL = item at Kew catalogued as *RAIL …* e.g. *RAIL 393/151* is a collection of LNE internal instructions. *RAIL 1005/265* = job lot dealing with opening dates of lines eventually part of LMS which seems to have been prepared in answer to questions from H.G. Lewin; only used where it gives company minutes or engineers' reports as source. The first 770 odd deal with individual companies; higher numbers more general information.

Ramsey = J. Rhodes, *Branch Lines to Ramsey*, Oakwood, 1986.

Raven = W.J.K. Davies, *The Ravenglass & Eskdale Railway*, D&C, 1968.

Reading = *The Reading Mercury*; **Reading.**

RCG = list of station openings, closures and renamings compiled from the Minutes of the Railway Clearing House Goods Managers' and Superintendents' Conferences. At Kew it is catalogued as *RAIL 1005/280*. It is a manuscript list, photocopies of which are available at York and Newton Abbot. 'RCG' means that the exact date is given. 'RCG ref' means that a more general reference is made; sometimes this type of entry looks like a catching up

exercise in which stations which other records show to have opened individually are here given in one batch; in any case, such entries were only made in January, April, July and October. Whilst it is a useful record, it has to be said that some of the dates given do not tally with information from local sources.

RCH = Railway Clearing House. Many publications – maps, Hand-book of Stations, lists of amendments to names, closures, opening dates. See *hb* and *hba* above and paragraphs on the RCH earlier in this section.

RCHS = Railway & Canal Historical Society.

RCHS Jour = Journal of the above.

Reid = *Reid's Monthly Timetable of the York, Newcastle, & Berwick Railway*, April 1849 (first issue, 1925 facsimile). Later was *Reid's Railway Guide*, covering the north-east.

RHD = W.J.K. Davies, *The Romney, Hythe & Dymchurch Railway*, Oakwood, 1988 edition.

Rhy = R.W. Kidner, *The Rhymney Railway*, Oakwood, 1995.

Rly Chron = *Railway Chronicle* (half-yearly report material from J. Gough).

Rly Gaz = *Railway Gazette*, various issues.

Rly Obs = *Railway Observer*, various issues.

Rly Times = *Railway Times* (half-yearly report material from J. Gough).

Rly World = *Railway World*, various issues.

RM = *Railway Magazine*: various issues (set at Newton Abbot). Most entries come from sections on 'What the Railways are doing', later 'Notes and News', most recently the regular lists of line updates. Please note that in the 1940s, the Magazine was issued every other month; an issue dated 'March and April' is given the reference *RM March*.

Robertson = C.J.A. Robertson, *Origins of the Scottish Railway System*, John Donald, 1983.

Robinson = *Robinson's Railway Guide/Timetable*, scattering of issues seen.

Ross = *The Ross Gazette*; **Hereford**.

Rounthwaite = T.E. Rounthwaite, *Ironstone Mines and Railways of Cleveland and Rosedale* (originally articles in *Railway Observer*, reprinted 1997 as book in *Industrial Archaeology of Cleveland* series).

Return/Rtn = Return to Parliament; see 'Returns to Parliament' in Section 3 for details – series RAIL 1053, Kew.

RtnT PP = Returns for July 1845 to June 1847 *(PP (937) LXIII, Return of Passenger and Goods Traffic …)*, House of Lords Record Office.

Rutland = *Railways of Rutland*, Rutland Local History Society, vol.3, 1980.

Ryde = R.J. Maycock & R. Silsbury, *The Piers, Tramways and Railways at Ryde*, Oakwood, 2005.

Rye & C = C. Judge, *The Rye & Camber Tramway*, Oakwood, 1995.

Ryedale = P. Howat, *The Railways of Ryedale*, Nelson, 1988.

S&D = P.J. Holmes, *Stockton & Darlington Railway 1825–1975*, First Avenue Publishing, Ayr, 1976.

S&D Pass = P. Holmes, *Stockton & Darlington Passenger Traffic*, author, 2000.

S Halts = R.W. Kidner, *Southern Railway Halts*, Oakwood, 1985.

S Spec = D.W. Winkworth, *Southern Special Traffic*, Irwell, 2000.

S Wales = *The South Wales Daily News* (R.A. Cooke).

S Yorks Joint = B.H. Elliott, *The South Yorkshire Joint Railway and the Coalfield*, Oakwood, 2002 edition.

Salisbury = *The Salisbury & Winchester Journal*; **Trowbridge**.

Scarborough = *The Scarborough Gazette* (B. Wilson).

Scot Cent = P. Marshall, *The Scottish Central Railway*, Oakwood, 1998.

Scott = *Scott's Railway Companion to The Newcastle & Carlisle Railway*. Dated 1837, probably for start of year but perhaps containing material of different dates.

SD Jt = R. Atthill, *The Somerset & Dorset Joint Railway*, Pan/D&C, 1970 edition.

SE = A. Gray, *The South Eastern Railway*, Middleton Press, 1990.

SEC = A. Gray, *The South Eastern & Chatham Railway*, Middleton, 1998.

Selkirk = *The Southern Reporter, Selkirk, Borders …*

Settle = timetable and note published by Settle – Carlisle Joint Action Committee Ltd, 2 July 1986 (information supplied by A. Brackenbury).

Sewell = G.W.M. Sewell, *The North British Railway in Northumberland*, Merlin, 1993 reprint.

Shepton = *The Shepton Mallet Journal*; **Taunton**.

Sherborne = *The Sherborne & Yeovil Mercury* (ancestor of *The Western Gazette*); **Taunton**. This and some of its successors are also available at a number of other Local Studies Libraries in the West of England.

Shrewsbury = *The Shrewsbury Chronicle* (B. Wilson).

Sidmouth = *The Sidmouth Observer & Visitors' List*; **Exeter**.

Sig inst = signalling instructions (B. Wilson) – gave details of changes such as new stations.

SIT = C.E. Lee, *The Swansea & Mumbles Railway*, Oakwood, 1988.

Skegness = A.J. Ludlam, *Railways to Skegnesss*, Oakwood, 1997.

SLS Jour = *The Journal of the Stephenson Locomotive Society*.

SMJ = J.M. Dunn, *The Stratford & Midland Junction Railway*, Oakwood, revised edition, undated (first published 1952).

SMJ Jordan = A. Jordan, *The Stratford & Midland Junction Railway*, OPC, 1982.

SMJ Riley = R.C. Riley & B. Simpson, *The Stratford & Midland Junction Railway*, Lamplight, 1999.

Sol J = S. Edgar & J.M. Sinton, *The Solway Junction Railway*, Oakwood Press 1990.

Som & W J = *The Somerset & Wilts Journal* (Frome based); **Taunton**.

Som Gaz = *The Somerset County Gazette*; **Taunton**.

Som Guard = *The Somerset Guardian & Radstock Observer*; **Taunton**.

Som H = *The Somerset County Herald*; **Taunton**.

Som Stand = *The Somerset Standard* (Frome area); **Taunton**.

Somerset = M. Oakley, *Somerset Railway Stations*, Dovecote, 1992.

Southport G = *The Southport Guardian* (J. Gilmour).

Southport Vis = *The Southport Visiter* [*sic*]; (J. Gilmour).

SR = R.H. Clark, *A Southern Region Chronology and Record, 1803–1965* (and appendix), Oakwood, 1964 (and 1975). Only used if more specific work not available – see *LBSC, LCD, SE*.

SRO = items derived from Scottish Record Office; all provided by people listed in the acknowledgements.

SS = N.T. Sinclair and I..S Carr, *The Railways of South Shields*, Tyne & Wear Museums, 1990.

Stamford = *The Stamford Mercury* (B. Wilson).

Stockport = *The Stockport Advertiser*; **Stockport and Manchester Central Libraries** (E. Bredee).

Stratford = *Stratford-upon-Avon Herald*; **Stratford-upon-Avon**.

Stroud J = *The Stroud Journal*; **Stroud**.

Stroud N = *The Stroud News*; **Stroud**.

SU = Bob Yate, *The Shropshire Union Railway*, Oakwood, 2003.

Surrey = A.A. Jackson, *The Railway in Surrey*, Atlantic, 1999.

Sweeney = D.J. Sweeney, *A Lancashire Triangle*, Triangle, 1996.

Swindon = *The Swindon Advertiser*; **Trowbridge**.

SY = D.L. Franks, *South Yorkshire Railway*, Turntable Enterprises, Leeds, 1971.

T = *The Times*; **Taunton Local Studies** (index available) – until early 2002 was at Bridgwater.

Talerddig = G. Briwant Jones, *Railways through Talerddig*, Gomer Press, 1992 impression.

Taunton = *The Taunton Courier*; **Taunton**.

Tavistock = *The Tavistock Gazette*; **Plymouth**.

Tayside = W.A.C. Smith & P. Anderson, *Illustrated History of Tayside's Railways*, Irwell, 1997.

Tenbury = K. Beddoes & W.H. Smith, *The Tenbury & Bewdley Railway*, Wild Swan, 1995.

Tewkesbury = *The Tewkesbury Register*; **Gloucester**.

Thames Haven = P. Kay, *The Thames Haven Railway*, author, 1999.

The Cambrian = newspaper of that name (P.R. Reynolds – some material direct, some via RCHS Chronology Group *Newsletter*).

Tiverton = *The Tiverton Gazette*; **Exeter** and **Tiverton Community College**.

Topham = *Topham's Patented Railway Timetables*. May 1848 to March 1850 seen (Bodleian); May 1848 to April 1849 are also at the British Library.

Torquay Dir = *The Torquay & Tor Directory*, later *The Torquay Directory & South Devon Journal*; **Torquay**.

Torquay T = *The Torquay Times*; **Torquay**.

Totnes = *The Totnes Times & Devon News*; **Exeter**.

Trains Illustrated, various issues.

Trewman = *Trewman's Exeter Flying Post*; **Exeter** (card index available).

Trowbridge = The Trowbridge Chronicle; **Trowbridge**.

True Line = The True Line, Magazine of Caledonian
Railway Association.

TTS = Journal of the Transport Ticket Society
(via D. Geldard).

Tuck = Tuck's Railway Shareholders Manual.

Tuck tt = Every Travellers Guide to the Railways, (only one
seen 1843, probably June).

TV = D.S.M. Barrie, *The Taff Vale Railway,* Oakwood,
1969 reprint.

Tyneside = A. Young, *The Suburban Railways of Tyneside,*
Martin Bairstow, 1999.

U = G. Croughton, R.W. Kidner & A. Young, *Private
and Untimetabled Railway Stations,* Oakwood, 1982.

Ug = D. Rose, *The London Underground: a Diagrammatic
History,* author, 1999 edition.

Van = L. Cozens, *Van and Kerry Railways,* author, 1953.

VoR = C.C. Green, *The Vale of Rheidol Railway,*
Wild Swan. 1986.

W Briton = The West Briton (Truro); **Redruth**.

W D Merc = The Western Daily Mercury; **Plymouth**.

W D Press = The Western Daily Press; **Bristol**.

W Fife = A.W. Brotchie & Harry Jack, *Early Railways of
West Fife,* Stenlake, undated (2007?).

W Fly P = The Western Flying Post (various additions
over the years); ancestor of *W Gaz;* **Taunton**.

W Gaz = The Western Gazette (Yeovil), various additions
to title in early days; Yeovil edition unless specified;
Taunton. Some editions only available at the County
Record Office, Obridge Road, Taunton.

W High = The Story of the West Highland, LNER, 1944.

W Lancs = J.E. Cotterall, *The West Lancashire Railway,*
Oakwood, 1982.

W Mid = C.R. Clinker, *The Railways of the West
Midlands, a Chronology 1808–1954,* Stephenson
Locomotive Society, introduction dated 1954.

W Morn News = Western Morning News; **Plymouth**.

W Som F P = The West Somerset Free Press, published at
Williton; **Taunton**.

*W Sussex = Going off the Rails: the Country Railway in
West Sussex,* West Sussex County Record Office, 1997.

Wales = H. Williams, *The Railways of Wales,* C. Davies
(Swansea), 1981.

Waterloo Times, Merseyside (J. Gilmour).

WCP = C.G. Maggs, *The Weston, Clevedon & Portishead
Light Railway,* Oakwood, 1990 edition.

Wellington = The Wellington Weekly News (originally
Corner's); **Taunton**.

Wells = The Wells Journal; **Taunton**.

Welshman = The Welshman (B. Wilson).

Wemyss = A.W. Brotchie, *The Wemyss Private Railway,*
Oakwood, 1998.

Wenlock = K. Jones, *The Wenlock Branch,* Oakwood, 1998.

Western Mail (The); **Plymouth**.

Westmorland = Westmorland Gazette & Kendal Advertiser
(B. Wilson).

Weston = The Weston Mercury; **Weston-super-Mare**.

*Weymouth = The Weymouth ,Portland & Dorchester
Telegram;* **Dorchester**.

Weymouth branch = V. Mitchell & K. Smith, *Branch Lines
in and around Weymouth,* Middleton, 1998 reprint.

WHH = Welsh Highland Heritage (newsletter of Welsh
Highland Heritage Group, via R. Maund).

Whishaw = F. Whishaw, *The Railways of Great Britain &
Ireland (1842),* 1969 reprint, Augustus M. Kelley,
New York. This was a contemporary description of
many of the early railways, mostly derived from
personal inspection – or so the author claimed.

Whitby = M. Bairstow, *Railways Around Whitby,* author,
2 volumes, 1989 (revised 1998) and 1996.

Whitchurch = The Whitchurch Herald (B. Wilson).

Whitland = M.R.C. Price, *The Whitland & Cardigan
Railway,* Oakwood, 1990 edition.

Wigan Examiner (part E. Bredee).

Wigan Observer (E. Bredee; J. Gilmour).

Wilts = The Wiltshire Independent (Devizes);
Trowbridge.

Wilts & Glos = The Wiltshire & Gloucestershire Standard;
Cirencester.

Wisbech = The Wisbech Advertiser (B. Wilson).

WL = J.B. Atkinson, *The West London Joint Railways,*
Ian Allan, 1984.

WMCQ = J.C. Boyd, *The Wrexham, Mold & Connah's
Quay Railway,* Oakwood, 1991.

Wolfe = C.S. Wolfe, *Historical Guide to the Romney, Hythe
& Dymchurch Railway,* RH&DR Association, 1976.

Wolverhampton = The Wolverhampton Chronicle
(M. Hale).

Woolmer = Woolmer's Exeter & Plymouth Gazette;
Exeter.

Worcester = The Worcester Herald (B. Wilson).

Wrexham = The Wrexham Advertiser (B. Wilson).

WSM = R. Sellick, *The West Somerset Mineral Railway,*
D&C, 1970 edition.

Wtt = working timetable – will always be one appropriate
to relevant company/BR Region; date given is when
came into force.

Wtt supp = supplement to above – these often gave
details of new station openings.

WW II = World War II Railway Study Group, *Bulletin,*
July & August 1997.

Wye = B. Handley & R. Dingwall, *The Wye Valley
Railway,* Oakwood, 1998.

*Wyld = Wyld's Guides to the London & Birmingham and
Liverpool & Manchester Railways.*

York = The York Courant (B. Wilson).

Yorks Gaz = The Yorkshire Gazette (B. Wilson).

Finally, mention has to be made of R.V. J. Butt's
Directory of Railway Stations, Patrick Stephens, 1995
(when part of the Haynes Group). This has many basic
faults. No means are provided for dealing with the
vagaries of early contractors' services; the author seemed
to be unaware of the lack of evidence for the earliest
services of many lines and simply assigned the line
opening date to all stations, when the reality is that
many opened later. Overall, the errors, omissions and
other inadequacies run into the thousands. It should be

added that his work covered ground not covered here, on Ireland, preservation lines and the like; comparison with *Johnson's Atlas & Gazetteer of the Railways of Ireland*, Midland Publishing, 1997 and *Ireland*, J.W.P. Rowledge, Atlantic Publishing, 1995 (issued as volume 16 of the D&C Regional History series) suggests even less accuracy there. Butt's book was used at an early stage to check dates given here and some corrections were made after reference to other sources; nothing, for obvious reasons, has been directly derived from it.

ATLASES

By far the best to use in conjunction with this work is Col. M. Cobb's, *The Railways of Great Britain, A Historical* Atlas, Ian Allan, 2003; except for a very few instances it includes all the regular stations listed in this book, shown on an outline of the one-inch Ordnance Survey. However, its lavish nature means that its availability might be limited (unlikely to be kept in print?), though a second, revised, edition has since been published (dated 2006 but issued in 2007); on balance it seems best to keep references in this book to the *Pre-Grouping Atlas* (see below).

Ian Allan have published a series of atlases, all using the same reference grid, but with some variation in enlargements provided. The scale used is such that all are cramped. They show the system at 1904 (reprint in book form of the Railway Clearing House map for that year), *Pre-Grouping Atlas*, (1922, based on Clearing House maps), 1947, 1955, 1965 and 1967; *Complete Atlas of Railway Station Names*, compiled by Tony Dewick, 2002 (here the ludicrous continued use of the same scale means that some areas are very difficult, even impossible, to disentangle); *Atlas of Train Operating Companies*, 2000; *Rail Atlas, 1890* (Tony Dewick); 2005. They have also produced, in book form: a reprint of Clearing House map of London of 1935; and *London Railway Atlas* (covering whole history) by J. Brown, 2005. They have begun a series designed to bring together all the factual material about railways in a particular area. The first two to be issued cover Norfolk & Suffolk and Kent & Sussex. Unfortunately in the first one there are very many discrepancies between the information given in the historical and map sections and that in the index and gazetteer; the second has fewer errors of this sort but is far from perfect.

S.K. Baker, *Rail Atlas of Great Britain & Ireland*, OPC / Ian Allan, shows the present position and is regularly re-issued in revised editions (most recent, 11th, 2007).

M.G. Ball, *British Railways Atlas*, Ian Allan, provides a pocket-sized version of the present system; it would seem to be the intention to revise and re-issue this regularly.

Thomas Cook's *Rail Map, Britain & Ireland*, gives full details of operating companies; fourth edition, 2005.

What is assumed to be the first of a series is: A. Mackintosh (editor), *As They Were, Book I, Southern England*, Offington Press, 2002. This is a reproduction of one-inch OS maps, designed to show railway system as it was in 1950s. This volume covers area south of line from Bristol to London.

R.A. Cooke, *Atlas of the Great Western Railway*, Wild Swan, revised edition 1997. This is centred on 1947 but does show stations closed before that time and added since; it covers the Great Western in its widest sense, including 1922–3 amalgamations. It is very accurate and detailed and it is unfortunate that no comparable works have been produced for other companies.

J. Jowett, *Railway Atlas*, Patrick Stephens, 1989. This is based on Railway Clearing House maps. It provides far more detail than the Ian Allan atlas listed in Section 4 but is no longer in print. The complex underlining used can be ignored by those who simply want to locate stations. Also *Jowett's Railway Centres*, vol.I, Patrick Stephens, 1993; *Jowett's Nationalised Railway Atlas*, Atlantic, 2000.

C.J. Wignall, *Complete British Railways Maps and Gazetteer 1825–1985*, OPC, revised edition 1985. Claims to include all lines and stations but there are many inaccuracies even in this revised edition.

Midland Railway System Maps (The Distance Diagrams) have been reprinted in 6 volumes, including an index and gradient diagrams, by the Cumbrian Railways Association (vol.1) and P. Kay (rest). They show the Midland Railway in great detail just before Grouping.

Table of Distances for the London, Brighton & South Coast Railway, January 1901, was reprinted by Ian Allan, no date given for reprint.

A very detailed National Series of Waterway, Tramway and Railway Atlases, photocopied and frequently revised was produced by G.L. Crowther of 224 South Meadow Lane, Preston, PR1 8JP. The various sections possess their own indexes but there is no overall national index.

North Eastern Railway Atlas 1922, S. Bragg, Industrialogical Associates, dated 2005, gives a very detailed picture of the North Eastern in its last independent year. An earlier work, *North Eastern Lines and Stations*, compiled by S. Bragg & E. Scarlett, North Eastern Railway Association, 1999, is essentially a list showing the lines and stations of the North Eastern at the end of 1922; some diagrams are also included.

The information obtained

Opening dates

The dates quoted are intended to be those when the station was first used by the ordinary fare-paying public, even if only a reduced (e.g. afternoon only) service ran that first day. Often there were also earlier ceremonial ('formal') occasions, when directors, chosen friends and local dignitaries travelled over the line. Quite a lot of these formal events are quoted in print as the public dates since contemporaries often cited only these. Indeed, this is one of the constants of railway history: *Bradshaw's Shareholders' Manual*, newspapers of all eras, and secondary sources, have all done this. Even today magazines devoted to railway matters often still fail to clarify the full significance of the dates they give. Many such errors have been corrected but some will have survived, especially in areas reliant on secondary sources.

Sunday dates can cause problems. Some Sunday opening dates have been copied from book to book down the years for stations, that as far as is known, never had a Sunday service. This has mostly, but not exclusively, occurred in cases where a first of the month was a Sunday. Some have been found and corrected; again, others probably still lurk. More difficult are cases where the station did have a Sunday service. Initially, there was much Victorian heart-searching, especially in Scotland, about Sunday train services so there would have been a reluctance to open lines on the Sabbath, with the accompanying celebrations. The policy followed has been to quote 'accepted' dates up to 1850, adding a note to the effect that it was a Sunday. After 1850, no comment has been added. The vast majority of stations affected were opened on the first day of a month and were additions to existing lines so that operationally it would have made sense to open them with the new timetable rather than wait a day. Primary evidence can be quoted in support of some of these openings. Some were perhaps held back but rather than add a lot of notes likely to turn out eventually to be unnecessary, it seems best to leave alone for the moment.

Whilst normally preference has been given to primary evidence, an exception has been made in the coverage of the Highland and Great North of Scotland Railways. The Societies devoted to the study of the histories of these companies have published lists where sources have been given for all items, the overwhelming majority of them from the local press. Whilst it would often have been possible to give *Times* references for these, at least as far as line openings are concerned, it would clearly have been perverse to do so. Many secondary works do give sources for at least some of their information, but none does so as comprehensively or sets it out in such a clear and readily accessible form.

If the source is described as e.g. *(Mid;T 3 May- line)* it means that the Midland Chronology gives the exact date for the station whilst *The Times* only covered the line opening; this approach has been used on the basis that as far as possible contemporary sources should be used; if these are incomplete, modern ones should be used to fill the gaps. *T/Derby Mercury* means that the information comes from the former, which acknowledged the latter as its source.

Where a newspaper report is given as the source it means that the item has been seen by the compiler or was provided by someone who knew it would be used in this book, and whose name is given after the paper in the list of sources. Where a secondary source quotes a press report of an opening, the source given is the book. Only where the sense demands reference to the paper, is full acknowledgement given. However, where a book includes a facsimile of an opening timetable or press advertisement of opening, that is cited as, e.g.: '*co n (= company's opening notice shown in) book's name*'.

As far as timetables are concerned, if a station is shown as 'first in *Brad* May 1856', it means that the April 1856 issue has also been seen and that the station was not present then. Occasionally a range of dates is given. If a station is shown as 'May/June/July 1856', it means that April has been seen and the station was absent; the May and June issues (or the relevant pages) were missing from the set used and the station was there in July.

However, more than 10,000 pieces of information have been either derived from, or checked against, *Bradshaw*. Though much has been double (or even triple) checked, it is highly unlikely that no errors or omissions have occurred. Furthermore, *Bradshaw* itself was dependent on companies sending up-to-date information in time for it to be included in the next issue. From common references in the book itself it is clear that this often did not happen. There are cases where other sources show that a new line or station was opened several months before it appeared there. There are also examples where it looks suspiciously as though revisions were made at intervals in a sort of catching-up exercise; changes such as the addition of an extra station or two coincide with alterations in the layout of tables and reorganisation of pagination rather more often than one would expect. These suspicious items were particularly prevalent during the hectic period of openings in the late 1840s. It is impossible to be sure whether *Bradshaw* or the railway companies were responsible – the writer suspects that both played a part.

Closing dates

The modern accepted convention is to quote as the closure date the first day a service should have run but did not do so. Nowadays the timetables start on a Sunday, so a quoted closure date will mean that the last train ran on the preceding Saturday (or perhaps Friday). However, from Nationalisation until recently the quoted date will normally have been a Monday and the last train will have run the preceding Friday, Saturday or Sunday but it was not always as simple as this. It seems to this compiler that it would have been preferable and more logical always to quote the date of the last train but the 'accepted' way is followed, partly because it is the one used by officialdom and partly because so much in print uses it that confusion would be caused by departing from it. Apart from some exceptions explained later, the dates used here are always those for the actual closure, calculated in accordance with the convention mentioned.
Some stations were initially 'temporarily closed' but never reopened; usually they were 'officially' closed years later. No mention is made of these later official dates since a station officially open but with no trains calling is of no use to anyone.

It should be pointed out that *Returns* usually operated on the principle of inclusive dates, so its closing dates were last days of use.

Initially, different companies' practice over station closures seems to have varied as much as their practices generally. The West Cornwall's notice of the closure of the Hayle to Redruth line for rebuilding in 1852 was phrased in the way that would be done today; however, that in *The Times* for the closure of the Gravesend to Rochester line for rebuilding in 1846 quoted the last day of use.

It would seem that, at first, stations were closed on any date and at any stage of the month. As the system grew, companies developed the practice of making the majority of the changes on the first of the month with a new timetable. The earlier paragraphs on 'Timetables' have explained how variable practice could be in this respect.

Many existing secondary sources (and perhaps even the Railway Clearing House) seem at times to have been confused by all this. Some attempt has been made here to unravel the tangle, but further work is needed. However, it should be stressed that normally only a matter of a day or two is involved.

After Nationalisation, the standard practice for all regions was to make changes on Mondays and to issue a standard form of closure notice. The fairly recent

change to Sunday starts for new timetables could in the future create problems of the sort explained later.

Various snags arise from the accepted way of dating closures. For a start, it is clear from examination of the evidence that it has not in reality always been followed and that some of the dates copied down the years were actually the last days of use; others seem to have been arrived at by adding one to a known last day of use, which gave the correct answer if the latter was a Sunday but created an absurdity if it was a Saturday since it resulted in a Sunday closure date for a line or station without a Sunday service (though there were circumstances in which this did certainly 'officially' happen as a result of Southern practice between the Wars). There are indications that the early nineteenth century usage of terms was not the same as today's (see the entry on *1844 December 1* in Section 5). The *Railway Gazette*, which has tended to be regarded as a semi-official source, probably contributed to the confusion. It is clear from analysis of lists it produced in the 1930s that it used a mixture of last days of use and official closure dates. *The Times* and the local press sometimes did quote the notices issued by the companies themselves but often only made brief mentions of closures. These can leave one wondering whether they meant the last day trains ran, or the official closure date, and thus fail to resolve the issue. Modern magazines devoted to railways are also sometimes at fault.

Another difficulty arises where closures were made with the introduction of a new timetable on the first of a month. Provided the first fell between Monday and Friday inclusive, there is no problem since the last train will clearly have run in accordance with the principles set out. Where it occurred on a Saturday or Sunday ambiguity can arise. If the first was a Saturday, did the company really close it then (i.e. last train on Friday) or was it a last day of use that historians have failed to correct to a Monday closure date? Sundays pose that problem, plus another one if the station concerned had no Sunday service. Where historians have spotted this type of closure they seem often to have resolved it by quoting the Monday (the 2nd) as the closure date. This compiler wonders whether in fact companies and their clerks were as finicky as this; he suspects that at least some of the time, especially before 1914, they simply quoted the date of the start of the new timetable as the closure date, regardless of niceties. Later, they do seem to have followed 'standard' practice. This problem is compounded by the fact that over time, the starting dates of new timetables were more frequently deferred or brought forward a day or two, so that the changes were made on a Monday. This was not done with any consistency; sometimes it was only done by a few companies. Thus dates like '2nd' or '31st' of a month should be regarded as suspect until the full story can be substantiated from reliable primary sources.

Throughout, where a station closed on a Monday, no comment is made. Closures on other days have the day of the week in brackets after them, so that e.g. (Tuesday) means that theoretically the last train should have run on a Monday. In the interests of consistency, Sunday dates have been given to all Southern services that are likely candidates. Ideally, information about whether there was a Sunday service or not should also be given. However, to do that from scratch would have taken a long time and required either a lot more space or the use of more symbols which, given the complexity of the information already included, might well have confused rather than enlightened the reader.

Some of the references used in support of the dates given are of the 'last day' kind, as long as they clearly support that date in accordance with the principles set out here. Ambiguous references are not used.

In cases where a station was served only on one or two days of the week, the date is given 'last day', thus avoiding some at least of the absurdities arising from the accepted practice.

In some cases, two sources are given; this normally occurs where the more immediate source gave notice well in advance and it thus seems desirable to give another source which confirms that it did actually close on the date given – there were cases where stays of execution were granted. Entries derived from timetables are shown: 'Last in *Brad* ....', if seen by the compiler but 'closed ...tt' if from elsewhere, since that is the way the sources used showed these (and the compiler usually has no means of knowing what timetable the source quoted used). This phrasing 'last in *Brad* ...' is also used in cases where a station later re-opened; it would be a waste of space to put 'last in the tt for the time being' or some such entry each time. Theoretically such stations would have had a closure date that was the first of the following month, unless they closed part way through a month. 'Last trains ...' covers those which remained in the timetable, without trains, after they had presumably been closed.

The same qualifications need to be added as for opening dates; there is a strong possibility that in some cases the service had ceased some time before it was omitted from *Bradshaw*.

Short-term omission from the timetable

Some stations were omitted from timetables for a few months only. These are shown: 'last in *Brad* ...; back ....'. Without corroborative evidence it is impossible to say whether they actually closed for a short time or remained open but were not included in the timetable because some clerk (almost certainly the railway company's, not the timetable publisher's) felt them not important enough for inclusion or wanted to save space.

Some companies, e.g. the Maryport & Carlisle, provided skeleton tables for some months, fully detailed ones for others. In such instances the fact that some stations went missing for a while is ignored.

Change of site

Where a station was removed to a new site, the information is given, as far as possible treating the new site as a continuation of the old station. Sometimes this is not possible since the new site was given a different name; cross-references are then given. In any case, the distinction between a re-sited station and a new one is one of the many grey areas of the subject. Sometimes the reader will find: 'New station ....': this is where the source used does not make it clear (the information might not be available anyway) whether the station was rebuilt on the same site or a different one. This aspect is one where there is the heaviest dependence on Clinker, who regarded a station as re-sited if the new location was more than 10 chains from the old. The local press was generally indifferent to such matters and timetables are rarely of any use for this purpose (they often gave distances but these were unreliable approximations). The vast majority of modern books simply copy Clinker.

Names

It seems appropriate to begin this section, about what is after all a secondary matter, with an apology about its length. However, so many unwarranted dogmatic assertions have been made that the compiler feels he has to justify his unconventional approach.

Many stations have carried more than one name over their lifetimes and it is clearly desirable that some indication of this should be given in a book claiming to detail station histories. Bluntly, there is no way simple answers that will satisfy everyone can be given. M.D. Greville, in an article in the RCHS *Journal* of September 1956, pp.66–7, effectively said this and the more this writer has tangled with the subject, the more he feels the same way, especially since he has collected ever-increasing numbers of contradictory dates given by now-dead respected railway historians; all attempts at finding definitive answers have usually led to more, not less, confusion.

Most books in print follow, or at least claim to follow, the principles set out by Clinker. He aimed to limit names to the official ones laid down by railway authorities and to ignore others, such as those invented by timetable publishers. He also tried to give exact dates for when names changed. However, he seems to have worked on the basis that at any one time there was only one name for a station and that when a name was changed it happened on an exact, ascertainable, date; occasionally he does give alternatives, with their sources, but this occurs only in a tiny proportion of the cases that could receive this treatment. Logically he should have been right but in actual life human beings, including railwaymen, do not always act in the tidy-minded ways that historians, struggling to produce order out of confusion, would like. Ideally, company timtables, *Bradshaw* and Clearing House records should always have told the same story. In practice they did not; the Clearing House, which, one would think, was supposed to reflect the companies' version, contained many differences from what was in the companies' timetables, even consistently using names that never appeared in any timetable seen by this compiler. One example was Ryhall & Belmisthorpe; all timetables seen contented themselves with Ryhall. Since the object of all types of history should be to record what did happen rather than give an edited version of what should have happened, some idea of the complications and contradictions that occurred needs to be given. The result is far removed from the simple and tidy answers all of us would prefer, but it reflects reality.

Also, Clinker's method resulted in a basic inconsistency. If names are to be validated and changes dated exactly, the only sources can be company records such as notices to staff that 'from day x, station a will be known as b'. He clearly obtained much information this way but unfortunately did not quote his sources so it is impossible now to differentiate these items from others. It is clear from comparison with other records that some of his dates were inferred: for example he dated the addition of (Oxon) to the existing Somerton station from the passenger opening of the Somerset one whilst GW records show that it was done earlier, when the latter opened for goods. Also, not all the necessary records exist; where they do, they can be contradictory, as he himself stated. Particularly for the early years, he had to fall back on timetables as the only practicable source. The result was a double standard: later material was subjected to more rigorous checks than earlier items. A publication devoted to one company, such as *The Midland Railway Chronology* can achieve much greater consistency by using its public timetables as the standard but no such means is available on a national level. The result is that for a single station one may have to use a mixture of company records, company and national timetables, and Clearing House records; since these often differed from one another in cases where direct comparison is possible, inconsistency in treatment is inevitable.

At first companies seem to have used 'X' to mean 'this is the station by which we provide a service to X'. Early timetables, for example the Liverpool and Manchester ones of March 1831, included amongst the general verbiage the information that the station was in Crown Street or Liverpool Road but that was almost certainly to help the would-be traveller find an unfamiliar building, not part of the station's name; they did not usually appear in general timetables. Such additions only became necessary as replacement or extra stations were provided in the same town. However, this book follows present accepted practice (which in itself contradicted much written about 'official' names by some of those involved) in treating them as though they were part of the name; it is simpler than adding 'this station was in ...' every time.

At first, usage seems to have been very casual and a single station could appear under several names in a very short period, especially if it was intended to serve an area containing several more-or-less equal-sized settlements rather than one obvious centre of population. The extreme case so far found is that of present-day Castleton. Early timetables contained at least six variants (none including 'Castleton'). A variation on this theme is that of rapid changes between two or three versions of a name. Much in print seizes on one of these changes and treats it as if it were definitive. It would seem more realistic to say 'was known early on as a/b/c ......', giving the variants. Even company records could be confusing: the Minute Books of the Stockton & Darlington regularly used more than one version of a name. Cargo Fleet / Cleveland Port, Beechburn / Howden, Staindrop / Winston, Spring Gardens / Lands and Lands / Evenwood were cases where they seem to have used names interchangeably. Stockton did duty in the timetable for two stations, much to the confusion of later historians; they appeared in the Minutes as Stockton / South Stockton and Guisborough Lane.

Where more than one station existed in a town or city, especially if the same company was involved, it sometimes became the practice to provide a helpful addition but this was not done in a uniform way: early LNW company timetables often had London, Euston, and Euston Square in different tables for the same station. Manchester, Liverpool and Edinburgh were amongst major centres where some tables in *Bradshaw* simply gave the city's name while others in the same issue added Waverley or whatever. Two companies using the same station did not always tell the same story. The Lancashire & Yorkshire and East Lancashire companies shared a terminus in Liverpool. Notices in the local press and tables in *Bradshaw* showed it as 'Liverpool' until just before they moved; then the Lancashire & Yorkshire added Borough Gaol to its station in both sources while the East Lancashire added Great Howard Street. They agreed that the new one was Exchange. This compiler suspects that this is another area where unplanned evolution rather than deliberate change was involved: what were originally intended as additions to help the traveller find the right station became 'official' parts of the name over time. Another, and later, example is provided by the Great Western: in the 1870s it briefly had two stations in Wells and Tucker Street was added in its company timetables and in *Bradshaw* to the newer one. When the unnecessary one was closed, the company tables (eventually) dropped the addition but *Bradshaw* kept it; 'Tucker Street' reappeared in official timetables after Nationalisation in order to distinguish it from the Somerset & Dorset station in Wells. Bolton Great Moor Street shows the limitations of the sampling method that has to be used. Great Moor Street was added early in *Bradshaw* and left there but company records say it was only added in 1924; for a long time the compiler believed that it was never used in the LNW's company tables but then discovered that it did appear (but in one table, one direction only) in 1856. For how long before and after is not known.

In the 1850s and 1860s there was an epidemic of adding 'Junction' to station names, especially in *Bradshaw*. These seem in many cases to have come from the companies since there was a tendency for several to have this addition at the same time: the main Lancashire & Yorkshire table had four in May 1852. Comparisons with company timetables suggest that these were perhaps helpful additions to warn the traveller that a change of trains might be necessary there, rather than true parts of the name; that would certainly be the case for such as Meigle Dundee Junction, which clearly meant 'change here for Dundee'. However, some did clearly become accepted parts of the name – but which?

Where stations changed their names frequently according to the timetable, especially where the change was from X to Y, back to X etc (names of the A & B variety were particularly prone to this), no attempt has been made to follow the contortions in detail. Apart from anything else, the sampling techniques that have to be used to enable the ground to be covered mean that short-lived changes are likely to be overlooked. The variations are listed but not dated.

Some minor changes were made at very different dates in different sources. According to Clinker, Bowland had Bridge added to its name from the May 1849 *Bradshaw*, losing it again in July 1862; however it was still included in the NB working timetable for 1 February 1868 and the Clearing House Hand-books did not drop 'Bridge' until near the end of the century. This is also one of the cases where a difference between the name in the index and in the body of *Bradshaw* persisted for many years. Other comparisons show

great disparities, but there is no pattern as to who made the changes first. All sources originally showed Queen's Ferry; by 1890 the Hand-books had Queensferry but *Bradshaw* was still making two words of it in 1938, though occasional earlier one-word versions have been seen. On the other hand Collumpton became Cullompton in the timetable in 1867 but not in the Hand-book until 1892. No attempt is made to date changes like these. Stalybridge and Thornfalcon were amongst those suffering the indignity of multiple variations in spelling; in both cases one- and two-word versions, with an additional 'e' in the middle were on offer, often more than one in the same issue of a timetable, even in up and down tables for the same line.

Some variations between sources would have been publishers' and compositors' ideas on how a name should be presented but the only explanation that sensibly fits much of the evidence is that different names for the same station were in use, perhaps informally, at the same time. The clearest evidence comes from the Hand-books, which often gave alternative names. Some were probably officially out-of-date names retained because they were still occasionally being used. Others were the result of dividing X & Y names to show the components separately. Yet others fit no obvious pattern and support the contention that alternatives were in concurrent use. In 1872, there were entries for both Child's Hill & Cricklewood and Cricklewood & Child's Hill, without any indication of which was the preferred version. There were sometimes entries for towns which did not have a station, such as Shaftesbury in Dorset; the intention was that parcels addressed to such places could be unloaded at the nearest railway station and taken on by road, but no indication was given in the books that the place lacked a railway station of its own. The aim seems to have been to provide a means for the accurate delivery of goods, however oddly addressed, not to lay down a standard set of names. By the end of the nineteenth century, the Hand-books had gone a long way, but by no means all of the way, towards establishing standard forms.

Bradshaw contributed to the confusion by adding extra words to help differentiate between stations in the same town. This would not have been necessary if the companies themselves had shown more regard for their customers and provided names themselves. Additions such as Manvers Street to Bath GW were certainly *Bradshaw*'s. These flourished from the late nineteenth century until Grouping or Nationalisation when officialdom at last acted. A complication here is that when, in late Grouping and early Nationalisation years, companies and British Rail Regions used *Bradshaw* to publish their timetables for them, 'unofficial' names came with them. Sometimes officialdom adopted the names already in use, sometimes it created new ones; there is a grey area where it seems that timetable names gradually slipped into official use. One such is Winchester Cheesehill, which Clinker seems to have accepted as the official name from opening. While *Bradshaw* called it Cheesehill Street from the start, neither the GW company timetable nor the Hand-books give their initial support, though by 1947 the GW was using Cheesehill. *Bradshaw* also gave shorter versions. The Hand-books show Callander Dreadnought as the passenger station for the town; the timetable did not include the addition. The latter also failed on occasion to amend names: Fawcett Street was attached to Sunderland long after it should have been removed.

Some variations were almost certainly due to the companies. In 1850 the same station is both Kendal Junction and Oxenholme Junction; this would seem to have been the result of two companies using a single station and sending their own versions of its name to the publisher. Later, there were other examples of this: the main line station at Templecombe was at one time differently described in the LSW and SD Jt tables, and in South Wales, Nelson and Llancai(a)ch were simultaneously in use for the same station; Redhill and the Aldershot / Ash area were particularly messy in this respect. It might be remembered that timetable publishers would have lacked both the detailed local knowledge needed to produce variations and the time required to edit and alter in depth; they provided a revised timetable every month without modern technology. In these circumstances we can safely assume that mostly they printed what they were sent.

If anyone still needs convincing of the complexity of the task of establishing names and an explanation of why this book takes refuge in inexact references, this final example, provided by sampling, might clinch matters. It concerns what is now Bristol Temple Meads. In the 1860s all sources seen just had Bristol. There was only one site, though a complex one. Passengers were left to work out for themselves whether they needed the Great Western station, the Bristol & Exeter or the through platform. Occasionally tables did specify 'the GW station' but for services which only a traveller totally ignorant of local geography would have attempted to catch from the Bristol & Exeter; no help was given in those vital cases where it was needed. In 1871 and 1887 *Bradshaw* had Bristol Temple Mead in both GW and Midland tables, but in 1876 and 1878 it was Bristol Temple Street. In 1902 the timetable issued by the GW itself had Bristol Temple Meads but that issued by the Midland in 1903 still showed Bristol Temple Mead. The Clearing House Hand-books for 1890 and 1895 called it Bristol Joint Passenger Station; the appendix for 1896/9 showed Temple Meads for passengers and goods, GW only (there was no Midland entry in the appendix); the 1904 book had Joint Station for passengers and confined Temple Meads to the GW goods station only; the 1938 book is the same; at some time between then and an amendment leaflet dated September 1939 the passenger station had become Bristol Temple Meads Joint. The Junction Diagrams added Temple Meads about 1900, apparently, but not

certainly, to the whole station. Though not strictly relevant here, it might be added that while for a long time no reference to Temple Meads appeared under 'Bristol' in the Hand-books, by 1890 there was an entry under 'T', with the explanation that it was the same as Bristol Goods: GW-Mid.

It is difficult to decide sometimes whether a name is a misprint or a printer's misreading of his copy (not all nineteenth century handwriting was copy-book copperplate) or an earlier spelling of a modern name. It needs here to be remembered that the spelling of place-names was still evolving during the Nineteenth Century; for example, Bridg(e)water appeared with and without the middle 'e' in general usage throughout that century. Some initially dismissed as printer's errors were later found to be what was really intended. Names such as Middlesbrough routinely became Middlesbro' and *The Times* was a leading user of forms like London-bridge; such variants are not included. Some variations included may seem to some to be too petty to be worthy of mention; indeed, it was tempting to omit some on these grounds. However, it was found impossible to define 'too petty' and anyway some people like the fullest possible picture. Some that were almost certainly errors, even a few obviously nonsense ones, are listed here to illustrate the arguments outlined above. Some of those religiously copied from book to book were almost certainly copying errors or the result of how a particular clerk thought a name should be spelled, rather than the company's ideas – but which? No attempt is made to lay down the law. Others may accept or reject as they choose.

To make matters worse, *Bradshaw* often changed a name in its index a little before or after it did so in the tables and it was joined in this by at least some company timetables seen (for example, the LNW's treatment of Fid(d)lers Ferry). From other evidence it is clear that no firm conclusion can be drawn about which was right, though it is inherently likely that the earlier is usually the right one. Throughout, the names in the tables in the body of the book have been used as standard; where earlier index versions have been detected, some such mention as 'earlier in the index' is made.

After all this, there is also the question of the timing of any change of name. A full answer for many stations would require: decision to change name made A, to take effect from B; appeared in timetables from C; name-boards on station changed D – or even up platform D, down platform E; changed on tickets from F; Clearing House records from G ....

At this point, another complication can be added. Companies seem sometimes to have printed on tickets names that were different from those in general use. Additionally, the using-up of old stock could mean that tickets bore station names that had long since been altered elsewhere.

Finally, it remains to outline the policy followed here. Exact dates for changes have now been added in cases where there is clear evidence, such as company or Clearing House notices or where a generally reliable source gives one where no contradictory evidence has been seen – in particular Clinker's post-1945 dates have mostly been used on the assumption that he had access to official records and many earlier ones have been used where there is generalised support from elsewhere: e.g. if he gave 1 May and a minute of the LNW Officers' Conference recommended the change at some time in the previous April. Only rarely is it pointed out that timetables, especially *Bradshaw*, made the change later; this happened so often that the result would be an often-repeated chorus. Many of the years quoted come from Clinker's book, but considerable efforts have been made to show that the dates given tally with the timetable and Clearing House information available.

While experience suggests that use of *Bradshaw* dates is generally a good guide, within a month or two, to the opening and closing of stations, it is of far more limited use when it comes to defining exact station names or the dates when these changed. Thus dates derived from there are quoted year-only and the same treatment has been given to dates where others have quoted a date clearly derived from timetables. The latter rarely specified 'company' tables or *Bradshaw* but, given the difficulties faced in finding runs of company tables, it is reasonable to assume that most came from *Bradshaw*. Mention is made, usually in general terms, of cases where the latter used a name before (often long before) officialdom apparently decided to adopt it. Where *Bradshaw* is the only source seen, year-only dates (or ranges of dates) are normally provided; even then, it should be borne in mind that the change might actually have occurred well before it appeared there, or the variation might have been one of *Bradshaw's* own – or an error. As a result, some information provided (including that on the addition or subtraction of 'Halt' from a name) is now given apparently less exactly than before. Even some of that derived from Clearing House sources is open to question: the late Jeoffrey Spence pointed out that sometimes the clerks used the date of the letter in which information was received from companies or the date a decision was taken, as though it were the date the change was actually made.

In the most shambolic cases no attempt is made to date variations. They are merely listed, usually at the end of the relevant entry, with perhaps a date giving an idea of when sanity prevailed.

Where names were of the 'X for Y' variety, the 'for Y' part is usually given in only a general way. Often mention is made that the version appeared in a company timetable in a particular year. This does not mean that it was the only time it appeared; it is done to try and give the reader some idea of which were sanctioned by companies and which might have been Clearing House or timetablers' concoctions. They are given because they help to show how places without stations were served, especially places of interest to tourists; they sometimes also reflected railway politics as one company added 'for X' to try and win custom from another's station at 'X'. It should be realised that there were far more of them than are here given, especially in the early years, where some tables listed many, presumably because the stations provided road-coach connections to the places concerned. Most of the 'for ...' variants have been placed at the very end of their entries; this avoids lengthy disruption to the flow of basic information and also makes it easier for those with no interest in this aspect to ignore unwanted information.

More exact treatment has been possible for stations on the Midland Railway because John Gough kindly supplied the writer with a full version of his sources, thus enabling him to specify what type of timetable is involved.

SECTION 4

The Stations

EXPLANATION

Far more information about many aspects is available in Section 3, Sources.

A separate GLOSSARY covering some of the terms used is included later.

Stations are listed in alphabetical order by place name. The 'nothing before something' principle used by librarians is followed here – thus:

HAY
HAY & X
HAY PARK
HAY-ON-WYE
HAYMARKET

Please note that many names (e.g. Queens Ferry / Queensferry) appeared in both one- and two-word forms in railway sources at different times.

Here, the last or present form is used; if you do not see the place you are looking for in one form, please look on or back to the other.

Suburban stations are listed under their own names. The name under which full details are given is normally the present name if it is still open or its name at closure. If a town or city has, or had, two or more stations where the place name is/was the first word of the station name (e.g. BATH SPA; BATH GREEN PARK), entries are preceded by an underlined heading, giving the place's name. Where the place's name is/was the second word, it is normally treated thus: SOUTH CROYDON is under 'S', with cross-reference under 'C'. Exceptions have been made for a few places where the complications make it seem sensible to put all its stations in one place; cross-references are provided for those where readers might initially look in the wrong place. Cross-references are also provided for alternative names where these are significantly different but not for minor differences of the 'BATH GW see BATH SPA' type, nor for cases where a name has appeared as both one and two words. Where 'HALT', 'SIDING' or 'PLATFORM' was part of a name, it is not included in the heading, but is mentioned in the text. Commas or brackets that were part of the name are usually omitted to avoid confusion; similarly, the possessive apostrophe is normally omitted. In both cases practice has been very variable both over time and region (St James being a leading victim). After a town or station name has been given once, initial letters only are used, unless ambiguity might result.

The organisation of entries is flexible, allowing each entry to be given in the way that seems most suitable. The components are explained below, but do not always appear in the order given.

Stations of the same name in different areas are generally distinguished by 'near ....' after the name; counties are only used if they actually formed part of the name (according to RCH sources or the body of a tt, not the index). This approach is used to avoid the need for alteration when local government boundaries are changed.

Company name – shown [...]. Normally, the company quoted is the one that operated the station at the end of 1922, or at closure if this was earlier. Following the usual custom, no reference is made to companies that were still legally independent but had their trains operated by another company. Stations not owned by a railway company (e.g. those provided by the government for munitions workers) are similarly ascribed to the company operating the service to and from then. Stations opened from 1923 to 1947 are ascribed to the company responsible for opening them. No reference is given for stations opened since nationalisation, unless they were opened by the London Underground or some other organisation not subject to British Railways. Exceptions have been made for operating companies that only lost their independence late, including all of those involved in amalgamations that were preliminaries to the main grouping. The London, Tilbury & Southend is shown, though by 1922 it was part of the Midland. The handling of the south east is more complicated. The South Eastern (SE) and the London, Chatham & Dover (LCD) in 1899 created the South Eastern & Chatham Railway Companies Managing Committee (SEC) to run their lines operationally as one, though they were still legally separate. Here SE and LCD are used for stations opened before the 'merger' and SEC for later ones. Stations now part of the London Underground are

given their present line names; if they were opened
by a 'surface' railway, that is also mentioned.
Abbreviations (list below) are used where frequent
reference has to be made to a company; where only
occasional mention is needed the name is given in full.
Names are sometimes given in a simpler form than
their full legal ones, especially where it was normal in
the nineteenth century to do this. Reference is made
occasionally to unusual arrangements, such as the
partitioning of the City of Glasgow Union between
North British and Glasgow & South Western in 1896.

Opening date. The date given is that when fare-paying
passengers were first carried on a train shown in the
ordinary public timetable. Non-timetable and
occasional stations and services are treated as seems
most appropriate to their circumstances and the
evidence available. The nature of the evidence is such
that even for public stations this has to be expressed in
different ways:

If the entry is simply 'op ...' it means that the source
quoted in brackets immediately after gives believable
evidence that the station really did open that day.

If it is 'op 1 May 1850 *(source – line)*', it means that the
quoted source only supplies the line date and not
details of intermediate stations. However, the station is
in the first timetable seen for the line, after and within
a month or two of its opening. The vast majority of
stations so shown will have opened on the date given.

With some early stations, the entry will be e.g.: 'line op
..., in early *Freeling*', which means that it was included
in a very early description of the line. Again, the vast
majority of these will have opened with their lines.

'Line op 1 May 1850, nd (= no detail), August 1851'
means either that no timetable prior to August 1851
has been seen or that the timetables seen did not give
full details until then, so that one cannot be sure
whether the station opened with the line or at some
time up to and including the date given after 'nd'.
Where other evidence has later come to light in cases
like this, it has shown that most did open with the line.
An awkward category is where short branches or
additional stretches of line were opened and initially
the timetable gave just the terminus of the new stretch,
adding one intermediate station a few months later.
These cases are far more difficult to judge than those
where several stations were included with the line and
only one added later. Another problem sometimes arose
when a new branch was opened, joining the main line
at a point away from existing stations so that a new
junction station had to be built. Sometimes this was not
shown at first, though it is clear from working arrangements that something had to exist at the junction.

'First in *Brad* June 1851' or something similar means it
is reasonably certain that it opened after its line and this
is the best available evidence for dating its appearance.

It must be emphasised that this will be an approximation;
whilst many stations did open on the first of the month
in which they were first included, others did not appear
in *Brad* for several months after opening and a few were
not included for years – or ever – presumably because
the companies did not think them worth a mention.
Far more rarely, stations were put in early.

'First trains May 1850' means previously included in
the timetable without any trains shown calling.

Closing date. The date given, following accepted
practice, is that of the first day when services would
normally have run but did not. In the vast majority of
cases, this will have been a Monday, with the last train
running the previous Friday, Saturday, or Sunday.
If there was a big gap between the date of the last train
and the official closure, the entry will be: 'Last train ....';
no reference will be made to the official date.

Where the date was not a Monday, the day of the week
is quoted in brackets after the date; this is done to
highlight issues fully explained in Section 3.
The commonest use after 1922 is (Sunday), for stations
on the Southern Railway, which normally began its
new timetables on Sundays. Days of the week are not
given when a closed station was immediately replaced
by another.

In most cases an exact date is available but a few dates
have had to be derived from timetables. These are
shown: 'Last in tt ....' or similarly. It should again be
borne in mind that these are approximations and that
some stations remained in the timetable after closure.
'Inertia?' is included where there is a suspicion that
there might have been a delay in removing the station.
'Last trains ...' means that the station was included in
later timetable(s) but no trains were shown calling.

Intermediate closures and re-openings are shown;
the same principles apply to these as to first openings
and final closures. Where timetables have had to be
quoted, it is: 'Last in tt ....; back in tt ....'. Especially
early on, it is unsafe to assume that a station closed just
because it was omitted from the timetable for a few
months; other evidence is needed to be certain.
Where the closure was clearly intended to be temporary
(as was the case with many stations closed in 1917 as
a war-time economy measure), or was a short one, the
phrasing will be 'clo...; reop (= re-opened)....' or a
variant based on timetables. If the closure was clearly
intended to be permanent, or the intention is not
known and the gap a long one, the uses are listed (a),
(b), etc. This is an area where many differences of
opinion will be found on the question of what should
and should not be included. Here, deliberate closures
for engineering works and closures resulting from
major structural failures are included up to 1994
whilst those resulting from strikes, accidents and
flooding are generally not.

Changes of site are mentioned, with details if known. As far as possible, where a station on a new site immediately replaced another, the replacement is normally treated as a continuation of that replaced, not as a new station. Where the replacement carried, or was later given, a different name, it is normally shown as a separate station. This method is followed regardless of distance between sites.

Name variations are shown. No attempt is made to lay down the law over what was 'official' and what not since the evidence seen suggests that usage was often variable amongst railwaymen themselves, perhaps depending on the circumstances in which a name had to be quoted. Practice seems to have become more exact over time, especially after the reorganisations of the twentieth century.

If part of the entry is 'CENTRAL added ...' it means the station opened as X and was renamed X CENTRAL on the date or in the year quoted. For reasons explained in Section 3, dating is often confined to a year-only basis or 'in the early years' or 'aot' used.

If a name variation is quoted as 'hb' or 'tt', it means that it was certainly in that source at some stage; it does not necessarily mean that this was the only place it appeared.

The name used for stations still open is that shown in tables in the body of the *Rail Times*. Different versions will sometimes be found – e.g. on station name-boards or tickets.

Other detail felt to be of interest is included, e.g.: if it was a station served only by market trains for all or part of its existence; if it had any use as a private station prior to, or after, its public existence; if it was a HALT, SIDING or PLATFORM; if it was at one time a request station of some sort, though it is likely than some halts not shown as request stops were in fact such – halts were often simply listed in footnotes, without any details about times and the like. Formal openings and pre-opening excursions are included if there was fairly wide public use. Where dated excursions are included they should usually be regarded as examples rather than as part of a complete history; sometimes the entry is just 'later excursions' and no attempt is made to date final use of a station since this would have been occasional and erratic and survival of the information depends on chance.

'**P**' is mostly used in cases where the only evidence is an entry in a Railway Clearing House Hand-book: this will mostly concern stations without a public timetabled service (often excursion stations). From 1877 the Hand-books had a series of columns showing the facilities available at the main locations. The inclusion of 'P' meant that passenger and/or parcel facilities should have been available. However, there were misprints and it was only in 1904 that stations handling only parcels (as well as goods and/or livestock) were

differentiated from those catering for passengers also, so that in the earlier books, 'P' might have meant 'parcels', not 'passengers'.

Map location – shown {...}. One possibility would have been to give Ordnance Survey six-figure references for all; however, finding these would have taken at least as long again as did the collection of the information presented here and, anyway, such references are no use to someone trying to find a station on a map not provided with the Ordnance Survey grid, or without access to a full set. Readers are initially referred to the atlases listed below, chosen because they are normally in print.

For stations still open see:

S.K. Baker's *Rail Atlas of Great Britain & Ireland*, OPC / Ian Allan;

M.G. Ball, *British Railways Atlas* (pocket-sized), Ian Allan or *Atlas of Train Operating Companies*, Ian Allan, 2000. The maps in British Rail's timetables showed all stations, though many areas were in diagrammatic form only.

For stations open about 1914 see:

British Railways Pre-Grouping Atlas & Gazetteer published by Ian Allan. Though the atlas is dated 1922, in practice the vast majority of stations closed during and just after the First World War were still included.

Provided that a station is shown on one (or more) of the four atlases mentioned immediately above, no reference to its location is given here. Where a station is not so shown, either because it closed before 1922, or both opened and closed after 1922, the location is explained, if possible, by reference to stations on the 1922 map: e.g. Yeo Mill is shown {East Anstey – Bishops Nympton} – i.e. it is between those two stations (which are in the Ian Allan Atlas). The reference stations may be shown with abbreviated names. Please remember to use the station's name in 1922 when seeking to find by this method. Where this is not possible, the reference will be {see map ...} and the station will be found on the appropriate map in Section 8. If *U* is used as a source, a six-figure OS reference will often be found there for the station concerned.

A fuller list of atlases is provided near the end of Section 3. Even though, between them, they show nearly all the stations included in this book, the number of atlases involved, and the difficulties likely to be met in trying to find copies of some of them, make it seem unreasonable to expect the reader to hunt for and through all of them. At the same time, the policy followed does provide a major saving of space.

GENERAL ABBREVIATIONS

* = see note later in the entry.

** after a date = see the note of that date in Section 5, where notes are in chronological order and may include material about the station and/or line's later history. Sources given there are not repeated in individual station entries.

\> = history continued below.

aot = at one time. Used where reliable exact dates have not been found.

clo = closed.

co ½ = information issued in a company half-yearly report or at a meeting following it.

co n = notice issued by the operating company, usually as a newspaper advertisement. Where a book or magazine article is cited, it means that the opening notice was reproduced in it. After 1948 the 'company' will be BR.

co tt = timetable issued by the company operating the line.

hb = Railway Clearing House Station Hand-book.

hba = Appendix to Railway Clearing House Station Hand-book.

HL = High Level }

LL = Low Level } used to distinguish between two stations, usually close together, in the same town or between two, perhaps separately run, parts of one station.

ng = narrow gauge station.

non-tt = station not in public timetables.

op = opened.

P = shown 'P' in RCH hand-book – see earlier in this section.

reop = reopened.

tt = timetable; please see earlier section for more exact information.

wtt = working timetable (for use of railwaymen, not the public); will always apply to relevant company.

Sources are given as far as possible for all items. They are normally shown: 1 May 1850 (*source*). However, where all items in a linked series of closures and re-openings come from the same source, this is only given once, at the end of the series.
Source abbreviations are explained in Section 3.
A date after a newspaper's name is the date of the newspaper; month and year are not given unless they are different from those of the opening date.

Since the material used has been accumulated over many years, much of it before there was any thought of publication, it has been found impossible to trace some of the sources. Where an opening date is involved, some attempt has been made to justify the date given, so the reference is: date *(?; first in tt …)*.

ABBREVIATIONS OF RAILWAY COMPANIES' NAMES

In most cases, the word 'Railway' needs to be added to the name given. The exceptions are those where 'Line', 'Tramway' or 'Committee' are given in the titles. For the most part, the abbreviations used are those given in Clinker's *Register*, since many readers will already be familiar with these. The main differences concern railways such as the Lynton & Barnstaple, where 'Lynton' still saves space but is more readily recognisable than 'LB'. Where companies are shown 'A/B', it means that the station in question was in some way jointly owned by A and B; separate listings for the various combinations are not given (there is a large number of them). Where 'A; B' is shown, it means that the two companies operated the station's services at different times. For more details on companies, see *Companies* or A. Warren's book listed at the end of Section 2; the former gives more information, the latter is restricted to the legal framework but is more accurate. For more on the complexities of joint ownership see the papers on this topic by various contributors in the RCHS *Chronology Group Newsletters, numbers 15 to 19.*

AN Jt	Ashby & Nuneaton Joint.
ANSW	Alexandra (Newport & South Wales) Docks & Railway.
Ax Jt	Axholme Joint.
Bak	Bakerloo Line.
BC	Bishops Castle.
BE	Bristol & Exeter.
BG	Birmingham & Gloucester.
BLCJ	Birkenhead, Lancashire & Cheshire Junction.
BM	Brecon & Merthyr.
BPGV	Burry Port & Gwendraeth Valley.
BR	British Railways (whilst nationalised).
BT	Blyth & Tyne.
BWA	Bideford, Westward Ho! & Appledore.
Cal	Caledonian.
Cam	Cambrian.
Camp	Campbeltown & Machrihanish Light.
CE	Clifton Extension Joint.
Cen	Central Line.
CGU	City of Glasgow Union.
CHP	Cromford & High Peak.
CKP	Cockermouth, Keswick & Penrith.
CLC	Cheshire Lines Committee.
CMDP	Cleobury Mortimer & Ditton Priors Light.
CO Jt	Croydon & Oxted Joint.
Croydon	Croydon Tramlink.
CVH	Colne Valley & Halstead.
CW Jc	Cleator & Workington Junction.
DA	Dundee & Arbroath (original and later Joint).
DB Jt	Dumbarton & Balloch Joint.

Dist	District Line (strictly Metropolitan District).
Dock	Docklands Light.
DPA	Dundee & Perth & Aberdeen Junction.
EA	East Anglian.
EC	Eastern Counties.
Ed & Dalk	Edinburgh & Dalkeith.
EG	Edinburgh & Glasgow.
EK	East Kent Light.
EU	Eastern Union.
EWYU	East & West Yorkshire Union.
Fur	Furness.
FYN	Freshwater, Yarmouth & Newport.
GBK Jt	Glasgow, Barrhead & Kilmarnock Joint.
GC	Great Central.
GC GI	Great Central (Grimsby & Immingham electric tramway).
GE	Great Eastern.
GJ	Grand Junction.
Glyn	Glyn Valley Tramway.
GN	Great Northern.
GNS	Great North of Scotland.
GP Jt	Glasgow & Paisley Joint.
GSW	Glasgow & South Western.
GU	Glasgow Underground.
GW	Great Western.
HB	Hull & Barnsley.
HC	Hammersmith & City Joint.
High	Highland.
IoW	Isle of Wight.
IWC	Isle of Wight Central.
Jub	Jubilee Line.
KB	Kilsyth & Bonnybridge Joint.
KE	Knot(t) End.
KES	Kent & East Sussex Light.
L&B	London & Birmingham.
LBSC	London, Brighton & South Coast.
LCD	London Chatham & Dover.
LM	Liverpool & Manchester.
LMS	London, Midland & Scottish.
LNE	London & North Eastern.
LNW	London & North Western.
LO	Liverpool Overhead.
LPJ	Lancaster & Preston Junction.
LPTB	London Passenger Transport Board.
LSW	London & South Western.
LTS	London, Tilbury & Southend.
LU	Lancashire Union.
LY	Lancashire & Yorkshire.
Lynton	Lynton & Barnstaple.
Manch	Manchester Metrolink.
MC	Maryport & Carlisle.
Met	Metropolitan Railway/Line
Met GNC	Metropolitan (Great Northern & City Section).
MGN	Midland and Great Northern Joint line.
Mid	Midland.
MK	Monkland & Kirkintilloch.
MS&L	Manchester, Sheffield & Lincolnshire.

MSJA	Manchester, South Junction & Altrincham.	SE	South Eastern.
MSWJ	Midland & South Western Junction.	SEC	South Eastern & Chatham.
N&B	Neath & Brecon.	SH Jt	Shrewsbury & Hereford Joint.
NB	North British.	SIT	Swansea Improvements & Tramways Company (Swansea & Mumbles).
NC	Newcastle & Carlisle.	SK	Swinton & Knottingley Joint.
NE	North Eastern.	SM	Shropshire & Montgomeryshire Light.
Newtyle	Dundee & Newtyle.	SMJ	Stratford-upon-Avon & Midland Junction.
Nidd	Nidd Valley Light.		
NL	North London.	SR	Southern.
Nor	Northern Line.	SSMWC	South Shields, Marsden & Whitburn Colliery.
Norfolk & S	Norfolk & Suffolk Joint.		
NS	North Staffordshire.	SW Jt	Severn & Wye Joint.
NSWJ	North & South Western Junction Joint.	SY	South Yorkshire (later part of GC).
NU	North Union / North Union Joint.	TFG Jt	Tottenham & Forest Gate Joint.
NWNG	North Wales Narrow Gauge.	TH Jt	Tottenham & Hampstead Joint.
OAGB	Oldham, Ashton & Guide Bridge Junction Joint.	TV	Taff Vale.
		TWM	Tyne & Wear Metro.
PDSW	Plymouth, Devonport & South Western Junction.	Vic	Victoria Line.
		VoR	Vale of Rheidol.
Picc	Piccadilly Line.	W Lancs	West Lancashire.
PLA	Port of London Authority.	WCE Jt	Whitehaven, Cleator & Egremont Joint.
PPW Jt	Portpatrick & Wigtownshire Joint.	WCP	Weston, Clevedon & Portishead Light.
PT	Port Talbot Railway & Docks.	WELCP	West End of London & Crystal Palace.
PW	Preston & Wyre (original and later Joint).	WH	Welsh Highland.
Raven	Ravenglass & Eskdale.	WL	West London Joint (including Extension).
RHD	Romney, Hythe & Dymchurch.	WMC	Wilsontown, Morningside & Coltness.
Rhy	Rhymney.	WMCQ	Wrexham, Mold & Connah's Quay.
RSB	Rhondda & Swansea Bay.	WP Jt	Weymouth & Portland Joint.
Rye & C	Rye & Camber Tramway.	WRG Jt	West Riding & Grimsby Joint.
S&D	Stockton & Darlington.	WS	West Sussex (Selsey Tramway).
Scot Cent	Scottish Central.	WSC Jt	Woodside & South Croydon Jt.
SD Jt	Somerset & Dorset Joint.	WSM	West Somerset Mineral.

GLOSSARY

Coach in the early days could cause the same problems of interpretation as 'omnibus', which see.

Depot was sometimes used in the early days for 'station', especially in Scotland.

Down trains are those from London; up trains towards. Cross-country lines need individual listing. As far as possible, the terms are avoided here – 'northbound', 'towards x' being used instead.

Exchange station. In theory, a station provided only for changing between main and branch line trains. Passengers could not be booked to or from such stations. Often there was no official public access. However, the possibility of local 'arrangements' should not be ruled out.

Flag station – see Signal station.

Formal openings: A common practice was to have a ceremonial opening. Most were held the day before the public opening though some were well before, the same day as, or several days after, the public one. Generally these are ignored – apart from anything else they sometimes applied to the line rather than individual stations.

Halt: simple stopping place, usually unstaffed, with basic provision of platform and, perhaps, minimal shelter. Originally spelled 'Halte' – the idea was copied from the continent. Company usage varied and was both erratic and inconsistent. Some (e.g. LNW) had halts but did not always call them that (*Bradshaw* often did). In the mid-1920s 'halt' was removed from the names of many ex-Lancashire & Yorkshire stops, but they seem still to have been (mostly, if not all) treated as halts; the 8 July 1935 tt had a note on the page containing the St Helens to Ormskirk service that certain trains did not stop at the halts but no 'halts' appeared in the tables or other notes. Halts, whether named as such or not, were frequently relegated to footnotes – but some were included in the tables themselves. The term was used from soon after 1900, when such stops were added to serve places not warranting the cost of proper stations; later the aim was to counter road competition. Many were simply extra stops on existing services but in some areas several were opened at close intervals and a special 'Rail Motor' service was laid on for them. Further complications are explained in notes on '1904' and '1905'. In later years cost-cutting meant that many stations became unstaffed. At first the Western Region generally added 'Halt' in the timetable but the North Eastern and Scottish did not. Thus *RM*, February 1960, said most stops on the Hornsea and Withernsea branches had been reduced to unstaffed halts but the timetable only included a symbol to show they were unstaffed; some on the Ballater line received similar treatment later

1960. Later in the 1960s 'Halt' was generally dropped from names. Oddly the handful that kept the title longest were in Scotland. Overall, usage appears to have been a lot less precise than some writers have claimed.

Incline was used to describe a stretch of line with a steep gradient. At first trains often had to be worked up and down such lines with the help of stationary engines, which meant a stop at top and bottom to attach and detach haulage cables. For safety reasons, passengers might be expected, officially at least, to walk the inclines. Some of these stops appeared in the timetables, often intermittently, others did not. The possibility existed for all to be unofficial joining or leaving points, though often few people lived nearby. Over time the inclines were replaced by more gently graded deviation lines, or ceased to cause operating problems as locomotive power increased.

Inspection. From 1840 the Board of Trade (or its replacement) had to be notified before a line could be opened to passengers and an Inspector (for a long time always a Royal Engineers officer) was sent to check on many aspects of safety. At first the report was advisory but the law was soon altered to allow officialdom to refuse opening if he recommended this. Any major faults found had to be rectified and the line re-inspected before it could open, though with lesser faults the authorities might be content with a written promise from the company to put the defects right. Failure to satisfy the Inspector frequently caused delays in opening. At first these requirements did not apply to stations opened after the line, but the law was later extended to include them. Sometimes ways around the law were found (see Section 5, '1844').

Narrow gauge was used initially to mean what would now be called 'standard' gauge, as opposed to Brunel's 'broad' gauge. In this work, 'standard' is used for 4 foot 8½ inch gauge, 'narrow' for lesser gauges.

Offset was used on some early Scottish railways in the way that 'Halt' was used later.

Omnibus was used in two ways in the early timetables, sometimes even in the same table. One referred to road services provided in connection with trains. The other equalled 'horse-drawn railway carriage'.

Passenger duty. Taxes were levied on private coaches and public stagecoaches, so it was inevitable that railways would also become liable. The tax was modified from time to time but not abolished until 1929. In the early years the fact that a particular railway company paid this tax is sometimes the only evidence available to show that passengers were carried.

'Platform' as part of a name: used for stops that ranked between stations and halts (which see, above). Usually one or two staff were available and parcels might be handled but accommodation was still very basic.

Request station – see Signal station.

'Siding' as part of a name. Generally 'siding' equalled some sort of provision for goods.
Some came to be granted passenger services, often of the one or two days a week variety; the 'facilities' would have been minimal – perhaps just platforms beside the running lines.

Signal station (alias Request station, Flag station). Trains only stopped (and in some cases still do stop) at some stations when there were (and are) passengers to be picked up or set down. The usual arrangement is that anyone wanting to alight informs the guard when joining the train or at the ordinary station immediately before the request stop, and that signals are used to halt trains when anyone needs to be picked up. Here, such stations are shown 'aot request'; the qualification for this reference is that for at least part of a station's life its entire week-day service was provided this way.
No attempt is made to date the period when they were request stops. To begin with, the majority of these were to be found on lines belonging (or later belonging) to the GE and the GN. Later they were mostly in the remoter parts of Wales or the Highlands and on lesser companies' lines.

Temporary terminus. Sometimes when railways were being built a length of line would be opened to a spot beside a main road where there was no intention of providing a permanent station. Road coaches would be laid on to take passengers to the next major town. This was usually done when a structure such as a tunnel or viaduct had to be completed before the next stretch could be opened and a lengthy delay in opening the already-built section would otherwise have occurred. Later such stations might be provided briefly if a line was cut by e.g. a tunnel collapse or by a dispute between companies over the use of a junction or station.

Ticket platform. At one time it was common practice to stop trains at a special platform just before major stations, especially termini, so that tickets could be collected or checked. Some appeared in the timetables, usually as places where people could alight only.
Less often, they were sited just after main stations and, even more rarely, available as joining points. Some developed into full stations. The possibility should be considered that passengers could also alight, if only by local arrangement, at some not listed; in this book they are only included if there is clear evidence that they could be so used.

Up trains: towards London; see also 'Down trains', above.

Workmen's services. On some lines cheap travel for workmen was provided on early morning and evening trains, either via special or normal services. The practice had its origins in the demolition of inner city residential areas to make room for lines and stations. The intention was that displaced workers would be compensated by cheap travel to and from their new, more distant, homes. In reality it did not work quite like that. The services mainly benefited skilled workers with secure jobs. The unskilled casual labourers, likely to be the main victims of the demolition, had to stay in the centres to be near whatever casual work was going, at whatever time it was offered, and, in any case, would not have been able to afford even the 'low' workmen's fares.

Traditional units are used:

Length: 22 yards = 1 chain
1760 yards or 80 chains = 1 mile.

Money: 12d (pence) = 1s or 1/- (shilling)
20s = £1.

STATIONS
A – Z

ABBEY
A TOWN [NB] op 4 September 1856** (*NB*); initially
ABBEYHOLME (*Brad*); then A; TOWN added 1889
tt (*Cl*); clo 7 September 1964 (*RM October*).
A JUNCTION [Cal] op 31 August 1870 (*co ½T 26 Sept*).
Clo 20 May 1921 (see 1920 April/May**).
A JUNCTION [NB] op 8 August 1870 (*D&C 14*);
clo 1 September 1921 (Thursday) (*RCG*) – stops still
shown until then in *Brad* (all-days August 1921) but
would seem to have been pointless after April/May 1921**.
Left in case Cal line reopened? Did trains actually call?
Sol J, p.21, says that from 1 July 1904 Cal switched to
NB Abbeyholme station, presumably closing own.
However RCH sources point (very roughly) in the
opposite direction.
RCH sources: *hb* 1895 showed both apparently using
same station, goods and passengers, 1904 separate
stations (NB passenger only, Cal also goods, livestock
and horseboxes). 1912 same (more clearly listed as
separate stations). 1922a (1918 previous seen) both
stations and Abbey Holme (physical) Junction closed;
1923a – junction reopened and Cal Junction station
reopened goods and livestock. Junction Diagams
initially just showed Abbey Holme Junction; about
1880 added station there; by 1903 NB had station
(ABBEY HOLME [JUNCTION?]) on junction, Cal
had A JUNCTION 5 chains south. Distance Books:
NB June 1907 Abbey Holme passenger station and
junction with Cal, Abbey Town 48 chains further on;
Cal October 1909 Abbey Holme junction with NB,
Abbey Junction 5 chains; both agreed that Kirkbride
Junction was 3m 63ch north of Abbey Holme Junction.
Brad and co tts seen all have Abbey Junction for the
station concerned.
Cl has A J [Cal] closed entirely 1 January 1917, reop
2 March 1919, with later goods information fitting the
above. *Sol J, p.58* reproduces NB notice dated
26 January 1917 saying goods closure of Cal branch
would be from 1 February. *Brad* 1917–9 sampled show
stops at A J in Cal table, though service was a much
reduced one; was Cal then using NB station?
Handbooks and appendices no guide since did not
show war-time closures.
ABBEY & WEST DEREHAM [GE]
op 1 August 1882 (*GE- line*) as A; became A for W D
1 January 1886 (*Cl; RCG ref Jan*), A & W D 1 July 1923
(*hbl 12th*); clo 22 September 1930 (*Cl*).
ABBEY FOREGATE – see SHREWSBURY.
ABBEY HOUSES see BEAUCHIEF.
ABBEY OF DEER [GNS] (non-tt): pilgrimages;

1930s, 1940s (*U*); PLATFORM; {Maud – Mintlaw}.
ABBEY WOOD [SE] op on or by 1 November 1849
(included in notice of alterations *T 29 October*, but not
in earlier notices seen); still open. Earliest co tt for line
has place for this occupied by HARROW ROAD, no
trains calling – intended name? (D. Banks); one word
until 1890 (*hb*); A W for the CRAYS (*Brad*, e.g. 1850).
ABBEY WOOD – see under FILTON.
ABBEYDORE [GW] op 1 September 1881**- line;
finally clo 8 December 1941.
ABBEYHILL [NB] op 1 May 1869 (*Rly Times 8th/
RCHS Journal July 1979*); clo 7 September 1964 (*Cl*).
At times ABBEY HILL (*hb*); about 1875–8 *Brad* called
it EDINBURGH A.
ABBEYHOLME [MC]: Macaulay's 1851 map
shows station just west of Leegate; not on 1854 map.
No supporting evidence for existence. See 1840** for
habits of MC; perhaps site between stations at which
trains called often enough to cause confusion for
someone drafting maps at a distance.
ABBOTS RIPTON [GN] op 2 November 1885
(based on *GN* – says 1st, but that a Sunday, no Sunday
service here – was first in *Brad* November); ABBOTTS
R until 1938 (*Cl*); clo 15 September 1958 (*RM October*).
ABBOTS WOOD JUNCTION [GW/Mid]
op November 1850 (*Mid*) as WORCESTER J;
renamed 1 March 1852 co tt (*Mid*); exchange only
but in public tt; clo 1 October 1855 (*Cl*);
{physical junction *IA*}.
ABBOTSBURY [GW] op 9 November 1885
(*W Gaz 13th*); clo 1 December 1952 (*W Gaz 5th*).
ABBOTSFORD FERRY [NB] first in *Brad* May
1856 – line op 5 April 1856 but A F not in op notice
Selkirk 5th, paper of 3 May (next issue) said passengers
now booked to 'BOLDSIDE (A.F.)';
clo 5 January 1931 (*Cl*).
ABBOTSHAM ROAD [BWA]:
line op 18 May 1901**; clo 28 March 1917**.
ABDIE: alias for LINDORES temp.
ABER [TV] – see ABERTRIDWR.
ABER near Caerphilly [Rhy] op 1 April 1908 (*Aber*)
as BEDDAU (BEDA, error, in *Brad*); became
A JUNCTION 17 September 1926 (*GW circ 3011*),
A 6 May 1968 (*Aberdare*); HALT until 1968/9; still open.
ABER near Bangor [LNW] op 1 May 1848 (*D&C 11;
co n T 2nd- line*); clo 12 September 1960 (*RM October*).
ABERAMAN [all TV]
First station of this name probably op 5 April 1847
(in co tt of that date, *RAIL 981/491*, assumed to be
opening tt as far as this station was concerned);

although in tt, more of a private station for Crawshay Bailey than a public one; last train ran 12 July 1856 (Saturday) (Aberdare).

Another station, TREAMAN, op nearby October 1848; re-sited about ¾ mile north January 1857; renamed A 1888/9 – authorised 26 October 1888 (Aberdare; RCG ref January 1889); clo 16 March 1964 (Cl).

ABERANGELL [Cam] op 30 September 1867 (co n Merioneth 5 October), when required – notice has ABERANGEL (and thus hb until 1882); clo 17 April 1901 (Wednesday) (Cl); reop 31 July 1911 (RCG); clo 1 January 1931** (Thursday) (Cl).

ABERAVON [RSB] {map 85}.

A SEA SIDE first in Brad April 1899 (listed March as newly opened, but not in body of book); clo 3 December 1962 (RM January 1963).

A Jubilee Road pre-opening (RAC).

A TOWN op 25 June 1885 (The Cambrian, 26th) as A; became A PORT TALBOT 1 December 1891 (RCG); PT 1895 tt (Cl; RCG ref April); A TOWN 1 July 1924 (GW circular 18 June); clo 3 December 1962 (RM January 1963).

ABERAYRON [GW] op 12 May 1911 (co n Lampeter); clo 12 February 1951 (Cl) – see 1951**.

ABERBARGOED [BM]

First station op 16 April 1866 (Cardiff T 20th- line) at 16m 16ch; ABER BARGOED at start; last in Brad October 1869; back March 1870; renamed A B & BARGOED 1 September 1905 (RCG) > Replaced 1 March 1909 by B & A/B & A B at 16m 26ch; renamed A 1 July 1924 (GW circular 18 June) > Replaced 30 September 1935 (co n dated 24th) by A, back at original site; aot request; clo 31 December 1962 (T 31st).

BARGOED & ABERBARGOED (under 'B') was [Rhy].

ABERBEEG [GW] op 23 December 1850**; clo 30 April 1962 (T 6 April).

ABERBRAN [N&B] op 14 September 1868 (N&B minutes – P. Rowledge); became HALT 1941/42 Brad, 1941/44a hb; clo 15 October 1962 (RM November).

ABERCAIRNY [Cal] op 21 May 1866**; clo 1 October 1951 (RM November). ABBERCAIRNY until 1890/1 Brad, ABERCAIRNEY early hb.

ABERCAMLAIS [N&B] (non-tt) private station: line op 3 June 1867 (T 5th), station included in pre-opening inspection report (P. Rowledge); HALT at clo 15 October 1962; {Devynock – Aberbran} (U).

Revd Garnons Williams had right to stop trains (GW Deed 25931, dated 18 September 1866).

ABERCANAID [GW/Rhy] op 1 April 1886 (GW- line); became A PENTREBACH 9 September 1913 (hbl 23 October); back to A 1 July 1924 (GW circular 18 June); last train 3 February 1951 – see 1951**.

ABERCARN [GW] op 23 December 1850**; re-sited on deviation about August 1867 (MT6/154/9, dated 8 August); clo 30 April 1962 (T 6 April).

ABERCARNE early – Brad to 1854 but still thus Monmouthshire co wtt November 1865.

ABERCHALDER [High; NB] op 22 July 1903**; clo 1 November 1911 (Wednesday),

reop 1 August 1913 (RM August); clo 1 December 1933 (Friday) (RM December).

ABERCORN – see PAISLEY.

ABERCRAVE [N&B] op 2 March 1891 (RCG) *; clo 12 September 1932 (Cl).

* = op 1882 according to N&B Gomer, at first non-tt use?

ABERCWMBOI [TV] op 26 December 1904 (Aberdare) as DUFFRYN CROSSING PLATFORM; became A PLATFORM 1906 tt (Cl); see 1904** for other name changes; first in hb 1938 as HALT; clo 2 April 1956 (Cl).

ABERCYNON

A NORTH op 3 October 1988 (free publicity service 2nd) (Aberdare); still open.

A SOUTH [TV] op 9 October 1840** as NAVIGATION HOUSE; became ABERDARE JUNCTION 1849 tt (Cl), ABERCYNON 1 December 1896 (hbl 28 January 1897); SOUTH added 1988; still open.

[Aberdare] initially had own station here, when name was ABERDARE JUNCTION; just north of main station, at/near present Abercynon North; op 6 August 1846; order to move it south alongside TV station given 23 March 1848; merged with TV station? (Aberdare).

Both ABERDARE JUNCTION stations reduced to exchange only after 29 October 1855 owing to dispute with landlord of nearby public house; full service again 1 May 1856 (Aberdare).

ABERDARE {map 86}.

ABERDARE op 3 October 1988 (free publicity service 2nd) (Aberdare); old HL reop; still open.

A HL [GW] op 24 September 1851**; HL added 1 July 1924 (GW circular 18 June); closed 15 June 1964** (RM August).

A LL [TV] op 6 August 1846 (Merlin 8th); LL added 1 July 1924 (GW circular18 June); clo 16 March 1964 (Cl).

Also see COMMERCIAL STREET; MILL STREET.

ABERDARE JUNCTION – see ABERCYNON.

ABERDEEN {map 7}

Line from south op to temporary terminus at FERRYHILL [Aberdeen] 1 April 1850 (Cal); replaced by >

A GUILD STREET [Cal] when line extended 2 August 1854 (GNS) >

Line from north op to A WATERLOO [GNS] 1 April 1856 (GNS) >

Both termini replaced by A JOINT [Cal/GNS] op 4 November 1867 (GNS); JOINT dropped 1938/9 Brad but 1952 according to ref RM October; still open.

Also see KITTYBREWSTER.

ABERDERFYN [GW] first in Brad October 1907; clo 22 March 1915** (Cl); HALT; {map 75}.

ABERDOUR [NB] op 2 June 1890 (D&C 6- line; inspected 16 April 1890 – W.T. Cochrane, Aberdour Railway Station Researched and Remembered, author, 2002); still open.

ABERDOVEY [Cam]

First station at Harbour op 24 October 1863 (T 28th); clo 14 August 1867.

Second: Savin, builder and early operator of line, used

siding from 21ch west of Ynyslas to Cerrig y Penrhyn, opposite harbour to ferry passengers and building materials across (shown, in truncated form, as FERRY in Col. Cobb's Atlas); no station or BoT sanction; this service ran until line along north bank of river Dovey supposed to open. Faulty tunnels led to BoT refusal for their use but rest of line and new station op 14 August 1867 *(co n Merioneth 17th)*, passengers being at first taken round faulty stretch by road *(Cam Coast)* – footnote to advertisement of excursion trains *(Merioneth 17th)* said arrangement was temporary, worked out with landowners (presumably while disputes settled); still open. 1877 *hb* had ABERDOVERY, corrected 1879a.

ABERDYLAIS [GW] op 24 September 1851★★; HALT from 1954; clo 15 June 1964 *(RM August)*. ABERDULASS *Brad*, amended before end of 1851.

ABEREDW [Cam] first in *Brad* November 1867; aot request; clo 31 December 1962 *(T 31st)*.

ABERERCH [Cam] first in *Brad* July 1884; HALT 1 May 1956 to 6 May 1968 *(Cl)*; aot request; still open.

ABERFAN [GW/Rhy] op 1 April 1886 *(GW- line)*; became A for MERTHYR VALE 15 October 1891 *(RCG)*, back to A 1 July 1924 *(GW circular 18 June)*; last train 3 February 1951 – see 1951★★.

ABERFELDY [High] op 3 July 1865 *(High)*; clo 3 May 1965 *(RM June)*.

ABERFFRWD [VoR] (ng) op 22 December 1902★★ (see for details); transferred to preservation 1989.

ABERFORD – see 1837 A★★.

ABERFOYLE [NB] op 1 August 1882 *(D&C 6)*; line first in *Brad* October; clo 1 October 1951 *(RM November)*.

ABERGAVENNY {map 91}
See 1829 A★★ for earliest 'service'.

ABERGAVENNY [GW] op 2 January 1854 *(T 29 December 1853- line)*; A MONMOUTH ROAD 19 July 1950 to 6 May 1968 tt *(Cl)*; still open.

A BRECON ROAD [LNW] op 1 October 1862 *(co ½ T 20 February 1863)*; clo 6 January 1958 *(RM February)*.

A JUNCTION [GW/LNW] existed to provide link between Hereford to Newport line, already open, and Abergavenny to Tredegar line, op 1 October 1862; however, opening tt *(LNW Officers)* showed A BRECON ROAD as eastern terminus of latter; A J was open on or by 1 January 1863, when present in GW wtt (P. Rowledge). Perhaps initially intended only as exchange, thus absence from public tt; first in *Brad* March 1864, then only in GW tables; added to LNW later. Re-sited 25 chains north 20 June 1870 *(LNW Officers 5523)*. Clo 9 June 1958 *(Cl)*. In LNW co tt 1864–70, at least: MERTHYR, TREDEGAR & A J.

ABERGELE & PENSARN [LNW] op 1 May 1848 *(D&C 11; co n T 2nd- line)*; still open. & P included intermittently, *Brad* and LNW co tt: *Brad* 1868/9 to 1882/3 (also *hbl ref January 1883*) and 1888/9 on; LNW co tt 1869/70 to 1870/74 and 1874/5 on. *Hb* just A 1883 on.

ABERGLASLYN [WH] (ng) op 1 June 1923 *(NGSC 2)* as NANTMOR; see 1922 July 31★★; renamed 9 July 1934 *(Cl)*; clo 28 September 1936 *(Cl)*; {map 76}.

ABERGWILI [LNW] op 1 June 1865★★; last trains shown March 1880 *Brad*; back June 1880; clo 9 September 1963 *(T 9th)*. ABERGWILLY/ ABERGWILLI early, settled 28 July 1893 *(LNW dates)*.

ABERGWYNFI [GW] op 22 March 1886 *(GW)*; clo 13 June 1960, when service diverted over new junction to Blaengwynfi *(RM July)*.

ABERGYNOLWYN [Talyllyn] (ng) op 1 October 1866★★; see 6 October 1950★★ *(Cl)*.

ABERKENFIG [Llynvi & Ogmore] first in *Brad* April 1869; last there January 1870; {just north of present Sarn}.

ABERLADY [NB] op 1 April 1898 *(RCG)*; clo 12 September 1932 *(co n, N Berwick)*.

ABERLLEFENI [Corris] (ng) op 25 August 1887 *(Corris)*; clo 1 January 1931 (Thursday) *(Cl)*. ABERLLEFENNY *hb* until 1908a.

ABERLOUR [GNS]
op 1 July 1863 *(GNS)*; clo 18 October 1965★★.

ABERMULE [Cam] op from Newtown 14 August 1860 mainly for workmen – stretch isolated from system *(Cam)*; full service 10 June 1861 *(Shrewsbury 14th)*; clo 14 June 1965 *(RM July)*.

ABERNANT
ABERNANT [GW] first in *Brad* June 1854; clo 31 December 1962 *(T 31st)*.

ABERNANT [LNW] – see under MARKHAM VILLAGE.

ABERNETHY near Perth {map 5}
Temp term **A ROAD** [Edinburgh & Northern] op 17 May 1848 *(co n Perthshire Courier 18th)*; clo when line extended to Perth via permanent >
ABERNETHY [NB] op 18 July 1848 *(co n, item Perthshire Courier 20th)*; clo 19 September 1955 *(RM October)*.

ABERNETHY near Aviemore
– see NETHY BRIDGE

ABERSYCHAN
A LL [GW] op 2 October 1854★★ *(GW- line)*; LL added 14 May 1885 *(hbl 29 June)*; clo 30 April 1962 *(T 6 April)*.

A & TALYWAIN JOINT [GW/LNW] op 1 May 1878 *(LNW Officers 18465)*; clo 5 May 1941 *(Cl)*.

ABERTAFOL [GW]
op 18 March 1935 *(Cl 29)*; HALT until 6 May 1968 *(GW H)*; aot request; clo 14 May 1984 *(RM June)*; {Aberdovey – Dovey Junction}.
According to *RM August 1983*, no trains called 28 May to 4 June and 16 July to 3 September 1983 because schools were on holiday and the only trains scheduled to call here ran during term only.

ABERTHAW
ABERTHAW [Barry]
op 1 December 1897 *(Colliery 3rd)*; A HL 1 July 1924 *(GW circular 18 July)* to 7 May 1945 *(Cl)*; clo 15 June 1964 *(RM August)*.

A LL [TV] op 1 October 1892 *(Western Mail, 3rd)*; LL added 1 July 1924 *(GW circular 18 July)*; clo 4 May 1926★★; reop 11 July 1927 *(Rly Gaz 11 July)*; clo 5 May 1930 *(Cl)*.

ABERTHIN [TV] op 1 May 1905 (*Cowbridge*);
see 1904★★; clo 12 July 1920 (*RCG*);
{Ystradowen – Cowbridge}.

ABERTILLERY [GW] op 23 December 1850★★;
re-sited about 200 yds north 1893/4;
clo 30 April 1962 (*T 6 April*).

ABERTRIDWR [Rhy] op 1 February 1894 (*Rhy*) as
ABER, renamed 26 June 1899 (*hbl 13 July*);
clo 15 June 1964 (*RM August*).

ABERTYSSWG [BM]
op 1 August 1905 (*RCG*); clo 14 April 1930 (*Cl*).

ABERYSTWYTH

ABERYSTWYTH [Cam/GW] (standard gauge)
op 23 June 1864 (*Camarvon 25th*); still open.
ABERYSTWITH in *Brad* until 1867 and *hb* until 1892a
(*RCG ref April 1893*); became A JOINT *hb* 1899a.

ABERYSTWYTH [VoR] (ng) op 22 December 1902★★
(see for line history); re-sited to north 31 July 1925 (*Cl*);
clo 17 April 1968 – services diverted to platform in
main station (*Cl*).

ABINGDON [GW] op 2 June 1856 (*GW*);
clo 9 September 1963 (*RM October*).

ABINGDON JUNCTION [GW] op 2 June 1856
(*GW*); (non-tt), exchange only for Abingdon branch;
clo 8 September 1873, branch extended north to
Radley, new junction station (*Cl*).

ABINGDON ROAD [GW] op 1 February 1908
(*Oxford Chron 31 January*); HALT; clo 22 March 1915
(*RCH*); {nearly 2 miles south of Oxford}.

ABINGDON ROAD as a junction station
– see CULHAM.

ABINGTON Cambridge – see PAMPISFORD.

ABINGTON near Lanark [Cal] op 15 February 1848
(*co ½ T 29 February- line*); clo 4 January 1965
(*RM February*).

ABOYNE [GNS] op 2 December 1859 (*GNS*);
clo 28 February 1966 (*RM March*).

ABOYNE CURLING POND [GNS] (non-tt):
occasional use; alias LOCH OF ABOYNE;
{Dess – Aboyne}; (*U*).

ABY [GN] op 3 September 1848 (*Boston 4th- line*) as
CLAYTHORPE; became A for C 1 November 1885
(*Cl/RCG ref October*) and thus GN co tt 1909, LNE tt
1933; clo 11 September 1961 (*RM September*).

ACCRINGTON [LY]
op 19 June 1848 (*Lancaster Guardian 17th*); still open.

ACH-NA-CLOICH [Cal] first in *Brad* June 1881;
clo 1 January 1917 (*RM February*); reop 1 March 1919
(*RCH*); aot request; clo 1 November 1965 (*Cl*).

ACHANALT [High] op 19 August 1870 (*High*); still
open. Aot request; ACHANAULT in *hb* until 1877.

ACHEILIDH CROSSING [High] (non-tt):
railwaymen, families; dates ?; {Lairg – Rogart}; (*U*).

ACHNASHEEN [High] op 19 August 1870 (*High*);
still open. *Brad* ? to 1955 but not *Murray* 1948:
A for KINLOCHEWE.

ACHNASHELLACH [High] op as private station
19 August 1870 (*High*); first in public co tt 1 May 1871
(*Lochalsh*); (first in *Brad* July 1871);
AUCHNASHELLACH tt until 1914 (*JS*) and *hb*
until 1898a; aot request; still open.

ACHTERNEED [High] op 19 August 1870 as
STRATHPEFFER (*High*); renamed 1 June 1885
(*Cl; RCG ref April*); clo 7 December 1964 (*Cl*).
Reop 8 February 1965, unadvertised, unstaffed, by
local arrangement (*Lochalsh*); no later information –
not in Baker's Atlas.

ACKERS CROSSING [NS]:
has been suggested there was a private station for
G.H. Ackers of Old Moreton Hall (see *Chron 30*);
{about ¾ mile north-east of Mow Cop}. This is unlikely:
Booklet 3 of *The Cheshire Ring Canal Walk*, refers to
road bridge built over canal by Ackers family for easy
access to Mow Cop (A. Brackenbury).

ACKLINGTON [NE]
op 1 July 1847★★ – line; still open.

ACKWORTH [SK] op 1 July 1879 (*Mid- wtt; co n
T 28 June- line*); clo 2 July 1951 (*RM September*);
later excursions, e.g. 3 August 1952 to Bridlington and
Scarborough (BR working notice).

ACLE [GE] op 12 March 1883; (*co n Norfolk News
10th* – G. Kenworthy; in *Brad* April and GE co tt May –
no April issue of latter); still open.

ACOCKS GREEN [GW] first in *Brad* June 1853;
A G & SOUTH YARDLEY 1878 tt (*W Mid*) to 6 May
1968 tt; still open.

ACREFAIR [GW] op 2 June 1862 (*GW- line*) as
CEFN MAWR; renamed 1863 (*Brad*); clo 18 January
1965★★. A LL in *hb* 1904 on (HL goods only).

ACROW: (non-tt)
HALT; Acrow Engineering workmen; op 1 April 1957
(*Rly Obs May*) – 27 March formal; clo 7 September
1964 (*U*); {Saffron Walden – Ashdon}.

ACTON London

A CENTRAL [NSWJ] op 1 August 1853
(*Mid; T 1st- line*) ★; CENTRAL added 1 January 1925
(*hbl January*); still open. A CHURCHFIELD ROAD
in *Brad* 1883 to 1925 (*JS*).

★ = line first in *Brad* October, this station not until December
– presumed case of 'nd'.

A GREEN – see CHISWICK PARK

A MAIN LINE [GW] op 1 February 1868
(*co n T 27 January*); M L added 26 September 1949
(*L corr*); still open. A ot A for LEAMINGTON PARK,
A HORN LANE *Brad*.

A TOWN [Dist] op 1 July 1879 as MILL HILL PARK
(*T 2nd*); renamed 1 March 1910 (*RCG*); [Picc] use
began 4 July 1932; still open.
Also see EAST A; NORTH A; SOUTH A; WEST A.

ACTON BRIDGE [LNW] near Runcorn op 4 July
1837 (*co n GJ*); BRIDGE added 1 July 1870
(*Cl; recommended LNW Officers 15 June*); still open.

ADAM STREET – see CARDIFF.

ADDERBURY [GW] op 6 April 1887 (*GW- line*);
clo 4 June 1951 (*T 4th*).

ADDERLEY [GW] op 20 October 1863
(*Rtn- line;* in co n for formal opening on 19th – *By GW*);
clo 9 September 1963 (*T 9th*).

ADDERLEY PARK [LNW]
op 1 August 1860 (*W Mid*); still open.

ADDIEWELL [Cal] op 1 July 1882 (? – first in *Brad*
July 1882); still open.

ADDINGHAM [Mid] op 16 May 1888 *(Mid)*; clo 22 March 1965 *(RM April)*.

ADDISCOMBE

ADDISCOMBE (a) [SE] op 1 April 1864 *(co ½ T 8 August)*; variously in *Brad* as CROYDON A ROAD, C A, A C, settled as A 13 June 1955 *(Cl)*; first in *hb* as ADDISCOMB ROAD CROYDON, then (1872) ADDISCOMBE ROAD; in SEC co tt 1914 as A R, C; clo 1 June 1997** for conversion >

ADDISCOMBE (b) [Croydon] op 23 May 2000 *(RM Feb 2001)*; about ½ mile east of (a); still open.

ADDISON ROAD
– see KENSINGTON OLYMPIA

ADDLESTONE [LSW]: line op 14 February 1848 *(co n T 7th)*, nd, April 1848; still open.

ADISHAM [LCD] op 22 July 1861 *(LCD)*; still open. *Brad* ? to 1955/6, SEC co tt 1914 and *hb* 1904 on: A for WINGHAM.

ADLESTROP [GW] op 4 June 1853 *(Glos Chron 4th- line)* as ADDLESTROP & STOW ROAD; & S R dropped 1 March 1862 *(Cl)*; spelling altered 1 July 1883 *(hbl 31 December)*; clo 3 January 1966 *(RM February)*.

ADLINGTON CHESHIRE [LNW] op 24 November 1845**; CHESHIRE added body of tt 1984, index much earlier; still open.

ADLINGTON LANCS [LY] op 22 December 1841 *(LY)*; last in *Brad* August 1843; back January 1844; LANCS added 1938/9 *(Brad)*; still open.

ADMASTON [Shrewsbury & Wellington]: first in *Brad* September 1849 (Shrewsbury to Stafford table); last there November 1849; back June 1850; aot request; became HALT 30 June 1952 *(Cl)*; clo 7 September 1964 *(RM October)*. At first erratically A SPA *(Brad)*; often trains only shown on Stafford line early on – perhaps tt does not tell full story.

ADMIRALTY PLATFORM
– see KEYHAM; KILLINGHOLME.

ADOLPHUS STREET – see BRADFORD.

ADVIE [GNS] op 1 July 1863 *(GNS)*; re-sited ¾ mile west 1 September 1868 *(Cl)*; clo 18 October 1965**.

ADWICK op 11 October 1993 *(BLN 718)*; near earlier Carcroft; still open.

AFON WEN [Cam]
op 2 September 1867** *(Cam; co ½ T 10 October- line)*; clo 7 December 1964 *(RM March 1965)*.
At times one word: thus LNW co tts seen 1874 to 1921 and LMS tt 1930; according to *JS* thus *Brad* 1904 to 1922; also thus *hb* 1912 and 1925.

AGECROFT [LY]: line opened 29 May 1838**; station for Kersal Moor Racecourse, probably initially race days only; by 1843 racegoers were using Pendleton (Bridge) *(race)*; first in *Brad* as public station October 1857; in LY table of signals 1857; last in *Brad* January 1861; alias A BRIDGE; {Pendleton – Clifton Junction}.

AIGBURTH [CLC] op 1 June 1864 *(CLC)* as MERSEY ROAD; renamed M R & A 1879/80 *(Brad)*; clo 17 April 1972 *(RM May)*; reop, as A, 3 January 1978 *(AZ; Daily Telegraph 3rd- line)*; still open.

AIKBANK [MC] op 10 February 1845; clo 2 February 1848 (probably); see 1840**; {map 20g}.

AINDERBY [NE]: line op 6 March 1848 *(NE)*, nd, July 1848 *(Topham)*; clo 26 April 1954 *(T 20th)*.

AINSDALE

AINSDALE [LY] op 24 July 1848**; still open. Perhaps suffered at least one short closure in early days.

A BEACH [CLC] op 19 June 1901 *(RCG)* as SEASIDE for A; renamed 1 January 1912 *(RCG)*; clo 1 January 1917 *(T 23 December 1916)*; reop non-tt for races at Aintree in March 1919 *(CLC Portrait)*, to public 1 April 1919 *(RCH)*; clo 7 January 1952 *(RM February)*.

AINSWORTH ROAD [LY] op 1 January 1918 *(LY)*; HALT; clo 21 September 1953 *(RM November)*.

AINTREE

AINTREE [LY] op 2 April 1849 *(Southport Vis 7th)*; became A SEFTON ARMS 1951/2 *(Brad)*, back to A 6 May 1968; still open.
Included extra-long platforms for race meetings *(AB)*.

A CENTRAL [CLC] op 13 July 1880 as A RACECOURSE, race use only *(U)*; became public station as A 1 September 1884 *(CLC)*; CENTRAL added 20 August 1951 *(Cl)*; clo to public 7 November 1960 *(RM December)*; race use to Grand National of 26 March 1966 *(Rly Obs May, p.149)*, probably last use.

A RACECOURSE [LY] (non-tt): op ?; (in *hb* 1883, but only added to junction diagram 1901/09); certainly used 27 March 1890 *(AB)*; A CINDER LANE until 18 May 1910 *(AB)*; clo 31 March 1962, Grand National day, presumed last use (R. Gell, *An Illustrated Survey of Liverpool's Railway Stations*, Heyday, 1985). Further east on this branch a special train was stabled for use as grandstand by railway officials – to 1967 at least *(AB)*.
Also see FAZAKERLEY.

AIRBLES op 15 May 1989 *(RM July)*; still open.

AIRDRIE {map 16}

AIRDRIE [Cal] op 1 June 1886 *(Cal)*; reduced 1 January 1917 to being terminus of service to Newhouse, operating detached from system; reconnected to system 1 March 1919, with reopening of line through Whifflet; clo 3 May 1943 *(Cl)*.

AIRDRIE [NB] op 11 Aug 1862 *(MK)*; A SOUTH until 3 March 1952 *(Cl; RM ref April)*; still open. *Hb*: A SOUTHSIDE 1865a, A SOUTH 1867.

A HALLCRAIG (STREET?) [NB] op 26 December 1844**; clo 1 June 1871 *(notice in wtt, BR/TT(S)/52/14A SRO)*. *Brad* added H Street 1852; later entries suggest should have been H Station. *Hb* early entries for A NORTH, HALL CRAIG, A OLD, often as alternatives. Also see 1840 August 5**.

A LEA END [MK]: several short-lived services from 1828 to 1843 (see 1828 B**).

COMMONHEAD A NORTH [NB] op 5 August 1840** as Airdrie station of Slammanan; not in *Brad* until January 1864 but *MK* quotes 1858 passengers' complaints about effects of nearby pig farm; A N added 1 June 1886 *(Cl)*; clo 1 May 1930 *(Cl)*.

AIRMYN [NE] op 1 May 1912 *(NE corr- line)*; A & RAWCLIFFE until 12 June 1961 *(RM April)*; clo 15 June 1964 *(T 25 March)*.

AIRTH [Cal]
first in *Brad* July 1852 as CARNOCK ROAD;
became A ROAD 1865 tt *(Cl/JS)*,
A 1866 *(Brad)*; aot request; clo 20 September 1954
(RM November).

AKELD [NE] op 5 September 1887 *(NE- line)*;
clo 22 September 1930★★ *(T 10 July)*.

AKEMAN STREET [GC] op 2 April 1906
(RCG; T 3rd- line); clo 7 July 1930 *(RAIL 393/151)*.

ALBANY PARK [SR]
op 7 July 1935 *(sig n 25/1935)*; still open.

ALBERT EDWARD DOCK
– see under PERCY MAIN.

ALBERT PARK
– see WITHINGTON & WEST DISBURY.

ALBERT ROAD Devonport [LSW]
op 1 October 1906 *(SR)*; HALT;
clo 13 January 1947 *(Cl)*; {map 114}.

ALBERT ROAD BRIDGE [LSW/LBSC]
op 1 July 1904 *(LBSC)*; HALT, though not so shown
LSW co tt 7 June 1914 or *Brad* July 1914, – was shown
as rail-motor served; clo 10 August 1914 *(RM June
1931)*; {East Southsea branch}.

ALBERTA PLACE Penarth [TV] op 19 September
1904 *(Penarth)*; see 1904★★; clo 6 May 1968 *(Cl)*.

ALBION [LNW] op 2 May 1853 *(Wolverhampton
27 April)* – (1st a Sunday); clo 1 February 1960
(RM March).

ALBRIGHTON [GW] op 13 November 1849
(see 1849★★); still open.

ALCESTER [Mid]
op 17 September 1866 *(Mid; Rtn- line)*;
clo 1 October 1962 (buses to 17 June 1963) *(Cl)*.

ALDAM JUNCTION [SY]: in *Brad* January to
October 1855 and September 1856 to September 1859
(both inclusive); trains only shown calling September
1856. Almost certainly error. *SY* includes what looks
like wtt but was issued to public. This says all trains
between Westwood and Aldam Junction one way,
Westwood and Blackburn Junction other, must be
accompanied by travelling porter for section (to ensure
only one train could get onto single line section).
Aldam and Blackburn Junctions were shown in station
list, no trains stopping (clearly they had to). *SY* suggests
they were included to increase public confidence about
safety. Times could not be shown in public tt, otherwise
people would try to catch trains; probably understood
locally but looks confusing in *Brad*, without explanatory
note. {Smithley – Wombwell}.

ALDEBURGH [GE] op 12 April 1860 *(T 16th)*;
ALDBOROUGH/ALDEBOROUGH until 1 June
1875 *(RCG)*, though ALDE... form not seen *Brad*;
clo 12 September 1966 *(RM September)*.

ALDEBY [GE] op 4 December 1854 *(Ipswich Mercury
2nd, 9th – G. Kenworthy)*; clo 15 May 1858★★;
reop 1 June 1859 *(T 2nd)*; clo 2 November 1959
(RM December).

ALDERBURY JUNCTION [LSW] (non-tt)
exchange, railwaymen; op February 1872 *(U)*;
in *hb* 1872 (no facilities then shown), 1877 'P',
no entry 1883; 9 October 1920 and 14 July 1924 wtts

show Saturday only stop, towards Salisbury only,
for wives going to market; clo 4 May 1964 *(U)*;
{physical junction *IA*}.

ALDERHOLT – see DAGGONS ROAD.

ALDERLEY EDGE [LNW] op 10 May 1842
(fare table, *co n Stockport 13th*) as A;
became A & CHORLEY 1853 tt *(Cl)*,
A E 1875/6 *(RCG ref January 1876)*; still open.

ALDERMASTON [GW] op 21 December 1847
(GW; Hants Chron 25th- line); HALT 2 November
1964 to 5 May 1969 tt *(Cl)*; still open.

ALDERMINSTER – see 1833 B★★.

ALDERSGATE (STREET) – see BARBICAN.

ALDERSHOT [LSW]
ALDERSHOT op 2 May 1870 *(SR; co n T 30 April-
line)*; still open. Chaotic variety of names *Brad* and *hb* –
A TOWN; A TOWN & CAMP; A for TOWN and
CAMP; A TOWN SOUTH CAMP; A T for S C – not
always same in different tables in same month.
Government Sidings here used (non-tt) for military
tattoos – dates ? *(U)*.
Also see ASH; NORTH CAMP.

ALDGATE
ALDGATE [Met] op 18 November 1876; initially just
shuttle to and from previous terminus at Bishopsgate
(later Liverpool Street) *(T 14th)*; through service began
4 December *(co n T 29 November)*, though earlier notice
had advertised this for 1st; still open.
A EAST [Met/Dist] op 6 October 1884 *(T 4th)*;
re-sited east 31 October 1938 *(Cl)*; still open.
Commercial Road before opening *(L)*.

ALDIN GRANGE – see BEARPARK.

ALDRIDGE [Mid] op 1 July 1879 *(Mid; LNW
Record- line)*; clo 18 January 1965 *(RM March)*.

ALDRINGTON [LBSC] op 3 September 1905
(LBSC) as DYKE JUNCTION, renamed 17 June
1932 *(JS)*; HALT until 5 May 1969 *(SR App)*;
still open.

ALDWARKE – see PARKGATE.

ALDWYCH [Picc] op 30 November 1907 as
STRAND *(T 16th)*, renamed A 1 May 1915 *(hbl 15th)*;
clo and converted to air raid shelter 22 September 1940
(Sunday) *(RM February 1941)*; reop 1 July 1946
(RM September); clo 3 October 1994 (last train
30 September) *(RM November)*. Normally just shuttle
to/from Holborn, but late 1907 to 1910, probably, one
late evening theatre-goers' train to Finsbury Park *(Ug)*;
e.g. in *Brad* August 1908 and July 1909.

ALEXANDRA DOCK
ALEXANDRA DOCK [LO] op 6 March 1893★★;
clo 31 December 1956 *(T 29th)*.
ALEXANDRA DOCK [LNW] op 5 September 1881
(Waterloo Times 3rd) as ATLANTIC DOCK;
renamed 10 September 1881 *(Cl, RCG ref October)*;
clo 31 May 1948 *(LNW Record)*.

ALEXANDRA PALACE [both GN]
ALEXANDRA PALACE (a) op 1 May 1859 *(L)* as
WOOD GREEN; at times W G A PARK or
W G for A P until 18 March 1871 *(Cl)*; renamed
A PALACE 17 May 1982 *(RM July)*; still open.
ALEXANDRA PALACE (b) op 24 May 1873 *(co n*

T 22nd); closed when fire destroyed Palace main building early afternoon 9 June 1873; banqueting hall, cricket and archery pavilions undamaged and caterers said would continue in business in these. By 14 June Park had been reopened and GN were running extra trains to Wood Green, later A P (a), near park's entrance, at such short intervals as traffic would require. On 16 June line to A P reopened (items T 10th, 11th; GN notices T 14th, 16th); service to end of August 1873 (GN).
Later clo/reop 9 times: end August 1873*/1 May 1875, November 1876 tt*/10 May 1877*, August 1882 tt/ April 1885 tt, September 1885/June 1887 tt, September 1887 tt/12 May 1888, November 1888 tt/June 1889 tt, August 1889 tt / March 1891 tt, April 1892 tt/1 April 1898 (Cl), 29 October 1951/7 January 1952 (T 18 December 1951). Finally clo 5 July 1954 (RM July). Was A PARK 1891–2 use.
* = November 1876 – late October bankruptcy action being taken against company running Palace – last advertisements for events there were for 18 November (T of that date); 10 May 1877 (Palace co n T 8th – called it HL).
ALEXANDRA PARADE Glasgow [NB*] first in Brad November 1877, when terminus, as A PARK; renamed 1 July 1923 (hbl 12th, T 27 August); clo 1 January 1917, except for workmen's services (RM February); reop 2 June 1919 (RCH); still open. Sometimes GLASGOW A P in tts.
* = [CGU] until 1896.
ALEXANDRA PARK – see A PARADE (Glasgow); WILBRAHAM ROAD (Manchester).
ALEXANDRIA [DB Jt] op 15 July 1850**; still open. A & BONHILL 1936a on according to hb but not thus Brad or BR Scottish Region tts 30 June 1952 and 11 September 1961.
ALFORD near Aberdeen [GNS] op 21 March 1859 (GNS); clo 2 January 1950 (RM February).
ALFORD near Langport [GW] op 1 July 1905 (RAIL 253/482); HALT; clo 10 September 1962 (Som Gaz 15th).
ALFORD TOWN near Lincoln [GN] op 3 September 1848 (Boston 4th- line); TOWN added 1 July 1923 (hbl 12th); clo 5 October 1970 (T 16 July).
ALFRETON
A & SOUTH NORMANTON [Mid] op 1 May 1862 wtt (Mid); & S N added 7 November 1891 (RCG); clo 2 January 1967 (Mid).
ALFRETON op 7 May 1973 as A & MANSFIELD PARKWAY (RM July), same site as A & S N; renamed 29 May 1994 tt (AB, Chron); still open.
ALGARKIRK & SUTTERTON [GN]
op 17 October 1848 (co n T 16th); clo 11 September 1961 (RM September). At first in Brad as A, SWINESHEAD & DONNINGTON (and thus in opening notice, T 16th); then SUTTERTON, SWINESHEAD & D; then SUTTERTON, A & SWINESHEAD; was A & SUTTERTON in GN opening tt for extension 7 August 1850, reproduced RM September 1910; Topham got all four place names into his version; at times just A in hb.
ALL SAINTS [Dock] op 31 August 1987 (T 1 September); still open.

ALL SAINTS – see under CLEVEDON.
ALL STRETTON [SH Jt] op 29 February 1936 (T 24th)*; clo 4 January 1943, reop 11 March 1946 (LMS/GW Joint Officers 21 August); HALT; clo 9 June 1958 (Cl).
* = Cl 29 also gave this date, but GW H, a later book gave 21st; in this instance 29th is preferred because T of 24th said 'will open on Saturday' and Saturday was a common opening day for halts in this area; Friday openings were very rare.
ALLANFEARN [High] op 7 November 1855 (High) as CULLODEN; renamed 1 November 1898 (RCG); clo 3 May 1965 (RM June).
ALLANGRANGE [High] op 1 February 1894 (High); clo 1 October 1951 (RM November).
ALLENDALE [NE] op 1 March 1869 (NC) as CATTON ROAD; renamed 1 May 1898 (RCG); clo 22 September 1930 (T 10 July). NE co tt November 1880, from Hexham only: C R for A.
ALLENS WEST [LNE] first in wtt 4 October 1943 as URLAY NOOK HALT for munitions workers at naval depot; renamed A W H before/with 22 May 1944 wtt (RM); made public and HALT dropped 4 October 1971 (Rly Obs November); still open.
Urlay Nook level crossing, about ½ mile west would have been likely stopping-place in horse-drawn S&D days.
ALLERTON Liverpool
ALLERTON [LNW] op 15 February 1864 (LNW Officers); clo 1 August 2005 for reconstruction as part of Liverpool South Parkway (AB).
Initially A & GARSTON (hb); LNW co tts A for G 1869, A for G & WOOLTON (1882), though still A for G some tables; thus until 6 May 1974 (BR notice). Also see WEST ALLERTON.
ALLERTON see HOPPERTON.
ALLERWASH [NC] op 28 June 1836; prob clo about start of January 1837 (see 1836 B**).
ALLESLEY GATE / LANE – see TILE HILL.
ALLHALLOWS COLLIERY [MC] (non-tt): in use 1922–3; miners; {Baggrow – Mealsgate} (U).
ALLHALLOWS-ON-SEA [SR]
op Tuesday 17 May 1932 (A.A. Jackson, RCHS Journal 148 p.227) – used for Whitsun excursions from 14th (sig inst 19/1932 – to be ready for passenger traffic on 14th); clo 4 December 1961 (T 8 November); {on short branch to north from Stoke Junction, between Middle Stoke and Grain Crossing}.
RCH dist 9 August 1933 said had opened as ALL HALLOWS-on-S, later amended, but not seen thus elsewhere.
ALLOA {map 6}.
ALLOA (a) [NB] op 28 August 1850 (Stirling Journal 30 August); A NORTH/N A 1875 tt (Cl) to 1882 (Brad); clo 7 October 1968 (RM October).
ALLOA (b) op 19 May 2008 (public trains operated by Scottish Railway Preservation Society Railtours on 15th, formal opening day; still open. (G. Borthwick – local press and handouts; RM July).
A FERRY [Stirling & Dunfermline] op 3 June 1851 (Clackmannan Advertiser 7th); clo 1 July 1852 (Cl), when line from Alloa to Stirling opened, making ferry crossing redundant.

A JUNCTION [Cal] op 2 September 1850
(Alloa Advertiser 7th); last in *Brad* November 1865.
SOUTH ALLOA [Cal] op 2 September 1850
(Alloa Advertiser 7th); SOUTH added 1854 tt *(Cl)*;
clo 1 October 1885 *(RCG)*, line diverted to NB station.
At times A S.
N.b. **A NORTH** clo 1885 *(Cl)* was a ferry-only station,
opposite SOUTH A.
ALLOWAY [GSW] op 17 May 1906 *(RCG)*;
clo 1 December 1930 *(Cl)*. Later use – *Butlin's* mentions
Sunday School party from Troon 16 June 1948.
ALLT-Y-GRAIG [LMS] op 1 February 1929 *(Cl 29)*;
ALT-Y-CRAIG until 8 July 1929 *(Cl)*; aot request;
clo 22 September 1930 *(Cl)*; {Meliden – Dyserth}.
ALLTDDU [GW] op 23 September 1935 *(T 20th)*;
HALT; aot request; {Strata Florida – Tregaron};
clo 22 February 1965 *(Cl)*.
ALMELEY [GW] first in *Brad* June 1875 (could not
be opened with line, 3 August 1874, because BoT
demanded alterations – *co ½ T 9 September 1874)*;
clo 1 January 1917 *(GW notice dated 22 December 1916)*;
reop 11 December 1922 *(GW Mag January 1923)*;
clo 1 July 1940 *(Cl)*.
ALMONDBANK [Cal]
op 1 January 1858 *(Tayside- line)*; clo 1 October 1951
(RM November). ALMOND BANK in *hb* until 1890.
ALNE [NE] op 31 March 1841 *(co n E Cos Her 25th-
line)*; clo 5 May 1958 *(RM June)*.
ALNESS
ALNESS (a) [High] op 23 March 1863 *(High)*;
clo 13 June 1960 *(RM July)*.
ALNESS (b) op 7 May 1973 *(RM July)*; still open.
ALNMOUTH [NE] prob op 1 October 1850, with
Alnwick branch, replacing Lesbury (which see). Op as
BILTON, ALNWICK *(Brad)*; became B JUNCTION
1852 *(Brad)*, B 1 November 1891 co tt *(JS)*,
ALNMOUTH 1 May 1892 *(RCG)*; still open.
ALNWICK [NE] op 1 October 1850 *(NE Maps)*;
re-sited short distance north 5 September 1887 *(Cl)*;
clo 29 January 1968 *(RM March)*.
ALPERTON op by [Dist] 28 June 1903 *(RCG)* as
PERIVALE-A; renamed A for P/A (P) 7 October 1910
(RCG/hbl 27th); A by 1938 *(hb)*; transferred to [Picc]
4 July 1932; still open.
Dist ticket: A for WEMBLEY and P *(JB)*.
ALPHINGTON [GW] op 2 April 1928 *(GW H)*;
HALT; clo 9 June 1958 *(T 5th)*; {map 115}.
ALRESFORD near Winchester [LSW] op 2 October
1865 *(Salisbury 7th)*; aot request; clo 5 February 1973
(Hants Chron 9th).
ALRESFORD ESSEX [GE] op 8 January 1866
(T 10th- line); ESSEX added body of tt 30 September
2001 (earlier in index); still open.
ALREWAS
ALREWAS [LNW] op 9 April 1849 *(LNW- line)*;
clo 18 January 1965 *(RM March)*.
ALREWAS [Mid] – see CROXALL.
ALSAGER [NS] op 9 October 1848 *(NS-K; co ½
T 3 February 1849)*; still open. A RODE HEATH 1889
tt *(Cl)* to 2 April 1923 co tt *(JS)*.
ALSAGER ROAD [NS] op 1 July 1889 tt *(NS)*

as TALK & A R; renamed 1 November 1902 *(RCG)*;
clo 27 April 1931 *(Cl)*.
ALSCOT PARK – see 1833 B★★.
ALSOP-EN-LE-DALE [LNW] op 4 August 1899
(LNW Officers 39077, 39103); clo 1 November 1954
(T 1 October). Later occasional winter emergency use
(Cl) and ramblers' excursions, last 29 May 1960 *(AB)*.
LNW co tts, LMS co tt 1930:
A-en-le-D for DOVEDALE.
ALSTON [NE]
op 21 May 1852★★; clo 3 May 1976 *(RM May)*.
ALTCAR & HILLHOUSE [CLC] op 1 September
1884 *(CLC)*; clo 1 January 1917 *(T 23 December 1916)*;
reop non-tt for races at Aintree in March 1919 *(CLC
Portrait)*, to public 1 April 1919 *(RCH)*;
clo 7 January 1952 *(RM February)*.
ALTCAR RIFLE RANGE [LY]:
Prior to opening, LY agreed to stop all trains at Hightown
(ordinary station) when required, letting Volunteers
travel at reduced fares (letter, 14 August 1860, LY
minutes, *RAIL 343/56)*. Op 29 October 1860
(Ormskirk 1 November); available to spectators as well
as competitors. Not in *Brad* until August 1862
(minutes show use June to September that year);
mainly summers only but some winter use early years
(e.g. December 1864, Saturdays only, and December
1865, all days for Volunteers). Originally on siding;
this put out of use by fire in November 1869.
New ordered to be ready for start of next season *(RAIL
series 343)*. RCG said it clo 2 October 1921 – end of use
for that season? Last all day summer trains 1 to 25 Sept.
1927 *Brad*; last summer Saturdays 1 to 22 September
1930; last entry, no trains, June 1931 (still shown LMS
wtt 28 September 1936, without trains); aot request.
Perhaps other use as required – e.g. later special troop
trains. *LNW Record* refers to removal of station,
mid-1936. Op as HIGHTOWN SIDING; became
H NEW SIDING 1865 tt, H RIFLE STATION 1871 tt,
A RIFLE STATION 1886 tt *(C/W)*, A R R 1886
(Cl; RCG ref July) but 1895/6 *(Brad)*.
(See L.M. Cook, *The Story of Altcar Rifle Range*, author,
1989, for basic story).
ALTHORNE [GE] op 1 July 1889 *(RCG)*;
ALTHORN until 1889 tt *(JS)*, 1895 *(hb)*; still open.
ALTHORP PARK [LNW]
op 1 December 1881 *(LNW Officers 22843, 22911)*;
clo 13 June 1960 *(RM July)*.
ALTHORPE [GC] op 1 October 1866 *(GC; Rtn- line)*;
re-sited on deviation 21 May 1916 *(RCG)*;
A & KEADBY 1890 to 1894 *(Brad)*; became A for K,
GUNNESS & BURRINGHAM 21 May 1916
(dist 19 April 1920) and thus LNE tt 1933 and *Brad*
to 1955; still open.
ALTNABREAC [High]
op 28 July 1874 *(High)*; aot request; still open.
ALTNAGOURACH – see 1957★★.
ALTOFTS [Mid] op 1 September 1870 *(Mid)* as
A & WHITWOOD; renamed 4 May 1970 co tt *(Mid)*;
clo 14 May 1990 *(Mid)*.
ALTON near Basingstoke [LSW]
ALTON op 28 July 1852 *(Hants Chron 31st)*; re-sited

just east 2 October 1865 when line extended to Winchester *(Cl)*; became A for SELBORNE 5 July 1926 *(hbl July)* and thus to *Brad* 1955; still open.

ALTON PARK, alias TRELOARS HOSPITAL / CRIPPLES HOME (non-tt): op ? (inspected 14 April 1910); regular service Thursdays; clo 11 September 1932 *(Basingstoke)*. Certainly used for delivery of patients (photograph *S Halts*), perhaps also visitors; although item *T 12 September 1932* said Basingstoke to Alton would be retained for goods while Alton Park line would be taken up completely, *dist t supp dated 9 August 1933* gave amended distance to "Treloar's, Lord Mayor, Cripples' Home", resulting from obstruction to line between Bentworth and Alton; according to *Hosp* annual Founder's Day special ran until outbreak of war in 1939; {on branch from Alton}.

ALTON HEIGHTS JUNCTION [Cal] (non-tt): workmen from 1893 or earlier *(U)*; still in wtt 15 September 1952, not wtt 17 June 1957; {Lesmahagow – Coalburn}

ALTON TOWERS [NS] op 13 July 1849 *(NS-K; T 11th- line)*; TOWERS added 1954 *(Cl)*; clo 4 Jan. 1965 *(RM March)*. GE co tt 1909: A for A T.

ALTRINCHAM
ALTRINCHAM (a) [MSJA] op 20 July 1849**; at first separate stations for here and Bowdon; both replaced by >
ALTRINCHAM (b) [MSJA] op 4 April 1881* *(MSJA)* as A & BOWDON; renamed 6 May 1974 *(BR notice)*; [Manch] op 15 June 1992 to terminal platforms already existing here station *(RM August)*; still open for both. Also see BROADHEATH.
* = GC dates gives clo of portion of line to Bowdon as 3rd, and (typescript version only) op of new as 4th. Likely that 3rd (Sunday) was last day of use of Bowdon, 4th (Monday) first of new station.

ALVA [NB] op 3 June 1863 *(D&C 15)*; clo 1 November 1954 *(RM December)*.

ALVECHURCH [Mid] op 1 November 1859 tt *(Mid)*; re-sited to north 14 March 1993 (19th ceremonial) *(BLN 712 p.242)*; still open.

ALVELEY COLLIERY [GW] (non-tt): miners; op 1940; still in use March 1959, as A HALT; also variously, A C HALT, A C SIDINGS (information from stationmaster at Bewdley 24 March 1959 and BR Birmingham District additional services pamphlet Good Friday 27 March 1929 – R. Maund); {Hampton Loade – Highley} *(U)*.

ALVERSTONE [IWC]: line op 1 February 1875 *(Hants Chron 6th)*; station probably later, first in *Brad* June 1876 (see 1875**); aot request; clo 6 February 1956 *(Southern Daily Echo 6th)*.

ALVERTHORPE [GN] trains first shown in *Brad* November 1872; clo 5 April 1954 *(RM May)* – 'excursions will continue'.

ALVES [High] op 25 March 1858 *(High)*; clo 3 May 1965 *(RM June)*.

ALVESCOT [GW] op 15 January 1873 *(Chelt Exp 18th)*; clo 18 June 1962 *(T 18 May)*.

ALYTH [Cal] op 2 September 1861 *(Newtyle)*; clo 2 July 1951 *(RM August)*.

ALYTH JUNCTION [Cal] op 1861 (see 1831 B**) as MEIGLE, renamed 1 November 1876 *(RCG)*; clo 4 September 1967 *(RM September)*; {map 8}.

AMBERGATE [Mid] op 11 May 1840 *(Mid; co n T 2nd- line)*, north of Toadmoor Tunnel *(Cl)*; replaced by station at south junction 1 June 1863; replaced again by triangular station 10 December 1876 *(Mid)*; still open. Erratically AMBER GATE early and A JUNCTION (some tables until 1893/4) in *Brad*.

AMBERLEY [LBSC] op 3 August 1863**; still open.

AMBERSWOOD for HINDLEY [LNW] op 1 January 1872 *(LNW Officers 6927, 7546, in tt Wigan Observer 5th)*; clo 1 March 1872 (Friday) *(Cl; LNW Officers 7681 – order given, without exact date, 14 February)*. Name as in sources cited for opening.

AMBLE
AMBLE [NE]: According to *Brad Sh 1880* this op 2 June 1879; however *Nhumb Young* gives February 1879 (then in NE wtt). Intended opening February but inspection problems delayed? Line first in *Brad* July, which would support June date. Originally workmen's service? *RCG* list has trio of entries which befog the issue: For 'April' (which could cover any time thereabouts) – Amble station, open G&M.
'July' two entries – Amble branch etc closed G; Amble branch (inc Broomhill) open P. No reference to goods reopening seen – (already goods use for 30 years). Did they have to close line to all traffic briefly in order to improve to passenger standards, resulting in garbled messages? Clo 7 July 1930 *(Cl)*.
Non-tt: miners' service Broomhill Colliery to Amble about 1894 to 1927. Exact details of sites used unknown (see B. Rippon, *The Amble Branch*, Kestrel, 2007).

AMERSHAM [Met/GC] op 1 September 1892 by Met *(co n Foxell)*; GC use began 15 March 1899; still open. At times A & CHESHAM BOIS: *hbl ref 22 January 1922* said had become this; & C B dropped BR tt 7 May 1973 but much earlier by Underground *(L says about 1934)*.

AMESBURY [LSW] op 1 October 1901 for military use *(SR)*; op to public 2 June 1902 *(W Gaz, Wilts & NE Somerset edition, 6th)*; see 1951**; clo 30 June 1952 *(RM August)*.

AMISFIELD [Cal] op 1 September 1863 *(co ½ T 25 March 1864- line)*; 1928/9 *Brad* note added that closed for day at 5.30 p.m., then used as halt; note removed 1934/5; clo 19 May 1952 *(RM June)*.

AMLWCH [LNW] op 3 June 1867 *(LNW)*; clo 7 December 1964 *(RM March 1965)*.

AMMANFORD [GW]
AMMANFORD (a) op 1 May 1850**- line; originally CROSS INN; renamed 1 July 1883 *(hbl 31 December)*; clo 18 August 1958 *(T 11th)*.
AMMANFORD (b) first in *Brad* May 1861 as DUFFRYN; renamed TIRYDAIL 1 July 1889 *(hbl 11th)*, A & T 1960 *(Cl)*, A 7 May 1973 *(Cl)*; HALT 6 September 1965 to 5 May 1969 *(Cl)*; still open.
A COLLIERY op 1 May 1905 *(GW H)*; HALT; clo 18 August 1958 *(T 11th)*.

AMOTHERBY [NE] op 1 June 1853**; clo 1 January 1931 (Thursday) *(T 5 December 1930)*; later excur, e.g. 27 July 1964 *(Whitby)*.

AMPLEFORTH [NE] op 1 June 1853★★;
clo 5 June 1950 *(Cl)*.

AMPRESS (non-tt) op 1 October 1956 *(RM March 1957)*; workmen; originally A WORKS HALT *(hb)*; last trains ran 6 October 1989, date of factory closure *(Southern Evening Echo* – E. Vaughan); {on Lymington branch}.

AMPTHILL

AMPTHILL [Mid] op 13 July 1868 *(T 14th)*; clo 4 May 1959 *(RM June)*.

AMPTHILL [LNW] – see MILLBROOK.

ANCASTER [GN] op 15 June 1857★★; still open.

ANDERSTON

A CROSS [Cal] op 10 August 1896 *(RCG)*; clo 3 August 1959 *(Cl)*. Sometimes GLASGOW A C in tts and Cal ticket thus *(JB)*.

ANDERSTON op 5 November 1979, same site as above *(RM December)*; still open.

ANDOVER [LSW]

ANDOVER op 3 July 1854 *(Salisbury 8th)*; A JUNCTION 6 March 1865 to 1964 *(SR App)*; still open.

A TOWN op 6 March 1865 *(Salisbury 11th- line)*; clo 7 September 1964 *(Andover Advertiser 31 July)*.

ANDOVER ROAD – see MICHELDEVER.

ANDOVERSFORD

ANDOVERSFORD [GW] op 1 June 1881 *(Bristol Merc 2nd)*. Though MSWJ trains ran through here from 1891, it was not included in MSWJ tables in *Brad* until October 1904; since an extra minute was then added to timings of trains stopping there, it would seem to have been an addition then rather than something previously happening but not included in tt (e.g. exchange only use). Clo 15 October 1962 *(RM November)*.
In MSWJ tables was A JUNCTION from start; J added GW tables in *Brad* and GW co tts later; dropped from *Brad* 1960, though this had been only station for here since 1927.

A & DOWDESWELL [MSWJ] op 1 August 1891 *(Chelt Exam 29 July)* as D; renamed 1 October 1892 *(hbl 27th)*; clo 1 April 1927 (Friday) *(wtt supp)*.

ANERLEY [LBSC] op 5 June 1839 *(co n T 6th)*; initially A BRIDGE (thus op tt *T)*; by first detail in *Brad* (about June 1840) was A (near Westow Hill, Norwood); explanation dropped 1841; still open.

ANGARRACK {map 111}
Line op 23 May 1843★★ ran through here but no evidence for station seen (line clo 16 February 1852).

ANGARRACK [West Cornwall] op 11 March 1852 with rebuilt line *(co n R Cornwall Gaz 12th)*; last in *Brad* October 1853 – since also disappeared from local press tt at same time, likely that clo 1 November, with new tt.

ANGEL [Nor] op 17 November 1901 *(T 16th)*; see 1922★★; still open.

ANGEL ROAD [GE] op 15 September 1840 as EDMONTON *(T 16th)*; last in *Brad* December 1842; back June 1843; became WATER LANE 1 March 1849 *(L)*, A R 1 January 1864 *(L)*; still open. At times *Brad* added JUNCTION or called it W L ENFIELD JUNCTION / A R EDMONTON; settled as A R 1883 *(JS)*.

ANGERTON [NB] op 23 July 1862 *(NB)*; clo 15 September 1952★★ *(RM October)*.

ANGLING CLUB COTTAGE [NB] (non-tt): op 1898; still in LNE Sectional Appendix November 1947. Trains only stopped when told by station-masters at Clovenfords and Thornielee either side of this PLATFORM; passengers to be set down told station-masters, those to be picked up had to give prior warning; members of Edinburgh Angling Club could get special tickets to/from here; non-members had to pay to/from station beyond/before.

ANGMERING [LBSC] op 16 March 1846 *(LBSC; T 17th- line)*; still open. A &/for A-ON-SEA 1917 to 1955 *(Brad)*; ticket A for EAST PRESTON and RUSTINGTON *(JB)*.

ANLABY ROAD Hull [NE] op 1 June 1853 *(G&S)*; clo end September 1854 *(G&S)*; {map 63}.

ANN STREET [LNW]
op 1 October 1911★★ *(LNW Cl)*; clo 18 June 1951 *(RM August)*; {Appleton – Widnes LNW}. LMS ticket for A S CROSSING *(JB)*.

ANNAN

ANNAN [GSW] op 23 August 1848 *(Dumfries 23rd-line)*; still open.

A SHAWHILL [Cal] op 1 October 1869, locally advertised service to Kirtlebridge, but not nationally advertised until 8 March 1870 *(Sol J)*; see 1921 April/May★★; SHAWHILL added 2 June 1924★★; clo 27 April 1931 *(Cl)*.
Also see NEWBIE JUNCTION.

ANNBANK [GSW]
op 1 September 1870 *(co ½ T 13 September- line)*; clo 10 September 1951 *(RM October)*.

ANNESLEY

ANNESLEY [Mid] op 1 July 1874 *(Mid)*; clo 6 April 1953 *(RM May)*.

A COLLIERY SIDINGS PLATFORM [Mid] (non-tt) was used by miners from 1 March 1882 to ?; {south of main station} *(Mid)*.
[GC/LNE] op two (non-tt) stops for railwaymen by July 1923, {Hollinswell – Hucknall}:
A SIDINGS (in yard★), clo 16 September 1956, and A SOUTH JUNCTION HALT (on main line★), clo 10 September 1962 *(U)*.
★ = evidence from 6 May 1946 wtt.

ANNFIELD PLAIN [NE] op I February 1894 *(RCG)*; clo 23 May 1955 *(RM July)*.
At first A P NEW *(hb)* – original was goods only.

ANNIESLAND [NB] op 15 March 1886 *(co ½ T 19 March- line)* as GREAT WESTERN ROAD; renamed 9 January 1931 *(Cl)*; still open.
LNE co tt 1933, *Murray* 1948 and *Brad* to 1955: A for KNIGHTSWOOD. A ot GLASGOW A in tts.

ANNITSFORD [NE]:
A (a) first in *Brad* April 1860 as DUDLEY; became D COLLIERY 1 September 1874 *(RCG)*; renamed A 1 April 1878★ *(JS)*; replaced 16 chains south 8 July 1878 *(Cl)* by >
A (b), clo 15 September 1958 *(RM October)*.
★ *RCG* gives 8 July as renaming date but *Brad* May 1878 has A, late D C.

ANSDELL & FAIRHAVEN [PW] first in *Brad*
October 1872 as A; re-sited 15 chains west 10 October
1903 *(Cl)*; & F added 25 January 1906 *(RCG)*;
aot request; still open.

ANSTON [GC/Mid] op 20 May 1912 *(GC dates)*;
clo April 1926 *(Cl)*, reop 25 July 1927 *(T 21st)*,
finally clo 2 December 1929 *(Cl)*;
used for works outings in 1950s and 1960s.

ANSTRUTHER [NB]
ANSTRUTHER (a) original terminus op 1 September
1863 *(D&C 15)* >
ANSTRUTHER (b) through station on line to Boarhills
op 1 September 1883; clo 6 September 1965 *(co n East of
TJ)*. Was A NEW *(hb)*. Became A for CELLARDYKE
Brad 1933/4 and thus to 1963/4 tt.
Tt and account of opening in *Fifeshire Journal 6 Sept*
show that both stations were in use together for some
months; turning facilities were not immediately available
at new one. *Brad* September 1883 shows the
Anstruther & St Andrews trains running through
Anstruther to Pittenweem, which the local paper called
the junction station (it was thus for passengers wanting
to go west); in this table now shown as Anstruther &
St Andrews Company station, old as NB station in
separate table. Through running began in December
and old station now closed* but Brad kept separate
tables for services either side for here for some time.
* = A. Hadjucki et al, *The Anstruther & St Andrews Railway*,
Oakwood, 2009, cite internal North British notice dated
21 December 1883 which said trains 'now run' to the new
station and old only used for goods.

APEDALE; APEDALE JUNCTION (non-tt):
Midland Coal Coke & Iron Co's workmen's trains
worked over LMS (ex NS) branch between these points
– certainly operating 9 July 1923 wtt *(RAIL 57/1)*;
from the wtt it appears that A J was the southern
terminus of this service from A, which would leave
open the question of what then happened to the
miners; perhaps at one time these trains ran to/from
Newcastle (R. Maund); {A J was between Liverpool
Road Halt and Knutton Halt}.

APPERLEY BRIDGE [Mid] op 16/30 July 1846
(Mid); clo 22 March 1965 *(T 23rd)*. Variously A, A B
early; became A & RAWDON 1 October 1890 *(RCG)*,
A B & R 20 December 1890 *(hbl 29 January)*
but 1 May 1893 co tt *(Mid)*, A B 12 June 1961
(RM April). Engineering, 20 April 1900, said would be
re-sited 300 yards nearer Leeds; ever done ?

APPIN [Cal] op 24 August 1903 *(Brad Sh 1904- line)*;
clo 28 March 1966 *(RM June – photo caption)*.
Non-tt: *BR Scottish Region Special Traffic Notices* show
stops at milepost 82, between here and Duror, for
workmen, weeks beginning 24 June and 29 July 1957.

APPLEBY near Penrith
APPLEBY [Mid] op 1 May 1876 *(Mid; co n T 1st- line)*;
A WEST 1 September 1952 to 5 May 1968 *(Mid)*;
see 1989 October 16**; still open.
A EAST [NE] op 9 June 1862**; EAST added 1952;
clo 22 January 1962 *(RM February)*.

APPLEBY LINCS [GC]
op 1 October 1866 *(GC; Rtn- line)*; LINCS added

1 July 1923 *(hbl 12th)*; clo 5 June 1967 *(Cl)*.

APPLEDORE near Bideford [BWA] op 1 May 1908
(Trewman 2nd); clo 28 March 1917**.

APPLEDORE KENT [SE] op 13 February 1851
(co n T 13th); KENT added in body of tt 12 May 1980
(index earlier); still open.

APPLEFORD [GW]
APPLEFORD (a) op 12 June 1844 *(co n GW)*; last in
Brad Feb. 1849.
APPLEFORD (b) op 11 September 1933 *(Cl 29)*;
HALT until 5 May 1969 *(GW H)*; still open.

APPLETON [LNW]: for line op see 1832 B**, nd,
June 1852; clo 18 June 1951 *(RM August)*.

APPLEY BRIDGE [LY] op 9 April 1855 *(Southport
Vis 5th)*; still open. According to paper, nameboard had
been painted 'Apply' when some local expert pointed
out error and they did a rapid repaint.

APSLEY [LMS] op 26 September 1938
(LNW Record); still open.

ARBIRLOT [DA] op 1 February 1900 *(Dundee- line)*;
clo 1 January 1917 *(Cl)*; back in *Brad*, Saturdays only,
September 1917; reop fully 1 January 1918 *(RCH)*;
clo 2 December 1929 *(Cl)*.

ARBROATH {map 2}
ARBROATH [Aberdeen]. Horse-drawn service from
Leysmill to harbour began 24 November 1838;
replacement station for locomotive haulage in Catherine
Street op 3 January 1839 (see 1838 October 8**) >
A LADYLOAN [DA] op 8 October 1838**, from
Dundee *(T 12th/Glasgow Courier)* >
Both replaced by [DA] temporary, on through line,
op 1 February 1848 *(co n RM February 1953)*;
replaced by permanent >
A JOINT [DA] op 14 December 1858 (N. Ferguson,
Arbroath & Forfar Railway, Oakwood, 2000);
JOINT dropped ?; still open.
Aot *hb*, *Brad* and *Intelligible tt* had A KEPTIE / KEPTI,
Brad until 1864; JOINT not seen there.

ARBUCKLE [NB]: line op 5 August 1840 but station
later 1840s *(MK)*; earliest tt reference July 1848
(Topham, its first detail for line); last in *Brad* October
1862; removal premature? Monkland minute of
9 October 1862: agreed to remove this, substituting
Whiterigg and Rawyards, either side
(SRO BR/MNK/1/4), so only limited time for
November opening.

ARCHER STREET – see under ROSEHILL.

ARCHWAY [Nor] op 22 June 1907** as
HIGHGATE; became A H 11 June 1939,
H A 19 January 1941 *(L)*, A 1947; still open.

ARDDLEEN [Cam] first in *Brad* February 1862;
originally Mondays, Wednesdays, Saturdays and
Welshpool Fair days; all days April 1865; HALT from
1954 tt *(Cl)*; clo 18 January 1965 *(RM March)*.

ARDEER [LMS] (non-tt): ICI workmen;
op by July 1926; clo 3 October 1966;
PLATFORM, originally A WORKS P;
{branch from Stevenston} *(RM January 1958; U)*.

ARDGAY [High] op 1 Oct 1864 *(High)* as BONAR
BRIDGE; renamed 2 May 1977 *(RM July)*; still open.
At first A (B B) *(hb)*.

ARDINGLY [LBSC] op 3 September 1883 *(LBSC; Hants Chron 8th- line)*; clo 28 October 1963 *(Cl)*.

ARDLEIGH [GE] op 15 June 1846 *(co n Moffat)*; clo 6 November 1967 *(RM December)*.

ARDLER [Cal] op 24 February 1837 *(Newtyle)*; clo 6 September 1847 (see 1837 B★★); reop 2 August 1848; clo 11 June 1956 *(RM April)*; {map 8, 9}.

ARDLEY [GW] op 1 July 1910 *(RCG; co ½ T 6 August- line)*; became HALT 1 August 1955; clo 7 January 1963 *(Cl)*.

ARDLUI [NB]
op 7 August 1894 *(T 7th)*; still open. LNE tt 1933, hb and tt to 1965: A (HEAD OF LOCH LOMOND)/A (L L).

ARDROSSAN
For earliest service see 1834★★.
[Ardrossan/GSW] Service began 17 August 1840★★; TOWN and HARBOUR stations not separately identified in tt for many years; both early *Brad* and *Murray* did have notes referring to trains to Ardrossan 'direct' in connection with steamers to Belfast; hb, e.g. 1929, made three of it: PIER, HARBOUR, 'Station' (later TOWN) >

A HARBOUR; op as A PIER, became WINTON PIER GSW co tt May 1909 *(GSW)* but 2 June 1924★★ according to *RM* list and *Cl*, A HARBOUR 6 March 1967 tt; clo 3 August 1986 for electrification work; buses until new station op 15 September 1986 *(BLN 583, pp. 97, 101)*; still open.

A TOWN: TOWN added 28 February 1953 *(JS, based on BR commercial circular)*; clo 1 January 1968 *(Cl)*; reop 19 January 1987 *(BLN 552)*; still open.
Brad 1853 and hb 1862, 1877: A PRINCES STREET.

A SOUTH BEACH [GSW] op 1 January 1883 *(GSW)*; enabled trains to Largs to stop here for A without going to Town and reversing; still open.

A NORTH [Cal] op 4 September 1888 *(Cal)* as A; became A TOWN 1 October 1906 *(Cl)*; clo 1 January 1917 *(RM February)*; became A N 1924; reop 1 February 1919 *(Cl)*; clo 4 July 1932 *(Cl)*.

A MONTGOMERIE PIER [Cal] op 30 May 1890 *(Cal)* as A PIER; clo 1 January 1917 *(RM February)*; reop 1 February 1919 *(Cl)*; renamed 2 June 1924★★, but *Brad* using M P from 1903 *(Cl)*; not used during Second World War; reop 16 June 1947 *(RM September)*, using new spur from ex-GSW line west of Kilwinning; summers only in later years *(hb)*; last train 25 September 1967 *(Cl)*.

ARDSLEY
ARDSLEY [GN] op 5 October 1857 *(T 5th)*;
A JUNCTION *Brad* 1850s to 1880s;
clo 2 November 1964 *(Cl)*.
Also see STAIRFOOT.

ARDWICK
ARDWICK [GC]; first trains shown in *Brad* January 1843; still open.
ARDWICK [LNW] first in *Brad* June 1878; mainly a ticket platform (already in use for this) but also used for alighting, towards Manchester only; clo 15 December 1902 *(LNW Officers 40823)*; {Longsight – Manchester}.
[LY] probably had exchange platform here 1852–3.
ARENIG [GW] op 1 November 1882 *(D&C 11)*;

clo 4 January 1960 *(RM March)*.

ARGOED [LNW]: line op 19 June 1865 *(LNW)*; first evidence from wtt 1 February 1866 (first in *Brad* April 1866); became HALT 29 September 1941 *(LNW Record)*; clo 13 June 1960 *(RM July)*.

ARGYLE STREET Glasgow op 5 November 1979 *(RM December)*; short distance west of earlier Glasgow Cross *(C/W)*; still open.

ARGYLE STREET Swansea [SIT] first found in *The Cambrian* August 1878 tt (see 1860 July 25★★); for a while 1879/81 known as SEA BEACH; last in *Brad* February 1910 (back April 1910 only – error?); also omitted from hb 1912. Back in hb 1938 (not present 1936a) but *Brad* much later (not June 1956, in January 1957); clo 6 January 1960★★; A HALT *(RCH)* but A STREET (tts); {map 88}.

ARGYLL COLLIERY [Camp] (non-tt): ticket here to Campbeltown *(JB)*; western terminus before line opened to passengers; later left on short branch to north, just before Machrihanish *(Camp p. 43)*.

ARISAIG [NB] op 1 April 1901 *(RCG)*; still open.

ARKHOLME [Fur/Mid] op 6 June 1867 *(Mid)*; clo 12 September 1960 *(RM October)*.
Became A for KIRKBY LONSDALE 1 December 1869 co tt *(Mid)* and closed thus.

ARKLEBY [MC] op 1840★★; full service last shown July 1852 *Brad*; Fridays only, towards Carlisle continued, last shown November 1852; {Bulgill – Aspatria, map 20g}.

ARKSEY [GN] op 6 June 1848★★ *(LY)* as STOCKBRIDGE; became A & S 1850 tt, A 1854 tt *(Cl)* in GN usage but LY kept longer to S *(JS)*; clo 5 August 1952 (Tuesday) *(RM September)* – trainless bank holiday intervened.

ARKWRIGHT STREET – see Nottingham.

ARKWRIGHT TOWN [GC] op 9 March 1897 (8th formal) *(GCR Society Journal, Spring 2003)*; AT DUCKMANTON until 1898 tt *(JS)*; clo 3 December 1951 *(RM January 1952)*.
Aot hb gave D as alternative name.

ARLECDON [CW Jc] op 3 July 1883, all days, *(D&C 14 date for Oatlands)*; last in *Brad* December 1883; reop 5 October 1912 *(RCG)*, Saturdays only; last public use December 1916; miners used until 1 January 1927 *(U)*. A for ROWRAH *(hb)*.

ARLESEY
ARLESEY op 3 October 1988 (free use 1st) *(BLN 596; H.P. White, RCHS Journal, March 1989)*; still open.
A & HENLOW [GN] op 7 August 1850 *(T 6th, 8th covered line but omitted this station; is in co n RM September 1910)*; op as A & SHEFFORD ROAD *(co n RM September 1910)*; became A 1893 tt *(Cl)*, A & S R 1895 tt *(Cl)*, A & H 1 March 1933 *(Cl)* – according to *Brad notices 1934* was previously A & S R for H; clo 5 January 1959 *(RM February)*.
Usually ARLSEY 1851–60 *(JS)*.
A SIDING – see THREE COUNTIES.
ARLEY near Kidderminster [GW] op 1 February 1862★★; clo 9 September 1963 *(T 9th)*.
ARLEY & FILLONGLEY [Mid] op 1 November 1864 *(Mid)*; & F added 1 March 1867 co tt *(Mid)*; clo 7 November 1960 *(RM December)*.

62

ARLEY COLLIERY SIDING(S) [Mid] (non-tt):
miners; at least 1917 to 1945 *(Mid)*;
{east of Arley & Fillongley}.

ARMADALE [NB] op 11 August 1862 *(MK)*;
clo 9 January 1956 *(RM February)*.

ARMATHWAITE [Mid] op 1 May 1876 *(Mid; co n*
T 1st- line); clo 4 May 1970 *(RM June)*; reop for regular
weekend Dales Rail services 3 April 1976 *(AB)*,
fully 14 July 1986 *(Settle)*; still open.

ARMITAGE [LNW] op 1 December 1847 *(W Mid)*;
clo 13 June 1960 *(RM July)*.

ARMLEY

A CANAL ROAD [Mid] op late September or
1 October 1847 – minute of 22 September ordered
opening *(Mid)*; C R added 25 September 1950 *(Cl)*;
clo 22 March 1965 *(RM April)*. A for FARNLEY &
WORTLEY in *hb* 1895 to 1949a.

A MOOR [GN] op 1 August 1854 *(GN; T 1st- line)* as
A & WORTLEY; renamed 25 September 1950 *(Cl)*;
clo 4 July 1966 *(RM July)*.

ARNAGE [GNS] op 18 July 1861 *(GNS)*;
clo 4 October 1965 *(Rly Obs November)*.

ARNOS GROVE [Picc] op 19 September 1932
(T 16th, 20th); still open.

ARNSIDE [Fur] first in *Brad* August 1858; still open.

ARPLEY – see WARRINGTON.

ARRAM [NE] first in *Brad* September 1855; still open.

ARROCHAR & TARBET [NB]
op 7 August 1894 *(T 7th)*; still open.

ARSENAL [Picc] op 15 December 1906 *(co n T 14th)*
as GILLESPIE ROAD; renamed A HIGHBURY HILL
31 October 1932 *(T 26th)*; H H gradually out (on map
long after omitted *Brad*); see 1922**; still open.

ARTHINGTON [NE] op 10 July 1849 *(D&C 8;*
T 9th- line) as POOL; renamed 1852 tt *(Cl)*; re-sited
1 February 1865, on opening of Otley branch *(Cl)*;
A JUNCTION from then/soon after to 1 May 1893 *(Cl)*;
clo 22 March 1965 *(RM April)*.

ARTHOG [Cam] op 28 March 1870 *(Cam)*;
clo 18 January 1965**.

ARUNDEL [LBSC]

A & LITTLEHAMPTON op 16 March 1846 *(T 17th)*;
at LYMINSTER, about half way Littlehampton /
Arundel; *Brad* and *hb* used 3 names indiscriminately,
sometimes in combination – *T* contrived to include
3 versions (but 'LEEMINSTER') in brief item on line
opening; clo 1 September 1863 (Tuesday) *(H.V. Borley,*
RCH Journal March 1962/West Sussex Gazette).

ARUNDEL op see 3 August 1863**; still open.
Also see FORD.

ASBY [WCE] (non-tt): purpose and dates ?;
{Wright Green – Rowrah} *(U)*.

ASCOT [LSW]

ASCOT op 4 June 1856 *(co n T 3rd)*;
A & SUNNINGHILL 1 February 1857 to 10 July
1921 *(Cl)*; still open.
Also two race platforms (non-tt):

A RACE PLATFORM op 13 June 1911 *(race)*; on north
side of line, to west of station; connected to main by
footpath and by special passage to racecourse; in use
1974 but probably not long after *(AB)*.

A WEST, about a mile further west; first used before
1899 *(race)*; until 1960s also used by Bertram Mills's
circus, which had winter quarters nearby; 'abolished'
January 1974 after several years' disuse *(AB)*.

ASCOTT-UNDER-WYCHWOOD [GW]
op 4 June 1853 *(Glos Chron 4th- line)*;
-U-W added 1 February 1880 *(Cl, RCG ref January)*;
aot request; HALT 24 May 1965 to 5 May 1969 *(Cl)*;
still open.

ASFORDBY [Mid] op 1 September 1846 *(Mid)* as
KIRBY; renamed 1 December 1857 wtt* *(Mid)*;
clo 2 April 1951 *(RM May)*. ASHFORDBY in *Brad* ?
to 1861 *(JS)*.
* = until 1 May 1903 was in co tt as A late K *(Mid)*.

ASH near Aldershot; chaotic area for names.

ASH [SE] op 20 August 1849 *(SR; Hants Chron 25th-*
line); still open. Variously ASH & ALDERSHOT(T),
ALDERSHOT (ASH), ASH JUNCTION,
ASH for A GREEN *(Brad)*.

A GREEN [LSW] op 8 October 1849 *(SR; Hants Chron*
13th- line); intermittently A/AG; HALT from
1 December 1926 *(Cl)*; clo 4 July 1937 (Sunday) *(Cl)*.

A VALE [LSW] op 2 May 1870 *(SR; co n T 30 April-*
line) as NORTH CAMP & A V; variously later
ALDERSHOT N C & A V, ALDERSHOT A V for N C /
for N C & SOUTH FARNBOROUGH, A V & S F
(Brad, RCH records); settled as A V 13 June 1955 *(JS)*;
still open.

ASH STREET: see under SOUTHPORT.

ASH TOWN near Canterbury [EK] op 16 October
1916 *(co n EK)*; only footpath access; clo 1 November
1948** *(RM January 1949)*.

ASHBOURNE

ASHBOURNE [NS] op 31 May 1852 *(T 26 May,*
1 June); replaced to north by >

ASHBOURNE [LNW/NS] op 4 August 1899 *(LNW*
Record); clo 1 November 1954 *(T 1 October)*;
see 1962 August 5**. A JOINT in *hb* 1900a.

ASHBURTON [GW] op 1 May 1872 *(Trewman 8th)*;
clo 3 November 1958 *(RM December)*.

ASHBURY [LSW] op 20 January 1879**;
clo 3 October 1966 *(Cornish & D P 8th)*.
Became A & NORTH LEW 1884/5, A 1888/9,
A & N L 1890, A for N L 1923, A 1955 *(Brad)*.
LSW co tt 1914: A & N L. Hb 1938: A for NORTHLEW.

ASHBURYS [GC] first in *Brad* July 1855; still open.
GC co tt 1903, LNE tt 1933,
LMS tt 1947: A for BELLEVUE.

ASHBY MAGNA [GC] op 15 March 1899
(GC; T 16th- line); clo 5 May 1969 *(Cl)*.

ASHBY ROAD – see BARDON HILL.

ASHBY-DE-LA-ZOUCH [Mid] op 1 March 1849
(Mid); -de-la-Z added *hb* 1867, but *Brad* and co tt
1924/5; clo 7 September 1964 *(RM October)*.
Branch line platform op 1 January 1874 *(T 2nd)*;
clo 22 September 1930 *(Mid)*.

ASHCHURCH

ASHCHURCH (a) [Mid] op 24 June 1840 *(Chelt Chron*
27th); clo 15 November 1971 *(RM December)*.
A for TEWKESBURY *Brad* e.g. 1861 and thus again
October 1961 *hba*.

ASHCHURCH (b) op 30 May 1997 *(Rly Obs December)*; still open.

ASHCOTT [SD Jt] op 28 August 1854★★; clo 7 March 1966 *(Shepton 11th)*. Spelling ASHCOT until 1905 *(Brad)*; A & MEARE in *Brad* 1867 to 1894; A for M LMS tt 1947 *(Brad* print*)*.

ASHDON [GE] op 14 August 1911 (P. Paye, *The Saffron Walden Branch*, OPC, 1981); HALT; clo 7 September 1964 *(RM September)*. Ticket as SAFFRON WALDEN A *(JB)*.

ASHEY [IWC]

ASHEY op 20 December 1875 (see 1875★★); clo 21 February 1966 *(RM March)*. A for NUNWELL e.g. *Brad* 1911.

A RACECOURSE (non-tt) on branch from Ashey: April 1882 *(race)* to ?; station made from piles of sleepers erected and dismantled as necessary. Probably last used 1925; substantial alterations 1926 when Ashey ceased to be crossing place (T. Cooper) but perhaps some sort of stop until racecourse abandoned 1929 after grandstand destroyed in fire *(AB)*.

GREEN LANES: (non-tt); temporary station 5–12 August 1899 for Volunteer Camp; all stopping trains to call, two minutes after Ashey or four minutes after Ryde St Johns Road *(IoW Obs)*.

ASHFIELD op 3 December 1993 *(BLN 725)*; still open.

ASHFORD near Maidstone

A INTERNATIONAL [SE] op 1 December 1842 *(co n T 1st)* as A; enlarged, partly op 4 September 1995 *(RM November)*, fully op 8 January 1996, when became A I, *(RM March)*; still open. A JUNCTION 1851/2 to 1900/1 *(Brad)* – SE co tt 1864 had A J for main line, A to Hastings; became A KENT 9 July 1923 *(hbl 26 April)*.

ASHFORD [LCD] op 1 July 1884 *(LCD)*; clo 1 January 1899 *(Cl)*. From December 1891 *Brad* LCD trains from Maidstone shown stopping at both own and SE stations. Made redundant by creation of SEC; all used ex-SE station.

ASHFORD BOWDLER [SH Jt] first in *Brad* December 1854; clo 1 November 1855 (Thursday) *(Cl supp 2)*; {Ludlow – Woofferton}.

ASHFORD MIDDLESEX [LSW] op 22 August 1848 *(co n T 21st)*; M added 9 July 1923 *(hbl 26 April)*; back to A 12 June 1961 tt, to A SURREY 12 May 1980 tt, to A M again 24 May 1998 tt; still open.

ASHINGTON [NE]

ASHINGTON first in *Brad* June 1878 as HIRST for A; renamed 1 October 1889 *(RCG)*; on line to North Seaton, ex-BT; clo 2 November 1964 *(RM January 1965)*.

A COLLIERY JUNCTION in wtt by December 1871 (A. Young), first in *Brad* January 1877; Saturdays only; on East Coast Main Line between Pegswood and Longhirst; last in tt June 1878 (though still indexed July); added 'P' hb 1879a, not thus 1883.

ASHLEIGH ROAD Swansea [SIT] first in *Brad* April 1929 (with electrification 2 March 1929?); clo 6 January 1960★★; {map 88}. Also see 1860 July 25★★.

ASHLEY near Altrincham [CLC] op 12 May 1862 *(T 7th, 12th)*; aot request; still open. A for ROSKERNE in *Brad* 1903 but not thus GC co tt.

ASHLEY & WESTON [LNW]: line op 1 June 1850 *(co ½ T 22 February 1851)*, nd, May 1851; op as MEDBOURNE BRIDGE, renamed 1 January 1880 *(LNW Officers)*; clo 18 June 1951 *(RM August)*; later railwaymen's use – shown in use, Fridays only, 30 June 1952 wtt. A & W for M in *Brad* ? to closure but not thus LMS tt 1930.

ASHLEY HEATH [SR] op 1 April 1927 *(Rly Gaz 22 April 1927)*; HALT – included 1929 hb as station, Halt added 1938 but Halt in *Brad* from start; clo 4 May 1964 *(Hants Chron 9th)*; {Ringwood – West Moors}.

ASHLEY HILL [GW] op 13 June 1864 *(GW ac)*; clo 23 November 1964 *(Bristol E P 21st)*.

ASHOVER BUTTS [Ashover] (ng) op 7 April 1925 *(RM October)*; clo 14 September 1936★★ *(Cl)*; later excur *(U)*; {map 59}.

ASHPERTON [GW] op 13 September 1861 *(Hereford T 14th)*; clo 5 April 1965 *(Cl)*.

ASHTEAD [LSW/LBSC] op 1 February 1859★★; still open.

ASHTON near Bristol [BE] prob op mid-/late-June 1852★; clo 1 February 1856 (see article, M. Hutson, RCHS *Journal*, November 2002, p.144–5); Long Ashton op nearby 1926.

★ = orders to provide station and stop trains from this date given 7 April *(RAIL 75/17)*, but no confirmation done on time; first in *Brad* August.

ASHTON near Exeter [GW] op 9 October 1882 *(Torquay Dir 11th)*; clo 9 June 1958 *(T 5th)*.

ASHTON & HOOLEY HILL – see GUIDE BRIDGE.

ASHTON GATE [GW] op 1 October 1906 *(Bristol NWR)* – 15 September 1906 given by *RCG* and *dist t supp 14 August 1908* was date opening authorised; clo August 1914, reop 18 September 1920 for football use *(Cl corr – Bristol notes)*; fully public again 23 May 1926 *(RCH)*; originally PLATFORM, just A G 1928 tt, HALT from 29 October 1962 *(Cl)*; clo 7 September 1964 *(W D Press 7th)*. Later occasional use – e.g. 29 Sept. 1970 *(RM Dec.)* and football special from Leeds 16 February 1974 *(IU)*. {Portishead branch, south of Clifton Bridge}. Always PLATFORM hb.

ASHTON HALL [LNW] (non-tt) private station op as MR STARKIE'S PLATFORM; meeting of LNW Special Committee 17 August 1883 gave authority for stopping trains for the convenience of J.P.C. Starkie (sometime MP for North East Lancashire) and his family, subject to his paying costs of proper platform, indemnifying company against risk, and agreeing stops could cease if it wished *(RAIL 410/116, minute 54927)*; transferred to Lord Ashton 15 June 1920 and clo 7 July 1930 *(LNW dates but only gives authority for closure)*; HALT at clo. {Lancaster – Conder Green}.

ASHTON MOSS – see ASHTON-UNDER LYNE.

ASHTON-IN-MAKERFIELD [GC] op 3 January 1900 *(RM January)*; clo 3 March 1952 *(RM April)*;

used for race meetings on five occasions in 1975 – first on 24 May* *(RM September)*, last 4 October, via new chord line from ex-LNW at Golborne (C.H.A. Towneley & J.A. Peden, *Industrial Railways of St Helens, Widnes & Warrington, Part I*, Industrial Railway Society, 1999, p.69).
* = book cited says 22nd (Thursday) but *RM* date checked against *T* for racing date and found correct.

ASHTON-ON-MERSEY – see SALE.

ASHTON-UNDER-HILL [Mid] op 1 October 1864 *(Worcester 8th)*; clo 17 June 1963 *(RM July)*.

ASHTON-UNDER-LYNE
(A and A-u-L often used indiscriminately); {map 53}.
A & HOOLEY HILL – see GUIDE BRIDGE.
A MOSS [OAGB] op 26 August 1861 *(GC; Rtn- line)*; last in *Brad* February 1862.
A-u-L [LY] op 13 April 1846**; A CHARLESTOWN 1868/9 *(LNW co tt)* to 6 May 1968 *(Cl)*; still open.
A OLDHAM ROAD [OAGB] op 26 August 1861 *(GC; Rtn- line)*; clo 4 May 1959 *(RM June)*.
Later excur – e.g. 15 Aug. 1960 (to Weston-super-Mare), 22 August 1960 (to Hereford) *(AB)*.
A PARK PARADE [GC] op 23 December 1845 *(GC)*; clo 5 November 1956 *(RM December)*.
Brad P P added one table 1870, others later.
Also see DUKINFIELD.

ASHURST KENT [LBSC] op 1 October 1888 *(co n T 28 September)*; K added 21 September 1996 *(National Fares Manual)*; still open.

ASHURST NEW FOREST [LSW] op 1 June 1847 *(Dorset Chron 20 May, 3 June)* as LYNDHURST ROAD; renamed 24 September 1995 tt *(RM November)*; still open.

ASHWATER [LSW] op 21 July 1886 *(Tavistock 23rd)*; clo 3 October 1966 *(Cornish & D P 8th)*; still open.

ASHWELL near Oakham [Mid] op 1 May 1848 *(Mid; co ½ T 21 August- line)*; clo 6 June 1966 *(RM July)*.

ASHWELL & MORDEN [GN] op 21 October 1850 *(co n T 18th)*; & M added 1 April 1920 *(Cl – but hbl ref 29 January 1920)*; still open.

ASHWELLTHORPE [GE] op 2 May 1881 *(RCG)*; clo 11 September 1939 *(G&S)*.

ASKAM [Fur] first in *Brad* March 1851 as IRELETH GATE, Sundays only; at one stage Thursdays also; last in *Brad* November 1857, Sundays only; reop 1 April 1868, all days (M. Peascod, *Chron February 2002*), as I; renamed 1 January 1875 *(RCG)*; still open.

ASKERN [LY] op 6 June 1848** *(LY)*; clo 10 March 1947 *(Cl)*; later excursions, using northbound platform at least 1971 to 29 July 1984 *(IU)*.

ASKRIGG [NE] op 1 February 1877 *(York Guardian 3rd)* and in *Brad* February 1877 as terminus of extension, staying there until further extension, to Hawes, added July 1878; clo 26 April 1954**.

ASLOCKTON [GN]
op 15 July 1850 *(in July tt, Henshaw)*; still open.

ASPALL & THORNDON [Mid-Suffolk Light] op 29 September 1908 *(T 28th- line)*; clo 28 July 1952 *(T 28th)*. A & T for DEBENHAM co tts, *hb*.

ASPATRIA [MC]
ASPATRIA op 12 April 1841 *(D&C 14)*; also see 1840**; aot request; still open.

LNW co tt 1882: A for ALLONBY; {map 20g}.
Also see NO 5 PIT SIDING.

ASPLEY GUISE [LNW] op 30 October 1905**; clo 1 January 1917 *(T 22 December 1916)*; reop 5 May 1919 *(RCH)*; still open.

ASTLEY [LNW] op 1844/5 *(LM)* – see 1830 September 17**; clo 7 May 1956 *(Cl)*.

ASTLEY BRIDGE [LY] op 15 October 1877 *(LY)*; clo 1 October 1879 (Wednesday) *(Cl)*; {goods IA}.

ASTON Birmingham [LNW]
first in *Brad* November 1854; still open.
A JUNCTION LNW co tts at least until 1899.

ASTON BOTTERELL [CMDP] op 21 November 1908**; at first in *Brad* as A B SIDING HALT; {Stottesdon – Burwarton}; clo 26 September 1938 *(T 9 August)*.

ASTON CANTLOW [GW] op 18 December 1922 *(GW Mag January 1923)*; HALT; clo 25 September 1939 *(Cl)*; Workers' service ran about July 1941 to last train, Saturday 1 July 1944 *(GW wtt; letter from Maudslay Motors Ltd to R. Maund)*; {Bearley – Great Alne}.

ASTON ROWANT [GW] op 15 August 1872 *(GW- line)*; clo 1 July 1957 *(RM August)*.

ASTON-BY-STONE [NS] op 1 November 1901 *(RCG)*; clo 6 January 1947 *(RM January 1950)*.

ASTWOOD [GW] op 18 May 1936 *(Cl 29)*; HALT; clo 25 September 1939 *(Cl)*; {Worcester – Fernhill Heath}.

ASWARBY & SCREDINGTON [GN] op 2 January 1872 *(insp rpt MT6/91/2; co ½ T 12 February- line)* as S; renamed 1 February 1875 *(Cl; hbl ref January)*; clo 22 September 1930** *(Cl)*. *Brad* made S for OSWARBY of it early. A FOR S *hb* 1875a to closure.

ATHELNEY [GW] op 1 October 1853 *(Taunton 5th)*; clo 15 June 1964 *(W Gaz 19th)*.

ATHERLEIGH [LMS] op 14 October 1935 *(LNW Record)*; clo 29 March 1954 *(BR clo notice Sweeney)*; wakes week use certainly 1957 (last day 11 July) *(AB)*; {West Leigh – Atherton Bag Lane}.

ATHERSTONE [LNW] op 15 September 1847 *(co n T 13th)*; see 2004 May 23**; still open.

ATHERTON
ATHERTON [LY] op 2 July 1888** *(in tt July)*; A CENTRAL until 15 June 1965 tt, when dropped; still open.
A BAG LANE [LNW] op 13 June 1831** as B L; A pre 1847 *(Cl)*; A B L 2 June 1924 *(Rly Gaz 23 May)*; clo 29 March 1954 *(BR clo notice Sweeney)*; wakes week use certainly 1957 (last day 11 July) *(AB)*.

ATLANTIC DOCK – see ALEXANDRA DOCK.

ATLANTIC PARK HOSTEL [SR] (non-tt); HALT; setting down only; reception centre for emigrants to USA from 30 October 1929 to ?; Southampton Airport Parkway here later *(U)*.

ATTADALE [High]: originally private station, op 1875/7; by December 1877 owner had given public permission to use *(Lochalsh)*; added 'P' 1878/9a *hb*, as A PLATFORM; not in *Brad* until July 1880; aot request; in *hb* A P (1879a), A (1893), A HALT (1938) still open.

ATTENBOROUGH [Mid]
A GATE first in *Brad* December 1856 *(Mid)*;
clo 1 November 1858 co tt *(Mid)*.
Reop as **ATTENBOROUGH** 1 September 1864 *(Mid)*;
CHILWELL from 19 April 1937 to 27 September 1937
(Mid); still open.

ATTERCLIFFE
ATTERCLIFFE [GC] first in *Brad* July 1871;
aot request; clo 26 September 1927 *(Cl)*.
A ROAD [Mid] op 1 February 1870 *(co n T 22 January)*;
clo 30 January 1995 *(Mid)*.

ATTIMORE HALL [GN] first in *Brad* May 1905;
last shown June 1905 but with note that motor-car
service was subject to alteration so perhaps closed
before 1 July (Saturday); {map 72}.

ATTLEBOROUGH [GE] op 30 July 1845
(co n Norfolk); still open.

ATTLEBRIDGE [MGN] op 2 December 1882
(MGN); clo 2 March 1959 *(T 2nd)*.

AUCHALLANDER [NB] (non-tt) PLATFORM;
purpose ?; op by 1929; clo ? *(U)*; included in *hb*
1925–56 (inclusive) but no facilities shown;
{Bridge of Orchy – Rannoch}.

AUCHENCASTLE [Cal] (non-tt): railwaymen and
families; op 3 January 1900; clo after 1926;
also see 1966**; {Beattock – Elvanfoot} *(U)*.

AUCHENDINNY [NB] op 2 September 1872 *(T 4th)*;
clo 5 March 1951 *(RM May)* – see 1951**.
In *Brad* about 1900 as A for MILTON BRIDGE and
GREENLAW BARRACKS.

AUCHENGRAY [Cal] op 15 February 1848
(Balerno; co ½ T 29 February- line); clo 18 April 1966 *(Cl)*.

AUCHENHEATH [Cal] op 1 December 1866
(Cal- line); clo 1 October 1951 *(RM November)*.

AUCHENMADE [Cal] op 4 September 1888 *(Cal)*;
clo 1 January 1917 *(RM February)*; reop 1 February
1919 *(RCH)*; clo 4 July 1932 *(Cl)*.

AUCHINCRUIVE [GSW]
AUCHINCRUIVE first in *Brad* March 1871;
clo 10 September 1951 *(RM October)*.
East of here A COLLIERY PLATFORM (non-tt)
used by miners from 1898 *(U)*; shown closed from
Monday 3 March 1947 *(LMS wtt notice 5 April)*.

AUCHINDACHY [GNS] op 21 February 1862
(GNS) as BOTRIPHNIE; renamed October 1862 tt
(Cl); clo 6 May 1968 *(RM July)*.

AUCHINLECK
AUCHINLECK (a) [GSW] op 9 August 1848 *(GSW)*;
clo 6 December 1965 *(RM January 1966)*.
AUCHINLECK (b) op 14 May 1984 *(RM July)*; still open.

AUCHLOCHAN [Cal] (non-tt)
HALT/PLATFORM used by workmen from ? –
notified as ready for inspection 23 September 1907
(MT6/1650/7 – D. Stirling); added 'P' 1944a *hb* as a
HALT, 'closed' May 1957a; {north of Coalburn}.

AUCHMACOY [GNS] op 2 August 1897 *(GNS)*;
clo 31 October 1932 *(RM December)*.

AUCHNAGATT [GNS] op 18 July 1861 *(GNS)*;
clo 4 October 1965 *(Rly Obs November)*.

AUCHNAGOOL [High] (non-tt) PLATFORM;
op by 6 August 1874; original use by goods trains
Mondays and Thursdays for 'those connected with the
works' (notice *RCHS Journal* November 1977, p.110);
clo ?; {Forsinard – Altnabreac}.

AUCHNASHELLACH – see ACHNASHELLACH.

AUCHTERARDER [Cal] op 23 May 1848**;
clo 11 June 1956 *(RM April)*.

AUCHTERHOUSE [Cal] op 16 December 1831
(Newtyle); re-sited on deviation 1 November 1860 *(Cl)*;
clo 10 January 1955 *(T 28 December 1954)*; {map 9}.

AUCHTERLESS [GNS] op 5 September 1857
(GNS); clo 1 October 1951 *(RM November)*.

AUCHTERMUCHTY [NB] op 8 June 1857**;
clo 5 June 1950 *(RM July)*.

AUDENSHAW [LNW] {map 53}.
AUDENSHAW (a): station always A op 1 November
1883* *(LNW Officers 25368)*; clo 1 May 1905 *(RCG)*.
* = in *Brad* for a few months after line op 1 March 1882 but
no trains calling; back, with trains, November 1883.
AUDENSHAW (b): op as HOOLEY HILL GUIDE
BRIDGE 1 November 1887 *(LNW Officers 29786)*;
clo 1 January 1917 *(T 22 December 1916)*;
reop 3 October 1921 *(alterations, LNW co tt)*; renamed
2 June 1924 *(Rly Gaz 23 May)*; clo 25 September 1950
(RM October).

AUDLEM [GW] op 20 October 1863 *(Rtn- line;*
in co n for formal opening on 19th – *By GW)*;
clo 9 September 1963 *(T 9th)*.

AUDLEY & BIGNALL END [NS] op 28 June 1880
(NS); & B E added 9 July 1923 *(Cl; hbl ref 26 April)*;
clo 27 April 1931 *(Cl)*.

AUDLEY END [GE] op 30 July 1845 *(co n T 26th- line)*
as WENDEN (modern maps show Wendens Ambo
nearby); renamed 1 November 1848 *(Cl)*; still open.
Topham 1849: A E for WALDEN. EC tts 1851, 1854:
A E for SAFFRON WALDEN.

AUGHTON PARK [LY]
op 1 May 1907 *(Ormskirk 2nd)*; still open.

AULDBAR ROAD [Cal]: line op 4 December 1838
(see 1838**), nd, in use by 25 February 1841
– date of company's reply to BoT about level crossings;
clo 11 June 1956 *(RM April)*. Wtt showed one down
passenger train calling until line closure, 4 September
1967; probably linked to business use by local game
dealer so passenger use cannot be guaranteed *(True Line,*
April 2004, p.15). A R for LETHAM in *Brad* to 1955
but not thus LMS tt 1930 nor *Murray* 1948.

AULDEARN [High] op 9 December 1895 *(High)*;
clo 6 June 1960 *(Cl)*. *High Pamph* says op 1871 – earlier
private use?

AULDGIRTH [GSW]: line op 15 October 1849 and
this probably op with it, though not in *Brad* until May
1850*; clo 3 November 1952 *(RM December)*.
* = inspection report dated 24 September, advising refusal to
open, said signal arrangements at an un-named level crossing
3m 60ch from Dumfries, which was to be used as a roadside
station, were incomplete; 10 October – now complete, can open.

AULTMORE [High] op 1 August 1884 *(High Pamph)*
as FORGIE; renamed 1 January 1899 *(hbl 26th)*;
clo 9 August 1915 *(Cl)*.

AUTHORPE [GN] 3 Sept. 1848 *(Boston 4th- line)*;
clo 11 September 1961 *(RM September)*.

AVIEMORE [High] op 3 August 1863 *(High)*;
still open. See 1957★★.
AVINGTON [GW] (non-tt): army camp;
op 20 October 1918; clo December 1920;
{branch from Winchester} *(U)*.
AVOCH [High] op 1 February 1894 *(High)*;
clo 1 October 1951 *(RM November)*.
AVON LODGE [LSW] (non-tt) private for Earl of
Egmont; op 3 November 1862; clo 30 September 1935
(RM October 1903; U); included *hb* 1904–29, without
facilities; {map 125}.
AVONBRIDGE [NB] op 5 August 1840★★;
clo 1 May 1930 (Thursday) *(Cl)*.
AVON BRIDGE in *hb* 1867 and 1872.
AVONCLIFF [GW] op 9 July 1906 *(wtt supp)*;
HALT until 5 May 1969 *(GW H)*; aot request; still open.
AVONMOUTH: see M. Vincent, *Lines to Avonmouth*,
OPC, 1979; {map 121}
AVONMOUTH [CE] (original terminus from Clifton,
later Hotwells) op 6 March 1865 *(Bristol T 7th)*, line at
first detached from system; clo to public 1 October 1902
(Joint Officers' Minute, 20th) but advertised workmen's
service to 15 May 1903 (last train) *(Cl)*.
AVONMOUTH [CE] op 1 September 1885 *(Mid)*;
op A DOCK JOINT; became A 6 May 1968 tt *(offic)*;
still open.
A DOCK [CE] op for workmen ? (work on dock began
26 August 1868); public use began ? – dock opened
24 February 1877 *(Mid)*, but station not in tt until
October 1877 (even then, perhaps prematurely –
re-inspection necessary, took place 26 October) *(Mid)*;
1885 station based on this; part clo, dates as 1865 station.
A DOCKS [GW] op 9 May 1910 *(W D Press 10th)*;
clo 22 March 1915 *(Cl)*.
Boat trains used a succession of non-tt stations owned
by Bristol Port Authority. A DOCK EAST PIER was
used from 1901 until replaced by A DOCK ROYAL
EDWARD, 20 April 1910 *(inspection report dated 13 May)*;
this was re-sited in 'S'Transit Shed 1941, after original
destroyed by enemy action; clo 26 August 1964 *(U)*.
Some workmen's use also.
AVONWICK [GW] op 19 December 1893
(Totnes 16th, 23rd); clo 16 September 1963 *(Cl)*.
AWE CROSSING [Cal] (non-tt): at times HALT;
railwaymen and schoolchildren; stops for
schoolchildren shown 15 September 1952 wtt.
{Falls of Cruachan – Taynuilt}.
AWRE (Junction) [GW] op 1 April 1869 (replaced
Gatcombe, clo now – *Cl*); clo 10 August 1959 *(Cl)*.
GW co tts 1874, 1932: A for BLAKENEY.
JUNCTION added 1904 *(hb)* but not seen thus in any
GW co tt or *Brad*.
AWSWORTH [GN] op 1 November 1880 *(RCG)*;
clo 7 September 1964 *(RM October)*.
AXBRIDGE [GW] op 3 August 1869 *(Shepton 6th)*;
clo 9 September 1963 *(Weston 13th)*.
AXMINSTER [LSW] op 19 July 1860★★; still open.
A for LYME REGIS & SEATON from ? until 6 May
1974 *(BR notice)*.
AYCLIFFE [NE] op 19 June 1844 *(co n T 24 May- line)*;
clo 2 March 1953 *(RM April)*.

AYCLIFFE LANE – see HEIGHINGTON.
AYLESBURY
AYLESBURY [GW] op 1 October 1863 *(GW co n T 30
September)*; aot A TOWN >
AYLESBURY [Met] temp term in Brook Street
op 1 September 1892 *(co n Foxell)* >
[Met/GC and GW/GC Joint] op 1 January 1894
(RCG) replacing two above. Essentially, Met line
extended to expanded 1863 station. Met use ceased
11 September 1961; main line services continue.
Variously A JOINT, A TOWN, settled as A 1965 tt.
AYLESBURY [Aylesbury & Buckingham] temp term
op 23 September 1868 *(Rtn)*; clo 1 November 1868,
when line extended to 1863 station *(Cl supp 2)*.
A HIGH STREET [LNW] opening: *T 29 May* – directors
had decided to open to public 11 June 1839; *notice,
T 6 June* – would open to public on 10th and gave tt;
item T 12th described opening day – first train ran on
10th at about time given, used by members of general
public, who came straight back; free 'experimental
trips' all through day; did those on first train go free and
any wanting to travel according to tt find something at
about time they wanted?; directors' special ran from the
junction about 4.30pm. Overall 11 June seems to be
best op date to use (also see letter, H.V. Borley, *RCHS
Journal, vol. II, no. 2, p. 15)*. Re-sited 16 June 1889
(LNW Officers 30930) – slight extension of line (Borley).
H S added 25 September 1950 *(RM October)* but in
Brad from 1905/6; clo 2 February 1953 *(LNW Record)*.
Brad called it STATION STREET 1867 to 1904 and
HIGH STREET 1905 to 1915/6; in both cases usually
only one table, one way.
A VALE PARKWAY op 14 December 2008 tt
(Chiltern Railways 'Latest News' 15 September);
formal 15th *(RM March 2009)*; still open.
Also see SOUTH AYLESBURY.
AYLESBURY JUNCTION – see CHEDDINGTON.
AYLESFORD [SE] op 18 June 1856 *(SE; T 17th- line)*;
still open.
AYLESHAM [SR]: op 1 July 1928★ *(sig inst 24/1928)*;
HALT until 6 November 1967; still open.
★ = *Brad 9 July* tt – 'see subsequent announcements for opening
date', trains first shown August – result of having to send
information to printer some time in advance? but *Rly Gaz 20
July* says 'has been brought into use', which also implies delay.
AYLSHAM
A NORTH [MGN] op 5 April 1883 *(MGN; T 9th- line)*
as A TOWN; TOWN dropped by 1901 *(Brad)*,
NORTH added 27 September 1948 *(RM November)*;
clo 2 March 1959 *(T 2nd)*.
A SOUTH [GE] op 1 January 1880 *(GE)*;
SOUTH added 27 September 1948 *(RM November)*;
clo 15 September 1952 *(RM October)*.
AYNHO [GW]
AYNHO op 2 September 1850 *(co n T 31 August)*;
became A for DEDDINGTON★ 1 May 1910 *(RCG)*;
clo 2 November 1964 *(BR WR circular 20 October)*.
★ = version in GW sources seen; *RCG* made
DODDINGTON of it.
A PARK op 1 July 1910 *(GW H; co ½ T 6 August- line)*;
PLATFORM; clo 7 January 1963 *(Cl)*. RCH sources

suggest PLATFORM added shortly after opening (*dist ref 11 December 1911*); *Brad* dropped it 1933/4.

AYOT [GN] op 2 July 1877 *(RCG)* as AYOTT ST PETERS; spelling amended and ST P dropped 1878 tt *(Cl, JS)*; clo 26 September 1949 *(RM September)*.

AYR [GSW]

AYR (1) op 5 August 1839 *(co ½ 1110/149)*; most trains were transferred to (2) from 7 August 1856. Finally clo 1 July 1857 (Wednesday) according to *GSW* and *Cl*, but some all-weekday trains each way in Dalmellington and Maybole table were still shown *Brad* December 1859; they called at both this station and (2), being given 10 minutes for this section (reversal would have been needed). January 1860 service reduced to a Tuesday only train, to Ayr N Side; other way to S Side only. February 1860 Tuesday only service just to and from 'Ayr'; this was last shown April – clearly market service since given extra time for journey.

AYR (2) op 7 August 1856** *(GSW; co ½ T 3 September- line)*; original temporary, permanent 1 July 1857 *(GSW)*; replaced, 14 chains south by >

AYR (3) op 12 January 1886 *(GSW)*; still open. *GSW* says that (1) was A NORTH SIDE,

(2) A TOWNHEAD or SOUTH SIDE until 1 July 1857, when became just A, though TOWNHEAD still in some general use. *Brad* only used NORTH SIDE and SOUTH SIDE in tables where both were involved; TOWNHEAD not seen there at all.

A NEWTONHEAD op 1 October 1864 *(GSW)*; southbound only; last in tt April 1866 (indexed for some time afterwards) but *GSW* says clo 1 April 1868; is type of stop that might well have had longer life than shown by tt – ticket platform? At/near later Newton-on-Ayr?

AYR ROAD – see DALSERF

AYSGARTH [NE] op 1 February 1877 *(York Guardian 3rd)*; clo 26 April 1954** *(T 20th)*.

AYTON near Berwick [NB] op 22 June 1846 *(First; co n T 23rd- line)*; clo 5 February 1962 *(BR NER supplement to wtt 7 May 1962)*.

AYTON – see GREAT AYTON.

AYTON JUNCTION [NE] only appeared in *Brad* April and May 1868; {Nunthorpe – (Great) Ayton}; line via latter op 1 April 1868; only trains on that line are shown as calling; tt error? – passing time from working tt wrongly added?

A BYE-LAW.

Guard. "SMOKING NOT ALLOWED, GENTS."

Swell. "O! AH! WHAT'S THE FINE?"

Guard. "A SHILLING, READY MONEY, TO THE GUARD, SIR. FORTY SHILLINGS TO THE COMPANY, PAYABLE BY INSTALMENTS AND AT YOUR OWN CONVENIENCE."

BACHAN – see 1957★★.

BACHE op 9 January 1984 *(RM February)*,
as replacement for Upton-by-Chester; still open.

BACK OF LAW – see DUNDEE.

BACK O' LOCH [LNE] op 21 September 1925
(Rly Gaz 25th); HALT; clo 7 September 1964 *(Cl)*;
{Lenzie Junction – Kirkintilloch}.

BACKNEY [GW] op 17 July 1933 *(Cl 29)*; HALT;
clo 12 February 1962 *(RM March)*;
{Ross-on-Wye – Fawley}.

BACKWORTH {map 26}.

BACKWORTH (a) [BT]: station that opened as
HOLYWELL, {Seghill – Prospect Hill}:
line op 28 August 1841 *(NE)*, nd, 1 October 1847 *(co n
BT)*; renamed 1860 tt *(Cl)*; clo 27 June 1864 *(Cl)*.

BACKWORTH (b) [NE]: station that opened as
HOTSPUR: op 27 June 1864 *(co ½ T 22 August- line)*;
renamed 1865 tt *(Cl)*; clo 13 June 1977 *(Cl)*.
See NORTHUMBERLAND PARK [TWM] for later
station nearby.

BACON'S HOUSE SIDING [LMS]: (non-tt);
wtts for 22 September 1930 and 1932 show stops here
by passenger trains; 1932 stops by 8.09am from
Bletchley and 4.40pm from Banbury; 1938 and 1942
only morning train called; by 1948 none; passenger use
cannot be guaranteed (R. Maund, *Chron April 2008)*;
{Fulwell & Westbury – Water Stratford}

BACTON [GW]: shown in footnotes of co tt as
B ROAD, request, by May 1889 (W.H. Smith,
The Golden Valley Railway, Wild Swan, 1993, pp.24–5)
–continuous use ?; op (as full station?), as B,
1 November 1901 *(wtt supp)*; clo 8 December 1941.
See 1881 September 1★★ for line history.

BACUP [LY] op 1 October 1852 *(co ½ T 8 February
1853)*; clo 5 December 1966 *(RM February 1967)*.

BADGWORTH [Mid] op 22 August 1843 *(Mid)*;
last in *Brad* October 1846; {Cheltenham – Gloucester}.

BADMINTON [GW] op 1 July 1903 *(Bristol T 2nd)*;
clo 3 June 1968 *(T 3rd)*. Duke of Beaufort could stop
any train *(GW Deed 11580, dated 7 December 1899)*;
need for special Act of Parliament to rescind this kept
B open after others nearby closed.

BADNALL WHARF [LMS] (non-tt) munitions
workers; 1940s; {Norton Bridge – Standon Bridge}
(WW II).

BAG HILL / BAGHILL – see PONTEFRACT.

BAG LANE – see ATHERTON.

BAGGROW [MC] op 26 December 1866 *(D&C 14)*;
clo 22 September 1930 *(LNW Record)*.

BAGILLT [LNW] first in *Brad* January 1849
(P. Baughan, *Chester & Holyhead Railway*, vol.1, D&C
1972); re-sited 1871; clo 14 February 1966 *(RM April)*.
Usually BAGILT at first.

BAGLAN

BAGLAN op Sunday 2 June 1996 *(Rly Obs August)* –
3rd ceremonial; on different line from B Sands; still open.

B SANDS [GW] op 1 May 1933 *(Cl 29)*; HALT;
clo 26 September 1938, reop 29 May 1939 *(Cl)*;
clo 25 September 1939 *(Cl)*;
{Briton Ferry – Aberavon Sea Side}.

BAGSHOT [LSW] op 18 March 1878 *(co n T 15th)*;
still open.

BAGULEY [CLC] op 1 December 1865 *(Stockport 1st)*;
clo 30 November 1964 *(RM March 1965)*.

BAGWORTH {map 62}.

BAGWORTH [Mid] op 18 July 1832 *(Mid)* ★;
see 1847 December★★; replaced on deviation line by >

B & ELLISTOWN [Mid] op 27 March 1848 *(Mid)*;
& E added 1 October 1894 *(hbl 25th)*;
clo 7 September 1964 *(RM October)*.

B INCLINE HOUSE [Leicester & Swannington]:
'stopping place' *(Leic)*, ¾ mile beyond B
(line op 18 July 1832); probably soon closed.

B STAUNTON ROAD [Leicester & Swannington]
was original terminus of service op 18 July 1832 *(Mid)*;
no station; would have 'closed' when line extended,
27 April 1833.

★ = a special train was run for public use in the afternoon,
following formal opening on 17th (C.R. Clinker, *Leicester &
Swannington Railway*, Avon Anglia, 1977).

BAILDON [Mid] op 4 December 1876 *(Mid)*;
clo 5 January 1953 *(RM February)*, reop 28 January
1957, clo 29 April 1957 *(Mid)*, reop 5 January 1973
(RM March); clo 25 July 1992 for electrification work,
reop 8 September 1992 *(Mid)*; still open.

BAILEY GATE [SD Jt] op 1 November 1860
(Dorset Chron 8th) as STURMINSTER MARSHALL;
renamed 1863 *(R App)*; clo 7 March 1966
(Shepton 11th). B G for S M in Mid co tts 1894, 1903
and *Brad* to 1955.

BAILIFF BRIDGE [LY] op 1 March 1881 *(LY)*;
clo 2 April 1917 *(Cl)*.

BAILLIESTON

BAILLIESTON (a) [Cal] op 8 January 1866 *(Cal- line)*;
clo 5 October 1964 *(RM November)*.

BAILLIESTON (b) op 4 October 1993 *(AZ)*,
¼ mile west of earlier station; still open.

BAINTON [NE] op 21 April 1890 *(RCG)*;
clo 20 September 1954 *(RM October)*.

BAINTON GATE [Mid] op 1 November 1854 co tt
(Mid); last in *Brad* July 1856; {Uffington – Helpston}.

BAKER STREET

BAKER STREET [Bak] op 10 March 1906 *(T 12th)*;
additional platform added 20 November 1939 for
opening of Stanmore arm of Bakerloo; still open.

BAKER STREET [Met] op 10 January 1863 *(co n
Portfolio)*; still open. Swiss Cottage line plats added
13 April 1868 *(T 10th)*; B S EAST early *(hb)*; still open.

BAKER STREET [Jub] op 1 May 1979 *(RM July)*;
in part based on 1939 addition to Bakerloo; still open.

BAKEWELL [Mid] op 1 August 1862 wtt *(Mid)*;
clo 6 March 1967 *(RM April)*. *Brad* ? to 1955:
B for HADDON HALL and CHATSWORTH.

BALA [GW]
BALA (a) op 1 April 1868 (*Carnarvon 4th*) *;
{Bala Junction – Llanuwchllyn}; replaced by >
BALA (b) op 1 November 1882 (*GW*) on Festiniog line;
clo 18 January 1965★★.

* = pre-opening excursion from Llandrillo to point just short
of station 31 December 1867 (*Carnarvon 11 January 1868*).

B JUNCTION op 1 November 1882 (*GW*); advertised
as exchange only but there was public access from road;
in *hb* 1890 and 1895 as 'P', omitted 1904, back 1938,
no facilities shown; clo 18 January 1965★★.

B LAKE first in *Brad* starting 8 July 1935★; on site of
1868 station and served as station for Bala on summer
Sundays, one train each way from Ruabon to
Barmouth (Bala itself had no Sunday service); HALT;
last used 24 September 1939 (*Cl* – confirmed by letter
to R. Maund, 10 February 1965); excursion from
Stoke 4 August 1963 (*AB*).

* = according to *Cl* it was ready for use 5 February 1934
so perhaps excursion use that year.

BALADO [NB] op 1 May 1863 (*D&C 15; T 4th- line*)
as CLEISH ROAD; renamed 1878 (*RCG ref July*);
clo 15 June 1964 (*RM July*).

BALBEUCHLY [DPA; Cal] {map 9}
Line op 16 December 1831 (*Newtyle; see 1831 B*★★);
stops at B FOOT and B TOP (of incline).
Once tt coverage became regular, **B FOOT** was last in
Brad March 1853; back July 1854, Fridays only; last
July 1855; however, the needs of incline haulage meant
that trains would always have had to stop there.
B TOP clo 1 November 1860, when incline bypassed
by deviation (*G&S*).

BALCHRISTON LEVEL CROSSING [GSW]
op 17 May 1906 (M. Cobb, *Chron*); never included in
tt and only in *hb*, as B SIDING, after clo to passengers;
clo 1 December 1930 (*Cl*); {Knoweside – Glenside}.

BALCOMBE [LBSC] op 12 July 1841 (*co n T 9th*);
still open.

BALDERSBY [NE] op 1 June 1848 (*co ½ T
30 August- line*); B GATE in tt 1855 to 1863 (*JS, Cl*);
clo 14 September 1959 (*RM September*).

BALDERTON [GW] op 1 July 1901 (*RAIL 253/482*);
clo 3 March 1952 (*Cl*).

BALDOCK [GN] op 21 October 1850 (*co n T 18th*);
still open.

BALDOVAN & DOWNFIELD [Cal]
op 16 December 1831 (*Newtyle; see 1831 B*★★);
at first FLOUR DEPOT ST MARYS ROAD OFFSET;
soon B; & D added 1 September 1905 (*RCG*);
clo 10 January 1955 (*T 28 December 1954*); {map 9}.

BALDRAGON [Cal] op 16 December 1831
(*Newtyle; see 1831 B*★★); initially OFFSET;
clo 1 January 1917 (*RM February*); reop 1 February
1919 (*RCH*); clo 10 January 1955 (*T 28 December
1954*); {map 9}.

BALDWINS [GW] use as workmen's stop began
3 October 1910; probably no platforms – minutes
say Halt brought into use 9 November 1910, as
CRYMLYN BURROWS (*GW and RSB minutes*);
in GW co tt 10 July to 30 September 1911, probably in
error; first in *Brad* December 1922 but officially op to

public 24 November 1925 (*hbl 56*); HALT;
clo 11 September 1933 (*Cl*); {Jersey Marine – Danygraig}.

BALERNO [Cal] op 1 August 1874 (*co n Balerno*);
clo 1 November 1943 (*LNW Record*).

BALFRON [NB] op 26 May 1856★★;
clo 1 October 1951 (*RM November*).

BALGOWAN [Cal] op 21 May 1866★★;
clo 1 October 1951 (*RM November*).

BALGREEN [LNE] op 29 January 1934 (*Cl 29*);
on site of part of EDINBURGH EXHIBITION [NB];
HALT; clo 1 January 1968 (*Cl*).

BALHAM
BALHAM [LBSC] op 1 December 1856 (*T 31 October,
28 November*); re-sited 1863; B & UPPER TOOTING
from 9 March 1927 (*SR*) to 6 October 1969 (*L*);
still open.
BALHAM [Nor] op 6 December 1926 (*L*); see 1922★★;
still open.

BALLACHULISH [Cal]
BALLACHULISH op 24 August 1903 (*Brad Sh 1904*);
clo 28 March 1966 (*RM June* – photo-caption).
Became B & GLENCOE 1905 tt (*Cl*), B (G) for
KINLOCHLEVEN 1907/8 (*Brad*) and thus Cal tt
1913 and *hb* 1938; B G for BRIDGE of COE 1914/15
(*Brad*); B 1955 – but still note that it was station for
Glencoe and Kinlochleven.
B FERRY op 24 August 1903 (*Brad Sh 1904- line*);
clo 1 January 1917 (*RM February*); reop 1 March 1919
(*RCH*); clo 28 March 1966 (*RM June* – photo-caption).

BALLATER [GNS] op 17 October 1866 (*GNS*);
clo 28 February 1966 (*RM March*).
Included a private waiting room built for Queen Victoria.
LNE tt 1933 and *Brad* until 1955: B for BALMORAL
and BRAEMAR.

BALLATHIE [Cal] op 2 August 1848 (*Rtn- line*);
originally all days; last in *Brad* October 1849;
back February 1850, Fridays only; April/June 1850
to Tuesdays and Fridays; last in *Brad* July 1868;
{goods *IA*}. In 1862 *hb* as B SIDING.

BALLENCRIEFF [NB] op 22 June 1846★★- line;
clo 1 November 1847 (*Cl*); {Longniddry – Drem}.

BALLIFURTH FARM op 15 June 1959 (*GNS*);
HALT; aot request; clo 18 October 1965★★;
{Nethy Bridge – Grantown West}. September 1959 *hbl*
BALLINFURTH; corrected December 1959 *hbl*.

BALLINDALLOCH [GNS] op 1 July 1863 (*GNS*);
clo 18 October 1965★★.
Brad ? to 1938/9: B for TOMINTOUL.

BALLINGHAM [GW] op 1 September 1908 (*RCG*);
clo 2 November 1964 (*Cl*).
Pre-op Carey Road Bridge (*RAC*).

BALLINLUIG [High] op 1 June 1863 (*High*);
clo 3 May 1965 (*RM June*).

BALLOCH [DB Jt]
Line op 15 July 1850★★. Initially *Brad* just showed
BALLOCH, as did *Murray* April 1852. First specific
reference to B PIER in *Brad* was September 1858
(present by 1 April 1858 co tt), but it was early regular
practice not to give town and pier stations separately.
Scottish Railway Gazette, describing line at opening said
passengers would be carried onto pier and could step

straight onto steamers – it did not mention any 'town'
station – oversight? – or that a later addition?
Ticket *(JB)*, perhaps pre-1858, exists for B-WHARF.
'Town' station became B CENTRAL 30 June 1952
(Cl), was re-sited 24 April 1988, just short of original,
to avoid level crossing *(BLN 607)*; renamed B 15 May
1989; still open. PIER mostly summer use only;
clo 29 September 1986 *(RM October* – last train
Sunday, 28th).

BALLOCH [High] – see 1957**.

BALMORE [NB] first in *Brad* April 1886;
clo 2 April 1951 *(RM May)*.

BALMOSSIE op 18 June 1962 *(RM August)*;
HALT until 16 May 1983 tt; still open; {map 4}.

BALNACOUL [High] op 23 October 1893 *(High)*
as B PLATFORM; just B by January 1894, finally
B HALT 1928/9 *(Brad)* – *hb* dropped PLATFORM
1904; clo 14 September 1931 *(RM November)*.
LMS tt 22 September 1930 said this station would be
used as a Halt.

BALNACRA LEVEL CROSSING GATEHOUSE
(non-tt): railwaymen's wives; op 3 December 1951 *(U)*;
still in use, Saturdays only, 14 May 1979 wtt and
14 May 1984 wtt but not present 12 May 1986 wtt,
nor 1987/8 wtt; {Achnashellach – Strathcarron}.

BALNAGUARD [LMS] op 2 December 1935
(Cl 29); clo 3 May 1965 *(RM June)*; HALT in *hb* but
not seen thus *Brad*; {Ballinluig/Grandtully}.

BALNE [NE] op 2 January 1871 *(T 3rd)*;
clo 15 September 1958 *(RM October)*.

BALQUHIDDER [Cal] op 1 June 1870 *(Callander;
Rtn- line)* as LOCHEARNHEAD; renamed B 1 May
1904 *(hbl 28 April)*, when new Lochearnhead opened
(under 'L'); extended 1 May 1905, for trains on line to
St Fillans (J Thomas, *The Callander & Oban Railway*,
D&C, 1966); clo 28 September 1965**.

BALSHAM ROAD [Newmarket] op 4 April 1848
(co n T 3rd- line); clo 1 July 1850**; reop 9 September
1850 *(co n T 6th)*; clo 9 October 1851** (Thursday)
(Cl); {map 70}.

BALSHAW LANE & EUXTON [LNW]
op 2 September 1895 *(RCG)* as replacement for
Euxton; clo 6 October 1969 *(Cl)*; later reop as E B L.

BALSPORRAN – see 1957**.

BAMBER BRIDGE [LY]: line op 1 June 1846
(Rtn PP), nd, February 1847; still open.

BAMFORD [Mid]
BAMFORD op 25 June 1894 *(RCG; Mid notice bound
with RAIL 963/63)*; still open.
B SIDING HALT built 1935 for transfer of passengers
to Sheffield Water Board line (see Section 7) but in the
event buses used instead and halt never used *(U)*.

BAMFURLONG [LNW] op 1 April 1878 *(LNW
Officers 18365)*; clo 27 November 1950 *(RM Jan. 1951)*.

BAMPTON DEVON [GW] op 1 August 1884
(Tiverton 5th); DEVON added 1911 *(Cl* – but not in *hb)*;
clo 7 October 1963 *(W Som F P 12th)*.

BAMPTON OXON – see BRIZE NORTON.

BANAVIE [NB]
BANAVIE op 1 April 1901 *(RCG)*; still open.
Originally BANAVI in *hb*.

B PIER op 1 June 1895 *(RCG)*; PIER added 1 April
1901 *(hbl 25th)*; at/soon after extension of line via
Banavie reduced to summer use only, though
sometimes an extended summer (October 1904 *Brad*
says last trains 7 and 8 October). At times all days, both
ways, but usual pattern one train Monday, Wednesday
and Friday to Fort William, one Tuesday, Thursday
and Saturday from Fort William. Actual last train ran
Saturday 2 September 1939 *(Cl)*; but planned end was
last from Pier 15 September, last to it 16 September
(Brad). Station nameboard remained B.

BANBURY
BANBURY [GW] op 2 September 1850 *(co n T 31
August)*;
still open. Became B BRIDGE STREET 1886/7,
B GENERAL 1950/1 *(Brad)*;
G dropped 11 September 1961 tt.

B MERTON STREET [LNW] op 1 May 1850
(co n T 1st); clo 2 January 1961 *(RM February)*.
In *Brad* first as B, then B MELTON ROAD 1867 to
1878/81; became B MERTON STREET 1887/8;
but *hb* only B to B M S 1956.

BANCHORY [GNS] op 8 September 1853 *(GNS)*;
re-sited 20 chains west when line extended to Aboyne,
2 December 1859 *(Cl)*; clo 28 February 1966
(RM March).

BANDEATH [Cal] (non-tt): Naval Depot; dates ?;
{Airth – South Alloa} *(U)*.

BANDON [LBSC] op 11 June 1906 *(L)*; HALT;
clo 7 June 1914 *(Cl)*; {Waddon – Wallington}.

BANFF [GNS]
BANFF op 30 July 1859**, temp term probably near
later GOLF CLUB HOUSE (which see); replaced by
permanent 1 May 1860 *(GNS)*; B HARBOUR until
1928 tt *(Cl)*; clo 6 July 1964 *(RM July)*.

B BRIDGE op 1 July 1872 *(GNS)*, as replacement for
Macduff B; clo 1 October 1951 *(RM November)*.

BANGOR GWYNEDD [LNW] op 1 May 1848
(co n T 2nd); G added in body of tt 14 May 1984;
still open. *Brad*: B for BEAUMARIS to its last issue
(1961) but not thus BR LM tt 1957.
24, 25 and 26 April 1848 there were pre-opening
excursions to view Britannia Bridge *(co n T 24th)*.
Line across bridge to Llanfair op 18 March 1850 *(T 19th)*.

BANGOR-ON-DEE [Cam] op 2 November 1895
(Wrexham 2nd, 9th); clo 10 June 1940**,
reop 6 May 1946 *(T 16 March)*; clo 10 September
1962 *(RM October)*.

BANGOUR op 19 June 1905 *(RCG)*; private hospital
service but advertised and operated by [NB];
clo 1 August 1921 (PB Russell, *RM September 1981*;
Brad support). Perhaps special use before 1905 *(U)*.

BANK
BANK [Cen] op 30 July 1900 *(T 25th)*; see 1922**;
still open.
BANK [Nor] op 26 February 1900**; see 1922**,
still open. First in *Brad* as CITY OR MONUMENT,
then CITY; BANK by January 1901.
BANK [Waterloo & City] op 8 August 1898 *(T 9th)*, as
CITY – in *Brad* as THE CITY STATION (MANSION
HOUSE) until 1900 and *hb* as MANSION HOUSE

CITY until 1938; renamed B 18 October 1940 *(SR)*;
clo 8 August 1992, reop 6 September 1992 *(BLN 689)*;
clo 28 May 1993, reop 19 July 1993 *(RM September)*.
Op by LSW; transferred from BR to London
Underground 1 April 1994 *(RM October)*; still open.
BANK [Dock] op 29 July 1991 *(RM Sept.)*; still open.
Also see KING WILLIAM STREET; MONUMENT.
BANK HALL [LY] op 1 July 1870 *(Liverpool 1st)*;
still open. LY ticket as B H STREET *(JB)*.
BANKEND [Cal] (non-tt): in use by workmen by
27 February 1920, when accident there (D. Stirling,
BoT accident reports); clo ?; {beyond Coalburn}.
BANKFOOT near Newcastle [TWM]
op 10 May 1981 *(Tyneside)* on site of earlier Kenton Bank;
clo 1 September 1991 for engineering work on line
extension *(BLN 681)*; reop 17 November 1991
(RM January 1992); still open.
BANKFOOT near Perth [Cal] op 7 May 1906
(RCG); see 1921 April/May★★; clo 13 April 1931 *(Cl)*.
BANKHEAD near Aberdeen [GNS] op 1 July 1887
(GNS); clo 5 April 1937 *(RM January 1938)*.
BANKHEAD near Lanark [Cal] first in *Brad*
November 1867; clo 12 September 1932; reop 17 July
1933 *(Cl)*; clo 4 June 1945★★.
BANKNOCK [KB] op 2 July 1888 *(RCG)*;
clo 1 February 1935 (Friday) *(RM March)*.
BANKS [LY] op 20 February 1878 *(Southport Vis
20th)*; clo 7 September 1964 *(RM October)*.
BANNISTER GREEN [GE] op 18 December 1922
(RM April 1923); HALT; clo 3 March 1952
(RM April); {Felsted – Rayne}.
BANNOCKBURN [Cal] op 1 March 1848 *(co ½ T
2 September- line)*; clo 2 January 1950 *(RM February)*.
BANSTEAD [LBSC] op 22 May 1865 *(co n T 20th)*;
B & BURGH HEATH 1 June 1898 *(hbl 28 April)* to
August 1928 *(hbl October)*; still open.
BANWELL – see PUXTON & WORLE.
BAPTIST END [GW] op 21 August 1905 *(GW H)*;
HALT; clo 15 June 1964 *(RM July)*;
{Netherton – Windmill End}.
BARASSIE
BARASSIE [GSW]: see 1847 March 1★★; still open;
was B JUNCTION 1862 to 1880s *(hb* only*)*.
B WORKSHOPS [LMS] (non-tt) on branch from here,
in use by railwaymen in 1926 *(U)*; still in use 24 June
1966 *(Rly Obs August)*; not in wtt May 1969.
BARBERS BRIDGE [GW] op 27 July 1885
(Glos Chron 1 August- line); clo 13 July 1959 *(RM August)*.
BARBICAN [Met] op 23 December 1865
(T 22nd, 23rd) as ALDERSGATE STREET;
became A 1 November 1910 *(L)*, then A S & B/A & B
(sources differ) 1923, B 1 December 1968 *(RM January
1969)*; 'Widened Lines' platforms op 1 March 1866,
clo 22 March 2009, last use 20th *(RM May)*; original
still open.
BARBON [LNW] op 16 September 1861
(co n 14 Lancaster Gaz 14th); clo 1 February 1954 *(T 1st)*.
Intermittent use for Casterton School and in bad
weather continued into the 1960s (e.g. 1963 when
snow closed Settle & Carlisle route). Last ramblers'
excursion 26 August 1962 *(AB)*.

BARCALDINE [Cal] first in *Brad* July 1914;.
Last in *Brad* ending 24 September 1939, back June
1948; not in LMS tt 7 May 1945; in LMS summer tt
1946 *(Callander)* but not in LMS tt 6 October 1947.
Was it closed during Second War, then reopened
summer only at first? – certainly in *Brad* October 1949.
Orig SIDING; HALT from 1960 *(Brad)*.
Clo 28 March 1966 *(RM June* – photo caption*)*;
{Benderloch – Creagan}.
BARCOMBE [LBSC]
BARCOMBE op 1 August 1882 *(LBSC; Hants Chron
5th- line)*; NEW B until 1 January 1885 *(Cl)*;
clo 30 May 1955★★.
B MILLS op 18 October 1858 *(LBSC; co ½
T 26 February 1859- line)*; MILLS added 1 January
1885 *(Cl)*; rail service clo 24 February 1969 (unsafe
bridge), but bus service to 4 May 1969 *(RM March,
June)*. LBSC ticket for OLD B *(JB)*.
BARDNEY [GN] op 17 October 1848 *(co n T 16th)*;
clo 5 October 1970 *(T 16 July)*.
Became B for WRAGBY 1853/4, B & W 1867 *(Brad)*
and in one table remained thus until 1882, even after
W had station of own.
BARDON HILL [Mid]: Friday market service first
worked to Leicester 22 February 1833; a specially-built
first- and second-class composite kept for this for use
on stretch of line beyond Bagworth incline; in theory
passengers walked up/down incline, from/to trains on
lower level but in practice they seem to have ridden
on waggons (C.R. Clinker, *The Leicester & Swannington
Railway*, AvonAnglia, 1977).
Service perhaps not regular.
Op fully 27 April 1833 *(Mid)* as ASHBY ROAD;
renamed 1 January 1847 *(Cl)*; see 1847 December★★;
perhaps clo 1 March 1849, reop 1 September 1849 *(Mid)*;
clo 12 May 1952 *(RM July)*.
BARDON MILL [NE]: line op 18 June 1838 *(T 21st)*,
nd, May 1848 *(Topham)*; see 1836 B★★; still open.
BARDOWIE [NB] op 1 June 1905 *(RCG)*;
clo 20 July 1931 *(Cl)*.
BARDSEY [NE] op 1 May 1876 *(NE- line)*;
clo 6 January 1964 *(Cl)*.
BARE LANE [LNW] op 8 August 1864
(co n Lancaster 6th) as POULTON-LE-SANDS;
renamed later 1864; clo 8 February 1994 for
engineering work in connection with new Morecambe
(RM June); reop 6 June 1994 *(RM October)*; still open.
BARGANY COLLIERY [GSW] (non-tt):
PLATFORM; miners; in use 1926;
{Dailly – Killochan} *(U)*.
BARGEDDIE
BARGEDDIE (a) [NB] first in *Brad* February 1871★
as CUILHILL; renamed 1 April 1904 *(hbl 28th)*;
clo 1 January 1917 *(RM February)*; reop 1 February
1919 *(RM February)*; clo 26 September 1927 (based
on *Cl* – has 24th, a Saturday, probably last day).
★ = line op 23 November 1870 *(Glasgow Herald 24th*, which
says it had been announced that passengers would be booked
from Cuilhill but arrangements were not quite complete*)*.
BARGEDDIE (b) op 4 October 1993 *(AZ)*; on site of
earlier Drumpark; still open.

BARGOED

BARGOED [Rhy] op 31 March 1858 *(co ½
T September- line)*; B & ABER BARGOED 1 June 1905
(RCG) to 1 July 1924 *(GW circular 18 June)*; still open.
Aot *Brad* made one word of A B.

B COLLIERY HALT [BM] (non-tt): in use by 1926;
clo 31 December 1962; {south of Bargoed} *(U)*.
B TOP OR WESTYARD was in *hb* 1925 'P',
but no facilities 1929 – was this same as above entry?
Also see ABERBARGOED.

BARHAM [SE] op 4 July 1887 *(SE)*;
clo 1 December 1940 (Sunday) *(Cl)*.

BARKING op by [LTS] 13 April 1854 *(L;T 13th- line)*;
use by [Dist] began 2 June 1902 ceased 1 October 1905,
resumed 1 April 1908; use by [Met] began 4 May 1936;
still open.

BARKING ROAD – see CANNING TOWN

BARKINGSIDE op by [GE] 1 May 1903 *(RCG;
co ½ T 21 July- line)*; clo 22 May 1916★★ *(T 2nd)*,
reop 1 July 1919 *(T 20 June)*; last steam train ran
Saturday 29 November 1947; buses until reop by [Cen]
31 May 1948 *(Clay)*; still open. Until 1917a *hb* made
two words of it.

BARKSTON [GN] op 1 July 1867 *(GN)*;
BARKSTONE until 1917 tt *(Cl; ref RM December)*;
aot request; clo 7 February 1955
(BR ER signalling notice).

BARLASTON [NS] first in tt *(Topham)* July 1848;
re-sited 21 September 1852; op as B, became
B TITTESOR 1896/8 *(Brad)*, B & T 1923 ? *(hbl ref
26 April)*; B 1 May 1972 *(Cl)*; see 23 May 2004★★.

BARLEITH [GSW; LMS] private use by June 1904
(U); first in public tt June 1927; HALT in *Brad*
except for 1933/4 to 1954 (but HALT 1938 *hb*);
clo 6 April 1964 *(RM May)*; {Hurlford – Galston}.

BARLOW [NE] op 1 May 1912 *(RCG)*;
clo 15 June 1964 *(T 25 March)*.

BARMBY [HB] op 1 February 1897 *(RCG)*;
clo 1 January 1932 (Friday) *(RM January)*;
excursion 14 October 1933 during Hull Civic Week
(RM February 1934, pp.153–4).

BARMING [LCD] op 1 June 1874 *(T 2nd)*; still open.

BARMOUTH [Cam]

B FERRY op 3 July 1865 *(Cam)*; replaced by B, below;
Fairbourne here later.

BARMOUTH op 3 June 1867 *(Cam)*, service horse-
drawn until 10 October 1867★; still open.
★ = *Brad* showed B JUNCTION as terminus until November
1867 (B present but trainless). *Co notices Merioneth 1 June,
12 October* confirm above; former said arrangements had been
made to take passengers to Barmouth over bridge [not yet
passed by BoT for locomotive haulage] instead of by ferry and
offered alternative of walking along footpath over it, enjoying
magnificent views; did not give exact date for start but
following Monday, 3rd, would have been logical.

B JUNCTION – see MORFA MAWDDACH.

BARNACK [GN] op 9 August 1867 *(GN)*;
clo 1 July 1929 *(Cl)*.

BARNARD CASTLE [NE]

BARNARD CASTLE (a) op 9 July 1856★★; clo 1 May
1862, when (b) became through station for all passengers.

BARNARD CASTLE (b) op 8 August 1861 as terminus
of 'extension', initially operated as detached line;
clo 30 November 1964 *(RM December)*.
Note that for a while there were two stations here,
passengers presumably being left to walk between
them. *RAIL 667/65*: 'the continuance of two stations at
that place resulting in considerable inconvenience
to the public', they agreed to close old station at end
of month (April).

BARNBOW [NE] (non-tt): munitions workers;
in use by 7 October 1915 (HALT has been erected
for workmen travelling from Leeds direction – *RAIL
527/2191* – D. Geldard); clo 1924 *(U)*;
{Garforth – Cross Gates}.

BARNBY DUN

BARNBY DUN [GC] op 1 July 1856 *(GC;T 28 June-
line)*; replaced by new station on deviation 1 October
1866 *(Cl; Rtn- line)*; clo 4 September 1967 *(Cl)*.
Also see BRAMWITH, below.

BARNBY MOOR & SUTTON [GN] first in *Brad*
July 1850, as S & B M; became S September 1850 tt *(Cl)*,
B M & S 16 November 1909 *(RCG)*;
clo 7 November 1949 *(Cl)*.

BARNEHURST [SE] op 1 May 1895 *(RCG)*;
still open.

BARNES London [LSW]

BARNES op 27 July 1846 *(T 23rd)*; still open.

B BRIDGE op 12 March 1916 *(L)*; still open.
By 1872 passengers were dropped on bridge so they
could use it as stand for watching Oxford and
Cambridge Boat Race; earliest use seen is for race of
23 March 1872 *(co n T 22nd)*; that year also used
for London v Atlanta Club of New York race, 10 June
(co n T 9 May); specials restricted to ticket holders only.
Practice ceased when station op; had to walk to bridge
from there *(S Spec)*.

BARNES - see STOBS.

BARNET – see HIGH BARNET; NEW BARNET.

BARNETBY [GC] op 1 November 1848
(GC; Stamford 7th- line); still open.
B JUNCTION in *Brad* briefly until 1852 and *Topham*.

BARNHAM near Bognor [LBSC] op 1 June 1864
(LBSC) as B JUNCTION; became B SUSSEX 7 July
1929 *(Cl)*; S dropped 1930/1 *(Brad)*; still open.

BARNHAM near Thetford [GE] op 1 March 1876
(T 2nd); clo 8 June 1953 *(T 8th)*.

BARNHILL – see PERTH.

BARNHILL Glasgow [NB★] op 1 October 1883
(Glasgow); clo 1 January 1917 *(RM February)*,
reop 2 June 1919 *(RCH)*; still open.
Sometimes B GLASGOW in tts.
★ = [CGU] until 1896.

BARNHILL ANGUS [Cal] first in *Brad* October
1874; A added 30 June 1952 *(Cl)*;
clo 10 January 1955 *(T 28 December 1954)*.

BARNOLDSWICK [Mid] op 13 February 1871
(J. Gough, from *Craven Pioneer 18th; Rtn*)
– 8th, usually quoted, is error begun by *Brad Sh*;
clo 27 September 1965 *(RM November)*.

BARNSBURY [NL] op 10 June 1852 as
CALEDONIAN ROAD *(L)*; aot noted in *Brad* as

'The Cattle Market Station'; renamed 1 July 1870 *(L)*; clo 21 November 1870, replaced to the east by station later renamed C R *(NL Circular 80)*; {map 101}.

BARNSLEY
BARNSLEY [LY] op 1 January 1850 *(co ½ T 22 Feb.)*; renamed B LOW TOWN 2 June 1924 *(Rly Gaz 23 May)*, B EXCHANGE 1 August 1924 *(Cl)*; reverted to B 13 June 1960 *(RM June)*; still open.

B COURT HOUSE [GC/Mid] op 2 May 1870 *(RCG)*; last train 15 April 1960 *(Cl)*. C H was in *T* item on opening, local press and *Brad* from start, but added to Mid co tt after July 1912 *(Mid)*.

SUMMER LANE [GC] op 1 November 1855 *(GC)* as BARNSLEY, terminus for that town; clo February 1857, when line extended to LY station – extension shown *Brad* February (in anticipation?), formal opening 12th (delayed?) (R. Maund, *Chron October 2008*) reop 1 February 1867 *(Cl)*; for clo see 1959**; later excur *(U)*.
Also see CUDWORTH.

BARNSLEY ROAD – see under PENISTONE.

BARNSTAPLE
BARNSTAPLE [LSW] op 1 August 1854 *(Trewman 3rd)*; link to GW op 1 June 1887 but this station not immediately included in tables; by August 1889 was in GW table as B JUNCTION (but J not added in LSW table until 1892/3 *Brad*); later B for ILFRACOMBE and BIDEFORD; just B from 6 May 1974 *(BR notice)*; still open.

B TOWN [LSW] op 20 July 1874 *(N Devon J 23rd)* as QUAY, renamed 1886 tt *(Cl)*; re-sited 11 chains nearer Ilfracombe on 16 May 1898, to serve Lynton line also (below) *(Cl)*; clo 5 October 1970 *(N Devon J 8th)*; B TOWN & QUAY 1877 *(hb)*.

B TOWN [LSW, Lynton ng platform] op 16 May 1898 *(N Devon J 19th)*; clo 30 September 1935**.
Just B TOWN in *hb*, which treated it as separate station, even when main was B T & Q.

B VICTORIA ROAD [GW] op 1 November 1873 *(W Som F P 8th)*; V R added 26 September 1949 *(Cl)*; clo 13 June 1960 *(N Devon J 16th)*, service diverted to B (Junction).
Also see PILTON.

BARNSTON – see STORETON.

BARNSTONE [GN/LNW] op 1 September 1879 *(LNW Officers 20028)*; from 1897 tt *(Cl)* to 1 August 1897 *(RCG)* was BARNSTON; clo 7 December 1953 *(T 7th)*.

BARNT GREEN [Mid]: first in *Brad* May 1844; still open. 1857 to 1868 was B G for REDDITCH, then B G for LICKEY INCLINE in co tts *(Mid)*.

BARNTON [Cal] op 1 March 1894 *(Edin)* as CRAMOND BRIG; renamed B for C B 1 April 1903 *(hbl 23rd)* and thus Cal co tt 1913 and LMS tt 1947; clo 7 May 1951 *(RM June)*.

BARNTON GATE – see DAVIDSONS MAINS.

BARNWELL near Northampton [LNW] op 2 June 1845 *(LNW co n)*; erratically BARNEWELL *Brad* and LNW co tts to 1870s or later; clo 4 May 1964 *(RM June)*.

BARNWELL JUNCTION near Cambridge [GE]

op 2 June 1884 *(GE- line)*; served by Fordham branch trains only; clo 18 June 1962 *(RM August)*.

BARONS COURT
BARONS COURT [Dist] op 9 October 1905 *(RCG)*; still open.

BARONS COURT [Picc] op 15 December 1906 *(co n T 14th)*; still open.

BARONS LANE [GE] op 10 July 1922 *(D&C 5)*; HALT; clo 11 September 1939 *(G&S)*; {Cold Norton – Maldon}.

BARRAS [NE] first in *Brad* February 1862 (only goods trains shown in working tt at line opening, 8 August 1861); clo 22 January 1962 *(RM February)*.

BARRASFORD [NB]: line op 1 December 1859 *(NC)*, nd, June 1860; clo 15 October 1956 *(T 21 September.)*.

BARRHEAD
BARRHEAD [GBKJt] op 27 September 1848 *(GSW; Rtn- line)*; still open.

B CENTRAL [GSW] op 1 October 1902 *(RCG)*; clo 1 January 1917 *(RCH)*.

B NEW [Cal] built 1902 for a suburban service that was never provided; {Glenfield – Patterton}; *(U)*.

BARRHILL [GSW] op 19 September 1877**; clo 7 February 1882, reop 16 February 1882, clo 12 April 1886, reop 14 June 1886 *(Cl)*; still open.

BARRMILL [GBK Jt] op 26 June 1873 *(GSW- line)*; clo 5 November 1962 *(RM October)*.

BARROW FOR TARVIN near Chester [CLC] op 1 May 1875 *(CLC)* as T & B; renamed 1883 *(Cl; RCG ref October)*; clo 1 June 1953 *(RM July)*.

BARROW HAVEN [GC] op 8 April 1850 *(GC)*; aot request; clo 1 June 1981, reop 24 June 1981 *(RM October)*; still open.

BARROW HILL [Mid]
BARROW HILL [Mid] op 1 November 1888 *(RCG)*; replaced STAVELEY and op under that name; renamed B H & S WORKS 1 June 1900 *(hbl 12 July)*; final name 18 June 1951 *(Mid)*; clo 5 July 1954 *(Cl)*. Later excursions for open days at Barrow Hill Shed; last of these 1983 *(Mid)*.

ROUNDHOUSE HALT (non-tt) op 28 April 2001 for use internal shuttle and excursions from national network (R. Maund, from display board there); still in use.

BARROW-IN-FURNESS [Fur]
BARROW op August 1846**; at first in *Brad* as B PIER; not known if this was station usually described as 'at Rabbit Hill' or whether latter was replacement for it; 'Rabbit Hill' replaced by >
B 'Strand' on 29 April 1863 *(Cl)*; replaced again by >
B CENTRAL on 1 June 1882 *(Cl)*; -in-F added in body of *Brad* 1957/8 (earlier in index); still open.

B RAMSDEN DOCK op 1 June 1881 *(Fur)*; originally R D, altered 1 June 1882; regular boat train traffic ceased on outbreak of war 1914 and never resumed; used for occasional excursions and boats until 1936 *(SLS/Manchester Loco Society Rail Tour Notes, 27 August 1961)*.

B SHIPYARD (non-tt): workmen's station; op 1 May 1899 (M Peascod, *Chron*, February 2002); clo 3 July 1967; alias ISLAND ROAD; {Roose – Ramsden Dock} *(U)*.

SALTHOUSE (non-tt) op May 1920 for summer Saturday shuttle service to Piel; not a success; discontinued next year (M. Andrews, *Furness Railway in and around Barrow*, Cumbrian Railway Assn, 2003). Also see PIEL.

BARROW-ON/UPON-SOAR
B-ON-S & QUORN [Mid] op 5 May 1840 *(co n Lee)* as BARROW; -on-S added 1 May 1871 co tt *(Mid)*, & Q added 1 July 1899 *(hbl 13th)*; clo 4 March 1968 *(Cl)*.
B UPON S op 30 May 1994, about ¼ mile south of above *(RM August)*, on former goods lines; still open.

BARRS COURT JUNCTION
– see under HEREFORD.

BARRY [GNS] – see GLENBARRY.

BARRY South Wales [Barry]
BARRY op 8 February 1889 *(Barry)*; still open.
B DOCKS op 20 December 1888 *(Barry)*; still open.
B DOCK in *hb* until 1908a.
B ISLAND op 3 August 1896 *(RCG)*; still open.
B PIER op 27 June 1899 *(Barry)*; connected with steamer services, mostly Campbell's, seasonal use; last train for steamers 11 October 1971 *(RM February 1972)*; occasional steamers called 1972 and 1973 but no railway connection (M.A. Tedstone, *The Barry Railway Steamers*, Oakwood, 2005).
BARRY LINKS near Dundee [DA]: DEYHOUSE first found in *Brad* October 1843, but this was first time it gave any detail for this line, which had opened 6 October 1838**; not in *Tuck* about June 1843, which did give detail, but this is not conclusive given nature of its early service, which was Tuesdays and Fridays only. D was last in *Brad* July 1851. After a month's gap, BARRY appeared in same place, September 1851, full use; same site; LINKS added 1 April 1919 *(RCG)*; still open.
BARRY REVIEW PLATFORM – see BUDDON.
BARTLOW [GE] op 1 June 1865 *(GE Journal January 1992)*; clo 6 March 1967 *(RM April)*.
BARTON – see DOWNHOLLAND.
BARTON & BROUGHTON [LNW] op about November 1840, as replacement for Broughton *(LPJ)* – no detail for this line in *Brad* until January or February 1848, when BROUGHTON; renamed 1861 *(Cl; JS)*; clo 1 May 1939 *(T 27 April)*.
BARTON & HALSALL – see MOSSBRIDGE.
BARTON & WALTON [Mid] op 12 August 1839 *(Mid; co n T 8th- line)*; clo 5 August 1958 *(RM September)*.
BARTON HILL [NE]:
line op 8 July 1845**; HILL added June 1853 co tt *(JS)*; clo 22 September 1930** *(T 10 July)*.
BARTON MOSS [LNW]: line op 17 September 1830**; 1 March 1831 co tt includes REIDS FARM; perhaps early name for B M, perhaps nearby stop soon replaced by it*; B M was listed September 1831; November 1832 abandoned for Lambs Cottage *(LM)*; by 19 October 1839 back in tt (perhaps other short term changes). Re-sited 60 chains east 1 May 1862 *(Cl)*; clo 23 September 1929 *(Cl)*.
* = H. Jack pointed out that J.S. Walker's *Accurate Description* of the LM says: 'On passing the 24th mile post ... a large part

of the [Barton] Moss has been thrown into cultivation ... About a mile distant are several cottages ... and in one of them ... resides Mr Reed, the skilful and active manager of an extensive and productive farm formed on the before profitless waste'. An advertisement for a buyer or tenant for WARTON MOSS FARM *(Dumfries, 14 July 1840)* said that passengers could be booked to and from farm. From description, station would appear either to have been Barton Moss or another nearby stop.
BARTON STACEY [GW] (non-tt): HALT; army camp; op ?; clo 2 December 1940 *(wtt supp)*; {Whitchurch – Sutton Scotney}.
BARTON-LE-STREET [NE] op 1 June 1853**; clo 1 January 1931 (Thursday) *(T 5 December 1930)*; later excursions, e.g. 27 July 1964 *(Whitby)*.
BARTON-ON-HUMBER [GC] op 1 March 1849 *(GC)*; -on-H added body of *Brad* 1925/6 (index earlier, intermittently); clo 1 June 1981, reop 24 June 1981 *(RM October)*; still open.
BASCHURCH [GW] op 14 October 1848 *(Shrewsbury)*; clo 12 September 1960 *(Cl)*.
BASFORD [LNW]: line op 4 July 1837; not in earliest descriptions of line; op by 8 August 1838, when mentioned in co minutes *(RAIL 220/2)*; clo 1 July 1875 (Thursday) *(LNW Officers 13009)* – replaced by Betley Road; {Crewe – Betley Road}.
BASFORD near Nottingham.
B NORTH [GN] op 1 February 1876 *(GN)* as NEW B; renamed B & BULWELL 1 August 1876, B N 21 September 1953 *(Cl)*; clo 7 September 1964 *(RM October)*. *RCG ref August 1876*: NEW BURFORD (error) for DOBPARK and BULWELL.
B VERNON [Mid] op 2 October 1848 *(Mid)*; VERNON added 11 August 1952 *(Cl)*; clo 4 January 1960 *(RM February)*; later excur; workmen used until 4 November 1963 *(U)*.
Also see NEW BASFORD [GC].
BASILDON op 25 November 1974 *(RM January 1975)*; still open.
BASHALL & CO'S SIDING [LY/LNW]: shown 'P' 1877 *hb*, same as FARINGTON MILL – but not shown 'P' under latter. Presumed error.
BASINGSTOKE
BASINGSTOKE [LSW] op 10 June 1839 *(Salisbury 17th)*; still open. B JUNCTION 1854 to 1858/9 *(Brad)*.
BASINGSTOKE [GW] op 1 November 1848 *(Hants Chron 4th)*; clo and trains diverted to LSW station 1 January 1932 *(RM January)*; one platform absorbed into LSW station *(Cl)*.
Stop at WORTING ROAD BRIDGE used 29 July 1900 as starting point of contractor-arranged pre-opening trip on Basingstoke & Alton *(Basingstoke)*.
BASON BRIDGE [SD Jt] op 28 August 1854**; clo 7 March 1966 *(Shepton 11th)*.
BASSALEG
BASSALEG [BM] op 14 June 1865 *(co n Newport 17th)*; clo 31 December 1962 *(T 31st)*.
B JUNCTION [GW] op 23 December 1850**, as RHYMNEY JUNCTION; renamed B J 1858 tt; clo 1 January 1917 *(GW notice dated 22 December 1916)*, reop 3 March 1919 *(GW circ 2653)*; back to B J 1 July 1924 *(GW circular 18 June)*; clo 30 April 1962 *(T 6 April)*.

At times R J for B and MACHEN *(Brad)*; at times
spelled BASSALLEG *(Brad, hb, 1865 wtt)*.
BASSENTHWAITE LAKE [CKP] op 2 January
1865 *(co ½ T 28 February- line; in op tt Cockermouth)*;
clo 18 April 1966 *(Cl)*.
BAT & BALL [LCD] op 2 June 1862 *(T 3rd)*,
originally temporary station; permanent, probably to
west (original line went due south into what became
goods yard – R. Hellyer), op when line extended
1 August 1869; clo 1 January 1917 *(RM February)*,
reop 1 March 1919 *(T 24 February)*; still open.
Opened as SEVENOAKS; became S B & B 1869 tt *(JS)*,
B & B 5 June 1950 *(SR)*.
BATH
B GREEN PARK [Mid] op 4 August 1869★
(Bath Chron 5th); G P added 18 June 1951 *(Cl)*;
clo 7 March 1966 *(Shepton 11th)*.
Was B QUEENS SQUARE *(Brad,* and SR tt August
1939 – but latter printed by *Brad)*; *Brad* added this in
SD Jt table soon after opening of extension to Bath, in
Mid table 1882/3, dropped 1942/3.

★ = *Bath Chron* describes station that was unfinished (normal)
but clearly intended to be permanent; item *28 April 1870* is
mainly about new goods station that would open 2 May but
mentions <u>extensions</u> to platforms (one of 240 feet) then under
way; thus 5 May 1870 is probably better interpreted as date
when extensions were completed, rather than a re-siting.
(For more detail see C.G. Maggs, *The Mangotsfield to Bath
Line*, Oakwood, 2005).

B SPA [GW] op 31 August 1840 *(Bristol Stand 3rd)*;
SPA added 1949/50 *Brad*; still open.
B MANVERS STREET 1883 to 1904/5 *(Brad)*.
BATH ROAD [NSWJ] op 8 April 1909 *(L)*;
clo 1 January 1917 *(T 26 September 1916)*; 'HALT' –
see 1905★★; {Hammersmith & Chiswick branch}.
BATHAMPTON [GW] op 2 February 1857 *(GW)*;
clo 3 October 1966 *(W D Press 3rd)*.
BATHFORD [GW] op 18 March 1929 *(Bath Chron
16th)*; HALT; clo 4 January 1965 *(RM February)*;
{Box – Bathampton}.
BATHGATE
BATHGATE op 24 March 1986 *(RM May)*; re-sited
version of earlier Upper, nearer to town centre, on part
of old Motive Power Depot site; still open.
B LOWER [NB] op 1 March 1856 *(co n Falkirk
Herald)*, without BoT approval; soon closed – probably
by 13 March, when BoT appointed inspector
(MT 12/2), though advertisement for service still in
paper of that date (inertia?), certainly by 20 March
(date of co minute 'has closed'). Reop 7 July 1856
(SRO BR/MNK/1/2); clo 1 May 1930 (Thursday) *(Cl)*.
In co wtts B MONKLAND at first; LOWER probably
added when NB took over.
B UPPER [NB] op 12 November 1849 *(Rtn)*; see 1851
November 29★★; clo 9 January 1956 *(RM February)*.
B E&G in co wtts at first; UPPER probably added by NB.
BATLEY {map 55}.
BATLEY [GN] op 1 November 1864 *(GN)*;
clo 7 September 1964 *(Cl)*.
BATLEY [LNW] op 18 September 1848 *(D&C 8)*;
still open.

Also see UPPER BATLEY.
BATLEY CARR [GN] op 12 April 1880 (both *GN
vol. II p.118* and *LNW Officers 20652* say line between
Batley and Dewsbury was opened now, in one piece,
not in two sections, as given by *D&C 8)*;
clo 6 March 1950 *(Cl)*.
BATTERSBY [NE]: logically op 1 April 1868 as
junction for line opened via (Great) Ayton *(NE maps)*;
initially tt apparently gives Ingleby as connection point;
first certain tt ref, as INGLEBY JUNCTION,
is *Brad* January 1869, Ayton line table; not added
Whitby line table until June 1874;
renamed B JUNCTION 30 September 1878
(Cl; RCG ref October), B 1 May 1893 *(Cl)*; still open.
BATTERSEA {map 109}.
BATTERSEA [WL] op 2 March 1863 *(LSW co n T 4th)*:
clo 14 September 1940 *(wtt supp)*.
B PARK [LBSC] (a) op 1 October 1860 *(co n T 1st)* as B;
PARK added 1 July 1862 *(Cl)*;
at times B P & STEAMBOAT PIER *(L)*;
clo 1 November 1870 (Tuesday) *(Cl)*.
February 1863 *Brad* – LCD using, with note that their
trains called for passengers to/from Railway Pier by river
steamboats which ran at frequent intervals. After closure
1870 was kept as booking-point for steamboat
passengers, who presumably had to walk along bridge
to Grosvenor Road (M. Searle, *Chron, July 2004)*.
B PARK [LBSC] (b) op 1 May 1867 *(L)* as YORK ROAD;
became Y R & B P 1 November 1870 *(L)*, B P & Y R
1 January 1877 *(RCG)*, B P 1 June 1885 *(L; RCG ref
July)*; still open.
B PARK ROAD [LCD] op 1 May 1867 *(T 2nd)*
as B P YORK ROAD; renamed 1 November 1877 *(L)*;
clo 3 April 1916 *(T 11 March)*.
B PIER STAFF HALT (non-tt) op for railway staff
15 May 2000 *(BLN 393)*; still in use.
Also see QUEENSTOWN ROAD.
BATTLE [SE] op 1 January 1852 *(SE)* (in *Brad*
November 1851, error – omitted December);
clo 8 March 1855 (collapse of Mountfield Tunnel),
reop 30 June 1855 *(Cl)*; still open.
BATTLESBRIDGE [GE] op 1 July 1889 *(RCG)*;
still open.
BATTY GREEN – see RIBBLEHEAD.
BATTYEFORD [LNW] op 1 October 1900
(LNW Officers 39764) as B & MIRFIELD;
renamed 2 May 1910 *(hbl 28 April)*;
clo 5 October 1953 *(RM November)*.
BAWDRIP [SD Jt] op 9 July 1923 *(Bridgwater Merc 4th)*:
HALT; clo 1 December 1952 *(Bridgwater Merc 2nd)*;
{Bridgwater – Cossington}.
BAWTRY [GN] op 4 September 1849 *(T 4th)*;
clo 6 October 1958 *(RM November)*; later excursions –
e.g. to Bridlington 3 April 1961 *(AB)*.
BAXENDEN [LY] op 17 August 1848 *(LY)*;
clo 10 September 1951 *(RM October)*.
BAY HORSE [LNW] op 26 June 1840 *(LPJ)*;
clo 13 June 1960 *(RM July)*.
BAYFORD [LNE] op 2 June 1924 *(T 29 May)*;
clo 11 March 1973 (tunnel repairs), reop 7 May 1973
(Cl); still open.

BAYNARDS [LBSC] op 2 October 1865 *(T 3rd)*;
clo 14 June 1965 *(Cl)*.

BAYSWATER [Met]
op 1 October 1868 *(T 16, 30 September)*; still open.
In *Brad* first shown as B; was B QUEENS ROAD from
1906/7 to 1912/13 and from 1927/9 until 1946/7, when
became B QUEENSWAY (according *RM November*
this was 1 September 1946); still thus October 1949.
In *hb* was B Q R from start to 1925 when became
B Q R & WESTBOURNE GROVE and still thus
1929; 1938 B; *hb* 1949a said now B QUEENSWAY
and still thus 1956.
At one time was QUEENS ROAD (BAYSWATER)
at station (painting W.S. Sickert about 1916 and map
issued by [Met] 1921/4 – J. Savage).
Always was B on Underground Maps.

BEACH ROAD [BWA]: line op 18 May 1901**;
clo 28 March 1917**; {Northam – Westward Ho!}.

BEACH STREET Swansea [SIT] first in *Brad* May
1882 (see 1860 July 25**); last there October 1885;
but in *hb* 1883, 1890, 1895; {map 88}.

BEACHLEY JUNCTION [GW] (non-tt):
workmen's service began 18 November 1918 *(U)*;
discontinued 25 October 1920 *(wtt supp)*;
{Woolaston – Chepstow}.

BEACONSFIELD

BEACONSFIELD [GW/GC]
op 2 April 1906 *(T 5 March)*; still open. Became
B for PENN 1911/12 *(Brad)*; thus in LNE tt 1927,
GW tt 1932, *hb* 1938 and *(Brad)* until 1955.
B GOLF – see SEER GREEN.
BEAG FAIR SIDING [GW] first in *Brad* April 1878;
aot request; clo 1 January 1883 *(Rtn)*; {map 81}.
B SIDING *(hb)*.

BEAL [NE]: line op 29 March 1847**, nd,
August 1847; clo 29 January 1968 *(RM March)*.

BEALINGS [GE] op 1 June 1859 *(T 2nd- line)*;
clo 17 September 1956 *(RM September)*.

BEAM BRIDGE [BE] op 1 May 1843 *(Taunton 3rd)*;
temporary terminus between Wellington and Whiteball
Tunnel, providing connection with road service to
Exeter pending completion of tunnel.
Removed from tt when line extended 1 May 1844.
'Accepted version' is that was passenger only.
However, GW minutes *(RAIL 250/120 on)* show it was
used for goods and continued to be so after that closure,
at least until early 1847 and was served by 9.30am
ex Paddington and 2pm ex Exeter, which included
passenger carriages. However, it is unlikely that,
officially at least, passengers could still use it.
It was included in table of charges for goods traffic
(27 February 1845) but (-) in column used for 3rd class
passenger fares, which were included with this table.

BEAMISH [NE] op 1 February 1894 *(RCG)*;
clo 21 September 1953 *(RM October)*.

BEANACRE [GW] op 29 October 1905 *(GW H)*;
HALT; clo 7 February 1955 *(Cl)*.
Hb 1938: BEARACRE; corrected 1941a.

BEARLEY [GW] op 10 October 1860
(W Mid; T 11th- line); HALT 21 June 1965 to 6 May
1968 *(Cl)*; still open.

BEARPARK [NE] op 1 June 1883 *(G&S)* as
ALDIN GRANGE; renamed 1 May 1927 *(hbl July)*;
clo 1 May 1939 *(Cl)*; used for miners' galas until 1954
or later *(U)*. According to *Brad* was A G for B prior
to renaming.

BEARSDEN [NB] op 28 July 1863 *(Glasgow- line)*;
still open.

BEARSTED [LCD] op 1 July 1884 *(LCD)* – RCG
says goods July, passengers October, but in *Brad* July;
B & THURNHAM 1 July 1907 *(hbl 3rd)* to 12 May
1980; still open.

BEASDALE [NB] op 1 April 1901 as private station
for Arisaig House *(U)*; op to public 6 September 1965
(U); aot request; still open.
In *hb* 1904, no indication was private; 1946 May *hba*
shown 'closed' – use not continuous?
NB wtt alterations for 6 February 1922 have note
(probably regular fixture) that any train could be
stopped at written request of Sir Arthur Nicholson of
Arisaig or his manager or factor; requests could be
made to person in charge at Beasdale Platform or
station-masters at Lochailort or Arisaig – in first case
had to telegraph to one of others.

BEATTOCK [Cal].
BEATTOCK op 10 September 1847 *(co n T 7th, where
was B BRIDGE)*; clo 3 January 1972 *(RM March)*.
B SUMMIT (non-tt) used by railwaymen and families
from 3 January 1900 *(U)*; in use 30 June 1952 wtt;
also see 1966**; {Beattock – Elvanfoot}.

BEAUCHIEF [Mid] op 1 February 1870
(Mid; co n Mining 19th- line) as ABBEY HOUSES;
renamed BEAUCHIEFF 1 April 1870;
& ABBEY DALE added 1 June 1874 co tt; ...FF to ...F
1 May 1888 co tt; settled as B 19 March 1914 *(Mid)*;
clo 2 January 1961 *(RM February)*.

BEAUFORT
BEAUFORT [LNW] op 1 March 1864 *(co ½ T August 12-
line)*; clo 6 January 1958 *(BR notice, December 1957)*.
LNW co tt 1864 (not 1868): B for EBBW VALE .
BEAUFORT [GW], (non-tt) miners; open by 1886;
clo 2 October 1961; {beyond Ebbw Vale} *(U)*.

BEAULIEU ROAD [LSW]
BEAULIEU ROAD (a) line op 1 June 1847 *(Salisbury
5th- line)*; this shown, with trains, in *Brad* July 1847,
first time line included; however, according to *Fawley*
(no source given) it op 9 August 1847. Since company
had not wanted station here (forced by Commissioners
of Woods & Forests), might well have been delay – note
reluctance at Southampton Blechynden; not mentioned
in description of journey over line *(T 17 May)* – but not
the only omission. Last in *Brad* February 1860.
BEAULIEU ROAD (b) op 1 November 1895 *(RCG)*;
same site; still open.

BEAULY near Inverness
BEAULY (a) [High] op 11 June 1862 *(High)*;
clo 13 June 1960 *(RM July)*.
BEAULY (b) op 15 April 2002 but did not appear in
official documents as 'in use' until 27 April *(Rly Obs June,
p.252)*; still open.

BEAUMONTS [Mid] op 9 August 1905 *(Mid)*;
HALT; clo 16 June 1947**;

{Hemel Hempsted – Redbourn}.
'Notices' panel in *Brad* 8 July 1929 (previous seen July 1928) says had been renamed from B CROSSING HALT to B HALT, but former not seen in tt – save space? error?

BEAVERS HILL [GW] op 1 May 1905 *(GW H)*; HALT; according to *Brad* clo in winter from 1908 (last shown September) though possible that service for workmen at Pembroke Dock continued; clo 21 September 1914 *(GM's report 12 January 1917)*; reop 1 December 1923; clo 15 June 1964 *(Cl)*; {Manorbier – Lamphey}.

BEBINGTON [Birkenhead] op 23 September 1840 *(Birkenhead)*; B & NEW FERRY 1 May 1895 *(Cl; RCH dist ref 31 August)* to 6 May 1974 *(BR notice)*; still open. Early often BEBBINGTON *(Brad; Robinson)*.

BEBSIDE [NE] op 3 August 1850 *(BT)* as COWPEN LANE; renamed 1860 tt *(Cl)*; clo 2 November 1964 *(RM January 1965)*.

BECCLES [GE] op 4 December 1854 *(Rtn– line)*; clo 15 May 1858** , reop 1 June 1859 *(T 2nd)*; still open. B JUNCTION 1859/60 to 1865/7 *(Brad)*

BECKENHAM

B HILL [LCD] 1 July 1892 *(L)*; still open.
B JUNCTION [WELCP] op 1 January 1857 *(L; co ½ T 9 February– line)*; JUNCTION added 1 April 1864 *(L)*; still open. B JOINT 1872 to 1925 *(hb)*.
B ROAD – see PENGE [WELCP].
Also see NEW BECKENHAM.

BECKERMET [WCE Jt]

BECKERMET op 2 August 1869 *(D&C 14*; line date supported by *co ½ T 11 August* which says 1 August, but that a Sunday, no Sunday service); clo 7 January 1935 *(LNW Record)*; later excur *(RM)*; reop to workmen 11 March 1940 *(U)*, to public 6 May 1946 *(RM July)*; clo 16 June 1947**; certainly not in use according to 23 May 1949 wtt (R. Maund); perhaps Sellafield UKEA workers' use about 1953 to 1965 *(WW II)*.
B MINES (non-tt) used by miners from 15 January 1912 to after 1923; {branch from Egremont} *(U)*.

BECKFOOT [Raven] (ng) op 20 November 1876 *(Raven; co yearly T 26 March 1877– line)*; clo 1 December 1908**; reop 20 April 1916 *(Cl)*; see 1960**.

BECKFORD [Mid] op 1 October 1864 *(Worcester 8th)*; clo 17 June 1963 *(RM July)*.

BECKHOLE(S) [NE] Spelling varied, apparently randomly rather than altering at particular times; BECK HOLE(S) also seen.

BECKHOLE(S) (a) on stretch of Whitby & Pickering op 26 May 1836, though *NE pp. 270–1* says by 18 July 1835 people could charter own 'excursion trains' (horse-drawn) to here from Whitby; not found in any tt nor shown on Macaulay's maps of time, though trains had to stop here for incline haulage – any station as such? BECK HOLES listed 1862 *hb*; 1866a 'closed', no later entry. Incline replaced 1 July 1865 *(NE)*. See 1835 B**.

BECKHOLE(S) (b) first in *Brad* July 1908 as BECKHOLES, terminus of summer only rail-motor service, on remnant of earlier incline line, so probably at

same site as (a) or near; clo end of summer 1914 *(Cl)*.
BECKINGHAM [GN/GE] op 15 July 1867 *(GN/GE; GN co ½ T 19 August– line)*; clo 2 November 1959 *(RM December)*.

BECKTON

BECKTON [GE] op 18 March 1874 *(L)*; clo 29 December 1940 *(Cl)*, but see 1940 September 8**. Earlier Gas Co workmen's service (non-tt) began 17 March 1873; according to *hb*, where added 'P' 1874/5a, B GASWORKS was separate station, on extension from public one; still in *hb* 1895, not 1904. No support elsewhere – others (e.g. *L*) say workers used GE station and trains. Section on workmen's tickets in GE co tt 4 October 1914 suggests ordinary station used then.
BECKTON [Dock] op 28 March 1994**; still open.
B PARK [Dock] op 28 March 1994**; at/near old Central; still open.

BECONTREE op by [LMS] 28 June 1926 *(Rly Gaz 2 July)* as GALE STREET; renamed 18 July 1932 *(Mid)*; HALT until 12 September 1932 *(Cl)*; [Dist] service added 12 September 1932; BR service ended 12 June 1961 *(Mid)*; transferred to LPTB 26 April 1970 *(Mid)*; still open.

BEDALE [NE] op 1 February 1855 *(co ½ T 23 Feb.)*; clo 26 April 1954 *(T 20th)*. Excur use 1980s *(U)*.

BEDDAU near CAERPHILLY – see ABER.
BEDDAU near Llantrisant [TV] first in *Brad* July 1910; see 1904**; clo 31 March 1952 *(Cl)*.

BEDDGELERT [WH] (ng) op 1 June 1923 (see 1922 July 31**); clo 28 September 1936 *(Cl)*; {map 76}.

BEDDINGTON LANE

BEDDINGTON LANE [LBSC] first in *Brad* February 1856 (line op 22 October 1855 but this station not mentioned in original inspection report – *Bylines August 1998)*. LANE added 1887 *Brad*; HALT 1919 to 1923 *Brad*; clo 1 June 1997** for conversion to >
BEDDINGTON LANE [Croydon] op 30 May 2000 *(Rly Obs July)*; still open.

BEDE [TWM] op 24 March 1984 *(Tyneside)*; still open.

BEDFORD

BEDFORD [Mid] op 1 February 1859 *(Mid)* *; realigned late 1978; renamed B MIDLAND ROAD 2 June 1924 *(Rly Gaz 23 May)*, B M 8 May 1978, B 16 May 1988 tt *(Mid)*; still open.
B ST JOHNS [LNW] op 18 November 1846**; ST J added 2 June 1924 *(Rly Gaz 23 May)*; re-sited 1 August 1862 *(Cl)*; again re-sited, 250 yards north, 14 May 1984 *(RM May)*; still open.
* = from 8 May 1857 until 1 February 1859 Mid used LNW station here.

Non-tt:
7 and 8 October 1858 (other times also?) one train each way to/from Bletchley stopped about a mile short of LNW station for benefit of race-goers; no facilities – passengers left 'to stride, straddle and leap' from carriage steps to rails and cross track (letter *T 12th*).
Two temporary stations for BEDFORD AGRICULTURAL SHOW, 13 to 17 July 1874,

inclusive *(notices T 7th)*. Map in *The Engineer, 3 July 1874* shows sites. LNW immediately west of point where Mid crossed over LNW line (Kempston & Elstow here later); Mid about 1,500 yards south-west of crossing point.

BEDFORD LEIGH – see LEIGH.

BEDHAMPTON [LBSC] op 1 April 1906 *(LBSC)*; HALT until 5 May 1969 *(SR App)*; still open.

BEDLAY [MK]: line op 10 December 1849 *(MK)*, station with line but only Wednesday and Saturday service; closed at the end of the month; {Map 16}. See 1844 December 26** for other services that went through this area and might have stopped here.

BEDLINGTON [NE] op 3 August 1850 *(BT)*; clo 2 November 1964 *(RM January 1965)*. B JUNCTION 1860 to 1865/6 *(Brad)*.

BEDLINOG [Taff Bargoed Joint]
BEDLINOG op 1 February 1876 *(S Wales 31 January-line)*; clo 15 June 1964 *(RM August)*.
B COLLIERY JUNCTION (non-tt) miners; 1897 to 1915 *(U)* and 1938 *(U)* to 1955 at least (shown still in 13 June 1955 wtt); {Bedlinog – Nantyffyn}.
Branch to another non-tt miners' station,
B WORKMAN'S PLATFORM; op after 1915; clo 1928/38 *(U)*.

BEDMINSTER [GW] first in *Brad* June 1871; re-sited 27 May 1884 *(GW Bristol Diary)*; still open.

BEDWAS [BM] op 14 June 1865 *(co n Newport 17th)*; clo 31 December 1962 *(T 31st)*.

BEDWELLTY PITS [LNW]: line op 19 June 1865; first in *Brad* June 1871, however in use earlier. *LMS S Wales p.85* shows working tt for 1 February 1866; this has passenger service for B LOWER both ways and miners' service from B UPPER to Tredegar. Originally in *hb* as BEDWELTY, later BEDWELLTY, then B P; became HALT 1936 *(Brad)*; clo 13 June 1960 *(RM July)*.

BEDWORTH
BEDWORTH (a) [LNW] op 2 September 1850**; clo 18 January 1965 *(RM March)*.
BEDWORTH (b) op 16 May 1988 – ordinary trains called during 'publicity day' 14th *(BLN 587)*; see 23 May 2004**; still open.

BEDWYN [GW] op 11 November 1862 *(co n Marlborough 8th)*; HALT 2 November 1964 to 5 May 1969 *(Cl)*; still open.
GREAT B pre-op *(GW ac)*.

BEECHBURN [S&D; NE]; {map 30}.
BEECHBURN's history cannot be separated from that of HOWDEN with any certainty.
Line op early 1844, probably initially market service only, full use 1845 (see 1843**, reference to Crook). Earliest station mention so far found is of HOWDEN, minutes of 14 February 1845, when it seems to have been regarded as station, but without facilities (soon remedied). In co tt September 1847, trains calling both ways. Never in *Brad*.
Clo by 20 December 1847 when plans for converting waiting-room into a tenement agreed *(RAIL 667/52)*.
Topham May 1848 (earliest of series seen) has BEECHBURN, no Howden; BEECHBURN had replaced Howden in next co tt seen (June 1848) and

was first in *Brad* July 1848, as addition to stations previously shown.
All three tables showed service towards Bishop Auckland only. Minutes show that cabin from Shildon was ordered to be moved to Beechburn to serve as a waiting-room and that station was still incomplete in January 1849, but a station incomplete a year or two after opening was not unusual on the S&D.
On 14 August 1855 improvements to HOWDEN station were authorised, suggesting it had re-opened, but S&D use of names was so casual that they might have meant Beechburn.
Minutes of 25 November 1868 say had agreed to reopen Howden; no reopening date found.
BEECHBURN's service became two way April or May 1869.
Cl said HOWDEN was renamed BEECHBURN 16 April 1869.
OS map (see D&C reprint) shows two stations in this area, one just north of Howden at Beechburn Colliery, the other just south. *The Imperial Atlas*, Bartholomew, late 1860s, names northern one Beechburn Colliery, southern one North Beechburn, probably not official names. Alias 'Bitchburn'.
Likeliest explanation: original stop was southern one, Howden; replaced by northern, Beechburn, late 1847. In 1869 Howden was reopened and name 'Beechburn' transferred to it.
What is not yet clear: did original Howden briefly re-open at any time between 1847 and 1869? There were clearly worries about safety owing to gradient hereabouts – its steepness was reason given when S&D twice refused earlier to re-open Howden.
BEECHBURN clo 8 March 1965 *(RM April)*.
B for HOWDEN-LE-WEAR in LNE tt 1933 and thus *Brad* and BR tts to closure.

BEECHES – see CARSHALTON.

BEESTON near Leeds [GN] first in *Brad* February 1860; clo 2 March 1953 *(Cl)*; later excur *(U)*.

BEESTON near Nottingham [Mid] op 4 June 1839 *(Mid)*; still open.

BEESTON CASTLE & TARPORLEY [LNW]: line op 1 October 1840**, nd, June 1842; originally B; CASTLE added 1 October 1868 *(Cl; LNW Officers 16 September 'in future')*, & T added January 1873 *(Cl; LNW Officers 18 December 1872 – 'to be altered')*; clo 18 April 1966 *(Cl)*.

BEESTONTOR [NS] (ng) op 29 June 1904**; clo 12 March 1934 *(LNW Record)*.

BEIGHTON
BEIGHTON [GC] op 12 February 1849 *(GC; T 12th-line)*; last in tt February 1852 (line clo); back in tt (line reop) March 1854; re-sited 6 chains north 1 November 1893 *(GC dates)*; clo 1 November 1954 *(Cl)*.
BEIGHTON [North Midland] op mid June 1840 – in local press notice 22 June, not in previous week *(Mid)*; last in *Brad* December 1842*;
{Woodhouse Mill – Killamarsh}.
* = *Tuck*, about June 1843 says that would be reopened Tuesdays, Saturdays, Sundays; no evidence on whether did or not.

BEITH

B NORTH [GSW] op 21 July 1840 *(GSW)*; NORTH added 2 June 1924**; clo 4 June 1951 *(RM July)*.
B TOWN [GBK Jt] op 26 June 1873 *(GSW)*; TOWN added 28 February 1953 *(Cl)*;
clo 5 November 1962 *(RM October)*.

BEKESBOURNE [LCD] op 22 July 1861 *(LCD)*; still open.

BELASIS LANE [LNE] first in *Brad* May 1928; clo 14 June 1954 *(Cl)*; HALT until 1937 tt; workmen's use to clo with effect from 6 November 1961 *(BR NER wtt supplement 7 May)*;
{Billingham – Haverton Hill}.

BELFORD [NE]: line op 29 March 1847**, nd, August 1847; clo 29 January 1968 *(RM March)*.

BELGRAVE & BIRSTALL [GC] op 15 March 1899 *(GC; T 16th- line)*; clo 4 March 1963 *(RM March)*.
See 2007 July 4** for later use.

BELGRAVE ROAD – see LEICESTER.

BELL BUSK [Mid] op 30 July 1849 *(T 28 July & 1 September)*; clo 4 May 1959 *(RM June)*.
B B for MALHAM in *Brad* from 1850; co tt dropped 'for M' 1 May 1889 *(Mid)* but *Brad* kept until 1955.

BELLAHOUSTON

BELLAHOUSTON (a) [GP Jt] op 6 November 1843 *(GSW)* – never in *Brad* but in *Murray* by September 1844; clo 1845 *(GSW)*; Ibrox here later.

BELLAHOUSTON (b) [GSW] op 1 July 1885 *(GSW; co ½ 1110/149- line)*; clo 1 January 1917* except workmen *(Cl)*; reop fully? (still workmen only tt September 1919, full service August 1920 tt); clo 20 September 1954 *(RM November)*.
* = still shown in *Brad* without indication that it was workmen only but timings clearly fitted that usage.

B PARK [LMS] first in *Brad* 2 May 1938; for Glasgow Exhibition *(LNW Record)*; clo 1 January 1939 (Sunday) *(Cl)*; {Bellahouston – Crookston}.

BELLE VUE Manchester [GC/Mid] op 1 September 1875 *(GC dates)*; entrance re-sited and platforms shortened 27 March 1986; still open.

BELLE VUE Warthill [Sand Hutton] (ng) op 4 October 1924**; last train 1 March 1930**; {map 40}.

BELLEPORT SIDING [High] (non-tt): Admiralty; op 20 November 1917; clo ?;
{Alness – Invergordon} *(High)*.

BELLFIELD [Cal] (non-tt): PLATFORM; workmen; advised to BoT as ready for inspection 2 December 1912 *(MT 29/74)*; clo 1922 or earlier *(U)*; {Coalburn – Auchlochan}.

BELLGROVE [NB*] op 23 November 1870**; still open. B STREET, later B for CATTLE MARKET *(hb 1926)*; RCH dist ref 23 July 1915 said 'STREET' had been dropped, but never seen thus in *Brad*.
Sometimes B GLASGOW in tts.
* = op by [CGU]; later [CGU/NB]; 1896 [NB] only.

BELLINGHAM London [LCD] op 1 July 1892 *(L)*; still open.

BELLINGHAM NORTH TYNE [NB] op 1 February 1861 *(NC- line)*; NT added 21 September 1926 *(hbl Oct.)*; clo 15 October 1956** *(T 21 Sept.)*.

BELLSHILL

BELLSHILL [Cal] op 1 May 1879 *(Cal- line)*; still open.

BELLSHILL [NB] op 1 May 1879 *(Hamilton 3rd)*; clo 1 January 1917 except for workmen's service *(RM February)*; reop 2 June 1919 *(RCH)*; clo 10 September 1951 *(RM October)*.
Also see MOSSEND.

BELLSIDE – see CLELAND; OMOA.

BELMONT near Durham [NE] op 15 April 1844 *(Durham County Advertiser 19th- line)*; clo 1 April 1857 (Wednesday) *(Cl)*.
B JUNCTION from 1852 *(Brad)* – perhaps closed thus; {map 32}.

BELMONT near Epsom [LBSC] op 22 May 1865 *(L; co n T 20th- line)* as CALIFORNIA; renamed 1 October 1875 *(RCG)*; still open.

BELMONT [LMS] op 12 September 1932 *(RM October)*; clo 5 October 1964 *(RM November)*; {on Stanmore ex-LNW branch}.

BELPER [Mid] op 11 May 1840 *(Mid; co n T 2nd- line)*; replaced 10 March 1878 by new station 54 chains north at King Street *(Mid)*; still open.

BELSES [NB] op 29 October 1849** as NEW B; NEW dropped 1862 *Brad* but still in wtt 1868; clo 6 January 1969 *(RM February)*. LNE tt 1933, *Brad* and BR tts until 1963/4: B for ANCRUM and LILLIESLEAF.

BELSIZE PARK [Nor] op 22 June 1907**; still open.

BELSTON JUNCTION [GSW] (non-tt): HALT; purpose ?; perhaps in use 1904; {Drongan – Ochiltree} *(U)*.

BELSTONE CORNER
– see SAMPFORD COURTENAY.

BELTON near Crowle [Ax Jt] op 2 January 1905 *(RCG)*; clo 17 July 1933 *(RM September)*.
In *hb* as B for WEST BUTTERWICK.

BELTON & BURGH [GE] op 1 June 1859 *(T 2nd)*; & BURGH added 1 July 1923 *(hbl 12th)*; clo 2 November 1959 *(RM December)*.

BELTONFORD [NB]: see 1846 June 22**; {East Linton – Dunbar}.

BELTRING [SEC] op 1 September 1909 *(SEC)* as B & BRANBRIDGES HALT; HALT dropped 5 May 1969 *(SR App)*; & B dropped 12 May 1980; still open.

BELUNCLE [SEC] first in tt July 1906 *(SEC)*; HALT; clo 4 December 1961 *(T 8 November)*.

BELVEDERE [SE] trains first shown March 1859 *Brad*; still open.

BEMBRIDGE [IoW] op 27 May 1882 *(Rtn)*; clo 11 February 1951, reop 22 March 1951 *(IoW 1923 and see 1951**)*; 21 September 1953 *(Cl)*.

BEMPTON [NE]: line op 20 October 1847**, nd, May 1848 *(Topham)*; still open.

BEN RHYDDING [Otley & Ilkley] op privately 1 August 1865*; bought by Mid and op to public 1 July 1866 *(Mid)*; clo for electrification 25 July 1992, reop 8 September 1992; still open.
* = in *Brad* August 1865 with first entry for line, presumably in error; omitted next month.

BENDERLOCH [Cal] op 24 August 1903
(Brad Sh 1904- line); clo 28 March 1966
(RM June – photo-caption).
BENFIELDSIDE – see BLACKHILL; CONSETT.
BENFLEET [LTS] op 1 July 1855 *(co n T 28 June)*;
re-sited to west 10 December 1911 *(Cl)*;
B for CANVEY ISLAND 11 July 1927 to 14 May
1984 tt *(Mid)*; still open.
BENGEWORTH [Mid] op 1 October 1864
(Worcester 8th); clo 8 June 1953 *(Mid)*.
BENINGBROUGH [NE] op 31 March 1841
(co n E Cos Her 25th- line) as SHIPTON;
renamed 1 December 1898 *(hbl 26 January 1899)*;
clo 15 September 1958 *(RM October)*.
BENSHAM [NE] op 1 November 1892 *(RCG)*;
clo 5 April 1954 *(RM May)*.
BENTHAM [North Western; Mid]
BENTHAM (alias HIGH B/B HIGH/B HIGHER)
op 2 May 1850, as terminus for time being. Inspection
report dated 29 May 1850 *(Rtn)*, prior to line opening
through (would happen 1 June 1850 – *T 3rd)*, shows
HIGH B as already in existence; distance given, 4 miles
15 chains to Clapham also fits HIGH B better than
Low B. Still open as B.
LOW B was on stretch opened 2 May 1850 but it is not
known whether station existed then, perhaps for market
only use. Earliest known appearance, in a special tt for
Saturday Lancaster market service, was in *Lancaster*
1 June 1850, in addition to tt for daily service: LOW B
was shown there as well as B HIGH. This tt was last
included in paper of 21 September 1850. However,
market service might have continued since LOW B
(as well as HIGH B) was in *Brad*, full service November
1851; last shown July 1853; company records show that
it was closed by 4 August 1853 (J. Gough).
Brad just showed B at first. After July 1853 for a while
it had LOW B in one direction, HIGH B in the other,
before settling for HIGH; eventually HIGH dropped
and then just B (1 May 1876 co tt, *Mid)*.
BENTLEY
B SOUTH YORKS op 27 April 1992 *(BLN 682)*;
still open.
B CROSSING [GN/GC] (non-tt) workmen; at least
1914 to 1943; also excur; {Doncaster – Carcroft} *(U)*.
BENTLEY near Alton [LSW] first in *Brad* July 1854;
still open.
BENTLEY near Ipswich
BENTLEY [GE] op 15 June 1846 *(EC- line)*;
clo 7 November 1966 *(RM January 1967)*.
Was B JUNCTION 1849 to 1878 *(Brad)* and also thus
EC co tt 1854 (not 1851).
B CHURCH [EU] first in *Brad* October 1853; on
Hadleigh branch; intended as alternative station for
Bentley, ready for when this would be bypassed by
spur taking branch northwards; diversion scheme was
dropped and station closed (or was entry in tt
premature and station never provided? – *Hadleigh* says
unable to substantiate existence from minutes).
According to tt trains stopped for passengers who had
tickets for 8 miles and over (i.e. journey that involved
travel over main line); this ruled out local use to

Hadleigh, though this was far closer to village than
station on main line. Most call it B C CROSSING but
not so *Brad*, where it was last included December 1853.
BENTLEY near Wolverhampton [Mid]:
op 1 November 1872 *(Mid; co n T 1st- line)*;
clo 1 October 1898 (Saturday) *(Mid)*.
BENTLEY GREEN – see GREAT BENTLEY.
BENTON {map 26}.
BENTON [NE] op 27 June 1864 *(co ½ T 22 August-
line)*; replaced 1 March 1871 *(Cl)* by new B to east;
Clinker calls first LONG B but not so shown in tt, *hb*,
Macaulay's maps. Replacement clo 23 January 1978
(RM March) for conversion >
BENTON [TWM] op 11 August 1980 *(RM August)*;
still open.
B SQUARE [NE] op 1 July 1909 *(RCG)*;
clo 20 September 1915 *(RCH; T 18th* referred to coming
closure of 'Ponton Square')*. Palmersville here later.
Also see FOREST HALL.
BENTS [NB] first in *Brad* February 1865;
clo 1 May 1930 (Thursday) *(Cl)*.
BENTS – see NETHERBURN.
BENTWORTH & LASHAM [LSW] op 1 June 1901
(co n Basingstoke); clo 1 January 1917 *(T 22 December
1916)*; reop 18 August 1924 *(T 14th, 16th)*;
clo 11 September 1932 (Sunday) – based on SR
practice + *Cl*.
BERE ALSTON [LSW] op 1 June 1890 *(W D Merc
2nd)* as BEER A; altered 18 November 1897 *(RCG)*;
still open.
BERE FERRERS [LSW] op 1 June 1890 *(W D Merc
2nd)* as BEER FERRIS; altered 18 November 1897
(RCG); aot request; still open.
BERKELEY [SW Jt] op 1 August 1876 *(Mid; Bath
Chron 3rd- line)*; clo 2 November 1964 *(Mid)*.
BERKELEY ROAD [Mid] op 8 July 1844 *(Bristol T
13th)*; at first DURSLEY & BERKELEY in *Brad* table
of times (altered June 1845), but B R in fares;
clo 4 January 1965 *(Mid)*. Aot *hb* made a separate
station of B R JUNCTION for SW Jt services;
deleted 1944a *hb*.
BERKHAMSTED [LNW] op 16 October 1837
(co n T 11th); new station about ¼ mile north 1874/5 *(Cl)*;
still open. Early usually BERKHAMPSTEAD/
BERKHAMSTEAD in *Brad, Topham, Robinson*.
LNW co tt: to final spelling 1852/1864;
at least 1891–1908 B for CHESHAM.
Hb to final spelling 1891a.
BERKSWELL [LNW]: for op see October 1844**;
op as DOCKERS LANE, renamed BERKSWELL
1 January 1853 *(Cl)*, B & BALSALL COMMON
1 February 1928 *(hbl January)*, reverted to B 1955
(Brad body – but index later)*; still open.
BERMONDSEY
BERMONDSEY [Jub] op 17 September 1999 *(RM
March 2000)*; still open.
Also see SOUTH BERMONDSEY; SPA ROAD.
BERNEY ARMS [GE] line op 1 May 1844
(T 14 April); this probably later; was in *Brad* June, when
line first included but not in notices in *Norfolk Chronicle*
until Saturday 25 May (G. Kenworthy); at first

Wednesdays and Saturdays (market days) 'when there are passengers'; last in *Brad* November 1844; back September 1845, all days; last May 1848; back February 1851, Mondays, Wednesdays and Saturdays; all days again November 1868; aot request, even when full service; still open.
HALT in 1938 *hb* but not seen thus tts.
BERRINGTON [GW] near Shrewsbury:
op 1 February 1862**; clo 9 September 1963 *(T 9th)*.
BERRINGTON & EYE [SH Jt] op 6 December 1853 *(Hereford T 6th- line)*; clo 9 June 1958 *(Cl)*.
BERRY BROW
BERRY BROW (a) [LY]: line op 1 July 1850 *(T 8th)*, nd, January 1851; clo 4 July 1966 *(RM July)*.
Until 1877 one word *(hb)*.
BERRY BROW (b) op 9 October 1989 *(RM December)* – 300 yards south of (a) *(C/W)*; still open.
BERRYLANDS [SR] op 16 October 1933 *(RM December)*; still open. SR tt 1947 and *hb* 1938: B for SURBITON HILL PARK.
BERVIE – see INVERBERVIE.
BERW ROAD [TV]
BERW ROAD (a) op 17 October 1904 *(GW H)*, on Merthyr line; clo 1 July 1906 *(Cl)*, replaced, after gap, by >
BERW ROAD (b) op July 1908 *(Cl)**, on Nelson line; see 1904** for name matters; clo 12 September 1932 *(RM October)*.
** = but internal company notice dated 10 September 1907 says ready for opening and inspection report is dated 27 February 1908 so perhaps op earlier.
BERWICK near Lewes [LBSC] op 27 June 1846 *(LBSC; Hants Chron 4 July- line)*; still open.
B SUSSEX 12 May 1980 tt to 11 May 1987 tt *(C/W)*.
BERWICK-UPON-TWEED [NB – note that NE were users, paying rent, not part-owners] op 22 June 1846 *(co n T 23rd)*; -upon-T added 1 January 1955 *(Cl)*; still open.
Temporary bridge across Tweed, linking Berwick and Tweedmouth, op 10 October 1848 *(NE maps)*; permanent Royal Border Bridge op, single line, 1 August 1850, principally for visitors to meetings at Edinburgh of the Society for the Advancement of Science *(T 22 July 1850; RM September 2000)*; full formal opening 28 August 1850 *(NE)*.
BERWIG [GW] op 1 May 1905 *(GW H)*; clo 1 January 1917 *(GW notice dated 22 December 1916)*; reop 2 April 1917 *(Cl)*; HALT; clo 1 January 1931 (Thursday) *(T 20 December 1930)*; {map 75}.
BERWYN [GW] op 8 May 1865 *(D&C 11)*; HALT from 1954 tt *(Cl)*; clo 14 December 1964**.
Mr Tottenham was given right to stop trains by *GW Deed M15799 dated 26 August 1861*.
BESCAR LANE [LY] op 9 April 1855 *(Southport Vis 5th)*; e.g. 1863 and 1865 *Brad* shown as stop for ticket collection on some trains to Southport, normal service others; still open.
BESCOT [LNW]
B BRIDGE op 4 July 1837 *(T 6th)*, on GJ main line. Shown as WALSALL by 19 October 1839 *(Brad)*, W BESCOTT B in *Freeling* 1841. When South Staffs

line opened to Walsall proper, 1 November 1847, this station reverted to B/B BRIDGE but still confusion – note in new table: 'To prevent mistakes, parties ought to ask for South Staffordshire tickets to the town of Walsall'. Last in *Brad* July 1850.
Wood Green Old Bescot same site later.
B STADIUM: initially no station on main line at junction with Walsall branch when latter opened. It opened as B 1 May 1850 (with line from Dudley – *Brad; Neele*); JUNCTION added August 1850, dropped 1895/6 *(Brad)* – LNW co tt used it, not always all tables, until 1883/1908; renamed B S by Sir Stanley Matthews 16 August 1990 *(M. Hale)*; still open. Main line trains did not at first use B J – *Neele* implies that both stations briefly existed together, separate services. B J first shown in main line table August 1850 tt, when it replaced B Bridge.
BESFORD [Mid] op November 1841** *(Mid)*; last in tt August 1846; {Wadborough – Defford}.
BESSACARR [GN/GE] (non-tt): HALT; golfers; op 1911 *(GE Journal September 1975)*; in use before inspection? – this was 16 January 1912, and report said was on Lincoln side of Level Crossing no 382 *(MT6/2061/7)*; clo 1914 *(U)*; {Doncaster – Finningley}.
BESSES O'TH' BARN
BESSES O'TH' BARN (a) [LMS] op 1 February 1933 *(T 18 January)*; clo 17 August 1991 *(BLN 660)* for conversion >
BESSES O'TH' BARN (b) [Manch] op 6 April 1992; still open.
BESTWOOD
B & ARNOLD – see DAYBROOK.
B COLLIERY [GN] op 2 October 1882 *(GN)* as B; C added intermittently tt; clo 14 September 1931 *(Cl)*.
BETCHWORTH [SE] op 4 July 1849 *(SR; Hants Chron 7th- line)*; still open.
BETHESDA [LNW] op 1 July 1884 *(LNW Officers 26299)*; clo 3 December 1951 *(RM January 1952)*; later excur *(U)*.
BETHNAL GREEN
BETHNAL GREEN [Cen] op 4 December 1946 *(T 5th)*; still open.
BETHNAL GREEN [GE] op 24 May 1872 *(co n T 23rd)*; replaced Mile End just prior to opening of Stoke Newington line (Mile End was beyond junction for latter); still open. B G JUNCTION until 1895/6 *(Brad)*, thus GE co tt (e.g. 1882), and *hb* until 1944a.
BETLEY ROAD [LNW] op 1 July 1875 *(LNW Officers 13009)*; replaced Basford; clo 1 October 1945 *(LNW Record)*.
BETTISFIELD [Cam] op 4 May 1863 *(Oswestry 6th)*; clo 18 January 1965 *(RM March)*.
BETTWS – see DERRY ORMOND.
BETTWS GARMON [WH] (ng) op 15 August 1877 *(NGSC 2; Rtn- line)*; clo 1 November 1916 *(G&S)*; reop 31 July 1922**; aot request; clo 28 September 1936 *(Cl)*; {map 76}.
BETTWS LLANGEINOR [PT] first in *Brad* February 1900; clo 12 September 1932 *(RM October)*.
BETWS-Y-COED [LNW] op 6 April 1868 *(Carnarvon 11th)*; BETTWYS-y-C until 1953 tt *(Cl)*;

still open. *Brad*? to 1955: B-y-C for CAPEL CURIG, but not thus LMS tt 1930.

BEULAH [GW] op 24 September 1928 *(GW H)*; HALT; clo 25 October 1937★★; {map 81}.

BEVERLEY [NE]: line op 7 October 1846★★, nd, May 1848 *(Topham)*; still open.

BEVERLEY ROAD [HB] op 27 July 1885 *(op tt NER I)*; clo 14 July 1924 *(Cl)*. Usually HULL B R.

BEWDLEY [GW] op 1 February 1862★★; clo 5 January 1970 *(RM February)*.

BEXHILL
BEXHILL [LBSC] op 27 June 1846 *(LBSC; Hants Chron 4 July- line)*; B CENTRAL 9 July 1923 *(hbl 26 April)* to 1968/1972 tt; still open.
B WEST [SEC] op 1 June 1902 *(SEC notice 39/1902)*; clo 1 January 1917 *(T 18 December 1916)*, reop 1 March 1919 *(T 24 February)*; B-ON-SEA 1920 *(Cl)* to 9 July 1923 *(hbl 26 April)*; WEST added November 1929 *(hbl 22 January 1930)*; clo 15 June 1964 *(Cl)*.

BEXLEY [SE] op 1 September 1866 *(L; co ½ T 24 August- line)*; still open.

BEXLEYHEATH [SE] op 1 May 1895 *(RCG)*; BEXLEY HEATH until 1903/4 *(Brad)*; still open.

BICESTER
B NORTH [GW] op 1 July 1910 *(RCG; co ½ T 6 August)*; NORTH added 26 November 1949 *(Cl)* to 5 May 1969 tt and presumably reinstated when Town (re)opened; still open.
B LONDON ROAD [LNW] op 1 October 1850 *(co n T 21 September)*; L R added 1954 *(Cl)*; clo 1 January 1968 *(RM January)*. See next entry.
B TOWN op 11 May 1987 *(Oxford Mail 11th)*; reopening of London Road; still open.

BICKERSHAW & ABRAM [GC] op 1 April 1884 *(Wigan Observer 2nd, item and tt)*; clo 2 November 1964 *(RM December)*.

BICKLEIGH [GW] op 22 June 1859 *(RAIL 631/6; Tavistock tt 24th)*; clo 31 December 1962★★.

BICKLEY [LCD] op 5 July 1858 *(Bromley Record August)* as SOUTHBOROUGH ROAD (but co n in paper called it 'The Southborough Station' and later complained about existence of two stations with same name); renamed 1 October 1860 *(Cl)*; still open. SE co tt 1864: B for CHISLEHURST.

BIDDENDEN [KES] op 15 May 1905 *(RCG)*; clo 4 January 1954 *(T 28 October 1953)*.

BIDDICK LANE [NE] first in *Brad* February 1864 (see 1862 March★★); Saturdays only; last in *Brad* January 1869; {map 34}.

BIDDULPH [NS] op 1 June 1864 *(co ½ T 5 August)* as GILLOW HEATH; renamed 1 May 1897 *(hbl 29 April)*; clo 11 July 1927 *(Cl)*.

BIDEFORD
BIDEFORD [LSW] op 2 November 1855 *(co ½ T 28 February 1856 – N Devon J 2nd only covered formal op of 29 October)*; new station 30 chains further on, ready for extension to Torrington, 10 June 1872 *(Cl)*; clo 4 October 1965 *(Bideford 8th)*; later excur *(U)*. For brief reopening see 1968 January★★. LSW tt 1914: B for WESTWARD HO [*sic*];

Brad? to 1955 B for HARTLAND.

B QUAY; **B STRAND ROAD** {Bideford – Abbotsham Road}; **B YARD**, alias THE YARD {next after Strand Road}: all [BWA], op 18 May 1901★★; clo 28 March 1917★★.

Temporary terminus by Art School, [BWA]: see 18 May 1901★★.

BIDFORD-ON-AVON [SMJ] first in *Brad* May 1881; -on-A added 1 July 1909 *(hbl 7th)*; clo 19 February 1917 *(RAIL 1005/282)*; reop 1 January 1919 *(Cl)*; clo 16 June 1947★★.

BIDSTON [Wirral] op 2 July 1866 *(D&C 10)*; clo 4 July 1870★★ – still in *Brad* August but table marked 'no information'; reop 1 August 1872; last trains June 1890 *Brad*; reop 18 May 1896 *(Cl)*; still open.

BIELDSIDE [GNS] op 1 June 1897 *(GNS)*; clo 5 April 1937 *(RM January 1938)*.

BIG FLEET VIADUCT [LMS] (non-tt): wtt 6 May 1946 shows one call each way to pick up/set down railwaymen; {Gatehouse of Fleet – Loch Skerrow}.

BIGBY ROAD BRIDGE [MS&L] op March 1852 *(GC)*; Thursdays only; last in *Brad* August 1882; {Barnetby – Howsham}.

BIGGAR [Cal] op 6 November 1860★★; clo 5 June 1950 *(RM July)*; school use to 14 August 1950 *(U)*.

BIGGLESWADE [GN] op 7 August 1850 *(T 6th, 8th)*; still open.

BIGLIS/B JUNCTION – see CADOXTON.

BIGSWEIR – see ST BRIAVELS.

BILBROOK [GW] op 30 April 1934 *(wtt supp)* as BIRCHES & BILBROOK; HALT until 6 May 1968 *(GW H)*; renamed BILBROOK 6 May 1974 *(BR notice)*; still open.

BILBSTER [High] op 28 July 1874 *(High)*; clo 13 June 1960 *(RM July)*. *Hb*: 1875a BILBESTER, corrected 1879à.

BILLACOMBE [GW] op 17 January 1898★★; finally clo 6 October 1947.

BILLERICAY [GE] op 1 January 1889 *(D&C 3- line)*; still open.

BILLING [LNW] op 20 December 1845 co tt *(?; first in Brad January 1846)*; B ROAD until 1 April 1883 *(Cl)*; clo 6 October 1952 *(RM December)*.

BILLINGBOROUGH & HORBLING [GN] op 2 January 1872 *(Insp rpt MT6/91/2; co ½ 12 February- line)*; clo 22 September 1930★★ *(Cl)*. At first B in hb, amended *hbl ref April 1927*; in *Brad* B January 1872, before trains shown on line, B & H thereafter.

BILLINGE GREEN [LNW] op 1 October 1914 *(LNW Officers 44461)*; HALT; clo 2 March 1942 *(LNW Record)*.

BILLINGHAM [NE]
See 1835 A★★ for first known service (Stockton to Port Clarence 'trains' passed through here).
B: line from Stockton to Hartlepool op 10 February 1841★★ *(NE maps)*, nd, May 1842; -ON-TEES added 1 October 1926 *(hbl October)* ★; replaced by new station (just B) about ¾ mile nearer Hartlepool 7 November 1966 *(RM December)*; still open. B JUNCTION from

1 March 1870 according to *Cl*, and certainly thus
Brad in 1871, but 1 March 1878 co tt *(JS)*,
until 1 May 1893 *(Cl)*.
★ = but 21 September according to *RAIL 153/191* – date of
decision?

BILLINGSHURST [LBSC] op 10 October 1859★★;
still open.

BILSON {map 94}.

BILSON temp sta for Cinderford [SW Jt]
op 1 September 1876 *(Ross 7th)*; clo 5 August 1878 –
replaced by Cinderford *(Mid)*. Local press called it
Cinderford; in *Brad* as B (C).

BILSON [GW] op 3 August 1907 *(GW H; Glos Chron
10th- line)*; in *Brad* as B (CINDERFORD) HALT;
clo 6 April 1908 except for miners' trains, reop 2 April
1917 *(Cl)*; clo 1 October 1920 (Friday) *(Cl)*; miners'
trains to 1930 or later *(U)*.

BILSTHORPE (non-tt): Colliery Yard (about 2 miles
north of Farnsfield), no station, used May 1956 for
annual outing of Colliery Institute Members'
Children's Fund to Cleethorpes (via Farnsfield,
Rolleston Junction and Lincoln) (R. Brettle).

BILSTON [GW]

B CENTRAL op 14 November 1854 *(T 15th)*;
CENTRAL added 19 July 1950 *(Cl)*;
clo 6 March 1972 *(RM April)*. In *hb* successively as
B BROAD GAUGE, B MAIN, B & ETTINGSHALL.

B WEST op 1 July 1854 *(W Mid; co ½ T 28 August- line)*;
WEST added 19 July 1950 *(Cl)*; clo 30 July 1962
(RM September). In *hb* successively B NARROW
GAUGE, B WEST MIDLAND, B & DEEPFIELDS.

BILTON / B JUNCTION – see ALNMOUTH.

BINEGAR [SD Jt] op 20 July 1874 *(Shepton 24th)*;
clo 7 March 1966 *(Shepton 11th)*.

BINGHAM near Nottingham [GN] op 15 July 1850
(T 18th); still open.

BINGHAM ROAD London

BINGHAM ROAD (a) [WSC Jt] op 1 September 1906
(L); HALT; clo 15 March 1915 *(Cl)* – RCH gives
1 May but last trains March tt.

BINGHAM ROAD (b) [SR] reop as station 30 September
1935 *(T 26th)*; clo 16 May 1983 *(BLN 456 corr)*.

BINGHAM ROAD Nottingham [GN/LNW]
op 1 September 1879 *(LNW Officers 20028)*;
clo 2 July 1951 *(RM September)*.

BINGLEY [Mid] op 16 March 1847 *(Mid)*;
re-sited about 400 yards south at noon 24 July 1892
(Mid); still open.

BINTON [SMJ] op 2 June 1879 *(Stratford 6th)*;
clo 16 June 1947★★.
Hb 1910a became B for WELTON-ON-AVON
and WESTON-ON-AVON.

BIRCH VALE [GC/Mid] first in *Brad* May 1868;
clo 5 January 1970 *(Cl)*.

BIRCHES & BILBROOK – see BILBROOK.

BIRCHFIELD near Elgin [GNS] first in *Brad*
January 1871; became PLATFORM 1904 *Brad*;
last in *Brad* May 1930, back May 1939 (probably did
close rather than just omitted from tt since in new
openings list of June 1939), now B HALT; aot request;
clo 7 May 1956 *(RM June)*.

BIRCHGROVE Cardiff [GW] op 10 June 1929 *(Cl 29)*;
HALT until 5 May 1969 *(GW H)*; still open.

BIRCHGROVE Swansea [Mid] op by 7 April 1866,
when in tt in *The Cambrian* – perhaps in use earlier
(Mid); Saturdays only; clo March 1875★★.

BIRCHILLS [LNW] first in *Brad* March 1858,
Tuesdays and Saturdays; all days June 1858; became
HALT 1909 (?) – served only by motor-cars thereafter,
see 1905★★; clo 1 January 1916 (Saturday) *(RCH)*.

BIRCHINGTON-ON-SEA [LCD] op 5 October
1863 *(LCD; T 5th- line)*; -on-S added 1878 tt *(Cl)*;
still open.

BIRCHWOOD op 6 October 1980 *(Rly Obs December)*;
still open.

BIRDBROOK [CVH]
Line through here opened 11 May 1863
(see HAVERHILL [CVH]) but no station then
provided. On 17 June Board agreed to provide a
temporary station at WHITLEY while they worked out
the best place for one to serve the district between
Yeldham and Haverhill. No date has been found for
opening of this; 'Whitley' never appeared in *Brad*.
19 August they accepted request of deputation of locals
to build station to serve New England, to be called
BIRDBROOK (both N E and B appeared in later
minutes). Again, no exact date has been found for its
opening (and thus closure of Whitley); first seen in tt for
1 September 1863 in *Halstead Gazette* (Oakwood book
on line), not in June tt of paper (first *Brad* October
1863), though it may be that earliest appearance(s)
really applied to a still-in-use Whitley (decision made
13 August would make September opening of
permanent unlikely). At 22 October 1863 and several
successive board meetings they discussed provision of
extra banking for Birdbrook; this *might* indicate that
station was unfinished, but the dilatory way in which
matter was deferred from meeting to meeting makes it
more likely that they were concerned with improvement to an existing station – as was almost standard for
the time, the line had opened with various bits of work
still to be done (Haverhill station was 'temporary').
The Directors' Report (given at board meeting of
18 February 1864) is first certain confirmation that
station had been provided *(RAIL 128/1, 2)*.
Macaulay's map of 1863 shows a station called
RIDGWELL; likeliest explanation of this is that he
knew there was a station thereabouts but did not know
its name, looked at a map and decided that this was
likeliest place (same map shows Yeovil Junction as
Stolford – station is beside the village of Stoford).
1865 map shows Birdbrook.
Clo 1 January 1962 *(T 17 November 1961)*.

BIRDINGBURY [LNW] first in *Brad* February 1853;
clo 15 June 1959 *(RM July)*.

BIRDWELL [GC] first in *Brad* January 1855 as
HANGMANS STONE; next month
B & HOYLAND; COMMON added 1 January 1894
(hbl 25th); renamed B 18 June 1951 *(Cl)*;
clo 7 December 1953 *(RM January 1954)*.

BIRKBECK [SR]
op 2 March 1930 *(sig/inst 11/1931)*; still open.

BIRKDALE

BIRKDALE [LY] op 24 July 1848**; B PARK 1854 tt to 1865 tt (but still B P in index for some time) *(Cl)*; still open.

Site of first station not known for certain but road crossing next north of Gilberts Crossing likeliest. 13 November 1848 Board discussed closing this and Hightown because of poor takings. Minutes 26 December suggest they had moved station to Gilbert's Crossing (on later Peel Lane) about a month previously; nothing said about Hightown but new site for Birkdale would have been within easy reach of potential custom from former. 3 August 1852 orders were given to open 'forthwith' the new [third] station at Birkdale, on present site, well to north. It is not clear whether it was an immediate replacement or whether there was a gap. If Hightown did close, nothing so far found about reopening. *(RAIL 372 series,* J. Gilmour).

B PALACE [CLC] op 1 September 1884 *(CLC)*; clo 1 January 1917 *(T 23 December 1916)*; re-op non-tt for races at Aintree in March 1919 *(CLC Portrait)*, fully 1 April 1919 *(RCH)*; clo 7 January 1952 *(RM February)*.

BIRKENHEAD {map 46}.

BIRKENHEAD [Chester & Birkenhead] op 23 September 1840 *(GW)*; just B in table but Station at Grange Lane in notes *(Brad)*; omnibus provided for link to Monks Ferry and ferry to St Georges Pier Head Liverpool – all rail passengers got ferry free but third class did not get omnibus; replaced by >

B MONKS FERRY [Birkenhead] op 23 October 1844 *(GW)*; replaced in turn by >

B WOODSIDE [Birkenhead] op 31 March 1878 *(Brad Sh 1880)* – first used Sunday p.m.; clo 5 November 1967 (Sunday) – last train 4th; on and after 5th trains used Rock Ferry *(RM December)*.

B TOWN [Birkenhead] op 1 January 1889 *(LNW Record)*; clo 7 May 1945 *(LMS/GW Joint Officers 8 January 1946)*. *Hb*: 1904 B TOWN GRANGE ROAD; later entries suggest G R was goods part.

B DOCKS [Wirral] op 2 July 1866 *(D&C 10)* as D; clo 4 July 1870**, reop 1 August 1872 as B D *(Cl)*; replaced by >

B NORTH [Wirral] op 2 January 1888*, when through passenger services were introduced, as B DOCKS (until 1895 tt B D for BIDSTON HILL, *JS*); renamed B NORTH 1 May 1926 *(hbl April; LMS circular 27 March)* or 17 September 1926 *(GW circular 3011)*; still open.

* = 1 April 1878 was when line linked to that of Mersey Docks & Harbour Board (T.B. Maund, letter *RCHS Journal July 1993* + later direct information).

B CENTRAL [Mersey] op 1 February 1886 *(T 2nd- line)*; still open.

B PARK [Mersey/Wirral] op 2 January 1888 *(D&C 10)*; still open.

HAMILTON SQUARE [Mersey] op 1 February 1886 *(T 2nd- line)*; additional lower level platform added 9 May 1977 on burrowing junction line, to allow trains to West Kirby and New Brighton to avoid flat crossing; still open.

Hoylake & Birkenhead Rail & Tramway company owned street tramway from DOCKS to Woodside Ferry, sold to Birkenhead Tramways in October 1879 *(Companies)*. This appeared in *Brad* by June 1875 to August 1878/January 1879; some journeys were noted as 'express', with no intermediate stops; even after sale, times to/from ferry continued to be included in main table (in such a way that made Docks look like through railway station).

Hb 1877 gave EGERTON DOCK 'P' under letter 'E' but not in its entry under Birkenhead – assumed error. Also see GREEN LANE; ROCK FERRY; ROCK LANE.

BIRKENHEAD JUNCTION GOLF PLATFORM – see CHESTER.

BIRKENSHAW & TONG [GN] op 20 August 1856 *(T 7th, 21st)*; & T added later 1856/early 1857 *(Brad)*; clo 5 October 1953 *(RM November)*.

BIRMINGHAM

{map 99 – LNW and Mid services only}.

B VAUXHALL [GJ] temporary terminus from Liverpool and Manchester op 4 July 1837 *(T 6th)*; replaced, on extension of line, by >

B CURZON STREET [GJ] op 19 November 1838 *(GJ)* >

B CURZON STREET [L&B] op from Rugby 9 April 1838 *(T 11th)*; through passengers at first brought here from Vauxhall by omnibus until 1 October 1838 when carriages were transferred through to GJ line *(T 1st/Liverpool Standard)*; >

CURZON STREET stations were termini, side by side, both entered from east, effectively functioning as one. According to description in *T 24 August 1839* L&B and GJ trains were running into each others' stations to facilitate forwarding of passengers. Mid used L&B from 17 August 1841 *(Brad)*. C S added to name in tt 1852 *(Cl)*. Excursion station built here in early 1870s.

LNW Officers 10205 and *10344* show that for Birmingham Onion Fair in 1873 LNW trains to/from south used it (late September or early October) and intention had been for Mid to use as well but time too short to arrange this; they planned to do it in 1874 (no confirmation seen). Bank Holiday use to 22 May 1893, especially to and from Sutton Coldfield *(U)*.

However, for regular services both replaced by >

B NEW STREET [LNW/Mid]: temporary platform at western end for Stour Valley trains from Wolverhampton op 1 July 1852 *(T 2nd)*; full station op 1 June 1854 when LNW (included both GJ and L&B) services diverted there; N S added to name November 1852 tt *(W Mid)*; Mid services followed on 1 July 1854* and CURZON STREET then closed.

At NEW STREET, the Midland op their own side 8 February 1885 and station made Joint 1 April 1897. Still open.

* = during June 1854, Mid passengers going on to ex-GJ line taken by omnibus from Curzon Street to New Street.

B CAMP HILL [BG] op from Cheltenham direction 17 December 1840 *(co n Chelt Exam 16th)*; service diverted to Curzon Street 17 August 1841 *(Mid)*; reop for passengers on night goods trains November 1841** *(Mid)*; finally clo ?

B LAWLEY STREET [Mid] op from Derby direction
10 February 1842 *(Mid)*; trains diverted to CURZON
STREET 1 May 1851 *(Cl)*.
B GRANVILLE STREET [Mid] op from King's Norton
3 April 1876 *(Mid)*; trains diverted to NEW STREET
1 July 1885 *(Mid)*.
B SNOW HILL [GW] op from Banbury 1 October
1852 *(T 27 September)*; S H in inspection report,
15 September 1852 but not added tt until 1858;
clo 6 March 1972 *(RM April; BR pamphlet)*;
reop 5 October 1987 *(BR LMR pamphlet)*; still open.
Unofficial tts called it LIVERY STREET or GREAT
CHARLES STREET *(W Mid)*.
B MOOR STREET [GW] op 1 July 1909 to provide
extra capacity for local services *(T 7th)*; terminus
replaced by through station 28 September 1987
(RM November – last from old 26th); still open.
For later through stations at CAMP HILL;
LAWLEY STREET; VAUXHALL: see under 'C'; 'L';
'DUDDESTON' (op as Vauxhall).
BIRMINGHAM INTERNATIONAL
op 26 January 1976 *(Rly Obs March)*; still open.
BIRNAM - see DUNKELD
BIRNIE ROAD [NB] first in *Brad* November 1866;
Fridays only; SIDING in *Brad*, NB and LNE co tts;
aot request; last use September 1951
(line clo 1 October – *RM November*).
BIRSIEKNOWE [Cal] (non-tt): workmen's
PLATFORM; advised ready for BoT inspection
17 May 1912 *(MT 29/74)*; actual dates of use ?;
{Giffen – Brackenhills} (D. Stirling).
BIRSTALL [LNW]
(BIRSTAL until 1 April 1907 – *hbl 25th*)
BIRSTALL op 30 September 1852 *(RAIL 1005/265)*;
clo 15 April 1917 *(RCH)* – but *Brad* April shows
'service suspended' (trains March) – *RCH* error?
last minute brief reprieve after information sent to *Brad*?
Became B LOWER after passenger closure.
B TOWN op 1 October 1900 *(LNW Officers 39764)*
as UPPER B; renamed 8 July 1935 *(LNW Record)*;
clo 1 August 1951 *(wtt supp)*.
BIRSTWITH [NE] op 1 May 1862 *(T 5th)*;
clo 2 April 1951 *(T 7 March)*.
BIRTLEY [NE] op 1 December 1868 *(NE- line)*;
clo 5 December 1955 *(Cl)*.
BISHOP AUCKLAND {map 31} [S&D; NE]
Original terminus at SOUTH CHURCH [S&D]
op 19 April 1842 *(RAIL 667/13)*. Minutes of 22 April
show that trains on first day were steam-hauled but that
on 20th they changed to horse-power; since horses
found it difficult to judge their footing in the dark of
tunnel, they ordered return to steam-haulage.
Only on that day did they give orders for the building of
a temporary coach station. On 4 November 1842 they
agreed to alterations, suggesting that they saw it as
a long-term station >
Line extended to permanent B A 30 January 1843
(see 1843★★) >
S C stayed open for a while – coach connection from
here to Rainton maintained. Closed by 18 October
1844, when orders were given to convert station into

railwaymen's cottages and reading room. A logical
closure date would have been 19 June 1844, when
opening of line from the north to Darlington would
have made coach connection redundant (see entry on
RAINTON); however, no confirmatory evidence seen.
S C still shown on OS map about 1855 (now in
converted state?).
NE opened a temporary terminus in Tenter Street
1 April 1857 *(co ½ T 17 August)* >
S&D and NE stations replaced by Joint about
December 1857; reorganised in same area 2 December
1867 and 1905 (made triangular); reduced to one
platform 6 June 1986 *(Modern Railways, September,
photo-caption)*; still open.
BISHOPBRIGGS [NB] op 21 February 1842
(co n T 19th); early in *Brad* as BISHOP(S)BRIDGE/
BISHOP-BRIGGS; initially a 'temporary' station
(i.e. had to prove worth to survive); still open.
BISHOPS CASTLE [BC] op 1 February 1866★★;
finally clo 20 April 1935.
BISHOPS CLEEVE [GW] op 1 June 1906
(Chelt Chron 2nd); clo 7 March 1960 *(RM April)*.
BISHOPS LYDEARD [GW] op 31 March 1862
(W Som F P 5 April); clo 4 January 1971 *(Som Gaz 8th)*.
See 2007 July 20★★.
BISHOPS NYMPTON & MOLLAND [GW]
op 1 November 1873 *(W Som F P 1st, 8th)* as M;
renamed 1874/5 *(Brad)*; clo 3 October 1966
(Som Gaz 7th).
BISHOPS ROAD – see LONDON PADDINGTON.
BISHOPS STORTFORD
BISHOPS STORTFORD [GE] op 16 May 1842 *(co n
T 7th)* ; still open. B S in inspection report and in co tt
by 1843 but S in *Brad* until 1845.
Hb 1862 (only): BISHOP S.
HOCKERILL (BISHOPS STORTFORD) [Northern
& Eastern]: notices in *T* advertised excursions to here
for Newmarket Races, 9 and 11 October 1843;
15 and 28 October 1844; perhaps other times.
Probably this was alternative name for main station,
used because Hockerill was name much better known
in racing circles. Just possible line beyond Bishops
Stortford was sufficiently ready for trains to go a little
further to point where Hockerill Road crossed line and
that passengers transferred to road there – notices imply
travellers would mostly take own horses and carriages
with them by train and use them for rest of the way.
BISHOPS WALTHAM [LSW] op 1 June 1863
(Hants Teleg 6th); clo 1 January 1933 (Sunday)
–based on SR practice; last train 31 December 1932
(Hants Chron 7th).
BISHOPSBOURNE [SE] op 1 July 1889 *(SE)*;
clo 1 December 1940 (Sunday) *(Cl)*.
BISHOPSGATE {map 107}
For early terminus see under LONDON.
BISHOPSGATE [GE] op 4 November 1872 *(L)*;
B LL until 1 November 1875 *(Cl)*; clo 22 May 1916★★
(T 2nd). Until Liverpool Street opened it was a
temporary terminus for trains from Hackney Downs,
(P. Kay, *GER in Town & Country, vol. III*, Irwell, 1996).
See LIVERPOOL STREET for [Met] station.

BISHOPSTOKE – see EASTLEIGH.

BISHOPSTON ROAD – see BLACKPILL Swansea.

BISHOPSTONE

BISHOPSTONE (a) [LBSC] op 1 June 1864 *(LBSC)*; HALT from 1 August 1922 *(Cl)*; clo 26 September 1938; reopened as B BEACH HALT April 1939 and then used summer only *(SR Halts)*; unlikely that any public trains called after end September 1939 (planned clo for year) – perhaps war caused earlier clo; perhaps use later by servicemen working on coastal defences (A.A. Jackson, *Chron January 2004)*. Shown clo in index to June 1941 *Brad*.

BISHOPSTONE (b) [SR] op 26 September 1938 *(RM November)*, nearer Seaford than (a); still open.

BISHOPTON [Cal] op 31 March 1841**; still open.

BISLEY CAMP [LSW] (non-tt): first (Royal) train 12 July 1890; opened 14 July 1890 for National Rifle Association's Range *(U)*; later Army Camp use, last train 19 July 1952 *(RM September)*; ticket for CAMP, issued by Military Railway *(JB)*; {branch from Brookwood} *(U)*.
For continuation beyond here as military line see Section 7:2, Blackdown Camp.

BISPHAM – see LAYTON.

BITTAFORD [GW] op 18 November 1907 *(dist t supp)* – RCG and *GW working tt* say 4th, but probably delayed for some reason; PLATFORM; clo 2 March 1959 *(RM April)*.

BITTERLEY [LNW/GW] (non-tt): *Joint Officers Committee* reported 21 November 1905 coach in use for carrying workmen from Ludlow to carry out alterations here; {Clee Hill line}.

BITTERNE [LSW] op 5 March 1866 *(Salisbury 10th- line)* as B ROAD; renamed 20 September 1896 *(RCG)*; still open.

BITTON [Mid] op 4 August 1869 *(Bath Chron 5th)*; clo 7 March 1966 *(Shepton 11th)*.

BLABY [LNW] op 1 January 1864 *(Leic; LNW Officers- line)*; clo 4 March 1968 *(Cl)*.

BLACK BANK [GE] first in *Brad* September 1851 as LITTLE DOWNHAM; renamed 1853 tt *(Cl)*; aot request; clo 17 June 1963 *(RM August)*. Early BLACKBANK *(hb)*.

BLACK BULL [NS] op 1 June 1864 *(co ½ T 5 August- line)*; clo 11 July 1927 *(Cl)*. In *Brad* 1873 to 1886 as B B CHILDERPLAY *(JS)*; according to *RCG* renamed from B B for BIDDULPH & CHELL to B B 1 May 1897; in NS co tt October 1914 as B B BRINDLEY FORD (and thus *Brad* 1886–1923). Aot *hb* made one word of it.

BLACK DOG [GW] op with line 3 November 1863, or soon after, as private station for Lord Lansdowne *(U)*; in *hb* by 1904 as B D SIDING; according to *RM July 1941* no restrictions on use at that time, and no reason for omission from tt; Lord Lansdowne provided building on plaform and station-master's house and allowed public use but banned provision of name-board; first in public tt starting 15 September 1952 as a HALT; clo 20 September 1965 *(RM October)*; {Calne branch}.

BLACK ISLAND [High] (non-tt): PLATFORM probably op mid-June 1904 for Scottish Horse Camp

(minutes of 26 April gave approval); officially clo 11 April 1959 *(High Rly Soc Journal 1993)*; {Struan – Blair Atholl}. Added 'P' 1941a *hb*; not in 1956 *hb*.

BLACK LANE – see RADCLIFFE.

BLACK LION CROSSING [GW] op to public 1 January 1906**; HALT; finally clo to public 22 September 1924; {map 86}.

BLACK ROCK [GW] op 9 July 1923 *(GW H)*; HALT; clo 13 August 1976 (Friday) – had become unsafe *(Cl)*; {Portmadoc – Criccieth}.

BLACK TANK – see 1957**.

BLACKBURN

BLACKBURN [LY] op 1 June 1846 *(Rtn PP)*; still open.

B DARWEN ROAD [East Lancs] op 3 August 1847 *(Rtn- line)*; clo 30 November 1852 but Whitsun use for many years after *(C/W*, from W.D. Tattersall, *Bolton, Blackburn … Railway*, Oakwood, 1973, p.60)*.
Surviving goods later B BOLTON ROAD

BLACKBURN FORGE [North Midland] op 1 November 1838; clo 25 March 1839 *(Mid)*.

BLACKBURN JUNCTION [SY] in *Brad* from October 1854 to October 1857 and June 1858 to September 1859 (both inc) at 3 miles from Sheffield, but no trains ever shown calling (see ALDAM JUNCTION for explanation).

BLACKDYKE [NB] line op 4 September 1856 *(Brad Sh 1863)*; this stop first in *Brad* October (line shown September), Saturdays only; full service May 1928 tt; sometimes BLACK DYKE(S); became HALT 1920/1 *Brad*; clo 7 September 1964 *(RM October)*.

BLACKFORD [Cal] op 23 May 1848**; clo 11 June 1956 *(BR n Ed Sub)*.

BLACKFORD HILL [NB] op 1 December 1884 *(Edin)*; clo 1 January 1917 *(RM February)*; reop 1 February 1919 *(RM February)*; clo 10 September 1962 *(RM September)*.

BLACKFRIARS

BLACKFRIARS [Dist] op 30 May 1870 *(T 31st)*; covered way to main line station op 13 November 1886; still open. At first in *hb* as B BRIDGE, and ticket thus *(JB)*.

BLACKFRIARS and **B BRIDGE** main line – see LONDON.

BLACKGRANGE [Stirling & Dunfermline] only shown with trains in *Brad* November 1852; still present, trainless, December; error? {Cambus – Causewayhead}.

BLACKHALL near Motherwell [NB] op 1 October 1864 *(D&C 6- line)*; clo 1 November 1893 (Wednesday) *(RCG)*; {map 16}.

BLACKHALL near Hartlepool:
B COLLIERY [LNE] op 24 July 1936 *(RM September)*; clo 4 May 1964 *(Cl)*; HALT until 1936/7 *(Brad)*; {B Rocks – Horden}.
B ROCKS [NE] first in *Brad* July 1907; until 1919 summer Wednesdays and Saturdays only; clo 4 January 1960 *(Cl)*. *RCG* says op 1 October 1919 – full use/provision of proper station?

BLACKHEATH

BLACKHEATH [SE] op 30 July 1849**; still open.

B HILL [LCD] op 18 September 1871 *(co n T 16th)*; clo 1 January 1917 *(T 28 December 1916)*.

BLACKHILL [NE] op 2 December 1867 *(Consett)* as BENFIELDSIDE; renamed CONSETT 1 November 1882 *(RCG)*, C & BLACKHILL 1 May 1885 *(hbl 23 April)*, BLACKHILL 1 May 1896 *(RCG)*; clo 23 May 1955 *(RM July)*.

BLACKHORSE ROAD

BLACKHORSE ROAD [Mid/TFG] op 9 July 1894 *(RCG)*; moved 200 yards west 14 December 1981 *(Mid)*; BLACK HORSE ROAD until 12 May 1980 tt *(Mid)*; still open.

BLACKHORSE ROAD [Vic] op 1 September 1968 *(T 2nd)*; still open.

BLACKMILL [GW] op 12 May 1873 *(co ½ T 7 August)*; clo 5 May 1958 *(RM June)*.
BLACK MILL until 1895/6 *(Brad)*.

BLACKMOOR [Lynton] (ng) op 16 May 1898 *(N Devon J 19th- line)*; clo 30 September 1935★★.

BLACKPILL Swansea [SIT]
BLACKPILL op 25 July 1860★★ as BLACKPILL ROAD AND BISHOPSTON ROAD (misleadingly some tts made it look like two stops, but *The Cambrian* of 22 January 1875 has BLACKPILL OR BISHOPSTON ROAD, clearly joint name); often just one half of name used – much variation; initially usually BLACK PILL in all forms; resited on deviation 26 August 1900; clo 6 January 1960★★; {map 88}.
BLACK PILL AND COLLIERY BRANCH (non-tt) – see end of 1860 July 25★★.

BLACKPOLE [GW] (non-tt);
GM's report, 16 November 1917 said work in hand for workmen's platform at Small Arms Factory; used until about 1920 *(U)* and from 9 November 1941 *(GW wtt supplement)* to about 1946 *(U)*; aot HALT; {Worcester – Fernhill Heath}.

BLACKPOOL

B CENTRAL [PW] op 6 April 1863 *(LY)* as B; became B HOUNDS HILL 1872 tt *(JS)*, B C 1878 tt *(Cl)*; clo 2 November 1964 *(BR WR circular 12 October)*.

B NORTH [PW] op 29 April 1846 *(LY)* as B; became B TALBOT ROAD 1872 tt *(JS)*, B N 17 March 1932 *(LNW dates)*; still open.

B PLEASURE BEACH op 13 April 1987 *(RM June)*; still open.

B SOUTH [PW] op 30 May 1903 *(RCG)*; original station on direct line; platforms on coastal line added 14 July 1916, to replace South Shore; still open. At first SOUTH SHORE WATERLOO ROAD, became B W R 1914 *(RCH ref July)*, B S 17 March 1932 *(LNW dates)*.

SOUTH SHORE LYTHAM ROAD [PW] op 6 April 1863 *(LY)* as S S; L R added 30 May 1903 *(hbl 9 July)*; clo 14 July 1916 (Friday) *(Cl)* – see B South, above. Note: Blackpool not part of name.

BURLINGTON ROAD [PW] op 1 October 1913 *(D&C 10)*; clo 1 October 1915 (Friday); reop by August 1919 ('has been reop', *RM August* – no trains July 1919 *Brad)*; clo 11 September 1939 *(Cl)*. HALT in *hb*.

BLACKROD [LY]: line op 4 February 1841 and opening notice in *Bolton Chronicle* of 6 February

includes this in fare list as 'Horwich and Blackrod station', its original name★; became H JUNCTION 14 February 1870, B & H J 11 February 1873 *(Cl)*, B 16 April 1888 *(Cl; hbl ref 26 April)*. Still open.
★ = despite fact that inspection report said station not ready and company letter, dated 1 February 1841 *(Rtn)*, said would not be used for present.

BLACKSBOAT [GNS] op 1 July 1863 *(GNS)*; clo 18 October 1965★★.

BLACKSTON (JUNCTION) [NB] first in *Brad* January 1863; B JUNCTION 1865/7 to 1890 *(Brad)*; clo 1 May 1930 (Thursday) *(Cl)*.
In *hb* until was BLACKSTONE, then BLACKSTON; *hbl ref January 1925* said had become B J but still B *Brad*.

BLACKTHORN [GW] op 1 July 1910 *(RCG; co ½ T 6 August- line)*; clo 8 June 1953 *(RM August)*.

BLACKWALL

BLACKWALL [GE] op 6 July 1840 *(co n T 29 June)*; see 1849 March 31★★; clo 4 May 1926★★ *(Cl)*.

BLACKWALL [Dock] op 28 March 1994★★; still open.

BLACKWATER near Aldershot [SE] op 4 July 1849 *(SR; Hants Chron 7th- line)* as B; later B & SANDHURST *(Brad 1851-2 but thus 1850 Topham)*; became B & YORK TOWN 1897 tt *(Cl)*, B & CAMBERLEY for SANDHURST COLLEGE 1 June 1913 *(hbl 24 April)*, B HANTS 9 July 1923 *(hbl 26 April)*; HANTS dropped ?; still open.

BLACKWATER IoW [IWC]: line op 1 February 1875 (see 1875★★); station probably later – first in *Brad* June 1876; IoW added 9 July 1923 *(hbl 26 April)*; aot request; clo 6 February 1956 *(Southern Daily Echo 6th)*. Tickets for B CROSSING *(JB)*.

BLACKWELL [BG; Mid]
Probable sequence (J. Gough):
BLACKWELL (a) op 5 June 1841 at 52m 54ch; clo ?
BLACKWELL (b) op November 1841★★ as TOP OF LICKEY INCLINE at 53m 15ch; renamed ?; clo 18 April 1966 *(Cl)*.

BLACKWELL MILL [Mid] (non-tt): used by railwaymen and families; first in working tt 1 November 1874; still there until line clo 6 March 1967; {Millers Dale – Buxton} *(Mid)*.

BLACKWOOD near Crumlin [LNW] op 19 June 1865 *(co n Newport 17th)*; clo 13 June 1960 *(RM July)*.

BLACKWOOD near Lanark [Cal] op 1 December 1866 *(Cal)* as terminus; replaced by through station on Stonehouse to Lesmahagow line 1 July 1905 *(RM November)*; clo 4 October 1965 *(BR notice, True Line July 2006)*.

BLACON [GC] op 31 March 1890 *(RCG)*; clo 9 September 1968 *(RM October)*.

BLAENAU FFESTINIOG

At first B FESTINIOG. *Brad* made change to B FFESTINIOG 1950/1 in GW table, LNW later – 1951/2 LNW table had B FEST... in body, with note giving distance to GW B FFEST...
Standard gauge stations:
BLAENAU FFESTINIOG [LNW] op 22 July 1879 *(Brad Sh Eng 1880)*, temporary at tunnel mouth; replaced by exchange with narrow gauge, op 1 April

1881 *(Neele)*; B F NORTH 18 June 1951 to 6 May
1968 *(BLN)*; replaced ¼ mile east by >
B F after 9.50am departure, 22 March 1982
(RM May) – planned for 5 January 1982 but delayed
by bad weather; still open. Is on same site as old GW
(next entry); according to *RM* op as B F CENTRAL
but just B F in tt – *RM* assumed back to old name?
Re-siting involved use of connection between old LNW
and GW lines opened 20 April 1964 for goods traffic
to Trawsfynydd Power Station.
B F CENTRAL [GW] op 10 September 1883
(hbl 31 December); CENTRAL added 18 June 1951 *(Cl)*;
clo 4 January 1960 *(RM March)*.
Narrow gauge stations {map 78}:
DINAS [Festiniog] op 6 January 1865 *(D&C 11)*;
clo August 1870 *(Cl)*. Passengers carried free and at
own risk for some months before official opening;
free use 5 January after formal opening *(Festiniog)*.
DUFFWS [Festiniog] first in *Brad* January 1866 as
DIFFWYS; amended 1867/9; clo 1 January 1923,
reop 1 January 1925 *(Cl)*; clo 1 June 1931 *(Cl)*.
In *hb* as DIFFWYS, later DUFFWS B F TOWN;
ticket for DIPHWYS *(JB)*.
B F **exchange** with GW [Festiniog] op 10 September
1883 *(D&C 11)*; trains last shown June 1939 *Brad*
though remained trainless to line clo 18 Sept. 1939**.
B F **exchange** with LNW [Festiniog] op 1 April 1881
(D&C 11); clo 18 September 1939**.
In *Brad* last two covered by one entry, B F JUNCTION,
until separate times provided 1889/90; use of both
intermittent in last years (see 1923 January 1**).
Note that 'Blaenau' not included in names of Dinas
and Duffws in *Brad*.
BLAENAU [Festiniog & Blaenau] op 30 May 1868**;
last train 5 September 1883 *(NGSC)*; replaced by
B F Central, standard gauge.
BLAENAVON
BLAENAVON [LNW] op 18 December 1869 *(LNW
Officers 4939)*; clo 5 May 1941 *(Cl)*.
B LL [GW] op 2 October 1854**; LL added 19 July
1950 *(Cl)*; clo 30 April 1962 *(T 6 April)*.
BLAENCORRWG – see NORTH RHONDDA.
BLAENGARW [GW]: miners used from 1877 *(U)*;
op (new station) to public 26 May 1902 *(RCG)*;
clo 9 February 1953 *(T 23 January)*.
BLAENGWYNFI [RSB] op 2 June 1890 *(GW)*;
became request 1965/8 tt – regarded as Halt?;
clo 26 February 1968 – tunnel unsafe *(Cl)*.
BLAEN-GWYNFI/BLAEN GWYNFI until 1936
(Brad). Hb until 1904 had B-GWNFY and tickets
thus *(JB)*
BLAENPLWYF [GW] op 12 May 1911
(co n Lampeter); HALT;
clo 12 February 1951 *(Cl)* – see 1951**.
BLAENRHONDDA [RSB] op 2 July 1890
(co ½ T 21 August); BLAEN-RHONDDA until 1936/7
(Brad); became request 1965/8 tt – regarded as Halt?;
clo 26 February 1968 – tunnel unsafe *(Cl)*.
BLAGDON [GW] op 4 December 1901 *(Wells 5th)*;
clo 14 September 1931 *(RM December)*.
BLAGUEGATE – see SKELMERSDALE.

BLAINA [GW] op 23 December 1850**;
clo 30 April 1962 *(T 6 April)*.
BLAIR ATHOLL [High] op 9 September 1863
(High); B ATHOLE until 7 September 1893 *(RCG)*;
still open. See 1957**. Hb: 1866 B ATHOLE;
1872 B ATHOL; 1894a B ATHOLL.
BLAIRADAM [NB] op 20 June 1860
(Tayside; co ½ T 28 September- line); in *Brad* but often
described as private (for Blairadam House);
clo 22 September 1930 *(Cl)*.
BLAIRGOWRIE [Cal] op 1 August 1855 *(co ½ T
7 September)*; clo 10 January 1955 *(T 28 December 1954)*.
BLAIRHILL [NB] first in *Brad* December 1888 as
DRUMPELLIER & GARTSHERRIE, though
BLAIRBRIDGE in BoT inspection report;
became BLAIRHILL & G 1 February 1899 *(JS)*,
B 6 May 1968 tt; still open.
BLAISDON [GW] op 4 November 1929 *(Cl 29)*;
HALT, though SIDING in hb 1956; clo 2 November
1964 *(Cl)*; {Grange Court – Longhope}.
BLAKE HALL op by [GE] 24 April 1865
(L; co n T 24th- line); its line treated as part of [Cen] from
25 September 1949 *(T 26th)* but not legally transferred
until 18 November 1957, when electric services began
(D&C 3); clo 2 November 1981 *(BLN 424)*.
BLAKE STREET [LNW] op 15 December 1884
(W Mid; LNW Officers 26784- line); still open.
BLAKEDOWN [GW] first in *Brad* April 1853 as
CHURCHILL & B; renamed 6 May 1968 *(Cl)*;
still open. Initially C in hb; 1904 C & B.
BLAKENEY [Forest of Dean Central]: 'P' in hb 1877
to 1895; almost certainly parcels only (thus shown 1904).
BLAKESLEY [SMJ] op 1 July 1873 *(SMJ; Chelt
Exam 9th- line)*; clo 1 August 1877 (Wednesday) *(Cl)*;
reop 2 March 1885**; clo 7 April 1952 *(RM May)*.
BLANDFORD FORUM [Dorset Central; SD Jt]
Temporary terminus at **B St Marys** op 1 November 1860
(Dorset Chron 8th); replaced 42 chains further on,
when line extended to Templecombe, by >
BLANDFORD FORUM op 10 September 1863**;
FORUM added 21 September 1953 *(Rly Obs November)*;
clo 7 March 1966 *(Shepton 11th)*.
B CAMP (non-tt) army; 1915– 19;
{branch from Blandford} *(U)*.
BLANEFIELD [NB] first in *Brad* February 1868;
clo 1 October 1951 *(RM November)*.
BLANKNEY & METHERINGHAM [GN/GE]
op 1 August 1882 *(GN/GE)*;
clo 11 September 1961 *(RM September)*.
Later reopened as METHERINGHAM, which see.
BLANTYRE
BLANTYRE [Cal]: line op 10 September 1849**, nd,
July 1853; still open.
Also see HIGH BLANTYRE.
BLAYDON [NE] op 10 March 1835** *(N&C)*;
clo 3 September 1966 for engineering work,
reop 1 May 1967 *(Cl)*; still open. *Scott* 1837 has B for
fares but STELLA OR B in details of tt; text suggests B.
BLEADON & UPHILL [GW] first in *Brad*
November 1871; op as U, renamed 1872 *(Brad)*;
clo 5 October 1964 *(Cl)*.

BLEAN & TYLER HILL [SEC] op 1 January 1908
(P. Laming, photo-caption, *Railway Archive November
2004, p.95*) *; HALT; just T H 1912 tt to 1915 tt *(Cl)*;
clo 1 January 1931 (Thursday) *(T 4 December 1930)*.
* = *Hart* says not in local press tt until 13 June; was in *Brad*
January.

BLEASBY [Mid] in co tts from December 1848,
Wednesdays only; Saturday service added November
1849 – was mentioned in note to Nottingham–Codnor
Park table, not in Lincoln–Derby, where it belonged
(Mid) – first in *Brad* March 1850; all days July 1863;
still open. B GATE until 1889 RCH Distance Books *(JS)*.

BLECHYNDEN – see SOUTHAMPTON.

BLEDLOW [GW]
BLEDLOW op 1 August 1862 *(GW ac)*;
clo 7 January 1963 *(RM January)*.
B BRIDGE op 1 September 1906 *(GW H)*; HALT;
clo 1 July 1957 *(RM August)*.

BLENCOW [CKP] op 2 January 1865
(co n T 28 February- line; in op tt Cockermouth);
clo 3 March 1952 *(RM April)*; reop 2 July 1956
(RM August); clo 6 March 1972 *(RM March)*.
Brad ? to 1952: B for GREYSTOKE, but not thus
LMS tt 1930.

BLENHEIM & WOODSTOCK [GW]
op 19 May 1890 *(Oxford Chron 24th)*;
clo 1 March 1954 *(T 1st)*.
Hb: 1892a W & B, corrected 1894a.

BLENKINSOPP HALL [NE] (non-tt): private;
op 18 June 1838; clo 1875; (see 1836 B**)
{Haltwhistle – Greenhead} *(U)*.

BLETCHINGTON [GW] op 2 September 1850
(co n T 31 August) as WOODSTOCK;
renamed W ROAD 1851 tt, KIRTLINGTON 1855 tt
(Cl), B 11 August 1890 *(hbl 23 October)*;
clo 2 November 1964 *(BRWR circular 12 October)*.

BLETCHLEY [LNW] op after 2 November 1838,
when co minutes refer to arrangements being made for
station there, but on or before 20 June 1839 when in co
tt *(Lee)*; still open. B & FENNY STRATFORD
1841-6 *Brad* but just B in *Tuck* 1843;
B JUNCTION 1851/2 to 1869/70 in *Brad* and thus
LNW co tt at least until 1868, in some tables.

BLIDWORTH & RAINWORTH [Mid] op 3 April
1871 *(Mid)* as R; renamed B 1 May 1877 *(Mid)*,
B & R 27 April 1894 *(hbl 11 July)*; clo 12 August 1929
(T 13th). Advertised excursion in special notice
1 August 1962 *(IU)*.

BLISWORTH [LNW] op 17 September 1838 *(T 18th)*;
moved ½ mile north by 1853 *(Cl)*; clo 4 January 1960
(RM February). B JUNCTION, some tables, *Brad*
1851/3 to 1895/6 and LNW co tt 1852–64 at least.
BLISWORTH [SMJ] op 1 May 1866** ; clo 7 April
1952 *(Cl)*; according to *hba* May 1948 this was 'closed'
– had trains been diverted to LNW station or was this
an error? Originally *hb* treated as one station.

BLOCHAIRN – see GARNGAD.

BLOCKLEY [GW]
op 4 June 1853 *(Glos Chron 4th- line)*;
clo 3 January 1966 *(RM February)*.

BLODWELL JUNCTION [Cam] op 6 January 1904
(RCG) on site of previous Llanyblodwell;
clo 15 January 1951 *(Cl)* – see 1951**; {map 80} .

BLOOMSBURY (& NECHELLS) [LNW]
op 1 August 1856 *(W Mid)*; clo 1 March 1869
(alterations notices LNW co tt March 1869;
LNW Officers 3994 – can be closed after 28th inst);
replaced by Vauxhall (later renamed Duddeston);
{Aston – Vauxhall & Duddeston}.
At times B & NECHELS *(Brad)*; just B in LNW tts
seen, including March 1869, cited above.

BLOORS SIDING – see 1833 May**.

BLOWERS GREEN [GW] op 1 March 1878
(hbl 20 June), 17 chains north of NETHERTON,
which it replaced; originally in *Brad* as N, soon
DUDLEY SOUTH SIDE & N, B G 1 August 1921
(RCG) *; clo 30 July 1962 *(RM September)*.
* = *hbl 15 July* said renamed from N.

BLOWICK [LY] op 1 April 1870 *(Ormskirk 7th)* as
COP END; renamed 1871 *(Cl; RCG ref April 1872)*;
clo 25 September 1939 *(LNW Record)*.

BLOXHAM [GW] op 6 April 1887 *(GW- line)*;
clo 4 June 1951 *(T 4th)*.

BLOXWICH
BLOXWICH (a) [LNW] op 1 Feb 1858 *(W Mid; T 1st-
line)*; clo 18 January 1965 *(RM March)*.
BLOXWICH (b) op 17 April 1989 *(BLN 609)*; still open.
B NORTH op 2 October 1990 *(RM December)*,
free trains first day; still open.
Originally to be BROAD LANE but 'renamed' before
opening *(AB, Chron)*; ticket exists under that name *(JB)*.

BLUE ANCHOR [GW] op 16 July 1874 *(Som H 18th)*;
clo 4 January 1971 *(Som Gaz 8th)*. See 2007 July 20**.

BLUE ANCHOR LANE – see 1835 June 9**.

BLUE PITS – see CASTLETON.

BLUESTONE [MGN] op 5 April 1883 *(MGN;
T 9th- line)*; clo 1 March 1916 (Wednesday) *(RCG)*;
{Corpusty – Aylsham}.

BLUNDELLSANDS & CROSBY [LY]
op 24 July 1848** *(Southport Vis 22nd, 29th)* as C, on
north side of level crossing at Mersey Road, on different
plot than agreed. At least one short closure in early days
(see note). Re-sited 250 yards north, to south side of
level crossing on newly built Blundellsands Road,
using materials from old Southport Eastbank Street,
1 June 1852. Re-sited again on north side of
Blundellsands Road level crossing in 1865, initially
B for C; exact date not known – between 7 January,
when platforms reported not ready, and 2 November,
when ordered to be renamed B & C 'forthwith',
but *Brad* changed from C to C & B December 1865 /
January 1866 (to B & C 1877/8); Local Board for Great
Crosby had decided, 30 August 1865, to protest about
intended change, so perhaps not yet open. Extensively
rebuilt, work completed May 1882. Still open.
(Much detail from *Liverpool, Southport & Crosby co
minutes*, J. Gilmour.)
Aot BLUNDELL SANDS *(hb)*.

BLUNHAM [LNW] op 7 July 1862 *(co n T 7th- line)*;
clo 1 January 1968 *(RM January)*.

BLUNSDON [MSWJ] op 1 September 1895
(MSWJ); Sundays only after 10 July 1922;
last used 28 September 1924 *(Cl)*.

BLUNTISHAM [GE] op 10 May 1878 *(GE- line)*;
clo 2 February 1931★★ *(RM March)*; later excur *(U)*.

BLYTH [NE] op 3 May 1847★★; new station to west
1 May 1867 *(NhumbYoung)*; clo 2 November 1964
(RM January 1965).

BLYTHBURGH [Southwold] (ng) first in *Brad*
December 1879; aot request; clo 12 April 1929★★.
GE co tts 1882, 1914 and *Brad* to closure:
B for WANGFORD.

BLYTHE BRIDGE [NS] op 7 August 1848;
BLYTH B until 1907 *(Cl; hbl ref 3 July)*; still open.

BLYTON [GC] op 2 April 1849 *(Lincs Times 3rd)*;
clo 2 February 1959 *(RM March)*.
Became B for CORRINGHAM 1885 ? *(RCG ref July)*
and thus GC co tt 1903, LNE tt 1933 and *Brad* to 1955/6.

BO'NESS [NB] op 1 March 1856 *(co n Falkirk
Herald)*, without BoT approval; soon closed – probably
by 13 March, when BoT appointed inspector *(MT 12/2)*
though advertisement for service still in paper of that
date (inertia?); certainly clo by 20 March (Monkland
minute of that date – 'has closed'). Service restarted
10 June 1856 *(SRO BR/MNK/1/2)*; clo 7 May 1956
(RM June).

BOARHILLS [NB] op 1 September 1883 *(Fifeshire
Journal 6th)*; clo 1 January 1917 *(RM February)*;
reop 1 February 1919 *(RM February)*;
clo 22 September 1930 *(Cl)*.

BOARS HEAD [LY&LU Joint/LNW]
op 1 December 1869★★; clo 31 January 1949 *(RM May)*.

BOAT OF GARTEN [GNS/High]
op 3 August 1863 *(High)*; clo 18 October 1965★★.

BOAT OF INSCH – see KINCRAIG.

BOATYARD CROSSING [LY] op 3 June 1912 *(LY)*;
clo 1 October 1913 (Wednesday)
(SouthportVisiter 25 September – will close 30th);
{on Tarleton branch, from Hesketh Bank}.

BOBBERS MILL – see RADFORD Nottingham.

BODDAM [GNS] op 2 August 1897 *(GNS)*;
clo 31 October 1932 *(RM December)*. Specials ran
during Second War but were replaced by buses before
its end (GNS Society's *Review*, August 2005).

BODFARI [LNW] op 6 September 1869★★;
clo 30 April 1962 *(RM June)*.

BODIAM [KES] op 2 April 1900 *(RM July)*;
clo 4 January 1954 *(T 28 October 1953)*; hop-pickers
to 1958 (from Robertsbridge end of line) *(U)*.
Brad and SEC co tt 1914: B for STAPLECROSS.
Hb 1904: B for S and EWHURST.

BODMIN {map 113}
BODMIN [Bodmin & Wadebridge; LSW]:
line op 1 October 1834★★ but operated on 'stop anywhere'
principle so impossible to say when first fare-paying
passengers were carried from BODMIN itself – earliest
passengers probably taken fromWenford Junction,
outside Bodmin; clo 1 November 1886 for line
reconstruction *(R Cornwall Gaz 29 October)*; on line
reop, replaced nearby by >
B NORTH [LSW] op 1 November 1895 *(Cornish &*

D P 2nd); NORTH added 26 September 1949 *(Cl)*;
HALT at clo 30 January 1967 *(Cornish & D P 4 Feb.)*.

BODMIN [Cornwall]: first station on main line to serve
Bodmin was **RESPRYN**, private station used
temporarily by public until proper one ready;
R op 4 May 1859★★; in *Brad* was BODMIN ROAD;
press description of ceremonial opening called it
B R station at Respryn. Kept as private station until
October 1864 or later *(Cl)*, but for public use
replaced by >

B PARKWAY [GW] op 27 June 1859 *(GW)*
as B ROAD; renamed 5 November 1983 *(19 March
1984 wtt supplement)*; still open

B GENERAL [GW] op 27 May 1887 *(GW –Cornish
Tel, 2 June, only covered formal opening of 26 May)*;
GENERAL added 26 September 1949 *(Cl)*;
clo 30 January 1967 *(Cornish & D P 4 February)*.

BODORGAN [LNW] first in tt *(Topham)* May or
June 1849; aot request; still open.

BOGFIELD – see CARLISLE.

BOGNOR REGIS
For first station see WOODGATE.
BOGNOR REGIS [LBSC] op 1 June 1864 *(co ½ T 25
July)*; destroyed by fire 1898; temporary replacement;
permanent new station 1902; REGIS added July 1929
(hbl 23 October); still open.

BOGSIDE near Irvine
BOGSIDE [GSW]: racegoers' use began after 1885 *(race)*;
first in *Brad* June 1894; initiallyTuesdays,Thursdays
and Saturdays only; all days June 1914; reverted to
Saturdays only for part at least of First World War;
at one stage, one of its trains was labelled "the golfers'
train"; aot request; was B RACECOURSE/RACE
COURSE 30 June 1952 to 14 June 1965 *(Cl)*;
clo 2 January 1967 *(Cl)*.

B MOOR [Cal] in use by June 1900 *(U)*; first in public
tt October 1901; noted in tt as golfers' station until
clo 1 January 1917 – according to co wtt July 1907
application for train to stop had to be made to
station-master at Irvine or Kilwinning; reop, daylight
only, 1 February 1919; MOOR added 2 June 1924★★;
clo 28 July 1930 *(Cl)*. According to *Cl* became HALT
1924, but not thus *Brad* July 1929 or hb 1929.

BOGSIDE FIFE [NB]: line op 28 August 1850
(co ½ T 1 October), nd, June 1851 (not in notice *Stirling
Journal 30 August* so probably did open after line);
FIFE added 1933/4 *Brad*;
clo 15 September 1958 *(RM October)*.

BOGSTON [Cal] first in *Brad* September 1878;
clo 1 January 1917 *(RM February)*;
reop 1 March 1917 *(Cl)*; still open.

BOLD [St Helens] first in *Brad* November 1856;
last January 1858; {St Helens Junction –Widnes}.

BOLDON {map 25}
BOLDON [York, Newcastle & Berwick]: line op 16
April 1835★★, nd, about August 1841 *(Robinson)* – not
in *Brad* until August 1844; last there December 1853.

B COLLIERY – see BROCKLEY WHINS.

BOLHAM [GW] op 23 April 1928 *(Tiverton 24th)*;
HALT; clo 7 October 1963 *(W Som F P 12th)*;
{Bampton –Tiverton}.

BOLLINGTON [GC/NS] op 2 August 1869 *(Macclesfield – co n 31 July, item 7 August)*; clo 5 January 1970 *(Cl)*.

BOLSOVER

BOLSOVER [Mid] op 1 September 1890 *(Mid)*; clo 28 July 1930 *(LNW Record)*; but unadvertised service ended 14 August 1931 tt *(Mid)*. Pre-war excursions to at least 27 July 1939; half-day excursion to Bridlington and Scarborough 26 July 1949; surviving goods renamed B CASTLE 25 September 1950; used 28 July 1978 for Queen's Jubilee, then yearly August excursions organised by Miners' Welfare 1978–81; also PTA excursion 15 November 1980 to Liverpool Street *(Mid)*.
B SOUTH [GC] op 9 March 1897 (8th formal) *(GCR Society Journal, Spring 2003, p.12)*; SOUTH added 25 September 1950 *(Cl)*; clo 3 December 1951 *(RM January 1952)*.

BOLTON

BOLTON [LY] op 29 May 1838**; became B TRINITY STREET 1895/6 *Brad* but probably officially same date as Great Moor Street – hbl ref 24 April 1924; reverted to B 6 May 1968 *(AB)*; 8 March 1987 buildings on main overbridge closed, replaced by single storey building alongside main road – slightly longer walk for passengers (R. Herbert, aot Operations Manager at Preston, via B. Wilson); still open. Early on known as BRIDGEMAN STREET / BRADFORD SQUARE *(Bolton)*; B JUNCTION 1852 to 1854/6 in occasional table *(Brad)*.
BOLTON GREAT MOOR STREET [LNW] (a) op 13 June 1831**; G M S added 1849 *Brad*, but 2 June 1924 *(LNW dates,* supported by co tts, though isolated appearances in LNW co tt – e.g. 1856, in one table, one way only); original station at street level. Replaced by temporary >
BOLTON CROOK STREET [LNW] op 1 August 1871 *(Bolton; LNW Officers 6917,* 16 April 1871 – 'consequent upon the erection of a new station in a few days, the present passenger station at Bolton would be closed and a temporary opened in the goods yard at Crook Street' – probably in warehouse alongside Chandos Street); would allow level crossing in Crook Street to be replaced by bridge. This was replaced by >
BOLTON GREAT MOOR STREET [LNW] (b) op 28 September 1874 *(Bolton;* Bert Holland, *Plodder Lane for Farnworth,* Triangle, 2001, p.19); this was on approximately the same site as (a) but 10 feet higher; clo 29 March 1954 *(BR clo notice Sweeney)*. Wakes week use to 1959 [RCTS railtour on 4 April 1959 was described as last passenger train] *(AB)*.
BOLTON ABBEY [Mid] op 16 May 1888 *(Mid)*; clo 17 June 1940, reop 17 March 1941 *(Mid)*; clo 22 March 1965 *(RM April)*.
BOLTON JUNCTION – see KENYON JUNCTION.
BOLTON PERCY [NE]: line op 30 May 1839 *(T 7th)*, nd, June 1840; clo 13 September 1965 *(T 4th)*.
BOLTON-LE-SANDS [LNW]: op by 7 August 1847, when first in tt *Lancaster Gaz*; -le-S added 1861 in body of *Brad* but in index by 1853; clo 3 February 1969 *(Cl)*.
BOLTON-ON-DEARNE [SK Jt] op 1 July 1879 *(Mid; co n T 28 June- line)* as HICKLETON;

became B-on-D 1 November 1879, B-on-D for GOLDTHORPE 15 January 1924, B-on-D 12 June 1961 *(Mid)*; still open. B-upon-D 1883 on *(hb)*.
BONAR BRIDGE – see ARDGAY.
BONCATH [GW] op 31 August 1886 (see note on Cardigan); clo 10 September 1962 *(Cl)*.
BOND STREET London
BOND STREET [Cen] op 24 September 1900 *(L)*; see 1922**; still open. Davies Street pre-opening *(L)*.
BOND STREET [Jub] op 1 May 1979 *(RM July)*; still open.
BOND STREET Swansea [SIT] first seen in tt *(The Cambrian)* November 1878 – see 1860 July 25**; last seen *(Brad)* December 1879; {map 88}.
BONDS MAIN COLLIERY [GC] (non-tt) PLATFORM; miners; op 13 March 1900 *(GC dates)*; clo ?; {Grassmoor – Heath}.
BO'NESS – see after BLYTON.

BONNINGTON

BONNINGTON [NB]: line op 20 May 1846 *(D&C 6)*, nd, October 1847 (often omitted from *Brad* in years immediately following); clo 1 January 1917 *(RM Feb.)*; reop 1 April 1919 *(RCH)*; clo 16 June 1947**.
BONNINGTON [Cal] (never opened) – see 1903**.

BONNYBRIDGE {map 11}

BONNYBRIDGE [Cal] op 2 August 1886 *(Cal)*; see 1921 April/ May**; clo 28 July 1930 *(Cl)*; later excur *(U)*.
BONNYBRIDGE [NB] op 1 May 1870 *(?;* first in *Brad* May); B HIGH 8 June 1953 *(Cl; RM ref April)* to 14 June 1965 *(Cl)*; clo 6 March 1967 *(Cl)*.
B CENTRAL [KB] op 2 July 1888 *(RCG)*; clo 1 February 1935 (Friday) *(RM March)*.

BONNYRIGG [NB]

For first station see BROOMIEKNOWE.
BONNYRIGG op 1 August 1855 *(Peebles)*; B ROAD 1866 tt to 1 August 1868 *(Cl –* and thus 1867 *hb)*; clo 10 September 1962 *(RM September)*.

BONT NEWYDD [Nantlle] (ng)

See 1829 B** for earliest service.
Official service began 11 August 1856; clo 12 June 1865 *(Cl)*.
BONTNEWYDD near Dolgellau [GW] op 4 August 1868 *(Carnarvon 11th)*; clo 18 January 1965**.
BONWM [GW] op 21 September 1935 *(T 20th)*; HALT; clo 14 December 1964**; {Carrog – Corwen}.
BOOKHAM [LSW] op 2 February 1885 *(co n T 31 January)*; still open. Op notice called it B COMMON and tickets exist thus but only B *Brad*.
BOOSBECK [NE] op 1 November 1878 *(S&D)*; clo 2 May 1960 *(RM June)*.
BOOT [Raven] (ng) op 20 November 1876 *(co yearly T 26 March 1877)*; clo 1 December 1908**, reop April 1917 *(Cl)*; clo end summer season 1918 *(Raven p.56)*.
BOOTHFERRY PARK – see HULL.
BOOTLE near Barrow-in-Furness [Fur] op 8 July 1850**; aot request; still open.
BOOTLE Liverpool
B BALLIOL ROAD [LNW] op 5 September 1881 *(Waterloo Times 3rd)* as BALLIOL ROAD; BOOTLE added 1 January 1891 *(RCG)*; clo 31 May 1948 *(LNW Record)*.

Note in LNW co tt May 1900 that Balliol Road and LY stations adjacent; passengers to/from Southport change 'except they travel by the through trains'.

MARSH LANE [LY] trains first shown in *Brad* December 1850 and tt for 2 December 1850 (*Liverpool Journal 7th*) but presumably already open – engineer's report 8 October 1850 (*RAIL 372/10*) says 'As the traffic is now very great the platforms should be properly lighted in the evening'; on north side of Marsh Lane, by level crossing; replaced by >

B NEW STRAND [LY] op 11 April 1886 (*Bootle Times 10th*), on south side, on embankment, as MARSH LANE & STRAND ROAD; clo by enemy action, 19 May 1941, reop 12 July 1943 *(Cl)*; renamed 6 March 1967 *(Cl)*; still open.

B VILLAGE [LY] trains first shown in *Brad* December 1850 and tt for 2 December 1850 (*Liverpool Journal 7th*) but presumably already open – engineer's report made same comment as for Marsh Lane, above; on south side of Merton Road; op as MERTON ROAD and still shown thus 1851 LY Distance Diagram but decision to rename taken 19 October 1850, to prevent their passengers being kidnapped to the E Lancs station at Bootle (B Lane/Kirkdale) (*RAIL 372/2 p.92*); replaced by >

B ORIEL ROAD [LY] op 1 May 1876 (*Liverpool 2nd*) on north side of Merton Road;
O R added 2 June 1924 *(JS)*; still open.
Rly Gaz made LIVERPOOL B O R of it.

B LANE – see KIRKDALE.
Also see CANADA DOCK.
Aot *hb* showed BOOTLE TIMBER DEPOT at Liverpool Canada Dock as 'P' but entry under CANADA DOCK was for goods only so presumably former was error.

BORDER OFFSET shown on Macaulay's maps 1851 to at least 1860s; with that name should have been a 'halt' but no evidence of passenger use found – perhaps just a goods siding; {Arbroath – Leysmill}.

BORDESLEY [GW] first in *Brad* June 1855; re-sited 14 chains south 7 March 1915 *(Cl)*; from 2003 national tt sparse service shown but local *Centro tt* shows many calling Saturdays when Birmingham City at home; from 20 May 2007 general tt only showed Saturday stop, northbound only; still open.

BORDON [LSW] op 11 December 1905 *(RCG)*; clo 16 September 1957 – last train early a.m. on Monday 16th (*Hants Chron 21st*).
During First War leave trains ran onto Longmoor Military Railway just north of here.

BOREHAM HOUSE [GE] (non-tt) private; originally stopped at level crossing, no platform or other facilities (line op 29 March 1843); no station until 1859/1874; for Sir J. Tyrrell; agreement ended with his death 19 September 1877; station removed day after funeral {Chelmsford – Hatfield Peverel} (article, H. Paar, *RCHS Journal September 1979, p.113–5*).

BOROUGH [Nor] op 18 December 1890 (*L; co ½T 14 February 1891- line)*, as GREAT DOVER STREET; renamed 1900/1 (*Brad*); see 1922**; still open.

BOROUGH ROAD [LCD] op 1 June 1864 *(L)*; clo 1 April 1907 *(RCG)*.

BOROUGH GREEN & WROTHAM [LCD] op 1 June 1874 *(T 2nd)* as W; became W & B G by January 1875, W 1926, W & B G 1933/4 *(Brad)*; settled as B G & W 18 June 1962 *(Cl)*; still open.

BOROUGHBRIDGE [NE] op 17 June 1847 *(NE)*; new station when line extended to Knaresborough 1 April 1875 *(Cl)*; clo 25 September 1950 (*RM November*). NE co tt July 1880 contained both one- and two-word versions of name.

BORROBOL [High] first in *Brad* September 1876 and in 1877 *hb*, though according to *High* no platforms provided until 1880; aot request; clo 29 November 1965 *(Cl)*. B PLATFORM until 10 September 1962 *(Cl)* but in *hb* was at first PLATFORM, 1904 B, and, according to *hb* 1944a, then renamed from B to B HALT.

BORROWASH [Mid] op 4 June 1839 *(Mid)*; re-sited ½ mile west, west of road overbridge, 1 May 1871 *(Mid)*; became B & OCKBROOK 1 May 1898 co tt *(Mid)*, back to B 1 April 1904 *(hbl 28th)*; clo 14 February 1966 *(RM April)*. *Brad* until 1955 but not LMS tt 1930: B for O.

BORTH [Cam] op 1 July 1863 (*co ½T 28 August*); still open.

BORWICK [Fur/Mid] op 6 June 1867 *(Mid)*; clo 12 September 1960 (*RM October*).

BOSCARNE EXCHANGE PLATFORMS op 15 June 1964 *(Cl 29)*; clo 18 April 1966, reop 2 May 1966 *(Cl)*; clo 30 January 1967 (*Cornish & D P 4 February*); {map 113}.

BOSCOMBE [LSW]
For first station of this name see POKESDOWN.
BOSCOMBE op 1 June 1897 (*Poole 27 May*); clo 4 October 1965 (*RM October*).

BOSHAM [LBSC] op 15 March 1847 (*LBSC; Salisbury 20th- line*); still open.

BOSLEY [NS]: excursion to fete here 10 August 1849; public op 1 September 1849 (*Churnet*); clo 7 November 1960 *(T 7th)*.

BOSSALL [Sand Hutton] (ng) op 4 October 1924**; last train 1 March 1930**; {map 40}.

BOSTON [GN] op 2 October 1848 (*Stamford 3rd*); still open.
A July 1859 excursion ran to goods depot for easier transfer of passengers to steamers for Skegness (*Skegness*) – others?

BOSTON LODGE [Festiniog] (ng) first in *Brad* 9 July 1928; intermittent use (see 1923 January 1**); aot request; briefly shown as PORT MEIRION (trains only shown under this name in 11 September 1933 *Brad*); HALT; trains last shown May 1935 but remained, trainless, last included 3 July 1939 (*Brad*); line clo 18 September 1939**; {map 76}.
In *Brad* 1930/1 and 1935 as B L for PORTMEIRION and GWYLLT FLOWER GARDENS.

BOSTON MANOR op by [Dist] 1 May 1883 (*L; Rtn-line*) as B ROAD for BRENTFORD and HANWELL; renamed B M for B and H 11 December 1911 *(RCG)*; [Picc] added 13 March 1933 *(T 14th)*; 'for B and H' dropped 1938 *hb*; [Dist] ceased 10 October 1964; still open for [Picc].

BOTANIC GARDENS Glasgow [Cal] op 10 August 1896 *(RCG)*; clo 1 January 1917 *(RM February)*, reop 2 June 1919 *(RCH)*; clo 6 February 1939 *(LNW Record)*.

BOTANIC GARDENS Hull [NE] op 1 June 1853 as CEMETERY, clo November 1854; reop September 1866 tt as CEMETERY GATES *(G&S)*; renamed B G 1 November 1881 *(Cl; RCG ref October)*; clo 19 October 1964 *(Cl)*. Became HALT 4 January 1960 according to *RM January* but not seen thus *Brad* though note then added that no staff were in attendance.

BOTHLIN VIADUCT [MK] op 26 December 1844**; clo by 23 March 1846 *(MK)*; {map 16}.

BOTHWELL

BOTHWELL [Cal] op 1 March 1877 *(Cal)*; according to *Cl*, reduced to workmen only 1917 to 1919, but full service shown *Brad*; clo 5 June 1950 *(Cl)*.

BOTHWELL [NB] op 1 April 1878 *(Hamilton 6th)*; clo 1 January 1917 except for workmen *(RM February)*; reop 2 June 1919 *(RCH)*; clo 4 July 1955 *(RM August)*.

B PARK [NB] (non-tt): miners; dates?; {Bellshill – Bothwell} *(U)*.

BOTLEY [LSW] op 29 November 1841** *(Salisbury 6th- line)*; HALT from 14 July 1968 *(Hants Chron 20th)* to 5 May 1969 *(SR App)*; still open. B & BISHOPS WALTHAM/B for BW in *Brad* 1846 to 1863 and in *hb* 1862.

BOTOLPHS BRIDGE [RHD] (ng) first trains shown in *Brad* November 1927 (see 1927 July 16**); HALT; request; last in *Brad* April 1931 but clo 1939 (and destroyed by Captain Howie) *(Wolfe)*.

BOTRIPHNIE – see AUCHINDACHY.

BOTT LANE [LY] first in *Brad* October 1906; see 1905** (b); clo 3 December 1956 *(RM December)*; {Nelson – Colne}.

BOTTESFORD

BOTTESFORD [GN] op 15 July 1850 *(T 18th)*; still open.

B SOUTH [GN/LNW] op 15 December 1879 *(LNW Officers 410/594 pp. 4421–2 and minute 20332)*; until 1880 in tt as B NEW; clo 1 May 1882 *(Cl)*; {Cotham – Redmile}.

BOTTISHAM & LODE [GE] op 2 June 1884 *(GE- line)*; & L added 22 April 1897 *(RCG)* or 1 May 1897 *(hbl 29 April)*; clo 18 June 1962 *(RM August)*.

BOTTOM OF SUTTON INCLINE
– see ST HELENS JUNCTION.

BOTTOM OF WHISTON INCLINE
– see HUYTON QUARRY.

BOUGHROOD & LLYSWEN [Cam] op 21 September 1864 *(D&C 11; co n Hereford J 24th- line)*; & L added 1 October 1912 *(hbl 24th)*; clo 31 December 1962 *(T 31st)*.

BOUGHTON near Newark [GC] op 9 March 1897 (8th formal) *(GCR Society Journal, Spring 2003, p. 12)*; clo 19 September 1955 *(BR ER internal notice August)*.

BOUGHTON near Worcester [GW] op 31 March 1924 *(GW H)*; HALT; clo 5 April 1965 *(Cl)*; {Henarth – Bransford Road}.

BOUNDS GREEN [Picc] op 19 September 1932 *(T 16th, 20th)*; still open.

BOURNE

(a) [GN] op 16 May 1860 *(co n Bourne)*; clo 2 March 1959 *(T 2nd)*. BOURN from May 1872 co tt *(Cl)* to 1 July 1893 *(RCG)*, but hb 1872 to 1890 and *Brad* 1872 to 1894.

(b) line from Spalding [Spalding & Bourn–Midland & Eastern] op 1 August 1866 to a temporary station east of level crossing east of GN station *(MT6 40/4)*; date when trains went on to GN station and temporary closed yet to be found; however August *Brad* shows arrival and departure times at Bourne that suggest through service and certainly would not have given time for passengers to change between stations – only one or two minutes – tt given in anticipation of move?

BOURNE BRIDGE [Newmarket] op 4 April 1848 *(co n T 3rd- line)*; clo 1 July 1850**; reop 9 September 1850 *(co n T 6th- line)*; clo 9 October 1851**; {map 70}. EC co tt May 1851: BOURN B.

BOURNE END [GW] op 1 August 1854 *(co n T 31 July)* as MARLOW ROAD; renamed 1 January 1874 *(Cl)*; still open.

BOURNEMOUTH [LSW] {map 125}

BOURNEMOUTH op 14 March 1870 *(Poole 17th)*; replaced by >

BOURNEMOUTH op 20 July 1885 *(W Gaz 24th)*; became B EAST 1875 *(Brad)*, renamed B CENTRAL 1 May 1899 *(hbl 27 April)*, CENTRAL dropped 10 July 1967 *(SR App)*; still open. B E HOLDENHURST ROAD 1882/3 to 1915, some tables, *Brad*.

B WEST op 15 June 1874 *(W Gaz 19th)*; clo 4 October 1965 *(RM Oct.)*; *Brad* first added WEST in SD Jt table; B W QUEENS ROAD some tables 1882/3 to 1915.

BOURNVILLE near Birmingham [Mid] op 3 April 1876 as STIRCHLEY STREET *(Mid)*; renamed S S & B 4 March 1880, B & S S 1 July 1888 co tt *(Mid)*, B 1 April 1904 *(RCG)*; still open.

BOURNVILLE MON South Wales [GW] op to miners July 1897 as TYLERS ARMS PLATFORM *(U)*; op to public and renamed B M 30 October 1933 *(co notice dated 'October')*; HALT added GW co tt by 5 October 1942 but *Brad* 1946; clo 30 April 1962 *(T 6 April)*; {Abertillery – Blaina}.

BOURTON – see FLAX BOURTON.

BOURTON-ON-THE-WATER [GW] op 1 March 1862 *(Wilts 8th)*; clo 15 October 1962 *(RM November)*.

BOVEY [GW] op 4 July 1866 *(GW; W D Merc 5th- line)*; clo 2 March 1959 *(Express & E 2nd)*. Ticket for B TRACEY *(JB)*.

BOVINGTON CAMP [LSW] (non-tt): Army; goods only First War *(LSW)*; passengers 1940s *(U)*; {branch from Wool}.

BOW London; {map 108}

BOW [EC]: line op 20 June 1839, nd, 15 November 1840, when mentioned in report of accident *(T 17th)* *; probably replaced by MILE END, which see, or clo soon after that opened. Probably just east of later Victoria Park & Bow interchange.

* = slight conflicts between journalist's version in *T* and official statement issued by EC and N&E, also included in *T 17th*. Former says train did not stop at Bow, but did stop just beyond to set down passenger and then stopped again to pick up passenger running after it; latter said first stop was in station; in any event, it suggests somewhat flexible operating practices. (Light engine belonging to N&E ran into back of EC train in middle of all of this).

B & BROMLEY [Blackwall] op 31 March 1849★★; clo 26 September 1850 (*L*); alias OLD FORD; replaced by >

BOW [NL] op 26 September 1850 (*T 12 October*); re-sited 1 December 1870 (*L*); clo 15 May 1944 (bus until 23 April 1945) (*Cl*).

B CHURCH [Dock] op 31 August 1987 (*T 1 Sept.*); still open.

Also see VICTORIA PARK & BOW.

BOW ROAD

BOW ROAD [GE] op 1 October 1876 (*L*); re-sited about ¼ mile north 4 April 1892 (*Cl*); clo 21 April 1941 (Sunday) (*T 15th*); reop 9 December 1946 (probably – *Cl*); clo 6 January 1947, reop 6 October 1947 (*Cl*); clo 7 November 1949 (*T 31 October*).

BOW ROAD [Dist/Met] op 11 June 1902 by [Dist] (*RCG*); [Met] added 30 March 1936; still open.

BOW [LSW] op 1 November 1865 (*Trewman 1st*); clo 5 June 1972 (*Cornish & D P 11th*).

DEVON added later years, in tt index only.

BOW BRICKHILL [LNW] op 30 October 1905★★; clo 1 January 1917 (*T 22 December 1916*); reop 5 May 1919 (*RCH*); still open.

BOW STREET [Cam] op 23 June 1864 (*Carnarvon 25th*); clo 14 June 1965 (*RM July*).

BOWBRIDGE CROSSING [GW] op 1 May 1905 (*GW H*); HALT; clo 2 November 1964 (*W D Press 2nd*).

BOWDON [MSJA]

BOWDON : minutes 18 September 1849 said would open 22nd, local paper said opened 23rd (Sunday); aimed to open for Wakes Week so at first used temporary station. Permanent probably opened about January 1850 (perhaps 1st) since appointment of station-master effective from then. Did not get BoT approval since believed already covered; inspection made 28 June 1850 (*MSJA; H. Paar, Chron October 2003*). Mileages given in *Returns*: line shown as 9m 12½ch at 31 July 1850, 9m 26ch at 31 December 1850 (late inspection probably responsible for discrepancy); clo 4 April 1881, replaced by ALTRINCHAM & B, short distance north, which see for source of date.

B PEEL CAUSEWAY – see HALE.

BOWER [High] op 28 July 1874 (*High*); clo 13 June 1960 (*RM July*).

BOWERS [LNE] op 15 December 1934 (*Cl 29*); in tt but mostly workmen; HALT until 3 May 1937 (R. Rockett, *Leeds, Castleford & Pontefract Junction Railway*, M. Bairstow, 2003); clo 22 January 1951 (*Cl*) – see 1951★★; {Ledston – Kipax}.

BOWES [NE] op 8 August 1861 (*co op tt*); clo 22 January 1962 (*RM February*).

BOWES BRIDGE [Brandling Junction] op 18 June 1842 (*Consett*); only appeared in *Brad* August 1844; on line to TANFIELD MOOR, which see for details of service; {map 27}.

BOWES PARK [GN] op 1 November 1880 (*RCG*); still open.

BOWESFIELD JUNCTION/LANE – see under STOCKTON.

BOWHOUSE [NB]: line op 5 August 1840 but station later 1840s (*MK*); certainly in existence by July 1848, when in *Topham*, earliest detail seen for line; clo 1 May 1930 (Thursday) (*Cl*).

BOWKER VALE

BOWKER VALE (a) [LMS] op 26 September 1938 (*LNW Record*); clo 17 August 1991 (*BLN 660*) for conversion to >

BOWKER VALE (b) op by [Manch] 6 April 1992 (*BLN 681*); still open.

BOWLAND [NB] op 1 August 1848★★; clo 7 December 1953 (*RM January 1954*). B BRIDGE in tt 1849 to 1862 (*Cl*) but still that in NB wtt 1868 and *hb* until 1898a.

BOWLING near Bradford; {map 54}

BOWLING [GN] op 1 August 1854 (*GN; T 1st - line*); clo 1 February 1895 (Friday) (*Cl*).

B JUNCTION [LY] op 1 February 1902 (*RCG*); clo 2 April 1917 (*Cl*); reop 5 May 1919 (*RCH*); clo 3 December 1951 (*RM February 1952*).

BOWLING near Glasgow

BOWLING [Cal] op 1 October 1896 (*RCG; Colliery 2nd - line*); clo 1 January 1917 (*RM February*); some trains back in *Brad* August 1917 – timings suggest workmen's service, but not so noted; fully reop 1 February 1919 (*RCH*); clo 5 February 1951 (*Cl*) – see 1951★★. B BAY in opening notice (*TrueLine*).

BOWLING [NB] op 15 July 1850★★; re-sited 31 May 1858 when line to Glasgow opened (*Cl*); still open.

BOWMANHILL BALLAST [High] (non-tt): 1922 to about 1946; railwaymen?; {Rafford – Forres} (*High*).

BOWNESS [Cal] op 8 March 1870 (*Cal*); for clo see 1921 April/May★★.

BOX [GW]

BOX op 30 June 1841 (*GW; Wilts 8th - line*); clo 4 January 1965 (*RM February*).

B MILL LANE op 31 March 1930 (*hbl 75*); HALT (but PLATFORM *hb* 1936a, still 1956); clo 4 January 1965 (*RM February*); {Corsham – Box}.

BOXFORD [GW] op 4 April 1898 (*co n Ephemera*); clo 4 January 1960 (*RM February*).

BOXHILL

B & WESTHUMBLE [LBSC] op 11 March 1867 (*co n T 11th*) as WEST HUMBLE; renamed BOX HILL & BURFORD BRIDGE 1 November 1870 but 1896–1904 tt reverted to B H (*JS*); became BOXHILL & W 15 September 1958 (*RM October*); still open. 1868 LBSC co tt: W H for B B. *Brad* ? to 1955/6: Boxhill & B Bridge for Mickleham. Also see DORKING.

BOXMOOR – see HEMEL HEMPSTEAD.

BOYCES BRIDGE [GE] op 20 August 1883★★; clo 2 January 1928 (*Cl*). GE in tt 1914: B B DEPOT.

BOYNE HILL – see MAIDENHEAD.

BRACEBOROUGH SPA [GN] op 16 May 1860 (*co n Bourne*); aot request; became HALT 19 February 1934 (*Cl* date for unstaffed – *Brad* added HALT 1933/4); clo 18 June 1951 (*RM July*).

BRACKENHILLS [Cal] op 1 September 1906
(RCG); clo 1 December 1930 *(Cl)*.

BRACKLEY

BRACKLEY [LNW]: line op 1 May 1850 *(co n T 1st)*, nd,
July 1850; clo 2 January 1961 *(RM February)*. Only B
in *Brad* but tickets for B TOWN *(JB)* – according to *Cl*
TOWN added 1 July 1950 to goods only.

B CENTRAL [GC] op 15 March 1899
(GC; T 16th- line); clo 5 September 1966 *(RM October)*.
Until 1904 B in *hb*.

BRACKNELL [LSW] op 9 July 1856 *(co n T 7th)*;
still open. Rebuilt 1975– ?; up platform temporarily
moved eastwards into former goods yard (see
photograph, V. Mitchell & K. Smith, *Branch Lines
around Ascot*, Middleton, 1989).

BRADBURY [NE] op 19 June 1844
(co n T 24 May- line); clo 2 January 1950 *(Cl)*.

BRADFIELD [GE] first in *Brad* January 1856;
aot request; clo 2 July 1956 *(RM August)*.

BRADFORD {map 54}

BRADFORD (ADOLPHUS STREET) [GN] temporary
op 1 August 1854 *(T 1st; D&C 8, p.80)*; permanent
1 June 1855 *(co ½ T 28 May)*; just B in *Brad*; clo 7 January
1867 – line extended to (EXCHANGE) *(T 7th)*.

B MARKET STREET [Mid] op 1 July 1846 *(Mid)*;
Brad 1867 added note that B was 'on the corner of
Market Street', 1875 just B M S; replaced by >

B FORSTER SQUARE [Mid] op 2 March 1890 *(Mid)*;
at first B MARKET STREET in *Brad*;
F S added 2 June 1924 *(Rly Gaz May)*; platforms
re-sited alongside and at end of previous platforms,
last trains Saturday 9 June 1990, buses instead on
Sunday, new station op 11th *(Rly Obs September)*;
still open.

B INTERCHANGE [LY] op 9 May 1850 *(T 13th)* as B;
became B EXCHANGE *hb* 1890 but 1901/2 *(Brad)*;
replaced about 200 yds south 14 January 1973
(Sunday) on part of site of former Bridge Street Goods
(RM March); became INTERCHANGE 16 May
1983; still open.
Also see MANCHESTER ROAD [GN].

BRADFORD PEVERELL & STRATTON [GW]
op 22 May 1933 *(GW Mag July)*; HALT;
clo 3 October 1966 *(W Daily Press 3rd)*;
{Grimstone – Dorchester}.

BRADFORD-ON-AVON [GW] op 2 February
1857 *(GW; Bath & Chelt 4th- line)*; -on-A added 1899
(Cl) but thus *hb* 1877; still open.

BRADING [IoW]

BRADING op 23 August 1864 *(Salisbury 27th- line)*;
clo 1 January 1967 for electrification, reop 20 March
1967 *(RM May)*; still open. B JUNCTION 1882 to
1923 *(Brad)*, 1912 to after 1938 *(hb)*. *Brad* ? to 1955/6:
B for YAVERLAND, THE ROMAN VILLA and
NUNWELL.
Also see YARBRIDGE.

BRADLEY near Huddersfield [LNW] op 2 August
1847 *(co ½ T 25 August- line)*; re-sited at junction
1 August 1849; clo 6 March 1950 *(Cl)*.
Hb 1862 and 1867: B WOOD.

BRADLEY & MOXLEY [GW] op 10 June 1862

(M. Hale, *Chron 3*); clo 1 May 1915 (Saturday) *(Cl)* –
RCH says clo 29 March but last trains shown April tt;
{Bilston – Wednesbury}.

BRADLEY FOLD [LY] first trains January 1849 tt
(line op 20 November 1848, station in tt December
but no trains calling); clo 5 October 1970 *(Cl)*.
LMS tt 1930 and 1947: B F for LITTLE LEVER
(for L L added 1 April 1921, *RCG,* but 10 May 1921,
hbl 15 July).

BRADNOP [NS] op 5 June 1905 *(D&C 7)*;
clo 30 September 1935 *(RM November)*.

BRADSHAW LEACH – see PENNINGTON.

BRADWELL [LNW] op 2 September 1867
(MT 29/28); clo 7 September 1964 *(RM October)*.

BRAEMORE – see BREAMORE.

BRAESIDE [NB] op early March 1916 as
CROMBIE HALT, officially for workers at Royal
Ordnance Depot, but also unauthorised public use;
officially op to public as B HALT on 1 March 1921
(Scottish Record Office NB/8/174 – H Jack);
Cl says clo August 1926 but *W Fife* does not suggest it
closed before the line – see CHARLESTOWN.

BRAFFERTON [NE] op 17 June 1847 (line date *NE*;
station included in inspection report dated 19th);
clo 25 September 1950 *(RM November)*.

BRAIDWOOD [Cal] first in tt *(Topham)* August 1848;
clo 2 July 1962 *(RM August)*.
JS: perhaps op as HARESTANES, perhaps that was
pre-op name – from *Lizar's Guide to the Caledonian*, 1848.

BRAINTREE

BRAINTREE [GE] op 2 October 1848 *(EC)*;
see 1850 August 19★★; new station on extension to
Bishops Stortford 22 February 1869 *(Cl)*; became
B & BOCKING 19 October 1910 *(hbl 27th)*, back to B
6 May 1968 tt; still open.

B FREEPORT op 8 November 1999 *(GE Society,*
quoting *Customer Services release 371)*; still open.

BRAITHWAITE [CKP] op 2 January 1865
(co ½ T 28 February- line; in op tt Cockermouth);
clo 18 April 1966 *(Cl)*.

BRAMBER [LBSC] op 1 July 1861 *(LBSC; co ½
23 January 1862- line)*; clo 7 March 1966 *(RM March)*.

BRAMBLEDOWN [SEC] first in *Brad* June 1907;
HALT; clo 4 December 1950 *(T 4th)*.

BRAMCOTE [Mid] (non-tt): private; on 1873
Distance Diagram; closed by 13 August 1894;
{Radford – Trowell} *(Mid)*.

BRAMFORD [GE] op 24 December 1846 *(EC- line)*;
original station burnt down 1 August 1911;
new on opposite, south, side of road bridge, op 1912
(GE Journal April 2001); clo 2 May 1955 *(Cl)*.

BRAMHALL [LNW]: op 24 November 1845★★;
still open.

BRAMLEY near Leeds

BRAMLEY (a) [GN] op 1 August 1854 *(GN; T 1st- line)*;
clo 4 July 1966 *(RM July)*.

BRAMLEY (b) op 12 September 1983 *(RM November)*;
still open.

BRAMLEY & WONERSH [LBSC] op 2 October
1865 *(T 3rd)*; & W added 1 June 1888 *(hbl 26 April)*;
clo 14 June 1965 *(Cl)*.

BRAMLEY HANTS [GW] op 1 May 1895 *(RCG)*;
HANTS added 1980 body of tt, index much earlier;
still open. B for SILCHESTER from 1 May 1910 *(RCG)*
to 1955 *(Brad)*.

BRAMPFORD SPEKE [GW] op 1 May 1885
(Wellington 7th); clo 1 January 1917 *(GW notice dated
22 December 1916)*; reop 1 January 1919
(GW Mag April); became HALT 1 October 1923 *(Cl)*;
clo 7 October 1963 *(W Som F P 12th)*.

BRAMPTON near Carlisle

BRAMPTON [NE] op 19 July 1836 *(NC- line; in Scott
1837; see 1836 B★★)*; still open. Op as MILTON;
renamed B 1 September 1870 *(Cl)* – according to *TTS
June 1978, p.18*, changed in tt August but official notice
says 1 September; became B JUNCTION 1885
(RCG ref January, but not in co tt until May 1885)*;
B 1 November 1891 co tt *(JS)*; B JUNCTION
1 August 1913 *(Cl)*; B CUMBERLAND 18 March
1971 *(Cl)*; by 1976 just B in body of tt; B CUMBRIA
14 May 1984 tt (index earlier). In tt in *Scott 1837* was
M for B.

B FELL [NC]: line op 19 July 1836 (see 1836 B★★);
clo ? ; unlikely any 'station' as such.

B TOWN [NE] op formally Friday 15 July 1836
(B. Webb & D. Gordon, *Lord Carlisle's Railway*, RCTS,
undated); miners' service started soon after by mine
owner (also see Section 7); initially horse-drawn from
junction to local coal depots, though on day of annual
Brampton Agricultural Show used steam engines
normally used for coal trains and borrowed coaches
from NE to carry more passengers; regular service
from proper station at Brampton began 4 July 1881;
poor support meant clo 1 May 1890 *(RM January,
February 1910)*. Reop, by NE, 1 August 1913 *(RCG)*;
clo 1 March 1917 (Thursday), reop 1 March 1920 *(Cl)*;
clo 29 October 1923 *(Cl)*.

BRAMPTON SUFFOLK [GE] op 4 December
1854 *(Ipswich Mercury 2nd, 9th*, G. Kenworthy)*;
clo 15 May 1858★★; reop 1 June 1859 *(T 2nd)*;
SUFFOLK added 1 June 1928 *(hbl April)*, dropped
14 June 1965 tt, added again to body of tt 14 May 1984
(C/W); still open.

BRAMPTON (others) – see BUCKDEN;
NEWCASTLE-UNDER-LYME; PITSFORD &
BRAMPTON.

BRAMSHOT [SR] op 10 May 1913 for golfers *(U)*;
BRAMSHOTT HALT in *hb* 1936; first in *Brad*
October 1938; clo 6 May 1946 *(Cl)*; always noted as
'platform adjoining Bramshot Golf Course', request
stop for members of golf club, available to and from
Woking direction only; not indexed; tt note was not
changed, but after mid 1939 probably used only
by people connected with camp built over it;
T 16 August 1939 item shows then that it was only
in use for workmen building Cove Militia camp.

BRAMWITH [MS&L] op 1 July 1856
(GC; T 28 June- line); clo 1 October 1866 *(Cl)*.

BRAMWITH [GN/GC] (non-tt): occasional
excursions from about 1870s to about 1901;
originally BARNBY DUN; renamed about 1888
{Hampole – Stainforth} *(GN I, p.161)*.

BRANCEPETH [NE] op 1 April 1857
(co ½ T 17 August- line); clo 4 May 1964 *(Cl)*.

BRANCHTON op 5 June 1967 as replacement for
Upper Greenock *(Cl 29)*; still open.

BRANDLESHOLME ROAD [LY] op 3 July 1905
(Manchester Guardian 30 June); see 1905★★ (b);
clo 5 May 1952 *(RM June)*.

BRANDON [GE] op 30 July 1845 *(co n T 23rd)*;
B NORFOLK from 1 July 1923 *(hbl 12th)* to 1 March
1925 *(hbl April)*; still open.

BRANDON & WOLSTON [LNW]
probably op 17 September 1838 when L&B opened
throughout; not in *Freeling* nor other very early
descriptions; is in *T 18th* – and see Hampton-in-Arden
LNW; &W added at or about time new station built,
almost same site, 29 October 1879 *(Cl; LNW Officers
recommended 11 September)*; clo 12 September 1960
(RM October).

BRANDON COLLIERY [NE] first in *Brad* July 1861,
Saturdays only; full service March 1878;
at first B SIDING/SIDINGS, became B 1 March 1878
co tt *(JS)* but 1868 *Brad*; COLLIERY added 1 July
1896 *(RCG)*; clo 4 May 1964 *(Cl)*; {in *IA* as B}.

BRANKSOME [LSW] op 1 June 1893 *(Poole 1st)*;
still open.

BRANSFORD ROAD [GW] op 1 September 1860
(GW); clo 5 April 1965 *(Cl)*

BRANSTON near Burton-on-Trent [Mid]
op 1 October 1889 *(RCG)*; clo 22 Sept. 1930 *(Mid)*.

BRANSTON & HEIGHINGTON [GN/GE]
op 1 August 1882 *(GN/GE)* as H & B; renamed 1884 tt
(JS); clo 3 November 1958 *(BRWR circular 18 October)*.

BRANSTY – see WHITEHAVEN.

BRANTHWAITE [WCE Jt] op 2 April 1866
(D&C 14); clo 13 April 1931 *(LNW Record)*.

BRASTED [SE] op 7 July 1881 *(T 8th)*;
became HALT 19 September 1955 *(Cl)*, though not
thus hb 1956; clo 30 October 1961 *(T 21 August)*.

BRATTON FLEMING [Lynton] (ng) op 16 May
1898 *(N Devon 19th- line)*; FLEMING added 1899 tt
but had been agreed June 1898 *(Cl)*; became HALT
16 June 1931 *(JS)*; clo 30 September 1935★★.

BRAUGHING [GE] op 3 July 1863 *(Hertford 4th)*;
clo 16 November 1964 *(T 14 October)*.

BRAUNSTON near Leicester [Mid] op 1 June 1850
co tt *(Mid)*; replaced by Kirby Muxloe 1 July 1859 co tt
(Mid); {map 62}.

BRAUNSTON near Rugby.

B & WILLOUGHBY [GC] op 15 March 1899
(GC; T 16th- line); op as W; became W for DAVENTRY
1 October 1899 *(hbl 26th)*, B & W for D 1 January 1904
(RCG), B & W 1922/3 *(hbl ref 25 January 1923)*;
clo 1 April 1957 *(RM May)*.

B LONDON ROAD [LNW] op 1 August 1895
(LNW Officers 36165, 36425); L R added 1 July 1950
(Cl); clo 15 September 1958 *(LNW Record)*.

BRAUNTON [LSW] op 20 July 1874 *(N Devon J
23rd)*; clo 5 October 1970 *(N Devon J 8th)*. LSW co tt
1914, *Brad* to 1955/6: B for SAUNTON SANDS.

BRAYSTONES [Fur] op 19 July 1849★★; aot request;
still open.

BRAYTON [MC]: originally a private station, op ?
(with line 2 December 1844?); op to public 1 March
1848 (D&C 14); clo 5 June 1950 (RM July);
see 1840★★; {map 20g}. Also see HEATHFIELD.

BRAYTON GATES – see SELBY.

BREADSALL [GN] op 1 April 1878 (GN);
clo 6 April 1953 (RM May).

BREAMORE [LSW] op 20 December 1866 (Som &
W J 22nd- line); clo 4 May 1964 (Hants Chron 9th).
BRAEMORE Brad until 1875 and intermittently
thus hb until 1904.

BREAN ROAD [GW] op 17 June 1929
(Bridgwater Merc 19th); HALT; clo 2 May 1955 (Cl);
{Bleadon – Brent Knoll}. GW co tt 1932 and Brad
to closure: B for B SANDS and LYMPSHAM.
GW ticket as PLATFORM (JB).

BREASTON – see SAWLEY.

BRECHIN [Cal] op 1 February 1848 (co n RM
February 1953); clo 4 August 1952 (RM September).

BRECK ROAD [LNW] op 1 July 1870 (LNW
Officers 5542); clo 31 May 1948 (LNW Record).

BRECON
See 1826★★ for early 'services'.
B WATTON [BM] op 23 April 1863 – 1 May, given by
Brad Sh was delayed formal opening (BM p.19);
replaced by >
B (FREE STREET) [BM] op 1 March 1871
(RAIL 1005/282); used by BM and Midland from
opening, Mid Wales from 1 May 1871 and N&B
from 1872; clo 31 December 1962 (T 31st).
Brad occasionally said B F S early but usually
B JOINT/B NEW JOINT; from 1917/18 plain B.
B MOUNT STREET [N&B] op 3 June 1867;
near Brecon Barracks, intended only to be temporary
(T 5th); clo 6 March 1872 – trains to Free Street
(BM p.30, N&B Gomer, supported by Brad May 1872,
which has B Joint).

BREDBURY [GC/Mid] op 1 September 1875
(GC dates); still open.

BREDICOT [Mid] op November 1845 (Mid); clo ?
(line lost stopping passenger service 1 October 1855,
but lack of mention of this station in tt suggests it might
have closed well before then);
{Spetchley – Dunhampstead, both in IA goods}.

BREDON [Mid] op 24 June 1840 (Chelt Chron 27th);
clo 4 January 1965 (Cl).

BREICH [Cal] op 9 July 1869 (T 12th- line); still open.

BREIDDEN [Shrewsbury & Welshpool]
op 27 January 1872 (co n Shrewsbury 31st) as
MIDDLETOWN; renamed M HILLS 1 June 1919
(RCG), B 1 February 1928 (hbl January);
clo 12 September 1960 (Cl).

BRENDON HILL – see 1865 September 4★★.

BRENT near Totnes [GW] probably op 15 June
1848★★; clo 5 October 1964 (Cl).

BRENT CROSS London [Nor] op 19 November
1923 (T 17th); CROSS added 20 July 1976
(RM September); still open.

BRENT KNOLL [GW] op 1 November 1875
(Weston 30 October); clo 4 January 1971 (RM January),
by when only one, up, train Mondays to Fridays only.

BRENTFORD
BRENTFORD [LSW] op 22 August 1849 (co n T 22th);
B CENTRAL 5 June 1950 (Cl) to 12 May 1980 tt
(C/W); still open.
BRENTFORD [GW] op 1 May 1860 (co n T 27 April);
clo 22 March 1915 except for workmen (GM's report
12 January 1917); reop 12 April 1920 (wtt supp);
see 1921 April/May★★; clo 4 May 1942 (hbl 17).
Both inspection report and T, 10 July 1859, description
of line, refer to Excursion Platform, beyond main GW
station; intention was to provide ferry connection to
Kew. No evidence ever actually used – perhaps swept
away in Dock changes before line op to passengers.

BRENTFORD ROAD – see GUNNERSBURY.

BRENTHAM [GW] op 1 May 1911 (RCH);
clo 1 February 1915★★; reop 29 March 1920 (Cl);
see 1921 April/May★★; for clo see 15 June 1947★★.
Opening reference in Dist op reference 11th and GW
ticket (JB) have B PLATFORM. In that op reference
and GW co tt 1932 was B for NORTH EALING;
from 1932 to closure B for N E and GREYSTOKE
PARK in Brad.

BRENTOR [LSW] op 1 June 1890 (W D Merc 2nd);
clo 6 May 1968 (Cornish & D P 11th).

BRENTWOOD [GE] op 1 July 1840 (co n T 29 June);
was B & WARLEY 1 November 1882 (Cl; RCG ref
October) to 20 February 1969 (Cl); still open.

BRETFORTON – see WESTON-SUB-EDGE.

BRETTELL LANE [GW] op 20 December 1852
(W Mid; T 20th- line); clo 30 July 1962 (RM September).
Originally BRETTEL L; later, early 1880s, both GW
and LNW co tts sometimes BRETTLE L;
RCH dist ref 12 February 1896 said BRETELL form
had been adopted.

BRICKET WOOD [LNW]: this and Park Street both
op 5 May 1858 (co n, British Railway Journal, Spring
1988); there were not enough passengers for both so
P S clo at start of June 1858; on 1 August 1858 P S
reop and B W closed except for picnic parties, who
had to give a few hours notice to station-master at
St Albans; local pressure led to reop (British Railways
Journal, Spring 1988), first in Brad July 1861. Still open.
BRICKETT W in op notice and Brad on and off
until 1878.

BRICKLAYERS ARMS – see LONDON.

BRICKYARD [LNW] (non-tt): HALT; according to
Ox & Camb company records show existence of this
¼ mile from Bow Brickhill; mentioned in connection
with halts opened 1 December 1905★★ but no other
details given.

BRIDESTOWE [LSW] op 12 October 1874
(Trewman 14th- line); HALT at clo 6 May 1968
(Cornish & D P 11th).

BRIDGE near Canterbury [SE] op 1 July 1889 (SE);
clo 1 December 1940 (Sunday) (Cl).

BRIDGE NO 16 (non-tt): see end of 1835 B★★;
note that this is in U as BRIDGE NO 60.

BRIDGE 110, 111, 130 – see under KILLIN
(GLENOGLEHEAD).

BRIDGE 774 [LNE] (non-tt): used by workmen at
least 1923–5; {Wickford – Rayleigh} (U).

BRIDGE END – see CAERGWRLE.

BRIDGE OF ALLAN

BRIDGE OF ALLAN (a) [Cal] op 1 June 1848 *(Scot Cent)*; north of overbridge; clo 1 November 1965 *(Cl)*.
BRIDGE OF ALLAN (b) op 13 May 1985 *(Rly Obs July)*; south of overbridge; still open.
BRIDGE OF DEE [GSW] op 18 April 1864 *(GSW)*; clo 26 September 1949 *(Cl)*.
BRIDGE OF DUN [Cal]: line op 1 February 1848 *(co n RM 1953)*, nd, May 1848 *(Topham)*; clo 4 September 1967 *(RM September)*. B O D JUNCTION 1849 to 1882 (index later) *(Brad)*.
BRIDGE OF EARN [NB] op 18 July 1848 *(co n, item Perthshire Courier 20th)*; re-sited ¼ mile north 1 February 1892 *(Cl)*; clo 15 June 1964 *(RM July)*.
BRIDGE OF ORCHY [NB] op 7 August 1894 *(T 7th)*; still open.
BRIDGE OF WEIR [GSW]
BRIDGE OF WEIR (a) op 20 June 1864 *(GSW)*; clo 18 May 1868 *(Cl)*.
BRIDGE OF WEIR (b) op 23 December 1869, new site, when line reop, extended to Greenock *(Cl)*; clo 10 January 1983 *(Rly Obs March)*.
BRIDGE STREET Glasgow
BRIDGE STREET [GU] op 14 December 1896★★; still open.
Also see under GLASGOW.
BRIDGEFOOT near Banff [GNS] op 1 October 1913 *(GNS)*; HALT; aot request; clo 6 July 1964 *(RM July)*; {Ladysbridge – Banff}.
BRIDGEFOOT near Workington [WCE Jt] op 2 April 1866 *(D&C 14)*; clo 13 April 1931 *(LNW Record)*.
BRIDGEFORD [GJ] op 4 July 1837 *(co n GJ)*; clo 10 September 1840★★.
Great Bridgeford here/near later.
BRIDGEND South Wales
See 1828 A★★ for possible early service.
BRIDGEND [GW] op 19 June 1850★★; still open.
BRIDGEND [Llynvi & Ogmore], terminus adjoining GW, op 25 February 1864 *(Cardiff T 26th)*; trains diverted to GW 1873 *(Cl)*.
BRIDGEND near Kirkintilloch [MK]: see 1844 December 26★★; listed by *MK* as stop on 10 December 1849 service – does not rule out earlier use; clo 10 December 1851★★; {map 16}.
BRIDGENESS [NB] (non-tt): workmen; dates ?; {beyond Bo'ness} *(U)*.
BRIDGES near St Austell – see LUXULYAN.
BRIDGETON {map 15}
BRIDGETON [Cal] op 1 April 1879 *(Cal)*; clo 1 November 1895 (Friday) *(RCG)*.
BRIDGETON [NB] op 1 June 1892 *(Glasgow)*; originally B CROSS, renamed B CENTRAL 1954, B 14 June 1965 *(Cl)*; clo 5 November 1979 *(Cl supp 2)*, when replaced by >
BRIDGETON op 5 November 1979 *(Cl supp 2)*, on the Argyle line; site of old B CROSS Cal; still open.
B CROSS [Cal] op 1 November 1895 *(RCG;T 2nd- line)*; clo 5 October 1964 *(RM November)*; see entry immediately above.

BRIDGNORTH [GW] op 1 February 1862★★; clo 9 September 1963 *(T 9th)*. Erratically BRIDGENORTH early GW co tt, *Brad, hb.*
BRIDGWATER
BRIDGWATER [GW] op 14 June 1841 *(Taunton 16th)*; still open. B GENERAL 1949/50 to 1952/3 *(Brad)*. GW co tt and *Brad* kept to BRIDGEWATER until about 1870, long after local paper had become *Bridgwater Mercury*; hb altered 1904.
B NORTH [SD Jt] op 21 July 1890 *(Bridgwater Merc 23rd)*; NORTH added 26 September 1949 *(Cl)*; clo 1 December 1952 *(Bridgwater Merc 2nd)*. Always 'Bridgwater' in tts seen although company was the 'Bridgewater'.
Both at times B for SPAXTON in *Brad*.
BRIDLINGTON [NE] op 7 October 1846★★; still open.
BRIDPORT [GW]
BRIDPORT op 12 November 1857 *(W Fly P 10th)*; clo 5 May 1975 *(Cl)*. B RADPOLE ROAD 1886/7 to 1901/2 *(Brad)*.
B EAST STREET op 31 March 1884 *(W Gaz 4 April)*; clo 1 January 1916 (Saturday) *(Cl)*; reop 7 July 1919 *(GW circ 2672)*; clo 11 April 1921; reop 11 July 1921 *(Cl)*; clo 22 September 1924, intended for winter *(GW Mag November)*; but reop 6 October 1924 *(wtt supp)*; clo 22 September 1930 *(Cl)*.
B WEST BAY: dates as EAST STREET; aot B HARBOUR *(hb)*.
BRIERDENE [NE]: built 1914 on Seaton Sluice line but idea of passenger service abandoned *(U)*.
BRIERFIELD [LY] op 1 February 1849 *(LY; co ½ T 3 February- line)* as MARSDEN; renamed 1857; still open. Aot B for MARSTON *(RCG)*.
BRIERLEY HILL [GW] op 1 December 1858 *(Brierley)*; clo 30 July 1962 *(RM September)*.
BRIERY BOBBIN MILL [LMS] (non-tt): HALT used by workers; op soon after 1922; clo 17 November 1958 – mill had ceased production a week earlier; {Threlkeld – Keswick} *(Lakeland)*.
BRIGG [GC] op 1 November 1848 *(Stamford 7th)*; still open. Became Saturdays only, three trains each way, 4 October 1993 (A. Brackenbury, *Chron January 2004*).
BRIGHAM [LNW] op 28 April 1847 *(Whitehaven Herald 1 May)*; clo 18 April 1966 *(Cl)*.
BRIGHOUSE
BRIGHOUSE (a) [LY] op 5 October 1840 *(co n Leeds 3rd)*; re-sited 15 chains west 1 May 1893 *(Cl)*; clo 5 January 1970 *(RM January)*. LY co tt 1899, LNE tt 1933 B for RASTRICK and thus at least to 1967 tt.
BRIGHOUSE (b) op 28 May 2000 *(RM July 2000)*; still open.
BRIGHTLINGSEA [GE] op 18 April 1866 *(co n Brightlingsea)*; clo 15 June 1964 *(RM July)*.
BRIGHTON [LBSC] op for Shoreham branch 12 May 1840★★; op for London trains 1841 *(T 22nd)*; was B CENTRAL 1887/8 *(Brad)*, to B 30 September 1935 *(SR)*; still open. Pre-1887 *Brad* had B GENERAL, in Kemp Town table only.
BRIGHTON ROAD [Mid] op 1 November 1875 *(Mid)*; clo 27 January 1941 *(Mid)*.

BRIGHTSIDE [Mid] op 1 November 1838 *(Mid)*;
new station 29 May 1898 *(Mid)*; clo 30 January 1995
(BLN 745).

BRILL

BRILL [Met/GC] op March 1872 (see 1871★★);
Met use from 1 December 1899; clo 1 December 1935
(Sunday) *(RCH)*.

B & LUDGERSHALL [GW] op 1 July 1910
(RCG; co ½ T 6 August- line); clo 7 January 1963 *(Cl)*.

BRIMINGTON [GC] op 4 June 1892 *(RCG)* as
SHEEPBRIDGE & B; renamed 18 June 1951 *(Cl)*;
clo 2 January 1956 *(Cl)*.
Hb 1894a: S & BRIMMINGTON; corrected 1904.

BRIMLEY [GW] op 21 May 1928 *(GW H)*; HALT;
clo 2 March 1959 *(Express & E 2nd)*;
{Bovey – Heathfield}.

BRIMSCOMBE [GW]

BRIMSCOMBE op 1 June 1845 *(co n Bristol T 10 May)*;
clo 2 November 1964 *(W D Press 2nd)*.
At first BRIMSCOMB; became B near CHALFORD
1850/1, BRIMSCOMBE for C 1890/1 *(Brad)*.
GW co tts followed same general pattern but had
added final 'E' by 1874. *Hb* added 'E' 1904, no
additions to name.

B BRIDGE op 1 February 1904 *(Stroud N 5th)*;
HALT; clo 2 November 1964 *(W D Press 2nd)*.

BRIMSDOWN [GE] op 1 October 1884 *(L)*;
still open. Became B for ENFIELD HIGHWAY
1 November 1910 *(hbl 26 January 1911)*;
thus GE co tt 1914, LNE tt 1933 and *Brad* to 1955.

BRIMSTONE BOTTOM [MSWJ] (non-tt):
workmen; dates ?; {Ludgershall – Tidworth} *(U)*.

BRINDLE HEATH [LY] (non-tt): races, certainly
1913 and 1934 *(U)* (but only horses and attendants –
AB); *hbl ref 12 July 1917* said had been renamed
PENDLETON B H: {Pendleton – Clifton Junction}.

BRINDLEY HEATH [LMS] op 3 August 1939 for
Bank Holiday specials from Air Force Base, returning
17 August; op to public 26 August 1939 *(LNW Record)*;
clo 6 April 1959 *(RM May)*; {Hednesford – Rugeley}.

BRINKBURN [NB] op 1 November 1870 *(Nhumb)*;
HALT at clo 15 September 1952★★.

BRINKLOW [LNW] op 1 December 1847 *(W Mid)*
as STRETTON; renamed 1 January 1870 *(Cl)*
but 1 February 1870 *(LNW dates)* – had been
recommended by *LNW Officers 15 December 1869*;
clo 16 September 1957 *(LNW Record)*.

BRINKWORTH [GW] op 1 July 1903 *(Bristol T 2nd)*;
clo 3 April 1961 *(RM May)*.

BRINNINGTON op 12 December 1977
(RM February 1978); still open.

BRINSCALL [LU/LY] op 1 December 1869★★;
clo 4 January 1960 *(RM February)*.

BRISCO [Lancaster & Carlisle] op 17 December
1846 *(D&C 14)*; last in *Brad* December 1852,
replaced by Wreay, to south.

BRISLINGTON [GW] op 3 September 1873
(Bristol T 4th- line); clo 2 November 1959 *(Shepton 6th)*.

BRISTOL {map 121}.

B PARKWAY op 1 May 1972 *(T 26th)*; still open.

B ST PHILIPS [Mid] op 2 May 1870 *(Bristol T 3rd)*;

clo 21 September 1953 *(W D Press 21st)*. At opening
local press referred to station at Whipping-cat-hill.

B TEMPLE MEADS [GW/Mid]:
B [GW] op 31 August 1840 *(Bristol Stand 3 September)*;
also used by BE, with reversal, when it opened its line
to Bridgwater 14 June 1841.
[BE] op own station, adjoining, but at right angles in
1845 (reported nearly complete about August 1845,
GW); through platform also added then.
Main part became Joint GW/Mid 19 June 1865
(BE also partner later). Rebuilt as one, completed
1 January 1878. T STREET/MEAD/MEADS added
in different sources at different times; see *Section 3,
The information obtained, Names* for fuller treatment.
Original terminal portion clo 6 September 1965 *(Cl)*.
Through part still open.
Non-tt: winter 1949 and summer 1957 wtts include
stops for staff at DOCTOR DAYS BRIDGE
JUNCTION (for signalman?); MARSH POND
{Carriage sidings on line to Brislington, near St Philips
Marsh}; ST PHILIPS MARSH {goods *IA*}; STOKE
GIFFORD {marshalling yard, site later used for Bristol
Parkway}. Trains concerned were mixture of specials
and ones publicly advertised between Lawrence Hill
and Filton Junction stations. Start and end not known
but public tt shows trains fitting this pattern by July
1939 (not October 1937) and contains them still in tt
beginning 10 September 1962. According to an old
Bath Road driver (via B. Wilson) there were no
platforms and service had begun before public
admitted to Lawrence Hill – Filton Junction section.

BRISTOL ROAD Weston-super-Mare [WCP] first in
Brad July 1912; clo 20 May 1940 *(Bridgwater Merc 22nd)*.
Ticket for B R (Worle) *(JB)*.

BRITANNIA near Bacup [LY] op 1 December 1881
(LY); clo 2 April 1917 *(Cl)*; later workmen's use *(U)*.

BRITANNIA [GW] (non-tt): HALT;
Naval College and workmen at least 1902 to 1917 *(U)*
as STEAM FERRY CROSSING; summer 1949, 1953
and 1957 wtts show several trains calling for Royal
Navy personnel at KINGSWEAR CROSSING;
by summer 1959 had become B CROSSING and calls
shown at least until 15 June to 10 September 1962 wtt;
see 1972 November 1★★. {Churston – Kingswear}.

BRITANNIA BRIDGE [LNW] first in *Brad* July
1851; replaced by Menai Bridge 1 October 1858
(co n Carnarvon 25 September).

BRITHDIR [Rhy] first in *Brad* May 1871;
GEORGE INN until 1 October 1891 *(hbl 29th)*;
still open.

BRITISH MUSEUM [Cen] op 30 July 1900
(L; T 25th- line); replaced by Holborn Kingsway
25 September 1933 *(Cl)*.

BRITISH RHONDDA [GW] op 27 August 1906
(wtt supp); HALT; platform on down side only – up
trains had to reverse across to it; replaced 1 May 1911
by Pontwalby, 18 chains to the north *(Cl)*

BRITISH STEEL – see REDCAR.

BRITON FERRY {map 85}.

BRITON FERRY op 1 June 1994 *(Rly Obs August)*;
2 chains nearer Neath than old B F West, below; still open.

B F EAST [RSB] op 14 March 1895 *(GW; Colliery 22nd-line)*; EAST added 1 July 1924 *(GW circular 18 June)* >
B F WEST [GW] op 2 September 1850 *(The Cambrian 30 August)*; WEST added 1 July 1924 *(GW circular 18 June)* >
Services for EAST and WEST diverted to new
BRITON FERRY [GW], 616 yds nearer Neath than old West, 16 September 1935 *(GW notice NW 1082)*; this clo 2 November 1964 *(Cl)*.
Also see 1865★★.
BRITON FERRY ROAD [GW] op 1 August 1863 *(GW; co ½ T 17 August- line)*; clo 1 March 1873 (Saturday), reop 1 October 1880 *(RAIL 1005/282)*; clo 28 September 1936 *(T 14th)*.
BRIXHAM [GW] op 27 February 1868 *(S Devon Minutes 28th, RAIL 631/8)* ★; clo 12 February 1951, reop 9 April 1951 (see 1951★★) *(Rly Obs* May via A. Brackenbury, *Chron July 2003)*; clo 13 May 1963 *(RM June)*. Pre op B TOWN *(GW ac)*.
★ = free trips formal opening day, 1 January 1868 – inspection problems delayed public op *(Brixham)*.
BRIXHAM ROAD – see CHURSTON.
BRIXTON
BRIXTON [LCD] op 6 October 1862 *(T 7th)*; see 1866★★; B & SOUTH STOCKWELL 1 May 1863 to 9 July 1934 *(L)*; still open.
BRIXTON [Vic] op 23 July 1971 *(T 24th)*; still open. Also see EAST BRIXTON.
BRIXTON ROAD Plymouth [GW] op 17 January 1898★★; finally clo 6 October 1947.
BRIXWORTH [LNW] op 16 February 1859 *(LNW- line)*; clo 4 January 1960 *(RM February)*.
BRIZE NORTON & BAMPTON [GW] op 15 January 1873 *(Chelt Exp 18th)* as BAMPTON; became BAMPTON OXON 1884 *(RCG ref October)* but *Brad* 1906/7, B N & B 1 May 1940 *(Cl)*; clo 18 June 1962 *(T 18 May)*.
B N for BAMPTON in *Chelt Exp*.
BROAD CLYST [LSW] op 19 July 1860★★; clo 7 March 1966 *(Chard 3rd)*.
At first BROADCLYST in *hb* – *hbl* ref *26 April 1923* said name now two words but always thus in *Brad*.
BROAD GREEN [LNW]: line op 17 September 1830★★, nd, 1 March 1831 co tt; still open.
BROAD LANE – see BLOXWICH NORTH.
BROAD MARSTON [GW] op 17 October 1904 *(GW H)*, but not in *Brad* until February 1905; HALT; clo 14 July 1916 (Friday) *(RCH)*; {Honeybourne – Long Marston}.
BROAD STREET – see LONDON.
BROADBOTTOM [GC] op 11 December 1842★★ as B; became MOTTRAM 1845 tt *(Cl)*, M & B 1 July 1884 *(Cl; RCG ref July)*, B for CHARLESWORTH 1 January 1954 *(JS)*, B 1955 *(Brad)*; still open.
BROADFIELD [LY] op 13 September 1869 *(LY corr)*; clo 5 October 1970 *(Cl)*.
BROADHEATH ALTRINCHAM [LNW] op 1 November 1853★★ as A; variously B A, A B, B in different sources 1850s to 1880s, including LNW co tts; renamed (settled?) 25 February 1884 *(LNW dates)*; clo 10 September 1962 *(Cl)*.

BROADLEY [LY] op 1 November 1870 *(LY- line)*; clo 16 June 1947★★.
BROADSANDS [GW] (non-tt): excursions; summers 1928 and 1929; {Paignton – Brixham} *(U)*.
BROADSTAIRS [LCD] op 5 October 1863 *(LCD; T 5th- line)*; still open.
BROADSTONE near Poole [LSW] op 2 December 1872 *(Dorset Chron 5th)*; initially POOLE, then variations of P and B with/without JUNCTION/NEW, then B DORSET, settled as B 1956; clo 7 March 1966 *(Shepton 11th)*.
BROADSTONE near Clevedon [WCP]: *RCG ref* December 1917, but not in *Brad* until July or August 1918; aot request; clo 20 May 1940 *(Bridgwater Merc 22nd)*; {Kingston Road – Ham Lane}.
BROADWAY near Stratford-upon-Avon [GW] op 1 August 1904 *(Chelt Chron 30 July)*; clo 7 March 1960 *(RM April)*.
BROADWAY/BROADWEY near Weymouth – see UPWEY.
BROCK [LNW] first in *Brad* August 1849 as replacement for Roebuck (see note there); clo 1 May 1939 *(T 27 April)*.
BROCKENHURST [LSW] op 1 June 1847 *(Dorset Cron 20 May, 3 June)*; still open.
Became B & LYMINGTON 1847, B 1849, B JUNCTION 1856/9, B 1887/9 in *Brad*, which called it BROKENHURST until 1849 and from 1876/7 to 1887/9. *Topham*: BROKENHURST & LYMINGEN 1848, corrected by 1850.
BROCKETSBRAE [Cal] op 1 December 1866 *(Cal)*; was LESMAHAGOW 1 June 1869 *(Cl)* to 1 June 1905 *(RCG)*; clo 1 October 1951 *(RM November)*. At first BROCKETS BRAE *(hb)*.
BROCKFORD & WETHERINGSETT [Mid-Suffolk Light] op 29 September 1908 *(T 28th- line)*; clo 28 July 1952 *(T 28th)*.
BROCKHOLES [LY]: line op 1 July 1850 *(T 8th)*, nd, January 1851; still open. B JUNCTION in some tables at least 1851 to 1878 *(Brad)*.
BROCKHURST – see FORT BROCKHURST.
BROCKLEBANK DOCK [LO] op 6 March 1893★★; clo 31 December 1956 *(T 29 September)*.
BROCKLESBY [GC] op 1 November 1848 *(GC; Stamford 7th- line)*; clo 4 October 1993 *(BLN 715)*.
BROCKLEY [LBSC] op 6 March 1871 *(L)*; still open. LBSC co tt 1912 and *Brad* ? to 1955/6: B for UPPER NEW CROSS and NUNHEAD.
BROCKLEY LANE [LCD] first in *Brad* June 1872: clo 1 January 1917 *(T 28 December 1916)*.
BROCKLEY WHINS {maps 24, 25}.
BROCKLEY WHINS (a) [Brandling Junction]: 9 March 1840 to 19 June 1844 there was a platform just west of later station, used solely for dividing/joining trains from/to South Shields, Gateshead and Wearmouth (see *NE pp. 415–6)*. Mentioned in *Robinson August 1841*: 'To prevent disappointment in case the trains [from Wearmouth] should not arrive at Brockley Whinns in time for the Brandling Junction trains, spare engines and carriages will be kept at that station, to convey passengers to their respective destinations'.

BROCKLEY WHINS (b) [NE] op 19 June 1844 *(NE)*; sometimes BW JUNCTION in *Brad* when it was part of East Coast Main Line; was BOLDON COLLIERY 1 March 1926 *(hbl April)* to 8 July 1991 tt *(AB Chron)* > New down platform March 2002 *(Rly Obs June)*; all transferred to [TWM] 31 March 2002**; still open.

BROCKMOOR [GW] op 11 May 1925 *(RM June)*; HALT; clo 31 October 1932 *(RM January 1933)*; {map 96}. Pre-op: Moor Lane *(RAC)*.

BROCKWEIR [GW] op 19 August 1929 *(co n dated 'August')*; HALT; clo 5 January 1959 *(T 5th)*; {Tintern – St Briavels}.

BRODIE [High] op 22 December 1857 *(High)*; clo 3 May 1965 *(RM June)*.

BRODSWORTH COLLIERY [GC/GN] (non-tt): miners; dates ?; {branch from Carcroft} *(U)*.

BROMBOROUGH
BROMBOROUGH [Birkenhead] first in *Brad* June 1846; still open.
B RAKE op 30 September 1985 *(Birkenhead)*; still open.
BROMFIELD near Carlisle [Cal] op 1 March 1873 *(RCG)*; BROOMFIELD until 1 November 1895 *(RCG)*; aot request; for clo see 1921 April/May**.
BROMFIELD near Ludlow [SH Jt] op 21 April 1852 *(co ½ T 17 August- line)*; clo 9 June 1958 *(Cl)*; later race use, e.g. 22 September 1960 *(BR handbill)* and 29 April 1965 from Manchester *(AB)*.
BROMFLEET – see BROOMFLEET.

BROMFORD FORGE
BROMFORD FORGE [Birmingham & Derby Junction] op 16 May 1842 *(W Mid)*; last in *Brad* May 1843; {map 99}.
B BRIDGE RACECOURSE [Mid], same site as above, op 9 March 1896 *(RCG)*; in *hb* 1904–56, for race traffic only; racecourse clo 28 June 1965 *(RM July)*, station perhaps earlier – excursion leaflets April & May 1965 were for New Street and Snow Hill *(AB)*.
BROMHAM & ROWDE [GW] op 22 February 1909 *(RAIL 253/482)*; HALT (thus *Brad* and GW co tt 1932, but staffed until 5 November 1951, *Cl*); clo 18 April 1966 *(RM May)*. Wraggs Wharf pre op *(RAC)*

BROMLEY near Dudley [GW] op 11 May 1925 *(RM June)*; HALT; clo 31 October 1932 *(RM January 1933)*; {map 96}.

BROMLEY South London
B NORTH [SE] op 1 January 1878 *(L)*; NORTH added 1 June 1899 *(hbl 13 July)*; still open.
B SOUTH [LCD]: op 5 July 1858 *(Bromley Record, monthly, 2 August*; both *Brad* and *Intelligible tt* showed this station with first entry for line and left it there); SOUTH added 1 June 1899 *(hbl 13 July)*; still open.
BROMLEY CROSS near Bolton [LY] op 12 June 1848 *(LY; RAIL 1005/265- line)*; still open.

BROMLEY-BY-BOW
BROMLEY-BY-BOW op by [LTS] 31 March 1858 *(co n T 30th)*; re-sited about 6 chains west 1 March 1894 *(L)* – fire had badly damaged station 20 October 1892; new platforms were west of St Leonards Road, buildings on old site, connected to new platforms by subway under road.

[Dist] service began 2 June 1902, [Met] 30 March 1936; main line service clo 27 October 1940; -by-B added 1967; transferred to LPTB 1 January 1969; still open. Also see SOUTH BROMLEY.

BROMPTON near Northallerton [NE] op 25 May 1852**; clo 6 September 1965 *(Cl)*.

BROMPTON ROAD London
BROMPTON ROAD [Picc] op 15 December 1906 *(co n T 14th)*; clo 14 May 1926 by General Strike; unlike others, did not reop until 4 October 1926 *(T 4th; Clay)*; clo 30 July 1934 *(Cl)*; {South Kensington – Knightsbridge}.
Also see GLOUCESTER ROAD.
BROMPTON ROAD – see CATTERICK.

BROMSGROVE [Mid] op 24 June 1840 *(Chelt Chron 27th)*; still open.

BROMSHALL [NS] op 7 August 1848**?; clo 1 January 1866 *(Cl)*.

BROMSHALL CROSSING [LMS] (non-tt): op 14 May 1942; clo September 1942; workmen building Ordnance Depot; {Leigh – Uttoxeter} *(WW II)*.

BROMYARD [GW] op 22 October 1877 *(Berrows 27th)*; clo 7 September 1964 *(Cl)*.

BRONDESBURY [LNW]
BRONDESBURY op 2 January 1860 *(T 2nd)* as EDGEWARE ROAD KILBURN; became EDGWARE ROAD 1 November 1865 *(JS, from company minutes)*, E R & B 1 January 1872 *(L; LNW Officers recommended 13 December 1871)*, B E R 1 January 1873 *(L)*, B 1 May 1883 *(L)*; still open.
B PARK op 1 June 1908 *(LNW Officers 42316)*; still open.

BRONGWYN – see BRYNGWYN.

BRONWYDD ARMS [GW] first in *Brad* October 1861; clo 22 February 1965 *(Cl)*.

BROOK STREET [GW] op 1 May 1905 *(GW H)*; HALT; clo 22 March 1915**; {map 75}.

BROOKFIELD [MC] temp term op 2 December 1844 *(D&C 14)*; clo 10 February 1845 when line extended to Low Row *(Cl)*; see 1840**; {map 20g}.

BROOKHAY [South Staffordshire] first trains shown in *Brad* June 1849; last December 1849.

BROOKLAND [SE] op 7 December 1881 *(SR)*; HALT at clo 6 March 1967 *(RM April)* – shown as halt in *Brad* 1923/4 to 1934/5 and from 1954.

BROOKLANDS
BROOKLANDS (a) [MSJA] op 1 December 1859 *(MSJA)*; clo 27 December 1991 *(BLN 671)* for conversion >
BROOKLANDS (b) [Manch] op 15 June 1992 *(RM August)*; still open.

BROOKMANS PARK [LNE] op 19 July 1926 *(T 13th)*; still open.

BROOKSBY [Mid] op 1 September 1846 *(Mid)*; clo 3 July 1961 *(RM August)*.

BROOKWOOD
BROOKWOOD [LSW] op 1 June 1864 *(SR corr)*; still open. At first B WOKING NECROPOLIS, became B N 1868 (and thus LSW co tt 1914), B 1916 *(Brad)*, B for BISLEY CAMP March 1930 *(hbl 29 April)* to 1955 *(Brad)*.

B CEMETERY [Brookwood Necropolis]:
special train for consecration 7 November 1854;
op for use 13 November 1854; clo 15 May 1941;
served by trains carrying funeral parties from special
station near Waterloo; separate NORTHERN
(Nonconformist and Roman Catholic) and
SOUTHERN (Church of England) stations.
(See J.M. Clarke, *The Brookwook Necropolis Railway*,
Oakwood, 1995.)

BROOM CRAIG: see under LARGS.

BROOM JUNCTION [Mid/SMJ] op 2 June 1879 as
unadvertised exchange – covered by *Stratford 6th*, which
says there was a building for use of those changing there
but 'the natives have to go to Wixford or Salford Priors
to get their tickets before they can get into the train on
their own platform'; made public 1 November 1880
(Mid); clo 1 October 1962, but buses to 17 June 1963
(Cl). At first B in *hb*, corrected 1908a.

BROOME [LNW] op 6 March 1861
(D&C 11; Hereford J 13th- line); aot request; still open.
At first BROOM; then BROOME & ASTON 1863/4
to 1867 *(Brad)*.

BROOMFIELD ROAD [Cal] op 1 November 1865
(co ½ T 3 November- line); initially both ways; reduced to
trains towards Montrose only August 1868/July 1869 tt;
last in tt November 1877; {physical junction *IA*}.
Sometimes B R JUNCTION *Brad, hb*.

BROOMFLEET [NE]: see 1840 July 2**; first
specific mention *Tuck* about June 1843; originally
market days (Tuesday) only; at first BROMFLUT,
then BROMFLEET in *Brad*, altered 1851 tt *(Cl)*;
see note for possible short closures; full use October
1907 *(Brad)*; aot request; still open.

BROOMHILL near Aviemore [High] op 3 August
1863 *(High)*; clo 18 October 1965**.
LMS tt 1930, *Murray* 1948 and *Brad* to 1955:
B for NETHY BRIDGE.

BROOMHILL near Alnmouth

BROOMHILL [NE] op 2 June 1879 ? (see Amble);
clo 7 July 1930 *(Cl)*.
Non-tt: miners' service Broomhill Colliery to Amble
about 1894 to 1927. Exact details of sites used unknown
(see B. Rippon, *The Amble Branch*, Kestrel, 2007).

BROOMHOPE [NB] (non-tt): platform for Vickers
weapon-testing site, early 1900s to 1952;
{Reedsmouth – Woodburn, just south of Hindhaugh}
(Sewell).

BROOMHOUSE [NB] first in *Brad* December 1878;
clo 1 January 1917 *(RM February)*; reop 2 June 1919
(RCH); clo 26 September 1927 (based on *Cl*, who has
24th, a Saturday, probably last day).

BROOMIEKNOWE [NB] op 15 April 1867
(Edin; T 18th- line) as BONNYRIGG;
renamed 1 August 1868 *(Cl)*; clo 1 January 1917
(RM February); reop 1 April 1919 *(RCH)*;
clo 10 September 1951 *(RM October)*.

BROOMIELAW [NE; LNE]: private use from 8 July
1856 *(U)*; op to public 9 June 1942 *(Cl 29*; first shown
'P' *hb* 1944a); clo 30 November 1964 *(RM December)*.

BROOMIELAW HARBOUR: this was the
terminus of the Polloc & Govan, from Rutherglen.

According to *Cal* it opened 1842 to goods and
'unknown' to passengers, implying that there was
a passenger service. According to *D&C 6* its formal
opening was 22 August 1840 and it remained 'little
more than a colliery tramway'. The *Returns* always
show it as not used for passemgers. In 1846 it became
part of the Caledonian; part of its track was lifted as
a result of an Act of 1867. If any passenger service
was operated (some sort of workmen's?), it would
have been very short-lived. It was on the south bank
of the Clyde, between the General Terminus and the
line to Glasgow Central HL.

BROOMLEE [NB] op 4 July 1864 *(Selkirk 7th)* as
WEST LINTON (but just L in paper); renamed
October 1864 *(Brad; RCG ref October)*; clo 1 April
1933**. NB co tt 1900, LNE tt 1933: B for W L.

BRORA [High] op 1 November 1870**; still open.

BROTHERTON [NB] (non-tt):
trains could be stopped on written request of Mrs Scott;
order could only be given by stationmasters at
Johnshaven and (Inver)Bervie, either side; in use 1901
(NBR Study Group Journal 73).

BROTTON [NE] op 1 April 1875 *(NE- line)*;
clo 2 May 1960 *(RM June)*.

BROUGH [NE] op 2 July 1840 *(Hull- line)*;
re-sited east of footbridge 1904; still open.

BROUGHTON near Peebles [Cal] op 6 November
1860**; clo 5 June 1950 *(RM July)*.

BROUGHTON near Preston [LPJ] op 26 June 1840
(LPJ); clo about November 1840 *(LPJ)*; replaced by
station later renamed Barton & Broughton.

BROUGHTON & BRETTON [LNW]
op 14 August 1849 *(D&C 11; co ½ T 16 August- line)*;
op as BROUGHTON; became BROUGHTON HALL
1861 *(Cl)*, B & B 1 July 1908 *(hbl 23 April)*;
clo 30 April 1962 *(RM June)*; workmen used until
9 September 1963 *(wtt, B Pask, TTS February 1966, p. 47)*.

BROUGHTON ASTLEY [Mid] op 30 June 1840
(Mid; co n T 27th- line); clo 1 January 1962 *(RM Feb.)*.
ASTLEY was only intermittently included in name in
the 1840s; comparison of tables suggests that limitation
of space was responsible; it was dropped again
1 October 1870 co tt *(Mid)* – but already 1868/9 in *Brad*,
where the change (index as well as body) coincided with
transfer to a separate local table; it was restored
15 September 1879 *(Mid)*; sometimes hyphenated

BROUGHTON CROSS [LNW]: op 28 April 1847
(Whitehaven Herald 1 May); clo 2 March 1942
(LNW Record). B C for GREYSOUTHERN in op
notice, paper cited, and thus *Brad* to closure.

BROUGHTON GIFFORD [GW] op 29 October
1905 *(GW H)*; HALT; clo 7 February 1955 *(Cl)*.

BROUGHTON LANE [GC] op 1 August 1864
(GC); clo 3 April 1956 (Tuesday) *(supplement to Brad)*
– trainless Bank Holiday intervened.

BROUGHTON SKEOG [PPW Jt]: orders to provide
station given in co minutes 21 December 1877;
first in *Brad* May 1878 – a little late?
Last in *Brad* November 1885; aot request; {map 17}.
In *hb* 1883 as B S SIDINGS (but 'P' only facilities);
1890 no facilities shown; 1895 no entry.

BROUGHTON-IN-FURNESS [Fur]
op by 26 February 1848 (see 1846 August★★); original
was a terminus, used by coast line trains and requiring
reversal; replaced by through station on Coniston
branch 1 June 1859 *(Cl)*; -in-F added 1928 tt
(Cl; hbl ref April); clo 6 October 1958 *(Cl)*.

BROUGHTY FERRY {map 4} [DA]
BROUGHTY FERRY (on main line): op 8 October
1838★★; still open.
BROUGHTY PIER (on branch): op 17 May 1848
(Dundee); its branch originally faced Dundee; diverted
1 May 1851 to face Forfar; clo 1 June 1878 (Saturday),
replaced by Tay Bridge; reop 1 Feb 1880, following
collapse of first bridge; clo 20 June 1887 when
replacement bridge opened.
At first all national tts seen called both just B F;
aot *hb* had third station, B F JUNCTION, presumably
branch platforms at main line station. Local tts and *hb*
just B at first and NB ticket thus *(JB)*.

BROWNDOWN [LSW] op 12 May 1894 *(Hants Teleg
19th)*; clo 31 August 1914, reop 1 October 1914 *(Cl)*;
aot request; became HALT 1910 *(Brad)* and in *hb*
1910a 'cancelled' (at that time halts not included there);
clo 1 May 1930 (Thursday) *(Cl)*.

BROWNHILLS
BROWNHILLS [LNW]: first trains shown in *Brad* June
1849; B HIGH STREET 2 June 1924 *(Rly Gaz 23 May)*
to 1 August 1930 *(hbl 22 October)*;
clo 18 January 1965 *(RM March)*.
B WATLING STREET [Mid] op 1 July 1884 *(Mid)*;
W S added 2 June 1924 *(Rly Gaz 23 May)*;
clo 31 March 1930 *(Mid)*.
BROXBOURNE [GE] op 15 September 1840 *(T 16th)*;
B & HODDESDON from 1 March 1900 *(hbl 26 April)*
to 4 May 1970 tt; re-sited 100 yards north 3 November
1960 (A. Brackenbury, *Chron October 2008*); still open.
Aot B JUNCTION (1850/2 to ?), B for H *(Brad)*;
B for H and HAILEYBURY (e.g. GE co tt 1882).

BROXBURN
BROXBURN [EG] first in *Brad* August 1843; last
October 1844; back June 1848; clo 12 November 1849
(Cl); {Ratho – Linlithgow}. Possibly also passenger
services by goods trains – see 1842 February 21★★.
Also see DRUMSHORELAND.
BROXTON [LNW] op 1 October 1872
(Whitchurch 5th); clo 16 September 1957 *(RM October)*.
BRUCE GROVE [GE] op 22 July 1872 *(L)*; still open.
Aot B G for TOTTENHAM *(hb* 1877 to 1904),
B G (T) *(Brad,* index only, 1875 to 1891/2).

BRUCKLAY [GNS]
BRUCKLAY op 24 April 1865 *(GNS)*;
clo 4 October 1965 *(Rly Obs November)*.
Also see MAUD.

BRUNDALL
BRUNDALL [GE] op 1 May 1844 *(T 14th- line)*;
still open.
B GARDENS [LNE] op 1 August 1924 (notice *Eastern
Daily Press*, 1 August – 'is now open' – G. Kenworthy);
HALT in *hb*, and tt until 6 May 1968; still open.
Tt in *Norwich Mercury* of 27 April 1844 showed
SURLINGHAM FERRY, 5 miles from Norwich,

on this site; a reference in the same paper in May says
'not in use' so it may be that this never opened
(G. Dow, *First Railway in Norfolk*, LNER pub, 1947 ed;
J.M. Cooper, *GE Journal April 1993)*; was included in
inspection report dated 12 April 1844.

BRUNSTANE op 3 June 2002, formal next day
(RM August); still open.

BRUNSWICK
For terminus see LIVERPOOL.
BRUNSWICK op 9 March 1998 *(RM May)*; still open.
B DOCK [LO] op 6 March 1893★★;
clo 31 December 1956 *(T 29 September)*.

BRUTON [GW] op 1 September 1856 *(Wells 6th)*;
still open.

BRYMBO {map 75}
BRYMBO [WMCQ] op 1 August 1889 *(RCG)*;
clo 1 March 1917 (Thursday) *(RCG)*.
BRYMBO [GW] op 24 May 1882 *(D&C 11*, which
also says perhaps earlier brief use about 1866);
clo 27 March 1950 *(RM May)*.
B WEST CROSSING [GW]
op 20 March 1905 *(GW H)*; HALT;
clo 1 January 1931 (Thursday) *(T 20 December 1930)*.
BRYN near Maesteg [PT] op 14 February 1898
(GW- line); clo 11 September 1933 *(Cl)*.
BRYN near Wigan [LNW] op 15 November 1869★★,
still open. Op as BRYNN; became BRYNN for
ASHTON-IN-MAKERFIELD 20 November 1899★
(LNW dates), BRYN for A-in-M 18 December 1906★
(LNW dates), B 5 May 1975 *(RM July)*.
★ = perhaps date recommended by LNW Officers.
BRYN TEIFY [GW] first in *Brad* August 1869
as CROSS INN LLANFIHANGEL;
renamed NEW QUAY ROAD 1874 *(Cl; RCG ref July)*,
BT 20 October 1916 *(hbl 12 July 1917)*;
clo 22 February 1965 *(Cl)*.
BRYN-Y-GWYNON [GW] (non-tt), alias BRYNNA:
PLATFORM; miners; agreement for provision made
4 April 1918 *(GM's report 11th)*; clo ?;
{Llanharan – Pencoed}.

BRYNAMMAN
B EAST [Mid] op 2 March 1868 *(Mid)*; EAST added
1950 *(Mid)*; clo 25 September 1950 *(Mid)*.
B WEST [GW] op 20 March 1865 *(co n Carmarthen
17th)*; WEST added 1950 *(Cl)*; clo 18 August 1958
(T 11th). RCH evidence suggests no GW station until
1890s but press, 1865, refers to a station and one is
shown on LNW plan for 1872 (printed 1873) at
Carmarthen Record Office; J.H. Davies, *History of
Pontardawe and District*, V. Davies, Llandybie, 1967,
refers to new GW station 25 June 1886 – perhaps slight
extension of line?

BRYNCELYNOG [GW] op 13 March 1939
(co n dated 'March'); HALT; clo 4 January 1960
(RM March); {Cwm Prysor – Trawsfynnydd}.

BRYNDERWEN – see TALYLLYN.
BRYNGLAS [Tallyllyn] (ng) first in *Brad* July 1872;
see 6 October 1950★★ *(Cl)*.

BRYNGWYN [NWNG] (ng) op 15 August 1877
(NGSC2; Rtn- line); clo 1 January 1914 *(Cl)*.

BRYNGWYN near Llangymynech [Cam] first in *Brad* May 1865, Wednesdays and Thursdays only; full use June 1867; originally BRONGWYN; became BRYNGWYN FLAG STATION 1869/70, B 1877/8 *(Brad)*, when moved from notes to table; aot request; shown as HALT in *hb* 1938 and 1956, but not in tt; clo 18 January 1965 *(RM March)*.

BRYNKIR [LNW] op 2 September 1867** *(co ½ T 10 Oct.- line)*; clo 7 December 1964 *(RM March 1965)*.

BRYNMAWR [LNW] op 1 October 1862**; clo 30 April 1962 *(T 6 April)*. LNW co tt: 1864 to 1882 at least B for NANTYGLO/B for N and BLAINA.

BRYNMENYN [GW] op 12 May 1873 *(co ½ T 7 Aug.- line)*; originally BRYNMENIN (thus *Brad*, *hb* until 1890 and GW co tt 1874), altered 1886 *(Cl; RCH dist ref 26 May 1886)*; clo 5 May 1958 *(RM June)*.

BRYNMILL [SIT]: line op 25 July 1860**, nd, May 1866; op as WATER WORKS /WATERWORKS ROAD; renamed BRYN MILL ROAD 1878 (Dickson), 1885 (SIT) in tts in *The Cambrian*, BRYNMILL ROAD 1885/6, B 1893/4 *(Brad)*; clo 6 January 1960**; {map 88}.

BRYNTEG COLLIERY [N&B] (non-tt) alias B & NANTYCEFN: HALT; miners; in use 1930; {Dillwyn – Seven Sisters} *(U)*.

BUBWITH [NE]
BUBWITH : op 1 August 1848**; clo 20 September 1954 *(RM October)*; later excur *(U)*.
B HIGH FIELD – see HIGH FIELD.

BUCHANAN STREET
B S [GU] op 14 December 1896**; still open. For terminus see GLASGOW.

BUCHANSTONE [GNS] op 1 December 1854 *(GNS)*; clo 1 October 1866 *(GNS)*; {Oyne – Insch}.

BUCHLYVIE [NB] op 26 May 1856**; clo 1 October 1951 *(RM November)*.

BUCKDEN [Mid] op 1 March 1866 *(Mid; co n T 27 February- line)* as BRAMPTON; renamed 1 February 1868 *(Mid)*; clo 15 June 1959 *(RM July)*.

BUCKENHAM [GE] op 1 May 1844 *(T 14 April- line*; included in inspection report); aot request; from 20 May 2007 tt reduced to Saturday and Sunday only; still open.

BUCKFASTLEIGH [GW] op 1 May 1872 *(Trewman 8th)*; clo 3 November 1958 *(RM December)*.

BUCKHAVEN [NB] op 8 August 1881 *(Fifeshire Journal 11th)*; clo 10 January 1955 *(T 28 December 1954)*.

BUCKHILL COLLIERY [CW Jc] (non-tt): HALT; miners; early 1920s? *(U)*. See photograph in *Cumbrian Railways* by J. Marsh & J. Garrett, Sutton, 1999, which shows passenger train at platform; {Camerton – Great Broughton}.

BUCKHURST HILL op by [GE] 22 August 1856 *(L; co n T 22nd- line)*; transferred to [Cen] 21 November 1948 *(T 20th)*; still open.

BUCKIE
BUCKIE [High] op 1 August 1884 *(High Pamph)*; clo 9 August 1915 *(Cl)*.
BUCKIE [GNS] op 1 May 1886 *(GNS)*; clo 6 May 1968 *(RM July)*.

BUCKINGHAM [LNW] op 1 May 1850 *(co n T 1st- line)*; clo 7 September 1964 *(RM October)*.

BUCKLEY [WMCQ]
BUCKLEY (a) op 1 May 1866 *(T 7th)*; clo 31 March 1890, reop June 1893 tt *(Cl)*; last in *Brad* February 1895.
BUCKLEY (b) op 31 March 1890 *(RCG)* as B JUNCTION; renamed 6 May 1974 *(BR notice)*; still open.

BUCKLEY'S SIDING – see 1833 May**.

BUCKNALL & NORTHWOOD [NS] op 1 June 1864 *(co ½ T 5 August- line)*; clo 7 May 1956 *(RM June)*. Non-tt, as B: last use for football trains (Stoke City) 23 April 1960 *(BR doc)*; still wakes week use at 19 August 1961 *(BR handbill)*; last use probably 11 August 1962 – not mentioned in 1963 leaflet *(AB)*. LMS tt 1947: B & N for HANLEY.
Diagram in *NS*, *p.78*, shows 'old station' north of B & N, suggesting that at some stage it was re-sited <u>nearer</u> Stoke-on-Trent. No answer found. On Airey's Lancashire District Maps of 1873, 1895 and 1905 it is 1 mile 43 chains south of Milton Junction; *Brad* April 1885 has it 2½ miles from Stoke, January 1894 2¾ miles, suggesting move <u>away</u> from Stoke (often *Brad* only gave fares not mileages and latter only roughest of guides even when given).

BUCKNELL [LNW] op 6 March 1861 *(D&C 11; Hereford J 13th- line)*; HALT 6 September 1965 to 5 May 1969 *(Cl)*; still open. Hb 1862 BUCKNALL; 1865a corrected.

BUCKPOOL [GNS] op 1 May 1886 *(GNS)* as NETHER BUCKIE; renamed 1 January 1887 *(Cl)* – decision made 25 November 1886 *(GNS)*; clo 7 March 1960 *(Cl)*.

BUCKSBURN [GNS] op 20 September 1854 *(GNS)* as BUXBURN; altered 1 January 1897 *(hbl 28th)*, but April 1897 tt *(JS)*; clo 5 March 1956 *(RM April)*.

BUDDON [DA] op as BARRY REVIEW PLATFORM for military (in *hb* 1890, no facilities shown); became BUDDON 1 June 1893 *(RCG)*; but *hb* 1895 BARRY R SIDING; *hb* 1904 BARRY LINKS BUDDON SIDING; first in *Brad* July 1910; only intermittently present – not March 1911, July 1912, November 1913 but present July and August 1914; clo 1 September 1914, but in tt to June 1915 *(Cl)*; later military use e.g. trains to here shown in special notice for 1-8 July 1939 *(IU)* – *hb*: 1944a and 1956 WAR DEPT B SIDING (for military camp only).

BUDE [LSW] op 10 August 1898 *(W Morn News 14th)*; clo 3 October 1966 *(Cornish & D P 8th)*.

BUDLEIGH SALTERTON [LSW]
BUDLEIGH SALTERTON op 15 May 1897 *(Sidmouth 19th)* as S; renamed 27 April 1898 *(hbl 7 July)*; clo 6 March 1967 *(Express & E 6th)*.
Also see EAST BUDLEIGH.

BUENOS AYRES – see MARGATE.

BUGLE [GW] op 20 June 1876 *(R Cornwall Gaz 24th)*; aot request; still open.

BUGSWORTH – see BUXWORTH.

BUILDWAS [GW] op 1 February 1862**; clo 9 September 1963 *(T 9th)*. B JUNCTION until 1865/7 *(Brad)*.

BUILTH ROAD

BUILTH ROAD [LNW] op 1 November 1866 *(co ½ T 13 February 1867)*; B R HL 1950 to 6 May 1968 tt *(official)*; still open.

B R LL [Cam] op 1 November 1866 (presumed – first in *Brad* November, when LNW line with which it provided connection was first shown); clo 31 December 1962 *(T 31st)*. Initially, and erratically, B R JUNCTION, then CENTRAL WALES J, LLECHRYD CW J/L J *(Brad)*; B R (L) in LNW co tt 1885; became B R 1 May 1889 *(hbl 25 April)* but already thus in *hb* 1867; LL added 1950 *(Cl)*.

BUILTH WELLS [Cam] op 21 September 1864 *(co n Hereford J 24th)*; WELLS added 1865 *(Brad)*; clo 31 December 1962 *(T 31st)*.

BUITTLE [GSW] first in *Brad* July 1862; Wednesdays only, to and from Maxwelltown and Dumfries only; last trains September 1894; B at MILL of B in 1877 *hb*; {Dalbeattie – Castle Douglas}.

BULFORD near Salisbury [LSW]

BULFORD op 1 June 1906 *(RCG)*; see 1951**; aot request; clo 30 June 1952 *(RM August)*.

B CAMP (non-tt): on Bulford branch, beyond public station; used intermittently 1906 to 1963 *(U)*.

BULFORD – see CRESSING.

BULKINGTON [LNW] op 15 September 1847 *(co n T 13th)*; clo 18 May 1931 *(LNW Record)*.

BULL & BUSH [London Electric (Northern Line)]: built 1907 between Hampstead and Golders Green but service never provided; alias NORTH END; *(U)*.

BULLCROFT COLLIERY [GC/GN] (non-tt): miners; in use 1914? *(U)*; probably known locally as SKELLOW – if so, in use 1920s (see *TTS* January 1992); {Hampole – Stainforth}.

BULLERS O' BUCHAN [GNS] op 1899 *(GNS)*; in *hb* 1904; first in *Brad* June 1905*; originally PLATFORM; became HALT 1914 *(Brad)*; clo 31 October 1932 *(RM December)*.

* = GNS wtt 1 July 1905 shows as request stop for which passengers had to buy ticket to station beyond (Longhaven or Cruden Bay).

BULLGILL [MC] op 1840**; clo 7 March 1960 *(RM April)*. At first BULL GILL; thus in co tt for 25 May 1841 *(RM February 1928)* and *Brad* until 1895/6. *Brad* ? to 1955: B for ALLONBY; {map 20g}.

BULLO CROSS [GW] op 3 August 1907 *(GW H; Glos Chron 10th- line)*; HALT; clo 3 November 1958 *(T 21 October)*; {map 94}.

BULMERS SIDINGS (non-tt): used 24 April 1971 for Open Day *(U; JB)*; {Credenhill – Hereford}.

BULVERHYTHE – see ST LEONARDS.

BULWELL

BULWELL op 23 May 1994 *(BLN 733)*; near site of old B Market, south side of Highbury Road Bridge; still open.

B COMMON [GC] op 15 March 1899 *(GC; T 16th- line)*; clo 4 March 1963 *(RM March)*.

B FOREST [GN] op 1 October 1887 *(GN)*; clo 23 September 1929 *(RAIL 393/151)*.

B HALL [GC] op 24 May 1909 *(GC dates)* – not in *Brad* until July 1911; HALT; clo 5 May 1930 *(RAIL 393/151)*.

B MARKET [Mid] op 2 October 1848 *(Mid; RAIL 1005/265- line)*; MARKET added 11 August 1952 *(Cl)*; clo 12 October 1964 *(RM November)*.

BUNCHREW [High] op 11 June 1862 *(High)*; clo 13 June 1960 *(RM July)*.

BUNGALOW TOWN [LBSC] op 1 October 1910 *(SR)*; HALT; clo 1 January 1933 (Sunday) *(Cl)*. Shoreham Airport here later.

BUNGAY [GE] op 2 November 1860**; clo 5 January 1953 *(T 5th)*.

BUNSALL – see 1833 May**.

BUNTINGFORD [GE] op 3 July 1863 *(Hertford 4th)*; clo 16 November 1964 *(T 14 October)*.

BURDALE [NE] op 1 June 1853 *(NE- line)*; clo 5 June 1950 *(Cl)*.

BURDETT ROAD [GE] op 11 September 1871 *(L)*; clo by bomb damage 29 December 1940, reop 5 January 1941, actually clo again by air raid 10 April 1941 (21st 'official') (J.E. Connor, *Stepney's Own Railway*, Connor & Butler, 1984).

BURES [GE] op 2 July 1849 *(T 5th- line)*; *Brad* included it in July 1849 but soon changed to nd tables for line so cannot be certain of early continuity; still open.

BURGESS HILL [LBSC] op 21 September 1841 – not in tt until March 1842 but mentioned in line inspection report *(Rtn)*; clo 2 October 1843 *(co n T 2nd)*; back in tt May 1844; still open.

BURGH-BY-SANDS [NB] op 22 June 1854 *(D&C 14; Rtn- line)*; -by-S added 1 July 1923 *(hbl 12th)*; clo 7 September 1964 *(RM October)*.

BURGH-LE-MARSH [GN]: op 3 September 1848 *(Boston 4th- line)*; -le-M added 1 July 1923 *(hbl 12th)*; clo 5 October 1970 *(T 16 July)*.

BURGHCLERE [GW] op 4 May 1885 *(Hants Chron 2nd)*; clo 4 August 1942**; reop 8 March 1943; clo 7 March 1960 *(Hants Chron 5th)*.

BURGHFIELD DEPOT [GW] (non-tt): for Royal Ordnance Factory; op 28 November 1941 *(GW wtt appendix 5 January 1942)*; still in use 18 June 1951 wtt; shown 'suspended' 8 June 1953 wtt so probably then recently closed (R. Maund); {branch from junction between Reading and Mortimer}.
Ticket *(JB)* for B FACTORY JUNCTION (from Reading West, 9 November 1941) – but no station there.

BURGHEAD [High] op 22 December 1862 *(High)*; new station 10 October 1892 when line extended to Hopeman *(High)*; clo 14 September 1931 *(RM November)*. Evening excursion from Inverness 1 July 1939 *(IU)*. Hb: BURGH HEAD until 1877.

BURLESCOMBE [GW] op 1 May 1867 *(Wellington 2nd)*; clo 5 October 1964 *(Som Gaz 5 September)*. 1895 (only) BURLESCOMB in *hb*.

BURLEY PARK op 28 November 1988 *(Harrogate)*; at/near site of earlier Royal Gardens; still open.

BURLEY-IN-WHARFEDALE [Otley & Ilkley] op 1 August 1865 *(Mid- wtt; co ½s T 15, 18 August- line)*; -in-W added 1922/3; clo 25 July 1992 for electrification, reop 8 September 1992 *(Mid)*; still open.

BURLINGTON ROAD – see BLACKPOOL.

BURLISH [GW] op 31 March 1930 *(Cl 29)*;
HALT until 6 May 1968 *(Cl)*; clo 5 January 1970
(RM February); {Bewdley – Stourport}.

BURMARSH ROAD [RHD] (ng) line op 16 July
1927**, which see for history until after Second War;
omitted from tt after end of 1947 summer service
but briefly re-op during 1950 *(Wolfe, p.20)*.
Variously B for EAST DYMCHURCH, D BAY,
B R HALT *(Wolfe)*.

BURN [GW] op 26 January 1929 *(Tiverton 29th)*;
HALT; clo 7 October 1963 *(W Som F P 12th)*;
{Cadeleigh – Up Exe}. B H for BUTTERLEY in
GW internal *opening notice no.9* and tts to closure.

BURN HOUSE – see FOUNTAINHALL.

BURN NAZE [PW] op 1 February 1909 *(D&C 10)*;
see 1905** (a/b); clo 1 June 1970 *(Cl)*.
Ticket as B N LEVEL CROSSING *(JB)*.

BURNAGE [LNW] op 1 July 1910 *(LNW Officers
42899)*; still open.

BURNBANK [NB]: line op 1 April 1878; station
included in *Brad* April but this was premature –
Hamilton 6 April did not include it in list of stations
opened with line; same paper 13 May – 'We understand
that a new station is about to be erected at Craighead' –
this is only one that would fit; actual op date?
Op as GREENFIELD, renamed 1 May 1902
(hbl 24 April); clo 1 January 1917 except for workmen
(RM February); reop 2 June 1919 *(RCH)*;
clo 15 September 1952 *(RM October)*.

BURNBY – see NUNBURNHOLME.

BURNESIDE [LNW] op 21 April 1847 *(D&C 14)*.
Last in *Brad* January 1855 (closed to public as
economy measure but trains continued to stop for
Mr Cropper, owner of paper mill here and director
of Lancaster & Carlisle, who paid £50 per year – Dick
Smith, *The Kendal & Windermere Railway*, Cumbrian
Railways Association, p.36); reop 1 March 1857;
a Mr Steele leased station and made it available to
public at his financial risk – whether it would be
available for a year only or permanently would depend
on response (presumably favourable). He even provided
cheap returns (4d) to Kendal and back on Saturdays
for working classes. (Notice, item *Westmorland 21 Feb.)*.
From 1 October 1915 name briefly altered to
BURNESHEAD by LNW to avoid confusion with
Burnside [Cal]; local protests caused rapid return to
original (J. Mellentin, *Kendal & Windermere Railway*,
Dalesman, 1980, p.56). Aot request. Still open.

BURNGULLOW [GW] op 1 February 1863
(Cornwall) but not in tt *R Cornwall Gaz* until 6 March
1863 *(Brad April)*; re-sited 11 chains west 1 Feb. 1896
(GM's report 22 January); clo 14 September 1931 *(Cl)*.

BURNHAM [GW] op 1 July 1899 *(RCG)*
as B BEECHES; clo 2 April 1917 *(GM's report)*;
reop 3 March 1919 *(RCH)*; became B BUCKS
1 September 1930 *(hbl 22 October)*, B 5 May 1975 *(Cl)*;
still open.

BURNHAM MARKET [GE] op 17 August 1866
(T 18th); MARKET added 1 June 1883
(GE notice of alterations for June – G. Kenworthy);
clo 2 June 1952 *(RM June)*.

BURNHAM-ON-CROUCH [GE] op 1 July 1889
(RCG); on-C added August 1889 tt *(JS)*; still open.

BURNHAM-ON-SEA [SD Jt] op 3 May 1858
(Bridgwater Merc); initially *Brad* showed it as terminus
of separate branch from Highbridge [BE], not as
extension of Somerset Central; usually just B until
1917 *(RCG ref October)*; clo 29 October 1951
(Bridgwater Merc 30th); many advertised excursions
later – 1961 handbills show summer Wednesdays and
Saturdays; last 8 September 1962 *(SD Jt)*.

BURNHILL [NE] op 4 July 1859 *(RAIL 667/395)*;
BURN HILL JUNCTION until 1893/4, when became
B H, to one word 1908 *(Brad)*; clo 1 May 1939 *(Cl)*.
Hb made two words of it in 1904 (only).

BURNLEY [LY]
B THORNEYBANK op 12 November 1849
(RAIL 1005/265); replaced short distance north by >
B MANCHESTER ROAD (a) op November 1866 *(LY
– 'would open 1 November if ready')*;
clo 6 November 1961 *(RM December)*.
B MANCHESTER ROAD (b) op 29 September 1986;
still open.
B BARRACKS op 18 September 1848 *(LY)* as
BURNLEY; clo 1 February 1849 (Thursday) *(Cl)* *;
back in tt September 1851 as B B; still open.
* = still in *Topham*, with trains, March 1850 – inertia? still open
then? – stayed open 1849–51?
B CENTRAL op 1 December 1848 *(LY)* as B;
became B BANK TOP 1871 tt, B C 2 October 1944
(Cl); still open.

BURNMILL – see LEVEN.

BURNMOUTH [NB] first in *Brad* July 1848 (see
1846 June 22**); clo 5 February 1962 *(BR NER wtt
supplement 7 May)*.

BURNSIDE [Cal] op 1 August 1904 *(RCG)*;
still open.

BURNSTONES [NE] (non-tt): probably used to end
of line, 3 May 1976, by general public – served line-side
hamlet distant from nearest station; no platform;
{Lambley – Slaggyford} (A.Young.)

BURNT FEN – see SHIPPEA HILL.

BURNT MILL – see HARLOW.

BURNT OAK [Nor] op 27 October 1924
(RM December); still open. B O WATLING according
to *L* but not seen thus *Brad* or *hb*.

BURNTISLAND [NB] op 20 September 1847**;
originally a terminus; for through running on opening
of Forth Bridge the line was replaced 2 June 1890,
platforms to north, buildings same; still open.
Hb 1892a added B NEW; 1895 both B and B NEW 'P';
1904 one entry, B.

BURRATOR [GW] op 4 February 1924, non-tt, to
public 18 May 1925 *(GW Plymouth area records)*;
HALT though PLATFORM in *Brad* until 1928/9,
daylight only; clo 5 March 1956 *(T 5th)*.
{Princetown branch}. B & SHEEPSTOR on station
nameboard (photo *BackTrack June 2006)*.

BURRELTON [Cal] op 2 August 1848 *(Rtn- line)* as
WOODSIDE; renamed W & B 1 October 1905
(hbl 26th), B 1 September 1927 *(hbl October)*;
clo 11 June 1956 *(RM April)*.

BURRINGTON [GW] op 4 December 1901
(*Wells 5th*); clo 14 September 1931 (*RM December*).
BURROW & TWYFORD – see JOHN O'GAUNT.
BURRY PORT [BPGV] op to public 2 August
1909★★; clo 21 September 1953 (*T 16th*).
BURSCOUGH [LY]
B BRIDGE op 9 April 1855 (*SouthportVis 5th*); still open.
B JUNCTION op 2 April 1849 (*SouthportVis 7th*);
J added 1855/6 *Brad* but 1890 *hb*; still open.
BURSLEDON [LSW] op 2 September 1889
(*RCG; Hants Teleg 7th- line*); still open.
BURSLEM [NS]
For first station see LONGPORT.
BURSLEM op 1 December 1873 (intended 1 November
but BoT not satisfied so delay) (A. Baker, *The Potteries
Loop*, Trent Valley Publications); clo 2 March 1964
(*RM April*). 1867–98 B LONGPORT (*Brad*).
BURSTON [GE] op 2 July 1849 (*T 5th*);
clo 7 November 1966 (*RM January 1967*).
BURSTWICK – see RYEHILL.
BURTON & HOLME [LNW] op 22 September 1846
(*co n Lancaster 26th*); clo 27 March 1950 (*RM May*).
BURTON AGNES [NE]: line op 7 October 1846★★,
nd, May 1848 (*Topham*); clo 5 January 1970 (*Cl*).
BURTON CONSTABLE – see ELLERBY.
BURTON DASSETT [SMJ] (non-tt):
HALT/PLATFORM: army camp use 1 December
1909 to 1912, at latest, and mid 1930s to ? (*U*) – not in
wtt 23 September 1929; still in wtt 10 September 1951
– stop when required for Engineer's Department
workmen (R. Maund); {Fenny Compton – Kineton,
at/near earlier Warwick Road} (*U*).
BURTON JOYCE [Mid] op 4 August 1846 (*Mid*);
still open.
BURTON LATIMER [Mid] op 8 May 1857
(*Mid; co ½ T 13th*); op as ISHAM; became I & B L
1859 (*Brad*), B L for I 1 October 1923 co tt (*Mid*);
clo 20 November 1950 (*RM January 1951*).
BURTON POINT [GC] op 1 August 1899 (*GC dates*);
clo 5 December 1955 (*RM February 1956*).
Became B P for BURTON and PUDDINGTON
1 May 1900 (*hbl 26 April*) and thus LNE tt 1933 and
Brad to closure.
BURTON SALMON [NE] op 11 May 1840 (*NE*);
clo 14 September 1959 (*RM September*).
BURTON-ON-TRENT
BURTON-ON-TRENT [Mid] op 12 August 1839
(*Mid; co n T 8th- line*); re-sited 7 chains south 29 April
1883 (*Mid*); -on-T added 1877 in *hb* but only 1 July
1903 in co tt (*Mid*); still open. B JUNCTION, some
tables early *Brad*. B-on-T STATION STREET (*hb,
Brad, LNW co tt 1900, GN co tt 1909, NS co tt 1910*) but
this was strictly only the goods station (*Mid*).
Also see HORNINGLOW.
BURWARTON [CMDP] op 21 November 1908★★;
clo 26 September 1938 (*T 9 August*). According to *Cl*
always treated as HALT and this added to name
1 October 1923, but always in body of table in *Brad*
and not 'Halt' 1906 when others were so tagged.
BURWELL [GE] op 2 June 1884 (*GE- line*);
clo 18 June 1962 (*RM August*).

BURY
BURY [LY] op 28 September 1846 (*LY; Rtn PP- line*);
re-sited on new line March 1980 – last train from old
14th, first from new 17th, bus service from Whitefield
over week-end (*RM May*). *Brad* first added BOLTON
STREET to some tables by 1862 but not seen early
1880s in any tables; added again 1888/9; dropped
3 May 1971 (*Cl*). In *hb* successively as B HIGH (1862),
B HL (1872), B EAST LANCS HL,
B BOLTON STREET (1925). 1980 station was
B INTERCHANGE. Clo 17 August 1991 (*BLN 660*)
for conversion to >
BURY [Manch] op 6 April 1992 (*BLN 681*); still open.
B KNOWSLEY STREET [LY] op 1 May 1848
(*co n Manchester 3rd*) as B; *Brad* added MARKET
PLACE occasionally from 1866 but in early 1880s
it was just B; K S regularly added 1888/9 (locally
always this); clo 5 October 1970 (*Cl*).
In *hb* as B LOW (1862), B LL (1872), B K S (1925).
BURY LANE – see GLAZEBURY.
BURY ST EDMUNDS [GE]
BURY ST EDMUNDS op 24 December 1846 (*EC*);
original temporary station replaced by permanent to
west mid-November 1847 after bridge built across main
road (*GE Society Journal April 2001*); still open.
Variously also B, B JUNCTION early *Brad*.
BURY EASTGATE op 9 August 1865 (*T 10th- line*);
clo 1 May 1909 (Saturday) (*Cl*); used July 1914 for
Suffolk Agricultural Show (*GE Journal October 1996*);
{Bury St Edmunds – Welnetham}.
BUSBY near Kilmarnock [GSW] first in *Brad*
September 1848; clo 15 April 1850 (*Cl*).
Crosshouse here later.
BUSBY near Motherwell [Cal] op 1 January 1866
(*T 5th*); still open. *Murray* 1948 and *Brad* ? to 1955:
B for CARMUNNOCK.
BUSH HILL PARK [GE] op 1 November 1880 (*L*);
still open.
BUSHBURY [LNW] op 2 August 1852 (*W Mid*),
exchange only; full use recommended 16 June 1856
(*LNW Officers 378*); clo 1 May 1912 (Wednesday)
(*RCG*); intermittently B JUNCTION in *Brad* until
1872/3 and LNW co tts, also *hb* 1867; {goods *IA*}.
BUSHEY [LNW] op 1 December 1841, probably,
(*L*); B & OXHEY 1 December 1912 (*RCG*) to
6 May 1974 (*BR notice*); still open.
Also [Bak] use 16 April 1917 to 27 September 1982.
BUSHEY PARK – see TEDDINGTON.
BUTLERS HILL [GN] op 2 October 1882 (*GN*);
clo 14 September 1931 (*Cl*).
BUTLERS LANE op 30 September 1957 as
'experimental station' (*LNW Record*); HALT until
April 1963a *hb*; clo 20 October 1991 for rebuilding;
reop 23 March 1992 (*RM May*); still open.
BUTLINS PENYCHAIN – see PENYCHAIN.
BUTTERLEY [Mid] op 1 May 1875 (*Mid*);
became B for RIPLEY and SWANWICK 29 July 1935
(*LNW Record*); clo 16 June 1947★★; advertised Saturday
and Sunday summer services 1951 (*18 June 1951 wtt*);
Saturdays 18 June 1960 to 9 September 1961 (last use);
ramblers' special to Matlock and Buxton called 14 April

1963 *(AB)*; other excursions to at least 17 May 1964 *(Mid)*.

BUTTERTON [NS] (ng) op 29 June 1904★★; clo 12 March 1934 *(LNW Record)*.

BUTTINGTON [Cam – Shrewsbury & Welshpool] first in *Brad* November 1860, as CEFN; renamed December 1860 *Brad*; clo 12 September 1960 *(Cl)*.

BUTTS LANE [LY] op 18 December 1909 *(Southport Vis 4th)*; see 1905★★ (b); clo 26 September 1938 *(RM November)*.

BUXBURN – see BUCKSBURN.

BUXTED [LBSC] op 3 August 1868 *(T 4th)*; still open.

BUXTON

BUXTON [Mid] op 1 June 1863 *(co n T 29 May)*; clo 6 March 1967 *(RM April)*.

BUXTON [LNW] op 15 June 1863 *(LNW Officers)*; still open.

Often treated as one station, e.g. *hb* 1927a on.

Also see HIGHER BUXTON.

BUXTON LAMAS [GE] op 8 July 1879 *(GE)*; clo 15 September 1952 *(RM October)*.

BUXWORTH [Mid] op 1 February 1867 *(Mid- wtt; T 2nd- line)*; BUGSWORTH until 4 June 1930 *(hbl 9 July)*; clo 15 September 1958 *(LNW Record)*.

BWLLFA DARE [GW/TV] (non-tt): miners; op ?; clo by September 1938; {beyond Nantmelyn} *(U)*.

BYERS GREEN [NE] {map 33}

BYERS GREEN (a): line through here op November 1845★★; Saturdays only; first *Brad* reference August 1848, following omission of B G (b); last in *Brad* April 1867; {Spennymoor – B G (b)}.

BYERS GREEN (b) first in *Brad* November 1845★★, (as TODDLES, corrected 1846 *Brad* to TODHILLS / TOD HILLS); Saturdays only; last July 1848; back August 1865 (still T H), apparently eastbound only; last April 1867. Reop, all days, 1 June 1878 *(Auckland Chronicle 7th)* as B G; replaced by >

BYERS GREEN (c) on through line to Bishop Auckland op 1 December 1885; clo 4 December 1939 *(Cl)*.
The branch also carried workmen: report of accident on 11 August 1853 when goods train collided with carriage containing Whitworth Colliery workmen (described as 'passengers' in BoT summary, *RAIL 1053/10)*. According to *T 13th* train was provided because of lack of cottages near the colliery and it ran from Thinford Junction; did it start there or was it where it left the main line? – if former did other trains stop there to make connection? Service began ? This was probably the end of the service since all twelve in carriage (which was being propelled) were killed or badly injured. Colliery shown on Page Bank branch from Spennymoor; disappeared from Airey/RCH maps between 1894 and 1904.
See SPENNYMOOR for possible later use.

BYFIELD [SMJ] op 1 July 1873 *(SMJ; Chelt Exam 9th- line)*; clo 1 August 1877 (Wednesday); reop 2 March 1885★★; clo 7 April 1952 *(RM May)*.

BYFLEET

BYFLEET & NEW HAW [SR] op 10 July 1927 *(sig inst 6th)* as WEST WEYBRIDGE; renamed 12 June 1961 *(hbl May)*; still open.

Also see WEST BYFLEET.

BYKER

BYKER (a) [NE]: workmen used from 1884 *(U)*; in NE wtt October 1898 as B PLATFORM; op to public 1 March 1901 *(RCG)*; clo 5 April 1954 *(Cl)*.

BYKER (b) [TWM] op 14 November 1982 *(Tyneside)*; still open.

BYNEA [GW] op 1 May 1850★★; HALT from 1959/60 *(Brad)* to 5 May 1969 *(Cl)*; aot request; still open.

C

CADBURY ROAD [WCP] op 7 August 1907
(Bristol T 8th); clo 20 May 1940 *(Bridgwater Merc 22nd)*.
Originally in *Brad* and *hb* as C LANE WESTON-IN-
GORDANO, later C R W-in-G *(hbl ref 3 July 1912)*.
CADDER YARD [NB] (non-tt): railway staff;
op 1899/1903; clo after summer 1959, when in wtt;
{Lenzie – Bishopbriggs} *(U)*.
CADELEIGH [GW] op 1 May 1885 *(Wellington 7th)*
as C & BICKLEIGH; renamed 1 May 1906
(hbl 26 April); clo 7 October 1963 *(W Som F P 12th)*.
CADISHEAD [CLC]
CADISHEAD (a) op 1 September 1873 *(CLC; MS&L
co ½ T 21 Jan. 1874- line)*; clo 1 August 1879 *(GC dates)*.
CADISHEAD (b) op, after gap, 29 May 1893 on
deviation line *(Cl)*; clo 30 November 1964 *(RM March)*.
CADMORES LANE CHESHUNT [Northern &
Eastern] probably op 22 November 1841 (see 1841**);
last in *Brad* May 1842; {at 14m 32ch, north of present
Cheshunt, which is at 13m 72ch}.
CADOXTON – see NEATH.
CADOXTON
CADOXTON [Barry] op 20 December 1888 *(Barry)*;
still open.
CADOXTON [TV] op 8 July 1889 as BIGLIS
JUNCTION; renamed February 1890 *Brad*; terminus
acting as interchange with Barry station (long walk)
until TV line extended to Barry Railway, 22 May 1890;
this station then closed *(Penarth)*.
CADOXTON TERRACE [GW] op 18 March 1929
(wt supp); HALT; clo 15 October 1962 *(RM November)*;
{Neath – Cilfrew}.
CAE HARRIS – see DOWLAIS.
CAEDYAH – see CLOY.
CAERAU [GW] op 1 April 1901 *(RCG)*; aot request;
clo to public 22 June 1970 but school use to 15 July
1970 *(RM September)*.
CAERGWRLE
CAERGWRLE [WMCQ] op 1 March 1873 *(Wrexham
1st)* as BRIDGE END; renamed C CASTLE 1 January
1899 *(hbl 26th)*, C C & WELLS 1 October 1908 *(RCG)*,
C 6 May 1974 *(BR notice)*; still open.
Also see HOPE.
CAERLEON [GW] op 21 December 1874
(County Obs 26th); clo 30 April 1962 *(T 6 April)*.
CAERNARVON {map 77}
CARNARVON QUAY – see 1829 B**.
CAERNARVON [LNW] op 1 July 1852 *(T 9th)*;
CARNARVON until 27 March 1926 *(hbl April)*;
clo 5 January 1970 *(Cl)*.
CARNARVON CASTLE [Nantlle] (ng) op 11 August
1856; clo 12 June 1865 for line conversion to standard
gauge; line reop from C Pant, below.
CARNARVON MORFA [LNW] op 1 July 1869 from
Llanberis *(Carnarvon 3rd)* >

CARNARVON PANT [LNW] op from south
2 September 1867** *(co ½ T 10 October)* >
MORFA and PANT clo when lines extended to main.
LNW Record (loose at front) has notice of luncheon
at Victoria Hotel, Llanberis, to celebrate opening of
C Town Line 5 July 1870, special that day, ordinary
trains starting 6th; minute 13 July 1870 *(LNW Officers)*
says both closed on 5 July (last day?). This occurred
despite inspection problems which meant full formal
authority to open necessary connections was only
received 3 January 1871.
CAERPHILLY [Rhy]
CAERPHILLY op 31 March 1858 *(co ½ T 1 September-
line)*; re-sited 1 April 1871 *(Mining Journal 8th)*;
still open; {map 92}.
C WORKS (non-tt), on branch from C used by
railwaymen 1902 to June 1963 *(U)*.
CAERSWS
CAERSWS [Cam] op 5 January 1863**; still open.
Ref hbl 12 July 1917 said (perhaps at distant time) been
renamed from C JUNCTION; not seen thus *Brad*.
CAERSWS [Van] op 1 December 1873**; last in *Brad*
July 1879 (August 'service suspended').
CAERWENT FACTORY [GW] (non-tt):
GW Signal Department Plan dated 14 June 1946
shows line from C F PLATFORM;
{Caerwent branch, Portskewett – Severn Tunnel
Junction; see *RAC Atlas map 52*}.
CAERWYS [LNW] op 6 September 1869**
(Mining 4th); clo 30 April 1962 *(RM June)*.
CAFFYNS [Lynton] (ng) first in *Brad* 14 July 1924;
HALT, principally for golf club; clo 30 September
1935**; {Woody Bay – Lynton}.
CAIRNBULG [GNS] op 1 July 1903 *(GNS)*;
op as INVERALLOCHY; renamed after one month
(GNS) – was I in list of stations opened 1 July *(RCG)*,
but C on opening day according to *hbl 29 October*;
clo 3 May 1965 *(RM May)*.
CAIRNEY [Ed & Dalk]: on map of March 1844;
no other information; see 1831 A**; {map 18}.
CAIRNEYHILL [NB] op 2 July 1906 *(RCG)*;
clo 7 July 1930 *(Cl)*.
CAIRNHILL BRIDGE see 1828 B**; {map 16}
CAIRNHILL BRIDGE (a) [MK] op summer 1832
(MK); clo by mid-October 1832 *(MK)*.
CAIRNHILL BRIDGE (b) [Monklands] op by
10 December 1849 *(MK)*; clo 1 January 1850
(Tuesday) *(MK)*.
CAIRNIE JUNCTION [GNS] op 1 June 1898
(GNS); initially exchange only, in footnotes, not
indexed *(Brad)*; aot C PLATFORM; advertised as
public station 14 June 1965; clo 6 May 1968 *(RM July)*.
In *Brad* as NEW EXCHANGE PLATFORM C J,
then E P C J, then C J.
CAIRNTABLE [LMS] first in *Brad* 24 September
1928; op as HALT; 'halt' dropped 1933/4, back 1937
(Brad) but not in *Murray* 1948; clo 3 April 1950
(RM June).
CAISTER [MGN]
C CAMP: see 17 July 1933**; summers only; HALT;
{Caister – Great Ormesby}.

C-ON-SEA op 7 August 1877 *(MGN; T 9th- line)*;
-on-S added 1 January 1893 *(hbl 27 October 1892)*;
clo 2 March 1959 *(T 2nd)*.

CALBOURNE & SHALFLEET [FYN] op 20 July
1889**; clo 21 September 1953 *(T 21st)*. Op as C & S;
became C for S 1907/8, C for S and BRIGHTSHAM
1912/13; back to C & S 1924/5 *(Brad)*.

CALCOTS [GNS] op 12 August 1884 *(GNS)*;
clo 6 May 1968 *(RM July)*.

CALDARVAN [NB] op 26 May 1856** as
KILMARONOCK; renamed 1877 tt *(Cl; RCG ref
January 1877)*; clo 1 October 1934 *(RM October)*.

CALDER [Cal] op 1 June 1886 *(Cal)*; clo 1 January
1917 *(RM February)*; reop 1 March 1919 *(RCH)*;
clo 3 May 1943 *(Cl)*.

CALDER BRIDGE [Dearne Valley] (non-tt):
purpose ?; in use 1943;
{Wakefield Kirkgate – Crofton South} *(U)*.

CALDER IRONWORKS [MK] op June 1831
(see 1828 B**); probably short-lived *(MK)*; {map 16}.

CALDERBANK [Cal] op 1 September 1887 *(Cal)*;
see 1921 April/May**; clo 1 December 1930 *(Cl)*.

CALDERCRUIX [NB] op 11 August 1862 *(MK)*;
clo 9 January 1956 *(RM February)*.

CALDERPARK op 5 July 1951 *(RM September* – 'for
Glasgow Zoo'); HALT; clo 4 July 1955 (RM *August)*;
{Mount Vernon NB – Uddingston West}.

CALDERSTONES HOSPITAL [LY] (non-tt):
originally planned for civilian use but taken over for war
wounded; first patients arrived May 1915; returned
to civilian control 1921, when became mental hospital;
no record of later passenger use *(Hosp)*;
{branch from Whalley}.

CALDERWOOD GLEN [Cal] (non-tt): excursions;
op 11 February 1907 *(RCG)*; clo September 1939 *(U)*;
served estate belonging to Scottish Co-operative
Wholesale Society; only available for parties of at least
200 *(RM May 1907)*; 'P' before/with *hb* 1910a to
1944a; {East Kilbride – Hamilton West}.

CALDICOT [GW] op 12 September 1932 *(co n dated
'September')*; HALT until 5 May 1969 *(GW H)*;
still open.

CALDON LOW [NS] op 1 July 1905, originally for
quarrymen and families *(Archive Magazine 20)*;
HALT; clo 30 September 1935 *(LNW Record)*.
Aot passengers for here had to hold Waterhouses tickets
(co tt October 1910).

CALDWELL see UPLAWMOOR.

CALDY [Birkenhead] op 1 May 1909 *(Birkenhead)*;
clo 1 February 1954 *(RM March)*.

CALEDONIAN ROAD
CALEDONIAN ROAD [Picc] op 15 December 1906
(co n T 14th); still open.

CALEDONIAN ROAD (non-tt), on branch from
Holloway, used for Motorail services 30 May 1960 to
15 September 1968 (last train) *(L)*.

C R & BARNSBURY [NL] op 21 November 1870
(NL Circular 80); op as B, replacing earlier station of
that name (see under 'B'); renamed 22 May 1893
(L; RCG ref July); still open; {map 101}.

CALIFORNIA near Epsom – see BELMONT.

CALIFORNIA near Yarmouth [MGN]:
see 1933 July 17**; summers only; HALT;
{Caister – Great Ormesby}.

CALIFORNIA – see CATTERICK BRIDGE.

CALLANDER [Cal] op 1 July 1858 *(co n T 3rd)*;
new station 1 June 1870 on extension to Killin;
clo 1 November 1965 *(Rly Obs November)*.
C DREADNOUGHT in *hb* (C reserved for goods)
but not in tts; *hb* 1936a passenger and goods now C.

CALLERTON
CALLERTON [NE] op 1 June 1905 *(RCG)*;
clo 17 June 1929 *(Cl)*.

C PARKWAY [TWM] op 17 November 1991 *(Tyneside)*;
still open. Immediately south of NE station.

CALLINGTON [PDSW] op 2 March 1908
(W Morn News 3rd) as C ROAD; clo 7 November 1966
(Cornish & D P 12th). Pre-opening Kelly Bray.
Was C R for STOKE CLIMSLAND 1 October 1909
(RCG) until 1955 *(Brad)*; thus *hb* 1938.

CALLOWLAND – see WATFORD NORTH.

CALNE [GW] op 3 November 1863 *(Bath & Chelt 4th)*;
clo 20 September 1965 *(RM October)*.

CALSTOCK [PDSW] op 2 March 1908
(W Morn News 3rd- line; in tt Corn & Dev P 7th);
aot request; still open.

CALTHWAITE [LNW] first in *Brad* November 1854;
originally Tuesdays & Saturdays; full use June 1855;
clo 7 April 1952 *(RM May)*.

CALVELEY [LNW] line op 1 October 1840**;
first found (1842) as HIGHWAYSIDE; C before end
of 1845; clo 7 March 1960 *(RM April)*.

CALVERLEY & RODLEY [Mid] op between
16 and 30 July 1846 *(Mid)*; clo 22 March 1965
(RM April). C BRIDGE until 1847/8 *Brad* and thus
on Junction Diagram (e.g. 1877) but not co tt *(Mid)*;
& R added 1 October 1889 *(JS)*.

CALVERT [GC] op 15 March 1899 *(GC; T 16th- line)*;
clo 4 March 1963 *(RM March)*.

CAM [Mid] op 17 September 1856**;
clo 10 September 1962 *(W D Press 10th)*.

CAM & DURSLEY op 29 May 1994 *(RM June)*;
150 yards north of earlier Coaley; still open.

CAMBER SANDS [Rye & C] (ng) op 13 July 1908
(Rye & C); no winter service after 1925;
clo 4 September 1939 *(Cl)*.

CAMBERLEY [LSW] op 18 March 1878 *(co n T 15th)*;
C & YORK TOWN until 1923; still open.
Was C & YT for SANDHURST from 1890?
(hbl ref 24 April) to 1923 and then C for YT and S
(hbl ref 26 April); ? to 1955 C for S in *Brad*.

CAMBERWELL [LCD] op 6 October 1862 *(T 7th)*;
C NEW ROAD 1 May 1863 *(Cl)* to 1 October 1908
(hbl 29th); clo 3 April 1916 *(T 11 March)*.

CAMBERWELL GATE – see WALWORTH ROAD.

CAMBORNE [GW] op 23 May 1843**;
clo 16 February 1852; reop 11 March 1852; still open.

CAMBRIDGE [GE]
CAMBRIDGE op 30 July 1845 *(co n T 26 July)*; still open.
Aot C JUNCTION 1851/2 to 1879/80 in some tables
in *Brad*, where 1867 to 1875 was C HILLS ROAD
in LNW and GN tables

Special stations for Agricultural Show:
1894 *(GE Journal)*; north of main station, north of Mill Road Bridge.
4 to 8 July 1922 (inc) *(Camb Ag; RM September 1922)*; on GE main line, south of main station, just south of junction with LNW, entrance from Trumpington Road.

CAMBRIDGE HEATH [GE] op 27 May 1872 *(co n T 25th)*; clo 22 May 1916** *(T 2nd)*; reop 5 May 1919 *(RCH)*; clo by fire 27 July 1984, reop September 1984; clo 17 February 1986 for rebuilding; reop 16 March 1986 *(London's Local)*; still open.

CAMBUS [NB]: line op 1 July 1852 *(D&C 15)*, nd, August 1854; clo 7 October 1968 *(RM October)*. *Hbl 25 January 1900* said had become C for TULLIBODY 1 December 1899 and was thus in NB co tt 1900, LNE tt 1930, *Brad*/BR tts to 1963/4; but 'for T' deleted *hba* May 1948.

CAMBUS O'MAY [GNS] op 4 October 1875 *(RCG; first Brad October)*; aot request; became HALT 1934/5 *(Brad)*; clo 28 February 1966 *(RM March)*.

CAMBUSAVIE [High] op 2 June 1902 *(High)*; PLATFORM *(Brad)*, HALT *(hb)*, just C *(Murray* 1948); aot request; clo 13 June 1960 *(T 8th)*.

CAMBUSLANG [Cal] op 1 June 1849 *(T 5th- line)*; still open.

CAMBUSNETHAN [Cal] op 1 October 1901 *(RCG)*; clo 1 January 1917 *(RCH; Cal wtt July 1921)*; {Wishaw Central – Newmains}.
Note that this became a terminus after line to Newmains was closed by colliery subsidence, October 1906 (see article by R. Hamilton, *True Line 82*).

CAMDEN {map 101}
CAMDEN [LNW]: until 1844 most trains into and out of Euston switched between cable and locomotive haulage here (line had op 20 July 1837). Some sort of ticket collecting arrangements here from start – letter *T 29 July 1837* complained of being stopped half an hour for this 'on the approach to the extremity of the Regents Park'; use might not have been continuous – description of journey, *T 24 August 1839* says tickets collected at Watford; certainly ticket platform here by 21 May 1840, when it was suggested that existing wooden shed for ticket collectors should be replaced by brick building *(RAIL 384/21)*. Thus locals might have been allowed to join or leave trains here, especially the latter.
Some early writers hint at this – *Whishaw* refers to it as stopping place, on a par with The Aylesbury Junction (later Cheddington); others, e.g. *Drake*, refer to it solely as goods station.
Op to passengers 1 November 1851 *(L)*.
Replaced 1 May 1852 by station more convenient for locals (first site determined by operational needs); aot C CHALK FARM in some tables; replaced again, 140 yards nearer Willesden, 1 April 1872 by station later renamed CHALK FARM (which see); first kept for some time as ticket platform. Name usage flexible: in LNW co tt 1863 as C for the Dock Line, 1867 as C for the North London Line; in 1868 said, 'Passengers must change carriages at Chalk Farm (Camden Ticket Platform)'; *Brad* same – probably ticket platform part was carry-over from past, since

original would have been inconvenient for changing. At first passengers for NL alighted here and joined NL trains at Hampstead Road (eventually PRIMROSE HILL, which see); arrangement ceased when NL extended to join LNW 2 June 1879 *(Neele)*.

C ROAD [Mid] op 13 July 1868 *(T 14th)*; clo 1 January 1916 (Saturday) *(RCG)*.

C TOWN [NL] op 7 December 1850 *(T 5 December, co ½ T 26 February 1851)*; C ROAD 1853 to 1 July 1870 *(Cl)*; replaced by >

C ROAD [NL] op 5 December 1870 as C TOWN *(NL Circular 81)*; renamed 25 September 1950 *(RM October)*; still open.

C TOWN [Nor] op 22 June 1907**; still open.

CAME BRIDGE – see MONKTON & CAME.

CAMELFORD [LSW] op 14 August 1893 *(W Morn News 15th)*; clo 3 October 1966 *(Cornish & D P 8th)*. LSW tt 1914 and *Brad* to 1955 C for BOSCASTLE and TINTAGEL.

CAMELON – see FALKIRK.

CAMELS HEAD [LSW] op 1 November 1906 *(RM December)*; HALT; clo 4 May 1942 *(Cl)*; {map 114}.

CAMERON BRIDGE [NB] op 10 August 1854 *(Fifeshire Journal 10th)*; clo 6 October 1969 *(Cl)*.

CAMERON TOLL [NB] (non-tt) op 4 July 1899 (Tuesday) for Highland Agricultural Show; clo 'at end of week' *(NB letter, MT6/890/3)*; {west of Duddingston} (D. Stirling).

CAMERTON near Bath [GW] op 1 March 1882* *(W Gaz Friday 3rd, third edition)*; clo 22 March 1915; reop 9 July 1923 *(Bristol notice S61153)*; clo 21 September 1925 *(Cl)*.
* = according to *GW Ency* and *Somerset* 1 March was goods opening, passenger 1 April (also given by *Brad Sh)*. *W Gaz* inconclusive: 'The Camerton branch opened for public traffic on Wednesday. A large mineral traffic over the line is expected'. Not included in *Brad* until April but added to weekly tt in *The Frome Times* 15 March.

CAMERTON near Whitehaven [LNW]: op 28 April 1847 *(Whitehaven Herald 1 May)*; clo to public 3 March 1952 *(RM April)*; to workmen 18 April 1966.

CAMERTON COLLIERY [CW Jc] (non-tt): HALT; op 24 March 1887, clo by October 1923 *(Ironmasters)*; {Seaton – Great Boughton}.

CAMP – see BISLEY CAMP.

CAMP HILL {map 99}.
For original terminus see under BIRMINGHAM.
CAMP HILL [Mid] through station op by December 1844, when first in *Brad* – but that was also first tt appearance for stations known to have been in existence for some time previously; C H & BALSALL HEATH December 1867 co tt *(Mid)* to 1 April 1904 *(hbl 28th)*; clo 27 January 1941 *(Mid)*.
Macaulay's maps to about mid-1865 and inset on Fullarton's map of about 1855 show C H to east of road to Stratford, north of junction with what had become branch to goods station (old C H terminus). Probably errors resulting from assuming that had been built alongside terminus. Earliest Junction Diagram (dated 1867 but probably drawn earlier) has C H

14 chains south of junction (in 1890s altered to 17 chains). Accident report of 26 June 1845 shows that policeman was stationed about ¼ mile south of junction, which would have put him in about right place to keep eye on station eventually closed 1941 (P. Jacques, quoting *Midland Record No.16*).
Date on station featured in V.R. Anderson and G.K. Fox, *Midland Railway Architecture*, OPC, 1985, said to be 1867; probably new station on same site, extended to south (thus increased distance), with RCH taking a while to catch up.

CAMPBELTOWN [Camp] (ng)
op 18 August 1906**; clo by May 1932.

CAMPDEN – see CHIPPING CAMPDEN

CAMPERDOWN – see LOCHEE WEST.

CAMPERDOWN JUNCTION – see DUNDEE.

CAMPSIE GLEN [NB] op 1 July 1867 (*D&C 6- line*); clo 1 January 1917 (*RM February*); reop 1 February 1919 (*RM February*); clo 1 October 1951 (*RM November*).

CAMPSIE JUNCTION – see LENZIE.

CANADA DOCK
CANADA DOCK [LNW] op 1 July 1870** as BOOTLE; renamed 1881 tt (*JS*); clo 5 May 1941 by enemy action (*Cl*).
CANADA DOCK [LO] op 6 March 1893**; clo 31 December 1956 (*T 29 September*).

CANADA WATER
CANADA WATER [East London line] op 19 August 1999 (*LRR 21*); clo 23 December 2007**.
CANADA WATER [Jub] op 17 September 1999 (*RM March 2000*); still open.

CANARY WHARF
CANARY WHARF [Dock] op 2 April 1991 for people working on the development; op to public 12 August 1991 (*RM Oct.*); clo by bomb on 9 February 1996 (*T 10th*); reop 9 March 1996 (*RM June 1997*); still open.
CANARY WHARF [Jub] op 17 September 1999 (*RM March 2000*); still open.
CANLEY [LMS] op 30 September 1940 (*LNW Record*); HALT until 6 May 1968 tt; still open.
Pre-op Fletchampstead.

CANNING Liverpool [LO] op 6 March 1893** as CUSTOM HOUSE; renamed 1947/8 (*Brad*); clo 31 December 1956 (*T 29 September*).

CANNING TOWN London
CANNING TOWN [GE] op 14 June 1847 (*L; co ½ T 13 August- line*) as BARKING ROAD; renamed 1 July 1873 (*L*); re-sited to north 1888 (*L*); clo 29 May 1994 for Jublilee line extension; (*BLN 734*); new station op 29 October 1995, south of previous (*BLN 734*); clo 10 December 2006 – last train Saturday 9th (*RM February 2007*). GE co tt 1882, 1914: C for B R.
CANNING TOWN [Dock] op 5 March 1998 (*LRR July 1998*); still open.
CANNING TOWN [Jub] op 14 May 1999 (*LRR July 1999*); still open.

CANNOCK
CANNOCK (a) [LNW] op 1 February 1858 (*T 1st*); clo 18 January 1965 (*RM March*).
CANNOCK (b) op 10 April 1989 (cheap introductory service 8th) (*BLN 605*); still open.

CANNON STREET London
For main line station see LONDON.
CANNON STREET [Met/Dist] op 6 October 1884 (*T 4th*); still open.
Also see MANSION HOUSE.

CANNON STREET ROAD [Blackwall] op 21 August 1842 (*L*) – a Sunday but was added to existing service (first in *Brad* September); last in *Brad* December 1848; {map 108}.

CANONBIE [NB] first in *Brad* May 1862, as CANOBIE; altered 1 February 1904 (*hbl 28 January*); clo 15 June 1964 (*RM July*).

CANONBURY
CANONBURY [NL] op 1 September 1858 (*L*) as NEWINGTON ROAD & BALLS POND; renamed 1 July 1870 (*JS*); replaced by new station short distance west 1 December 1870 (*NL Circular 81*); still open.
GE co tt 1882: C & N R {map 101}.

C & ESSEX ROAD – see ESSEX ROAD.

CANONS PARK op by [Met] 10 December 1932 (*T 10th*); C P EDGWARE at first, E dropped 1933/9 (sources differ – *Brad* dropped from table 1939/40 but kept in index until it ceased to give detail for LT stations; *RCH dist ref 22 February 1939*); transferred to [Bak] 20 November 1939, transferred again, to [Jub] 1 May 1979; still open.

CANTERBURY
CANTERBURY [Canterbury & Whitstable; SE] op 4 May 1830**; clo 6 February 1846. Line later reop from C West.
C EAST [LCD] op 9 July 1860 (*T 9th*); EAST added 1 June 1899 (*hbl 13 July*); still open.
C WEST [SE] op 6 February 1846 (*co n T 2nd*) *; WEST added 1 June 1899 (*hbl 13 July*); still open.
Also see MARGATE [SE].
* = but although *T* item included tt, item in *Kentish Gazette 10th* made it look like formal only.
Non-tt: Royal Agricultural Society Show held here 4–7 and 9–12 July 1860 in grounds of Hales's Place, a little east of C [SE]. First four days seem to have been principally for machinery trade; special siding provided for machinery and stock. For the last four it was possible for visitors to alight either at C or SHOWGROUND STATION; all had to return from 'City' station. (*co n T 5th; items T 7th, 9th*).
Also see SOUTH CANTERBURY.

CANTERBURY ROAD – see WINGHAM.

CANTLEY [GE] op 1 May 1844 (*T 14 April- line*); last in *Brad* September 1847; back January 1851; aot request; still open.

CAPE [RSB] (non-tt): HALT/PLATFORM; workmen; dates ?; {Jersey Marine – Court Sart} (*U*). C P shown hb 1895, no facilities; not included 1904.

CAPEL [GE] op 2 September 1847**; aot request; clo 29 February 1932 (*T 27th*).

CAPEL BANGOR [VoR] (ng) op 22 Dec. 1902** (see for line history); transferred to preservation 1989.

CAPEL CELYN [GW] op 1 December 1930 (*Cl 29*); HALT; clo 4 January 1960 (*RM March*).

CAPEL COLBREN JUNCTION
– see COLBREN JUNCTION.

CAPEL IFAN COLLIERY [BPGV] (non-tt):
see PENTREMAWR COLLIERY.

CAPENHURST [Birkenhead] op 1 August 1870
(Birkenhead); still open.

CARADOG FALLS [GW] op 5 September 1932
(Cl 29); HALT; clo 14 December 1964★★;
{Trawscoed – Strata Florida}.

CARBIS BAY [GW] op 1 June 1877
(Cornish Tel 29 May); still open.

CARBUIE – see 1957★★.

CARCROFT & ADWICK-LE-STREET [WRG Jt]
op 1 March 1866 *(GN)* as A; became A & C January
1867 tt, A-le-S & C March 1867 tt, C & A-le-S 1 May
1880 *(JS; Cl)*; clo 6 November 1967 *(RM December)*.
Also see ADWICK.

CARDENDEN [NB: op 4 September 1848
(co n Perthshire Courier 31 August); still open.
Became C for BOWHILL February 1908 *(RCG)*
and still thus *hb* 1956 but not seen thus in *Brad*.

CARDIFF {map 84}.

C QUEEN STREET [TV] op 9 October 1840★★;
Q S added [Barry] table 1890, as addition to
(explanation of?) C [TV], others 1891/3 *(Brad)*; still open.

C BAY [TV]: line op 9 October 1840★★; this station not
open by time of inspection of Merthyr extension
(op 21 April 1841) *(Rtn)*. *Brad* did not give detail until
December 1844, when this was mentioned, in footnotes,
where it was said passengers could be conveyed from
terminus to Cardiff station, to be booked there; one of
company's carriage would leave terminus 15 minutes
before advertised time of leaving Cardiff. When added
to table in *Brad* was C BUTE DOCK; became
C DOCK/DOCKS 1845 *(Brad)*, C BUTE ROAD
1 July 1924 *(GW circular 18 June)*, C B 26 September
1994 *(AB, Chron)*; still open.

C CENTRAL [GW] op 19 June 1850★★; originally C;
became C GENERAL 1 July 1924 *(GW circ 2197,
18 June)* – but already in use some tables in *Brad* 1922;
renamed C C 9 May 1973 *(RM April)*; still open.

C RIVERSIDE [GW] op 14 August 1893 *(GW)*;
R first seen *Brad* 1894/6; amalgamated into Central
28 October 1940 *(Cl)*.

C CLARENCE ROAD [GW] op 2 April 1894 *(GW)*;
clo 16 March 1964 *(Cl)*.

C ADAM STREET [Rhy] op 31 March 1858
(co ½ T 1 September); replaced by >

C PARADE [Rhy] op 1 April 1871 *(T 5th)* as C;
CROCKHERBTOWN added *Brad* 1872 when
Rhymney trains moved from own table to LNW one,
dropped 1888 tt *(Cl)*; became C P 1 July 1924
(GW circular 18 June); clo 16 April 1928
(C/W – J. Morris from *Western Mail* – trains used
Sunday 15th), then its services diverted to Queen Street.
Also aot service (non-tt) for railway staff to
EAST DOCK LOCO SHED, beyond Adam Street *(U)*.

CARDIGAN [GW] op 31 August 1886 by local
company and handed over to GW for regular service on
1 September 1886 *(Whitland)*; clo 10 September 1962
(Cl). GW co tt 1932: C for GWBERT-ON-SEA.

CARDINGTON [Mid]
CARDINGTON op 8 May 1857 *(Mid; co ½ T 13 August-*

line); clo 1 January 1962 *(RM January)*; later use for
Air Force base *(U)* – *hb* September 1962a says closed
but still special RAF passenger trains.

C WORKMEN'S PLATFORM (non-tt): op about
September 1917 (work to be completed on Saturday
22 September); clo 3 October 1921;
{Cardington – Bedford} *(Mid)*.

CARDONALD [GP Jt] first in *Brad* September 1879,
on site of earlier Moss Road; still open.

CARDONNEL [GW] op 1 June 1905 *(GW H)*;
HALT; clo 28 September 1936 *(T 14th)*;
{Neath – Swansea}.

CARDRONA [NB] op 1 October 1864 *(Peebles;
T 5th- line)*; clo 5 February 1962 *(RM February)*.

CARDROSS near Dumbarton [NB]
op 31 May 1858 *(T 7 June)*; still open.

CARDROSS – see PORT of MENTEITH.

CARESTON [Cal] op 1 June 1895★★;
clo 4 August 1952 *(RM September)*.

CARFIN
For first station of this name see HOLYTOWN.

CARFIN [LMS] op 1 Oct 1927 *(Rly World June 1975)*,
at or near site of earlier Newarthill; originally opened
for pilgrims to Holytown *(RM March 1935)*;
HALT until 16 May 1983 tt; still open.

CARGILL [Cal] op 2 August 1848 *(Rtn- line)*;
clo 11 June 1956 *(RM April)*.

CARGO FLEET [NE]: line op 5 June 1846★★.
Earliest references found: 29 April 1847 instructions
were given to provide name-board for CLEVELAND
PORT and 15 March 1848 a platform was ordered for
CARGO FLEET. Present in earliest tt seen for line,
co tt September 1847. First there and *Brad* as C P;
S&D minutes generally called it C F from 1848 but not
renamed in tt until 1867 *(Cl)*; references in minutes,
1851 and 1865, suggest it might have been slightly
re-sited as a result of one or both of their discussions;
replaced by new station about ¼ mile west 9 November
1885 *(Cl)*; clo 22 January 1990 *(BLN 625)*; {map 43}.

CARHAM [NE]: line op 27 July 1849 *(NE)*, nd,
July 1851; clo 4 July 1955 *(RM August)*.

CARISBROOKE [FYN] op 20 July 1889★★;
became HALT 1920/1 *Brad*; clo 21 September 1953
(T 21st). *Brad* ? to closure: is station for Castle.

CARK [Fur] op 1 September 1857★★ *(Fur)*; still open.
Variously CARK, C & CARTMEL, C-IN-CARTMEL
(briefly, about 1885) in *Brad*; reverted to CARK
13 May 1984 tt. *Hb* originally CARK, then 1883
(preceded by *RCG ref 1882*) to 1904 inclusive C-in-C,
then C & C *(RCG ref July 1906)*.
Furness co tt 1910: C & C.

CARLIN HOW – see SKINNINGROVE.

CARLINGHOW [LNW] op 1 April 1872 *(LNW
Officers 7815)*; according to *RCH* clo 15 April 1917
but *Brad* and *ABC tt* show last trains March;
April 'service suspended'.

CARLISLE (all not otherwise attributed below from
D&C 14 and *Cl*); {map 20}
Line from Newcastle op to **C LONDON ROAD** [NC; NE]
19 July 1836 *(N.C. MacLean)* ★; clo 1 January 1863,
trains diverted to C Citadel. Still shown 'P' in *hb* until

1895 – occasional special use? inertia?

* = reference to temporary ROME STREET in *NC* seems to have resulted from misunderstanding – visitor to line just before opening referred to London Road as 'a neat little building in the Gothic style'; temporary station <u>was</u> used for official opening train but contemporary accounts suggest this was exceptional event; *Scott, 1837*, has L R.

<u>Trains from Maryport</u> arrived at **C BOGFIELD** [MC] (alias WATER LANE) 10 May 1843**;
this was replaced by >

C CROWN STREET [MC] op 30 December 1844; some trains diverted to London Road in 1848; clo 17 March 1849, when rest diverted. Maryport trains again diverted, to Citadel, 1 June 1851.

<u>Trains from London</u> arrived 17 December 1846, at first using London Road, via reversal. By 10 September 1847, opening of the line to Beattock, they had been diverted to C Joint/Citadel.

[NB] trains arrived at **C CANAL** from Port Carlisle 22 June 1854, Silloth trains added 4 September 1856; this clo 1 July 1864 – trains diverted to Citadel. However, NB services from Scotch Dyke had used Citadel from opening of service on 29 October 1861.

CARLISLE [Cal/LNW] op on or by 10 September 1847 (G Body, *Great Railway Battles*, Silver Link 1994 and *Cal* say Lancaster & Carlisle use from 1 September but *D&C 14* says perhaps not until Caledonian line opened on 10th); description of opening of Caledonian line *(Scottish Railway Gazette 11th* implies 10th – arrangements for some companies not completed but Lancaster & Carlisle and Caledonian 'will be accommodated from the outset'; still open.
Hb: 1862 C, 1872 C CITADEL JOINT, 1904 C CITADEL; still thus 1956.
JOINT and CITADEL inconsistently applied in tts seen.

CARLTON near Nottingham [Mid] op 4 August 1846 *(Mid)*; became C & GEDLING 1 November 1871 *(Mid)*, C & NETHERFIELD for G and COLWICK 1 November 1896 *(hbl 29 October)*, C & N 7 May 1973 tt *(Mid)*, CARLTON 6 May 1974 *(BR notice)*; still open.

CARLTON MAIN COLLIERY [Mid] (non-tt): op 2 February 1885 wtt; in 1903 wtt as C EXCHANGE SIDINGS PLATFORM; clo 1913 *(Mid)*.

CARLTON/CARLTON IRONWORKS
– see REDMARSHALL; STILLINGTON.

CARLTON COLVILLE – see OULTON BROAD

CARLTON TOWERS [HB] op 27 July 1885 *(op tt NER I)*; T added 1 July 1922 *(hbl 13th)*; clo 1 January 1932 (Friday) *(RM January)*; excursion 14 October 1933 during Hull Civic Week *(RM February 1934, pp 153-4)*; non-tt workmen's use during WW2.

CARLTON-ON-TRENT [GN] op 15 July 1852**; -on-T added 1 March 1881 *(Cl)*; clo 2 March 1953 *(RM April)*.

CARLUKE {map 16}
C & LANARK [Wishaw & Coltness; Cal] op 8 May 1843 (see 1835 C**); for clo see 1848**.
Much in print calls this STIRLING ROAD, but this name only seen in *Cal*; perhaps became this after passenger closure? *Brad*: 1843 L, C; 1844 C, coach

connection to L; thus to the end. *Murray* September 1844: C & L. 1932 RCH Map of Glasgow etc has NEWMAINS S R Goods – any possibility of confusion?

CARLUKE [Cal] op 15 February 1848 *(co ½ T 29 February- line)*; still open.

CARMARTHEN [GW]
CARMARTHEN op 1 March 1860 *(GW)*; clo 31 December 1860; reop 15 August 1861 *(Rtn)*; replaced by new station 18 chains south 1 July 1902 *(RM September)*; still open. C TOWN in *hb* 1883 and LMS ticket thus.

C JUNCTION op 11 October 1852 *(T 12th)*; J added 1 July 1860 *(Cl)*; clo 27 September 1926 *(Cl)*. C J ROAD in *hb*, 1895 only.

CARMONT [Cal] first in *Brad* September 1855 as NEW MILL OFFSET; became NEWMILL SIDING 1866 tt, N 1891 tt *(Cl)*, C 1 October 1912 *(hbl 24th)*; at first Saturdays only, later, e.g. December 1901, Thursdays; full use January 1910; aot request; clo 11 June 1956 *(RM April)*.

CARMYLE
CARMYLE (a) [Cal] op 8 January 1866 *(Cal- line)*; clo 5 October 1964 *(RM November)*.
CARMYLE (b) op 4 October 1993 *(BLN 712)*; still open.

CARMYLLIE [DA] op 1 February 1900 *(Dundee)*; clo 1 January 1917 *(Cl)*; back in *Brad*, Saturdays only, September 1917; fully reop 1 January 1918 *(RCH)*; clo 2 December 1929 *(Cl)*.

CARN BREA {map 111}
CARN BREA (a) [West Cornwall] op 23 May 1843**; clo 16 February 1852.
CARN BREA (b) [GW] op 25 August 1852 *(Cornwall*; included in tt for 25 August, opening date for stretch on to Truro, in *Penzance 1 September)* – note station op after line had reopened; POOL 1854 *(Cl)* to 1 November 1875 *(RCG)*; clo 2 January 1961 *(RM February)*. Aot *hb* C BRAE (probably error).

CARNABY [NE]: line op 7 October 1846**, nd, May 1848 *(Topham)*; clo 5 January 1970 *(Cl)*.

CARNARVON – see CAERNARVON for all stations serving the town.

CARNBROE IRONWORKS [Wishaw & Coltness]: line op for minerals 25 January 1834 (see 1835 C**) and passenger services mentioned there might have stopped here; in October 1844 co tt quoted in *True Line 49*; never in *Brad*, not in *Murray* September 1844; thus very short lived or only of local importance (workmen's station?); clo ? – *Pigeon* suggests clo in July 1845 (based on intention to move, given in management committee's minutes) or, less likely, in 1847 when line was improved ready for Caledonian take-over; {Whifflet Cal – Mossend}.

CARNE POINT (non-tt): used for regattas 1977 *(U)* and 1994; {on Fowey branch}.

CARNFORTH
CARNFORTH [Fur/LNW] op 22 September 1846 *(co n Lancaster 26th)*; both C and C-YEALAND 1849 to 1864 *(Brad, Murray)*; main line platforms clo 4 May 1970 *(Cl)*; branch platforms still open.
Addition of YEALAND to name probably clerical error – see YEALAND.

CARNFORTH [Fur/Mid] op 6 June 1867 to temporary station *(Mid)*. Line extended 1 July 1868 to Furness main line to Barrow; station, perhaps exchange only, provided at junction to give connections between Fur and Mid lines (named as C F&M JUNCTION *Brad*, but not Mid co tt). Mid boat trains via Wennington probably only stopped at exchange and went straight on towards Barrow and Piel; other Mid trains backed from F&M into LNW station. Some Fur trains also stopped at exchange. Clo 2 August 1880; new curve allowed trains from Wennington to run straight into new bay platform at LNW station *(D&C 14)*.

CARNO [Cam] op 5 January 1863★★; clo 14 June 1965 *(RM July)*.

CARNOCK ROAD – see AIRTH.

CARNOUSTIE [DA] op 8 October 1838★★; replaced by new station east of level crossing 1900; still open.

CARNTYNE [NB] first in *Brad* June 1888; clo 1 January 1917 *(RM February)*; reop 1 April 1919 *(RCH)*; still open. NB co tt 1900: C for WESTMUIR and TOLLCROSS in one table.

CARNWATH [Cal] op 15 February 1848 *(Balerno; co ½ T 29 February - line)*; clo 18 April 1966 *(Cl)*.

CARPENDERS PARK [LNW] op 1 April 1914 *(RCH)*; clo 1 January 1917 *(T 22 December 1916)*; reop 5 May 1919 *(RCH)*; replaced by new station 231 yards south 17 November 1952 *(Cl)*; still open. Also [Bak] from reop to 27 September 1982. LNW co tt 1921, LMS tt 1930 and *Brad* to 1955: C P for OXHEY GOLF CLUB.

CARR LANE [KE] first in *Brad* July 1921; clo 31 March 1930 *(Cl)*. See 1905★★ (c) – was HALT in co wtt 1922; {Preesall – Pilling}.

CARR MILL [LNW] op 1 January 1896 *(LNW Officers 36535)*; clo 1 January 1917 *(T 22 December 1916)*.

CARRBRIDGE [High] op 8 July 1892 *(High Pamph)*; still open. At first usually CARR BRIDGE – to one word 16 May 1983 tt, but thus *hb* 1899a to 1925.

CARREGHOFA [GW] op 11 April 1938 *(T 8th)*; HALT; clo 18 January 1965★★; {Llanymynech – Llantsantffraid}.

CARRHOUSE [NE] op 1 July 1858 *(Durham Chronicle 2nd)*; clo 1 October 1868 (Thursday) *(Cl)*; minutes show that it was only on 17 June 1858 that S&D Secretary was ordered to approach owners of land needed for station – original arrangements?; {map 28}. In some books shown as CARR HOUSE but always one word in *Brads* seen.

CARRINGTON [GC] op 15 March 1899 *(GC; T 16th- line)*; clo 24 September 1928 *(Cl)*.

CARROG [GW] op 8 May 1865 *(D&C 11)*; clo 14 December 1964★★.

CARRON [GNS] op 1 July 1863 *(GNS)*; clo 18 October 1965★★. *Brad* ? to 1938/9 C for ARCHIESTOWN.

CARRON DOCK: [NB] (non-tt): used for Carron & Co's and other passenger steamers; op 3 May 1887; clo 30 September 1920; used again for Forces in Second War; {branch, Falkirk area}. (NB Railway Study Group *Journal*, 87, p.29).

CARRONBRIDGE [GSW] op 1 March 1851 *(GSW)*; clo 7 December 1953 *(RM January 1954)*. CARRON BRIDGE until 1860 *(GSW)*, 1875 *(Brad)*, 1890 *(hb)*.

CARSEBRECK [Cal] (non-tt): for Caledonian Curling Society meetings; used 25 times in period 1853 to 1935 *(Scot Cent)*; alias CURLING POND, CURLING CLUB; shown 'P' in *hb*; one (final?) use was 24 December 1935 *(Away)* – but perhaps later use, perhaps kept in *hb* in case of that – *1936a* 'P' removed, 1938 present without facilities, *1941a* spelling amended from CARSBRECK, *1944a* 'closed'.

CARSHALTON [LBSC] For first station see WALLINGTON. **CARSHALTON** op 1 October 1868 *(T 28 September)*; still open.

C BEECHES op 1 October 1906 *(L)* as BEECHES HALT; replaced by station (now C B) east of over-bridge 29 March 1925 *(sig inst 6/1925)*; still open.

CARSTAIRS [Cal] op 15 February 1848 *(D&C 6; co ½ T 29 February - line)*; still open. C JUNCTION in *Brad* until 1903 and thus Cal co tt 1859.

CARTERHATCH LANE [GE] op 12 June 1916 *(RM July)*; HALT; clo 1 July 1919★★; {Churchbury – Forty Hill}. C L for ENFIELD HIGHWAY *(Brad)*.

CARTERS CROSSING [NS] (non-tt): for employees at NS Stoke Works, which was 300 yards from crossing; from October 1907 train to Stoke called here (no return service); not even unmanned halt; still served July 1916 according to wtt; by 1921 service ended (B. Jeudah, *Railway Archive, December 2002*); {Fenton – Stoke}.

CARTERTON [GW] op 2 October 1944 *(Cl 29)*; clo 18 June 1962 *(T 18 May)*; {Alvescot – Bampton}.

CARTSDYKE [Cal] first in *Brad* July 1870; still open. Cal co tt 1913 but not LMS tt 1930: C for JAMES WATT DOCK.

CARVILLE [NE] For first station of this name see WALLSEND. **CARVILLE** op 1 August 1891 *(RCG)*; clo 23 July 1973 *(RM August)*.

CARWAY COLLIERY [BPGV] (non-tt): SIDING used by miners from 1898 *(U)*; still shown wtt 15 September 1952; {Glyn Abbey – Pontyates}.

CASHES GREEN [GW] first in *Brad* March 1931; HALT; clo 2 November 1964 *(W D Press 2nd)*.

CASSILLIS [GSW] op 13 October 1856 *(GSW- line)*; clo 6 December 1954 *(RM January 1955)*.

CASSINGTON [GW] op 9 March 1936 *(GW notice dated 'February')*; HALT; re-sited from south to north of road bridge after 1945; clo 18 June 1962 *(T 18 May)*; {Yarnton – Eynsham}.

CASTLE ASHBY & EARLS BARTON [LNW] op 2 June 1845 *(co op tt)* as C A WHITE MILL (but just C A in *hb*); renamed May 1869 tt *(Cl; recommended LNW Officers 14 April, where was from C A & W M)*; clo 4 May 1964 *(RM June)*.

CASTLE BAR PARK [GW] op 1 May 1904
(RM June); HALT until 5 May 1969 *(GW H)*; still open.
CASTLE BROMWICH [Mid]
op 10 February 1842 *(Mid)*; clo 4 March 1968 *(Cl)*.
CASTLE BYTHAM [Mid]
op 4 April 1898 *(RCG)*; clo 2 March 1959 *(T 2nd)*.
CASTLE CAEREINION [Cam] (ng)
op 6 April 1903 *(D&C 11)*; clo 9 February 1931 *(Cl)*.
CASTLE CARY near Yeovil [GW] op 1 September
1856 *(Wells 6th)*; still open. At times all sources seen,
including GW co tt 1859: C CAREY.
CASTLE DONINGTON & SHARDLOW [Mid]
op 6 December 1869 *(Mid)*; & S added 1 May 1898
co tt *(Mid)* – *hbl 11 July 1901* and *RCG* said 15 June
1901 but *Brad* also altered in 1898; clo 22 September
1930 *(Cl)*; still in use for excursions at 10 August 1961
(BR handbill) and 1 August 1962 *(IU)*.
Until 1890 C DONNINGTON in *hb*.
CASTLE DOUGLAS [GSW]
CASTLE DOUGLAS op 7 November 1859 *(Dumfries
5th)*; clo 14 June 1965 *(RM July)*.
C D ST ANDREW op 7 March 1864 *(Kirkcudbright 11th)*;
temporary station, acting as terminus for branch to
Kirkcudbright – BoT had refused to pass junction
connecting branch to main station. Trains ran through
to main station 15 August 1864 but, according to *GSW*,
this station was not closed until 1 December 1867.
However, it was only in tt from April 1867 to
December 1867 (inclusive), which might indicate
a brief reopening rather than continuity (when
terminus tt just treated it as C D).
Variously shown as ST ANDREW(S)/ST A ROAD.
CASTLE EDEN [NE]: line op 1 May 1839 *(see 1836
A**)*, nd, January 1843 *(co tt)*; clo 9 June 1952**.
CASTLE EDEN COLLIERY – see HESLEDEN.
CASTLE GRANT [High] (non-tt): PLATFORM for
Grant family estate; op 1863 *(U)*; in 1938 *hb* 'P' as
C G HALT; 1949a *hb* 'closed'; {Grantown – Dava}.
CASTLE HEDINGHAM – see SIBLE.
CASTLE HILL – see FILLEIGH near Barnstaple;
WEST EALING, London.
CASTLE HOWARD [NE]:
op 8 July 1845**; clo 22 September 1930**.
CASTLE KENNEDY [PPW Jt]
op 1 July 1861 *(GSW)*; clo 14 June 1965 *(RM July)*.
CASTLE MILL [Glyn] (ng) {map 79}
C M (a) op 1 April 1874 *(Glyn)*;
clo 1 April 1886 (Thursday).
C M (b) op 15 March 1891 *(Glyn)*;
clo 7 April 1933**.
CASTLE PIT [GW/Rhy] (non-tt): miners; 1897 to
1915 at least; {Abercanaid – Troedrhiw} *(U)*.
CASTLE STUART [High] (non-tt): private; dates ?;
'P' in *hb* 1938; *hb* 1949a 'closed';
{Allanfearn – Dalcross}.
CASTLEBYTHE [GW] op 24 September 1928
(GW H); HALT; clo 25 October 1937**; {map 81}.
CASTLECARY near Falkirk [NB] op 21 February
1842 *(co n T 19th)*; clo 6 March 1967 *(Cl)*.
CASTLEFORD
CASTLEFORD [NE]: line op 1 July 1840 *(North*

Midland co n T 27 June), nd, December 1841; re-sited
about 3 chains west 1871; was C CENTRAL 15
September 1952 to 20 February 1969 *(Cl)*; still open.
C CUTSYKE [LY] first *Brad* tt March 1860;
CUTSYKE added 15 September 1952 *(Cl)*;
clo 7 October 1968 *(RM October)*.
CASTLEMILK [Cal] (non-tt): possible early station
for a railway director (line op 10 September 1847);
{Lockerbie – Ecclefechan} *(True Line)*.
CASTLETHORPE [LNW] op 1 August 1882
(LNW Officers 23694); clo 7 September 1964 *(RM Oct.)*.
CASTLETON [LY] op 15 September 1839
(LY appendix) – Sunday but did have Sunday service;
still open. *Brad*: 19 October 1839 BLUE PITS,
April 1840 HEYWOOD & B P BRIDGE, March 1841
H one version but H & B P another, April 1841 (sheet)
B P, 1853 B P JUNCTION. Other early sources
included other variations, e.g. BLUE PITTS and
BLUEPITS. Settled as C 1 November 1875 *(RCG)*.
CASTLETON MOOR [NE] op 1 April 1861 *(NE)*;
MOOR added 14 June 1965 tt; still open.
CASTOR [LNW] first in *Brad* April 1847;
clo 1 July 1957 *(RM July)*].
CATCLIFFE [GC] op 30 May 1900 *(RCG; co ½ T
4 August- line)*; clo 11 September 1939 *(Cl)*.
CATERHAM [SE] op 5 August 1856 *(co ½ T 30 Aug.)*;
new station 1 January 1900 *(Cl)*; still open.
CATERHAM JUNCTION – see PURLEY.
CATFIELD [MGN] op 17 January 1880 *(T 21st)*;
clo 2 March 1959 *(T 2nd)*.
CATFORD
CATFORD [LCD] op 1 July 1892 *(L)*; still open.
C BRIDGE [SE] op 1 January 1857
(L; co ½ T 9 February- line); still open.
CATHAYS
CATHAYS op 3 October 1983 *(wtt supp)*, 7 chains
south of previous Woodville Road; still open.
Non-tt: temporary departure platform here, inspection
report dated 10 August 1863 *(RAC)*; for those going to
the National Eisteddfod; held at Swansea, starting
1 September; route?
C WOODVILLE ROAD – see WOODVILLE ROAD.
CATHCART [Cal] op 25 May 1886 *(Cal)*;
re-sited on circle line 18 March 1894 *(Cl)*; still open.
CATHCART ROAD – see GUSHETFAULDS.
CATON [Mid] op 17 November 1849 *(co n Lancaster
17th)*; clo 1 May 1961 *(RM June)*.
CATRINE [GSW] op 1 September 1903 *(RCG)*;
clo 1 January 1917 *(RM February)*; according to *RCH*
reop 10 February 1919, but *Brad* showed trains again
January 1919; clo 3 May 1943 *(Cl)*.
CATTAL [NE] op 30 October 1848**; still open.
CATTERICK
C BRIDGE [NE] op 10 September 1846 *(co n Catterick)*;
clo 3 March 1969 *(RM March)*.
A line ran from station at **C B BROMPTON ROAD**
(public platform – J.P. McCricken, *NE Express, August
1986*) to Catterick Camp. This line opened in 1915.
It appeared in *Brad* from December 1918, with the
following stops:
CALIFORNIA, last shown November 1919;

CENTRAL, last shown April 1920 (May 'service suspended');
SCOTTON, last shown January 1919.
Military use of the line continued, worked by LNER from 1923 *(U)*. Daily recreational service for troops from Camp Centre to Brompton Road began February 1944; some services running through to Darlington by 22 May 1944; summer 1961 wtt showed week-end trains (non-tt Camp to Darlington, no intermediate stops within camp) to or from Sheffield, Birmingham, Gloucester, Bristol and King's Cross; last train to Camp Centre ran 26 October 1964, by when service was early Monday mornings only. (J.P. McCrickard, entry dated 12 March 2002 in *Bylines*; R. Maund.)
CATTISTOCK [GW] op 3 August 1931 *(Cl 29)*; HALT; clo 3 October 1966 *(W D Press 3rd)*; {Evershot – Maiden Newton}.
CATTLE MARKET: on site of later Maiden Lane [NL]; market opened 15 June 1855 *(NL co ½ T 13 Aug.)*, but no reference to any passenger use then; LNW notice *(T 2 July 1855)* advertised extra Monday and Friday market trains to Caledonian Road station of NL, 'within a few minutes walk' of new Metropolitan Cattle Market' and in *Brad* Caledonian Road was noted as station for here – this would have been the case for most passengers. However, in *Brad*, footnote added March 1863 that a train from Windsor LSW ran to Cattle Market station in Maiden Lane but returned from Cattle Siding in Maiden Lane but returned from Cattle Siding in Maiden Lane (any significance? – arrival/departure sides of station?); this service clearly began considerably earlier since it was included in *The Intelligible Railway Guide* for June 1858. Detailed company tts show trains also took portion to Reading on return and that those with return tickets could return to Windsor from Waterloo if they wished.
(D. Geldard; M.H. Hughes, *Chron October 2003*).
Last in *Brad* November 1866 – cannot be guaranteed that this was the end of it.
CATTON ROAD – see ALLENDALE.
CAULDCOTS [NB] first in *Brad* October 1883; clo 22 September 1930 *(Cl)*.
CAUSELAND [GW] op 11 September 1879 *(Cornish T 13th- line)*; ★; clo 3 November 1990 for flood prevention work, reop 19 November 1990 *(RM January 1991)*; still open. HALT in *hb* 1938 and 1956, and on GW ticket *(JB)* but not in *Brad* until 1952; aot request; HALT dropped 5 May 1969.
★ = last in *Brad* November 1881 and shown as 'closed' December 1881, when replaced by Sandplace; back June 1888, and then listed in new openings panel; according to G. Beale, *Liskeard & Looe Branch*, Wild Swan, 2000 and M. Messenger, *Caradon & Looe*, Twelveheads, 2001, they intended to close this when Sandplace opened but public pressure kept it open. GW tts of this era ignored existence of branch – Menheniot was shown as 'for Looe'.
CAUSEWAY CROSSING [BWA]:
line op 18 May 1901★★, nd, March 1902 *Brad*; alias THE CAUSEWAY; clo 28 March 1917★★.
CAUSEWAYEND near Wigtown [PPW Jt]:
orders to open given 22 May 1875, receipts shown June

(company minutes); in *hb* as C SIDING (but 'P' only); aot request; last in *Brad* November 1885; {map 17}.
CAUSEWAYEND near Linlithgow [NB]
op 5 August 1840★★; re-sited at least once, probably twice – original south of canal, probably different site for service to Linlithgow, certainly north of canal for service to Bo'ness (D Stirling); clo 1 May 1930 (Thursday) *(Cl)*.
CAUSEWAYHEAD [Carlisle & Silloth]
first in *Brad* November 1856; Saturdays only; originally CAUSEY HEAD *(Brad)*, amended 1857; last in *Brad* April 1859.
CAUSEWAYHEAD near Stirling [NB] op 1 July 1852 *(D&C 15- line)*; clo 1 January 1917 *(RM Feb.)*; reop 1 February 1919 *(RM February)*; after October 1949, before/with 5 June 1950 *Brad* reduced to service towards Stirling only; clo 4 July 1955 *(Cl)*.
NB co tt 1900: C for BRIDGE OF ALLAN.
CAVE – see NORTH CAVE; SOUTH CAVE.
CAVENDISH [GE] op 9 August 1865 *(GE- line)*; clo 6 March 1967 *(RM April)*.
CAWDOR – see KILDRUMMIE.
CAWOOD [NE] op 16 February 1898 *(co n Cawood)*; clo 1 January 1930 (Wednesday) *(Cl)*; occasional excursions until about 1945/6 *(Cawood)*.
CAWSTON [GE] op 1 September 1880 *(RCG)*; clo 15 September 1952 *(RM October)*.
CAYTHORPE [GN] op 15 April 1867 *(GN; co ½ T 19 August- line)*; clo 10 September 1962 *(RM October)*.
CAYTON [NE]: line op 7 October 1846★★, nd, May 1848 *(Topham)*; clo 20 September 1915 *(T 18th)*; back in tt June 1921; reduced to Saturdays only after 1 July 1940 co tt alterations, before/with December 1940 *Brad*; clo 5 May 1952 *(RM June)*.
CEFN near Wrexham [GW] first in *Brad* July 1849, replacing RHOSYMEDRE, 20 chains north of it *(RAC)*; clo 12 September 1960 *(Cl)*.
CEFN – see BUTTINGTON; KENFIG HILL.
CEFN COED [BM/LNW] op 1 August 1867★★ *(BM; Cardiff T 27 July- line)* as CEFN (originally in *hb* as CEFN COED CYMMER); COED added 1 May 1920 *(hbl 22 April)*; HALT in *Brad* 1933/4 to 1934/5; clo 13 November 1961 *(T 8th)*.
CEFN COED COLLIERY [GW] op 8 September 1930 *(Cl 29)*; HALT; clo 15 October 1962 *(RM Nov.)*; {Crynant – Cilfrew}.
CEFN CRIB [West Midland] first in *Brad* February 1860; last trains October 1860; {Pontypool – Crumlin}.
CEFN MAWR – see ACREFAIR.
CEFN TILLA op 14 June 1954 *(Cl 29)*; HALT; clo 30 May 1955★★; {Usk – Llandenny}.
CEFN-ONN [Rhy] first in *Brad* October 1915★, only footpath access; originally C-ON; HALT until 5 May 1969 *(GW H)*; spelling altered 12 May 1980 tt; clo 29 September 1986 *(BLN 546)*.
★ = perhaps op earlier – ready for inspection 18 June 1915, reported in order 6 August 1915 *(MT6/2360/6)*.
CEFN-Y-BEDD near Wrexham [WMCQ]
op 1 May 1866 *(T 7th)*; still open.
CEFN-Y-BEDD – see CILMERI.
CEINT [LNW] op 1 July 1908 *(RCG; LNW Officers 42318- line)*; clo 22 September 1930 *(Cl)*.

CELLULOID SIDING [PT] (non-tt):
blank workman's ticket dated 190. exists *(JB)*;
engineer's report 15 March 1917 *(RAIL 1057/1528)*
said platform for German prisoners had been completed
– keep apart from British workers?; {*RAC* atlas, p.154:
English Celluloid Co's Siding at 1m 45ch}.

CELTIC [PT]
CELTIC (non-tt): miners' HALT; op ?; clo by September
1938; {Celtic Lower – Bettws Llangeinor} *(U)*.
C LOWER (non-tt): miners' PLATFORM, earlier
CWM CEDFYW RHONDDA HALT; op ?;
clo after 1930; {Celtic Halt – Lletty Brongu} *(U)*.

CELYNEN [GW]
C NORTH (non-tt): miners' HALT; op 10 August 1936
(GW notice 1279); clo 30 April 1962 *(U)*;
{Newbridge – Crumlin LL}.
C SOUTH op 14 August 1933 *(GW notice dated
'August')*; HALT; SOUTH added 1936 *(Cl)*;
clo 30 April 1962 *(T 6 April)*; {Newbridge – Abercarn}.

CEMENT MILLS [IWC] (non-tt but public):
HALT; mainly for factory workers but also used by
fishermen and locals; opened by January 1870; rebuilt
and shelter provided after April 1898 (decision then
taken) (V. Mitchell & K. Smith, *Branch Lines to Newport*,
Middleton 1985); clo 21 February 1966 *(U)*;
{Newport – Mill Hill}.

CEMETERY [Rhy] (non-tt):
in *hb* 1872; 'has been closed' *hbl 27 May 1898*;
{Cardiff Adam Street – Caerphilly – see *RAC*}.

CEMETERY/C GATES
– see BOTANIC GARDENS Hull.

CEMETERY ROAD [LNW/Rhy] (non-tt): HALT;
purpose ?; op ?; clo by September 1928;
{Rhymney – Rhymney Bridge} *(U)*.

CEMMAES [Cam] op 30 September 1867 *(co n
Merioneth 5 October)* as CEMMES, stop as required;
clo 17 April 1901 (Wednesday); reop 31 July 1911
(RCG) as CEMMAES; clo 1 January 1931★★
(Thursday) *(Cl)*.

CEMMES ROAD
CEMMES ROAD [Cam – main] op 5 January 1863★★;
clo 14 June 1965 *(RM July)*.
CEMMES ROAD [Cam – Mawddwy] op 30 September
1867 *(co n Merioneth 5 October)*; clo 17 April 1901 (Wed.)
(G&S). (Line reop 31 July 1911 from main station.)

CENTRAL Royal Albert Dock [PLA] op 3 August
1880 *(co n T 31 July*, which shows it as terminus of
shuttle from Custom House, pending further
arrangements); became HALT 1 November 1933
(R. Green, *Chron January 2006*); clo 9 September
1940★★. GE co tt 1914: ROYAL ALBERT DOCK C.
CENTRAL CROYDON [LBSC] op 1 January 1868
(co n T 1st); clo 1 December 1871 (Friday); reop 1 June
1886 *(Cl)*; clo 1 September 1890 *(co n LRR October
2000)*. Often described as Croydon Central during
second use but not seen thus *(hb* lists all Croydon
stations under 'Croydon').

CENTRAL WALES JUNCTION
– see BUILTH ROAD.

CERIST [Van] op 1 December 1873★★- line;
last trains shown October 1875 *(Brad)*; trains again

September 1876; Tuesdays only; request stop,
originally in *hb* as C SIDING; last in *Brad* July 1879
(August 'service suspended') – but still 'P' in *hb* 1895
(not 1904); {goods *IA*}.

CERNEY – see SOUTH CERNEY.

CERRIG Y PENRHYN – see ABERDOVEY.

CESSNOCK [GU]
op 14 December 1896★★; still open.

CHACEWATER [GW] first in *Brad* November 1853
and tt *Penzance* 2 November 1853 – likely that it op
1 November with new tt; clo 5 October 1964 *(Cl)*.
Intelligible tt 1858: C SEVEOCK.

CHADWELL HEATH [GE]
op 11 January 1864 *(co n T 11th)*; still open.
Became C H for BECONTREE 1927? *(hbl ref October)*
and thus LNE tt 1933 and *Brad* to 1955.

CHAFFORD HUNDRED op 30 May 1995
(ceremonial 29th) *(GE News, Autumn)*; still open.

CHALCOMBE ROAD [GC] op 17 April 1911
(GC dates); HALT (but PLATFORM in *hb*);
clo 6 February 1956 *(RM March)*.

CHALDER [WS] op 27 August 1897 *(D&C 2- line)*;
clo 20 January 1935★★.

CHALFONT & LATIMER [Met/GC]
op 8 July 1889 by Met *(L; LNW Record- line)* as C ROAD;
GC use began 15 March 1899; renamed 1 November
1915 *(hbl 27 January 1916)*; still open.

CHALFORD [GW] op 2 August 1897 *(Stroud N 6th)*;
clo 2 November 1964 *(W D Press 2nd)*.

CHALK FARM {map 101}
CHALK FARM [NL] – see PRIMROSE HILL.
CHALK FARM [LNW] op 1 April 1872 *(LNW Officers
7672*, which also refers to start of through traffic to
Willesden) as CAMDEN C F, replacing earlier station
of this name; renamed 1876; in e.g. 1882 LNW co tt
referred to C F NL Platforms and C F LNW Platforms;
clo 10 May 1915 *(RCG)*.
CHALK FARM [Nor] op 22 June 1907★★; still open.
Pre-op Adelaide Road *(L)*.

CHALKWELL [LMS]
op 11 September 1933 *(LNW Record)*; still open.

**CHALLOCH JUNCTION GOLFERS
PLATFORM** [PPW Jt] (non-tt): used 1894 to
October 1918 at latest *(U)*; {physical junction *IA*}.

CHALLOW [GW]
op 20 July 1840 *(co n Bristol Stand 23rd)* as
FARINGDON ROAD; renamed 1 June 1864 *(GW ac)*;
clo 7 December 1964 *(Cl)*. At times early *Brad* and *hb*
made FARINGTON–FARRINGDON R of it.

CHALVEY [GW] op 6 May 1929 *(T 7th)*; HALT;
clo 7 July 1930 *(Cl)*; {Slough – Windsor}.

CHAMBERS CROSSING [GW]
op 17 October 1904 *(GW H)* – but not in *Brad* until
February 1905; HALT; clo 14 July 1916 (Friday)
(RCH); {Milcote – Stratford}.

CHAMPION HILL – see EAST DULWICH.

CHANCERY LANE [Cen] op 30 July 1900
(L; T 25th- line); 1934 renamed C L GRAYS INN *(L)*,
though not seen thus in *Brad*; G I gradually dropped;
see 1922★★; still open.

CHANDLERS FORD
CHANDLERS FORD (a) [LSW] first in *Brad* February 1848; clo 5 May 1969 *(Cl)*. Until 1852 one word in *Brad*, though two from start in *Topham*.

CHANDLERS FORD (b): op Sunday 18 May 2003 *(Rly Obs August, p. 362)*; still open.

CHANNEL TUNNEL SIDINGS [SE] (non-tt): workmen; in use 1899; {Folkestone Warren – Dover} *(U)*.

CHANTERS LANE [BWA] – see THE LANE.

CHAPEL BRIDGE [Monmouthshire] first in *Brad* May 1855; clo 1 July 1876 (Saturday) *(RAIL 253/228)*; {Cross Keys – Llanbradach}. Cwmcarn near here later.

CHAPEL LANE [SM] first in *Brad* August 1920; request; finally clo 6 November 1933.
See 1866 August 13** (Criggion branch) for line history.

CHAPEL STREET Prestatyn [LNW] op 29 January 1906 (T. Thomson, *The Prestatyn & Dyserth Railway*, North Clwyd Railway Association, 1978); clo 22 September 1930 *(Cl)*; {Dyserth branch}.

CHAPEL TOWN
– see TURTON & EDGEWORTH.

CHAPEL-EN-LE-FRITH
CHAPEL-EN-LE-FRITH [LNW] op 15 June 1863 *(LNW Officers)*; C-en-le-F SOUTH 2 June 1924 *(Rly Gaz 23 May)* to 6 May 1968 *(Cl)*; still open.

C-EN-LE-F CENTRAL [Mid] op 1 February 1867 *(Mid; T 2nd- line)*; CENTRAL added 2 June 1924 *(Rly Gaz 23 May)*; clo 6 March 1967 *(RM April)*.

CHAPELHALL [Cal] op 1 September 1887 *(Cal)*; see 1921 April/May**; clo 1 December 1930 *(Cl)*.

CHAPELTON [LSW] probably op 8 June 1857 *(Brad June* says 'will open 8th inst.'; in *tt 11 June Trewman)*; initially all days, including Sundays; April 1858 reduced to Tuesdays and Fridays as C SIDING; briefly back to full service end May to early June for Bath & West Show at Barnstaple *(Trewman)*; October 1858 reduced to Fridays only; last in tt *N Devon J* 19 April 1860 (but *Brad* August 1860 – inertia?); reop 1 March 1875 *(LSW)* but not back in *Brad* until June 1875, all days. Variously early: CHAPPLETOWN; CHAP(P)ELTOWN; settled as CHAPELTON on reopening 1875; HALT 2 January 1966 to 5 May 1969 *(Cl)*; altered to CHAPLETON 29 September 1996 in National Fares Manual (D. Steggles, *Chron*) – error?, reverted 20 May 2001 tt *(AB Chron)*. Aot request. Still open.

CHAPELTOWN near Sheffield
CHAPELTOWN [Mid] op 1 July 1897 *(RCG)*; C SOUTH 18 June 1951 *(Mid)* to 20 February 1969 (BR ER commercial circular of that date 'forthwith' – *JS)*; re-sited 200 yards nearer the town 2 August 1982 *(RM August)*; still open.

C CENTRAL [GC] op 4 September 1854 *(GC; co ½ T 1 September -line)* as C; renamed C & THORNCLIFFE June 1895 *(Cl; RCG ref April)*, C CENTRAL 18 June 1951 *(Cl)*; clo 7 December 1953 *(RM January 1954)*.

CHAPPEL & WAKES COLNE [GE] op 2 July 1849 *(T 5th- line)* as CHAPPEL; renamed 1 October 1914 *(hbl 29th)*; still open.

CHARD
C CENTRAL [GW/LSW] op 11 September 1866 *(W Fly P 14th)* as C; became C JOINT 1879 *(SR)*; JOINT dropped 1 March 1928 *(hbl April)*; CENTRAL added 26 September 1949 *(Cl)*; clo 5 February 1951 *(Chard 3rd)*, reop 7 May 1951 *(Chard 5th)* – see 1951**; clo 10 September 1962 *(Chard 15th)*.

C JUNCTION [LSW] op 19 July 1860**; branch plats added and clo, dates as for C Central; originally C ROAD, renamed 1872 tt *(Cl)*; aot C R J *(hb)*; clo 7 March 1966 *(Chard 3rd)*.

C TOWN [LSW] op 8 May 1863 *(Taunton 13th)* as C; even when line opened through to the GW, this remained a terminus until through platform added about 1871; clo 1 January 1917 *(Express & E 29 December 1916)*.

Brad for a while managed to make three entries of Central and Town after opening of link to GW: C NEW (called first), C TOWN, C [GW] – presumably error of some kind, later C TOWN, C NEW; latter became C JOINT 1879/80.

CHARFIELD [Mid] op 8 July 1844 *(Bristol T 13th)*; renamed C for WOOTTON-UNDER-EDGE 1 July 1879 co tt *(Mid)*; clo 4 January 1965 *(Cl)*.

CHARING [LCD] op 1 July 1884 *(LCD)*; still open.

CHARING CROSS London
For main line station see under LONDON.

CHARING CROSS [Bak] op 10 March 1906 *(L;T 12th-line)* as TRAFALGAR SQUARE; see 1922**; 1 May 1979 renamed C C, becoming part, with ex-Strand, of interchange station *(L)*; still open.

CHARING CROSS [Jub] op 1 May 1979 *(RM July)*; clo after last train on Friday 19 November 1999 (effectively replaced by Westminster on extension to Stratford) but retained for occasional use to relieve congestion *(RM March 2000)*.

CHARING CROSS [Nor] op 22 June 1907**; became C C STRAND 6 April 1914 *(hbl 23rd)*, S 1 May 1915 *(hbl 15 July)*; see 1922**; clo 17 June 1973 for rebuilding; reop 1 May 1979 as C C *(L)*; still open.
Also see EMBANKMENT.

CHARING CROSS Glasgow [NB] op 15 March 1886 *(Glasgow; co ½ T 19 March- line)*; still open. Sometimes GLASGOW C C in tts.

CHARLBURY [GW] op 4 June 1853 *(Glos Chron 4th- line)*; still open.

CHARLESFIELD [NB] (non-tt): HALT; workmen; op 10 August 1942 *(MT29/96/60)*; clo by June 1961 *(U)*; {St Boswells – Belses}.

CHARLESTOWN near Dunfermline
For earliest service see 1833 A**.

CHARLESTOWN [NB] op 1 September 1894 *(D&C 15)*; clo 1 November 1926 *(Cl)*. Cl date would have given last train Saturday October 30; *W Fife* suggests that perhaps lasted a week longer – last 6 November.

CHARLESTOWN – see ASHTON-U-LYNE

CHARLTON near Bristol [GW] op 9 May 1910 *(W D Press 10th)*; HALT; clo 22 March 1915 *(RCH)*; workmen's use continued *(GM's report 12 January 1917)* – until ?; {map 121}.

CHARLTON near Hexham [NB] op 1 February 1861 *(NC- line)*; clo 1 October 1862 (Wednesday) *(Cl)*; {Bellingam – Tarset}. In *hb* as CHARLETON.

CHARLTON near Oxford [LNW] op 9 October 1905 *(Oxford Chron 6th)*; see 1905**; clo 1 January 1917 *(T 22 December 1916)*; reop 5 May 1919 *(RCH)*; clo 25 October 1926 *(Cl)*.

CHARLTON near Woolwich [SE] op 30 July 1849**; C JUNCTION 1877/8 to 1928/9 *(Brad)*; still open.

CHARLTON KINGS [GW] op 1 June 1881 *(Bristol Merc 2nd)*; clo 15 October 1962 *(RM Nov.)*.

CHARLTON MACKRELL [GW] op 1 July 1905 *(Langport 1st, 8th)*; clo 10 September 1962 *(Som Gaz 15th)*.

CHARLTON MARSHALL [SD Jt] op 9 July 1928 *(W Gaz Bournemouth edition 22 June)*; HALT; clo 17 September 1956 *(T 13th)*; used after closure by pupils of Claysmore Preparatory School at start and end of term *(School's website)*; {Blandford – Spetisbury}. Pre-opening C M (Parkhill Road) *(Rly Gaz 6 July)*.

CHARTHAM [SE] first trains shown in tt November 1859; still open.

CHARTLEY [GN] op 23 December 1867 (P. Jones, *The Stafford & Uttoxeter Railway*, Oakwood, 1981; *T 13th- line*) as STOWE; renamed 3 October 1874 *(Cl; RCG ref October)*; trains ceased to be shown from start of LNE emergency tt 2 October 1939.

CHARWELTON [GC] op 15 March 1899 *(GC; T 16th- line)*; clo 4 March 1963 *(RM March)*.

CHASSEN ROAD [CLC] op 10 September 1934 *(RM November)*; still open.

CHAT MOSS – see 1830 September 17**.

CHATBURN [LY] op 22 June 1850**; new station about 100 yards north 2 June 1879 *(Cl supp)*; clo 10 September 1962 *(T 5 July)*. *Hb* 1877: C & HORROCKSFORD.

CHATELHERAULT op 12 December 2005**; short distance north of earlier Ferniegair; still open.

CHATHAM {map 129}

CHATHAM [LCD] op 25 January 1858**; still open.

C CENTRAL [SE] op 1 March 1892 *(SE)*; CENTRAL added?; clo 1 October 1911 (Sunday) *(RCG)*.

C DOCKYARD – see Section 7: 2.

CHATHILL [NE] op 29 March 1847 *(Newcastle Journal 3 April)*; still open.

CHATTERIS [GN/GE] op 1 March 1848**; clo 6 March 1967 *(RM April)*.

CHATTERLEY [NS] first in *Brad* January 1864, as TUNSTALL; renamed 1873 in *Brad*, where C for T until 1881; clo 27 September 1948 *(Cl)*.

CHAUL END [GN] (non-tt): HALT; munitions workers; 1914 to about 1919; {Luton – Dunstable} *(U)*.

CHEADLE near Stoke-on-Trent [NS] op 1 January 1901 *(RCG)*; clo 17 June 1963 *(RM July)*. Later excursions, e.g. to Liverpool 4 August 1963; football to Stoke 1963/4, last 18 April 1964 *(AB)*.

CHEADLE near Stockport

CHEADLE [Manchester & Birmingham] op 10 May 1842 (fare table, *co n Stockport 13th*); replaced by >

C HULME [LNW] op 24 November 1845 *(LNW; co ½ Rly Chron 7 March 1846- line)* slightly nearer Stockport, at junction with line to Macclesfield; HULME added 1 March 1866 *(Cl)*; still open.

CHEADLE [LNW] op 1 August 1866 *(LNW Officers*

1356); clo 1 January 1917 *(T 22 December 1916)*.

C HEATH [Mid] op 1 October 1901 *(RCG)*; C H for STOCKPORT 1 May 1902 co tt to 14 June 1965 co tt ('for' omitted 1 October 1908 co tt) *(Mid)*; clo 2 January 1967 *(T 8 December 1966)*.

CHEADLE [CLC] op 1 December 1865 *(Stockport 1st)*; clo 30 November 1964 *(RM March 1965)*.

CHEAM [LBSC] op 10 May 1847 *(T 8th/Globe)*; still open.

CHECKER HOUSE [GC] op 1 April 1852 *(GC)*; aot request; clo 14 September 1931 *(Cl)*.

CHEDDAR [GW] op 3 August 1869 *(Shepton 6th)*; clo 9 September 1963 *(Weston 13th)*.

CHEDDINGTON [LNW] logically op 10 June 1839 with Aylesbury branch; in footnotes co tt 20 June 1839 *(Lee)* as THE AYLESBURY JUNCTION; shown as C early 1840, with full list of fares in *RAIL 384/21*; not present in *Brad* until April 1844, when only southbound trains shown; it should be noted that some Aylesbury trains operated from Tring (see working tt for May 1841 in *Harrow*) – even so, unlikely that *Brad* told whole story. Still open.

C JUNCTION 1850 to 1869/70 *Brad* and LNW co tts 1852 and 1864 (but not 1868).

CHEDDLETON [NS]

CHEDDLETON op 1 September 1849 *(Churnet)*; clo 4 January 1965 *(RM March)*; later excur *(U)*.

C ASYLUM – see LEEK BROOK.

CHEDWORTH [MSWJ] op 1 October 1892 *(MSWJ)*; replaced 1902; HALT at clo 11 September 1961 *(T 9th)*.

CHEE DALE: HALT; summer Sundays 5 July to 13 September 1987 plus a Bank Holiday Monday (13 times in all); later use prevented by Health & Safety Executive – line's signalling not up to passenger standard (A. Brackenbury, quoting retired signalling engineer); for ramblers in Peak District.

CHEESEWRING – see 1844**.

CHELFHAM [Lynton] op 16 May 1898 *(N Devon J 19th- line)*; became HALT 1910 *(Brad)*; clo 30 September 1935**.

CHELFORD [LNW] op 10 May 1842 (fare table, *co n Stockport 13th*); still open. LNW co tt 1852: C for KNUTSFORD and NANTWICH. LNW co tt 1864, LMS tt 1930 and *Brad* always (last issue 1961), but not BR LM tt 1957: C for K.

CHELL JUNCTION [NS] (non-tt): interchange point with Whitfield Colliery Co's line (see Section 7:4); op 3 November 1890, clo 1923 (A. Baker, *Illustrated History of Stoke & North Staffs Railway*); in *U* as HALT; {Ford Green – Black Bull}.

CHELLASTON & SWARKESTONE [Mid] op 1 September 1868 *(co n Melbourne)*; clo 22 September 1930 *(Mid)*; still in use for excursions at 10 August 1961 *(BR handbill)* and 1 August 1962 *(IU)*. Always C & S *(Mid co tt)* but C until 15 June 1901 *(hbl 11 July)*.

CHELLASTON EAST JUNCTION [LMS] (non-tt): forces leave tickets *(JB)* – one 'C E J for Ashby Military Railway', another 'C E J for Melbourne Military Railway'. *Melbourne*, p.91, refers to Army's 'four days a week recreational trains to Derby' but gives no details.

CHELMSFORD [GE]

CHELMSFORD op 29 March 1843 *(T 30th)*; new station about 200 yards south 1856 *(Cl)*; still open.
Non-tt (a): Royal Agricultural Society Show held on Walk-field 15–18 July 1856. Special siding for implements, cattle and those accompanying but general public seemed to have used ordinary station, nearby *(co n T 15th; item T 16th)*.
Non-tt (b): 4 August 1860 a Grand Review of Yeomanry Cavalry and Volunteer Rifle Corps and Sham Fight was held in grounds of Hyland's Park, just south of here. From notice would appear that special trains ran from London and Colchester direct to Hyland's for Volunteers but all had to use ordinary station for return *(co n T 1st)*.

CHELSEA & FULHAM [WL] op 2 March 1863 *(LSW co n T 4th)*; & F added 1 January 1903 *(RCG)*; clo 14 September 1940 *(wtt supp)*.

CHELSFIELD [SE]
op 2 March 1868 *(L; co ½ T 21 August- line)*; still open.

CHELTENHAM
(where relevant, SPA added 1 February 1925 – *hbl April*).
C SPA [Mid] op 24 June 1840 *(Chelt Chron 27th)*; still open. Local press called it LANSDOWN at opening; C QUEENS ROAD L in *Brad* from 1867 to 1925; C L in *hb* 1892a, but not in *Mid tt* until 1 February 1925; renamed C S 6 May 1968 tt *(off)*.
C SPA MALVERN ROAD [GW] op 30 March 1908 *(Chelt Exam 1 April)*; clo 1 January 1917 *(GW notice dated 22 December 1916)*; reop 7 July 1919 *(GW circ 2672)*; clo 3 January 1966 *(RM February)*.
C SPA ST JAMES [GW] op 23 October 1847 *(Bath & Chelt 27th)* as C; re-sited to the east 9 September 1894 *(Cl supp 2)*; ST J added 11 May 1908 *(hbl 9 July)* but *Brad* had C ST J SQUARE 1867 to 1910; clo 3 January 1966 *(RM February)*.
C HIGH STREET [GW] op 1 October 1908 *(Chelt Exam 1st)*; HALT; clo 30 April 1917 *(Cl)*; {north of Malvern Road}.
C HIGH STREET [Mid] op 1 September 1862 *(Chelt Chron 2nd)* as C TEWKESBURY ROAD BRIDGE; renamed next month; clo 1 July 1910 (Friday) *(RCG)*; {north of Lansdown}.
C LECKHAMPTON [GW] op 1 June 1881 *(Bristol Merc 2nd)* as L; renamed C SOUTH & L 1 May 1906 *(hbl 26 April)*, C L 1952 *(Cl)*; clo 15 October 1962 *(RM November)*.
C RACECOURSE [GW] (non-tt): race meetings; op 13 March 1912 *(race)*; line closed 25 March 1968, just after race meeting of 21 March, *(RM May; AB)* but reop 16 March 1971 *(AB)* to here for occasional use, last 18 March 1976 *(BLN 320 p.76)*; reop again in April 2003 for race excursions by Gloucestershire Warwickshire Railway (Preservation) *(AB)*; {Cheltenham – Bishops Cleeve}.
Pre-opening Evesham Road Bridge *(RAC)*.

CHEPSTOW
CHEPSTOW [GW] op 19 June 1850** from Cardiff direction *(Cl)*. For race meetings: extension to up

platform, 'No.3 Platform', used both ways, separate entrance; into use 1926 (report for 1926 *GW Mag January 1927*); certainly used until 1941 *(race)*.
C EAST [South Wales] temp station op 19 September 1851 from Gloucester direction *(Gloucester J 20th)*. Gap between two existed until bridge op 19 July 1852 *(Gloucester J 17th)*; C EAST then closed.

CHEQUERBENT [LNW]
CHEQUERBENT : line op 13 June 1831**, nd, mid 1846 when in *Huish List*; not in *Brad* until May 1847. New station on deviation 2 February 1885 *(LNW Officers 26900)*. Clo 3 March 1952 *(RM April)*. *Hb* 1890 on, LNW co tt 1908, LMS tt 1930 and *Brad* to closure: C for HULTON PARK.
C SIDING (non-tt): miners; dates ?; {branch from near C} *(U)*.
CHERITON [SEC] op 1 May 1908 *(SEC)*; HALT; used by Elham Valley trains and summer motor cars to Sandgate; clo 1 December 1915, reop 14 June 1920, clo 1 February 1941, reop 7 October 1946 *(Cl)*; clo 16 June 1947** – but *sig inst 22/1947* makes it look as if permanent closure intended then; {west of Shorncliffe Camp}.
CHERITON ARCH – see FOLKESTONE.
CHERRY BURTON [NE] op 1 May 1865**- line; clo 5 January 1959 *(RM February)*.
CHERRY HINTON [EC]: line op 9 October 1851**, in opening tt, local press, but no trains calling; first in *Brad* August 1852; perhaps case of nd; last trains *Brad* March 1854; spelling is that in *Brad* and EC co tt 1854. {map 70}.
CHERRY LANE – see DONCASTER.
CHERRY TREE near Blackburn [LY] first in *Brad* November 1847; still open.
CHERTSEY [LSW] op 14 February 1848 *(co n T 7th)*; re-sited opposite side of road on extension to Virginia Water 1 October 1866 *(Cl)*; still open.
CHESHAM [Met/GC] op 8 July 1889 by Met *(LNW Record)*; still open. GC/main line use began 1 March 1906, ended 16 October 1967.

CHESHUNT
CHESHUNT [GE] op Whit Sunday 31 May 1846 *(co n T 28th)*; re-sited about 150 yards south 1 October 1891 or a little earlier *(Cl)*; still open.
Also see CADMORES LANE.

CHESSINGTON [SR]
C NORTH op 28 May 1939 *(T 27th)*; still open.
C SOUTH op 28 May 1939 *(T 27th)*; still open.
Hb 1941a: C S for CHESSINGTON ZOO, but not seen thus *Brad*.

CHESTER
CHESTER [BLCJ] terminus from Birkenhead op in Brook Street 23 September 1840 *(D&C 10)* >
CHESTER [Chester & Crewe] terminus op 1 October 1840 *(GW)* >
Both replaced by C Joint [GW/LNW] 1 August 1848 *(GW)*; see map in *Birkenhead* for details of sites; aot C GENERAL; still open. GENERAL was added gradually – in *hb* 1872, in some tables *Brad* 1890s, but co tts later; dropped 6 May 1970 tt.
LNW co tt August 1856 (and other times?) had line

showing arrival at 'ticket stage' Chester for Mail trains only, from Holyhead only. Were passengers allowed to alight? – if not, why in public tt?

C LIVERPOOL ROAD [GC] op 31 March 1890 *(RCG)*; clo 3 December 1951 *(RM January 1952)*.

C NORTHGATE [CLC] op 1 May 1875 *(CLC)*; clo 6 October 1969 *(RM January 1970)*.
During race meetings other sites used – 1874 advertised that return excursion to Worcester would start from **C COAL EXCHANGE YARD** *(Berrows 9 May)*.
C GOLF CLUB was served by non-tt platforms.
One near later Wrexham Junction was in use 1891 to 1895, when it was replaced by one near Chester East Junction, as **C JUNCTION GOLF CLUB PLATFORM**; extra platform provided at Birkenhead Junction 18 May 1896 (as **BIRKENHEAD JUNCTION GOLF PLATFORM**) *(U)*; survivors clo 26 September 1927 *(RAIL 393/151 – Passenger Supt Circ PM 330)*.

CHESTER ROAD [LNW] first in *Brad* December 1862; still open. *Brad* ? to 1955: C R for OSCOTT COLLEGE, but not thus LMS tt 1930.

CHESTER-LE-STREET [NE]
CHESTER-LE-STREET (a) op 16 April 1835**; alias DURHAM TURNPIKE – provided connection with road services; last in *Brad* December 1853; back March 1862; last January 1869; {map 34}.
CHESTER-LE-STREET (b) op 1 December 1868 *(NE- line)*; still open.

CHESTERFIELD
CHESTERFIELD [Mid] op 11 May 1840 *(Mid; co n T 2nd- line)*; re-sited about 100 yards north 2 May 1870 *(Cl)*; renamed C ST MARYS 25 September 1950, C MIDLAND 18 June 1951, C 7 September 1964 *(Mid)*; still open.
C CENTRAL [GC] op 4 June 1892 *(RCG)*; CENTRAL added 1 November 1907 *(hbl 24 October)*; clo 4 March 1963 *(T 27 February)*.
C MARKET PLACE [GC] op 9 March 1897 (8th formal) *(GCR Society Journal Spring 2003, p.12)*; M P added 1 January 1907 *(Cl)*; clo 3 December 1951 *(RM January 1952)*.

CHESTERFIELD ROAD (Ashover) (ng) op 7 April 1925 *(RM October)*; clo 14 September 1936** *(Cl)*; {map 59}.

CHESTERFORD – see GREAT CHESTERFORD.

CHESTERTON [EC] op 19 January 1850 as a flag station *(Cambridge Chronicle 19th- Tony Kirby)*, though not in *Brad* until June 1850; last in *Brad* October 1850; {north of Cambridge at junction with line to St Ives}.

CHESTERTON LANE
op 2 February 1959 *(Wilts 7th)*; HALT; clo 6 April 1964 *(W D Press 6th)*; {Kemble – Cirencester}.

CHESTFIELD & SWALECLIFFE [SR] op 6 July 1930 *(LCD)*; HALT until 5 May 1969 *(SR App)*; still open.

CHETNOLE [GW] op 11 September 1933 *(Cl 29)*; HALT until 5 May 1969 *(GW H)*; aot request; still open.

CHETTISHAM
CHETTISHAM [GE] op 14 January 1847 *(Herapath 16th- line)*; CHITTISHAM until 1 August 1901 *(hbl*

24 October)*; aot request; clo 13 June 1960 *(RM July)*.
Also see ELY.

CHEVENING [SEC] op 16 April 1906 *(SEC)*; HALT; clo 30 October 1961 *(T 21 August)*.
At first C BRIDGE HALT (tt).

CHEVINGTON [NE] first in *Brad* October 1870; clo 15 September 1958 *(RM October)*. C JUNCTION 1882 to 1893/4 in *Brad,* and thus NE co tt 1880.

CHEW MOOR [LY] first in *Brad* January 1851; last July 1851; {Bolton – Lostock Lane}.

CHICHESTER
CHICHESTER [LBSC] op 8 June 1846 *(Hants Chron 13th)*; original terminus east of road replaced when line extended to Havant, 15 March 1847 *(Cl)*; still open. LBSC co tt 1912: C for SELSEY.
Brad 1936 to 1955: C for BRACKLESHAM BAY, EAST & WEST WITTERING and SELSEY.
CHICHESTER [WS] op 27 August 1897 *(D&C 2)*; clo 20 January 1935**.
CHICHESTER [TWM] op 24 March 1984 *(Tyneside)*; still open.

CHICKENLEY HEATH [GN] op 2 July 1877 *(RCG)*; clo 1 July 1909 (Thursday) *(notice of alterations, GN co tt 1 July)*; {map 55}.

CHIGWELL op by [GE] 1 May 1903 *(RCG)*; last steam train ran Saturday 29 November 1947 *(Clay)*; buses until reop by [Cen] 21 November 1948 *(T 20th)*; still open.

CHIGWELL LANE/ROAD – see DEBDEN.

CHILCOMPTON [SD Jt] op 20 July 1874 *(Shepton 24th)*; clo 7 March 1966 *(Shepton 11th)*. LMS tt 1930: C for DOWNSIDE.

CHILDS HILL – see CRICKLEWOOD.

CHILDWALL [CLC] op 1 December 1879 *(CLC)*; clo 1 January 1931 (Thursday) *(Cl)*.

CHILHAM [SE]
op 6 February 1846 *(SE; co n T 2nd- line)* – but see note on CANTERBURY WEST; still open.

CHILLINGHAM ROAD [TWM] op 14 November 1982 *(Tyneside)*; still open

CHILSWORTHY [PDSW] op 1 June 1909 *(SR)*; aot request; clo 7 November 1966 *(Cornish & D P 12th)*. HALT in *hb* 1938 and 1956 and on BR ticket *(JB)* but not in *Brad*.

CHILTERN GREEN [Mid] op 13 July 1868 *(T 14th)*; renamed C G for LUTON HOO 1 December 1891 *(RCG)*; clo 7 April 1952 *(RM May)*. In early years John Shaw Leigh of mansion called The Hoo had right to stop all trains except expresses not stopping between London and Bedford, for self, family and visitors, at ten minutes notice (article, Midland Society Journal, 30).

CHILTON [CMDP] op 21 November 1908**; at first C SIDING HALT in *Brad,* HALT omitted from table about 1908 but still indexed as such; clo June 1917 *(Cl)*; {Cleobury Town – Stottesdon}.

CHILVERS COTON [LNW] op 2 September 1850**; clo 18 January 1965 *(RM March)*.

CHILWELL – see ATTENBOROUGH.

CHILWELL ORDNANCE DEPOT [LMS] (non-tt): op 1940 – station inside depot (C.J. Perkins & R. Padgett, *The Midland Railway in Nottingham*, vol.III,

Furlong Press, 2002); clo 4 November 1963 (U);
{branch from Attenborough}.

CHILWORTH [SE] op 20 August 1849 (co n T 18th);
renamed C & ALBURY 1864 (Brad and thus SE co tt
April 1864), reverted to C 12 May 1980 (Cl); still open.

CHINA QUARRY [Glyn] (non-tt): workmen; dates ?;
{Glynceiriog – Pandy} (U).

CHINGFORD [GE] op 17 November 1873 (L);
re-sited to north 2 September 1878 (Cl); still open.

CHINLEY [Mid] op 1 February 1867 (Mid- wtt;
T 2nd- line); re-sited further north 1 June 1902 (Mid);
still open.

CHINNOR [GW] op 15 August 1872 (GW- line);
clo 1 July 1957 (RM August).

CHIPPENHAM [GW]
op 31 May 1841 (Bath Chron 3 June); still open.
C JUNCTION 1853 to 1858 in Brad.

CHIPPING CAMPDEN [GW] op 4 June 1853
(Glos Chron 4th- line) as CAMPDEN; renamed 1952;
clo 3 January 1966 (RM February).

CHIPPING NORTON [GW]
op 10 August 1855 (T 11th); re-sited when line
extended to King's Sutton 6 April 1887 (Cl);
clo 3 December 1962 (RM January 1963).

CHIPPING NORTON JUNCTION
– see KINGHAM.

CHIPPING SODBURY [GW] op 1 July 1903
(Bristol T 2nd); clo 3 April 1961 (RM May).

CHIPSTEAD [SE] first train 9 November 1897 (L);
C & BANSTEAD DOWNS 1898 (Brad) to 9 July
1923 (hbl 26 April); still open.

CHIRK
CHIRK [GW] op 14 October 1848 (Shrewsbury 13th);
still open. Mr Biddulph awarded right to stop trains
by GW Deed 4329G, dated 23 August 1850.
CHIRK [Glyn] (ng) op 15 March 1891 (Glyn);
clo 7 April 1933★★; {map 79}.

CHIRMOR(R)IE [LMS] (non-tt): Railwaymen,
families; in use 1926, 1938; {Barrhill – Glenwhilly} (U).

CHIRNSIDE [NB]: for op see 1849 August 15★★;
clo 10 September 1951 (RM October).

CHISELDON [MSWJ; GW]
CHISELDON op 27 July 1881★★; clo 11 September
1961 (T 9th). Ticket for CHISLEDON (JB).
C CAMP: platform put up here to deal with
demobilisation after First World War (MSWJ);
op as public station 1 December 1930 (N Wilts
28 November – also mentions earlier use); HALT;
clo 11 September 1961 (T 9th); {south of Chiseldon}.

CHISLEHURST [SE] op 1 July 1865 (co ½ T 23 Aug.);
C & BICKLEY PARK until 1 September 1866 (Cl);
replaced by new station on extension to Sevenoaks,
soon after 2 March 1868 (SE); still open.

CHISLET [SEC] first in Brad June 1920;
C COLLIERY HALT until 5 May 1969 (SR App);
clo 4 October 1971 (RM November).

CHISWICK
CHISWICK [LSW] op 22 August 1849 (co n T 22nd);
became C & GROVE PARK 1 November 1872 (Cl),
C for G P 1920/1 (RCG ref January 1921),
C 1955 (Brad); still open.

C PARK [Dist] op 1 July 1879 (L;T 2nd- line) as
ACTON GREEN; renamed C P & A G 1887,
C P 1 March 1910 (RCG); still open.

CHITTENING [GW] {map 121}
C FACTORY (non-tt): workmen; op 5 March 1917
(RAC); {Avonmouth – Pilning} (U); replaced★ by >
C PLATFORM op 13 November 1918★ (wtt supp),
non-tt; clo 11 October 1923 (wtt supp);
reop 27 October 1941, still non-tt (U);
clo 1 August 1946, reop 25 August 1947 (workmen)
(RAC); first in Brad November 1947, but not officially
public until 31 May 1948 (RAC);
clo 23 November 1964 (Bristol E P 21st).
★ = Notice dated 1 February 1917 said men would be picked
up from ballast where opening had been made in fence and
board 'ROCKINGHAM' put up (RAC, see GW atlas).
Perhaps replaced C F, perhaps both briefly in use together,
until C P opened.

CHOLLERFORD – see HUMSHAUGH.

CHOLLERTON [NB]: line op 1 December 1859
(NC), nd, June 1860; clo 15 October 1956 (T 21 Sept.).

CHOLSEY [GW] op 29 February 1892 (co n Reading
27th); replaced Moulsford; op as C & M;
renamed 6 May 1974 (BR notice); still open.

CHOPPINGTON [NE] op 1 April 1858 (BT;T 3rd-
line; in inspection report); reduced to one train daily,
towards Morpeth, after 6 October 1947, before/with
31 May 1948 BR NE tt; clo 3 April 1950 (Cl).

CHORLEY
For temporary station at RAWLINSON BRIDGE
see under 'R'.
CHORLEY [LY] op 22 December 1841 (LY corr);
still open.
C ROYAL ORDNANCE FACTORY PLATFORM
(variations – R O F HALT C, BR LM wtt 1951),
later C HALT [LMS] (non-tt): op 24 January 1938 –
'not for public' (LNW Record); clo 31 August 1964 (U);
{Chorley – Leyland}.

CHORLEYWOOD [Met/GC] op 8 July 1889 by Met
(L; LNW Record- line); as CHORLEY WOOD;
GC trains added 15 March 1899;
renamed C W & CHENIES 1 November 1915 (hbl
27 January 1917); & CHENIES dropped 1950/1 (Brad)
to one word 1987 BR tt; still open.
Underground maps dropped '& Chenies' 1937/40 and
used one word version from 1964/8.

CHORLTON-CUM-HARDY [CLC] op 1 January
1880 (RCG); clo 2 January 1967 (T 8 December 1966).

CHOWBENT
– see ATHERTON BAG LANE; HOWE BRIDGE.

CHRISTCHURCH [LSW] {map 125}
Originally served by CHRISTCHURCH ROAD
– see HOLMSLEY.
CHRISTCHURCH op 13 November 1862 (Dorset Chron
20th); replaced by new station on coast line 30 May
1886 (W Gaz, Hants edition, 28th); still open. LSW co tt
1914, SR tt 1947: C for SOUTHBOURNE-ON-SEA.

CHRISTIAN MALFORD [GW]
op 18 October 1926 (GW H); HALT; clo 4 January
1965 (RM February); {Chippenham – Dauntsey}.

CHRISTON BANK [NE]: line op 1 July 1847★★, nd,

August; clo 5 May 1941, reop 7 October 1946 *(RM January 1947)*; clo 15 September 1958 *(RM October)*.

CHRISTOW [GW] op 1 July 1903 *(Trewman 4th)*; clo 9 June 1958 *(T 5th)*.

CHRISTS HOSPITAL [LBSC] op 28 April 1902 *(LBSC)* as C H WEST HORSHAM; renamed 1968/72 tt; still open.

CHRYSTON [MK]: see 1828 B★★; first known use in second half of 1839; clo 1840 or soon after *(MK)*; {map 16}.

CHRYSTON ROAD – see GARNKIRK.

CHUDLEIGH [GW]

CHUDLEIGH op 9 October 1882 *(Torquay Dir 11th)*; clo 9 June 1958 *(T 5th)*.
Non-tt: emergency platform on Trusham side of station for use when trains unable to pass floods *(Exeter notice 28 September 1932)*.

C KNIGHTON op 9 June 1924 *(GW H)*; HALT; clo 9 June 1958 *(T 5th)*; {south of Chudleigh}.

C ROAD – see HEATHFIELD near Exeter.

CHURCH & OSWALDTWISTLE [LY] op 19 June 1848 *(LY; Lancaster Guardian 17th- line)*; & O added 1 January 1895 *(hbl 11th)*; still open.

CHURCH BRAMPTON [LNW] op 13 May 1912 *(RCG)*; clo 1 January 1917 *(T 22 December 1916)*; reop 5 May 1919 *(RCH)*; clo 18 May 1931 *(T 12th)*. Mainly for members of Northamptonshire Golf Club – official quoted by *The Times* explained closure by saying golfers now went by car.

CHURCH FENTON [NE]: probably a station on line op 30 May 1839 (F. Dean, *NE Express November 1990*), replaced when line to Spofforth, which branched off here, opened 10 August 1847. First certain reference *Topham*, May 1848; still open. C F JUNCTION 1850 to 1893/4 in some tables *(Brad)*, and in NE co tt 1880.

CHURCH MANOR WAY [SEC] op 1 January 1917 *(SEC sig notice 32/1917)*; HALT; clo 1 January 1920 (Thursday) *(Cl)*; {Abbey Wood – Plumstead}.

CHURCH ROAD Birmingham [Mid] op 3 April 1876 *(Mid)*; clo 1 January 1925 (Thursday) *(Mid)*.

CHURCH ROAD near Machen [BM] op 14 June 1865 *(co n Newport 17th)*; clo 16 September 1957 *(Cl)*.

CHURCH ROAD [CW Jc]
– see under HARRINGTON.

CHURCH ROAD GARSTON [LNW]
– see under GARSTON.

CHURCH SIDING [Wotton] op March 1872 (see 1871★★), but hb did not add 'P' until 1878/9a; last in *Brad* August 1894.

CHURCH STRETTON [SH Jt] op 21 April 1852 *(co ½ T 17 August- line)*; re-sited 5 chains south 23 May 1914 *(Cl)*; still open.

CHURCH VILLAGE [TV] op 1 October 1887 *(Llantrisant)*; became HALT 14 March 1932 *(Cl)*; clo 31 March 1952 *(Cl)*.

CHURCH'S HILL op 2 February 1959 *(Wilts 7th)*; HALT; clo 6 April 1964 *(W D Press 6th)*; {Culkerton – Rodmarton}.

CHURCHBURY [GE] op 1 October 1891 *(RCG)*; clo 1 October 1909 (Friday) *(RCG)*; reop 1 March 1915 *(Cl)*; clo 1 July 1919★★. Southbury here later.

CHURCHDOWN

CHURCHDOWN (a) [BG] op 9 August 1842 *(BG; company minute 27 September, 'has been open five weeks', J. Gough)*; clo 27 September 1842 *(BG)*.

CHURCHDOWN (b) [GW/Mid] op 2 February 1874 *(Gloucester J 31 January)*; clo 2 November 1964 *(Cl)*.

CHURCHILL – see BLAKEDOWN.

CHURCHTOWN [LY]
op 20 February 1878 *(Southport Vis 20th)*; clo 7 September 1964 *(RM October)*. C for BOTANIC GARDENS *Brad* 1899, but just C LY co tt then.

CHURN [GW] op 6 July 1888 for National Rifle Association competitions *(U)*; continued in occasional use for army camps after Rifle competitions moved to Bisley 1890. Examples of early specials for Volunteers' Camps – 2 August 1895 from Wolverton, Aylesbury and Buckingham for 1st Bucks, 3 August 1895 from Bedford for Beds Volunteers *(LNW Officers)*. Intermittently in *Brad* (wtts same basic pattern): May 1905 to October 1905; May 1906 to September 1907; 1908 to 1913 summer only (May to September); May 1914 to December 1916. Still shown, trainless, to mid 1922. Back August 1928, permanently, with note trains only called during daylight hours. Unlikely to be full story – presumably full use throughout First World War; also problem in that *RAIL 253/482* says it reop 8 May 1915, but trains already shown – perhaps now properly staffed for extra use? Hb, 1904–1929 has note that only used when camp open. Aot request.
Clo 4 August 1942★★; reop 8 March 1943 *(Cl)*; hb 1956 said was HALT but not thus any tt seen; clo 10 September 1962 *(RM October)*.

CHURSTON [GW] op 14 March 1861 *(Trewman 20th)* as BRIXHAM ROAD; renamed by 12 March 1868, when *GW ac* said 'has been renamed'. See 1 November 1972★★. C FERRERS pre-op *(Brad)*.

CHURWELL [LNW] op 18 September 1848 *(D&C 8)*; clo 1 January 1917 *(T 22 December 1916)*; reop 1 March 1920 *(Cl)*; clo 2 December 1940 *(LNW Record)*. Cottingley nearby later.

CHWILOG [LNW] op 2 September 1867★★ *(D&C 11; co ½ T 10 October- line)*; C for NEVIN 1 April 1900 *(LNW dates)* to 1 June 1909 *(RCG)*; clo 7 December 1964 *(RM March 1965)*. *Brad* ? to 1955: C for FOUR CROSSES and NEVIN; not thus LMS tt 1930.

CHWRELA – see TREVOR.

CILCEWYDD
Two temporary platforms, C EAST and C WEST, op 17 January 1994 after line cut by floods; last used 26 February 1994, then line reopened *(RM May)* {Welshpool – Forden}.

CILFREW [N&B] first in *Brad* December 1888; originally Wednesdays and Saturdays only; full use January 1892 *Brad*. Inspection report of 24 May 1893 said platform rotten, no proper passenger accommodation and no authority had been given for a public service so should not have been in *Brad*. Company apologised, claiming to have overlooked fact that stop was for miners only. Original PLATFORM replaced by proper station 1 May 1895 *(MT 707/11; RAIL 1005/280)*, though *Brad* dropped 'Platform'

before/with December 1894 issue;
clo 15 October 1962 (RM November).
CILFYNYDD [TV] op 1 June 1900 (RCG);
clo 12 September 1932 (Cl).
CILIAU-AERON [GW] op 12 May 1911
(co n Lampeter) as C; -AERON added later 1911/12
(RCG ref January 1912); op as HALT; in Brad became
station 1936, HALT again 1939; spelling as in Brad.
Clo 12 February 1951 (Cl) – see 1951**.
CILMERI [LNW] op 11 March 1867 (LNW Officers)
as CEFN-Y-BEDD; renamed CILMERY July 1868 tt
(Cl; LNW Officers recommended 17 June);
HALT 31 August 1936 to 5 May 1969 (Cl); spelling
altered 12 May 1980 tt (Cl); aot request; still open.
CINDERFORD [SW Jt] {map 94}
For first station serving Cinderford, see BILSON,
first entry. This was replaced by >
CINDERFORD_, op 5 August 1878 (Glos Chron 10th);
in turn replaced by >
station in tts (Brad and Mid co) as C NEW, op 2 July
1900 (Ross 5th); NEW dropped 1911/12 Brad – was it
helpful information rather part of name?;
clo 3 November 1958 (T 21 October).
CIRENCESTER
C TOWN [GW] op 31 May 1841 (Bath Chron 3 June);
TOWN added 1 July 1924 (GW circular 18 June);
clo 6 April 1964 (W D Press 6th). C SHEEP STREET
in Brad from 1886 until 1924.
C WATERMOOR [MSWJ] op 18 December 1883
(Bath Chron 20th); W added 1 July 1924
(GW circular18 June) – but Brad using since 1886;
clo 11 September 1961 (T 9th).
CITY - see BANK.
CITY AIRPORT [Dock]
– see LONDON CITY AIRPORT.
CITY ROAD [City & South London, which was later
part of Nor] op 17 November 1901 (T 16th);
clo 9 August 1922 (Cl) – closure, on a Wednesday, was
for line reconstruction but this station did not reopen
when the line did; {Angel – Old Street}.
CITY THAMESLINK – see under LONDON.
CLACHNAHARRY [High] op 1 April 1868 (High);
clo 1 April 1913 (Tuesday) (RCG), trains still in Brad
April – inertia?; {Inverness – Bunchrew}.
CLACKMANNAN [NB]
C ROAD, op 28 August 1850 (notice, item Stirling
Journal 30th); ROAD added 1 January 1894 (hbl 25th);
clo 1 January 1917 (RCH); reop 2 June 1919 (RCH);
clo 1 December 1921 (RCG).
C & KENNET op 18 December 1893 (D&C 15- line);
clo 7 July 1930 (Cl).
CLACTON-ON-SEA [GE] op 4 July 1882 (T 6th) –
date in GE as well as T, but description in latter raises
suspicion of formal, not public, opening;
op as C-on-SEA; renamed C-on-S & SOUTHCLIFFE
22 June 1909 (hbl 7 July), C-on-S & HOLLAND-on-SEA
12 September 1932 (T 19 August), CLACTON
20 February 1969 (Cl); C-on-S 20 May 2007 tt;
still open. Brad and hb at first CLACKTON.
CLANDON [LSW] op 2 February 1885 (co n T 31 Jan.);
C & RIPLEY until 1910 (RCH dist ref 12 September

1910); still open. Hb 1900a: C for SEND;
1938 on C for NEWLANDS CORNER. SR tt (Brad
printings) 1939, 1947 C for BURNT COMMON,
NEWLANDS CORNER, EAST CLANDON and
RIPLEY. Brad: C for RIPLEY ? to 1955.
CLAPHAM London {map 109, 110}.
C & NORTH STOCKWELL [LCD; see 1866**]
op 25 August 1862 (co n T 23rd); & N S added 1 May
1863 (L); alias C ROAD/C ROAD & N S/C TOWN;
clo 3 April 1916 (T 16 March). See C High Street, below.
C HIGH STREET [LBSC; see 1866**]
op 1 May 1867 (LBSC); clo 16 May 1926 (perhaps last
day), reop 20 September 1926 (RM November);
still open. In effect, this was LBSC part of C & North
Stockwell, above; named thus until 27 September 1937
(L), when became C; H S added 1989.
C COMMON [Nor] op 3 June 1900 (T 4th);
see 1922**; still open.
C COMMON [LSW] op 21 May 1838 (Salisbury 28th)
as WANDSWORTH; renamed 1846 tt (Cl; JS);
replaced by >
C JUNCTION [LSW/LBSC/WL] op 2 March 1863*
(co n T 4th); still open. Brad 1911, SR tt 1947: note
added – 'mid-Battersea, 1¼ miles from Clapham'.
* = assumes station op with West London Extension;
LNW notice covers that line opening; strict interpretation
of LSW notice of replacement of C Common by this would
imply change made 1st.
C NORTH [Nor] op 3 June 1900 (T 4th- line) as
C ROAD; see 1922**; renamed 13 September 1926
(hbl January 1927); still open.
C SOUTH [Nor] op 13 September 1926 (T 14th);
still open.
CLAPHAM NORTH YORKS [Mid] op 30 July
1849 (T 28 July, 1 September); NY added body of tt
1984/1987, index earlier; still open.
CLAPTON [GE] op 1 July 1872 (L); still open.
CLAPTON ROAD Portishead [WCP] op 7 August
1907 (Bristol T 8th); aot request; clo 20 May 1940
(Bridgwater Merc 22nd).
CLARBESTON ROAD [GW] op 2 January 1854
(co ½ T 26 August- line); perhaps briefly CROSS INN at
start (Cl); re-sited to west 27 July 1914 – old destroyed
by fire 9 July 1907 (GM's report) – old patched-up
meanwhile?; aot request; still open.
CLARE [GE] op 9 August 1865 (GE- line);
clo 6 March 1967 (RM April).
CLARENCE DOCK Liverpool [LO] op 6 March
1893**; clo 31 December 1956 (Cl).
According to RM April 1906 clo 5 March 1906; if it did
so, soon reop - in Brad May–August (inclusive) 1906.
CLARENCE ROAD – see CARDIFF.
CLARENCE YARD - see under GOSPORT.
CLARKSTON near Airdrie; {map 16}
CLARKSTON [MK] op summer 1832 (see 1828 B**);
clo by mid-October 1832 (MK).
C LANARK [NB] op 11 August 1862 (MK);
LANARK added 8 June 1953 (Cl; ref RM April);
clo 9 January 1956 (RM February).
CLARKSTON on East Kilbride Line [Cal]
op 1 January 1866** as C; became C for EAGLESHAM

1 July 1877 *(RCG)*, C & STAMPERLAND 5 May 1952 *(Cl)*, back to C 7 May 1973 *(Cl)*; still open. At first CLARKSTONE *(hb)*; C for E ? to 1955 at least *(Brad)* but not *Murray* 1948.

CLASHAID – see 1957**.

CLATFORD [LSW]
op 6 March 1865 *(Salisbury 11th- line)*; clo 7 September 1964 *(Andover Advertiser 31 July)*.

CLAUGHTON [North Western] first appeared in note on market trains added to 1 June 1850 tt in *Lancaster*, Saturday only, to and from Lancaster; market note last appeared in paper of 21 September 1850 but service might have continued since station appeared in *Brad* November 1851, full use; last there July 1853 (company records show closed by 4 August – J. Gough); {Hornby – Caton}.

CLAVERDON [GW] op 10 October 1860 *(W Mid; T 11th- line)*; re-sited west of overbridge 2 July 1939 *(Cl)*; still open.

CLAXBY & USSELBY [GC] op 1 November 1848 *(GC)* as U; renamed 1 July 1897 *(hbl 29 April)*; clo 7 March 1960 *(RM April)*.

CLAY CROSS
CLAY CROSS [Mid] op 6 April 1841** (in *Brad* about July 1840 but omitted from next issue seen, so July entry presumed to be error); clo 2 January 1967 *(Mid)*. *Brad*: C C for NORTH WINGFIELD ? to 1955.

C C & EGSTOW [Ashover] (ng) op 7 April 1925 *(RM October)*; clo 14 September 1936** *(Cl)*; {map 59}.

CLAY LANE [Ashover] (ng) op 7 April 1925 *(RM October)*; request; clo 14 September 1936** *(Cl)*; {map 59}.

CLAYDON near Buckingham [LNW]
op 1 October 1850 *(co n T 21 September)*; clo 1 January 1968 *(RM January)*.

CLAYDON near Ipswich [GE] op 24 December 1846 *(EC- line)*; clo 17 June 1963 *(RM August)*.

CLAYGATE [LSW] op 2 February 1885 *(co n T 31 January)*; still open. C & CLAREMONT until 1913 *(RCG dist ref 10 March)*, then C for CLAREMONT until 1955 *(Brad)* and thus *hb* 1938.

CLAYPOLE [GN] op 15 July 1852**; clo 16 September 1957 *(RM October)*.

CLAYTHORPE – see ABY.

CLAYTON near Bradford [GN] op 14 October 1878 *(GN; T 15th- line)*; clo 23 May 1955**.

CLAYTON – see FRICKLEY.

CLAYTON BRIDGE [LY] op 13 April 1846**; clo 7 October 1968 *(RM November)*.

CLAYTON WEST [LY] op 1 September 1879 *(RCG)*; clo 24 January 1983 *(BLN 456)*.

CLEADON LANE – see EAST BOLDON.

CLEARBROOK [GW] op 29 October 1928 *(GW annual report)*; HALT; clo 31 December 1962 *(T 28th)*; {Shaugh Bridge – Yelverton}. *Hb* 1938 (only): C PLATFORM.

CLEATOR MOOR
C M EAST [WCE Jt] op 1 July 1857 *(D&C 14; co ½ T 1 September- line)*; re-sited on deviation 19 April 1866; EAST added 2 June 1924 *(Rly Gaz 23 May)*; clo 13 April 1931 *(LNW Record)*; workmen used

11 March 1940 to 8 April 1940 *(U)*.
C M WEST [CW Jc] op 1 October 1879 *(D&C 14; Rtn- line)*; WEST added 2 June 1924 *(Rly Gaz 23 May)*; clo 13 April 1931 *(LNW Record)*.

CLECKHEATON
CLECKHEATON [LY] op 18 July 1848 *(co ½ T 7 Sept.)*; C CENTRAL 2 June 1924 *(Rly Gaz 23 May)* to 12 June 1961 *(Cl)*; clo 14 June 1965 *(RM June)*.
C SPEN [LNW] op 1 October 1900 *(LNW Officers 39764)*; SPEN added 2 June 1924 *(Rly Gaz 23 May)*; clo 5 January 1953 *(RM March)*; later excur *(U)*.

CLEDFORD BRIDGE [LNW]
op 2 January 1911 *(LNW Cl)*; HALT in *Brad*; clo 2 March 1942 *(LNW Record)*.

CLEETHORPES [GC] op 6 April 1863 *(Grimsby … Advertiser 11th)*; still open.

CLEEVE [Mid] op 14 February 1843 *(Mid)*; clo 20 February 1950 *(RM May)*.

CLEGHORN [Cal] op 15 February 1848 *(co ½ T 29 February- line)* as LANARK; renamed C JUNCTION 1 January 1855 *(Cl; thus Cal co tt 1859)*, C 1 April 1864 *(Cl)*; clo 4 January 1965 *(RM February)*.

CLEISH ROAD – see BALADO.

CLELAND [Cal]
CLELAND (a) op 15 May 1867 *(G&S)*; clo 1 January 1917 *(RM February)*; reop 2 June 1919 *(RCH)*; see 1921 April/May**; clo 1 December 1930 *(Cl)*.
CLELAND (b) op 9 July 1869 *(T 12th- line)* as BELLSIDE; renamed B for OMOA 1873 *(RCG ref July)*, OMOA 1 October 1879 *(Cl)*, C 1 October 1941 *(Cl)*; still open.

CLENCHWARTON [MGN] op 1 March 1866 *(T 2nd)*; clo 2 March 1959 *(T 2nd)*.

CLEOBURY MORTIMER
CLEOBURY MORTIMER [GW] op 13 August 1864 *(Worcester 13th)*; clo 1 August 1962**.
CLEOBURY MORTIMER [CMDP] op 21 November 1908**; clo 26 September 1938 *(T 9 August)*. In *hb* as C M JUNCTION.
C TOWN [CMDP] op 21 November 1908**; HALT added 1 October 1923, but always treated as such *(Cl)*; clo 26 September 1938 *(T 9 August)*.

CLEOBURY NORTH CROSSING [CMDP]
op 21 November 1908**; HALT – this omitted in table from about 1916 but still indexed as that *(Brad)*; clo 26 September 1938 *(T 9 August)*; {Burwarton – Ditton Priors}.

CLEVEDON
CLEVEDON [GW] op 28 July 1847 *(co ½ T 2 Sept)*; became HALT June 1963 tt; clo 3 October 1966 *(W D Press 3rd)*.
CLEVEDON [WCP] op 1 December 1897 *(Bristol T 2nd)*; clo 20 May 1940 *(Bridgwater Merc 22nd)*.
C ALL SAINTS [WCP] op 1917 *(RCG mention August, first in Brad October)*; clo 20 May 1940 *(Bridgwater Merc 22nd)*.
C EAST [WCP] op 7 August 1907 *(Bristol T 8th)*; clo 20 May 1940 *(Bridgwater Merc 22nd)*.
CLEVEDON ROAD – see YATTON.
CLEVELAND BRIDGE – see GRIMSBY.
CLEVELAND PORT – see CARGO FLEET.

CLEVELEYS – see THORNTON.

CLIBURN [NE] op 9 June 1862**, in first tt for line; clo 17 September 1956 *(RM October)*. Wtts 15 June 1959 and 2 November 1959 show 8.30pm Penrith to Darlington calling Fridays only here to set down and at C CROSSING to take up railway staff; nothing other way.

CLIDDESDEN [LSW]
op 1 June 1901 *(co n Basingstoke)*; clo 1 January 1917 *(T 22 Dec. 1916)*; reop 18 August 1924 *(T 14th, 16th)*; clo 1 September 1932 (Sunday) – *Cl* + SR practice.

CLIFF COMMON

CLIFF COMMON [NE]: line op 1 August 1848**; C C GATE until 1864 tt *(Cl)*; clo 20 September 1954 *(RM October)*; later excur *(U)*.

CLIFF COMMON [Derwent Valley] op 21 July 1913 *(NE Staff Magazine 1913)*; after January 1918 *Brad*, before/with May 1918 had lost Tuesday service; August or September 1919 reduced to Mondays and Saturdays; between August 1924 and July 1925 to Mondays only (most trains terminated at Skipwith); clo 1 September 1926** (Wednesday) *(RM Oct.)*. Aot CLIFFE C *(hb)*.

CLIFFE near Gravesend [SE] op 1 April 1882 *(SE)*; clo 4 December 1961 *(T 8 November)*.

CLIFFE – see HEMINGBROUGH.

CLIFFE PARK [NS] op 1 May 1905 *(RCG)* as RUDYARD LAKE; renamed 1 April 1926 *(hbl April)*; became HALT 28 September 1936 *(Cl)*; clo 7 November 1960 *(T 7th)*.

CLIFFE VALE [NS] first in *Brad* March 1865; last July 1865; {Stoke-on-Trent – Newcastle}.

CLIFFORD [GW] op 27 May 1889 *(GW- line)*; clo 8 December 1941.
See 1881 September 1** for line history.

CLIFFORD [SMJ] (non-tt): RAF base; Second World War; {Ettington – Stratford} *(WW II)*.

CLIFTON near Ashbourne [NS] op 31 May 1852 *(T 26 May, 1 June)*; clo 1 November 1954 *(T 1 October)*; later excur *(U)*. Became C (MAYFIELD) / C for M 1894 until closure *(Brad)*, and thus LNW, NS and LMS tts at least 1909–30.

CLIFTON Bristol
For first station see HOTWELLS.

C BRIDGE [GW] op 18 April 1867 *(co n Bristol T 17th)*; clo 7 September 1964 *(W D Press 7th)*.

C DOWN [CE] op 1 October 1874 *(Mid; Bristol T 2nd- line)*; still open. Hb 1875a gave WHITELADIES ROAD as alternative.

CLIFTON near Manchester [LY] first in *Brad* May 1847* as C; renamed/corrected to C JUNCTION June 1847; JUNCTION dropped 6 May 1974 *(BR notice)*; still open.
* = previously a Clifton, alias Dixon Fold, was in *Brad*, but timings show name now transferred to this station at junction (see 1838 May 29**).

CLIFTON near Penrith
C & LOWTHER [LNW] op 17 December 1846 *(D&C 14)*; & L added 1 February 1877 *(RCG, LNW Officers recommended 16 January)*; clo 4 July 1938 *(RM August)*. Earl of Lonsdale could stop any train.

C MOOR [NE] op 1 August 1863 *(NE Maps- line)*;

MOOR added 1 September 1927 *(hbl October)*; clo 22 January 1962 *(RM February)*.

CLIFTON MILL [LNW] op 1 December 1864 *(?; first in Brad February 1865)*; aot request; clo 6 April 1953 *(Cl)*. *Brad*? to closure noted it as C-on-Dunsmore.

CLIFTON ROAD BRIGHOUSE [LY] op 1 March 1881 *(LY)*; clo 14 September 1931 *(LNW Record)*.

CLIFTON-ON-TRENT [GC] op 15 December 1896 *(GC)*; clo 19 September 1955 *(BR ER internal notice August)*.

CLIFTONVILLE – see HOVE.

CLIPPENS [GSW] (non-tt):
in use 1918 without BoT approval by oil workmen; *(Engineering, 18 February 1898, Chron)*; {Elderslie – Houston & Crosslee}.

CLIPSTON & OXENDON [LNW] op 1 June 1863 *(LNW Officers 285)*; CLIPSTONE & OXENDEN until November 1879 – Revd Parker of Oxford then told LNW spelling was wrong and *LNW Officers 14 October* recommended change; clo 4 January 1960 *(RM Feb.)*.

CLIPSTONE CAMP: line op 13 June 1916, passenger service began? Built by War Office, taken over by GC 17 December 1917; shared route of line to Clipstone Colliery (J.C. Fareham, *Clipstone Camp …*, author c.1997). First in *Brad* November 1917; last there July 1920, when note states 'will be discontinued on 10th inst' – Saturday, therefore last day?; {branch from Mansfield GC}.

CLIPSTONE COLLIERY [Mansfield] (non-tt): SIDING; dates ?; {Edwinstowe – Mansfield} *(U; see map GC III p.294)*.

CLITHEROE

CLITHEROE (a) [LY] op 22 June 1850**; re-sited about 10 chains north 1893/4 *(Cl)*; clo 10 September 1962 *(T 8th)*.

CLITHEROE (b) reop for excursions 8 April 1978 *(D&C 10)*; regular week-end summer services began 19 May 1990 *(AZ)*; fully reop 29 May 1994 *(RM June)* – one train on Sunday, full service Monday 30th; still open.

CLOCK FACE [LNW]

CLOCK FACE first in *Brad* November 1856; clo 18 June 1951 *(RM August)*.

C F COLLIERY (non-tt): miners; in use 1923; {Clock Face – Union Bank Farm} *(U)*.

CLOCK HOUSE [SE] op 1 May 1890 *(SE)*; still open. Pre-op Penge Road *(SE)*.

CLOCKSBRIGGS [Cal]: line op 4 December 1838 (see 1838**), nd, by February 1841 (report of accident *T 22nd/Scotsman*); clo 1 January 1917 *(RM February)*; reop 2 June 1919 *(RCH)*; became HALT 1926 *(Brad)*; LMS tt 1930 – this station will be used as a halt; HALT dropped 12 September 1932 body of *Brad* but still in index for a while; clo 5 December 1955 *(Rly Gaz 16th)*.

CLOGWYN [Snowdon Mountain] (ng; rack)
op 6 April 1896**; still open.

CLOSEBURN [GSW]
op 15 October 1849 *(Glasgow Herald 19th/Glasgow Courier)*; clo 11 September 1961 *(Cl)*.

CLOUGH FOLD [LY] op end of 1870 *(?; in Brad January 1871)*; clo 2 April 1917 *(Cl)*; back October 1919 *Brad*; clo 5 December 1966 *(RM February 1967)*.

CLOUGHTON [NE] op 16 July 1885 *(T 16th)*;
clo 8 March 1965 *(T 19 January)*.

CLOVENFORDS [NB] op 18 June 1866 *(NB)*;
clo 5 February 1962 *(RM February)*.

CLOWNE (originally CLOWN in tt for both companies;
hb 1904 to 1929 had 'CLOWN or CLOWNE'; co tts and
Brad added 'E' inconsistently until settled 18 June 1951.)

C & BARLBOROUGH [Mid] op 1 November 1888
(RCG); originally CLOWN; & B added 4 July 1938
(Mid); clo 5 July 1954 *(Cl)*; summer weekend to/from
Blackpool continued – last train 18 August 1962
(BR ER tt).

C SOUTH [LDEC] op 9 March 1897 (8th formal)
(GCR Society Journal, Spring 2003, p.12);
clo 11 Sept. 1939 *(G&S)*; excursion to Cleethorpes
3 August 1952 *(BR working notice)*; later summer
Saturday use, reop 17 June 1961, clo 8 September 1962
(wtts). Goods became C SOUTH 18 June 1951; not
known if this name used for passengers 1961–2.

CLOY [GW] op 1 July 1932 *(GW Mag August)*;
HALT; clo 10 June 1940** ; reop 6 May 1946 *(Cl)*;
clo 10 September 1962 *(RM October)*;
{Overton-on-Dee – Bangor-on-Dee}.
Earlier was Caedyah Halt (non-tt) *(RAC)*.

CLUBMOOR [CLC] op 14 April 1927 *(CLC)*;
clo 7 November 1960 *(RM December)*;
{West Derby – Aintree}.

CLUNDERWEN [GW] op 2 January 1854
(co ½ T 26 August- line) as NARBERTH ROAD;
renamed CLYNDERWEN 1 December 1875,
CLUNDERWEN 12 May 1980 *(Cl)*; HALT 6 Sept.
1965 to 5 May 1969 *(Cl)*; aot request; still open.
GW co tt 1859: N R for TENBY and CARDIGAN.

CLUNES [High] first in *Brad* October 1863;
clo 13 June 1960 *(RM July)*.

CLUTTON [GW] op 3 September 1873 *(Bristol T
4th- line)*; clo 2 November 1959 *(Shepton 6th)*.

CLYDACH near Abergavenny [LNW]: first in *Brad*
January 1864, but *LNW MTA minutes, 6 August 1863*,
said would be ready by mid-September so perhaps op
earlier. Clo 6 January 1958 *(BR notice December)*.
HALT in tt from 1930/34 but not in *hb*.

CLYDACH COURT [TV] first in *Brad* July 1917,
but, according to *Nelson*, inspected 16 October 1915 so
perhaps op earlier; see 1904** ; clo 28 July 1952 *(Cl)*.

CLYDACH VALE [GW] (non-tt): miners; at least by
1902 *(U)*; still in 1925 wtt appendix; {beyond Penygraig}.

CLYDACH-ON-TAWE

CLYDACH [GW] (non-tt), later C-on-T NORTH
(goods only); excursion 9 July 1939 *(U)* and GW ticket
for half-day excursion to Porthcawl *(JB)* – same event?;
{branch from Felin Fran}.

C-ON-T SOUTH [Mid] op March 1875** as
CWM CLYDACH; renamed C-on-T 1 October 1901
(Mid, from working notices); SOUTH added January
1950 *(JS)*; clo 25 September 1950 *(RM November)*;
{map 88}. Pre-opening Ynistanglwys (M. Hale).

CLYDEBANK

CLYDEBANK [NB] op 17 May 1897 *(RCG)*;
clo 1 January 1917 *(RM February)*; reop 2 June 1919
(RCH); C CENTRAL until 14 June 1965 *(Cl)*; still open.

C EAST [NB] op 1 December 1882** ;
EAST added 17 May 1897 *(RCG)*; clo 14 September
1959 *(RM September)*.

C RIVERSIDE [Cal] op 1 October 1896 *(RCG; Colliery
2nd- line)*; R added 28 February 1953
(Cl; ref RM April); clo 5 October 1964 *(RM November)*.

CLYNDERWEN see CLUNDERWEN.

CLYNE [GW] op 1 June 1905 *(?; first in Brad June)*;
HALT; clo 15 June 1964 *(RM August)*.

CLYST ST MARY & DIGBY [LSW] op 1 June 1908
(Trewman 30 May); HALT; clo 27 September 1948
(Cl); {map 115}. Digby & Sowton nearby later.

COALBROOKDALE

COALBROOKDALE (a) [GW] op 1 November 1864
(GW); became HALT 1958/9 *Brad* and so shown on
BR ticket *(JB)*; clo 23 July 1962 *(RM August)*.

COALBROOKDALE (b) (non-tt) summer weekends,
visitors to Ironbridge Museum, first train 19 July 1987
(first two planned did not run – *BLN 565*), last Sunday
2 September 1990 *(BLN 634)*; alias IRONBRIDGE
GORGE.
Also see under TELFORD

COALBURN [Cal] op 2 November 1891 *(RCG)*;
clo 4 October 1965 *(BR notice, The True Line July 2006)*.

COALEY [Mid] op 17 September 1856** *(co n Glos
Chron 20th)* as DURSLEY JUNCTION; became C J
1 October 1870 *(Mid; RCH dist ref 16 December)*,
C 1888 tt *(Cl)*; clo 4 January 1965 *(Mid)*.
C JUNCTION in *hb* 1872 on. Mid co tt 1903 and
LMS tt 1930: C for D. *Brad*: C 1888 and later.

COALPIT HEATH [GW] op 1 July 1903 *(Bristol T
2nd)*; clo 3 April 1961 *(RM May)*.

COALPORT

COALPORT [GW] op 1 February 1862** ;
clo 9 September 1963 *(T 9th)*.

COALPORT (EAST) [LNW] op 10 June 1861** ;
clo 2 June 1952 *(RM August)*. EAST not seen *Brad*,
but was in *Rly Gaz* that reported closure *(C/W)*.

COALVILLE

C EAST [LNW] op 16 April 1883 *(Leic; LNW Officers
24577- line)*; became just C 1 May 1905 *(hbl 27 April)*,
C LNW May 1910 *(LNW dates)*, again C E 2 June 1924
(Rly Gaz 23 May); clo 13 April 1931 *(LNW dates PCC)*.
Hb – always C E.

C TOWN [Mid] op 27 April 1833 *(Mid)* as LONG
LANE; see 1847 December** ; renamed C 1848 *(Brad)*;
TOWN added 2 June 1924 *(Rly Gaz 23 May)*;
clo 7 September 1964 *(RM October)*.

C MANTLE LANE (non-tt): used for Freight Depot
Open Days – certainly 31 May 1981, 5 June 1983 and
1 September 1985 *(IU)* and 1 June 1986 *(JB)*;
diagram with 1981 and 1983 showed shuttle from
Derby using temporary platform on Down Goods Line
No.2 within depot {Coalville Town – Swannington}.

COALYBURN – see MACBIE HILL.

COANWOOD [NE] op 19 July 1851 *(NC)*, as
SHAFTHILL, terminus for the time being; see 1852
May 1** ; last in *Brad* May 1853; back December 1862;
re-sited 1877/8 *(NC)*; renamed 1 March 1885 *(Cl)*;
clo 3 May 1976 *(RM May)*. HALT on BR ticket *(JB)*
but 1961 tt merely note that unstaffed.

COATBRIDGE

For earliest MK/Monkland stations hereabouts see HOWES; SOUTH END.

COATBRIDGE [Monkland] op 10 December 1849 (see 1844 December 26★★); clo 10 December 1851 (Wednesday) *(MK)*; {map 16}.

C CENTRAL [Cal] first in *Brad* January 1843, fare list, though according to *MK* Cal did not open own independent line until February; CENTRAL added 8 June 1953 *(Cl; ref RM April)*; still open.

C CENTRAL [NB] op 26 October 1871 *(D&C 6)*; perhaps at/near 1849 Monkland station; clo 1 January 1917 except for workmen *(RM February)*; reop 2 June 1919 *(RCH)*; clo 10 September 1951 *(RM October)*.

C SUNNYSIDE [NB] op 1 December 1863 *(MK)*; still open.

COATDYKE [NB] first in *Brad* December 1890; still open.

COATHAM LANE [S&D] (non-tt): about 1858 to ?; private for Mrs Newcomen of Kirkleatham Estate, Wednesday only *(L. Crowther's atlas)*; {east of Redcar}.

COBBETTS LANE – see 1835 June 9★★.

COBBINSHAW [Cal] first in *Brad* October 1874; re-sited 37 chains south 4 October 1875 *(Cl)*; clo 18 April 1966 *(Cl)*.

COBHAM & STOKE D'ABERNON [LSW] op 2 February 1885 *(co n T 31 January)*; still open. Op notice called it S d'A & C and tickets exist thus but in *Brad* always C & S d'A until became C for S d'A *(RCH dist ref 10 March 1913*; and thus LSW co tt 1914)*; back to C & S d'A 9 September 1951 *(Cl)*.

COBORN ROAD [GE] op 1 February 1865 *(L)* as OLD FORD; renamed 1 March 1879 *(Cl)*; re-sited a little west 2 December 1883 *(Cl)*; clo 22 May 1916★★; reop 5 May 1919 *(RCH)*; clo 9 December 1946 *(T 15 November* – 'will be closed after 1.20am on December 9th')*. GE co tt 1882, LNE tt 1933: C R for O F.

COBRIDGE [NS] op 1 October 1874 *(RCG)*; clo 2 March 1964 *(RM April)*.

COCHRANE MILL – see MILLIKEN PARK.

COCKBURNSPATH [NB] op 22 June 1846 *(First; co n T 23rd- line)*; clo 18 June 1951 *(RM July)*.

COCKER BAR [LY] first in *Brad* September 1851; clo 1 November 1859 *(Preston Pilot 5th)*; replaced by Midge Hall.

COCKERHAM CROSS [KE]: line op Monday 5 December 1870 *(Rtn- line)*; station originally Thursdays & Saturdays only; last train 9 March 1872; line reop Monday 17 May 1875 *(Cl)*; from August 1877 Fridays as well; became all-day station July 1923/14 July 1924 *Brad*, and HALT now added, though presumably always treated as one (see 1905★★); aot request; clo 31 March 1930 *(LNW Record)*. Alias C CROSSING, which might have been correct name throughout – shorter form appeared in *Brad* when moved from notes to body of table – space saving?

COCKERMOUTH [CKP/LNW]

First station was terminus from west, op 28 April 1847 *(co ½ T 5 August)* ★. Line from east opened 2 January 1865 *(co ½ T 28 February)*, to station that became through one. Agreement had been reached in January

1864 that both would use latter *(Lakeland)* but *D&C 14* says that probably lines were not immediately linked and both in use together until first clo 1 July 1865. Separate tables for lines to east and west in *Brad* until October 1866, when through table provided; however, timings suggest through services possible by August 1865. Clo 18 April 1966 *(Cl)*.

Became C for BUTTERMERE 14 November 1932 *(hbl February 1933)*.

★ = On formal opening date, 27 April, in addition to directors' special there was a trip from Workington open to all – allegedly 1,500 took advantage *(Whitehaven Herald 1 May)*.

COCKETT [GW] first in *Brad* May 1871; clo 15 June 1964 *(Cl)*.

COCKFIELD FELL [NE]

For first service through here see 1834 March 24★★ and LANDS. At times S&D used COCKFIELD and LANDS interchangeably – minute of 17 October 1860 *(RAIL 667/64)* has marginal heading 'footbridge at Lands' but entry reads 'footbridge to be erected at Cockfield' (people there would build bridge, S&D contributing £5).

COCKFIELD FELL op 1 August 1863 *(RAIL 667/167- line)*; effectively replaced Lands, but some overlap in use; FELL added 1 July 1923 *(hbl 12th)*; clo 15 September 1958 *(Cl)*.

COCKFIELD SUFFOLK [GE] op 14 November 1870 *(Bury & Norwich Post 15th)*; SUFFOLK added 1 October 1927 *(hbl October)*; clo 10 April 1961 *(RM May)*.

COCKFOSTERS [Picc] op 31 July 1933 *(T 1 August)*; still open.

COCKING [LBSC] op 11 July 1881 *(co n W Sussex)*; became HALT 23 May 1932 *(Cl)*; clo 7 July 1935 (Sunday) *(RM September)*.

CODFORD [GW]

CODFORD op 30 June 1856 *(W Fly P 1 July)*; clo 19 September 1955 *(RM November)*.

C CAMP (non-tt): army; op October 1914; line taken over by Military Camp Railways (Southern Command) 3 June 1916; ran to KNOOK CAMP *(RAC)*; clo 1 January 1923 *(GW goods circular 26th)*; {branch from Codford}.

CODNOR PARK

C P & IRONVILLE [Mid] op 6 September 1847 *(Mid)* as C P; missing from co tt December 1851, back 1 January 1852 tt★ *(Mid)*; & I added 17 Nov. 1898 *(hbl 26 January 1899)*; clo 2 January 1967 *(Mid)*.

★ = likely that it was intended only to be a temporary terminus, to be replaced by Pye Bridge but public outcry led either to it being retained or reopened after brief closure *(Mid)*.

C P & SELSTON – see JACKSDALE.

CODSALL [GW] op 13 November 1849 (see 1849★★); CODSAL until 1855 *(Brad)*; still open.

COED ELY [GW] op 13 July 1925 *(Cardiff Divisional Report 1925)*; clo 9 June 1958 *(T 5th)*; {Llantrisant – junction south of Tonyrefail}. Pre op: Thomastown *(RAC)*.

COED POETH [GW] op 15 November 1897 *(Wrexham 20th)*; clo 1 January 1931 (Thursday) *(T 20 December)*; {map 75}.

COED TALON [LNW] op 1 January 1892 *(Wrexham 2nd, 9th)*; clo 27 March 1950 *(RM May)*.

COEDPENMAEN [TV] op 1 June 1900 *(RCG)*; clo 1 June 1915 (Tue.) *(Cl)*; {Cilfynydd – Berw Road}.

COEDYMOETH COLLIERY [Rhy] (non-tt): trains calling October 1902 wtt and 20 June 1920 tt; facilities?; {Brithdir – Bargoed}.

COFTON [BG]
Temporary terminus, **C FARM**, op 17 September 1840 *(co n Chelt Exam 30th)*; clo 17 December 1840 when line extended to Birmingham *(Mid)*.
COFTON probably op November 1841★★, with the other 'police stations' (J. Gough); probably same site as C Farm; clo after December 1843 *(Mid)*.

COGAN [Barry] op 20 December 1888 *(Barry)*; initially terminus from Barry (result of TV/Barry politics), passengers going further walked to Penarth Dock and continued journey from there; line op through to Cardiff 14 August 1893 *(Penarth)*; still open.

COGIE HILL [KE]: line op Monday 5 December 1870 *(LNW Record- line)*; this station originally Thursdays & Saturdays only; last train 9 March 1872; line reop Monday 17 May 1875 *(Cl)*; from August 1877 Fridays as well; alias C H CROSSING / C H HALT (see note on Cockerham Cross, above); aot request; July 1923/14 July 1924 *Brad* became all-days station (see 1905★★); clo 31 March 1930 *(Cl)*.

COLBREN JUNCTION [N&B] op 10 November 1873 *(G&S)* as CAPEL COLBREN J; renamed 1874 tt *(Cl)*; clo 15 October 1962 *(RM November)*.

COLCHESTER
COLCHESTER [EC; GE] op 29 March 1843 *(T 30th)*; aot C NORTH *(hb)*; still open.
COLCHESTER [EU]: EU line op to Colchester 15 June 1846 *(Rtn PP)*, at first using EC station. Dispute resulted in EU building own, op 1848 on opposite, eastern, side of road bridge; short-lived (K.A. Frost, *Back Track, January 2000, p.15)*.
C TOWN [GE] op 1 March 1866 *(GE)* as ST BOTOLPHS; renamed 15 July 1991 *(AB, Chron)*; still open.

COLD BLOW LANE – see NEW CROSS GATE.

COLD MEECE [LMS] (non-tt): ordnance factory workers; op about May 1941 *(WW II)*; last train 27 June 1958 *(RM August)*; {branch from Swynnerton Junction, between Norton Bridge and Stone}.

COLD NORTON [GE] op 1 October 1889 *(co n, back of November 1889 GE co tt at Newton Abbot)*; clo 11 September 1939 *(G&S)*.
Hb 1890: C N for PURLEIGH and STOKE MARIES.

COLD ROWLEY – see ROWLEY.

COLDHAM first in *Brad* February 1858 as PEAR TREE HILL (EC wtt 1 September 1856 shows only train calling was a goods); renamed 1 September 1876 *(RCG)*; aot request; clo 7 March 1966 *(RM February)*. GE co tt 1882, LNE tt 1933: C for PT H.

COLDHARBOUR [GW] op 23 February 1929 *(Tiverton 26th)*; HALT; clo 9 September 1963 *(Express & E 9th)*; {Tiverton Junction – Uffculme}. Until 1956 hb made two words of it.

COLDSTREAM [NE]: line op 27 July 1849 *(NE)*, nd, July 1851; originally CORNHILL; renamed 1 October 1873 *(RCG)* – but *Brad* and *Murray* had CORNHILL for COLDSTREAM earlier; clo 15 June 1964 *(RM July)*.

COLE [SD Jt] op 3 February 1862★★; clo 7 March 1966 *(Shepton 11th)*. In op tt *Shepton*, LSW co tt 1914 and *Brad* to 1955: C for BRUTON.

COLE GREEN [GN] first in *Brad* December 1858; aot request; clo 18 June 1951 *(RM July)*.

COLEBURNS [GNS] op 5 June 1863 *(GNS)*; request; last in tt April 1867 but did not clo until 1871 *(GNS)*. At times COLEBURN in *hb*, after passenger use; PLATFORM sometimes added; {map 3}. Later private use (1925/6 certainly – *U*).

COLEFORD
COLEFORD [GW] op 1 September 1883 *(GW)*; clo 1 January 1917 *(GW notice dated 22 December 1916)*.
COLEFORD [SW Jt] op 9 December 1875★★; clo 8 July 1929 *(RM August)*. GW co tt 1902, Mid co tt 1903: C for STAUNTON.

COLEFORD JUNCTION [SW Jt] (non-tt):
Trains joined/divided but no official public boarding or alighting, except:
(a) unadvertised September 1878 to 1 November 1879 *(Mid/Cl)*.
(b) Minute 5 February 1896 – old, dilapidated platform here, David & Slant's workmen were trespassing on lines to board trains whilst being joined/divided; decided to provide platform and path to allow workmen to travel to Milkwall and Coleford 3rd class; minute 11 April 1906 – joint committee agreed to withdraw facilities *(RAIL 241/6, 241/18)*; {Parkend – Speech House}.

COLEHAM EXCURSION
– see under SHREWSBURY.

COLEHOUSE LANE [WCP] op 1 December 1897 *(Bristol 2nd- line)*; aot request; clo 20 May 1940 *(Bridgwater Merc 22nd)*.

COLESHILL [Mid]
COLESHILL (a) op 12 August 1839 *(Mid; co n T 8th- line)*; from 1 November 1849 to 1 December 1872 was C HAMPTON LINE in co tt *(Mid)*; clo 1 January 1917 *(T 29 December 1916)*; surviving goods later Maxstoke.
COLESHILL (b) op 10 February 1842 *(Mid)* as FORGE MILLS; on main line; renamed F M for C 1 November 1849 co tt *(Mid)*, F M 1 April 1904 *(hbl 28th)*, C 9 July 1923 *(hbl 26 April)*; clo 4 March 1968 *(Mid)*.
C PARKWAY op 19 August 2007 *(RM October)*; on site of (b); still open.

COLFIN [PPW J] op 28 August 1862 *(co n 20th)*; clo 6 February 1950 *(RM March)*.

COLINDALE [Nor] op 18 August 1924 *(T 18th)*; still open.

COLINTON [Cal] op 1 August 1874 *(co n Balerno)*; clo 1 November 1943 *(LNW Record)*.

COLLEGE Glasgow
– see GLASGOW HIGH STREET.

COLLESSIE [NB]: line op 20 September 1847★★; nd, May 1848 *(Topham)*; clo 19 September 1955 *(RM October)*.

COLLETTS BRIDGE – see 1883 August 20★★.

COLLIERS WOOD [Nor] op 13 September 1926
(T 14th); still open.
COLLIERY ROAD [Camp] (ng)
first in *Brad* May 1927; request; last October 1927 –
but see 1906 August 18**; {Drumlemble – Lintmill}.
COLLIERY WORKS PLATFORM
– see SHAKESPEARE CLIFF.
COLLINGBOURNE [MSW]; GW]
COLLINGBOURNE op 1 May 1882 *(MSWJ; W Gaz
5th- line)*; clo 11 September 1961 *(T 9th)*.
C KINGSTON op 1 April 1932 *(Cl 29)*; HALT at clo 11
September 1961 *(T 9th)*; {north of Collingbourne}.
COLLINGHAM [Mid] op 4 August 1846 *(Mid)*;
still open.
COLLINGHAM BRIDGE [NE] op 1 May 1876
(NE- line); clo 6 January 1964 *(Cl)*. Lord Leconfield
could stop all trains.
COLLINGTON [LBSC] op 11 September 1905
(LBSC) as C WOOD HALT; clo 1 September 1906
(Saturday) *(Cl)*; back in *Brad* June 1911 as WEST
BEXHILL HALT; renamed C HALT 1 November
1929 *(Cl)*; HALT dropped 5 May 1969 *(Cl)*; still open.
COLLINS GREEN [LNW]: line op 17 Sept. 1830**;
nd, March 1831 co tt; clo 2 April 1951 *(RM May)*.
COLLISTON [Cal] op 24 Nov. 1838 (see 1838**);
clo 5 December 1955 *(RM January 1956)*.
COLLYWELL BAY – see SEATON SLUICE.
COLNBROOK
COLNBROOK [GW] op 9 August 1884 *(L)*;
clo 29 March 1965 *(RM April)*.
C ESTATE op 1 May 1961 *(RM June 1965)*; HALT;
clo 29 March 1965 *(RM April)*.
Ticket for C ESTATES *(JB)*.
COLNE near Burnley [LY/Mid] op 2 October 1848
(RAIL 1005/265); still open.
COLNE – see EARLS COLNE; WHITE COLNE.
COLNEY HATCH [GN]
COLNEY HATCH – see NEW SOUTHGATE.
C H CEMETERY (non-tt): funerals; op 10 July 1861;
clo 3 April 1863; perhaps used during cholera epidemic
1866–7; alias NEW SOUTHGATE C;
{branch from New Southgate} *(LRR October 1999)*.
COLTFIELD [High] op 22 December 1862 *(High)*
as WARDS; renamed 1 January 1865 *(JS)*;
became PLATFORM 1895/6 *(Brad)*; aot request;
clo 14 September 1931 *(RM November)*. 1865–8 was
COLTFIELDS in *Brad* – probably error *(JS)*.
COLTISHALL [GE] op 8 July 1879 *(GE- line)*;
clo 15 September 1952 *(RM October)*.
COLWALL [GW]
op 13 September 1861 *(Hereford T 14th)*; still open.
COLWICH [LNW] op 15 September 1847
(co n T 13th); clo 3 February 1958 *(RM March)*.
COLWICK – see NETHERFIELD.
COLWYN [LNW]
C BAY first in *Brad* October 1849; BAY added 1 August
1876 *(JS; RCG ref October)*; still open. Original was
primitive structure in field east of Glan-y-Don Crossing;
known locally as Pwllychrochan, after estate owned by
Lady Erskine, who had sold land for it and had easy
access; later re-sited further west. (D. Thomas,

Memories of Old Colwyn, Bridge Books, 2000).
Also see OLD COLWYN.
COLYFORD [LSW] op 16 March 1868 *(Trewman
18th- line)*; clo 7 March 1966 *(RM April)*.
COLYTON [LSW]
COLYTON op 16 March 1868 *(Trewman 18th- line)* as
C TOWN; renamed 1890 tt *(Cl)*; clo 7 March 1966
(RM April).
Also see SEATON JUNCTION.
COLZIUM [KB] op 2 July 1888 *(RCG)*; clo 1 March
1917 (Thursday) *(Cal wtt 11 July 1921)* – RM February
says clo 1 January, but *Brad* January shows trains on
NB service, not Cal.
COMBE near Oxford [GW] op 8 July 1935 *(Cl 29)*;
HALT until 5 May 1969; aot request; still open.
COMBE HAY [GW] op 9 May 1910 *(W D Press 10th)*;
HALT; clo 22 March 1915 *(RCH)*; reop 9 July 1923
(Bristol notice S1153); clo 21 September 1925 *(Cl)*.
COMBE ROW [WSM] op 4 September 1865**;
clo 8 November 1898**; {map 117}.
Various aliases: COOMROW in inspection reports,
including correspondence from company, *(MT6/35/10)*;
W Som F P had COOMBE ROW in op tt,
COMBE-ROW in description;
Brad at times COMBERROW, COMBEROW.
COMBPYNE [LSW] op 24 August 1903 *(Chard 29th)*;
clo 29 November 1965 *(Chard 3 December)*.
COMELY PARK – see DUNFERMLINE.
COMMERCIAL DOCKS London [SE]
op 1 May 1856 *(co n T 17 April)*;
clo 1 January 1867 (Tuesday) *(Cl)*; {map 105}.
COMMERCIAL STREET [TV]
op 26 November 1904 *(Aberdare)*; see 1904**;
last trains June 1912 tt; {map 86}.
COMMINS COCH [GW] op 19 October 1931
(Cl 29); HALT; clo 14 June 1965 *(RM July)*;
{Cemmes Road – Llanbrynmair}.
COMMONDALE [NE] first in *Brad* December 1882;
C SIDING until 1891 tt *(JS)*; still open.
COMMONDYKE [GSW] op 1 October 1897 *(RCG)*;
clo 3 July 1950 *(RM August)*.
COMMONHEAD AIRDRIE NORTH
– see AIRDRIE.
COMPSTALL – see MARPLE.
COMPTON near Newbury [GW] op 13 April 1882
(T 10th- line); clo 4 August 1942**; reop 8 March 1943;
clo 10 September 1962 *(RM October)*.
COMPTON near Wolverhampton [GW]
op 11 May 1925 *(RM June)*; HALT;
clo 31 October 1932 *(RM January 1933)*; {map 96}.
COMRIE [Cal] op 1 June 1893 *(RCG)*;
clo 6 July 1964 *(RM June)*.
CONCLE – see RAMPSIDE.
CONDER GREEN [LNW] op 5 November 1887
(LNW Officers 29856), Saturdays only; from October
1911 all days but usually noted as only available to/from
Lancaster; aot request; clo 7 July 1930 *(Cl)*.
Hb: 1890 and 1895 private, no facilities shown; 1904
still private, 'P' added; 'private' deleted 1927a.
Not marked 'private' in any LNW co tt and *Brad* seen.
CONDOVER [SH Jt] op 21 April 1852

(co ½ T 17 August- line); clo 9 June 1958 *(Cl)*.

CONGLETON [NS]
op 9 October 1848 *(co ½ T 3 Feb 1849)*; still open.
CONGLETON UPPER JUNCTION [NS] only in
Brad June 1864, only branch line trains calling (branch
had op 1 June 1864, *NS*); perhaps tt error – e.g. passing
time at physical junction translated into station;
{physical junction *IA*}.
CONGRESBURY [GW] op 3 August 1869
(Shepton 6th); clo 9 September 1963 *(Weston 13th)*.
CONINGSBY [GN] op 1 July 1913 *(RCG; in tt July)*;
clo 5 October 1970 *(T 16 July)*.
CONISBROUGH [GC] op 10 November 1849
(GC; T 13th- line); moved 150 yards west 1890s *(Cl)*;
CONISBOROUGH until 1950 *(Cl)*; still open.
CONISHEAD PRIORY [Fur] op 27 June 1883 *(Fur)*;
last in *Brad* June 1916 (one train each way daily),
July 'service suspended'. {branch south from Cark &
Cartmel}. At times just PRIORY, e.g. co tt 1914,
hb 1890s; *Brad* just C in table (space?).
CONISTON [Fur] op 18 June 1859 *(Kendal Mercury
25th)* as C LAKE; renamed 1914 tt *(Cl)*, but *hb* 1904;
clo 6 October 1958 *(LNW Record)*.
CONNAHS QUAY
CONNAHS QUAY [LNW] op 1 September 1870 *(LNW
Officers 5691)*; clo 14 February 1966 *(RM April)*.
Also see SHOTTON.
CONNAUGHT ROAD [PLA] op 3 August 1880
(R. Green), though not in opening notice *(T 31 July)*
and not in *Brad* until November 1880;
clo 9 September 1940★★.
GE co tt 1914: ROYAL ALBERT DOCK C R.
CONNEL FERRY [Cal] op 1 July 1880 *(T 2nd- line)*;
still open. C F JUNCTION on station nameboard.
CONON [High] op 11 June 1862 *(High)*;
clo 13 June 1960 *(RM July)*.
CONONLEY
CONONLEY (a) [Mid] op about December 1847 *(Mid)*;
clo 22 March 1965 *(RM April)*.
CONONLEY (b) op 20 April 1988, using same platforms
(Mid); still open.
CONSALL [NS] op 3 March 1902 *(co n Churnet)*;
clo 4 January 1965 *(RM March)*.
CONSETT [NE] {map 28}.
CONSETT (a) op 1 September 1862 *(NE)*; replaced by >
CONSETT (b) op as Benfieldside 2 December 1867;
finally BLACKHILL (which see for full details).
CONSETT (c) op 17 August 1896 *(RCG)*;
clo 23 May 1955 *(RM July)*.
CONSTABLE BURTON [NE] op 19 May 1856
(RCG- line); clo 26 April 1954 *(T 20th)*.
CONWAY PARK op 22 June 1998; still open.
CONWIL [GW] op 3 September 1860 *(GW)*;
clo 31 December 1860; reop 15 August 1861 *(Rtn)*;
CONWYL until 1864 *(Brad)*; clo 22 Feb. 1965 *(Cl)*.
CONWY
CONWAY [LNW] op 1 May 1848 *(D&C 11;
co n T 2nd- line)*; clo 14 February 1966 *(RM April)*.
CONWY op 29 June 1987 (local signalman,
D.A. Roberts, via B. Wilson – 27th was formal);
east of earlier; still open.

CONWAY MORFA [LNW] (non-tt): op 12 May 1894
as C MARSH *(LNW dates)* – 'Platform for Volunteers'
in inspection report *MT6/654/11, 6 April 1894*;
new site 2 May 1901 as C MORFA; in *hb* 1895, deleted
as 'P' August 1929 *(LNW dates)*; later excur *(U)*;
{Conway – Penmaenmawr}.
COODEN BEACH [LBSC] op 11 September 1905
(LBSC) as C GOLF CLUB; renamed 1910 *(JS)*;
HALT until 7 July 1935 *(SR)*; still open.
COOKHAM [GW]
op 1 August 1854 *(co n T 31 July)*; still open.
COOKSBRIDGE [LBSC]
first in *Brad* January 1851; still open.
COOKS BRIDGE until 1885 tt *(Cl)*, 1877 *hb*.
COOLE PILATE [GW] op 17 August 1935 *(T 7th)*;
HALT; clo 9 September 1963 *(T 9th)*;
{Nantwich – Audlem}.
COOMBE near Croydon
C LANE [WSC Jt] op 10 August 1885 *(L)*; in April
1915 *Brad* reduced to southbound service only, one
Monday to Friday plus one extra, Wednesday only;
December 1915 further reduced, to Wednesday only
train; that last shown February 1916.
C ROAD [SR] op 30 September 1935 *(T 26th)*,
same site as C Lane; clo 16 May 1983 *(BLN 456 corr)*.
Also see NEW MALDEN.
COOMBE JUNCTION HALT near Liskeard [GW]:
platform was available for alighting from opening of
Looe line 11 Sept. 1879, but not advertised *(RM
March 1899)* – gave easier interchange with main
Liskeard station than going on to Moorswater;
advertised platform op 15 May 1901 *(W Morn News
16th- line)*; op as C JUNCTION; HALT 1952 *(Brad)*
to 6 May 1968 tt *(offic)*, when JUNCTION also
dropped; clo 3 November 1990 for flood prevention
work, reop 19 November 1990 *(RM January 1991)*;
J HALT restored 17 May 2008 *(RM July)*; still open.
COOMBES HOLLOWAY [GW] op 1 July 1905
(GW H); HALT; moved from down to up side of
single line April 1913 *(Cl)*; clo 5 December 1927 *(Cl)*;
{Old Hill – Halesowen}.
COOPER BRIDGE [LY] first in *Brad* about March
1841 – not in op tt *Leeds* nor earliest *Brad* for line,
which had opened 1 October 1840;
clo 20 February 1950 *(RM May)*.
C B JUNCTION 1852 to 1868/9 *(Brad)*.
COP END – see BLOWICK.
COP LANE – see PENWORTHAM.
COPGROVE [NE] op 1 April 1875 *(NE- line)*;
STAVELEY in the inspection report,
C & S in June *Brad*, first time line shown;
renamed C 1 November 1881 *(Cl; RCG ref October)*;
clo 25 September 1950 *(RM November)*.
COPLAND ROAD – see IBROX.
COPLEY [LY] first in *Brad* November 1855;
clo 20 July 1931 *(LNW Record)*.
COPMANTHORPE [NE]: line op 30 May 1839
(T 7 June), nd, about June 1840 (also mentioned by
Whishaw); clo 5 January 1959 *(RM February)*.
COPPENHALL [GJ] op 4 July 1837 *(co n GJ)*;
clo 10 September 1840★★; {Crewe – Minshull Vernon}.

COPPER PIT [GW] first in *Brad* February 1915; see April/May 1921**; PLATFORM; clo 11 June 1956 *(T 8th)*.
COPPER WORKS JUNCTION [PT] (non-tt): *Engineer's Report* of 15 March 1917 said workmen's platform nearly completed *(RAIL 1057/1528;* {south of Margam steelworks – see *RAC Atlas p.141*}.
COPPERAS HILL [CW Jc] op 2 June 1913 *(RCG)*; last in tt June 1921; {map 21}.
COPPERHOUSE {map 111}
COPPERHOUSE (a) [West Cornwall] op 23 May 1843**; on original line; clo 16 February 1852.
COPPERHOUSE (b) [GW] op 1 July 1905 *(GW H)*; on 1852 deviation line; HALT; clo 1 May 1908 (Friday) *(wtt supp)*.
COPPLESTONE [LSW] op 1 August 1854 *(Trewman 13 July, 3 August)*; aot request; still open.
COPPULL [LNW]: line op 31 October 1838 *(co n Manch G 27th- line)*, nd, 19 October 1839 tt; re-sited 150 yards west 2 September 1895 *(Cl)*; clo 6 October 1969 *(Cl)*.
SPENDMOOR in press account of opening *(JS)*; at first COPPUL in *Brad, Robinson*.
COPPULL HALL [LNW] (non-tt): collier's ticket from Wigan to C H, Pearson Knowles Coal & Iron Co *(JB)*; mine concerned probably Chisnall Hall (sinking began 1891, first coal January 1900); {shown as Hicbibi Siding, 1m. 7ch. south of Coppull on RCH maps of time}; (see 1904 *hb*; C.H.A. Towneley, F.D. Smith and J.A. Peden, *The Industrial Railways of the Wigan Coalfield, Part II*, Runpast, 1992, pp.411–14).
CORBRIDGE [NE] op 10 March 1835** *(NC- line; in Scott 1837)*; still open.
CORBY
CORBY (a) [Mid] op 1 March 1880 *(Mid)* as C & COTTINGHAM; renamed WELDON 1 Nov. 1880 *(RCG)*, W & COTTINGHAM 1 Nov. 1881 *(RCG)*, CORBY & W 1 May 1937 *(Mid)*, CORBY 4 March 1957 *(Cl)*; clo 18 April 1966 *(Mid)*.
CORBY (b): occasional use from 1 July 1984; fully op, experimentally, 13 April 1987 *(Mid)*; clo 4 June 1990 *(BLN 633)*.
CORBY (c) op 23 February 2009 *(RM April)*; still open.
CORBY [NE] (non-tt): shown 'P' in 1877 *hb*; only 11 chains from Wetheral but on other side of viaduct so perhaps something for staff, perhaps error, perhaps duplicate entry for Wetheral – *Scott* has W or C, tts sometimes W for C; {Wetheral – How Mill}.
CORBY GLEN [GN] op 15 July 1852** as C; renamed C LINCS 3 May 1937, C G 16 June 1947 *(hba May 1947)*; clo 15 June 1959 *(RM July)*.
CORFE CASTLE [LSW] op 20 May 1885 *(SR; W Gaz first edition 22 May- line)*; clo 3 January 1972 *(RM January)*.
CORFE MULLEN [SD Jt] op 8 July 1929 *(W Gaz Bournemouth edition 5th)*; HALT; C M EAST END in *Brad* (omitted from table 1950/1 but left in index) and *hb*; clo 17 September 1956 *(T 13th)*; {Bailey Gate – Broadstone}.

CORKERHILL [GSW; LMS] op non-tt for railwaymen and families 1 December 1896 *(U)*; first in *Brad* December 1923; HALT until 1933/4 *Brad*; clo 10 January 1983 *(Rly Obs March)*; reop 30 July 1990 – trains at half-fare Saturday & Sunday 28 & 29 July *(BLN 636)*; still open.
CORKICKLE – see WHITEHAVEN.
CORNBOROUGH [BWA] first in *Brad* October 1911 (see 1901 May 18**); clo 28 March 1917**; {Abbotsham Road – Westward Ho!}.
CORNBROOK
CORNBROOK (a) [MSJA] op 1 June 1856 *(MSJA)*; last trains in tt April 1865.
CORNBROOK (b) [Manch] op 6 December 1999; interchange only, between line to Altrincham and that to Broadway; became normal station with outside access, 2 Sept. 2005 *(AB)*; still open.
CORNHILL near Keith [GNS] op 30 July 1859** *(GNS)*; clo 6 May 1968 *(RM July)*.
CORNHILL – see COLDSTREAM.
CORNHOLME [LY] first in *Brad* July 1878; clo 26 September 1938 *(RM November)*.
CORNWOOD [GW] prob op late August 1852 *(Ex to NA; in tt Plymouth* 'corrected to 1 September') as C ROAD; renamed 1864 tt *(Cl)*; clo 2 March 1959 *(RM April)*.
CORPACH [NB] op 1 April 1901 *(RCG)*; still open.
CORPORATION BRIDGE – see GRIMSBY.
CORPUSTY & SAXTHORPE [MGN] op 5 April 1883 *(MGN; T 9th- line)*; clo 2 March 1959 *(T 2nd)*.
CORRINGHAM [Corringham] op 29 June 1901**; first in *Brad* October 1948; clo 3 March 1952 *(Cl)*. Never shown 'P' in *hb*.
CORRIS [Corris]
For first service see 1874**.
CORRIS op 4 July 1883 *(Corris)*; clo 1 Jan. 1931 (Thur) *(Cl)*. Cambrian tt 1904: C for CADER IDRIS and TALYLLYN LAKE.
CORROUR [NB; LNE] op, non-tt, 7 August 1894, for Sir J.S. Maxwell's shooting estate (J. Thomas, *The West Highland Railway*, D&C 1984); July 1896 and February 1922 wtts say any train can be stopped at request of Sir J Maxwell on 'reasonable notice' to nearest station-master or signalman at Corrour. Op to public 11 September 1934 *(Cl 29)*; still open. In *hb* 1904 on without indication of private status.
CORRWG MERTHYR NAVIGATION COLLIERY [PT] (non-tt): in use for Whitworth Colliery Co – minutes 27 Nov. 1908 *(RAIL 242/3)*; see 1920** for later use; alias TORYBANWEN COLLIERY/WHITWORTH; HALT; {branch from Tonmawr}.
CORSEHILL [Cal] (non-tt): quarrymen; op by 1888; clo by July 1926; {Kirtlebridge – Annan} *(U)*.
CORSHAM [GW] op 30 June 1841 *(Wilts 8 July)*; clo 4 January 1965 *(Bath Chron 9th)*.
CORSTORPHINE
For first station of this name see SAUGHTON.
CORSTORPHINE [NB] op 1 February 1902 *(RCG)*; clo 1 January 1968 *(Cl)*.

CORTON [Norfolk & S] op 13 July 1903 *(co n Norfolk & S)*; clo 4 May 1970 *(RM May)*.

CORWEN

CORWEN [Corwen & Bala; GW] op 8 May 1865 *(GW)*; initially used by Llangollen & Corwen trains; C & B's own trains started 16 July 1866; clo 14 December 1964★★.

CORWEN temp from Denbigh [Denbigh, Ruthin & Corwen] op 6 October 1864 *(D&C 11)*; service extended to above when that was made available 1 September 1865 *(Pratt)*.

CORYATES [GW] op 1 May 1906 *(Bristol NWR)*; HALT; clo 1 December 1952 *(W Gaz 5th)*.

CORYTON [Cardiff] op 1 March 1911 *(RCG)*; re-sited south of road overbridge when part of line clo 20 July 1931; now terminus *(Cardiff)*; became C HALT 1 July 1924 *(GW circular 18 June)* – but thus in *Brad* from start; C HALT GLAM 17 Sept. 1926 *(GW circular 3011)*, C 5 May 1969 *(GW H)*; still open. At first PLATFORM *(hb)*.

CORYTON near Tavistock [GW] op 1 July 1865 *(W D Merc 4th- line; in tt Tavistock 8th)*; clo 31 December 1962★★.

CORYTON near Tilbury [Corringham] op 29 June 1901★★ as KYNOCHTOWN; renamed 1921; first in *Brad* October 1948; clo 3 March 1952 *(Cl)*. Never shown 'P' in *hb*.

COSELEY [LNW] op 10 March 1902 *(co ½ Rly Times 9 August)*; op as DEEPFIELDS & C, replacing earlier station of that name, which see; became C D 25 August 1952 *(W Mid)*; C 10 May 1968; still open.

COSFORD [GW] op 17 January 1938 *(co n 23, dated 14th)* as C AERODROME HALT for workmen only; op to public 31 March 1938 *(Cl 29)* – but in *Brad* March; renamed 28 October 1940 *(hbl September)*; still open.

COSHAM [LSW/LBSC] op 1 September 1848 *(Hants Adv 2nd)*: still open.

COSSEY/COSTESSEY – see DRAYTON.

COSSINGTON [SD Jt] op 21 July 1890 *(Bridgwater Merc 23rd)*; clo 1 Dec. 1952 *(Bridgwater Merc 2nd)*.

COSSINGTON GATE [Mid] company minutes of 21 October 1845 ordered provision of platforms; first evidence for stops *Brad* December 1845; Saturdays only. Closure resulted when replacement of level-crossing by bridge meant man would have to be kept there only for a station whose receipts for five months ending May 1873 were £3 0 7d; co notice dated 'September' 1873 said 'will be closed after Saturday September 27th and no trains will call there after that date' (J. Gough); {Syston – Sileby}.

COTEHILL [Mid] op 1 May 1876 *(Mid; co n T 1st- line)*; clo 7 April 1952 *(RM May)*.

COTHAM [GN] op 14 April 1879 *(RCG)*; clo 2 April 1917 *(Cl)*; reop 1 April 1919 *(RCH)*; clo 11 September 1939 *(Cl)*.

COTHERSTONE [NE] op 13 May 1868 *(Darlington 16th)*; clo 30 November 1964 *(RM December)*. COTHERSTON *hb* 1904 to 1910a, *Brad* 1906 to 1914.

COTTAM [GC] first in *Brad* December 1850; permanent station (same site?) 1853; clo 2 November 1959 *(RM December)*.

COTTINGHAM [NE] line op 7 October 1846★★, nd, May 1848 *(Topham)*; still open.

COTTINGLEY op 25 April 1988 *(BLN 584)*, near earlier Churwell; still open.

COTTINGWITH [Derwent Valley] op 21 July 1913 *(NER Staff Mag 1913)*; clo 1 September 1926★★ (Wednesday) *(RM October)*.

COUGHTON [Mid] op 4 May 1868 *(Mid)*; clo 30 June 1952 *(Mid)*.

COULSDON

C NORTH [LBSC] op 5 November 1899 *(L)* as STOATS NEST for CANE HILL; renamed COULSDON & SMITHAM DOWNS 1 June 1911 *(NE dist amdt 1911/16)*, C WEST 9 July 1923 *(hbl 26 April)*, C NORTH 1 August 1923 *(Cl)*; clo 3 October 1983 *(RM March 1984)*. *Brad* ? to 1955 C N for CANE HILL. *Hb* 1904 S N; 1912 S N & C H; 1925 C N.

C SOUTH [SE] op 1 October 1889 *(RCG)* as C; renamed C & CANE HILL 1896 tt *(Cl)*, C EAST 9 July 1923 *(hbl 26 April)*, C SOUTH 1 August 1923 *(Cl)*; still open. Also see KENLEY.

COULTER [Cal] op 6 November 1860★★; clo 5 June 1950 *(RM July)*.

COUND [GW] op 4 August 1934 *(T 25 July)*; HALT; 5 October 1942 co tt says trains call daylight only; clo 9 September 1963 *(T 9th)*; {Cressage – Berrington}.

COUNDON near Bishop Auckland [NE] op 1 December 1885 *(NE- line)*; clo 4 Dec. 1939 *(Cl)*. Also see SPENNYMOOR (for possible later use.)

COUNDON ROAD near Coventry [LNW] op 2 September 1850★★; COUNDEN R until 1 Nov. 1894 *(Cl)*; clo 18 January 1965 *(RM March)*.

COUNTER DRAIN [MGN] first trains in tt September 1866; clo 2 March 1959 *(T 2nd)*.

COUNTESS PARK [NB] op 1 December 1859 *(NC)*; temporary terminus; clo 1 February 1861 when line extended to Thorneyburn *(Cl)*.

COUNTESTHORPE [Mid]: line through opened 30 June 1840 but unlikely any stop then. *Allen's Guide* to line includes tt for 7 September 1840 and no stop shown; description simply refers to trains passing here. Earliest evidence is *Robinson*, about August 1841, showing Sat. stop at C GATE-HOUSE; it was also in notes in *Brad* at about this time, but mentions were erratic (e.g. not in December 1842 Companion, nor in July 1845). Earliest mention found in local press (where tables were irregularly included) is in tt *Leicester Journal* 10 June 1842, Saturday stop; by 1 March 1844 *(tt Leicester Journal)* stops Wednesdays and Saturdays. Minutes of company's Committee of Management show that they ordered station, full use, to be included in tts for March 1846. *Leicestershire Mercury* tts from 18 October 1844 call it C but *Brad* August 1845 still C G-H. It is likely that the lack of continuous reference was owing to clerical vagaries rather than irregular use of stop. (Press and company information from J. Gough.) Clo 1 January 1962 *(RM February)*.

COUNTY MARCH – see 1957★★.

COUNTY SCHOOL [GE] op 1 March 1884
(GE Journal April 2002);
clo 5 October 1964 *(RM September)*.

COUPAR ANGUS [Cal] op 24 February 1837 (see 1837 B★★); clo 6 September 1847 *(Rtn)*; reop 2 August 1848 *(Cl)*; clo 4 September 1967 *(RM September)*.
C A JUNCTION 1858/9 to 1882 *(Brad)*.

COURT SART [RSB]
op 14 March 1895 *(Colliery 22nd- line)*;
clo 16 September 1935 *(GW notice NW 1082)*.

COVE [GW] op 9 June 1924 *(Tiverton 10th)*; HALT;
clo 7 October 1963 *(W Som F P 12th)*;
{Tiverton – Bampton}.

COVE BAY near Aberdeen [Cal] op 1 April 1850
(Cal- line); BAY added 1 October 1912 *(hbl 24th)*;
clo 11 June 1956 *(RM April)*.

COVENT GARDEN [Picc] op 11 April 1907
(RM May) – in *Brad January 1907,* and on map in
advertisement for line opening *(T 14 December 1906)*,
both presumably in anticipation; still open.

COVENTRY [LNW] op 9 April 1838 *(T 11th)*;
original station replaced by 1840; still open.
C JUNCTION in LNW co tt 1856.

COW BANK – see SEACROFT.

COWBIT [GN/GE] op 2 September 1867★ *(GN)*;
clo 11 September 1961 *(RM September)*.
★ = GN minutes say op 1st, but that a Sunday, no Sunday service.

COWBRIDGE [TV] op 18 September 1865 *(T 20th)*;
re-sited on extension to Aberthaw 1 October 1892 *(Cl)*;
clo 26 November 1951 *(RM January 1952)*.

COWCADDENS [GU] op 14 December 1896★★;
still open.

COWDEN [LBSC]
op 1 October 1888 *(co n T 28 September)*; still open.

COWDENBEATH [NB]
C OLD: op 4 September 1848 *(co n Perthshire Courier 31 August)*; OLD added 1 June 1890 *(Cl)*;
clo 31 March 1919 *(Cl)*. Engine based at Kelty worked
miners' trains which called here long after public closure
(Locos of LNER Part 8B, RCTS, 1971). C JUNCTION
1862 to 1890 *(Brad)*.
COWDENBEATH op 2 June 1890 *(G&S)*;
C NEW until 14 June 1965 tt; still open.

COWES [IWC] op 16 June 1862 *(Hants Adv 21st)*;
clo 21 February 1966 *(RM March)*. Noted 1939 and
1947 in SR tt as nearest station for Osborne House.

COWLAIRS [NB] op by 1 April 1858 co tt, when only
trains from Glasgow shown; first in *Brad* July 1859.
However, from line opening 21 February 1842 trains
between here and Glasgow Queen Street were cable
hauled; also note in *Brad* says all down trains stop at
ticket platform; thus possibly earlier use hereabouts,
though sites probably different. Clo 7 September 1964
(Cl). A o t C JUNCTION station nameboard.

COWLEY near Uxbridge [GW] op 1 October 1904
(RCG); clo 10 September 1962 *(RM October)*.

COWPEN [Stockton & Hartlepool]: possible early
station; no tt evidence seen; see 1841 February 10★★.

COWPEN LANE – see BEBSIDE.

COWTON [NE] op 31 March 1841 *(co n E Cos Her 25th- line)*; clo 15 September 1958 *(RM October)*.

COX GREEN [NE] first in *Brad* November 1854 as
COXGREEN CROSSING; CROSSING dropped 1857
tt *(Cl)*; two words July 1931 co tt *(JS)*; clo 4 May 1964 *(Cl)*.

COXBANK [GW] op 23 June 1934 *(GW H)*; HALT;
clo 9 September 1963 *(T 9th)*; {Audlem – Adderley}.

COXBENCH [Mid] op 1 September 1856
(Mid; T 12th- line); clo 1 June 1930 (Sunday) *(Mid)*.

COXHOE [NE] {map 33}
COXHOE op 11 July 1835 (see 1835 A★★); clo November
1837; reop 20 June 1838; clo 1 April 1902 (Tuesday)
(RCG).
C BRIDGE: line op 13 October 1846 *(NE maps)*, nd,
August 1847; BRIDGE added 1860 *Brad*, by January
1861 NE co tt; clo 9 June 1952★★.

COXLODGE [NE] op 1 June 1905 *(RCG)*;
clo 17 June 1929 *(Cl)*. Fawdon at/near later.

COXWOLD [NE] op 1 June 1853★★; clo 2 February
1953 *(RM March)*; later excur for shopping and
football *(RM February 1955)*.

CRABLEY CREEK [NE] probably op between June
1843 and July 1844 Tuesdays only; see 1840 July 2★★
for details of opening and later service.

CRADLEY HEATH [GW] op 2 March 1863 *(RAIL 1089/7)* as C; became C H & C 1 July 1899 *(hbl 13th)*,
C 6 May 1968, C H 1 June 1981 tt *(Cl)*; still open.

CRADOC [N&B] op 1 March 1877 *(N&B Minutes –
P. Rowledge; not in Brad until November 1877)*;
clo 15 October 1962 *(RM November)*.

CRAGG MILL [NE]: included in 1857 list of NE
stations in Clinker Collection (as CRAG MILL) and
on first edition OS map of about 1866 as CRAGMILL
(S. Bragg); passenger use then cannot be guaranteed –
perhaps non-tt market stops; in operation by February
1871, when in wtt (A. Young); first in *Brad* November
1875; Tuesdays & Saturdays; last there October 1877,
and hb 1878a 'closed'; {Belford – Smeafield}.
Also see 1847 March 29★★.

CRAIG HOUSES (non-tt): railwaymen's wives;
op 3 December 1951; used to 1972 or later;
{Glencarron – Achnashellach} *(U)*.

CRAIG MERTHYR COLLIERY (non-tt):
see GRAIG MERTHYR – correct spelling.

CRAIG-Y-NOS PENWYLLT [N&B] op 3 June
1867 *(D&C 12; T 5th- line)* as P; renamed 1 February
1907 *(hbl 24 January)*; clo 15 Oct. 1962 *(RM Nov.)*.
Until 1919 it included private waiting room for Dame
Adeline Patti, later restored as a museum.

CRAIGELLACHIE
For first station of this name see DANDALEITH.
CRAIGELLACHIE [GNS] op 1 July 1863 *(GNS)* as
STRATHSPEY JUNCTION; renamed C JUNCTION
1 June 1864 *(Cl)*, C 1897/8 *(Brad)*, but already thus hb
1872; clo 6 May 1968 *(RM July)*.

CRAIGENDORAN [NB]
Station on lower line op 15 May 1882 *(D&C 6)*,
C PIER in *Brad* until 1922/3, then C; still open.
C West Highland platforms (separate station in hb)
op 7 Aug. 1894 *(T 7th)*, C in *Brad*; clo 15 June 1964 *(Cl)*.
From 1922/3, *Brad* just used C for both but wtt
(e.g. 4 May 1936 and 17 June 1963) continued to show
C PIER as separate.

CRAIGLEITH [Cal] op 1 August 1879 *(RCG)*; became C for BLACKHALL 1 July 1922 *(hbl 13th)*; clo 30 April 1962 *(RM May)*; {map 19}.

CRAIGLOCKHART [NB] op 1 June 1887 *(D&C 6)*; clo 1 May 1890, replaced for duration by Edinburgh Exhibition NB; reop 1 January 1891 *(Cl)*; clo 1 January 1917 *(RM February)*; reop 1 February 1919 *(RM Feb.)*; clo 10 September 1962 *(BR n Ed Sub)*.

CRAIGLON BRIDGE [GW] op 1 February 1932 *(Cl 29)*; HALT; clo 21 September 1953 *(BRWR notice August)*; {Pembrey – Pinged}.

CRAIGMYLE [GNS] (non-tt): private for Craigmyle House; op ?; clo 1887; {Glassel – Torphins} *(GNS)*.

CRAIGNACAILLEICH★ [Cal] (non-tt): PLATFORM; railwaymen, schoolchildren; at least 1922 *(U)* to summer 1959 wtt, which shows 5.15pm Glasgow–Oban calling all Saturdays to set down railway employees; {Callander – Strathyre}.
★ = spelling from ticket *(JB)*.

CRAIGO [Cal] first in *Brad* February 1851; clo 11 June 1956 *(RM April)*.

CRAIL [NB] op 1 September 1883 *(Fifeshire Journal 6th)*; clo 6 September 1965 *(co n East of T J)*.

CRAKEHALL [NE] op 19 May 1856 *(RCG- line)*; clo 1 March 1917 (Thursday) *(RCH)*; back in *Brad* November 1921; clo 26 April 1954 *(T 20th)*.

CRAMLINGTON [NE]: op 1 March 1847★★ *(co n Newcastle Journal 27 February)*; still open.

CRAMOND BRIG – see BARNTON.

CRANBROOK [SE] op 4 September 1893 *(SR)*; clo 12 June 1961 *(T 12th)*.

CRANFORD [Mid] op 1 March 1866 *(Mid; co n T 27 February- line)*; clo 2 April 1956 *(RM May)*.

CRANK [LNW] first in *Brad* April 1858; became HALT 1940 *(Brad)*; clo 18 June 1951 *(RM August)*.

CRANLEIGH [LBSC] op 2 October 1865 *(T 3rd)*; CRANLEY to 1867 tt *(Cl)*; clo 14 June 1965 *(Cl)*. 1938 *hb*: C for EWHURST.

CRANLEY GARDENS [GN] op 2 Aug. 1902 *(RCG)*; clo 29 October 1951, reop 7 January 1952 *(T 18 December 1951)*; clo 5 July 1954 *(RM July)*.

CRANMORE [GW] op 9 November 1858 *(GW; in tt Shepton 12th)*; clo 9 September 1963 *(Weston 13th)*.

CRATHES [GNS]

C CASTLE PLATFORM (non-tt) op 8 September 1853 *(GNS)*; at 13m 76ch; replaced by >

CRATHES (public) op 1 January 1863 *(GNS)*; at 14m 25ch; clo 28 February 1966 *(RM March)*. Until 1914 Burnett family could stop any train. *RM Oct. 1960* said had become HALT; not thus BR tts.

CRAVEN ARMS [SH Jt] op 21 April 1852 *(co ½ T 17 August- line)*; C A & STOKESAY from 1879 *(LNW circular 30 July – 'in future')* to 6 May 1974 *(BR notice)*; still open. C A JUNCTION 1862 to 1879 *(Brad)*, and thus LNW co tts 1864 to 1874 at least.

CRAWFORD [Cal] op 1 January 1891 *(RCG)*; clo 4 January 1965 *(RM February)*.

CRAWLEY near Durham [S&D] op 1 September 1845 *(S&D; see 1843★★)*; clo 31 October 1845 (Friday); reop 1 April 1846 *(G&S)*; last in *Brad* December 1846; see PARK HEAD for possible later service; {map 30}.

CRAWLEY near Horsham [LBSC] op 14 February 1848 *(Hants Chron 12th)*; re-sited slightly nearer London 28 July 1968 *(Cl)*; still open.

CRAY [N&B] first in *Brad* February 1870; clo 15 October 1962 *(RM November)*.

CRAYFORD [SE] op 1 September 1866 *(L; co ½ T 24 August- line)*; still open.

CREAGAN [Cal]
op 24 August 1903 *(D&C 15, chapter- line)*; clo 28 March 1966 *(RM June – photo caption)*.

CREDENHILL [Mid] op 30 June 1863 *(Hereford J 27th)*; clo 31 December 1962 *(T 31st)*.

CREDITON [LSW]
op 12 May 1851★★ *(Trewman 15th)*; re-sited on extension of line to Barnstaple 1 August 1854 *(Cl)*; still open.

CREECH ST MICHAEL [GW] op 13 August 1928 *(Som Gaz 18th)*; HALT, though this at first omitted *hb*; clo 5 October 1964 *(Cl)*; {Durston – Creech junction}.

CREEKMOOR [SR]
op 19 June 1933 *(Poole 22nd)*; HALT; clo 7 March 1966 *(Shepton 11th)*; {Poole – Broadstone}.

CREETOWN [PPW Jt] op 12 March 1861 *(Galloway 15th)*; clo 14 June 1965 *(RM July)*.

CREIGIAU [Barry] op 16 March 1896 *(dist t supp 13 April)*; clo 10 September 1962 *(Cl)*.

CRESSAGE [GW] op 1 February 1862★★; clo 9 September 1963 *(T 9th)*.

CRESSING [GE]: line op 2 October 1848 *(EC)*, nd, February 1850; see 1850 August 19★★; op as BULFORD; renamed 1 February 1911 *(RCG)*; aot request; still open.

CRESSINGTON [CLC]
op non-tt April 1872 *(D&C 10)*; first in public tt April 1873; C & GRASSENDALE 1877 *(Cl; RCG ref Jan.)* to clo 17 April 1972 *(RM May)*; reop 3 January 1978 as C *(AZ; Daily Telegraph 3rd- line)*; still open.

CRESSWELL near Stoke-on-Trent [NS] op 7 August 1848★★; clo 7 November 1966 *(RM January 1967)*.

CRESWELL

CRESWELL – see ELMTON

C & WELBECK [GC] op 1 June 1897 *(GC dates)*; &W added 1 September 1897 *(hbl 28 October –original RCG entry was C for W)*; clo 11 Sept. 1939 *(G&S)*.
C DERBYS op 25 May 1998 *(BLN 821)*, on same site as earlier ELMTON & C; 'fun day' 24 May; still open.

CREW GREEN [SM] op 2 June 1871 *(D&C 11)* as CREWE G; spelling amended 1920 *(Cl; hbl ref 24 April 1921)*; finally clo October 1932 *(Cl)*. See 1866 August 13★★ (Criggion branch) for full details.
Became C G for COEDWAY and ALDERBURY added 1 January 1918 *(hbl 24th)* and thus *Brad* to closure.

CREWE

CREWE [GJ; LNW] op 4 July 1837 *(T 6th)*; still open.
C JUNCTION some tables 1851/2 to 1885/6 *(Brad)*, LNW co tt 1864, but not 1868; C BRIDGE in one opening description *T 6th*.

CREWE [Manchester and Birmingham] terminus op 10 Aug. 1842 *(GJ co n T 9th- line)*; separated from GJ line by gate, opened to allow passage of through trains; about 1846 absorbed into main station.
Also [LMS] non-tt station on branch from here, used

by railway workmen from 1923; variously C WORKS, CARRIAGE WORKS, WISTASTON ROAD; clo 24 April 1989 (BLN 632).

CREWKERNE [LSW] op 19 July 1860**; still open. Early *Brad* was C for BRIDPORT/for BEAMINSTER and BRIDPORT, then C for BEAMINSTER until 1929/30 but just C in LSW co tt 1914.

CREWS HILL [GN] op 4 April 1910 (wtt notice NLRHS Journal 41); still open.

CRIANLARICH
CRIANLARICH [NB] op 7 August 1894 (T 7th); C UPPER 1951 tt (JS) to 1964/8 tt; still open.
C LOWER [Cal] op 1 August 1873 (Cal- line); LOWER added 1953 (JS); clo 28 September 1965**.

CRIBBWR FAWR COLLIERY
– see under PORT TALBOT

CRICCIETH [Cam] op 2 September 1867** (Cam; Carnarvon co ½ T 10 October- line); still open.

CRICK – see KILSBY & CRICK; WELTON.

CRICKLADE [MSWJ] op 18 December 1883 (Bath Chron 20th); clo 11 September 1961 (T 9th).

CRICKLADE ROAD LEVEL CROSSING: (non-tt); shown both ways for staff service in Bristol District wtt 12 June 1961 – error? work in locality?; {Highworth branch, Stanton – Hannington} (IU).

CRICKLEWOOD [Mid] op 2 May 1870 (Mid) as CHILDS HILL & C; renamed 1 May 1903 (hbl 23 April); still open.

CRIEFF [Cal] op 14 March 1856 (Tayside); re-sited on extension of line to Comrie 1 June 1893 (Cl); clo 6 July 1964 (RM July). Later specials ran, probably for cadets attending summer camp in this area. Wtts show: 8.45am to Edinburgh on Friday 31 July 1964; 9.15pm to Liverpool and 10.45pm to Wigan on Saturday 15 August 1964 (G. Borthwick).

CRIEFF JUNCTION – see GLENEAGLES.

CRIGGION [SM]
CRIGGION op 2 June 1871 (D&C 11); finally clo Oct. 1932 (Cl). See 1866 August 13** (Criggion branch) for full details.
C QUARRY SIDINGS is listed by RCG at 1912 reop, with same facilities as C and in hb, added 1914a; shown as between Criggion and Kinnerley but RAC has Quarries beyond Criggion. Not in RCH distance diagrams; presumably persistent error.

CRIGGLESTONE [LY] op 1 January 1850 (LY; co ½ T 22 February- line); C WEST 2 June 1924 (Rly Gaz 23 May) to 12 June 1961 (RM April); clo 13 September 1965 (T 4th).

CRIMDON – see HART.

CRIMPLE [NE] first in *Brad* November 1867; last May 1869; {physical junction IA}.

CRIMSTONE [NB]: line op 15 August 1849** and C probably op with it; clo by May 1852, first time *Brad* gave line details (was in Edinburgh tt Feb 1850). Alias CRUMSTANE.

CROESOR JUNCTION [WH] (ng): stops shown in wtt by 14 July 1924 (WHH 5, 25); in co tt 26 Sept. 1927 (NGSC 2); see 1922 July 31**; clo 28 September 1936 (Cl); {map 76}.

CROFT near Leicester [LNW] op 1 November 1877 (LNW Officers 17900); clo 4 March 1968 (Cl).

CROFT near Darlington; {map 36} Early [S&D] – see 1825**: co notice of 16 October 1826 (S&D) says Union Coach will use Black Swan Inn, near Croft branch.
CROFT [S&D], on branch, op end September 1833; decision to discontinue service taken 13 December 1833 – actually clo ?; reop 1 February 1837 when William Walton was given a year's contract to run service (S&D Pass); replaced by >
C SPA [NE], on main line, op 31 March 1841 (S&D Pass; co n E Cos Her 25th- line); SPA added 1 Oct. 1896 (hbl 29th); served by Richmond line branch trains only after 15 September 1958; clo 3 March 1969 (RM March).

CROFT BANK – see HAVENHOUSE.

CROFTFOOT [LMS] first in *Brad* April 1931; still open.

CROFTHEAD
– see: FAULDHOUSE & C [NB], 1845–1930; KENNISHEAD [GBK Jt], 1840 – present; NEILSTON [GBK Jt], 1855–1966.

CROFTON near Wakefield [LY] op 1 November 1853 (LY); clo 30 November 1931 (LNW Record).
CROFTON [MC] (non-tt): see 1843 May 10**; private station, built for Sir M.H. Brisco of Crofton Hall; op about 1856 [buildings?]; officially clo 1954 but already out of use; hb added 1899a, still 'P' 1925, goods only 1929; {Curthwaite – Wigton} (RM October 1903; U).

CROFTON PARK London [LCD] op 1 July 1892 (L); still open. Hb 1904: C P for LADYWELL.

CROFTON SOUTH [Dearne Valley] (non-tt): in use 1942–3; purpose ?; {Calder Bridge – Ryhill} (U).

CROMBIE – see BRAESIDE.

CROMDALE [GNS] op 1 July 1863 (GNS); clo 18 October 1965**.

CROMER
CROMER [MGN] op 16 June 1887 (RCG); C BEACH until 30 October 1969 (Cl); still open.
C HIGH [GE] op 26 March 1877 (T 27th); HIGH added 27 September 1948 (RM November); clo 20 September 1954 (RM October).
C LINKS [Norfolk & S] op 14 May 1923 (D&C 5; in *Brad* June); HALT; clo 7 April 1953 (RM May); {Overstrand – Cromer}.

CROMFORD
For [C & High Peak] service – see 1833 May**.
CROMFORD [Mid] op 4 June 1849 (Mid; T 5th- line); still open. C for WIRKSWORTH 1894 *Brad*, but not Mid co tt.

CRONBERRY [GSW] op 1 May 1876 (RCG); clo 10 September 1951 (RM October).

CROOK [NE] probably op early 1844, market only (see 1843**) (first in *Brad* July 1844); full use January 1845 tt. 30 December 1843: orders given to build temporary station here, designed for later conversion into railwaymen's cottages. 15 July 1846: orders given to send redundant platform from Stockton, to fill the need for one here. When line was extended to Tow Law 1 September 1845 station was left on a stub line; map evidence shows still so in mid-1850s. 22 September 1856: minutes said building of new station was to be proceeded with *(RAIL 667/62)*; no exact op date found. Clo 8 March 1965 *(RM April)*.

CROOK OF DEVON [NB] op 1 May 1863 *(D&C 15; T 4th- line)*; clo 15 June 1964 *(RM July)*. *Hb* 1904 C of D for FOSSOWAY.

CROOK STREET – see under BOLTON.

CROOKSTON [GSW]
op 1 July 1885 *(co ½ 1110/149- line)*; clo 1 January 1917 *(Cl)*; reop 10 February 1919 *(RCH)*, but only back in tt May 1923 (relevant table previously nd); clo 10 January 1983 *(RM March)*; reop 30 July 1990 – trains at half-fare Saturday & Sunday 28th & 29th *(BLN 636)*; still open.

CROPREDY [GW]
op 1 October 1852 *(GW; T 27 September- line*, in inspection report; clo 17 September 1956 *(Cl)*.

CROSBY – see BLUNDELLSANDS.

CROSBY GARRETT [Mid] op 1 May 1876 *(Mid; co n T 1st- line)*; clo 6 October 1952 *(Cl)*.

CROSS GATES near Leeds [NE]: line op 22 Sept. 1834**; in co tt 1835, but not *Brad* before 1840, nor in *Whishaw*; still open. *Hb*: one word until 1877.

CROSS GATES – see FORD & CROSSGATES.

CROSS HANDS near Bristol [GW]
op 9 July 1928 *(W D Press 7th)*; HALT; clo 23 November 1964 *(Bristol E P 21st)*; {map 121}.

CROSS HANDS near Llanelli – see 1887**.

CROSS INN near Llantrisant [TV] op 6 September 1869 *(Cardiff T 11th)*; clo 31 March 1952 *(Cl)*.

CROSS INN (others) – see AMMANFORD; BRYN TEIFI; CLARBESTON ROAD.

CROSS KEYS near Risca [GW]
CROSS KEYS (a) first in *Brad* September 1851; clo 30 April 1962 *(T 6 April)*.
CROSSKEYS (b) op Saturday 7 June 2008 *(South Wales Argus* via internet and M. Preskett)*; still open. Spelling as in paper, *Rail Times* makes two words of it.

CROSS KEYS – see GLANAMMAN.

CROSS LANE [LNW]: line op 17 September 1830**, nd, 1 March 1831 co tt; clo 20 July 1959 *(RM August)*. C L BRIDGE in early co tt.

CROSS SLACK [PW] first in *Brad* June 1870; last November 1873; replaced by St Annes-on-Sea.

CROSSENS [LY] op 20 February 1878 *(Southport Vis 20th)*; clo 7 September 1964 *(RM October)*.

CROSSFLATTS
op 17 May 1982 *(RM June)*; still open.

CROSSFORD [GSW] op 1 March 1905 *(RCG)*; clo 3 May 1943 *(RM January 1944)*.

CROSSGATEHALL [NB] op 1 August 1913 *(Edin)*; HALT; clo 1 January 1917 *(RM February)*; reop 1 February 1919 *(RM February)*; clo 22 September 1930 *(Cl)*; {Smeaton – Ormiston}.

CROSSGATES FIFE [NB]
op 4 September 1848 *(co n Perthshire Courier 31 August)*; FIFE added 1 July 1923 *(hbl 12th)*; clo 26 September 1949 *(RM January 1950)*.

CROSSHARBOUR & LONDON ARENA [Dock]
op 31 August 1987 *(T 1 September)*; & L A added 14 August 1995 *(AB Chron)*; clo by bomb during evening of 9 February 1996 *(T 10th)*;

reop 15 April 1996 *(Rly Obs June)*; still open.

CROSSHILL near Ayr [GSW] op 24 May 1860 *(co ½ T 3 September- line)*; reduced to Tuesdays only August 1861 *Brad*; last trains shown March 1862.

CROSSHILL Glasgow [Cal] op 1 March 1886 *(Cal)*; clo 1 January 1917 *(RM February)*; reop 1 April 1919 *(RCH)*; still open.

CROSSHILL & CODNOR [Mid] op 2 June 1890 *(RCG)*; clo 1 January 1917 *(T 29 December 1916)*; reop 3 May 1920 *(Mid)*; clo 4 May 1926**.

CROSSHOUSE [GSW] trains first shown April 1873 *Brad*; at/near site of earlier Busby; clo 18 April 1966 *(RM May)*.

CROSSLEE – see HOUSTON.

CROSSMICHAEL [PPW Jt] op 12 March 1861 *(Galloway 15th)*; clo 14 June 1965 *(RM July)*. Two words in *hb* until 1877.

CROSSMYLOOF [GBK Jt] op in June 1888 *(Cal;* first in *Brad* July)*; still open.

CROSSROADS – see DUNDEE.

CROSSWAYS [GW] op 8 April 1929 *(wtt supp)*; HALT; clo 12 February 1951 *(Cl)* – see 1951**; {Ciliau Aeron – Llanerch Aeron}.

CROSTON

CROSTON [LY] op 2 April 1849 *(Southport Vis 7th)*; still open.

C ROYAL ORDNANCE DEPOT [LMS] (non-tt): for workmen building Ulnes Walton WD Depot; op 27 January 1941; clo July/August 1941; {Croston – Midge Hall} *(WW II)*.

CROUCH END [GN]
op 22 August 1867 *(L; co n T 22nd- line)*; clo 29 October 1951, reop 7 January 1952 *(T 18 December 1951)*; clo 5 July 1954 *(RM July)*.

CROUCH HILL [TH Jt] op 21 July 1868 *(L; co ½ T 30 September- line)*; clo 31 January 1870**; reop 1 October 1870 *(Cl)*; still open.

CROW PARK near Newark [GN] op 1 November 1882 *(GN)*; clo 6 October 1958* *(RM November)*.
* = appears to be one of those stations whose service faded away; August 1951 *Brad* shows one train each way, weekdays at least; by 15 September 1952 weekday service northbound had been withdrawn; thereafter tts checked always show a Sunday train northbound and a weekday train southbound during the summer (present 4 May 1953, 11 June 1956 and August 1958; absent 4 February 1957 and February 1958). GN co tt 1909, and *Brad* to 1955: C P for SUTTON-ON-TRENT.

CROW PARK [LSW] (non-tt): workmen; op about July 1918; HALT; clo by July 1920; {Bursledon – Swanwick} *(U)*.

CROW ROAD [Cal] op 1 October 1896 *(RCG; Colliery 2nd- line)*; clo 6 November 1960**.

CROWBOROUGH [LBSC]
op 3 August 1868 *(T 4th)* as ROTHERFIELD; renamed C 1 August 1880 *(Cl)*, C & JARVIS BROOK 1 May 1897 *(RCG)*, C 12 May 1980 tt *(Cl)*; still open.

CROWCOMBE [GW] op 31 March 1862 *(W Som F P 5 April)*; C HEATHFIELD until 1 Dec. 1889 *(hbl 23 January 1890)* but already just C in B&E wtt 1886; clo 4 January 1971 *(Som Gaz 8th)*. See 2007 July 20**.

CROWDEN [GC] op 1 July 1861 *(GC)*; clo 4 February 1957 *(RM March)*. *Hb* 1890 (only): CROWDON.

CROWHURST [SEC] op 1 June 1902 *(RCG)*; still open.

CROWLAND – see POSTLAND; ST JAMES DEEPING.

CROWLANDS [LNE (ex-GE)]: station built about 1930 between Chadwell Heath and Romford but never provided with service *(U)*.

CROWLE

CROWLE [GC] op 13 September 1859 (P. Scowcroft, *Chron*); C CENTRAL 1 July 1923 *(hbl 12th)* to 20 February 1969 *(Cl)*; still open. GC co tt 1903: C for EPWORTH and BELTON (and still thus 1923).

CROWLE [Ax Jt] op 10 August 1903 *(RCG)*; clo 17 July 1933 *(RM September)*.

CROWN POINT – see under NORWICH.

CROWN STREET – see under SILVERDALE.

CROWTHORNE [SE] op Saturday 29 January 1859 as WELLINGTON COLLEGE; that day only train was special for those going to see Queen Victoria open the College *(co n T 27th)*;
op fully 31 January or 1 February *(co n T 1 February – 'now open')*; re-sited ½ mile north early on *(C/W* – V. Mitchell & K. Smith, *Country Branch Lines between Reading and* Guildford, Middleton, 1988) – *SE, p. 68*, refers to expenditure of £1,500 on 'improvements' in 1860 (occasion of removal?); renamed 17 June 1928 *(hbl July)*; still open.
According to *RCH dist ref 30 November 1907* had been renamed from W C for SANDHURST to W C for CROWTHORNE but former not seen in *Brad*, where it had become W C for C 1895/6; it became C 17 June 1928 *(hbl July)*.

CROXALL [Mid] *(op* 15 June 1840 *(Mid)* as OAKLEY & ALREWAS; renamed O 1 November 1849 co tt *(Mid)*, February 1849 *Brad (JS)*, C 1956 *(Brad)*; clo 9 July 1928 *(Mid)*. *Tuck* June 1843: O.

CROXDALE [NE] first in *Brad* May 1876; clo 26 September 1938 *(RM November)*.

CROXLEY

CROXLEY [Met/LNE] op 2 November 1925 *(T 2nd)* as C GREEN; only Met after 4 May 1926; renamed 23 May 1949 *(Cl)*; still open.

C GREEN [LNW] op 15 June 1912 *(T 7th)*; after 17 May 1993 only one train each way per day, early morning; last train Friday 22 March 1996 *(RM November)*. Allegedly temporary closure for bridge repair but last replacement road service ran 26 September 2003 *(Silverlink Train Services Ltd letter dated 1 October 2004 – via R. Maund)*.

CROY [NB] op 21 February 1842 *(co n 19th)*; at first 'trial' station; still open.

CROYDON – see CENTRAL, EAST, SOUTH, WEST CROYDON. Early tts tended to show indiscriminately as e.g. SOUTH C / C SOUTH.

CRUCKTON [SM]: listed with line op 14 April 1911 *(RCG)* and shown 'P' 1912 *hb* but co tt reproduced *RM September 1911* says 'not yet open'; first trains shown *Brad* October 1913; nature of line such that might have op earlier; aot request; clo 6 November 1933 *(Cl)*.

CRUDEN BAY [GNS] op 2 August 1897 *(GNS)*; clo 31 October 1932 *(RM December)*.
Later excursions – e.g. St Mary's Church, Ellon's Sunday School Trip late 1933; also specials Second War, though replaced by road transport before end of war (GNS Society's *Review* August 2005).

CRUDGINGTON [GW] op 16 October 1867 *(Rtn- line)*; clo 9 September 1963 *(T 9th)*.

CRUMLIN

C LL [GW] op 23 December 1850**; LL added 1 September 1881 *(RCG dist 31 July 1882)*; clo 30 April 1962 *(T 6 April)*.

CRUMLIN [Newport, Abergavenny & Hereford], temporary station pending completion of viaduct, op 20 August 1855**. Replaced by >

C HL [GW] op 15 October 1857, after line had been opened through *(Star of Gwent 17th – RAC)*; HL added 1 September 1881 *(RCG dist 31 July 1882)*; clo 15 June 1964 *(RM August)*.

C VALLEY(S) COLLIERY (non-tt) [GW]: PLATFORM; miners; application for facilities noted by Traffic Committee 6 January 1921; clo 6 November 1961 *(U)*; {Hafodyrynys – Pontypool}.

CRUMLIN BURROWS [RSB] (non-tt): HALT; op 9 November 1910 *(RSB/GW Officers' Conference minutes, 243/2 – M. Hale)*; clo ?; {C B Colliery shown by *RAC* about ¼ mile north-east of Jersey Marine}.

CRUMPSALL

CRUMPSALL (a) [LY] op 1 September 1879* *(Manchester 2nd)*.
clo 17 August 1991 *(BLN 660)* for conversion to >
CRUMPSALL (b) [Manch] op 6 April 1992 *(BLN 681)*; still open.
* = perhaps used 30 August – see HEATON PARK – paper said stretch of line as far as Heaton Park was used then.

CRUMSTANE – see CRIMSTONE.

CRYMMYCH ARMS [GW] op 12 July 1875 *(GW)*; clo 10 September 1962 *(Cl)*.

CRYNANT [N&B]

CRYNANT op 3 June 1867 *(T 5th- line)*; clo 15 October 1962 *(RM November)*.

C COLLIERY (non-tt): miners; dates ?; {Crynant – Crynant New Colliery} *(U)*.

C NEW COLLIERY (non-tt): HALT; miners; at least 1938 to 1954; {Crynant Colliery – Brynteg} *(U)*.

CRYSTAL PALACE

CRYSTAL PALACE [LBSC] op 10 June 1854 *(co n T 9th)*; C P LL 1933/4 *(Brad)* to 13 June 1955 *(Cl)*; still open. *Hb* made two of it: C P EAST on line from Sydenham; C P WEST from Norwood; added LL 1938.
Notice T 14 March 1855 – on and from 12 March additional accommodation for local traffic will be provided by extra 19 weekday trains to and from the WESTOW HILL station at the Crystal Palace, as if W H was some sort of extension/overflow to main station; notice *T 29 June 1855* says weekday trains use C P, Sunday W H; *Brad*, e.g. January 1856, has note that Sunday trains run to WESTOW HILL (timing same as weekdays). Street map suggests this perhaps just short of main station – originally two stops, one for direct entry, another for the grounds, run together with extension of

line 1 December 1856? or (more likely?) two names for same station? Note omitted by January 1857 *Brad*.

C P HL & UPPER NORWOOD [LCD]
op 1 August 1865 *(co n T 31 July)* as C P HL; & U N added 1 November 1898 *(RCG)*, HL not always included thereafter; clo 1 January 1917 *(RM February)*; reop 1 March 1919 *(T 24 February)*; clo 22 May 1944 *(T 22 April)*; reop 4 March 1946 *(RM May)*; clo 20 September 1954 *(T 20th)*. Tickets *(JB)* show even greater variety of names, including addition of SOUTH SIDE on some SEC examples.

CRYTHAN [South Wales Mineral] (non-tt): PLATFORM; miners; op ?; clo by September 1938; {Tonmawr – Briton Ferry} *(U)*.

CUDDINGTON [CLC]
op 22 June 1870 *(CLC)*; still open.

CUDWORTH
CUDWORTH [Mid] op 1 July 1840 *(Mid; co n T 27 June-line)* as BARNSLEY; renamed C for B 1 August 1854 co tt *(Mid)*, C 1 May 1870 co tt *(Mid)*; re-sited slightly south about 1854 *(Mid)*; clo 1 January 1968 *(RM Feb.)*.
CUDWORTH [HB] op 27 July 1885 *(co ½ T 21 August)*; clo 2 October 1905 – services to Mid station *(Cl)*.

CUERDLEY [St Helens] first in *Brad* March 1856; last January 1858; {Fidlers Ferry – Widnes}.

CUFFLEY [GN] op 4 April 1910 *(wtt notice NLRHS Journal 41)*; C & GOFFS OAK 25 May 1910 *(hbl 28 April)* to 18 March 1971 *(Cl)*; still open.

CUILHILL – see BARGEDDIE.

CULCHETH
CULCHETH [GC] op 1 April 1884 *(Wigan Observer 2nd, item and tt)*; clo 2 November 1964 *(RM December)*. Also see 1846 April 13★★.

CULGAITH [Mid] op 1 April 1880 *(Mid)*; clo 4 May 1970 *(RM June)*.

CULHAM [GW] op 12 June 1844 *(co n dated 17th)* as ABINGDON ROAD; renamed 2 June 1856 *(Cl)*; still open.

CULKERTON [GW]
op 2 December 1889 *(Stroud N 6th)*; clo 5 March 1956 *(Cl)*; reop as HALT 2 February 1959 *(Wilts 7th)*, though *Brad* did not add 'Halt' until May 1959; clo 6 April 1964 *(W D Press 6th)*.

CULLEN [GNS] op 1 May 1886 *(GNS)*; clo 6 May 1968 *(RM July)*.

CULLERCOATS {map 26}
CULLERCOATS (a) [NE] op 27 June 1864 *(co ½ T 22 August- line)*; re-sited on deviation 3 July 1882 *(Cl)*; clo 10 September 1979 *(Cl supp 2)* for conversion to >
CULLERCOATS (b) [TWM] op 11 August 1980 *(RM August)*; still open.

CULLINGWORTH [GN]
op 7 April 1884 *(GN)*; clo 23 May 1955★★.

CULLODEN
For first station of this name see ALLANFEARN.
C MOOR [High] op 1 November 1898 *(High)*; clo 3 May 1965 *(RM June)*. *Brad* ? to 1955, but not LMS tt 1930, *Murray* 1948 nor *hb*: C M for CROY.

CULLOMPTON [GW] op 1 May 1844 *(Taunton 8th)*; clo 5 October 1964 *(Som Gaz 5 September)*.
At first COLLUMPTON (tts, *hb*) but CULLUMPTON

in op n for South Devon, 30 May 1846 *(Exeter to Newton Abbot)*, CULLOMPTON in op description *(Trewmans)*; *Brad* to present form 1867, *hb* 1892a.

CULMSTOCK [GW] op 29 May 1876 *(Culm V)*; HALT at closure 9 September 1963 *(Express & E 9th)*.

CULRAIN [High] op 1 July 1870 *(High)*; still open.

CULROSS [NB] op 2 July 1906 *(RCG)*; clo 7 July 1930 *(Cl)*. Used 21–22 June 1992, 10–22 Aug. 1992, town's history celebration (D. Lindsay).

CULTER [GNS] op 8 September 1853 *(GNS)*; clo 28 February 1966 *(RM March)*.

CULTS [GNS] op 8 September 1853 *(GNS)*; new station early 1855 *(Cl)*; clo 28 February 1966 *(RM March)*. Had become C HALT according to *RM October 1960* but not thus in any tt seen.

CULWORTH [GC] op 15 Mar. 1899 *(GC; T 16th- line)*; clo 29 September 1958 *(LNW Record)*.

CUMBERLAND STREET [GSW]
op 20 August 1900 *(RCG)* as EGLINTON STREET; renamed 2 June 1924 *(Cl)*; often shown in tts as GLASGOW E S/C S; clo 14 February 1966 *(Cl)*.

CUMBERNAULD [Cal]
CUMBERNAULD (a) op 7 August 1848 *(co n T 7th-line)*; trains last shown October 1849 *Brad*.
CUMBERNAULD (b) first in *Brad* May 1870; still open.

CUMBERNAULD ROAD – see STEPPS.

CUMMERSDALE [MC] first in *Brad* October 1858; originally Saturdays only; all days May 1879; clo 18 June 1951 *(Cl)*. After closure one workmen's train, morning and evening, Monday to Friday *(Rly Obs August 1951, p.180)*; this ceased ?.
In *hb* 1862 as C DEPOT, 1877 goods only, 1890 'P'.

CUMMERTREES [GSW]
op 23 August 1848 *(Dumfries 23rd- line)*; clo 19 September 1955 *(RM October)*.

CUMMINGSTON [High] op 10 October 1892 *(High)*; clo 1 April 1904 *(Cl)* but last trains shown June 1904 *Brad* – inertia?; {Burghead – Hopefield}.

CUMNOCK [GSW]
CUMNOCK (a) op 20 May 1850 *(T 24th- line)* as OLD C; renamed 10 January 1955 *(Cl)*; clo 6 December 1965 *(RM January 1966)*.
CUMNOCK (b) op 1 July 1872 *(co ½ T 18 September-line)*; clo 10 September 1951 *(RM October)*.
Also see NEW CUMNOCK.

CUMWHINTON [Mid]
op 1 May 1876 *(Mid; co n T 1st- line)*; clo 5 November 1956 *(RM December)*. *Brad* ? to 1955 but not LMS tt 1930 nor *hb*: C for WETHERAL.

CUNNINGHAMHEAD [GSW]: line op 4 April 1843 *(co ½ 1110/149)*, nd, September 1844 *(Murray)* – in *Brad* July 1845, first time orthodox table provided; op as STEWARTON; clo 22 May 1848 *(Cl)*; back in tt November 1850; renamed 1 September 1873 *(Cl; RCG ref July)*; clo 1 January 1951 *(RM February)*.

CUPAR [NB] op 20 September 1847★★; still open.

CURLING POND – see CARSBRECK.

CURRIE [Cal] op 1 August 1874 *(co n Balerno)*; clo 1 November 1943 *(LNW Record)*.

CURRIEHILL

CURRIEHILL (a) [Cal] op 15 February 1848 *(Balerno; co ½ T 29 February - line)* as CURRIE; renamed 1 May 1874 *(Cl; RCG ref July)*; clo 2 April 1951 *(RM May)*. Cal co tt 1913: CURRIE HILL.

CURRIEHILL (b) op 5 October 1987 *(BLN 572)*; still open.

CURRY MARSH [LMS] (non-tt); op 1 January 1923; clo 1927; alias HALT No.2; workers at Miners' Safety Factory; {Thameshaven branch} *(Thameshaven)*.

CURTHWAITE [MC]: for op see 10 May 1843★★ (and 1840★★ for line habits); in *Tuck* about June 1843 so probably op with line; clo 12 June 1950 *(RM October)*. {map 20g}.

CUSTOM HOUSE London

CUSTOM HOUSE [GE]★ op 26 November 1855 *(co n T 26th)*; hb made separate GE and London & St Katherine's Dock stations of it; clo 29 May 1994 in connection with Jubilee line extension *(BLN 734)*; reop 29 October 1995 *(RM Feb. 1996)*; clo 10 Dec. 2006 – last train Saturday 9th *(RM February 2007)*. GE co tt 1882, 1914: VICTORIA DOCK C H.
★ = belonged to GE, also used by PLA.

CUSTOM HOUSE [Dock] op 28 March 1994★★; still open.

CUSTOM HOUSE Liverpool – see CANNING.

CUTHLIE [DA] op 1 February 1900 *(Dundee- line)*; clo 1 January 1917 *(Cl)*; back in *Brad* September 1917, Saturdays only; reop fully 1 January 1918 *(RCH)*; clo 2 December 1929 *(Cl)*.

CUTLERS GREEN [GE] op 1 April 1913 *(T 1st)*; HALT; clo 15 September 1952 *(RM October)*.

CUTNALL GREEN [GW] first in *Brad* 9 July 1928; clo 5 April 1965 *(Cl)*; {Hartlebury – Droitwich}. Became HALT 1952 *(Brad)* and so shown BR ticket *(JB)* but not in *hb*. Hampton Lovett pre-opening *(RAC)*.

CUTSYKE – see CASTLEFORD.

CUTTY SARK [Dock] op 3 December 1999 *(LRR 22)*; still open.

CUXTON [SE] op 18 June 1856 *(SE; T 17th- line)*; still open.

CWM [GW] op 19 April 1852 *(co n Merlin 16th)*; in *Merlin* as Cymmerthych *(Star of Gwent* Cwmmertych, 1854)*; clo 30 April 1962 *(T 6 April)*.

CWM BARGOED [Taff Bargoed Joint] op 1 February 1876 *(S Wales 31 January- line)*; clo 15 June 1964 *(Cl)*.

CWM BLAWD – see 1887★★.

CWM CLYDACH – see CLYDACH-ON-TAWE.

CWM CYMMER – see CYMMER.

CWM PRYSOR [GW] op 1 September 1902 *(dist t supp 657)*; HALT from 1953 tt *(Cl)* but thus 1938 hb; aot request; clo 4 January 1960 *(RM March)*.

CWM-Y-GLO [LNW] op 1 July 1869 *(Carnarvon 3rd)*; for clo see 1939 September★★.

CWMAMAN [GW] {map 86}
C COLLIERY and C CROSSING:
Op to public 1 January 1906★★; both HALTS; see 1921 April/May★★; finally clo to public 22 Sept. 1924 *(Cl)*.

CWMAVON (GLAM)
C GLAM [RSB] op 25 June 1885 *(The Cambrian 26th)*;

GLAM added 1 January 1902 *(hbl 23rd)*; clo 3 December 1962 *(RM January 1963)*. Hb: CWM AVON until 1904, and RSB ticket thus *(JB)*.

C YARD [GW] (non-tt); miners; see 1920★★; {Tonygroes – Maesmelyn}. Alias MAESMELYN *(RAC)*.

CWMAVON MON [GW] op 2 October 1854★★; MON added 1 January 1902 *(hbl 23rd)*. According to *GW circular 2653*, it reop 3 March 1919; any closure would have been brief – trains still shown February 1919 *Brad* (had 'closure' been temporary reduction to halt? tt continued entries inertia? left because reopening expected soon?). Became HALT 8 June 1953 *(Cl)*; hb 1941a had said it was now Halt but hbl January 1942 said 'read C MON', so 1941 presumably error. Clo 30 April 1962 *(T 6 April)*.

CWMBACH [GW]
CWMBACH (a) op 12 July 1914 *(GW H)*; HALT; clo 15 June 1964 *(Cl)*.

CWMBACH (b) op 3 October 1988 *(Aberdare)* – free publicity service on 2nd; still open.

C COLLIERY (non-tt): 1899 to ?; {adjoining public station} *(RAC)*.

CWMBRAN
CWMBRAN (a) [Monmouthshire] op 1 July 1852 *(Merlin 2nd)*; originally C WORKS *(Brad)*, WORKS soon dropped; replaced on new line by >

CWMBRAN (b) [GW] op 1 August 1880 *(co n Merlin 31 July)*; clo 30 April 1962 *(Cl)*.

CWMBRAN (c) op 12 May 1986 *(RM April)*; south of old Lower Pontnewydd; still open.
Also see UPPER PONTNEWYDD.

CWMCARN [GW]
op 2 March 1925 *(GW Mag January 1926)*; clo 30 April 1962 *(T 6 April)*; {Cross Keys – Llanbradach}. Near site of earlier Chapel Bridge, but exact site of latter had been bypassed by deviation line *(RAC)*.

CWMDU [PT] op 9 June 1913 *(RCG)* – four months before inspected; replaced GARTH (which see); clo 12 September 1932 *(RM October)*.

CWMFFRWD [GW] op 13 July 1912 co tt *(GW H)*; HALT; clo 30 April 1962 *(T 6 April)*.

CWMFFRWDOER [GW]
op 13 July 1912★★; clo 5 May 1941 *(Cl)*.

CWMGORSE [GW]: station built about 1923 between Clydach and Gwaun-cae-Gurwen but never provided with service *(U)*.

CWMLLYNFELL [Mid] op non-tt 7 Dec. 1896 as GWAUN-CAE-GURWEN COLLIERS PLATFORM *(Mid)*; renamed C and made public 1 July 1909 *(RCG)*; clo 25 September 1950 *(RM November)*.

CWMMAWR [BPGV] op 29 January 1913 *(D&C 12)*; clo 21 September 1953 *(T 16th)*.

CWMMERTYCH – see CWM

CWMNEOL [GW]
op 1 January 1906★★; see 1921 April/May★★; HALT; clo 22 September 1924 *(Cl)*; {map 86}.

CWMRHYD-Y-GAU [GW] (non-tt): HALT; miners; op 14 January 1935 *(wtt supp)*; clo by October 1945 *(U)*; {Pontwalby – Glyn Neath}.

CWMSIFIOG [BM; GW]
CWMSIFIOG (a), at 17m 21ch, op 1 February 1908

(RCG) as C & BRITHDIR; renamed 1 July 1924
(GW circular 18 June); clo to public 5 July 1937;
reop 6 December 1937 for miners (non-tt) as
C COLLIERY HALT (co n dated 30 November);
clo 31 December 1962 (U).

CWMSIFIOG (b) replacement public C HALT,
at 17m 50ch, op 5 July 1937 (co n dated 'July');
clo 31 December 1962 (T 31st); {Gwys – Ystalyfera}.

CWMTWRCH WELL [LMS] op 16 December
1935*; HALT; clo 25 September 1950 (RM Nov.).
* = op from weekly engineering notice; LMS handbill, cited by
Rly Gaz 27th said 14th, which was formal op (J. Gough).

CYFARTHFA [GW/Rhy] (non-tt): workmen; at least
1897 to 1915; {branch from Abercanaid} (U).

CYFRONYDD [Cam] (ng) op 6 April 1903 (D&C 11);
aot request; clo 9 February 1931 (Cl).

CYMMER

C AFAN [RSB] op 2 November 1885 (GW) as C,
temporary; replaced 1888; renamed CWM CYMMER
1 July 1924 (GW circular 18 June), CYMMER AFAN
17 September 1926 (GW circular 3011); amalgamated
with C General as C A January 1950 (Cl); became
request 1965/8 tt; clo to general public 22 June 1970
but school use to 14 July 1970 (last train) (RM Sept.).

C CORRWG [GW] op to public March 1918** (see for
full details); CORRWG added 17 Sept. 1926 (GW
circular 3011); clo to public 22 September 1930 (Cl).

C GENERAL [GW] op 19 July 1880 (Maesteg) as C;
became C for GLYNCORRWG 1 July 1924
(GW circular 18 June) – but already this in GW co tt

April 1891 (dropped at some point between?),
C G 1926 (Brad; hbl ref January 1927) amalgamated
with C Afan, above, January 1950;
line through here clo 13 June 1960.

CYMMERTYCH – see CWM.

CYNFAL [Talyllyn]: HALT; added hba May/Sept. 1946;
not in Brad; public or private? (hb rarely distinguished
in later years); see 1950 October 6**;
{Towyn Pendre – Rhydyronen}.

CYNHEIDRE – see 1887**.

CYNGHORDY [LNW]
op 8 June 1868 (LNW Officers); aot request; still open.

CYNONVILLE [RSB]: originally men at old pit
joined/alighted direct from lineside, north of here;
RSB Traffic Manager's Report, 11 September 1902 said
up side platform had been provided and down side
should be (£25 from second-hand materials).
GW/RSB minutes, 2 June 1910, authorised platforms for
here at CYNON NEW PIT, later CYNONVILLE;
minutes 25 October 1912 recommended provision of
waiting-room and booking-office since demand had
arisen from ordinary passengers; in co public tt 10 July
to September (inclusive) 1911, perhaps in error;
first in Brad October 1912 – all suggests slippage
from workmen's to public station; HALT;
clo 2 January 1956 (Cl).

CYNWYD [GW] op 16 July 1866 (D&C 11; Rtn- line);
clo 14 December 1964**.

CYPRUS [Dock] op 28 March 1994**; still open.

SYMPATHY.

Passenger (in a whisper, behind his paper, to Wilkins, who had been "catching it" from the Elder Lady). "MOTHER-'N-LAW?"
Wilkins (in still fainter whisper). "YE'." *Passenger.* "GOT JUST SUCH 'NOTHER!" [*They console together at the next Buffet.*

D

DACRE [NE] op 1 May 1862 *(T 5th)* as D BANKS; renamed 1866 tt *(Cl)* but 1890 *hb*; clo 2 April 1951 *(T 7 March)*.

DAGENHAM
D DOCK [LTS] op 1 July 1908 *(RCG)*; still open.
D EAST op by [LTS] 1 May 1885 *(Mid)*; EAST added 1 May 1949 *(Mid)*; [Dist] use from 2 June 1902 to 1 October 1905 and 12 September 1932 on; BR use ended 12 June 1961 *(Cl)*; still open.
D HEATHWAY op by [LMS] 12 September 1932 *(L)* as H; renamed 1 May 1949 *(Mid)*; only used by LT trains; to LTPB 1 January 1969; still open.
DAGGONS ROAD [LSW] op 1 January 1876 *(LSW;* in tt *Salisbury 1st)*; op as ALDERHOLT; renamed DAGGENS ROAD 1 May 1876 *(Cl)*; spelling amended 1903/4 *(Brad)*, 1904 co tt *(JS)*; clo 4 May 1964 *(Hants Chron 9th)*.
DAILLY [GSW] op 24 May 1860 *(co ½ T 3 September- line)*; clo 6 September 1965 *(RM September)*.
DAILUAINE [LNE] op 18 November 1933 *(GNS)*; HALT; aot request; clo 18 October 1965★★; {Aberlour – Carron}.
DAIMLER [LNW; LMS] op to workmen 19 March 1917 *(LNW Record)*; first in public tt 11 June 1956; HALT; clo 18 January 1965 *(RM March)*; {Coundon Road – Foleshill}.
DAIRSIE [NB] op 17 May 1848 *(co n Perthshire Courier 18th- line)*; clo 20 September 1954 *(RM Nov.)*.
DAIRY HOUSE – see THE AVENUE.
DAISY BANK & BRADLEY [GW] op 1 July 1854 *(W Mid; co ½ T 28 August- line)*; clo 1 January 1917 *(GW notice dated 22 December 1916)*, reop 3 February 1919 *(RCH; GW Mag April)*; & B added 1919; clo 30 July 1962 *(RM September)*. DAISEY BANK until 1866 *(Brad)* – index later, 1898a *(hb)*.
DAISY FIELD [LY] first in *Brad* November 1851; clo 2 April 1917 *(Cl)*; reop 5 May 1919 *(RCH)*; clo 3 November 1958 *(LNW Record)*.
Spelling as in LY co tt 1 May 1899 and *Brad* Aug. 1958. *Hb* at first DAISEY FIELD, then DAISY FIELD; 1908a DAISYFIELD *(LNW Record* thus at closure). Aot *Brad* index: DAISEY F.
DAISY HILL [LY] op 1 October 1888 *(Lancs Chesh- line)*; still open.
DALANREOCH – see 1957★★.
DALBEALLIE – see KNOCKANDO.
DALBEATTIE [GSW] op 7 November 1859 *(Dumfries 5th)*; clo 14 June 1965 *(RM July)*.
DALCHONZIE [Cal] op 15 July 1903 *(Railways of Upper Strathearn, p.105)*; always PLATFORM *(Brad)*; HALT *(hb* 1938); aot request; clo 1 October 1951 *(RM November)*.
DALCROSS [High] op 7 November 1855★★; clo 3 May 1965 *(RM June)*.

DALE BANK [Ashover] (ng) op 7 April 1925 *(RM October)*; request; clo 14 September 1936★★ *(Ashover)*; {map 59}.
DALEGARTH [Raven] (ng) op 22 March 1920 *(Raven)*; probably re-sited November 1926 when line extended to new terminus *(Cl)*; see 1960★★. *Hb*: 1925 BOOT, 1938 B D, 1949a D.
DALGETY BAY
op 28 March 1998 *(BLN 823)*; still open.
DALGUISE [High]
op 1 June 1863 *(High)*; clo 3 May 1965 *(June)*.
DALHOUSIE [NB]
op 1834 (see 1831 A★★); at SOUTH ESK until 1847 tt *(Cl)*; clo 1 August 1908 (Saturday) *(RCG)*; replaced by Newtongrange; {map 18}.
DALKEITH [NB] op 1839 (see 1831 A★★); clo 1 January 1917 *(RM February)*; reop 1 October 1919 *(Cl)*; clo 5 January 1942 *(Cl)*; {map 18}.
DALMALLY [Cal]
op 1 May 1877 *(co ½ T 11 September)*; still open.
DALMARNOCK
DALMARNOCK (a) [Cal] op 1 November 1895 *(RCG; T 2nd- line)*; clo 5 October 1964 *(RM November)*.
DALMARNOCK (b) op 5 November 1979 *(RM December)*, same site as (a); still open.
DALMELLINGTON [GSW] op 7 August 1856★★; clo 6 April 1964 *(RM May)*.
DALMENY [NB] {map 13}
DALMENY (a) op 1 March 1866 *(co ½ March 1866)*; replaced by new station on Forth Bridge line >
DALMENY (b) op 5 March 1890 as FORTH BRIDGE; renamed later 1890 tt (reported in Dunfermline press 28 June – *JS)*; still open. *Hb* 1892, NB co tt 1900 and *Brad* to 1919: D for SOUTH QUEENSFERRY.
DALMUIR
D PARK [NB] op 31 May 1858 *(T 7 June)*; re-sited 11 chains west 17 May 1897 *(Cl)*; PARK added May 1952 *(Cl; ref RM October)*; still open. Aot D JUNCTION *(hb)*.
D RIVERSIDE [Cal] op 1 October 1896 *(RCG; Colliery 2nd- line)*; RIVERSIDE added May 1952 *(Cl; ref RM July)*; clo 5 October 1964 *(RM November)*.
DALNACARDOCH [High] (non-tt): purpose ?; op 1 May 1905; clo ?; {Dalnaspidal – Struan} *(U)*.
DALNASPIDAL [High] first in *Brad* June 1864; clo 3 May 1965 *(RM June)*.
DALRADDY CROSSING [High] (non-tt); railwaymen, families; dates ?; {Kincraig – Aviemore} *(U)*.
DALREOCH [DB Jt]
first in *Brad* May 1852; still open.
DALRY [GSW] op 21 July 1840 *(GSW)*; still open.
DALRY JUNCTION [GSW] first in *Brad* November 1850; last December 1859. Murray April 1852 shows times but no fares – exchange only? Possibility of later non-tt use?
DALRY ROAD [Cal]: op 2 July 1900 *(RCG)*; clo 30 April 1962 *(RM May)*.
DALRYMPLE [GSW] op 1 November 1856 *(GSW)*; clo 6 December 1954 *(RM January 1955)*.
DALRYMPLE JUNCTION
– see MAYBOLE JUNCTION.

DALSERF [Cal] op 1 December 1866 *(Cal- line)* as AYR ROAD; renamed 1 July 1903 *(hbl 9th)*; clo 1 October 1951 *(RM November)*.

DALSTON near Carlisle [MC] op 10 May 1843**; also see 1840**; aot request; still open; {map 20g}.

DALSTON London

D JUNCTION [NL] op 1 November 1865 *(T 2nd)*; clo 30 June 1986 – last train Friday 27th *(RM Sept.)*.

D KINGSLAND op 16 May 1983 *(Rly Obs July)*; still open. BR ticket for D K ROAD *(JB)*. Also see KINGSLAND.

DALTON near Barrow-in-Furness [Fur] op August 1846**; intermittent early use; still open.

DALTON – see ERYHOLME.

DALVEY [Inverness & Aberdeen Junction] temporary terminus just west of Forres op 22 Dec. 1857 *(High)*; clo 25 March 1858, when line extended to Elgin *(Cl)*.

DALVEY near Grantown

DALVEY [GNS] op 1 July 1863 *(GNS)*; clo 1 September 1868 (Tuesday) *(Cl)*. Same site as/near D Farm?

D FARM op 15 June 1959 *(RM August)*; HALT; request; clo 18 October 1965**; {Advie – Cromdale}.

DALWHINNIE [High] op 9 September 1863 *(High)*; still open.

DAMEMS [Mid] op 1 September 1867 *(Mid)*; clo 23 May 1949 *(RM September)*.

DANBY [NE] op 2 October 1865 *(co ½ T Feb. 1866- line)*; still open.

DANBY WISKE [NE]

DANBY WISKE (a): line op 31 March 1841**, nd, about August 1841; last in *Brad* June 1842.

DANBY WISKE (b) op 1 December 1884 *(NE Hoole)*; clo 15 September 1958 *(RM October)*.

DANDALEITH [GNS] op 23 December 1858 – date given by *T 29th*, *Brad Sh*, and Sir M. Barclay Harvey in his history of the GNS; Vallance's history of the line (D&C 1989) gives this date on p.40 but in the appendix says 24 December; *GNS* also gives 24th, but this is rare example of date not given a contemporary source. Op as CRAIGELLACHIE; renamed 1864; aot request; HALT status from 1931, though staffed *(GNS)*; after 7 June 1953 *Brad*, before/with November 1953, reduced to one train, to Elgin, per day; clo 5 March 1962 *(RM April)*.

DANE ROAD

DANE ROAD (a) [LMS/LNE] op 20 July 1931 *(Cl 29)*; D R SALE until 1935/6 *(Brad)*; clo 27 December 1991 *(BLN 671)* for conversion to >

DANE ROAD (b) [Manch] op 15 June 1992 *(RM August)*; still open.

DANESCOURT op 4 October 1987**; still open.

DANYGRAIG

DANYGRAIG [RSB] op 14 March 1895 *(Colliery 22nd- line)*; aot Dan-y-graig *(hb)*; re-sited to east 7 May 1899, when RSB opened own line to Swansea (see *RAC* atlas); replaced, on GW line alongside, by >

DANYGRAIG [GW] op 11 September 1933 *(Cl 29)*; HALT; clo 28 September 1936 *(T 14th)*.

DANZEY [GW] op 1 July 1908 *(RCG; T 2nd- line)*; still open. D for TANWORTH until 1966/68 tt (and thus GW co tt 1932, 1947).

DARBY END [GW] op 21 August 1905 *(GW H)*; HALT; clo 15 June 1964 *(RM July)*; {Old Hill – Windmill End}].

DARCLIFFE/DARKCLIFFE – see DOVECLIFFE.

DARCY LEVER [LY] first in *Brad* January 1849; clo 29 October 1951 *(Cl)*.

DARESBURY [Birkenhead] op 18 December 1850 *(D&C 10)* as MOORE; renamed 5 April 1861 *LNW dates)*; clo 7 July 1952 *(Cl)*.

DARFIELD [Mid] op 1 July 1840 *(Mid; co n T 27 June- line)*; re-sited 45 chains north 30 June 1901, new station opening at noon *(Mid)*; clo 17 June 1963 *(RM June)*.

DARLASTON [LNW]

DARLASTON (a) op 4 July 1837 *(T 6th)* as D; renamed JAMES BRIDGE 14 September 1863 *(JS, W Mid)*, J B for D 1 November 1887 *(W Mid)*, D & J B March 1889 co tt *(W Mid)*, D 1 December 1913 *(hbl 29 Jan. 1914)*; clo 18 January 1965 *(RM March)*.

DARLASTON (b) op 14 September 1863 *(LNW Officers)*; clo 1 November 1887 (Tuesday) *(LNW Record)*; {on loop between D (a) and Wednesbury}.

DARLEY near Harrogate [NE] first in *Brad* Feb. 1864; clo 2 April 1951 *(T 7 March)*.

DARLEY DALE [Mid] op 4 June 1849 *(Mid; T 5th- line)*; moved from south to north of level crossing 1873/4 *(Mid)*; DALE added 1890; clo 6 March 1967 *(RM April)*. LMS tt 1947 (Brad printing): D D for WINSTER.

DARLINGTON {map 36}

DARLINGTON [NE] op 31 March 1841 *(co n E Cos Her 25th)*; re-sited slightly west 1 July 1887 *(Cl)*; D BANK TOP October 1868 *(Brad)* to September 1934 tt *(JS)*; still open.

NORTH ROAD [S&D; NE] first regularly served 10 October 1825 *(poster S&D)*; original arrangements varied (see 1825**); in co notice 16 October 1826 *(S&D)* Talbot Inn given as enquiry point for Union coach; probably first fixed station was on west side of North Road, re-sited 1842 *(Cl)*. (Building of temporary replacement station authorised 15 May 1840; almost immediately planning for permanent station began; 1 April 1842 they arranged for road to new station to be 'for the present' through goods yard of old one, suggesting that new nearly ready – *RAIL 667/11,12,13)*; still open. Originally D, then became D N R October 1868 tt *(JS)*, N R September 1934 tt *(JS)*. For a long time *hb* called it D HOPE TOWN OR NORTH ROAD; eventually separated into D N R, passenger, and D H T, goods.

RISE CARR ROLLING MILLS (non-tt): shown 'P' 1912 *hb*; probably error – deleted 1914 appendix. For special station for 1925 Centenary see last paragraph of 1825**.

DARNALL [GC] op 12 February 1849 *(GC; T 12th- line)*; erratically DARNAL in *Brad* until 1855; still open. Was D for HANDSWORTH from 1 July 1896 *(hbl 9th)* (thus LNE tt 1933 and *hb* 1938) until 1955 *(Brad)*.

DARRAN & DERI [Rhy] op 1 September 1868 *(D&C 12- line)*; DARRAN until 1905 *(Brad)*; clo 31 December 1962 *(T 31st)*.

DARRAS HALL [NE] op 1 October 1913
(NER Staff Mag 1915); clo 17 June 1929 *(Cl)*.
DARSHAM [GE] op 1 June 1859 *(T 2nd)*; still open.
D for YOXFORD in GE co tt 1914, LNE tt 1933 and
Brad ? to 1955 but not thus *hb* 1938.
DARTFORD [SE] op 30 July 1849★★; still open.
1870 became D JUNCTION, 1871 D J for
FARNINGHAM; D 1879/80 *(Brad)*.
DARTMOUTH [GW]: see KINGSWEAR.
DARTMOUTH ARMS – see FOREST HALL.
DARTON [LY]
op 1 January 1850 *(LY; co ½ T 22 Feb.- line)*; still open.
DARVEL [GSW] op 1 June 1896 *(co ½ 1110/149)*;
clo 6 April 1964 *(RM May)*.
DARWEN
DARWEN [LY]: line op 3 August 1847 *(LY; Rtn- line)*,
nd, May 1848 *(Topham)*; op as OVER DARWEN;
renamed 1 December 1883 *(Cl; RCG ref January
1884)*; still open.
Also see LOWER DARWEN.
DATCHET [LSW] op 22 August 1848 *(co n T 24th)*;
still open. Originally DATCHETT, *Brad* and *Topham*.
DAUBHILL [LNW]: line op 13 June 1831★★, nd, mid
1846 *(Huish List)*; replaced on deviation 2 Feb. 1885
by station later renamed RUMWORTH & D *(Cl)*.
DAUNTSEY [GW] op 1 February 1868 *(Wilts 23 Jan.)*;
clo 4 January 1965 *(RM February)*.
DAVA [High] op 1 November 1864 *(High)*;
clo 18 October 1965★★.
DAVENPORT [LNW]
op 1 March 1858 *(?; first in Brad* March)*; last trains
September 1859; back January 1862; still open.
DAVENTRY [LNW] op 1 March 1888 *(LNW Officers
30089, 30105)*; clo 15 September 1958 *(LNW Record)*.
DAVIDSONS MAINS [Cal] op 1 March 1894 *(Edin)*
as BARNTON GATE; renamed 1 April 1903 *(hbl 23rd)*;
clo 7 May 1951 *(RM June)*.
DAVIE'S DYKE [WMC] op 2 June 1845★★;
last in *Brad* April 1848 (but see 1848★★); {map 16}.
DAVIOT [High] op 19 Juy 1897 *(High)*;
clo 3 May 1965 *(RM June)*.
DAWLEY & STIRCHLEY [LNW]
op 10 June 1861★★ as S; renamed 1 July 1923 *(hbl 12th)*;
clo 2 June 1952 *(RM August)*.
S for D in LNW co tts until at least 1909.
DAWLISH [GW]
DAWLISH op 30 May 1846 *(Trewman 4 June)*; still open.
D WARREN prob op 1 August 1905 *(Ex & NA; first in
Brad* October)*; re-sited 17 chains north 23 Sept. 1912
(GW Mag November); clo 1 January 1917 *(Express & E
29 December 1916)*; reop 5 May 1919 *(RCH)*; still open.
Early THE W, W HALT, THE W PLATFORM.
DAWSHOLM
DAWSHOLM [Cal] op 1 October 1896 *(RCG)*;
clo 1 May 1908 (Friday) *(RCG)*; {map 15}.
Also see KELVINDALE.
DAYBROOK [GN] op 1 February 1876 *(GN)*;
BESTWOOD & ARNOLD until 1876 tt *(Cl)*;
clo 4 April 1960 *(Cl)*. RCH sources give various
combinations of D and B (PARK); LNE tt 1933,
1947 – D for A.

DDUALLT [Festiniog] (ng) first in *Brad* May 1879;
in last years tt suggests intermittent use; aot request;
last trains shown in *Brad* ending 25 September 1938;
left, trainless, to line closure 18 September 1939★★.
DEADWATER [NB] op privately by March 1877 as
D FOOT CROSSING *(U)*; op to public as D 1 March
1880 *(NC)*; became HALT 9 September 1955
(RM October); clo 15 October 1956★★.
DEAL [Dover & Deal Joint/SE]★
op 1 July 1847 *(co n T 30 June)*; still open.
★ = as 1895 *hb* – later [SEC].
DEAN [LSW]
op 1 March 1847 *(W Fly P 6th- line)*; still open.
DEAN LANE [LY] op 17 May 1880 *(Manchester 17th)*
as D L NEWTON HEATH; renamed 7 May 1973 *(Cl)*;
still open.
DEANSGATE [MSJA] op 20 July 1849★★ as
KNOTT MILL; renamed K M & D 1882 *(RCG ref
April)*, D 3 May 1971; still open.
Often KNOT M, all sources, early. MSJA special ticket
for Wembley: MANCHESTER K M *(JB)*.
DEANSIDE [GP Jt]
op 1 June 1903 *(RCG)*; clo 1 January 1905 (Sunday)
(RCG); {Cardonald – King's Inch}.
DEARHAM [MC]
DEARHAM op 1 June 1867 *(D&C 14)*;
clo 29 April 1935 *(LNW Record)*.
D BRIDGE op 1840★★; aot request; BRIDGE added
intermittently in early years; clo 5 June 1950 *(RM July)*;
{map 20g}.
DEBDEN op by [GE] 24 April 1865 *(L; co n T 24th-
line)* as CHIGWELL ROAD;
renamed C LANE 1 December 1865 *(Cl)*; clo 22 May
1916★★ *(T 2nd)*, reop 3 February 1919 *(RCG)*;
renamed D 25 September 1949 *(Cl)*; transferred to
[Cen] 25 September 1949 *(T 26th)*; still open.
DECHMONT
DECHMONT (a) [EG] first in *Brad* October 1850,
Wednesdays only; last December 1861.
DECHMONT (b) op 19 June 1905 *(RCG)*; on a private
hospital line but trains advertised and publicly available,
worked by [NB]; clo 1 August 1921 (P.B. Russell, *RM
Sept. 1981)*; {Uphall to Bangour branch}.
DEE STREET op 6 February 1961 *(GNS)*;
clo 28 February 1966 *(RM March)*; {Banchory – Glassel}.
DEE-SIDE [GW] (non-tt): HALT; in use 1913;
purpose ?; {Berwyn – Glydyfrdwy} *(U)*.
DEEPCAR [GC] op 14 July 1845 *(GC)*; clo 15 June
1959 *(RM July)*; later excur *(U)*. DEEP CAR in *Brad*
until 1865/6 (index earlier). GC co tt 1903, LNE tt
1933, *Brad* to 1955: D for STOCKSBRIDGE.
DEEPDALE / D STREET – see PRESTON.
DEEPDENE – see DORKING.
DEEPFIELDS & COSELEY [LNW] op 1 July
1852 *(W Mid; T 2nd- line)* as D; & C added August
1854 co tt *(W Mid)*; replaced ¼ mile south 10 March
1902 *(W Mid)* by station later renamed COSELEY.
DEFFORD [Mid] op 24 June 1840 *(Chelt Chron 27th)*;
clo 4 January 1965 *(Mid)*. D for PERSHORE in *LMS
list* 1933, but not seen thus elsewhere.

DEFIANCE [GW]

D WEARDE op 1 March 1905 *(April wtt supp)*; HALT; replaced on different alignment by >

DEFIANCE op 1 August 1905 (date of realignment from GW records – *RAC*); became PLATFORM 1 May 1906 *(Cl)*; clo 27 October 1930 *(Cl)*; used in strawberry season to 1954 *(U)*.

DEGANWY [LNW] op 1 May 1866 *(LNW Officers 1037, 18 April, 'recommended')*; DEGANWAY until 1870 *Brad*, 1875/82 LNW co tt, but DEGANWY 1867 *hb*, DEGANAWAY 1872; aot request; still open.

DEIGHTON

DEIGHTON (a) [LNW], Kirkburton branch, op 1 September 1871 *(LNW Officers 6933)*; clo 28 July 1930 *(Cl)*.

DEIGHTON (b), main line, op 26 April 1982 *(RM June)*; still open.

DELABOLE [LSW] op 18 October 1893 *(Cornish & D P 21st)*; clo 3 October 1966 *(Cornish & D P 8th)*.

DELAMERE [CLC]
op 22 June 1870 *(CLC)*; still open.

DELNY [High]
op 1 June 1864 *(High)*; DELNEY until 1865/6 *Brad*, and thus *hb* 1865a; clo 13 June 1960 *(RM July)*.

DELPH [LNW]
op 1 September 1851 *(Huddersfield 6th)*; clo 2 May 1955 *(T 11 March)*.

DEMONS BRIDGE [LNE] (non-tt)
op 14 December 1941 *(Cl 29)*; ordnance factory workers; 4 May 1942 wtt showed trains from Grangetown and Hartlepool; absent from working BR NER wtt by October 1945 *(WWII)*; trains also from Saltburn and Seaham at other times; {Stillington – Shildon}.
In *U* see HEIGHINGTON.

DENABY

DENABY [Dearne] first in *Brad* December 1913; HALT (see 1912 June 3**); clo 1 January 1949 (Sat.) *(RM March)*; all trains still called for railway staff according to 18 June 1951 wtt, where shown as HALT. LMS tt 1930 and *Brad* to closure:
D for CONISBOROUGH and MEXBOROUGH.

D & CONISBOROUGH [HB] op 1 December 1894 *(RCG)*; clo 1 February 1903 (Sunday) *(RCG)*.

DENBIGH [LNW] op 5 October 1858 *(T 7th)*; original temporary station replaced by permanent December 1860 *(LNW)*; clo 30 April 1962 *(RM June)*; later excur *(U)*.

DENBIGH HALL [L&B] temporary terminus op 9 April 1838 *(T 11th)*; clo when line extended for full use 17 September 1838 *(co n T 17th)*.

DENBY [Mid]
op 1 September 1856 *(Mid; T 12th- line)* as SMITHY HOUSES; became DENBEY 1 November 1856 wtt *(Mid)*, DENBY 1 February 1878 co tt *(Mid)*; clo 1 June 1930 (Sunday) *(Cl)*; later excur *(U)*.

DENBY DALE [LY]: line op 1 July 1850 *(T 8th)*, nd, January 1851; D D & CUMBERWORTH 1883/4 *(Brad)* to 12 June 1961 *(RM April)*; still open.

DENHAM [GW/GC]
DENHAM op 2 April 1906 *(T March 5)*; still open.
Became D for HAREFIELD 1 October 1907 *(hbl 24th)*, and thus LNE tt 1933, GW tt 1947 and *hb* 1938, until

1955 *(Brad)*, apart from brief period about 1928/30, when just D.

D GOLF CLUB op 22 July 1912 *(GC dates)*; PLATFORM until 20 September 1954 tt *(GW H)*; still open.

DENHEAD [DA] op 1 February 1900 *(Dundee- line)*; clo 1 January 1917 *(Cl)*; reop, Saturdays only, September 1917 *Brad*; reop fully 1 January 1918 *(RCH)*; clo 2 December 1929 *(Cl)*.

DENHOLME [GN] op 1 January 1884 *(GN)*; clo 23 May 1955**.

DENMARK HILL (see 1866**).
[LBSC platforms] op 13 August 1866 *(T 14th)*.
[LCD platforms] op 1 December 1865 *(co n T 1st)*.
All still open.

DENNY [Cal]
op 26 March 1858 *(co ½ report, T 22 March*, said proposed to open 26 March. Report of meeting at Perth on 26th, *T 29th*, said government certificate had been received and trains were running); clo 28 July 1930 *(RM Sept.)*.
Connection to Larbert for excursion to Blackpool shown in special train notice 1 July 1939 *(IU)*.

DENNYLOANHEAD [KB] op 2 July 1888 *(RCG)*; clo 1 February 1935 (Friday) *(RM March)*.

DENSTONE [NS] op 1 August 1873 *(NS-K)* as D CROSSING; renamed 2 April 1923 co tt *(JS)*; aot request; clo 4 January 1965 *(RM March)*.

DENT [Mid] op 6 August 1877 *(Mid)*; clo 4 May 1970 *(RM June)*; probably used by trial charter excursion that ran 9 June 1974 *(AB)*; reop weekend Dales Rail 3 May 1975 (P.W. Robinson, *Cumbria's Lost Railways*, Stenlake, 2002); reop fully 14 July 1986 *(Settle)*; see 1989 October 16**; still open. Excur while closed *(U)*.

DENTON [SEC] first in *Brad* July or August 1906 as D HALT; D ROAD 1914 tt to 1919 tt, then D HALT again *(Cl)*; clo 4 December 1961 *(T 8 November)*; {Gravesend – Hoo Junction}.

DENTON near Manchester [LNW] first in *Brad* February 1851; reduced to only one train per week, northbound, Fridays 11 May 1992 tt – to avoid costs of closure procedures; altered to Saturdays only 18 May 2003 tt; to one Fridays, southbound only 23 May 2004 tt; to one northbound, Saturday only February 2007 tt; one northbound Fridays 14 December 2008 tt.

DENVER [GE] op January 1847 *(EC*; first in *Brad* then); beyond the then terminus of full service, as D ROAD GATE, Tuesdays & Saturdays only; full service 26 October 1847 as D when line extended; clo 1 February 1870 (Tuesday), reop 1 July 1885 *(Cl)*, now only used by branch trains to Stoke Ferry; aot request; clo 22 September 1930 *(Cl)*.

DENVILLE – see WARBLINGTON.

DEPTFORD [SE] op 8 February 1836 *(Herapath March)*; original temporary terminus replaced 24 December 1838 when line extended to Greenwich *(Cl)*; clo 15 March 1915 *(RCH)*; reop 19 July 1926 *(sig/inst 24/1926)*; still open.

DEPTFORD BRIDGE [Dock]
op 20 November 1999 *(RM January 2000)*; still open.

DEPTFORD ROAD – see SURREY QUAYS.

DERBY

DERBY [Midland Counties] temporary station from
Nottingham op 4 June 1839 *(Mid)* >

DERBY [Birmingham & Derby Junction] temporary
op 12 August 1839 *(co n T 8th)* >

Both temporaries replaced by permanent **DERBY** [Mid]
op 11 May 1840 *(Mid)*; D MIDLAND 25 September
1950 *(Mid)* to 6 May 1968 *(JS)*; still open.

D STATION STREET 1867 to 1904/6 *(Brad)*.

D FRIAR GATE [GN] op 1 April 1878 *(GN)*;
F G added 1881 tt *(Cl)*; clo 7 Sept. 1964 *(RM Oct.)*.

NOTTINGHAM ROAD [Mid] op 1 September 1856
wtt *(Mid)*; clo 6 March 1967 *(RM April)*.

D RACECOURSE SIDING [GN] (non-tt);
op 16 March 1885 for horses and attendants only *(race)*;
used to 1938 at least *(U)*; {Breadsall – Friar Gate}.

D RAMSLINE (non-tt): HALT; op 20 January 1990
(AZ) for football supporters; only used four times
(BLN 813), all in first season; however, included in
lease to Central Trains dated 17 September 1995
(R. Maund); alias BASEBALL GROUND.

DERBY ROAD Ipswich [GE]
op 1 May 1877 *(Rtn- line)*; still open.
At times IPSWICH D R in *hb* and early ticket thus *(JB)*.

DEREHAM

DEREHAM [Norfolk] op 15 February 1847
(co n Ephemera); station in Norwich Road. >

DEREHAM [Lynn & Dereham] op 11 September
1848, station in Swan Lane. >

Relations between companies bad. Probably concentrated
on one station, D [GE], 1849 *(GE Journal October 1979)*.
This clo 6 October 1969 *(RM October)*; later excur *(U)*.

DERKER
op 30 September 1985 *(AZ)* and just D in tt supplement
of that date, but in 12 May 1986 and 29 September
1986 tts only was D-ROYTON *(AB, Chron)*; still open.

DERRY ORMOND [GW] op 1 September 1866
(D&C 11) as BETTWS; renamed 1873/4 *(RCG ref
January 1874)*; clo 22 February 1965 *(Cl)*.

DERSINGHAM [GE] op 3 October 1862 *(T 6th)*;
clo 5 May 1969 *(RM July* – photo caption)*.

DERWEN [LNW] op 6 October 1864 *(D&C 11)*;
clo 2 February 1953 *(RM March)*.
At first BRYN seems to have been alternative name in
some circles: *hb* 1865a has entry B, same as D and early
ticket has B or D *(JB)*.

DERWENTHAUGH – see GATESHEAD.

DERWYDD ROAD [GW] op 26 January 1857
(Carmarthen 23rd); aot request; clo 3 May 1954 *(Cl)*.

DESBOROUGH & ROTHWELL [Mid]
op 8 May 1857 *(Mid; co ½ T 13 August- line)* as D;
for R added 1 October 1857 co tt *(Mid)*, altered to
D & R 1 November 1899 *(hbl 25 January 1900)*;
clo 1 January 1968 *(RM February)*.

DESFORD [Mid]
op 18 July 1832 *(Mid)* as D LANE; renamed by
26 April 1833 *(Mid* – from local press)*; resited about
150 yards west 27 March 1847 *(Cl)*; see 1847
December★★; clo 7 September 1964 *(RM October)*.

DESS [GNS] op 2 December 1859 *(GNS)*;
clo 28 February 1966 *(RM March)*. *RM October 1960*

said had become HALT but not seen thus any tt.

DETTON FORD SIDING [CMDP]
op 21 November 1908★★; clo 26 September 1938
(T 9 August;); {Cleobury Town – Stottesdon}.

DEVILS BRIDGE [VoR] (ng) op 22 December
1902★★ (see for full detail); to preservation 1989.

DEVIZES [GW] op 1 July 1857 *(Bath & Chelt 8th)*;
clo 18 April 1966 *(RM May)*.

DEVONPORT {map 114}

DEVONPORT [GW] op 4 May 1859★★;
D ALBERT ROAD 26 September 1949 *(Cl)* to 6 May
1968 *(offic)*; still open.

D KINGS ROAD [LSW] op 17 May 1876
(W D Merc 18th); K R added 26 September 1949 *(Cl)*;
clo 7 September 1964 *(Cl)*.

D & STONEHOUSE until 1916 *(Brad)* but just D in
LSW co tt 1914.

[LSW] boat trains: first America Line vessel arrived
9 April 1904; services ceased from 28 May 1910 – poorly
patronised, now agreement by which GW handled
traffic (see PLYMOUTH MILLBAY DOCKS);
perhaps later naval specials *(LSW)*. NEW QUAY and
OCEAN QUAY added 1910a *hb*; strangely, 1912 *hb*
has line to STONEHOUSE POOL with O Q and N Q
as intermediate 'stations' (all three 'P'); same to 1929;
1938 and 1956 books only show O Q (at Stonehouse
Pool) – inertia? double entering? available if wanted?
See *Kittridge* – no mention of renewal of use after 1910.
Also see DOCKYARD.

DEVONS ROAD [Dock]
op 31 August 1987 *(T 1 September)*; still open.

DEVONSHIRE STREET MILE END
– see LONDON.

DEVYNOCK & SENNYBRIDGE [N&B]
op 3 June 1867 *(T 5th- line)*; & S added 1 August 1913
(hbl 23 October); clo 15 October 1962 *(RM November)*.

DEWSBURY {map 55}

DEWSBURY [LNW] op 18 September 1848 *(D&C 8)*;
D WELLINGTON ROAD from 2 June 1924
(Rly Gaz 23 May) to 20 February 1969 *(Cl)*; still open.

D CENTRAL [GN] op 9 September 1874 *(GN)*;
replaced 12 April 1880 on extension to Batley
(GN – see BATLEY CARR)*; CENTRAL added 1951
(Cl); clo 7 September 1964 *(Cl)*.

D MARKET PLACE [LY] op 1 April 1867 *(Yorkshire
Post 2nd)*; clo 1 December 1930 *(Cl)*.
M P added 2 June 1924 *(Rly Gaz 23 May)* but *Brad*
included in at least one table from start/soon after and
thus LY co tt 1912.
Also see THORNHILL.

DEYHOUSE – see BARRY LINKS.

DIAL HOUSE – see 1883 August 20★★.

DICCONSON LANE & ASPULL [LY]
first in *Brad* May 1869, as D's L; became D L 1870
(Brad); & A added 1 July 1895 *(hbl 11th)*;
clo 2 April 1917 *(Cl)*, reop 5 May 1919 *(RCH)* as
HALT; clo 1 February 1954 *(RM March)*.

DIDCOT

D PARKWAY [GW] op 12 June 1844 *(co n dated 17th)*;
PARKWAY added 29 July 1985 *(RM October)*; still open.

D JUNCTION in *Brad* 1844/5 to 1858/9, GW co tt to

1891/1902 (not always all tables), *hb* 1877 to 1904.

D DEPOT [GW/BR?] (non-tt): 18 June 1951 wtt shows one Monday–Friday train each way from/to Oxford; start? end? {branch from Foxhall Junction, Didcot}.

DIDSBURY [Mid] op 1 January 1880 *(RCG)*; clo 2 January 1967 *(T 8 December 1966)*.

DIGBY near Sleaford [GN/GE] op 1 August 1882 *(GN/GE)*; clo 11 September 1961 *(RM September)*.

DIGBY & SOWTON op 29 May 1995 *(BLN 758)*; about 300 yards south of earlier Clyst St Mary; still open.

DIGGLE [LNW] op 1 July 1850 *(T 8th- line)* and this in July tt; clo 7 October 1968 *(RM November)*.

DILLWYN alias D & BRYNTEG [N&B] (non-tt): HALT/PLATFORM; miners; op by September 1928; clo 15 October 1962; {Crynant – Brynteg} *(U)*.

DILSTON CROSSING [NC] – see 1836 B**; {Hexham – Corbridge}

DILTON MARSH [GW] op 1 June 1937 *(RM Aug.)*; HALT until 5 May 1969 *(GW H)*; clo 6 March 1994 *(BLN 726)*; reop 30 April 1994 *(BLN 733)*; still open.

DINAS near Caernarfon

D CAERNARVON [LNW] op 15 August 1877 *(LNW Officers 17506*)*; D JUNCTION 1912 *(RCH ref July)* to 26 September 1938 *(hbl October)*, when became D C; clo 10 September 1951 *(RM October)*.
* = minutes called it station at LLANWNDA JUNCTION – not known if name actually applied, e.g. for short time after opening.

D JUNCTION [WH] (ng) op 15 August 1877 *(NGSC2; Rtn)*; clo 1 November 1916, reop 31 July 1922** *(Cl)*; clo 28 September 1936 *(Cl)*.

DINAS – see under BLAENAU.

DINAS MAWDDWY [Cam] op 30 September 1867 *(co n Merioneth 5 November)*, stop when required; clo 17 April 1901 (Wed.), reop 31 July 1911 *(RCG)*; clo 1 January 1931** (Thursday) *(Cl)*.
Schools excursions to Aberystwyth until 1939 (G. Williams, article, *GW Journal 59*). *Brad* and *Brad Sh* initially spelled this and company MOWDDY, but *Merioneth notice* called station just D and spelled company MAWDDWY.

DINAS POWYS [Barry] op 20 December 1888 *(Barry)*; still open. At first DINAS POWIS; altered to DYNAS POWYS 1898/9, DINAS POWIS 1922 *(Brad)*; settled 12 May 1980 tt. *Hb* always DINAS POWIS.

DINAS RHONDDA [TV] replaced Pandy on 2 August 1886 *(hbl 15 December)*; clo 1 April 1917 (Sunday); back in *Brad* July 1919; still open. RHONDDA first added 1 November 1927 *(hbl January 1928)*, omitted 12 May 1980 *(C/W)*, back 28 May 2000 tt *(AB Chron)*.

DINGESTOW [GW] op October 1857**; DINASTOW 1866 to 1868 *(Brad)* and *hb* thus 1867 (only); clo 30 May 1955** *(Cl)*.

DINGLE PARK ROAD [LO] op 21 December 1896 *(LO)*; clo 31 December 1956 *(T 29 September)*.

DINGLE ROAD [TV] op 1 March 1904 *(Penarth)*; see 1904**; ceased to be HALT 5 May 1969 *(GW H)*; still open.

DINGWALL [High] op 11 June 1862 *(High)*; still open.

DINMORE [SH Jt] op 6 December 1853**; clo 9 June 1958 *(Cl)*.

DINNET [GNS] op 17 October 1866 *(GNS)*; clo 28 February 1966 *(RM March)*.

DINNINGTON & LAUGHTON [South Yorkshire Joint] op 1 December 1910** *(RCG)*; clo April 1926 *(Cl)*; reop 25 July 1927 *(T 21st)*; clo 2 December 1929 *(Mid)*. Two pre-opening excursions 20 June 1910, one to Doncaster for miners' rally, the other Wesleyan Sunday School outing to Cleethorpes *(S Yorks Joint)*.

DINSDALE [NE] op 1 July 1887 *(RCG)*; replaced Fighting Cocks; still open.

DINTING

DINTING (a) op as GLOSSOP 25 Dec. 1842 *(co n Manchester Guardian 24th)*; *GC dates* says 24th – was this a directors' trip (other sections on this line received formal openings the day before the public) or might it have been one of those cases where some trains ran a day earlier than advertised? Renamed D 9 June 1845 *(Cl)*; clo 1 February 1847 and name transferred to >

DINTING (b) op 9 June 1845 as GLOSSOP JUNCTION, ¾ mile east of above; renamed D February 1847 tt *(JS)*, G & D 10 July 1922 *(hbl 13th)*, D 26 October 1938 *(hbl October)*. Still open.
Based on *GC* and *Brad* September 1846, which includes both DINTING and GLOSSOP JUNCTION on main line, both with times and fares, and has note that trains left GLOSSOP ten minutes before advertised departure time from G Junction.
Also see E.M. Johnson, *Scenes from the Past, Woodhead Part 1*, Foxline, 1996.

DINTON [LSW] op 2 May 1859 *(Salisbury 7th)*; clo 7 March 1966 *(RM April)*.

DINWOODIE [Cal] first in *Brad* May 1853; clo 13 June 1960 *(RM July)*.

DIRLETON [NB] op 17 June 1850 *(Edin)*; clo 1 February 1954 *(RM March)*.

DISLEY [LNW] op 9 June 1857 *(Stockport 5th)*; still open.

DISS [GE] op 2 July 1849 *(T 5th)*; still open.

DISTINGTON [CW Jc] op 1 October 1879 *(D&C 14; Rtn- line)*; clo 13 April 1931 *(LNW Record)*.

DITCHAM PARK – see WOODCROFT.

DITCHFORD [LNW] op 2 June 1845 *(co op tt)*; clo 1 November 1924 (Saturday) *(RM December)*; railwaymen and families used to June 1952 or later *(U)*.

DITCHINGHAM [GE] op 2 March 1863 *(D&C 5; T 5th- line; included in inspection report)*; aot request; clo 5 January 1953 *(T 5th)*.

DITTON [LNW]: line op 1 July 1852 *(T 10th)*, nd, August 1852; re-sited about 250 yards west 1 May 1871 *(LNW Officers 6555)*; D JUNCTION until 9 May 1973 *(Cl)*; clo 29 May 1994 *(RM September)*.

DITTON MARSH – see ESHER.

DITTON PRIORS [CMDP] op 21 November 1908**; HALT from 1 October 1923 – but already treated as such; clo 26 September 1938 *(T 9 August)*.

DIXON FOLD [LY] op 29 May 1838** (in 11 June 1838 tt quoted by *Bolton*); continuous use in early years not certain; is in September 1845 tt, first with detail since July 1843, as CLIFTON (supported by timings and OS evidence, L. Crowther). May 1847 tt this name was transferred to another station, which see under CLIFTON (now 8/10 minutes to Stoneclough, previously 5), no sign of D F; perhaps D F remained open but omitted from *Brad*; in *Topham* May 1848 (first issue) but not back in *Brad* until July 1848. Clo 2 August 1926 by coal crisis, reop 7 March 1927 *(Cl)*; clo 18 May 1931 *(Cl)*.

DOBCROSS [LNW] op 1 January 1912 *(LNW Officers 43577)*; clo 2 May 1955 *(T 11 March)*. HALT according to *hb* 1938 and not included there previously (usually sign of Halt) – see 1905★★.

DOCKERS LANE – see BERKSWELL.

DOCKING [GE] op 17 August 1866 *(T 18th)*; clo 2 June 1952 *(RM June)*.

DOCKYARD Devonport [GW] op 1 June 1905 *(GW H)*; HALT until 5 May 1969 *(GW H)*; aot request; still open; {map 114}.
Devonport Tunnel pre-op *(RAC)*.

DOCTOR DAYS BRIDGE JUNCTION – see under BRISTOL.

DODDERHILL [BG] op November 1841★★ *(Mid)*; clo 5 March 1844? *(Mid)*.

DODDINGTON & HARBY [GC] op 1 January 1897 *(RCG)*; clo 19 September 1955 *(BR ER internal notice August)*.

DODNOR [IWC] (non-tt): platform between Newport and Cement Mills; exact dates ?; certainly used in WW1 by men from Camp Hill prison sent to work on island's defences; (A. Stroud, *Yesterday's Papers, Volume Two ... from The Isle of Wight County Press*, Oakwood, 2008).

DODWORTH
DODWORTH (a) [GC] op 1 July 1854 *(co ½ T 26 July)*; for clo see 1959★★ (except for special excursions, *RM August)*.
DODWORTH (b) op 15 May 1989, same site as (a) *(RM July)*; still open.

DOE HILL [Mid] op 1 May 1862 wtt *(Mid)*; clo 12 September 1960 *(T 12th)*.

DOG LANE – see DUKINFIELD.

DOGDYKE [GN]: decision to have a station made in April 1849 *(GN)*; first tt evidence May or June 1849 *(Topham)*; clo 17 June 1963 *(RM July)*.

DOLARDDYN CROSSING [Cam] (ng): line op 6 April 1903; not known if this there at outset. Co working tt July 1904 (OPC 1977 reprint) says: 'On Mondays all Up and Down trains will stop at the Crossing at Dolarddyn to pick up or set down passengers to or from Welshpool. Passengers must take Cyfronydd tickets. Trains will also stop at Dolarddyn on other days for picnic parties'. Became regular daily stopping place 16 March 1929 *(wtt evidence – TTS, March 1966, p.86)*, first in *Brad*, full use, 8 July 1929; aot request; clo 9 February 1931 *(Cl)*; {Castle Ceireinion – Cyfronydd}.

DOLAU [LNW] op 1 December 1865★★– line; HALT 6 September 1965 to 5 May 1969 *(Cl)*; still open.

DOLCOATH [GW] op 28 August 1905 *(GW H)*; HALT; clo 1 May 1908 (Friday) *(wtt supp)*; {map 111}.

DOLDDERWEN CROSSING [Corris] (ng): occasional stop *(NGMW)*; not in *Brad*; line clo 1 January 1931.

DOLDOWLOD [Cam] op 21 September 1864 *(D&C 11; co n Hereford J 24th-line)*; clo 31 December 1962 *(T 31st)*.

DOLEHAM [SEC] op 1 July 1907 *(SEC)*; GUESTLING until 1908 *(Brad)*; HALT until 5 May 1969 *(SR App)*; still open.

DOLGARROG [LNW] op 18 December 1916 *(LNW Officers 44979)*; clo 26 October 1964 *(RM Dec.)*; reop 14 June 1965 *(Cl)*; aot request; still open. Also see Section 7:5.

DOLGELLAU
DOLGELLAU [GW] line op 4 August 1868 from Bala *(Carnarvon 15th)* but station not in final location because had been delays in buying land needed; declared complete 18 August *(Pratt)*; clo 18 January 1965★★. Originally DOLGELLY; altered to DOLGELLEY 24 June 1896 *(Cl; RCH dist ref 30 January 1897)*, to DOLGELLAU June 1960 (W.G. Rear & N.G. Jones, *Scenes from the Past, 9, the Llangollen Line ...*, Foxline, 1990).

DOLGELLY [Cam] temporary terminus, wooden platform at west end of goods yard, op 21 June 1869 from Barmouth★ *(Cam)*; clo when line extended to meet GW, work completed in January 1872 *(Pratt)*.
★ = *Carnarvon 19 June* confirms existence of temporary and need to walk between stations but does not give opening date.

DOLGOCH
DOLGOCH [Talyllyn] (ng) first in *Brad* August 1867 – not in original inspection report (see 1866 October 1★★); see 1950 October 6★★.

D QUARRY SIDING [Cam] (non-tt): co notice, week ending 2 March 1918 said train had gone from Whittington to here and back with prisoners of war (spent day working at quarry?).

DOLLAR [NB] op 3 May 1869 *(Rly Times 8th/RCHS Journal July 1979)*; clo 15 June 1964 *(RM July)*.

DOLLIS HILL op by [Met] 1 October 1909 *(RCG)*; [Bak] added 20 November 1939; Met last use 7 Nov. 1940 *(Ug)*; transferred to [Jub] 1 May 1979; still open. Became D H & GLADSTONE PARK 1931 *(L; RCH dist ref 19 October 1931)* but 1932/3 *(Brad)*; reverted 1933 *(L)* but *RCH dist ref 22 February 1939* and *Brad* still D H & G P 1948, when it ceased to give details of LT services.

DOLPHINTON
DOLPHINTON [Cal] op 1 March 1867 *(Cal)*; clo 12 September 1932, reop 17 July 1933 *(Cl)*; clo 4 June 1945★★.

DOLPHINTON [NB] op 4 July 1864 *(Selkirk 7th)*; clo 1 April 1933★★.

DOLSERAU [GW] op 8 February 1935 *(Cl 29)*; HALT; clo 29 October 1951 *(Cl)*; {Bontnewydd – Dolgellau}. Hb 1938: D for TORRENT WALK HALT, but not seen thus *Brad*.

DOLWEN [Cam] op 2 September 1859 *(Cam)*; became HALT 1957 *(Brad)*; clo 31 Dec. 1962 *(T 31st)*.

DOLWYDDELAN [LNW] op 22 July 1879 *(Brad Sh Eng 1880– line)*; aot request; still open.

Spelling DOLWYDDELEN in use by June 1880 (Brad), at request of Lady Willoughby (LNW Officers 19539); reverted to ...AN 1980 tt.

DOLYGAER [BM] op 19 March 1863★★; clo 31 December 1962 (T 31st). Aot Dol-y-gaer (hb). HALT in hb 1938 and 1956 and on BR ticket (JB) but not in tt.

DOLYHIR [GW] op 25 September 1875 (GW- line); clo 5 February 1951 (RM October) – see 1951★★. Originally DOLYHIR OR DOLHIER (hb); Brad at first DOLYHIER, to DOLYHIR 1882/3.

DOLYWERN [Glyn] (ng) op 15 March 1891 (GlynV) as replacement for Queens Head Inn on line reopening; clo 7 April 1933★★; {map 79}.

DON STREET Aberdeen [GNS] op 1 August 1887 (GNS); clo 5 April 1937 (RM January 1938).

DONCASTER:
[GN] temporary station op 7 September 1848; replaced to north (much dispute about exact distance) 16 (probably) September 1850. D CENTRAL 1 July 1923 (hbl 12th) to January 1951 tt (JS); still open. Line from Swinton [SY, at first operated by Mid] opened 10 November 1849 (GC;T 13th- line). All contemporary sources give 'Doncaster' as terminus and suggest that there was only one Doncaster station late 1849/early 1850 but modern works such as GC and SY say it used a temporary terminus, CHERRY TREE (LANE). A possible (likely?) explanation is provided by the six-inch OS map of Doncaster, published 1854 (before the Midland had a goods station there – opened 1857), which shows CHERRY TREE STATION, apparently without any outside access, about half-way between Doncaster South Junction and the Junction which provided a southern 'bypass' for Doncaster (the later Hexthorpe Junction was well to the west of this). If the GN temporary was south of, or partially on, the junction it would have been difficult, or even impossible, for Swinton trains to call there. In that case it would have made sense for temporary platforms to be built beside it for the SY service, to all appearances part of the GN station. This would explain the lack of evidence for the closure of CHERRY TREE since the Swinton trains would automatically have been able to use the permanent station when it opened, or soon after if work needed to be done on the junction – certainly SY was paying rent for the use of GN station from 1 January 1851. This would explain why the GN service to Barnsley, started 1 July 1851, used main station (SY). St Leger excursion trains certainly used CHERRY TREE 16–19 September 1851 (and perhaps had done so in 1850). No reliable evidence exists for later use of CHERRY TREE until 1852 by the Midland. (Based on article Early Days at Doncaster Railway Station, by P.L. Scowcroft, RCHS Journal, March 1990, p.5 on, plus additional information from J. Gough.)

Racing, especially St Leger
Various sites were used over the years:
Platform at Cherry Tree Junction, initially for third-class passengers from Sheffield (1851 on), Shakespeare and

Marshgate Sidings (1859 on), by 1867 Loco Sidings, Marshgate Horse Dock, Cherry Tree Goods Sidings and St James Sidings. (See article by P. Scowcroft, RCHS Journal, November 1983, p.266–75).
Example of notice that SHAKESPEARE SIDINGS would be used 16, 18, 19 Sept. 1863 (St Leger Week) for specials to/from London was in The Times on the 7th. Ticket (JB) exists; SOUTH DOCK (1899). Also see Away (p.85–7).

JAMES BRIDGE [GC], previously Cherry Lane, used starting with St Leger meeting of 5 to 8 September 1899; after opening of GC line to London, they were able to run excursions from many places (RM October 1899); used as ST J B 13 September 1923 (JB); still in use St Leger Week 1955 for all specials from Sheffield, Manchester and west (Rly Obs October 1955, p.319); station still there 1971 but use then not certain (AB).

WORKS PLATFORM DECOY SIDING D [GN] (non-tt): when wagon shops moved to Carr, about 1¾ miles south-east of Doncaster in 1889 (works completed February, workmen's platform ready April – GN), a shuttle service from Central was provided for workers; in July 1939 wtt as RED BANK; certainly still operating 25 September 1954; works closed 1965 (B. Wilson; LNE ticket, JB). Also see EDLINGTON; HEXTHORPE.

DONIBRISTLE [LNE] (non-tt):
HALT for Admiralty workmen; op 2 March 1942 (LNE circular ST3074 of 27 January); clo 2 November 1959 (U); added 'P' 1944a hb, December 1959a 'temporarily closed', January 1962a 'closed'; {Inverkeithing – Aberdour}.

DONIFORD HALT: see 2007 July 20★★.

DONINGTON ROAD [GN/GE] op 6 March 1882 (GN/GE); clo 11 September 1961 (RM September).

DONINGTON-ON-BAIN [GN]
op 1 December 1876 (RCG;T 28 November- line); DONNINGTON-on-B until 1 January 1877 (Cl); clo 11 September 1939★★, reop 4 December 1939; clo 5 November 1951 (RM December).

DONISTHORPE [AN Jt] op 1 May 1874 (LNW notice T 1st); clo 13 April 1931 (LNW dates PCC).

DONNINGTON [LNW] op 1 June 1849 (Shrewsbury 8th); LNW Officers 5972, 6443 show that change to D WOOD was recommended 16 November 1870, reversion to D decided 19 April 1871; clo 7 September 1964 (RM October).

DONYATT [GW] op 5 May 1928 (Chard 5th); HALT; clo 5 February 1951 (Chard 3rd), reop 7 May 1951 (BR notice Chard 5th) – see 1951★★; clo 10 September 1962 (Chard 15th).

DORCHESTER
D SOUTH [LSW] op 1 June 1847 (Salisbury 5th); originally a terminus, through trains having to reverse; through westbound platform added 5 May 1879, eastbound 28 June 1970; SOUTH added 26 Sept. 1949 (Cl); still open.
D WEST [GW] op 20 January 1857 (W Fly P 27th); WEST added 26 September 1949 (Cl); still open.
DORE [Mid] op 1 February 1872 (Mid) as D & TOTLEY; renamed 18 Mar. 1971 (Mid); still open.

DORKING

DORKING [LBSC] op 11 March 1867 *(co n T 11th)*;
D NORTH 9 July 1923 *(hbl 26 April)* to 6 May 1968
(A.A. Jackson); still open.

D DEEPDENE [SE] first in *Brad* December 1850 as
BOX HILL & LEATHERHEAD ROAD;
renamed B H 1851 tt *(Cl)*; clo 1 January 1917 *(RM Feb.)*;
reop 1 January 1919 *(Cl)*; renamed DEEPDENE
9 July 1923 *(hbl 26 April)*; DORKING added 11 May
1987 (A.A. Jackson); still open.

D WEST [SE] op 4 July 1849 *(Hants Chron 7th)* as D;
became D TOWN 9 July 1923 *(hbl 26 April)*,
D WEST 1987 (A.A. Jackson); still open.

DORMANS [LBSC] op 10 March 1884 *(Hants Chron
15th- line*; included in inspection report *MT 6/1908/3)*;
still open. According to *hbl 26th* became D PARK 1
January 1899 – not seen thus in any tt.

DORNOCH [High]
op 2 June 1902 *(High)*; clo 13 June 1960 *(T 8th)*.

DORNOCK – see EASTRIGGS.

DORRIDGE [GW] op 1 October 1852 *(W Mid;
T 27 September- line)* as KNOWLE (but D in inspection
report); renamed K & D 1 July 1899 *(hbl 13th)*,
K 6 May 1968 *(Cl)*, D 6 May 1974 *(BR notice)*; still open.

DORRINGTON [SH Jt] op 21 April 1852
(co ½ T 17 August- line); clo 9 June 1958 *(Cl)*.

DORSTONE [GW] op 1 September 1881**;
finally clo 8 December 1941. Annual excursions 1950
to 1952 (e.g. *T 18 August 1950)*.

DORTON [GW] op 21 June 1937 *(RM August)*;
HALT; clo 7 January 1963 *(Cl)*. Also see POLLICOTT.

DOSELEY [GW] op 1 December 1932 *(Cl 29)*;
HALT; clo 23 July 1962 *(RM August)*.

DOUBLEBOIS [GW] first in *Brad* June 1860 (and in
tt *R Cornwall Gaz* 8 June); clo 5 October 1964 *(Cl)*.

DOUGLAS – see HAPPENDON.

DOUGLAS WEST [Cal] op 1 October 1896 *(RCG)*;
clo 5 October 1964 *(RM October)*.

DOULTING [GW] (non-tt): op ?; clo by 1906 *(U)*;
quarry workers?; {Shepton Mallet – Cranmore}.

DOUNE [Cal] op 1 July 1858 *(Cal; co n T 3rd- line)*;
clo 1 November 1965 *(Rly Obs November)*.

DOUSLAND [GW] op 11 August 1883
(Tavistock 17th); clo 5 March 1956 *(T 5th)*.

DOVE BANK – see UTTOXETER.

DOVE HOLES [LNW]
op 15 June 1863 *(LNW Officers)*; still open.

DOVECLIFFE [GC]
op 4 September 1854 *(GC; co ½ T 1 Sept- line)*;
first in *Brad* as SMITHLEY, DARLEY MAIN &
WORSBOROUGH *(GC* says S FOR ..., but no 'for'
Brad); DARCLIFFE October 1859, DARKCLIFFE
December 1859, DOVECLIFFE March 1860;
clo 7 December 1953 *(RM January 1954)*.
Hb used various combinations of above.
GC co tt 1903: D for D M and W. LMS tt 1933 and
Brad ? to closure: D for W.

DOVENBY [MC] (non-tt): private station for
Ballentine-Dykes of Dovenby Lodge;
op 1867 (P. Anderson, *British Railways Illustrated*, July
2002, p.470); added 'P' to hb 1896/9; see *RM October*
1903; clo 29 April 1935 *(LNW Record)*;
{Dearham – Papcastle}. M&C ticket for D LODGE *(JB)*.

DOVER {map 133}

D ADMIRALTY PIER [SE]: First used by SE. *Hasenson*
says its line to Pier was opened at the end of October
1860 and then became possible for travellers to step
straight from train to ship. *SE* says failed inspection in
November 1861 and refers to *Hasenson's* mention of
track needing to be relaid almost immediately; however,
Hasenson was writing about a second set of rails and
implication is that LCD's was opening delayed. Station
not in *Brad* until February 1862 and earliest mention
seen in SE notices in *T* is in paper of 26 September
1862 – even then, not always mentioned later. LCD
line opened 30 August 1864 *(Hasenson*, supported by
undated LCD notice, *T 2 September* – 'Pier now open'
and correspondence in *T December*, which referred to
three months use by both companies – complaints
about way public access restricted). Clo August 1914
(Cl). *Brad* only included 'ADMIRALTY' 1870 to
1879/80.

D HARBOUR [LCD] op 1 November 1861 *(T 2nd)*;
originally a temporary station; permanent not completed
by February 1865 *(SE)*; became D TOWN & H 1863,
reverted to D H 1 June 1899 *(hbl 13 July)*;
clo 10 July 1927 (Sunday) *(Cl)*.

D PRIORY [LCD] op 22 July 1861 *(co n T 22nd)*;
still open. D TOWN (P) in *Brad* until 1863.

D TOWN [SE] op 7 February 1844 *(co n T 5th)*;
inspection report, dated 1 February, *(T 8th)* shows that
temporary station would have been used at first – even
that not erected at time of inspection; TOWN added
SE co tt December 1861 *(JS)* but 1 June 1899
(hbl 13 July); clo 12 January 1877 by landslip,
reop 12 March 1877 *(Cl)*; originally terminus;
platforms on through line op 1 October 1885;
clo 14 October 1914 (Wednesday) *(RCH)*.

D WESTERN DOCKS [SEC] op for military use
2 February 1915 as D ADMIRALTY PIER;
renamed D MARINE 5 December 1918 *(SR)*;
op to public 18 January 1919 *(LCD)*; renamed D W D
1979 tt; at times boat trains only; clo 25 September 1994,
though continued to be used by unadvertised trains to
Faversham, last running 19 November 1994; after that,
classified as empty stock movements *(BLN 746)*.

D PRINCE OF WALES PIER [SEC] (non-tt)
boat trains; 1903 to 1914 *(U)*.
Also see SHAKESPEARE CLIFF.

DOVER STREET – see GREEN PARK.

DOVERCOURT [GE]: line op 15 August 1854**, nd,
October; became HARWICH D 15 March 1883 *(JS)*,
H D BAY 1 May 1913 *(hbl 24 April)*, D B 1926 *(Brad)*,
D 14 December 1972 *(Cl)*; still open.
At first DOVER COURT *(hb)*. RCH sources seen
omitted 'HARWICH' but this was in GE co tt 1914.

DOVEY JUNCTION [Cam] op 14 August 1867
(Merioneth 17th); originally GLAN D J; booking office
clo 1 January 1902 for a time since council would not
provide access road, but station remained open;
became D J 1 July 1904 *(hbl 7th)*; still open.

DOWDESWELL – see ANDOVERSFORD.

DOWLAIS

D CAE HARRIS [Taff Bargoed Joint]
op 1 February 1876 *(S Wales 31 January)*; clo 15 June 1964 *(RM August)*. D Cwm Cinnel Street pre-op *(RAC)*.
According to *GW circular 18 June 1924* would become D CAEHARRIS on 1 July, but this form not in GW co tt 1932, nor seen *Brad*, but was in 1925 *hb*, and tickets thus.
D CENTRAL [BM] op 23 June 1869 *(BM)*;
CENTRAL added 1 July 1924 *(GW circular 18 June)*;
October 1939 *Brad* 'service suspended' (operating August 1939); still suspended January 1940;
trains December 1940; from 30 June 1952 advertised as workmen's trains though carried all comers;
'clo' 2 May 1960 but continued unadvertised until last, Friday 6 May 1960 *(RM July; Chron 6)*.
D HIGH STREET [LNW] op 11 May 1885 *(S Wales 6th)* *;
H S added June 1893 tt *(JS* – supported by *Brad* – still D January 1893); clo 6 January 1958 *(BRWR notice December 1957)*.
* = *LNW Officers 27026* said would open 4 May provided inspection satisfactory; *LNW Record* gave 4 May as opening, no proviso; *LNW Officers* gave 11 May for Dowlais Top and Penywern widening, presumably linked to opening of this station; 11th confirmed by *hbl 30 September*.
Dowlais Iron Company's line from **D JUNCTION** on TV line to **D IRONWORKS** op 21 August 1851 *(T 23rd)*; line owned by ironworks company, operated by TV. Closure resulted from accident 27 December 1853, when coach ran down incline before rope was attached; at that time not clear whether TV was still responsible for operating service or iron company had taken over for itself *(Cardiff & M G 31 December 1853, 7 and 14 January 1854)*. One fact is difficult to fit into picture: *Return* shows 22 passengers carried in first half of 1854. Perhaps service briefly resumed after accident; perhaps the 22 really travelled at end of previous year and were carried over into 1854 by accounting procedures. *Brad* showed trains up to and including May 1854 – inertia? did they hope to reopen service? Not just workers' service: *Returns* show that they carried 2,149 passengers, including 158 first-class, in second half of 1853.
1938 *hb* has 'P' for Guest, Keen & Baldwin's New Washery; probably error – 1944a 'delete'.
Also see PANT.

DOWLAIS TOP

DOWLAIS TOP [BM] op 1 August 1867** *(BM, body of book; Cardiff T 27 July- line)*; clo 31 December 1962 *(T 31st)*.
DOWLAIS TOP [LNW] op 1 January 1873 *(LNW Officers 8645, 8919)*; clo 11 May 1885, replaced by D HIGH STREET (see above).
DOWLOW [LMS] op to workmen first half of 1920, to public 4 November 1929 *(U)*; HALT;
clo 1 November 1954 *(T 1 October)*.
DOWN STREET [Cen] op 15 March 1907 *(L)* *;
clo 22 May 1932 *(Cl)*. At first D S MAYFAIR according to some sources, but not thus *Brad* 1907.
* = note on Covent Garden also applies here.
DOWNFIELD CROSSING [GW]
op 12 October 1903 *(Stroud N 16th)*; HALT;
clo 2 November 1964 *(W D Press 2nd)*.

DOWNHAM MARKET [GE]
op 27 October 1846 *(co n D&C 5)*;
MARKET added 12 May 1981 tt; still open.
DOWNHOLLAND [LY] op 2 September 1887 *(Southport Guard 8th)* as BARTON;
renamed 2 June 1924 *(Rly Gaz 23 May)*;
clo 26 September 1938 *(RM November)*.
DOWNTON [LSW] op 20 December 1866 *(SR; Som & W J 22nd- line)*; clo 4 May 1964 *(Hants Chron 9th)*.
DR DAYS BRIDGE – see under BRISTOL.

DRAX

DRAX [HB] op 27 July 1885 *(op tt NER I)*;
clo 1 January 1932 (Friday) *(RM January)*.
Excursion 14 October 1933 during Hull Civic Week *(RM February 1934, pp. 153–4)*.
DRAX [NE] op 1 May 1912 *(RCG)* as D HALES until 12 June 1961 *(RM April)*; clo 15 June 1964 *(T 25 Mar.)*.
DRAYCOTT near Cheddar [GW] op 5 April 1870 *(Shepton 8th)*; clo 9 September 1963 *(Weston 13th)*.
DRAYCOTT & BREASTON [Mid]
op 1 April 1852 co tt *(Mid)*; & B added 7 August 1939 *(hbl September)*; clo 14 February 1966 *(RM April)*.
DRAYCOTT CAMP [MSWJ] (non-tt);
army camp; September 1914 to 1931 at latest;
{branch from Chiseldon} *(U)*.
DRAYTON near Chichester [LBSC] op 8 June 1846 *(LBSC; Hants Chron 13th- line)*;
clo 1 June 1930 (Sunday) *(Cl)*.
DRAYTON near Norwich [MGN]
op 2 December 1882 *(MGN)* as COSTESSEY & D;
renamed 1 February 1883 *(Cl)*; clo 2 Mar. 1959 *(T 2nd)*.
Was D for COSSEY from 1883 (thus Mid co tts), D for COSTESSEY about 1905 and thus later LMS and LNE tts and *Brad* to 1955.
DRAYTON GREEN [GW]
op 1 March 1905 *(GW Mag March 1908)*;
HALT until 5 May 1969 *(GW H)*; still open.

DRAYTON PARK

DRAYTON PARK (a) [Met GNC] op 14 February 1904 *(L)*; clo 5 October 1975 (Sunday) for reconstruction *(T 30 August)* >
DRAYTON PARK (b) [BR] op 16 August 1976 *(T 16th)*; still open.
DREGHORN [GSW] op 22 May 1848 *(co ½ T 23 August- line)*; last in *Brad* October 1850;
back May 1868; clo 6 April 1964 *(RM May)*.
DREM [NB] op 22 June 1846 *(First; co n T 23rd- line)*;
still open. D JUNCTION until 1890 *(Brad)*.
DRIFFIELD [NE] op 7 October 1846 *(NE maps)*;
still open. D JUNCTION 1864/5 to 1890 *Brad* and thus NE co tt 1880.
DRIGG [Fur] op 19 July 1849**; still open.
Brad 1850s to 1955 but not LMS tt 1930 nor *hb*:
D for WASTWATER.
DRIGHLINGTON [GN] op 20 August 1856 *(T 7th, 21st)*; D & ADWALTON until 12 June 1961 *(RM April)*;
clo 1 January 1962 *(Cl)*.

DROITWICH

D ROAD [Mid] op 24 June 1840 *(Chelt Chron 27th)*;
ROAD added 10 February 1852 *(Cl)*;
clo 1 October 1855 *(Cl)*; {goods *IA*}.

D SPA [GW] op 18 February 1852 *(GW; Rtn- line;* in inspection report)*;* SPA added 1 October 1923 *(hbl 25th);* still open.

DROMORE – see GATEHOUSE OF FLEET.

DRONFIELD

DRONFIELD (a) [Mid] op 1 February 1870 *(Mid; co n Mining 19 February- line);* clo 2 January 1967 *(Mid);* later excur and e.g. 15–19 February 1972 owing to bad weather and gritters' strike *(Mid).*

DRONFIELD (b) op 5 January 1981 *(T 5th);* still open.

DRONGAN [GSW] first in *Brad* March 1875; clo 10 September 1951 *(RM October).*

DRONLEY [Cal] op 1 November 1860 *(Dundee);* clo 10 January 1955 *(T 28 December 1954).* 1863 *Brad* DRONLEY (index), DRONLY (table); latter altered 1866 *(JS).*

DROXFORD [LSW] op 1 June 1903 *(Hants Teleg 5th);* clo 7 February 1955 *(Hants Chron 12th).* LSW co tt 1914, *Brad* to closure and *hb* always: D for HAMBLETON *(RCH dist ref 31 May 1917 for change to this).*

DROYLSDEN [LNW/LY]: see 13 April 1846★★; clo 7 October 1968 *(RM November).* Hb: originally DROYLESDEN; 1883 separate entries for LNW and LY; 1890 D JOINT; 1904 D.

DRUM [GNS] first in *Brad* January 1854; clo 10 September 1951 *(RM October).*

DRUMBURGH [NB]: logically op as junction station 4 September 1856★★ *(D&C 14- line)* – not in *Brad* until October (line there September) but in notice used for note; clo 4 July 1955 *(RM September).*

DRUMCHAPEL [NB] first in *Brad* May 1890; still open.

DRUMCLOG [Cal] op 1 May 1905 *(RCG);* clo 1 July 1909 (Thursday), reop 1 November 1909 *(Cl);* clo 1 January 1917 *(Cal wtt 11 July 1921);* reop 4 December 1922 *(Cl).* 1930/1 *Brad* note added: closed for day at 6 p.m., then used as halt; note removed 1933/4. Clo 11 September 1939 *(Cl).*

DRUMDOW [GSW] (non-tt): HALT; at least 1922 to 1928; purpose ?; {Trabboch – Annbank} *(U).*

DRUMFROCHAR op 24 May 1998 *(RM August);* still open.

DRUMGELLOCH op 15 May 1989 *(RM July);* still open.

DRUMLEMBLE [Camp] (ng) op 18 August 1906★★; request; clo by May 1932 *(Camp).*

DRUMLITHIE [Cal] op 1 November 1849 *(co ½ T Nov 27- line; in Topham December 1849,* first time line included); clo 11 June 1956 *(RM April).*

DRUMMUIR [GNS]

DRUMMUIR op 21 Feb. 1862 *(GNS);* clo 6 May 1968 *(RM July).*

D CURLERS' PLATFORM (non-tt) op about December 1884; clo ? *(GNS).*

DRUMPARK [LMS] op 1 May 1934 *(LNW Record);* clo 5 October 1964 *(RM November);* {Langloan – Baillieston}. Bargeddie (b) here later.

DRUMPELLIER – see BLAIRHILL.

DRUMRY op 6 April 1953 *(RM May);* still open.

DRUMSHORELAND [NB] op 12 November 1849 *(Rtn- line)* as BROXBURN; see 1851 November 29★★; became D for B 1 May 1870 *(JS)* and thus *Murray* 1948 and *Brad* to closure; clo 18 June 1951 *(RM July).*

DRUMVAIACH CROSSING [LMS] (non-tt): schools; about 1927 to ?; {Callander – Doune} *(U).*

DRWS-Y-NANT [GW] op 4 August 1868 *(Carnarvon 15th);* clo 18 January 1965★★.

DRYBRIDGE near Ayr See 1818★★ for first service through here.

DRYBRIDGE [GSW] first in *Brad* July 1847; see 1847 March 1★★ for temporary closures; clo 3 March 1969 *(Cl).*

DRYBRIDGE near Buckie [High] first in *Brad* May 1885; PLATFORM; aot request; clo 9 August 1915; {Keith – Buckie}. Intended to reopen as Letterfourie, but did not *(High).*

DRYBROOK {map 94}

DRYBROOK [GW] op 4 November 1907 *(GW H);* HALT; clo 7 July 1930 *(RM August).*

D ROAD [SW Jt] op 23 September 1875★★; clo 8 July 1929 *(RM August).*

DRYMEN [NB] op 26 May 1856★★; clo 1 October 1934 *(RM October).*

DRYSLLWYN [LNW]: see 1865 June 1★★; first in *Brad* November 1868; last September 1873, in table marked 'no recent information', but 'P' in 1877 *hb;* indexed in May 1875 LNW co tt but no reference in body of book; back in *Brad* June 1880, towards Lland(e)ilo only; both ways by July 1881 *(Brad)* and July 1882 (LNW co tt); aot request; clo 9 September 1963 *(T 9th).* HALT on GW ticket *(JB)* but no tt or *hb* support seen.

DUBTON [Cal]: line op 1 February 1848 *(co n RM February 1953),* nd, May *(Topham);* clo 4 August 1952 *(RM September).* D JUNCTION 1849 to 1882 (index later) in *Brad,* D J for HILLSIDE 1890 in *hb.*

DUCKMANTON – see ARKWRIGHT TOWN.

DUDBRIDGE [Mid] op 4 February 1867 *(Stroud J 9th);* D for STROUD until 1 July 1886 co tt *(Mid);* clo 16 June 1947★★.

DUDDESTON [LNW] op 1 March 1869 (alterations notices LNW co tt March 1869; *LNW Officers 3994)* as VAUXHALL, replacing Bloomsbury & Nechells and Lawley Street (1854 station); renamed V & D 1 November 1889 *(RCG),* D 6 May 1974 *(BR notice);* still open. 21 chains west of earlier terminus – see BIRMINGHAM VAUXHALL.

DUDDING HILL [Mid] op 3 August 1875 *(Mid);* clo 2 July 1888, reop 1 March 1893 co tt *(Mid);* clo 1 October 1902 (Wednesday) *(Cl).* Hb called it WILLESDEN & DUDDEN HILL, later variations, but company did not *(Mid).* Became D H for CHURCH END WILLESDEN 1 February 1876 co tt, D H 1 May 1878 co tt, D H for WILLESDEN and NEASDEN 1 June 1880 co tt *(Mid).*

DUDDINGSTON & CRAIGMILLAR [NB] op 1 December 1884 *(Edin);* clo 10 September 1962 *(BR n Ed Sub).* Addition of & CRAIGMILLAR was erratic; it was added 1885 to 1953/4 in *Brad,* was in *hb*

1890 on, NB co tt 1900, *Murray* 1948 (but not *Brad* at that time) and clo notice.

DUDLEY
DUDLEY [LNW] op 1 May 1850 *(Worcester 4th)*, temporary station; extended to permanent after a few months *(W Mid)*; clo 6 July 1964 *(RM August)*.
DUDLEY [GW] op 20 December 1852 *(T 20th)*; local service between Wolverhampton and Stourbridge withdrawn 30 July 1962 *(RM September)*; used by Old Hill and Birmingham Snow Hill services until 15 June 1964 (ex-LNW, should have closed same day but delayed for three weeks) (M. Hale).
There were later Zoo excursions – photo of one, 3 August 1964 *(Dudley)*.
D SOUTH SIDE & NETHERTON
– see BLOWERS GREEN.
DUDLEY COLLIERY [NE]: see ANNITSFORD.
DUDLEY HILL [GN] op 20 August 1856 *(T 7th, 21st)*; re-sited about 30ch north, for line to Low Moor, 1 October 1875 *(Cl)*; clo 7 April 1952 *(Cl)*.
DUDLEY PORT [LNW]:
DUDLEY PORT op 1 July 1852 *(W Mid;T 2nd- line)*; still open. At times D P JUNCTION (thus LNW co tt 1885), later D P HL in *Brad* and LNW co tt 1909.
D P LL op 1 May 1850 *(W Mid;T 2nd- line)*; clo 6 July 1964 *(RM August)*. LNW co tt: D P JUNCTION, one table at least, to 1883 or later.
DUFFIELD [Mid] op 6 April 1841★★; re-sited a little to south on opening of Wirksworth branch, 1 October 1867 *(Cl)*; still open.
DUFFIELD GATE [NE]: line op 1 August 1848★★; first certain reference in tt June 1849 *(Topham)*, when Monday only; first specific reference in *Brad* November 1850; all days November 1851; last there June 1870; back May 1871, Mondays only, when GATE/GATES added; last trains shown in February 1890, though still in *Brad*, trainless, to April.
DUFFRYN – see AMMANFORD; DYFFRYN.
DUFFRYN CROSSING
DUFFRYN CROSSING [GW] op 12 July 1914 *(GW H)*; HALT; clo 2 April 1917 *(RCH)*.
Also see ABERCWMBOI.
DUFFRYN MILLS [PT] (non-tt); HALT used by funeral parties; op 14 February 1931; use ceased by September 1936; {Port Talbot – Bryn}.
DUFFRYN RHONDDA [RSB] miners' use by 1898 *(U)*; in co tt 10 July to 2 October 1911, perhaps in error, as D R PLATFORM; first in *Brad* October 1912 as D R HALT; clo 3 December 1962 *(RM January 1963)*; workmen's service withdrawn from 7 November 1966 *(RM January 1967)*.
DUFFTOWN [GNS] op 21 February 1862 *(GNS)*; clo 6 May 1968 *(RM July)*; occasional later use *(Hurst)*. Became D for TOMINTOUL 1933/4 according to notices in *Brad*.
DUFFWS – see BLAENAU.
DUIRINISH [High] op 2 November 1897 *(High)*; aot request; still open. HALT in *hb* 1938, not seen thus elsewhere.
DUKE OF WELLINGTON JUNCTION
– see 1883 August 20★★.

DUKE STREET Glasgow [NB]★ first in *Brad* October 1883; clo 1 January 1917 *(RM February)*; reop 2 June 1919 *(RCH)*; still open. Sometimes GLASGOW D S in tts.
★ = [CGU] until 1896.
DUKERIES JUNCTION
[GC] and [GN] stations both op 1 June 1897 *(RCG)*; both clo 6 March 1950 *(RM April)*.
Early both TUXFORD JUNCTION / T DUKERIES J / T EXCHANGE.
DUKINFIELD {map 53}
D & ASHTON [LNW] op 2 October 1893 *(co ½ Rly Times 10 February 1894)*; clo 25 September 1950 *(LNW Record)*.
D DOG LANE [MS&L] op 17 November 1841 *(GC; Rtn- line)*; clo 23 December 1845 (Tuesday) *(Cl)*.
DOG LANE [MS&L], near site of above entry, op 1 May 1846 *(GC)*; clo 1 November 1847 *(Cl)*.
D CENTRAL [GC] op 23 December 1845 *(GC)*; CENTRAL added 1954 *(Brad)*; clo 4 May 1959 *(RM June)*.
DULLATUR [NB] first in *Brad* March 1876; clo 5 June 1967 *(Cl)*.
DULLINGHAM [GE] op 4 April 1848 *(co n T 3rd- line)*; clo 1 July 1850★★; reop 9 September 1850 *(co n T 6th)*; aot request; still open.
DULVERTON [GW] op 1 November 1873 *(W Som F P 1st, 8th)*; clo 3 October 1966 *(Som Gaz 7th)*.
DULWICH – see WEST DULWICH.
Also see EAST and NORTH DULWICH.
DUMBARTON
D CENTRAL [DB Jt] op 15 July 1850★★- line; new station 31 May 1858; CENTRAL added 3 March 1952 *(Cl)*; still open. 1858/9 to 1894 D JUNCTION in *Brad* (and thus co tt 1858); then DUNBARTON (and indexed for this spelling); corrected 1896/7 *(Brad)*; D JOINT *(hb 1899a)*.
D EAST [Cal] op 1 October 1896 *(RCG; Colliery 2nd- line)*; still open.
DUMBRECK op 30 July 1990 *(BLN 636)*, near earlier Bellahouston; still open.
DUMFRIES [GSW] op 23 August 1848 *(Dumfries 23rd)*; at first temporary station; extended to permanent 15 October 1849, re-sited again, 15 chains north, in September 1859 *(co ½ 1110/149)*; still open.
DUMFRIES HOUSE [GSW] op 1 July 1872 *(co ½ T 18 September- line)*; clo 13 June 1949 *(Cl)*.
DUMGOYNE [NB] op 1 July 1867 *(D&C 6- line)* as KILLEARN; renamed K OLD 1 October 1882 *(Cl)*, DUMGOYN HILL 1 April 1896 *(hbl 23rd)*, DUMGOYNE 28 September 1897 *(hbl 28 October)*; clo 1 October 1951 *(RM November)*.
DUMPTON PARK [SR] op 19 July 1926 *(LCD)*; still open. Was D P for EAST RAMSGATE 12 March 1927 *(SR; hbl April – 'March' and thus hb 1938 and SR tt 1947)* until 1955 *(Brad)*.
DUNBALL [GW]: orders for station given 19 Feb. 1873 *(RAIL 75/45)*; first in *Brad* June 1873; became HALT 18 June 1962 tt (but *hbl ref October 1961)*; clo 5 October 1964 *(Cl)*.

DUNBAR [NB]
op 22 June 1846 *(First; co n T 23rd- line)*; still open.
DUNBLANE [Cal] op 23 May 1848**; still open.
DUNBRIDGE – see MOTTISFONT & D.
DUNCHURCH [LNW] op 2 October 1871
(LNW notice of alterations for October, T 30 September)
– *LNW Officers 7125* said 1st but this was a Sunday;
there was a Sunday service on line but presumably
this station had to wait until the Monday;
clo 15 June 1959 *(RM July)*.
DUNCRAIG [High] op privately 2 November 1897
(High); wtt appendix 1 May 1920 says stops on
personal application of Mr Fletcher; made public
23 May 1949 *(Cl 29)*; since 7 December 1964 only
intermittently advertised, sometimes locally only.
According to *The Times*, 15 December 1975, trains
were then calling regularly for Duncraig Castle College,
run by Highland Regional Council for girls taking
domestic science; aot request; still open.
Hb has it as HALT 1938 (no indication that not public)
and 1956, dropped 1962a; but PLATFORM in tt until
10 September 1962 *(Cl)*.
DUNDEE {maps 4, 9}.
At first *Brad* called all just 'Dundee'; additions were
made on dates given below and were frequently first
added in some tables only. Some of the names cited
below seem to have either been local ones or created by
later historians to help identify sites concerned.
Newtyle line (see 1831 B**): op 16 December 1831
from **D TOP OF LAW**; intermittently included in *Brad*.
Line [DPA] extended to **D WARD STREET** 3 April
1832 *(co n Dundee)*; clo 10 June 1861 (date of opening
of deviation line). In *Brad* as D until 1853, then D WARD;
Cornwall's Scottish tt 1860: D WARD STREET.
Also on this line – **D BACK OF LAW** [DPA] op May
1833 *(Newtyle)*; intermittently in *Brad*; last shown July
1855. Perhaps this and Top of Law were alternative
names for same site – see 1831 B**.
Further out was **CROSSROADS** [DPA], op 3 April
1832 *(Newtyle)*; intermittently in *Brad*; last shown
April 1853, but added to Macaulay's maps between
1851 and 1854 and left there until deviation line
opened in 1861.
Line from Arbroath [DA] op to **D CRAIGIE**
8 October 1838**; replaced on extension of line by >
D ROODYARDS op 3 June 1839 *(Tayside)*; replaced on
further extension of line* by >
D DOCK STREET/TRADES LANE
op 2 April 1840 *(Dundee)*; replaced on yet another
extension of line by >
D EAST op 14 December 1857 *(Dundee)*; op as D,
became EAST 1848 tt, DOCK STREET 1856 tt,
EAST 1866 tt *(JS)*; clo 5 January 1959 *(Cl)*.
* = *Whishaw*, 1840, listed ROODYARDS as an intermediate
station so perhaps it was kept briefly beyond the extension of
line to Dock Street; part of its site was included in later
Stannergate *(Cl)*.
Line from Perth [Cal] to **D WEST** op 24 May 1847
(Perthshire Courier 27th); op as D, became D WEST
1848 tt, D WEST STREET 1853 tt,
D UNION STREET 1856 tt, D WEST again 1866 tt

(JS); clo 3 May 1965 *(RM May)*.
Tay Bridge line [NB] op to **DUNDEE** 1 June 1878
(T 1st); D TAY BRIDGE until 15 April 1966 tt; still open.
Also:
D CAMPERDOWN JUNCTION [DA]: February and
March 1880 tt shown in station list, but blank space for
times ('arrangements incomplete' as result of becoming
joint); one train shown calling on way to Dundee April
and May; June still present, trainless; probably tt error.
D ESPLANADE [NB] first in *Brad* May 1889;
clo 1 January 1917 *(RM February)*; reop 1 February
1919 *(RM February)*; clo 2 October 1939, when
requistioned by War Department *(Cl)*.
Later used for Royal Highland Show at Magdalen
Green for a few days in 1957 *(Tayside p. 83)*.
D NINEWELLS JUNCTION [Cal] logically would have
op 10 June 1861 with diversion of Newtyle line, but not
in *Brad* until June 1864; last there October 1865.
DUNFERMLINE
For early service to Charlestown see 1833 A**.
D TOWN [NB] op 1 November 1877 *(Edin)* as
D COMELY PARK; became D LOWER 1890
('adopted' 4 March, *JS*), D 1968/76 tt, D LOWER
again May 1987 tt, D 4 May 1988 tt; D TOWN
26 January 2000 *(AB Chron)*; still open. Rebuilt 1889,
mostly on same site but extended eastwards slightly
(H. Jack); became a through station 5 March 1890.
D UPPER [NB] op 13 December 1849 *(D&C 15)*;
UPPER added 1890 tt *(Cl)*; clo 7 October 1968
(RM October).
D QUEEN MARGARET op 26 January 2000 *(Rly Obs
March 2000)*; still open.
DUNFORD BRIDGE [GC] op 14 July 1845 *(GC)*;
clo 5 January 1970 *(RM March)*.
Perhaps at first temporary station west of road bridge
(C/W, based on inspection report).
DUNGENESS
DUNGENESS [SE] op 1 April 1883 *(SE)*; clo 4 July
1937 (Sunday) *(SR sig inst 1937/32)*; {map 130}.
DUNGENESS [RHD] (ng) op August 1928 *(RHD)*;
D LIGHTHOUSE later 1928 *(Brad)* to reopening
1947; see 1927 July 16** for later history.
DUNHAM near Swaffham [GE]
op 11 September 1848 *(EC- line; in Topham October)*
as LITTLE D; renamed 1851 tt *(Cl)*; aot request;
clo 9 September 1968 *(RM November)*.
DUNHAM near Altrincham
DUNHAM [Warrington & Stockport] first in *Brad*
December 1853 (but see 1853 November 1**); last
there April 1855.
D MASSEY [LNW] first in *Brad* December 1853 as
WARBURTON (but see 1853 November 1**);
renamed W & D June 1856, D October 1856,
D M 1861 *(Cl)*; clo 10 September 1962 *(RM September)*.
DUNHAM HILL [Birkenhead]
op 18 December 1850 *(D&C 10)*; HILL added 1861 tt
(Cl); clo 7 April 1952 *(RM May)*.
DUNHAMPSTEAD [Mid] op November 1841**
(Mid); clo 1 October 1855 *(Cl)*.
DUNKELD & BIRNAM [High] op 7 April 1856
(High); name often changed – variously D, B & D, D & B

(sources not agreed) – settled 13 May 1991 tt
(AB Chron); still open

DUNKELD ROAD – see STRATHORD.

DUNKERTON [GW]
DUNKERTON op 9 May 1910 *(W D Press 10th)* >
D COLLIERY HALT op 9 October 1911 *(GW H)* >
Both clo 22 March 1915 *(RCH)*; reop 9 July 1923
(Bristol notice S1153); clo 21 September 1925 *(Cl)*.

DUNLAPPIE – see STRACATHRO.

DUNLOP [GBK Jt] op 27 March 1871 *(GSW- line)*;
clo 7 November 1966 *(Cl)*, reop 5 June 1967
(RM September); still open.

DUNMERE [LSW] op 1 June 1906 *(W Briton 4th)*;
HALT; clo 30 January 1967 *(Cornish & D P 4 Feb.)*;
{map 113}. Ticket: D JUNCTION H *(JB)*.

DUNMOW [GE]
op 22 February 1869 *(EC;MT 6/56/8)*;
clo 3 March 1952 *(RM April)*; last excursion August
Bank Holiday 1964 *(Bishops Stortford)*.

DUNNERHOLM(E) GATE [Fur]:
according to *D&C 14*, stop Askam – Kirkby-in-Furness;
on line op August 1846; no other reference found.
Area is Dunnerholme on later OS maps; in descriptive
part of Linton's *Handbook of the Whitehaven & Furness
Railway*, 1852, but no mention of station; however,
Ireleth treated same way and no mention at all of Roose
(later Askam) and Rampside. Perhaps casual stop –
see 1840** for early MC practices, perhaps copied
by other companies in this area.
Hb 1872 and 1877 had D SIDING; facilities not shown.

DUNNING [Cal] op 23 May 1848**;
clo 11 June 1956 *(RM April)*.

DUNNINGTON [Derwent Valley]
DUNNINGTON and **D HALT** both op 21 July 1913
(NE Staff Mag 1913); clo 1 September 1926**
(Wednesday) *(RM Oct.)*. *Hb* showed first as D for KEXBY,
and ticket thus *(JB)*.

DUNPHAIL [High]
op 3 August 1863 *(High)*; clo 18 October 1965**.

DUNRAGIT [PPW Jt]
op 1 July 1861 *(GSW)*; clo 14 June 1965 *(RM July)*.

DUNROBIN CASTLE [High]
op 1 November 1870 *(High)*; became private station
for Duke of Sutherland 19 June 1871; use often
seasonal – e.g. 9 August to 21 October 1897 *(RCG)*;
public allowed to use later years; aot request;
clo 29 November 1965 *(Cl)*; in hb 1938 as D HALT,
private. Later Royal Scotsman land cruise train made
Monday stops; reop for locally advertised summer
excursions July 1984; formally reop, summers only,
30 June 1985 *(BLN 516)*; that year excursions
Wednesdays, regular service Sundays; back in public tt,
all days, summers only, 17 May 1993, when CASTLE
added (but nameboard later); still open.
Privately owned (Sutherland Estates) – see item by
R. Maund, *Chron January 2008*.

DUNS [NB] op 15 August 1849 *(D&C 6)* as DUNSE;
altered 1883 tt *(Cl)*, 1890 *(hb)*; clo 10 September 1951
(RM October).

DUNSBEAR [SR] op 27 July 1925 *(Bideford 28th)*;
HALT, though included *hb* 1926a and 1929 as though

station; clo 1 March 1965 *(Express & E 1st)*; {map 116}.

DUNSCORE [GSW] op 1 March 1905 *(RCG)*;
clo 3 May 1943 *(RM January 1954)*.

DUNSFORD [GW]
op 16 January 1928 *(co n Heathfield to Exeter)*;
HALT; clo 9 June 1958 *(T 5th)*.

DUNSLAND CROSS [LSW] op 20 January 1879**;
clo 3 October 1966 *(Cornish & D P 8th)*.

DUNSTABLE
D TOWN [GN] op 3 May 1858; replaced by new station
late 1860s for opening of completed line *(Hatfield)*;
was D CHURCH STREET from 1860 *(Brad)* to
1 January 1927 *(hbl Jan.)*; clo 26 April 1965 *(RM May)*.
D NORTH [LNW] op 29 May 1848. LNW Traffic &
Coaching Minutes *(RAIL 410/142)*, 31 May:
'The Manager reported <u>the result</u> [compiler's
underlining] of the opening of the Dunstable line' and
difficulties caused by the incline. No reference at next
meeting 14 June. *31 May only makes sense if line was
already open by that date. RAIL 1005/265 and Brad
Share*, 1850 retrospective on line openings, give 29 May.
Notice issued by LNW in *The Times* said would open
1 June, date used by modern works in print; same notice
(dated 24 May) in *Bedford Mercury Saturday 27 May
1848*. Presumably a case of opening early. Re-sited
about 100 yards north January 1866 *(Cl)*;
NORTH added 25 September 1950 *(RM October)*;
clo 26 April 1965 *(RM May)*.

DUNSTALL PARK [GW] op 1 December 1896
(W Mid); clo 1 January 1917 *(GW notice dated
22 December 1916)*; reop 3 February 1919 *(RCH;
GW Mag April)*; clo 4 March 1968 *(Cl)*.

DUNSTER [GW] op 16 July 1874 *(Som H 18th)*;
clo 4 January 1971 *(Som Gaz 8th)*. See 2007 July 20**.

DUNSTON
Rudimentary service provided by Brandling Co on
Tanfield branch; dates ? *(NE Express April 1992)*.
D-ON-TYNE [NE] op 1 January 1909 *(RCG)*;
clo 1 May 1918, reop 1 October 1919 *(Cl)*;
clo 4 May 1926 *(Cl)*; later used for World War II
evacuation specials *(Dunston)*.
DUNSTON op 1 October 1984 *(Dunston)*; still open.

DUNSYRE [Cal] op 1 March 1867 *(Cal- line)*;
clo 12 September 1932*, reop 17 July 1933 *(Cl)*;
clo 4 June 1945**.
* = *Brad* confirms that whole branch was closed.

DUNTON GREEN [SE]
op 2 March 1868 *(SE; co ½T 21 August- line)* as
D G & RIVERHEAD; renamed 1 July 1873 *(Cl)*;
still open.

DUNURE [GSW] op 17 May 1906 *(RCG)*;
clo 1 December 1930 *(Cl)*.

DUNVANT [LNW] first in *Brad* April 1868 (not in
line inspection report); clo 15 June 1964 *(RM August)*.

DURHAM [NE]; {map 32}
DURHAM (GILESGATE) op 15 April 1844 *(Durham
County Advertiser, 19th)*; just D in *Brad* (it was the only
Durham station at that time); replaced by >
DURHAM op 1 April 1857 *(Durham; co ½T 17 August-
line)*; still open.

D ELVET op 24 July 1893 *(RCG)*; clo 1 January 1931 (Thursday) *(T 5 December 1930)*; used by ambulance trains WWII and circus trains (animals, equipment and personnel) 1940s and 1950s (A. Chadwick, article in *BackTrack* February 2007, pp.110–11) and miners' galas to 18 July 1953 *(U)*.

DURHAM TURNPIKE
– see CHESTER-LE-STREET.

DURLEY [LSW]
op 23 December 1909 *(Hants Chron 25th)*; HALT; clo 1 January 1933 (Sunday) *(Hants Chron 7 January)*.

DURNSFORD ROAD – see WIMBLEDON.

DUROR [Cal] op 24 August 1903 *(D&C 15, chapter-line)*; clo 28 March 1966 *(RM June – photo caption)*.

DURRINGTON-ON-SEA [SR]
op 4 July 1937 *(Cl 29)*; still open.

DURSLEY
DURSLEY [Mid] op 17 September 1856★★; clo 10 September 1962 *(W D Press 10th)*.
Also see BERKELEY ROAD; COALEY.

DURSTON [GW] op 1 October 1853 *(Som H 8th)*; clo 5 October 1964 *(Cl)*. *Brad* intermittently D JUNCTION until 1879/80; not seen thus co tts.

DUXFORD (non-tt): used for Ciba Geigy works outings 1983 and 15 June 1984 (A. Rush); {Whittlesford – Great Chesterford}.

DYCE
DYCE (a) [GNS] op 20 September 1854; moved ¼ mile north on opening of line to Mintlaw 18 June 1861; closed 6 May 1968 *(RM July)*. D JUNCTION 1862/3 to 1897/8 *(Brad)*.
DYCE (b) op 15 September 1984 on same site as station closed 1968 *(RM October)*; still open.

DYFFRYN ARDUDWY [Cam]
op 10 October 1867 *(Cam; Merioneth 12th- line)* as D; renamed D-ON-SEA 1 July 1924 *(GW circular 18 June)*, D A 1 June 1948 *(Cl)*; aot request; still open.

DYKE [LBSC]
DYKE – see THE DYKE.
D GOLF CLUB (non-tt): PLATFORM, later HALT; op ?; clo 1 January 1939; {Rowan – The Dyke} *(U)*.
D JUNCTION – see ALDRINGTON.

DYKEBAR [Cal]
D built about 1902 between Paisley East and Barrhead New for suburban service that never materialised *(U)*.
D HOSPITAL (non-tt): used about end World War I according to *(U)* but railway probably only used for goods deliveries *(Hosp)*; {branch near Paisley}.

DYMCHURCH [RHD]
DYMCHURCH (ng) op 16 July 1927★★; see note for later history.
D SCHOOL (ng) first in *Brad* December 1929; last June 1930; see 1927 July 16★★.

DYMOCK [GW] op 27 July 1885 *(Glos Chron 1st)*; clo 13 July 1959 *(RM August)*.

DYNEA [ANSW] op 1 September 1904★★- line; became HALT 1 July 1924 *(GW circular 18 June)*; clo 17 September 1956 *(RM October)*.

DYNEVOR – see SKEWEN.

DYSART [NB] op 20 September 1847 *(Edinburgh Advertiser 21st)*; clo 6 October 1969 *(Cl)*.

DYSERTH [LNW] op 28 August 1905 *(RCG)*; clo 22 September 1930 *(Cl)*.

"THE OTHER WAY ABOUT."

Irate Passenger (as Train is moving off). "WHY THE — DIDN'T YOU PUT MY LUGGAGE IN AS I TOLD YOU—YOU OLD —"
Porter. "E—H. MAN! YER BAGGAGE ES NA SIC A FULE AS YERSEL. YE'RE I' THE WRANG TRAIN!"

EAGLESCLIFFE [NE] op 25 May 1852★★;
often said op 25 January 1853, (when service to South
Stockton was added) but in *Brad* June 1852 with line
to North Stockton; still open.
Op as E; became E JUNCTION later 1852/1853,
PRESTON J 1854 *(Brad)*, E J 1 February 1878 *(RCG)*
and thus NE co tt 1880 and *Brad* to 1893/4.

EAGLESHAM ROAD – see THORNTONHALL.

EALING

E BROADWAY [GW] op 1 December 1838 *(L)*;
B added 1875 *Brad* but 1900a *hb*; still open.
Joint GW/Dist service began 1 March 1883;
from 1 October 1885 GW only.

E BROADWAY [Dist] op 1 July 1879 *(T 2nd)*; B added
1890 *hb* but 1903 *Brad*; still open.

E BROADWAY [Cen] op 3 August 1920 *(T 4th)*;
still open.

Combined entrance 13 November 1966 *(L)*.

E COMMON [Dist] op 1 July 1879 *(T 2nd- line)*;
E & WEST ACTON 1886 *(L; RCG ref October)* to
1 March 1910 *(RCG)*; [Picc] use began 4 July 1932
(L); still open.
Also see NORTH, SOUTH, WEST EALING.

EARBY [Mid] op 2 October 1848 *(Mid- Brad; RAIL
1005/265- line)*; clo 2 February 1970 *(RM February)*.

EARDINGTON [GW]
op 1 June 1868 *(?; first in Brad June 1868)*; became
HALT 1952 *(Brad)*; clo 9 September 1963 *(T 9th)*.

EARDISLEY [Mid] op 30 June 1863 *(Hereford J 27th)*;
clo 31 December 1962 *(T 31st)*.

EARITH BRIDGE [GE] op 10 May 1878 *(GE- line)*;
clo 2 February 1931★★.

EARLESTOWN [LNW]: line op 17 September
1830★★, nd. VIADUCT is in co tt 1 March 1831;
early name for E or earlier stop close by?
First in *Brad* as NEWTON JUNCTION;
renamed WARRINGTON J 1852 tt *(Cl)*,
E J 1861 tt *(JS)*; E 5 June 1950 *(Cl)* though LMS
tickets thus earlier *(JB)*. Still open.

EARLEY [SE]
first in *Brad* November 1863; still open.

EARLS COLNE [CVH] first in *Brad* September
1882 as FORD GATE; renamed COLNE 1 May 1889
(hbl 25 April), E C 1 May 1905 *(hbl 27 April)*;
clo 1 January 1962 *(T 17 November 1961)*.

EARLS COURT

EARLS COURT [Dist] op 30 October 1871 *(L)*; destroyed
by fire 30 December 1875; temporary replacement at
once; new to west 1 February 1878; still open.

EARLS COURT [Picc] op 15 December 1906
(co n T 14th); still open.

EARLSFIELD [LSW] op 1 April 1884 *(L)*; still open.
Was E & SUMMERS TOWN later 1884 *(L)*,
then E for S 1 June 1902 LSW co tt *(JS)* but 1913 *(Brad)*
to 1955 *(Brad)*.

EARLSHEATON [GN]
op 9 September 1874 *(GN)*; clo 8 June 1953 *(Cl)*.

EARLSMILL – see KEITH TOWN.

EARLSTON [NB] op 16 Nov 1863 *(co ½ T 4 April
1864)*; clo 13 August 1948★★.

EARLSWOOD SURREY [LBSC] first in *Brad*
August 1868; SURREY added 12 May 1980 tt (index
much earlier); still open.

EARLSWOOD WEST MIDLANDS [GW]
op 1 July 1908 *(RCG; T 2nd- line)*;
E LAKES until 6 May 1974 *(BR notice)*;
W M added 1979/87 tt; still open.

EARLYVALE GATE [Peebles] first in *Brad* June 1856;
market trains only, various combinations of Tuesday,
Wednesday and Thursday stops; last in *Brad* February
1857; {Leadburn – Eddleston}.

EARSHAM [GE] op 2 November 1860★★;
clo 22 May 1916★★, reop 1 August 1919 *(RCG)*;
aot request; clo 5 January 1953 *(T 5th)*.

EARSWICK [NE]: line op 4 October 1847★★, nd,
May 1848 *(Topham)* as HUNTINGTON;
renamed 1 November 1874 *(Cl; RCG ref October)*;
clo 29 November 1965 *(RM December)*.

EASINGTON near Sunderland [NE]
op 1 July 1913 *(RCG)*; clo 4 May 1964 *(Cl)*.

EASINGTON – see GRINKLE.

EASINGWOLD [Easingwold]: free trips for
schoolchildren formal op day 25 July 1891;
op to public 27 July 1891 (K.E. Hartley, revised
N. Redman, *The Easingwold Railway*, Oakwood, 1991)
– though *York Evening Press 25th* suggests wider public
use on 25th; clo 29 November 1948 *(T 27th)*.

EASSIE [Cal] op 4 June 1838 *(Tayside)*; last in tt
October 1847 (but see 1837 B★★); reop 2 August 1848
(Rtn- line); clo 11 June 1956 *(RM April)*.

EAST ACCESS – see GLASCOED.

EAST ACTON [Cen]
op 3 August 1920 *(T 4th)*; still open.

EAST ANSTEY [GW] op 1 November 1873
(W Som F P 1st, 8th); clo 3 October 1966 *(Som Gaz 7th)*.

EAST BARKWITH [GN]
op 1 December 1876 *(RCG; T 28 November- line)*;
clo 11 September 1939★★, reop 4 December 1939;
clo 5 November 1951 *(RM December)*.

EAST BOLDON [NE]: line op 19 June 1839 *(co n
Newcastle Journal 22nd)*, nd, March 1864, but on Bell's
Map of Great Northern Coalfield 1850 (M. Cobb);
op as CLEADON LANE, renamed 1 October 1898
(hbl 27th); transferred to [TWM] 31 March 2002★★;
still open.

EAST BRIXTON [LBSC – see 1866★★] op 13 August
1866 *(T 14th)* as LOUGHBOROUGH PARK;
renamed L PARK & B 1870 tt *(Cl)*, E B 1 January 1894
(RCG); clo Wednesday 19 May 1926 (perhaps last day?),
reop 20 September 1926 *(RM November 1926 p.418)*;
clo 5 January 1976 *(T 8 November 1975)*.

EAST BUDLEIGH [LSW] op 15 May 1897
(Sidmouth 19th) as B; EAST added 27 April 1898
(hbl 7 July); clo 6 March 1967 *(RM April)*.

EAST CROYDON

EAST CROYDON [LBSC] op 12 July 1841 *(co n T 9th)*
as C; became C EAST 1850 tt *(L)*; E C 1 May 1862
(co minutes, *JS*), E C MAIN 1 June 1909 *(R M June)*,
E C when comined with next; still open.
E C NEW [LBSC] op 1 May 1862 *(L)* for locals;
became E C LOCAL 1 June 1909 *(RM June)*;
combined with main July 1924 *(L)*.
Alias C NEW/NEW C.
EAST CROYDON [Croydon] op 11 May 2000; still open.
EAST DIDSBURY [LNW] op 1 May 1909 *(LNW
Officers 42501 + appendix)*; E D & PARRS WOOD
until 6 May 1974 *(BR notice)*; still open.
EAST DULWICH [LBSC] op 1 October 1868
(T 28 September) as CHAMPION HILL;
renamed 1 June 1888 *(hbl 26 April)*; still open.
EAST END – see EAST FINCHLEY.
EAST ENTRANCE
– see under IMMINGHAM DOCK.
EAST FARLEIGH [SE]
first in *Brad* June 1845; aot request; still open.
EAST FINCHLEY op by [GN] 22 August 1867
(L; co n T 22nd- line) as EAST END F; renamed
1 February 1887 *(Cl; RCG ref January)*; transferred to
[Nor] 3 July 1939; still open.
EAST FORTUNE [NB] first in *Brad* July 1848
(see 1846 June 22★★); clo 4 May 1964 *(RM June)*.
EAST GARFORTH
op 1 May 1987 *(BLN 581)*; still open.
EAST GARSTON [GW] op 4 April 1898 *(co n
Ephemera)*; clo 4 January 1960 *(RM February)*.
EAST GRANGE [NB]: line op 28 August 1850
(co ½ T 1 October), nd, June 1851; not included in
notice *Stirling Journal 30 August* and added to
Macaulay's maps 1851/1854 so probably did open after
line; clo 15 September 1958 *(RM October)*.
In *Brad* at first as EASTGRANGE, CULROSS &
TORRYBURN, became EAST GRANGE,
C & T 1878 tt, E G for C 1886, E G 1909 *(JS)*;
variations in other tts.
EAST GRINSTEAD [LBSC]
EAST GRINSTEAD first station op 9 July 1855 *(Hants
Chron 14th)* – many carried free on first train; replaced
by new station on extension to Tunbridge Wells
1 October 1866; replaced 15 October 1883★ by >
E G HL: some Three Bridges to Tunbridge Wells trains
called at partially complete platform from 1 August
1882, for passenger exchange to LL, and at 1866
station, 300 yards further on, for local use
(D. Coe, article, *Signalling Record Society Journal*,
July/August 2003). Completed station op 15 October
1883★; clo 2 January 1967 *(RM February)*.
★ = *RAIL 1057/3050* says 1866 station 'finally ceased to be
used for passenger traffic on October 14th 1883 [last day],
when present commodious station was opened'.
E G LL op 1 August 1882 *(LBSC; Hants Chron 5th- line)*;
still open as E G.
HL and LL added erratically in *Brad*.
EAST HALTON [GC]
op 1 May 1911 *(co n New Holland)*; became HALT 2
August 1948 *(Cl)*; clo 17 June 1963 *(RM June)*.

EAST HAM op by [LTS] 31 March 1858 *(co n T 30th)*;
[Dist] use added 2 June 1902;
[Met] use added 30 March 1936; still open.
EAST HARTLEPOOL – see HARTLEPOOL.
EAST HORNDON – see WEST HORNDON.
EAST INDIA [Dock] op 28 March 1994★★; still open.
EAST INDIA DOCK (ROAD) – see POPLAR.
EAST KILBRIDE [Cal] op 1 September 1868 *(Cal)*;
still open. Originally K *(hb)* and Brad.
EAST LANGTON [Mid]
op 2 October 1876 *(Mid)*; EAST added 1 May 1891
(hbl 23 April); clo 1 January 1968 *(RM February)*.
EAST LEAKE [GC] op 15 March 1899
(GC; T 16th- line); clo 5 May 1969 *(Cl)*.
EAST LINTON [NB]
op 22 June 1846 *(co n T 23 June- line)*; EAST added
1864 tt *(Cl)*; clo 4 May 1964 *(RM June)*.
EAST MALLING [SEC] decision to provide station
taken October 1912 *(SEC)*; first in *Brad* May 1913;
HALT until 5 May 1969 *(SR App)*; still open.
EAST MIDLANDS PARKWAY
op 26 January 2009 *(RM March)*; still open.
EAST MINSTER-ON-SEA [SEC]
first in *Brad* July 1902; clo 4 December 1950 *(T 4th)*.
In *hb* 1938 as HALT; not seen thus *Brad*.
EAST NEWPORT – see NEWPORT-ON-TAY.
EAST NORTON [GN/LNW] op 15 December 1879
(Leic; LNW Record- line); clo 7 December 1953 *(T 7th)*.
Workmen used until last train 18 May 1957 – treated as
excursion so others could travel *(Henshaw)*.
EAST PILTON [LMS]
op 1 Dec. 1934 *(Cl 29)*; clo 30 April 1962 *(RM May)*;
{Davidsons Mains – Craigleith}.
HALT in *Brad* December 1936/July 1937 to
September 1937/July 1938; in *hb* as HALT until 1944a.
EAST PUTNEY: station initially owned by [LSW]
but first used 3 June 1889 by [Dist] *(L)*;
LSW own use began 1 July 1889 *(L)*; LSW platforms
clo 5 May 1941 *(Cl)*; Dist use continues.
EAST RUDHAM [MGN]
op 16 August 1880 *(GN)*; EAST added 1 March 1882
(Cl); clo 2 March 1959 *(T 2nd)*.
EAST SOUTHSEA [LSW/LBSC]
op 2 July 1885★★; EAST added 1896 tt *(Cl)*;
re-sited nearby soon after railcars introduced, 1 July 1904
(Cl); clo 10 August 1914 *(RM June 1931)*.
EAST STREET – see BRIDPORT.
EAST TILBURY [LMS] op 7 September 1936
(T 2nd); HALT until February 1949 *(Mid)*; still open.
EAST VILLE [GN] op 2 October 1848 *(Stamford 3rd)*
as EV & NEW LEAKE; renamed 1852 tt *(Cl)*;
clo 11 September 1961 *(RM September)*.
EAST WINCH [GE] op 27 Oct. 1846 *(co n D&C 5)*;
aot request; clo 9 September 1968 *(RM November)*.
EAST WOOLWICH – see WOOLWICH ARSENAL.
EAST WORTHING [LBSC]
op 3 September 1905 *(LBSC)* as HAM BRIDGE;
became H B for E W 1933/4 *(Brad)*, E W 23 May 1949
(JS); HALT until 5 May 1969; still open.
EASTBOURNE [LBSC]
op 15 May 1849★★; new station 1866 *(Cl)*; still open.

EASTBROOK
op 24 November 1986 *(BLN 552)*; still open.
EASTBURY [GW] op 4 April 1898 *(co n Ephemera)*;
HALT from 1934 tt *(Cl)*; clo 4 January 1960 *(RM Feb.)*.
EASTCHEAP – see MONUMENT.
EASTCHURCH [SEC] op 1 August 1901 *(RCG)*;
clo 4 December 1950 *(T 4th)*.
EASTCOTE op by [Met] 26 May 1906 *(L)*;
[Dist] added 1 March 1910; Met transferred to [Picc]
23 October 1933 *(L)*; HALT until 1934/5 *(Brad)*;
still open.
EASTER ROAD [NB] op 1 December 1891 *(Edin)*;
clo 1 January 1917 *(RM February)*; reop 1 February
1919 *(RM February)*; clo 16 June 1947★★.
EASTER ROAD HALT (non-tt):
football supporters; op 8 April 1950 *(RM June)*;
used for detraining only – return from Waverley.
In *hb* 1956 as E R PARK HALT, football excursion
traffic only; December 1959a 'closed'; but probably
last used 4 January 1964 *(Chron 56)*
{on Leith Central branch}.
EASTERHOUSE [NB]
op 23 November 1870★★; still open. NB co tt 1900,
LNE tt 1933: E for BAILLIESTON.
'For B' deleted *hb* 1949a but kept in *Brad* until 1955.
EASTFIELD DEPOT (non-tt):
used for Open Days 16 and 17 September 1972 *(U; JB)*;
{Cowlairs – Bishopbriggs}.
EASTFIELDS – see under MITCHAM.
EASTGATE –in-Weardale [NE] op 21 October 1895
(RCG); clo 29 June 1953 *(RM August)*.
EASTHAM RAKE
op 3 April 1995 *(Birkenhead)*; still open.
EASTHAVEN [DA] op 8 October 1838★★;
clo 4 September 1967 *(RM November)*.
EAST HAVEN in *Brad* until 1902/4 (one way at a time
in body, index earlier), *hb* until 1895.
EASTHOPE [GW] op 4 April 1936 *(T 24 March)*;
HALT; clo 31 December 1951 *(T 31st)*.
EASTLEIGH [LSW] op 29 November 1841?★
as BISHOPSTOKE; became E & B 1889 tt *(JS;
RCG ref July)*, E for B 9 July 1923 (and thus *hb* 1938),
E 1955 *(Brad)*; still open.
Brad added JUNCTION 1847/8 to 1854/6.
★ = op date Gosport branch; first in *Brad* December 1841, not
in any earlier tt seen in *Salisbury* (tts only printed occasionally);
mentioned as if new in branch inspection report *(Rtn)*.
Also see 1839 June 10★★.
EASTOFT [Ax Jt] op 10 August 1903 *(RCG)*;
clo 17 July 1933 *(RM September)*.
EASTON [Easton & Church Hope]
op 1 September 1902 *(Weymouth 5th)*;
from 11 November 1940 to 1 January 1945 used
summer only *(Cl; Brad* January 1944 – service will
begin 3 April); clo 3 March 1952 *(RM March)*.
EASTON COURT [Tenbury Joint] op 1 August 1861
(T 3rd- line); last in *Brad* October 1862; back April 1865;
clo 31 July 1961 *(Tenbury p. 190)*.
Became E C for LITTLE HEREFORD 1 November
1889 *(RCG)* and thus GW co tt and *Brad* to closure.

EASTON LODGE [GE]
op 2 September 1895 *(Bishops Stortford)*; aot request;
HALT at closure 3 March 1952 according to *RM April*,
but not seen thus *Brad*.
EASTREA [GE] first in *Brad* October 1847;
aot request; clo 1 August 1866 (Wednesday) *(Cl)*.
EASTRIGGS [GSW] op 23 August 1848
(Dumfries 23rd- line) as DORNOCK; last in *Brad*
October 1854; reop 2 January 1865 *(Cl)*; renamed 1 May
1923 *(Cl)*; clo 6 December 1965 *(RM Jan. 1966)*.
EASTRINGTON
EASTRINGTON [NE] op 2 July 1840 *(Hull 10th)*;
SOUTH E 1 July 1922 *(hbl 13th)* to 12 June 1961 *(RM
April)*; still open.
Also see NORTH EASTRINGTON.
EASTRY [EK]
EASTRY op 16 October 1916 *(op n E Kent)*; only
footpath access; clo 1 November 1948★★ *(RM January
1949)*. Became E JUNCTION according to *RCG ref
1920*, but E for SANDWICH in opening notice and
only that version seen in *Brad*.
E SOUTH first in *Brad* 11 July 1927; aot request;
clo 1 November 1948★★ *(RM January 1949)*.
EASTWOOD near Rochdale [LY] op 28 December
1840★★; clo 3 December 1951 *(RM January 1952)*.
EASTWOOD & LANGLEY MILL [GN]
op 1 August 1876 *(GN)*; clo 7 January 1963
(RM February). Initially E ROAD & L M in *hb* (only).
EATON [BC] first in *Brad* March 1866, Fridays only;
to all days August 1866; aot request; finally clo 20 April
1935. See 1866 February 1★★ for line history.
EBBERSTON [NE]
op 1 May 1882 *(Scarborough 4th- line)* as WILTON;
renamed 1 April 1903 *(hbl 23rd)*; clo 5 June 1950 *(Cl)*.
EBBSFLEET & CLIFFSEND [SEC]
op 1 May 1908 *(SEC)*; HALT; clo 1 April 1933
(Saturday) *(T 24 March)*; {Minster – St Lawrence}.
EBBSFLEET INTERNATIONAL op for Eurostar
19 November 2007 *(RM January 2008)*; still open.
EBBW JUNCTION [GW] (non-tt):
railway staff and ordnance factory workers;
rail-motor service began 17 July 1915; last ran Friday
28 November 1919 *(wtt supps)*; {Newport – Marshfield}.
EBBW VALE
EV HL [LNW] op 2 September 1867 *(LNW Officers*
says 1st, but a Sunday, no service); HL added 23 May
1949 *(Cl)*; clo 5 February 1951 *(Cl)* – see 1951★★.
EV LL [GW] op 19 April 1852 *(co n Merlin 16th)*;
LL added 19 July 1950 *(Cl)*; clo 30 April 1962 *(T 6 April)*.
E V PARKWAY op 6 February 2008 *(RM April)*;
still open.
EBCHESTER [NE] op 2 December 1867 *(Consett)*;
see 1951★★; clo 21 September 1953 *(RM October)*.
EBDON LANE [WCP] op 1 December 1897
(WCP; Bristol T 2nd- line); aot request;
clo 20 May 1940 *(Bridgwater Merc 22nd)*.
EBLEY CROSSING [GW]
op 12 October 1903 *(Stroud N 16th)*; HALT;
clo 2 November 1964 *(W D Press 3rd)*.
ECCLEFECHAN [Cal] op 10 September 1847
(co n True Line); clo 13 June 1960 *(RM July)*.

ECCLES

ECCLES [LNW]: line op 17 September 1830**, nd,
1 March 1831 co tt. Still open.

ECCLES [Manch] op 21 July 2000 *(RM September)*;
still open.

ECCLES ROAD [GE] op 30 July 1845 *(co n Norfolk)*;
E in *Brad* 1847 to 1849; still open.

ECCLESFIELD

ECCLESFIELD [SY] first in *Brad* November 1854;
last trains August 1856, though remained, trainless, for
a while after. Later E EAST nearby.

E EAST [GC] op 1 August 1876 *(GC dates)*;
EAST added 25 September 1950 *(Rly Obs October)*;
clo 7 December 1953 *(RM January 1954)*.

E WEST [Mid] op 1 July 1897 *(RCG)*;
WEST added 25 September 1950 *(Rly Obs October)*;
clo 6 November 1967 *(RM December)*; later excur *(U)*.

ECCLESHALL – see MILLHOUSES.

ECCLESHILL [GN] op 15 April 1875 *(D&C 8;*
first in *Brad* May 1875); clo 2 Feb. 1931 *(RM March)*.

ECCLESTON PARK [LNW]
op 1 June 1891 *(LNW Officers 32507)*; still open.

ECKINGTON near Worcester [Mid]: op 24 June 1840
(Chelt Chron 27th); clo 4 January 1965 *(Cl)*.
Aot E WEST, staff usage *(Cl)* and LMS ticket thus.

ECKINGTON & RENISHAW

ECKINGTON [Mid] op 11 May 1840 *(Mid; co n T 2nd-
line)*; re-sited 14ch north 13 September 1874 *(Mid)*;
renamed E & RENISHAW 10 April 1886 *(Mid)*;
clo 1 October 1951 *(RM November)*; later excur *(U)*.
Aot E NORTH, staff usage *(Cl)*, though there was
RCG ref January 1886 which said renamed from this.
Also see RENISHAW CENTRAL.

ECTON [NS] (ng)
op 29 June 1904**; clo 12 March 1934 *(LNW Record)*.
E for WARSLOW in NS co tt 1910 and *Brad*.

EDALE [Mid] op 25 June 1894 *(RCG)*; still open.

EDDERTON [High] op 1 October 1864 *(High)*;
clo 13 June 1960 *(RM July)*.

EDDLESTON [NB] op 4 July 1855 *(Peebles; co ½
T 22 Oct.- line)*; clo 5 February 1962 *(RM February)*.

EDEN PARK [SE] op 29 May 1882 *(L)*; still open.

EDENBRIDGE

EDENBRIDGE [SE] op 26 May 1842 *(co n T 13th,
20th)*; still open. EDEN BRIDGE until 1877 *(hb)*.

E TOWN [LBSC] op 2 January 1888 *(co ½ dated
25 January 1888)*; TOWN added 1 May 1896 *(RCG)*;
still open.

EDENHAM [Edenham & Little Bytham]
op 8 December 1857**; finally clo 17 October 1871
though still in *Brad* until February 1872.

EDGBASTON – see MONUMENT LANE.

EDGE HILL [LNW]: something had to exist
hereabouts from line op 17 September 1830**;
was point where carriages transferred from locomotive
to stationary engine haulage; furthermore,
Walker's *Accurate Description ... [*of LM] said that
most passengers would be brought here by free
omnibus from the offices in Dale Street;
this arrangement does not seem to have lasted very long.
Proper station probably op 15 August 1836 with

Liverpool Lime Street (mention at General Meeting of
27 July, *T 29 July*) – would have been to north of
anything existing previously since line to Lime Street
diverged from the old just on Manchester side of
Edge Hill; still open.

EDGE LANE

EDGE LANE [LNW] op 1 July 1870*;
clo 31 May 1948 *(LNW Record)*.
* = included, with trains, in tt for line opening *(LNW Officers
5542)* and date is given by *Liverpool Mercury 1 July* but not in
Brad until November, though rest of line there July – reason not
known; also see 1870 July 1**.
Also see STRETFORD.

EDGEBOLD [SM]
op 13 August 1866** *(co n RM May 1903)* as
HANWOOD ROAD; renamed 1 April 1921 *(hbl 24th)*;
aot request; finally clo 6 November 1933 *(Cl)*.

EDGELEY – see STOCKPORT.

EDGERLEY [SM]
op 16 June 1927 *(hbl 65)*; clo 6 November 1933 *(Cl)*.

EDGWARE

EDGWARE [GN] op 22 August 1867 *(co n T 22nd)*;
clo 11 September 1939 *(Cl)* – replacement bus service
for holders of rail tickets until 18 May 1941 (letter,
H.V. Borley, *RCHS Journal XVI, no. 1, p. 13*).
Became E for CANONS PARK 1933/4 *(Brad)* thus
LNE tt 1927 and *Brad* to closure.

EDGWARE [Nor] op 18 August 1924 *(T 18th)*; still open.

EDGWARE ROAD

EDGWARE ROAD [Met] op 10 January 1863 *(co n
Portfolio)*; [Dist] added 1 November 1926; still open.

EDGWARE ROAD [Bak] op 15 June 1907 *(RM July)*;
clo for rebuilding 25 June 1990, reop 28 January 1992;
still open.
Also see BRONDESBURY.

EDINBURGH {map 18}

To begin with, mostly just E in all tts seen. Additions to
name made erratically and inconsistently, sometimes
different ones for different routes in same issue of tt.

North British

E ST LEONARDS: for op by [Ed & Dalk] see 1831 A**;
last in tt October 1847; reop 1 June 1860,
clo 1 October 1860 *(D&C 6)*. Just St L, early *Brad*.

[EG] line op from Glasgow to **HAYMARKET**
21 February 1842 *(The Scotsman 23rd)*; this was
originally EDINBURGH in *Brad*; presumably renamed
when line extended to Waverley (it became H in *Brad*
June 1847); last in *Brad* October 1848, though still in
Topham until May 1849 (last), by when reduced to one
up train per day; back in *Brad* October 1856
Wednesday only, November 1865 fully; still open.

EDINBURGH [NB]: line from Berwick op 22 June
1846 *(co n T 23rd)* to station known variously as E,
E NORTH BRIDGE, E GENERAL, E WAVERLEY
BRIDGE, E W G; settled as E WAVERLEY 1860s
(Brad), just E from 18 April 1966 tt *(Cl)*.
Line from Glasgow extended to this station 17 May 1847
(Edinburgh Advertiser 18th, Edinburgh Weekly Journal 19th).
Initially NB and EG portions run separately; various
rebuildings and enlargements, helped by amalgamation
of two companies in 1865, led to union; still open.

[NB] line op from Trinity & Newhaven to
E SCOTLAND STREET 31 August 1842 *(Rtn)*;
extended to >
E PRINCES STREET op 17 May 1847 *(Edinburgh Advertiser 18th)* – called it CANAL STREET
but *Brad* just E until 1850/3 when became E P S >
Services diverted to WAVERLEY 22 May 1868,
and S S and P S [NB] closed *(T 25th)*.
<u>Caledonian</u>
Line from Carstairs to **E LOTHIAN ROAD** op
15 February 1848 *(co ½ T 29 February)*;
L R added 1850/3 *(Brad)*, only in notes in Cal co tt
1859; diverted to >
E PRINCES STREET op 2 May 1870 *(T 2nd)*;
clo 6 September 1965 *(T 6th)* – services to Waverley.
<u>Later</u>
E PARK op 4 December 2003 (formal 8th)
(RM February 2004, p.59); still open
<u>Also</u> special stations for events held in Edinburgh:
E EXHIBITION [Cal] op 1 May 1890 *(Balerno)*;
{Merchiston – Slateford}; clo 3 November 1890 *(Cl)*.
E EXHIBITION [NB] (a) op 1 May 1890 *(Balerno)*;
near Craiglockhart, which it replaced for the duration
of the Exhibition; clo 1 January 1891 (Thursday) *(Cl)*.
See plan *Ed Sub p.164* for details of above two.
E EXHIBITION [NB] (b) op 1 May 1908 *(RCG)*;
two platforms on Corstorphine branch and one on
eastbound main line, saving passengers from Glasgow
direction going into Edinburgh and back; *(RM June
1908, p.511)*; clo 1 November 1908 (Sunday) *(RCG)*.
Balgreen on branch part later.
E MEADOWBANK (non-tt) only used for major events
at stadium; first public use 14 June 1986 *(RM August)*;
used 24 July to 2 August 1986 inclusive for
Commonwealth Games (shuttle service from Waveley)
(Special Traffic Notice); a few hundred yards west of
earlier Piershill (D. Lindsay).
ST MARGARETS, alias **MEADOWBANK**, alias
QUEENS PARK [NB]: royal trains, railwaymen;
op 1850; clo by 1906; {Waverley – Portobello} *(U)*.
HAYMARKET TM DEPOT: service from Waverley to
here for open days, certainly used 24 August 1984
(D. Lindsay, personal knowledge).
EDINGTON & BRATTON [GW]
op 1 October 1900 *(RCG; W Gaz 5th- line)*;
clo 3 November 1952 *(Cl)*.
EDINGTON BURTLE [SD Jt]
op 28 August 1854** as E ROAD (thus *Brad* and
GW co tt 1859); became E 1864 *(Brad)*; E JUNCTION
21 July 1890 *(Cl)*, E B 30 November 1952 *(SR App)*;
clo 7 March 1966 *(Shepton 11th)*.
EDLINGHAM [NE]
op 5 September 1887 *(NE- line)*; became HALT 1926
(Brad); clo 22 September 1930** *(T 10 July)*.
EDLINGTON [Dearne] op 3 June 1912** *(LY)*;
clo 10 September 1951 *(RM November)*; excursion
19 July 1966 for local British Legion Social Club *(JB)*;
{goods *IA*}. Was E & WARMSWORTH until day of
passenger opening *(hbl 3 July)*;
E for BALBY (DONCASTER) in LMS tt 1930
and thus *Brad* to closure.

EDMONDTHORPE & WYMONDHAM [Mid]
op 1 May 1894 *(RCG; insp rept MT6/638/6)*;
clo 2 March 1959 *(T 2nd)*.
EDMONTON
E GREEN [GE] op 22 July 1872 *(L)* as LOWER
EDMONTON; renamed L E HL 1 July 1883,
E G 28 September 1992 tt *(AB Chron)*; still open.
Also see ANGEL ROAD; LOWER EDMONTON.
EDROM [NB]: line op 15 August 1849**;
in *Brad* May 1852 when it first gave detail for line;
clo 10 September 1951 *(RM October)*.
EDWALTON [Mid] op 2 February 1880 *(RCG)*;
clo 28 July 1941 *(LNW Record)*. Excursion to Dudley
27 July 1958 *(RM November, p.765)*.
EDWINSTOWE [GC]
op 15 December 1896 *(GC; Brad Sh)*; clo 2 January 1956
(RM February) but summer Saturday services to e.g.
Skegness until 5 September 1964 *(Cl)*; later excur –
one called Whit Monday, 3 June 1963 *(AB)*, another
(to Skegness) 12 Aug. 1972 *(Rly World June 1974, p.262)*.
EDZELL [Cal] op 8 June 1896 *(RCG)*;
clo 27 April 1931 *(Cl)*; reop 4 July 1938 *(Rly Obs July,
p.274)*; clo 26 September 1938 *(G&S)*.
EFAIL FACH [PT] (non-tt): see 1920**;
{Cwmavon (Glam) Yard – Tonmawr Junction}.
EFAIL ISAF [Barry] op 16 March 1896
(dist t supp 13 April); clo 10 September 1962 *(Cl)*.
E I & LLANTWIT VARDRE 1912 to 1935/6 *(Brad)* –
GW ticket *(JB)* for E I & L VARDE.
EFFINGHAM JUNCTION [LSW]
op 2 July 1888 *(SR)*; still open.
EGGESFORD [LSW]
op 1 August 1854 *(Trewman 13 July, 3 Aug)*; still open.
E for CHUMLEIGH in *Brad*? to 1955.
EGGINTON
EGGINTON [NS] first in *Brad* October 1849 (in
September WILLINGTON had been in its place, no
trains shown; same in *co n Churnet*); EGGINGTON
until 1873/4 *(Brad)*; replaced about ¼ mile west by >
E JUNCTION [GN/NS] op 1 July 1878 *(Cl)*;
clo 5 March 1962 *(RM March)*.
Note that this was after GN line had opened – at first its
trains had no stop here. In *hb* as E JOINT until 1956.
EGHAM [LSW] op 4 June 1856 *(co n T 3rd)*; still open.
Became E for ENGLEFIELD GREEN 17 July 1902
(hbl 23 October); thus LSW co tt 1914, *hb* 1938, and
Brad to 1955.
EGLINTON STREET
EGLINTON STREET [Cal] op 1 July 1879 as
replacement for Glasgow South Side *(Cal)*;
clo 1 February 1965 *(RM March)*.
Also see CUMBERLAND STREET [GSW].
EGLOSKERRY [LSW] op 1 October 1892 *(Cornish
& D P 4th)*; clo 3 October 1966 *(Cornish & D P 8th)*.
EGREMONT [WCE Jt]
op 1 July 1857 *(co ½ T 1 September)*; clo 7 January 1935
(LNW Record); later excur *(RM)*; reop 11 March 1940
for workmen *(U)*, 6 May 1946 for public *(RM July)*;
clo 16 June 1947**; in use by 23 May 1949 wtt for
Sellafield workmen, clo 6 September 1965;
occasional later schools use to 3 March 1969 *(Cl)*.

EGTON [NE] op 2 October 1865 *(co ½ T 14 February 1866- line)*; still open. Intermittently E BRIDGE *(hb)* and thus *Brad* 1881–92 but not NE co tt *(JS)*.

ELBURTON CROSS [GW] op 17 January 1898★★; omitted from internal op notice dated 13th, in *Ephemera*, but in description of opening in paper cited in note and in *Brad* Feb; finally clo 6 October 1947. According to *hbl May 1942* it had been renamed E C from E; not seen as E in *Brad* – did it reopen for workmen under that name?

ELDERSLIE [GSW]
first in *Brad* August 1875; clo 14 February 1966 *(Cl)*.

ELEPHANT & CASTLE
ELEPHANT & CASTLE [LCD] op 6 October 1862 *(T 7th)*; original temporary station in New Kent Road replaced February 1863 *(Cl)*; still open.

ELEPHANT & CASTLE [Nor] op 18 December 1890 *(L; co ½ T 14 February 1891- line)*; see 1922★★; still open.

ELEPHANT & CASTLE [Bak] op 5 August 1906 *(T 4th)*; see 1922★★; still open.

ELFORD [Mid]
op 1 July 1850 *(Mid)* as HASELOUR; became H & E 1 November 1855 wtt *(Mid)*, E & H 1 September 1864 wtt *(Mid)*, H 1 April 1904 *(hbl 28th)*, E 5 May 1914 *(hbl 14 July)*; clo 31 March 1952 *(RM May)*.

ELGIN {map 3}
ELGIN [GNS] op 10 August 1852★★ *(GNS)*.
ELGIN [High] op 25 March 1858 *(High)*.
Two later combined; ex-GNS part clo 6 May 1968 *(RM July)*; ex-High part still open.

ELHAM [SE] op 4 July 1887 *(SE)*;
clo 1 December 1940 (Sunday) *(Cl)*.

ELIE [NB] op 1 September 1863 *(D&C 15- line)*;
clo 6 September 1965 *(closure notice East of T J)*.

ELING JUNCTION – see TOTTON.

ELLAND [LY]
first in *Brad* about April 1841 (not in line op tt *Leeds*); re-sited about 200 yards east 1 August 1865 *(Cl)*;
clo 10 September 1962 *(RM August)*.

ELLENBROOK [LNW]: op 1 September 1864★★;
clo 2 January 1961 *(RM January)*.
Became E for BOOTHSTOWN 1 May 1890 *(RCG)* and thus LNW co tt 1921, LMS tt 1930 and *Brad* to closure.

ELLERBY [NE]
ELLERBY (a) E op 28 March 1864 *(NE- line)* as MARTON; renamed BURTON CONSTABLE 1 August 1864 *(Cl)*, E 1 January 1922 *(hbl 26th)*; became HALT 4 January 1960 *(RM January)*;
clo 19 October 1964 *(Cl)*. Not seen as Halt in *Brad* but note added 1960 that no staff were in attendance.

ELLERBY (b), always ELLERBY: first in *Brad* September 1864; Tuesdays only; last trains shown July 1902 *(RCG says clo 1 July, so perhaps should be 'last use June + tt inertia')*; {Skirlaugh – Ellerby (a)}.

ELLERDINE [GW] op 7 July 1930 *(Cl 29)*; HALT; clo 9 September 1963 *(T 9th)*; {Crudgington – Peplow}. Bailey's Bridge pre-op *(RAC)*.

ELLESMERE [Cam] op 4 May 1863 *(Oswestry 6th)*;
clo 18 January 1965 *(RM March)*.

ELLESMERE PORT [Birkenhead]
op 1 July 1863 *(D&C 10; LNW co ½ T 14 August- line)*

as WHITBY LOCKS; renamed 1 September 1870 *(Cl; RCH dist ref 16 December)*; still open.

ELLINGHAM [GE] op 2 March 1863 *(T 5th- line; included in inspection report)*; according to *Jowett's Railway Centres* (vol.I, Patrick Stephens, 1993) was clo May 1916, reop August 1916, though not so shown *Cl* or items in *The Times* 5 April and 1 and 2 May 1916 – also continuously in *Brad*; aot request;
clo 5 January 1953 *(T 5th)*.

ELLIOT COLLIERY (non-tt):
Agreement dated 4 November 1899 in GW Deeds Office refers to workmen's trains Rhymney Bridge / Elliot Colliery; no details of site or route are known.

ELLIOT COLLIERY [BM] alias E PIT; PLATFORM / HALT; miners; op by September 1926; clo 31 December 1962; {Cwmsifiog – New Tredegar} *(U)*.

ELLIOT JUNCTION [DA]
ELLIOT JUNCTION first in *Brad* October 1866;
clo 1 January 1917 *(Cl)*; back in *Brad* September 1917, Saturdays only; from 1 January 1918 served all days by Carmyllie branch trains, which started from Arbroath; main line stops resumed 1 February 1919 (given by *RCH* as reop date); clo 4 September 1967 *(RM Nov.)*. In *hb* 1867 (only) as E & KELLYFIELD J.

E J LIGHT RAILWAY PLATFORM op 1 February 1900, used by Carmyllie branch trains if platform in main station was not available; clo with branch?

ELLON [GNS] op 18 July 1861 *(GNS)*;
clo 4 October 1965 *(Rly Obs November)*.

ELM BRIDGE [GE] op 20 August 1883★★;
clo 2 January 1928 *(Cl)*. GE co tt 1914: E B DEPOT.

ELM PARK op by [LMS] 13 May 1935 *(Mid)* but only [Dist] trains used it; transferred to LPTB 1 January 1969; still open.

ELM ROAD CROSSING – see 1883 August 20★★.

ELMERS END
ELMERS END [SE] op 1 April 1864 *(L; co T 8 August- line)*; still open.

ELMERS END [Croydon] op 30 May 2000; still open.

ELMESTHORPE [LNW] op 1 January 1864 *(Leic; LNW Officers- line)*; clo 4 March 1968 *(Cl)*.
Became E for BARWELL and EARL SHILTON 1 February 1904 *(RCG)* and thus LNW tt 1909, LMS tt 1930 and BR tt at least to 1964.

ELMHAM – see NORTH ELMHAM.

ELMORE [LSW] op 11 April 1910 *(SR)*; HALT;
clo 31 August 1914, reop 1 October 1914 *(Cl)*;
clo 1 May 1930 (Thursday) *(Cl)*.

ELMS BRIDGE [GW] op 27 November 1933 *(co n dated 'November')*; HALT; clo 30 May 1955★★; {Dingestow – Raglan}.

ELMSTEAD WOODS [SEC] op 1 July 1904 *(RCG)*; WOODS added 1 October 1908 *(RCG)*; still open.

ELMSWELL [GE]
op 24 December 1846 *(EC- line)*; still open.

ELMTON & CRESWELL [Mid] op 1 June 1875 *(Mid)*; originally CRESSWELL; E & added 10 April 1886 *(Mid)*, spelling altered 1 May 1887 co tt *(Mid)*;
clo 12 October 1964 *(RM November)*.
See CRESWELL DERBYSHIRE for later station on this site.

ELRINGTON [NE] op 1 March 1869 *(NC)*;
became HALT 1 September 1926 *(N'humb Young)*;
clo 22 September 1930 *(T 10 July)*.

ELSECAR

ELSECAR [Mid] op 1 July 1897 *(RCG)* as
E & HOYLAND; renamed 17 March 1971 *(Cl)*;
still open.

ELSECAR [GC] (non-tt): built 1870 for Earl
Fitzwilliam; used for carrying his guests to St Leger –
example of one such 12–15 September 1871 *(SY p.52)*;
also used by villagers going to coast in summer months
(GC Society Journal December 1988, p.12).

ELSENHAM [GE] op 30 July 1845 *(co n T 26th- line)*;
re-sited north 1846 to avoid incline *(C/W –* from
correspondence with H Paar*)*; still open.
Thaxted line platform op 1 April 1913,
clo 15 September 1952.

ELSHAM [GC] op 1 October 1866 *(GC; Rtn- line)*;
clo 4 October 1993 *(BLN 715)*.

ELSLACK [Mid]: decision for station taken 3 Nov.
1848; first in *Brad* December 1848, perhaps
prematurely – not in Mid co tt until 1 January 1849
(J. Gough); clo 3 March 1952 *(RM April)*.

ELSON [GW] op 8 February 1937 *(Cl 29)*; HALT;
clo 10 June 1940★★, reop 6 May 1946 *(Cl)*;
clo 10 September 1962 *(RM October)*;
{Ellesmere – Overton-on-Dee}.

ELSTED [LSW]
op 1 September 1864 *(SR; co ½ 13 February 1865- line)*;
clo 7 February 1955 *(Hants Chron 12th)*.
ELSTEAD in *hb* 1872; 1898a should read ELSTED.

ELSTREE & BOREHAMWOOD [Mid]
op 13 July 1868 *(T 14th)*; & BOREHAMWOOD
added 1 June 1869 co tt *(Mid)*, back to E 1 April 1904
(hbl 28th); & BOREHAMWOOD added 21 September
1953 tt *(Mid)*, removed 6 May 1974 *(Mid)*;
back 1987/1993 tt; still open.

ELSWICK [NE] op 2 September 1889 *(RCG)*;
clo 2 January 1967 *(RM January)*.

ELTHAM

E PARK [SEC] op 1 July 1908 *(RCG)* as
SHOOTERS HILL & E P;
renamed 26 September 1927 *(hbl October)* >
E WELL HALL [SE] op 1 May 1895 *(RCG)* as W H;
renamed W H for NORTH ELTHAM 1 October 1916
(hbl 26th), E W H 26 September 1927 *(hbl October)* >
Both replaced by ELTHAM 17 March 1985, after
early a.m. Sunday trains had used E P and E W H
(intended 2 March but delayed by bad weather)
(BLN 509); E still open.
Also see MOTTINGHAM; NEW ELTHAM.

ELTON near Peterborough [LNW] first in *Brad*
January 1847; clo 7 December 1953 *(RM January 1954)*.

ELTON & ORSTON [GN]: op 15 July 1850
(July co tt, Henshaw); & O added 1924/5 *(Brad)*; still open.
Had been E for O until 1899/1900 *(Brad)*.

ELTRINGHAM – see MICKLEY.

ELVANFOOT [Cal] first in *Brad* April 1848;
clo 4 January 1965 *(RM February)*.

ELVERSON ROAD [Dock]
op 20 November 1999 *(RM January 2000)*; still open.

ELVET – see DURHAM.

ELVINGTON near Canterbury [EK] op 16 October
1916 *(co n EK)* as TILMANSTONE COLLIERY;
renamed T C HALT 1921, T 1925, E 1927 *(Brad)*;
clo 1 November 1948★★; {already E in *IA*}.

ELVINGTON near Selby [Derwent Valley]
op 21 July 1913 *(NER Staff Mag 1913)*;
clo 1 September 1926★★ (Wednesday) *(RM October)*.
Hb: E for SUTTON and ticket thus *(JB)*.

ELY near Cambridge

ELY [GE] op 30 July 1845 *(co n T 26th)*; clo (replacement
bus) for resignalling Sat. 11 April to Friday 8 May 1992
(inclusive) *(BR tt brochure)* – see next entry; still open.
Was E JUNCTION 1850s to 1870s, some tables *(Brad)*.

ELY: temporary station on site of earlier Chettisham
and informally called that but officially described as
'a station near Ely' (Tony Kirby) so would not have to
use official closure procedure once no longer needed:
used odd days 5 October to 29 December 1991,
regularly during 1992 closure for resignalling of main
station (above).

ELY MAIN LINE near Cardiff [GW]
op 2 September 1850 *(The Cambrian 30 August)*;
E for LLANDAFF until 1 July 1924 *(GW circular
18 June)*; clo 10 September 1962 *(Cl)*.

EMBANKMENT

EMBANKMENT [Dist] op 30 May 1870 *(T 31st)* as
CHARING CROSS; renamed C C E 4 August 1974
(L), E 12 September 1976 *(L)*; still open.

EMBANKMENT [Bak] op 10 March 1906 *(L;T 12th-
line)*; see 1922★★. Originally single platform on loop at
then 'terminus'; extra line and platform (southbound)
added when line extended 13 September 1926 – now
through station; still open. Originally E; became
CHARING CROSS E 6 April 1914 *(L)*, C C 1 May
1915 *(hbl 15 July)*, then 1974 and 1976 as above.

EMBANKMENT [Nor] op 6 April 1914 *(T 6th)* as
CHARING CROSS E; then 1915, 1974, 1976 as above;
see 1922★★; still open.

EMBLETON [CKP]
op 2 January 1865 *(co ½ T 28 February- line; in op tt
Cockermouth)*; clo 15 September 1958 *(LNW Record)*.

EMBO [High]
op 2 June 1902 *(High)*; clo 13 June 1960 *(T 8th)*.

EMBSAY [Mid] op 1 October 1888 *(RCG)*;
clo 22 March 1965 *(RM April)*.

EMERSON PARK [LTS] op 1 October 1909 *(RCG)*;
HALT until 6 May 1968 *(Mid)*; still open.
Aot one nameboard read E P & GREAT NELMES.

EMNETH [GE]:
line op 1 February 1848★★, nd, May 1848 *(Topham)*;
aot request; clo 9 September 1968 *(RM November)*.

EMSWORTH [LBSC]
op 15 March 1847 *(Salisbury 20th)*; still open.

ENDON [NS] op 1 November 1867 *(NS-K)*;
clo 7 May 1956 *(RM June)*; last football use 23 April
1960 *(BR doc)*; still in use for wakes weeks at 19 August
1961 *(BR handbill)*; last probably 10 August 1963
(no leaflet for 1964 found) *(AB)*.

ENFIELD

E CHASE [GN] op 1 April 1871 *(L)*; re-sited when line extended to Cuffley 4 April 1910 *(wtt notice NLRHS Journal 41)*; CHASE added 1 July 1923 *(hbl 12th)*; still open.

E LOCK [GE] first in *Brad* April 1855 as ORDNANCE FACTORY; renamed E L for ENFIELD HIGHWAY 1 April 1886 *(L)*; re-sited south of level crossing 1890/1 *(Cl)*; renamed E L for ENFIELD WASH 1 November 1910 *(RCG)* and still thus LNE tt 1933 and *hb* 1938; 'for EW' dropped 1955 *(Brad)*; still open.

E TOWN [GE] op 1 March 1849 *(T 2nd)*; TOWN added 1 April 1886 *(Cl)*; still open.

E WEST – see OAKWOOD.

ENGLISH BRIDGE – see SHREWSBURY.

ENTHORPE [NE]
op 21 April 1890 *(RCG)*; clo 20 September 1954 *(RM October)*. Later race excursions *(AB)*.

ENTWISTLE

Temp [Bolton, Blackburn, Clitheroe & West Yorkshire] station at WHITTLESTONE HEAD op 12 June 1848 *(LY; RAIL 1005/265- line)* >
Permanent E [LY] op 1 August 1848 *(LY)*; aot request; still open.
Logically W H should have closed 1 August 1848 but *Brad* and *Topham* include both in August 1848 tt – error or were both briefly open together?

ENZIE [High]
op 1 August 1884 *(High)*; clo 9 August 1915 *(Cl)*.

EPPING op by [GE] 24 April 1865 *(co n T 24th)*; to [Cen] 25 September 1949 – *T 26th*; still open.

EPSOM

EPSOM [LSW] op 1 February 1859**; still open.
E HIGH STREET in *Brad* 1874/5 to 1883/4.

E DOWNS [LBSC] op 22 May 1865 *(co n T 20th)*; re-sited 300 yards back along line, first trains using late evening of 13 February 1989 *(RM May – intended earlier in day but signalling problems caused delay)*; still open. Early LBSC notices *(T)* often carried exhortation to travellers to make sure they asked specifically for E Downs.

E TOWN [LBSC] op 10 May 1847 *(co n T 4th)*; TOWN added 1870 in some tables, to differentiate from E Downs and dropped about 1900 when E Downs given separate table; added again 9 July 1923 *(Cl)*; station clo at 12.45am on Sunday 3 March 1929 *(T 4th)*. Ex-LBSC service now used rebuilt ex-LSW station – previously through without stopping.

EPWORTH [Ax Jt] op 2 January 1905 *(RCG)*; clo 17 July 1933 *(RM September)*.

ERDINGTON [LNW]
op 2 June 1862 *(W Mid; T 2nd- line)*; still open.

ERIDGE [LBSC]
op 3 August 1868 *(T 4th)*; still open.

ERITH [SE] op 30 July 1849**; still open.

ERROL [Cal] op 24 May 1847 *(Perthshire Courier 27th)*; clo 28 September 1985 (Saturday) *(BLN 522)*; used by special trains one day a year from 1992 – e.g. 3 October 1993 *(BLN 716)*.

ERWOOD [Cam]
op 21 September 1864 *(D&C 11; co n Hereford J 24th- line)*; clo 31 December 1962 *(T 31st)*.

ERYHOLME [NE]
op 10 September 1846 *(co n Catterick)* as DALTON; renamed 1 May 1901 *(hbl 25 April)*; clo 1 October 1911 (Sunday) *(RCG)*; LNE NE Area wtts show Monday, Thursday, Friday and Saturday stops by Richmond branch trains for railwaymen; reopened for Air Force Base use (authorised by LNE Emergency Board 17 February 1944 – *RAIL 390/1872*); winter 1945/6 wtt showed additional calls for RAF personnel only; BR NER wtts 12 June 1961 and 11 September 1961 show stops both ways for railwaymen and families all days except Sundays (R. Maund); end of use by RAF and railwaymen ?; D JUNCTION in *Brad* until 1893/4 and NE ticket thus; {goods *1A*}.

ESCOMBE – see 1843**.

ESCRICK [NE]
op 2 January 1871 *(T 3rd)*; clo 8 June 1953 *(RM July)*.

ESGAIRGEILIOG [Corris] (ng)
For first service through here see 1874**.

ESGAIRGEILIOG first in *Brad* May 1884 (passed fit by BoT inspector on 6 March 1884); clo 1 January 1931 (Thursday) *(Cl)*.

ESHER [LSW]
op 21 May 1838 *(Salisbury 28th)*; still open.
First in *Brad* as E & HAMPTON COURT, but DITTON MARSH in opening notice in *T 16th*; renamed E & CLAREMONT 1844 tt *(Cl)*, E for C 1912/3 *(RCG ref Oct. 1912)* (and thus LSW co tt 1914), E for SANDOWN PARK 1934 *(SR App)*, E 13 June 1955 *(SR App)*. Initially, *Freeling* had DITTON MARSH in line description, E & H C in fare table.
20 April 1882 platforms were added immediately west of main station for racegoers returning from Sandown Park to London *(S Spec; AB)*; clo 18 October 1965 *(U)*.

ESHOLT [Mid] op 4 December 1876 *(Mid)*; clo 28 October 1940 *(LNW Record)*.

ESKBANK & DALKEITH [NB] first in tt July 1849 *(Topham)* as GALLOWSHALL; renamed G E, then E 1850 tt *(Cl)*, E & D 1951/2 *(Brad)*; clo 6 January 1969 *(RM February)*.

ESKBRIDGE [NB] op 1 July 1874 *(Edin)*; clo 1 January 1917 *(RM February)*; reop 2 June 1919 *(RCH)*; clo 22 September 1930 *(Cl)*. Early ESK BRIDGE *(hb)*, E JUNCTION *(Brad)*.

ESKDALE GREEN [Raven] (ng) op 20 November 1876 *(Raven; co annual report T 26 March 1877- line)*; clo 1 December 1908** (Tuesday), reop 27 March 1916 *(Cl)*; see 1960**.

ESKETT [WCE Jt]: op 1 February 1864**; for clo see 1874 June**; {map 22}.

ESKMEALS [Fur]
op 8 July 1850**; clo 3 August 1959 *(RM August)*.

ESPLANADE – see under DUNDEE.

ESSENDINE [GN]
op 15 July 1852**; clo 15 June 1959 *(RM July)*.

ESSEX ROAD

ESSEX ROAD (a) [Met GNC] op 14 February 1904 *(L)*; CANONBURY & E R 20 July 1922 *(Cl; hbl ref*

25 Jan. 1923) to 11 July 1948 *(Cl)*; clo 5 October 1975
(Sunday) for reconstruction *(T 30 August)* >
ESSEX ROAD (b) [BR] op 16 August 1976 *(T 16th)*;
still open.
ESSLEMONT [GNS] op 18 July 1861 *(GNS)*;
clo 15 September 1952 *(RM October)*.
ESTON {map 43}
ESTON [NE], on main line, first in *Brad* June 1853,
though it was only 19 June 1857 that platforms were
reported completed *(RAIL 667/62)*; perhaps re-sited
1864/5 (tenders for new station 'near the junction'
accepted 16 November 1864 – *RAIL 667/105*);
was SOUTHBANK/SOUTH BANK 1 December 1877
(LNW circ 672) to 1 May 1882 *(Cl; RCG ref April)*;
clo 22 November 1885 (Sunday) *(Cl)*, when replaced
by E Grange, later renamed Grangetown.
ESTON [NE], on branch, op 1 January 1902 *(RCG)*;
clo 11 March 1929 *(Cl)*.
E GRANGE – see GRANGETOWN.
E MINES: on private line from Eston Junction, on main
line, to Eston Depot of Bolckow Vaughan; agreement
for workmen's service reached 17 February 1851,
operated by S&D for 10/- per day. Market trips to
Middlesbrough on Saturdays first agreed 10 May 1852;
probably occasional break in service; at times ran to
'top' of BV's line, at times to junction only; if latter,
firm took over for rest of way, using own engines and
carriages borrowed from NE. Initiative originally from
Middlesbrough tradespeople, who paid S&D 13/- per
week for running train (S&D got fares as well); when
they pulled out in November 1853, fare raised from 3d
to 4d (S&D minutes; *S&D Pass*). This service appeared
in *Brad* from December 1870 to February 1873
(inclusive), Saturdays only. In *hb* 1872 (facilities?),
1877 and 1880 ('P' only); not 1890.
ETCHINGHAM [SE] first in *Brad* November 1851;
still open.
ETHERLEY [NE]: line op early 1844 (see 1843★★,
reference to Crook), originally market days only;
first firm evidence for existence in company minutes
15 April 1847 (alterations to existing station), first tt
evidence September 1847 co tt. Re-sited by 16 October
1867, when considering conversion of old station into
cottages *(RAIL 667/76)*; first edition OS 6 inch map
shows station 20 chains further from Bishop Auckland
than later site (S. Bragg). Clo 8 March 1965 *(RM April)*;
later use as Witton Park. E & WITTON PARK in *Brad*
1852 to 1879/80 and co tt ? to 1 July 1871 *(JS)*.
ETRURIA [NS]
op 9 October 1848 *(co ½ T 3 February 1849- line)*;
original station north of site of later Hanley Junction;
re-sited on south side of road bridge 2 August 1874
for safer public access to Hanley branch platform;
23 May 2004 tt reduced to service northbound
(replacement buses other way); clo 1 October 2005
(Saturday – last train Friday 30 September
(T 1 October; RM October p. 74). Used 20 July 2006
when overhead line problems meant passengers
alighted here and sent on to Crewe by road
(J. McCrickard, *Chron 50 p. 17*). NS co tt 1910 and
Brad 1887/9 to 1922/3: E for BASFORD.

ETTERIDGE CROSSING [High] (non-tt):
Perhaps 'halt' here in early days (line op 1863)
– oral family evidence but no documentary support
(Highland Railway Society Journal, Spring 2003, pp. 14–15).
See 1957★★; {Dalwhinnie – Newtonmore}.
ETTINGSHALL ROAD & BILSTON [LNW]
op 1 July 1852 *(W Mid; T 2nd- line)*; clo 15 June 1964
(RM July). In *hb* 1862 (only) as E & B.
ETTINGTON [SMJ] op 1 July 1873 *(Stratford 4th)*;
clo 1 August 1877 (Wednesday), reop 2 March 1885★★;
clo 7 April 1952 *(RM May)*. Originally to be Eatington
(as village name then spelled) but railway used spelling
that fitted local pronunciation; *Stratford* journalist much
piqued by this. Became E for WELLESBOURNE
according to *hb* 1910a and thus *LMS list* 1933, but not
LMS tt 1930.
ETWALL [GN] op 1 April 1878 *(GN)*; lost trains
with start of LNE emergency tt 2 October 1939;
excursions to at least 11 August 1961 *(BR handbill)*.
EUSTON
E main – see under LONDON.
EUSTON [Nor] City line platforms op 12 May 1907
(L); see 1922★★; still open.
EUSTON [Nor] Charing Cross line platforms op
22 June 1907★★; still in use.
EUSTON [Vic] op 1 December 1968 *(T 2nd)*; still open.
E ROAD – see WARREN STREET.
E SQUARE [Met] op 10 January 1863 *(co n Portfolio)*
as GOWER STREET; renamed 1 November 1909
(RCG); still open.
EUXTON
EUXTON [LNW] op 31 October 1838 *(co n Manch G
27th)*. Opening notice calls it E LANE; it and Wigan
were only intermediate stops for fast trains when stretch
to Preston opened. Clo 2 September 1895 *(RCG)* –
replaced by Balshaw Lane & E, ¾ mile south.
First in *Brad* as E LODGE; E by time details regularly
given there, also thus *Robinson* 1841.
EUXTON [LY] op 22 June 1843 *(Rtn- line)*; clo 2 April
1917 *(Cl)*. According to *RCH dist 15 December 1911* it
had at some point been renamed from E JUNCTION
but not seen thus *Brad*.
E BALSHAW LANE op 15 December 1997
(BLN 814); still open.
EVANTON [High] op 23 March 1863 *(High)* as NOVAR;
renamed 1 June 1937 *(Cl)*; clo 13 June 1960 *(RM July)*.
EVENWOOD {map 31}
See 1834 March 24★★ for earliest service here.
EVENWOOD [NE] op 13 October 1858★★; original
station on Lands branch; continued to be served by
latter's trains after Barnard Castle line opened, until
re-sited on new line May 1864 *Brad*; clo 14 October
1957 *(RM Dec.)*.
Hb 1912 showed 'P' against PIT CLOSE COLLIERY;
presumed misprint, deleted *hb* 1916a.
EVERCREECH [SD Jt]
E JUNCTION op 3 February 1862★★; JUNCTION
added 20 July 1874 *(Cl)*; clo 7 March 1966 *(Shepton
11th)*. E for DITCHEAT in op tt *Shepton*;
E J for CASTLE CARY in Mid co tt 1894, and thus
Brad ? to 1955.

E NEW op 20 July 1874 *(Shepton 24th)*;
clo 7 March 1966 *(Shepton 11th)*.
Originally E VILLAGE in *Brad*, altered September 1874;
E NEW VILLAGE in *hb* 1875a.

EVERINGHAM [NE]: line op 1 August 1848★★;
station op as HARSWELL GATE, Tuesdays only;
full use November 1851 *Brad*; renamed 1 September
1874 *(RCG)*; clo 20 September 1954 *(RM October)*.

EVERSHOT [GW] op 20 January 1857 *(W Fly P 27th)*;
became HALT 7 September 1964; clo 3 October 1966
(W D Press 3rd). EVERSHOTT in GW co tt 1859, but
not seen thus *Brad*.

EVESHAM

EVESHAM [GW] op 3 May 1852★★; still open.

EVESHAM [Mid] op 1 October 1864 *(Worcester 8th)*;
clo 17 June 1963 *(RM July)*.

EVESHAM ROAD CROSSING [GW]
op 17 October 1904 *(GW H)*; HALT; clo 14 July 1916
(Friday) *(RCH)*; {Milcote – Stratford-upon-Avon}.

EWELL near Epsom

E EAST [LBSC] op 10 May 1847 *(T 8th/Globe)*;
EAST added 9 July 1923 *(hbl 26 April)*; still open.
Was E for WORCESTER PARK 1871 to 1936/7
(Brad) and thus LBSC co tt 1912.

E WEST [LSW] op 4 April 1859 *(L; co n T 5th- line)*;
WEST added 9 July 1923 *(hbl 26 April)*; still open.

EWELL near Dover – see KEARSNEY.

EWESLEY [NB] op 1 November 1870 *(Nhumb)*;
HALT at clo 15 September 1952 *(RM October)*.

EWOOD BRIDGE & EDENFIELD [LY]
op 28 September 1846 *(LY; Rtn PP- line)*;
& EDENFIELD added 1891/2 *(Brad)*;
clo 5 June 1972 *(RM August)*.

EXETER

E CENTRAL [LSW] op 19 July 1860★★ as E QUEEN
STREET; renamed 1 July 1933 *(hbl July)*; still open.

E ST DAVIDS [GW] op 1 May 1844 *(Taunton 8th)*; still
open. St D added one table *Brad* 1854/6 but not in
S Devon opening notice 30 May 1846, B&E co tt 1877,
nor GW co tt until 1891/1902; *hb* 1862 had E in main
entry with cross-reference St Davids at Exeter,
1873 E St D.

E ST THOMAS [GW] op 30 May 1846 *(GW)*; initially
just St T or St T E; clo 2 April 1917 *(Trewman 31
March)*; reop 3 March 1919 *(GW circ 2653)*; still open.
Initially only available to/from stations on South Devon

line (to/from Plymouth): S Devon tt for November 1848
(Plymouth Reference Library) says no passenger can be
booked by down trains (westbound) to St T, nor by up
trains from it.

EXHIBITION – see EDINBURGH;
MANCHESTER ART TREASURES;
WEMBLEY; WHITE CITY.

EXHIBITION CENTRE Glasgow: op 5 November
1979 *(RM December)*, on site of earlier Stobcross;
op as FINNIESTON, renamed E C 1986; still open.

EXMINSTER [GW] probably op late August 1852
(Ex to NA), in tt 'corrected to 1 September 1852'
(Plymouth); clo 30 March 1964 *(Cl)*.

EXMOUTH [LSW]
op 1 May 1861 *(Trewman 1st, second edition)*;
re-sited just short of original, first used by first train
afternoon of 2 May 1976 *(RM August)*; still open.

EXNING ROAD [GE] op 20 November 1922
(RM April 1923); HALT; clo 18 June 1962 *(RM Aug.)*.

EXTON [LSW] op 1 May 1861 *(Trewman 1st, second
edition- line)* as WOODBURY ROAD;
renamed 15 September 1958 *(RM October)*;
HALT 28 February 1965 to 5 May 1969 *(Cl)*;
aot request; still open.

EYARTH [LNW] op 6 October 1864 *(D&C 11)*;
clo 2 February 1953 *(RM March)*.

EYDON ROAD [GC] op 1 September 1913
(GC dates); always HALT in *Brad* but PLATFORM *(hb)*;
clo 2 April 1956 *(RM May)*.

EYE [GE] op 2 April 1867 *(T 3rd)*;
clo 2 February 1931 *(RM March)*.

EYE GREEN [MGN] op 1 August 1866 *(Mid wtt
D&C 5)*; GREEN added 1 October 1875 *(RCG)*;
clo 2 Dec. 1957 *(Cl)*. Became E G for CROWLAND
1921/2? *(RCG ref January 1922)* and thus LMS tt
1930, LNE tt 1933 and *Brad* to closure.

EYEMOUTH [NB] op 13 April 1891 *(RCG)*;
clo 13 August 1948 by floods, reop 29 June 1949
(D. Lindsay, Chron); clo 5 February 1962 *(Cl)*.

EYNSFORD [LCD] op 1 July 1862 *(LCD)*; still open.
Originally in *Brad* and *hb* as EYNESFORD;
also ticket thus *(JB)*.

EYNSHAM [GW] op 14 November 1861 *(GW- line)*;
clo 18 June 1962 *(T 18 May)*.

EYTHORNE [EK] op 16 October 1916 *(co n EK)*;
clo 1 November 1948★★.

FACH GOCH – see 1950 October 6★★.

FACIT [LY]
op 1 November 1870 *(LY)*; clo 16 June 1947★★.

FAENOL BACH – see KINMEL CAMP.

FAILSWORTH [LY]
op 1 April 1881 *(Oldham E Stand 2nd)*; still open.

FAIRBOURNE [Cam] op 1 July 1897 *(RCG)*
on site of earlier Barmouth Ferry; still open.

FAIRFIELD near Buxton [LNW]
op 16 December 1907 *(?; first in Brad January 1908)*;
golfers, alighting, up side only; HALT at clo (and thus *hb*),
11 September 1939 *(LNW Record)*.
Photograph of one-sided station here, *LMS Magazine
January 1935*, p.37. In *Brad* 1909, LNW tt 1909 and
LMS tt 1930 as F for GOLF LINKS.

FAIRFIELD Manchester [GC]
op 17 November 1841 *(GC; Rtn- line)*;
re-sited 17 chains east 2 May 1892 *(GC dates)*; still open.
Became F for DROYLSDEN 1888? *(RCG ref April)*,
and thus in GC co tt 1903 and LNE tt 1933,
until 6 May 1974 *(BR notice)*.

FAIRFIELDS [Forth & Clyde] first in *Brad* June 1861;
SIDING, Fridays only; last October 1866 – *Cl* has
clo 20 October (Saturday) – would mean last train 19th;
{Port of Menteith – Kippen}.

FAIRFORD [GW] op 15 January 1873 *(Chelt Exp
18th)*; clo 18 June 1962 *(T 18 May)*.

FAIRLIE [GSW]
FAIRLIE op 1 June 1880 *(RCG)*; became F TOWN
30 June 1952, F HIGH 2 March 1953 *(Cl: RM ref
April)*, back to F 1968/1976 tt; still open.
F PIER op 1 July 1882 *(co ½ 1110/149)*;
last train 1 October 1971 (Thursday) *(D&D)*.

FAIRLOP op by [GE] 1 May 1903 *(RCG; co ½
T 21 July)*; last steam train ran Saturday 29 November
1947 *(Clay)*; buses until reop by [Cen] 31 May 1948
(T 1 June); still open.

FAIRWATER op 4 October 1987★★; still open.

FAKENHAM
F EAST [GE] op 20 March 1849 *(EC)*; EAST added
27 September 1948 *(RM November/December)*;
clo 5 October 1964 *(RM September)*.
F WEST [MGN] op 16 August 1880 *(E D Press 16th)*;
locally known as station 'at Hempton'; F TOWN until
1898/9 *(Brad)*, then F; WEST added 27 September
1948 *(RM Nov./Dec.)*; clo 2 March 1959 *(T 2nd)*.

FALCONWOOD [SR]
op 1 January 1936 *(SR sig inst 47/1935)*; still open.

FALKIRK {map 11}
CAMELON (a) [EG], on line via F High; first in *Brad*
November 1843; last October 1844.
F CAMELON (b) [NB], on line via F High,
op 15 June 1903 *(RCG)*; clo 1 January 1917 *(RM Feb.)*;
reop 1 February 1919 *(RM February)*; clo 4 September
1967 *(Cl)*. Layout of *hb* such that impossible to decide
whether it was regarded as F C or C F.
CAMELON (c) op 25 September 1994 *(BLN 738)*,
at/near site of (b); still open.
F GRAHAMSTON [NB] op 1 October 1850 *(James)*;
still open. Variously and erratically F, F G and G F in
Brad until became F G 1 February 1903 *(hbl 29 Jan.)* –

e.g. in January 1870 F G to Perth, G to Grangemouth.
In NB co tt 1900 as F (G).
F HIGH [NB] op 21 February 1842 *(co n T 19th)*;
HIGH added 1 February 1903 *(hbl 29 January)*;
clo 9 March 1980 for tunnel repairs, reop 8 December
1980 *(RM February 1981)*; still open.

FALKLAND ROAD [NB]: op 20 September 1847★★;
clo 15 September 1958 *(RM October)*; perhaps opened
as NEW INN.

FALLGATE [Ashover] (ng) op 7 April 1925 *(RM
October)*; clo 14 September 1936★★ *(Cl)*; {map 59}.

FALLODON [NE] (non-tt): built for Earl Grey; op ?
(line op 1 July 1847); used 30 July 1930 for excursion
to Liberal Association Garden Party *(LNE notice,
Nhumb Young)*; clo about 1935 *(U)*;
FALLODEN 'P' in *hb* from 1895; 1912 'private' added;
1926a 'read FALLODON'; same 1938; absent 1956;
{Chathill – Christon Bank}.

FALLOWFIELD [GC] op 1 October 1891 *(RCG)*;
clo 7 July 1958 *(LNW Record)*. Became F for
WITHINGTON and DIDSBURY 1 November 1910
(RCG); thus LNE tt 1933 and *Brad* to closure.

FALLS OF CRUACHAN
FALLS OF CRUACHAN (a) [Cal] used, non-tt, by
sightseers from 1 October 1893 *(Callander)*; first in
Brad July 1908; summers only; clo end summer 1965
(based on *Cl* – clo 1 November 1965).
It had an erratic existence – possibly non-tt use in
addition to dates given. Probably closed during WWI –
not included in *Brad* July 1919; September 1920 shows
service from Oban only; August 1921 both ways.
LMS co tt 30 September 1935: served by Saturdays
only 9.35pm from Oban and 11.25pm to Oban
(sightseers??). Probably closed during WWII – not
present *Brad* June 1941 or July 1945 (nor LMS tt
7 May 1945); August 1946, one train from Oban
1 June to 28 September inclusive; not present August
1948; August 1950 indexed but not in body of book;
not present, BR (Scot) tt 25 September 1950; August
1951 *Brad* Saturdays only and thus e.g. 30 June 1952
and 17 June 1963. In 15 September 1952 wtt shown as
stop alternate Saturdays for railwaymen's wives (was this
the usual winter service?). HALT according to *hb*;
ticket as PLATFORM *(JB)*; in *Brad* in notes so
perhaps inferior status taken for granted.
FALLS OF CRUACHAN (b) op 20 June 1988
(R. Hamilton, *True Line, April 2003, p.37)*; summers
only; still open.

FALLSIDE [Cal] first in *Brad* August 1872;
clo 1 January 1917 *(RM February)*, reop 1 May 1919
(RCH); clo 3 August 1953 *(RM September)*.

FALMER [LBSC]
op 8 June 1846 *(LBSC; Hants Chron 13th- line)*;
re-sited about ½ mile west 1 August 1865 *(Cl)*; still open.

FALMOUTH

F DOCKS [GW] op 24 August 1863 *(R Cornwall Gaz 28th)* as F; clo 7 December 1970, when line cut back to new terminus (below); reop 5 May 1975 *(RM June)*, still F; DOCKS added October 1988 tt; still open.

F TOWN op 7 December 1970 *(RM February 1971)* as F, 42 chains nearer Truro than above; renamed THE DELL when original station reop, F TOWN October 1988 tt; still open.

FALSTONE [NB] op 2 September 1861 *(NC)*; clo 15 October 1956** *(T 21 September)*.

FAMBRIDGE – see NORTH FAMBRIDGE.

FANGFOSS [NE]: line op 4 October 1847**, nd, May 1848 *(Topham)*; clo 5 January 1959 *(RM Feb.)*.

FAREHAM [LSW] op 29 November 1841** *(SR; Salisbury 6 December- line)*; still open. F JUNCTION in *Brad* until 1853.

FARINGDON near Oxford [GW] op 1 June 1864 *(co n T 30 May)*; clo 31 December 1951 *(RM March 1952)*. FARRINGDON in *hb* until 1879a.

FARINGDON ROAD – see CHALLOW.

FARINGTON near Preston [NU]

FARINGTON op 31 October 1838 *(LY; co n Manch G 27th- line)*; FARRINGTON LODGE in *Brad* 1839, then often FARRINGTON, standardised *Brad* 1850s, *hb* 1879a; clo 7 March 1960 *(RM April)*.

F MILL – see BASHALL & CO's SIDING.

FARLEY [GW] op 24 October 1934 *(T 20th)* *; HALT; clo 23 July 1962 *(RM August)*.

* = *Cl 29* and *GW H* say op 27th – perhaps last minute delay? / *T* error? – *T* clearly said would open 'next Wednesday' but 27th, a Saturday, much more in accordance with practice in this area.

FARLINGTON [LBSC] op 26 June 1891 as F RACE STATION *(RCG)*; alias PORTSMOUTH R S (served Portsmouth Park Racecourse) *(U)*; out of use between 28 June 1894 and 25 April 1899, when no races were held here *(AB)*; in *hb* 1904 and 1912 'P'; closed for races 1914; racecourse became ammunition dump and station used by workmen 14 August 1914 to 1917 and 1922 to 1927 *(U)*; reop, now public, 17 June 1928 *(T 23 April)* as F HALT; clo 4 July 1937 (Sunday) *(RM June)*.

FARNBOROUGH

F MAIN [LSW] op 24 September 1838 *(co n T 20th)*; MAIN added 12 May 1980 tt *(Cl)*; still open. *Brad* 1859: F for ALDERSHOT.

F NORTH [SE] op 4 July 1849 *(Hants Chron 7th)*; NORTH added 9 July 1923 *(hbl 26 April)*; still open. *Brad* 1849: F for FRIMLEY. SR tt 1947 F N for FRIMLEY.

FARNCOMBE [LSW] op 1 May 1897 *(RCG)*; replaced Godalming Old; still open.

FARNELL ROAD [Cal]: line op 1 February 1848 *(co n RM February 1953)*, nd, May 1848 *(Topham)*; clo 11 June 1956 *(RM April)*.

FARNHAM [LSW] op 8 October 1849 *(Hants Chron 13th)*; still open.

FARNINGHAM HOME FOR LITTLE BOYS [LCD] (non-tt): first used 11 October 1870; clo ? (demolished 1939); {Farningham Road – Fawkham} *(RM June 1962 p.441)*.

FARNINGHAM ROAD [LCD]

op 3 Dec 1860 *(T 4th & 7th)* as F; became F & SUTTON-AT-HONE 1 April 1861, back to F 1 August 1861, to F R 1869 tt, F & S-at-H 1872 *(Cl)*; settled as F R 5 May 1975 in body of tt (but index later); still open.

FARNLEY & WORTLEY [LNW]

WORTLEY op 5 October 1848 *(D&C 8)*; renamed W & FARNLEY 1 February 1877 *(RCG)*; replaced by >
New station op 1 March 1882 *(LNW Officers 23189)*, as W & F; renamed F & W 1891 tt *(JS; RCG ref April)*; clo 3 November 1952, but facilities kept for incoming Leeds United fans *(RM December)*, until ?; still used by a few stopping trains to pick up/set down railway workmen *(Rly Obs October 1960, p.317)*; {map 56}.

FARNSFIELD [Mid] op 3 April 1871 *(Mid)*; clo 12 August 1929 *(T 13th)*; later excur *(U)*.

FARNWORTH near Bolton [LY]

Line op 29 May 1838**; this station was in local press tt for 11 June 1838 cited by *Bolton*; not in *Brad* 19 October 1839; present by October 1845 as HALSHAW MOOR; early indiscriminately TUNNEL, F, H M and various combinations; F & H M from 1870 tt to 6 May 1974 *(BR notice)*; still open.

N.b. at the end of 1845 stations named Farnworth and Halshaw Moor were open together.

See MOSES GATE for the other Farnworth.

FARNWORTH near Widnes

F & BOLD [LNW]: for line op see 1832 B**, nd, June 1852; & BOLD added 1 February 1890 *(hbl 24 April)*; clo 18 June 1951 *(RM August)*. Also see WIDNES.

FARRINGDON near Alton [SR]

op 15 May 1931 *(Cl 29)*; FARINGDON PLATFORM until 8 July 1934 *(JS)*; HALT 1938 *hb*, but not *Brad*; clo 7 February 1955 *(Hants Chron 12th)*.

FARRINGDON London [Met]

op 10 January 1863 *(co n Portfolio)* as F STREET; new station op 23 December 1865, though old did not clo until 1 March 1866 when widened lines platforms op *(L)*; became F & HIGH HOLBORN 26 January 1922 *(L; hbl ref 25 January 1923)*, F 21 April 1936 *(L; hbl ref May)*; still open. F STREET OR CITY in *hb* 1863a (only).

FARRINGTON GURNEY [GW]

op 11 July 1927 *(co n W D Press 9th)*; HALT; clo 2 November 1959 *(Shepton 6th)*.

FARTHINGHOE [LNW]

first in *Brad* October 1851; clo 3 November 1952 *(Cl)*.

FARWORTH: see 1835 B**.

FASLANE [LNE] (non-tt): PLATFORM; workmen on Loch Sloy HEP scheme; op 26 August 1945; clo later 1940s; {Rhu – Shandon} *(U)*.

FAULDHOUSE [Cal]

op 9 July 1869 *(Edin; T 12th- line)*; F NORTH 3 March 1952 to 7 May 1973 *(Cl)*; still open.

FAULDHOUSE & CROFTHEAD [NB]

op 2 June 1845**; last in *Brad* April 1848 (but see 1848**); back August 1850; last December 1852; reop 1 October 1864 *(Cl)*; op as C, became C for F 1 June 1899 *(hbl 13 July)*, F & C 1 September 1906 *(hbl 25 October)*; clo 1 May 1930 (Thursday) *(Cl)*.

FAVERSHAM [LCD]
op 25 January 1858**; still open.

FAWDON [TWM] op 10 May 1981 *(Tyneside)*;
at/near earlier Coxlodge; still open.

FAWKHAM (ROAD) – see LONGFIELD.

FAWLEY near Hereford [GW]
op 1 June 1855**; clo 2 November 1964 *(Cl)*.

FAWLEY near Southampton [SR] op 20 July 1925
(T 20th); clo 14 February 1966 *(RM February)* – last
train Friday, 11th. F HANTS until 1955 *(Brad)* but
not treated as part of name in *hb* 1938; {map 128}.

FAYGATE [LBSC]
op 14 February 1848 *(Hants Chron 12th)*;
FAY GATE until 5 December 1953 *(Cl)*; still open.

FAZAKERLEY [LY] op 20 November 1848
(LY; co n Manch G 18th- line); works in print say op as
SIMONSTONE; was AINTREE when first in *Brad*
December 1850; renamed F 1860 *(Brad)*; still open.

FEARN [High] op 1 June 1864 *(High)*; still open.

FEATHERSTONE
FEATHERSTONE (a) [LY] op 1 April 1848 *(LY;
co ½ T 7 September- line)*; clo 2 January 1967 *(Cl)*;
used by rugby supporters at least until May 1975 *(U)*.
FEATHERSTONE (b) op 11 May 1992 *(RM June)*;
still open.

FEATHERSTONE PARK [NE]
op 19 July 1851 *(NC)*; PARK added 1 January 1902
(hbl 23rd); clo 3 May 1976 *(RM May)*.
Became HALT in *Brad* 1933/4 until 1936/7; not thus
in *hb* 1938; perhaps also halt of sorts later – note added
Brad 1960 that was unstaffed (see COANWOOD).

FEERING [LNE] op 1 January 1934 (P. Paye,
The Tollesbury Branch, OPC, 1985); HALT;
clo 7 May 1951 *(T 8th)*; {Kelvedon – Inworth}.

FELIN FACH [GW] op 12 May 1911 *(co n Lampeter)*
as YSTRAD CARDIGANSHIRE; renamed 1 January
1913 *(hbl 23rd, which gave previous name as Y)*;
clo 12 February 1951 *(Cl)* – see 1951**.

FELIN FOEL – see 1887**.

FELIN FRAN [GW] op 2 January 1922 *(GW H)*;
HALT; clo 11 June 1956 *(T 8th)*.

FELIN HEN [LNW] op 1 July 1884 *(D&C 11;
LNW Officers 26999- line)*; became HALT 1939
(Brad); clo 3 December 1951 *(RM January 1952)*.

FELINDYFFRYN [GW] op 10 June 1935 *(Cl 29)*;
HALT; clo 14 December 1964**.

FELIXSTOWE [GE] {map 71}
FELIXSTOWE op 1 July 1898 *(T 2nd)* as F TOWN;
TOWN dropped 20 February 1969 *(Cl)*; still open.
F BEACH op 1 May 1877 *(GE; first in Brad June)*;
in *Brad* as F TOWN; became F BEACH 1 July 1898
(RCG); summers only from 2 November 1959 (also
used for a few Sundays either side of strict summer tt);
clo 11 September 1967 *(Cl)*.
F PIER first in *Brad* July 1877*; clo 11 September
1939, reop 3 June 1946 *(RM November)*;
clo 2 July 1951 *(RM August)*.
* = inspection report for line, dated 28 April, says extension
to Pier incomplete; that saying extension satisfactory dated
8 June (both *MT 29/38*).

For brief period mid-1930s shuttle operated between wooden
platform south of station level-crossing and PIER (R. Adderson
& G. Kenworthy, *Branch Lines to Felixstowe and Aldeburgh*,
Middleton, 2003).

FELLGATE [TWM]
op 31 March 2002 *(Rly Obs May)*; still open.

FELLING
FELLING [NE]: line op 5 September 1839 *(Newcastle
Journal 7th)*, nd, February 1843*; re-sited west
18 November 1896 *(Cl)*; clo 5 November 1979 *(Cl)* for
conversion >
FELLING [TWM] op 15 November 1981 *(Tyneside)*;
still open.
* = *T 27 February 1843* referred to attempt at derailing train
near Parkhouse, between Gateshead and 'Felton' station,
presumably this one, but not in *Brad* until September 1856.

FELMINGHAM [MGN] op 5 April 1883 *(MGN;
T 9th- line)*; clo 2 March 1959 *(T 2nd)*.

FELSTED [GE] op 22 February 1869 *(GE- line;
MT 6/56/8)*; FELSTEAD until 5 June 1950 *(Cl)*;
clo 3 March 1952 *(RM April)*; last excursion Bank
Holiday Monday 1964 *(Bishops Stortford)*.
LNE tt 1933: FELSTEAD for LITTLE DUNMOW
and thus *Brad* to 1950.

FELTHAM [LSW]
op 22 August 1848 *(T 24 July, co n T 21 Aug.)*; still open.

FEN DITTON [GE]
op 20 November 1922 *(RM April 1923)*; HALT;
clo 18 June 1962 *(RM August)*; {Barnwell – Quy}.

FENAY BRIDGE & LEPTON [LNW]
op 7 October 1867 *(Huddersfield 12th)*; & L added
1 September 1897 *(RCG)*; clo 28 July 1930 *(Cl)*.

FENCEHOUSES [NE]: line op 9 March 1840
(NE maps), nd, about August 1841 *(Robinson)*;
sometimes FENCE HOUSES early (NE wtt 1861 two
words in main table, one in branch); clo 4 May 1964 *(Cl)*.

FENCHURCH STREET – see LONDON.

FENCOTE [GW]
op 1 September 1897 *(co n Ephemera)*;
clo 15 September 1952 *(RM November)*.

FENISCOWLES [LY/LU]
op 1 December 1869**; clo 4 January 1960 *(RM Feb.)*.
In *Brad* as above in LY tables but FENNISCOWLES
in LNW tables until 1872 and LNW ticket thus *(JB)*.
In LNW co tt to FENISCOWLES in index 1875/82,
but body 1891/1900.

FENITON [LSW]
op 19 July 1860** as F; renamed OTTERY ROAD
1 July 1861 *(Cl)*, OTTERY ST MARY February 1868
tt *(JS)*, O R & F April 1868 tt *(JS)*, SIDMOUTH
JUNCTION 6 July 1874 *(Cl)*; clo 6 March 1967,
still S J *(Express & E 6th)*; reop 3 May 1971 *(RM March)*
as F; still open. 1867 *hb*: entries for F and O R.

FENNANT ROAD [GW] first in *Brad* October 1907;
HALT; clo 22 March 1915**; {map 75}.

FENNS BANK [Cam] op 4 May 1863 *(Oswestry 6th)*;
clo 18 January 1965 *(RM March)*.

FENNY COMPTON
FENNY COMPTON [GW] op 1 October 1852 *(GW;
T 27 September- line; in inspection report)*;
clo 2 November 1964 *(BRWR circular 12 October)*.

FENNY COMPTON [SMJ]: line op 5 June 1871
(Oxford Chron 10th); probably op own station 1 July
1873, with next stretch of line★; clo 1 August 1877 (Wed.)
(Cl); reop 2 March 1885★★; clo 7 April 1952 *(Cl)*.
According to *Cl* this was F C WEST but not seen thus
Brad or *hb*.
★ = according to *Brad Sh 1874*, line up to GW station; *Oxford
Chron* did not specify this but did say op in connection with
GW trains there; *hb* does not give separate SMJ reference until
hb 1874/5a. Stratford 16 June 1871 said Joint station to be built
(never was), implying temporary arrangement.

FENNY STRATFORD [LNW]
op 18 November 1846★★- line; still open.

FENTON [NS]
FENTON op 1 August 1864 *(NS-K)*; re-sited slightly
nearer Stoke-on-Trent 31 October 1906 *(Cl)*;
clo 6 February 1961 *(Cl)*: later wakes week use, last
probably 11 August 1962 – not mentioned in 1963
leaflet *(AB)*.
F MANOR first in *Brad* October 1889; clo 7 May 1956
but still available for excursions *(RM June)*.

FERGUSLIE [Cal] (non-tt): excursion station near
Paisley St James *(U)*; shown 'P' in 1890 *hb*, amended to
goods only in appendix 1891/2.

FERNDALE [TV] op as private station for D. Davis &
Sons in 1868; they ran train for own employees and at
one stage allowed public use but stopped this when
local population grew and there was a danger of their
own workers being crowded out; then public used
guards vans on mineral trains until the antics of a drunk
stopped that; clo 13 March 1875; op to public 5 June
1876 *(Cardiff T 10th)*; clo 15 June 1964 *(RM August)*.

FERNHILL op 3 October 1988 *(Aberdare)*,
free publicity service on 2nd; still open.

FERNHILL COLLIERY [TV] (non-tt): miners;
1875 to ?; {beyond Treherbert} *(U)*.

FERNHILL HEATH [GW] op 18 February 1852
(Rtn- line) ★ as FEARNALL H; renamed 1 July 1883
(RCH dist 31 December); clo 5 April 1965 *(Cl)*.
Brad at first FEARNEL H some tables.
★ = inspection report 15 January said 'Fernal Heath' was not
to be used for present but re-inspection necessary so would
have been able to open with line – in *Brad* March.

FERNIEGAIR [Cal] op 1 December 1866 *(Cal)* as
northern terminus of line detached from system, coach
connection to Hamilton; linked to system 1 April 1868
by line via Motherwell Bridge (which see); link diverted
to Hamilton 2 October 1876, with new station at F;
clo 1 January 1917 *(Cal wtt 11 July 1921)*; {map 16}.
See CHATELHERAULT for later station nearby.

FERRIBY [NE] op 2 July 1840 *(Hull 10th)*; still open.

FERRY near Chichester [WS]
op 1 August 1898 *(D&C 2)*; F SIDING until 1911
(Brad); clo 20 January 1935★★.

FERRY near Wisbech [MGN]
op 1 August 1866 *(Mid op working tt D&C 5)*;
clo 2 March 1959 *(T 2nd)*; {map 66}.

FERRYBRIDGE [SK] op 1 May 1882 *(RCG)*;
clo 13 September 1965 *(T 4th)*. For a long time
indiscriminately FERRY BRIDGE/F B JUNCTION;
to F for KNOTTINGLEY 1 June 1901 *(hbl 11 July)*,

and thus LNE tt 1933, *hb* 1938, and *Brad* to 1955.

FERRYHILL
Two companies' services ran through here; not known
if separate stations; both later [NE].
[Clarence] – see 1835 A★★; first *Brad* evidence
November 1844.
[York, Newcastle & Berwick] service began 19 June 1844
(co n T 24 May- line); clo 6 March 1967 *(RM March)*.
Early indiscriminately FERRY HILL/F H JUNCTION.

FERRYHILL – see ABERDEEN.

FERRYPORT-ON-CRAIG – see TAYPORT.

FERRYSIDE [GW] op 11 October 1852 *(T 12th- line)*;
aot request; still open.

FERSIT [LNE] op 1 August 1931 *(Cl 29)*; HALT;
clo 31 December 1934 *(Cl)*; {Tulloch – Corrour}.

FESTINIOG {map 78}
FESTINIOG [Festiniog & Blaenau] (ng) op from north
30 May 1868★★; last train 5 September 1883.
FESTINIOG [GW] op from south 1 November 1882
(GW); clo 4 January 1960 *(RM March)*.
This was standard gauge replacement for the above but
for a while both stations open together, as termini of
separate services. Through service to north began
10 September 1883.

FFAIRFACH [GW] op 26 January 1857 *(Carmarthen
23rd)*; HALT from 1 May 1961 *(RM June)* to 5 May
1969 *(Cl)*; aot request; still open.

FFOCHRIEW PITS [GW/Rhy] (non-tt):
alias FOCHRIW PITS/COLLIERY; used at least 1897
to 1928 by miners; {branch from Cwm Bargoed} *(U)*.

FFRIDD GATE [Corris] (ng)
For first service through here, see 1874★★.
FFRIDD GATE first in *Brad* July 1887; aot request;
clo 1 January 1931 (Thursday) *(Cl)*.

FFRITH [Wrexham & Minera Joint] op 2 May 1898
(Wrexham 7th); clo 27 March 1950 *(RM May)*.

FFRONFRAITH – see FRONFRAITH.

FIDLERS FERRY & PENKETH [LNW]
op 1 February 1853 *(T 16th- line)* as FIDLERS F;
& PENKETH added 1864 tt *(JS)*;
became FIDDLERS F & P 1881 tt *(JS)*,
FIDLERS F & P 26 January 1921 *(LNW dates)*;
clo 2 January 1950 *(LNW Record)*.
LNW dates contains letter from the Clerk to Penketh
Parish Council, dated 4 December 1920: Fidlers Ferry
seems to have derived name from a tenant of Ferry
Tavern. No record of ferry being used by a Fiddler or
Fiddlers [should that be a *fiddler* …?]. In all books
belonging to Parish of Penketh it is 'Fidlers Ferry'.
P.S. John Fidler was tenant of Ferry Hotel 1794–1802.

FIGHTING COCKS [NE]: line opened 10 October
1825 (see 1825★★), nd; in *Whishaw* 1840 and *Robinson*
(notes) about August 1841, as F C, and thus in report
of accident 25 June 1842; first in *Brad* November 1846,
as MIDDLETON & DINSDALE; renamed F C
1 September 1866 *(Cl)*; clo 1 July 1887 *(Cl)*,
replaced by Dinsdale on deviation; {map 36}.

FILEY
FILEY [NE] op 7 October 1846★★; still open.
F HOLIDAY CAMP [LNE]: Perhaps use by general
public towards end of 1946 season (November) –

certainly intention, and by special train Monday
21 October 1946 provided by Sir Billy Butlin for guests
at opera put on at camp. Certainly used by campers
3 May 1947 (10 May delayed formal opening).
Generally Saturdays only during season, but experimental
Wednesday service, locally advertised, ran to/from Hull
21 July to 25 August 1976 (Butlin's).
Road train to Butlin's via private subway.
Last train Saturday 17 September 1977 (Cl).

FILLEIGH [GW]
op 1 November 1873 (W Som F P 1st, 8th) as
CASTLE HILL; renamed 1 January 1881 (Cl;
RCG ref January); clo 3 October 1966 (Som Gaz 7th).

FILTON {map 131}
FILTON [GW] op 8 September 1863 (co n W D Press
7th); re-sited slightly north 4 October 1886;
F JUNCTION 1 May 1910 (Cl) to 6 May 1968 tt;
effectively replaced by F Abbey Wood but retained
token service, Sats only, until last train 31 May 1997.
F ABBEY WOOD op 11 March 1996 (Bristol E P
11th); still open.
F HALT [GW] op 9 May 1910 (W D Press 10th);
clo 22 March 1915 (RCH); workmen's use continued
(GM's report 12 January 1917); until ?
Also see NORTH FILTON (later on site used by F Halt).
FIMBER – see SLEDMERE.

FINCHLEY
F CENTRAL op by [GN] 22 August 1867 (L; co n
T 22nd- line) as F & HENDON; renamed F 1 February
1872 (Cl; RCG ref January), F CHURCH END 1 Feb.
1894 (hbl 26 April); F C 1 April 1940 (hbl March);
transferred to [Nor] 14 April 1940; still open.
Also see EAST FINCHLEY; WEST FINCHLEY.

FINCHLEY ROAD
FINCHLEY ROAD op by [Met] 30 June 1879 (T 3 July);
aot alias F R SOUTH HAMPSTEAD (ug, but not
seen thus Brad). [Bak] added 20 November 1939
(T 18th); transferred to [Jub] 1 May 1979. Still open.
FINCHLEY ROAD [Mid] op 13 July 1868 (T 14th)
as F R & ST JOHNS WOOD; renamed 1 September
1868 wtt (Mid); re-sited on new passenger lines
3 February 1884 (Mid); clo 11 July 1927 (Mid)
F R & FROGNAL [LNW] op 2 January 1860 (T 2nd);
& F added 1 October 1880 (L; LNW Officers
recommended 16 September); still open.
F R & F FOR ST JOHNS WOOD in Brad, but not any
other sources seen.
FINDHORN [High] op 18 April 1860 (Findhorn);
clo 1 February 1869 (Rtn); {map 3}.
FINDOCHTY [GNS] op 1 May 1886 (GNS);
clo 6 May 1968 (RM July).
FINEDON [Mid] first in Brad July 1857;
clo 2 December 1940 (LNW Record).
FINGASK [GNS] op by 2 September 1867 (GNS),
though not in Brad until July 1870; probably originally
MUIRTOWN (GNS); became F PLATFORM 1907/8,
F HALT 1924/5 (Brad); aot request;
clo 2 November 1931 (RM December).
FINGHALL LANE [NE]
op 19 May 1856 (RCG- line); clo 26 April 1954
(T 20th); occasional use 1984 to 1988 as F.

FINMERE [GC]
op 15 March 1899 (GC; T 16th- line); became
F for BUCKINGHAM 1 July 1899 (hbl 27 April) and
thus GC co tt 1903; reverted to F 1913/14? (RCG ref
January 1914); clo 4 March 1963 (RM March).

FINNIESTON
FINNIESTON [NB] op 15 March 1886 (Glas; co ½
T 19 March- line); clo 1 January 1917 (RM February).
At times GLASGOW F in tts.
Also see EXHIBITION CENTRE.
FINNINGHAM [GE] op 2 July 1849 (EC; T 5th- line) *;
clo 7 November 1966 (RM January 1967).
* = 7 June 1848 was goods opening (EC).
FINNINGLEY [GN/GE] op 15 July 1867 (GN/GE;
GN co ½ T 19 August- line); clo 11 September 1961
(RM September); later excur, royal trains (U).
Temporary platform here/near 19 September 1981,
RAF air display (RM September); used again as F HALT
for display 4 September 1982 (AB), and 17 September
1983 and, as F, 1 September 1984 (IU).

FINSBURY PARK
FINSBURY PARK [GN] op 1 July 1861 (co n dated
28 June) as SEVEN SISTERS ROAD; renamed
1869/70 (JS, L, Cl give different dates, 1 August 1869,
15 November 1869, 1 January 1870; there was an RCG
ref January 1870); still open. According to L and JS was
S S R HOLLOWAY until renaming but not seen thus
Brad (space?).
FINSBURY PARK [Met GNC] op 14 February 1904
(L); clo 4 October 1964 (Sunday) (RM October) >
Replaced by BR service, from Moorgate, which began
8 November 1976, using new tunnel and alignment to
ex-GN station; still open.
For reuse of tunnels see >
FINSBURY PARK [Picc] op 15 December 1906 (co n
T 14th); southbound line diverted through old Met
GNC northbound tunnel 3 October 1965 and own
southbound tunnel closed (but see next); still open.
FINSBURY PARK [Vic] op 1 September 1968 (T 2nd);
northbound platform was ealier Picc southbound,
southbound old Met GNC southbound; still open.
FINSTOCK [GW] op 9 April 1934 (co n, undated);
HALT until 5 May 1969 (GW H); closed for three weeks
during February 1993 for platform modifications
(RM May); aot request; still open.
FIRBECK COLLIERY [S Yorks Joint] (non-tt):
excursions from July 1929 (to Blackpool) until 1966
(S Yorks Joint); {branch from just south of Tickhill}.
FIRSBY [GN]
op 3 September 1848 (Boston 4th- line); clo 5 October
1970 (T 16 July). Op as F, SPILSBY & WAINFLEET
(at times in Brad as F, S &c); became F & S 1854/6,
F for S 1863/4, F 1868/9 (Brad).
FISHBOURNE SUSSEX [LBSC] op 1 April 1906
(LBSC); HALT until 5 May 1969 (SR App);
SUSSEX added body 1980 tt (index earlier); still open.
FISHERROW [NB]: for op see 1831 A**; clo ?;
replaced by Musselburgh, which op 14 July 1847;
{map 18}.
FISHERSGATE [LBSC] op 3 September 1905
(LBSC); HALT until 5 May 1969 (SR App); still open.

FISHGUARD [GW]

F & GOODWICK op 1 July 1899★ *(Carmarthen Weekly Reporter 7th)* as G; renamed 1 May 1904 *(hbl 29 April)*; clo 6 April 1964 *(Cl)*; workmen used to 3 August 1964 *(U)*. Motorail seasonal use 19 June 1965 to 16 Sept. 1972 (inclusive) *(BR publicity; wtts)*.

★ = J.P. Morris, *The North Pembroke & Fishguard Railway*, Oakwood, 1969 said op 1 August (1 July goods) but in a later book, *The Railways of Pembrokeshire*, H.G. Walters of Tenby, 1981, p.125, he says first passenger train left here 1 July, date used by most, but supporting detail is same as earlier work, only 10 passengers on it. Not in *Brad* until August; perhaps source of confusion.

F HARBOUR [GW] op 30 August 1906 *(T 31st)*; still open.

FISHPONDS [Mid]

FISHPONDS (a) first in *Brad* October 1849; Thursdays & Saturdays only; last there September 1850. Earlier use: schoolchildren's excursion picked up and set down here in September 1846 *(Gloucester Journal 12 September*, via J. Gough).

FISHPONDS (b) op by 21 March 1866 *(Clifton Chronicle of that date*, a Wednesday, 'Midland Railway has opened a station at Fishponds'); first in *Brad* April 1866 as STAPLETON; renamed FISH PONDS 1 January 1867 *(Mid)*, became one word 1910 *hb* appendix, but 1 May 1939 LMS tt *(C/W)*, though as late as 1959 *Brad* was using two-word form in one table, one-word form in another; clo 7 March 1966 *(Cl)*.

FISKERTON [Mid] op 4 August 1846 *(Mid)*; still open. Was F for SOUTHWELL 1 January 1850 co tt to May 1860 *Brad (Mid)*.

FITTLEWORTH [LBSC] op 2 September 1889 *(co n W Sussex)*; clo 7 February 1955 *(co n W Sussex)*.

FITZWILLIAM

FITZWILLIAM (a) [LNE] op 1 June 1937 *(RM August)*; HALT until 16 June 1947 *(Cl)*; clo 6 November 1967 *(RM December)*.

FITZWILLIAM (b) op 1 March 1982 *(RM June)*; still open.

FIVE MILE HOUSE [GN] op 17 October 1848 *(co n T 16th)*; clo 1 December 1850 *(Cl)*; trains still shown in December (inertia?); reop 1 September 1865 *(Cl)*; clo 15 September 1958 except for summer Saturday and Sunday advertised anglers' trains to/from Sheffield and Rotherham *(RM October)*, last used 6 September 1964 *(Cl)*.

FIVE WAYS

FIVE WAYS (a) [Mid] op 1 July 1885 *(Mid)*; through station which replaced Granville Street terminus (see BIRMINGHAM); clo 2 October 1944 *(LNW Record)*.

FIVE WAYS (b) op 8 May 1978 *(RM July)*; still open.

FLADBURY [GW] op 3 May 1852★★; clo 3 January 1966 *(RM February)*.

FLAG STATION – see GLANLLYN

FLAMBOROUGH [NE]: line op 20 October 1847★★, nd, May 1848 *(Topham)*; at first MARTON, renamed 1 July 1884 *(Cl)*; clo 5 January 1970 *(Cl)*. *Topham* 1849, NE co tt 1880: M for F. *Brad* 1858–9

had it successively as M for F, M from F, M or F: 'This would appear to be nonsense' *(JS)*.

FLAX BOURTON [GW] op 1 September 1860 *(BE minutes: RAIL 75/33)* as B; renamed 1 September 1888 *(Cl; RCG ref October)*; re-sited ¼ mile west 2 March 1893 *(Cl)*; clo 2 December 1963 *(Cl)*.

FLAXTON [NE]: line op 8 July 1845★★; clo 22 September 1930★★.

FLECKNOE [LNW] op 1 August 1895 *(LNW Officers 36165, 36425)*; clo 1 August 1917 (Wednesday), reop 1 March 1919 *(Cl)*; clo 3 November 1952 *(Cl)*.

FLEDBOROUGH [GC] op 15 December 1896 *(GC; Brad Sh)*; clo 19 September 1955 *(BR ER internal notice August)*.

FLEET near Basingstoke [LSW] first in *Brad* February 1848, as FLEETPOND; renamed 1 July 1869 *(Cl)*; re-sited 1904; still open.

FLEET near Spalding [MGN] op 1 November 1862 *(Linc R & S Merc 4th)*; aot request; clo 2 March 1959 *(T 2nd)*.

FLEETWOOD [PW]

FLEETWOOD (a) op 16 July 1840 *(co n T 13th)*; re-sited 13 February 1851 (M. Cobb, via *The Journal of the Engine Shed Society*, Summer 2006); in *Brad* as F DOCK STREET from August 1852 *(JS)* to 1876/7. Re-sited 15 July 1883; replaced 18 April 1966 *(Cl)* by >

FLEETWOOD (b) which had op 1 December 1885 for down trains only as WYRE DOCK; up trains began to call 1 May 1901 *(LNW dates*, which called it W D HALT – anachronistic?); renamed 1966 on closure of (a); clo 1 June 1970 *(Cl)*.

Note added June 1880/July 1881 *(Brad)* that some trains ran direct to/from **QUAY**; omitted Aug./Dec. 1882. However, that was not end of this.

LY co tt 1 May 1899, in pages on steamer services to Belfast, said that passengers and their luggage passed direct from train to steamer by a covered way; also thus in LNW co tts to 3 October 1921 at least; still in LMS tt 22 September 1930, for trains to Isle of Man.

See photograph of 'post-1910 period' train in article by R.B.O. Brindle, *(LY Society Journal)*, where he says that at one time boat trains ran to special timber platform beside shipping berths. Ceased ?

FLEMINGTON [Cal] op 2 March 1891 *(RCG)*; clo 4 January 1965 *(RM February)*.

FLETCHING – see SHEFFIELD PARK.

FLEUR-DE-LIS

FLEUR-DE-LIS [GW] op 29 March 1926 *(co n dated 'March')*; PLATFORM; clo 31 December 1962 *(T 31st)*; {Maesycwmmer – Pengam}.
Also see PENGAM Mon [BM].

FLIMBY [LNW]: line op 19 January 1846 *(Whitehaven Herald 20 March 1847* – dealing with next stretch), nd, May 1848 *(Topham)*; aot request; still open.

FLINT [LNW] op 1 May 1848 *(D&C 11; co n T 2nd- line)*; still open.

FLITWICK [Mid] op 2 May 1870 *(Mid)*; still open .

FLIXTON [CLC] op 1 October 1873 *(CLC)*; still open.

FLORDON [GE] op 12 December 1849 *(T 11th- line)*;

clo 7 November 1966 *(RM January 1967)*.

FLORDEN in tt until 1875 *(JS)* and *hb* until 1883.

FLORENCE COLLIERY [NS] (non-tt): miners;
op ?; clo 1923; {branch from Trentham} *(U)*.

FLORISTON [Cal]
first in *Brad* May 1853; clo 17 July 1950 *(Cl)*.

FLOUR DEPOT ST MARYS ROAD
– see BALDOVAN.

FLOW MOSS [LM] op after autumn of 1832, but
before 1 September 1838 *(Drake)*; see 1830 September
17**; clo by 29 October 1842 *(Railway Times* of that
date – 'now abandoned').

FLOWERY FIELD
op 13 May 1985 *(D&C 10)*; still open.

FLUSHDYKE [GN] first in *Brad* March 1865;
near original Ossett, but at higher level *(GN)*;
clo 5 May 1941 *(Cl)*. Aot in *hb* as FLUSH DYKE.

FOCHABERS
F TOWN [High] op 23 October 1893 *(High)*;
TOWN added 1 July 1894 *(hbl 11th)*;
clo 14 September 1931 *(RM November)*.
Also see ORBLISTON JUNCTION; SPEY BAY.

FOCHRIW [BM] first in *Brad* September 1867 as
terminus for the time being of service from Dowlais
Top; strictly, this was illegal service since enabling Act
stipulated that this section should not open to
passengers until branch to Merthyr opened (would
happen 1 August 1868); clo 31 December 1962 *(T 31st)*.
Hb early also had FOCHRHW, FOCHRIW OR
VOCHRIW. Tkt: FOCHRIEW *(JB)*.

FOCKERBY [Ax Jt] op 10 August 1903 *(RCG)*;
clo 17 July 1933 *(RM September)*.

FOGGATHORPE [NE]
op 1 August 1848**- line; F GATE until 1864 *(Cl)*;
clo 20 September 1954 *(RM October)*; later excur *(U)*.

FOLESHILL [LNW] op 2 September 1850**;
clo 18 January 1965 *(RM March)*.

FOLEY PARK [GW] op 2 January 1905 *(GW H)*;
re-sited from south to north of single line 1925 to make
way for West Midland Sugar Co's factory; HALT until
6 May 1968 *(Cl)*; clo 5 January 1970 *(RM February)*;
{Kidderminster – Bewdley}.

FOLKESTONE [SE]
FOLKESTONE temporary station 28 June 1843
(co n T 24th); replaced by >
FOLKESTONE permanent (eventually **F EAST**)
op 18 December 1843 *(SE)*; variously and intermittently
FOLKESTONE, F OLD, F JUNCTION,
F J SHORNCLIFFE, FOLKESTONE; became
F EAST 10 September 1962 *(SR)*;
clo to public 6 September 1965 *(RM July)*; railway staff
still use. SE co tt 1864, in summary table: F J described
as station for SANDGATE & SHORNCLIFFE CAMP.
F CENTRAL op 18 August 1884 *(SE)* as CHERITON
ARCH; renamed RADNOR PARK 1886 *(SR)*, F C 1
June 1895 *(RCG)*; still open.
Brad ? to 1955: F C for SANDGATE.
F WEST op 1 February 1881 *(SE)*, as
SHORNCLIFFE CAMP, replacing an earlier station
of that name, which see under 'S'; renamed S 1926,
F W 10 September 1962 *(SR)*; still open.

F HARBOUR op 1 January 1849 *(SE)*; passengers
alighted on the Pier and walked across swing bridge;
rails across the swing bridge 1850; new Pier 16 August
1861 but passengers still had to walk to F H *(SE)*;
clo 29 November 1915, reop 1 March 1919 *(Cl)*;
regular service ceased 2 October 2000 *(BLN 917)*;
excursions to 30 May 2002 and again from 28 Sept.
2003; last special 14 March 2009 *(RM May)*.

ART TREASURES EXHIBITION (non-tt):
the Exhibition opened on Saturday, 22 May 1886 and
closed Saturday night, 30 October; its opening times
included Sunday afternoons. To begin with, all visitors
used existing stations: on opening day the dignitaries
came by special train to Folkestone Junction [later
F East] and many of the public came by other specials.
(T 24 May, 1 November). On 31 May the General
Manager of the SE wrote to the BoT saying that they
wished to open for occasional passenger excursions
a short branch to the Exhibition, up to then only used
for goods; he asked for prompt action 'as the Excursions
will soon commence and we are anxious to run the trains
right up to the Building'. On 8 June Major General
Hutchinson reported that he had inspected it and saw
no objection to opening provided stringent conditions
were met. The line was one purpose-built for the
Exhibition; about 1,500 yards long, starting from
sidings on the south side of the line at Shorncliffe
[thus in report, later Folkestone West] and running
south-east to the site, immediately north of Bouverie
Road; it had been built without an Act of Parliament
since it was entirely on private land apart from crossing
two public roads on the level. Hutchinson said the BoT
could not sanction the use of the crossings but he
implied that there was no objection to them provided
they were careful. His suggested conditions included
that trains should come to a complete stop before
crossings, should not exceed 6mph, a platform should
be provided at the Exhibition end and the line should
be removed after the Exhibition's closure.
On the 9th the Board wrote giving its agreement,
provided the conditions were met; it played safe by
saying it had 'no objection to' (the usual 'sanction' was
crossed out) the use and including, 'as it is only to be
used for a short time I presume no objection will be
made with regard to the level crossings' – does this
translate 'alright unless the locals object'? *(MT6/408/8)*.
Art Exhibitions notice in *T, 9 June*, says 'Excursion
trains from London daily, and from all parts of Kent,
Surrey, and Sussex now running'. Does not specify use
of special station (mixture of special trains and excursion
tickets by regular services? 'occasional' equals 'daily'?)
SE co ½ referred to extra revenue but did not mention
special station; no SE adverts seen. {map 134}.

FOLKESTONE WARREN [SE; SEC; SR]:
FOLKESTONE WARREN (a): first in *Brad* September
1888, Dover to Sandgate local table; next month place
strangely taken by F Harbour, no trains. Accords with
story in *SE* that Lord Raglan objected to picnic parties,
brought by trains, trespassing on his land, so station
abruptly closed; however dates do not tally.
Year misprint in *SE*?

FOLKESTONE WARREN (b) op 1 June 1908 *(SEC)*;
HALT, summer use only (e.g. 1910 May to September);
initially in Sandgate table but in last year moved to
Elham Valley table. *RCG* says clo September 1915,
though it was last in tt November 1915 (both mentions
almost certainly inertia, given earlier history and
function as picnic station).
FOLKESTONE WARREN (c) first in *Brad* June 1924;
HALT; clo 25 September 1939 *(Cl)*.
Also much non-tt use at various times: military camp,
doctor, Channel Tunnel workmen; railwaymen *(U)*.
FONTBURN [NB]: perhaps unofficial use by 1896
for quarry and railway workers and families;
temporary Platform op 12 January 1903 as
WHITEHOUSE SIDING, for reservoir workers;
briefly in *Brad* (present June 1903 to November 1903
or later – there just W) but removed on BoT protest
that it had not been officially passed; renamed a month
before it officially op 1 June 1904 as F *(Nhumb Young)*;
clo 3 October 1921 *(RCG)*; reop 21 November 1921
(RCG) as HALT; clo 15 September 1952** *(RM Oct.)*.
Reid still called it WHITEHOUSE in 1907.
FOOTPATH CROSSING – see SUNNY WOOD.
FORD near Worthing [LBSC] op 8 June 1846
(LBSC; Hants Chron 13th- line) as ARUNDEL;
renamed F for ARUNDEL 1850 tt, F JUNCTION
1863 *(Cl)*, F SUSSEX 9 July 1923 *(hbl 26 April)*,
F 1955 *(Brad)*, though *hb* 1938 did not treat SUSSEX
as part of name; still open.
FORD Liverpool [LY] op 1 July 1906 *(Wigan Observer
4th)*; clo 2 April 1951 *(RM May)*.
FORD Plymouth; {map 114}
FORD [GW] op 1 June 1904 *(W Morn News 1st, 2nd)*;
initially and finally public HALT; PLATFORM from
23 May 1906 (which *RCG* gave as op date) to 10 July
1922 *(Cl)*; clo 6 October 1941 *(Cl; temporarily out of use
– GW wtt supplement 5 January 1942)*.
FORD [LSW] op 1 June 1890 *(W D Merc 2nd)*; was
F DEVON 9 July 1923 *(hbl 26 April)* to 1955 *(Brad)*;
clo 7 September 1964 *(Cl)*.
Hb 1938 did not treat DEVON as part of name.
FORD & CROSSGATES [SM] op 13 August
1866**, as CROSS GATES; reopened 1911 as F & C;
finally clo 6 November 1933 *(Cl)*.
FORD BRIDGE [SH Jt]
first in *Brad* September 1854; clo 5 April 1954 *(Cl)*.
FORD GATE – see EARLS COLNE.
FORD GREEN & SMALLTHORNE [NS]
first trains shown in *Brad* July 1864; & S added 1887/8
(Brad); clo 11 July 1927 *(Cl)*; still weeks use
(as F G) at 19 August 1961 *(BR handbill)*; last probably
10 August 1963 – no leaflet for 1964 found *(AB)*.
FORD HOUSES [LMS] (non-tt):
for R.O.F. Featherstone; op 5 August 1941;
clo by about 1945; {Bushbury – Four Ashes} *(WW II)*.
FORDEN [Cam] op 10 June 1861 *(Cam)*;
aot request; clo 14 June 1965 *(RM July)*.
FORDHAM [GE]
op 1 September 1879 *(Bury Free Post 6th* – B. Wilson);
F & BURWELL until 2 June 1884 *(RCG)*;
clo 13 September 1965 *(T 11 August)*.

FORDINGBRIDGE [LSW]
op 20 December 1866 *(Som & W J 22nd- line)*;
clo 4 May 1964 *(Hants Chron 9th)*.
FORDOUN [Cal]:
line op 1 November 1849 *(co ½ T 27 November)*, nd *Brad*,
in *Topham* December 1849, first time it included table
for this line; clo 11 June 1956 *(RM April)*.
BR Scottish Region Special Traffic Notice shows stops
scheduled here 30 July 1957 for school parties to/from
Drumtochy Castle.
FOREST GATE [GE] op 1840 *(L)* – first in *Brad*
about March 1841; clo 1 June 1843 (Sunday) – omitted
from list of stations in co notice of alterations for June
(T 31 May); reop Whit Sunday, 31 May 1846
(co n T 28th); still open. GE co tt 1882, 1914 and *Brad*
to 1955: F G for UPTON.
FOREST HALL {map 26}
FOREST HALL (a) [NE] first in *Brad* February 1856 as
BENTON; renamed 1 December 1874 *(Cl; RCG ref
January 1875)*; clo 15 September 1958 *(RM October)*.
FOREST HALL (b) [BT] op 27 June 1864 *(co ½
T 22 August- line)*; clo 1 March 1871 (Wednesday) *(Cl)*.
FOREST HILL [LBSC] op 5 June 1839 *(co n T 6th)*;
DARTMOUTH ARMS until 3 July 1845 *(JS, from
company minute)*; still open.
Was F H for LORDSHIP LANE from 1877/8 to
1942/3 *(Brad)*; still thus SR tt 1947 (printed by
Bradshaw), but not in Bradshaw's own tt.
FOREST MILL [NB] op 28 August 1850 *(notice &
item Stirling Journal 30th)* as KINCARDINE; renamed
1 January 1894 *(hbl 25th)*; clo 22 September 1930 *(Cl)*.
FOREST ROW [LBSC]
op 1 October 1866 *(co n T 1st)*; clo 2 January 1967
(RM February). *Brad* ? to 1955: F R for ASHDOWN
FOREST and ASHDOWN PARK.
FORFAR
FORFAR Play Field* [Arbroath & Forfar; Aberdeen]
op 4 December 1838 (see 1838**); replaced by >
FORFAR [Scottish Midland Junction; Cal] op 2 August
1848 *(Rtn)*; originally F JOINT; clo 4 September 1967
(RM Sept.).
* = local name; F in *Brad*.
FORGANDENNY [Cal] op 23 May 1848**- line;
clo 11 June 1956 *(RM April)*.
FORGE CROSSING [GW]
op 9 March 1929 *(wtt supp)*; HALT; clo 5 February
1951 *(RM October)* – see 1951**; {Titley – Presteign}.
FORGE MILLS – see COLESHILL.
FORGE VALLEY [NE] op 1 May 1882 *(Scarborough
4th- line)*; clo 5 June 1950 *(Cl)*.
FORGIE – see AULTMORE.
FORMBY [LY] op 24 July 1848 *(Southport Vis 22nd,
29th)* as F & ALTCAR; intermittently thus until 1866
tt *(JS)*; still open.
FORMBY POWER STATION [LY] (non-tt):
used by workmen at least 1917 to 1943 *(U)*
– certainly still in LMS wtt, with trains, 4 May 1942;
{Formby – Altcar Rifle Range}.
FORNCETT [GE]:
line op 12 December 1849 *(T 11th- line)*, nd, Feb. 1850;
clo 7 November 1966 *(RM January 1967)*.

FORRES
See DALVEY for early temporary terminus.
FORRES [High] op 25 March 1858 *(High)*;
re-sited as triangular station 3 August 1863 when Perth
line opened *(Cl)*; still open.
FORRESTFIELD [NB] op 11 August 1862 *(MK)*;
clo 22 September 1930 *(Cl)*. FORESTFIELD in *Brad*
1864 to 1873, [Monkland] ticket thus *(JB)*.
FORSINARD [High]
op 28 July 1874 *(High)*; still open.

FORT AUGUSTUS
FORT AUGUSTUS [High; NB] op 22 July 1903**;
clo 1 November 1911 (Wednesday), reop 1 August 1913
(RM August); clo 1 December 1933 (Friday) *(RM Dec.)*.
F A PIER [High] op 22 July 1903**; summer only;
clo 1 October 1906 *(Cl)*; {beyond Fort Augustus}.
FORT BROCKHURST [LSW]
first in tt November 1865 (J. Alsop, article, *Railway
Archive, November 2004, p.5)*; FORT added 23 Nov.
1893 *(RCG)*; clo 8 June 1953 *(RM July)*. Shown as
F B JUNCTION in handbill tt of 1908 *(Railway
Archive)* and thus *Brad* some tables 1898 to 1909.

FORT GEORGE
FORT GEORGE [High] op 1 July 1899 *(High)*;
clo 5 April 1943 *(Cl)*; troop trains continued to use line
until it was completely abandoned in 1958 (M. Pearson,
The Iron Road to Whisky Country, Wayzgoose/GNS
Society, 2002).
Also see GOLLANFIELD.
FORT GOMER [LSW] op 12 May 1894 *(Hants Teleg
19th)* as PRIVETT; became F G 1909 tt *(Cl)*; HALT
1910 *(Brad)*; clo 31 August 1914, reop 1 October 1914
(Cl); aot request; clo 1 May 1930 (Thursday) *(Cl)*.
FORT MATILDA [Cal] op 1 June 1889 *(Cal)*;
clo 5 February 1973 for tunnel repairs, reop 20 April
1973; clo 3 October 1993 (Sunday) *(BLN 718)*; reop
27 March 1995 *(BLN 752)*; still open.
FORT WILLIAM [NB] op 7 August 1894 *(T 7th)*;
re-sited about ½ mile north 9 June 1975 *(RM August)*;
still open. Was F W for BALLACHULISH
GLENCOE and KINLOCHLEVEN 1 May 1909
(hbl 9 July) (thus LNE tt 1933), to 1992 tt.
FORTEVIOT [Cal]
op 23 May 1848**- line; clo 11 June 1956 *(RM April)*.
FORTH BRIDGE – see DALMENY.
FORTROSE [High] op 1 February 1894 *(High)*; clo
1 October 1951 *(RM November)*.
FORTY HILL [GE] op 1 October 1891 *(RCG)*;
clo 1 October 1909 (Friday) *(RCG)*;
reop 1 March 1915 *(Cl)*; clo 1 July 1919** (Tuesday)
(Cl). Turkey Street on this site later.
FORYD [LNW]
FORYD (a) op 5 October 1858 *(op tt Clwyd)* on
Denbigh line; replaced by >
FORYD (b) op 20 April 1885 *(Cl)* on coast line; clo 2
July 1917 (see KINMEL CAMP), reop 1 July 1919
(Cl); clo 5 January 1931 *(Cl)*; Kinmel Bay here later.
F PIER (non-tt) use began August 1859, to connect
with steamers to Liverpool; re-sited nearer river mouth
1 October 1865 *(LNW; Brad Sh 1866)*; unlikely use
regular; ended ?

FOSS CROSS [MSWJ] op 1 August 1891 *(Chelt Exam
29 August)*; clo 11 September 1961 *(T 9th)*.
FOTHERBY [GN]
F GATE HOUSE first in *Brad* September 1863; Fridays
only; last used Friday 28 June 1872 *(GN I, p.34)*.
FOTHERBY op 11 December 1905 *(GN)*; same site?;
see 1905** (d); aot request; clo 11 September 1961
(RM September).
FOULIS [High] op 23 March 1863 *(High)*;
FOWLIS until 20 March 1916 *(hbl 27 April)*;
clo 13 June 1960 *(RM July)*. *Hb* reverted to FOWLIS
in 1929, amended 1936a; not then seen thus *Brad*.
FOULRIDGE [Mid] op 2 October 1848 *(Mid;
RAIL 1005/265- line)*; clo 5 January 1959 *(RM Feb.)*.
At first in *Brad* as FAULRIDGE; altered 1849.
FOULSHAM [GE] op 1 May 1882 *(GE- line)*;
clo 15 September 1952 *(RM October)*.
FOUNTAIN BRIDGE [BM] first in *Brad* October
1908**; HALT; down service only – see Waterloo for
up service; clo 17 September 1956 *(RM October)*.
FOUNTAINHALL [NB] op 1 August 1848 **- line
as BURN HOUSE; renamed 1849 *(Brad)*;
became F JUNCTION 2 July 1901 *(Cl; hbl ref 23rd)*
but 17 July 1902 *(RCG)*; back to F 1959 *(Cl)*;
clo 6 January 1969 *(RM February)*. RCH at times
FOUNTAIN HALL and [NB] ticket thus *(JB)*.
FOUR ASHES [LNW]
op 4 July 1837 *(co n GJ)*; clo 15 June 1959 *(RM July)*.
FOUR CROSSES [Cam]
op 1 May 1860 *(Cam; co ½ T 9 August- line)*;
clo 18 January 1965 *(RM March)*.
FOUR LANE ENDS [TWM]
op 11 August 1980 *(RM August)*; still open.
At/near Benton of 1864 to 1871.
FOUR OAKS [GW] op 16 October 1937 *(T 13th)*;
HALT; clo 13 July 1959 *(RM August.)*;
{Newent – Dymock}.
FOUR OAKS near Sutton Coldfield [LNW]
op 15 December 1884 *(W Mid; LNW Officers 26784-
line)*; still open.
FOURSTONES [NE]
probably op about start of January 1837 (see 1836 B**);
clo 2 January 1967 *(RM January)*.
FOWEY [GW] op 20 June 1876 *(R Cornwall Gaz 24th)*;
clo 1 January 1940, reop 9 February 1942,
clo 24 August 1942, reop 3 October 1942,
clo 2 May 1944 (Tuesday), reop 2 October 1944 *(Cl)*;
clo 4 January 1965 *(W Briton 7th)*.
FOXFIELD [Fur] op 1 August 1858 *(D&C 14)*;
aot request; still open. F JUNCTION until 1893/4 *Brad*
but *hb* until September 1957a
FOXTON [GE]
first in *Brad* June 1852; aot request; still open.
FRAMLINGHAM [GE] op 1 June 1859 *(T 2nd)*;
clo 3 November 1952 *(RM December)*; later ramblers'
excur *(U)*; *RM August 1957, p.555* has picture of special
train 4 May 1957 from Liverpool Street for a wedding
party; last school use 2 May 1958 (portion of 3.33pm
from Liverpool Street to Yarmouth South Town
detached at Ipswich and forwarded from there).
FRAMPTON – see GRIMSTONE.

FRANKLAND [NE] first in *Brad* March 1861;
originally Saturdays, later alternate Saturdays only;
last in *Brad* July 1877; {map 32}.
F SIDING until 1868 *Brad*.

FRANKTON [Cam] first in *Brad* January 1867;
became HALT before/with BR (WR) wtt of 13 June
1955; clo 18 January 1965 *(RM March)*.

FRANSHAM [GE]
op 11 September 1848 *(EC- line; in Topham* October);
aot request; clo 9 September 1968 *(RM November)*.

FRANT [SE] op 1 September 1851
(SE; Hants Chron 6th- line); still open.

FRASERBURGH [GNS] op 24 April 1865 *(GNS)*;
clo 4 October 1965 *(Rly Obs Nov.)*. *Brad* ? to 1938/9:
F for ROSEHEARTY and NEW ABERDOUR,
but not thus LNE tt 1933.

FRATTON [LSW/LBSC] op 2 July 1885**; still open.
Became F & SOUTHSEA 4 July 1905 for LSW use,
1 October 1910 for LBSC *(JS)*; back to F 1 December
1921 *(RCG)*. 1890 to 1908a F JUNCTION in *hb*.

FREMINGTON [LSW]
op 2 November 1855 *(N Devon 29 October, co ½
T 28 February 1856)*; clo 4 October 1965 *(Bideford 8th)*.

FRENCH DROVE & GEDNEY HILL [GN/GE]
op 2 September 1867 *(GN)* – GN minutes say op 1st
but that a Sunday and no Sunday service; & G H added
4 July 1938 *(Cl)*; clo 11 September 1961 *(RM Sept.)*.

FRESHFIELD [LY]
first in *Brad* April 1854 and in tt *Southport Vis* 6 April
1854 (not in its tt 30 March); still open.

FRESHFORD [GW] op 2 February 1857 *(GW;
Bath & Chelt 4th- line)*; still open.

FRESHWATER [FYN]
op 20 July 1889**; clo 21 September 1953 *(T 21st)*.
LBSC co tt June 1912: F for TOTLAND BAY. *Brad* ?
to closure: F for T B, ALUM BAY and THE NEEDLES.

FRIAR WADDON MILK PLATFORM [GW]:
(non-tt) perhaps passenger use for all/part of period
1932 to 1952 (B.L. Jackson, *The Abbotsbury Branch*,
Wild Swan, 1989, pp.62 and 98).

FRICKLEY [SK Jt]
op 1 July 1879 *(Mid; co n T 28 June)* as CLAYTON;
renamed 1 November 1882 *(RCG)*; clo 8 June 1953
but excursion facilities retained *(RM July)*.

FRIDEN – see 1833 May**.

FRIEZLAND [LNW]
op 1 July 1886 *(RCG; LNW Officers 28684* – 'local
service'); clo 1 January 1917 *(RCH)*.

FRIMLEY [LSW]
op 18 March 1878 *(co n T 15th)*; still open.

FRINTON-ON-SEA [GE]:
section of line through here op 17 May 1867, to
Walton-on-Naze; inspection report *(MT29/208)* said
was only intermediate station, platforms unfinished,
not to be used until June; *hb* 1872, 1877, 1883 shows as
'stopping place', without facilities. Presumably early
'halt' – no similar *hb* entry seen. First in *Brad* July 1888
as F; F-ON-SEA 1888 tt to 20 February 1969 *(Cl)* and
from 20 May 2007 tt; still open.

FRIOCKHEIM [Cal]: line op 4 December 1838
(see 1838**), nd, in use by 25 February 1841 – date of

company's reply to BoT about level crossings, though
not in tt *(Tuck)* until about June 1843; clo 5 December
1955 *(RM January 1956)*. F JUNCTION until 1849
Brad and *Topham*.

FRIOG (non-tt): railway workmen; op about 1960;
clo ?; {Llwyngwril – Fairbourne} *(U)*.

FRISBY [Mid] op 1 January 1847 *(Mid)*;
at first market service only (J. Gough); full service by
June 1849 when first in *Brad*; clo 3 July 1961 *(RM Aug.)*.

FRITTENDEN ROAD [KES] op 15 May 1905 *(RCG)*;
aot request; clo 4 January 1954 *(T 28 October 1953)*.

FRITWELL & SOMERTON [GW] first in *Brad*
April 1854 as S; became S OXON 12 February 1906
(RAIL 253/482), F & S 1 October 1907 *(hbl 24th)*;
clo 2 November 1964 *(BRWR circular 12 October)*.

FRIZINGHALL
FRIZINGHALL (a) [Mid] op 1 February 1875 *(Mid)*;
clo 22 March 1965 *(RM April)*.

FRIZINGHALL (b) op 7 September 1987, same site
(wtt supp); still open.

FRIZINGTON [WCE Jt]
op 1 July 1857 *(co ½ T 1 September)*; clo 13 April 1931
(LNW Record); workmen 11 March 1940 to 8 April
1940 *(U)*.

FROCESTER [Mid] op 8 July 1844 *(Bristol T 13th)*;
clo 11 December 1961 *(Cl)*.

FRODINGHAM & SCUNTHORPE [GC]
op 1 October 1866 *(GC; Rtn- line)*; & S added 1886
(Cl; RCG ref October); re-sited west of old Brigg Road
level crossing *(GC)*, new op 2 January 1888 *(GC dates)*;
briefly reverted to F about 1920 to 1922 according to
RCH dist refs 19 April 1920, 13 October 1922;
clo 11 March 1928 *(Cl; Rly Gaz 16 March* says closed day
previous to new being brought into use on 11th), when
replaced by a new station 1 mile west, which was later
renamed S & F. *Hb* 1866a made FRADINGHAM of it.

FRODSHAM [Birkenhead]
op 18 December 1850 *(D&C 10)*; still open.

FROGHALL – see KINGSLEY & FROGHALL.

FROME [GW]
op 7 October 1850 *(Som H 12th)*; still open.

FRONFRAITH [Cam]
first in *Brad* 9 July 1923; HALT according to some
sources but not thus *Brad*, though in *hb* 1929 as
F SIDING, no facilities shown, which suggests was
treated as halt; aot request; clo 9 February 1931 *(Cl)*.
Spelling used is that given by *Brad, hb* 1929,
Bartholomew's Directory and *1955 OS (1 inch)*.

FRONGOCH [GW] op 1 November 1882 *(GW- line)*;
clo 4 January 1960 *(RM March)*.

FROSTERLEY [NE] op 3 August 1847**;
clo 29 June 1953 *(RM August)*; [NE].

FUGAR BAR [Brandling Junction]
op 18 June 1842 *(Consett)*; not present when line in
Brad 1844 for only time, but, nature of service on this
line, and lack of detailed information means it is no
proof it had closed by then (see TANFIELD MOOR
for known line details); {map 27}.

FULBAR STREET – see under RENFREW.

FULBOURNE [GE] line op 9 October 1851**, in
opening tt, local press, but no trains calling; first in *Brad*

August 1852 – perhaps case of nd; aot request;
clo 2 January 1967 *(RM February)*.
Later used for Sunday School excursion for celebration
of 1,300th anniversary of Ely Cathedral on 15 May
1973 (Tony Kirby). At first FULBOURN, *Brad*
(intermittently until 1880/1); thus EC co tt 1854.
FULHAM BROADWAY [Dist]
op 1 March 1880 *(L)* as WALHAM GREEN;
renamed 1 March 1952 *(L)*; still open.
FULLARTON – see MEIGLE.
FULLERTON [LSW]
FULLERTON op 6 March 1865 *(Salisbury 11th- line)*;
F BRIDGE until 1871 tt *(Cl)*; replaced by >
FULLERTON op 2 February 1885, to south, ready to
serve as junction with Hurstbourne line *(LSW II,
p.194)*; F JUNCTION 1889 tt to 7 July 1929 *(Cl)*;
clo 7 September 1964 *(Andover Advertiser 31 July)*.
FULWELL near Teddington [LSW]
op 1 November 1864 *(co n T 27 October)*; still open.
Became F (NEW HAMPTON) 1874 *(L)*,
F for HAMPTON HILL 1887 *(L)*; 1908/9 *Brad* added
note that it was station for UPPER TEDDINGTON;
in LSW co tt 1914, and *hb* 1938 it was
F for U T and H H; reduced to F 1955 *(Brad)*.
FULWELL & WESTBURY [LNW] op 1 August
1879 *(LNW Officers 19885)* as W CROSSING;
renamed 1 October 1880 *(Cl – LNW Officers
recommended 16 Sept.)*; clo 2 January 1961 *(RM Feb.)*.

FULWOOD – see RIBBLETON.
FURNACE – see 1887★★.
FURNESS ABBEY [Fur] op August 1846★★;
early use intermittent; clo 25 September 1950 *(RM Oct.)*.
F A JUNCTION until 1853/6 in *Brad*.
FURNESS VALE [LNW] first in *Brad* December 1857;
VALE added 1862 tt *(JS)*; still open.
FURZE PLATT [GW] op 5 July 1937 *(RM August)*;
HALT until 5 May 1969 *(GW H)*; still open.
FUSHIEBRIDGE [NB] first in *Brad* September 1847,
in notes; notice in *Edinburgh Advertiser, 13 July* had shown
Gorebridge as terminus of stretch to be op on 14th; so
F only intended as temporary, beyond then 'terminus',
for coach connection? – omitted from *Brad* September
1848 when extension to Bowland included (clo 4 August
1848?); back in tt May or June 1849 *(Topham)*. Clo
4 October 1943 *(Cl)*, though workmen used to 1 January
1959 *(U)*. FUSHIE BRIDGE in *hb* until 1877.
FYLING HALL [NE]
op 16 July 1885 *(T 16th)*; last trains shown September
1915 *Brad*★, October present without trains, November
'temporarily closed'; reop 18 September 1920
(RM October); became HALT 5 May 1958 *(RM June)*;
clo 8 March 1965 *(T 19 January)*.
★ = according to *Cl* clo 1 November but *T 18 September*
included it in list of stations to be closed on 20 September.
FYVIE [GNS] op 5 September 1857 *(GNS)*;
clo 1 October 1951 *(RM November)*.

PLEASANT!

Scene—A bleak Scottish Moor. Time—New Year's Day. Train gradually stops.

Excited Passenger. "NOW, THEN, GUARD, WHAT ARE YOU STOPPING HERE FOR?"

Philosophical Guard. "FACT IS, THE WATTERS GANE AFF THE BILE. HOOEVER, IT'S JIST POSSIBLE TH' EXPRESS BEHIN'LL BE LATE."

A very common accident at the time was for a following train to run into a stationary one ahead.

G

GADLYS ROAD [TV] (non-tt): PLATFORM;
miners; op 12 July 1914; clo 1 April 1949; alias
G R BRIDGE (ticket thus *JB*);
{branch from Aberdare LL} *(Aberdare)*.
GAERWEN [LNW] first in *Brad* January 1849
(P. Baughan, *Chester & Holyhead Railway*, vol.1, D&C,
1972); clo 14 February 1966 *(RM April)*.
G JUNCTION *Brad* 1865/6 to 1899; LNW wtt 1908
and [Anglesey Central] ticket thus *(JB)*.
GAGIE [LMS] op 2 September 1935 *(Cl 29)*;
clo 10 January 1955 *(T 28 December 1954)*;
{Monikie – Kingennie}. HALT in 1938 *hb* and on
LMS ticket *(JB)* but not seen thus *Brad*.
GAILES [GSW]: shown 'P' in *hb* 1890 but not
included on RCH map of Scotland 1891; first in *Brad*
June 1893 but in January 1894 (earliest presently
available) shown with only one stop, northbound;
perhaps had been in use for some years previously and
not considered worth inclusion in tt; according to *GSW*
it opened 1 June 1893, but this might have been derived
from tt. Still one way only April 1895. By July 1896 it
had a full service. Clo 2 January 1967 *(Cl)*.
GAILEY [LNW] op 4 July 1837 *(co n GJ)* as
SPREAD EAGLE; renamed 1 August 1881
(LNW dates; LNW Officers recommended 12 July);
clo 18 June 1951 *(RM August)*.
GAINFORD [NE] op 9 July 1856★★- line;
clo 30 November 1964 *(RM December)*.
GAINSBOROUGH
G CENTRAL [GC] op 2 April 1849 *(Lincs Times 3rd)*;
CENTRAL added 1 July 1923 *(hbl 12th)*;
became Saturdays only, 4 October 1993 tt
(A. Brackenbury, *Chron*); still open.
G LEA ROAD [GN/GE] op 15 July 1867 *(GN/GE;*
co ½ T 19 August- line); op as G, renamed G NORTH
1 July 1923 *(hbl 12th)*, G L R 1 December 1923
(hbl 14 February 1924); still open.
GAIRLOCHY [High; NB] op 22 July 1903★★;
clo 1 November 1911 (Wednesday) *(Cl)*;
reop 1 August 1913 *(RM August)*;
clo 1 December 1933 (Friday) *(RM December)*.
GAISGILL [NE]
op 8 August 1861 *(co op tt)*; clo 1 December 1952 *(Cl)*.
GALASHIELS [NB]
op 20 February 1849 *(D&C 6- line)*; clo 6 January 1969
(RM February). Shown as G JUNCTION 1856/7 to
1882/3 main line, 1892/3 Peebles loop *(Brad)*.
GALE STREET – see BECONTREE.
GALGATE [LNW]
op 26 June 1840 *(LPJ)*; clo 1 May 1939 *(T 27 April)*.
GALLIONS
GALLIONS [PLA]: inspection report dated 30 October
1880 (called it G REACH) shows one train each way
already running (R. Green); first in *Brad* November

1880; re-sited 275 yards east, on diverted line,
12 December 1886; re-sited again, to east 1924/5;
clo 9 September 1940★★. GE co tt 1882, 1914:
ROYAL ALBERT DOCK G; tickets thus and
GALLEONS *(JB)*.
G REACH [Dock] op 28 March 1994★★; still open.
GALLOWGATE
– see under GLASGOW and 1967 June 5★★.
GALLOWSHALL – see ESKBANK.
GALSTON [GSW] op 9 August 1848 *(GSW)*;
clo 6 April 1964 *(RM May)*.
GAMLINGAY [LNW] op 7 July 1862 *(T 7th- line)*;
clo 1 January 1968 *(RM January)*.
GAMMER LANE – see RIBBLETON.
GANTON [NE]: op 8 July 1845★★; clo 22 September
1930★★; used again for Ryder Cup Golf 12 to 17
September 1949 *(Cl)*.
GANTS HILL [Cen]
op 14 December 1947 *(T 17th)*; still open.
GARA BRIDGE [GW] op 19 December 1893
(Totnes 16th, 23rd); clo 16 September 1963 *(Cl)*.
GARELOCHHEAD [NB]
op 7 August 1894 *(W High; T 7th- line)*; still open.
GARFORTH
See 1837 A★★ for service to Aberford.
GARFORTH [NE]: line op 22 September 1834★★
(NE), nd, 19 October 1839 tt; still open.
GARGILL – see GARTSHERRIE.
GARGRAVE [Mid] op 30 July 1849 *(T 28 July, 1 Sept.)*;
still open. G for MALHAM in *Brad* 1863 to 1878/9;
not thus Mid sources *(Mid)*.
GARGUNNOCK [NB] op 26 May 1856★★;
clo 1 October 1934 *(RM October)*.
GARLIESTOWN {map 17}
GARLIESTOWN (a) [Wigtownshire] op 2 August 1875
(company minutes 29 September); replaced by >
GARLIESTOWN (b) [PPW Jt] op 3 April 1876 *(Little*
SW Scotland; co n Kirkcudbright 14th – 'now open');
clo 1 March 1903 (Sunday) *(RM April)*.
Line between Wigtown and here appears to have
suffered short closure in 1876. *Brad* August (only) just
shows a service between Newton Stewart and Wigtown;
other stations absent from the index; oddly, this was
included in New Openings list – clearly misinterpretation
– should have listed Wigtown to Garliestown as a
Closure. Note that the surviving goods had become
GARLIESTON by 1910 *(hba)*.
Also see MILLISLE.
GARMOUTH [GNS] op 12 August 1884 *(GNS)*;
clo 6 May 1968 *(RM July)*.
GARN-YR-ERW [LNW] op 1 February 1913
(LNW Officers 43959); clo 5 May 1941 *(Cl)*.
1912 July 13★★ applies here; was HALT in *hb*.
GARNANT [GW]
op 1 May 1850★★; re-sited ½ mile west 20 March 1865
(Carmarthen 17th, with notice of opening of extension
to Brynamman); clo 18 August 1958 *(T 11th)*.
Platforms for Gwaun-Cae-Gurwen line, shown as
G HALT, added 1 January 1908 *(GW)*;
clo 2 April 1917 *(Cl)*; reop 7 July 1919 *(GW circ 2672)*;
see 1921 April/May★★; clo 4 May 1926★★.

GARNDIFFAITH [LNW]
op 13 July 1912★★ *(LNW Cl)* as SIX BELLS;
renamed 2 October 1922 *(RCG)*; clo 5 May 1941 *(Cl)*.
HALT in *Brad* and *hb* but not LNW co tt nor LMS tt
1930; 'Motor Halt' according to *LNW dates*.

GARNEDDWEN near Bala [GW] op 9 July 1928
(GW H); HALT; clo 18 January 1965★★;
{Llanuwchllyn – Drws-y-Nant}.

GARNEDDWEN [Corris] (ng)
first in *Brad* November 1887; aot request, daylight only;
clo 1 January 1931 (Thursday) *(Cl)*.

GARNGAD [NB]★ op 1 October 1883 *(Glasgow)*;
clo 1 March 1910 (Tuesday) *(Cl)* – *RCG* says 31 March
(Thursday) but last in *Brad* February; {map 15}.
BLOCHAIRN for first fortnight *(MK)*.
At times GLASGOW G in tts.
★ = [CGU] until 1896.

GARNKIRK [Cal]: line op 1 June 1831,
stop by 1837 *(Garnkirk)*; at first CHRYSTON ROAD,
later G WORKS (thus *Murray September 1844*);
G when first detail appeared in *Brad*, 1847/8;
clo 7 March 1960 *(Cl)*.
G for C in *Brad* but not *Murray* 1948.

GARNOCK [LMS] (both non-tt)
EAST and WEST op 8 January 1940; closed about
1945, EAST probably first; for ICI explosives workers?;
{Bogside – Kilwinning} *(WW II)*.

GARNQUEEN [Monklands] op 10 December 1849
(MK) – perhaps earlier use (see 1828 B★★);
clo 10 December 1851★★ (Wed.) *(MK)*; {map 16}.

GARROWHILL [LMS] op 16 March 1936 *(RM May;*
HALT until 11 September 1961 tt; still open.

GARRY BRIDGE – see 1957★★.

GARSCADDEN op 7 November 1960★★; still open.

GARSDALE [Mid] op 1 August 1876 *(Mid)* as
HAWES JUNCTION; renamed H J & G 20 January
1900 *(Mid)*, G 1 September 1932 *(Mid)*;
clo 4 May 1970 *(RM June)* but still excursions; trial
charter excursion 9 June 1974 *(AB)*; reop for Dales
Rail summer use 3 May 1975 (P.W. Robinson, *Cumbria's
Lost Railways*, Stenlake, 2002); reop fully 14 July 1986
(Settle); see 1989 October 16★★; still open.

GARSINGTON BRIDGE [GW]
op 1 February 1908 *(Oxford Chron 31 January)*;
HALT; clo 22 March 1915 *(RCH)*;
{Wheatley – Littlemore}. Morris Cowley here later.

GARSTANG
G & CATTERALL [LNW] op 26 June 1840 *(LPJ)*;
& C added 1881 (recommended *LNW Officers 18 Jan.*);
clo 3 February 1969 *(Cl)*.
Tickets for G & C JUNCTION/G JUNCTION *(JB)*.
G TOWN [KE] op 5 December 1870 *(LNW Record -
line)*; clo 11 March 1872, reop 17 May 1875 *(Cl)*;
TOWN added 2 June 1924 *(Rly Gaz 23 May)*;
clo 31 March 1930 *(LNW Record)*.

GARSTANG ROAD [KE] first in *Brad* October 1923;
see 1908★★ (d); clo 31 March 1930 *(LNW Record)*;
{Cockerham – Pilling}.

GARSTON Liverpool
G MERSEYSIDE [CLC] op 1 April 1874 *(CLC)* as G;
clo 17 April 1972 *(RM May)*, reop 3 January 1978 as

G LANCS *(Daily Telegraph 3rd)*; became G M 14 May
1984 BR tt (index much earlier); clo 11 June 2006
(Merseyrail leaflet) – replaced by Liverpool South
Parkway. BR ticket for G CENTRAL *(JB)*.
G DOCK [LNW] op 1 July 1852 *(T 10th)*;
clo 15 April 1917★ (Sunday) *(Cl)*; reop 5 May 1919
(RCH); clo 16 June 1947★★. Aot G DOCKS *(hb)*.
G CHURCH ROAD op 1 March 1881 *(LNW Officers
21780, 21840)*; clo 15 April 1917★ (Sunday) *(Cl)*;
reop 5 May 1919 *(RCH)*; clo 3 July 1939 *(LNW Record)*.
Alias C R G.
★ = already shown 'service suspended' April 1917 *Brad*
– last minute temporary reprieve?

GARSTON HERTFORDSHIRE
op 7 February 1966 *(RM March)*; still open.

GARSWOOD [LNW]:
op 15 November 1869★★; still open.

GARTCOSH
GARTCOSH (a) [Cal]: line op 1 June 1831, nd, stop by
1837 *(Garnkirk)*; clo 5 November 1962 *(RM October)*.
GARTCOSH (b) op 9 May 2005, at 97m 31ch (previous
at 97m 29ch) *(Rly Obs June, August)*; still open.

GARTH near Builth [LNW]
op 11 March 1867 *(LNW Officers)*; still open.

GARTH near Maesteg
GARTH [PT] first in *Brad* March 1899; clo 9 June 1913
(Cl; RAIL 1005/280 gives 7th, last day) – buildings
destroyed by arson 21 May 1911, station stayed in use;
local council asked for replacement to be at CWMDU,
which see *(Welsh Railway Archive May 2003, p.156)*.
G MID GLAMORGAN op 28 September 1992
(RM December); on different line from earlier, about
¼ mile north of earlier Troedyrhiew Garth; still open.

GARTH & SUN BANK – see SUN BANK.

GARTH & VAN ROAD [Van] op 1 December 1873★★;
last in *Brad* July 1879 (August 'service suspended');
excursion trains once or twice a year in 1880s,
children continued to be taken to school *(Van)*;
still shown 'P' *hb* 1895; {goods *IA*}.

GARTLY [GNS] op 20 September 1854 *(GNS)*;
clo 6 May 1968 *(RM July)*.
Brad 1911: G for LUMSDEN and STRATHDON.

GARTMORE [NB]
op 1 August 1882 (line *D&C 6*); line not in *Brad* until
October; clo 2 January 1950 *(Cl)*.

GARTNESS [NB]
op 26 May 1856★★; clo 1 October 1934 *(RM October)*.

GARTON [NE] op 1 June 1853 *(NE- line)*;
clo 5 June 1950 *(Cl)*; see 1953★★.

GARTSHERRIE {map 16}
The following assumes that there was one station here,
used at first by two companies; however, exact
arrangements unknown, perhaps separate stations.
Line op 1 June 1831. Some sort of stop must have
existed from start, since it was end of Garnkirk & Glasgow
(later Cal) stretch of line; passengers taken on further
by MK; inn beside line op for use of travellers by 7 July
1832 *(Garnkirk)*; see 1828 B★★; originally GARGILL
(and thus in report of accident 9 June 1842); renamed
by time first in *Brad*, 1848. Monklands use ended
1 January 1850 *(MK)*. Cal clo 1 January 1917 *(RCH)*;

reop 1 March 1919 (RCH); 1931/1932 Brad note added
that this station would be used as a halt;
became G HALT 1933; back to G 1934/5;
clo 28 October 1940 (Cl). Aot G JUNCTION in Brad.
GARVE [High] op 19 August 1870 (High); still open.
GASCOIGNE WOOD [NE]:
line op 30 May 1839 (T 7 June), nd, 19 October 1839
Brad; see 1834 September 2** (for clo and reop);
clo 1 January 1902 (Wednesday) (Cl); 1940s wtts
showed stops for railwaymen's wives all days both ways
except Sundays (e.g. LNE wtts 5 Oct. 1942, 1 October
1945, 31 May 1948) (R. Maund); according to U used
by railwaymen until 2 November 1959;
{physical junction IA}.
At first YORK J; became OLD J 1850; MILFORD
OLD J April 1867 co tt (JS), GW J 1 November 1879
(Cl; RCG ref October), GW 1893/4 (Brad).
GATCOMBE [GW] first in Brad August 1852;
replaced by Awre Junction 1 April 1869 (Cl).
Always G PURTON PASSAGE (Brad; hb);
thus GW co tt 1865, not 1859.
GATE HELMSLEY – see HOLTBY.
GATEACRE [CLC] op 1 December 1879 (CLC);
clo 17 April 1972 (RM May).
G & WOOLTON on 1887 Junction Diagram;
G for W Mid co tt 1894, LMS tt 1930, and hb still 1956
but Brad dropped 'for W' 1938/9.
GATEHEAD
See 1818** for first service to run through here.
GATEHEAD [GSW] op 1 March 1847**;
clo 3 March 1969 (Cl).
GATEHOUSE OF FLEET
GATEHOUSE OF FLEET [PPW Jt] first in Brad
September 1861 as DROMORE/D for G; names
alternated until settled 1 January 1912 (hbl 25th);
clo 5 December 1949 (RM January 1950);
reop 20 May 1950 (Cl) but not in public tt (e.g. not in
BR Scot R tt 25 September 1950); Fridays and
Saturdays only 30 June 1952 wtt; back in Brad after that
of November 1953, before/with that of March 1954;
thereafter variety of Monday, Friday and Saturday
services; lost last eastbound service 18 June 1962 tt;
HALT by 1960 wtt but not thus even in last public tt.
Last wtt for line, 7 September 1964, shows unadvertised
stops both ways – eastbound Fridays and Saturdays,
westbound Fridays and Mondays. Clo 14 June 1965
(RM July).
Also see TARFF.
GATESHEAD {map 27}
DERWENTHAUGH [NC; NE] op 1 March 1837 (NE),
as stop on way to Redheugh, below; clo 30 August 1850.
November 1852 tt showed start of Redheugh to Swalwell
Colliery service which stopped at junction just short of
D but did not use station. June 1853 Brad showed
replacement service, Tuesdays and Saturdays, from
Newcastle via Blaydon (reversal) which stopped at D
and then reversed at junction (just beyond from this
direction), in order to reach Swalwell. Reduced to
Saturdays only Newcastle to D July 1853 Brad; last
there February 1868.
REDHEUGH [NC] op 1 March 1837 (NE maps);

acted as south-of-the-Tyne terminus for NC, with ferry
link to station at 'The Close'. Lost function as ferry
station for Newcastle October/November 1839 when
NC extended to station near Shot Tower but remained
in use for local needs. Omitted from Brad about
February 1841, back January 1842; given lack of detail
in NC tables cannot be taken as proof of brief closure;
on return at first only in notes, some trains asterisked
to show they carried portions to/ from here as well as
Newcastle. From 18 June 1842 when the Newcastle &
Darlington Junction reached Oakwellgate its usefulness
increased again when Brandling Junction/Newcastle &
Darlington Junction started free service down the inline
from their Gateshead station (NE maps; Return of
accident on 31 October 1844). A notice reproduced in
NC MacLean refers to a service starting on 23 March
1843, presumably a later addition to/alteration of the
service; this states that service was free – perhaps to
avoid problems over inspection? Only in July 1844 did
NC table in Brad start to reflect this – 'GATESHEAD'
replaced 'REDHEUGH' in table but timings left alone;
in October 1844 timings adjusted to include time taken
on incline link. Clo 30 August 1850 – result of opening
of Newcastle Central. Back in Brad November 1852 as
terminus of Tuesday and Saturday service to Swalwell
Colliery, which operated detached from system; last
shown May 1853.
OAKWELLGATE [Newcastle & Darlington Junction]
op 5 September 1839 from Wearmouth and South
Shields (co n dated 3rd); clo 2 September 1844 when
service diverted to Greenesfield, which was already
open (Cl). Brad 1844: G station, OAKWELL GATE.
GREENESFIELD [York, Newcastle & Berwick]
op 19 June 1844 (18th formal) as terminus for main
line service to south (co n T 24 May); clo 30 August
1850 (Cl), service concentrated on East.
G (EAST)* [NE] op 30 August 1850 (NE) – but some
sort of arrangement presumably needed here when
service across Tyne began 1 November 1848 – see note
at end of Newcastle-on-Tyne entry; clo 23 November
1981 (last train Sunday 22nd) – just G at closure
(BLN 435); replaced by TWM station.
G WEST* [NE] op 1 December 1868 (NE- line);
clo 1 November 1965 (RM November).
* = Brad added EAST and WEST 1872/3, and then only in
main line table; hb only one entry for both, 'G', until 1904.
GATESHEAD [TWM] op 15 November 1981 (Tyneside);
still open.
G STADIUM [TWM] op 15 November 1981 (Tyneside);
still open. Intended name was OLD FOLD and ticket
issued under that name (JB).
Also see METRO CENTRE
GATESIDE [NB] op 15 March 1858**; aot request;
clo 5 June 1950 (RM July).
GATEWEN [GW] op 1 May 1905 (GW H); HALT;
clo 1 January 1931 (Thursday) (T 20 December 1930);
{map 75}.
GATHURST [LY]
op 9 April 1855 (co n Southport Vis 5th); still open.
Became G for SHEVINGTON in Brad 1934/5, and hb
1936a; back to G 5 May 1975 (RM July).

GATLEY [LNW]
op 1 May 1909 (*LNW Officers 42501 + appendix*);
still open. Became G for CHEADLE 1 February 1911
(*RCG*) and thus LNW co tt 1921, LMS tt 1930;
reverted to G 6 May 1974 (*BR notice*).

GATWICK
GATWICK: *U* includes station clo to public in 1876; no
tt or other supporting evidence seen.
G RACECOURSE [LBSC] op non-tt 7 October 1891
(*RCG*); appeared in *Brad* June 1907 as G, apparently
full public station; last in *Brad* November 1907,
reverting to non-tt racecourse use; R added *hb*
1936a/1938; in use until 15 June 1940 (last); later used
for this 24 April 1948 (*AB*) and 10 July 1948 for air
pageant (B.Pask, *Chron April 2009*); site used for >
G AIRPORT (b), public station, 28 May 1958
(*Crawley Observer* …; R. Maund); still op.
G AIRPORT (a) [SR] had op 30 September 1935
(*SR sig inst 35/1935*) as TINSLEY GREEN FOR G A;
renamed 1 June 1936 (*SR*); closed 28 May 1958,
name transferred to G A (b), above.
GAVELL – see TWECHAR.
GAYTON ROAD [MGN]
op 1 July 1887 (*GN*); clo 2 March 1959 (*T 2nd*).
GEDDINGTON [Mid]
op 1 March 1880 (*Mid*); clo 1 November 1948 (*Mid*).
GEDLING [GN]
G & CARLTON op 1 February 1876 (*GN*);
clo 4 April 1960 (*Cl*). Only seen as G & C in *Brad*,
but *hb* 1876a had G, & C added 1877.
G COLLIERY (non-tt): PLATFORM; miners;
built May 1906; clo before 1940; {Daybrook – Gedling}
(A. Henshaw, *The Great Northern Railway in the East
Midlands, vol.1*, RCTS, 1999, p.60).
GEDNEY [MGN]
op 1 July 1862 (*Linc R & S Merc 4th*); aot request;
clo 2 March 1959 (*T 2nd*).
GELDESTON [GE] op 2 March 1863 (*T 5th- line*;
included in inspection report); clo 22 May 1916
(*T 2 May*); reop 14 September 1916 (*RCG*) as HALT;
ceased to be HALT 2 October 1922; aot request;
clo 5 January 1953 (*T 5th*).
GELDESTONE in *hb* until 1904.
GELLI near Treherbert
GELLI [TV] first in *Brad* October 1906; see 1904**;
last November 1912; later non-tt use (*U*); {in IA}.
Also see YSTRAD RHONDDA.
GELLI CEIDRIM [Llanelly] first in *Brad* November
1851 (perhaps in use earlier); then omitted (result of
lack of detail in tt then? intermittent use?), included
again April 1852 on; same mileage as Cross Keys (later
Glanamman), one minute between stops; aot request;
last in *Brad* December 1861; {Glanamman – Garnant}.
GELLI FELEN [LMS] op 6 September 1933 (*RM
November*); HALT; clo 6 January 1958 (*BRWR notice
December 1957*); {Brynmawr – Clydach}.
GELLY MILL – see MACDUFF.
GELLYRHAIAD CROSSING [GW] (non-tt):
PLATFORM; miners; service approved 27 June 1912
by GWR Traffic Committee; began ?; ended ?;
{Hedreforgan – junction to east) (*RAC*).

GENERAL POST OFFICE – see ST PAULS.
GEORGE INN – see BRITHDIR.
GEORGE LANE – see SOUTH WOODFORD.
GEORGEMAS JUNCTION [High]
op 28 July 1874 (*High*); still open.
JUNCTION omitted 1913/14 to 1923 (*Brad*).
GEORGETOWN
GEORGETOWN [Cal] op 31 March 1841** as
HOUSTON; renamed 1 May 1926 (*hbl April*);
clo 2 Feb. 1959 (*Cl*).
True Line 87, has article on station here during WWI,
work on factory starting 25 September 1915.
Says Cal built station and operated lines connected
with factory – was this station the terminus of internal
line (see 7:2, Bishopton ROF) or a separate workers'
station on main line?
GERARDS BRIDGE [LNW]
op 3 February 1858 (*Ormskirk 4th*);
clo 1 August 1905 (Tuesday) (*LNW Officers 41559*);
{St Helens – Moss Bank}. GERRARDS B in *Brad* until
late 1850s; still thus LNW co tt 1864.
GERRARDS CROSS [GW/GC]
op 2 April 1906 (*T 5 March*); still open.
GETHIN PIT [GW/Rhy] (non-tt); PLATFORM; in
use about 1920?; {Troedyrhiw – Abercanaid} (*U*).
GIDEA PARK [GE] op 1 December 1910 (*RCG*)
as SQUIRRELS HEATH & G P;
renamed G P & S H 1 October 1913 (*hbl 23rd*),
G P 20 February 1969 (*Cl*); still open.
GIFFEN [Cal] op 4 September 1888 (*Cal*) as
KILBIRNIE JUNCTION; renamed 1 October 1889
(*hbl 24th*); clo 4 July 1932 (*Cl*). Seen as G JUNCTION
only in *hb*, 1890 to 1912 (inclusive).
GIFFNOCK [Cal] op 1 January 1866**; still open.
GIFFORD [NB]
op 14 October 1901**; clo 3 April 1933**.
GIGGLESWICK [Mid] op 30 July 1849 (*T 28 July,
1 September*) as SETTLE; renamed S OLD 1 May 1876
co tt (*Mid*), G 1 November 1877 (*RCG*); still open.
GILBERDYKE [NE] op 2 July 1840 (*Hull 10th*) as
STADDLETHORPE; renamed 7 January 1974
(*BR ER alterations leaflet of that date*); still open.
GILBEYS COTTAGES op 15 June 1959 (*GNS*);
HALT; request; clo 18 October 1965**;
{Carron – Knockando}.
GILDERSOME
GILDERSOME [LNW] op 1 October 1900 (*LNW
Officers 39764*); clo 1 August 1917 (Wednesday),
reop 5 May 1919 (*RCH*); clo 11 July 1921 (*RCG*).
G WEST [GN] op 20 August 1856 (*T 7th, 21st*); WEST
added 2 March 1951 (*Cl*); clo 13 June 1955 (*Cl*).
GILESGATE – see DURHAM.
GILESTON [Barry]
op 1 December 1897 (*Glam; Colliery 3rd- line*);
clo 15 June 1964 (*RM August*).
GW co tt 1932: G for ST ATHAN and the LEYS;
also BR ticket thus (*JB*).
GILFACH FARGOED [Rhy] first in *Brad* April 1908;
HALT until 5 May 1969 tt; still open.

GILFACH GOCH [GW]
GILFACH GOCH op 9 May 1881 *(Brad Sh 1882)*;
clo 5 March 1928, reop 26 March 1928 *(Cl)*; GOCH
added 30 June 1928 *(hbl July)*; clo 22 September 1930
(Cl); used by workmen's trains to Tremains platform;
began by March 1941, ended by June 1947 (special
notices); later excursions *(U)*.
G G COLLIERS PLATFORM (non-tt): op after 1915;
probably clo with above, 22 September 1930 – not in
July 1931 and later wtts;
{60 chains beyond G G}.
GILGARRAN [WCE Jt] (non-tt): HALT; shown on
OS map about 1925, on Cleator & Workington Junction
south-east of junction at Distington; no other information.
GILLESPIE ROAD – see ARSENAL.
GILLETTS CROSSING [PW] op 1 October 1913
(LNW Cl); clo 1 October 1915 (Friday) *(Cl)*, reop by
August 1919 *(RM August* 'has reopened' – no trains
July 1919 *Brad)*; HALT; clo 11 September 1939 *(Cl)*.
GILLING [NE]
op 1 June 1853** - line; clo 2 February 1953 *(RM March)*;
later military and school (until 28 April 1964 – *Whitby)*;
RM February 1955 refers to shopping and football
excursions; ramblers' specials to 27 July 1964 *(Away)*.
NE co tt 1880, LNE tt 1933 and *Brad* to closure:
G for AMPLEFORTH COLLEGE.
GILLINGHAM DORSET [LSW]
op 2 May 1859 *(W Fly P 3rd)*;
DORSET added 9 July 1923 *(hbl 26 April)*; still open.
LSW co tt 1914: G for MERE and thus *Brad* until 1923.
GILLINGHAM KENT [LCD] op 24 June 1858 as
NEW BROMPTON, in time for Chatham races
(E Kent notice T 21st); in 1886 *Brad* became N B G,
but N B & G 1904 *(hb)*; became G 1 October 1912
(hbl 24th); KENT added 9 July 1923 *(Cl)*; still open.
Brad dropped KENT from body of tt 1955 but it was
restored in 14 June 1965 tt, having remained in index
and sometimes been used in table headings in the
interval; was G K in *hb* 1938.
GILLOW HEATH – see BIDDULPH.
GILMANSCROFT [GSW] (non-tt): daily workmen's
train from Muirkirk, stopping at intermediate stations,
G JUNCTION and G COLLIERY; dates ?; *(GSW
Society Journal 38, p.44)*; {Junction was 26 chains from
Auchinleck; it was the end of a branch, which served
several collieries, 1m 78ch beyond – was stop at
Junction to allow miners from opposite direction to
join trains here?}.
GILMERTON [NB]
op 23 July 1874**; clo, except for workmen's services,
1 January 1917 *(RM February)*; fully reop 2 June 1919
(RCH); clo 1 May 1933 *(RM March)*.
GILMOUR STREET – see PAISLEY
GILNOCKIE [NB]
op 2 November 1864 (R.B. McCartney, *The Railway to
Langholm …*, private, 1981 – based on reop date of
Langholm branch since tickets issued to station-master
here in October 1864) but not in *Brad* until October
1865; clo 15 June 1964 *(RM July)*.
Hb 1866a, NB co tt 1900, *Murray* 1948 and *Brad*/BR
tts to closure: G for CLAYGATE.

GILSHOCHILL
op 3 December 1993 as LAMBHILL *(BLN 725)*;
renamed 24 May 1998 *(RM August)*; still open.
GILSLAND [NE]: line op 19 July 1836 (see 1836 B**),
nd, in *Scott* 1837; originally ROSE HILL (body) /
ROSEHILL (index) *(Brad)*; renamed 1 May 1869 *(Cl)*;
clo 2 January 1967 *(RM January)*.
Scott 1837: R for G in tt, R H text.
GILWERN [LNW] first in *Brad* April 1863 but *LNW
MTA Minutes Engineer's Reports 27 January 1863* say
supposed to be ready in 3 or 4 weeks, 6 August say has
been open for five months, suggesting actual opening
late February/early March; became HALT 1932/3 *(Brad)*;
clo 6 January 1958 *(BRWR notice December 1957)*.
GIPSY HILL [LBSC]
op 1 December 1856 *(T 31 October, 28 Nov.)*; still open.
Alias GYPSY HILL *(L)*. Became G H for UPPER
NORWOOD 1911/12 *(RCG ref January 1912)* and
thus LBSC co tt 1912, *hb* 1938 and *Brad* until 1955.
GIRTFORD [LMS]
op 1 January 1938 *(T 8 December 1937)*; first appeared
in *Brad* July 1938 as a HALT, though *notices* for that
month implied it had just been renamed to that;
clo 17 November 1940 (Sunday) *(Cl)*; {Sandy – Blunham}.
GIRVAN [GSW]
G OLD op 24 May 1860 *(co ½ T 3 September)*; OLD
added 5 October 1877; clo 1 April 1893 (Saturday) *(Cl)*.
GIRVAN op 19 September 1877** as G NEW; NEW
dropped 1 April 1893; clo 7 February 1882 (Tuesday),
reop 1 August 1883, clo 12 April 1886, reop 14 June
1886, clo 2 September 1886, reop 14 July 1890 *(Cl)*;
still open.
GISBURN [LY] op 2 June 1879 *(Lancs Chesh)*;
clo 10 September 1962 *(T 5 July)*. *Brad* ? to 1950/1 but
not LMS tt 1930: G for BOLTON-BY-HOWLAND.
GLADSTONE DOCK
GLADSTONE DOCK [LO] op 16 June 1930 *(RM
August)*; clo 31 December 1956 *(T 29 September)*.
GLADSTONE DOCK [LY] op 7 September 1914
(RCG); clo 7 July 1924 *(Cl)*. Became HALT 1916 *(Brad)*.
GLAIS [Mid] op 21 February 1860 *(Mid; Mining
Journal 25th- line)*; re-sited on deviation March 1875**;
clo 25 September 1950 *(RM November)*; {map 88}.
GLAISDALE [NE] op 2 October 1865 *(co ½
T 14 February 1866- line)*; still open.
GLAMIS [Cal] op 4 June 1838 *(Tayside)*; last in *Brad*
July 1846 (but see 1837 B**); reop 2 August 1848
(Rtn- line); clo 11 June 1956 *(RM June)*.
GLAMMIS/GLAMMISS early.
GLAN CONWY [LNW]
op 17 June 1863 *(LNW Officers)* as
LLANSAINTFFRAIDD; renamed G CONWAY
1 January 1865 *(Cl)*; clo 26 October 1964 *(RM Dec.)*;
reop 4 May 1970 *(T 8 April)*; spelling altered 12 May
1980 *(BLN 392)*; aot request; still open.
GLAN LLYN [GW] op 4 August 1868 *(Carnarvon 11th)*
as private station for Sir W. W. Wynn but unofficial
public use with his consent; in paper as 'a flag station
at Glanllyn'; in *hb* as SIR WATKIN'S, later FLAG
STATION; first in *Brad* 20 September 1926 as F S;
officially public 14 September 1931 *(GW H)*; became

F S HALT 4 July 1938 *(Cl –* from *Brad?)* but still F S
in GW wtt 28 September 1938; renamed G L HALT
25 September 1950 *(Cl)*; clo 18 January 1965★★;
{Llanderfel – Llanuchllyn}.

GLAN-YR-AFON near Llanidloes [GW]
op 16 January 1928 *(Oswestry area notice 13th)*;
HALT *(Brad)*; clo 31 December 1962 *(T 31st)*;
{Tylwch – Pantydwr}. In *hb* 1938 as PLATFORM.

GLANAMMAN [GW] first in *Brad* May 1851
(perhaps op earlier since no detail given for a while
previously) as CROSS KEYS; renamed 1 December
1884 *(RCH dist 12 February 1885)*; aot request;
clo 18 August 1958 *(T 11th)*.

GLANDWYFACH – see 1867 September 2★★.

GLANDYFI [Cam]
GLANDYFI op 1 July 1863 *(Cam; co ½ T 28 August– line)*
as GLANDOVEY (GLAN-DOVEY in *Brad* until
1880/1, GLAN DOVEY in *hb*); renamed 1 July 1904
(hbl 7th); clo 14 June 1965 *(RM July)*.

GLANDOVEY JUNCTION – see DOVEY JUNCTION.

GLANRAFON [VoR] (ng) op 7 May 1904 *(VoR)*;
see 1902 December 22★★ (for line history);
HALT until 6 May 1968 *(Cl)*; to preservation 1989.

GLANRAFON [NWNG] (non-tt): quarrymen;
op ?; clo 31 October 1916;
{Snowdon Ranger – South Snowdon} *(U)*.

GLANRHYD [Vale of Towy Joint]
first in *Brad* May 1858; clo 20 July 1931 *(Cl)*,
reop 19 December 1938 as HALT *(GW notice dated
'December')*; aot request; clo 7 March 1955 *(LMS/GW
Joint Officers 22 September)*. Aot Glan-rhyd in *hb*.

GLANTON [NE] op 5 September 1887 *(NE– line)*;
clo 22 September 1930★★ *(T 10 July)*.

GLANYLLYN [Cardiff] op 1 March 1911 *(RCG)*;
clo 20 July 1931 *(GW goods circular 13th –* after last
train 18th).

GLANYRAFON near Oswestry [Cam]
op 1 September 1904 *(RCG)*; aot request; HALT;
clo 15 January 1951 *(Cl)* – see 1951★★.

GLAPWELL [Mid]
GLAPWELL (public station) op 22 August 1892 *(Mid)*;
clo 28 July 1930 *(LNW Record)*.

GLAPWELL (non-tt), alias G COLLIERY SIDING(S):
op 1 September 1886 wtt; clo 14 September 1931 wtt;
{Palterton – Glapwell} *(Mid)*.

GLASBURY-ON-WYE [Mid] op 19 September 1864
(co n Hereford J 24th); -on-WYE added 1 February
1894 *(RCG)*; clo 31 December 1962 *(T 31st)*.

GLASCOED [GW]
GLASCOED (public) op 16 May 1927 *(co n dated 'May')*;
HALT; originally platform on downside of single line,
moved to up 22 April 1938 *(Cl)*; clo 30 May 1955★★
(wtt 8 June 1953 shows only served by public trains so
probably fully closed); {Usk – Little Mill Junction}.
Non-tt stations for Ordnance workers, first two on
main line, third on a branch:
G EAST ACCESS; HALT; op 3 January 1943 *(RAIL
250/450)*; alias E A ROAD HALT; clo by mid-1953 –
23 May 1949 wtt shows only used by one train each
way (combined Newport/Blaenavon sections) and that
absent 8 June 1953 wtt – relevant train to G R O F.

G WEST ACCESS; HALT; op 12 June 1941 for
workmen's train; 18 June 1941 service by public trains
added *(GW Superintendent of line's letter)*; before/with
23 May 1949 wtt was G CROSSING HALT;
by 8 June 1953 wtt only stops by public services shown
so probably fully clo 30 May 1955, with Usk line service.
G ROYAL ORDNANCE FACTORY; first trains with
construction workers ran to level crossing at Glascoed
24 May 1938 (no platform); probably later temporary
platforms until station op 6 October 1940 *(RAC)*;
clo 24 April 1961.
Also see WERN HIR.

GLASGOW {map 15}
*Some stations in addition to those listed below were at one
time shown in tt as 'GLASGOW xxx'. Those not listed here
will be found under their own initial letters, as will all on the
Glasgow Subway.*
Most Glasgow stations were just 'GLASGOW' in early tts.
The additions given below were added mostly about
1850 or later, often at first only in tables where there
were two possibilities for a particular service.
G BRIDGE STREET [Cal] op 14 July 1840 *(GSW)*;
permanent buildings op 4 April 1841 *(GSW)*;
clo 1 March 1905 (Wednesday) *(RCG)*.
CLYDE PLACE: Col. Cobb's Atlas shows a [Cal]
station of this name between BRIDGE STREET and
CENTRAL, just south of the river, open 1879 to 1889.
However, no reference to this has been seen in any
timetable or Clearing House publication. The map of
Glasgow in Bacon's 'Atlas of the British Isles', undated
but last census 1881, shows BRIDGE STREET right
alongside Clyde Place (street) with no room for anything
between there and the river. The likely explanation is to
be found in Brand's Chronology; in this there were
many instances of the same information being given
double or multiple entries under different letters of the
alphabet. Under 'C': 'Clyde Place (Glasgow) opened
for passengers' ... 1 July 1879. Under 'B': 'Bridge Street
Station (as remodelled) opened for passengers' ...
12 July 1879. Given the map evidence, and lack of
mentions elsewhere, it would seem that these two
entries referred to the same station (or two parts of one
station), though the different dates cannot be explained
with certainty – for different stages of the work?
G BUCHANAN STREET [Cal] op 1 November 1849
(T 6th); clo 7 November 1966 *(RM January 1967)*.
G CENTRAL [Cal] op 1 August 1879 *(Glas)*; still open.
Aot G C HL GORDON STREET *(hb)*;
G C HL in *Murray* 1948.
G CENTRAL LL [Cal] op 10 August 1896 *(RCG)*; *RM
February 1899* says permanent station now open and
temporary closed – does not give exact date or any
details about site; clo 5 October 1964 *(RM November)*;
reop 5 November 1979 *(RM December)*; still open, since
1979 both levels of G Central treated as single station.
G COLLEGE – see G HIGH STREET.
G DUNLOP STREET [CGU] op 12 October 1870
(minute of 19th, *SRO BR/CGU/1/5)*;
absorbed into G ST ENOCH, 1 May 1876.
G GALLOWGATE [GSW]★ op 19 December 1870 for
NB service to Coatbridge (minute of 26th,

SRO BR/CGU/1/5); clo 1 April 1871 (Saturday), service diverted to College (later High Street) (minute of 3rd, *SRO BR/CGU/1/6)*; reop 17 May 1871 (minute of 22nd, *SRO BR/CGU/1/6)*, with start of hourly Bellgrove to Shields Road service; additional service 1 June 1871 when through Edinburgh to Greenock trains began (minute of 3rd, *SRO BR/CGU/1/6)*;
clo to public 1 October 1902 (Wednesday) *(RM Nov.)*. Included in *Brad* December 1904 with Renfrew Wharf, workmen's service (see 1967 June 5**); last in tt September 1926 *(G&S)*.
* = [CGU] until 1896.

G GALLOWGATE CENTRAL [NB] op 1 June 1892 *(Glas)*; clo 1 January 1917 *(RM February)*.

G GORBALS [GBK Jt] op 1 September 1877 *(GSW)*; clo 1 June 1928 (Friday) *(Cl)*.

G HIGH STREET [NB]* op 1 April 1871 *(D&C 6)* as COLLEGE, a terminus; replaced at lower level by new station (still C) on through line 15 March 1886 *(D&C 6; co ½ T 19 March- line)*; renamed 1 January 1914 *(hbl 29th)*; still open.
* = COLLEGE originally shown in RCH sources (error?) as [CGU/NB Joint]. *Brad Sh* shows that ground for station belonged to CGU and that might have led RCH to think that NB station, built on rented land was part CGU property; shown as [NB] only by 1883.

G LONDON ROAD [Cal] op 1 April 1879 *(Cal)*; clo 1 November 1895 (Friday) *(RCG)*.

G MAIN STREET [GSW]: fares agreed 27 April 1871 so likely opening date is either 1 April 1871 with start of Dunlop Street to Govan service (opening date given by minute of 3rd; minute agreeing fares could have been confirmation of what was already in operation) or 17 May 1871 with start of hourly Bellgrove to Shields Road service. First in *Brad* June 1871 when latter first added to Glasgow–Coatbridge service; not added to Govan table until January 1872. This would initially suggest 17 May 1871 as opening date, with trains on Govan and other relevant services added later; however CGU co tt includes it in Govan table by September 1871. Replaced 20 August 1900 *(RCG)* by station later renamed Cumberland Street.

G QUEEN STREET [NB] op 21 February 1842 *(Scotsman 23rd)*; still open. G Q S HL in *Murray* 1948.

G QUEEN STREET LL [NB] op 15 March 1886 *(Glas; co ½ T 19 March)*; still open.

G ST ENOCH [GSW]* op 1 May 1876 *(GSW)*; clo 27 June 1966 *(Cl)*. Later use: 4 July 1966 for King's Troop Royal Horse Artillery to Kensington Olympia for Royal Tournament *(Rly Obs August p. 266)*.
* = [CGU] until 1883 (transferred before split between NB and GSW).

G SOUTH SIDE [GBK Jt] op 27 September 1848 *(Rtn)*; clo 1 October 1877 *(Cl)*.

G SOUTH SIDE [Cal] op 1 June 1849 *(T 5th)*, as G GUSHETFAULDS; became G S S November 1849 *(Brad)*; terminus for Hamilton trains, which were diverted to Bridge Street 1 July 1879 (Tuesday) *(Cl)*; replaced by EGLINTON STREET [Cal] – under 'E'.

G TOWNHEAD (alias ST ROLLOX) [Cal] op 1 June 1831 *(MK)*; replaced by Buchanan Street 1 November

1849 *(Cl)* – see under 'S' for later ST ROLLOX through station.

GLASGOW CROSS [Cal] op 1 November 1895 *(RCG; T 2nd- line)*; clo 5 October 1964 *(RM November)*. Argyle Street near later.

GLASGOW GREEN [Cal] op 1 November 1895 *(RCG; T 2nd- line)*; clo 1 January 1917 *(RM February)*; reop Monday 2 June 1919 *(RCH)*; clo 2 November 1953 *(RM December)*.

GLASSAUGH [GNS] op 1 April 1884 *(GNS)*; clo 21 September 1953 *(RM November)*.

GLASSEL [GNS] op 2 December 1859 *(GNS)*; clo 28 February 1966 *(RM March)*. According to *RM October 1960* had become a HALT but not thus in *Brad*.

GLASSFORD [Cal] op 2 February 1863** *(Cal)*; in *Brad* became HALT 1933, reverted to G 1937/8 and thus to closure (but became HALT *hb* 1944a); clo 1 October 1945 *(RM March 1946)*.

GLASSHOUGHTON
op 21 February 2005 *(Rly Obs April)*; still open.

GLASSON near Carlisle [NB]:
line op 22 June 1854 *(D&C 14; Rtn- line)*, nd, in August *Brad* as a request stop all days; omitted March 1858 (error?); back April 1858 Saturdays only; all days again June 1884; clo 1 January 1917 *(Cl)*, reop 1 February 1919 *(RM Feb)*; August 1921 *Brad* includes PORT CARLISLE line, but without trains. Trains were shown September 1920 and July 1922. Another casualty of 1921 April/May**?
Clo 1 June 1932 (Wednesday) *(T 3 March)*.

GLASSON DOCK near Lancaster [LNW]
op 9 July 1883 *(LNW Officers 24972)*; clo 7 July 1930 *(Cl)*. LNW co tt July 1883 said it was 'expected' that this would open on 2nd; clearly a short delay.
G D PLATFORM on 1928 Junction Diagram.

GLASTERLAW

GLASTERLAW (a) [Scottish North Eastern]:
line op 1 February 1848 *(co n RM February 1953)*, nd, May *(Topham)*; last in tt March 1849.

GLASTERLAW (b) [Cal] first in *Brad* September 1880, initially Saturdays only, to Montrose only; August 1882/ July 1883 one all days from Montrose, also extra 'Mn' (= Mondays only?) to Montrose; certainly by April 1885 all days, both ways; clo 2 April 1951 *(RM May)*. Aot G JUNCTION in *Brad*.

GLASTONBURY & STREET [SD Jt]
op 28 August 1854**; see 1859 March 16**; & S added 1885 *(RCG ref October)*; clo 7 March 1966 *(Shepton 11th)*.

GLAZEBROOK [CLC] op 1 September 1873 *(MS&L co ½ T 21 January 1874)*; still open.

GLAZEBURY & BURY LANE [LNW]:
line op 17 September 1830**, nd, 1 March 1831 co tt; clo 7 July 1958 *(RM August)*. Op as B L, renamed G 1878 *(RCG ref April)*, G & B L 1883/4 *(Brad)*.

GLEMSFORD [GE]
first in *Brad* July 1866; clo 6 March 1967 *(RM April)*.

GLEN – see GREAT GLEN.

GLEN DOUGLAS [NB]:
at first non-tt; line opened 7 August 1894; not in NB wtt July 1896; note (probably regular fixture) in wtt

alterations 6 February 1922 that any of five trains each
way could be stopped on request, clearly by any traveller;
according to *U* was for use by railwaymen and families,
school teacher, occasional visitors; wtts 11 June 1956
and 13 June 1959 also show trains both ways, none
noted as 'not advertised'; op to public 12 June 1961 *(U)*;
aot PLATFORM/HALT; clo 15 June 1964 *(RM July)*.
Wtt 6 March 1967 shows Thursday and Saturday stops
for domestic purposes *(IU)*; Wtt 7 May 1973 stop
Thursdays only for domestic purposes, Saturdays only
for track walker (G. Borthwick);
{Whistlefield – Arrochar}.

GLEN FALLOCH [LNE] (non-tt):
workmen Loch Sloy HEP; op 10 April 1946;
clo later 1940s; {Ardlui – Crianlarich} *(U)*.

GLEN PARVA – see under WIGSTON.

GLENBARRY [GNS]
op 1 October 1859 *(GNS)* as BARRY; last in *Brad*
October 1863*; back September 1870; renamed 1872
Brad; aot request; clo 6 May 1968 *(RM July)*.

* = *GNS* does not show closure so perhaps remained open
but not included in tt – latter rearranged at relevant time.

GLENBIRNIE – see GLENBURNIE.

GLENBOIG [Cal] first in *Brad* February 1880;
clo 11 June 1956 *(RM April)*.

GLENBUCK [Cal] first in *Brad* October 1875;
clo 4 August 1952 *(RM September)*.

GLENBURNIE [Edinburgh & Northern]
op 9 December 1847 *(Tayside)* as a temporary terminus;
clo 17 May 1848 *(co n Perthshire Courier 18th)*; {map 5}.
In tt as GLENBIRNIE but this was probably
mis-spelling by tt printers – estate shown on 1850s map
is GLENBURNIE and NB wtt later used this version
(D. Lindsay), as did *Edinburgh Advertiser*, which only
mentioned opening 'shortly'.

GLENCARRON [High]: approval given for station
9 May 1871 *(High)*, though not in *Brad* until August
1873 (earliest use as private station?); PLATFORM
until 10 September 1962 *(Cl)*; aot request;
clo 7 December 1964, but later unadvertised use –
revenue shown *(High; Lochalsh)*.
Hb 1938 showed as HALT.

GLENCARSE [Cal] op 24 May 1847 *(Perthshire
Courier 27th)*; clo 11 June 1956 *(RM April)*.

GLENCORSE [NB] op 2 July 1877 *(Edin)*; clo 1 May
1933 *(RM March)*. GLENCROSS in early *Brad* and
RCG ref January 1878 for alteration/correction.

GLENCRUITTEN SUMMIT [LMS] (non-tt):
railwaymen, schools; op ?; clo after 1938;
{Connel Ferry – Oban} *(U)*.

GLENDON & RUSHTON [Mid] op 8 May 1857
(Mid; co ½T 13 August- line) as R; renamed 1 March
1896 *(hbl 23 April)*; clo 4 January 1960 *(RM February)*.

GLENEAGLES [Cal]
op 14 March 1856, with Crieff branch *(Tayside)*, as
CRIEFF JUNCTION; renamed 1 April 1912 *(RCG)*;
still open.

GLENELLRIG [Monkland]: line op 5 August 1840
but this station later in the 1840s *(MK)*; early tts nd,
first found July 1848 *(Topham)*; clo 1 January 1850
(Tuesday) *(Cl)*; {Slamannan – Avonbridge}.

GLENESK [NB] first in *Brad* October 1855;
originally trains shown both ways, last northbound
train shown January 1861; then southbound only until
clo (does tt tell full story? Unadvertised exchange use?);
clo 1 November 1874 (Sunday) *(Cl)*;
unadvertised use to at least 1886 *(U)*;
{Millerhill – junction with line to Dalkeith}.
In *Brad* at first as G for LASSWADE;
became G JUNCTION for L 1859/61, G J 1869/70.

GLENFARG [NB]
op 2 June 1890 *(Tayside)*; clo 15 June 1964 *(RM July)*.

GLENFIELD [Mid] op 18 July 1832 *(Mid)*; see 1847
December**; re-sited east of level crossing 1875 *(Mid)*;
clo 24 September 1928 *(Mid)*.
Used 1 July 1938 for educational excursion to
Port Sunlight and 2 July 1938 for British Legion one
to Mablethorpe *(Rly Obs August p.266)*.

GLENFIELD [Cal]: perhaps built about 1902
between Barrhead New and Stanely for suburban
service that never materialised *(U)*.

GLENFINNAN [NB] op 1 April 1901 *(RCG)*;
still open. LNE tt 1933, *Murray* 1948 and BR tts to
17 May 1982: G for LOCH SHIEL.

GLENFOOT – see under TILLICOULTRY.

GLENGARNOCK
GLENGARNOCK [GSW] op 14 June 1841 co tt *(GSW)*
as KILBIRNIE; became G & K 1888 *(RCG ref April)*,
G 1 June 1905 *(hbl 27 April)*; still open.
G HIGH [Cal] op 2 December 1889 *(RCG)*;
HIGH added 2 June 1924**; clo 1 December 1930 *(Cl)*.

GLENLOCHY CROSSING [LMS] (non-tt):
railwaymen and families; op ?; clo? – still shown
15 September 1952 wtt. {Tyndrum – Dalmally}.

GLENLUCE [PPW Jt] op 12 March 1861 *(Galloway
15th)*; clo 14 June 1965 *(RM July)*.

GLENOGLEHEAD – see KILLIN.

GLENROTHES WITH THORNTON
op 11 May 1992 *(RM June)*; still open.

GLENSIDE [GSW]
op 17 May 1906 *(RCG)*; clo 1 December 1930 *(Cl)*.

GLENWHILLY [GSW] op 19 September 1877**;
clo 7 February 1882 (Tuesday), reop 16 February 1882,
clo 12 April 1886, reop 14 June 1886 *(Cl)*;
clo 6 September 1965 *(RM September)*;
later use by railwaymen *(U)*.

GLOBE ROAD & DEVONSHIRE STREET [GE]
op 1 July 1884 *(L)*; clo 22 May 1916**;
{Bethnal Green – Coborn Road – just east of earlier
London Devonshire Street – see maps in P. Kay,
GE in Town & Country, part 3, Irwell, 1996}.

GLOGUE [GW] op 12 July 1875 *(Whitland)*;
clo 10 September 1962 *(Cl)*.

GLOSSOP
GLOSSOP [GC] op 9 June 1845 *(GC)*; G CENTRAL
10 July 1922 *(hbl 13th)* to 6 May 1974 *(BR notice)*;
still open.

G JUNCTION – see DINTING.

GLOUCESTER {map 95}
GW expected that Birmingham – Gloucester – Bristol
line would become part of GW; however, it became
part of Mid instead.

[**Birmingham & Gloucester**] op 4 November 1840
(Bath & Chelt 10th) >
[**Bristol & Gloucester**] was originally operated by GW;
service began 8 July 1844, using platform added to
station above >
Station became **GLOUCESTER** [Mid]; replaced by
through station 12 April 1896 *(Mid)*; renamed
G EASTGATE 1951 >
[**GW**] arrived from Swindon 12 May 1845, initially
using Bristol & Gloucester platform; own station
op with line to South Wales 19 September 1851
(Gloucester J 20th); renamed G CENTRAL 1951 >
EASTGATE and CENTRAL combined 26 May 1968
as G *(Mid)*; old Mid part closed 1 December 1975
(Cl); GW part still open.
G 'T' STATION [GW] op 23 October 1847 with
Gloucester avoiding line *(T 25th)*;
clo 19 September 1851 *(Cl)*.
GLOUCESTER ROAD
GLOUCESTER ROAD [Met] op 1 October 1868
(T 16th, 30th September); sometimes BROMPTON G R
until 1903 *(Brad)*; [Dist] service began 12 April 1869;
still open.
GLOUCESTER ROAD [Picc] op 15 December 1906
(co n T 14th); clo 30 August 1987, reop 21 May 1989
(ug); still open.
GLYN ABBEY [BPGV]
op 2 August 1909** as PONTNEWYDD;
renamed 1910 tt *(Cl)*; HALT until 1913, when moved
from notes to table in *Brad* and again from 3 May 1943
(Cl); clo 21 September 1953 *(T 16th)*.
GLYN COLLIERY [TV] (non-tt): approval for
station given 26 April 1892; clo by September 1928;
{branch from Treferig, in *IA*, goods} *(U)*.
GLYN NEATH [GW] op 24 September 1851**;
clo 15 June 1964 *(RM August)*.
GLYNCEIRIOG [Glyn] (ng) {map 79}
NEW INN G op 1 April 1874 *(GlynV)*;
clo 1 April 1886 *(Cl)*.
GLYNCEIRIOG op 15 March 1891 *(Cl)*; reopening of
above; clo 7 April 1933**.
GLYNCORRWG [GW] op to public March 1918**
(see for full details); clo to public 22 September 1930 *(Cl)*.
GLYNDE [LBSC] op 27 June 1846 *(LBSC; Hants
Chron 4 July- line)*; still open.
GLYNDYFRDWY [GW]
op 8 May 1865 *(D&C 11)*; clo 14 December 1964**.
GLYNE GAP [LBSC]
op 11 September 1905 *(LBSC)*; HALT; last in tt
September 1915; {Bexhill – St Leonards}.
GLYNHEBOG COLLIERY SIDING [BPGV]
(non-tt): miners used from about 1898 *(U)*; still in use
15 September 1952 wtt; {Pontyberem – Cwmmawr}.
GLYNRHONWY [LNW]: only evidence found is in
LNW Officers, minute of 13 July 1870; G is included,
one train each way per day, in tt proposed for Llanberis
line, following opening of Carnarvon Town Line.
Line through G had op 1 July 1869. Not found in *Brad*,
where timings suggest still in use both ways May 1872,
reduced to one train from Llanberis January 1873.
LNW co tt timings suggest April 1870 that most trains

were stopping here on way to Llanberis; January 1874
none either way (though *Brad* April 1874 suggested
one still stopping – presumably inertia); in *hb* as siding,
latterly for slate company; {Llanberis – Cwm-y-glo}.
GLYNTAFF [ANSW]
op 1 September 1904**; clo 5 May 1930 *(Cl)*.
GNOSALL [LNW]
op 1 June 1849 *(Shrewsbury 8th)*;
clo 7 September 1964 *(RM October)*.
At times GNOSSAL, GNOSAL *(hb, Brad)*; LNW co tt
altered from GNOSAL to GNOSALL in body 1864/70
but index still using earlier form in 1883.
GOATHLAND [NE]
GOATHLAND (a): line op 26 May 1836 (see 1835 B**).
Omitted from *Brad* October 1857; back April 1858, in
footnotes as terminus of Saturday afternoon service
from Whitby; shown fully again November 1863;
however, throughout this period trains had to stop
hereabouts to join/leave incline haulage; April 1858
entry probably only included because G was terminus
– presumably at least one train took people to Whitby.
GOATHLAND (b): New station on deviation line 1 July
1865, op as G MILL; MILL dropped 1 November
1891 *(Cl)*; clo 8 March 1965 *(T 19 January)*;
occasional later severe weather use *(U)*.
GOATHLAND (c): 20 May 2007 tt included this,
service from Whitby (not Mondays and Fridays), run
by North Yorkshire Moors Railway; still included.
G SUMMIT – see end of 1835 B**.
GOBOWEN [GW]
op 14 October 1848 *(Shrewsbury 13th)*; still open.
GODALMING [LSW]
G OLD op 15 October 1849 *(Hants Chron 20th)*;
OLD added on opening of G NEW; clo 1 May 1897
(Cl); replaced by FARNCOMBE.
GODALMING op 1 January 1859 *(SR corr; T 1st- line)*;
G NEW until 1 May 1897 *(RCG)*; still open.
GODLEY
GODLEY station at the Toll Bar [Sheffield, Ashton-
under-Lyne & Manchester] op 17 November 1841 *(Rtn)*;
temporary terminus; clo 11 December 1842 *(GC dates)*
when line extended – 10th was last day; no immediate
replacement.
G EAST [CLC/GC] op 1 February 1866 *(CLC)*
as G JUNCTION; J dropped 6 May 1974 *(Cl)*;
EAST added 7 July 1986, when effectively replaced by
next entry; after that only token service (one train per
week to Manchester, often in footnotes only) until last
train ran Saturday 27 May 1995 *(BLN 754)*.
GODLEY op 7 July 1986 *(BLN 543)*; still open.
GODMANCHESTER [GN/GE] op 17 August 1847
(EC co ½ T 13 August) as HUNTINGDON / H JOINT
and acted as its station; service from St Ives reduced to
horse-drawn one from October 1849 to December
1849 *(Companies)*; renamed G 1 May 1882 *(Mid)*;
clo 15 June 1959 *(RM July)*.
GODNOW BRIDGE [GC]
first in *Brad* November 1859; Saturdays only;
last February 1917; {Medge Hall – Crowle}.
GODREAMAN [GW]
op to public 1 January 1906**; HALT;

see 1921 April/May**; re-sited 2 January 1922; finally clo to public 22 September 1924; {goods IA}.

GODSHILL [IWC] op 20 July 1897 *(SR; Rtn- line)*; aot request; became HALT 1928/9 *(Brad)*; clo 15 September 1952 *(T 6 August)*. *Brad ?* to closure: G HALT for SANDFORD.

GODSTONE [SE] op 26 May 1842 *(co n T 13th, T 20th)*; clo 25 July 1992 for work on Bletchingley Tunnel in connection with electrification, reop 31 August 1993 *(Network SouthEast North Downs pamphlet – RMd)*; still open.

GODSTONE ROAD – see PURLEY.

GODWINS [Mid] op 9 August 1905 *(Mid)*; HALT; clo 16 June 1947**.

GOGAR [NB] first in *Brad* July 1842; see 1842 February 21**; clo 22 September 1930 *(Cl)*.

GOGARTH [GW] op 9 July 1923 *(GW H)*; HALT until 6 May 1968 *(GW H)*; clo 14 May 1984 *(RM June)*; {Dovey Junction – Aberdovey}.
In 1983 there were no trains 28 May to 4 June and 16 July to 3 September; schools on holiday; trains scheduled to call here ran term time only *(RM August)*.

GOITRE [GW] first in *Brad* starting 9 July 1923; clo 9 February 1931 *(Cl)*; {Abermule – Kerry}.
Not Halt in *Brad* but only in *hb* 1929 as G SIDING, which suggests it was treated as one.

GOLANT [GW] op 1 July 1896 *(Cornwall; W Brit 9th – 'now a station at G')*; clo 2 April 1917 *(RCH)*, reop 1 November 1917 *(Cl)*; see 1921 April/May**; clo 1 January 1940 *(hbl L 50)*, reop 9 February 1942 *(hbl L 17)*, clo 24 August 1942, reop 3 October 1942, clo 2 May 1944 (Tuesday), reop 2 October 1944 *(Cl)*; became HALT 1938 *hb*, 1952 *Brad*; clo 4 January 1965 *(W Briton 7th)*.

GOLBORNE

G NORTH [GC] op 3 January 1900 *(RM January)*; NORTH added 1 January 1949 *(RM March)*; clo 3 March 1952 *(RM April)*.

G SOUTH [LNW]: line op 3 September 1832, station probably later *(C to C)* – certainly by 19 October 1839 *Brad*, where GOLBOURNE GATE; soon altered to GOLBORNE; SOUTH added 1 January 1949 *(RM March)*; clo 6 February 1961 *(Cl)*.

GOLCAR [LNW] op 1 August 1849 *(co ½ T 18 August- line; in co tt for 1 August, Stockport 3rd)*; clo 7 October 1968 *(RM November)*.

GOLDEN GROVE [LNW] op 1 June 1865**; clo 9 September 1963 *(T 9th)*.

GOLDEN HILL Pembroke [GW] op 1 July 1909 *(RCH)*; PLATFORM; clo 5 February 1940 *(Cl)*.

GOLDEN HILL near Preston – see LEYLAND.

GOLDEN SANDS [RHD] (ng) (non-tt) HALT used only for holiday camp, op 1948 *(Wolfe)*; see 1927 July 16** for later history of line.

GOLDENHILL near Stoke-on-Trent – see NEWCHAPEL.

GOLDERS GREEN [Nor] op 22 June 1907**; still open.

GOLDHAWK ROAD [HC] op 1 April 1914 *(RCG)*; still open.

GOLDSBOROUGH [NE] first in *Brad* Feb. 1850;

originally GOULDSBOROUGH (amended 1853 *Brad* but *hb* 1899a); clo 15 September 1958 *(RM Oct.)*.

GOLDTHORPE

GOLDTHORPE op 16 May 1988 *(Mid)*; still open.

G & THURNSCOE [Dearne] op 3 June 1912**; clo 10 September 1951 *(RM November)*.
Was renamed from HICKLETON two days before passenger traffic added to existing goods *(hbl 13th)*.

GOLF CLUB HOUSE [GNS] op 1 October 1913 *(GNS)*; request; originally all year use; by December 1920 reduced to May to November (inc), by end to May to September (inc) *(GNS)*; HALT; clo 6 July 1964 *(RM July)*; {Banff – Ladysbridge}.
Hb: at first G H HALT, amended May 1961a.

GOLF LINKS [Rye & C] (ng) op 13 July 1895**; no winter service after 1925; clo 4 September 1939 *(Cl)*; {Rye – Camber}.

GOLF STREET Carnoustie op 7 November 1960 *(RM May 1961)*; at first trains southbound only; northbound added 11 September 1961 *(BR Scottish Regional tt)*; HALT until 16 May 1983; still open.

GOLFA [Cam] (ng) op 6 April 1903 *(D&C 11)*; aot request; clo 9 February 1931 *(Cl)*.

GOLLANFIELD [High] op 7 November 1855** as FORT GEORGE; renamed GOLLANFIELD JUNCTION 1 July 1899 *(hbl 13th)*, G 1959; clo 3 May 1965 *(RM June)*.

GOLSPIE [High] op 13 April 1868 *(High)*; aot request; still open.

GOMERSAL [LNW] op 1 October 1900 *(LNW Officers 39764)*; clo 5 October 1953 *(RM November)*.

GOMSHALL [SE] op 20 August 1849 as G *(co n T 18th)*; still open.
At first in *Brad* as G & SHEIRE/G & S HEATH*; became G & SHERE 1897/8 *(Brad)*; just G from 12 May 1980 tt *(Cl)*.
* = *Brad* did not give station detail for this line until some time after it opened; likely that SHE(I)RE added after closure of station there.

GOODGE STREET [Nor] op 22 June 1907** as TOTTENHAM COURT ROAD; renamed 9 March 1908 *(L)*; still open.

GOODMANS CROSSING – see 1883 August 20**.

GOODMAYES [GE] op 8 February 1901 *(RCG)*; still open.

GOODRINGTON SANDS [GW] op 9 July 1928 *(GW H)*; HALT; SANDS added 24 September 1928 *(GW H)*. Usually closed in winter; clo end summer 1928, reop 25 March 1929 (J.R. Pike, *Paignton, Torquay, a Bibliographical* Guide, Borough of Torbay, 1974, p.18); not after October 5th *(22 September 1930 Brad)*; but no restriction 12 Sept. 1932; trains calling January 1936 and January 1941; no trains GW co tt 6 October 1941 and later winter tts seen – e.g. until Sunday 29 September 1952 (inclusive) and commencing Sunday 3 May 1953.
See 1972 November 1**; {Paignton – Churston}.
According to 'notices' panel *Brad* July 1938 had been renamed from G-ON-SANDS HALT to G S HALT; always G S in tables – error?

GOODWICK – see FISHGUARD.

GOOLE

GOOLE [LY] op 1 April 1848 *(co ½ T 7 September)*;
service diverted to NE station 1 October 1879
(Wednesday) *(Cl)*.

GOOLE [NE] op 2 August 1869 *(T 2nd)*; still open.
Hb 1956 showed it as G TOWN, name confined in
1938 issue to goods use; not seen thus *Brad*, though
according to *RM April* TOWN dropped 12 June 1961.

GOONBELL [GW] op 14 August 1905**;
HALT clo 4 February 1963 *(W Briton 4th)*.

GOONHAVERN [GW] – details as Goonbell.

GOOSEPOOL – see 1825**.

GOOSTREY [LNW]
op 1 September 1891 *(LNW Officers 32907)*; still open.

GORBALS – see GLASGOW.

GORDON [NB] op 16 November 1863 *(co ½
T 4 April 1864- line)*; clo 13 August 1948**.

GORDON HILL [GN] op 4 April 1910 *(wtt notice
NLRHS Journal 41)*; still open.

GOREBRIDGE [NB] op 14 July 1847 *(co n
Edinburgh Advertiser 13th)*; clo 6 January 1969
(RM February). Until 1872 GORE BRIDGE in *hb*.

GORGIE EAST [NB] op 1 December 1884 *(Edin)*;
EAST added May 1952 *(Cl; ref RM July)*;
clo 10 September 1962 *(BR n Ed Sub)*.

GORING & STREATLEY [GW] op 1 June 1840
(GW; co n T 30 May- line); & S added 9 November
1895 *(hbl 23 January 1896)*; still open.

GORING-BY-SEA [LBSC]
op 16 March 1846 *(LBSC; T 17th- line)*;
-by-S added 1 April 1908 *hbl 23rd)*; still open.

GORLESTON-ON-SEA [Norfolk & S]
G LINKS first in *Brad* March 1914; clo 1 May 1918,
reop 21 October 1919 after agreement with golf clubs
(GE Journal October 2003); HALT until 6 May 1968
(Cl); clo 4 May 1970 *(RM May)*;
{Hopton – Gorleston}.
G NORTH op 13 July 1903 *(co n Norfolk & S)*;
clo 5 October 1942 *(T 25 September)*.
GORLESTON-ON-SEA op 13 July 1903 *(co n Norfolk
& S)*; clo 4 May 1970 *(RM May)*.

GORNAL [GW] op 11 May 1925 *(RM June)*; HALT;
clo 31 October 1932 *(RM January 1933)*; {map 96}.
G Crossing pre-op *(RAC)*.

GORS-Y-GARNANT [GW]
op 1 January 1908 *(GW H)*; HALT;
clo 2 April 1917 *(Cl)*; reop 7 July 1919 *(GW circ 2672)*;
see 1921 April/May**; clo 4 May 1926**.

GORSE LANE Swansea – see ST GABRIELS.

GORSEINON [LNW] op 14 December 1867
(The Cambrian 20th) as LOUGHOR COMMON;
renamed G for L 1 February 1868 *(RCH dist 19th)*;
'for L' dropped 1874/5 *(Brad)*; clo 15 June 1964 *(RM
August)*. Also G ROAD in local press.

GORTAN/GORTON [NB] (non-tt):
op ? wtt for West Highland, July 1896, shows one stop
each way on Fridays only by passenger trains – to
Glasgow one called 7.56 a.m., to pick up and 8.12pm
other way to set down; at 12.53 a goods to Fort William
shown as dropping provisions for workmen here on
Tuesdays and Fridays.

T, 26 August 1938, described remote setting.
Then: 'Until last Easter a morning and afternoon train
stopped especially at Gorton Box to take the
[railwaymen's] children to and from Rannoch, but this
little school has become overcrowded so the LNER
have provided a carriage body which has been placed
on the platform by Gorton Box and fitted up with
chairs and desks and at Easter this year a young woman
teacher was appointed by the educational authorities of
Argyll County Council and now gives lessons at what
must be one of the most unusual schools in Great Britain'.
Trains now stopped for teacher; still 'P' 1956 *hb*;
still in use December 1968; crossing place closed by
1975, ending need for school *(U)*;
{Bridge of Orchy – Rannoch}.

GORTON [GC] op 23 May 1842 *(GC)* as G;
re-sited about 200 yards east 26 August 1906 *(GC dates)*,
as G & OPENSHAW; renamed G 6 May 1970 tt;
still open.

GORTONS BUILDINGS – see WEASTE.

GOSBERTON [GN/GE] op 6 March 1882 *(GN/GE)*;
clo 11 September 1961 *(RM September)*.

GOSFORTH

See SOUTH GOSFORTH; WEST GOSFORTH.
G SHEDS (non-tt): regular service between here and
Newcastle for railwaymen shown 11 March 1940 wtt
and succeeding war years.

GOSPEL OAK

GOSPEL OAK [LNW] op 2 January 1860 *(T 2nd)* as
KENTISH TOWN; renamed 1 February 1867 *(L)*;
still open. LNW co tt 1869, LMS tt 1930 and *Brad*/BR
tts to 7 May 1973: G O for HIGHGATE.

GOSPEL OAK [TH Jt] platforms op 4 June 1888* *(Mid)*;
regular service ceased 1 November 1925, began again
1 June 1926, finally ceased 6 September 1926; bank
holiday service last ran 7 August 1939; also used by
football specials to Northumberland Park for
Tottenham Hotspur's home games. Evidence from
ticket dated 22 October 1932 and club's Handbooks.
Likely that last use was for game on 26 August 1939
last home game before war intervened. (B. Pask).
On 5 January 1981 service from Barking rerouted
to terminate here instead of Kentish Town;
bay platform added.
* = in 1868 platforms partly built here but not used (K.A. Scholey,
Railways of Camden, Camden Historical Society, 2002).

GOSPORT [LSW]

GOSPORT op 29 November 1841**; clo 8 June 1953
(RM July); also used for naval reviews *(S Spec)*.

G CLARENCE YARD (non-tt): on extension from
Gosport for Queen Victoria's trips to Portsmouth and
the Isle of Wight. First used 13 September 1845 by
special train from London carrying Ministers to Privy
Council meeting *(T 5th)*. Even royal lines could open
in incomplete state – later 1845 Lords of the Admiralty
were considering plans for an appropriate royal
reception room *(T 22 December)*.
Examples of use: 23 April 1856 for Queen's visit to
review Fleet at Spithead *(T 24th)*, for outward journey
described in WOOLWICH DOCKYARD entry.
Used by Queen Victoria's Funeral Train 2 December

1901 (see *RM February 1901*; article by GP Neele, *RM December 1906*, for further details).

GOSPORT ROAD & ALVERSTOKE [LSW]
op 1 June 1865 *(SR corr)* as STOKE(S) ROAD;
became G R 8 November 1866 *(JS)*, G R & A 1893 *(Cl)*;
clo 1 November 1915 *(RCH)*; {map 127}.

GOSWICK [NE]
first in *Brad* November 1870 as WIND MILL HILL;
renamed 1 January 1898 *(hbl 27th)*; clo 5 May 1941,
reop 7 October 1946 *(RM January 1947)*;
clo 15 September 1958 *(RM October)*.
In *hb* as WINDMILL HILL.

GOTHERINGTON [GW]
op 1 June 1906 *(Chelt Chron 2nd)*; became HALT
1 January 1941 *(RM March)*; clo 13 June 1955 *(Cl)*.

GOUDHURST [SE] op 1 October 1892 *(SE)* as
HOPE MILL for G and LAMBERHURST;
renamed G 1 December 1892 *(Cl; RCG ref Jan. 1893)*;
clo 12 June 1961 *(T 12th)*.

GOURDON [NB] op 1 November 1865 *(co ½
T 3 November- line)*; clo 1 October 1951 *(RM Nov.)*.

GOUROCK [Cal] op 1 June 1889 *(Cal)*;
clo 5 February 1973 for tunnel repairs, reop 20 April
1973; clo 3 October 1993 (Sunday) *(BLN 718)*;
reop 27 March 1995 *(BLN 752)*; still open.

GOVAN
GOVAN [GP Jt] op 2 December 1868 *(GSW)*;
clo 1 July 1875 (Thursday), reop 1 March 1880,
clo April 1899 *Brad*, back May 1902, last May 1906,
back February 1911; clo 9 May 1921 *(Cl)*;
see 1967 June 5**.
GOVAN [GU] op 14 December 1896**; still open.

GOVILON [LNW] op 1 October 1862**;
clo 6 January 1958 *(BRWR notice December 1957)*.
GOVILAN in *Brad* until 1872, *hb* until 1890.

GOWER ROAD Swansea – see GOWERTON
GOWER STREET London
– see EUSTON SQUARE.
GOWER STREET Swansea – see SWANSEA.

GOWERTON
GOWERTON [GW] op 1 August 1854 *(The Cambrian
28 July)* as GOWER ROAD; renamed GOWERTON
8 June 1886 *(Cl)*; G NORTH 1950 *(Cl)* to 6 May
1968 tt *(offic)*; still open.
G SOUTH [LNW] op 14 December 1867
(The Cambrian 20th) as GOWER ROAD; renamed
GOWERTON 1 July 1886 *(RCH dist 25 August)*,
G S 1950 *(Cl)*; clo 15 June 1964 *(RM August)*.

GOXHILL [GC]
op 1 March 1848 *(co n GC)*; still open.

GOXHILL ROAD – see WASSAND.

GRACE DIEU [LNW] op 2 April 1907 *(LNW Cl)*;
clo 13 April 1931 *(LNW dates PCC)*. See 1905** (a).

GRAFHAM [Mid] op 1 March 1866 *(Mid; co n
T 27 February- line)*; GRAFFHAM until 1 February
1877 *wtt (Mid)*; clo 15 June 1959 *(RM July)*.

GRAFTON & BURBAGE [MSWJ] op 1 May 1882
(W Gaz 5th); clo 11 September 1961 *(T 9th)*.

GRAHAMSTON – see under FALKIRK.

GRAIG MERTHYR COLLIERY: (non-tt):
miners; ? to 1960s; {line from Pontard(d)ulais} *(U)*.

Often wrongly spelled (including in earlier version
of this book) CRAIG M.

GRAIN {Middle Stoke – Port Victoria}.
G CROSSING [SEC] first in *Brad* July or August 1906;
HALT; substituted 11 June 1951 by bus until
replacement ready – next entry; line shortened by
about 300 yards for oil refinery expansion.
GRAIN op Monday 3 September 1951 *(SR sig inst
1/1951*, which dated to 2nd – but no Sunday service
here); clo 4 December 1961 *(Cl)*.

GRAINSBY [GN] op 11 December 1905 *(GN)*;
see 1905** (d); clo 1939 *(Cl)* – trains shown October
1939 *Brad* but not January 1940 (still shown, trainless,
until 1941).

GRAMPOUND ROAD [GW] op 4 May 1859**;
clo 5 October 1964 *(Cl)*.

GRANBOROUGH ROAD
[Aylesbury & Buckingham; Met/GC] first in *Brad*
December 1868; see 27 March 1874**; [Met] use
began 1 July 1891; GRANDBOROUGH ROAD until
6 October 1920 *(Cl; RCG ref October)*; aot request;
clo 6 July 1936 *(RM July)*.

GRAND SLUICE [West Lancs] (non-tt): *Liverpool &
Southport Daily News*, 12 to 16 December 1878 carried
notice that trains would stop here for benefit of skaters;
line crossed Sluice about half-way between Crossens
and Banks.

GRAND SURREY CANAL – see 1835 June 9**.

GRANDTULLY [High]
op 3 July 1865 *(High)*; clo 3 May 1965 *(RM June)*.

GRANGE [GNS] op 5 January 1857 *(GNS corr)*;
clo 6 May 1968 *(RM July)*.

GRANGE COURT [GW] isolated entry October
1853 *Brad*, without trains; actually op 1 June 1855**;
clo 2 November 1964 *(Cl)*.
Aot G C JUNCTION *(hb, Brad)*, one word GW co tt.

GRANGE HILL op by [GE] 1 May 1903 *(RCG)*;
last steam train ran Saturday 29 November 1947 *(Clay)*;
buses until reop by [Cen] 21 November 1948 *(T 20th)*;
still open. From July 1912 *(hbl 24 October)* to ? was
G H for CHIGWELL ROW (thus GE co tt 1914,
LNE tt 1933) to 1947 clo *(Brad)* or later.

GRANGE LANE [GC] first in *Brad* June 1855;
clo 7 December 1953 *(RM January 1954)*.

GRANGE PARK [GN] op 4 April 1910 *(wtt notice
NLRHS Journal 41)*; still open.

GRANGE ROAD [LBSC] op 2 April 1860 *(LBSC)*;
aot request; clo 2 January 1967 *(RM February)*.
Became G R for CRAWLEY DOWN and TURNERS
HILL 14 February 1912 *(hbl 25 April)* and thus LBSC
co tt later 1912, *hb* 1938; 'for ...' dropped 1955 *(Brad)*.

GRANGE-OVER-SANDS [Fur]
op 1 September 1857** *(Fur)*; initially, and
intermittently later, just G; still open.

GRANGEMOUTH [Cal] op 1 November 1861
(Falkirk Herald 7th); clo 29 January 1968 *(RM March)*.
Also platforms for Carron Line's ships to London;
original at Carron Dock (arrangements approved by
BoT 6 June 1889); replaced by one at new Grange Dock
(1907), different route from main station *(MT 6/1715/1)*;
not continuous use – at times replaced by road

connection; perhaps lasted until WW1 (all D. Stirling).
Non-tt: 1 January 1918 to well on into 1918 workers'
trains to platforms at Mine Depot here, run at
Admiralty insistence (*True Line July 2005*, from
E. Pratt, *British Railways and the Great War*).
GRANGESTON [LMS] (non-tt): HALT;
Ordnance workers; op 15 December 1941 *(WW II)*;
clo ?; added 'P' *hb* 1949a, shown closed May 1957a;
{Killochan – Girvan}.
GRANGETOWN near Penarth [TV] op 29 May
1882 *(GW Minutes RAIL 250/33 – RAC)*; still open.
GRANGETOWN until 1890s *(Brad, hb)*.
GRANGETOWN near Middlesbrough [NE]
op 22 November 1885 (S&D) as ESTON GRANGE,
replacing earlier station, listed under ESTON;
renamed 1 January 1902 *(RCG)*; clo 25 November 1991
(last train 24th) (RM December); {map 43}.
GRANITE QUARRY [Glyn] (non-tt):
workmen; dates ?; alias HENDRE QUARRY;
{end of Glyn Valley line} *(U)*.
GRANTHAM [GN]
GRANTHAM op 15 July 1850; service diverted to
station below 15 July 1852*; later called Old Wharf.
* = presumed from opening date of next station – or did some
trains continue to use until through express service began,
1 August 1852?
GRANTHAM op 15 July 1852** *(Newark; T 20th- line)*;
still open.
GRANTON
GRANTON [NB] op 19 February 1846 *(Edin)*;
clo 1 January 1917 *(RM February)*, reop 1 February
1919 *(RM Feb.)*; clo 2 November 1925 *(RM Jan. 1926)*.
G GASWORKS [Cal] (non-tt): used by workmen at
least 1902 to 1942 *(U)*.
GRANTON ROAD [Cal] op 1 August 1879 *(RCG)*;
clo 30 April 1962 *(RM May)*.
GRANTOWN-ON-SPEY
G-O-S EAST [GNS] op 1 July 1863 *(GNS)*;
clo 18 October 1965**.
G-O-S WEST [High] op 3 August 1863 *(High)*;
clo 18 October 1965**.
Both: -on-S added 1 June 1912 *(hbl 3 July)*,
EAST/WEST 5 June 1950 *(Cl)*.
GRANTSHOUSE [NB]: line op 22 June 1846**,
nd, September; clo 4 May 1964 *(RM June)*.
GRANTS HOUSE *Brad* and e.g. NB co tt 1900;
to one word 1915 *(Cl)*.
GRANVILLE STREET – see BIRMINGHAM.
GRAPPENHALL ROAD – see LATCHFORD.
GRASSCROFT [LNW] op 1 January 1912 *(LNW
Officers 43577)*; clo 16 July 1917, reop 1 January 1919
(Cl); clo 2 May 1955 *(T 11 March)*. HALT *(hb)*.
GRASSINGTON & THRESHFIELD [Mid]
op 30 July 1902* *(RCG)*; & T added soon after op;
clo 22 September 1930 *(Cl)*; ramblers' excursions to
14 April 1968 (probably last) – now just 'G' *(AB)* .
* = four public trains at ordinary fares ran in afternoon 29th,
following formal opening (notices in *Midland Railway Society
Journal No. 20*).
GRASSMOOR [GC] op 1 November 1893
(GC dates); clo 28 October 1940 *(Cl)*.

GRASSMOOR COLLIERY [Mid] (non-tt):
op 1 January 1874 wtt *(Mid)*; clo 9 November 1927;
{branch from Clay Cross} *(Mid)*.
GRATELEY [LSW]
op 1 May 1857 *(W Fly P 5th)*; still open.
GRAVELLY HILL [LNW]
op 2 June 1862 *(W Mid; T 2nd- line)*; still open.
Hb 1862: GRAVILLY HILL, corrected 1863a.
GRAVESEND
GRAVESEND [SE] op 10 February 1845**;
clo 14 December 1846 (Sunday) for line rebuilding
(co n T 27 November – last train will run 13th);
reop 23 August 1847 *(co n T 20th)*; new station op
30 July 1849 *(Cl)*; G CENTRAL 1 June 1899 *(hbl July)*
to 14 June 1965 *(Cl)*; still open.
G WEST [LCD] op 10 May 1886 *(Kent Messenger 15th)*
as G; renamed G WEST STREET 1 June 1899
(hbl July), GW 26 September 1949 *(Cl)*;
clo 3 August 1953 *(RM September)*.
G WEST PIER [LCD] (non-tt):
used by boat trains from ? until 1914 *(U)*.
Also see Section 7, Non-rail.
GRAYRIGG
GRAYRIGG (a) [Lancaster & Carlisle] op by 15 July
1848, when first in weekly tt *Lancaster Gaz*;
clo 1 November 1849 (Thursday) *(Cl)*.
GRAYRIGG (b) [LNW] op 1 November 1861 *(co n
Lancaster Obs)*, two miles east of (a); clo 1 February
1954 *(RM March)*.
GRAYS [LTS] op 13 April 1854 *(Mid; T 13th- line)*;
still open. Alias G THURROCK early *(L)* – only seen
index *Brad* 1858/9 to 1865/6, not tables.
GRAYTHORP [NE] (non-tt):
Gray's shipyard workers; HALT; about 1920 to 1923;
{Seaton Snook branch}.
GREAT ALNE [GW]
op 4 September 1876 *(W Mid; Rtn- line)*;
clo 1 January 1917 *(GW notice dated 22 December 1916)*,
reop 18 December 1922 *(GW Mag January 1923)*;
clo 25 September 1939 *(GW goods circular 13 November)*;
later workmen's use, about July 1941 to Saturday 1 July
1944 (last) *(U)*.
GREAT AYTON [NE] op 1 April 1868 *(NE- line)*;
GREAT added 1874 *Brad*; still open.
GREAT BARR [LNW]
op 1 October 1862 *(LNW Officers)* as G B,
then HAMSTEAD & G B December 1862 tt *(JS)*,
G B 1 May 1875 *(LNW notices of alterations)*;
replaced by station, south of bridge, later renamed
HAMSTEAD, 25 March 1899 *(Cl)*.
Hb: G BAR & H 1863a.
GREAT BENTLEY [GE]
op 8 January 1866 *(T 10th- line)* as B GREEN;
renamed 1 May 1878 *(Cl; RCG ref July)*; still open.
GREAT BRIDGE
G B NORTH [LNW] op 1 May 1850 *(T 2nd)*;
NORTH added 1 July 1950 *(Cl)*; clo 6 July 1964
(RM August).
G B SOUTH [GW] op 1 September 1866 *(W Mid)*;
clo 29 November 1915 *(wtt supp)*, reop 5 January 1920
(GM's report 8th); see 1921 April/May**;

SOUTH added 1 July 1950 *(Cl)*; clo 15 June 1964 *(RM July)*.

GREAT BRIDGEFORD [LNW] op 1 December 1876 *(LNW Officers 16602)*, at/near site of earlier Bridgeford; clo 8 August 1949 *(RM September)*; railwaymen's use continued at least to mid 1952 *(U)*.

GREAT BROUGHTON [CW Jc] first in *Brad* September 1908; Saturdays only; last trains shown November 1908; according to article in *RM September 1912, p.223 on*, excursions and specials were then stopping there occasionally; in *hb* shown 'P' 1895 to 1912; 1922a 'closed' – end of excursions?; {goods *IA*}.

GREAT CENTRAL – see MARYLEBONE.

GREAT CHESTERFORD [GE] op 30 July 1845 *(co n T 26th- line)*; GREAT added 1 June 1875 *(RCG)*; still open.

GREAT COATES

GREAT COATES [GC] op 1 March 1848 *(co n GC)*; still open.

G C LEVEL CROSSING [GC GI] op 15 May 1912 *(RCG)*; clo 3 July 1961 *(co n G&I)*.

GREAT DALBY [GE/LNW] op 15 December 1879 *(Leic; LNW Record- line)*; clo 7 December 1953 *(T 7th)*.

GREAT DOVER STREET – see BOROUGH.

GREAT GLEN [Mid] op 8 May 1857 *(Mid; co ½ T 13 August- line)*; GREAT added 18 January 1897 *(Mid; hbl ref 28 January)*; clo 18 June 1951 *(RM August)*.

GREAT GRIMSBY – see GRIMSBY.

GREAT HARWOOD [LY] op 15 October 1877 *(Blackburn T – op two days before advertised date)*; clo 2 December 1957 *(RM January 1958)*. Certainly excursions Easter 1962 *(AB)*; used Wakes Weeks until 1963 (LY Society, *The North Lancs Loop – Branch Line Series No.10)*.

GREAT HAYWOOD [NS] op 6 June 1887 *(NS-K)*; reduced to one up train daily, no down trains with tt alterations of 28 July 1941 (J. Gough); HALT at clo 6 January 1947 *(RM January 1950)* – but not shown thus *Brad*.

GREAT HORTON [GN] op 14 October 1878 *(GN; T 15th- line)*; clo 23 May 1955**. *Hb* 1935a: renamed G H for LIDGET GREEN; though it remained thus in *hb*, not seen in *Brad*.

GREAT HOUGHTON [Dearne] op 3 June 1912**; GREAT added 24 August 1912 *(hbl 24 October)*; HALT; clo 10 September 1951 *(RM November)*.

GREAT LINFORD [LNW] op 2 September 1867 *(Rtn- line)*; GREAT added LNW co tt February 1884 *(C/W)*; clo 7 September 1964 *(RM October)*.

GREAT LONGSTONE [Mid] op 1 June 1863 *(Mid; co n T 29 May- line)* as L; became G L for ASHFORD 1 October 1913 co tt *(Mid)* and thus to closure; clo 10 September 1962 *(RM Sept.)*; condition of closure was that a hospital sister could continue to use when necessary *(T 18 May)*; certainly used 26 April 1966 (R. Maund); last available for her use Saturday 4 March 1967.

GREAT MALVERN [GW] op 25 May 1860 *(GW)*; still open. Many tts, including GW co tts, at times had M, M G.

GREAT MARLOW – see MARLOW.

GREAT MISSENDEN [Met/GC] op 1 September 1892 *(co n Foxell)*; Met use from opening, ended 11 September 1961; GC use began 15 March 1899; still open for ex-GC services.

GREAT ORMESBY [MGN] op 7 August 1877 *(T 9th)*; GREAT added 1 January 1884 *(Cl; RCG ref January)*; clo 2 March 1959 *(T 2nd)*.

GREAT PONTON [GN] op 15 July 1852**; clo 15 September 1958 *(Cl)*.

GREAT PORTLAND STREET [Met] op 10 January 1863 *(co n Portfolio)* as P ROAD; renamed 1 March 1917 *(hbl 12 July)*; still open. In *hb*, but not *Brad*, was G P S &/for REGENTS PARK 1923a until 1938.

GREAT SHEFFORD [GW] op 4 April 1898 *(co n Ephemera)* as WEST S; renamed November 1900 tt *(Cl; RCH dist ref 5 Dec.)*; clo 4 January 1960 *(RM February)*.

GREAT SOMERFORD [GW] op 18 December 1877 *(Bath Chron 20th- line)*; GREAT added 1 January 1903 *(RCG)*; HALT from 22 May 1922 *(Cl)*; clo 17 July 1933, when Malmesbury branch diverted to Little Somerford *(Bristol notice S1562)*; {map 122}.

GREAT WESTERN ROAD – see ANNIESLAND.

GREAT YARMOUTH

Railways have rarely until recently included GREAT – first BR National tt to do so was 15 May 1989 tt (A. Young).

GREAT YARMOUTH [GE] op 1 May 1844 *(T 14 April)*; Y VAUXHALL 1864/5 *(Brad)* to 3 May 1971 tt *(BLN 174)*; still open.

Y BEACH [MGN] op 7 August 1877 *(T 9th)*; BEACH added 1882/3 *(Brad)*; clo 2 March 1959 *(T 2nd)*.

Y SOUTH TOWN [GE] op 1 June 1859 *(T 2nd)*; S T added 1864/5 *(Brad)*; clo 4 May 1970 *(RM May)*.

GREATHAM [NE]: line op 10 February 1841** *(S&D)*; although not in *Brad* until January 1847, it was in inspection report dated 6 September 1841 *(Rtn)*; clo 25 November 1991 (last train 23rd) *(RM December)*.

GREATSTONE(-ON-SEA)

GREATSTONE-ON-SEA [SR] op 4 July 1937 *(SR sig inst 32/1937)*; HALT from 14 June 1954 *(Cl)*; clo 6 March 1967 *(RM April)*; {map 130}.

GREATSTONE [RHD] (ng) op 24 May 1928 *(RHD)* as G DUNES; D dropped later 1928 *Brad*; see 1927 July 16** for remainder of history.

GREEN BANK near Coalbrookdale [GW] op 12 March 1934 *(Cl 29)*; HALT; clo 23 July 1962 *(RM August)*.

GREEN LANE [Mersey] op 1 February 1886 *(D&C 10; T 2nd- line)*; still open. G L for LAIRDSIDE on nameboard by autumn 2002.

GREEN LANES

– see HARRINGAY STADIUM; NOEL PARK.

GREEN PARK

GREEN PARK [Jub] op 1 May 1979 *(RM July)*; still open.

GREEN PARK [Picc] op 15 December 1906 *(co n T 14th)*; as DOVER STREET (thus in *Brad*); see 1922**;

renamed 18 September 1933 when entrance re-sited (*T 18th, 19th* – called it new station); still open. *Hb* 1910a said it had opened as D STREET ST JAMES; altered 1935a.

GREEN PARK [Vic] op 7 March 1969 *(T 8th)*; still open.

GREEN ROAD [Fur]
first in *Brad* June 1852; aot request; still open.

GREENBANK [CLC]
op 22 June 1870 *(CLC)* as HARTFORD & G; renamed 7 May 1973 *(Cl)*; still open.
Line through here op to passengers 1 March 1870, for local service Acton Bridge to Northwich *(LNW)*; *Brad* showed this line October and November 1869, with a stop here; clearly error since December table was replaced by notice 'line expected to open soon'. When trains were shown again, March/April 1870, no stop was shown here.

GREENESFIELD – see under GATESHEAD.

GREENFAULDS
op 15 May 1989 *(RM July)*; still open.

GREENFIELD near Hamilton – see BURNBANK.

GREENFIELD near Huddersfield [LNW]
op 1 August 1849 *(co ½ T 18 August- line; in co tt for 1 August, Stockport 3rd)*; still open.

GREENFORD

GREENFORD [GW] op 1 October 1904 *(RCG)*; see 1921 April/May** for temporary loss of local service; June 1949 *Brad* still showed full use, but table heading warned that service was subject to alteration in July; before/with October 1949 *(Brad)* nearly all trains terminated at [Cen] station, only occasional through trains, varying over time, used [GW]; fully clo 17 June 1963 *(Cl)*; later excur *(U)*.

GREENFORD [Cen] op 30 June 1947 *(T 1 July)* by GW for Cen use; transferred to London Transport 1 January 1948; still open.
Also see SOUTH GREENFORD.

GREENHEAD [NE] op 19 July 1836 *(NC)*; clo 2 January 1967 *(RM January)*.

GREENHILL {map 11}

GREENHILL [Cal] op 1 March 1848 *(co ½ T 4 September-line)*; clo 18 April 1966 *(Cl)*.
At first G JUNCTION in Cal tables but CALEDONIAN JUNCTION, G LOWER J / LOWER G in Scottish Central tables *(Brad)*; *Murray* April 1852 also had CALEDONIAN JUNCTION so companies presumably responsible for this usage – best described as descriptive?
Also see UPPER GREENHILL.

GREENHITHE FOR BLUEWATER [SE]
op 30 July 1849**; for B added 1998/2000 tt; new station 14 March 2008 (photograph *RM May*); still open.

GREENLAW [NB] op 16 November 1863 *(co ½ T 4 April 1864- line)*; clo 13 August 1948**.

GREENLOANING [Cal]
op 23 May 1848**- line; clo 11 June 1956 *(RM April)*.
Cal co tt 1913, LMS tt 1930, *Murray* 1948: G for BRACO and thus to closure in *Brad*.

GREENMOUNT [LY] op 6 November 1882 *(LY)*; clo 5 May 1952 *(RM June)*.

GREENOCK

G BRIDGE STREET [Cal] op 31 March 1841** as G; became G CATHCART STREET 1877/8, G B S 1878/9 *(Brad)*; replaced on extension to Gourock by >

G CENTRAL [Cal]: op 1 June 1889 *(Cal)* as G CATHCART STREET; renamed 1 October 1898 *(RCG)*; still open.

LYNEDOCH G [GSW] op 23 December 1869 *(T 25th-line)* as L; became L G 1898 tt; clo 2 February 1959 *(RM March)*. G LYNEDOCH STREET *(hb)*.

G PRINCES PIER [GSW] op 23 December 1869 *(T 25th)* as G ALBERT HARBOUR; renamed 1 May 1875 *(JS)*; re-sited 100 yards north 25 May 1894 *(Cl)*; clo 2 February 1959 *(RM March)*; boat trains used to 20 November 1965 *(BLN 49)*.

G WEST [Cal] op 1 June 1889 *(Cal- line)*; still open.
Also see I B M; UPPER GREENOCK.

GREENODD [Fur] op 2 June 1869 *(Fur)*; reduced to summer only from 26 September 1938; clo 16 September 1940, reop 3 June 1946 *(Cl)*; clo 30 September 1946 *(Cl)*.

GREENS OF DRAINIE [Morayshire; GNS]
op 4 June 1853 *(GNS corr)*; last in *Brad* November 1859 but not actually closed until 1898 *(GNS)* – continuous use?; {map 3}.

GREENS SIDING [GW] first in *Brad* July 1903; clo 8 December 1941. In *hb* was G S 1908a (under Westbrook), G S HALT 1938 (under 'G') but not seen thus *Brad*, but with a name like G S likely to have been treated as one; {Clifford – Westbrook}.

GREENWAY [GW] op 1 April 1937 *(co n dated 'March')*; HALT; clo 13 July 1959 *(RM August)*; {Dymock – Ledbury}.

GREENWICH

GREENWICH [SE] op 24 December 1838 *(co n T 22nd)*; permanent station 12 April 1840 *(SE)*; still open. G PARK in *hb* 1877, amended (corrected?) 1879a.

GREENWICH [Dock] op 20 November 1999 *(RM January 2000)*; still open.

G PARK [LCD] op 1 October 1888 *(L)*; PARK added 1 July 1900 *(RCG)*; clo 1 January 1917 *(T 28 December 1916)*.
Also see MAZE HILL; NORTH GREENWICH.

GREETLAND [LY]
first in *Brad* February 1846 (but January table blank – 'arrangements incomplete') as NORTH DEAN; renamed G & N D 1 January 1883 *(Cl; RCG ref Jan.)*, G 22 December 1886 *(hbl 28 January 1887)* or 1 January 1887 *(RCG)* *; clo 10 September 1962 *(Cl)*.
N D JUNCTION 1852 to 1883 *(Brad)*.
* = should former have read 'will be renamed 1 January ...'? or was latter derived from timetable?

GREGSON LANE [LY] (non-tt): For workers at Brindle Mill which opened in 1895; also used by locals, especially for holiday specials. Originally G L Sidings; 'Halt' well established by 1909; tickets had to be bought from Bamber Bridge or Hoghton, whose station-masters notified trains of need to stop at Halt. Mill closed 1932 and Halt into disuse. Reopened in Second World War; finally closed ? – after 1 August

1952 (date on copy of ticket, provided by D. Geldard); {78 chains west of Hoghton}.

Also see article by F. Elliot, LY Society's *Platform*, no.22.

GRESFORD [GW] op 4 November 1846 *(co n GW)*; became G for LLAY 1923? *(hbl ref 12 July)* and thus GW co tt 1932; became HALT 1955 *(Brad)*; clo 10 September 1962 *(Cl)*; {map 75}.

GRESKINE [Cal] (non-tt): railwaymen and families; op 3 January 1900; clo after 1926 *(U)*; also see 1966★★; {Beattock – Elvanfoot}.

GRESLEY [Mid]
op 1 March 1849 *(Mid)*; re-sited east of road bridge about 1869 *(Mid)*; clo 7 September 1964 *(RM October)*.

GRESTY [LNW] op 2 January 1911 *(LNW Cl)*; clo 1 April 1918 *(RCH)*. HALT in July 1921 *RCH* list giving its closure date – see 1905★★.

GRETNA

GRETNA [Cal] op 10 September 1847 *(co n True Line)*; clo 10 September 1951 *(RM December, corr)*.
G JUNCTION 1849 to 1862/3 *Brad* and in Cal co tt 1859.
G [NB] op 1 November 1861 *(NB)*; clo 9 August 1915 *(RCG)*.
G GREEN (a) [GSW] op 23 August 1848 *(Dumfries 23rd)*; GREEN added 1852 tt; clo 6 December 1965 *(RM January 1966)*.
G GREEN (b) op 20 September 1993 *(BLN 712)*; short distance north of (a); still open.

GRETTON near Cheltenham [GW] op 1 June 1906 *(Chelt Chron 2nd)*; HALT; clo 7 March 1960 *(RM April)*.

GRETTON near Kettering [Mid]
op 1 March 1880 *(Mid)*; clo 18 April 1966 *(Cl)*.

GREYHOUND LANE – see STREATHAM.

GRIFFITHS CROSSING [LNW] first in *Brad* June 1854; HALT at clo 5 July 1937 *(RM August)*.

GRIMES HILL – see WYTHALL.

GRIMESTHORPE BRIDGE – see SHEFFIELD.

GRIMETHORPE

GRIMETHORPE [Dearne] op 3 June 1912★★; HALT; clo 10 September 1951 *(RM November)*.

G COLLIERY [Mid] (non-tt): HALT; miners; op 21 February 1916 *(Midland Special Traffic Notice 547, RAIL 963/107)*; clo at or by 7 March 1927 *(LMS notice of that date – not shown as suspended in January notice RAIL 957/12)*; {Mid branch from Storrs Mill Junction, Cudworth – trains ran to/from Barnsley via Cudworth}.

GRIMOLDBY [GN] op 17 October 1877 *(RCG)*; clo 5 December 1960 *(RM January 1961)*.

GRIMSARGH [Preston & Longridge]:
GRIMSARGH line op 2 May 1840★★, nd, July 1848; clo 2 June 1930 *(LNW Record)*.
Also see 7:6 Hospitals

GRIMSBY [GC] {map 64}
G DOCKS: inspection report 7 December 1854 said line from town to Docks in use some time for goods but so incomplete that approval for passenger use refused. 30 January 1855: company withdrew notice of passenger opening – line not yet ready for inspection *(Rtn)*. Station here actually op 6 April 1863 *(Grimsby ... Advertiser 11th)*. Still open.

G TOWN op 1 March 1848 *(co n GC)*; TOWN added 1900; still open. GREAT G in description *T 12 April*

1849 and *Brad* to about 1900; then G T, though occasionally just 'G'.

G PIER (non-tt): MS&L notice *(T 13 May 1852)* says new dock will be opened for steamers and ships [freight] on 27 May at noon. Clear PIER station would be available then – main line of railway extends to edge of low water landing-stage, 'where a passenger station is [compiler's underlining] built and to which passenger trains will run in connection with the boats'. Exact date of first use not known – said subsequent advertisements would give details, but none found. Certainly likely that was in use by mid-August since half-yearly report (and meeting) *(T 20, 26 August)* say steam packets running to Hamburgh [sic], Rotterdam and Antwerp. clo ? – no evidence of use 1880s or later.
Non-tt: report of 7 December 1854 referred to (very incomplete) CLEETHORPE [ROAD? – there is a mention of junction at C R as intermediate station; presumably nothing ever came of this.

Tramways
G PYEWIPE ROAD [GC] used by workmen from May 1906 *(U)*; op to public 3 January 1910 *(RCH)*; clo 15 May 1912 *(Cl)*; effectively replaced by next two >
G CLEVELAND BRIDGE [GC GI]
op 15 May 1912 *(RCG)*; clo 3 July 1961 *(co n G&I)*.
G CORPORATION BRIDGE [GC GI] op 15 May 1912 *(RCG)*; clo 1 July 1956 (Sunday) *(co n G&I)*.
These stops on town section of Grimsby & Immingham, shown in e.g. LNE tt 1933: YARBOROUGH STREET; STORTFORD STREET; JACKSON STREET; BOULEVARD RECREATION GROUND.

GRIMSTON [Mid] op 2 February 1880 *(RCG)*; clo 4 February 1957 *(T 4th)*.

GRIMSTON ROAD [MGN] op 16 August 1879 *(T 18th)*; clo 2 March 1959 *(T 2nd)*}.

GRIMSTONE & FRAMPTON [GW]
op 20 January 1857 *(W Fly P 27th)*; clo 3 October 1966 *(W D Press 3rd)*. First in *Brad* as F, became G for F August 1857, G September 1857, G & F before/with January 1859.

GRINDLEFORD [Mid]
op 25 June 1894 *(RCG)*; still open.

GRINDLEY [GN] op 23 December 1867 *(GN; T 23rd- line)*; clo 4 December 1939 *(Cl)*.

GRINDLEY BROOK [LMS]
op 4 July 1938 *(LNW Record)*; HALT; clo 16 Sept. 1957 *(LNW Record)*; {Whitchurch – Malplas}.

GRINDON [NS] (ng) op 29 June 1904★★; clo 12 March 1934 *(LNW Record)*.

GRINKLE [NE] op 3 December 1883 *(Rtn- line)* as EASINGTON; renamed 1 April 1904 *(hbl 28th)*; clo 11 September 1939 *(Cl)*.

GRISTHORPE [NE]:
line op 7 October 1846★★, nd, May 1848 *(Topham)*; clo 16 February 1959 *(RM March)*.

GROESFAEN COLLIERY/COLLIERS [BM] (non-tt): PLATFORM; agreement for workers' trains to/from Pengam dated 20 June 1919 *(GW deeds office)*; clo 31 December 1962 *(U)*; {Bargoed – Darran}.

GROESFFORDD [GW] op 8 September 1934 *(T 6th)*; HALT; clo 31 December 1962 *(T 31st)*.

GROESLON

For first service see 1829 B★★.

GROESLON [Nantlle] (ng) op 11 August 1856;
clo 12 June 1865, for conversion to standard gauge
(G&S) >

GROESLON [LNW] op 2 September 1867★★
(co ½ T 10 October- line); clo 7 December 1964 *(RM March 1965)*.

GROESWEN [ANSW] op 1 September 1904★★;
became HALT 1 July 1924 according to *GW circular 18 June* but always thus *Brad*; clo 17 September 1956
(RM October).

GROGLEY [LSW] op 1 June 1906 *(W Briton 4th)*;
HALT; clo 30 January 1967 *(Corn & D P 4 February)*;
{map 113}.

GROOMBRIDGE [LBSC] op 1 October 1866
(co n T 1st); clo 8 July 1985 *(RM June)*.

GROSMONT [NE]:
for op see 1835 B★★; originally TUNNEL INN;
renamed by time detailed tts first provided in 1848;
still open. Whitby & Pickering ticket for TUNNEL *(JB)*

GROSVENOR ROAD

GROSVENOR ROAD [LBSC] op 1 November 1870
(L) – in *Brad* by April 1870, no trains shown;
G R & BATTERSEA PIER until 1890 *(Brad)*;
clo 1 April 1907 *(RCG)*.
See BATTERSEA PARK.

GROSVENOR ROAD [LCD] op 1 November 1867
(co n T 29 October); clo 1 October 1911 (Sunday) *(RCG)*.
Both previously used as ticket platforms (op January 1867) *(L)*.

GROTTON & SPRINGHEAD [LNW] first in *Brad*
December 1857; & S added 1 May 1900 *(hbl 26 April)*;
clo 2 May 1955 *(T 11 March)*.

GROVE FERRY & UPSTREET [SE] first in *Brad*
July 1846, though *SE* implies op with line, 14 April
1846, as very basic station, with permanent later;
& U added 1954; clo 3 January 1966 *(RM Nov. 1965)*.

GROVE PARK [SE]
op 1 November 1871 *(L)*; still open.

GROVESEND [LNW] op 1 January 1910
(LNW Officers 42725); clo 6 June 1932 *(Cl)*.

GUARD BRIDGE [NB] op 1 July 1852
(co ½ T 4 November- line); clo 6 September 1965 *(Cl)*.

GUAY [High]
op 1 June 1863 *(High)*; clo 3 August 1959 *(Cl)*.

GUEST KEEN ... – see DOWLAIS, last entry.

GUESTLING – see DOLEHAM.

GUESTWICK [MGN] op 19 January 1882 *(MGN)*;
clo 2 March 1959 *(T 2nd)*.

GUIDE BRIDGE [GC] op 17 November 1841
(GC; Rtn- line) as ASHTON & HOOLEY HILL;
renamed A 1842, G B 1845 tt; still open.
G B JUNCTION some tables at least 1853–81 *(Brad)*.

GUILDFORD [LSW]
GUILDFORD op 5 May 1845 *(co n T 1st)*; still open.
G JUNCTION 1852/3 to 1858/9 *(Brad)* but *RCG ref January 1921* for dropping of JUNCTION.
Temporary station at St Catherines Tunnel op 23 March
1895 *(U)*; clo 1 April 1895 *(U)*.
Also see LONDON ROAD GUILDFORD.

GUISBOROUGH [NE]
op 25 February 1854 *(co ½ T 25 August)*;
clo 2 March 1964 *(RM April)*.

GUISBOROUGH LANE
– see STOCKTON [S&D].

GUISELEY [Mid]
op 1 August 1865 *(Mid- wtt; co ½ T 11 August- line)*;
clo for electrification 25 July 1992 *(BLN 689)*;
reop 8 September 1992; still open.

GULLANE [NB]
GULLANE op 1 April 1898 *(RCG)*;
clo 12 September 1932 *(co n N Berwick)*.
G PRIVATE GOLF CLUB PLATFORM (non-tt): ticket
25 April 1900 *(JB)*; in NB 1 April 1914 wtt alterations
as P G C PLATFORM. Perhaps alternative name for
LUFFNESS (which see), perhaps extra stop between
there and Gullane – OS map shows string of courses
thereabouts.

GUNNERSBURY op by [LSW] 1 January 1869
(co n T 24 December 1868) as BRENTFORD ROAD;
renamed 1 November 1871 *(L)*; [Dist] use began
1 June 1877; [Met] used 1 October 1877 to 1 January
1907; LSW use ended 5 June 1916; still open.

GUNNESS & BURRINGHAM [GC]
op 2 August 1869 *(GC dates)*; clo 21 May 1916
(Sunday) *(Cl)*; {in IA, goods}.

GUNNISLAKE [PDSW]
op 2 March 1908 *(W Morn News 3rd)*; clo 31 Jan. 1994
(RM June); new station short of old op 9 June 1994
(BLN 890) – planned for 2nd but delayed; still open.

GUNTON [GE] op 29 July 1876 *(T 29th)*; still open.

GUPWORTHY – see 1865 September 4★★.

GUSHETFAULDS

GUSHETFAULDS [Cal] op 6 April 1885 as
CATHCART ROAD *(Cal)*; renamed 1 July 1886 *(Cl; RCG ref July)*; clo 1 May 1907 (Wednesday) *(RCG)*.
At times GLASGOW C R, tts.
Also see GLASGOW SOUTH SIDE [Cal].

GUTHRIE [Cal] op 4 December 1838 (see 1838★★);
clo 5 December 1955 *(RM January 1956)*.
G JUNCTION 1849 to 1882/3 *(Brad)*.

GUYHIRNE [GN/GE] op 2 September 1867★ *(GN)*;
clo 5 October 1953 *(RM November)*.
★ = GN minutes say 1st but that a Sunday and no Sunday service.

GWAELODYWAEN COLLIERY [BM] (non-tt):
op ?; clo by June 1954; {Pengam – Bargoed} *(U)*.

GWAUN-CAE-GURWEN

GWAUN-CAE-GURWEN [GW] op 1 January 1908
(GW H); HALT; clo 2 April 1917 *(Cl)*, reop 7 July
1919 *(GW circular 2672)*; see 1921 April/May★★;
clo 4 May 1926★★. Included 'P' in hb 1912 to 1938 –
and not shown as halt.

GWAUN-CAE-GURWEN [Mid] shown 'P' only in *hb*
1899a (cumulative since 1895) – assumed error,
amended to 'G' only 1904.

G-C-G COLLIERS – see CWMLLYNFELL.

GWENDRAETH COLLIERY [BPGV] (non-tt):
ticket 18 February 1911 *(JB)*; {Glyn Abbey – Pontyates
– or on branch between these? – see *RAC* Atlas}.

GWERNYDOMEN [BM] first in *Brad* October
1908★★; HALT; clo 17 September 1956 *(RM October)*.

GWERSYLLT {map 75}
GWERSYLLT [WMCQ] op 1 May 1866 *(T 7th)*;
still open. G & WHEATSHEAF in *hb* 1883 on but not
thus *Brad*.
G HILL [GW] op 1 May 1906 *(GW H)*; HALT;
clo 1 January 1931 (Thursday) *(T 20 December 1930)*.
GWINEAR {map 111}
Tt and local press evidence seen gives no support to
there being a station for Gwinear on the original Hayle
to Redruth line (see 1843 May 23★★).
G ROAD [GW] first in *Brad* November 1853 (also in
tt Penzance 2 November) – likely that op 1 November
with new tt; clo 5 October 1964 *(Cl)*.
1890–1912 G R JUNCTION *(hb)*.

GWYDDELWERN [LNW] op 6 October 1864
(D&C 11); clo 2 February 1953 *(RM March)*.
GWYS [Mid] op 2 March 1868 *(Mid)*;
clo 25 September 1950 *(RM November)*.
GYFEILLON [TV] op 5 June 1905 *(RM July)*;
see 1904★★; last in *Brad* July 1918.
GYPSY LANE
op 3 May 1976 *(Rly Obs July 1976)*; still open.

"A SOFT ANSWER," ETC.

Stout Lady Passenger (wincing—he had trod on her best corn). "PHEW!—CLUMSY—"
Polite Old Gent. "VERY SORRY, MY DEAR MADAM, BUT IF YOU HAD A FOOT LARGE ENOUGH
TO BE SEEN, SUCH AN ACCIDENT COULDN'T OCCUR!"

H

HABROUGH [GC] op 1 March 1848 *(GC)*; still open.
HACHESTON [LNE] op 9 April 1923 *(GE Journal April 1983)*; though service that included this HALT began in November 1922 (P. Paye, *The Framlingham Branch*, Oakwood, 2008); clo 3 November 1952 *(RM December)*; {Marlesford – Parham}.
HACKBRIDGE [LBSC]
op 1 October 1868 *(T 28 September)*; still open.
HACKNEY
HACKNEY [NL] op 26 September 1850 *(T 12 October, co ½ T 26 February 1851)*; re-sited 1 December 1870 *(NL Circular 81)*; clo 15 May 1944 but replacement bus service to 23 April 1945 *(Cl)*.
H CENTRAL op 12 May 1980 *(RM July)*; still open.
H DOWNS [GE] op 27 May 1872 *(co n T 25th)*; still open. H D JUNCTION most tables until 1897/8 *(Brad)*.
H WICK op 12 May 1980 *(RM July)*; still open.
HADDENHAM
HADDENHAM [GW/GC] op 2 April 1906 *(T 5 March, 3 April)*; clo 7 January 1963 *(Cl)*. H (BUCKS) in LNE co tt 1927.
H & THAME PARKWAY op 5 October 1987 *(wtt supp)*; about 0.4 miles north of earlier H; still open.
HADDENHAM CAMBS [GE] op 16 April 1866 *(T 16th)*; CAMBS added 1 July 1923 *(hbl 12th)*; clo 2 February 1931** *(RM March)*; later excur *(U)*.
HADDINGTON [NB] op 22 June 1846 *(co n T 23rd)*; co 5 December 1949 *(clo n Haddington)*.
HADDISCOE [GE] {map 73}
First station was on line from Reedham to Lowestoft, op 1 July 1847 *(co ½ T 6 September)*; at first *Brad* lacked detail; this station first shown January or February 1848; line from Halesworth also used it from 4 December 1854 until 15 May 1858** >
When line from Halesworth was reopened, 1 June 1859 *(T 2nd)*, it now passed east of Haddiscoe and exchange only station, ST OLAVES JUNCTION, was opened where lines crossed *(MT6/240/13)*; new interchange 1 May 1879 *(GE Journal April 2001)*;
St O J was renamed HERRINGFLEET JUNCTION 1 November 1891 *(RCG)* >
9 May 1904 original HADDISCOE (H JUNCTION 1854/5 to 1859 *Brad*) replaced, with the exchange station by a two level public station 700 yards east of this, H HL and H LL *(RCG; GE Weekly Engineering Notice 456)** >
HL clo 2 November 1959 *(RM December)*; LL still open as H.
* = officialdom saw 1904 events as renaming of (HL) and replacement of (LL) by new station.
HADFIELD [GC] op 8 August 1844 *(GC)*; still open. H & TINTWISTLE 1862/3 to 1880/1 *(Brad)*; became H for HOLLINGWORTH 12 October 1903 *(hbl 29th)*; thus LNE tt 1933, *hb* 1938 and *Brad* to 1955.

HADHAM [GE] op 3 July 1863 *(Hertford 4th)*; clo 16 November 1964 *(T 14 October)*.
HADLEIGH [GE] op 2 September 1847** *(EC)*; clo 29 February 1932 *(T 27th)*.
HADLEY [LNW] op 1 June 1849 *(Shrewsbury 8th)*; clo 7 September 1964 *(RM October)*.
HADLEY WOOD [GN]
op 1 May 1885 *(L)*; still open.
HADLOW ROAD [Birkenhead] op 1 October 1866 *(Birkenhead; LNW co ½ 13 February 1867- line)*; clo 17 September 1956 *(RM October)*.
Became H R for WILLASTON 22 July 1910 *(LNW dates)*; thus *hb* 1938 but not seen *Brad*.
HADNALL [LNW]
op 1 September 1858**; clo 2 May 1960 *(RM June)*.
HADNOCK [GW]
op 7 May 1951 *(Cl 29)*; HALT; clo 5 January 1959 *(T 5th)*; {Symonds Yat – Monmouth}.
HADRIAN ROAD [TWM]
op 14 November 1982 *(Tyneside)*; still open.
HAFOD [TV] op 30 August 1861 tt, at 18m 8ch *(RAC)*; replaced by Trehafod, 17 October 1892 at 14m 72ch *(RAC)*. HAVOD until 1890 tt *(Cl)*.
HAFOD GARREGOG [WH] (ng) {map 76}
HAFOD GARREGOG (a): stopping place op 1 June 1923; 9 July 1923 name transferred to >
HAFOD GARREGOG (b): op 1 June 1923 as YNYSFERLAS, renamed 9 July 1923 *(WHH)*; aot request; clo 28 September 1936 *(Cl)*.
See 1922 July 31**; *NGNC II, p.16; WHH 12, 20.*
HAFOD RUFFYDD [WH] (ng)
op 1 June 1923 (see 1922 July 31**); aot request; clo 28 September 1936 *(Cl)*; {map 76}.
WH ticket for H RYFFYDD *(JB)*.
HAFOD-Y-LLYN [WH] (ng)
op 1 June 1923 (see 1922 July 31**); aot request; clo 28 September 1936 *(Cl)*; {map 76}.
HAFOD-Y-LLYN [Festiniog] (ng)
op 6 January 1865* *(D&C 11)*; replaced by Tan-y-Bylch, ½ mile north, July 1872 tt. At first HAVOD-Y-L *(hb)*.
* = passengers free, own risk for some months previously; free use 5th after formal opening *(Festiniog)*.
HAFODYRYNYS [GW]
op 1 January 1913 *(GW working tt; in Brad January)*; PLATFORM; clo 15 June 1964 *(Cl)*; {Pontypool – Crumlin}.
GW notice of 3 August 1932 said treat as Halt from 8th but not so shown *Brad* or BR tt September 1962.
HAG FOLD op 11 May 1987 *(BLN 555)*; still open.
HAGGERLEASES [S&D] {map 31}
For first services in this area see 1834 March 24**; these intermittent. One example: on 18 March 1836 orders were given for arranging a coach (horse-drawn) to 'Hagger Lease's Lane' (co minutes).
Purely passenger services almost certainly ceased 1847 when rail service to West Auckland ended, but *NE* (p.527–8) quotes 1854 press description of a chiefly coal train with passenger waggons near rear.
H first in *Brad* April 1859; then and May shown as terminus of one train per day, outwards; June – one each way per day; last trains shown August 1859.

HAGGERSTON [NL]
op 2 September 1867 *(L)*; clo 6 May 1940 *(T 2nd)*.
Pre-op De-Beauvoir Town *(North London Railway Source Book*, NL Historical Society, 1998).

HAGLEY [GW] first in *Brad* June 1857; still open.

HAGLEY ROAD [LNW] op 10 August 1874 *(LNW Officers 11616, 11692)*; clo 26 November 1934 *(Cl)*.

HAIGH [LY] op 1 January 1850 *(LY; co ½ T 22 Feb.- line)*;
clo 13 September 1965 *(T 4th)*.

HAILES [Cal] op 16 November 1908, mainly for golfers though available to all, first advertised 26 September 1927 *(Balerno)*; according to LMS tt 22 September 1930, this PLATFORM would only be used as a HALT and in *Brad* as HALT (from 1928) – also thus *hb*; clo 1 November 1943 *(LNW Record)*; {Colinton – junction with main line}.

HAILSHAM [LBSC]
op 15 May 1849**; clo 9 September 1968 *(T 9th)*.

HAINAULT [GE]
op 1 May 1903 *(L; co ½ T 21 July- line)*;
clo 1 October 1908 (Thursday) *(Cl; GE minutes July –* Superintendent recommended closure at end of September); non-tt use during public closure: note in March 1927 wtt shows that could be used by employees of Messrs Hughes and public to and from certain stations 'on application' and holders of tickets to station beyond could join or alight here *(London Local, p.294)*. Reop to public 3 March 1930 *(RM April)*; last steam train ran Saturday 29 November 1947 *(Clay)*; buses until reop by [Cen] 31 May 1948 *(T 1 June)*; still open.

HAINTON STREET [GN] op 11 December 1905 *(GN)*; see 1905** (d); trains still both ways October 1939 *Brad*; before/with January 1940, no trains; trains (to Grimsby only) restored co tt alterations 1 July 1940; thus to clo 11 September 1961 *(RM September)*.
(IA makes one of this and Weelsby Road but *Brad*, e.g. 1922 reprint, shows separate.)

HAIRMYRES [Cal] op 1 September 1868 *(Cal- line)*;
still open. *Brad* to 1955 but not LMS tt 1930, *hb* 1938, *Murray* 1948: H for EAGLESHAM.

HALBEATH [NB]: line op 13 December 1849 *(D&C 15)*, and this probably opened with it*;
clo 1 January 1917 *(RM February)*;
reop 1 April 1919 *(RCH)*; clo 22 September 1930 *(Cl)*.
* = Not in *Edinburgh & District tt* December 1849 (Dunfermline was); was included February 1850 (January 1850 not seen); was mentioned in inspection report dated 6 December 1849.

HALBERTON [GW] op 5 December 1927 *(Tiverton 13th)*; HALT; clo 5 October 1964 *(Som Gaz 5 September)*; {Tiverton branch}.

HALE [CLC] op 12 May 1862 *(T 7th, 12th)* as BOWDON PEEL CAUSEWAY; became P C 1 January 1899 *(hbl 26th)*, HALE 1 January 1902 *(hbl 23rd)*; still open. According to *hb* 1908a had become H for ALTRINCHAM and BOWDON.

HALE END – see HIGHAMS PARK.

HALEBANK [LNW]:
line op 1 July 1852 *(T 10th)*, nd, August (line included July); op as HALEWOOD ROAD;
renamed HALEBANK for HALE 1 November 1874

(LNW General Managers' Circular, 21 October),
HALEBANK 1895 *(Cl)*; clo 1 January 1917 *(T 22 December 1916)*; reop 5 May 1919 *(RCH)*;
clo 15 September 1958 *(LNW Record)*.

HALESOWEN [GW] op 1 March 1878 *(co ½ T 23 February)*; clo to public 5 December 1927 *(Cl)*;
workmen used again 31 March 1928 to Friday 29 August 1958 (last train); also excur *(U)*.

HALESOWEN JUNCTION HALT
– see LONGBRIDGE (c).

HALESWORTH
HALESWORTH [GE] op 4 December 1854 *(Rtn)*;
last train 15 May 1858**; new station 20ch south op 1 June 1859 *(T 2nd)*; still open. H JUNCTION 1880/1 to 1893/4 *(Brad)*. GE co tt 1889, and *Brad*/BR tt until 1964/67: H for SOUTHWOLD but not thus *hb* 1938, 1956.

HALESWORTH [Southwold] (ng) op 24 September 1879 *(T 24th)*; clo 12 April 1929**.

HALEWOOD
HALEWOOD (a) [CLC] first in *Brad* May 1874;
clo 17 September 1951 *(RM December, corr)*.

HALEWOOD (b) op 16 May 1988 *(BLN 587)*; still open.
Also see HALEBANK.

HALFWAY [Snowdon Mountain] (ng; rack):
line op 6 April 1896** *(NGNC 1)*, nd, May 1898;
still open.

HALFWAY [Rye & C] (ng) op 13 July 1895**;
no winter service after 1925; clo 1929.

HALIFAX
HALIFAX [LY] op 1 July 1844 *(Halifax Guardian 8th –* B. Wilson); new stations 7 August 1850 (temporary wooden one ¼ mile north of original) and 24 June 1855 (double platform structure) *(Cl)*; still open.
Cl restics H SHAW SYKE to first but S S in *hb* until 1895 (last); probably result of RCH habit of entering separate goods/passenger stations as one.
H in *Brad* until about 1890; then still H in LY tables but H OLD STATION in GN/LNE tables, and on their tickets *(JB)*. H OLD in LY co tt 1899 and H Old Station in GE co tt 1909 (was it meant to be descriptive rather than part of name?).
H TOWN 30 September 1951 *(RM January 1952)* to 12 June 1961 *(RM April)*.

H NORTH BRIDGE [Halifax & Ovendon]
op 25 March 1880 *(GN)*; clo 23 May 1955**.

H ST PAULS [Halifax High Level] op 5 September 1890 *(RCG)*; clo 1 January 1917 *(RCH)*.
Excursions until 1939 *(GN Society Journal 151)*.
Before opening in September *Brad*, no trains, as H HL.
Also see PELLON.

HALKIRK [High]
op 28 July 1874 *(High)*; clo 13 June 1960 *(RM July)*.

HALL DENE – see SEAHAM.

HALL GREEN [GW]
op 1 July 1908 *(RCG; T 2nd- line)*; still open.

HALL HILLS [LNE] (non-tt): sleeper depot workmen;
op by summer 1937; 16 June 1947 wtt suggests service by engine and brake van rather than carriage;
workmen's trains still shown summer 1949 wtt;
{Boston – Langrick}.

HALL I' TH' WOOD op 29 September 1986
(BLN 552); ½ mile south of earlier The Oaks; still open.
HALL ROAD [LY]
op 1 October 1874 *(LY Board Minutes 6th)*; still open.
HALLATON [GN/LNW] op 15 December 1879
(Leic; LNW Record- line); clo 7 December 1953 *(T 7th)*;
workmen used to 20 May 1957 *(U)*.
HALLATROW [GW] op 3 September 1873
(Bristol T 4th- line); clo 2 November 1959 *(Shepton 6th)*.
HALLCRAIG (STREET) – see AIRDRIE.
HALLEN [GW] op 9 May 1910 *(W D Press 10th)*,
at 116m 08ch; HALT; clo 22 March 1915 *(RCH)*
except for workmen *(GM's report 12 January 1917)*;
re-sited (at 116m 18ch) and reop for workmen
15 March 1917 *(Bristol notice S1007)*;
clo October 1918 *(U)*; {map 121}.
HALLIFORD – see UPPER HALLIFORD.
HALLILOO [SE] (non-tt): PLATFORM; farm,
school parties; op about 1856; clo by 1899;
{Whyteleafe South – Caterham} *(U)*.
HALLING [SE] op 1 March 1890 *(SE)*; still open.
HALLINGTON [GN] op 1 December 1876 *(RCG;*
T 28 November- line); clo 11 September 1939**,
reop 4 December 1939; clo 5 November 1951 *(Cl)*.
HALLOON – see ST COLUMB ROAD.
HALMEREND [NS] op 28 June 1880 *(NS)*;
clo 27 April 1931 *(Cl)*. 1883 hb : HALMER END.
HALSALL [LY] op 2 September 1887 *(Southport*
Guard 8th); clo 26 September 1938 *(RM November)*.
Hb: 1890 H for ORMSKIRK; 1912 H.
HALSHAW MOOR – see FARNWORTH.
HALSTEAD near Colchester [CVH] op 16 April 1860
(T 13th); clo 1 January 1962 *(T 17 November 1961)*.
HALSTEAD – see KNOCKHOLT.
HALTON [Birkenhead] first in *Brad* August 1851,
as RUNCORN ROAD; became R 1858 *(RCG ref Sept.)*,
R ROAD again 1861/2 *(Brad)*, H 1869 *(RCH dist ref*
June); clo 7 July 1952 *(Cl)*.
HALTON near Lancaster [Mid]
op 17 November 1849 *(co n Lancaster 17th)*;
clo 3 January 1966 *(RM February)*.
HALTON DIAL [NE]: see 1834 September 22**;
not known whether existed before line closed 1840;
first seen January 1851 *Brad*, full service; last there
November 1858; back February 1859, now Saturdays
only; last February 1864; {Leeds – Cross Gates}.
At first H D BRIDGE, later H, settled 1852.
HALTON HOLGATE [GN]
op 1 May 1868 *(GN; Stamford 15th- line)*; aot request;
clo 11 September 1939 *(G&S)*.
HALTWHISTLE [NE]
op 18 June 1838 *(T 21st- line)*; see 1836 B**; still open.
HALWILL [LSW] op 20 January 1879**
clo 3 October 1966 *(Cornish & D P 8th)*.
Op as H & BEAWORTHY, became H JUNCTION
1887 tt *(Cl)*, H for B 1922 *(RCG ref July)* and thus
Brad to 1955.
HAM BRIDGE – see EAST WORTHING.
HAM GREEN [GW] op 23 December 1926
(RM March 1927); HALT; clo 7 September 1964
(W D Press 7th); {Clifton Bridge – Pill}.

HAM LANE [WCP]
op 1 December 1897 *(WCP; Bristol T 2nd- line)*;
clo 20 May 1940 *(Bridgwater Merc 22nd)*.
HAM MILL [GW] op 12 October 1903 *(Stroud N 16th)*;
HALT; H M CROSSING until 1957 *(Cl)*;
clo 2 November 1964 *(W D Press 2nd)*.
HAM STREET [SE] op 13 February 1851
(co n T 13th); H S & ORLESTONE 1 February 1897
(hbl 29 April) to 3 May 1976 tt; still open.
HAMBLE [SR] op 18 January 1942 *(Southampton*
District notice, 14th); HALT until 5 May 1969 *(SR App)*;
still open.
HAMBLETON [NE]:
line op 22 September 1834 *(NE)*, nd, 19 October 1839
Brad; clo 14 September 1959 *(RM September)*; later use
when engineering work prevented stop at Selby *(U)*
– certainly 28/9 March 1975 and 29 July 1980 *(IU)*.
HAMILTON
HAMILTON [NB] op 1 April 1878 *(Hamilton 30 March)*;
clo 1 January 1917, except for workmen *(RM February;*
reop 2 June 1919 *(RCH)*; clo 15 September 1952
(RM October). Aot H TERMINUS, later
H CADZOW STREET in *Brad*, settled as H 1882.
H WEST [Cal] op 10 September 1849**;
tt suggests that clo 14 July 1876, when Central op,
and reop 2 October 1876, with link to Ferniegair –
WEST now added; still open.
H CENTRAL [Cal] op 14 July 1876 *(Hamilton 15th)*;
still open.
Also see PEACOCK CROSS.
HAMILTON SQUARE – see BIRKENHEAD.
HAMMERSMITH
HAMMERSMITH [HC]* op 13 June 1864 *(GW n*
T 10th); re-sited on extension of line southwards
1 December 1868 *(Cl)*; still open.
HAMMERSMITH [Dist]* op 9 September 1874
(T 10th); clo 20 January 1882 (Friday) by fire,
reop 23 August 1882 *(L)*; still open.
HAMMERSMITH [Picc] op 15 December 1906 *(co n*
T 14th); still open.
Dist and Picc share entrance; HC separate.
H & CHISWICK [NSWJ] op 8 April 1858 *(L)*;
& C added 1 July 1880 *(L)*;
clo 1 January 1917 *(T 26 December 1916)*.
H GROVE ROAD* [LSW] op 1 January 1869
(co n T 24 December 1868); clo 5 June 1916 *(RCH)*.
Also Met use 1 October 1877 to 1 January 1907.
Ticket: THE GROVE *(JB)*.
* = *Brad*: HC, Dist and LSW at first H. GROVE ROAD added
to LSW later 1869/70; also added to HC 1874/5. BROADWAY
was added to Dist and HC 1875 (replacing G R in latter).
1882/3 became H BEADON ROAD, BROADWAY [HC] and
H KING STREET, BROADWAY [Dist]; by 1904 both
reduced to H. GROVE ROAD was used in LSW co tt 1914
but seems to have been error of some sort: *The A to Z of Victorian*
London, H. Margary's reprint of Bacon's 1888, London Atlas
shows the relevant street as 'The Grove' and A.A. Jackson's
book on the Metropolitan states that the HC's 1868 station's
entrance was in The Grove.

HAMMERTON [NE]: line op 30 October 1848 *(NE)*, nd, April 1849 *(Reid)*; KIRK H in *Brad* until 1850, but just H in *Reid* and *Topham*; still open.

HAMMERWICH [LNW] first trains shown in tt June 1849; clo 18 January 1965 *(RM March)*.

HAMPDEN PARK [LBSC] op 1 January 1888 *(LBSC)* as WILLINGDON; renamed 1 July 1903 *(hbl 7th)*; still open. LBSC co tt 1912, *hb* 1938 and *Brad*? to 1955: H P for W. BR added SUSSEX to name 12 May 1980 tt *(C/W)*, dropped 1993/5.

HAMPOLE [WRG Jt] op 1 January 1885 *(GN)*; clo 7 January 1952 *(RM March)*.

HAMPSTEAD

HAMPSTEAD [Nor] op 22 June 1907**; still open. Pre-op Heath Street *(L)*.

H HEATH [LNW] op 2 January 1860 *(T 2nd)*; clo 4 December 1984 when line blocked by collapse, on 2nd, of retaining wall *(RM April 1985)*; reop 15 April 1985; still open.

H ROAD [NL] op 9 June 1851 *(L)*; replaced 5 May 1855 by station to west *(Cl)*, which was later renamed Chalk Farm, then (1950) PRIMROSE HILL, which see; {map 101}.

Also see SOUTH HAMPSTEAD; WEST HAMPSTEAD.

HAMPSTEAD NORRIS [GW] op 13 April 1882 *(T 10th- line)*; clo 4 August 1942**, reop 8 March 1943 *(Cl)*; clo 10 September 1962 *(RM October)*.

HAMPSTHWAITE [NE] first in *Brad* September 1866; clo 2 January 1950 *(Cl)*.

HAMPTON [LSW] op 1 November 1864 *(co n T 27 October)*; still open.

HAMPTON COURT [LSW] op 1 February 1849 *(T 30 January)*; still open. In *Brad* became H C & EAST MOULSEY 1869, H C for E MOULSEY 1897/8, H C for E MOLESEY 1903/4; ? to 1955 was H C for EAST and WEST MOLESEY. 1904 *hb*: H C & E MOLESEY. Aot extra platform for excursions and race specials *(AB)*.

HAMPTON LOADE [GW] op 1 February 1862**; clo 9 September 1963 *(T 9th)*. At first H, tt and local press – *Brad* added L in March 1862.

HAMPTON ROW [GW] op 18 March 1907 *(wtt supp)*; HALT; clo 29 April 1917 (Sunday) *(RCH)*.

HAMPTON WICK [LSW] op 1 July 1863 *(L; co ½ T 10 August- line)*; still open.

HAMPTON-IN-ARDEN

HAMPTON-IN-ARDEN [LNW] probably opened 17 September 1838, when L&B opened throughout (in *T 18th* line description, though orders to provide only given 20 August – *company minutes*); re-sited about 30 chains east 1 September 1884 *(LNW Officers 26408)*; -in-ARDEN added July 1886 co tt *(W Mid)* but 4 October 1904 *(LNW dates)*, supported by *hb* 1908a; still open. LNW co tt 1852: H JUNCTION.

HAMPTON [Mid] op 12 August 1839 *(co n T 8th)*; was H JUNCTION 1 November 1849 co tt to 1 December 1872 co tt *(Mid)*; clo 1 January 1917 *(T 29 December 1916)*.

HAMSTEAD

HAMSTEAD [LNW] op 25 March 1899 *(W Mid)* as GREAT BARR, replacing an earlier station of that name; renamed 6 May 1974 *(BR notice)*; still open. *Brad*? to end (1961): G B for H, but not thus BR LM tt 1957. Also see GREAT BARR & HAMSTEAD.

HAMWORTHY [LSW] {map 125} Two stations op 1 June 1847 *(Dorset Chron 20 May, 3 June)*. One op as POOLE JUNCTION, became H JUNCTION 2 December 1872, H 1 May 1972 *(Cl)*; still open. *Hb*: 1894a became H & NEW POOLE J, 1895 H & P J. Other op as POOLE, became H 2 December 1872 *(Cl)*; clo 1 July 1896 (Wednesday) *(RCG)*.

HANBOROUGH [GW] op 4 June 1853 *(Glos Chron 4th- line)*; HANDBOROUGH until 28 September 1992 *(AB)*; still open. LNW co tt 1856, GW co tt: 1865 H JUNCTION for BLENHEIM; 1902 H for B and thus *Brad* until 1957/8 but not *hb* 1938, 1956. 1854–61 trains divided here for Euston and Oxford.

HANDFORTH [LNW] op 10 May 1842 (in fare table, *co n Stockport 13th*); still open.

HANDSWORTH

HANDSWORTH [GW] op 14 November 1854 *(T 15th)*; H & SMETHWICK until 6 May 1968 *(Cl)*; clo 6 March 1972 *(RM April)*.

H WOOD [LNW] op 1 January 1896 *(LNW Officers 36535)*; clo 5 May 1941 *(LNW Record)*.

HANFORD ROAD [NS] prob op 28 March 1910 *(RCG date for Trentham Park)*; HALT; clo 1 May 1913 (Thursday) *(Cl)*; {Trentham Park branch}.

HANGER LANE op by [GW] 30 June 1947 *(T 1 July)*; to [Cen] 1 January 1948; still open.

HANGMANS STONE – see BIRDWELL.

HANLEY [NS] op 13 July 1864 *(co ½ T 5 August)*; re-sited 1 December 1873 when line extended to Burslem, which see; clo 2 March 1964 *(RM April)*.

HANNINGTON [GW] op 9 May 1883 *(Swindon 12th)*; clo 2 March 1953 *(T 20 February)*; trains for employees at Swindon Works until last Friday 3 August 1962 *(Back Track June 2003)*.

HANWELL [GW] op 1 December 1838 *(L)*; H & ELTHORNE 1 April 1896 *(RCG)* to 6 May 1974 *(BR notice)*; still open. Joint GW/District service began 1 March 1883; from 1 October 1885 GW only.

HANWOOD [Shrewsbury & Welshpool] op 14 February 1861 *(D&C 11)*; clo 12 September 1960 *(Cl)*.

HANWOOD ROAD – see EDGEBOLD.

HAPPENDON [Cal] op 1 April 1864 *(Cal)* as DOUGLAS; renamed 1 April 1931 *(Cl)*; clo 5 October 1964 *(RM October)*.

HAPTON [LY] first in *Brad* May 1862; still open.

HARBORNE [LNW] op 10 August 1874 *(LNW Officers 11616, 11692)*; clo 26 November 1934 *(Cl)*.

HARBURN [Cal] op 15 February 1848 *(Balerno; co ½ T 29 February- line)*; clo 18 April 1966 *(Cl)*. Originally WEST CALDER & TORPHIN, later W C & H in *Brad*, then erratically

H/W C/H for C, settled as H about 1870;
aot H or W C (hb); *Murray* 1852 H for WESTER.

HARBY & STATHERN [GN/LNW]
op 1 September 1879 *(LNW Officers 20028)* as S;
renamed 1 November 1879 *(Cl)*;
clo 7 December 1953 *(T 7th)*.

HARDINGHAM [GE]
line op 15 February 1847 *(EC)*, nd, February 1848;
clo 6 October 1969 *(RM October)*.

HARDLEY [SR] (non-tt): HALT; oil workmen;
op 3 March 1958 *(Rly Obs April)*; clo 5 April 1965
(letter *RM April 1966, p.230)*; {Fawley – Hythe}.

HARE PARK & CROFTON [WRG Jt]
first in *Brad* November 1886; clo 4 February 1952 *(Cl)*.

HARECASTLE – see KIDSGROVE.

HAREFIELD – see SOUTH HAREFIELD.

HARESFIELD [Mid] op 29 May 1854 *(Mid;*
Gloucester J 3 June- line); clo 4 January 1965 *(Mid)*.

HARKER [NB]
op 29 October 1861★★; clo 1 November 1929 (Friday)
(Cl); later non-tt Ordnance Depot use 1936 to 1941?
and 1 March 1943 to 6 January 1969 *(Cl 29; U)*
– stop shown in wtt notice 5 April 1947.

HARLECH [Cam] op 10 October 1867 *(Cam; co n*
Merioneth 12th- line); still open.

HARLESDEN
HARLESDEN [LNW] op 15 June 1912 *(T 14th)*;
[Bak] use began 16 April 1917 *(RM May)*; still open.
HARLESDEN [Mid] op 3 August 1875 *(Mid)* as
HARROW ROAD for STONEBRIDGE PARK and
WEST WILLESDEN; became H R for S P and
HARLESDEN February 1876 co tt, HARROW ROAD
1 May 1878 co tt, HARROW ROAD for S and
HARLESDEN 1 November 1880 co tt, S P for WW
and HARLESDEN 1 July 1884 *(Mid)*; clo 2 July 1888,
reop 1 March 1893 co tt *(Mid)*; renamed
HARLESDEN for WW and S P 1 February 1901
(RCG); clo 1 October 1902 (Wednesday) *(RCG)*.
Other variations used elsewhere – e.g. hb 1894a, 1895
omitted 'WEST'.

HARLESTON [GE] op 1 December 1855 *(EC- line)*;
see 1860 November 2★★; clo 5 January 1953 *(T 5th)*.
At first in hb as HARLESTONE.

HARLING ROAD [GE] op 30 July 1845 *(co n Norfolk)*;
H until 1849 tt *(Cl)*; still open.

HARLINGTON near Doncaster [Dearne]
op 3 June 1912★★; clo 10 September 1951 *(RM Nov.)*.

HARLINGTON BEDS [Mid]
op 13 July 1868 *(T 14th)*; still open.
Became H for TODDINGTON 1 October 1889
(RCG), H BEDS 1 November 1927 *(hbl October)*.
Brad dropped 'for T' 1955.

HARLOW [GE]
H MILL op 9 August 1841 *(co n T 30 July)*; MILL added
1960; still open.
H TOWN probably op 22 November 1841, with earlier
special use 9 and 10 September 1841 (see 1841★★);
in mid-1843 it was still alternative stop to Harlow and
Roydon but by the end of 1843 some trains were
stopping here and at one/both of the others; still open.
Early NETTESWELL; BURNT MILL, N; B M & N

(NETTLESWELL *Brad*); & N dropped 1843 tt *(Cl)*;
renamed H T 13 June 1960 *(RM July)*; still open.

HARMSTON [GN] op 15 April 1867 *(GN)*;
clo 10 September 1962 *(RM October)*.

HAROLD WOOD [GE] op 1 February 1868 *(L)*;
aot request; still open. Heril Wood pre-opening *(L)*.

HAROLDS MOOR [SIT] first in *Brad* December
1878; see 1860 July 25★★; last in *Brad* May 1896;
in hb 1883 to 1895 (inclusive); {map 88}.

HARPENDEN
HARPENDEN [Mid] op 13 July 1868 *(T 14th)*;
H CENTRAL 25 September 1950 to 18 April 1966
(Mid); still open.
H EAST [GN] op 1 September 1860 *(GN; co n T 1st-*
line); EAST added 25 September 1950 *(RM October)*;
clo 26 April 1965 *(RM May)*.

HARPERLEY [NE]
On Bell's Map of Great Northern Coalfield 1850
(perhaps goods only) (M. Cobb).
HARPERLEY (a) first in *Brad* March 1861; last May
1864.
HARPERLEY (b) op 1 November 1892 *(NE Hoole)*;
clo 29 June 1953 *(RM August)*.

HARPUR HILL – see 1833 May★★.

HARRIETSHAM [LCD]
op 1 July 1884 *(LCD)*; still open.

HARRINGAY
HARRINGAY [GN] op 1 May 1885 *(L)*; H WEST
18 June 1951 to 27 May 1971 *(Cl)*; still open.
HARRINGAY [TH Jt] op 1 June 1880 *(Mid)* as
GREEN LANES; renamed H P G L 30 August 1884
(Mid; RCG ref July), H PARK in co tt by April 1910 but
9 June 1951 official records *(Mid)*, H STADIUM
27 October 1958 *(RM December)*, H EAST 14 May
1990 *(BLN)*, H GREEN LANES 8 July 1991 *(AB*
Chron); still open.

HARRINGTON
HARRINGTON [LNW] op 18 May 1846 *(LNW;*
Whitehaven Herald 20 March 1847, in account of
opening of next stretch); aot request; still open.
H CHURCH ROAD [CW Jc] first in *Brad* November
1913; clo 31 May 1926 *(Cl)*; used by workmen until
1 April 1929 *(Cumbria)*.
Also see HIGH HARRINGTON.

HARRINGWORTH [Mid]
op 1 March 1880 *(Mid)*; clo 1 November 1948 *(Mid)*.

HARROGATE [NE] {map 42};
early sometimes HARROWGATE.
See SPOFFORTH and STARBECK for early stations
serving Harrogate.
HARROGATE (a) op 20 July 1848 *(Herapath 29th/Yorks*
Gazette 22nd); in most modern works is H BRUNSWICK,
but only H in *Brad*; clo 1 August 1862 (Friday) *(Cl)*.
HARROGATE (b) op 1 August 1862 *(T 4th)*; still open.

HARROW
H & WEALDSTONE [LNW] op 20 July 1837
(co n T 19th); & W added 1 May 1897 *(hbl 29 April)*;
still open. Also used by [Bak] 16 April 1917 to
27 September 1982★★ and 4 June 1984 *(Ug)* to present.
H-ON-THE-HILL [Met/GC] op 2 August 1880 by
Met *(T 2nd)*; -on-the-H added by 1890 *(hb)* but 1 June

1894 (Cl); GC use began 15 March 1899; still open.
H ROAD – see HARLESDEN.
Also see NORTH HARROW; SOUTH HARROW;
SUDBURY HILL; WEST HARROW.
HARSTON [GE] op 1 April 1852 (D&C 5- line);
aot request; clo 17 June 1963 (RM August).
HARSWELL GATE – see EVERINGHAM.
HART [NE] first in Brad July 1871 as CRIMDON;
renamed October 1871; clo 28 July 1941,
reop 7 October 1946 (RM January 1947);
suffered gradual dilution of service: all days at reop
but soon reduced to summer only; still winter trains
6 October 1947 LNE tt; none October 1949 Brad.
After August 1948 Brad, before/with August 1950
further reduced, to Saturdays and Sundays only (1950
until 3 September, inclusive); clo 31 August 1953 (Cl).
HARTFIELD [LBSC] op 1 October 1866 (co n T 1st);
clo 2 January 1967 (RM February).

HARTFORD
HARTFORD [LNW] op 4 July 1837 (T 6th); still open.
Brad ? to end (1961) and BR LM tt to 1957/62:
H for NORTHWICH but not thus hb 1938, 1956.
Also see GREENBANK.
HARTHOPE [Cal] (non-tt): railwaymen and families;
op 3 January 1900; clo after 1926;
{Beattock Summit – Ruttonside} (U).
HARTINGTON [LNW]
op 4 August 1899 (LNW Officers 39077, 39103);
clo 1 November 1954 (T 1 October), later emergency
winter use (U); see 1962 August 5**.
HARTINGTON COLLIERY [Mid]:
non-tt; at some point Saturdays only service for miners;
notice with November 1888 public tt says that trains
will not pick up/set down at sidings adjacent to colliery
on Saturdays – passengers now to go to/from
Netherthorpe (later Staveley Town) and Staveley
(later Barrow Hill) stations; {branch from between
Staveley Town and Barrow Hill} (Mid).
HARTINGTON ROAD Brighton [LBSC]
op 1 January 1906 (LBSC); HALT; clo 1 June 1911
(Thursday) (Cl); {Lewes Road – Kemp Town}.
HARTLEBURY [GW] op 3 May 1852**; still open.
H JUNCTION 1862 to 1894 (Brad) and thus
GW co tt 1865.
HARTLEPOOL all lines ultimately part of [NE];
(based on Hartlepool plus information from S. Bragg);
{map 35}.
[Hartlepool Dock & Railway]: first service provided by
contractors, first licence issued 21 July 1836 (see 1836
A**), to dock area, exact site unknown; company began
own service 1 May 1839, again initial terminus
unknown; by 1841 a station had been built at the
NE corner of Victoria Dock; re-sited about 1880
(perhaps 6 June 1880 when other station, below,
opened). This station clo to public 16 June 1947**,
though school trains continued to 20 March 1964 (U).
In Brad 1862 to 1894/8 shown as EAST H in some tables,
especially those including both Hartlepool stations.
[Stockton & Hartlepool] service began 10 February
1841** from Middleton (perhaps sometimes used as
name for it, especially locally), with 'halt' at STRANTON.

Harbour improvements meant line had to be cut.
According to a literal interpretation of writings
of local historians sequence then was:
About April 1846 line cut back to STRANTON,
now used as a temporary terminus;
About June 1847 new temporary terminus opened on
west side of South Street, needing spur from point just
south of STRANTON, which would then have closed;
Between early 1848 and 1851 new terminus built on
Victoria Terrace, opposite the Customs House.
About September 1853 this was again replaced, by
terminus in Mainsforth Terrace. A local paper said new
station was expected to open on 1 September, but that
was a month before and no evidence has been found
that it actually did so.
On the face of it, seems unlikely they should have
moved their station so often and it may be that in reality
the 1846 and 1847 'stations' were same one since no
map evidence has been found for 1847 one, though its
life was so short that no maps might have been made
during, or have survived from, its period of existence;
furthermore, many 'stations' of that era were such
primitive affairs that it would often have been possible,
literally, to move them from one site to another.
From July 1846 to July 1847 (inclusive) Brad has
references to 'STRANTON' that clearly have to be
interpreted as 'The Hartlepool station at Stranton';
name WEST HARTLEPOOL first appeared in
February 1848 tt (Cl). These name changes would fit
full listing given, but naming of stations was then such a
haphazard business that this cannot be relied upon fully.
Thereafter, its history is much clearer: it was again
re-sited 6 June 1880; WEST dropped from name
26 April 1967 (Cl); still open as HARTLEPOOL.
Tts (e.g. Brad 1872 and NE co tt 1880) often
indiscriminate, having EAST H/WEST H in one table,
H E/H W in another.
HARTLEY [NE] op 3 May 1847**- line;
re-sited to north in 1851 (BT); clo 2 November 1964
(RM January 1965). Originally H PIT and thus
intermittently to 1858 tt (JS), later briefly, about 1863,
H JUNCTION (Brad).
HARTON ROAD [GW] op 16 December 1867
(GW- line); ROAD added 1881? (ref RCH dist 31 July);
clo 31 December 1951 (T 31st).
HARTS HILL & WOODSIDE [GW]
op 1 April 1895 (RCG); clo 1 January 1917 (GW notice
dated 22 December 1916); {Round Oak – Dudley}.
Aot HARTSHILL & W (hb).
HARTSHILL & BASFORD [NS]
op 1 May 1905 (NS); HALT; clo 20 September 1926
(Cl); {Stoke-on-Trent – Newcastle-under-Lyne}.
HARTWOOD [Cal] initially in use 'by signal' – for
workmen?; op to public 1 May 1889 (W.A.C. Smith,
Rly World June 1975); still open.
HARTY ROAD [SEC] first in Brad June 1907;
HALT; clo 4 December 1950 (T 4th).
HARVINGTON [Mid] op 17 September 1866
(Mid; Rtn- line); clo 1 October 1962, but buses to
17 June 1963 (Cl).

HARWICH

H TOWN [GE] op 15 August 1854**; originally single platform close to quayside, betweeen West Street and George Street; had to be replaced because in direct line of access to new GE Continental Pier, built 1864. Old station clo in March 1865 and a new op 1 December 1865, slightly inland, 300 yards south (arrangements in between?); TOWN added 1 March 1883 *(GE Journal Special No.2*, September 1979). Still open.

In 1864 (at least) boat trains ran along quayside (M. Harris, article, *Steam Days*, June 2000).

Co n T 4th said on and after 15 May 1877 Rotterdam Boat Express would run direct onto Pier here; wording suggests new arrangement (not in equivalent 1876 notice), though 'uniformed interpreter' who accompanied passengers from London to Cologne was already in post. Pier soon dropped from notices – assumed or discontinued?

H INTERNATIONAL [GE] op by 15 March 1883 (date of closure of old line, *GE Soc Journal 93*; supported by *co n T 5th* giving warning of time alteration for Boat Train on 15th) as PARKESTON QUAY; sometimes H P Q (e.g. GE co tt 1889, 1914); H I PORT 28 May 1995 *(AB Chron)*, on opening of new passenger terminal *(D&C 5)* – PORT soon omitted, in practice even before 24 September 1995 tt *(AB)*; still open.

H PARKESTON QUAY WEST [LNE] first in *Brad* September 1934 (either prematurely, or station was in use before formal op 1 October 1934, described in *T 2 October)*; steamer passengers only *(hb)*; officially clo 1 May 1972 but already out of use *(U)*.

HARWORTH COLLIERY SIDINGS (non-tt): used for works outings 30 May 1965 (to Cleethorpes) and 4 June 1967; {branch from Tickhill & Wadworth} *(U; JB)*.

HASELOUR – see ELFORD.

HASLAND NO 9 PIT SIDING [Mid] (non-tt) op by 5 March 1913; clo ?; {Clay Cross – Chesterfield} *(Mid)*.

HASLEMERE [LSW] op 1 January 1859 *(SR; co n T 1st- line)*; still open. H for HINDHEAD in *Brad* 1929/30 to 1955 but not *hb* 1929, 1938.

HASLINGDEN [LY] op 17 August 1848 *(LY)*; clo 7 November 1960 *(RM December)*.

HASSALL GREEN [NS] op 17 April 1905 *(RCG)*; after December 1926 *Brad*, before/with August 1927 reduced to Thursdays and Saturdays; clo 28 July 1930 *(Cl)*.

HASSENDEAN [NB] first in *Brad* March 1850*; clo 6 January 1969 *(RM February)*.

* = line through here opened 29 October 1849 *(Scottish Railway Gazette 3 Nov.)*; journal said that station was planned for here.

HASSOCKS [LBSC] op 21 September 1841 *(T 22nd- line)*; H GATE until 1881; still open. *Brad* ? to 1955: H for HURSTPIERPOINT.

HASSOP [Mid] op 1 August 1862 *(Mid)*; clo 17 August 1942 *(Cl)*. 1870 to 1906/7 H for CHATSWORTH in *Brad*, but not thus Mid co tt.

HASTINGS

HASTINGS [SE] op 13 February 1851 *(co n T 13th)*; still open. For difficulties met by LBSC when they tried to use this station, see *Great Railway Battles* – details given at end of Section 2.

Also see ST LEONARDS.

HASWELL [eventually NE] Station op for goods by [Hartlepool Railway & Docks] 23 November 1835; first passenger service horse-drawn, provided by contractors from dock area at Hartlepool, first licence issued 21 July 1836 (see 1836 A**).

First regular passenger service provided from Sunderland by [Durham & Sunderland], using Hartlepool station, April or May 1837 *(NE)*.

Hartlepool Railway began own regular service 1 May 1839**.

Original station a terminus, requiring change of trains or reversal for through travel; replaced by through station 1 November 1877 *(Cl)*.

Clo 9 June 1952** *(RM August)*.

HATCH [GW] op 11 September 1866 *(W Fly P 14th)*; clo 5 February 1951 *(Chard 3rd)*, reop 7 May 1951 *(Chard 5th)* – see 1951**; clo 10 September 1962 *(Chard 15th)*.

HATCH END [LNW] op 8 August 1842 *(P.G. Scott)* as PINNER; renamed P & H E 1 February 1897 *(hbl 29 April)*, H E for P 1 February 1920 *(hbl 29 Jan.)*, H E 11 June 1956 *(L)*; still open. Also [Bak] use 16 April 1917 to 27 September 1982.

HATFIELD near Hertford; {map 72}

HATFIELD [GN] op 7 August 1850 *(T 6th, 8th)*; still open.

H HYDE [GN] first in *Brad* May 1905; last June 1905 (with note, 'subject to alteration', so perhaps did not last the month); {Hatfield – Cole Green}.

HATFIELD near Chelmsford

HATFIELD [EC] first in *Brad* December 1844; last February 1849 (had been destroyed by fire).

H PEVEREL [GE] op 1 March 1878 *(Cl, note 1600)*, on same site; H PEVERIL until 1879/80 *(Brad)*; still open.

HATFIELD – see SIGGLESTHORNE.

HATFIELD & STAINFORTH [GC] op 1 October 1866 *(GC; Rtn- line)*, replacing earlier STAINFORTH; S & H until 28 September 1992 tt *(AB Chron)*; still open.

HATHERLEIGH [SR] op 27 July 1925 *(Bideford 28th)*; clo 1 March 1965 *(Express & E 1st)*; {map 116}.

HATHERN [Mid] op 17 February 1868 *(Mid)*; clo 4 January 1960 *(RM February)*.

HATHERSAGE [Mid] op 25 June 1894 *(RCG)*; still open.

HATTERSLEY op 8 May 1978 *(D&C 10)*; still open.

HATTON near Aberdeen [GNS] op 2 August 1897 *(GNS)*; clo 31 October 1932 *(GNS)*.

HATTON near Dundee [Dundee, Perth & Aberdeen] op 16 December 1831 (see 1831 B**); last in *Brad* October 1865; {maps 8, 9}.

HATTON near Warwick [GW] op 1 October 1852 *(W Mid; T 27 September- line*; in inspection report) still open. *Hb*: H JUNCTION 1904 to 1944a; not thus *Brad*.

HATTON CROSS [Picc] op 19 July 1975 *(RM July)*; still open.

HAUGHLEY

H ROAD [EU] op 24 December 1846 *(EC- line)*;
clo 9 July 1849* *(Cl)*; {Haughley – Elmswell}.
HAUGHLEY [GE] op 2 July 1849* *(Cl;T 5th- line)*;
closed 2 January 1967 *(RM February)*.
Opened as H JUNCTION (and thus EC co tt 1851),
then H ROAD J 1866 tt, H ROAD 1878 tt, H 1890 tt
(JS); became H WEST 1 July 1923 *(hbl 12th)*;
H, when combined with other September 1932 tt *(Cl)*;
* = both stations open together for a week.
HAUGHLEY [Mid-Suffolk Light] op 29 September 1908
(T 28th) [1932 – see above; this part clo November 1939,
service to main (P. Paye, *Mid-Suffolk Light Railway*,
Wild Swan, 1986, p.72).
HAUGHTON near Shrewsbury [GW]
op 22 September 1934 *(Cl 29)*; HALT;
clo 12 September 1960 *(Cl)*; {Baschurch – Rednal}.
HAUGHTON near Stafford [LNW] op 1 June 1849
(Shrewsbury 8th); clo 23 May 1949 *(RM September)*.

HAVANT

HAVANT [LBSC] op 15 March 1847 *(Salisbury 20th)*;
still open.
H NEW [LSW] op 1 January 1859 *(co n T 1st)*;
temporary terminus between Havant and Rowlands
Castle, provided as result of dispute with LBSC,
passengers being taken on to Portsmouth by omnibus;
although line opened through to Portsmouth
24 January 1859, this was kept as LSW Havant station
at least until end of month. Notice of through use
(T 21st) said all trains would stop at Havant New to set
down and pick up; notice about cheap fares *(T 27th)*
specified New. Notices for February merely 'Havant'.
However, inter-company relations such that 'New'
perhaps taken for granted. Through services suspended
with effect from 9 June 1859 after LBSC had won
injunction *(co n T 11th)*; again just 'Havant' but highly
unlikely LBSC would have allowed use of 'main' since
it would have meant use of their station yard by
omnibuses taking passengers on to Portsmouth;
LSW vol.1, p.147 says LSW had to stop its trains 'before
Havant'. During this dispute LSW did run excursions
along LBSC line to Chichester, reversing at Havant,
for Goodwood Races 27–8 July; these would not have
competed with LBSC since they started from Clapham
Common *(co n T 23rd)*. Through services resumed
8 August 1859 *(co n T 4th)* and this then closed?
HAVENHOUSE [GN] op 28 July 1873 *(GN)* as
CROFT BANK; renamed 1900 (1 October according
to *hbl 12 July*, but 1 August, *Cl, JS* – latter looks better
fit); see 1962 November 11**; aot request; still open.
HAVENSTREET [IWC]: line op 20 December 1875;
station later – first in *Brad* June 1876 (see 1875**);
partially re-sited when rebuilt and crossing loop
installed 1926 (T. Cooper); aot request;
HAVEN STREET until 9 June 1958 *(Cl)*;
clo 21 February 1966 *(RM March)*.
HAVERFORDWEST [GW]
op 2 January 1854 *(co ½ T 26 August)*; still open.
GW co tt 1932: H W for ST DAVIDS.

HAVERHILL

HAVERHILL [GE] op 1 June 1865 *(GE Journal
January 1992)*; H NORTH 1 July 1923 *(hbl 12th)* to
1952; clo 6 March 1967 *(RM April)*.
HAVERHILL [CVH] op 11 May 1863 (a Monday)
*(T 29 April, 11 May; Herapath 16 May/Essex Telegraph
12 May)* *. Clo 14 July 1924 *(Cl)* – from 1865 CVH
trains had used main if connections had to be made.
* = co ½ dated 19 August said had opened on 10th, date used
by all seen in modern print. Likely explanation is that excursions
were run from Haverhill on the Sunday. Board minutes of
13 May said these carried over 600 passengers; did not give exact
date but context would fit this interpretation *(RAIL 128/1, 2)*.
HAVERSTOCK HILL [Mid]
op 13 July 1868 *(T 14th)*; clo 1 January 1916 (Saturday)
(RCG); {Kentish Town – Finchley Road}.
HAVERTHWAITE [Fur]
op 1 September 1869 *(D&C 14)*; reduced to summers
only from 26 September 1938; clo 16 September 1940,
reop 3 June 1946 *(Cl)*; clo 30 September 1946 *(Cl)*.
HAVERTON HILL [NE] first in *Brad* November
1872; clo to public 14 June 1954 *(Cl)*, but workmen
until clo with effect from 6 November 1961 *(BR NER
wtt supplement 7 November – RMd)*.

HAWARDEN

HAWARDEN [WMCQ] op 31 March 1890 *(RCG)*;
still open.
H BRIDGE [LNE] op 22 September 1924
(RM November); HALT until 1954 *(Brad)*; still open.

HAWES

HAWES [Mid/NE] op 1 June 1878*; see 1954 April 26**
(refers to closure of line from here to Northallerton);
clo 16 March 1959 *(RM April)*, by when only one train
each way per day (to/from Garsdale).
* = generally dated (e.g. by *NE*) as op 1 October 1878 with
line through here opening as one; however *Brad* shows line op
in instalments to passengers as well as goods. *Richmond & Ripon
Chronicle 8 June* said it had opened on 1st without advance publicity.
HAWES JUNCTION – see GARSDALE.
HAWICK [NB] op 29 October 1849**;
re-sited on extension to Newcastleton 1 July 1862 *(Cl)*;
clo 6 January 1969 *(RM February)*.
HAWKESBURY LANE [LNW] op 2 September
1850**; clo 18 January 1965 *(RM March)*.

HAWKHEAD

HAWKHEAD (a) [GSW] op 1 May 1894 *(GSW)*;
clo 1 January 1917 *(Cl)*; reop 10 February 1919 *(RCH)*
– not back in *Brad* until June 1923, but table for its line
lacked detail until then; clo 14 February 1966 *(Cl)*.
HAWKHEAD (b) op 12 April 1991 *(BLN 657)*;
new site, west of overbridge; still open.
HAWKHURST [SE]
op 4 September 1893 *(SE)*; clo 12 June 1961 *(T 12th)*.
HAWKMOOR – see PULLABROOK.
HAWORTH [Mid] op 15 April 1867 *(Mid)*;
clo 1 January 1962 *(RM March)*.
HAWSKER [NE] probably op 16 July 1885*;
clo 8 March 1965 *(T 19 January)*.
* = *T 16th* confirmed line date and listed all stations on stretch
then opened except this one, probably omitted in error – was
with rest in August *Brad*.

HAWTHORN TOWER [LNE] (non-tt): HALT;
op 4 July 1936 for King George's Jubilee Trust children's
holiday camp *(T 9th)*; clo at end of summer 1939;
hb included 1938, 1944a 'closed'; {Easington – Seaham}.

HAWTHORNDEN – see ROSEWELL.

HAXBY [NE] op 8 July 1845★★, May 1848 *(Topham)*;
clo 22 September 1930★★.

HAXEY

H & EPWORTH [GN/GE] op 15 July 1867 *(GN/GE;
GN co ½ T 19 August- line)*; & E added 1884 tt *(Cl)*;
clo 2 February 1959 *(RM March)*.

H JUNCTION [Ax Jt] op 2 January 1905 *(RCG)*;
clo 17 July 1933 *(RM September)*.

H TOWN [Ax Jt] op 2 January 1905 *(RCG)*; clo 17 July
1933 *(RM September)*. H T for OWSTON FERRY
hb 1910a, when first included but not seen thus *Brad*.

HAY LANE – see WOOTTON BASSETT.

HAY PARK LANE – see KNARESBOROUGH.

HAY-ON-WYE

For earliest service see 1826★★.

HAY-ON-WYE [Mid] op 11 July 1864 *(Hereford J 16th)*;
-on-W added 13 June 1955 *(Cl)*;
clo 31 December 1962 *(T 31st)*.

HAYBURN WYKE [NE] op 16 July 1885 *(T 16th)*;
perhaps re-sited, from south to north of level crossing,
about 1899/1900; clo 1 March 1917 (Thursday),
reop 2 May 1921 *(Cl)*; clo 8 March 1965 *(T 19 January)*.

HAYDOCK [GC]

HAYDOCK op 3 January 1900 *(RM January)*;
clo 3 March 1952 *(RM April* – racecourse station,
below, would remain open). In *Brad* May 1899,
pre-opening, as ST HELENS BLACKBROOK.

H PARK RACECOURSE (non-tt); op 10 February
1899 *(GC dates)*; specials ran up to and including
5 October 1963 (via Lowton St Marys) *(BR handbill)*,
thereafter bus from Wigan;
{Golborne – Ashton-in-Makerfield}.

HAYDON BRIDGE [NE]
op 28 June 1836 *(NC)*; new station when line extended
18 June 1838 *(Cl)*; still open.

HAYDONS ROAD [LSW/LBSC]
op 1 October 1868 *(L; co n T 1 October- line)* as
HAYDENS LANE; altered 1 October 1889 *(Cl;
RCG ref October)*; clo 1 January 1917 *(T 22 December
1916)*; reop 27 August 1923 *(RM October)*; still open.

HAYES & HARLINGTON near Slough [GW]
op 2 May 1864 *(co n T 27 April)* as HAYES;
& HARLINGTON added 22 November 1897 *(Cl;
ref RCH dist 23 March 1898)*; still open.
Joint GW/District service began 1 March 1883;
from 1 October 1885 GW only.

HAYES KENT [SE] op 29 May 1882 *(L)*;
KENT added 1964/6 tt; still open.
Brad 1913/14 to 1955, but not *hb*: H for KESTON.

HAYFIELD [GC/Mid]
op 1 March 1868 *(Mid)*; clo 5 January 1970 *(Mid)*.

HAYLE {map 111}.

HAYLE [Hayle; West Cornwall] op 23 May 1843★★;
clo 16 February 1852, for line rebuilding.

HAYLE [GW] op 11 March 1852 *(co n R Cornwall Gaz
12th)*; still open.

HAYLE RIVIERE BRIDGE [Hayle; West Cornwall?]
op 23 May 1843★★; clo/trains ceased to stop
16 February 1852 – or earlier?

HAYLES ABBEY [GW] op 24 September 1928
(GW H); HALT; clo 7 March 1960 *(RM April)*;
{Toddington – Winchcombe}. H Bridge pre-op *(RAC)*.

HAYLING [LBSC]

H ISLAND op 17 July 1867 *(SR)*; last in *Brad*
December 1868 (January 1869 'discontinued');
back August 1869 as SOUTH H; H I again 1 June 1892
(hbl 7 July); clo 4 November 1963 *(Cl)*.
Also see NORTH HAYLING.

HAYMARKET – see EDINBURGH.

HAYMARKET Newcastle [TWM]
op 11 August 1980 *(RM August)*; still open.

HAYWARDS HEATH [LBSC]
op 12 July 1841 *(co n T 9th)*; still open.
H H for CUCKFIELD in *Brad* 1906/7 to 1955 but not *hb*.

HAYWOOD [Cal]: line op 1 March 1867, nd,
November 1867 (only intermediate station on branch);
see 1921 April/May★★; clo 10 September 1951
(RM October). HEYWOOD in *Brad* until 1874/5;
hb made same change 1875a.

HAZEL GROVE

HAZEL GROVE [LNW] op 9 June 1857 *(Stockport 5th)*;
still open.

HAZEL GROVE [Mid] op 1 July 1902 *(RCG)*;
clo 1 January 1917 *(RCH)*.

HAZELWELL [Mid] op 1 January 1903 *(notice
Railway Archive 9, p. 30)*; clo 27 January 1941 *(Mid)*.

HAZELWOOD [Mid] op 1 October 1867 *(Mid)*;
clo 16 June 1947★★. HAZLEWOOD until 1904 *hb*.

HAZLEHEAD BRIDGE [GC]
op 1 May 1846 *(GC)*; last in *(Brad)* October 1847;
back in tt *(Topham)* January 1849, when BRIDGE
added; clo 6 March 1950 *(RM April)*.

HEACHAM [GE] op 3 October 1862 *(T 6th)*;
clo 5 May 1969 *(RM July-* photo-caption).

HEADCORN

HEADCORN [SE] op 31 August 1842 *(co n T 27th)*;
still open.

HEADCORN [KES] op 15 May 1905 *(RCG)*;
clo 4 January 1954 *(T 28 October 1953)*.
Always H JUNCTION *(Brad, hb)*.

HEADINGLEY [NE] op 10 July 1849 *(D&C 8;
T 9th- line)* as H & KIRKSTALL;
& K dropped 1852/3 *(Brad)*; still open.

HEADLESS CROSS [WMC] op 2 June 1845★★
(Lewin); last in *Brad* December 1852 but see 1848★★;
{map 16}.

HEADS NOOK [NE] first in *Brad* September 1862;
perhaps earlier non-tt use *(NC)*; clo 2 January 1967
(RM January).

HEADS OF AYR

HEADS OF AYR (a) [GSW] op 17 May 1906 *(RCG)*;
clo 1 December 1930 *(Cl)*.

HEADS OF AYR (b): according to *G&S* there was a
station [LMS] op 4 July 1932, one mile nearer Turnberry
than (a) for a holiday camp and was used this summer
only. However, no other source seen supports this;
indeed, *RM September 1932, p. 230*, says that while the

line reopened, Turnberry was the only intermediate station involved.

HEADS OF AYR (c) [LMS] op 17 May 1947 *(RM November)* – probably official since camp not opened to public until 4 June (possible staff use, but unlikely); not in public tt until 31 May 1948; Saturdays only; was on site given for (b); last train to camp 7 September 1968; last return train Saturday 14 September 1968 *(RM Aug.)*.

HEADSTONE LANE [LNW]
op 10 February 1913 *(RCG; T 8th- line)*; still open.
Also [Bak] use 16 April 1917 to 27 September 1982.

HEALD GREEN [LNW] op 1 May 1909
(LNW Officers 42501 + appendix); still open.

HEALEY HOUSE [LY] op 5 July 1869 *(LY- line)*;
clo 23 May 1949 *(RM September)*.

HEALING [GC]
op 1 April 1881 *(GC dates)*; still open.

HEANOR

HEANOR [GN] op 1 July 1891 *(GN)*; public clo 1 May 1928 *(RAIL 393/151)*, but still used by workmen at Nottingham factory; back in public tt 2 October 1939 – error; service withdrawn 2 December 1939 (last day) *(RM March 1941)*. GN co tt 1909: H for SMALLEY.

HEANOR [Mid] op 2 June 1890 *(RCG)*; clo 1 January 1917 *(T 29 December 1916)*; reop 3 May 1920 *(Mid)*; clo 4 May 1926**.

HEAP BRIDGE

HEAP BRIDGE on main line – see PIMHOLE.

HEAP BRIDGE on branch from Bury Knowsley Street [LY] (non-tt): workmen; op 9 September 1874; clo ? *(U)*.

HEAPEY [LY/LU] op 1 December 1869**;
clo 4 January 1960 *(RM February)*.

HEATH near Chesterfield [GC] op 2 January 1893 *(RCG)*; clo 4 March 1963 *(T 27 February* – 'will be specially opened for holidays and excursions')*.

HEATH near Cardiff

HEATH (HL) [Rhy] first in *Brad* October 1915;
still open.

HEATH (LL) [Cardiff] op 1 March 1911 *(RCG)*;
still open.

HL and LL added 1 July 1924 *(GW circular 18 June)*;
same date both became HALTS, until 5 May 1969 *(GWH)*.
Hb 1912–29 called [Cardiff] stop H PLATFORM.

HEATH HALL [LMS] (non-tt): HALT; in use by workmen 1926 *(U)*; added 'P' hb 1941a, still present 1944a, not 1956; {Dumfries – Lockerbie}

HEATH PARK [Mid] op 9 August 1905 *(Mid)*;
HALT; clo 16 June 1947**. In *LMS List* 1933 as H P HALT for BOXMOOR; not seen thus elsewhere.

HEATH TOWN near Wolverhampton [Mid]
op 1 November 1872 *(Mid; co n T 1st- line)*;
clo 1 April 1910 (Friday) *(RCG)*.

HEATHER & IBSTOCK [AN Jt]
op 1 September 1873 *(LNW Officers 10205, 10207)*;
& I added 1 September 1894 *(hbl 25 October)*;
clo 13 April 1931 *(LNW dates PCC 192)*.

HEATHEY LANE [LY]
op 1 March 1907 *(Southport Guard 20th)*; see 1905** (b);
clo 26 September 1938 *(RM November)*.

HEATHFIELD near Carlisle [MC]
op 2 December 1844; clo 1 March 1848, probably;
ticket dated 1846 exists (photocopy seen); see 1840**,
{map 20g}.

HEATHFIELD near Eastbourne [LBSC]
op 3 April 1880 (M. Welsh, *Steam Days*, November 1997); clo 14 June 1965 *(Cl)*.

HEATHFIELD near Exeter [GW]
op 1 July 1874 *(Woolmer 3rd)* as CHUDLEIGH ROAD,
though paper called it station at Jew's Bridge;
renamed 1 October 1882 *(Cl; RCG ref October)*;
clo 2 March 1959 *(Express & E 2nd)*.

HEATHROW

H JUNCTION op 19 January 1998 *(RM April)*;
temporary station on branch from Paddington; service suspended 31 January 1998 owing to damage to wheels from sharp curvature of track; restarted 3 February 1998; clo 25 May 1998 (last use Saturday 23rd) – replaced by next two entries.

H TERMINALS 1-2-3, on branch from Paddington,
op 25 May 1998* *(RM August)*; still open.

H TERMINAL 4, on branch from Paddington,
op 25 May 1998* *(RM August)*; technical problems so ceased early first day; restarted next day; still open.

* = reduced fares charged until after formal opening of the line on 23 June.

H TERMINALS 1-2-3 [Picc] op 16 December 1977
(T 17th) as H CENTRAL; renamed H C T 1-2-3
3 September 1983, CENTRAL dropped 12 April 1986 *(ug)*; still open.

H TERMINAL 4 [Picc] op 12 April 1986 *(Rly Obs June)*;
clo 21 October 1994, reop 4 December 1994
(BLN 746); still open.

H TERMINAL 5: op 27 March 2008; still open.

HEATHWAY – see DAGENHAM.

HEATLEY & WARBURTON [LNW]
op 1 November 1853**- line; & W added 1856/7 *(Brad)*;
clo 10 September 1962 *(RM September)*.

HEATON near Newcastle [NE]:
earliest line through here, to North Shields, op 22 June 1839**; probably op after line – not in Whishaw's list of stations for this line, 1840; not in main line table *(Brad)* June 1853 (main line had op 1 July 1847) but on Macaulay's map 1851; in *Brad* by July 1854;
re-sited 1 April 1887 *(Nhumb Young)* – moved from east to west of overbridge (S. Bragg, *RCHS Journal*, November 1991); clo 11 August 1980 *(RM October)*.
H JUNCTION 1877, 1883 *(hb)*.

HEATON near Stockport

H CHAPEL [LNW] first in *Brad* January 1852;
H C & HEATON MOOR 1 January 1916 *(hbl 27th)*
to 6 May 1974 *(BR notice)*; still open.

H MERSEY [Mid] op 1 January 1880 *(RCG)*;
clo 3 July 1961 *(RM August)*.

H NORRIS [LNW] op 4 June 1840 *(Manchester Guardian 6th* – G. Boyes) as STOCKPORT, for which it was temporary terminus; still station for Stockport when line extended over viaduct and through Stockport proper 10 May 1842; when trains started calling at Stockport Edgeley on 15 February 1843, the company's notice in the *Stockport Advertiser* of 10th made it clear that the first station would also continue in use; confusingly, 'Stockport' was used for both and it was some time before differential fares came into effect; there was some debate about which of the two should become the main one for the town; only on 3 June 1843 did *The Railway Times* say that Edgeley was to be the principal one and that the turntable there was being moved from the 'Heaton Norris side' (J. Gough); the earliest tt use of HEATON NORRIS as name so far found was in August 1843 (*Brad*), when it first included a separate local table; clo 2 March 1959 (*RM April*).

HEATON LODGE [LNW]
op 2 August 1847 (*co ½ T 25 August- line*); clo 31 October 1864 (*Cl*); still in tt November, inertia?; {physical junction shown *IA*}.
H L JUNCTION until 1849 (*Brad*).

HEATON PARK
HEATON PARK (a) [LY] used for special trains for Volunteer Review here 30 August 1879 (3,650 Volunteers and 4,000 others carried), full opening 1 September 1879 (*Manchester 2 September*); clo 17 August 1991 (*BLN 660*) for conversion >
HEATON PARK (b) [Manch] op 6 April 1992 (*BLN 681*); still open.

HEBBURN
HEBBURN (a) [NE] op 1 March 1872 (*co ½ T 9 February- line*); clo 1 June 1981 (*RM June*) for conversion to >
HEBBURN (b) [TWM] op 24 March 1984 (*Tyneside*); still open.

HEBDEN BRIDGE [LY]
op 5 October 1840 (*co n Leeds 3rd*); still open.

HEBRON [Snowdon Mountain] (ng; rack)
op 6 April 1896**; H CHAPEL until 1901 (*Brad*); still open.

HECK [NE] op 2 January 1871 (*T 3rd*); clo 15 September 1958 (*RM October*).

HECKINGTON [GN]
op 13 April 1859 (*GN*); still open.

HECKMONDWIKE
HECKMONDWIKE [LY] op 18 July 1848 (*LY; co ½ T 7 September- line*); originally east of level crossing at SE 216231; when road replaced by one that went under line new station provided west of this at SE 214232, op 9 August 1888 (J. Dilnot, *The Cleckheaton Branch*, LY Society, 1986) – goods not moved; H CENTRAL 2 June 1924 (*Rly Gaz 23 May*) to 12 June 1961 (*RM April*); clo 14 June 1965 (*RM June*). *Rly World, September 1978, p. 515*, mentions excursion from here to Scarborough 18 June 1978.
H SPEN [LNW] op 1 October 1900 (*LNW Officers 39764*); SPEN added 2 June 1924 (*Rly Gaz 23 May*); clo 5 October 1953 (*RM November*).
Before SPEN added, was briefly H NORTH (*LNW dates*) but no tt support seen.

HEDDON-ON-THE-WALL [NE] first in *Brad* July 1881* (*RCG ref 'July'*); clo 15 September 1958 (*RM October*). From H-on-W to H-on-the-W 1903 tt (*JS*).
* = *NC* says op 15 May 1881 but that was a Sunday.

HEDGE END used 6 May 1990 for Solent Gala day; fully op 14 May 1990 (*RM July*); still open.

HEDGELEY [NE] op 5 September 1887 (*NE- line*); clo 22 September 1930** (*T 10 July*).

HEDNESFORD
HEDNESFORD (a) [LNW] line op 7 November 1859 (*co ½ 14 February 1860*) but according to *Cl corr* this station only passed by BoT in December 1859, service first shown co tt January 1860; clo 18 January 1965 (*RM March*). *Brad* 1933/4 to 1955 and *hb* 1938 tt: H for CANNOCK CHASE.
HEDNESFORD (b) op 10 April 1989; cheap introductory service on Gala Day 8th (*BLN 605; BR pamphlet 3/89 L04098*); still open.

HEDON
HEDON [NE] op 27 June 1854 (*co ½ T 4 September- line*); clo 19 October 1964 (*Cl*). According to *RM January* became HALT 4 January 1960; not seen thus tt but note added there that no staff were in attendance.
H RACECOURSE [NE] (non-tt): op 24 August 1888 (*race*); horse-racing; 11 meetings 1888–95, four 1908–9 (*AB*).
H HALT [LNE] (non-tt): old Racecourse reop for speedway; op 14 August 1948 (*RM November*); Saturday only; last used 23 October 1948; {Hedon – Marfleet}.

HEELEY [Mid] op 1 February 1870 (*Mid; co n Mining 19 February- line*); clo 10 June 1968 (*Mid*).

HEIGHINGTON [NE]:
line op April 1826 (see 1825**); trains shown in tt for winter 1837/8 (*S&D Pass*); only on 3 January 1840 was gatekeeper here authorised to 'ticket passengers' – presumably no station as such yet; at times early AYCLIFFE LANE, A & H (e.g. co tt 1847); became A 1 July 1871 (*Cl*); settled 1 September 1874 (*RCG*); still open. Note that workmen's trains ran to/from this station from/to Darlington and Durham as well as to/from those included under SIMPASTURE.

HEIGHINGTON
– see BRANSTON & HEIGHINGTON.

HEIGHINGTON R.O.F.
– see DEMONS BRIDGE; SIMPASTURE.

HELE & BRADNINCH [GW]
op 1 May 1844 (*Taunton 8th*); & B added 1867 (*Brad*); clo 5 October 1964 (*Cl*).

HELENSBURGH [NB]
H CENTRAL op 31 May 1858 (*T 7 June*); CENTRAL added 8 June 1953 (*Cl; ref RM April*); still open.
H UPPER op 7 August 1894 (*T 7th*); still open.

HELLESDON [MGN] op 2 December 1882 (*MGN*); clo 15 September 1952 (*RM November*).

HELLIFIELD [Mid] op 30 July 1849 (*T 28 July, 1 September*); re-sited 35 chains north 1 June 1880 (*Mid*); still open. 1880 station aot H NEW *Brad* but not Mid co tt – informative, not part of name?

HELLINGLY [LBSC]
HELLINGLY op 3 April 1880 (M. Welsh, *Steam Days*, November 1997); clo 14 June 1965 (*Cl*). Until 1904 HELLINGLEY (*hb*).
H ASYLUM (non-tt): patients, visitors, staff; op about 1900; clo 1931 (*Course*).

HELMDON
HELMDON [GC] op 15 March 1899 (*GC; T 16th- line*); clo 4 March 1963 (*RM March*).

Became H for SULGRAVE 1 January 1928 *(hbl Jan.)*; thus LNE tt 1933, *hb* 1938 and *Brad* to 1955.

H VILLAGE [SMJ] op 1 June 1872 *(SMJ; co ½ T 14 August- line)*; VILLAGE added 1 July 1950 *(Cl)*; clo 2 July 1951 *(RM September)*.

HELMSDALE

HELMSDALE [High] op 16 May 1871 – though through services did not start until 19 June, the West Helmsdale service was almost certainly now extended to here *(High)*; still open. See 1957**.

Also see WEST HELMSDALE.

HELMSHORE [LY] op 17 August 1848 *(LY)*; clo 5 December 1966 *(RM February 1967)*.

HELMSLEY [NE] op 9 October 1871 *(Yorks Gaz 14th)*; clo 2 February 1953 *(RM March)*; later football and shopping excursions *(RM February 1955)*; *Whitby* gives example of an excursion 27 July 1964. Prior to opening special took Lord Feversham's party to York on Saturday 30 September 1871 *(T 2 October)* – clearly private trip not formal opening.

HELPRINGHAM [GN/GE] op 6 March 1882 *(GN/GE)*; clo 4 July 1955 *(RM August)*.

HELPSTON [Mid] op 2 October 1846 *(Mid)*; clo 6 June 1966 *(RM July)*. Spelled HELPSTONE until 1 May 1877 co tt, was H for MARKET DEEPING 1 July 1858 co tt to 1 May 1912 co tt *(Mid)*; still thus *LMS List* 1933, but not in LMS tt 1930.

HELSBY

HELSBY [Birkenhead] first in *Brad* September 1852; still open.

H & ALVANLEY [CLC] op 22 June 1870 *(CLC)*; clo 1 May 1875 (Saturday) *(Cl)*; reop 3 May 1934 for summer Thursdays and Sundays from Birkenhead to Northwich and Knutsford, service to summer of 1939; daily use to/from Hooton for BICC workmen shown by 8 July 1935 LMS wtt, added 28 September 1936 in GW public tt for round trip from Hooton. Thursday and Sunday services ran until outbreak of war; workmen's advertised until 22 May 1944; continued unadvertised until advertised again public 9 September 1963 (R. Maund from relevant tts).

Clo 6 January 1964 *(Cl)*; H until 1949/51 {goods *IA*}.

HELSTON [GW] op 9 May 1887 *(Cornish Tel 12th)*; clo 5 November 1962 *(W Briton 8th)*.

HEMEL HEMPSTEAD

HEMEL HEMPSTEAD [LNW] op 20 July 1837 *(co n T 19th)* as BOXMOOR; later variously and erratically (LNW co tts and *Brad*) B & H H, B for H H, H H & B; sometimes HEMPSTED; settled 1963/4; still open.

H HEMPSTED [Mid] op 16 July 1877 *(T 18th)*; clo 16 June 1947**.

Was H HEMPSTEAD until co wtt 1 June 1880 *(Mid)*.

HEMINGBROUGH [NE] op 2 July 1840 *(Hull 10th)* as CLIFF/CLIFFE; renamed 1 September 1874 *(Cl; RCG ref October)*; closed 6 November 1967 *(RM December)*.

HEMSBY [MGN]

Main station op 16 May 1878 *(MGN)*; closed 2 March 1959 *(T 2nd)*.

Temporary station to Martham op 15 July 1878 on opposite side of road to main one *(GN)*; company lacked powers for level crossing so opened this to enable line to open on to Martham (does not say how they got the train across).

Temporary station to south sanctioned October 1878; minimised distance walked between stations *(GN)*.

In July 1879, company gained powers for crossing and both temporary stations closed.

HEMSWORTH

HEMSWORTH [WRG Jt] op 1 February 1866 *(GN; T 3rd- line)*; clo 6 November 1967 *(RM December)*.

H & SOUTH KIRKBY [HB] op 1 July 1891 *(RCG)*; clo 1 January 1932 (Friday) *(RM January)*; excursion 14 October 1933 during Hull Civic Week *(RM February 1934, pp. 153–4)*.

HEMYOCK [GW] op 29 May 1876 *(Wellington 1 June)*; clo 9 September 1963 *(Express & E 9th)*.

HENBURY [GW] op 9 May 1910 *(W D Press 10th)*; in theory closed 22 March 1915 *(RCH)* except for workmen but note in RCH list of July 1921 said 'Season Ticket and Ordinary Passengers are conveyed'; advertised to public again 10 July 1922 *(Cl)*; clo 23 November 1964 *(Bristol E P 21st)*

HENDFORD

For original terminus see under YEOVIL.

HENDFORD [GW] op 2 May 1932 *(W Gaz 6th)*; HALT, used mostly by Westlands workers; slightly west of earlier terminus (shown as GW goods in *IA*); clo 15 June 1964 *(W Gaz 12th, 19th)*.

HENDON

HENDON [Mid] op 13 July 1868 *(T 14th)*; still open.

H CENTRAL [Nor] op 19 November 1923 *(T 17th)*; still open.

H FACTORY [Mid] (non-tt): PLATFORM; op 19 May 1918; clo 1919; {branch from Hendon} *(Mid)*.

HENDRE QUARRY – see GRANITE QUARRY.

HENDREFORGAN [GW] op 1 September 1875 *(GW)*; clo 5 March 1928, reop 26 March 1928 *(Cl)*; clo 22 September 1930 *(Cl)*; used by later workmen's trains to/from Gilfach Goch, which see.

HENDREFORCHAN until 1880/1 *(Brad)*.

HENDY – see 1950 October 6**.

HENFIELD [LBSC] op 1 July 1861 *(LBSC; co ½ T 23 January 1862- line)*; clo 7 March 1966 *(RM March)*.

HENGOED

HENGOED [Rhy] op 31 March 1858 *(co ½ T 1 Sept.- line)* as H; was H & MAESYCWMMER 1 June 1905 *(hbl 13 July)* to 6 May 1968 *(offic)*; LL added 1 July 1924 to 6 May 1968 tt; still open.

In turn RHYMNEY J (H), R J, R OR H J, H J, H OR RHYMNEY JUNCTION, H J & R J, in *Brad* until 1906/7.

HENGOED HL [GW] op 5 January 1858 *(RAIL 253/367)* as RHYMNEY JUNCTION; became H & MAESYCWMMER 1 July 1906 *(hbl 12th)*, H HL 1 July 1924 *(GW circular 18 June)*; clo 15 June 1964 *(RM August)*.

Successively H (WEST MIDLAND JUNCTION), H J, H OR R J, R J, R J & H J in *Brad* until 1905/6.

HENHAM [GE] op 1 April 1913 *(T 1st)*; HALT; clo 15 September 1952 *(RM October)*.

HENIARTH [Cam] (ng) op 6 April 1903 *(D&C 11)*;
H GATE until 1 February 1913 *(hbl 23 January)*;
aot request; clo 9 February 1931 *(Cl)*.
HENLEY-IN-ARDEN [GW]
HENLEY-IN-ARDEN (a) op 6 June 1894 *(Stratford 8th)*,
on branch; replaced by through station on main line >
HENLEY-IN-ARDEN (b) op 1 July 1908 *(Cl)*; still open.
HENLEY-ON-THAMES [GW]
op 1 June 1857 *(Berkshire 6th)*;
-on-T added 1894 *(hbl 8 October)*; still open.
HENLLAN [GW] op 1 July 1895 *(RCG)*;
clo 15 September 1952 *(RM November)*.
HENLOW CAMP [Mid]
op 8 May 1857 *(Mid; co ½ T 13 August- line)*;
CAMP added 1 March 1933 *(Cl)*;
clo 1 January 1962 *(RM January)*.
HENSALL [LY]
op 1 April 1848 *(LY; co ½ T 7 September- line)*; still open.
HENSTRIDGE [SD Jt] op 10 September 1863**;
clo 7 March 1966 *(Shepton 11th)*.
HENWICK [GW]
op 25 July 1859** as WORCESTER H (it was
Worcester terminus of the line for the time being);
W soon dropped; clo 5 April 1965 *(Cl)*.
HEOLGERRIG [GW/LMS]
op 31 May 1937 *(GW co n dated 26th)*; HALT;
clo 13 November 1961 *(T 8th)*; {Merthyr – Cefn Coed}.
HEPSCOTT [NE] op 1 April 1858 *(BT; T 3rd- line*; in
inspection report); after 6 October 1947 *Brad*,
before/with 31 May 1948 tt reduced to one train daily,
towards Morpeth; clo 3 April 1950 *(Cl)*.
HERBERT TOLL GATE [Glyn] (ng)
op 1 April 1874 *(Glyn)*; last in tt September 1881;
{map 79}. *Hb* 1879a: HERBERT T G.
HERCULANEUM DOCK [LO] op 6 March
1893**; re-sited on extension to Dingle 21 December
1896 *(Cl)*; clo 31 December 1956 *(T 29 September)*.
HEREFORD {map 93}
For earliest service see 1829 A**.
HEREFORD [SH Jt] op 6 December 1853**; at first,
and at times later, H BARRS COURT; still open.
H BARTON [GW] op 2 January 1854 *(T 29 Dec.)*;
clo 2 January 1893 *(RAIL 1005/208)*.
H MOORFIELDS [Mid] 30 June 1863 *(Hereford J 27th)*;
clo 1 April 1874 (Wednesday) *(Mid)*.
BARRS COURT JUNCTION [GW/LNW]
first in *Brad* September 1864; last May 1868 (according
to *U* was in GW co tt at least April 1864 to October
1868). Service only shown southbound, initially one
weekday plus 2 Sunday trains; at the end one Sunday.
{map 93}.
Trains to/from Gloucester always used Barrs Court.
Trains on Joint line to/from Shrewsbury could initially
use either Barton or Barrs Court, some having portions
for both, divided/joined at Barrs Court Junction.
Trains to/from Newport had initially to use Barton,
also used by Worcester trains; those to/from Brecon
used Moorfields. From 1 December 1857 some
Newport trains used Barrs Court. The opening of the
'Hereford Loop' (see map) on 1 August 1866 *(Joint
GW/LNW notice, Hereford Journal 28 July)* allowed

trains to/from Shrewsbury, Newport and Worcester all
to use Barrs Court, though some Worcester and
Newport trains continued to use Barton and some
Shrewsbury ones to have both Barton and Barrs Court
portions. When section of line south from Barton to
western end of new loop closed to passenger traffic is
not known; December 1866 tt shows one train each
way; wtt September 1867 shows coaches for Newport
being taken by Pilot engine from Barrs Court Junction
to Barton; *Brad* last shows service from Barton to
Newport May 1868; only services then left using
Barton, as a terminus, were some of Midland's services
from beyond Worcester. From 1 November 1872
Midland coaches were taken to Worcester by GW trains.
Services from Moorfields were diverted to Barton
1874; all Midland and associated services were diverted
to Barrs Court 1893.
There were also local connecting services, full details
unknown. 1866 notice quoted refers to 'a Pilot Train'
taking passengers on weekdays between Barrs Court
and Brecon & Merthyr line; whether this involved
reversal to Moorfields or some sort of exchange
arrangement at junction west of Moorfields not known;
at least sometimes through carriages were transferred
this way. Arrangements might have begun when Brecon
line opened in 1864 – opening notice says trains will run
in connection with LNW and GW trains at Hereford,
though might have been bus connection at first.
See articles by C.R. Clinker in RCHS *Journal* July and
November 1982 for legal aspects.
ROTHERWAS FACTORY [LNW/GW Joint] (non-tt):
alias R F SIDINGS; from 26 January 1917 to after
9 March 1918 (facsimile of ticket so dated *GW book*)
trains for workers at munitions factory. One wtt notice,
headed 'Workpeople's Trains', included separate trains
for 'Work Girls', 'Workmen', 'Soldiers'. Trains ran from
Hereford Barrs Court, journey taking five minutes;
connections provided at least for Ross and Credenhill
(Ray Gaston and late John Morris of Signalling Record
Society, via B. Wilson). Workmen's trains again at least
by 2 October 1944 wtt to 1946 *(RAC)*;
{Rotherwas physical junction shown *IA*}.
HEREFORD JUNCTION: according to *Byles*
exchange platform (non-tt) south of Pontypool;
line op 2 January 1854; platform op then ? clo ?
HERIOT [NB] op 1 August 1848**- line;
clo 6 January 1969 *(RM February)*.
HERMITAGE [GW] op 13 April 1882 *(T 10th- line)*;
clo 4 August 1942**, reop 8 March 1943;
clo 10 September 1962 *(RM October)*.
HERMITAGE FOOT [NB] appeared only in *Brad*
June 1862, when no trains were yet shown for its stretch
of line, though line opened 2 June. Omitted July when
trains were shown. Perhaps indicated a stop for benefit
of workmen on line since service on this stretch seems
initially to have been mostly for their benefit (see entry
on Riccarton Junction); {Steele Road – Newcastleton}.
HERNE BAY [LCD] op 13 July 1861 *(co n T 15th)*;
H B & HAMPTON-ON-SEA 1880/1 *(Brad)* to 1951
(Cl); still open.
HERNE / HERNE BRIDGE – see HURN.

HERNE HILL [LCD]
op 25 August 1862 *(co n T 23rd)*; still open.
HERON QUAYS [Dock] op 31 August 1987
(T 1 Sept.); clo during 9 February 1996 by IRA bomb
(T 10th), reop 22 April 1996 *(Rly Obs June)*; still open.
HERRIARD [LSW]
op 1 June 1901 *(co n Basingstoke)*; clo 1 January 1917
(T 22 Dec. 1916), reop 18 August 1924 *(T 14th, 16th)*;
clo 11 September 1932 (Sunday) – *Cl* + SR practice.
HERRINGFLEET JUNCTION
– see HADDISCOE.
HERSHAM [SR]
op 28 September 1936 *(SR sig inst 34/1936)*; still open.
HERTFORD {map 74}
H EAST [GE] op 31 October 1843 *(T 2 November)*;
re-sited 27 February 1888 *(Hertfordshire Mercury
3rd March – B. Wilson)*; EAST added 1 July 1923
(hbl 12th); still open. H RAILWAY STREET 1883/4
to 1923 *(Brad)*.
H NORTH [GN] op 1 March 1858 *(GN)*; NORTH
added 1 July 1923 *(hbl 12th)*; passenger service cut back
from original terminus to through station 2 June 1924
(Cl); still open. GN co tt 1909: H for HAILEYBURY.
H COWBRIDGE 1882/3 to 1923 *(Brad)*.
HERTINGFORDBURY [GN]
first in *Brad* December 1858; clo 18 June 1951 *(RM July)*.
GN notice of alterations for July 1861 *(T 29 June)* said
new passenger station would open here – brief closure
overlooked? – some sort of upgrading, previously
regarded as 'halt'? – latter unlikely since in January 1859
Brad all trains shown as stopping but in February 1863
it and Cole Green, only other intermediate station,
request stops. Or (most likely?) clerical
misunderstanding after GN absorbed line.
HESKETH BANK [LY] op 20 February 1878
(SouthportVis 20th); clo 7 September 1964 *(RM October)*.
Brad: H B & TARLETON at op (and thus *hb* until
1890), became H B for T 1882, H B 1911/12;
but just H B in LY co tt 1899.
HESKETH PARK [LY] op 20 February 1878
(SouthportVis 20th); clo 7 September 1964 *(RM October)*.
At first H P SOUTHPORT in *hb*.
HESLEDEN [NE]: line op 1 May 1839 (see 1836**),
nd; added to Macaulay's map between 1851 and 1854,
though not in *Brad* until February 1858;
CASTLE EDEN COLLIERY until 1 February 1891
(RCG); clo 9 June 1952** *(RM August)*.
HESLERTON [NE]:
op 8 July 1845**; clo 22 September 1930**.
HESSAY [NE] line op 30 October 1848, nd, first in tt
(Reid) April 1849, first issue of this tt; clo 20 September
1915 *(T 18th)*; back in *Brad* June 1919, Saturdays only,
for York passengers only; full use August 1921 / July 1922;
aot request; clo 15 September 1958 *(RM October)*.
HESSLE [NE] op 2 July 1840 *(Hull 10th)*; still open.
HESSLE ROAD [NE] op 1 June 1853 *(NE- line)*;
clo October 1853 *(Cl)*; {map 63}.
HEST BANK [LNW] op 22 September 1846
(co n Lancaster 26th); clo 3 February 1969 *(Cl)*.
HESTON – see HOUNSLOW CENTRAL.

HESWALL
HESWALL [Birkenhead] op 19 April 1886 *(co ½
Herapath 14 August)*; clo 17 September 1956 *(RM Oct.)*.
HESWALL [GC] op 2 May 1898 *(GC dates)* as
H HILLS; renamed 7 May 1973 *(Cl)*; still open.
HETHERSETT [GE] op 30 July 1845 *(co n Norfolk)*;
last in *Brad* September 1847; back January 1852;
aot request; clo 31 January 1966 *(Cl)*.
HETTON [NE]: line op 6 November 1837 *(NE)*, nd,
May 1848 *(Topham)*; clo 5 January 1953 *(RM March)*.
HEVER [LBSC]
op 1 October 1888 *(co n T 28 September)*; still open.
HEVERSHAM [Fur]
op 1 July 1890 *(RCG)*; clo 4 May 1942 *(LNW Record)*.
HEWORTH
HEWORTH main line op 5 November 1979 *(Rly Obs
February 1980)* as replacement for Felling and Pelaw,
which both clo then for coversion to TWM; still open.
HEWORTH [TWM] op 15 November 1981; still open.
See 2002 March 31**; continues to be served by ex-BR
and TWM trains.
HEXHAM [NE]
op 10 March 1835** *(NC)*; see 1836 B**; still open.
HEXTHORPE [SY]
op 1 February 1850 *(GC)*; last in tt February 1855.
HEYFORD [GW]
op 2 September 1850 *(co n T 31 August)*; still open.
HEYS CROSSING [LY] first in *Brad* September
1911 but perhaps op late in that month – *Ormskirk
28th* says 'now open' (no mention in previous paper,
21st); see 1905** (b); clo 18 June 1951 *(wtt supp)*.
HEYSHAM PORT [Mid]
op 11 July 1904 *(Morecambe & Heysham Times 13th)*;
for local service to/from Morecambe; long distance
services began 1 September 1904, when shipping
services transferred from Morecambe; re-sited to east
4 May 1970 *(Cl)*; clo 6 October 1975, except for
occasional use by boat train passengers; reop 11 May
1987 *(Mid)*; H in public tt, *Brad* and on station
nameboard (photograph dated 1960 on back cover of
M. Bairstow, *The 'Little' North Western Railway*, author,
2000) but H HARBOUR in wtt until 1917 (R. Bond)
and tickets generally bore this name *(JB)*;
H SEA TERMINAL on reopening (owners' version but
in tt); clo 8 February 1994, reop 16 December 1994;
still open. Officially from H HARBOUR to H PORT
11 December 1994, but already this in 11 May 1992 tt
(AB Chron).
HEYTESBURY [GW] op 30 June 1856
(W Fly P 1 July); clo 19 September 1955 *(RM Nov.)*.
HEYWOOD
HEYWOOD [LY] op 15 April 1841 *(LY)*; re-sited 1 May
1848 on extension to Bury *(Cl)*; clo 5 October 1970 *(Cl)*.
Also see CASTLETON.
HEYWOOD – see HAYWOOD.
HICKLETON
H & THURNSCOE [HB] op 23 August 1902 *(RCG)*;
clo 8 April 1929 (last train 6th) *(NE Express, June 2003)*;
excursion 14 October 1933 during Hull Civic Week
(RM January 1934, pp.153–4).
Also see BOLTON-ON-DEARNE.

HIGH BARNET
op by [GN] 1 April 1872 *(co ½ T 12 August)*;
transferred to [Nor] 14 April 1940 *(T 15th)*; still open.
HIGH BENTHAM – see BENTHAM.
HIGH BLAITHWAITE [MC]
op 1 October 1878 *(G&S)*; clo 1 August 1921 *(Cl)*.
HIGH BLANTYRE [Cal] op 2 February 1863**;
clo 1 October 1945 *(RM March)*.
HIGH BROOMS [SE] op 1 March 1893
(SE sig notice 10/1893) as SOUTHBOROUGH;
renamed 21 September 1925 *(Cl; hbl ref October)*;
still open.
HIGH FIELD [NE] first in *Brad* January 1859;
BUBWITH H F until 1 December 1873 *(Cl)*;
clo 20 September 1954 *(RM Oct.)*. *RCG*: HIGHFIELD.
HIGH HALDEN ROAD [KES]
op 15 May 1905 *(RCG)*; HALT;
clo 4 January 1954 *(T 28 October 1953)*.
HIGH HALSTOW [SEC] first in *Brad* July or August
1906; HALT; clo 4 December 1961 *(T 8 November)*.
HIGH HARRINGTON [CW Jc] op 1 October 1879
(D&C 14; Rtn- line); clo 13 April 1931 *(Cl)*.
HIGH LANE [GC/NS] op 2 August 1869
(Macclesfield – co n 31 July, item 7 August);
clo 5 January 1970 *(Cl)*.
HIGH MARISHES – see MARISHES ROAD.
HIGH PEAK JUNCTION – see 1833 May**.
HIGH ROCKS [LBSC] op 1 June 1907 *(LBSC)*;
HALT; clo 16 October 1939, reop 15 June 1942 *(Cl)*;
clo 5 May 1952 *(RM June)*.
HIGH ROYDS [SY] existed about July to September
1856 *(GC,* quoting evidence from local press tt; not in
Brad); {Dovecliffe – Westwood}.
HIGH SHIELDS [NE] {map 25}
The first station in High Shields was called South
Shields, which see.
17 December 1842 *(Brandling Junction co n)* above
replaced by two stations, new South Shields and first
to be named HIGH SHIELDS; in op notice latter is
'Station at Grewcock's Corner';
clo 1 June 1981 *(RM June)*.
HIGH STOOP [S&D]: probably early staff halt,
though public use cannot be ruled out.
On 11 December 1867 Engineer reported he was
providing wooden shed for station and gatekeeper's cabin
here, cost of which would be 'trifling', in connection
with Tow Law deviation line; included in *hb* 1862
(facilities not then shown) to 1956 (no public facilities
shown when these were included in later books);
on early OS map as H SOUK; see 1843**; {map 30}.
HIGH STREET – see GLASGOW.
HIGH STREET KENSINGTON [Met]
op 1 October 1868 *(T 16, 30 September)*; K H S until
1894/6 *(Brad)*; Dist use also from 3 July 1871;
still open. Pre-opening just K *(L)*.
HIGH WESTWOOD [NE]
op 1 July 1909 *(RCG)*; clo 4 May 1942 *(Cl)*.
HIGH WYCOMBE [GW/GC] op 1 August 1854
(co n T 31 July); re-sited 1 October 1864 *(Cl)*; still open.
HIGH added intermittently 1861/3 on *(Brad, hb)*.
HIGHAM near Gravesend [SE]: line opened

10 February 1845**; station later – *Canterbury Journal
15 February* said station 'in contemplation' *;* for early
line closure – see under Gravesend; first seen July 1848
(Topham); clo/reop as Gravesend, which see; earliest tt
mention July 1848 *(Topham)*; still open.
* = original inspection report also said station intended here
but report of tunnel inspection dated 9 August 1845 implies
that had been provided by then.

HIGHAM FERRERS
HIGHAM FERRERS [Mid] op 1 May 1894 *(RCG)*;
H F for IRTHLINGBOROUGH 1 July 1902
(hbl 23 October) to 1 October 1910 *(hbl 1st)*;
clo 15 June 1959 *(RM July)*; later special use – e.g. *BR
handbill* showed through trains to Blackpool Central,
Manchester Central, St Pancras and Scarborough
Saturday 5 August 1961; Saturdays over local holiday
fortnight to at least 1 to 15 August 1964 *(RM November)*.
H F for I in Mid co tt 1903; by 1909 *Brad* gave joint
entry in index for Mid and LNW stations as H F & I,
but in table Mid was 'for'. *Hb*: 1904 H F & I; 1912 H F.
Also see IRTHLINGBOROUGH.
HIGHAM SUFFOLK [GE] op 1 April 1854 **;
SUFFOLK added ? – not in body of 15 June 1964 tt,
perhaps one of those where was added index only;
aot request; clo 2 January 1967 *(RM February)*.
HIGHAM-ON-THE-HILL [AN Jt]
op 1 September 1873 *(LNW Officers 10205, 10207)*;
clo 13 April 1931 *(LNW dates PCC 192)*.
Just HIGHAM in opening wtt; not seen thus elsewhere.
HIGHAMS PARK [GE] op 17 November 1873 *(L)*
as HALE END; became H PARK 1 October 1894
(RCG), H P & H END 1 May 1899 *(hbl 13 July)*,
H PARK 20 February 1969; still open.
Brad and hb 1895/6 made H P (H E) of it – their way of
saying H P, late H E ?
HIGHBRIDGE
HIGHBRIDGE [BE; GW] op 14 June 1841 *(Taunton
16th- line)*; until 1879/80 successively H,
H near BURNHAM, H JUNCTION near B, H J in
Brad, &/for BURNHAM-ON-SEA added intermittently;
H WEST 1950 tt to 1952 *(Cl)*; >
HIGHBRIDGE [Somerset Central; SD Jt]:
line op 28 August 1854**, using platform at BE station;
op own station May 1862 *(SD Jt)*; tickets exist for
H EAST *(JB)* >
Two combined 30 June 1952 *(C/W)*; ex-SD Jt part
clo 7 March 1966 *(Shepton 11th)*; ex-GW part still open.
HIGHBURY {map 101 – main only}
H & ISLINGTON [NL] op 26 September 1850
(T 12 October, co ½ T 26 February 1851); variously I,
I or H, H until settled 1 July 1872 *(L)*; still open.
H & ISLINGTON [Met GNC] op 28 June 1904 *(L)*;
& I added 20 July 1922 *(ug)*; clo 5 October 1975
(Sunday) for reconstruction *(T 30 August)* >
HIGHBURY [BR] op 16 August 1976 *(T 16th)*;
still open.
H & ISLINGTON [Vic] op 1 September 1968 *(T 2nd)*;
still open.
HIGHCLERE [GW] op 4 May 1885 *(Hants Chron
2nd)*; clo 4 August 1942**, reop 8 March 1943;
clo 7 March 1960 *(Hants Chron 5th)*.

HIGHER BUXTON [LNW] op 1 June 1894 *(RCG; LNW Officers 35402- line)*; clo 2 April 1951 *(RM May)*.
HIGHER POYNTON [GC/NS]
op 2 August 1869 *(Macclesfield – co n 31 July, item 7 Aug.)*; HIGHER added 13 April 1930 *(hbl 29th)*; clo 5 January 1970 *(Cl)*. *Brad* 1882/3 to 1898/9 called it 'P Top Station, New Road'. GC co tt 1903 and *Brad*: P for LYME PARK.
HIGHFIELD ROAD [GC] first in *Brad* May 1905; HALT; clo 1 March 1917 (Thursday) *(RCH)*; {map 75}.
HIGHGATE [CKP] (non-tt): PLATFORM; to enable children from isolated area to go to school at Threlkeld plus other occasional use; op 17 August 1908; no nameboards allowed to be put up; petition at end of 1918 for public use declined by BoT; clo at end of December term 1928; {Threlkeld – Troutbeck} *(Lakeland/Cockermouth)*.
HIGHGATE London
HIGHGATE [GN] op 22 August 1867 *(L; co n T 22nd- line)*; clo 29 October 1951, reop 7 January 1952 *(T 18 December 1951)*; clo 5 July 1954 *(RM July)*.
HIGHGATE [Nor] was LL portion of GN station; used as air-raid shelter; trains stopped for this purpose from September 1940; op for normal service 19 January 1941 *(RM March)*; still open.
Also see ARCHWAY.
HIGHGATE ROAD
HL portion [TH Jt] op 21 July 1868 *(L; co ½ T 30 September- line)*; clo 31 January 1870**, reop 1 October 1870 *(Cl)*. Most use ended 1 October 1915 but a few Mid trains started from here until 1 March 1918 *(Mid)*. Was H R for PARLIAMENT HILL November 1894 to 1 July 1903 co tt *(Mid)*.
LL portion [Mid] op 17 December 1900 *(RCG)*. GE also used (service from Gospel Oak) until 1 October 1915.
All clo 1 March 1918 (Friday) *(RCH)*.
HIGHLANDMAN [Cal] first in *Brad* July 1856; clo 1 January 1917 *(RM February)*, reop 1 February 1919 *(RCH)*; aot request; clo 6 July 1964 *(RM July)*.
HIGHLEY [GW]
op 1 February 1862**; clo 9 September 1963 *(T 9th)*. HIGLEY in *Brad* until 1863/4.
HIGHTOWN Liverpool
HIGHTOWN [LY] op 24 July 1848**; still open. H in opening press tt, no detail at first in *Brad*; certainly H & INCE by 1852; became H 1861 *(Brad)*; HIGH TOWN *(hb)*.
Also see ALTCAR RIFLE RANGE.
HIGHTOWN [GW] first in *Brad* 9 July 1923; HALT; clo 10 June 1940**, reop 6 May 1946 *(T 16 March)*; clo 10 September 1962 *(RM October)*; {Marchwiel – Wrexham}.
HIGHWAYSIDE – see CALVELEY.
HIGHWORTH [GW] op 9 May 1883 *(Swindon 12th)*; clo 2 March 1953 *(T 20 February)*; trains for employees at Swindon Works until last, Friday 3 August 1962 *(Back Track June 2003)*.
HILDENBOROUGH [SE]
op 1 May 1868 *(SE; co ½ T 21 August- line)*; still open.

HILGAY [GE]: line op 26 October 1847; H probably opened later since not initially shown in any tt; first in tt *(Topham)* May 1848; H FEN until 1 October 1896 *(hbl 29th)*; aot request; clo 4 November 1963 *(T 12 October)*.
HILL END [GN]
op by March 1899 *(GN Rly Soc Newsletter 57)*; passengers set down on request to guard; for Hertfordshire County Mental Hospital; officially op to public from 1 August 1899 (H.V. Borley, *RCHS Jour 138, p.210)*; clo 1 October 1951 *(T 8 September)*.
HILLFOOT [NB] op 1 May 1900 *(RCG)*; still open.
HILLHEAD [GU]
op 14 December 1896**; still open.
HILLINGDON London op by [Met/Dist] 10 December 1923 *(L)*; H SWAKELEYS in *hb* 1935a but not *Brad*; HALT until 1934/5 *Brad*; Dist service replaced by [Picc] 23 October 1933; platforms re-sited about 3 chains nearer Uxbridge Sunday 28 June 1992, buildings completed later *(BLN 689)*; still open.
HILLINGTON near King's Lynn [MGN]
op 16 August 1879 *(T 18th)*; clo 2 March 1959 *(T 2nd)*. Mid co tt 1894, GN co tt 1909, LNE tt 1933: H for SANDRINGHAM and thus *hb* 1938 and *Brad* to 1955.
HILLINGTON near Glasgow [LMS]
H EAST op 19 March 1934 *(Cl 29)*; EAST added 1 April 1940 *(JS)*; still open. HALT 1938 *hb* and ticket thus *(JB)* but not in tt, though stop only in footnotes at first.
H WEST op 1 April 1940 *(RM June)*; WEST added 3 March 1952 *(Cl)*; still open. Though in tt was originally opened to serve new factories in the area *(WW II)*.
HILLSIDE near Montrose [NB]
op 1 May 1883**; clo February 1927 *(Cl)*.
HILLSIDE [LMS] near Southport: op 1 May 1926 *(Southport Vis 1st)*; still open. Was H SOUTHPORT on opening according to LMS circular 1 May 1926 *(RAIL 957/10)* and in *1938 hb*; just H in *Brad*, Network Rail tt 10 December 2006.
HILSEA [SR]: workmen began to use October 1937 *(U)*; op to public 2 November 1941 *(Southampton District notice 20 October)*; HALT until 5 May 1969 *(SR App)*; still open.
HILTON HOUSE [LY] first in *Brad* May 1869; clo 2 April 1917, reop 5 May 1919 *(RCH)*; clo 1 February 1954 *(RM March)*.
HIMLEY [GW] op 11 May 1925 *(hbl 56)*; clo 31 October 1932 *(RM January 1933)*; {map 96}.
HINCHLEY WOOD [SR]
op 20 October 1930 *(T 17th)*; still open.
HINCKLEY [LNW]
op 1 January 1862 *(co ½ T 29 April)*; still open.
HINDERWELL [NE]
op 3 December 1883 *(Rtn- line)*; clo 5 May 1958 *(RM May)*. LNE tt 1933: H for RUNSWICK BAY and thus *Brad* to closure but not in *hb* 1938, 1956.
HINDHAUGH [NB] (non-tt); iron miners; by 1866 to 1879; trains from Bellingham only, had to walk home in evening; {Reedsmouth – Woodburn, just north of Broomhope} *(Sewell)*.

HINDLEY

HINDLEY [LY] first in *Brad* January 1849; H NORTH
11 August 1952 to 16 May 1968 *(Cl)*; still open.
H GREEN [LNW]: op 1 September 1864**;
clo 1 May 1961 *(RM June)*.
H SOUTH [GC] op 1 April 1884 *(Wigan Observer 2nd,
item and tt)* as STRANGEWAYS & H;
renamed PLATT BRIDGE 1 January 1892 *(hbl 28th)*,
H S 1952 *(Cl)*; clo 2 November 1964 *(RM December)*.

HINDLOW

For earliest service see 1833 May**.
HINDLOW [LNW] op 1 June 1894 *(RCG; LNW Officers
35402- line)*; clo 1 November 1954 *(T 1 October)*; later
excur; see 1962 August 5**.
HINDOLVESTONE [MGN] op 19 January 1882
(MGN); clo 2 March 1959 *(T 2nd)*.
HINKSEY [GW] op 1 February 1908 *(Oxford Chron
31 January)*; HALT; clo 22 March 1915 *(RCH)*;
{Hinksey – Oxford}.
HINTON near Evesham [Mid] op 1 October 1864
(Worcester 8th); clo 17 June 1963 *(RM July)*. Not seen
as HALT, *Brad* or BR tt but BR ticket thus *(JB)*.
HINTON ADMIRAL [LSW]
op 6 March 1888 *(W Gaz first edition 9th)*;
ADMIRAL added 1 May 1888 *(Cl)*; still open.
LSW co tt 1914: H A for HIGHCLIFFE-ON-SEA
and thus *Brad* to 1955 but not in *hb* 1938.
HIPPERHOLME [LY]
op 7 August 1850 *(LY; T 5th- line)*; clo 8 June 1953
but facilities for excursions retained *(RM July)*.
HIRST – see ASHINGTON.
HIRWAUN [GW]
HIRWAUN op 24 September 1851**- line; HIRWAIN
until 1928 *(Cl)*; clo 15 June 1964 *(RM August)*.
H POND (non-tt): HALT; op 23 July 1941 for
Ordnance Factory; clo ?; reop for Trading estate ?;
clo 15 June 1964; {Hirwaun – Rhigos} *(U)*.
HIRWAUN TRADING ESTATE (non-tt):
U lists station on branch from H Pond but others say
existence unlikely – no primary evidence found.
HISTON [GE] op 17 August 1847 *(co ½ year 13 August-
line)*; aot request; clo 5 October 1970 *(RM October)*.
HITCHIN [GN]
op 7 August 1850 *(T 6th, 8th)*; still open.
HITHER GREEN [SE]
op 1 June 1895 *(RCG)*; still open.
HIXON [NS]: first in *Brad* December 1864;
reduced to one up train per day, no down service with
tt alterations of 28 July 1941 (J. Gough); clo 6 January
1947 *(RM January 1950)*. HALT in *hb* 1938 and at
clo according to *RM* but not thus *Brad*.
HOB HOLE – see OLD LEAKE.
HOCKERILL
HOCKERILL [GE] op 7 November 1910 for golf club,
but others used; initially not available to/from Bishops
Stortford (only short walk); passengers from Dunmow
direction had to buy ticket to Bishops Stortford; when
other halts on line opened 18 December 1922, tickets
issued by guard, including tickets to Bishops Stortford
(Bishops Stortford); HALT; clo 3 March 1952 *(RM April)*.
Also see BISHOPS STORTFORD.

HOCKLEY near Southend [GE] op 1 October 1889
*(co notice – at back of GE co tt starting November 1889,
at Newton Abbot)*; still open.
HOCKLEY near Birmingham [GW] op 14 November
1854 *(GW; T 13th- line)*; clo 6 March 1972 *(RM April)*.
HODNET [GW] op 16 October 1867 *(Rtn- line)*;
clo 9 September 1963 *(T 9th)*.
HOE FARM [WS] (non-tt):
private; aot HALT; op about 1897;
clo 20 January 1935; {Hunston – Chalder} *(U)*.
HOE STREET – see WALTHAMSTOW.
HOGHTON
HOGHTON [LY]: line op 1 June 1846 *(Rtn PP)*, nd,
February 1847; clo 12 September 1960 *(RM October)*.
H TOWER [East Lancashire] first in *Brad* August 1847;
last October 1848; {Hoghton – Pleasington}.
HOLBEACH [MGN] op 15 November 1858
(Linc R & S Merc 19th); clo 2 March 1959 *(T 2nd)*.
HOLBECK
Station opened here 1 July 1855 *(GN co n T 2nd)*.
Notice clearly states that both GN and NE trains will
be using; *Brad* confirms. GN would have used HL
platforms, NE LL ones. Not in NE list of stations later
1850s so perhaps a GN concern.
Joint Mid/NE LL station op 2 June 1862 *(Mid)*.
Hb made three of it: GN, Mid, NE.
All closed 7 July 1958 *(Cl)*.
At times H JUNCTION, e.g. early *Brad*, NE co tt 1880,
LY co tt 1899, *hb* 1872 to 1949a. HL and LL (officially?)
added to name 2 March 1951; earlier on tickets – LY
and LNE examples *(JB)* and in *Brad* from 1892/3 to
1915/16 (not consistently); added *hb* 1949a.
HOLBORN
HOLBORN [Picc] op 15 December 1906 *(co n T 14th)*.
Aldwych line platforms added 30 November 1907;
clo 22 September 1940 (Sunday) *(RM February 1941)*;
reop 1 July 1946 *(RM September)*; clo 3 October 1994.
Main still open.
Renamed H KINGSWAY 22 May 1933 *(L)*.
HOLBORN [Cen] op 25 September 1933 *(L)* as
H KINGSWAY, replacing British Museum; still open.
In both cases KINGSWAY gradually dropped – from
map about 1960 judging by maps in K Garland,
Mr Beck's Underground Map, Capital Transport, 1994.
Only seen as H in *Brad* – space?
H VIADUCT – see under LONDON.
HOLBORN HILL – see MILLOM.
HOLBURN STREET [GNS] op 2 July 1894 *(GNS)*;
clo 5 April 1937 *(RM January 1938)*.
HOLCOMBE BROOK [LY] op 6 November 1882
(LY); clo 5 May 1952 *(RM June)*.
HOLE [SR] op 27 July 1925 *(Bideford 28th)*;
clo 1 March 1965 *(Express & E 1st)*; {map 116}.
Station nameboard: H for BLACK TORRINGTON
(BackTrack November 2005, p. 651).
HOLEHOUSE (JUNCTION) [GSW] into use
2 December 1895 (D. Stirling, from wtt at SRO);
in *Brad* from 1937, always exchange only; only ever
shown as physical junction in *hb*; H in wtt,
H JUNCTION in *Brad*; clo 3 April 1950 *(RM June)*.
HOLEGATE BRIDGE – see YORK.

HOLIDAY CAMP – see ST MARYS BAY.

HOLKHAM [GE] op 17 August 1866 *(T 18th)*; aot request; clo 2 June 1952 *(RM June)*.

HOLLAND ARMS [LNW] op 8 March 1865 (source as Llangefni); clo 4 August 1952 *(RM September)*. 1867 only: HOLLANDS A *(hb)*.

HOLLAND PARK [Cen] op 30 July 1900 *(L;T 15th- line)*; still open.

HOLLAND ROAD [LBSC] op 3 September 1905 *(LBSC)*; HALT*; clo 7 May 1956 *(Cl)*. Hove (a) was on this site or close by earlier.
* = certainly thus February 1906 *(Brad)* but RCH only made it Halt with *hb* 1941a.

HOLLINWELL & ANNESLEY GOLF STATION [GC] op 1 November 1901 for golfers *(GC dates)*; clo 10 September 1962, by when used by railwaymen only; continuity of use not certain *(U)*.
Included in *Brad* November 1901 only (just as H & A), two trains each way, and op date given by *RCG* and *RM November* without qualification; perhaps original intention was public station but soon demoted to non-tt; shown 'P' in *hb* 1904 to 1956.

HOLLINGBOURNE [LCD] op 1 July 1884 *(LCD)*; still open.

HOLLINGWOOD COLLIERY [Mid]: non-tt; 2 August 1875 wtt shows service (not in July wtt), Saturdays only, to Chesterfield only; ended ?; {Staveley Town – Barrow Hill} *(Mid)*.

HOLLINWOOD [LY] op 17 May 1880 *(Oldham E P)*; still open.

HOLLOWAY

H & CALEDONIAN ROAD [GN]: at first a ticket platform; from 1852 passengers could alight but no porters available *(L)*; first in *Brad* November 1853; fully open 1 August 1856 *(co n T 31 July)*; & C R added 6 May 1901 *(RCG)*; clo 1 October 1915 (Friday) *(RCG)*.
RM September 1897: At last GN has stopped collecting tickets of passengers to Moorgate, Victoria and Woolwich at Holloway; practice had given local 'enterprising boys' free rides; could get on without challenge at Holloway and off at King's Cross York Road (no ticket collectors there).

H ROAD [Picc] op 15 December 1906 *(co n T 14th)*; still open. H in *Brad* until 1907/8.

H MOTORAIL (non-tt) op 30 May 1960; last used 15 September 1968 *(L)*.
Also see UPPER HOLLOWAY.

HOLLY BUSH South Wales [LNW] first in *Brad* August 1871; re-sited to south, 'into use Monday 31 August 1891' *(co ½ Rly Times 13 February 1892)*; HOLLYBUSH until 1 December 1899 *(LNW dates)*; clo 13 June 1960 *(RM July)*.

HOLLYBUSH near Ayr [GSW] op 7 August 1856**- line; clo 6 April 1964 *(RM May)*.

HOLLYM GATE [NE] first in *Brad* January 1855, as H ROAD GATE; 'ROAD' dropped 1856/7 *(Brad)*; service varied – at first Tuesdays & Fridays only; January 1856 all trains stopped by request; June 1859 and January 1861 Tuesdays and Fridays; March 1863 Tuesdays only; same when last in *Brad* August 1870; {Patrington – Withernsea}.

HOLME near Burnley [LY]: line op 12 November 1849**; clo 28 July 1930 *(Cl)*.

HOLME near King's Lynn [EA] first in *Brad* February 1847, where was H GATE until November 1847; Tuesdays and Saturdays only; last in *Brad* March 1853.

HOLME near Peterborough [GN] op 7 August 1850 *(T 6th, 8th)*; clo 6 April 1959 *(RM May)*.

HOLME HALE [GE] op 15 November 1875 *(T 17th- line)*; clo 15 June 1964 *(Cl)*. At first HOLM HALE *(hb)*.

HOLME LACY [GW] op 1 June 1855**; clo 2 November 1964 *(Cl)*. *Brad* and GW co tt provided all possible combinations of HOLM(E) LAC(E)Y; settled about 1893 *(RCH dist ref 20 October)*.

HOLME MOOR [NE]: op 1 August 1848**; MOOR added 1 July 1923 *(hbl 12th)*; clo 20 September 1954 *(RM October)*; later excur. Not seen as HYORKS in *Brad* or *hb*.

HOLMES near Rotherham [Mid]: line op 1 November 1838 *(Mid)*, nd, no mention in press account of opening (J. Gough) but in return *PP 1*, end April 1839, whose implication is that there from start; THE HOLMES until 1 January 1858 co wtt *(Mid)*; clo 19 September 1955 *(RM October)*.

HOLMES CHAPEL [LNW] op 10 May 1842 (fare table, *co n Stockport 13th*); still open.

HOLMFIELD [Halifax & Ovendon] op 15 December 1879 *(GN)*; clo 23 May 1955**.

HOLMFIRTH [LY] op 1 July 1850 *(T 8th)*; clo 3 December 1865 by collapse of viaduct; passengers taken by horse-bus until line reop 11 March 1867 *(LY)*; clo 2 November 1959 *(RM December)*; [LY].

HOLMGATE [Ashover] (ng) {map 59} op 7 April 1925 *(RM October)*; request; clo 14 September 1936** *(Cl)*.

HOLMSLEY [LSW] op 1 June 1847 *(SR; Salisbury 5th- line)*; CHRISTCHURCH ROAD until 13 November 1862 *(Cl)*; clo 4 May 1964 *(Hants Chron 9th)*.

HOLMWOOD [LBSC] op 1 May 1867 *(LBSC)*; still open. LBSC co tt 1868: H for LEITHE HILL. *Brad* until 1955 but not in *hb* 1929, 1938: H for LEITH HILL.

HOLSWORTHY [LSW] op 20 January 1879**; new on extension to Bude 10 August 1898 *(Cl)*; clo 3 October 1966 *(Cornish & D P 8th)*.

HOLT near Cromer [MGN] op 1 October 1884 *(MGN)*; original station temporary *(MGN)*; clo 6 April 1964 *(RM April)*.

HOLT JUNCTION near Trowbridge [GW] first in *Brad* September 1861 and in tt *Trowbridge 7 September*; no indication in either that not a fully public station, however early service was peculiar – GW co tt 1865 shows only one train to Trowbridge but all 6 (plus the Sunday train) stopping the other way; clo 18 April 1966 *(RM May)*. Often just H *(Brad, hb)*.

HOLTBY [NE]: line op 4 October 1847 *(NE corr)*, nd; first found in *Topham* June 1848 whilst rest of line there by May; thus perhaps did open after line; GATE HELMSLEY until 1 February 1872 *(Cl; RCG ref February)*; clo 11 September 1939 *(Cl)*.

HOLTON [GN]

H-LE-CLAY op 1 March 1848 (co n GC vol. I p. 120) as H-L-C & TETNEY; & T dropped 1850/1 (Brad); clo 4 July 1955 (RM August).

H VILLAGE op 11 December 1905 (GN); see 1905** (d); clo 11 September 1961 (RM September).

HOLTON HEATH [LSW]

H HALT (non-tt): platform up line only for men building Royal Naval Cordite Factory; op ? – building of factory started March 1915 (LSW).
Replaced to west by >

HOLTON HEATH op, still non-tt, 3 April 1916 (U); op unadvertised for ordinary trains April 1917 (Dorset); in Brad from that starting 14 July 1924 and now public according to LSW; however hb 1926a has 'P' to and from Admiralty Sidings only – qualification removed 1929/1938; still open.

HOLTON-LE-MOOR [GC] op 1 November 1848 (GC); -le-M added 1 July 1923 (hbl 12th); clo 1 November 1965 (RM December).

HOLYHEAD [LNW]

HOLYHEAD op 1 August 1848 (co n T 18 July) *; original temporary station near engine shed, opposite Port Dafach Road; replaced during week beginning 14 September 1851; third, really a reconstruction of second, putting it on both sides of harbour, op 17 June 1880 (P. Baughan, Chester & Holyhead Railway, vol. I, D&C, 1972; Davies & Rowlands, Holy Island, privately, 1986; LNW Officers 20945); still open.
* = public enjoyed free trips 1 April 1848, following arrival of train carrying officials and gentry on previous day (D. Lloyd Hughes & D.M. Williams, Holyhead – The Story of a Port, authors, 1967).

H ADMIRALTY PIER op 20 May 1851 (LNW); horse-drawn from main station until about 1860; clo 1 April 1925 (Wednesday) (RM June).
By 1866 quay at west side of harbour had been completed; its goods sheds used by passengers on LNW boats to Ireland (Historical Survey of Chester to Holyhead Railway, OPC, 1984). This ceased to be used after opening of 1880 extension to main station (Neele, pp. 241–2).

HOLYTOWN [Cal]

HOLYTOWN (a) op on or before 6 March 1835 (see 1835 C**); first appeared in Brad as HOLYTOWN, BELLSHILL (really H & B – Murray); became just H 1845 (Brad); clo 1 June 1882, replaced by Mossend, to north*.

HOLYTOWN (b) op 1 June 1880 (Cal-line) as CARFIN; renamed C JUNCTION 1 January 1882, H J 1 June 1882, H 1 October 1901 (Cl); still open.
* = 1864 and 1871 OS 6 inch maps show Holytown station south of junction between main line and line to later Carfin / Holytown, with separate platform on latter line. Misleadingly, Airey's map of about 1875 shows Holytown on the junction, where Mossend would be later. Has been assumed that date previously taken as that of renaming from Holytown to Mossend was really opening date of new station.

HOLYWELL – see BACKWORTH.

HOLYWELL near Rhyl [LNW]

H JUNCTION op 1 May 1848 (D&C 11; co n T 2nd-line);

JUNCTION added 1 July 1912 (hbl 3rd); clo 14 February 1966 (RM April).

H TOWN op 1 July 1912 (LNW Officers 43723); clo 6 September 1954 (T 2nd).

HOLYWOOD [GSW]
line op 15 October 1849 and this probably opened with it though not in Brad until May 1850*; first in Brad May 1850 as KILLYLUNG; renamed 28 October 1850 (Cl); clo 26 September 1949 (Cl).
* = inspection report dated 24 September, advising refusal of permission to open, said signal arrangements at 'Killielung' were incomplete; 10 October – now complete, can open.

HOMERSFIELD [GE]
op 2 November 1860**; clo 5 January 1953 (T 5th).

HOMERTON

HOMERTON (a) [NL] op 1 October 1868 (L); clo 15 May 1944 (buses in lieu until 23 April 1945) (Cl).

HOMERTON (b) op 13 May 1985 (AZ); still open.

HONEYBOURNE

HONEYBOURNE (a) [GW] op 4 June 1853 (Glos Chron 4th- line); clo 5 May 1969 (Cl).

HONEYBOURNE (b) op 25 May 1981 (RM July); still open.

HONING [MGN] first in Brad August 1882; clo 2 March 1959 (T 2nd). Mid co tt 1903, GN co tt 1909, LNE tt 1933, hb 1938 and Brad to 1955: H for WORSTEAD.

HONINGTON [GN] op 1 July 1857 (GN) – mentioned in T 15 June report for opening of line that day, but inspection report, 13 June 1857, says did not intend to use until 1 July (Rtn); aot request; clo 10 September 1962 (RM October); later used occasionally when engineering work prevented stop at Grantham (U).

HONITON [LSW] op 19 July 1860**; still open.

HONLEY [LY]:
line op 1 July 1850 (T 8th), nd, January 1851; still open.

HONOR OAK

HONOR OAK [LCD] op 1 December 1865 (co n T 1st); clo 1 January 1917 (RM February); reop 1 March 1919 (RCH); clo 22 May 1944 (T 22 April), reop 4 March 1946 (RM May); clo 20 September 1954 (T 20th).

H O PARK [LBSC] op 1 April 1886 (L); still open.

HOO JUNCTION STAFF HALT (non-tt): railwaymen; op 6 February 1956 (U); still shown as Staff Halt in Network Rail Sectional Appendix 1/141, reissued January 2005 (R. Maund); {Milton Range – Higham}

HOOK [LSW] op 2 July 1883 (Hants Chron 7th); still open. SR tt 1939, 1947: H for ODIHAM and thus Brad to 1955 but not in hb 1938.

HOOK NORTON [GW]
op 6 April 1887 (GW-line); clo 4 June 1951 (T 4th).
On two occasions in 1897 line was blocked by landslips and passengers walked between trains run to either side of blockage – 19 January (line clear 25th) and 20 February (22nd) (GM's report).

HOOKAGATE & REDHILL [SM]
op 14 April 1911 (RM September) as REDHILL; renamed H 1 April 1921 (hbl 24th), H & R 1927 (Brad) – index earlier; clo 6 November 1933 (Cl).

Hb 1912: RED HILL. 100 yards nearer to Shrewsbury than earlier Red Hill, which see.

HOOLE [LY] op 18 May 1882 *(Ormskirk 25th)*; clo 7 September 1964 *(RM October)*.

HOOLEY HILL – see AUDENSHAW.

HOOLEY HOUSE [London & Brighton]: temporary transfer point 30 October to 2 November (inclusive) 1841. Fall of earth in Merstham cutting blocked line and arrangements were made to carry passengers by road between Merstham and Hooley House (Coulsdon side of Merstham), 4 miles *(co notices T 29 October, 2 November)*. Perhaps already something here since original intention had been to open Brighton line to temporary terminus here *(T 18 September 1840 / Brighton Gazette)*.

HOOTON [Birkenhead]: line op 23 September 1840; station later 1840 – certainly by tt starting 15 December 1840 *(Freeling)*; still open.

HOPE

H CLWYD [WMCQ] op 1 May 1866 *(T 7th)* as CAERGWRLE; became H VILLAGE 1 January 1899 *(hbl 26th)*, H 6 May 1974 *(Cl)*; CLWYD added 1983/7 body of BR tt (index earlier); still open.

H & PENYFFORDD [LNW] op 14 August 1849 *(D&C 11; co ½ T 16 August- line)* as H; & P added 16 January 1912 *(hbl 25 April)*; clo 30 April 1962 *(RM June)*.

H EXCHANGE, HL [WMCQ] and **LL** [LNW], op 18 November 1867 *(WMCQ)*; at first in *hb* as H PASSENGER EXCHANGE; no outside access; no tickets issued; no proper provision even for exchange until platforms provided February 1868, when first in *Brad*; EXCHANGE dropped from name 1953/4 *(Brad)*; clo 1 September 1958 *(RM October)*.

H JUNCTION – see PENYFFORDD.

HOPE DERBYSHIRE [Mid] op 25 June 1894 *(RCG)* as H for CASTLETON; became H for C and BRADWELL 1 April 1895 *(RCG)*, H 14 June 1965 tt *(Mid)*; D added body of BR tt 1979/87 (index earlier); still open.

HOPE MILL – see GOUDHURST.

HOPEFIELD JUNCTION – see KINROSS.

HOPEMAN [High] op 10 October 1892 *(High)*; clo 1 January 1917 *(Cl)*, reop for limited school use 13 January 1917 *(GNS)*, fully reop 2 June 1919 *(RCH)*; clo 14 September 1931 *(RM November)*.
Special notice showed evening excursion from Inverness 1 July 1939 *(IU)*.

HOPESBROOK [Hereford, Ross & Gloucester] op 11 July 1853 *(Gloucester J 16th)*; temporary terminus, clo 1 June 1855**, when line extended to Ross; {Grange Court – Longhope}.

HOPPERTON [NE] op 30 October 1848** as ALLERTON; renamed 1 October 1925 *(Cl; hbl ref January 1926)*; clo 15 September 1958 *(RM October)*.

HOPTON [CHP] – see 1833 May**.

HOPTON HEATH [LNW] op 6 March 1861 *(D&C 11; Hereford J 13th- line)*; aot request; still open.

HOPTON-ON-SEA [Norfolk & S] op 13 July 1903 *(co n Norfolk & S)*; -on-S added 18 July 1932 *(Cl; RCH dist ref 5 June 1933)*; clo 4 May 1970 *(RM May)*.

HORAM [LBSC] op 3 April 1880 *(Steam Days November 1997)* as HOREHAM ROAD for WALDRON; variously H R & W, W & H R, W & HORAM/HORAM ROAD; settled 21 September 1953 *(Rly Obs November)*; clo 14 June 1965 *(Cl)*.

HORBURY

HORBURY [LY] op 5 October 1840 *(co n Leeds 3rd)*; H & OSSETT 25 March 1903 *(hbl 23 April)* to 18 June 1962 *(Cl)*; clo 5 January 1970 *(RM January)*.

H JUNCTION [LY] op 1 January 1850 *(co ½ T 22 February- line)*; replaced by >

H MILLFIELD ROAD [LMS] op 11 July 1927 *(RM July)*; clo 6 November 1961 *(RM November)*.

HORDEN [NE] op 1 September 1905 *(RCG)*; clo 4 May 1964 *(Cl)*.

HORDERLEY [BC] first in *Brad* March 1866; see 1866 February 1** for line history; aot request; clo 20 April 1935.

HOREB – see 1887**.

HOREHAM – see HORAM.

HORFIELD [GW] op 14 May 1927 *(W D Press 13th)*; PLATFORM until 1933; clo 23 November 1964 *(Bristol E P 21st)*; {map 121}.
According to 'notices' panel *Brad* August 1927 it had been renamed from H HALT to H; nothing seen between opening and August 1927 *Brad*.

HORHAM [Mid-Suffolk Light] op 29 September 1908 *(T 28th- line)*; clo 28 July 1952 *(T 28th)*.

HORLEY [LBSC] op 12 July 1841 *(co n T 9th)*; re-sited to south 31 December 1905 *(Cl)*; still open.

HORNBEAM PARK op 24 August 1992 *(Harrogate)*; still open.

HORNBY [Mid] op 17 November 1849 *(co n Lancaster 17th)*; clo 16 September 1957 *(LNW Record)*. H for KIRKBY LONSDALE in *Brad* 1851 to 1863 *(Mid)*.

HORNCASTLE [GN] op 11 August 1855 *(T 9th)*; clo 11 September 1939**, reop 4 December 1939; clo 13 September 1954 *(RM October)*.

HORNCHURCH op by [LTS] 1 May 1885 *(Mid)*; [Dist] use began 2 June 1902, ended 1 October 1905, restarted 12 September 1932; clo to ex-LTS trains 12 June 1961 *(Cl)*; Dist use continues.

HORNINGLOW [NS] op 1 August 1883 *(NS-K)*; clo 1 January 1949 (Saturday) *(RM March)*. GN co tt 1909, NS co tt 1910: BURTON (HORNINGLOW). Ticket *(JB)* for B-on-TRENT H.

HORN'S CORNER – see 1883 August 20**.

HORNSEA [NE]

H BRIDGE first in *Brad* July 1864; clo 19 October 1964 *(Cl)*.

H TOWN op 28 March 1864 *(NE)*; TOWN added 1950; clo 19 October 1964 *(Cl)*. *Hb* 1865a H SEA SIDE.

HORNSEY [GN] op 7 August 1850 *(T 6th, 8th)*; still open.

HORNSEY ROAD [TH Jt] op 1 January 1872 *(Mid n T 30 December 1871)*; clo 3 May 1943 *(LNE/LMS notice*, in *The Tottenham Joint Lines*, J.E. Connor, Connor & Butler, 1993). H R for HORNSEY RISE in Mid co tt 1 February 1880 to 1 July 1903 *(Mid)*.

HORRABRIDGE [GW] op 22 June 1859 *(Tavistock 21st, 24th)*; clo 31 December 1962★★.

HORRINGFORD [IWC]: intended to be opened in May 1872 but inspection unsatisfactory; despite refusal of permission, ran service to Sandown 28 June 1872; maintained briefly by contractor – clo by 27 July 1872 *(IWC)*. Authorised service began 1 February 1875 *(Hants Chron 6th- line)*;
clo 6 February 1956 *(Southern Daily Echo 6th)*.

HORSEBRIDGE [LSW]
op 6 March 1865 *(Salisbury 11th- line)*;
clo 7 September 1964 *(Andover Advertiser 31 July)*.

HORSEHAY & DAWLEY [GW] op 2 May 1859 *(Wenlock)* as H; became H (D) 1888/9, H & D 1908 *(Brad)*; clo 23 July 1962 *(RM August)*.

HORSFORTH [NE]
HORSFORTH op 10 July 1849 *(D&C 6;T 9th- line)*; still open. Known locally as CARR BRIDGE (J.H. Morfitt, *Horsforth & its History*, author).
H WOODSIDE first in *Brad* July 1850 as W; last there May 1853; back June 1857 as HW added; last there April 1864; at start and end service was Tuesdays & Saturdays only, towards Leeds so the possibility should be considered that it was one of those market services that continued but was omitted from *Brad* because clerk then sending information did not think it belonged there.

HORSHAM [LBSC]
op 14 February 1848 *(Hants Chron 12th)*; re-sited on mid-Sussex line 10 October 1859 *(Cl)*; still open.

HORSLEY [LSW] op 2 February 1885 *(co n T 31 January)*; still open. Originally H & OCKHAM in *Brad*, then H & O & RIPLEY, and various other combinations with 'for' instead of 'and'; these also found in *hb* but not necessarily at the same time. *Brad* ? to 1955: H for EAST H, WEST H, O and R, but *hb* 1938 content with H for O and R.

HORSMONDEN [SE]
op 1 October 1892 *(SR)*; clo 12 June 1961 *(T 12th)*.

HORSPATH [GW]
HORSPATH (a) op 1 February 1908 *(Oxford Chron 31 January)*; HALT; clo 22 March 1915 *(RCH)*.
HORSPATH (b) op 5 June 1933 *(Cl 29)*; HALT;
clo 7 January 1963 *(RM Jan.)*; {Wheatley – Littlemore}.

HORSTED KEYNES [LBSC] op 1 August 1882 *(LBSC; Hants Chron 5th- line)*; clo 28 October 1963 *(Cl)*.

HORTON – see PIDDINGTON.

HORTON KIRBY BOYS' HOME [LCD] (non-tt):
orphanage; alias HOME FOR LITTLE BOYS;
op 11 October 1870; clo by 1930; eastbound only;
{Farningham Road – Fawkham} *(U)*.

HORTON PARK [GN]
op 23 October 1880 *(RCG)*; clo 15 September 1952 *(RM October* – facilities will be kept for specials for cricket and football at Park Avenue).

HORTON-IN-RIBBLESDALE [Mid]
op 1 May 1876 *(Mid; co n T 1st- line)*;
-in-R added 26 September 1927 *(JS)*, since then intermittently; clo 4 May 1970 *(RM June)*; still excur; reop summer Dales Rail 1975 on; see 1989 October 16★★; fully reop 14 July 1986 *(Settle)*; still open.

HORWICH
HORWICH [LY] op 14 February 1870 *(LY)*;
clo 27 September 1965 *(RM November)*.
Hb 1872: H TOWN.
H PARKWAY op 30 May 2000 (A. Brackenbury, *Chron)*; still open.
Also see BLACKROD.

HOSCAR [LY]
The line through here opened 9 April 1855. A report of the inspection on the 4th *(Wigan Examiner 6th)* described the line and said 'a mile and a half or two miles beyond Newbrough [Newburgh/Parbold] is the Hoscar Moss Station ...'. However, no station for here was shown on Macaulay's Map of 1856, there was no reference in *hb* 1862 and 1867 and none appeared in *Brad* until November 1870; none was mentioned in the report of the same event in *The Southport Visiter, 5th*, which said there were six intermediate stations and then listed them. *Brad* date is supported by an item in *Ormskirk 3rd* which said it had opened on 1 November 1870. Was the 1855 mention a journalist's error such as a temporary arrangement for those building the line or for drainage works? a private station? goods only?
The Southport paper did say that railway staff were set down at their respective stations by the inspection train and 'we particularly compassionated the fate of one who was dropped somewhere in the middle of the Moss, like a Selkirk [Robinson Crusoe], alone and desolate in an unfrequented region' and it explained that Mr Scarisbrick had drained an extensive part of the moss land – was this a reference to Hoscar Moss? – if so, was it in continuous use until 1870?
It was H MOSS until 1 January 1900 *(hbl 25th)*; still open.

HOSPITAL – see PORTLAND.

HOTHFIELD [LCD] op 1 July 1884 *(LCD)*;
became HALT, but staffed 13 August 1937 *(Cl)*;
clo 2 November 1959 *(T 2 October)*. *Brad* ? to 1955 and SEC co tt 1914: H for WESTWELL HALT and thus *hb* 1938 (but HOTHWELL for ...).

HOTSPUR – see BACKWORTH.

HOTWELLS {map 121} [CE]
HOTWELLS op 6 March 1865 *(Bristol T 7th)* as CLIFTON; line at first detached from system; renamed C (H) 1888/9 *(Brad)*, H 1 September 1890 *(Cl; RCG ref January 1891)*; clo 19 September 1921 *(Bristol circular 31 August)*. Hbl of 29 January 1891 called it HOT WELLS.
H HALT op 14 May 1917 *(Mid)*; opened as an extra station, on the west side of the tunnel, to take longer trains than terminus would – latter kept as well; clo 3 July 1922 *(Mid)* – references in local press could be interpreted to mean that 1 July was official closure date, but Mid records make it reasonably clear that 1st was last day of use (J. Gough). At first H NEW STATION *(Brad)*, became H HALT 19 September 1921 tt.

HOUGH GREEN [CLC] first in *Brad* May 1874; still open. Mid co tt 1894, GC co tt 1903, LNE tt 1933 H G for DITTON and thus *hb* and until 6 May 1974 tt.

HOUGHAM [GN]
op 15 July 1852★★; clo 16 September 1957 *(RM October)*.
Until 1854/6 H & MARSTON in *Brad*.

HOUGHTON – see GREAT HOUGHTON.

HOUNSLOW {map 104 – Dist only}.

SMALLBERRY GREEN (temp terminus) [LSW]
op 22 August 1849 *(co n T 22nd)*; generally H in tts;
replaced by Isleworth and >

HOUNSLOW [LSW] op 1 February 1850 *(L)*;
aot H & WHITTON / H for W; settled 6 July 1930 as
H *(T 30 June)*; still open.

H CENTRAL [*] op 1 April 1886 *(L)*; still open.
HESTON-HOUNSLOW until 1 December 1925 *(L)*.
Hbl ref January 1926 said had become
HOUNSLOW C for HESTON but just H C *(Brad)*.

H TOWN [Dist] op 1 May 1883 *(Rtn)*; TOWN added
21 July 1884 *(ug)*; clo 1 April 1886 (Thursday),
reop 1 March 1903 *(Cl)*; replaced by through station
on main line >

H EAST [*] op 2 May 1909 *(L)*; H TOWN until
1 December 1925 *(L)*; still open.

H WEST [*] op 21 July 1884 *(L)*;
HOUNSLOW BARRACKS until 1 December 1925
(L); clo 12 July 1975, ready to be replaced by new
through station to north, opened 14 July 1975
(RM September); still open.

* = [Dist] op EAST, CENTRAL and WEST; [Picc] began to
use 13 March 1933 and now provides only service – Dist ceased
10 October 1964.

HOUSE O'HILL [LMS] op 1 February 1937
(RM March); HALT until 1937/8 *(Brad)*; clo 7 May
1951 *(RM June)*; {Davidsons Mains – Craigleith}.

HOUSTON

H & CROSSLEE [GSW] first in *Brad* March 1871;
early WINDYHILL, then CROSSLEE, H & C,
H for C, variations; settled as H 7 May 1973 *(Cl)*;
clo 10 January 1983 *(Rly Obs March)*.
Also see GEORGETOWN; UPHALL.

HOVE [LBSC]

HOVE (a) op 12 May 1840**- line; clo 1 March 1880
(Cl); Holland Road here/near later.

HOVE (b) op 1 October 1865 *(LBSC)* as
CLIFTONVILLE; renamed WEST BRIGHTON
1 July 1879 *(Cl; RCG ref July)*, H & W B 1 October
1894 *(RCG)*, H 1 July 1895 *(RCG)*; still open.

HOVETON & WROXHAM [GE] op 20 October
1874 *(T 21st)* as W; renamed 1984/7 tt; still open.

HOVINGHAM SPA [NE] op 1 June 1853**;
SPA added 1 October 1896 *(hbl 29th)*; clo 1 January
1931 (Thursday) *(T 5 December 1930)*;
later excursions – e.g. 27 July 1964 *(Whitby)*.

HOW MILL [NE] op 19 July 1836 *(NC; see 1836 B**)*;
clo 5 January 1959 *(RM February)*.

HOW WOOD near Watford
op 24 October 1988 *(Rly Obs January 1989)*; still open.

HOWDEN near Hull

HOWDEN [NE] op 2 July 1840 *(Hull 10th)*; NORTH
H 1 July 1922 *(hbl 13th)* to 12 June 1961 *(RM April)*;
still open.
Also see SOUTH HOWDEN.

HOWDEN near Bishop Auckland
– see BEECHBURN.

HOWDEN CLOUGH [GN]
op 1 November 1866 *(GN)*; clo 1 December 1952 *(Cl)*.
GN co tt 1909, LNE tt 1933, *hb* 1938 and *Brad* to
closure: H C for BIRSTALL.

HOWDON-ON-TYNE

HOWDON-ON-TYNE [NE] op 22 June 1839**;
on-T added 1 December 1875 *(RCG)*;
clo 11 August 1980 *(RM October)* for conversion to >

HOWDON [TWM] op 14 November 1982 *(Tyneside)*;
still open.

HOWE BRIDGE [LNW] op 1 September 1864**;
op as CHOWBENT; renamed 1 May 1901 *(RCG)*;
clo 20 July 1959 *(RM August)*.

HOWES [MK] first service through here, horse-drawn,
began 1 June 1831**, ceased calling February 1843
(MK); alias THE HOWES/SOUTH END; {map 16}.
Junction Diagram, e.g. 1870, shows Summerlee Iron
Works and Howe's Basin at the junction north of
Sunnyside.

HOWICK – see NEW LONGTON & HUTTON.

HOWNES GILL [S&D] first in *Brad* January 1857;
on western edge of ravine that meant traffic going
further (goods only) had to be hauled down/up inclines
by stationary engine; clo 1 July 1858 (Thursday) *(Cl)* –
opening of bridge across ravine enabled passenger
trains to go on. According to *S&D*, was replaced by
new platform on eastern side, clo 5 June 1868 with
service to Carr House. No certain evidence for this seen;
was in *hb* 1867 (not 1872), but perhaps inertia; not in
Brad, but that is not conclusive proof of non-existence;
{map 28}. HOWENS GILL in *Intelligible tt* 1858.

HOWSHAM [GC]
op 1 November 1848 *(GC* date for line; in *Brad*
November)*; clo 1 November 1965 *(RM December)*.

HOWWOOD

HOWOOD [Glagow, Paisley, Kilmarnock & Ayr]
op 21 July 1840 *(GSW)*; temporary terminus;
clo 12 August 1840 when next stretch of line op *(GSW)*.

HOWWOOD [GSW] op 1 December 1876 *(GSW)*;
same site as above; clo 7 March 1955 *(RM April)*.
Alias HOWOOD, HOW-WOOD *(hb)*
HOWWOOD STRATHCLYDE op 12 March 2001
(RM May); still open.

HOY [High] op 1 October 1874 *(RCG)*;
clo 29 November 1965 *(Cl)*. HALT in *hb* 1938 and
1956, dropped *hb* 1962a, but not seen thus in any tt.

HOYLAKE [Wirral]
op 2 July 1866 *(D&C 10)*; still open.

HUBBERTS BRIDGE [GN]
first in *Brad* June 1860; HUBBARDS BRIDGE until
October 1860; aot request; still open.

HUCKNALL

HUCKNALL op 17 May 1993 *(RM May)*; site of old
H BYRON; still open.

H BYRON [Mid] op 2 October 1848 *(Mid; RAIL
1005/265- line)*; re-sited 4 chains south 22 December
1895 *(Mid)*; BYRON added 11 August 1952 *(Cl)*;
clo 12 October 1964 *(RM November)*.

H CENTRAL [GC] op 15 March 1899 *(GC; T 16th-
line)*; H TOWN until 1 July 1923 *(hbl 12th*, which said
previously just H, though *hb* 1899a listed as H T)*;

clo 4 March 1963 *(RM March)*.
Excursion to Edwinstowe and Ollerton called here
Whit Monday, 3 June 1963 *(AB)*,
H TOWN [GN] op 2 October 1882 *(GN)*;
TOWN added 1 July 1923 *(hbl 12th)*; clo to public
14 September 1931 *(Cl)*, though railwaymen used to
1954 or later *(U)*.
HUDDERSFIELD [LY/LNW]
op 2 August 1847 *(co ½ T 25 August)*; still open.
HUGGLESCOTE [AN Jt]
op 1 September 1873 *(LNW Officers 10205, 10207)*;
clo 13 April 1931 *(LNW dates PCC 192)*.
HULANDS [LNE] (non-tt): quarry workmen; in use
by about 1935 (P. Walton, *Stainmore & Eden Valley
Railway*, OPC, 1992); certainly in wtt 11 March 1940
and 31 May 1948, but wtts 6 May 1946 and 31 May
1948 showed only services to set down on Darlington
to Penrith trains – perhaps long-running misprint since
stops other way were shown earlier; not in wtt 18 June
1961 (R. Maund); {Lartington – Bowes}.
HULL {map 63}
HULL [NE] op 8 May 1848 *(Herapath 13th)*; still open.
H PARAGON STREET / H P in *Brad* and co tts from
early 1850s to 1938/9 but inconsistently; 'Street' might
well have been error resulting from use of abbreviated
'St' versions internally – in 1880 NE co tt was 'Station'
in three places, 'Street' in one and plain 'Hull' in most.
H ALEXANDRA DOCK [HB] (non-tt): boat trains;
from 1885 *(U)*; last regular use 1908/9 (not inspected
by BoT for passenger use when signalling revised 1910);
perhaps used WWI for repatriating German prisoners
(NE Express June 2003); {branch from Beverley Road}.
H BOOTHFERRY PARK (non-tt): football supporters;
HALT; op 6 January 1951 *(RM March)*; specials
ceased end 1985/6 season *(BLN 966)*;
{loop line at Hull} *(U)*. Ticket B P *(JB)*.
H CANNON STREET [HB] op 27 July 1885 *(co ½
T 21 August)*; clo 14 July 1924 *(Cl)* – services diverted
to PARAGON.
H MANOR HOUSE STREET [York & North Midland]
op 2 July 1840 *(Hull 10th)*; clo 8 May 1848 – services
diverted to Paragon *(Cl)*; reop 1 June 1853 for local
service to Victoria Dock *(Cl)*; last in *Brad* September
1854. Was H KINGSTON STREET ? to 1853 tt *(JS)*;
thereafter 'H old station, M H S' in *Brad*.
H NEPTUNE STREET [HB] (non-tt): cattle market;
dates ?; {branch from Springbank junction} *(U)*.
H NEWINGTON [NE] (non-tt): op 8 October 1896;
perhaps origin was that local timber merchant,
Mr Jameson, built platform for invalid wife, using own
materials; later used for fairs; clo ?; {Hessle – Cottingham}.
H RIVERSIDE QUAY [NE] op 11 May 1907 *(NE maps,
but RCG gives 1 July 1909 – NE, p.763, says 'partially
opened' 1907; 1909 perhaps completion)*; first in *Brad*
July 1907 – special continental boat trains for Zeebrugge
steamship passengers only, Tuesdays, Thursdays and
Saturdays to Hull, Mondays, Thursdays and Saturdays
from Hull – later varied; clo August 1914, reop 15 May
1920 *(Cl)*; last in tt ending w.e.f. 27 September 1937,
which shows Wednesday and Saturday trains from
Paragon for Rotterdam and Hamburg steamers.

H VICTORIA DOCK [NE] op 1 June 1853 *(NE)*;
clo 1 June 1864 (Wednesday) – services diverted to
Paragon *(Cl)*. In 1877 *hb* DRYPOOL is shown 'P'
(Airey's name for Victoria Dock; probably error).
HULL JOINT DOCK: temporary non-tt station.
For opening of this, 26 June 1914 (ticket evidence,
D. Geldard).
Also see BEVERLEY ROAD and section 7 (non-rail).
For details of 1850s suburban services see article by
M.D. Greville, RCHS *Journal*, March 1956.
HULLAVINGTON [GW] op 1 July 1903
(Bristol T 2nd); clo 3 April 1961 *(RM May)*.
HULME END [NS] (ng) op 29 June 1904**;
clo 12 March 1934 *(LNW Record)*. NS co tt 1910 and
Brad to closure: H E for SHEEN and HARTINGTON.
HULTON: BR *Scottish Region Special traffic Notice*
shows train from 'HULTON' to Peterhead, arriving at
7.31am on Sunday 28 July 1957. The first entry is for
Kinnaber Junction, presumably where it entered
territory of area concerned. It looks like a forces' train –
precisely lists expected passengers as 29 first- and 285
second-class. 'Hulton' has not been identified; only
places found in Gazetteer are near Bolton. Perhaps
Little Hulton, closed 1954? perhaps misprint – e.g. for
Halton, closed 1952? Both very unlikely. Hilton
Junction, where taken over from another company?
HUMBERSTONE [GN]
op 1 January 1883 *(co n Leicester Mercury 6th)*;
clo 7 December 1953 *(T 7th)*, though workmen used to
29 April 1957 *(U)* and summer Saturday and Sunday
use continued to 9 September 1962, last train *(Cl)*.
HUMBERSTONE ROAD [Mid]
op 1 July 1875 *(Mid)*; clo 4 March 1968 *(Cl)*.
HUMBERTON [NE] (non-tt):
shown 'P' 1877 *hb*, H SIDING, no facilities 1883;
no evidence of passenger use found;
{Gatehouse at crossing 4m 2ch from Pilmoor Junction}.
HUMBIE [NB]
op 14 October 1901**- line; clo 3 April 1933**.
HUMPHREY PARK
op 15 October 1984 *(D&C 10)*; still open.
HUMSHAUGH [NB]
op 5 April 1858 *(T 5th)* as CHOLLERFORD;
renamed 1 August 1919 *(hbl 29 January 1920)*;
clo 15 October 1956 *(T 21 September)*.
HUNCOAT [LY]
op 18 September 1848 *(Herapath 23rd- line; nd Brad,
but in Topham November, first time it included line)*;
re-sited 37 chains nearer Accrington, date unknown;
still open.
HUNDRED END [LY] first in *Brad* July 1878 (also
in *11 July tt Oldham Adv*, tts irregularly included);
aot request; clo 30 April 1962 *(Southport Vis 1 May
– last train Sunday evening)*. At first H E GATE HOUSE;
became H E for MERE BROW and HOLMS 1882/3
(Brad); 1899 H E for M B *(Brad)* but H E in LY co tt.
HUNGERFORD [GW] op 21 December 1847
(Hants Chron 25th); re-sited on extension to Devizes
11 November 1862 *(Cl)*; HALT 2 November 1964 to
5 May 1969 *(Cl)*; still open.

HUNMANBY [NE]: line op 20 October 1847**, nd, May 1848 *(Topham)*; still open.

HUNNINGTON [Halesowen Joint] op 10 September 1883 *(Mid)*; clo to public April 1919 but workmen used to Friday 29 August 1958 (last train) *(Cl)*.

HUNSLET {map 56}
For H LANE, original terminus, see LEEDS.
Through station, H [Mid], op 1 April 1850 tt *(Mid)*; re-sited 25 chains north 14 September 1873 *(Mid)*; clo 13 June 1960 *(RM July)*.

HUNSTANTON [GE] op 3 October 1862 *(T 6th)*; clo 5 May 1969 *(RM July, photo-caption)*.

HUNSTON [WS] op 27 August 1897 *(D&C 2- line)*; clo 20 January 1935**.

HUNTINGDON {map 69}
For first [GE] station serving here, until 1883, see GODMANCHESTER.

HUNTINGDON [GN] op 7 August 1850 *(T 6th & 8th)*; H NORTH 1 July 1923 *(hbl 12th)* to 15 June 1964 *(Cl)*; still open.

H EAST [GN/GE] op 1 May 1883 *(GN/GE)*; EAST added 1 July 1923 *(hbl 12th)*; clo for main service 15 June 1959, but ex-GN Fridays only train ran to 11 September 1959 (last) (based on *Cl* – clo 18th); later military and excursion use *(U)*.
Hb and Junction Diagrams made two of this – GN/GE and Mid (dates of use same).

HUNTINGTON – see EARSWICK.

HUNTLEYS CAVE [LMS] (non-tt):
market ticket to Grantown-on-Spey (East) 29 May 1937 *(JB)*; *BR Scottish Region Special Traffic Notices* show stops here on 22 June and 21 September 1957 to take up and set down railwaymen's wives, presumably regular service; {'3 miles from Dava'}.

HUNTLY [GNS]
op 20 September 1854 *(GNS)*; still open.

HUNTS CROSS [CLC]
first in *Brad* May 1874; still open. GC co tt 1903, LMS tt 1930, LNE tt 1933: H C for MUCH WOOLTON but not seen thus *Brad* or *hb* 1929, 1938.

HUNTSPILL O D [GW] (non-tt):
op Thursday 17 October 1940 *(GW notice S 1851, 15 October)*; still in GW wtt supplement 5 January 1942; clo ?; alias PURITON DEPOT or PURITON ROF; {Dunball – Highbridge}.

HUNWICK [NE] op 1 April 1857 *(co ½ T 17 August- line)*; clo 4 May 1964 *(Cl)*.

HURDLOW
For first service see 1833 May**.
HURDLOW [LNW] op 1 June 1894 *(RCG; LNW Officers 35402- line)*; clo 15 August 1949 *(RM September)*; railwaymen's Saturday use shown 30 June 1952 wtt. LMS tt 1947: H for LONGNOR and MONYASH.

HURLFORD [GSW] op 9 August 1848 *(GSW- line)*; clo 7 March 1955 *(RM April)*.

HURN [LSW] op by Thursday 15 January 1863, when in tt *Poole*; clo 30 September 1935 *(Cl*, supported by *RM November*, but usual Southern practice would have given clo as Sunday 29th). HURN in 1863 *Poole* tt but at first HERNE in *Brad*. *Hb*: 1863a HURN, 1872 HERNE BRIDGE, HURN 9 June 1897 *(hbl 9 July)*.

HURST GREEN [CO Jt]
op 1 June 1907 *(LBSC)*; HALT until re-sited about 10 chains north 12 June 1961 *(hba May)*; still open.

HURST LANE [Ashover] (ng)
op 7 April 1925 *(RM October)*; request; clo 14 September 1936** *(Cl)*; {map 59}.

HURSTBOURNE [LSW] op 1 December 1882 *(Hants Chron 2nd)*; clo 6 April 1964 *(Cl)*.

HURWORTH BURN [NE] op 1 March 1880 *(NE maps- line)*; clo 2 November 1931 *(Cl)*.

HUSBORNE CRAWLEY [LNW] op 30 October 1905**; clo 1 January 1917 *(T 22 December 1916)*; reop 5 May 1919 *(RCH)*; clo 5 May 1941 *(LNW Record)*.

HUSKISSON
HUSKISSON [CLC] used for race traffic 13 and 14 July 1880 *(GN)*; public op 2 August 1880 *(RCG)*; clo 1 May 1885 (Friday) *(GC dates)*.
H CATTLE [CLC] (non-tt): ticket (to Bury St Edmunds) *(JB)*; for herdsman accompanying cattle?
H DOCK [LO] op by May 1896, first time *Brad* included line (see 1893 March 6**); clo 31 December 1956 *(T 29 September)*.

HUSTHWAITE GATE [NE] first in *Brad* February 1856; aot request; clo 2 February 1953 *(RM March)*.

HUTCHEON STREET [GNS] op 1 December 1887 *(GNS)*; clo 5 April 1937 *(RM January 1938)*.

HUTTON near Middlesbrough [NE]
HUTTON or **HUTTONS LANE**: evidence that station was here from about 1855: September 1855 accounts of [Guisborough] show receipts for it; press report of October 1859, census of 1861 (stationmaster here) and estate map of 1862 (shown on south side of level crossing, near present Newstead school, whence a lane formerly led to village) *(NE Express, August 1992)*; no tt evidence found but there is ticket *(JB)* from Middlesbrough 12 October 1871.
H GATE: probably on different site from H; originally private station for Sir E. Pease; first traffic receipts shown November 1856; first in *Brad* October 1858; last May 1864 (no facilities shown *hb* 1877); back July 1881; clo 1 October 1903 (Thursday) *(Cl)*; reop 1 January 1904 *(RCG)*; clo 2 March 1964 *(RM April)*.
H JUNCTION op 1 November 1878 *(S&D- line)*; reduced to one train daily, towards Middlesbrough after July 1885 *Brad*, before/with June 1886; last in *Brad* April 1891.

HUTTON & HOWICK – see NEW LONGTON.

HUTTON CRANSWICK [NE]: line op 7 October 1846**, nd, May 1848 *(Topham)*; still open.

HUTTONS AMBO [NE]: op 8 July 1845**; AMBO added 1 February 1885 *(Cl; RCG ref January)*; clo 22 September 1930**.

HUYTON [LNW]
HUYTON: line op 17 September 1830**, nd, 1 March 1831 co tt when shown as H LANE GATE; H LANE when first in *Brad* 1839; LANE dropped gradually – in LNW co tt 1852 H some tables, H L others; still open.
H QUARRY: line op 17 September 1830**, nd, 1 March 1831 co tt when this or nearby stop shown as BOTTOM OF WHISTON INCLINE; renamed, or replaced by, H Q by November 1837 (when mentioned

in accident report – P. Bolger, *Merseyside & District Railway Stations*, Bluecoat Press 1994)*;* clo 15 September 1958 *(LNW Record)*.

HYDE
H CENTRAL [GC/Mid]: early history from BoT report on goods accident here 28 May *(Return)* and *Hyde & Glossop Weekly News* (E. Bredee) – slight discrepancy. Both agree it opened 1 March 1858 (item in paper of 6th); BoT says opened without BoT sanction; was inspected early May 1858 and closed shortly after owing to 'incompleteness of the works'; reopened, with official approval on 26 May 1858. Paper says reopened on 28th (issue of Saturday 5 June said reopened on Friday) after being closed for a fortnight for 'repairs and other reasons that had been raised against the company running the new line'. It was shown in weekly tts in paper up to and including 8 May, omitted 15 and 22 May, back 29 May. Possible reason for difference is that 26 May was date on letter giving permission to reopen. Re-sited on extension to Marple 5 August 1862 *(Cl)*; CENTRAL added 17 September 1951 *(Mid)*; still open.
H NORTH [GC/Mid] first in *Brad* February 1863; H JUNCTION until 17 September 1951 *(Mid)*; still open.
Also see NEWTON FOR HYDE.
HYDE PARK CORNER [Picc] op 15 December 1906 *(co n T 14th)*; see 1922★★; still open.
HYDE ROAD [GC]
op 2 May 1892 *(GC)*; clo 7 July 1958 *(LNW Record)*.
HYKEHAM [Mid]: in tt 1847, but no trains calling; op 1 January 1849 co tt *(Mid)*; still open.

HYLTON
HYLTON [NE] op 1 June 1853 *(T 6th- line)*; clo 4 May 1964 *(Cl)*.
Also see SOUTH HYLTON.

HYNDLAND
HYNDLAND (a) [NB] op 15 March 1886 *(Glas; co ½ T 19 March)*; branch terminus; clo 'since 29 September', reop 26 October 1953 due to fire in embankment, much of which had to be dug out to extinguish fire *(RM December 1953, December 2003)*; sometimes GLASGOW H in tts; replaced by through station on line to Dumbarton by >
HYNDLAND (b) op 5 November 1960★★; still open.
HYTHE near Colchester [GE] op 8 May 1863 *(T 11th)*; still open.

HYTHE near Folkestone
HYTHE [SE] op 10 October 1874 (9th, given by co ½ T 20 January 1875, was formal op); clo 3 May 1943, reop 1 October 1945 *(Cl)*; clo 3 December 1951.
See B. Hert, *Hythe & Sandgate Railway*, Wild Swan, 1987. Op as H; became H KENT 21 September 1925 *(SR; hbl ref October)*, H for SANDGATE 1931 *(Brad notices ref August)*, H 2 July 1939 *(JS)*.
HYTHE [RHD] (ng) op 16 July 1927★★, which see for rest of its history. *Brad*: H KENT until 1946 reopening.
HYTHE (HANTS) [SR] op 20 July 1925 *(T 20th)*; clo 14 February 1966 *(RM February* – last train Friday, 11th); {map 128}. *Brad* dropped 'Hants' 1955.

THE END OF THE SEASON. AU REVOIR!

I B M op non-tt 9 May 1978 *(RM July)* for factory workers; HALT until 16 May 1983; in public tt 12 May 1986, but for authorised access to I B M only; alias GREENOCK I B M; still open

IBROX

IBROX [GP Jt] probably op 2 December 1868* on site of earlier Bellahouston; clo 6 February 1967 *(Cl)*.
* = first in *Brad* with Govan branch, which opened this date; at first only served by branch trains; main line service added July 1870 *(Brad)*. On RCH Junction Diagram 1870 shown as I or BELLAHOUSTON, platforms on branch only; main line platforms, site of earlier B not shown on diagrams until 1877/85.
IBROX [GU] op 14 December 1896** as COPLAND ROAD*; renamed ?; still open.
* = prior to 1938 was COPELAND R in *hb*.

I FOOTBALL GROUND (non-tt): op ?; clo about 1965; {on Govan branch} *(U)*.

ICKENHAM

op by [Met] 25 September 1905 *(L)*; [Dist] service added 1 March 1910 but transferred to [Picc] 23 October 1933; HALT until 1934/5 *(Brad)* and Met ticket thus *(JB)*; still open for Met and Picc services.

ICKLETON: *London Illustrated News* said station [EC] existed here and provided picture, between (Great) Chesterford and Whittlesford on line op 30 July 1845. *T* (29 July 1845) describes opening of line beyond Bishops Stortford. It does not include Ickleton, but does include LITTLEBURY (which see), placing this beyond (Great) Chesterford, appropriate relative place for Ickleton; in reality, Littlebury is south of Great Chesterford. Account unsatisfactory in other ways – stations on Hertford branch listed as though on main line. Possible explanation is that reporter celebrated too well and wrote report from fuzzy memory, helped by list of stations from timetable, without properly understanding latter. Despite its shortcomings, article does give very tentative support to existence of station that did not appear in *Brad* when it first included line, August 1845, or at any other time.

ICKNIELD PORT ROAD [LNW]
op 10 August 1874 *(LNW Oficers 11616, 11692)*; re-sited west of road bridge 1897 *(Cl)*; clo 18 May 1931 *(LNW Record)*.

IDE [GW] op 1 July 1903 *(RCG; Trewman 4th- line)*; clo 1 January 1917 *(Express & E 29 December 1916)*; reop 5 May 1919 *(RCH)*; clo 9 June 1958 *(T 5th)*; HALT from 1923/4 *(Brad)* and on ticket *(JB)* but not in *hb* 1938; later excur; {map 115}.

IDLE

IDLE [GN] op 15 April 1875 *(D&C 8; first in Brad May)*; clo 2 February 1931 *(RM March)*; later excur *(U)*.
IDLE [Mid] op by 1 September 1847 co tt *(Mid)* – line had opened late July; last in *Brad* September 1848.

IDMISTON [SR] op 3 January 1943 *(Cl 29)*; HALT; clo 9 September 1968 *(RM September)*; {Grateley – Porton}.

IDRIDGEHAY [Mid]
op 1 October 1867 *(Mid)*; clo 16 June 1947**.

IFFLEY [GW] op 1 February 1908 *(Oxford Chron 31 January)*; HALT; clo 22 March 1915 *(RCH)*; {Littlemore – Oxford}.

IFIELD [LBSC] op 1 June 1907 *(LBSC)* as LYONS CROSSING HALT; renamed I HALT 6 July 1907 tt *(SR)*; clo 1 January 1917 *(T 22 December 1916)*; reop 3 May 1920 *(Cl)*; HALT dropped 6 July 1930 *(Cl)*; still open.

ILDERTON [NE] op 5 September 1887 *(NE- line)*; clo 22 September 1930** *(T 10 July)*.

ILFORD [GE] op 20 June 1839 *(T 14th, 19th)*; still open. EC co tt 1854 (some tables), GE co tt 1889: I for BARKING.

ILFORD ROAD [TWM]
op 11 August 1980 *(RM August)*; still open.

ILFRACOMBE [LSW] op 20 July 1874 *(N Devon 23rd)*; clo 5 October 1970 *(N Devon 8th)*.

ILKESTON

I JUNCTION & COSSALL [Mid] op 6 September 1847 on main line as unadvertised exchange, I J; advertised 1 August 1858 co tt *(Mid)*; added to *Brad* 1864/5; re-sited 13 chains north 2 May 1870 *(Cl)* – but no support found from local press *(Mid)*; just ILKESTON 1870 to 1879, while branch clo; & C added 1 December 1890 *(hbl 29 January 1891)*; clo 2 January 1967 *(Mid)*.
I NORTH [GN] op 1 April 1878 *(GN)*; NORTH added 1954 *(Brad)* and BR ticket thus *(JB)*; clo 7 September 1964 *(RM October)*.
I TOWN [Mid] op 6 September 1847 *(Mid)*; clo 2 May 1870, reop 1 July 1879 co tt *(Mid)*, when TOWN added; clo 16 June 1947**.

ILKLEY [Otley & Ilkley] op 1 August 1865 *(co ½ T 11, 15 Aug.)*; clo 25 July 1992 for electrification, reop 8 September 1992; still open.

ILMER [GW/GC]
op 1 April 1929 *(wtt supp)*; HALT; clo 7 January 1963 *(Cl)*; {Princes Risborough – Haddenham}.

ILMINGTON – see 1833 B**.

ILMINSTER [GW]
op 11 September 1866 *(W Fly P 14th)*; clo 5 February 1951 *(Chard 3rd)*, reop 7 May 1951 *(Chard 5th)* – see 1951**; clo 10 September 1962 *(Chard 15th)*.

ILTON [GW] op 26 May 1928 *(Chard 26th)*; clo 5 February 1951 *(Chard 3rd)*, reop 7 May 1951 *(Chard 5th)* – see 1951**; HALT; clo 10 September 1962 *(Chard 15th)*; {Hatch – Ilminster}.

IMBER HOUSES (non-tt); alias IMEER H; railwaymen's wives; op 3 December 1951; clo 1972 or later; {Attadale – Strome Ferry} *(U)*.

IMMINGHAM [GC] {map 64}

I EASTERN JETTY (non-tt): boat trains; op 17 November 1913; clo 1939; {beyond I ROAD} *(U)*.

I DOCK op 5 December 1910**; temporary station; replaced 9 chains to east on an extension 17 November 1913 *(GC dates has two entries, presumably to be read together: Temporary halt removed and rebuilt in

permanent position on western side of lock pit,
November 1913; Extension from eastern boundary
of dock to lock pit opened 17 November 1913);
op as I WESTERN JETTY, renamed late 1919 /
early 1920 (*RCG ref January 1920*);
clo 6 October 1969 *(RM October)*.
(Non-tt): temporary platforms for a Sunday open day
at diesel depot and wagon maintenance shop; served
by shuttle service from Cleethorpes and Grimsby;
date unknown. (C.P. Boocock, article, *Railway World*,
June 1975, pp.232–6.)

Tramways

I ROAD op for workmen May 1906, to public 3 January
1910; HALT; clo 15 May 1912 *(Cl)*. Replaced by >
I TOWN [GC GI] op 15 May 1912 *(RCG)*;
clo 3 July 1961 *(co n G&I)*.
I DOCK [GC GI] workmen used from ? *(U)*;
op to public 17 November 1913 *(D&C 9)*;
clo 3 July 1961 *(co n G&I)*.
EASTERN ENTRANCE (to I Dock) [GC GI]:
first in *Brad* September or October 1916; last there
July 1920; request; see *G&I p.3*.
QUEENS ROAD: according to *RM August 1959, p.565*,
extension to here used by public for a week; however,
GC III p.242, says built but not used.
IMPERIAL COTTAGES op 15 June 1959 *(GNS)*;
HALT; request; clo 18 October 1965**;
{Carron – Knockando}.

IMPERIAL WHARF
17 May 2009 tt says date of opening not available
at time of going to press
{Clapham Junction – West Brompton}.

INCE near Wigan:
INCE [LY] first in *Brad* June 1863 (indexed earlier but
not in body of book); still open.
Also see LOWER INCE.
INCE & ELTON near Chester [Birkenhead]
op 1 July 1863 *(D&C 10; LNW co ½ T 14 August- line)*;
& ELTON added 17 April 1884 *(Cl; RCG ref April)*;
still open.
INCHBARE – see STRACATHRO.
INCHES [Cal] op 1 June 1874 *(Cal- line)*;
clo 5 October 1964 *(RM October)*.
INCHLEA CROSSING [High/LMS?] (non-tt):
railwaymen, families; dates ?; in 1920s and early 1930s
(after coming of LMS) wtt shows coal train stopped to
take signalman's children to and from school at
Kingussie (article J. Roake, *Highland Railway Journal
56)*; see 1957**; {Dalwhinnie – Newtonmore}.
INCHMAGRANACHAN CROSSING [High?]
(non-tt): railwaymen, families; dates ?;
{Dunkeld – Dalguise} *(U)*.
INCHTURE [Cal]
INCHTURE op 24 May 1847 *(Perthshire Courier 27th)*;
clo 11 June 1956 *(RM April)*.
I VILLAGE op 1 February 1848; service horse-drawn,
dependent on local initiative, effectively a roadside
tramway *(Dundee)*; not in *Brad* until April 1867,
after it had been acquired by the Caledonian;
clo 1 January 1917 *(Cl)*. See article by T. Edmonds,
RCHS Journal, March 1993.

INCLINE TOP near Abercynon [TV]
op 29 September 1841 *(Nelson)*, but not in *Brad* until
November 1845; no road access, no passenger shelter,
tickets bought at engine house;
alias TOP OF INCLINE; last in *Brad* December 1857.
INGARSBY [GN]
op 1 January 1883 *(co n Leicester Mercury 6th)*;
INGERSBY until 1939 tt *(Cl)*, but op notice
INGARSBY; clo 7 December 1953 *(T 7th)*,
but workmen's use continued to 29 April 1957.
GN co tt 1909, LNE tt 1933:
INGERSBY/INGARSBY for HOUGHTON and thus
hb 1938 and *Brad* to 1955.
INGATESTONE [GE]
Most from articles by N. Bowdidge in *GE Journal July
1989 and July 1996* and a series of letters, all headed
'Advertisement', in *T* (24 and 31 August, 15 and 22
September 1843).
Line op 29 March 1843; station not included in report
on opening *(T 30th)*; included in company tt 12 July
1843, but without trains (H. Paar, *Chron February 1996)*;
first in *Brad* December 1843. At first company was in
dispute with Lord Petre about positioning of station –
he wanted station in Old Hall Lane, company wanted it
in Stock Lane. In June Petre was still refusing agreement
to Stock Lane. On 15 July it was decided at a meeting
between villagers and company representatives that
station would be provided in Stock Lane. This was put
up and opened between 22 and 28 July – it only
consisted of steps leading down into cutting and two
platforms, nearby alms-house acting as booking-office;
booking-clerk said all parcels and goods traffic had
stopped with effect from 1 August, only six small parcels
having been handled between opening and then.
Affidavit sworn on 4 August by Petre's steward led to
stoppage of trains; further legal action on 7 August
resulted in trains using station again from 8 August, but
passengers had to alight on ground and walk up/down
slope of cutting – not allowed to use platform or steps.
Another break came early 1844 (minutes of February
say 'is discontinued'); from March to May 1844 *Brad*
included station but no trains calling, trains restored
June. On 9 February government inspector (Pasley)
gave opinion that unsafe for use; on 14 May he wrote
suggesting that reopening be allowed; he clearly felt that
Petre was being most unreasonable. In 1846 (plans
approved March) moved to site at Hall Lane, given by
Lord Petre. Still open.
INGESTRE [GN]
op 23 December 1867 *(GN; T 23rd- line)* as WESTON
(W-on-TRENT briefly 1869 *Brad*); renamed I 1870 tt
(Cl); clo 4 December 1939 *(Cl)*.
I for W in *Brad* from 1899/1900 and thus *hb* 1872 on.
INGHAM [GE]
op 1 March 1876 *(T 2nd)*; clo 8 June 1953 *(T 8th)*.
INGLEBY [NE]
op 1 April 1861 *(NE maps- line)*; clo 14 June 1954 *(Cl)*.
In *hb* 1877 (only): I for GREENHOW.
INGLEBY JUNCTION – see BATTERSBY.
INGLETHORPE HALL – see 1883 August 20**.

INGLETON

INGLETON [LNW] op 16 September 1861 *(co n Lancaster Gaz 14th)*; clo 1 January 1917 *(RCH)*.
INGLETON [Mid] op 30 July 1849 *(T 28 July, 1 Sept.)* as link with road service on to Milnthorpe on Lancaster & Carlisle; clo 1 June 1850 when line opened through to Lancaster; reop 1 October 1861 *(Cl)*; clo 1 February 1954 *(T 1st)*; later excursions – last ramblers' 20 September 1964 *(AB)*.
D&C 10: Mid station replaced soon after 1861 reopening. Initially connections between Mid and LNW inconvenient but through passenger service established by summer of 1862.
INGRA TOR [GW] op 2 March 1936 *(T 29 February)*; daylight only; HALT; clo 5 March 1956 *(T 5th)*; {Princetown branch}.
INGRESS ABBEY [SEC] (non-tt): PLATFORM; military hospital; used about 1915–18 *(Hosp)*; {branch from Greenhithe}.

INGROW

INGROW [Mid] op 15 April 1867 *(Mid)*; I WEST 2 March 1951 *(Mid)* to 12 June 1961 *(RM April)*; clo 1 January 1962 *(RM March)*.
I EAST [GN] op 7 April 1884 *(GN)*; EAST added 2 March 1951 *(Cl)*; clo 23 May 1955★★.
INNERLEITHEN [NB] op 1 October 1864 *(T 5th)*; clo 5 February 1962 *(RM February)*.
INNERPEFFRAY [Cal] op 21 May 1866★★- line; clo 1 January 1917 *(RM February)*; reop 2 June 1919 *(RCH)*; clo 1 October 1951 *(RM November)*.
INNERWICK [NB]: first in *Brad* July 1848 (but see 1846 June 22★★); clo 18 June 1951 *(RM July)*.
INSCH [GNS] op 20 September 1854 *(GNS)*; still open.
INSTOW [LSW] op 2 November 1855 *(N Devon 2nd* description of formal op on 29 October includes this; *co ½ T 28 February 1856* confirms public line op date); clo 4 October 1965 *(Bideford 8th)*.
INVERALLOCHY – see CAIRNBULG.
INVERAMSAY [GNS] op 5 September 1857 *(GNS)*; clo 1 October 1951 *(RM November)*.
INVERBERVIE [NB] op 1 November 1865 *(co ½ T 3 November)* as BERVIE; renamed 5 July 1926 *(hbl July)*; clo 1 October 1951 *(RM November)*.
INVERESK [NB]: line op 22 June 1846★★ *(co n T 23rd)*, nd, September 1846; op as MUSSELBURGH; renamed I 1847 tt *(Cl)*, I JUNCTION 1 October 1876 *(RCG)*, I 12 June 1890 *(Cl)*; clo 4 May 1964 *(RM June)*.
INVERGARRY [High; NB] op 22 July 1903★★; clo 1 November 1911 (Wednesday), reop 1 August 1913 *(RM August)*; clo 1 December 1933 (Friday) *(RM December)*. Private waiting room for visitors to Invergarry House.
INVERGLOY [High; NB] first in *Brad* June 1904 (see 1903 July 22★★); request; clo 1 November 1911 (Wednesday), reop 1 August 1913 *(RM August)*; clo 1 December 1933 (Friday) *(RM December)*. PLATFORM *(Brad)*, SIDING *(hb)*.
INVERGORDON [High] op 23 March 1863 *(High)*; still open.

INVERGOWRIE [Cal] op 24 May 1847 *(Perthshire Courier 27th)*; still open. INVERGOURIE in *Brad* until 1848, still this *Topham* 1849.
INVERKEILOR [NB] op 1 May 1883★★; INVERKEILLOR until 1896 tt *(JS)* and early *hb*; clo 22 September 1930 *(Cl)*.
INVERKEITHING [NB] {map 10} op 1 November 1877 *(Edin- line)*; re-sited 12 chains to north, 2 June 1890, for Forth Bridge Line, which by-passed original station *(W Fife)*; still open.
INVERKIP [Cal] op 15 May 1865 *(co n True Line 68)*; still open.
INVERLAIR – see TULLOCH.
INVERNESS [High] {map 1}
INVERNESS op 7 November 1855★★; when line to Dingwall op 11 June 1862 it used new terminal platforms beside the original and also entered from east so in effect now two termini side by side; still open.
I HARBOUR: first in *Brad* October 1863; last June 1867.
INVERSHIN [High] op 13 April 1868 *(High)*; aot request; still open.
INVERUGIE [GNS] op 3 July 1862 *(GNS)*; clo 3 May 1965 *(RM May)*.
INVERUGLAS [LNE] (non-tt): workmen, Loch Sloy HEP; op 29 October 1945; clo later 1940s; {Arrochar – Ardlui} *(U)*.
INVERURIE [GNS] op 20 September 1854 *(GNS)*; INVERURY until 1 May 1866 *(Cl)*; re-sited ½ mile north 8 February 1902; still open.
INWORTH [GE] op 1 May 1905 *(RCG)*; aot request; clo 7 May 1951 *(T 8th)*.
IPSTONES [NS] op 5 June 1905 *(D&C 7)*; clo 30 September 1935 *(RM November)*.

IPSWICH

IPSWICH [GE] op 15 June 1846★★; terminus; after line was extended, trains going northwards needed reversal. Replaced by through station op 1 July 1860 *(Cl)*; still open.
Also see DERBY ROAD.
IRCHESTER [Mid] op 8 May 1857 *(Mid; co ½ T 13 August- line)*; became I for HIGHAM FERRERS 1 November 1881, I for RUSHDEN and H F 1 October 1888, I 1 May 1894, on opening of Higham Ferrers branch *(Mid)*; clo 7 March 1960 *(RM April)*. In *LMS List* 1933 as I for WOLLASTON and BOZEAT.
IRELAND COLLIERY [Mid]: (non-tt); first in wtt for goods purposes July 1885; Saturday service began ? Notice with November 1888 public tt says that trains will not pick up/set down at sidings adjacent to colliery on Saturdays – passengers now to go to/from Netherthorpe (later Staveley Town) and Staveley (later Barrow Hill) stations; {branch from just south of Staveley Town} *(Mid)*.
IRELETH (GATE) – see ASKAM.
IRLAM [CLC]
IRLAM (a) first in *Brad* October 1873 (line shown September); became I & CADISHEAD on clo of C, 1 August 1879; replaced on deviation needed for Manchester Ship Canal by >
IRLAM (b) op 26 March 1893 *(Cl)* as I & C; became

I for C 1954; & C dropped 6 May 1974 *(BR notice)*;
still open.

IRLAMS O' TH' HEIGHT [LY]
op 1 July 1901 *(RCG)*; clo 5 March 1956 *(RM April)*.

IRON ACTON [Mid]
op 2 September 1872 *(Bristol Merc 7th)*;
clo 19 June 1944★★ *(LNW Record)*.

IRON BRIDGE
I B & BROSELEY [GW] op 1 February 1862★★ as
IRONBRIDGE; became I & B in Severn Valley table
1875 but still I in another until 1883/5 *(Brad)*,
I B & B 9 November 1895 *(hbl 23 January 1896)*;
clo 9 September 1963 *(T 9th)*.
Also see COALBROOKDALE.

IRONGRAY [GSW] op 1 March 1905 *(Dumfries 1st)*;
clo 3 May 1943 *(RM January 1944)*.

IRTHLINGBOROUGH
IRTHLINGBOROUGH [LNW] op 2 June 1845 *(co op n)*
as HIGHAM FERRARS *(Brad, Topham)*; became
H FERRERS 1852 *(Brad)*, H F & I 28 April 1885 *(Cl)*,
I 1 October 1910 *(LNW Officers 42958)*; clo 4 May
1964 *(Cl)*. LMS tt 1947: I for H F and thus to 1955
(Brad) but not *hb* 1929, 1938.
IRTHLINGBOROUGH [Mid]
– see HIGHAM FERRERS.

IRTON ROAD [Raven] (ng) op 20 November 1876
(co yearly T 26 March 1877- line); clo 1 December
1908★★; reop 1 October 1915 *(Cl)*; see 1960★★.

IRVINE
IRVINE [GSW] op 5 August 1839 *(co ½ 1110/149)*;
still open.
I BANK STREET [Cal] op 2 June 1890 *(Cal)*;
clo 1 January 1917 *(RM February)*; reop 1 February
1919 *(RCH)*; B S added 2 June 1924★★;
clo 28 July 1930 *(Cl)*.

ISFIELD [LBSC]
op 18 October 1858 *(LBSC; co ½ T 26 Feb. 1859- line)*;
clo 24 February 1969 – unsafe bridge, but bus
substitute to 4 May 1969 *(RM March, June)*.

ISHAM – see BURTON LATIMER.

ISLAND GARDENS [Dock] op 31 August 1987,
on site of earlier North Greenwich *(T 1 September)*;
clo during evening of 9 February 1996 by IRA bomb
(T 10th); reop 15 April 1996 *(Rly Obs June)*;
clo 11 January 1999 for work on Lewisham extension
(RM August); buses until new station, in tunnel,
op 20 November 1999 *(RM July 2000)*; still open. .

ISLEHAM [GE] op 1 April 1885 *(GE- line)*;
clo 18 June 1962 *(RM August)*.

ISLEWORTH [LSW]
op 1 February 1850 *(L)*; still open.
In *Brad* first as I; became I & SPRING GROVE 1854/5,
S G & I 1874/5, I & S G 1895/6, I for S G 1912/13,
1955 I; co tts varied – e.g. LSW wtt 1856 S G & I.

ISLINGTON – see HIGHBURY.

ISLIP
ISLIP (a) [LNW] op 1 October 1850 *(co n T 21 Sept.)*;
clo 1 January 1968 *(RM January)*.
ISLIP (b) op 15 May 1989 *(RM July)*; still open.

ITCHEN ABBAS [LSW] op 2 October 1865
(Salisbury 7th); clo 5 February 1973 *(Hants Chron 9th)*.

IVER [GW]
op 1 December 1924 *(wtt supp)*; still open.

IVYBRIDGE
IVYBRIDGE (a) [GW] op 15 June 1848★★;
clo 2 March 1959 *(RM April)*.
One word in opening description in press; IVY BRIDGE
in *Brad* until 1853/4; still I B in GW co tt 1859.
IVYBRIDGE (b) op 15 July 1994 *(W Morn News 16th)*;
about ¾ mile east of earlier station; still open.

JACKAMENTS BRIDGE [GW]
op 3 July 1939 *(Wilts 8th)*; HALT; clo 27 September
1948 *(Cl)*; {Kemble – Rodmarton}.
JACKFIELD [GW] op 3 December 1934 *(wtt supp)*;
HALT; re-sited 18 chains south 1 March 1954 owing
to threat of landslip *(Cl)*; clo 9 September 1963 *(T 9th)*;
{Coalport – Ironbridge}.
JACKDSALE [GN] op 1 August 1876 *(GN)*
clo 7 January 1963 *(RM Feb.)*. Op as CODNOR PARK;
became C P for IRONVILLE & JACKSDALE 22 May
1901 *(hbl 11 July)*; by GN co tt 1909 had been
renamed C P & SELSTON for I and J (still thus LNE
tt 1947); became J 1 July 1950 *(Cl)*.
Hb: 1876a C P, PYE HILL & SELSTON;
1877 C P & S; 1904 C P for I & J; 1956 J.
JACKWOOD SPRINGS:
– see TUNBRIDGE WELLS.
JAMES BRIDGE – see DARLASTON.
JAMES STREET Liverpool
JAMES STREET [LO] op 6 March 1893★★;
clo 31 December 1956 *(T 29 September)*.
For other station see LIVERPOOL.
JAMESTOWN [NB]
op 26 May 1856★★; clo 1 October 1934 *(RM October)*.
JARROW {map 24}
JARROW (a) [Springwell] op by August 1844★★;
probably more than one site used; replaced by >
JARROW (b) [NE] op 1 March 1872 *(co ½ T 9 Feb.)*,
when line along south bank of Tyne opened; clo 1 June
1981 *(RM June)* for conversion to >
JARROW (c) [TWM] op 24 March 1984 *(Tyneside)*;
still open.
JEDBURGH [NB]
op 18 July 1856★★; clo 13 August 1948★★.
JEDFOOT [NB] op 18 July 1856★★;
J BRIDGE until 1913 *(Brad)*; clo 13 August 1948★★.
JEFFERSTONE LANE – post-preservation name of
ST MARYS BAY; see last paragraph of 1927 July 16★★.
JERSEY MARINE [RSB] op 14 March 1895
(Colliery 22 March- line); clo 11 September 1933 *(Cl)*.
JERVAULX [NE] op 19 May 1856 *(RCG- line)* as
NEWTON-LE-WILLOWS; renamed 1 December
1887 *(LNW circular 672)*; clo 26 April 1954★★ *(T 20th)*.
JERVIS TOWN – see STREETLY.
JESMOND
JESMOND (a) [NE] op 27 June 1864 *(co ½ T 22 August-*
line); clo 23 January 1978 *(RM March)* for conversion
of line to [TWM] >
JESMOND (b) [TWM] op 11 August 1980 *(RM August)*
on different line; still open.
Also see WEST JESMOND.
JESSIE ROAD BRIDGE [LSW/LBSC]
op 1 October 1904 *(LBSC)*; HALT; clo 10 August
1914 *(RM June 1931)* {East Southsea branch}.
Not shown as HALT LSW co tt and *Brad* 1914
but was served by rail motor.
JEWELLERY QUARTER op 25 September 1995
(RM February 1996); still open.
JOAN CROFT [NE] (non-tt): HALT; for families of
crossing keepers to travel to and from market in
Doncaster; in use at least 1920 to 1955 (in wtt,

Saturdays only July 1939, various 1940s, June 1955,
so probably continuous use); {Arksey – Moss}
(also see R.N. Forsythe, *Steam Days*, September 2001).
JOCKS LODGE [NB] op by 1 September 1847,
when in co tt; last in *Brad* May 1848 *(Cl* gives 1 July
1848 as clo; not certain that wrong since tt for its line
then in state of flux); {map 18}.
JOHN O'GAUNT [GN/LNW]
op 15 December 1879 *(Leic; LNW Record- line)* as
BURROW & TWYFORD; renamed 1883
(RCG ref July); clo 7 December 1953 *(T 7th)*;
workmen's use continued to 29 April 1957 *(U)*.
JOHNSHAVEN [NB]
op 1 November 1865 *(co ½ T 3 November- line)*;
clo 1 October 1951 *(RM October)*.
JOHNSTON DYFED [GW]
op 15 April 1856 *(T 17th)* as J; became MILFORD
ROAD 1859 tt *(Cl)*, J 7 September 1863 *(GW ac)*,
J PEM 18 June 1928 *(Cl; ref Rly Gaz 29th)*,
J D 3 May 1976 tt *(Cl)*; aot request; still open.
JOHNSTONE
JOHNSTONE [GSW]: line op 21 July 1840 *(GSW)*,
nd, about November 1840; J HIGH 1951 tt to
10 September 1962 *(Cl)*; still open.
J NORTH [GSW]: short-lived passenger station at
Laigh Cartside Street op in April 1876, only known
from local press; platform built in summer of 1878;
no more known; lack of mention in area inspection
8 August 1888 suggests closed by then.
New station op 1 August 1896 (but not in *Brad* until
May 1897) (article, A. Swan, *Sou'West*, GSW Association
Newsletter, February 2004). Original terminus
replaced by through station on loop line 1 June 1905
(Cl; RM July- line); clo 7 March 1955 *(RM April)*.
JOHNSTOWN & HAFOD [GW] op 1 June 1896
(Wrexham 6th); clo 12 September 1960 *(Cl)*.
JOLLY SAILOR – see NORWOOD.
JOPPA [NB]: line op 14 July 1847 *(Ed & Dalk)*, nd,
1 September 1847 co tt (not in opening notice
Edinburgh Advertiser 13 July 1847 but tt there not in
standard form); omitted from *Brad* June 1848,
returned July or August 1855 but probably stayed
open, served by Musselburgh branch trains only, for
which *Brad* gave no detail during relevant period – still
in *Topham* March 1850 and in *Murray* April 1852;
re-sited, when Musselburgh branch diverted, 16 May
1859; clo 7 September 1964 *(Cl)*; {map 18}.
JORDANHILL [NB] first in *Brad* August 1887;
still open. Ticket JORDAN HILL *(JB)*.
JORDANSTON [GW]
op 1 October 1923 *(GW Mag Oct.)*; HALT; aot request,
daylight only; clo 6 April 1964 *(Cl)*; {map 81}.
JORDANSTONE [Cal] first in *Brad* October 1861;
clo 2 July 1951 *(RM August)*.

227

JUNCTION
– see MILFORD [NE]; WEAR VALLEY JUNCTION.
JUNCTION BRIDGE Edinburgh [NB]
op 1 May 1869 *(Rly Times 8th / RCHS Journal July 1979)* as J ROAD; clo 1 January 1917 *(RM February)*; reop 1 April 1919 *(RCH)*; renamed 1 July 1923 *(hbl 12th)*; clo 16 June 1947★★.
JUNCTION ROAD Edinburgh: see above entry.
JUNCTION ROAD London [TH Jt]
op 1 January 1872 *(Mid n T 30 December 1871)* as J R for TUFNELL PARK; 'for T P' dropped 1 July 1903 co tt *(Mid)*; clo 3 May 1943 *(LNE/LMS notice*, in *The Tottenham Joint Lines*, J.E. Connor, Connor & Butler, 1993).

JUNCTION ROAD Tenterden [KES] first in *Brad* January 1901; last trains shown May 1901, trains again June 1903; originally opened for shooting parties *(KES)*, so *Brad* may well not tell whole story; became HALT 1939 *(Brad)*; aot request; clo 4 January 1954 *(T 28 October 1953)*; hop pickers' specials to September 1957 or later *(U)*.
Aot J R for HAWKHURST *(Brad, hb, SEC co tt 1914)*.
JUNIPER GREEN [Cal]
op 1 August 1874 *(co n Balerno)*; clo 1 November 1943 *(LNW Record)*.
JUSTINHAUGH [Cal] op 1 June 1895★★; clo 4 August 1952 *(RM September)*.
Pre-opening reference in *hbl* 25 October 1894 as Oathlaw.

RETALIATION.

Workman (politely, to old Lady, who has accidentally got into a Smoking Compartment). "YOU
DON'T OBJECT TO MY PIPE, I 'OPE, MUM ?"

Old Lady. "YES, I DO OBJECT, VERY STRONGLY!"

Workman. "OH! THEN OUT YOU GET!!"

KEADBY [MS&L] op 13 September 1859**;
clo 2 November 1874 *(GC dates gives 1st but Sunday,
no Sunday trains – based on new tt?)*; {goods *IA*}.
KEARSLEY [LY] op 29 May 1838**;
early was RINGLEY/STONECLOUGH/S (R);
settled as S 1848 tt; renamed K & S 7 February 1894
(hbl 26 April), K 1 January 1903 *(RCH)*; still open.
KEARSNEY [LCD]
op 1 August 1862 *(co n T 1st)* as EWELL near DOVER;
renamed 1869 *(RCG ref April)*; still open. *Brad ?* to
1955: note that near/adjacent to River and Ewell.
Hb 1904 on and SEC co tt 1914: K for R and E.
KEEKLE COLLIERS [CW Jc] (non-tt):
PLATFORM for miners; op July 1910, clo 2 January
1911; reop June 1913, clo 1 October 1920;
{Moresby Junction – Cleator Moor} *(Ironmasters)*.
KEELE [NS] op 1 February 1870 *(co ½ Whitchurch
5 March)*; clo 7 May 1956 *(RM June)*.
At first in *hb* as K ROAD, altered 1898a.
K for LITTLE MADELEY and MADELEY HEATH
to clo *(Brad)*, but not in LMS tt 1933 nor *hb*.
KEELE PARK [NS] (non-tt): op 26 October 1896,
'excursions only' *(RCG)*, mainly for races;
last used 17–18 October 1906, after which races were
transferred to Uttoxeter *(AB)* – 5 March 1907 was
'official' clo; {Keele – Madeley Road}.
KEGWORTH [Mid]
op 5 May 1840 *(co n Lee)*; clo 4 March 1968 *(Cl)*.
KEIGHLEY [Mid]
op 16 March 1847 *(Mid)*; station replaced 6 May 1883
on opposite side of road from old *(Mid)*; still open.
KEINTON MANDEVILLE [GW]
op 1 July 1905 *(Langport 1st, 8th)*;
clo 10 September 1962 *(Som Gaz 15th)*.
KEITH
KEITH op by [GNS] 11 October 1856 *(GNS)*;
[High] part op 18 August 1858; K JUNCTION 1952/3
(Brad) to 12 May 1980; still open.
K TOWN [GNS]: in *Brad* March 1862, no trains calling;
trains first shown April 1862; op as EARLSMILL;
renamed 1 May 1897 *(RCG)*; clo 6 May 1968 *(RM July)*.
KELMARSH [LNW] op 16 February 1859
(LNW- line); clo 4 January 1960 *(RM February)*.
KELMSCOTT & LANGFORD [GW]
op 4 November 1907 *(RAIL 253/482)*;
clo 18 June 1962 *(T 18 May)*. PLATFORM in *Brad*
until 1908, *hb* until 1949a and thus tickets *(JB)* but not
in GW co tt, though sometimes in working instructions
(GW Halts).
KELSO [NB]
Temporary station at **WALLACE NICK** op 17 June
1850 *(co n Scotsman 15th)*; replaced by >
KELSO, op 27 January 1851 *(Grev Temp)*;
clo 15 June 1964 *(RM July)*.
KELSTON [Mid] op 1 December 1869 *(Mid)*;
clo 1 January 1949 (Saturday) *(RM March)*.
Brad 1871, Mid co tt 1894, LMS tt 1930 and *Brad* to
closure: K for SALTFORD. *Hb* added 'for S' 1914a.
KELTY [NB] op 20 June 1860 *(Tayside; co ½ T 28
September- line)*; clo 22 September 1930 *(Cl)*.

KELVEDON [GE]
KELVEDON op 29 March 1843 *(T 30th)*; still open.
K LL op 1 October 1904 *(GE notice Kelvedon)*;
clo 7 May 1951 *(T 8th)*.
KELVIN BRIDGE
KELVIN BRIDGE [Cal] op 10 August 1896 *(RCG)*;
clo 1 January 1917 *(RM February)*; reop 2 June 1919
(RCG); clo 4 August 1952 *(RM September)*.
KELVIN BRIDGE [GU] op 14 December 1896**;
still open.
KELVIN HALL
KELVIN HALL [Cal] op 1 October 1896 *(RCG)* as
PARTICK CENTRAL; renamed 15 June 1959 *(Cl)*;
clo 5 October 1964 *(RM November)*.
KELVIN HALL [GU] op 14 December 1896**;
PARTICK CROSS until 16 April 1980 reopening;
still open.
KELVINDALE (and loop for Anniesland to Maryhill
trains) op 26 September 2005 *(ScotRail tt amendment
pamphlet)*, official 28th; still open.
On/near site of earlier Dawsholm (which see).
Original intention was to call it Dawsholm but K used
to give it a better image *(Rly Obs, quoting Evening Times
of 29 March)*.
KELVINSIDE [Cal] op 1 April 1897 *(RCG)*;
clo 1 January 1917 *(RM February)*; reop 2 June 1919
(RCG); clo 1 July 1942 (Wednesday) *(Cl)*.
KEMBLE [GW] op for exchange only 12 May 1845
(GW); to public 1 May 1882, replacing Tetbury Road
(GW); still open. K JUNCTION in *Brad* until 1898/9;
always thus *hb*.
KEMNAY [GNS] op 21 March 1859 *(GNS)*;
clo 2 January 1950 *(RM February)*.
KEMP TOWN [LBSC] op 2 August 1869 *(LBSC*;
supported by *co n Alterations for August T 2nd* – 1st a
Sunday, no Sunday service); clo 1 January 1917
(T 22 December 1916); reop 10 August 1919 *(Cl)*;
clo 1 January 1933 – based on *Cl* (says 2nd) + SR practice.
KEMPSTON & ELSTOW [LNW]
op 30 October 1905**; see 1905** (a); & E added 1908;
clo 1 January 1917 *(T 22 December 1916)*; reop 5 May
1919 *(RCG)*; clo 5 May 1941 *(LNW Record)*.
See Bedford (Agricultural Show) for earlier station here.
KEMPSTON HARDWICK [LNW]
op 30 October 1905**; see 1905** (a);
clo 1 January 1917 *(T 22 December 1916)*;
reop 5 May 1919 *(RCG)*; still open.
KEMPTON PARK [LSW]:
at first non-tt for race meetings, op 18 July 1878 for
members only, 1890 to public also *(Surrey)*; originally
SUNBURY RACECOURSE; renamed 1891.
Added (under SUNBURY) in *hb* 1941a: 'P' open race
days only. Full public service began Monday 6 March
2006 (unadvertised previous day) – <u>before</u> appearance

in National tt (South West Trains e-mail 2 January 2007 to R. Maund); still open; {Hampton – Sunbury}.

KEMSING [LCD] op 1 June 1874 *(T 2nd)*; still open.

KEMSLEY [SR] op 1 January 1927 *(SR)*; HALT until 5 May 1969 *(SR App)*; still open.

KENDAL [LNW] op 22 September 1846 *(co n Manchester Guardian 26th)*; still open.

KENDAL JUNCTION – see OXENHOLME.

KENDRICK(S) CROSS – see RAINHILL.

KENFIG HILL [GW] op 1 August 1865 *(GW- line)*; CEFN until 1 August 1885 *(RCH dist 31 December)*; clo 5 May 1958 *(RM June)*.

KENILWORTH [LNW] op 9 December 1844 *(T 10th)*; clo 18 January 1965 *(RM March)*.

KENLEY [SE] op 5 August 1856 *(L; co ½ T 30 August- line)* as COULSDON; renamed December 1856 tt *(Cl)*; still open.

KENNETHMONT [GNS] op 20 September 1854 *(GNS)*; clo 6 May 1968 *(RM July)*.

KENNETT [GE] op 1 April 1854**; at first KENNET; aot request; still open.

KENNINGTON

KENNINGTON [Nor] op 18 December 1890 *(L; co ½ T 14 February 1891- line)*; Waterloo branch platforms added 13 September 1926; see 1922**; K NEW STREET until 1890 *(Brad)*; still open.

K ROAD – see LAMBETH NORTH.

Also see OVAL.

KENNISHEAD [GBK Jt]: line op 27 September 1848 *(Rtn)*, nd, June 1850; still open. Op as CROFTHEAD; later various combinations of KENNISHEAD / KINNISHEAD (JUNCTION) / THORNLIEBANK / & SPIERSBRIDGE / & SPIERS BRIDGE in *Brad, Murray*; settled 1859 *Brad* but perhaps later in Cal co tt.

KENNOWAY: on line to LARGOBEATH, which see; details same.

KENSAL GREEN op 1 October 1916 *(RCG)* by [LNW] for [Bak] use; LNW began own service 10 July 1922; still open.

KENSAL RISE [LNW] op 1 November 1861 *(L)* as K GREEN & HARLESDEN; replaced 1 July 1873 *(co n T 29 June)* by station that was originally called K G and was renamed K R 24 May 1890 *(RCG)*; still open.

KENSINGTON

KENSINGTON [WL] op 27 May 1844 *(T 24th)*; clo 1 December 1844**; {map 100}.

K OLYMPIA [WL] op 2 June 1862, belatedly, for Grand Exhibition of 1862 *(LNW co n T 4th)* – clearly new site, south of original; kept after Exhibition closed (stressed in *co n T 31 October*). Note that until Willesden Junction opened in 1866, main line connections were made at Harrow. [Met] use began 1 July 1864; [Dist] began 1 February 1872. Clo 21 October 1940 by enemy action. Later workers' (National Savings Bank Employees) services from Clapham Junction began ? (certainly in operation summer 1946). Used 19 December 1946 *(LNW Record)* until ? for Bertram Mills's Circus *(RM January 1947)*, when received present name; also from Earls Court for Exhibitions (separate platform op 3 March 1958).

Reop 1 April 1963 for diversions during Euston electrification; clo 15 June 1965 *(L)*. Reop 15 October 1967 for diversions during Paddington rebuilding; clo 20 December 1967 *(L)*. Motorail terminal opened 24 May 1966 *(RM July)*; clo ?. Token service to Clapham Junction publicly advertised from 5 May 1969. Workmen's services advertised 16 May 1983 tt. Reop fully 12 May 1986 (start of InterCity cross-London service) *(ug)*; still open. Op as K; ADDISON ROAD was added 1868/9 in LNW co tt: in *Brad* added 1868/9 in the Metropolitan table, 1870 in the LNW table; LMS tt 1930: K A R for OLYMPIA. Also see SOUTH KENSINGTON; WEST KENSINGTON.

KENT HOUSE [LCD] op 1 October 1884 *(LCD sig notice 59S/1884)*; still open. K H (BECKENHAM) in *Brad* until 1916; *hb* still thus 1956.

KENTALLEN [Cal] op 24 August 1903 *(D&C 6, chapter- line)*; clo 28 March 1966 *(RM June)*. Became K for FORT WILLIAM 1911/12? *(hbl ref 25 January 1912)* and thus Cal co tt 1913, LMS tt 1930. *Hb* back to K 1925. Only seen as K in *Brad*.

KENTISH TOWN

KENTISH TOWN [Mid] op 13 July 1868 *(T 14th)*; still open.

KENTISH TOWN [Nor] op 22 June 1907** *(co n T 21st)*; still open.

K T WEST [LNW] op 1 April 1867 *(L)*; WEST added 2 June 1924 *(T 16 May)*; clo by fire 18 April 1971 after service finished for that day *(RM July 1975)*; reop 5 October 1981 *(RM December)*; still open. Also see SOUTH KENTISH TOWN; GOSPEL OAK.

KENTON London.

KENTON [LNW] op 15 June 1912 *(T 14th)*; also [Bak] use from 16 April 1917 to 27 September 1982** and 4 June 1984 on *(Ug)*; still open. Became K for NORTHWICK PARK 1 October 1927 *(hbl October)* and thus LMS tt 1930, *hb* 1929 on and tts until 7 May 1973. Also see SOUTH KENTON.

KENTON [Mid-Suffolk Light] op 29 September 1908 *(T 28th)*; clo 28 July 1952 *(T 28th)*.

KENTON BANK [NE] op 1 June 1905 *(RCG)*; BANK added 1 July 1923 *(hbl 12th)*; clo 17 June 1929 *(Cl)*. Bankfoot [TWM] on same site later.

KENTS BANK [Fur] op 1 September 1857** *(Fur)*; last trains in *Brad* March 1858; back May 1859; still open.

KENWITH CASTLE [BWA]: line op 18 May 1901**; clo 28 March 1917**; {Bideford – Abbotsham Road}.

KENYON JUNCTION [LNW]: line op 17 September 1830**, nd, 1 March 1831 co tt; also see 1831 June 13*; clo 2 January 1961 *(RM Jan.)*. * = perhaps did not open until Bolton branch did. All early railway sources seen called it K J; Bolton J probably descriptive name in early line companions. LNW co tt 1852 called it K J; thereafter mixture of K and K J; *LNW dates* said renamed from K to K J 11 November 1895; always K J *Brad, hb.*.

KERNE BRIDGE [GW] op 4 August 1873**; clo 5 January 1959 *(T 5th)*. GW co tt 1902, 1932: K B for GOODRICH CASTLE; not thus 1942.

KERRY [Cam] op July 1863★★; reduced to Tuesdays only from emergency tt dated Thursday 5 May 1921 until ? by coal shortages – see 1921 April/May★★; clo 9 February 1931 *(Cl)*. Annual Sunday School excursion used line until 1939 *(Van)*.

KERSHOPE FOOT [NB] op 1 March 1862 *(NB)*; clo 6 January 1969 *(RM February)*.
1877 to 1890s one word *(hb)* and ticket thus *(JB)*.

KESWICK [CKP]
op 2 January 1865 *(co ½ T 28 February- line; in op tt Cockermouth)*; clo 6 March 1972 *(RM March)*.

KETLEY [GW]
KETLEY op 2 May 1859 *(Wenlock)*; clo 23 July 1962 *(RM Aug.)*.
K FORGE (non-tt): added *hb* 1873a (before facilities listed), shown 'P' 1877 and 1883 – omitted 1890; workmen's stop?; {Ketley – Lawley Bank}.
K TOWN op 6 March 1936 *(T 29 February)*; HALT; clo 23 July 1962 *(RM August)*; {Ketley – Lawley Bank}.

KETTERING [Mid] op 8 May 1857 *(T 9th)* – public use at reduced charges on formal opening day, 7th *(Herapath/Mid)*; became K for CORBY 4 May 1970 tt, K & C 5 May 1975 tt, K for C 2 May 1977, K 16 May 1988 tt *(Mid)*; still open.

KETTLE – see KINGSKETTLE.

KETTLENESS [NE] op 3 December 1883 *(Rtn- line)*; clo 5 May 1958 *(RM May)*.

KETTON & COLLYWESTON [Mid]
op 1 May 1848 *(Mid; co ½ T 21 August- line)*; & C added 8 July 1935 *(Mid)* – *Brad* briefly K for C; clo 6 June 1966 *(RM July)*.

KEW London.
KEW [NSWJ service but LSW owned site] op 1 August 1853 *(T 1st)*; most used ended 1 February 1862, when effectively replaced by Kew Bridge; one or two trains a week from Windsor to Caledonian Road for Metropolitan Cattle Market continued, last November 1866 *(Brad)*; {map 103}.
K BRIDGE [LSW] op 22 August 1849 *(co n T 22nd)*; BRIDGE added 1868/9 – 1 January 1869, when K GARDENS opened? *(JS)*; still open.
[NSWJ] platforms added 1 February 1862, clo 12 September 1940 *(L)*.
K GARDENS op by [LSW] 1 January 1869 *(co n T 24 December 1868)*; [Dist] use began 1 June 1877; [Met] also used 1 October 1877 to 1 January 1907; still open.

KEW GARDENS Southport [LY]
op 2 September 1887 *(Southport Guard 8th)*; clo 26 September 1938 *(RM November)*.

KEYHAM [GW]
KEYHAM op 2 July 1900 *(W Morn News 2nd)*; still open.
K ADMIRALTY PLATFORM (non-tt): used for Naval Dockyard, 1867 to 1954; {branch from above} *(U)*.

KEYINGHAM [NE]
op 27 June 1854 *(co ½ T 4 September- line)*: clo 19 October 1964 *(Cl)*. According to *RM January 1960* this became HALT on 4th; not seen thus *Brad* but note was added that no staff were in attendance.

KEYMER JUNCTION [LBSC]:
trains called from the start of Lewes line opening, 1 October 1847, though no proper station until late

1854 *(LBSC)* – first in *Brad* January 1862; platforms only on Lewes line; clo 1 November 1883, replaced by station later renamed Wivelsfield *(Cl)*.

KEYNSHAM [GW] op 31 August 1840 *(Bristol Stand 3 September)*; was K & SOMERDALE 1 February 1925 *(hbl April)* to 6 May 1974 *(BR notice)*; still open.

KIBWORTH [Mid]
op 8 May 1857 *(Mid; co ½ T 13 August- line)*; clo 1 January 1968 *(RM February)*.

KIDBROOKE [SE] op 1 May 1895 *(RCG)*; still open. *Hb* 1895 (only): KIDBROOK.

KIDDERMINSTER [GW]
op 3 May 1852★★; still open.

KIDLINGTON [GW] op 1 June 1855 *(co n T 31 May)*; op notice refers to WOODSTOCK ROAD station at LANGFORD LANE; first month only L L in *Brad*, next month W S, so perhaps last minute change of mind; renamed K 19 May 1890 *(hbl 10 July)*; clo 2 November 1964 *(BRWR circular 12 October)*. GW co tt 1902, 1947: K for BLENHEIM and thus *Brad* to 1957/8; not seen thus *hb*.

KIDSGROVE [NS]
KIDSGROVE op 9 October 1848 *(co ½ T 3 February 1849- line)* as HARECASTLE; then successively H JUNCTION, K JUNCTION, K J H early 1850s tt, became H 15 November 1875 *(JS)*, 'for K' back 1885/6 to 1923/4; became K CENTRAL 2 October 1944 *(RM Nov./Dec.)*, K 18 April 1966 tt; still open.
K LIVERPOOL ROAD op 15 November 1875 *(RCG)*; L R added 2 October 1944 *(LNW Record)*; clo 2 March 1964 *(RM April)*.
Note: double-entered *Cl*, under 'K' and 'L'.
K MARKET STREET op 1 July 1909 *(NS)*; HALT; clo 25 September 1950 *(RM October)*.

KIDWELLY
KIDWELLY [GW] op 11 October 1852★; aot request; still open.
★ = line op from *T 12th*; other stations on line listed but not this – error? – in *Brad* when line first included November, and in inspection report.
K FLATS [GW] (non-tt) op 6 August 1941 *(Cl 29)*; HALT; military depot; clo 11 November 1957 *(U)*; added *hb* 1949a, 'closed' December 1957a; {Kidwelly – Pembrey}.
K QUAY [BPGV] (non-tt): miners; dates ?; {branch from Trimsaran Road} *(U)*.

KIELDER FOREST [NB] op 1 January 1862 (M.D. Greville, list of openings in 1862, *RM January 1962*), as terminus for the time being; FOREST added 1 October 1948 *(Cl)*; clo 15 October 1956★★.

KILBAGIE [NB]
op 17 September 1894 *(NB)*; clo 7 July 1930 *(Cl)*.

KILBARCHAN [GSW]
op 1 June 1905 *(RCG)*; clo 27 June 1966 *(RM August)*.

KILBIRNIE
KILBIRNIE [GSW] op 1 June 1905 *(RCG)*; clo 27 June 1966 *(RM August)*.
K JUNCTION – see GIFFEN.
K SOUTH [Cal] op 2 December 1889 *(RCG)*; SOUTH added 2 June 1924★★; clo 1 December 1930 *(Cl)*. Also see GLENGARNOCK.

KILBOWIE

KILBOWIE [Cal] op 1 October 1896 *(RCG; Colliery 2nd- line)* as K ROAD; renamed 1 April 1908 *(hbl 9 July)*; clo 5 October 1964 *(RM November)*.

KILBOWIE [NB] first in *Brad* May 1879; clo 4 November 1907, replaced by Singer on a deviation *(Cl has 3rd but Monday needed)* – but see SINGER.

KILBRIDE – see EAST KILBRIDE.

KILBURN near Derby [Mid] op 1 December 1856 wtt *(Mid)*; clo 1 June 1930 (Sunday) *(Mid)*.

KILBURN London.

KILBURN op by [Met] 24 November 1879 *(T 22nd)* as K & BRONDESBURY/K-B; [Bak] began 20 November 1939; Met service ended 7 December 1940 (last use – *Ug*); renamed 1950; transferred to [Jub] 1 May 1979; still open.

K HIGH ROAD [LNW] op 1851/2 *; as K; renamed K & MAIDA VALE 1 June 1879 *(Cl)*; clo 1 January 1917 *(T 22 December 1916)*; reop 10 July 1922 *(T 10th)*; renamed K H R 1 August 1923 *(hbl 25 October)*; clo by fire 17 September 2004, reop 22 August 2005 *(LRR January 2006)*; still open.
* = in *Brad* November 1851, probably in error since omitted in December. *T 13 November 1851*: 'works at Kilburn proceeding with activity. It is believed it will be ready for opening in the early part of next month'; this was at least fourth progress report but no actual opening date so far found. Op December 1851 or early 1852 according to *L*. 'Will soon be completed' *(Herapath 6 March)* – already in use incomplete or later date needed? Back in *Brad* July 1852.

K PARK [Bak] op 31 January 1915 *(T 27th)*; still open.

KILCONQUHAR [NB] op 11 August 1857**; K & ELIE until 1863/4 *(Brad)*; clo 6 September 1965 *(closure notice East of T J)*.

KILDALE [NE] op 1 April 1861 *(NE maps)*; still open.

KILDARY [High] op 1 June 1864 *(High)*; PARKHILL until 1 May 1868 according to *Cl* (from tt?) but a minute of 5 December 1865 shows change then approved after request from GNS *(High)*; clo 13 June 1960 *(RM July)*.

KILDONAN [High] op 28 July 1874 *(High)*; aot request; still open.

KILDRUMMIE [Inverness & Nairn; High] op 1 December 1855 *(High)* as CAWDOR; renamed 1 January 1857 *(Inverness Courier/JS)*; last in *Brad* January 1858; continued as private PLATFORM for Earl of Cawdor; disused about 1880 *(U)*; {Gollanfield – Nairn}.

KILDWICK & CROSSHILLS [Mid] op by April 1848 *(Mid)* – line had op 8 September 1847; originally K, later K for/& CROSS HILLS; name settled 1884/5; re-sited 16 chains west 7 April 1889 *(Mid)*; clo 22 March 1965 *(RM April)*.

KILGERRAN [GW] op 31 August 1886 (see note on Cardigan); became HALT 1958 *(Brad)*; clo 10 September 1962 *(Cl)*.

KILGETTY [GW] op 5 September 1866 *(Cardiff T 7th- line)* as K & BEGELLY; renamed 1901 tt *(Cl)*; aot request; still open.

KILKERRAN [GSW] op 24 May 1860 *(co ½ T 3 September- line)*; clo 6 September 1965 *(RM September)*.

KILLAMARSH

KILLAMARSH [North Midland] op 6 April 1841**; clo 2 January 1843* *(Cl – last Brad December 1842)*.
* = *Tuck*, about June 1843 said would be reopened Tuesdays, Saturdays, Sundays; no evidence on whether did or not.

K CENTRAL [GC] op 1 June 1892 *(RCG)*; CENTRAL added 25 September 1950 *(Rly Obs Oct.)*; clo 4 March 1963 but 'will be opened specially for excursion and holiday use' *(T 27 February)*.

K WEST [Mid] op 21 July 1873 *(Mid)* on site of 1841 station; WEST added 25 September 1950 *(Rly Obs Oct.)*; clo 1 February 1954 *(RM March)*.
Also see UPPERTHORPE & KILLAMARSH.

KILLAY [LNW] op 14 December 1867 *(The Cambrian 20th)*; clo 15 June 1964 *(RM August)*.

KILLEARNAN – see 1957**.

KILLEARN

KILLEARN [NB] op 1 August 1882 *(D&C-line)*, line first in *Brad* October; op as K NEW; renamed 1 April 1896 *(hbl 23rd)*; clo 1 October 1951 *(RM October)*.

K OLD – see DUMGOYNE.

KILLIECRANKIE [High] op 1 July 1864 *(High)*; clo 3 May 1965 *(RM June)*.

KILLIN [Cal]

KILLIN (a) op 1 June 1870 *(Rtn)*; replaced, 1 April 1886 *(Cl)*, by (b) in public tt but kept as GLENOGLEHEAD CROSSING (non-tt); probably intermittent use, school trains (railwaymen's children) to line closure 28 September 1965** (last used 24th) (D. Stirling, personal knowledge).

KILLIN (b) op 1 April 1886 *(Cal)*; clo 28 September 1965**.

K JUNCTION op 1 April 1886 *(Cal)*; intended to be exchange only but pressure from locals meant they were soon able to use (ticket and receipt evidence – C. Hogarth, *The Killin Branch Railway*, Stirling Libraries; D. Stirling from company records at SRO); clo 28 September 1965**.
Non-tt: *BR Scottish Region Special Traffic Notices* 1957 show stops to take up railwaymen weekdays on weeks beginning 24 June and 29 July at Bridges 110 and 111 (both weeks) and 130 (22 June only) between here and milepost 16¼.
Also see LOCH TAY.

KILLINGHALL – see RIPLEY VALLEY.

KILLINGHOLME

KILLINGHOLME [GC] op 5 December 1910**; became HALT 1 September 1955 *(Cl)*; clo 17 June 1963 *(RM June)*.

K ADMIRALTY PLATFORM [GC] (non-tt): op 17 March 1913 *(GC dates)*; naval base; alias NORTH K (LNE ticket, *JB*); clo 17 June 1963 *(RM June)*; {East Halton – Killingholme}.

KILLINGWORTH [NE]

KILLINGWORTH: op 1 March 1847** *(co n Newcastle Journal 27 Feb.)*; clo 15 September 1958 'but will remain available for race specials and excursions'

(RM October); last really referred to next entry.

K SIDINGS PLATFORM (non-tt): race meetings; opened before October 1903 and remained in use until 1959 *(race)*.

KILLOCHAN [GSW]
op 24 May 1860 *(co ½ T 3 September- line)*;
clo 1 January 1951 *(RM February)*.

KILLYLUNG – see HOLYWOOD.

KILLYWHAN [GSW] op 7 November 1859
(Dumfries 5th); clo 3 August 1959 *(Cl)*; 17 June 1963
wtt showed one eastbound stop, Fridays only (perhaps only to deliver staff pay?) and still shown 7 September 1964 wtt (last for line).

KILMACOLM [GSW] op 23 December 1869
(T 25th- line); KILMALCOLM until 1 December 1904
(RCG); clo 10 January 1983 *(Rly Obs March)*.

KILMANY [NB] op 25 January 1909 *(RCG)*;
clo 12 February 1951 *(RM April)* – see 1951**.

KILMARNOCK
For earliest service see 1818** (terminus later
St Marnocks).

KILMARNOCK [GSW] op 4 April 1843 *(co ½ 1110/149)*;
still open.

KILMARONOCK – see CALDARVAN.

KILMAURS
KILMAURS (a) [GBK Jt] op 26 June 1873 *(GSW- line)*;
clo 7 November 1966 *(Cl)*.

KILMAURS (b) op 12 May 1984, nearer town centre
than (a) *(RM July)*; still open.

KILN LANE CROSSING
STALLINGBOROUGH [GC GI]
op 15 May 1912 *(RCG)*; alias NO 8 LOOP (ticket *JB*);
clo 3 July 1961 *(notice G&I)*.

KILNHURST
Neither *GC* nor *Brad* support existence of MS&L
station here before 1871.

K CENTRAL [GC] first in *Brad* September 1871;
CENTRAL added 25 September 1950 *(Rly Obs
October)*; clo 5 February 1968 *(Cl)*.

K WEST [Mid] op 6 April 1841**; last in *Brad* (North
Midland table) December 1842*; back (Doncaster –
Sheffield table, SY) October 1852 *(Mid)*;
WEST added 25 September 1950 *(Rly Obs October)*;
clo 1 January 1968 *(RM February)*.

* = *Tuck*, about June 1843 says that this would be reopened
Tuesdays, Saturdays, Sundays; no evidence whether did or not.

KILNWICK GATE [NE] (non-tt):
shown 'P' in *hb* 1877 (goods only 1883); no other
evidence for passenger use; {on Airey's Yorkshire Map,
1879, 1m 6ch north of Lockington}.

KILPATRICK
KILPATRICK [NB] op 31 May 1858 *(T 7 June)*;
still open. *Hb* 1910a on: K for OLD K; not seen thus
in *Brad*.
Also see OLD KILPATRICK.

KILSBY & CRICK [LNW]
op 1 December 1881 *(LNW Officers 22843, 22911)*;
clo 1 February 1960 *(RM March)*.

KILSYTH
KILSYTH [NB] op 1 June 1878 *(D&C 6)*; became
K OLD on opening of next (and thus NB co tt 1900)

and thus until 1 January 1936 *(JS,* based on *circular 297,
of 23 December 1935)*; clo 6 August 1951 *(Cl)*.
K NEW [KB] op 2 July 1888 *(RCG)*;
clo 1 February 1935 (Friday) *(RM March)*.

KILWINNING
For early service to Ardrossan see 1834**.
KILWINNING [GSW] op 23 March 1840 from Ayr
(GSW); still open. K JUNCTION 1852/3 to 1878/9 in
Brad (Ardrossan table).
K EAST [Cal] op 4 September 1888 *(Cal)*;
clo 1 January 1917 *(RM February)*; reop 1 February
1919 *(RCG)*; EAST added 2 June 1924**;
clo 4 July 1932 *(Cl)*.

KIMBERLEY
KIMBERLEY [Mid] op 1 September 1882 *(Mid)*;
clo 1 January 1917 *(T 29 December 1916)*.
K EAST [GN] op 1 August 1876 *(GN)*; EAST added
1955 tt; clo 7 September 1964 *(RM October)*.
Became K for WATNALL, NUTTALL and
GILTBROOK 1905/6 *(RCG reference January 1906)*
and thus GN co tt 1909 but just K for W in LNE tt
1933. Full version in *Brad* until 1955; also in *hb* 1938.

KIMBERLEY PARK [GE]:
line op 15 February 1847; not in *Brad* until July 1857
but *GE Journal July 1998* quotes evidence for station
being in existence at 12 December 1848 and in 1853
and wtt showing Saturdays only service September 1856;
possible explanation – initially private station for Lord
Wodehouse of Kimberley Park and locals allowed to
use market days; aot request; PARK added 1 July 1923
(hbl 12th); clo 6 October 1969 *(RM October)*;
later excursions *(U)*.

KIMBOLTON [Mid] op 1 March 1866 *(Mid; co n
T 27 February- line)*; clo 15 June 1959 *(RM July)*.

KINALDIE [GNS] op 1 December 1854 *(GNS)* *;
clo 7 December 1964 *(RM January 1965)*.
* = in *Brad* November 1854 (southbound only), probably
prematurely; both ways December.

KINBRACE [High]
op 28 July 1874 *(High)*; aot request; still open.

KINBUCK [Cal] op 23 May 1848 *(co n Perthshire
Courier 18th- line)*; clo 11 June 1956 *(RM April)*.

KINCARDINE near Alloa
KINCARDINE [NB] op 18 December 1893 *(RCG)*;
clo 7 July 1930 *(Cl)*.
Also see FOREST MILL.

KINCRAIG [High]
op 9 September 1863 *(High)* as BOAT OF INSCH;
renamed 1871; clo 18 October 1965**.

KINETON [SMJ] op 5 June 1871 *(Oxford Chron 10th)*;
clo 1 August 1877 (Wednesday), reop 2 March 1885**;
clo 7 April 1952 *(RM May)*.

KINFAUNS [Cal] op 24 May 1847 *(Perthshire Courier
27th)*; clo 2 January 1950 *(Cl)*.

KING EDWARD [GNS] op 4 June 1860 *(GNS)*;
clo 1 October 1951 *(RM November)*.

KING GEORGE V DOCK Glasgow [LMS] (non-tt):
troop trains in 1940s; {branch from Cardonald} *(U)*.

KING GEORGE V DOCK London
KING GEORGE V DOCK [PLA]
– see ROYAL GROUP OF DOCKS.

KING GEORGE V DOCK [Dock] op 2 December 2005
(formal 6th) *(LRR January 2006)*; still open.
KING TOR [GW] op 2 April 1928 *(wtt supp)*; HALT;
clo 5 March 1956 *(T 5th)*; {Princetown branch}.
KING WILLIAM STREET [City & South London]
op 18 December 1890★★; clo 26 February 1900★★.
Brad: at first CITY OR MONUMENT,
1891/3 changed to K W S (CITY STATION).
KINGENNIE [Cal] op 14 November 1870 *(Dundee)*;
clo 10 January 1955 *(T 28 December 1954)*.
KINGHAM [GW] op 10 August 1855
(T 11 August – date of line from this junction station)★
as CHIPPING NORTON JUNCTION;
renamed 1 May 1909 *(hbl 22 April)*; still open.
★ = Chipping Norton branch inspection report, 26 July 1855,
said only one station on line (i.e. C N itself) 'but a house has
been erected at the junction for the issue of tickets to
passengers, etc' *(Rtn)*.
KINGHORN [NB]:
op 20 September 1847★★; still open.
KINGS CLIFFE [LNW] op 1 November 1879 *(RCG)*;
clo 6 June 1966 *(RM July)*. All *Brad* and LNW co tts
seen shown as two words; *hb* always KINGSCLIFFE.
KINGS CROSS
For main line station see under London.
K C ST PANCRAS [Met] platforms used by Circle
op 10 January 1863 *(co n Portfolio)*; clo by enemy action
16 October 1940; new station to west op 14 March
1941 *(L)*; still open. 'Widened Lines' platforms op
17 February 1868; clo 14 May 1979 *(L)*;
reop later by BR – see LONDON KINGS CROSS.
K C ST PANCRAS [Picc] op 15 December 1906
(co n T 14th); still open.
K C ST PANCRAS [Nor] op 12 May 1907 *(L)*;
see 1922★★; clo 18 November 1987, reop 5 March
1989 *(Ug)*; clo 15 October 1995 by escalator fire,
reop 17 June 1996 *(BLN 781)*; still open.
K C ST PANCRAS [Vic] op 1 December 1968
(T 2nd); still open.
Where applicable, ST PANCRAS added 1920s/30s;
originally added as & ST P / for ST P. *Hb*: 1910a 'for';
1936a on '&'.
KINGS FERRY BRIDGE [SEC]
Temporary HALT (non-tt) existed south of the bridge;
for workmen building Ridham Dock; exact dates ?
– it was in use in December 1913 *(SEC)*.
Bridge, connecting Sheerness with 'mainland' closed
when ship collided with it 17 December 1922.
From 27 December passengers taken between
Sheerness and Port Victoria by steamer, thence by train.
Temporary platforms (K F B and K F B NORTH)
op as termini 1 March 1923 *(Marx)* – 'passengers will
walk the short distance between the Halt platforms'
(Brad April). Former already under construction as
permanent station for Ridham Dock workers; kept after
repairs finished, later renamed SWALE, which see.
K F B NORTH clo 1 November 1923 (Thursday) *(Cl)*.
KINGS HEATH [Mid] op November 1841 *(Mid)* as
MOSELEY; renamed 1 November 1867 *(RCH dist
22 January 1868)*; clo 27 January 1941 *(Cl)*.
KINGS INCH – see RENFREW.

KINGS LANGLEY [LNW] op about October 1839
(LNW Record entry added much later)*; minutes show
certainly op between 8 June 1838 (decision taken to
build station) and January 1840 (included in fare list),
but not in *Brad* until December 1841, (earlier *Robinson*);
K L & ABBOTS LANGLEY 1 October 1909 (LNW
co tt) to 6 May 1974 *(BR notice)*; still open.
KINGS LYNN [GE] op 27 October 1846 *(co n D&C 5)*
as LYNN; re-sited 28 August 1871 *(Cl)*;
renamed 1 January 1911 *(hbl 26th)*; still open. 1893
(only) *hb* had L CENTRAL for [Eastern & Midlands]
use, L for [GE]; 1912 (only) K L TOWN; {map 67}.
KINGS NORTON [Mid]
op 1 May 1849 co tt *(Mid)*; still open.
KINGS NYMPTON [LSW] op 1 August 1854
(Trewman 13 July, 3 August) as SOUTH MOLTON
ROAD (until 1868 S M one word in tt, *JS*);
renamed S M R CHUMLEIGH 1874 tt,
S M R 1906 tt *(JS)*, K N 1 March 1951 *(RM May)*;
aot request; still open. NEWNHAM in *Trewman's*
description of formal opening.
KINGS PARK Glasgow [LMS]
op 6 October 1928 *(Rly Gaz 12th)*; still open.
KINGS SUTTON [GW] op 1 June 1872 *(co n T 1st)*;
HALT 2 November 1964 *(BRWR circular 12 October)*
to 6 May 1968 *(Cl)*; still open.
KINGSWORTHY [GW] op 1 February 1909
(RCG); clo 4 August 1942★★, reop 8 March 1943;
clo 7 March 1960 *(Hants Chron 5th)*.
KINGSBARNS [NB] op 1 September 1883 *(Fifeshire
Journal 6th)*; clo 22 September 1930 *(Cl)*.
KINGSBRIDGE [GW] op 19 December 1893
(Totnes); *Totnes* mentioned at least three trains with
general use on formal opening day, 18th; implication is
that were free (no tickets issued) and non-stop to/from
Totnes; clo 16 September 1963 *(Cl)*.
GW co tt 1902, 1948: K for SALCOMBE; later entry
for bus connection; only seen as K in *hb*.
KINGSBRIDGE ROAD – see WRANGATON.
KINGSBURY Birmingham [Mid]
KINGSBURY op 12 August 1839 *(Mid; co n T 8th- line)*;
clo 4 March 1968 *(Mid)*.
K COLLIERY SIDINGS/PITS (non-tt): miners;
op by March 1914; in May 1922 wtt as K PIT;
clo 7 December 1928; {branch from Kingsbury} *(U)*.
KINGSBURY London
KINGSBURY op by [Met] 10 December 1932 *(T 10th)*;
transferred to [Bak] 20 November 1939;
transferred again, to [Jub], 1 May 1979; still open.
Also see NEASDEN.
KINGSCOTE [LBSC] op 1 August 1882
(Hants Chron 5th- line); clo 30 May 1955★★.
KINGSHOUSE [Cal] first in *Brad* June 1872
(Callander says op 1871; nature of service – request –
such that sort of station liable to be late in tt);
PLATFORM 1911 to 18 June 1962 tt index (but later
table); clo 28 September 1965★★. Cal co tt 1913 has
note that passengers for Braes of Balquhidder would be
set down by previous arrangement with station-master
at Strathyre and picked up if on platform. Shown as
K PLATFORM for BRAES OF BALQUHIDDER,

LOCH VOYLE, ROB ROY'S GRAVE in *Brad* to
1955, and on 1960 season ticket *(JB)* but just
K PLATFORM in *Murray* 1948.
HALT in *hb* 1938 to September 1962a.

KINGSKERSWELL [GW]
op 1 July 1853 *(Trewman 7th)*; clo 5 October 1964 *(Cl)*.

KINGSKETTLE [NB] op 20 September 1847**;
clo 1 January 1917 *(RM February)*; reop 1 February
1919 *(RM February)*; clo 4 September 1967 *(Cl)*.
KETTLE in op description and in *Topham*, June 1848
only. *RCH* at first made two words of it.

KINGSKNOWE
KINGSKNOWE (a) [Cal] op 15 February 1848* as
SLATEFORD; renamed KINGS KNOWES 1 January
1853 when new Slateford op; name amended later 1853
(Brad); clo 1 January 1917 *(RM February)*;
reop 1 February 1919 *(RCG)*; HALT in *Brad* 1930/1
to 1933/1934; clo 6 July 1964 *(RM July)*.
* = line op confirmed by *co ½ T 29 February*; station not found
in any tt until September 1848 *(Topham)*; *Balerno* says did open
with line but its incomplete state explains omission from tt then.
KINGSKNOWE (b) op 1 February 1971 *(Cl)*; still open.

KINGSLAND London
KINGSLAND [NL] op 9 November 1850 *(L)*;
clo 1 November 1865 (Wednesday) *(Cl)*, replaced by
Dalston Junction.
Also see DALSTON.

KINGSLAND near Hereford [GW]
op 20 August 1857**; clo 5 February 1951
(RM October) – see 1951**; reop 2 April 1951 *(Cl)*;
clo 7 February 1955 *(RM March)*.

KINGSLEY [LSW] op 7 March 1906 *(RM April)*;
HALT; clo 16 September 1957 *(Hants Chron 21st)*
– last train early a.m. 16th.

KINGSLEY & FROGHALL [NS]
op 1 September 1849 *(Churnet)* as F;
renamed May 1907 tt *(JS; RCG ref July)*;
clo 4 January 1965 *(RM March)*.

KINGSMUIR [Cal] op 14 November 1870 *(Dundee)*;
clo 10 January 1955 *(T 28 December 1954)*.

KINGSTON-on-Thames [LSW]
For first station of this name see SURBITON.
K op 1 July 1863 *(co ½ T 10 August)* as a terminus;
station on through lines op 1 January 1869 as K NEW;
aot pair HL, LL in *Brad*, sometimes with TOWN
added; two combined in station reconstruction 1935;
still open. According to *hbl 23rd* K NEW lost 'NEW'
1 April 1896.

KINGSTON CROSSING [GW]
op 1 September 1906 *(GW H)*; HALT; clo 1 July 1957
(RM August); {Chinnor – Aston Rowant}.

KINGSTON PARK [TWM]
op 15 September 1985 *(Rly Obs December)*; still open.

KINGSTON ROAD [WCP] line op 1 December
1897 *(Bristol T 2nd)*, nd, December 1899;
clo 20 May 1940 *(Bridgwater Merc 22nd)*.

KINGSTON-ON-SEA [LBSC] op 12 May 1840**;
absent from *Brad* about same time as YAPTON (which
see), but in *Topham* so probably tt vagary; -on-S added
1870; clo 1 April 1879 (Tuesday) *(Cl)*. 1883 *hb* showed
K WHARF as 'P'; presumably parcels only or error.

KINGSWEAR [GW]
KINGSWEAR : op 16 August 1864 *(W Morn News 17th)*;
see 1972 November 1**.
Pre-op in *Brad* as DARTMOUTH.
K CROSSING – see BRITANNIA.

KINGSWOOD [SE] first train 9 November 1897
(SE); K & BURGH HEATH until 1 December 1968
(Cl); still open.

KINGSWOOD – see LAPWORTH.

KINGSWOOD CROSSING [High] (non-tt):
railwaymen's wives; in use 1926;
{Murthly – Dunkeld} *(U)*.

KINGTHORPE [GN] op 1 December 1876 *(RCG;
T 28 November- line)*; clo 11 September 1939**,
reop 4 December 1939; clo 5 November 1951
(RM December). Initially in *hb* as KINGS THORPE,
later KING THORPE; settled 1890.

KINGTON [GW] op 20 August 1857**; re-sited on
extension to New Radnor 25 September 1875 *(Cl)*;
clo 5 February 1951 *(RM October)* – see 1951**;
reop 2 April 1951 *(Cl)*; clo 7 February 1955 *(RM March)*.

KINGUSSIE [High]
op 9 September 1863 *(High)*; still open.

KINLOSS [High] op 25 March 1858 *(High)*;
re-sited 18 April 1860 to east as junction station for
Findhorn branch; moved back to original site May
1904, probably; clo 3 May 1965 *(Cl)*; {map 3}.

KINMEL BAY [LMS] (non-tt)
op experimentally 4 July 1938 to 2 September 1938
(LNW Record); site of earlier Foryd (which see);
HALT; presumably also used next summer
– clo 2 September 1939 (Saturday) *(Cl)*.

KINMEL CAMP [LNW] (non-tt): military camp.
Line originally ran to Foryd station, joining from east
so reversal needed for journeys to Rhyl;
War Department took over line from contractor
7 August 1916; passenger service for troops began ?
Line diverted to join Vale of Clwyd line just before this
joined main line; initially link was via part of line to
harbour and double reversal, officially opened 14 June
1917 by GOC Western Command; 2 July 1917 soldiers'
trains diverted via this line to run to Rhyl and Foryd
then closed (later reopened); initial service 6 trains to
Rhyl, 7 back, daily, for troops' recreation. In January
1919 another diversion allowed direct running onto
Clwyd line. Original platform south of Abergele to
St Asaph road. By 7 February 1919 another station
had been added at FAENOL BACH, at end of short
branch to east, north of original. Closed ? (Foryd reop
1 July 1919) – camp dismantled 1920 on.
(P.G. Hindley, *The Kinmel Camp Railway*, in *Industrial
Railway Society Journal*, date ?).

KINNABER JUNCTION (non-tt): *BR Scottish Region
Special Traffic Notice* shows stop here for workmen week
beginning Monday 24 June 1957.

KINNERLEY JUNCTION [SM] op 13 August
1866** (see for full details) as K; JUNCTION added
at 1911 reop; clo 6 November 1933 *(Cl)*.

KINNERSLEY [Mid] op 1 September 1863
(co n Hereford J 5th); clo 31 December 1962 *(T 31st)*.

KINNERTON [LNW]
op 2 March 1891 *(LNW Permanent Way Committee minute of 18th)*; clo 30 April 1962 *(RM June)*.
KINNIEL [NB]: originally ticket platform (D. Stirling, *Steam Days, September 2002, p. 281)*; op 2 January 1899 *(NB notice, SRO BR/NBR/8/1238)*; clo 1 January 1917 *(RM February)*; reop 1 September 1919 *(Cl)*; clo 22 September 1930 *(Cl)*.
Alias KINNEIL (local spelling); hb 1922a changed to this; *Brad* altered in index 1928/9, not body of book.
KINNING PARK [GU]
op 14 December 1896**; still open.
KINROSS
KINROSS [Kinross-shire] temporary terminus op 20 June 1860 *(co ½ T 28 September)*; clo soon after 20 September 1860, when line extended to station later renamed Loch Leven *(Tayside)*; {Loch Leven – Blairadam}.
K JUNCTION [NB] op 20 August 1858 *(Kinross 28th)* as K; renamed HOPEFIELD 1860 tt [n.b. not H JUNCTION, *JS*], K J 16 October 1871 *(Cl; RCG ref October)*; re-sited 200 yards north 1890 *(Cl)*; aot request; clo 5 January 1970 *(RM January)*.
Also see LOCH LEVEN.
KINTBURY [GW]
op 21 December 1847 *(Hants Chron 25th- line)*; HALT 2 November 1964 to 5 May 1969 *(Cl)*; still open.
KINTORE [GNS] op 20 September 1854 *(GNS)*; clo 7 December 1964 *(RM January 1965)*.
KIPLING COTES [NE] op 1 May 1865**; clo 29 November 1965 *(RM December)*. RM June 1961 said would be unstaffed HALT from 12 June; not thus BR tts, but was note that no staff in attendance.
KIPPAX [NE]
op 12 August 1878 *(co ½ Herapath 15 February 1879- line)*; clo 22 January 1951 *(Cl)* – see 1951**.
KIPPEN [NB]
op 26 May 1856**; clo 1 October 1934 *(RM October)*.
KIPPS [MK] see 1828**; other early short-lived services through area might have called; {map 16}.
KIRBY – see ASFORDBY.
KIRBY near Pickering [NE] op 8 July 1845**; soon closed; back in tt November 1853; clo authorised 17 July 1858, last in *Brad* August but last in co tt 1 October *(Cl)*.
KIRBY CROSS [GE]
op 28 July 1866 *(T 30th)*; still open.
KIRBY MUXLOE [Mid]
first in *Brad* July 1859, replacing Braunston; clo 7 September 1964 *(RM October)*.
KIRBY PARK [Birkenhead] op 1 October 1894 *(RCG)*, as an 'experimental station' *(LNW Record)*; clo 5 July 1954 *(RM September)*; schools' use continued to 17 September 1956 *(U)*.
KIRBYMOORSIDE [NE] op 1 January 1874 *(Yorks Gaz 3rd)*; sometimes KIRBY MOORSIDE; clo 2 February 1953 *(RM March)*; later excursions for shopping and football *(RM February 1955)*; one 3 May 1964 *(Whitby)*.
KIRK HAMMERTON – see HAMMERTON.
KIRK SANDALL
op 13 May 1991 *(BLN 662)*; still open.

KIRK SMEATON [HB] op 27 July 1885 *(NER I)*; clo 1 January 1932 (Friday) *(RM January)*; later excursions to Hull Fair and Leeds football – e.g 14 October 1933 during Hull Civic Week *(RM January 1934)*, 28 February 1953 *(RM May)*.
KIRKANDREWS [NB]: line op 22 June 1854 *(Rtn)*, nd, August 1854; omitted from *Brad* September 1856 (space saving after op of Port Carlisle line and need to fit its stations in?); back October 1856; aot request; clo 7 September 1964 *(RM October)*.
KIRKBANK [NB]
op 18 July 1856** as OLD ORMISTON; renamed 20 May 1868 *(Cl; RCG ref July)*; clo 13 August 1948**.
KIRKBRIDE [NB]
op 4 September 1856** *(Brad Sh 1863- line)*; clo 7 September 1964 *(RM October)*.
KIRKBUDDO [Cal] op 14 November 1870 *(Dundee)*; clo 10 January 1955 *(T 28 December 1954)*.
KIRKBURTON [LNW] op 7 October 1867 *(Huddersfield 12th)*; clo 28 July 1930 *(Cl)*.
KIRKBY Liverpool
KIRKBY [LY] op 20 November 1848 *(LY; co n Manch G 18th- line)*; still open, as terminus of two separate services, opposite ways.
K ROYAL ORDNANCE FACTORY [LMS] (non-tt): HALT; op 9 December 1940, built on government property at its expense *(LNW Record)*; used at least until 1943 *(U)*; {branch from Kirkby}.
KIRKBY LONSDALE [LNW] op 16 September 1861 *(co n Lancaster Gax 14th)*; clo 1 February 1954 *(T 1st)*. Later use by schools' specials, beginning and end of terms, for Cressbrook School and boarders of Kirkby Lonsdale Grammar School (R. Western, *The Ingleton Branch*, Oakwood, 1990); also more generally 1963, when snow closed Settle to Carlisle line; last ramblers' excursion 26 August 1962 *(AB)*.
KIRKBY STEPHEN
KIRKBY STEPHEN [Mid] op 1 May 1876 *(Mid; co n T 1 May- line)* as K S; became K S & RAVENSTONEDALE 1 October 1900 *(RCG)*, K S WEST 8 June 1953 tt *(Mid)*, K S 6 May 1968 *(Cl)*; clo 4 May 1970 *(RM June)*; probably used by trial charter excursion 9 June 1974 *(AB)*; reop summer week-end Dales Rail 3 May 1975 (P.W. Robinson, *Cumbria's Lost Railways*, Stenlake, 2002); reop fully 14 July 1986 *(Settle)*; see 1989 October 16**; still open.
K S EAST [NE] op 8 August 1861 *(co op tt)*; EAST added 1958 *(Cl)*; clo 22 January 1962 *(RM Feb.)*.
KIRKBY THORE [NE] op 9 June 1862**; clo 7 December 1953 *(RM January 1954)*.
KIRKBY–in-Ashfield.
For earliest service hereabouts see 1832**.
K BENTINCK [GC] op 2 January 1893 *(RCG)* as K & PINXTON; renamed 1 March 1925 *(hbl April)*; clo 4 March 1963 *(RM March)*.
K IN ASHFIELD op 18 November 1996 – 'fun day' 17th *(Rly Obs December)*; still open.
K-IN-ASHFIELD CENTRAL [GC] op 2 April 1917 *(RCG)*; CENTRAL added 1 July 1923 *(hbl 12th)*; clo 2 January 1956 *(RM February)*; later excur and

advertised summer Saturday services to 8 September 1962 (last train) *(Cl)*. Excursion to Ollerton and Edwinstowe called Whit Monday 3 June 1963 *(AB)*.

K-IN-ASHFIELD EAST [Mid] op 2 October 1848 *(RAIL 1005/265)* as K; renamed K-in-A 1 January 1901 *(hbl 24th)*, K-I-A EAST 15 June 1959 *(Cl)*; clo 12 October 1964 *(RM Nov.)*, but workmen's trains, via Pye Bridge, continued to 6 September 1965 *(Mid)*.

KIRKBY-IN-FURNESS [Fur]: for op see 1846 August★★; early use intermittent; -in-F added 1928 *(hbl ref April)*; aot request; still open.

KIRKCALDY [NB] op 20 September 1847★★; still open. *Hb* 1862 KIRKALDY, amended 1867.

KIRKCONNEL [GSW] op 28 October 1850 *(T 26th- line)*; still open. *Hb* 1862 KIRKCONNELL, amended 1872.

KIRKCOWAN [PPW Jt] op 12 March 1861 *(Galloway 15th)*; clo 14 June 1965 *(RM July)*.

KIRKCUDBRIGHT [GSW] op 7 March 1864 *(Kirkcudbright 11th)*; clo 3 May 1965 *(RM May)*.

KIRKDALE [LY] op 20 November 1848 *(LY; co n Manch G 18th- line)*; as BOOTLE LANE; renamed 1 February 1876 *(RCG)* – *RAIL 343/216* says 11 January (date decision taken?); still open.

KIRKGATE – see WAKEFIELD.

KIRKGUNZEON [PPW Jt] op 7 November 1859 *(Dumfries 5th)*; clo 2 January 1950 *(RM February)*.

KIRKHAM ABBEY [NE]: op 8 July 1845★★; ABBEY added 1 June 1875 *(RCG)*; clo 22 September 1930★★.

KIRKHAM & WESHAM [PW] op 16 July 1840★★; re-sited 1890; & W added 1906 *(RCG ref October)*; still open. K JUNCTION 1856/7 to 1882/3 *(Brad)*;

KIRKHEATON [LNW] op 7 October 1867 *(Huddersfield 12th)*; clo 28 July 1930 *(Cl)*.

KIRKHILL [Cal] op 1 August 1904 *(RCG)*; still open.

KIRKINCH [Scottish Midland Junction]: line op 4 June 1838 *(Tayside)*, nd, July 1842; probably clo 1847 (see 1837 B★★); {maps 8, 9}.

KIRKINNER [PPW Jt] op 2 August 1875 *(Directors' Minutes 29 September)*; clo 25 September 1950 *(Cl)*; for brief intermediate closure see GARLIESTOWN; {map 17}.

KIRKINTILLOCH {map 16}

KIRKINTILLOCH [NB] op 5 July 1848 *(D&C 6- line)*; clo 7 September 1964 *(Cl)*.

K BASIN [Monklands]: intermittent short lived services (see 1828 B★★, 1844 December 26★★).

KIRKINTILLOCH, alias K JUNCTION, [Monkland] op 26 December 1844★★ *(MK)*; last use 26 July 1847 (Monday); perhaps should be regarded as part of station included as Lenzie, which see also.

KIRKLAND [GSW] op 1 March 1905 *(RCG)*; clo 3 May 1943 *(RM January 1944)*.

KIRKLEE [Cal] op 10 August 1896 *(RCG)*; clo 1 January 1917 *(RM February)*; reop 2 June 1919 *(RCG)*; clo 1 May 1939 *(T 27 April)*. Cal co tt 1913: K for NORTH KELVINSIDE; thus *Brad*, hb 1912.

KIRKLINGTON [Mid] op 3 April 1871 *(Mid)*; K & EDINGLEY from September 1871 *Brad (Mid)* to

1 April 1904 *(hbl 28th)*; clo 12 August 1929 *(T 13th)*.

KIRKLISTON [NB] op 1 March 1866 *(D&C 6- line)*; clo 22 September 1930 *(Cl)*.

KIRKNEWTON [Cal] op 15 February 1848 *(Balerno; co ½ T 29 February- line)* as K, renamed MIDCALDER & K April 1848 *(True Line 70, p.21)*, M 1849 *(Brad)*, K 17 May 1982 *(C/W)*; still open.

KIRKNEWTON near Kelso [NE] op 5 September 1887 *(NE- line)*; clo 22 September 1930★★ *(T 10 July)*.

KIRKPATRICK [Cal] op 10 September 1847 *(co n True Line 60)*; clo 13 June 1960 *(RM July)*.

KIRKSANTON CROSSING [Whitehaven & Furness Junction] first in *Brad* July 1854; last September 1857; {Millom – Silecroft}. Alias KIRKSEATON – heading as in *Brad*.

KIRKSTALL [Mid]

KIRKSTALL op 16/30 July 1846 *(Mid)*; new station opened 11am 5 July 1905 – route widening *(Mid)*; clo 22 March 1965 *(RM April)*.

K FORGE: (a) perhaps brief use about February/March 1852 when in co tt but use then cannot be guaranteed *(Mid)*; (b) op 2 July 1860 (1st a Sunday, no Sunday service); clo 1 August 1905 (Tuesday) *(RCG)*; {Kirkstall – Newlay}.

KIRKSTEAD – see WOODHALL JUNCTION.

KIRKTON BRIDGE [GNS] first in *Brad* June 1904; clo 3 May 1965 *(RM May)*. KIRTON B in *Brad* until 1908 and hb until September 1946a, but KIRKTON B in wtt 1 July 1905; PLATFORM until 1914 *(Brad)*, then request HALT – but not in hb until 1938, suggesting always a halt.

KIRKWOOD op 4 October 1993 *(AZ)*; about ¼ mile west of earlier Langloan; still open.

KIRRIEMUIR

KIRRIEMUIR [Cal] opening set for 20 November 1854 *(Dundee Courier 15th)* but BoT letter giving consent was dated 20th so perhaps delay★; co ½ T 7 September 1855 gave December 1854 for opening and not in *Brad* until January 1855; see 1951★★; clo 4 August 1952 *(RM September)*.

★ = BoT consent given in reply to letter sent by company on 15 November, saying that they had met conditions set by inspector (N. Ferguson, *Arbroath & Forfar Rly*, Oakwood 2000); circumstances such that they might have felt safe in going ahead.

K JUNCTION [Scottish North Eastern] op with above (presumed – in January *Brad* with branch); *Cornwall (January 1861)* shows one time, and fare, from Perth, nothing other way. last in tt July 1862; back July 1863; last June 1864★; perhaps essentially exchange station with longer existence than indicated by tt – still in *Brad* March 1865, towards Aberdeen only, no trains stopping; *BR Scottish Region Special Traffic Notice* shows stop here for workmen week beginning Monday 29 July 1957; {at physical junction}.

★ = disappearance from *Brad* then strictly impossible: shown with trains in June; July – table altered so no trains shown for here, but marked 'no recent information'.

KIRTLEBRIDGE [Cal]: line op 10 September 1847, station not in original co tt *(True Line 60)* so probably op after line – first in *Brad*

March 1848; moved about 1 mile north, probably by October 1869 *(True Line 60)*; clo 13 June 1960 *(RM July)*. *Brad* ? to 1955 but not LNE tt 1933 nor *Murray* 1948: K for EAGLESFIELD.

KIRTLINGTON – see BLETCHINGTON.

KIRTON near Boston [GN] op 3 April 1849 *(Loop)*; clo 11 September 1961 *(RM September)*.

KIRTON BRIDGE – see KIRKTON BRIDGE.

KIRTON LINDSEY [GC] op 2 April 1849★★ *(GC)*; clo 4 January 1992 for engineering work, reop 11 May 1992; reduced to Saturdays only, three trains each way, 4 October 1993 tt (A. Brackenbury, *Chron, January 2004)*.

KISSTHORNS [Sand Hutton] (ng) op 4 October 1924★★; last train Saturday 1 March 1930★★; {map 40}.

KITTYBREWSTER [GNS] op 20 September 1854 *(GNS)* as ABERDEEN K (it was then terminus for Aberdeen); re-sited as K 1 April 1856 when line to Aberdeen Waterloo opened and again 4 November 1867 (close to 1854 site) when line through Joint station opened *(GNS)*; clo 6 May 1968 *(RM July)*; {map 7}.

KIVETON BRIDGE [LNE] op 8 July 1929 *(Cl 29)*; still open.

KIVETON PARK [GC] op 17 July 1849 *(GC;T 18th- line)*; still open.

KNAPTON [NE]: op 8 July 1845★★; clo 22 September 1930★★.

KNARESBOROUGH {map 42}

KNARESBOROUGH [York & North Midland] temporary terminus in Hay/Haya Park Lane★; free train 13 July 1848 to York for agricultural show (authorities had refused permission to open so could not charge) *(Harrogate)*; op to public 30 October 1848★★; replaced by >

KNARESBOROUGH [NE] permanent op 21 July 1851 *(NE maps)*; still open.
★ = site uncertain. Possibilities: a) by level crossing at 368574; b) by under-bridge at 359575; latter more likely – ½ mile nearer town centre (S. Bragg).

KNEBWORTH [GN] op 1 February 1884 *(GN)*; still open.

KNIGHTON [LNW] op 6 March 1861 *(co n Hereford J 13th)*; HALT 6 September 1965 to 5 May 1969 *(Cl)*; still open. LNW co tt 1875: K for PRESTEIGN.

KNIGHTSBRIDGE [Picc] op 15 December 1906 *(co n T 14th)*; see 1922★★; still open.

KNIGHTWICK [GW] op 2 May 1874 *(Berrow's 9th- line)*; clo 7 September 1964 *(Cl)*.

KNITSLEY [NE] op 1 September 1862 *(Consett)*; clo 1 December 1915 (Wednesday) *(RCG)*, though trains still shown in *Brad* December (inertia?); reop 30 March 1925 *(T 28th)*; clo 1 May 1939 *(Cl)*; later use for miners' galas *(U)*.

KNOCK [GNS] op 30 July 1859★★; clo (goods and passengers) 1 July 1875 (Thursday) *(RCG)*; reop ? – *RCG* only gives goods reopening 'October' 1875, or was passenger closure an error? – present *Brad* June 1875, September to December 1875 and September 1876; clo 6 May 1968 *(RM July)*.

KNOCKANDO [GNS]

KNOCKANDO op 1 July 1899 *(GNS)* as DALBEALLIE; renamed 1 May 1905 *(hbl 27 April)*; clo 18 October 1965★★.

KNOCKANDO HOUSE (non-tt): HALT/PLATFORM; op 1869 *(GNS)*; private; HOUSE added 1905; clo 18 October 1965 *(U)*.

KNOCKHOLT [SE] op 1 May 1876 *(SR)* as HALSTEAD for K; renamed 1 October 1900 *(hbl 12 July)*; still open.

KNOOK CAMP – see CODFORD.

KNOTT END [KE] op 30 July 1908 *(T 31st)*; clo 31 March 1930 *(LNW Record)*.

KNOTT MILL – see DEANSGATE.

KNOTTINGLEY [LY/GN] op 1 April 1848 *(LY; co ½ T 7 September- line)*; still open. K JUNCTION in *Brad* 1851 to 1857/1859 in GN tables only. Became K for FERRY BRIDGE 1 November 1903 *(hbl 28 January 1904)* or 1 February 1904 *(RCG)*, and thus GN co tt 1909, LMS tt 1930. K for FERRYBRIDGE in *Brad*/BR tts until 1967/74 (but still 'for' index 1979).

KNOTTY ASH & STANLEY [CLC] op 1 December 1879 *(CLC)* as OLD SWAN & K A; renamed 1 November 1888 *(Cl; RCG ref January 1889)*; clo 7 November 1960 *(RM December)*.

KNOWESGATE [NB] op 1 July 1864 *(NB)*; KNOWES GATE until 1877 *(hb)*, 1908 tt *(Cl)*; clo 15 September 1952 *(RM October)*.

KNOWESIDE [GSW] op 17 May 1906 *(RCG; Brad May- will open 17th)*; aot request; clo 1 December 1930 *(Cl)*.

KNOWLE near Fareham [LSW] op 1 May 1907 *(SR)*; clo 12 August 1963, reop next day following official objection; clo 6 April 1964 *(Cl)*. Variously K HALT, K ASYLUM HALT, K PLATFORM, K HALT.

KNOWLE & DORRIDGE – see DORRIDGE.

KNOWLES LEVEL CROSSING [LY] op 3 July 1905 *(Manchester Guardian 30 June)*; clo 1 April 1918 *(Cl)*; {Tottington – Greenmount}.

KNOWLTON [EK] op 16 October 1916 *(co n EK)* as TILMANSTONE VILLAGE & K; renamed 1917 *(Brad)*; clo 1 November 1948★★ *(RM January 1949)*.

KNUCKLAS [LNW] op 1 December 1865★★; HALT 1 February 1956 to 5 May 1969 *(Cl)*; aot request; still open.

KNUTSFORD [CLC] op 12 May 1862 *(T 7th, 12th)*; re-sited on extension to Northwich 1 January 1863 *(Cl)*; still open.

KNUTTON [NS] op 1 May 1905 *(NS)*; HALT; clo 20 September 1926 *(Cl)*; {Newcastle – Silverdale}.

KNUTTON GATE HALT: [NS/LMS] (non-tt): Midland Coal Coke & Iron Co's workmen's trains shown operating in wtt 9 July 1923; {Apedale – Apedale Junction}.

KNYPERSLEY [NS] op 1 October 1914 *(RCG)*; HALT; clo 11 July 1927 *(Cl)*.

KYLE OF LOCHALSH [High] op 2 November 1897 *(High)*; still open.

KYNOCHTOWN – see CORYTON (Tilbury).

LACKENBY [S&D]: prob op with line to Redcar,
5 June 1846★★, or soon after; not found in any tt seen;
evidence is from S&D minutes, which show that they
were planning alterations to station on 15 March 1848
(building to be divided in two at cost of £10); also
shown on Macaulay's maps 1851 to at least mid-1860s
(also see D&C reprint of OS map for the area).
In *hb* 1862, 1867, 1872 (but no facilities then shown);
not 'P' 1877. Clo ? – probably early; {map 43}.

LACOCK [GW] op 16 October 1905 *(Devizes 19th)*;
HALT; clo 18 April 1966 *(RM May)*.

LADBROKE GROVE [HC]
op 13 June 1864 *(co n T 10th)*; op as NOTTING HILL;
later N H & L G (according to *L* alternative available
from 1869, *RCG ref* October 1880, *Brad* from 1888/9);
became L G 1 June 1919 *(L; RM July 1919* said had
become L G but was L G NORTH KENSINGTON
on nameboard); still open. *(RM July 1919)*.

LADE [RHD] (ng)
op 24 May 1928 *(RHD)*; see 1927 July 16★★ for many
details of use; HALT; last in *Brad* October 1930;
back October 1936; last end of summer 1947 but
stayed in use – shelter demolished about 1946,
replaced 1968; still in use when preservation group
took over *(Wolfe)*; SHIP INN on pre-op plans *(Wolfe)*.

LADMANLOW – see 1833 May★★.

LADYBANK [NB]
op 20 September 1847 *(Edinburgh Advertiser 21st)*;
L JUNCTION in *Brad* until 1924/5 and thus NB co tt
1900; still open.

LADYLANDS [NB]
first in *Brad* June 1861; originally Fridays only;
Saturdays only 1880s; Thursdays only last years;
L SIDING until 11 July 1927 *(Cl)*, then L PLATFORM;
clo 1 October 1934 *(RM October)* – last train
27 September; shown 'P' in *hb* 1877 and 1883 but 1890
on no facilities shown {Port of Menteith – Kippen}.

LADYSBRIDGE [GNS]
op 1 October 1859 *(GNS)*; clo 6 July 1964 *(RM July)*.
LADYS BRIDGE until 1886 tt *(Cl)*, 1904 *hb*.

LADYWELL [SE] op 1 January 1857 *(L; co ½
T 9 February-* line); still open. LADY WELL in *Brad*
until 1960 and thus SE co tt 1864.

LAGGAN FARM HOUSE [Cal] (non-tt):
used by anglers; dates ?; {Callander – Strathyre} *(U)*.

LAINDON [LTS] op 1 June 1888 *(Mid)*; still open.

LAIRA
For early [South Devon] temporary terminus at
L GREEN see PLYMOUTH.

LAIRA [GW] op 1 June 1904 *(W Morn News 1st, 2nd)*;
HALT; clo 7 July 1930 *(Cl)*; {map 114}.

LAIRG [High] op 13 April 1868 *(High)*; still open.

LAISTERDYKE [GN] op 1 August 1854
(GN; T 1st- line); clo 4 July 1966 *(RM July)*.
In *Brad* as LAISTER DYKE, at times L D JUNCTION
(GN table only, 1871 to 1882), until 1938/9; two words
LY co tt 1899 and LMS tt 1930; one word, *hb* 1949a.

LAKE Isle of Wight
LAKE (a) [IoW] (non-tt) (a) op April 1889 *(IoW CP 27th*
– opening of new County Cricket Ground took form of
athletic meeting; platform has been erected opposite

entrance). On 19 August 1889 used for Volunteer Sports
and visit of HRH Prince Henry of Battenburg (same
paper 17th, 24th). County Ground fell into disuse, at
least for matches of county status about 1902 but used
by Shanklin Home of Rest (later Shanklin Cottage
Hospital) until 1914 or later (Dr J. Mackett, via
T. Cooper); HALT in later days.

LAKE (b) op 11 May 1987 *(BLN 558)*; about ⅜ mile
north of (a) *(Railways Illustrated August 2005 p. 68)*;
still open.

LAKE [LSW] (non-tt):
op 22 June 1918; HALT; daily train to/from Christchurch
until 4 October 1920 *(LSW)*; shipyard workers;
{Hamworthy Junction – Hamworthy}.

LAKE SIDE – see WINDERMERE.

LAKENHEATH [GE] op 30 July 1845 *(co n Norfolk)*;
reduced to Saturdays and Sundays only 20 May 2007 tt;
still open. Opening co tt has THE HISS; L first time
detail given in *Brad*, September 1845.

LAMANCHA [NB] op 4 July 1864? – not mentioned
in *Selkirk 7th* item on line but was in *Brad* when line
first there August; perhaps opened a little after line;
clo 1 April 1933★★.

LAMB BRIDGE – see 1846 April 13★★.

LAMBETH NORTH [Bak]
op 10 March 1906 *(T 12th)* as KENNINGTON ROAD;
became WESTMINSTER BRIDGE ROAD 5 August
1906 *(L)*, L N 16 April 1917 *(hbl 12 July)*; see 1922★★;
clo 10 November 1996 for work under Thames *(RM
October 1997)*; reop 14 July 1997 *(RM February 1998)*;
still open.

LAMBHILL – see GILSHOCHILL.

LAMBLEY [NE] op 21 May 1852★★; clo 3 May 1976
(RM May). Ticket as HALT *(JB)* – see COANWOOD;
1961 tt merely says unstaffed.

LAMBOURN [GW] op 4 April 1898 *(co n Ephemera)*;
clo 4 January 1960 *(RM February)*.

LAMBS COTTAGE [LM] op between November
1832 and 1 September 1838 *(Drake)* – see 1830
September 19★★; use perhaps intermittent;
clo by 29 October 1842 *(Railway Times* of that date –
'now closed').

LAMESLEY [NE]
op 1 December 1868 *(NE- line)*; clo 4 June 1945 *(Cl)*;
later use for miners' galas *(U)*. May 1949 wtt shows
Fridays only stop; 1953 wtt shows stop for setting down
railway staff (no pick-up stop shown), which probably
ceased 2 November 1953 (R.N. Forsythe, *Steam Days*,
September 2001); stops to deliver wages?

LAMINGTON [Cal] first in *Brad* April 1848;
clo 4 January 1965 *(RM February)*.

LAMPETER [GW]
op 1 January 1866 *(GW)*; clo 22 February 1965 *(Cl)*.

LAMPETER ROAD – see LLANWRDA.

LAMPHEY [GW]
op 6 August 1863**; aot request; still open.
LAMPLUGH [WCE Jt] op 2 April 1866 *(D&C 14)*
as WRIGHT GREEN; renamed 14 August 1901
(hbl 24 October) – or was this date when change
authorised? *RCG* says 1 September – or was this
derived from tt?; clo 13 April 1931 *(LNW Record)*.
LAMPORT [LNW] op 16 February 1859 *(LNW- line)*;
clo 4 January 1960 *(RM February)*.
LANARK [Cal]
For first stations carrying this name see CARLUKE
and CLEGHORN.
LANARK op 5 June 1855 *(Cal)*; still open.
L RACECOURSE (non-tt): first used 9 August 1910
for airshow on racecourse; first race use 27 September
1910 *(AB)*; races and military traffic; added 1941a *hb*
as L RACE COURSE HALT; clo 27 September 1964
for races *(race)*; perhaps military use continued – kept
for goods until 15 January 1968 *(AB)*;
{Lanark – Sandilands}.
LANCASTER
LANCASTER [LPJ] op 26 June 1840 *(co n Lancaster
27th)*; alias L GREAVES or L PENNY STREET in
modern works but just L in *Brad*; clo 1 August 1849
(Wednesday) – trains diverted to L LNW, below *(LPJ)*.
(Non-tt): special militia trains departed from 'Old Station,
near the Barracks' after training; would have been the
goods facilities here (passenger station sold off some
years previously). One train ran Saturdays at least on
these dates (all advertised *Lancaster Guardian* or *Lancaster
Gazette* on days they ran): 7 May 1864, 27 May 1865,
12 May 1866, 16 May 1868, 20 May 1871.
LANCASTER [LNW] op 22 September 1846 from
Kendal *(Lancaster 26th)*; still open. Initially in *Brad* as
L NEW BAILEY; at times L CASTLE until 5 May
1969; LNW co tts only usually added this when needed
to distinguish from Mid station and *Brad* added some
tables by 1853, for same reason.
L GREEN AYRE [Mid] op 12 June 1848 *(Lancaster Gaz
17th)* as L, facilities ? (paper of 17th said a temporary
station was in use for opening, but engineer's report in
co ½ yearly, *Lancaster 2 September 1848*, said temporary
station was then in course of construction); became
L GREEN AREA 1 June 1850, L GREEN AYRE
1 November 1870 co tt *(Mid)*; clo 3 January 1966
(RM February). Original described as 'near the Green
Ayre' in contemporary booklet on line (J. Gough).
[V.R. Anderson & G.K. Fox in an article in *Back Track*,
Autumn 1987, p.130, say original station was on
St George's Quay but letter from North Western
Company to Railway Commissioners, dated 19 June
1848, makes it clear that extension towards Wennington
would make end-on junction with existing terminus
here (R. Bond).]
L FACTORY PLATFORM [Mid] (non-tt):
op 17 July 1916 *(Mid Excursion tt 31, RAIL 963/108)*;
still in Mid wtt 3 October 1921; deleted before/with
February 1922 notice (no notice issued January)
(RAIL 963/119, /122); {shown in 1917 at 32 chains east
of L G A in *The Midland's Settle & Carlisle Distance
Diagrams*, Cumbrian Railways Association, 1992}.

LANCASTER GATE [Cen]
op 30 July 1900 *(L;T 25th- line)*; still open.
LANCHESTER [NE] op 1 September 1862 *(Consett)*;
clo 1 May 1939 *(Cl)*; later use for miners' galas *(U)*.
LANCING [LBSC]
LANCING op 24 November 1845 *(T 26th)*; still open.
L WORKS PLATFORM (non-tt): op ?; railwaymen; clo
6 July 1964; {branch from Lancing} *(U)*.
LANDO [GW]
L HALT / PLATFORM / SIDING (non-tt): agreement
with R. Thorburn & Son for workmen's trains to/from
Swansea made 19 November 1915 *(GM's report
9 December)*; added *hb* 1949a as L PLATFORM;
clo 15 June 1964 *(U)*; {Pembrey – Kidwelly}
Also branches from here to at least three sites in Lando
Royal Ordnance Factory; in use 1940s *(U)*.
LANDORE [GW]
LANDORE op 19 June 1850**; originally ticket platform
but in *Brad*, note that passengers could be booked
to/from; TICKET PLATFORM dropped from name
1854 tt *(Cl)*; originally in fork of junction north of
Swansea; re-sited to east (9 May 1881 possible date)
(C/W); clo 2 November 1964 *(Cl)*. Aot L HL *(hb)*;
L JUNCTION *(Brad)* 1869/70 to 1898/9 and thus
GW co tt 1874 to 1891 or later.
L LL op 9 May 1881 *(GW- line)*; see 1921 April/May**;
clo 4 January 1954 *(Cl)*.
L DEPOT (non-tt:): open day 30 August 1980 *(U)*.
LANDS
See 1834 March 24** for earliest service [S&D].
LANDS [NE] op 13 October 1858**; originally all
days; reduced May 1864 to Thursdays and Saturdays
because Evenwood (which had been main station
on line to Lands) was now re-sited on a different line;
last in *Brad* May 1872; {map 31}.
Also see COCKFIELD FELL.
LANDYWOOD
LANDYWOOD (a) [LNW] op 2 March 1908 *(LNW
Cl; notice of alterations co tt March – 'now open')*;
clo 1 January 1916 (Saturday) *(Cl)*. Notice called it
Motor Stage at L, just L in body of tt; HALT in RCH
list of closures, 1921 – see 1905**.
LANDYWOOD (b) op 10 April 1989 *(BLN 609)* –
cheap introductory service 8th (Gala Day); same site as
(a)?; still open.
LANE – see THE LANE.
LANGBANK [Cal]
op between 31 March 1841** and July 1848, first tt
reference found *(Topham)*; still open. Until 1860s
intermittently LANG BANK in *Brad*, which first called
it L station near West Ferry [on Clyde].
LANGDON PARK [Dock]
op Monday 10 December 2007 (promotional use 8th
and 9th) *(BLN 12 January 2008)*; still open.
LANGFORD near Cheddar [GW]
op 4 December 1901 *(Wells 5th)*;
clo 14 September 1931 *(RM December)*.
LANGFORD near Salisbury [GW]
op 30 June 1856 *(W Fly P 1 July)*;
clo 1 October 1857 *(GW ac)*; {Wylye – Wishford}.

LANGFORD & ULTING [GE]:
line op 2 October 1848 *(EC)*, nd, February 1850;
see 1850 August 19★★; op as L, renamed 1 July 1923
(hbl 12th); aot request; clo 7 September 1964 *(RM Oct.)*.
LANGFORD LANE – see KIDLINGTON.
LANGHO
LANGHO (a) [LY] op 22 June 1850★★; clo 7 May 1956 *(Cl)*.
LANGHO (b) op 29 May 1994 *(RM June)* – one train
on Sunday, full service Monday 30th; still open.
LANGHOLM [NB] op 11 April 1864; problems with
Byreburn Viaduct meant that at first passengers had to
walk across and rejoin train at other side – service
'impeded' not suspended; after a few days, collapse of
viaduct meant line cut back to Canonbie and coaches
used; reop 2 November 1864 *(Eskdale & Lidderdale
Advertiser 20 April* – Ewart Library Dumfries and
R.B. McCartney, *The Railway to Langholm ...*, private,
1981). Clo 15 June 1964 *(RM July)*.
LANGLEY-on-Tyne [NE] op 1 March 1869 *(NC)*;
clo 22 September 1930 *(T 10 July)*.
Hb suggests that only goods was '-on-Tyne'.
LANGLEY near Slough [GW] first in *Brad* May 1846
as L MARSH; renamed L 1849 tt *(Cl)*, L BUCKS
1 September 1920 *(hbl 29 October)*, L 5 May 1975 *(Cl)*;
still open. Joint GW/Dist service began 1 March 1883;
GW only from 1 October 1885.
LANGLEY GREEN [GW] op 1 April 1867
(co n Brierley 30 March) as OLDBURY & L G (but just
L G in *GW ac* prior to opening); renamed L G when
re-sited about 10 chains east 1 May 1885 *(hbl 29 June)*;
renamed L G & ROOD END 9 October 1903 *(RCG)*,
OLDBURY & L G 6 January 1936, L G 6 May 1968
(Cl); still open.
LANGLEY MILL
L M & EASTWOOD [Mid] op 6 September 1847 *(Mid)*
as L M for HEANOR; renamed L M & E for H
1 November 1876 co tt *(Mid)* and thus *Brad* to closure;
clo 2 January 1967 *(Cl)*. Heanor line platforms op
1 October 1895; clo 1 January 1917; reop 3 May 1920;
clo 4 May 1926 *(Mid)*.
LANGLEY MILL op 12 May 1986 *(Mid)*; same site;
still open.
LANGLOAN [Cal] op 8 January 1866 *(Cal- line)*;
clo 5 October 1964 *(RM November)*.
LANGPORT [GW]
L EAST op 2 July 1906 *(Langport 7th)*;
clo 10 September 1962 *(Som Gaz 15th)*.
L WEST op 1 October 1853 *(Taunton 5th)*;
WEST added 1 July 1906 *(hbl 12 July)* – a Sunday,
so first trains under new name on 2nd;
clo 15 June 1964 *(W Gaz 12th, 19th)*.
LANGRICK [GN] op 17 October 1848 *(co n T 16th)*;
clo 17 June 1963 *(RM July)*.
LANGSIDE [Cal] op 2 April 1894 *(Cal)*;
was L & NEWLANDS 1 May 1899 *(RCG)* to 1961/2 tt;
still open.
LANGSTON [LBSC] op 17 July 1867 *(SR)*; last in
Brad December 1868 *(January 1869* 'discontinued');
back August 1869; initially LANGSTONE;
clo 4 November 1963 *(Cl)*.
LANGTON – see EAST LANGTON.

LANGTON DOCK [LO] op by May 1896 (see 1893
March 6★★); clo 5 March 1906 *(RM April)*.
LANGWATHBY [Mid] op 1 May 1876 *(Mid; co n
T 1st- line)*; LONGWATHBY until 1 October 1876
co tt *(Mid)*; clo 4 May 1970 *(RM June)*;
reop for summer Dales Rail 3 April 1976 *(AB)*;
fully reop 14 July 1986 *(Settle)*; still open. In *LMS List
1933* as L for PENRITH; not seen thus elsewhere.
LANGWITH
LANGWITH [Mid] op 1 June 1875 *(Mid)*;
clo 12 October 1964 *(RM November)*.
L JUNCTION – see SHIREBROOK NORTH.
L-WHALEY THORNS op 25 May 1998 *(BLN 821)*;
'fun day' 24 May; about ¾ mile north of station clo 1964;
still open.
L COLLIERY [Mid] (non-tt): op 4 November 1894;
miners; clo after 1945; {Langwith – Elmton} *(U)*.
LANGWORTH [GC]
op 18 December 1848 *(GC)*; clo 1 November 1965
(RM December). GC co tt 1903, LNE tt 1933 and *Brad*
to 1955, but not *hb*: L for WRAGBY.
LAPFORD [LSW]
first in *Brad* September 1855, first in tt *(Trewman)*
20 September 1855★; aot request; still open.
★ = at line opening (25 July 1854) letter from engineer to
BoT – do not intend to open for public traffic at present.
Brad premature or *Trewman* behind events?
LAPWORTH [GW]
first in *Brad* October 1854, as KINGSWOOD;
renamed 1 May 1902 *(hbl 24 April)*; still open.
LARBERT [Cal] op 1 March 1848 *(co ½ 4 September-
line)*; still open. L JUNCTION 1850/1 to 1856/9
(Brad). *Brad* ? to 1955, but not LMS tt 1930 nor *hb*:
L for STENHOUSEMUIR and CARRON.
LARGO [NB] op 11 August 1857★★;
clo 6 September 1965 *(closure notice East of T J)*.
LARGOBEATH COLLIERY (non-tt):
service from Cameron Bridge to this colliery on Lochty
goods branch; stop shown in working tt February 1913
(probably soon after start of service), March and May
1914; colliery closed by flooding later 1914.
LARGS [GSW]
LARGS op 1 June 1885 *(GSW)*; still open.
Private station (name ?) between here and junction
with Fairlie Pier line for I Kempt of Broomcraig;
exact dates unknown but early and short-lived
(GSW Association, Profile No. 5).
LARKHALL
LARKHALL [Cal] op 1 July 1905 *(RCG)*; L CENTRAL
until 14 June 1965 *(Cl)*; clo 4 October 1965 *(BR notice,
The True Line July 2006)*.
L EAST [Cal] op 1 December 1866 *(Cal- line)*; EAST
added 1 June 1905 *(hbl 13 July)*; clo 10 September 1951
(Cl). Became HALT *hb* 1941a but not seen thus *Brad*.
LARKHALL op 12 December 2005★★; still open.
LARTINGTON [NE] op 8 August 1861 *(co op tt)*;
clo 22 January 1962 *(RM February)*.
LASSWADE {map 18}
LASSWADE [NB] op 12 October 1868 *(Edin)*;
clo 10 September 1951 *(RM October)*.
L ROAD – see 1831 A★★.

LATCHFORD [LNW]
trains first shown December 1853 (but see 1853 November 1**) as L & GRAPPENHALL ROAD; renamed 1854 tt *(Cl)*; re-sited 9 July 1893 *(LNW Record)*, on deviation for Manchester Ship Canal; clo 10 September 1962 *(RM September)*.

LATCHLEY [PDSW]
op 2 March 1908 *(W Morn News 3rd)*; clo 7 November 1966 *(Cornish & D P 12th)*. HALT *hb* 1938 and 1956 and on ticket *(JB)*, but not in *Brad*.

LATHOL HALT
– see LONDON & THAMESHAVEN.

LATIMER ROAD [HC]
op 16 December 1868 *(L)*; still open.

LAUDER [NB] op 2 July 1901 *(Rtn)*; clo 12 September 1932 *(RM October)*.

LAUNCESTON
LAUNCESTON [GW] op 1 July 1865 *(W D Merc 4th)*; clo 30 June 1952 *(Cl)* – trains diverted to LSW station.
LAUNCESTON [LSW] op 21 July 1886 *(Tavistock 23rd)*; clo 3 October 1966 *(Cornish & D P 8th)*.
Hb 1956 made GW (then goods only) L NORTH, LSW L SOUTH; BR ticket for latter *(JB)* but not seen thus in any tt.

LAUNTON [LNW]: line op 1 October 1850**; clo 1 January 1968 *(RM January)*.

LAURENCEKIRK
LAURENCEKIRK (a) [Cal] op 1 November 1849 *(co ½ T 27 November- line)*; clo 4 September 1967 *(RM Sept.)*.
LAURENCEKIRK (b) op 17 May 2009 *(Today's Railways U.K., July 2009)*; still open.

LAURISTON [NB] op 1 November 1865 *(co ½ T 3 November- line)*; clo 1 October 1951 *(RM November)*.

LAVANT [LBSC]
op 11 July 1881 *(co nW Sussex)*; clo 7 July 1935 (Sunday) *(RM September)*; race special for Goodwood 26 July 1954, perhaps others, but most used Chichester *(AB)*.

LAVENHAM [GE] op 9 August 1865 *(T 10th- line)*; clo 10 April 1961 *(RM May)*.

LAVERNOCK [TV]
op 1 December 1887 *(Penarth)*; clo 6 May 1968 *(Cl)*.

LAVERTON [GW] op 14 August 1905 *(GW H)*; HALT; clo 7 March 1960 *(RM April)*.

LAVINGTON [GW] op 1 October 1900 *(RCG; W Gaz 5th- line)*; clo 18 April 1966 *(RM May)*.

LAW JUNCTION [Cal]: trains first shown December 1879 *Brad* (before op of line that made it junction station); clo 4 January 1965 *(RM February)*.

LAWLEY BANK [GW] op 2 May 1859 *(Wenlock)*; clo 23 July 1962 *(RM August)*.

LAWLEY STREET {map 99}
For original terminus see BIRMINGHAM.
LAWLEY STREET [LNW] through station op 1 October 1854 *(W Mid)*; clo 1 March 1869 (alterations notices LNW co tt March 1869; *LNW Officers 3994* – can be closed after 28th inst – last day?); replaced by Vauxhall (later renamed Duddeston).

LAWRENCE HILL [GW] op 8 September 1863 *(co n W D Press 7th)*; still open. Sometimes BRISTOL L H. Thus GW co tt 1932 and *Brad* from 1947 (in local tables only); B officially dropped 6 May 1974 *(BR notice)*.

LAWTON [NS]
op 3 July 1893 *(RCG)*; after December 1926 *Brad*, before/with August 1927 reduced to Thursdays and Saturdays only; clo 28 July 1930 *(Cl)*.

LAXFIELD [Mid-Suffolk Light] op 29 September 1908 *(T 28th)*; clo 28 July 1952 *(T 28th)*.

LAYERTHORPE – see YORK.

LAYTON LANCS [PW] first in *Brad* June 1868 as BISPHAM; renamed 4 July 1938 *(hbl July)*; still open.

LAZENBY [NE]: probably op with line 5 June 1846**; earliest reference found is in S&D minutes of 29 April 1847 (to be provided with name-board); earliest tt reference September 1847 co tt; last in *Brad* May 1864; present in *hb* 1862, 1867, 1872 (facilities not then listed), not 'P' 1877; {map 43}.

LAZONBY & KIRKOSWALD [Mid]
op 1 May 1876 *(Mid; co n T 1st- line)*; & K added 1 August 1895 *(hbl 24 October)*; clo 4 May 1970 *(RM June)*; reop summer Dales Rail 3 April 1976 *(AB)*, fully 14 July 1986 *(Settle)*; still open.

LEA [GN/GE]
op 1 August 1849 *(GN/GE)*; clo 1 December 1864 (Thursday) *(co n T 29 October)*, reop 15 July 1867; clo 6 August 1957 (Tuesday) *(RM September)* – trainless Bank Holiday Monday intervened.

LEA BRIDGE [GE] op 15 September 1840 *(T 16th)*; clo 8 July 1985 *(BLN 519)*. L B ROAD / LEABRIDGE ROAD / L B WALTHAMSTOW early – settled about 1871 *(Brad)*; EC co tt 1854: L B for W etc [sic] one way, L B for SNARESBROOK and WANSTEAD other way.

LEA GREEN
LEA GREEN (a) [LNW] line op 17 September 1830**, nd, 1 March 1831 co tt (when BOTTOM OF SUTTON INCLINE); at times SUTTON early; settled 1848 tt *(Cl)*; clo 7 March 1955 *(RM April)*.
LEA GREEN (b) op 17 September 2000 *(Rly Obs November)*; still open.

LEA HALL [LMS]
op 1 May 1939 *(T 27 April)*; still open.

LEA ROAD Preston [PW]: line op 16 July 1840**, nd, about March 1841 *(Freeling)*; initially market only, perhaps early use intermittent; ROAD not always added in early years; clo 2 May 1938 *(T 21 March)*.

LEADBURN [NB] op 4 July 1855 *(Peebles; co ½ T 22 October- line)*; clo 7 March 1955 *(RM April)*.

LEADENHAM [GN] op 15 April 1867 *(GN; co ½ T 19 August- line)*; clo 1 November 1965 *(RM December)*.

LEADGATE [NE]
op 17 August 1896 *(RCG)*; clo 23 May 1955 *(RM July)*.

LEADHILLS [Cal] op 1 October 1901 *(RCG)*; clo 2 January 1939 *(T 16 December 1938)*.

LEAGRAVE [Mid] op 13 July 1868 *(Mid)* – *T 14th* covered line but item omitted this station from description – probably journalist's error; still open. In *LMS List* 1933 as L for DUNSTABLE; not seen thus elsewhere.

LEAKE & WRANGLE – see OLD LEAKE.

LEALHOLM [NE] op 2 October 1865 *(co ½ T 14 February 1866- line)*; still open. NE tickets for LEALHOLME, LEALHOLME BRIDGE *(JB)*.

LEAMINGTON SPA (SPA added 26 July 1913, *RCH dist 29 December*).

LEAMINGTON SPA [GW] op 1 October 1852 *(W Mid; T 27 September- line; in inspection report)* as L; L GENERAL 25 September 1950 *(Cl)* to 1964/76 tt; still open. In *Brad* as L WARWICK OLD ROAD from 1887/8 to 1947/8.

L S AVENUE [LNW]: On 9 July 1852 Captain Huish reported that he had authorised the erection of a temporary station at Avenue Road *(RAIL 410/482)*; opened ? – *Leamington Courier* 17 July 1852 said would be completed 'in about six weeks from the present time'; no exact opening date found; at times just L. *Leamington Year Book* of 1853 said LNW had put up station within past year. Notice in *Leamington Courier* 28 January 1854 said omnibus connections would be made at AVENUE, not MILVERTON, since all trains would be despatched from there from 1 February (fits first appearance in *Brad*). Likely that still used Milverton as terminus – still in *Brad* and description of temporary hardly fits terminus. Paper of 3 March 1860 expected permanent AVENUE to be opened in April and existing 'miserable wooden erection' would be removed (via B. Wilson). Clo 18 January 1965 *(RM March)*. 'AVENUE' not always included in tts.

L S MILVERTON [LNW] op 9 December 1844 *(co n T 20 November)*; re-sited just south 13 October 1883 *(Cl)*; clo 18 January 1965 *(RM March)*. At times just M, or WARWICK, or W plus L and/or M; both *Brad* and LNW co tts often had two or three names for this station in different tables in the same issue.

LEAMSIDE [NE]: line op 15 April 1844 *(Durham County Advertiser 19th)*, nd, August 1844; re-sited about 7 chains south, pre 1920 *(Durham)*; clo 5 October 1953 *(RM November)*. Aot L JUNCTION 1860 to 1893/4 *(Brad)* and thus (one table only) NE co tt 1861.

LEASINGTHORNE [NE]
first in *Brad* June 1864 (see 1845 November★★); fortnightly Saturday market service terminus; last in *Brad* April 1867. In tt as L; map evidence suggests Westerton was different site (see *Cl*); {map 33}.

LEASON HILL [Scottish Midland Junction]: line op 4 June 1838 *(Tayside)*, nd, July 1842; probably clo 1847 (see 1837 B★★); {map 9}.

LEASOWE {map 46}.

L CROSSING [Hoylake] op 4 July 1870★★; clo 1 August 1872, when line to Birkenhead reopened.

LEASOWE [Wirral] op 5 May 1894 *(RCG)*; same site as above; still open.

LEASOWE ROAD – see WALLASEY.

LEATHERHEAD

LEATHERHEAD [LSW/LBSC] op 1 February 1859★★; it was replaced by two stations, each about ½ mile south >

LEATHERHEAD [LBSC] op 4 March 1867 *(LBSC)*; still open. L for MICKLEHAM in LBSC co tt 1912.

LEATHERHEAD [LSW] op 4 March 1867 *(SR)*; clo 10 July 1927 (Sunday) *(RM September)* – trains diverted to ex-LBSC station over new junction.

LEATHERHEAD ROAD – see BOX HILL.

LEATON [GW] op 14 October 1848 *(Shrewsbury 13th)*; clo 12 September 1960 *(Cl)*.

LECH-A-VUIE [NB] (non-tt): op with line 1 April 1901 (in *NB appendix* of that date; inspected with line, *MT6/1034/2*); still in existence 1 November 1947; daylight only; passengers wishing to use had to give prior notice to station master at Lochailort, who would make the necessary arrangements; they had to buy ticket to next station beyond (A. Simpson, *NB Study Group Journal*, Autumn 2000); according to ex-signalman Jim Archibald in the early 1970s it was a private halt for the local laird and his shooting-parties; the last use according to his memory was July or August 1973; some years later much of the platform was removed in track realignment *(Steam Railway, 347, 20 March 2008, p. 73)*. {Glenfinnan – Lochailort}.

LECHLADE [GW] op 15 January 1873 *(Chelt Exp 18th)*; clo 18 June 1962 *(T 18 May)*.

LECKHAMPTON – see CHELTENHAM.

LEDBURY [GW]
LEDBURY op 13 September 1861 *(Hereford T 14th)*; still open.

L TOWN op 26 November 1928 *(wtt supp)*; HALT; clo 13 July 1959 *(RM August)*; {Dymock – Ledbury}. Pre-opening Newtown *(RAC)*.

LEDSHAM
LEDSHAM [Birkenhead] op 23 September 1840 *(Birkenhead)* as SUTTON; renamed 1 July 1863, when Sutton given own station *(Cl)*; clo 20 July 1959 *(RM August)*.
Also see LITTLE SUTTON.

LEDSTON [NE]
op 12 August 1878 *(co ½ Herapath 15 February 1879- line)*; LEDSTONE until 1 July 1915 *(Cl)*; clo 22 January 1951 *(Cl)* – see 1951★★.

LEE near Lewisham [SE] op 1 September 1866 *(L; co ½ T 24 August- line)*; still open. *Brad* 1870/1 to 1955, SEC co tt 1914 and *hb*: L for BURNT ASH.

LEE-ON-THE-SOLENT [LSW]
op 12 May 1894 *(Hants Teleg 19th)*; clo 31 August 1914, reop 1 October 1914 *(Cl)*; clo 1 January 1931 (Thursday) *(T 4 December 1930)*.

LEEBOTWOOD [SH Jt] op 21 April 1852 *(co ½ T 17 August- line)*; clo 9 June 1958 *(Cl)*.

LEEDS {map 56}
Most stations at first in *Brad* as L; names mostly expanded in late 1840s, early 1850s; perhaps at first helpful description rather than part of name – e.g. July 1850 had 'Wellington Road station, opposite Exchange'.

LEEDS [LMS/LNE] op 2 May 1938 *(Mid)*; amalgamation of WELLINGTON and NEW; L CITY until 1 May 1975 tt; old Mid portion clo 13 June 1966 *(Mid)*; rest still open.

L CENTRAL [GN/LY/LNW/NE] op 18 September 1848 *(D&C 8)*; originally a temporary station, gradually transformed into permanent over next 9 years (D. Joy, *RCHS Journal*, 1976); last train 29 April 1967; next day services diverted to City *(RM May)*.

L HUNSLET LANE [Mid] op 1 July 1840 *(co n T 27 June)*; clo 1 March 1851 (Saturday) *(Mid)*; though Mid station, last used by LY trains.★

L MARSH LANE [NE] op 22 September 1834★★ (trial

trip 18th) *(York Courant)*; clo 1 April 1869 (Thursday) *(Cl)*.★

L NEW [LNW/NE] op 1 April 1869 *(T 2nd)*; combined with Wellington to form City 2 May 1938 *(Cl)*.

L WELLINGTON [Mid] op 1 July 1846 *(Mid)*; original temporary station replaced by permanent 1 October 1850 *(Mid)*; combined with New as City 2 May 1938 *(Cl)*.

L WELLINGTON STREET [GN] op 14 May 1850 *(GN)*; temporary terminus, really the goods station; clo 1 August 1854 (Tuesday) when service diverted to Central *(co n T 2nd)*; later at holiday times passenger trains ran from the goods yard to pleasure gardens at Headingley *(NE & Scottish Staff Magazine 1924)*.

L WHITEHALL op 26 September 1999 *(Rly Obs 849)*; temporary platform, regarded as part of station, used by trains to Manchester Airport during work on Leeds station (last train 23 February 2002) *(Rly Obs May p.205)* and for Goole trains in latter part of 2001 *(IU)*.

★ = For through replacements for Hunslet Lane and Marsh Lane see under 'H' and 'M'.

LEEGATE [MC] op 2 February 1848 *(D&C 14)*; clo 5 June 1950 *(RM July)*; see 1840★★; {map 20g}.

LEEK [NS]
LEEK op 13 July 1849 *(T 11th- line)*; clo 4 January 1965 *(RM March)*.

L BROOK: non-tt service for Cheddleton Hospital, alias Staffordshire County Asylum / Mental Hospital, alias St Edward's Hospital. Consisted of platforms on Stoke and Churnet Valley lines (sometimes referred to as CHEDDLETON JUNCTION) and a branch thence to hospital. Began for workmen by June 1895, who used it until May 1899; used for visitors and staff about 1904 to about 1920 *(Hosp)*; in *hb* 1904 on as LEEKBROOK SIDING, no facilities listed; clo 7 May 1956 *(RM June)*.

LEEMING BAR [NE]
op 6 March 1848 *(NE)* as L LANE; renamed 1 July 1902 *(hbl 10th)*; clo 26 April 1954 *(T 20th)*.

LEES [LNW] op 5 July 1856 *(LNW- line)*; clo 2 May 1955 *(T 11 March)*.

LEGACY [GW] op 1 October 1901 *(RCG – 'drop station for passengers')*; HALT on ticket *(JB)* but not in tt and not included in *hb* until 1922a; clo 1 January 1931 (Thursday) *(T 20 December 1930)*; {map 75}.

LEGBOURNE ROAD [GN]: op 3 September 1848 *(Boston 4th- line)*; ROAD added 1880 *(RCG ref April)*; clo 7 December 1953 *(RM January 1954)*.

LEICESTER
LEICESTER [Mid] op 5 May 1840 *(co n Lee)*; extra platform added July 1868 for visitors to Royal Agricultural Show and then kept as part of station *(Mid)*; L LONDON ROAD 12 June 1892 to 4 May 1970 *(Mid)*; still open. L CAMPBELL STREET in *Brad* June 1867 to November 1893 (inclusive) *(Mid)*.

L BELGRAVE ROAD [GN] op 2 October 1882 *(Leicester Mercury 2nd, 9th)*; clo to public 7 December 1953 *(T 7th)*, but one train each way per day for workmen until 29 April 1957 *(RM June)*; then summer Saturday and Sunday to Skegness, last Sunday 9 September 1962.

L CENTRAL [GC] op 15 March 1899 *(GC; T 16th- line)*; clo 5 May 1969 *(Cl)*.

L NORTH: see 2007 July 4★★.

L WELFORD ROAD [Mid]
op 4 November 1874 *(Mid)*; alighting only, Wednesdays and Saturdays only – early morning trains for market; last train, local from Nuneaton, called early February 1918, probably 6th (J. Gough).

L WEST BRIDGE [Mid] op 18 July 1832 *(Mid)*; W B added soon after opening; see 1847 December★★; replaced 13 March 1893 by station known locally as King Richard's Road; clo 24 September 1928 *(Cl)*. For **HUMBERSTONE ROAD** see under 'H'. 1904 *hb* had 'P' for L EAST (QUEEN STREET); error – was goods only.

LEICESTER SQUARE
LEICESTER SQUARE [Nor] op 22 June 1907 *(co n T 21st)*; still open.

LEICESTER SQUARE [Picc] op 15 December 1906 *(co n T 14th)*; still open.

LEIGH near Stoke-on-Trent [NS] op 7 August 1848★★; clo 7 November 1966 *(RM January 1967)*.

LEIGH near Manchester
LEIGH [LNW]: for op see 1864 September 1★★; op as BEDFORD L; renamed L & B 1 August 1876 *(Cl; RCG ref October)*, L 1 July 1914 *(hbl 14th)*; clo 5 May 1969 *(RM June)*. *Brad* made it into B & L September 1876, L & B next month – former probably error *(JS)*.

Also see WEST LEIGH.

LEIGH COURT [GW]
op 2 May 1874 *(Berrow's 9th- line)*; clo 7 September 1964 *(Cl)*. Initially L in *Brad* (briefly) and local press.

LEIGH KENT [SEC] op 1 September 1911 *(SEC)*; spelled LYGHE April 1917 to 13 June 1960; HALT until 5 May 1969 *(SR/SR App)*; KENT added body of BR tt 5 May 1976 (index earlier); still open.

LEIGH-ON-SEA [LTS]
op 1 July 1855 *(co n T 28 June)*; -on-S added 1 October 1904 co tt *(Mid)* and thus *Brad* from then but RCH only caught up 1938 *(hb)*; re-sited 46 chains west 1 January 1934 *(T 1 November 1933)*; still open.

LEIGHTON BUZZARD [LNW]:
line op 9 April 1838 *(T 11th)*, nd, *Freeling* later 1838; re-sited 8 chains south 14 February 1859 *(Cl)*; still open. While usually LEIGHTON early, e.g. *co n T 2 June 1838* called it L B; L B became normal form 1 July 1911 *(hbl 6th)*. L JUNCTION in *Brad* 1851/2 to 1869/70 and thus LNW co tt 1852 but not 1868.

LEIRE [LMS] op 2 March 1925 *(Mid)*; HALT clo 1 January 1962 *(RM February)*.

LEISTON [GE] op 1 June 1859 *(T 2nd)*; clo 12 September 1966 *(RM September)*.

LEITH {maps 18, 19}
Caledonian
L NORTH op 1 August 1879 *(RCG)* as L; became NORTH LEITH 1 August 1903 *(hbl 29 October)*, L N 7 April 1952 *(Cl)*; clo 30 April 1962 *(RM May)*.

L WALK (never opened) – see 1903★★.

North British
L CENTRAL op 1 July 1903 *(RM August)*★;

clo 7 April 1952 *(RM May)*.

* = *RCG* supports this in one place but gives 30 September in another; first in *Brad* July.

L WALK op 22 May 1868 *(T 25th)*; clo 1 January 1917 *(RM February)*; reop 1 February 1919 *(Cl)*; clo 31 March 1930 *(Cl)*. In 1870s *Brad*, some tables, made it EDINBURGH L W.

NORTH LEITH op 20 May 1846 *(D&C 6)*; *Brad* added NORTH 1868; clo 1 January 1917 *(RM February)*; reop 1 April 1919 *(RCG)*; clo 16 June 1947**.
Hb: 1862 L; 1872 L N; 1912 N L. *Tuck* 1843: THE SHORE, LEITH.

SOUTH LEITH: for op and possible short closure about 1847 see 1831 A**; (earliest tt reference found is *Tuck* about June 1843); originally just L; *Murray* April 1852 and *Brad* 1853 say 'per coach from Portobello' – presumably horse-drawn railway coach. Last in *Brad* July 1856 – line closed about then for improvement; back October 1859, now served from main line Portobello *(co ½ T 8 September* said line had been converted to locomotive haulage, already in use goods, passengers would follow in short time); last two way service in *Brad* April 1904 (three trains each way); May to September three to Leith only; October and November one to Leith; still present December, but no trains shown. SOUTH added *Brad* and *hb* as for NORTH L [NB].

LELANT
LELANT [GW] op 1 June 1877 *(GW* gives line; L in *Cornish Tel* description of formal opening); HALT 29 September 1958 to 5 May 1969 *(Cl)*; aot request; still open.

L SALTINGS op 29 May 1978 *(W Briton 1 June)*; still open.

LEMAN STREET [GE]
op 1 June 1877 *(L)*; clo 22 May 1916 *(T 2nd)*, reop 1 July 1919 *(T 20th)*; clo 7 July 1941 *(T 25 June)*.

LEMINGTON [NE] op 12 July 1875 *(NC)*; clo 15 September 1958 *(RM October)*.

LEMSFORD ROAD [LNE] (non-tt)
op 1 August 1942 *(U)*; workmen; HALT; clo 1 October 1951 *(T 8 Sept.)*; {Hatfield – Nast Hyde}.

LENHAM [LCD] op 1 July 1884 *(SR)*; still open.

LENNOXTOWN [NB]
LENNOXTOWN op 1 July 1867 *(D&C 6- line)* as L BLANE VALLEY; renamed on closure of L OLD; clo 1 October 1951 *(RM November)*.

L OLD op 5 July 1848 *(D&C 6)*; OLD added 1 July 1867; clo 1 October 1881 (Saturday) *(Cl)*.

LENTON [Mid] op 2 October 1848 *(Mid; RAIL 1005/265- line)*; clo 1 July 1911 (Saturday) *(RCG)*.

LENTRAN [High] op 11 June 1862 *(High)*; clo 13 June 1960 *(RM July)*. Reopened 27 to 29 March 1982 as temporary terminus during work on swing bridge at Clachnaharry. In *hb* 1863a (only) as LENTRAM.

LENWADE [MGN]
op 1 July 1882 *(MGN)*; clo 2 March 1959 *(T 2nd)*.

LENZIE [NB] {map 16}
KIRKINTILLOCH op 21 February 1842 *(co n T 19th)*; replaced by >
K 26 December 1844**, a little to the east, to serve as

interchange between EG and MK services; now MK had their station, different gauge alongside (see under KIRKINTILLOCH) >
K moved back to original site 5 July 1848 *(EG)* to serve as junction station for Campsie branch (regauging of MK meant its trains were running through to Glasgow, making 1844 interchange redundant);
now K JUNCTION. Renamed CAMPSIE JUNCTION 1849 tt, LENZIE J 1867 tt, L 1890 *(Cl)*, L J 1925/6 *(Brad)*, L 1951 *(Brad)*; still open.
Became L J for GARNGABER J 1 August 1917 according to *hbl 24 January 1918* and thus *hb* 1925 to September 1962a but not seen thus *Brad*.

LEOMINSTER [SH Jt] op 6 December 1853**; still open. L JUNCTION 1862 to 1895/6 in *Brad* and thus LNW co tt 1869 (one way) .

LEONARDS BRIDGE [LSW] (non-tt): passengers picked up and set down at passing loop but no platforms; first mention December 1857; ceased ?; {Ringwood – Wimborne}; (M. Hutson, *SW Circular*, April 1998).

LESBURY [York, Newcastle & Berwick] op 1 July 1847**; probably clo 1 October 1850 when Alnwick branch opened from Bilton, later Alnmouth. *Brad, Topham* and some maps of the time suggest Bilton was just renaming of Lesbury, delayed until May 1851 *Brad*. However, inspection report *(MT 6/9/49)* makes it clear that Lesbury was a mile or so north of junction; its continuance in tt and late arrival there of Bilton probably inertia. It is likely it was only intended as a temporary station, sited to provide link with road service to Alnwick; few people lived in immediate area, so no point in keeping it once railway open to Alnwick. One snag is that inspector said station at junction had only just been laid out, but there was two-month gap between inspection and opening; so time for something to be provided. Also, if branch had initially operated from Lesbury, with reversal (as timetables imply), it would have added significantly to journey times and tts do not show any reduction in timings when Bilton did eventually appear.
In *Brad* as L, [for?] ALNWICK.

LESLIE [NB] op 1 February 1861 *(co ½ T 8 October)*; clo 4 January 1932 *(Cl)*.

LESMAHAGOW
First station of this name – see BROCKETSBRAE.
LESMAHAGOW [Cal] op 1 July 1905 *(RCG)*; clo 4 October 1965 *(BR notice, The True Line July 2006)*.

LETCHWORTH GARDEN CITY [GN]: workmen used from 1903 *(U)*; op to public 15 April 1905 *(RM May)*; re-sited 18 May 1913 *(Cl)*; still open. G C intermittently added: was in GN co tt 1909 and LNE tt 1927; omitted body of *Brad* 1937 (index much earlier); restored 17 June 1999 tt *(AB Chron)*.

LETHAM
L GRANGE [NB]
op 1 May 1883**; clo 22 September 1930 *(Cl)*.

L MILL OFFSET is shown on Macaulay's Maps (added 1851/4, still present mid-1860s); with that name should have been passenger 'halt' but no evidence for such use exists; all other sources seen refer to it as goods siding.

LETHENTY [GNS] op 1 October 1856 *(GNS corr)*;
clo 2 November 1931 *(RM December)*.

LETTERSTON [GW]
op 11 April 1895 *(GW)*; clo 25 October 1937★★.

LEUCHARS [NB]
LEUCHARS op 1 June 1878 *(T 1st- line)* as L JUNCTION;
JUNCTION dropped 1968/76 tt; still open.
L OLD op 17 May 1848 *(Dundee- line)* as
L / L ST ANDREWS ROAD (latter in heading *Brad*
and in *Edinburgh tt December 1849)*;
became L JUNCTION 1 July 1852 *(Cl)*; clo 1 June
1878, replaced by station above; reop 1 December 1878
as L OLD *(Cl)*; clo 3 October 1921 *(RCG)*.

LEVEN
[Edinburgh, Perth & Dundee]
BURNMILL, temporary op 10 August 1854 *(Fifeshire
Journal 10th)* – formal 5th; replaced by >
LEVEN [NB] permanent op 11 August 1857★★;
clo 6 October 1969 *(Cl)*.

LEVENSHULME
LEVENSHULME [LNW]: op 24 June 1842 (co notice
Stockport Advertiser 24th – J. Gough); L & BURNAGE
1887/8 *(Brad)* to 1 July 1910 *(hbl 28 April)*; L NORTH
15 September 1952 *(JS)* to 18 June 1962 tt; still open.
L SOUTH [GC] op 2 May 1892 *(GC)*; SOUTH added
15 September 1952 *(JS)*; clo 7 July 1958 *(LNW Record)*.
LEVERTON [GC] first in *Brad* December 1850;
permanent station 1853; clo 2 November 1959
(RM December).

LEVISHAM [NE]
for op see 1835 B★★; clo 8 March 1965 *(T 19 January)*.

LEWES [LBSC] {map 132}
LEWES op 8 June 1846 *(Hants Chron 13th)* in Friars
Walk; permanent station 28 August 1846; re-sited
1 November 1857 and again 17 June 1889; still open.
L HAM op 8 June 1846 *(LBSC implies)*;
and **L PINWELL** op about 1 October 1847 *(LBSC)*.
Last two were effectively extensions of main station and
were absorbed with/before 1857 re-siting.

LEWES ROAD Brighton [LBSC]
op 1 September 1873 *(LBSC)*; clo 1 January 1917
(T 22 December 1916); reop 10 August 1919 *(Cl)*;
HALT added, probably on reopening – in *Brad* 1920;
clo 1 January 1933 (Sunday) – based on *Cl* (says 2nd)
+ SR practice.

LEWIEFIELD [LNE] op 3 July 1933 *(Cl 29)*;
HALT; clo 15 October 1956 *(T 21 September)*;
{Kielder – Plashetts}.

LEWISHAM
LEWISHAM [SE] op 30 July 1849★★; L JUNCTION
1 January 1857 *(L)* to 7 July 1929 *(Cl)*; still open.
Accident report in 1858 referred to L OLD, on North
Kent line, and L JUNCTION new station on Mid-Kent;
presumably regarded as one station by the SE.
LEWISHAM [Dock] op 20 November 1999 *(RM
January 2000)*; still open.
LEWISHAM ROAD [LCD] op 18 September 1871
(co n T 16th); clo 1 January 1917 *(T 28 December 1916)*.
LEWISTOWN [GW]
op 10 August 1942 *(hbl 18)*; HALT; clo 4 June 1951 *(Cl)*;
{Pontyrhyll – Pontcwmmer}.

LEWKNOR BRIDGE [GW] op 1 September 1906
(GW H); HALT; clo 1 July 1957 *(RM August)*;
{Aston Rowant – Watlington}.

LEYBURN [NE] op 19 May 1856 *(RCG)*;
clo 26 April 1954★★. Later excursions – e.g. Ramblers'
25 April 1981 *(IU)*. Reop for occasional use 1984–8.

LEYCETT [NS]
op 28 June 1880 *(NS)*; clo 27 April 1931 *(Cl)*.

LEYLAND [NU]
op 31 October 1838 *(LY; co n Manch G 27th- line)*;
still open. GOLDENHILL in early newspaper account
but not confirmed from railway sources *(JS)*.

LEYSDOWN [SEC] op 1 August 1901 *(RCG)*;
clo 4 December 1950 *(T 4th)*.

LEYSMILL [Cal] op 24 November 1838 (see 1838★★);
clo 5 December 1955 *(RM January 1956)*.

LEYTON
LEYTON op by [GE] 22 August 1856 *(L; co n T 22nd-
line)*; LOW LEYTON until 27 November 1867 *(Cl)*;
transferred to [Cen] 5 May 1947 *(T 6th)*; still open.
L MIDLAND ROAD [TFG Jt] op 9 July 1894 *(RCG)*;
M R added 1 May 1949 *(Mid)*; still open.

LEYTONSTONE
LEYTONSTONE op by [GE] 22 August 1856 *(L; co n
T 22nd- line)*; transferred to [Cen] 5 May 1947 *(T 6th)*;
still open.
L HIGH ROAD [TFG Jt] op 9 July 1894 *(RCG)*;
H R added 1 May 1949 *(Mid)*; still open.

LHANBRYDE [High] op 18 August 1858 *(High)*;
clo 7 December 1964 *(RM January 1965)*.

LICHFIELD [LNW]
LICHFIELD op 15 September 1847 *(co n T 13th)* >
L TRENT VALLEY JUNCTION would logically have op
9 April 1849 but not in *Brad* until July 1849 (perhaps at
first unadvertised exchange?) >
Both replaced 3 July 1871 *(LNW Officers 6776)* by
L TRENT VALLEY HL and **L TRENT VALLEY LL**.
HL clo 18 January 1965 *(RM March)*;
reop 28 November 1988 *(RM December)*.
Now treated as one station; still open.
L CITY op 9 April 1849 *(Shrewsbury 13th)*; re-sited
to south-west 3 November 1884 *(Cl)*; still open.
Neither LNW co tt nor *Brad* added CITY until 1870/1,
even though LNW had two stations for Lichfield
– in *Brad* added October 1871.

LIDDATON [GW] op 4 April 1938 *(co n dated 'March')*;
HALT; clo 31 December 1962★★; {Coryton – Lydford.

LIDFORD – see LYDFORD.

LIDLINGTON [LNW]
op 18 November 1846★★; still open.

LIFF [Cal] op 10 June 1861 *(Dundee)*;
clo 10 January 1955 *(T 28 December 1954)*.

LIFFORD
LIFFORD (a) [BG] op 17 December 1840 *(Mid; co n
Chelt Exam 16th- line)*; last in *Brad* November 1844.
LIFFORD (b) [Mid] op 1 June 1876 *(Mid)* on Selly
Oak line; replaced by >
LIFFORD (c) [Mid] op 28 September 1885 *(Mid)* on
Camp Hill line; clo 30 September 1940 *(LNW Record)*.
LIFTON [GW] op 1 July 1865 (line report *W D Merc
4th*, in tt *Tavistock 8th)*; clo 31 December 1962★★.

LIGHTCLIFFE [LY] op 7 August 1850
(LY;T 5th- line); clo 14 June 1965 *(RM June)*.

LIGHTMOOR [GW]

LIGHTMOOR (a) op 2 May 1859 *(Wenlock)*;
clo 1 November 1864 (Tuesday) *(Cl)*.

LIGHTMOOR (b) op 12 August 1907 *(GW H)* as
L PLATFORM; clo 1 January 1917 *(GW notice dated
22 December 1916)*; reop 23 June 1919 *(GW circular
2672)*; became HALT 6 February 1956 *(GW H)*;
clo 23 July 1962 *(RM August)*. RCH dist ref 29 December
1913 said had become (no date given) L JUNCTION,
but not seen thus in any tt.

LILBOURNE [LNW] op 1 November 1854 *(Leic)*;
clo 6 June 1966 *(RM July)*.

LILLIPUT ROAD Swansea [SIT]:
line op 11 November 1860, nd, May 1866 (see 1860
July 25★★); re-sited on deviation line 26 August 1900;
last in *Brad* November 1904; present *hb* 1867,
'cancelled' 1908a; {map 88}.

LIME KILN LANE – see TRANMERE.

LIMEHOUSE {map 108}.

LIMEHOUSE (a) [GE] op 6 July 1840 *(T 29 June,
10 July)*; see 1849 March 31★★; clo 4 May 1926★★.

LIMEHOUSE (b) [GE] op by 3 August 1840 *(L)* as
STEPNEY; see 1849 March 31★★; renamed
STEPNEY EAST 1 July 1923 *(hbl 12th)*, L 1983/7 tt;
clo for track remodelling 22 July 1994 *(BLN 740)*;
reop 12 September 1994; still open. Platforms on Bow
line clo ?, reop 17 July 1876 *(T 19th)*; item said work
had been going on for several months *(8 May* had said
same); replaced bridge over Commercial Road with
one carrying wider platforms – previous thought unsafe
(also see J.E. Connor, *Stepney's Own Railway*, 1987).

LIMEHOUSE [Dock] op 31 August 1987 *(T 1 Sept.)*;
still open.

LIMESIDE – see 1957★★.

LIMPET MILL [Aberdeen]
op 1 November 1849 *(co ½ T 27 November)*; temporary
terminus, clo 1 April 1850 when line completed to
Aberdeen *(Cl)*; {Muchalls – Stonehaven}.

LIMPLEY STOKE [GW]
op 2 February 1857 *(GW; Bath & Chelt 4th- line)*;
clo 3 October 1966 *(RM November)*.

LINACRE ROAD [LY]
op 1 June 1906 *(RCG)*; clo 2 April 1951 *(RM May)*.

LINBY

LINBY [GN] op 2 October 1882 *(GN)*;
clo 1 July 1916 (Saturday) *(RCG)*.

LINBY [Mid] op 2 October 1848 *(Mid; RAIL 1005/265-
line)*; clo 12 October 1964 *(RM November)*.

LINCOLN

LINCOLN [GN] op 17 October 1848 *(co n T 16th)*;
CENTRAL intermittently added – first added
25 September 1950 *(Rly Obs October)*, finally dropped
11 December 2005 tt *(AB)*; still open.
L HIGH STREET in *Brad* 1867 to 1924 *(JS)*,
but not GN co tt 1909.

L ST MARKS [Mid] op 4 August 1846 *(Mid)*;
ST M added 25 September 1950 *(Rly Obs October)*;
clo 12 May 1985 (Sunday) – had Sunday service
but last train Saturday *(BLN 517/8)*.

LINDAL

LINDAL [Fur] op 6 May 1851 *(D&C 14)*;
clo 1 October 1951 *(RM October)*.

L EAST – see ULVERSTON.

LINDEAN [NB] op 5 April 1856 *(co n Selkirk 4th)*;
notice referred to 'Gala Opening' but clearly full service
of fare-payers; Directors' experimental trip week
previously. Clo 10 September 1951 *(RM October)*.

LINDORES

LINDORES (a) [Edinburgh Northern], temporary
terminus, op 20 September 1847 *(Edinburgh Advertiser
21st)*; clo 9 December 1847, line extended to Glenbirnie
(Cl) {map 5}. [One in Ian Allan atlas is (b)]

LINDORES (b) [NB] op 25 January 1909 *(RCG)*;
different line; clo 12 February 1951 *(RM April)* – see
1951★★.

LINEFOOT [CW Jc] op 1 September 1908 *(D&C 14)*;
last in tt November 1908; {in *IA*}.

LINFORD – see GREAT LINFORD.

LINGFIELD [LBSC] op 10 March 1884 *(Hants Chron
15th- line*; included in inspection report of 16 February,
MT6/1908/3); enlarged 1894 for race use (course
opened 1890) with footbridge and covered way to
course (removed 1976/86) *(AB)*; still open.

LINGS COLLIERY [Mid] (non-tt):
op by 31 August 1874 wtt; clo 9 November 1927;
{near Clay Cross} *(Mid)*.

LINGWOOD [GE]
op 1 June 1883 *(GE- line)*; still open.

LINKSFIELD LEVEL CROSSING [GNS]
op 4 June 1853 *(GNS amdt)*; last in *Brad* November
1859 but actually clo 1898 *(GNS)* – continuous use?;
present *hb* 1867, 1872 (when facilities were not shown),
and 1877 (no facilities shown here); {map 3}.

LINLEY [GW] op 1 February 1862★★; clo 1 January
1917 *(GW notice dated 22 December 1916)*; reop 2 April
1917 *(GM's report)*; became HALT 10 September 1951;
clo 9 September 1963 *(T 9th)*.

LINLITHGOW

LINLITHGOW [NB] op 21 February 1842 *(co n T 19th)*;
see 1840 August 5★★; still open.
Also see BO'NESS; CAUSEWAYEND.

LINT MILL [Camp] (ng): line op 18 August 1906★★;
request; clo by May 1932.

LINTON near Cambridge [GE] op 1 June 1865
(GE Journal Jan. 1992); clo 6 March 1967 *(RM April)*.

LINTON – see EAST LINTON.

LINTZ GREEN [NE] op 2 December 1867 *(Consett)*;
see 1951★★; clo 2 November 1953 *(RM December)*.

LIONS HOLT – see ST JAMES'S PARK Exeter.

LIPHOOK [LSW]
op 1 January 1859 *(SR; co n T 1st- line)*; still open.

LIPSON VALE [GW] op 1 June 1904 *(W Morn News
1st, 2nd)*; HALT; after 7 July 1930 only used by ex-LSW
trains; clo 22 March 1942 (Sunday) as a fire risk
– area subject to bombing *(Cl)*.
In LSW co tt 1914 as PLYMOUTH LV; {map 114}.

LISCARD & POULTON [Wirral]
first in *Brad* October 1895 *(Wrexham, 15 June,
describing line opening, says this station was to follow)*;
clo 4 January 1960 *(RM February)*.

LISKEARD
LISKEARD [GW] op 4 May 1859**; Looe line
platforms added 15 May 1901; all still open.
L MOORSWATER [Liskeard & Looe] op 11 September
1879 *(Cornish T 13th)*; clo 15 May 1901 – trains diverted
to main *(W Morning News 16th)*. Also see 1844**.
LISS [LSW]
op 1 January 1859 *(SR; co n T 1st- line)*; still open.
LISVANE & THORNHILL
op 4 November 1985 *(Rly Obs January 1986)*;
effectively replaced Cefn-Onn – latter's closure
procedure so protracted that both open together for
a year; still open.
Pre-opening in 30 September 1985 tt as T *(AB Chron)*.
LITCHFIELD [GW] op 4 May 1885 *(Hants Chron
2nd)*; clo 4 August 1942**, reop 8 March 1943 *(Cl)*;
L HANTS 7 June 1909 *(hbl 7 July)* to 13 June 1955
(Cl); clo 7 March 1960 *(Hants Chron 5th)*.
LITTLE BYTHAM
LITTLE BYTHAM [GN] op 15 July 1852**;
clo 15 June 1959 *(RM July)*.
LITTLE BYTHAM [Edenham & Little Bytham]
op 8 December 1857**; finally clo 17 October 1871 *(Cl)*.
LITTLE DOWNHAM – see BLACKBANK.
LITTLE DRAYTON [GW] op 14 September 1935
(T 12th); HALT; clo 6 October 1941 *(Cl)*;
{Tern Hill – Market Drayton}.
LITTLE DUNHAM – see DUNHAM.
LITTLE EATON [Mid] op 1 September 1856 *(Mid;
T 12th- line)*; clo 1 June 1930 (Sunday) *(Mid)*.
LITTLE HULTON [LNW]
op 1 April 1875 *(LNW Officers 12593)*;
clo 29 March 1954 *(BR clo notice Sweeney)*.
LITTLE KIMBLE [GW]
op 1 June 1872 *(co n T 1st)*; still open.
LITTLE MILL near Alnwick [NE]:
earliest use (non-tt) was by Greys of Howick, given
right to trains here by agreement of 4 October 1847
(right rescinded on death of 4th Earl Grey in 1917);
first in public tt January 1861; clo 5 May 1941,
reop 7 October 1946 *(RM January 1947)*;
clo 15 September 1958 *(RM October)*.
LITTLE MILL near Pontypool [GW]
LITTLE MILL op 2 January 1854 *(T 29 December 1853-
line)*; see 1856 June 2**; clo 1 October 1861 *(co n
Hereford T)*.
L M JUNCTION op 1 May 1883 *(RAIL 253/228)*;
JUNCTION added 1 July 1883 *(Cl)*; only Monmouth
line trains called; clo 30 May 1955**.
GW co tt 1886: L M J (MON).
LITTLE ORMESBY [MGN]: see 17 July 1933**;
HALT; {Hemsby – Great Ormesby}.
LITTLE SALKELD [Mid] op 1 May 1876 *(Mid; co n
T 1st- line)*; clo 4 May 1970 *(RM June)*.
LITTLE SOMERFORD [GW] op 1 July 1903
(Bristol T 2nd); clo 3 April 1961 *(RM May)*; {map 122}.
LITTLE STEEPING [GN]
op 2 October 1848 *(Stamford 3rd)*;
clo 11 September 1961 *(RM September)*.
LITTLE STRETTON [SH Jt] op 18 April 1935
(wtt supp); HALT; clo 4 January 1943 *(hbl 19)*,

reop 11 March 1946 *(Joint Officers 21 August)*;
clo 9 June 1958 *(Cl)*; {Church Stretton – Marsh Brook}.
LITTLE SUTTON [Birkenhead] op 1 July 1863
(D&C 10; LNW co ½ T 14 August- line);
LITTLE added 19 October 1886 *(Cl; RCG ref October)*;
still open.
LITTLE WEIGHTON [HB] op 27 July 1885
(op tt NER I); clo 1 August 1955 *(RM September)*.
LITTLEBOROUGH [LY]
op 4 July 1839 *(T 11th)*; still open.
LITTLEBURY [EC line]: *GE Society Journal* included
a number of items on this: *July 1993* –photograph of
mystery buildings, looking like station; *April 1994* –
identified as Littlebury Siding; *October 1994* – evidence
(contradictory) about contract for station here.
When plans handed over to Railtrack in 1994 it was
noticed that a platform was shown here on old EC map;
interpreted as most likely having existed for navvies
working in area (G. Kenworthy). *The Times* included
Littlebury as a station in account of formal opening of
appropriate stretch but this was almost certainly an error.
As well as reasons given in entry for ICKLETON, there
was no reference to a station in any of the accounts of
accident here on 4 August 1845 (within a week of line
opening); all refer to Wenden and Chesterford as
stations either side of accident *(T 6th, 7th)*.
LITTLEHAM [LSW] op 1 June 1903 *(RCG; W Gaz
5th- line)*; clo 6 March 1967 *(RM April)*.
LITTLEHAMPTON
For first station for this area see ARUNDEL.
LITTLEHAMPTON [LBSC] op 17 August 1863 *(co ½
T 23 January 1864)*; still open.
LITTLEHAVEN [LBSC]
op 1 June 1907 *(LBSC)* as RUSPER ROAD CROSSING;
became L CROSSING July 1907 tt, L December 1907
tt *(Cl)*; clo 1 January 1917 *(T 22 December 1916)*;
reop 3 May 1920 *(Cl)*; HALT until 5 May 1969 *(Cl)*;
still open.
LITTLEMORE [GW]
LITTLEMORE op 24 October 1864 *(T 25th)*;
clo 7 January 1963 *(RM January)*.
Hb 1877 gave separate 'P' listing to **L ASYLUM**;
private siding at right angles to running lines, provided
by instruction of 1 September 1870 for Committee of
Visitors; used until ? (Committee continued to exist
under various names until 1 July 1968).
LITTLEPORT [GE]
op 26 October 1847 *(co n T 25th)*; still open.
LITTLETON & BADSEY [GW]
op 21 April 1884 *(RAC)*; clo 3 January 1966
(RM February). Pre-opening Blackminster *(RAC)*.
LITTLEWORTH [GN] op 17 October 1848 *(co n
T 16th)* as L & DEEPING FEN; & D F dropped 1857
(Brad); clo 11 September 1961 *(RM September)*.
LIVERPOOL {map 47}
All [LO] stations shown under own letter of the alphabet.
L BRUNSWICK [CLC] op 1 June 1864 *(CLC)*;
replaced by >
L CENTRAL [CLC] op Monday 2 March 1874*
(notice in Mid co tt March – J. Gough); HL (but this not
used in tt); clo 17 April 1972 *(RM May)*.

* = some sources including *MS&L co ½ T 23 July* say op 1 March – case where station op with new tt, first of month was Sunday, officialdom used tt date.

L CENTRAL [Mersey] op 11 January 1892 *(D&C 10)* as L C LL, terminus from West Kirby / New Brighton / Rock Ferry; clo 28 July 1975 for construction of new loop line *(Cl)*; reop 2 May 1977 as, terminus from Southport/Ormskirk/Kirkby; became through station 3 January 1978 on (re)opening of line to Garston *(Daily Telegraph 3rd)*, extended 16 May 1983 to Hunts Cross; still open.
Ticket exists for L BOLD STREET *(JB)*.

L CENTRAL DEEP LEVEL op 9 May 1977 *(T 9th)*; still open.

L (CROWN STREET) [LM] op 17 September 1830**; replaced by Lime Street 15 August 1836.
C S only used in explanatory text in co tt March 1831 – just L in table.

L GREAT HOWARD STREET / BOROUGH GAOL [LY/East Lancashire] op 20 November 1848 *(co n Manch G 18th)*; just L in *Brad* until April 1850, when B G added in LY tables and G H S in E Lancs table, presumably as help for passengers in forthcoming moves; same in press notices – E Lancs used it in notice *Liverpool Mail 7 April* for opening on 2nd of Liverpool, Ormskirk & Preston section of their line. Replaced for LY use by Exchange 13 May 1850 *(Liverpool Mercury 14th)*. E Lancs notice in that paper and *Liverpool Times of same date* said that all its trains would continue to call at Great Howard Street until further notice; its trains were first shown from Exchange July 1851 *Brad*. >

L EXCHANGE [LY] op 13 May 1850 *(T 14th)*; clo 30 April 1977 (Saturday) *(RM July)* – service diverted to Central (LL). In the LY opening notice in *The Liverpool Mercury (14th)* it was described as The New Station at the Exchange; in the tt in same paper was new Station Tithebarn-street. Also seen as L E & TYTHE BARN STREET, later L E & TTTHE B S in tt; BOROUGH GAOL on LY Distance Diagram 1851; official records of the Railway Commissioners show that this was a Siamese twin rather than single station: an award dated 10 June 1851 divided it into TITHE BARN and GAOL LANE. Unity would have resulted from amalgamation of companies in 1859, but note persistence of old names.

L JAMES STREET [Mersey] op 1 February 1886 *(T 2nd)*; eastbound platform replaced 9 May 1977 by platform on new loop line; still open.

L LIME STREET [LNW] op 15 August 1836 *(LM; stated at General Meeting 27 July that would open then – T 29 July)*; still open.
Brad added L S in some tables by the end of 1844, though have been called the 'New Lime Street station' at the Meeting cited; in some tables LNW co tt by 1852; probably at first descriptive rather than part of name.

L LIME STREET DEEP LEVEL op 30 October 1977 *(T 31st)*; still open.

L MOORFIELDS Low Level platforms op 2 May 1977 *(T 9th)*; Deep Level platforms op 8 May 1978 *(D&C 10)*; all still open.

L RIVERSIDE [Mersey Docks & Harbour Board]:

co ½ Rly Times 10 August 1895 says line brought into use for passengers 12 June, but station op by Mersey Docks & Harbour Board 10 July. *LNW, p.186*, says 12 June was special working, inaugural regular service 15 June. Temporary arrangements for first month? Boat train passengers only; clo by accident 21 October 1949, reop 27 March 1950 *(Cl)*; last train used 25 February 1971 *(Cl)*.

L ST JAMES [CLC] op 2 March 1874 *(CLC)*; clo 1 January 1917 *(RCG)*.

L SOUTH PARKWAY op 11 June 2006 *(Merseyrail leaflet)*; still open.
Also see Section 7, Non-rail.

LIVERPOOL ROAD Newcastle-under-Lyne [NS] op 1 May 1905 *(NS)*; HALT; clo 2 March 1964 *(RM April)*. NS co tt 1910: NEWCASTLE L R HALT.

LIVERPOOL ROAD – see KIDSGROVE.

LIVERPOOL STREET London.
For main line station see under London.

LIVERPOOL STREET [Met] op 12 July 1875* *(T 12th)* as BISHOPSGATE; renamed 1 November 1909 *(RCG)*; still open.
* = Met service had begun 1 February 1875, using platform in main; now switched to own station.

LIVERPOOL STREET [Cen] op 28 July 1912 *(T 29th)*; still open.

LIVERSEDGE
LIVERSEDGE [LY] op 18 July 1848 *(co n LY)*; L CENTRAL 2 June 1924 *(Rly Gaz 23 May)* to 12 June 1961 *RM April)*; clo 14 June 1965 *(RM June)*.

L SPEN [LNW] op 1 October 1900 *(LNW Officers 39764)*; SPEN added 2 June 1924 *(Rly Gaz 23 May)*; clo 5 October 1953 *(RM November)*.
LNW dates suggests it was briefly L LITTLETOWN before L SPEN.

LIVINGSTON
LIVINGSTON [NB] op 12 November 1849 *(Edin- line)*; see 1850 November 29**; clo 1 November 1948 *(Cl)*.
LIVINGSTONE in tt 1875 to 1925 *(Cl)* and thus *hb* 1862 until 1904.

L NORTH op 24 March 1986 *(RM May)*; same site as 1849 to 1948 station; still open.

L SOUTH op 6 October 1984 *(RM December)*; SOUTH added 24 March 1986; still open.

LLAFAR [GW] op 1 March 1932 *(Cl 29)*; HALT; clo 4 January 1960 *(RM March)*; {Arenig – Trawsfynydd}.

LLANABER [Cam] first in *Brad* July 1914; HALT until 6 May 1968 *(GW H)*; aot request; still open.

LLANARTHNEY [LNW] op 1 June 1865**; became HALT 1954 *(Brad)*; clo 9 September 1963 *(T 9th)*.

LLANBADARN [VoR] (ng) op 22 December 1902 ** (see for line history); to preservation 1989.

LLANBEDR
LLANBEDR [GW] op 9 July 1923 *(GW H)* as TALWRN BACH; HALT until 6 May 1968 *(GW H)*; renamed L 8 May 1978 *(GW H)*; aot request; still open.
Also see PENSARN.

LLANBEDR GOCH [LNW] op 24 May 1909 *(LNW Officers 42542)*; clo 22 September 1930**.

LLANBERIS

LLANBERIS [LNW] op 1 July 1869 *(Carnarvon 3rd)*; for closure see 1939 September★★. LNW co tt 1900, LMS tt 1930, and *Brad* 1903/4 to closure, but not *hb*: L for SNOWDON.

LLANBERIS [Snowdon Mountain] (ng; rack) op 6 April 1896★★; still open.

LLANBETHERY [TV] op 1 May 1905 *(Cowbridge)*; see 1904★★ (HALT in *IA*); clo 12 July 1920 *(RCG)*.

LLANBISTER ROAD [LNW] first in *Brad* June 1868 but perhaps in use earlier since it was at first only a market stop and table was now remodelled★; full use 1 December 1868 (given as op date by *LNW Officers 3727*); HALT 28 September 1964 to 5 May 1969 *(Cl)*; aot request; still open.
★ = *LNW Officers 1709* (13 December 1866) reported that Central Wales had put up platform here and proposed to stop trains Thursdays, for Knighton Market; one official deputed to inspect and report – no decision yet.

LLANBRADACH [Rhy]

LLANBRADACH op 1 March 1893 *(Rhy)*; still open.

L COLLIERY (non-tt): op by September 1928 *(U)*; miners; still in use 31 May 1948 wtt; {Llanbradach – Ystrad Mynach}.

LLANBRYNMAIR [Cam] op 5 January 1863★★; clo 14 June 1965 *(RM July)*.

LLANCAIACH [GW]
op 5 January 1858 *(RAIL 253/367)* as LLANCAICH (NELSON); became L & N 1865 *(Brad, GW table)* and thus GW co tt 1869; spelling of L altered 1872 *(hb)*, 1876 *(Brad)*, 1874/81 GW co tt; became L 1893/4 *(Brad)*; clo 1 July 1912 *(RAIL 253/482)* replaced by Nelson & Llancaiach, 13 chains nearer Quakers Yard. In GW/Rhy table in *Brad* always L JUNCTION.

LLANDAF [TV] op 9 October 1840★★ as LLANDAFF; was L for WHITCHURCH from 26 October 1896 *(hbl 29th)*; spelling altered and 'for W' dropped 12 May 1980 tt *(Cl)*; still open.

LLANDANWG [GW]
op 8 November 1929 *(GW H)*; HALT until 6 May 1968 *(GW H)*; aot request; still open.

LLANDARCY [GW]

LLANDARCY op 22 September 1924 *(hbl 53)*; PLATFORM; clo 4 October 1947 *(Cl)*; {Briton Ferry – Llangyfelach goods}.

L PRIVATE PLATFORM (non-tt): op 7 July 1919 as LONLAS, as result of *GW Agreement dated 3 July 1919* to run trains to/from Swansea East Dock for National Oil Refineries Ltd workmen; renamed about 1923; clo 4 May 1925 *(U)*; {Court Sart – Llandarcy}.

LLANDDERFEL [GW]
op 1 April 1868 *(Carnarvon 4th)*; LLANDERFEL until 27 October 1908 *(hbl 29th)*; clo 14 December 1964★★.

LLANDEBIE – see LLANDYBIE.

LLANDECWYN [GW]
op 18 November 1935 *(wtt supp)*; HALT until 6 May 1968 *(GW H)*; aot request; still open.

LLANDEILO

LLANDEILO [GW] op 26 January 1857 *(Carmarthen 23rd)*; LLANDILO until 1968/72 tt; still open. Local press called it station at Gurry Fach.

LLANDILO BRIDGE

LLANDILO BRIDGE [LNW] op 1 June 1865★★; clo 9 September 1963 *(T 9th)*.

LLANDENNY [GW]
op October 1857★★; clo 30 May 1955★★.

LLANDINAM [Cam] op 2 September 1859 *(Cam)*; clo 31 December 1962 *(T 31st)*.

LLANDOGO

See ST BRIAVELS.

L HALT [GW] op 9 March 1927 *(co n dated 'March')*; clo 5 January 1959 *(T 5th)*; {Tintern – St Briavels}.

LLANDOUGH [TV] op 13 June 1904 *(Penarth)*; see 1904★★; clo 3 June 1918 *(RCG)*; {Cardiff – Penarth Dock}.

LLANDOVERY [Vale of Towy Joint] op 1 April 1858 *(co ½ T 29 July)*; still open.

LLANDOW

LLANDOW [Barry] op 1 May 1915 (co instructions to staff – D. Steggles, *Chron*); HALT; clo 15 June 1964 *(RM Aug.)*.

L WICK ROAD [GW] op 19 April 1943 *(hbl 20)*; HALT; clo 15 June 1964 *(RM August)*; {Llantwit Major – Southerndown Road}. Pre-opening Glue Pot Bridge *(RAC)*.

LLANDRE [Cam] op 23 June 1864 *(Carnarvon 25th)* as LLANFIHANGEL; renamed 1 August 1916 *(hbl 26 October)*; clo 14 June 1965 *(RM July)*.

LLANDRILLO [GW] op 16 July 1866 *(GW; Rtn- line)*; clo 14 December 1964★★.

LLANDRINDOD [LNW] op 1 December 1865★★; was L WELLS from 1867 *(Brad)* but still L in index (and thus LNW co tt 1868) to 12 May 1980 tt *(Cl)*; HALT 30 December 1968 to 5 May 1969 *(Cl)*; still open. *Hb* added WELLS 1890.

LLANDRINIO ROAD [SM] op 2 June 1871 *(D&C 11)*; see 1866 August 13★★ (Criggion branch) for full details; finally clo October 1932.

LLANDUDNO [LNW]

LLANDUDNO op 1 October 1858 *(Carnarvon 2nd)*; new station 1 July 1903 *(RCG)*; still open.

L JUNCTION: op 1 October 1858 (included in tt for branch *Carnarvon 2 October*, but not in main line table until 30 October, for November service); first in *Brad* November (L itself there October). Some weeks prior to October 1859 branch trains worked from Conway (evidence of accident report); in April 1860 decided to develop JUNCTION as proper interchange, due to congestion at Conway. At times branch worked by horses (financial difficulties), certainly during winter of 1862; permanently loco-hauled by October 1863 when decided to ease curve at junction (all from *Carnarvon*). Re-sited on deviation 1 November 1897 *(co ½ Rly Times 12 February 1898)*; still open.

LLANDULAS

LLANDULAS [LNW] op 1 July 1889 *(co ½ Rly Times 10 August)*; clo 1 December 1952 *(RM January 1953)*. Also see LLYSFAEN.

LLANDYBIE [GW] op 26 January 1857 *(Carmarthen 23rd)* as LLANDEBIE; spelling altered 3 May 1971 *(Cl)*; still open

LLANDYSSUL [GW] op 3 June 1864 *(Cardiff T 10th)* as LLANDYSSIL; became LLANDYSSUL

17 December 1918 *(RCG)*; clo 15 September 1952
(RM November). [LLANDYSUL later, goods only.]
LLANELLI {map 82}
LLANELLI [GW] op 11 October 1852 *(T 12th)*;
LLANELLY until 1966 *(RM June – 'in future')*; still
open. In Llandovery table in *Brad* was L HIGH
STREET 1877/8 to 1906/7.

LLANELLY [Llanelly; GW] first in *Brad* April 1853;
beside South Wales, later GW, station; needed because
Llanelly was standard gauge line, South Wales broad;
clo 1 September 1879, service diverted over direct
route to main station *(S Wales 1st).*

LLANELLY DOCK [Llanelly; GW]
op 1 May 1850**; clo 1 September 1879 *(S Wales 1st)* –
trains diverted to main station.

LLANERCH AYRON [GW] op 2 October 1911 *(GWH)*;
HALT; clo 12 February 1951 *(Cl)* – see 1951**.

LLANERCHYMEDD [LNW]
op 1 February 1866 *(co ½ T 6 April)*; clo 7 December
1964 *(RM March 1965).* Spelling as co tt, BR tt, *Brad*,
tickets; LLANERCH-Y-MEDD was RCH version.

LLANFABON ROAD [TV]
op 10 October 1904 *(Nelson)*; see 1904**;
clo 12 September 1932 *(RM October).*

LLANFAIR CAEREINION [Cam] (ng)
op 6 April 1903 *(D&C 11)*; clo 9 February 1931 *(Cl).*

LLANFAIRFECHAN [LNW]
op 1 May 1860 (L. Hughes, *Llanfairfechan, a Pictorial
History*, Cyhoeddiad Mei (Pen-y-Groes), p.50);
aot request; still open.

LLANFAIRPWLL
LLANFAIR [LNW] op 1 August 1848 *(co n T 18 July)*;
clo 14 February 1966 *(RM April).*
Reop 29 May 1970 as **LLANFAIR P G** to serve as
temporary terminus following fire damage to Britannia
Bridge *(Cl)*; clo 31 January 1972 *(Cl).*
Reop 7 May 1973 as **LLANFAIRPWLL** *(Cl)*;
aot request; still open.

LLANFALTEG [GW] op 12 July 1875 *(Whitland)*;
clo 10 September 1962 *(Cl).*

LLANFAREDD [GW] op 7 May 1934 *(Cl 29)*;
HALT; clo 31 December 1962 *(T 31st).*

LLANFECHAIN [Cam]
first in *Brad* August 1865 (works authorised 12 October
1864); clo 18 January 1965 *(RM March).*
Became HALT 1941a *hb*, so shown 1956 *hb* and GW
ticket *(JB)*, but not in *Brad*, nor GW co tt 1942, 1947.

LLANFIHANGEL
– see LLANDRE; LLANVIHANGEL.

LLANFYLLIN [Cam]
op in July 1863**; clo 18 January 1965 *(RM March).*

LLANFYNYDD [Wrexham & Minera Joint]
op 2 May 1898 *(Wrexham 7th)*; clo 27 March 1950
(RM May).

LLANFYRNACH [GW] op 12 July 1875 *(Whitland)*;
clo 10 September 1962 *(Cl).*

LLANGADOG [Vale of Towy Joint] op 1 April 1858
(D&C 11; co ½ T 29 July- line); until 1959
LLANGADOCK *(Brad)*, but RCH made change *hb*
September 1958a; HALT 6 September 1965 to 5 May
1969 *(Cl)*; still open.

LLANGAMMARCH [LNW]
first in *Brad* September 1867; L WELLS 1883 tt *(JS;
RCG ref July)* to 12 May 1980 tt *(Cl)*; still open.

LLANGEDWYN [Cam] op 6 January 1904 *(RCG)*;
became HALT 1949a *hb* but not in *Brad*;
clo 15 January 1951 *(Cl)* – see 1951**.

LLANGEFNI [LNW]
op 8 March 1865* (G. Wynn Griffith, *The Day Before
Yesterday* – a history of nineteenth century Anglesey,
1988); permanent station, north of first, op 1 February
1866; clo 7 December 1964 *(RM March 1965).*
* = *LNW* says 12 March but that a Sunday and no Sunday
service.

LLANGEINOR
LLANGEINOR [GW] op 25 October 1886 *(Brad Sh
1887- line)*; clo 1 January 1917 *(GW notice dated
22 December 1916)*; reop 1 January 1919 *(GW Circular
2647)*; clo 9 February 1953 *(T 23 January).*
Also see BETTWS, for [PT] station .

LLANGELYNIN [GW] op 7 July 1930 *(GWH)*;
HALT until 6 May 1968 *(Cl)*; following decision that
not worth providing lighting ordered by Health & Safety
Executive for the platform, engineer insisted on closure
'as from Saturday 26 October 1991' (last train 25th)
(BLN 680, 682); {Tonfanau – Llwyngwril}.

LLANGENNECH [GW] op 1 May 1850**;
aot request; HALT from 1959 *(Brad)* to 5 May 1969
(Cl); still open. Originally single platform, west of level
crossing; when line doubled about July 1909, replaced
by platforms on each line, east of crossing; owing to
freak of chance, first was 3m 1ch from original Llandeilo
junction, second same distance from revised junction
(line remiled 7 July 1913) *(RAC).*

LLANGLYDWEN [GW] op 12 July 1875 *(Whitland)*;
clo 10 September 1962 *(Cl).*

LLANGOLLEN [GW] op 2 June 1862 *(Rtn)*;
re-sited 8 May 1865 *(D&C 11)*, when line extended;
clo 18 January 1965**.

LLANGOLLEN ROAD [GW]
op 14 October 1848 *(Shrewsbury 13th)*, to provide rail
connection with road service to Llangollen;
clo 1 July 1862 *(co n Shrewsbury 4th)*, though logically
should have clo when Llangollen branch op 2 June;
{Chirk – Cefn}. Whitehurst on nearby site later.

LLANGORSE LAKE [GW]
op 9 July 1923 *(GWH)*; HALT; clo 31 December 1962
(T 31st); {Trefeinon – Talyllyn}.

LLANGOWER [GW] op 10 June 1929 *(Chester
division annual report 1929)*; HALT; clo 18 January
1965**; {Llanderfel – Llanuwchllyn}.

LLANGWYLLOG [LNW] op 1 February 1866
(source as for Llangefni), though not in *Brad* until April
1866; clo 7 December 1964 *(RM March 1965).* Prior
to 1890 was LLANGWILLOG in *hb*.

LLANGYBI near Lampeter [GW] first in *Brad* August
1869 for markets and fairs; aot request; e.g. January
1874 trains stopped on Lampeter and Tregarron
market days and on Mondays; in 1875 all days service
began (one way January, both June, according to *Brad*);
clo 22 February 1965 *(Cl).*

LLANGYBI near Pwllheli [LNW]
first in *Brad* October 1870, Tuesdays only; all days
January 1872*; clo 7 December 1964 *(RM March 1965)*.
See 1867 September 2** for earlier trains through here.
In *hb* 1872 as L CROSSING.
* = *LNW Officers 7255*, 15 November 1871: considered
suggestion that market stop here should be transferred to
Rhosgill but decided to recommend keeping Llangybi and
stopping all days.

LLANGYFELACH [GW]
op 9 July 1923 *(hb amendment leaflet dated 25 October
1923)*; clo 22 September 1924 *(Cl)*; {*IA* goods}.

LLANGYNLLO [LNW] first in *Brad* March 1866;
as LLANGUNLLO; HALT 6 September 1965 to
5 May 1969 *(Cl)*; spelling altered 12 May 1980 tt *(Cl)*;
aot request; still open. Many sources say this opened as
Llyncoch but not thus in *Brad*; perhaps local name.

LLANGYNOG [Cam] op 6 January 1904 *(RCG)*;
clo 15 January 1951 *(Cl)* – see 1951**.

LLANGYNWYD [GW] first in *Brad* September 1865
as LLANGONOYD; new station 1897; clo 1 January
1917 *(GW notice dated 22 Dec. 1916)*; reop 1 January
1919 *(GW Circular 2657)*; name altered 1935 *(Cl)*;
reduced to schools only use 22 June 1970; aot request;
last school train 14 July 1970 *(RM September)*.

LLANHARAN
LLANHARAN (a) [GW] op 1 September 1899 *(RCG)*;
clo 2 November 1964 *(Cl)*.
LLANHARAN (b) op 10 December 2007 *(BLN
26 January 2008, corr)*; still open.

LLANHARRY [TV] first in *Brad* July 1871, where
was L POINT until 1875; re-sited 2 March 1891
(RCG); clo 26 November 1951 *(RM January 1952)*.

LLANHILLETH
LLANHILLETH (a) [Monmouthshire] first in *Brad*
August 1853; last there October 1861.
LLANHILLETH (b) [GW] op 1 October 1901 *(RCG)*;
clo 30 April 1962 *(T 6th)*.
LLANHILLETH (c) op Sunday 27 April 2008 *(Arriva
Trains Wales, via internet and M. Preskett)*; still open.

LLANIDLOES [Cam] op 2 September 1859 *(Cam)*;
re-sited by January 1862 – line extended to Joint
Llanidloes & Newtown and Mid Wales (later Cam)
station; clo 31 December 1962 *(T 31st)*.

LLANILAR [GW] op 12 August 1867 *(Merioneth 17th)*;
clo 14 December 1964**.

LLANION [GW] op 1 May 1905 *(GW H)*; HALT;
clo 1 October 1908 (Thursday) *(Cl)*;
{Pembroke – Pembroke Dock}.

LLANISHEN [Rhy]
op 1 April 1871 *(Rhy; T 5th- line)*; still open.

LLANMORLAIS [LNW] op 1 March 1884 *(LNW
Officers 25714)*; clo 5 January 1931 *(Cl)*.

LLANNERCH [LNW] (non-tt): private;
op 5 October 1858; clo December 1871;
{St Asaph – Trefnant} *(U)*.

LLANPUMPSAINT [GW] op 28 March 1864
(GW- line); clo 22 February 1965 *(Cl)*.

LLANRHAIADR near Ruthin [LNW]
op 1 March 1862 *(D&C 11; co ½ T 14th- line)*;
clo 2 February 1953 *(RM March)*.

LLANRHAIADR MOCHNANT [Cam]
op 6 January 1904 *(RCG)*; clo 15 January 1951 *(Cl)*
– see 1951**.

LLANRHYSTYD ROAD [GW] op 12 August 1867
(Merioneth 17th); clo 14 December 1964**.

LLANRWST
For first station here see NORTH LLANRWST.
L op 29 July 1989 *(BLN 616)*; originally built for
Eisteddfod; at 11 m 57 ch; still open.

LLANSAINTFFRAID – see GLAN CONWY.

LLANSAMLET
LLANSAMLET [Mid] op 21 February 1860 *(Mid;
Mining Journal 25th- line)*; clo March 1875**.
LLANSAMLET op 27 June 1994 *(BLN 735)*; between
two earlier GW sites, below, at 212 m 36 ch; still open.
L NORTH [GW] op 1 April 1852 *(The Cambrian
26 March)* at 211m 40ch; re-sited to west, at 212m 47ch,
1 January 1885 *(hbl 12 February)*; NORTH added
1950 *(Cl)*; clo 2 November 1964 *(Cl)*.

LLANSANTFFRAID near Oswestry [Cam]
op in July 1863**; LLANSAINTFFRAIDD until 1921
(RCG ref October); clo 18 January 1965 *(RM March)*.

LLANSILIN ROAD [Cam] op 6 January 1904 *(RCG)*;
clo 15 January 1951 *(Cl)* – see 1951**.

LLANSTEPHAN [GW] op 6 March 1933 *(Cl 29)*;
HALT; clo 31 December 1962 *(T 31st)*;
{Erwood – Boughrood}.

LLANTARNAM
LLANTARNAM (a) [Monmouthshire], on line to
Newport Mill Street, first in *Brad* May 1853; clo,
1 August 1880, when line diverted *(co n Merlin 30 July)*.
LLANTARNAM (b) [GW], on line to Newport High
Street, trains first shown August 1878 *Brad*;
clo 30 April 1962 *(T 6th)*.
Note: both stations briefly open together, not
differentiated by name in *Brad*.

LLANTRISANT (at first LLANTRISSANT)
LLANTRISANT [GW] op 19 June 1850**;
LLANTRISSANT until mid-1890s; clo 2 November
1964 *(Cl)*. Op notice, *Brad* for some years, GW co tt
1865: L for COWBRIDGE.
LLANTRISANT [TV] op 18 September 1865 *(T 20th)*;
amalgamated with GW August 1891 *(Cl)*.

LLANTWIT FARDRE [TV] op by January 1867,
when in co tt *(Nelson)* – not in *Brad* until June 1867.
FARDRE added 8 October 1936 *(Cl)*;
clo 31 March 1952 *(Cl)*.

LLANTWIT MAJOR
(a) [Barry] op 1 December 1897 *(Glam; Colliery 3rd- line)*;
clo 15 June 1964 *(RM August)*.
(b) op 12 June 2005 *(Rly Obs August)*; same site;
still open.

LLANUWCHLLYN [GW] op 4 August 1868
(Carnarvon 11th); clo 18 January 1965** *(RM March)*.

LLANVAIR [Newport, Abergavenny & Hereford]
op 2 January 1854 *(T 29 December 1853- line)*;
clo 1 October 1854 (Sunday) *(Cl)*;
{Nantyderry – Penpergwm}.

LLANVIHANGEL MON [GW]
op 2 January 1854 *(T 29 December 1853- line)*;
originally LLANFIHANGEL; spelling changed

1 January 1900 (hbl 26 October 1899); MON added
10 December 1910 (Cl; RCH dist ref December 1911);
clo 9 June 1958 (Cl).

LLANWERN [GW]
first in *Brad* October 1855; clo 12 September 1960 (Cl).

LLANWNDA
For earliest service see PWLLHELI ROAD, then name
for station here.
LLANWNDA [LNW] op 2 September 1867★★ (co ½
T 10 October- line); clo 7 December 1964 (RM March
1965). Shown as LLANWYNDA in tt with LNW Officers,
13 July 1870.

LLANWRDA [Vale of Towy Joint]
op 1 April 1858 (D&C 11; co ½ T 29 July- line) as
LAMPETER ROAD; HALT 6 September 1965 to
5 May 1969 (Cl); still open. Became L for PUMPSAINT
1 February 1868 (RCH dist 19th) and thus Brad until
1891/3.

LLANWRTYD [LNW] op 6 May 1867 (LNW Officers);
L WELLS until 12 May 1980 tt (Cl) – thus body of
Brad from start and LNW co tt 1868, though both just
L in index at start; still open.

LLANYBLODWELL {map 80}
LLANYBLODWELL (a) [Potteries, Shrewsbury &
North Wales] op 18 April 1870; see 1866 August 13★★;
finally clo 22 June 1880. Blodwell Junction here later.
LLANYBLODWELL (b) [Cam] op 6 January 1904
(RCG); clo 15 January 1951 (Cl) – see 1951★★.

LLANYBYTHER [GW]
op 1 January 1866 (GW- line; in tt for 12 January,
Milford); clo 22 February 1965 (Cl).

LLANYCEFN [GW]
op 19 September 1876 (S Wales 22nd- line);
clo 1 January 1883 (Rtn); reop 11 April 1895 (Cl);
clo 8 January 1917 (co n GW book); reop 12 July 1920
(GW Mag July); clo 25 October 1937★★; {map 81}.

LLANYMYNECH
LLANYMYNECH [Cam] op 1 May 1860 (Cam; co ½
T 9 August- line); clo 18 January 1965 (RM March).
LLANYMYNECH [SM] op 13 August 1866★★; finally
clo 6 November 1933 (Cl). L JUNCTION 1912 on (hb).
LLECHRYD – see BUILTH ROAD.

LLETTY BRONGU [PT] op 14 February 1898
(GW); clo 12 September 1932 (RM October).

LLIWDY [Corris] (ng) (non-tt): occasional stop;
see 1874★★; line clo 1 January 1931 (Thursday).

LLONG [LNW]
op 14 August 1849 (D&C 11; co ½ T 16 August- line);
clo 1 January 1917 (T 22 December 1916); reop 5 May
1919 (RCG); clo 30 April 1962 (RM June).

LLWYDCOED [GW] op 2 November 1853 (GW;
Cardiff & M J 5th- line); clo 31 December 1962
(T 31st). In hb as LLYDCOED (1862),
LLURYDCOED (1867), correct 1872.

LLWYNGWERN [Corris] (ng)
For first service through here, see 1874★★.
LLWYNGWERN first in Brad May 1884 (passed fit by
Inspector 6 March); clo 1 January 1931 (Thursday) (Cl).

LLWYNGWRIL [Cam] op 24 October 1863 (T 28th);
aot request; still open.

LLWYNYPIA [TV] first in Brad May 1871 as

LLWYNPIA; spelling amended 1883 (hb), 1908 (Brad);
still open. L & TONYPANDY until 9 March 1908
(RCG) but had been L for T in Brad.

LLYNCLYS [Cam] op 1 May 1860 (Cam; co ½
T 9 August- line); clo 18 January 1965 (RM March).

LLYS [GW]
op 4 June 1934 (Cl 29); HALT; clo 18 January 1965★★.

LLYSFAEN [LNW]
op 1 August 1862 (Llandulas) as LLANDULAS;
renamed 1 July 1889 (RCG); clo 5 January 1931 (Cl).

LOANHEAD [NB]
op 23 July 1874★★; clo 1 May 1933 (RM March).

LOBLEY HILL (non-tt): unofficial stop on line to
Tanfield Moor (which see for nature of service)
op 18 June 1842 (Consett).

LOCH AWE
LOCH AWE (a) [Cal] op 1 July 1880 (T 2nd- line);
clo 1 November 1965 (its stretch not affected by
landslide which closed some nearby prematurely).
LOCH AWE (b) op 1 May 1985 (BLN 508); still open.

LOCH EIL OUTWARD BOUND
op 6 May 1985 (BLN 516 corr); aot request; still open.

LOCH LEVEN [NB] op soon after 20 September
1860, goods opening (Tayside) as KINROSS;
renamed 16 October 1871 (Cl; RCG ref October);
clo 1 September 1921 (Thursday) (RCG).

LOCH OF ABOYNE – see ABOYNE.

LOCH TAY [Cal]
op 1 April 1886 (Cal) as LT KILLIN PIER;
K P dropped 1 October 1895 (RCG); see
1921 April/May★★; trains last shown June 1921 (but
likely that already closed); August 1921 (without trains)
says see p.855 for Loch Tay steamers; p.855 shows road
service to/from Killin; trains again March 1922 (Brad);
summer only at clo 9 September 1939 (Saturday) (Cl).

LOCHAILORT [NB]
op 1 April 1901 (RCG); aot request; still open.

LOCHANHEAD [GSW] op 7 November 1859
(Dumfries 5th); clo 25 September 1939 (Cl).

LOCHARBRIGGS [Cal]
op 1 September 1863 (co ½ T 25 March 1864- line);
clo 19 May 1952 (RM June).

LOCHBURN [NB]
first in Brad May 1890; clo 1 January 1917 (RCG).

LOCHEARNHEAD
For first station of this name see BALQUHIDDER.
LOCHEARNHEAD [Cal] (second of name) op 1 July
1904 (RCG) as terminus; became through station when
line extended to enlarged Balquhidder 1 May 1905;
clo 1 January 1917 (RCG); reop 6 January 1919 (RCG);
see 1921 April/May★★; clo 1 October 1951 (RM Nov.).

LOCHEE [Cal]
LOCHEE op 10 June 1861 (Dundee);
clo 10 January 1955 (T 28 December 1954).
L WEST op 10 June 1861 (Dundee) as VICTORIA;
renamed CAMPERDOWN 1 May 1862 (Cl),
LW 1 February 1896 (hbl 23 January);
clo 1 January 1917 (RCG).

LOCHEILSIDE [NB]
LOCHEILSIDE op 1 April 1901 (RCG); still open.
Above is only spelling seen Brad but hbl of 29 January

1914 suggests it had once been LOCHIELSIDE.
Non-tt: wtts 6 March 1967 and 7 May 1979 show stop
at milepost 13¾, between here and Glenfinnan, for
domestic purposes *(IU; G. Borthwick)*.
LOCHGELLY [NB]: op 4 September 1848
(co n Perthshire Courier 31 August); still open.
LOCHLUICHART [High]
op private for Lochluichart Lodge 19 August 1870,
as L LODGE; re-sited and made public station 1 July
1871 *(High)*; again re-sited, on deviation for HEP
scheme, 3 May 1954 *(Cl)*; aot request; still open.
LOHMABEN [Cal]
op 1 September 1863 *(co ½ T 25 March 1864- line)*;
clo 19 May 1952 *(RM June)*.
LOCHSIDE – see LOCHWINNOCH.
LOCHSKERROW [PPW Jt]:
non-tt for private and railwaymen's use by 1871, when
Saturday call in wtt; used for curling match in December
1875; 'P' in *hb* 1904 ('P' added since 1900); Saturday
call shown *LMS wtt notice* 5 April 1947; added to public
tt 13 June 1955 *(Cl 29)*; in tt was accompanied by note
'no public access'; removed from public tt 9 September
1963 *(Cl)*; last wtt for line, 7 September 1964, shows
unadvertised stops both ways that might have had
passenger use – line clo 14 June 1965. Much used
by anglers; passengers had to sign indemnity form
(Little SW Scot; Jack Hunter, *Galloway Byways,*
Dumfries and Galloway Library, 2006 pp.41-3).
HALT on LMS ticket *(JB)* and in *hb* 1938 on; just L in
Brad and BR tt 1962; aot LOCH SKERROW in *hb*;
{New Galloway – Gatehouse of Fleet}.
LOCHWINNOCH [GSW]
LOCHWINNOCH (a) op 12 August 1840 *(co n Glasgow
Herald 10th)*; renamed LOCHSIDE 1 June 1905 *(hbl
27 April)*; clo 4 July 1955. Reop 27 June 1966 *(AZ)*,
still LOCHSIDE, renamed LOCHWINNOCH
13 May 1985; still open.
LOCHWINNOCH (b) op 1 June 1905 *(RCG)*;
clo 27 June 1966 *(RM August)*; always Lochwinnoch.
LOCKERBIE [Cal]
op 10 September 1847 *(co n True Line)*; still open.
LOCKINGTON [NE]: line op 7 October 1846**, nd,
May 1848 *(Topham)*; clo 13 June 1960 *(RM July)*.
LOCKWOOD [LY]: line op 1 July 1850 *(T 8th)*, nd,
January 1851; still open.
LODDISWELL [GW]
op 19 December 1893 *(co n Kingsbridge)*; became HALT
6 February 1961; clo 16 September 1963 *(Cl)*.
LODGE – see THE LODGE.
LODGE FARM – see RAGLAN FOOTPATH.
LODGE HILL [GW] op 5 April 1870 *(Shepton 8th)*;
clo 9 September 1963 *(Weston 13th)*.
LOFTHOUSE & OUTWOOD
LOFTHOUSE & OUTWOOD [GN] first in *Brad*
October 1858; & O added 1865/6; clo 13 June 1960
(RM July
LOFTHOUSE & OUTWOOD [Methley Joint]
op 1 May 1876 *(D&C 8)* as L JOINT;
JOINT dropped 1881 tt; & O added 1888 tt *(Cl)*;
clo 17 June 1957 *(Cl)*. *Brad*, LY tables, first shown as L,
became L & WRENTHORPE 1859/60, back to L

1874/5, to L & O 1905/6.
Outwood nearby later.
LOFTHOUSE-IN-NIDDERDALE [Nidd]
used by reservoir workmen from 14 July 1904 *(U)*;
op to public 12 September 1907 *(Rtn)*;
clo 1 January 1930 (Wednesday) *(Cl)*.
LOFTUS [NE] op 1 April 1875 *(NE)* as;
clo 2 May 1960 *(RM June)*.
Note: was LOFTHOUSE before op to passengers.
LOGIERIEVE [GNS] op 18 July 1861 *(GNS)* as
NEWBURGH ROAD; renamed 1862 tt *(Cl)*;
clo 4 October 1965 *(Rly Obs November)*.
LOGIN [GW] op 12 July 1875 *(GW- line)*;
clo 10 September 1962 *(Cl)*.
LONDESBOROUGH [NE]:
line op 4 October 1847**, nd, May 1848 *(Topham)*;
originally SHIPTON & L; became S April 1864 co tt
(JS), L January 1867 co tt *(JS; RCG ref January)*;
clo 29 November 1965 *(RM December)*.
LONDESBOROUGH PARK [NE] (non-tt):
op ?; private for George Hudson; clo January 1867;
{Nunburnholme – Londesborough} *(U)*.
LONDESBOROUGH ROAD – see Scarborough.

LONDON

*Stations listed below are termini and major central area
stations served by surface lines. Suburban and all
Underground and Docklands stations are listed under
their initial letters.*
*Early timetables tended just to have 'LONDON' or
e.g. 'EUSTON' on its own. Hb 1862 had 12 entries,
all 'LONDON'; they were also provided with separate
entries, such as 'EUSTON' 'same as London', under 'E'.*
BISHOPS ROAD – see PADDINGTON.
BISHOPSGATE [GE] op 1 July 1840 *(co n T 29 June)*
when line extended from Devonshire Street;
op as SHOREDITCH, renamed by Act of 27 July 1846
(JS); trains diverted to Liverpool Street 1 November
1875 *(co n T 28 October)*; some use for relief trains until
about 1879; {map 107}. *Brad*, e.g. 1846-7, had
B WITHOUT in Colchester table and B NORTH in
1873 (probably incorrect additions, *JS*); in 1840 just
LONDON and 1841 on just S or B.
BLACKFRIARS [SE] op 11 January 1864
(L; co n T 9th- line); replaced by Waterloo East,
1 January 1869 *(co n T 23 December 1868)*; {map 106}.
BLACKFRIARS [LCD] op 10 May 1886
(Kent Messenger 15th) as ST PAULS; renamed
1 February 1937 *(RCH dist 5 January)*; still open.
BLACKFRIARS BRIDGE [LCD]
op 1 June 1864 *(co n T 30 May)*; clo 1 October 1885
(Thursday) *(Cl)*; {map 106}.
BRICKLAYERS ARMS [SE]
op 1 May 1844 *(T 2nd)*. See article by Canon Fellows,
RM 1944, pp. 209-12, 272-4: aim was to provide station
nearer West End, to which omnibus connections would
be provided; would also save SE and Croydon companies
need to pay tolls they considered too high, for using the
Greenwich's line to London Bridge. Diversion of traffic
caused the Greenwich to reduce tolls. Thus the Croydon

stopped using after 31 March 1845. SE continued to use; services from London Bridge and here were joined at 'New Cross' (letter *T 1 August 1845*) – was this writer's version of North Kent Junction, or point further out? At end of October 1846 ordinary SE passenger service withdrawn. They continued to attach passenger coach to 11pm goods from B A for people catching morning steamers from Folkestone and Dover; this last in tt January 1851.

Meanwhile, SE had tried to tap local traffic: from 1 September 1849 a shuttle service was run to North Kent Junction to connect with Greenwich and Kent trains (use detailed in *SE co ½ T 20 September*, which refers, not entirely accurately, to B A branch being 'opened' now to 'the junction station with the North Kent line').

21 August 1850 shunting engine hit a wagon into a pillar, bringing down roof *(T 22nd)*. SE notice, *T 22nd* said from 'this day' they would cease to use B A, report in next day's paper confirmed had done. Probably end of North Kent Junction. No reference to B L in SE notices of alterations for 16 October and 1 November, but notice in paper of 3 December does give fares and times from here to North Kent line and Greenwich; this suggests use again from start of December. Last in tt January 1852.

1856: special first-class trains from here so people from West End could go to Sandhurst 3 May (to see Queen lay foundation stone of Wellington College) and 2 June for fête there *(co notices T 1, 28 May)*.

Early excursions. Christmas Day 1856 to/from principal SE stations *(co n T 15 December)*. 1857: Easter 'Holydays' afternoon trips to Blackheath *(SE n T April)* and regular weekly Monday morning trips, third-class only, to Ramsgate and Margate for 3s 6d (including admission to Tivoli Gardens) from 4 May to end October, by when Folkestone and Dover also possible destinations. Seems to have been end of series – SE's Christmas 1857 excursions from London Bridge.

7 March 1863: special took Prince of Wales to Gravesend to collect Princess Alexandra, his future wife, and brought pair back *(T 9th)*.

Reop for excursions, Sundays only, 12 June 1932 *(T 10th)*; last Sunday 10 September 1939 (based on introduction of emergency tt on 11th); {map 105}.

BROAD STREET [NL]
op 1 November 1865 *(T 2nd)*; station demolished and replaced by temporary platform 1985; clo 30 June 1986 *(RM September* – last train Friday 27 June).
Often B S (CITY) in *Brad* and thus LNW co tt 1874.

CANNON STREET [SE]
op 1 September 1866 *(co n T 28 August)*; clo at 3pm on 5 June 1926 (Saturday) for electrification *(T 5th)*, reop 28 June 1926; clo 5 August 1974 for track remodelling, reop 9 September 1974 *(Cl)*; still open.

CHARING CROSS [SE]
op 11 January 1864 *(co n T 9th)* from temporary platform in Villiers Street for Greenwich and Mid-Kent services only; main line services 1 May 1864 *(co n 22 April)*; clo 5 December 1905 after roof collapse, reop 19 March 1906 *(RM April)*; clo 24 July 1993 for

track remodelling, reop 16 August 1993 *(RM July* – planned dates); still open.

CITY THAMESLINK
op 29 May 1990 as ST PAULS T;
renamed 30 September 1991 *(AB Chron)*; still open.

DEVONSHIRE STREET MILE END [EC]
op 20 June 1839 *(T 14th, 19th)*; services extended to Shoreditch (later Bishopsgate) on 1 July 1840 but this station kept open; still in use 15 November 1840, when mentioned in report of accident *(T 17th)* and at 11 April 1841, when a drunk fell off the platform here *(Return)*; never appeared in *Brad*; probably replaced by MILE END (see under 'M') or clo soon after that opened; later Globe Road just to west (maps in P. Kay, *GE in Town & Country*, pt 3, Irwell 1996); {map 107}.

EUSTON [LNW]
op 20 July 1837 *(co n T 19th)*; still open.
Early indiscriminately L, E and E SQUARE in LNW co tts; E-GROVE in *Times* 10 April 1838 description of opening of an extension to line. *Brad* had just L in tables until 1844, though quoted hackney fares from Euston in 1840.

FENCHURCH STREET [GE]:
opening advertised for 2 August 1841, but actual use began 29 July *(T 2 August/Observer)*, when service extended from Minories; see 1849 March 31**; still open.

HOLBORN VIADUCT [LCD]
op 2 March 1874 *(co n T 2nd)*; clo 29 January 1990 (last train Friday 26th) *(T 27th)*.

HOLBORN VIADUCT LL [LCD]
op 1 August 1874 *(T 4th)* as SNOW HILL; renamed 1 May 1912 *(hbl 25 April)*; clo 1 June 1916 (Thursday) *(RCG)*; {map 106}.

KINGS CROSS: [GN]
services opened 7 August 1850 *(T 8th)* to a temporary station usually shown as MAIDEN LANE, though GN called it K C; line was extended to permanent K C 14 October 1852 *(T 15th)*; this was also used as Mid terminus from 1 February 1858 to 1 October 1868*; still open.
Main line local station added 18 December 1874, later absorbed into main *(KC)*.

* = article by P.J. Wylde in *Midland Record no. 24* claims that Midland had a separate station, north of the Regents Canal, between the GN goods depot and potato station. A Midland station is certainly shown on the maps included in the article but this is much more likely to have been for goods of some description. All contemporary evidence supports the accepted view that the Midland used the GN station. In addition, the site shown would have been so inconvenient that one would have expected hostile comment in both the railway and public press, but none has been seen. A notice issued by the Midland in the *Bedfordshire Times* 7 July 1868 said that main line trains would continue to run from the GN station at King's Cross until further notice (F.G. Cockman, *The Railway Age in Bedfordshire*, Bedfordshire Historical Record Society vol.53, p.61, 1974).

K C YORK ROAD: platform provided 1863 *(KC)*; new station 4 March 1879 *(T 6th)* *; clo 8 November 1976 *(Cl)*; briefly reop 3rd to 5th March 1977 *(Cl)*.

* = *KC* has re-sited 4 March 1878 (copying error? – 4 March too much of a co-incidence).

LONDON continued

K C SUBURBAN op 1 February 1878 *(L)*; incorporated into main station 5 March 1977.

K C FUNERAL STATION (non-tt, but advertised): train for consecration of Cemetery ran 10 July 1861 *(Friends of National Railway Museum Newsletter, Summer 2000)*; op to funeral parties 11 July 1861. Initially operated daily; from 1 August 1861, Mondays, Wednesdays and Fridays; from 14 February 1862, Fridays only; from 31 August 1862 Sundays (now allowed for working men's funerals) and Wednesdays, with occasional variations; from 1 January 1863 only occasional trains; last known ran 3 April 1863. Station was north of main and trains with coffins and mourners were run to Cemetery at Colney Hatch. See M. Dawes, *LRR,* October 1999.

Other non-tt use: excursions to the Great International Exhibition of 1862 were run to the GN goods depot and Midland coal depot (A.A. Jackson, *London's Termini,* p.60).

KINGS CROSS THAMESLINK
op 11 July 1983 (15th formal) *(RM September p. 378)* as K C MIDLAND (in tt as K C M City Line); renamed 16 May 1988 *(BR leaflet)*; clo 9 December 2007 (last train 8th), replaced by platforms under St Pancras International *(RM February 2008)*.

LIVERPOOL STREET: [GE] op 2 February 1874 *(T 2nd)* for some suburban trains and 1 November 1875 *(co n T 28 October)* for full use, including those previously terminating at Bishopsgate LL; [Met] used platform in main station from 1 February 1875 until 12 July 1875, when it opened own station, but connection used for excursions until 1904, removed 1907 *(London's Termini)*; clo on 24 April 1993 by bomb which destroyed most of glass roof, reop 26th *(RM October)*; still open.

LONDON BRIDGE {map 105}
London & Greenwich: see 1835 June** for pre-opening trials nearby; from 10 October 1836 passengers bought tickets here and walked along line to Bermondsey Street (no station) to board trains *(co n T 3rd)*; station came into use 1 December 1836 though formal opening did not occur until 14 December *(co n T 13th)*.
London & Croydon: op own part 5 June 1839.
Later: July 1844 – station made Joint; L & Greenwich and SE used original L & Croydon part on north, L & Croydon and L & Brighton used original L & Greenwich plus a new part.
2 August 1850 – Joint station divided *(SE co ½ T 17 Sept.)*. According to *T 2 August 1850* LBSC and SE had temporary stations to cover period of demolition of old joint station and building of new separate ones. LBSC described as being at end of area being cleared and having all necessary booking offices and waiting rooms, SE as abutting onto Tooley Street.
3 January 1851 – separate SE (low level section; arrival platform in use from 9 December 1850) and LBSC stations.
Through platforms added 11 January 1864, with opening of line to Charing Cross.

Amalgamated into one station 1928 by SR. Still open. Sometimes TOOLEY STREET early *(Brad* until 1844, *Tuck* 1843, co notices in *The Times* issued by London & Croydon; but not seen thus in SE tables, where it was just L at first). Later 'City Terminus' often added to name. London & Brighton / LBSC tables just LONDON until 1844.

LUDGATE HILL [LCD]
op 21 December 1864 *(co n T 21st)*; temporary station replaced by permanent 1 June 1865 *(L; co n T 2nd – is now open)*; clo early Saturday afternoon 2 March 1929 *(T 4th;* A.A. Jackson, *Chron)*.

MAIDEN LANE – see under KINGS CROSS.

MARYLEBONE [GC]
op 15 March 1899 *(T 16th)*; briefly closed by bombing in 1940 – see NEASDEN (under 'N'); still open.

MINORIES [Blackwall]
op 6 July 1840 *(co n T 29 June)*; service extended to Fenchurch Street 29 July 1841 but this kept – omitted from *Brad* about September 1841, when Fenchurch Street first included, but back about October 1841, so probably remained open; clo 15 February 1849 (Thursday), reop 9 September 1849 *(Cl,* and see 1849 March 31**)*; clo 24 October 1853 *(Cl)*; {map 108}.

MOORGATE
op 8 November 1976; still open. (See under 'M' for earlier history).

NINE ELMS [LSW]
op 21 May 1838 *(Salisbury 28th)*; clo 11 July 1848 *(co n T 10th)* when line extended to Waterloo. Often VAUXHALL in tts and co notices. Replaced by Vauxhall (under 'V').
A Royal Station was built here in 1854; re-sited 1876; used by troop trains during Boer War *(RM February 1901)*; Airey's maps of London, 1877 and 1894, show 'private station' as terminus of short branch to south of through line (original to north of it); not present on 1910 map.

PADDINGTON [GW]
op 4 June 1838 *(T 4th)*; re-sited, departure platforms op 16 January 1854 *(co n T 11th)*, arrival platforms 29 May 1854 *(co n T 26th)*; still open.
This now includes BISHOPS ROAD [GW/HC], opened 10 January 1863 *(co n Portfolio)*; amalgamated into main station 10 September 1933; *hb* 1936a called it P SUBURBAN.

PIMLICO [LBSC]
op 29 March 1858 *(co n T 27th, 30th)*; clo 1 October 1860 on extension of line to Victoria; {map 109}. Earliest company notices in *The Times* called it BATTERSEA SLOANE STREET TERMINUS, later BATTERSEA; PIMLICO first seen 6 April.

ST PANCRAS INTERNATIONAL [Mid]
op 1 October 1868 *(co n T 23 September)* for express service; last train from original station ran Friday 9 April 2004; clo for rebuilding for Eurostar (10th, 11th trains terminated at Luton); replaced by temporary 300 yards north, first used Monday 12 April *(Daily Telegraph 10th)*. Mid suburban service had begun 13 July 1868, using King's Cross Met *(T 14th)*.
Eurostar portion opened 14 November 2007 *(Daily*

Telegraph 15th), when I added to name; platforms below station opened 9 December 2007, replacing King's Cross Thameslink *(RM February 2008)*; all still open.

ST PAULS – see BLACKFRIARS.

SHOREDITCH – see BISHOPSGATE.

SNOW HILL – see HOLBORN VIADUCT LL.

VICTORIA {map 109}
op by [LBSC] 1 October 1860 *(co n T 1st)*. Also used by [LCD] until they opened their own, 25 August 1862 *(co n T 23rd)*. Two stations amalgamated 1924 to form one that is still open. Often 'West End Terminus' added in *Brad*.
Special facilities, on Platform 17, for passengers going to Southampton to catch Empire Flying Boat services, entered from Airways House without using station entrance, were opened 6 June 1939 *(T 7th)*; ended by War?

WATERLOO [LSW]:
main op 11 July 1848 *(T 12th)*; Windsor, alias North, station op 3 August 1860; South, or Main Line Suburban, op 16 December 1878 *(co n T 16th)*; all combined 1 October 1912; still open.
Usually W BRIDGE early.
There was a through line from here to SE line from London Bridge to Charing Cross. Platform was over Waterloo Road, owned by SE. Passed by BoT for passenger traffic at same time as Charing Cross extension but trains did not use until 6 July 1865, start of service from Euston to London Bridge via Willesden, Kensington, Waterloo (this platform) and Blackfriars (1864 station) *(co n T 6th, T item 7th)*; in LNW tables in *Brad* was NEW W; aim was to provide link north to south without need to cross London by road; 1 February 1867 replaced by Willesden–Waterloo–Cannon Street service *(co n T 30 January)*; 1 December 1867 LNW service cut back, now Willesden to main Waterloo *(LNW Officers)* but LSW Kensington to Cannon Street continued; this ceased 1 January 1868 owing to refusal of SE to work trains through link to their line *(co n T 26 December 1867, item 30th)*, last train ran 31 December 1867; line kept for occasional special use – e.g. Royal specials detailed under Woolwich Dockyard ran over it; (also see D. W. Winkworth, *Back Track*, August 2000); {map 106}.

W INTERNATIONAL op 14 November 1994 *(RM February 1995)* – unadvertised trial services from 17 August 1994 ; sometimes regarded as a separate station, sometimes part of main; closed 14 November 2007 – last train Tuesday 13th, service diverted to St Pancras *(Daily Telegraph 15th)*.

W NECROPOLIS (non-tt): op 13 November 1854; for funeral trains to Brookwood, which see; re-sited 16 February 1902; clo 15 May 1941 *(U)*. LONDON NECROPOLIS CO on *hb* 1904 to 1938 (inclusive).

WATERLOO EAST [SE]
op 1 January 1869 *(co n T 23 December 1868)* as W JUNCTION; renamed W 7 July 1935 *(RM Sept.)*, W E 2 May 1977 *(L)*; clo 24 July 1993 for track remodelling, reop 16 August 1993 *(RM July* – gave planned dates, which were followed – *BLN 713)*; still open.

LONDON & THAMESHAVEN OIL WHARVES
[LTS] (non-tt): op 1 January 1923; workmen; prob clo 9 June 1958; {Thameshaven branch};
alias HALT NO.3 or LATHOL *(Thames Haven)*.

LONDON BRIDGE
For main line station, see under LONDON.

LONDON BRIDGE [Nor] op 26 February 1900**; see 1922**; still open.

LONDON BRIDGE [Jub] op 7 October 1999 *(RM March 2000)*; still open.

LONDON CITY AIRPORT [Dock]
op 2 December 2005 *(LRR January 2006)*; still open.

LONDON DOCKS
The following were shown 'P' in *hb*, inclusive dates given, presumably available for boat trains:

EAST INDIA DOCKS [GE] 1877–90;

WEST INDIA DOCKS [London & India Docks] 1904–56.
Also see ROYAL GROUP OF DOCKS (under 'R').

LONDON FIELDS [GE] op 27 May 1872 *(co n T 25th)*; clo 22 May 1916**; reop 1 July 1919 *(T 20th)*; clo 13 November 1981 by fire *(RM January 1982)*; reop 29 September 1986 *(RM December)*; still open.

LONDON ROAD BRIGHTON [LBSC]
op 1 October 1877 *(LBSC)*;
BRIGHTON added 9 July 1923 *(SR)*; still open.

LONDON ROAD GUILDFORD [LSW]
op 2 February 1885 *(co n T 31 January)*;
GUILDFORD added 9 July 1923 *(Cl)*; still open.
LSW ticket *(JB)* has G L R.

LONG ASHTON [GW] op 12 July 1926 *(Bristol notice S1243 – May wtt supp* had wrongly said would open 17 May); at or near earlier Ashton; PLATFORM until 23 September 1929 *(Cl)*; clo 6 October 1941 *(Cl)*; in *hb* 1938 as HALT; {Bedminster – Flax Bourton}.

LONG BUCKBY [LNW] op 1 December 1881 *(LNW Officers 22843, 22911)*; still open.

LONG CLAWSON & HOSE [GN/LNW]
op 1 September 1879 *(LNW Officers 20028)*; & H added 1884; clo 7 December 1953 *(T 7th)*.

LONG EATON [Mid] {map 60}
LONG EATON (a) op 6 September 1847 *(Mid)*; became TOTON for L E 1 October 1851 co tt, L E 1862 *(Mid)*; re-sited about ¼ mile south July 1863 *(Cl)*; clo 2 January 1967 *(Mid)*.
LONG EATON (b) op 3 December 1888 *(Mid)* as SAWLEY JUNCTION; became S J for L E 1 January 1933 *(hbl February)*, L E 6 May 1968 *(RM)*; still open.
L E JUNCTION op 4 June 1839 *(Mid)*; JUNCTION added about 1847; clo 1 May 1862 (Thursday) *(Mid)*.

LONG LANE – see COALVILLE.

LONG MARSTON [GW]
op 12 July 1859 (see STRATFORD-UPON-AVON, line from Honeybourne); clo 3 January 1966 *(RM Feb.)*.

LONG MARTON [Mid]
op 1 May 1876 *(Mid; co n T 1st- line)*;
clo 4 May 1970 *(RM June)*.

LONG MELFORD [GE]
op 9 August 1865 *(GE; T 10th- line)*; LONG added 1 February 1884 *(RCG)*; clo 6 March 1967 *(RM April)*.

LONG PRESTON [Mid]
op 30 July 1849 *(T 28 July, 1 September)*; still open.
LONG STANTON [GE]
op 17 August 1847 *(co ½ T 13 August- line)*; aot request;
clo 5 October 1970 *(RM October)*.
LONG SUTTON near Wisbech [MGN] op 1 July 1862
(Linc R & S Merc 4th); clo 2 March 1959 *(T 2nd)*.
LONG SUTTON & PITNEY near Langport [GW]
op 1 October 1907 *(GW II, p.226–7)*; clo 10 September
1962 *(Som Gaz 15th)*. HALT in *Brad* about 1908 to
1915 and thus in GW co tt 1911, but not 1932;
in *hb* 1912 on as L S & P, suggesting RCH did not
regard as a halt. & P not always added *Brad*.
LONGBECK op 13 May 1985 *(BLN 520)*; still open.
LONGBENTON
For station in *Cl* as LONG BENTON, see BENTON.
LONGBENTON [LNE] op 14 July 1947 *(Cl 29)*;
clo 23 January 1978 *(RM March)* for conversion >
LONGBENTON [TWM] on 11 August 1980 *(RM
August)*; still open. Planning documents at Kew and
1956 *hb* say HALT (A. Young) but not tt.
LONGBRIDGE
LONGBRIDGE (a) [Mid] op November 1841★★ *(Mid)*;
on main line; clo 1 May 1849 (Tuesday) co tt *(Mid)*.
LONGBRIDGE (b) [Mid] op, non-tt, 5 July 1915 *(Mid/
GW Officers 13th)*; added to *Brad* 20 September 1954;
first shown 'P' in *hb* 1956, as L RUBERY; clo 4 January
1960 *(Cl)*. On Halesowen branch 33 chains from
junction *(Midland System Maps 1915 amendment)*;
1918 amendments 'now' at 35 chains.
LONGBRIDGE (c) [Mid] (non-tt) op 1 July 1918 *(Mid
weekly notices at National Railway Museum)*; on main
line, 12 chains south of junction with Halesowen
branch *(System Map 1918)*; last train 25 February 1922.
RAIL 491/802, letters 16th on – had been provided for
wartime 'projectile', alias 'shell' factory; aot 1,000+
using special trains. Possibility of continued use by
Austin's but by 1922 they were able to recruit workers
locally and few using; Midland prepared to keep as
non-tt stop for ordinary trains but Austin's not prepared
to alter hours to fit. There were protests from e.g.
Lord Mayor of Worcester, concerned about level of
unemployment in his city. Internal letters usually called
it HALESOWEN JUNCTION HALT.
LONGBRIDGE (d) op 8 May 1978 *(Mid)*; same site as
1840s station; still open.
LONGCLIFFE – see 1833 May★★.
LONGCROSS [SR]: army camp use from about
1940; op to public 21 September 1942 *(Cl 29)*;
HALT until 5 May 1969 *(SR App)*; still open.
LONGDON near Shrewsbury [GW]
op 20 October 1934 *(Cl 29)*; HALT; clo 9 September
1963 *(T 9th)*; {Wellington – Crudgington}.
LONGDON ROAD near Moreton-in-Marsh
For first service through here see 1833 B★★.
LONGDON ROAD [GW] op 1 July 1889 *(Wilts 6th-
line)*; clo 8 July 1929 *(RM September)*. GW co tt 1902:
L R for ILMINGTON and always thus *hb*.
LONGDOWN [GW] op 1 July 1903 *(RCG; Trewman
4th- line)*; clo 9 June 1958 *(T 5th)*.

LONGFIELD
LONGFIELD [LCD] first in *Brad* June 1872 as
FAWKHAM ROAD; ROAD dropped by 1875 *(Brad)*;
became F for HARTLEY and L 1895/6 *(Brad)*, thus *hb*
and SEC co tt 1914; renamed L for F and HARTLEY
12 June 1961 *(SR)*, L 1968/72 tt (index sometimes
later); still open.
L HALT [SEC] op 1 July 1913 *(LCD)* – in *Brad* June
1913, prematurely?; clo 3 August 1953 *(RM Sept.)*.
Always L HALT for PINDEN and WESTWOOD in
Brad and thus SEC co tt 1914 but just L HALT *(hb)*.
LONGFORD & EXHALL [LNW]: op 2 September
1850★★; clo 23 May 1949 *(RM September)*.
LONGFORGAN [Cal]: line op 24 May 1847 *(Rtn PP)*,
nd, May 1848 *(Topham* – where it was
LONG FORGAN); not in list of fares at opening
(Scot Cent), nor included in tt with line op notice
(Perthshire Courier 27th), so probably opened after line;
clo 11 June 1956 *(RM April)*.
LONGHAVEN [GNS] op 2 August 1897 *(GNS)*;
clo 31 October 1932 *(RM December)*.
LONGHIRST [NE] op 1 July 1847★★ (in *Brad* with
line, August); clo 29 October 1951 *(Cl)*.
LONGHOPE [GW]
op 1 June 1855★★; clo 2 November 1964 *(Cl)*.
LONGHOUGHTON [NE] op 1 July 1847★★ (in *Brad*
with line, August); clo 5 May 1941, reop 7 October
1946 *(RM January 1947)*; clo 18 June 1962 *(RM July)*.
LONGMORN [GNS] op 1 March 1862 *(GNS)*;
aot request; clo 6 May 1968 *(RM July)*.
LONGNIDDRY [NB]: line op 22 June 1846★★; in
Brad September; still open. L JUNCTION until 1890
(Brad); LONG NIDDRY in *hb* 1862;
L for GULLANE in *Murray* 1948 but not *Brad*.
LONGPARISH [LSW] op 1 June 1885 *(Hants Chron
13th)*; LONG PARISH until 1 July 1890 *(SR)*;
clo 6 July 1931 *(Cl)*.
LONGPORT [NS]
op 9 October 1848 *(co ½ T 3 February 1849- line)* as
BURSLEM; became B (L) 1853 tt, B (L & TUNSTALL)
1857 tt, B (L) 1864 tt *(JS)*, L 1 October 1873 *(JS;
RCG ref January 1874)*; still open.
By 1875 was L for WOLSTANTON in *Brad* and thus
NS co tt 1910; for W dropped 1923 *(Brad)*.
LONGRIDGE [Preston & Longridge]
op 2 May 1840★★?; clo 2 June 1930 *(LNW Record)*.
LONGRIDGE near Wishaw [WMC]
op 2 June 1845★★; for clo/reop see 1848★★;
last in tt December 1852; {map 16}.
LONGRIGGEND [NB]
first in *Brad* November 1862 (perhaps prematurely –
see ARBUCKLE); clo 1 May 1930 (Thursday) *(Cl)*.
LONGSIDE [GNS]
op 3 July 1862 *(GNS)*; clo 3 May 1965 *(RM May)*.
LONGSIGHT
LONGSIGHT (a) [LNW] first in *Brad* May 1843,
replacing Rushford; clo 15 September 1958 but kept for
excursions to Belle Vue *(RM November)*; one from
Macclesfield Easter Monday 23 April 1962 *(AB)*.
LNW co tt 1852, 1908, LMS tt 1930, *Brad* and *hb* to
closure: L for BELLEVUE.

LONGSIGHT (b) (non-tt) op March 1980; railwaymen *(U)*; during resignalling work used by public at weekends from 23 July 1988, all days from 1 October 1988; reverted to staff only use on 17 October 1988; still open.

LONGSTONE – see GREAT LONGSTONE.

LONGSTOW [Mid]:
shown 'P' in *hb* 1890 (as LONG STOW), and 1895 (one word); 1904 goods only; assumed error (goods only in *Mid*); {Kimbolton – Grafham}.

LONGTON near Stoke-on-Trent [NS]
op 7 August 1848★★; still open.

LONGTON BRIDGE near Southport [LY]
op 18 May 1882 *(Ormskirk 25th)*;
BRIDGE added 1 January 1892 *(hbl 28th)*;
clo 7 September 1964 *(RM October)*.

LONGTOWN [NB] op 29 October 1861★★;
clo 6 January 1969 *(RM February)*.

LONGVILLE [GW] op 16 December 1867 *(GW- line)*;
clo 31 December 1951 *(T 31st)*.

LONGWITTON [NB]
op 1 November 1870 *(Nhumb)* as ROTHLEY;
until 1873 private station for Trevelyan estate, but in *Brad* (G.W.M. Sewell, *The North British Railway in Northumberland*, Merlin, 1991); renamed April 1875 tt *(Cl; RCG ref July)*; clo 15 September 1952★★.
Hb 1876a (only) LONG WITTON.

LONGWOOD [LNW]
op 1 August 1849 *(D&C 8; co ½ T 18 August- line)*;
was L & MILNSBRIDGE 1 July 1887 *(Cl)* to 12 June 1961 *(RM June)*; clo 7 October 1968 *(RM November)*.

LONLAS – see LLANDARCY.

LONMAY [GNS] op 24 April 1865 *(GNS)*;
clo 4 October 1965 *(Rly Obs November)*.

LONSDALE [non-tt] – see 1933 November 6★★.

LOOE [GW] op 11 September 1879 *(Cornish T 13th)*;
clo 3 November 1990 for flood prevention work, reop 19 November 1990 *(RM January 1991)*; still open.

LORDS [Met] op 13 April 1868 *(T 10 April, 3 August)* as ST JOHNS WOOD ROAD; ROAD dropped 1 April 1925 *(hbl April)*; renamed LORDS 11 June 1939 *(Cl)* ; clo 20 November 1939 *(Cl)*, replaced by new St Johns Wood Road; later use for cricket spectators – *(hb 1940a* for cricket only)*; still shown open as required for cricket 1956 *hb* –inertia?

LORDS BRIDGE [LNW] op 7 July 1862
(co n T 7th- line); clo 1 January 1968 *(RM January)*.

LORDSHIP LANE [LCD]
op 1 September 1865 *(L; co ½ T 22 August* – arrangements had been made to open, no date given); clo 1 January 1917 *(RM February)*; reop 1 March 1919 *(RCG)*; clo 22 May 1944 *(T 22 April)*; reop 4 March 1946 *(RM June)*; clo 20 September 1954 *(T 20th)*.
Brad 1868/9 to clo, SEC co tt 1914 and *hb* 1904 on: L L for FOREST HILL.

LOSEBY – see LOWESBY.

LOSSIEMOUTH [GNS] op 10 August 1852★★
(GNS); clo 6 April 1964 *(RM May)*.

LOSTOCK
L LANE [LU] and **L JUNCTION** [LY] (opening):
L LANE first in *Brad* November 1846; LY Distance Diagram 1851 shows it well west of junction, on way to

Horwich; in September 1852 *Brad* it was replaced by L JUNCTION, timing same, suggesting perhaps just renaming, but Diagram evidence makes it clear that was different site. In Februay 1856 L LANE returned, L JUNCTION still present >
L LANE clo 1 June 1879 (Sunday) *(Cl)*.
L JUNCTION clo 7 November 1966 *(RM Jan. 1967)*.

LOSTOCK op 16 May 1988 *(BLN 587)*; near earlier L Junction; platforms on Chorley line only; still open.
L PARKWAY in first tt and on platform indicator at Manchester *(AB Chron)*.

LOSTOCK GRALAM [CLC]
LOSTOCK GRALAM op 1 January 1863 *(CLC; co ½ T 26 February- line)*; GRALAM added later 1863 *(Cl)*; still open.

L TEMPORARY PLATFORM (non-tt): provided WW1 for workmen; service discontinued April 1919; {near L G} *(CLC Portrait)*.

LOSTOCK HALL
LOSTOCK HALL (a) [LY] op 2 April 1849 *(LY)*;
clo 6 October 1969 *(Cl)*. L H JUNCTION until 1851/2 in *Brad*.
LOSTOCK HALL (b) op 14 May 1984 *(RM August)*; still open.

LOSTWITHIEL [GW] op 4 May 1859★★; still open.
Hb 1877 and 1883 made separate GW (Cornwall) and Cornwall Minerals stations of this.

LOTH [High] op 1 November 1870 *(High)*;
clo 13 June 1960 *(RM July)*.

LOTHIAN ROAD – see EDINBURGH.

LOUDOUN ROAD [LNW]
op 3 June 1879★★; clo 1 January 1917 *(RCG)*.
South Hampstead same site later. LNW co tt 1882, *Brad* and *hb* always: L R for SWISS COTTAGE.

LOUDOUNHILL [GSW] op 1 May 1905 *(RCG)*;
clo 1 July 1909 (Thursday), reop 1 November 1909 *(Cl)*; clo 1 January 1917 *(RCG)*; reop 4 December 1922 *(Cl)*; clo 11 September 1939 *(Cl)*.
In 1938 *hb* as HALT; not seen thus *Brad*.

LOUDWATER [GW]
op 1 August 1854 *(co n T 31 July)*; clo 4 May 1970 *(Cl)*.

LOUGHBOROUGH
LOUGHBOROUGH [Mid] op 5 May 1840 *(co n Lee)*;
replaced north of road bridge 13 May 1872 *(Mid)*;
briefly L TOWN 1923, then L MIDLAND from 9 July 1923 until 4 May 1970 *(Mid)*; still open.

L CENTRAL [GC] op 15 March 1899 *(GC; T 16th- line)*; clo 5 May 1969 *(Cl)*. See 2007 July 4★★.

L DERBY ROAD [LNW] op 16 April 1883 *(LNW Officers 24577)*; clo 13 April 1931 *(LNW dates PCC 192)*.

LOUGHBOROUGH JUNCTION [LCD]
Platforms on Brixton line spur first in *Brad* October 1864 as L ROAD; renamed when rest opened; clo 3 April 1916 *(L)*.
Platforms on main line op 1 December 1872 *(T 2nd –* called it 'new station')*; still open.
Platforms on Cambria Road spur op 1 December 1872 *(T 2nd)*; clo 12 July 1925 *(L)*.

LOUGHBOROUGH PARK – see EAST BRIXTON.

LOUGHOR [GW]
op 11 October 1852 *(T 12th)*; clo 4 April 1960 *(Cl)*.

LOUGHOR COMMON – see GORSEINON.

LOUGHTON op by [GE] 22 August 1856 *(co n T 22nd)*; re-sited on extension to Ongar 24 April 1865, probably *(L)*; again re-sited 28 April 1940, 300 yards south of second site *(GE Journal July 2001)*; transferred to [Cen] 21 November 1948 *(T 20th)*; still open.

LOUGHTON SIDING(S) [LMS] (non-tt): in use at least 1946 to 1952; railwaymen; {Bletchley – Wolverton} *(U)*.

LOUTH [GN] op 1 March 1848 *(co n GC I p.120)*; clo 5 October 1970 *(T 16 July)*; later excursion *(U)*.

LOVERS LANE [BWA] op 1 May 1908 *(Trewman 2nd- line)*; clo 28 March 1917**.

LOVESGROVE [VoR] (ng) (non-tt): HALT; Cardiganshire Territorial Army Camp *(VoR)*; intermittent use 1910 to about 1939 *(U)*: {Glanrafon – Capel Bangor}.

LOW BENTHAM – see BENTHAM.

LOW FELL [NE] op 1 December 1868 *(NE- line)*; clo 7 April 1952 *(Cl)*.

LOW GILL [LNW]

LOW GILL (a) op 17 December 1846 *(D&C 14; co n Lancaster 12th- line)*; clo 1 November 1861.

LOW GILL (b), about ½ mile, for Ingleton branch op 16 September 1861 *(co n Lancaster Gaz 14th)* as L G JUNCTION; JUNCTION dropped after LNW co tt 1883 and from *Brad 1897/8*; clo 7 March 1960 *(RM April)*.

Note that both were briefly open together. *Co n Lancaster Obs 26 October 1861* said all Third Class trains would cease to call at 'Lowgill' on and after 1 November.

LOW LEYTON – see LEYTON.

LOW MARISHES [NE] – see 1845 July 8**; no tt evidence seen.

LOW MOOR [LY] op 18 July 1848 *(co ½ T 7 Sept.)*; clo 14 June 1965 *(RM June)*.

LOW ROW [MC] op 2 December 1844 *(D&C 14)*; clo 2 February 1848 *(D&C 14)*; see 1840**; {map 20g}.

LOW ROW [NE] op 19 July 1836 (see 1836 B**), in *Scott 1837*; clo 5 January 1959 *(RM February)*.

LOW STREET [LTS] first in *Brad July 1861*; clo 5 June 1967 *(Cl)*.

LOW WALKER – see WALKER.

LOW WHITE HEAPS – see PARK HEAD.

LOWCA [CW Jc] op 2 June 1913 *(RCG)*; clo 31 May 1926 *(Cl)*; workmen continued to use to 1 April 1929 *(U)*; {map 21}.

LOWDHAM [Mid] op 4 August 1846 *(Mid)*; still open.

LOWER DARWEN [LY]: line op 3 August 1847 *(Rtn)*, nd, May 1848 *(Topham)*; clo 3 November 1958 *(LNW Record)*.

LOWER EDMONTON

LOWER EDMONTON (LL) [GE] op 1 March 1849 *(T 2nd)* as E; renamed L E 1 July 1883 *(Cl)*; aot request; clo 11 September 1939 *(Cl)*. Also see EDMONTON GREEN.

LOWER INCE [GC] op 1 April 1884 *(Wigan Obs 2nd, item and tt)*; clo 2 November 1964 *(RM December)*.

LOWER LYDBROOK [SW Jt] op 23 September 1875**; clo 1 April 1903 *(RAIL 241/17)*.

LOWER MERTON – see MERTON PARK.

LOWER NORWOOD – see WEST NORWOOD.

LOWER PENARTH [TV] op 1 February 1897 *(Penarth)*; HALT from 1935 *(C/W; Brad)*; clo 14 June 1954 *(Cl)*.

LOWER PONTNEWYDD [GW] op 21 December 1874 *(C Obs Usk- line)*; clo 1 January 1917 *(GW notice dated 22 December 1916)*; reop 5 May 1919 *(RCG)*; LOWER added 1 April 1925 *(hbl October)*; clo 9 June 1958 *(Cl)*.

LOWER SYDENHAM [SE] op 1 January 1857 *(L; co ½ T 9 February- line)*; re-sited to south 1906 *(Cl)*; still open.

LOWESBY [GN] op 1 January 1883 *(co n Leicester Mercury 6th)*; LOSEBY until 1916 *(refs RM Dec., hbl 25 Jan. 1917)*; clo 7 December 1953 *(T 7th)*; workmen continued to use to 29 April 1957 (but service interrupted 8–31 December 1956 – Henshaw); later excur *(U)*.

LOWESTOFT

LOWESTOFT [GE] op 1 July 1847 *(co ½ T 6 September)*; L CENTRAL 13 July 1903 *(RCG)* to 3 May 1971; still open.

L NORTH [Norfolk & S] op 13 July 1903 *(co n Norfolk & S)*; clo 4 May 1970 *(RM May)*.

LOWSONFORD: according to letter from P.S. Boness, *RM November 1968, p.675*, there was a 'halt' here, on the GW's Henley-in-Arden branch; it was asserted in *RM June 2001, p.29* that it had been closed when the second station opened at Henley in 1908; branch dates 6 June 1894 to 1 January 1915. No contemporary evidence has been seen in support. (see A. Brackenbury, *Chron October 2008*)

LOWTHORPE [NE]: line op 7 October 1846**, nd, May 1848 *(Topham)*; clo 5 January 1970 *(Cl)*.

LOWTON

LOWTON [LNW] op 1 January 1847 *(D&C 10)*; early NORTH UNION JUNCTION / PRESTON JUNCTION; renamed L & P J 1 February 1877 *(RCG)*, L 1880 *(LNW Officers recommended 17 February – but they did not seem to be entirely sure whether it had been L & P J or P J & L)*; clo 1 January 1917 *(T 22 December 1916)*; reop 1 February 1919 *(Cl)*; clo 26 September 1949 *(RM September)*.

L ST MARYS [GC] op 1 April 1884 *(Wigan Obs 2nd, item and tt)*; clo 2 November 1964 *(RM December)*.

LUBENHAM [LNW] op 1 September 1869 *(LNW Officers 4523)*; clo 6 June 1966 *(RM July)*.

LUCAS TERRACE [LSW] first in *Brad October 1905*; HALT; clo 15 January 1951 *(T 12th)*, reop 2 July 1951 *(D&C 1)* – see 1951**; clo 10 September 1951 *(RM October)*; {map 114}.

LUCKER [NE]: line op 29 March 1847**, nd, August; clo 5 May 1941*, reop 7 October 1946 *(RM January 1947)*; clo 2 February 1953 *(RM March)*. * = 5 May 1941 wtt only shows call to set down news parcels but at least 6 October 1941 wtt to 6 May 1946 wtt one call daily northbound, and one Saturdays only to set down southbound.

LUCKETT [PDSW] op 2 March 1908
(W Morn News 3rd) as STOKE CLIMSLAND;
renamed 1 October 1909 *(RCG)*;
clo 7 November 1966 *(Cornish & D P 12th)*.

LUDBOROUGH [GN] op 1 March 1848 *(co n GC I
p.120)*; clo 11 September 1961 *(RM September)*.

LUDDENDENFOOT [LY]: line op 5 October 1840;
not in op tt *Leeds*; first in *Brad* about April 1841;
clo 10 September 1962 *(Cl)*. LUDDENDEN FOOT
in *Brad* until l865/6. LUDDENDEN in *Robinson* 1841.
Hb consistently to one word 1890.

LUDDINGTON [Ax Jt] op 10 August 1903 *(RCG)*;
clo 17 July 1933 *(RM September)*.

LUDGATE HILL – see LONDON.

LUDGERSHALL [MSWJ] op 1 May 1882 *(W Gaz
5th)*; separate troop platform added about 1899/1902;
clo 11 September 1961 *(T 9th)*; troop trains continue
to use *(U*; still shown Baker's atlas, 2007).

LUDLOW [SH Jt]
op 21 April 1852 *(co ½ T 17 August)*; still open.

LUFFENHAM [Mid] op 1 May 1848 *(Mid; co ½
T 21 August- line)*; clo 6 June 1966 *(RM July)*.

LUFFNESS
LUFFNESS [NB] (non-tt): op 1 September 1903,
clo 1 June 1931 *(N Berwick)*; golfers;
{Aberlady – Gullane}. In 1 April 1914 co alterations as
PRIVATE GOLF CLUB PLATFORM.
Also see GULLANE GOLF.

LUGAR [GSW] first in *Brad* January 1860; clo 3 July
1950 *(RM August)*. *Hb*: L JUNCTION 1872 only.

LUGTON
LUGTON [GBK Jt] op 27 March 1871 *(GSW- line)*;
clo 7 November 1966 *(Cl)*.
L HIGH [Cal] op 1 May 1903 *(RCG)*; clo 1 January
1917 *(RM February)*; reop 1 February 1919 *(RCG)*;
HIGH added 2 June 1924**; clo 4 July 1932 *(Cl)*.

LUIB [Cal] op 1 August 1873 *(Cal- line)*;
clo 28 September 1965**.

LUIB HOUSES (non-tt): perhaps initially L SUMMIT;
op/reop 3 December 1951; railwaymen's wives;
clo 1972 or later; {Achnasheen – Glencarron} *(U)*.

LULLINGSTONE: station built 1939 by [SR] but
intended opening 2 April 1939 *(U)* deferred when
approach of war stopped building of aerodrome it was
intended to serve. In *Brad* certainly July 1939 to June
1941, with trains shown but plus '*' (= opening date
would be advertised); before/with January 1942 trains
and '*' removed but station still shown; omitted May
1953/March 1954; {Swanley – Eynsford}.

LUMPHANAN [GNS] op 2 December 1859 *(GNS)*;
clo 28 February 1966 *(RM March)*.

LUMPHINNANS [NB]
NB wtt 1 May 1914 shows workmen's train stopping at
L NORTH PIT SIDING and L WEST and Factory
Workers' train stopping at L WEST, both from Kelty
to Dunfermline. Services also shown other way,
one being described as 'Passenger 3rd'.

LUNAN BAY [NB]
op 1 May 1883**; clo 22 September 1930 *(Cl)*.

LUNCARTY [Cal] op 2 August 1848 *(Rtn- line)*;
clo 18 June 1951 *(RM July)*.

LUNDIN LINKS [NB] op 11 August 1857**;
clo 6 September 1965 *(closure notice East of T J)*.

LUSTLEIGH [GW] op 4 July 1866 *(W D Merc 5th-
line)*; clo 2 March 1959 *(Express & E 2nd)*.

LUTHRIE [NB] op 25 January 1909 *(RCG)*;
clo 12 February 1951 *(RM April)* – see 1951**.

LUTON
LUTON [Mid] op 13 July 1868 *(T 14th)*;
L MIDLAND ROAD 25 September 1950 to 18 April
1966 *(Mid)*; still open.
L AIRPORT PARKWAY op 21 November 1999
(Rail, 1 to 14 December 1999); still open.
L BUTE STREET [GN] op 3 May 1858 *(GN)*;
B S added 25 September 1950 *(RM October)*;
clo 26 April 1965 *(RM May)*.
LUTON HOO [GN] op 1 September 1860
(GN; co n 1st- line) as NEW MILL END;
renamed L H for N M E 1 December 1891
(hbl 28 January 1892) and thus *Brad* to 1955, LNE co
tt 1927; aot request; clo 26 April 1965 *(RM May)*.

LUTTERWORTH
LUTTERWORTH [GC] op 15 March 1899 *(GC; T
16th- line)*; clo 5 May 1969 *(Cl)*.
Also see – ULLESTHORPE; WELFORD.

LUXBOROUGH ROAD – see 1865 September 4**.

LUXULYAN [GW]
op 20 June 1876 *(R Cornwall Gaz 24th)*;
BRIDGES until 1 May 1905*; aot request; still open.
* = date given by *hbl 27 April, RCG, GW circular 2012;* but
RAIL 253/482 says 13 April – latter date when change authorised?

LYBSTER [High]
op 1 July 1903 *(High)*; clo 3 April 1944**.

LYDBROOK
L JUNCTION [GW] op 4 August 1873**; JUNCTION
added 1 January 1899 *(hbl 26th)*, but thus in 1877 *hb*;
clo 5 January 1959 *(T 5th)*.
Also see LOWER LYDBROOK; UPPER LYDBROOK.

LYDD {map 130}
L TOWN [SE] op 7 December 1881 *(SE)*; TOWN
added 4 July 1937 *(Cl)*; clo 6 March 1967 *(RM April)*.
L-ON-SEA [SR] op 4 July 1937 *(SR sig inst 1937/2)*;
HALT from 20 December 1954 *(Cl)*; clo 6 March
1967 *(RM April)*. SR tt 1939 (and *hb* always):
L-on-S for DUNGENESS; thus *Brad* to 1955.

LYDFORD (LIDFORD until 3 June 1897, *hbl July*).
LYDFORD [GW] op 1 July 1865 *(W D Merc 4th- line;
in tt Tavistock 8th)*; clo 31 December 1962**.
LYDFORD [LSW] op 12 October 1874 *(Trewman 14th)*;
clo 6 May 1968 *(Cornish & D P 11th)*.
LSW ticket exists for LIDFORD JUNCTION *(JB)*
and *Brad* used this form until 1879/80 in LSW tables.

LYDHAM HEATH [BC]
op 1 February 1866**; finally clo 20 April 1935.

LYDIATE [CLC]
op 1 September 1884 *(CLC)*; clo 1 January 1917
(T 23 December 1916); reop non-tt for races at Aintree
in March 1919 *(CLC Portrait)*, to public 1 April 1919
(RCG); clo 7 January 1952 *(RM February)*.

LYDNEY
LYDNEY [GW] op 19 September 1851 *(T 20th)*;
L JUNCTION 1875 to 6 May 1968 *(offic)* >

L JUNCTION [SW Jt] op 23 September 1875★★;
re-sited alongside GW station 20 October 1879
(Gloucester J 18th) >
The two above merged 21 May 1955; SW Jt part
clo 26 October 1960★★; GW part still open as L.
L TOWN [SW Jt] op 23 September 1875★★;
clo 26 October 1960★★; still excursion use at 10 August
1961 *(BR pamphlet)*.
LYDSTEP [GW] existed by 1873 for excursions and
picnics; HALT; perhaps wider use informally but no
firm evidence *(Pembroke)*; officially op to public 1 May
1905 *(GW H)*; from autumn of 1908 (last in tt
September) was closed in winter, though use by
workmen at Pembroke Dock might have continued;
fully clo 21 September 1914 *(GM's report 17 January
1917)*, intended only for season but war prevented reop
next year; reop 9 July 1923 *(RCG)*; all year use again
then? – certainly by November 1926 *Brad*;
clo 2 January 1956 *(Cl)*.
LYE [GW] op 2 March 1863 ? (date given for Cradley
Heath by *RAIL 1089/7* – both first in *Brad* April);
still open.
LYGHE – see LEIGH KENT.
LYME REGIS [LSW] op 24 August 1903 *(Chard 29th)*;
clo 29 November 1965 *(Chard 3rd)*.
In *Brad* as L R for CHARMOUTH 1908/9 to 1929/30
but not thus LSW co tt 1914, nor *hb*.
LYMINGE [SE]
op 4 July 1887 *(SE)*; clo 3 May 1943, reop 7 October
1946 *(Cl)*; clo 16 June 1947★★ – but *SR sig inst 22/1947*
makes it look as if permanent closure intended then.
LYMINGTON [LSW]
L PIER op 1 May 1884 *(SR)*; clo 5 October 1992
(RM September); reop 22 November 1992 *(RM Dec.)*;
clo 8 January 1996, reop 18 February 1996 *(BLN 774)*,
still open.
L JETTY (non-tt) shown 'P' in *hb* 1877 and 1883
('extension from L'); according to *LSW, 2, p.151*, this was
opened 1 June 1861 and passengers suffered 'a long
rambling walk' to and from town. Thus, used by railway
passengers, but not railway served.
L TOWN op 12 July 1858★ *(Salisbury 17th)*;
extended about 200 yards to permanent station
19 September 1860 *(Cl)*; still open.
Brad ? to 1955: LT for MILFORD-ON-SEA; thus.
★ = several free trips on formal opening day, 8 May 1858;
although line passed BoT inspection on 11 May, LSW insisted
on extra sleepers before they would work line for Lymington
company *(LSW vol.1 p.98, vol.2 p.148)*.
LYMINSTER
For first station see ARUNDEL.
LYMINSTER [LBSC] op 1 August 1907 *(LBSC)*;
on opposite side of level crossing from station above;
HALT; last in *Brad* November 1914.
LYMM [LNW] op 1 November 1853★★;
clo 10 September 1962 *(RM September)*.
LYMPSTONE
L VILLAGE [LSW] op 1 May 1861 *(Trewman 1st, 2nd
edition)*; HALT 28 February 1965 to 5 May 1969 *(Cl)*;
VILLAGE added 3 May 1991 tt *(AB, Chron)*; still open.
L COMMANDO op 3 May 1976 *(Express & E 3rd)*;

in tt but available only for Royal Marines and closed
when nearby Camp is closed; request; still open.
LYNDHURST ROAD
– see ASHURST NEW FOREST.
LYNE [Cal] op 1 February 1864 *(co ½ T 3 March- line)*.
1922/3 *Brad* note added that station closed after 5pm
and would then be used as halt; 1932 *Brad* became
L HALT; 1939/1940 HALT dropped from *Brad* but
still in *Murray* 1948. Clo 5 June 1950 *(RM July)*.
LYNEDOCH – see GREENOCK.
LYNESIDE [NB]
op 29 October 1861★★ as WEST LINTON;
renamed LINESIDE 10 June 1870 *(Cl)*; spelling
altered 1871 tt *(Cl)*; clo 1 November 1929 (Friday) *(Cl)*.
LYNG [GW] op 24 September 1928 *(Langport 22nd)*;
HALT; clo 15 June 1964 *(W Gaz 12th, 19th)*;
{Durston – Athelney}.
LYNN
– see KINGS LYNN; SOUTH LYNN; WEST LYNN.
LYNTON & LYNMOUTH [Lynton] (ng)
op 16 May 1898 *(N Devon J 18th)*; op as LYNTON;
became L for L 1905 *(Brad)*, L & L 1921 *(Brad)*
but already L & L LSW co tt 1914, *hb* 1918a;
clo 30 September 1935★★.
LYON CROSS / LYONCROSS [Cal]:
road maps approx 1940s and 1950s show station here;
one planned about 1905 but growth of tram competion
meant service that would have used it was not provided;
{IA p.44, Patterton/Netherton goods} (D. Pedley; *AB*).
LYONS CROSSING – see IFIELD.
LYONSHALL [GW]
op 3 August 1874 *(co ½ T 1, 9 September- line)*;
clo 1 January 1917 *(GW notice dated 22 December
1916)*; reop 11 December 1922 *(GW Mag January
1923)*; clo 1 July 1940 *(Cl)*.
LYONS HALL in *Brad* until 1880/1; always thus *hb*
but *hbl July 1938* said change (undated) had been made.
LYTHAM [PW]
LYTHAM, terminus from Preston, op 17 February
1846 *(Railway Record 28th, LY)* >
LYTHAM, terminus from Blackpool op 6 April 1863
(LY) >
On 1 July 1874, the 1863 station was converted into
a through one and the 1846 station clo, its services
diverted to through one, which is still open.
Brad and LNW co tt (e.g. January 1874) added
STATION ROAD to 1863 one, until the other was
closed. LNW co tt referred to other as station
'on the coast line'.
L JUNCTION first in *Brad* June 1853★; last there
November 1853.
★ = unlikely that it op earlier, e.g. as unadvertised exchange
station, since the previous month showed 'Kirkham Junction'
and June 'Kirkham', suggesting that changes had previously
had to be made there. It allowed passengers from Lytham to
change to trains going from Preston to Blackpool and Fleetwood.
L DOCK – see WARTON DOCK.

MABLETHORPE [GN] op 17 October 1877
(co n Louth); clo 5 October 1970 *(T 16 July)*.

MACBIE HILL [NB]
op 4 July 1864 *(Selkirk 7th)* as COALYBURN;
renamed 25 May 1874 *(Cl; RCG ref July)*; clo 1 April
1933**. MACBIEHILL in *hb* 1904 on;
M H in *Brad* and LNE tt.

MACCLESFIELD

MACCLESFIELD terminus in Beech Lane [Manchester
& Birmingham] op 24 November 1845**; clo 13 July
1849 (B. Jeuda, *Railways of the Macclesfield District*,
Wyvern, Skipton, 1984, pp. 3 and 61).

M HIBEL ROAD [LNW/NS] op 18 June 1849
(Macclesfield 16th) – paper had notice for public op and
described formal on 14th, when there was widespread
public use, principally to let people visit 'the splendid
viaduct at North Rode'; first used by NS; joined by
LNW 13 July 1849; clo 7 November 1960 *(RM Dec.)*.
Brad added H B in one table 1875; long after it
remained M in table from Manchester.

M temporary terminus from Marple [MS&L/NS]
op 2 August 1869 *(Macclesfield – co n 31 July, item
7 August)*; *Brad* called this 'the New station';
replaced by >

MACCLESFIELD [GC/NS] op 1 July 1873 *(Macclesfield
5th)*; M CENTRAL until 11 September 1961 tt;
still open.

MACDUFF [GNS]

MACDUFF op 1 July 1872 *(GNS)*; clo 1 October 1951
(RM November).

M BANFF op 4 June 1860 *(GNS)*; alias GELLYMILL;
terminus replaced 1 July 1872 *(Cl)* by Banff Bridge,
through station, on extension of the line to Macduff.
Brad: 1861 B (but index M), 1863 B & M (and thus
hb 1862); 1867 M.

McCLAREN COLLIERY [BM] (non-tt):
miners' PLATFORM; in use 1930;
{New Tredegar – Abertwsswg} *(U)*.

McGRATH'S FARM [LM]: see 1830 September
17**; briefly stop instead of Barton Moss in 1830s.

MACHEN [BM] op 14 June 1865 *(co n Newport 17th)*;
clo 31 December 1962 *(T 31st)*.

MACHRIHANISH [Camp] (ng)

MACHRIHANISH op 18 August 1906**; clo by May
1932 *(Camp)*.

M FARM : see 1906 August 18**; first listed in *Brad*
September 1907; request; clo by May 1932 *(Camp)*.

MACHYNLLETH

MACHYNLLETH [Cam] op 5 January 1863**; still open.

MACHYNLLETH [Corris]: For first service see 1874**.
Station for steam service op 4 July 1883 *(Corris)*;
clo 1 January 1931 (Thursday) *(Cl)*.

MACMERRY [NB] op 1 May 1872 *(Edin)*;
clo 1 July 1925 (Wednesday) *(closure notice Haddington)*.
M GLADSMUIR *(hb)*.

MADDAFORD MOOR [SR]
op 26 July 1926 *(hbl 61)* HALT;
clo 3 October 1966 *(Cornish & D P 8th)*.
Brad ? to 1955: M M Halt for THORNDON.

MADDERTY [Cal]
op 21 May 1866**; clo 1 October 1951 *(RM November)*.

MADDIESONS CAMP [RHD] first in *Brad* June
1932; alias LITTLESTONE HOLIDAY CAMP/
ROMNEY SANDS; see 1927 July 16** for later history.

MADELEY near Telford.

MADELEY [GW] op 2 May 1859 *(Wenlock)*;
M COURT until 4 June 1897 *(RCG)*; clo 22 March
1915 *(RCG)*; reop 13 July 1925 *(RM September)*;
clo 21 September 1925 *(GW)*.

M MARKET [LNW]
op 10 June 1861**; clo 2 June 1952 *(RM August)*.

MADELEY near Stoke-on-Trent.

MADELEY [LNW] op 4 July 1837 *(T 6th)*;
clo 4 February 1952 *(RM March)*.

M ROAD [NS] first in *Brad* October 1870 as M;
became M MANOR May 1871 tt *(NS)*, M R August
1871 tt *(NS)*; clo 20 July 1931 *(LNW Record)*.

MAENCLOCHOG [GW]
op 19 September 1876 *(S Wales 22nd)*;
clo 1 January 1883 *(Rtn)*; reop 5 December 1884;
clo 31 March 1885, reop 21 March 1887;
clo 25 May 1887 (Wednesday), reop 11 April 1895 *(Cl)*;
clo 8 January 1917 *(co n GW book)*; reop 12 July 1920
(GW Mag July); clo 25 October 1937**.

MAENTWROG ROAD [GW] op 1 November 1882
(D&C 11); clo 4 January 1960 *(RM March)*.
Later use as TRAWSFYNNYDD.

MAERDY [TV]
op 18 June 1889 *(S Wales 19th)*; clo 15 June 1964
(RM August). MARDY in local press at start.

MAESBROOK [SM] op 13 August 1866** *(D&C 11)*;
finally clo 6 November 1933 *(Cl)*.

MAESMAWR [TV] op 30 October 1840;
clo 20 April 1841; reop, Saturdays only, April to July
(inc) 1845; {near present Trefforest Estate} *(RAC)*.

MAESMELYN
– see CWMAVONYARD (under CWMAVON GLAM).

MAESTEG

MAESTEG [GW] op 25 February 1864 *(Cardiff T 26th)*;
M CASTLE STREET 1 July 1924 *(GW circular 18 June)*
to 6 May 1968 *(offic)*; clo to public 22 June 1970;
school use continued, last train 14 July 1970 *(RM
September)*. *Hb* 1877 made Maes-teg of it.

MAESTEG op 28 September 1992 *(RM December)*;
old Castle Street, above, reopened; still open.

M EWENNY ROAD op 26 October 1992 *(BLN 695)*;
still open. Just E R on nameboard (P. Jeffries).

M NEATH ROAD [PT] op 14 February 1898 *(GW)*; N
R added 1 July 1924 *(GW circular 18 June)*;
clo 11 September 1933 *(Cl)*.
Also see 1828 A**.

MAESYCRUGIAU [GW]
op 1 January 1866 *(GW- line; in tt for 12 January, Milford)*;
clo 22 February 1965 *(Cl)*.
Maes-y-crugiau/Crugiau 1895 on *(hb)*.

MAESYCWMMER
MAESYCWMMER [BM] op 14 June 1865 *(co n Newport 17th)*; M & HENGOED 12 March 1906 *(hbl 26 April)* to 1 July 1924 *(GW circular 18 June)*; clo 31 December 1962 *(T 31st)*. Maes-y-cwmmer 1877 to 1890s *(hb)*.
Also see HENGOED.
MAGDALEN GATE [GE]:
line op 1 February 1848 *(GE)*, nd, July 1848 (probably did op after others on line – added late to *Topham* also); request; clo 1 August 1866 (Wednesday) *(Cl)*; {Magdalen Road – Middle Drove}.
MAGDALEN GREEN [Cal] first in *Brad* June 1878; clo 11 June 1956 *(RM April)*; used for a few days in 1957 for Highland Agricultural Show *(Tayside)*. Until 1904 MAGDALENE G *(hb)*.
MAGDALEN ROAD – see WATLINGTON.
MAGHULL [LY]
op 2 April 1849 *(Southport Vis 7th)*; still open.
MAGOR [GW]
first in *Brad* October 1851; clo 2 November 1964 *(Cl)*.
MAIDA VALE [Bak]
op 6 June 1915 *(L)*; see 1922★★; still open.
MAIDEN LANE
Main line terminus – see LONDON KINGS CROSS.
MAIDEN LANE [NL] op 1 July 1887 *(NL Circular 230)*; clo 1 January 1917 *(RCG)*; {map 101}.
MAIDEN NEWTON [GW]
op 20 January 1857 *(W Fly P 27th)*; still open.
MAIDENHEAD [GW]
For first station of this name see TAPLOW.
M BOYNE HILL op 1 August 1854 *(co n T 31 July)*; M WYCOMBE BRANCH in *Brad* until 1862 (and thus GW co tt 1859); {Maidenhead – Cookham}; replaced by >
MAIDENHEAD op 1 November 1871 *(co n T 25 Oct.)*; still open.
MAIDENS [GSW]
op 17 May 1906 *(RCG)*; clo 1 December 1930 *(Cl)*.
MAIDSTONE
M BARRACKS [SE] op 1 July 1874 *(SE)*; at first mainly military use; still open.
M EAST [LCD] op 1 June 1874 *(T 2nd)*; EAST added 1 June 1899 *(hbl 13 July)*; still open.
M WEST [SE] op 25 September 1844 – free trips 24th *(SE)*; WEST added 1 June 1899 *(hbl 13 July)*; still open.
MAIDSTONE ROAD – see PADDOCK WOOD.
MAIN STREET – see under GLASGOW.
MAINDY [TV]
first in *Brad* May 1907 as M NORTH ROAD PLATFORM; see 1904★★; N R dropped 1952 *(Cl)*; clo 15 September 1958 *(RM November)*; {Cardiff – Llandaff}.
MAINS CROSSING [PPW Jt]
op in June 1875: orders for station given 22 May; receipts shown in company records June as MAINS (OF PENNINGHAME) - perhaps to help identification on map rather than as intended name, but not in *Brad* until May 1878; aot request; last in tt November 1885; M CROSS in body of *Brad* (space?); M PLATFORM in *hb*; {map 17}.

MALDEN
M (& COOMBE) – see NEW MALDEN.
M MANOR [SR] op 29 May 1938 *(SR sig inst 22/1938)*; still open.
MALDON [GE]
M EAST & HEYBRIDGE op 2 October 1848 *(EC)*; see 1850 August 19★★; EAST added 1 October 1889 according to *hbl 24th* but in use in tt July 1889 *(Cl)*; & H added 1 October 1907 *(RCG)*; clo 7 September 1964 *(RM October)*.
M WEST op 1 October 1889 *(co notice – at back of November 1889 co tt at Newton Abbot)*; clo 22 May 1916★★; reop 1 August 1919 *(RCG)*; clo 11 September 1939 *(G&S)*.
MALINS LEE [LNW]
op 7 July 1862 *(SU; co n Shrewsbury 11th* 'now open', not in tt paper of 4th); clo ? (trains last shown March 1918 *Brad*); reop 1 February 1919 *(Cl)*; clo 2 June 1952 *(RM August)*. Notice *SU* shows as one word.
MALLAIG [NB] op 1 April 1901 *(RCG)*; still open.
MALLING
– see EAST MALLING; WEST MALLING.
MALLWYD [Cam] first in *Brad* August 1896 (company minutes show that only on 5 March 1896 was Secretary instructed to find cost of providing 'halt' here – Glyn Williams); clo 17 April 1901 (Wednesday) *(Cl)*; reop 31 July 1911 *(RCG)*; facilities first shown *hb* 1912; clo 1 January 1931★★ (Thursday) *(Cl)*.
MALMESBURY [GW] op 18 December 1877 *(Bath Chron 20th)*; clo 12 February 1951, reop 2 April 1951 *(Cl)*; clo 10 September 1951 *(T 10th)* – see 1951★★; {map 122}.
MALPAS [LNW] op 1 October 1872 *(Whitchurch 5th- line)*; clo 16 September 1957 *(LNW Record)*.
MALSWICK [GW] op 1 February 1938 *(Cl 29)*; HALT; clo 13 July 1959 *(RM August)*.
MALTBY [South Yorkshire Joint] op 1 December 1910★★ *(RCG)*; clo April 1926 *(Cl)*; reop 25 July 1927 *(T 21st)*; clo 2 December 1929 *(Mid)*.
There was later use: *The Times*, 6 February 1935 and *RM, May* said had been reopened at weekends; Saturdays services to Doncaster and Sheffield, ended 1937 *(S Yorks Joint)*.
MALTON [NE]: op 8 July 1845★★; still open.
MALVERN
M HANLEY ROAD [Mid] op 1 July 1862 *(Mid)*; M WELLS until 2 March 1951 *(Cl)* ★; clo 1 December 1952 *(T 1st)*.
★ = *Brad* added H R 1882/3 and LMS co tt 6 October 1947 showed this - but it was printed by Bradshaw.
M LINK [GW] op 25 July 1859★★; still open.
M WELLS [GW] op 25 May 1860 *(GW)*; clo 19 January 1861 by fire, reop 1 February 1864 *(Cl)*; clo 5 April 1965 *(Cl)*. Aot separate Hospital Platform. Was M W THE COMMON in *Brad* 1883 to 1947/8. LMS tt 22 September 1930 indexed this as M WALES. Also see GREAT MALVERN.
MANCHESTER {map 52}.
At first timetables often just had 'M'; fuller names appeared gradually, apparently initially only being added where confusion might occur. *Brad* 1840 had M

in railway tables but specified Liverpool Road, Oldham Road and Fairfield Road (= Travis Street) in table of hackney fares.

M AIRPORT op late evening 16 May 1993 *(BLN 707)*; still open.

M ART TREASURES [MSJA] op 5 May 1857 (assumed from date of Exhibition opening, *T 6th)*; Exhibition last day was 15 October 1857. Main service was shuttle from London Road in connection with trains from London, Oxford, Birmingham, Shrewsbury, Crewe, Macclesfield and Sheffield; also a through service from Chester, connecting there with GW services – see Walton Junction. Later use as M EXHIBITION (below).

M CENTRAL [CLC]: temporary station op 9 July 1877 *(Mid)*; replaced by permanent 1 July 1880 *(LNW Officers 21087)*; clo 5 May 1969 *(RM May)*. Both had entrances in Windmill Street; permanent slightly south-east of temporary (line NE-SW here) *(GN II p. 78; later map evidence E. Bredee)*.

M CRICKET & FOOTBALL (non-tt)
– see M EXHIBITION.

M DOCKS [LY] (non-tt): op 11 April 1898 as M RACECOURSE; certainly used 21 to 23 November 1901, last flat race meeting; perhaps used for National Hunt racing 1 & 2 January 1902 *(race)*; 'P' in *hb* 1904 and 1912 as M D, for general excursions until 1939 *(AB)*; {shown *IA*}.

M DUCIE BRIDGE (a) [LY] op late 1855 *(LY)*; merged with M Victoria 1877 *(LY)*.

M DUCIE BRIDGE (b) [LY] op 1 September 1879 *(D&C 10)*; clo 30 March 1884 (Sunday) *(Cl)*. Built to provide temporary extra capacity whilst M Victoria was being rebuilt.

M EXCHANGE [LNW] op 30 June 1884 *(LNW Officers 26313* – 'part' opened); completely op 4 May 1885 *(Brad Sh Eng 1886)*; connected to M Victoria in 1929 and management unified; old Exchange portion closed 5 May 1969 *(Cl)*.

M EXHIBITION [MSJA] used (non-tt) as E for Royal Agricultural Society July 1869 and 1897 *(MSJA)*. For Queen Victoria's Golden Jubilee first in *Brad* May 1887; clo October 1887. Also used from ? as OLD TRAFFORD CRICKET GROUND / O T C & FOOTBALL GROUND (and variations); in *Brad* summers 1862–6; advert for services to and from the CRICKET GROUND STATION 'on each day of the Matches at Old Trafford' on back of Lancashire County Cricket Club's scorecards 1926 (E. Bredee); in 1931 permanently opened as WARWICK ROAD (see under 'W'). Some at least of shorter usages seem to have been from temporary platforms near Warwick Road site.

M HOPE STREET: shown 'P' in 1883 *hb* –presumably parcels or error.

M LIVERPOOL ROAD [LM] op 17 September 1830★★; clo 4 May 1844 when service diverted to Victoria *(Cl)*. Co tt for March 1831 had M in timetable but referred elsewhere to company's station in Liverpool Road (explanatory?).

M MAYFIELD [LNW] op 8 August 1910 *(LNW Officers 42936)*; clo 28 August 1960 (Sunday) *(Cl)*.

M OLDHAM ROAD [Manchester & Leeds]
op 4 July 1839 *(T 11th)*; clo 1 January 1844 when service diverted to Victoria *(Cl)*. *Freeling* referred to station in Oldham Road as one for Leeds service.

M OXFORD ROAD [MSJA] op 20 July 1849★★; still open. *Co n Manch G 18th* specifies O R but *Brad* erratic – often just M.

M PICCADILLY [GC/LNW] op 10 May 1842 *(T 16th/Liverpool Mail)*; just M LNW co tt 1852; >

M PICCADILLY [MSJA] op 1 August 1849 *(GC)* > Two above at first M STORE STREET for MS&L, M LONDON ROAD (rest); *Brad* added L R 1844; merged 15 September 1958; renamed 12 September 1960 *(Cl)*; still open.

M PICCADILLY [Manch] op 20 July 1992 *(RM August)*; still open.

M (Travis Street) [Manchester & Birmingham] op 4 June 1840 *(Manchester Guardian 6th* – G. Boyes); clo 10 May 1842 when service extended to M London Road (later Piccadilly).

M UNITED FOOTBALL [CLC] (non-tt) op 4 September 1935 *(Cl 29)*; still used.

M VICTORIA [LY] op 1 January 1844 from Yorkshire *(LY)*, 4 May 1844 from Liverpool *(T 10th)*; briefly clo for rebuilding, reop 16 August 1993 *(RM October)*; still open. At first *Brad* called it HUNTS BANK in table, V in note about refreshment rooms; in July 1845 it was V in Preston & Wyre table, H B in Leeds table.

M VICTORIA [Manch] op 6 April 1992; still open. Also see SALFORD.

MANCHESTER ROAD [GN] Bradford:
op 14 October 1878 *(GN; T 15th– line)*; clo 1 January 1916 (Saturday) *(RCG)*.

MANEA [GE] op 14 January 1847 *(Herapath 16th- line)*; aot request; still open.

MANGOTSFIELD [Mid] first in *Brad* May 1845; re-sited 40 chains south 4 August 1869 tt after Bath branch op *(Mid)*; clo 7 March 1966 *(Shepton 11th)*.

MANLEY [CLC] op 22 June 1870 *(CLC)*; clo 1 May 1875 (Saurday) *(Cl)*; {goods *IA*}.

MANNINGFORD [GW] op 20 June 1932 *(GW Mag August)*; HALT; clo 18 April 1966 *(RM May)*; {Pewsey – Woodborough}.

MANNINGHAM [Mid] op 17 February 1868 *(Mid)*; aot request; clo 22 March 1965 *(RM April)*.

MANNINGTREE [GE]
op 15 June 1846 *(co n Moffat)*; still open. M JUNCTION during mid-1850s *(Brad)*.

MANOD [GW] op 10 September 1883 *(GW- line)* as replacement for Tyddyn Gwyn; clo 1 January 1917, reop 5 May 1919 *(RCG)*; became HALT 16 May 1955 and so shown on ticket *(JB)*; clo 4 January 1960 *(RM March)*.

MANOR HOUSE [Picc]
op 19 September 1932 *(T 16th, 20th)*; still open.

MANOR HOUSE STREET – see HULL.

MANOR PARK [GE] op 6 January 1873 *(L)*; still open. *Brad* 1895/6 to 1940, GE co tt 1914, LNE tt 1933: M P for LITTLE ILFORD. *Hb* 1895 M P & L I but 1904 M P.

MANOR POWIS COLLIERY [NB] (non-tt):
agreement made 7 and 16 March 1916 for train from
Stirling to here, calling at Causewayhead, six days per
week; dates of use ?

MANOR ROAD Wirral [LMS]
op 26 May 1941 (*LNW Record*); still open.

MANOR WAY [PLA] first in *Brad* July 1881 as
M ROAD; renamed June 1882 *Brad* original temporary
station replaced by new east of bridge, partly on diverted
line, after 4 December 1886, when BoT received
drawings of changes (R. Green); clo 9 September 1940★★.
GE co tt 1914: ROYAL ALBERT DOCK M W.

MANORBIER [GW] op 6 August 1863★★; aot request;
still open. GW co tt 1865: M for ST FLORENCE and
thus *Brad* until 1890/1. [Pembroke & Tenby] ticket for
MANORBEER (*JS*).

MANORS

M EAST [NE] op 30 August 1850 (*Cl*), replacing
Newcastle Carliol Square; EAST added 1 January
1909 (*RCG*) >

M NORTH [NE] op 1 January 1909 (*Cl*), replacing
Newcastle New Bridge Street >
Merged 20 February 1969 >
Old North part clo 23 January 1978; effectively
replaced by >

MANORS [TWM] op 14 November 1982 (*Tyneside*);
still open.
Platforms on line to Chathill (ex-M EAST) still open.
Aot RCH tended to lump Manors with Trafalgar
and/or Granary as one station with double or treble
name; eventually confined other names to goods.
NE co tt 1880, LNE tt 1933: NEWCASTLE M E/N.

MANSFIELD
For earliest service see 1832 A★★.

MANSFIELD op 20 November 1995 (*RM January
1996*) – 'fun day' 19th; on site of old Midland station;
still open.

M CENTRAL [GC] op 2 April 1917 (*RCG*); CENTRAL
added *Brad* 1953; clo 2 January 1956 but summer
Saturday services to e.g. Skegness continued until
8 September 1956 (last train) (*RM February 1956*);
even later summer Saturday use shown from wtt
15 June 1959 to that of 1964.

M TOWN [Mid] op 9 October 1849 (*Mid*); original
terminus replaced by through station 1 March 1872
(*Mid*); TOWN added 11 August 1952 (*Cl*);
clo 12 October 1964 (*RM November*).

MANSFIELD WOODHOUSE
MANSFIELD WOODHOUSE (a) [Mid] op 1 June
1875 (*Mid*); clo 12 October 1964 (*RM November*).
MANSFIELD WOODHOUSE (b) op 20 November
1995 (fun day 19th) as terminus from Nottingham;
became through station 25 May 1998 (P. Anderson &
J. Cupit, *An Illustrated History of Mansfield's Railways*,
Irwell, 2000); on, or slightly north of, site of (a); still open.

MANSION HOUSE [Dist] op 3 July 1871 (*co ½
T 31 July*); clo 30 October 1989 for building of office
block (*BLN 622*); reop 11 February 1991 (*BLN 653*);
still open. Cannon Street pre-opening (*L*).

MANSTON [NE]: line through here op 22 September
1834★★; not known whether there was station here

before it was first included in *Brad* January 1851;
clo 1 April 1869 (Thursday) (*Cl*).

MANTON [Mid] op 1 May 1848 (*Mid; co ½ T 21 Aug.*);
clo 6 June 1966 (*RM July*). M for UPPINGHAM until
1 October 1934 co tt (*Mid*). Hb: 1890 M & U,
1904 M for U, 1956 M.

MANUEL [NB]
MANUEL op 1 January 1866★; clo 6 March 1967 (*Cl*).
M LL op 1 January 1866★; clo 1 May 1933 (*Cl*).
★ = (*NB notice 26 December 1865*); no previous use as Bo'ness
Junction – physical junction was only now renamed that
(previously Slamannan Junction).
Hb names: M Edinburgh & Glasgow; M Monkland.

MARAZION [GW] op 11 March 1852 (*co n
R Cornwall Gaz 12th*); M ROAD until 1 October 1896
(*RCG*); clo 5 October 1964 (*Cl*).

MARBLE ARCH [Cen]
op 30 July 1900 (*L; T 25th- line*); see 1922★★; still open.

MARCH [GE] op 14 January 1847 (*Herapath 16th*);
re-sited 'a little west' 1886 (T. Bevis, *The Railway at March*,
locally, 1988); still open. M JUNCTION in some
tables *Brad* 1851 to 1879/80 and in EC co tt 1851.

MARCHINGTON [NS] first trains shown in *Brad*
February 1854; clo 15 September 1958 (*LNW Record*).

MARCHMONT [NB] op 16 November 1863 (*co ½
T 4 April 1864- line*); clo 13 August 1948★★.

MARCHWIEL
MARCHWIEL [Cam] op 2 November 1895 (*Wrexham
2nd, 9th*); clo 10 June 1940★★ (*Cl*), reop 6 May 1946
(*T 16 March*); clo 10 September 1962 (*RM October*).
M FACTORY LINE JUNCTION [GW]
– see 1940 June 10★★.

MARCHWOOD
MARCHWOOD [SR] op 20 July 1925 (*T 20th*);
clo 14 February 1966 (*RM March* – 'last train on
Friday', 11th); {map 128}.
Z Reservists were carried by through trains from
Waterloo to MARCHWOOD MILITARY SIDING;
certainly in July 1952 and on 17 May 1954 (*Fawley*);
other times?

MARDEN [SE]
op 31 August 1842 (*co n T 27th*); still open.

MARDEN PARK – see WOLDINGHAM.

MARDOCK [GE] op 3 July 1863 (*Hertford Mercury
4th*); aot request; clo 16 November 1964 (*T 14 October*).
At times MARDOCKS in RCH sources;
M for WAKESIDE in GE co tt 1882 and *Brad* 1880s.

MARFLEET [NE]
op 27 June 1854 (*co ½ T 4 September- line*);
clo 19 October 1964 (*Cl*). *RM January 1960* said it
would be a HALT from 4 January; not seen thus *Brad*
but note was added that no staff were in attendance.

MARGAM (not in *Brad* but locally advertised)
op 4 February 1948 for steel workers; served by Cardiff
to Swansea stopping trains and specials for shift workers,
including one from Treherbert via RSB line;
HALT (ticket *JB*); clo 2 November 1964 (M. Hale).

MARGARETTING [GE] (non-tt):
HALT; for munitions workers going to Chelmsford;
in wtt beginning 1 May 1918, perhaps in advance of
opening since works stated to be 'complete' 5 June

(though perhaps already in use in incomplete state);
closed with effect from 1 November 1921;
{Ingatestone – Chelmsford}; *(GE Journal* – B. Walsh
January 2000 and H. Paar October 2000).

MARGATE {map 131}
MARGATE [LCD] op 5 October 1863 *(T 5th)*;
became M & CLIFTONVILLE 1880 tt *(Brad* only? –
not in RCH sources), M WEST 1 June 1899 *(hbl 13
July)*; M 11 July 1926 *(hbl 13th)*; still open.
M EAST [LCD]: engineer's report dated 15 August
1864, in Kent Coast co ?, said new station had been
opened at the East End of Margate to accommodate
local traffic between there and Ramsgate; evidence
from *Thanet Advertiser* and *co tt* is that was in use from
1 August 1864 to end of October 1864 as
RAMSGATE ROAD*; trains stopped two minutes
before/after Buenos Ayres; EAST MARGATE in co tt
June to October (inclusive) 1866 (D. Banks) –
possibility of summer use 1865?; station first in *Brad*
July 1870; was EAST M until 1 June 1899 *(hbl 13 July)*;
clo 4 May 1953 *(RM June)*.
M SANDS [SE] op 1 December 1846 *(SE)* but
described as private opening by *Kentish Gazette 8th* –
public 2nd? SANDS added 1 June 1899 *(hbl 13 July)*;
clo 2 July 1926 (Friday) *(sig inst 21/1926)*.
M BUENOS AYRES*: evidence from *Thanet Advertiser*
and *co tt* (D. Banks) is that this name was in use from
1 August 1864 to end of October 1864. Perhaps this was
name used for LCD station to distinguish from SE's –
B A was name then used for its area. If this was so, why
was it only applied to local service (true of *co tt, Brad*
and *tts Thanet Advertiser*), and that only for a short time?
Another possibility is that it was east facing terminus
(see D&C OS reprint). Part of short-lived local service
from Margate to Ramsgate in competitive battle being
fought by the LCD and SE Companies? What was
station shown on D&C OS reprint if not B A? Station
built but not opened? *Herapath 4 July 1863*: understood
present platform [sic] is insufficient for holiday traffic
and so intend to lengthen forthwith – clue to this?
* = Station hand-books make a nonsense of B A and R R.
Appendix for 1865 added, under 'B', Buenos Ayres LCD,
[between] Margate and Herne Bay; shown same way up to
and including book of 1895, columns for facilities left blank
when these first included 1877; 1904, 1912 and 1925 shown
as 'same as Birchington-on-Sea'; omitted 1929. R R also added
under 'R' 1865, between Margate and Herne Bay; same 1872
when also entry for Margate East, between Margate and
Ramsgate; 1875 appendix R R 'closed'. Given tt version
neither R R nor B A could have been west of Margate.
MARINE COLLIERY [GW] (non-tt):
alias CWM COLLIERS; service began without facilities;
minutes of 18 December 1889 show agreement to
continue service and to allow company to put up platform
at Craig [= Graig] Fawr; clo 2 October 1961 *(U)*.
MARISHES
M ROAD [NE]: line op 8 July 1845**, nd, May 1848
(Topham); alias HIGH M early; clo 8 March 1965
(T 19 January).
Also see LOW MARISHES.
MARK LANE – see TOWER HILL.

MARKET BOSWORTH [AN Jt]
op 1 September 1873 *(LNW Officers 10205, 10207)*;
clo 13 April 1931 *(Cl)*. Programme of five excursions
in each of summers 1960 and 1961.
Excursion to Blackpool 13 August 1962 *(AB)*.
MARKET DRAYTON [GW] op 20 October 1863
(Rtn); clo 9 September 1963 *(T 9th)*.
MARKET HARBOROUGH op by [LNW] 29 April
1850 *(co n T 1 May)*; [Mid] used from 8 May 1857;
rebuilt 1884 to 1886 (completed 15 February 1886) –
now separate Mid and LNW platforms; ex-LNW
platforms clo 6 June 1966 *(Cl)*; ex-Mid still open.
MARKET RASEN [GC]
op 1 November 1848 *(GC)*; still open.
MARKET STREET – see KIDSGROVE.
MARKET WEIGHTON [NE]
op 4 October 1847 *(co ½ T 22 February 1848)*;
clo 29 November 1965 *(RM December)*.
MARKHAM COLLIERY [Mid] (non-tt):
op 1 September 1886 wtt *(Mid)*; miners;
clo 14 September 1931 wtt *(Mid)*;
{Staveley Town – Bolsover}.
MARKHAM VILLAGE [LNW]
Information from *RAC* unless indicated.
ABERNANT COLLIERS (non-tt): down platform
adjacent to colliery (at about 6m 72ch) and up platform
adjacent to northern wagon inlet (about 6m 44ch)
authorised 13 October 1896; op 1897?; >
M COLLIERS PLATFORM: name now used by *LNW
dates* for original up platform plus new temporary down
platform opposite it, op 19 April 1915; public allowed
to use from this date as temporary measure, footpath to
booking-office and waiting-shed provided. Replaced for
public and miners* by >
M VILLAGE op 1 February 1917 *(LNW Officers 44980)*,
at 6m 40ch; became HALT 5 May 1941 according to
hbl September but thus *Brad* from 1928/9; clo 13 June
1960 *(RM July)*; {Holly Bush – Argoed}.
* = not known when original down platform closed.
MARKINCH [NB]
op 20 September 1847 *(Edinburgh Advertiser 21st)*;
still open. M JUNCTION 1862 to 1904 or later in
Brad and thus NB co tt 1900.
MARKS TEY [GE] first in *Brad* December 1844;
still open. M T JUNCTION 1849 to 1878/9 *(Brad)*.
MARLBOROUGH {map 124}
M HL [GW] op 14 April 1864 *(Marlborough 16th)*;
HL added 1 July 1924 *(GW circular 18 June)*;
clo 6 March 1933, service diverted to LL *(RM May)*.
M LL [MSWJ]: special for Marlborough School 26 July;
op to public 27 July 1881**; LL added 1 July 1924
(GW circular 18 June); 1924; clo 11 September 1961
(T 9th); later school use, beginning and end of School
term – last 1 May 1964 (K. Robertson & D. Abbott,
The Marlborough Branch, Irwell, 1990, p.59).
MARLBOROUGH ROAD [Met] op 13 April 1868
(T 10 April, 3 August); clo 20 November 1939 *(Cl)*.
MARLESFORD [GE] line op 1 June 1859 *(T 2nd)*,
in *Brad* June but not mentioned in *Ipswich Journal
4 June* so perhaps delay (B. Wilson);
clo 3 November 1952 *(RM December)*.

MARLOW [GW]: formal op 27 June 1873;
also public use that day – 'hundreds of passengers took
a trial-trip [free?] to Marlow Road and back' *(Reading
5 July)*; clearly fare-paying public use 28th for regatta;
Rtn confused matters further by saying op 26th –
actually inspection date.
GREAT M until 14 February 1899 *(hbl 27 April)*;
re-sited nearby 10 July 1967 *(Cl)*; still open.
MARLOW ROAD – see BOURNE END.
MARLPOOL [GN] op 1 July 1891 *(GN)*;
clo 1 May 1928 *(RAIL 393/151)*. *Hb* 1904:
M for SHIPLEY HALL and thus *Brad* until 1915/6.
MARPLE
MARPLE temporary terminus at COMPSTALL
[MS&L], pending completion of viaduct, op 5 August
1862 *(Mid)*; clo 1 October 1865 (Sunday) *(Mid)* – kept
briefly after opening of permanent station >
MARPLE [GC/Mid] op 1 July 1865 *(Mid)*; still open.
Also see ROSE HILL MARPLE.
MARRON JUNCTION [LNW] op 2 April 1866
(D&C 14); after August 1878 tt, before/with August
1881 tt *Brad* added note that passengers not booked
to/from here – same in LNW co tt 1883; shown 'P' in
1877 *hb* but not later; clo to public 1 July 1897
(Thursday) *(Cl)*; railwaymen used until at least 1923 *(U)*.
MARSDEN near Huddersfield [LNW]
op 1 August 1849 *(co ½ T 18 August- line; in co tt for
1 August, Stockport 3rd)*; still open.
MARSDEN – see BRIERFIELD.
MARSDEN near South Shields [SSMWC]
MARSDEN (a) op 19 March 1888** *(SS)*; replaced
August 1926 by >
MARSDEN (b) op non-tt as WHITBURN COLLIERY,
May 1879; renamed and made public 9 April 1929
(see 1888 March 19**); clo 23 November 1953**.
In *hb* 1938 as M W C.
M COTTAGE op about 1900 *(SS)*; never in *Brad*;
HALT; clo 23 November 1953**; see 1888 March 19**.
MARSH BROOK [SH Jt] op 21 April 1852 *(co ½
T 17 August- line)*; clo 9 June 1958 *(Cl)*.
MARSH GIBBON & POUNDON [LNW]
op 2 August 1880 *(LNW Officers 21078)*;
clo 1 January 1968 *(RM January)*.
MARSH LANE Leeds; {map 56}.
For original terminus see LEEDS.
Through station [NE] op 1 April 1869 *(D&C 8; T 2nd-
line)*; clo 15 September 1958 *(RM October)*.
NE co tt 1880: LEEDS M L.
MARSH LANE
– see BOOTLE; NORTHUMBERLAND PARK.
MARSH MILLS [BE; GW]
Some sort of stop provided Friday 15 March 1861 so
that people of Plympton area could travel to Tavistock
market; not in tt; likely that was Fridays only (Tavistock
market day); at/near 1865 site – entailed walk to/from
Plympton (G.H. Anthony, *The Tavistock, Launceston
and Princetown Railways*, Oakwood, 1983 reprint).
Not known if continuity with >
Full passenger station op 1 November 1865
(co n W D Merc 25 October); clo 31 December 1962**.
MARSH POND – see under BRISTOL.

MARSH ROAD LEVEL CROSSING [GC GI]
op 15 May 1912 *(RCG)*; clo 3 July 1961 *(con G&I)*.
MARSHFIELD [GW] op 2 September 1850
(The Cambrian 30 August); clo 10 August 1959 *(Cl)*.
MARSKE [NE]
op 19 August 1861 *(RAIL 667/395- line)*; still open.
MARSTON – see MILLBROOK.
MARSTON [GW] {Pembridge – Titley}
M LANE first in *Brad* January 1863; last January 1864.
M HALT op 26 April 1929 *(Cl 29)*; same site as above;
clo 5 February 1951 *(RM October)* – see 1951**;
reop 2 April 1951 *(Cl)*; clo 7 February 1955 *(RM March)*.
MARSTON GATE [LNW] first in *Brad* November
1860; clo 2 February 1953 *(LNW Record)*.
MARSTON GREEN [LNW] for op see October
1844**; first in *Brad* January 1845; still open.
MARSTON MAGNA [GW] op 1 September 1856
(W Fly P 2nd- line); MAGNA added 9 May 1895
(hbl 11 July); clo 3 October 1966 *(W D Press 3rd)*.
MARSTON MOOR [NE] op 30 October 1848**;
MOOR added 1 October 1896 *(hbl 29th)*;
clo 15 September 1958 *(RM October)*.
MARTEG [GW]
op 18 May 1931 *(Cl 29)*; HALT; clo 31 December
1962 *(T 31st)*; {St Harmons – Rhayader}.
MARTELL BRIDGE [GW] op 1 January 1930
(RM March); HALT; clo 25 October 1937**; {map 81}.
MARTHAM [MGN] op 15 July 1878 *(MGN)*;
became M for ROLLESBY 1 November 1897
(hbl 28 October) and thus GE co tt 1909, LNE tt 1933
and *Brad* until 1955; clo 2 March 1959 *(T 2nd)*.
MARTIN MILL [Dover & Deal Joint]
op 15 June 1881 *(LCD notice dated 13th)*; still open.
MARTINS HERON
op 3 October 1988 *(Rly Obs December)*; still open.
MARTOCK [GW] op 1 October 1853 *(Taunton 5th)*;
clo 15 June 1964 *(W Gaz 12th, 19th)*.
MARTON near Leamington [LNW] first in tt *Rugby
Advertiser* 1 January 1852 (B Wilson); clo 15 June 1959
(RM July). At times M for SOUTHAM *(Brad)* and
thus LNW co tt 1891; finally to M 1 August 1895
(hbl 11 July).
MARTON near Middlesbrough [NE] op 25 February
1854 *(co ½ T 25 August- line)* as ORMESBY; renamed
17 May 1982; still open.
MARTON (others) – see ELLERBY;
FLAMBOROUGH; STOW PARK.
MARY TAVY & BLACKDOWN [GW]
op 1 July 1865 *(W D Merc 4th- line; in tt Tavistock 8th)*;
& B added 1906/7; clo 31 December 1962**.
MARYTAVY & B until 1908a *hb*, 1940 *Brad*.
MARYHILL
MARYHILL op 3 December 1993 *(BLN 725)*; same
site as M PARK; still open.
M CENTRAL [Cal] op 10 August 1896 *(RCG)*;
CENTRAL added 15 September 1952 *(Cl)*;
clo 5 October 1964 *(RM November)*. Had been
M Barracks pre-passenger use.
M PARK [NB] op 31 May 1858 *(T 7 June)*; clo 2 April
1951 *(RM May)*; but one early morning train continued
to be shown in *Brad* (Milngavie circular for Singer

workmen); PARK added 15 September 1952 (Cl);
wtt 13 June 1960 also one each way; reop fully
19 December 1960 (Cl); clo to public 2 October 1961
(Cl); workmen used to last train Friday or Saturday
28 or 29 February 1964.

MARYKIRK [Cal]: line op 1 November 1849*;
clo 11 June 1956 (RM April); Cl).
* = co ½ T 27 November gives line date; Brad did not give detail
until March 1850, but station was in Topham December 1849,
first time it included line.

MARYLAND [GE] op 6 January 1873 (L); M POINT
until 28 October 1940 (hbl January 1941); still open.

MARYLEBONE
For terminus see under LONDON.

MARYLEBONE [Bak] op 27 March 1907 (L) as
GREAT CENTRAL; renamed 16 April 1917 (hbl 12 July);
still open.

MARYPORT [MC]: for opening see 1840**;
re-sited 4 June 1860 (Cl); still open; {map 20g}.

MARYVILLE [NB] op 1 April 1878 (Hamilton 6th);
clo 1 February 1908 (Saturday) (Cl);
{Broomhouse – Uddingston West}.

MASBOROUGH – see ROTHERHAM.

MASBURY [SD Jt] op 20 July 1874 (Shepton 24th);
became HALT 1938 (SR); clo 7 March 1966 (Shepton
11th). MAESBURY in local press 1874.

MASHAM [NE] op 10 June 1875 (NE maps);
clo 1 January 1931 (Thursday) (T 5 December 1930).

MASSINGHAM [MGN] op 16 August 1879 (T 18th);
clo 2 March 1959 (T 2nd).

MATHRY ROAD [GW]
op 1 August 1923 (RAIL 253/482 dated 15 October 1923)
as M; soon renamed R for ST DAVIDS (hbl ref
15 October 1923): thus GW co tt 1932 and Brad to
1947/8; clo 6 April 1964 (Cl); {map 81}.
Pre-opening Heathfield Pembs (RAC).

MATLOCK [Mid]

MATLOCK op 4 June 1849 (Mid;T 5th- line);
M BRIDGE until 1 July 1905 (hbl 13 July); still open.
Mid co tt 1903: M B for the Hydros.

M BATH op 4 June 1849 (Mid;T 5th- line); clo 6 March
1967 (RM April); reop 27 May 1972 (Cl); still open.

MATTHEWSTOWN [TV] op 1 October 1914
(GW H); see 1904**; clo 16 March 1964 (Cl);
{Abercynon – Mountain Ash}.
Spelling as in tt but place and station nameboard
MATHEWSTOWN (M. Hale, Steam in South Wales 5,
Welsh Railways Research Circle, 1996).

MAUCHLINE [GSW] op 9 August 1848 (GSW- line);
clo 6 December 1965 (RM January 1966).
Was M for CATRINE 1877 to 1903.

MAUD [GNS] op 18 July 1861 (GNS) as BRUCKLAY;
renamed NEW MAUD JUNCTION 24 April 1865
(GNS), M J 1866 tt (Cl), M 21 September 1925 (Cl);
clo 4 October 1965 (Rly Obs November).

MAUDLAND(S) – see PRESTON.

MAUDS BRIDGE [MS&L] first in Brad November
1859; clo 1 October 1866 (Cl); {goods IA}.

MAULDETH ROAD [LNW] op 1 May 1909 (LNW
Officers 42501 + appendix) as M R for WITHINGTON
and thus LNW co tt October 1909, LMS tt 1930;

'for W' dropped 6 May 1974 (BR notice); still open.

MAWCARSE [NB] op 15 March 1858**;
M JUNCTION until 1955/9 (Brad and BR Scot tts
differ – from each other and in body/index within
themselves); aot request; clo 15 June 1964 (RM July).

MAXTON [NB]:
line op 17 June 1850 (Grev Temp), nd, June 1851;
see 1948 August 12**; clo 15 June 1964 (RM July).

MAXWELL PARK [Cal]
op 2 April 1894 (Cal); still open.

MAXWELLTOWN [GSW] op 7 November 1859
(Dumfries 5th); clo 1 March 1939 (Wednesday) (Cl);
still in 30 June to 14 September 1952 wtt for football
use; not in 1963 equivalent.

MAYBOLE [GSW]
op 13 October 1856 (GSW- line); re-sited when line
extended to Girvan 24 May 1860 (Cl); still open.

MAYBOLE JUNCTION [GSW]
op 13 October 1856 (GSW- line);
clo 31 December 1859 (GSW) *.
Later renamed Dalrymple J when goods only.
* = trains still shown December supporting GSW but its date
perhaps last day, rather than Cl (says clo 1 December); in any
case, type of station that might have survived as unadvertised
exchange.

MAYES CROSSING [LMS] (non-tt):
alias HALT NO.1; op 1 January 1923; for workers at
Thames Haven branch factories who lived at Stanford-
le-Hope; prob clo 9 June 1958 (Thames Haven).

MAYFIELD [LBSC] op 1 September 1880 (co ½
T January 1883- line); clo 14 June 1965 (Cl).

MAZE HILL [SE] op 1 January 1873 (co ½ T 17th);
still open. Opened as GREENWICH M H; became
M H & EAST GREENWICH 1 February 1878,
M H & GREENWICH PARK 1 July 1878,
M H for NATIONAL MARITIME MUSEUM 1937
(L) – but M H (E G) SEC co tt 1914;
settled as M H 1955 (Brad).

MEADOW WELL [TWM]
op 14 November 1982 (Tyneside) as SMITHS PARK;
renamed 10 October 1994 (AB, Chron); still open.

MEADOWBANK – see EDINBURGH.

MEADOWHALL

MEADOW HALL [GC] first in Brad May 1868;
M H & WINCOBANK 1 July 1899 (hbl 27 April) to
18 June 1951 (Cl); clo 7 December 1953 (RM Jan. 1954).

MEADOWHALL op 5 September 1990 (Barnsley line
platforms added 8th) (BLN 644); at/near earlier
Wincobank. [Sheffield Supertram] added 21 March
1994 (T 22nd) – calls it M INTERCHANGE.
Still open for both.
For [Mid] station see WINCOBANK.

MEALSGATE [MC] op 26 December 1866
(D&C 14); clo 22 September 1930 (LNW Record).
On map as through station but actually terminus of
separate services from Aspatria and Wigton.

MEASHAM [AN Jt] op 1 September 1873 (LNW
Officers 10205, 10207); clo 13 April 1931 (LNW dates
PCC 192); still excursions at 30 September 1961
(BR doc) – programme of five applied summers 1960
and 1961; excursion to Blackpool 13 August 1962 (AB).

MEASUREMENTS [LMS] op 18 July 1932 *(Cl 29)*; HALT; clo 2 May 1955 *(T 11 March)*.

MEATHOP [Fur] (non-tt): included in *Cumbria* without any detail; {Arnside – Grange-over-Sands}.

MEDBOURNE

MEDBOURNE [GN/LNW] op 2 July 1883 *(co n Leicester Mercury 7th)*; clo 1 April 1916 (Saturday) *(RCG)*.

M BRIDGE – see ASHLEY & WESTON.

MEDGE HALL [GC] first in *Brad* November 1859; clo 12 September 1960 *(RM October)*.

MEDINA WHARF [IWC] (non-tt): perhaps in use by 1882 (goods facilities provided November 1878): *A History of Newport Quay …*, Bill Shepard & Bill Greening, includes report of lad falling into water at wharf and going home to Newport by train, but does not specify station he left; local press reference 21 January 1910 to Jetty station for railway workmen – only users (T. Cooper); clo 21 February 1966 *(IoW)*.

MEDSTEAD & FOUR MARKS [LSW] first in *Brad* August 1868; & F M added 1 October 1937 *(Cl)*; clo 5 February 1973 *(Hants Chron 9th)*.

MEETH [SR] op 27 July 1925 *(Bideford 28th)*; HALT, though included *hb* 1926a and 1929 as M; clo 1 March 1965 *(Express & E 1st)*; {map 116}.

MEIGLE {map 8}

MEIGLE [Cal] op 2 September 1861 *(Newtyle)* as FULLARTON; renamed 1 November 1876 *(RCG)*; clo 2 July 1951 *(RM August)*.

M JUNCTION [Scottish North Eastern] op 2 August 1848 *(Rtn- line; see 1837 B**)*; last in *Brad* June 1861; replaced by Ardler Junction, later renamed Alyth Junction.

MEIKLE EARNOCK [Cal] op 2 February 1863 *(Cal; co ½ Herapath 26 September- line)*; clo 12 December 1943 (Sunday) *(Cl)*. Became HALT according to *hb* 1941a but not seen thus *Brad*; according to *Cl* unstaffed from March 1940.

MEIKLE FERRY [High] op 1 June 1864 *(High)*; clo 1 January 1869 *(Cl)* – still in *Brad* January – inertia?; {Edderton – Tain}.

MEINTHRINFA [VoR] (ng) (non-tt): HALT; stop near 8½ mile point for children at Miss Trotter's nursery school and a few grammar school pupils *(VoR)*; dates ?

MEIR [NS] op 12 May 1894 *(RCG)*; clo 7 November 1966 *(RM January 1967)*.

MEIROS COLLIERY [GW] (non-tt): in use 1890s for miners; {branch from Llanharan} *(U)*.

MELBOURNE [Mid] op 1 September 1868 *(co n Melbourne)*; clo 22 September 1930 *(Mid)*; later military use *(U)*.

MELCOMBE REGIS [WP Jt] op 30 May 1909 *(Weymouth 28th)* – excursion previous day stopped here; effectively addition to Weymouth station for Portland branch trains, saving them from having to reverse in/out of Weymouth; full service clo 3 March 1952 *(RM March)* but retained as summer Saturdays overflow for Weymouth until 12 September 1959 (last train). *Brad* at times: M R (WEYMOUTH).

MELDON [NB] op 23 July 1862 *(NB)*; clo 15 September 1952 *(RM October)*.

MELDON QUARRY [LSW] (non-tt):

HALT/PLATFORM; op about 1890; railwaymen, wives; clo 6 May 1968; {Okehampton – Bridestowe} *(U)*.

MELDRETH [GN] op 1 August 1851 *(co n T 2nd- line)*; M & MELBOURN 1 May 1879 *(Cl; RCG ref April)* to 18 March 1971 *(Cl)*; still open.

MELFORD – see LONG MELFORD.

MELIDEN [LNW] op 28 August 1905 *(RCG)*; clo 22 September 1930 *(Cl)*.

MELKSHAM

MELKSHAM (a) [GW] op 5 September 1848 *(Bath & Chelt 6th)*; clo 18 April 1966 *(RM May)*.

MELKSHAM (b) op 13 May 1985 *(RM June)*, at first one each way, Monday to Fridays, on experimental basis; still open.

MELLING [Fur/Mid] op 6 June 1867 *(Mid)*; clo 5 May 1952 *(RM July)*.

MELLIS [GE] op 2 July 1849 *(T 5th- line)*; clo 7 November 1966 *(RM January 1967)*.

MELLS ROAD [GW] op 1 March 1887 *(co n Som & W J 26 February)* *; ROAD added 16 November 1898 *(hbl 26 January 1899)*; became HALT 17 September 1956 *(Cl)*; clo 2 November 1959 *(Shepton 6th)*. M & BABINGTON in *hb* until 1899a.

* = *Som Standard* wrongly said would open 4th.

MELMERBY [NE] op 1 June 1848 *(co ½ T 30 August- line)* as WATH; renamed M for W 1852 tt *(JS)*; clo 6 March 1967 *(RM March)*. Aot M JUNCTION (some tables) *Brad* and NE co tt 1880.

MELROSE [NB] op 20 February 1849 *(D&C 6- line)*; clo 6 January 1969 *(RM February)*. Reid 1904: M for ABBOTSFORD but just M in NB co tt.

MELTHAM

MELTHAM [LY] op 5 July 1869 *(co n LY)*; clo 23 May 1949 *(RM September)*.

M MILLS (non-tt): PLATFORM; in use 1902; workmen; clo September 1934, but some special trains in WW2; {Healey House – Meltham}.

MELTON near Ipswich

MELTON (a) [GE] op 1 June 1859 *(T 2nd)*; clo 2 May 1955 *(RM June)*.

MELTON (b) op 3 September 1984 *(RM November)*; still open.

MELTON [NE]: alias M CROSSING; HALT; op by October 1920 *(U)*; workmen; mostly non-tt but was in tt towards the end – letter *RM September 1988, p. 599* says had been in footnotes of Table 39 for 'last two years' and it was certainly present 11 May 1987 tt, one train each way; last train 8 July 1989 *(BLN 611)*; {Brough – Ferriby}.

MELTON CONSTABLE [MGN] op 19 January 1882 *(MGN)*; clo 6 April 1964 *(RM April)*. Private platform and waiting room for Lord Hastings.

MELTON MOWBRAY

MELTON MOWBRAY [Mid] op 1 September 1846 *(Mid)*; original temporary station replaced by permanent 1 May 1848 *(Mid)*; originally MELTON; MOWBRAY added 1 November 1876 tt; became M M SOUTH 1923, M M MIDLAND 25 September 1950 tt *(Mid)*, M M TOWN 4 January 1954 *(Brad; C/W)* but TOWN added erratically thereafter; settled as M M 14 June 1965 tt *(Mid)*; still open.

MELTON MOWBRAY [GN/LNW] op 1 September 1879 *(LNW Officers 20028)*; clo 7 December 1953 *(T 7th)* but later summer Saturday and Sunday use to 9 September 1962 (last train) *(Cl)*. During later use became M M NORTH: thus in BR tt 16 September 1957 and wtt 18 June 1962 and on BR ticket *(JB)*.

MELVERLEY [SM] op 2 June 1871 *(D&C 11)*; see 1866 August 13** (Criggion branch) for full details; finally clo 6 November 1933.

MELYNCOURT [GW] op 1 June 1905 *(GW H)*; HALT; clo 15 June 1964 *(RM August)*.

MEMORIAL [Sand Hutton] (ng) op 4 October 1924** *(RM September)*; last train Saturday, 1 March 1930**; {map 40}.

MENAI BRIDGE [LNW]
op 1 October 1858 *(co n Carnarvon 25 September)* as replacement for Britannia Bridge; clo 14 February 1966 *(RM April)*. Aot M B for BEAUMARIS in *Brad* but not seen thus LMS or BR tts.

MENDLESHAM [Mid-Suffolk Light] op 29 September 1908 *(T 28th- line)*; clo 28 July 1952 *(T 28th)*.

MENHENIOT [GW] op 4 May 1859**; still open. GW co tt 1874: M for LOOE.

MENSTON [Mid]
MENSTON (a) op 1 March 1873 *(Mid)*; clo 1 March 1876. (b) effectively replaced it but both briefly open at same time – this still used for Sunday trains and joining/dividing *(Mid)*. M JUNCTION in *Brad*.
MENSTON (b) op 34 chains south 1 November 1875; clo 25 July 1992 for electrification *(BLN 689)*; reop 8 September 1992; still open.
Non-tt: aot line to local mental hospital carried passengers free (not officially authorized) (D. Pedley from local press).

MENSTRIE & GLENOCHIL [NB]
op 3 June 1863 *(D&C 15- line)*; clo 1 November 1954 *(Cl)*. Was M & G in all *Brad* issues sampled, NB co tt 1900 and LNE tt 1933. Hb added & G 1904; *hba* May 1948 said had become M for Tullibody but not seen thus *Brad*.

MENTHORPE GATE [NE]:
line op 1 August 1848**; first certain reference November 1851; clo 7 December 1953 *(RM Jan. 1954)*.

MEOLE BRACE [SM]
op 14 April 1911 *(RCG)*; clo 6 November 1933**.

MEOLS [Wirral] op 2 July 1866 *(D&C 10)*; still open.

MEOLS COP [LY]
op 2 September 1887 *(Southport Guard 8th)*; still open.

MEOPHAM [LCD] op Monday 6 May 1861 *(co n T 1st)*; still open. In opening notice as M ROAD.

MERCANTILE COLLIERY [PT] (non-tt): agreement signed 15 March 1899 between PT and Messrs Powley, Thomas & Co for train from Port Talbot Central at £1 per day for miners (who would pay no fares selves); no evidence of BoT approval; clo ?; {branch from Tonmawr} (M. Hale).

MERCHISTON [Cal] op 1 July 1882 *(D&C 6)*; clo 6 September 1965 *(RM September)*.

MERKLAND STREET [GU]
op 14 December 1896**; clo 21 May 1977.

Replaced by Partick when line reopened.

MERRYLEES [Mid] op 18 July 1832 *(Mid)*; see 1847 December**; re-sited 150 yards west of road overbridge 27 March 1848 *(Cl)*; originally MERRY LEES; clo 1 March 1871 (Wednesday) *(Cl)*; {map 62}.

MERRYTON op 12 December 2005**; still open.

MERSEY ROAD – see AIGBURTH.

MERSTHAM op 12 July 1841, originally request stop *(co n T 9th)*; on stretch of line op by London & Brighton, later transferred to SE; even after transfer only used by Brighton trains; Brighton notice dated 2 October 1843 *(T 2nd)* says M has been clo by SE so trains will no longer call; reop 4 October 1844 (Countess of Warwick had it reopened until new station ready); re-sited about ½ mile north, about 1845 *(SE)*; for time being only used by SE trains; still open.

MERSTONE [IWC]: line op 1 February 1875; this station probably later – first in *Brad* June 1876; see 1875**; re-sited from east to west of level crossing June 1895 *(IWC)*; aot request; M JUNCTION 1897/8 *(Brad)* to 1 October 1911 *(hbl 26th)*; clo 6 February 1956 *(Southern Daily Echo 6th)*.

MERTHYR TYDFIL
MERTHYR [TV] op 21 April 1841 *(Merlin 17th, 24th)*; clo 1 August 1877 (Wednesday) *(Cl)*, service diverted to GW station.
M ROAD [Vale of Neath] temporary station, with road connection to Merthyr, op 24 September 1851**; {Hirwain – Gelli Tarw physical junction}; replaced by >
M TYDFIL [GW] op 2 November 1853 *(GW)*; original replaced 1971 by one on new site in John Street; T added 1980; re-sited 200 yards short of original, in Court Street 14 January 1996 *(Monmouthshire Railway Society Journal, September 1996, p.27)*; still open. Aot M HIGH STREET in some tables – at first probably to help travellers find right station after diversion: GW tables were last to have H S added and first to lose again; some kept to 1927 *(Brad)*; also used in LNW co tts, e.g. 1883.
M VALE [TV] op 1 June 1883 *(S Wales 1st)*; still open.

MERTON
M ABBEY [LSW/LBSC] op 1 October 1868 *(L; co n T 1st- line)*; clo 1 January 1917 *(T 22 December 1916)*; reop 27 August 1923 *(RM October)*; clo 3 March 1929 (Sunday) *(T 23 February)*.
M PARK [LSW/LBSC] (LOWER M until 1 September 1887, *L*): M Abbey line platforms op 1 October 1868 *(L; co n T 1st- line)*; clo 1 January 1917, reop 27 August 1923 *(RM October)*; clo 3 March 1929 *(T 23 February)*. Mitcham line platforms added 1 November 1870 *(L)*; HALT in *Brad* 1918 to 1923/4 and on ticket *(JB)*; clo 1 June 1997** for conversion >
M PARK [Croydon] op 30 May 2000 *(RM July)*; still open.
Also see SOUTH MERTON.

MERTON ROAD – see BOOTLE VILLAGE.

METHERINGHAM
For first use of site see BLANKNEY & M.
METHERINGHAM op 6 October 1975 *(T 6th)*; above reop as M; still open.

METHIL [NB] op 5 May 1887 *(Wemyss)*;
clo 10 January 1955 *(T 28 December 1954)*.

METHLEY

M JUNCTION [LY] first in *Brad* March 1860;
clo 4 October 1943 *(LNW Record)*.

M NORTH [Mid] op 6 April 1841**; NORTH added
25 September 1950 *(Mid)*; clo 16 September 1957
(RM November).

M SOUTH [Methley Joint] op 1 May 1869 *(D&C 7)*;
SOUTH added 2 March 1951 *(Cl)*; clo 7 March 1960
(RM April).

METHVEN [Cal]

METHVEN op 1 January 1858 *(Tayside)*; see 1921 April/
May** – was JUNCTION available to public while this
was closed?; clo 27 September 1937 *(RM November)*.

M JUNCTION op 21 May 1866**; unadvertised
exchange 1889 to 27 September 1937, when it took
over role of closed branch station; clo 1 October 1951
(RM November). HALT at clo according to *RM* and
thus 1938 *hb* but not *Brad* (last seen August 1951).

METROCENTRE
op 3 August 1987 *(RM October)*; GATESHEAD M C
until 17 May 1993 tt *(AB Chron)* ; still open.

MEXBOROUGH [GC]

M JUNCTION first in *Brad* January 1850; replaced
30 chains east by >

MEXBOROUGH op 3 April 1871 *(GC)*, initially
M NEW in *Brad* (to advise passengers rather than as
part of name?); still open.
Hb showed both OLD and NEW as 'P' up to and
including 1890; in 1895 'P' shown only for NEW.

MEYRICK PARK [LSW]
op 1 March 1906 *(RM April)*; HALT;
clo 1 November 1917 (Thursday) *(Cl)*; {map 125}.

MICHELDEVER [LSW]
op 11 May 1840 *(tt Salisbury 9th)* as ANDOVER
ROAD; renamed 1856 tt *(Cl)*; still open. Local press
usage at the start: M *(Hants Advertiser)*, but A R
(Salisbury tt).

MICKLAM [CW Jc]
op 2 June 1913 *(RCG)*; clo 31 May 1926 *(Cl)*; used by
workmen until 1 April 1929 *(Cumbria)*; {map 21}.

MICKLE TRAFFORD

MICKLE TRAFFORD [Birkenhead] op 2 December
1889 *(Birkenhead)*; clo 2 April 1951 *(RM May)*.

M T EAST [CLC] op 1 May 1875 *(CLC)*;
EAST added 5 June 1950 *(Cl)*; clo 12 February 1951
(RM May) – see 1951**.

MICKLEFIELD [NE]:
line op 22 September 1834**; still open.

MICKLEHURST [LNW] op 1 July 1886 *(RCG;
LNW Officers 28684* – 'local service')*;
clo 1 May 1907 (Wednesday) *(Cl)*; {map 53}.

MICKLEOVER [GN] op 1 April 1878 *(GN)*;
lost trains with start of LNE emergency tt 2 October
1939; later excursions, e.g to Skegness *(Skegness p.192)*
and 1 August 1957 to Trentham Gardens *(AB)*.
GN co tt 1909: M for RADBOURNE and thus *Brad*
to closure (*hb* M for RODBOURNE, GN ticket
M for RADBURN, *JB*).

MICKLETHWAITE [MC]: only reference seen is in
Cl, which says in tt June 1845 (company tt? – not found
in *Brad* which then gave nd tables for this line); perhaps
casual stop – see 1840** for habits of MC at that time
{Wigton – Curthwaite}.

MICKLETON near Barnard Castle [NE]
op 13 May 1868 *(Darlington 16th)*;
clo 30 November 1964 *(RM December)*.

MICKLETON [GW] op 8 November 1937 *(T 4th)**;
HALT; clo 6 October 1941 *(Cl)*;
{Campden – Honeybourne}.
* = *GW H* says opened 11th; however, *T* said would open on
'Monday' and Monday was one of the standard opening days
for halts; mid-week openings were rare, though not unknown.
Perhaps last minute delay?

MICKLEY [NE]
first used, non-tt, as ELTRINGHAM(E) COLLIERY
(NC); first in *Brad* November 1859 for Saturdays only
market service from Newcastle; since this terminated at
Mickley, thus compelling reference in tt, it may be that
other trains stopped here and had been doing so before
1859; by closure, also one each way Tuesdays; last in
Brad June 1915; {Prudhoe – Stocksfield}.

MID CLYTH [High]
op 1 July 1903 *(High)*; clo 3 April 1944**.

MID FEARN [High] op 1 October 1864 *(High)*;
clo 31 March 1865 *(High)*, though still in *Brad* April
1865 (inertia?); {Bonar Bridge – Edderton}.
Later non-tt use: wtt appendix 1 May 1920 says most
trains would stop by request during times Mid-Fearn
Lodge was occupied; still in *hb* 1938 as M F HALT,
'P'; (in *U* as WEST F PLATFORM).

MIDCALDER – see KIRKNEWTON.

MIDDLE DROVE [GE]: line op 1 February 1848**,
nd, by May 1848 *(Topham)*; aot request;
clo 9 September 1968 *(RM November)*.

MIDDLE STOKE [SEC] first in *Brad* July or August
1906; HALT; clo 4 December 1961 *(T 8 November)*.

MIDDLESBROUGH [NE]:
formal op 27 December 1830 *(NE)*. Variety of dates in
print for public opening; S&D annual report said had
op to the public before the close of 1830 – but no
guarantee that its use of 'public' was same as this book's.
RAIL 667/395, very sketchy chronological record of
S&D, gives 1 January 1831 – perhaps 'conventional'
rather than actual date. See 1825**. Original terminus
was by Watson's Wharf; replaced in 1837 by station in
Commercial Street.
Company had continuing problem with people using
line from Stockton as footpath, even after steam
introduced for all traffic. To try to combat this they
allowed cheap travel by any coal train that happened
to be running and also provided a very cheap basic
service, run more or less on demand *(S&D Pass)*.
1837 station replaced by temporary (site unknown)
on op of extension to Redcar 5 June 1846**, replaced
again by permanent station in Sussex Street August
1847 (minutes contradictory over exact date);
re-sited slightly east 1 December 1877 *(Cl)*; still open.

MIDDLESBROUGH JUNCTION
– see STOCKTON S&D.

MIDDLETON [CHP] – see 1833 May★★.
MIDDLETON [LY]
MIDDLETON op 1 May 1857 (A. Brackenbury, *Chron 33*, citing T. Wray, *The Middleton Branch*, LY Society 1999)★; clo 7 September 1964 *(RM October)*.
In *hb* 1872 (only) as M TOWN.
★ = this is date given in list of LY openings drawn up in 1920 by company's Chief Engineer. 5 January 1857, given by most in print, including earlier versions of this book, seems to have resulted from someone unknown muddling figures, 1 5 1857 becoming 5 1 1857. Inspection reports also support May date.
M JUNCTION op 31 March 1842 *(LY)* as OLDHAM JUNCTION; renamed M 11 August 1842 *(Cl)*; M JUNCTION 1852 tt *(Cl)*; clo 3 January 1966 *(RM February)*.

MIDDLETON & DINSDALE
– see FIGHTING COCKS.

MIDDLETON NORTH [NB]
op 23 July 1862 *(NB)*; NORTH added 1 July 1923 *(hbl 12th)*; clo 15 September 1952★★.

MIDDLETON ROAD [Mid]
op 11 July 1904 *(Mid)* ★; alias M R BRIDGE; clo June 1905 *(Mid)*; {on Heysham branch}.
★ = not even in company tt; evidence from *RM September 1904* and ticket for 20 July 1904 *(JB)*.

MIDDLETON TOWERS [GE]
op 27 October 1846 *(co n D&C 5)*; aot request; TOWERS added 1 November 1924 *(RAIL 393/151)*; clo 9 September 1968 *(RM November)*.

MIDDLETON-IN-TEESDALE [NE] op 13 May 1868 *(Darlington 16th)*; -in-T added 1894 tt *(Cl)* but always in *hb*; clo 30 November 1964 *(RM December)*.

MIDDLETON-ON-LUNE [LNW]
op 16 September 1861 *(co n Lancaster Gaz)*; clo 13 April 1931 *(LNW dates PCC 192)*. According to *hbl July* was M WESTMORLAND from ? until 19 July 1926 but not seen thus *Brad* or LNW co tt.

MIDDLETON-ON-THE-WOLDS [NE]
op 21 April 1890 *(RCG)*; clo 20 September 1954 *(RM October)*.

MIDDLETOWN HILLS – see BREIDDEN.
MIDDLEWICH [LNW] op 1 July 1868 *(co ½ T 14 August- line)*; clo 4 January 1960 *(RM February)*.

MIDDLEWOOD
Both [GN/NS] and [LNW] op 1 April 1879 and were given improved services in June 1879 tt (B. Jeuda, *Railways of Macclesfield*, Foxline 1995)★ >
[GN/NS] was M JUNCTION in *Brad* until 1901/2; became M HIGHER 25 July 1951 *(Cl)*; clo 7 November 1960 *(RM December)*.
[LNW] op as M for NORBURY;
became N for HIGH LANE 1 July 1899 *(LNW dates)*, M LOWER 1951/2 *(Brad)* – actual date as for Higher?, M 6 May 1968 tt *(AB)*; still open.
★ = not surprising different dates in print – *LNW Officers*: 'would probably be opened' 1 November 1878 *(18949, 15 October)*; 'would be opened' 1 April 1879 *(19367, 18 February)*; finally 'would be opened' 1 June 1879 *(19613, 16 April)*; since they had already agreed on tt for station it would have been easy to put on some sort of service earlier.

MIDFORD
MIDFORD [SD Jt] op 20 July 1874 *(Shepton 24th)*; clo 7 March 1966 *(Shepton 11th)*.
MIDFORD [GW] op 27 February 1911 *(Bristol NWR)*; HALT; clo 22 March 1915 *(RCG)*.

MIDGE HALL [LY]
op 1 November 1859 *(Preston P 5th)* as replacement for Cocker Bar; clo 2 October 1961 *(RM November)*.
MIDGHAM [GW] op 21 December 1847 *(GW; Hants Chron 25th- line)* as WOOLHAMPTON; renamed 1 July 1873 *(Cl; RCG ref April)*; HALT 2 November 1964 to 5 May 1969 *(Cl)*; still open.

MIDHURST
MIDHURST [LBSC] op 15 October 1866 *(LBSC)*; re-sited 23 chains east on op of line to Chichester 11 July 1881 *(Cl)*; clo 7 February 1955 *(BR notice W Sussex)*; ramblers' special 8 June 1958 *(RM August 1958, photo facing p. 515)*.
MIDHURST [LSW] op 1 September 1864 *(co ½ T 13 February 1865)*; clo 13 July 1925 *(Cl)*, when lines were linked so that all could use ex-LBSC station.

MIDSOMER NORTON
M N & WELTON [GW] op 3 September 1873 *(Bristol T 4th- line)* as W; renamed W & M N 2 May 1898 *(hbl 7 July)*, M N & W 1 May 1904 *(hbl 28 April)*; clo 2 November 1959 *(Shepton 6th)*.
GW co tt 1881: W for M N.
M N & WELTON SOUTH [SD Jt] op 20 July 1874 *(Shepton 24th)*; & W added 16 October 1898 *(hbl 27th)*; became M N & W UPPER 26 September 1949 *(Cl)*; M N & W SOUTH 1950/1 *(Brad)*; clo 7 March 1966 *(Shepton 11th)*.

MIDVILLE [GN] op 1 July 1913 *(RCG)*; clo 5 October 1970 *(T 16 July)*. *Brad* October 1939 shows it reduced to 1 train daily, towards Firsby; probably change to this made 11 September, when a number of temporary closures were made in this area; November tt showed one train each way.

MILBORNE PORT [LSW] op 7 May 1860 *(W Fly P 15th)*; HALT from 1960 *(Brad)* and thus BR SR tt 12 September 1960; clo 7 March 1966 *(Chard 3rd)*.

MILCOTE [GW]
op 12 July 1859 (see STRATFORD-UPON-AVON, Honeybourne line); new platforms north of level crossing (old buildings kept) about 9 May 1908 *(Cl)*; clo 3 January 1966 *(RM February)*. At first M, WESTON & WELFORD in *Brad*; became just M in *Brad* 1864/March 1865 but GW co tt June 1865/1869. *Hb* 1862 M & WESTON, 1904 on M for WESTON-ON-AVON and WELFORD-ON-AVON.

MILDENHALL
MILDENHALL [GE] op 1 April 1885 *(GE- line)*; clo 18 June 1962 *(RM August)*.

M DROVE/ROAD – see SHIPPEA HILL.
M GOLF – see WORLINGTON.

MILDMAY PARK [NL] op 1 January 1880 *(T 2nd, NL Circular 158)*; clo 1 October 1934 *(T 26 September)*.

MILE END
MILE END [GE] probably effectively replaced LONDON DEVONSHIRE STREET M E and BOW (both of which see – it was about half way between the

two). The Eastern Counties line opened through here 20 June 1839 but the first certain* appearance of the line in *Brad* was in a sheet dated 'April 1841' *(RAIL 903/535)*; it would seem unlikely that stations so close would have been open at same time but the scanty evidence is contradictory. M E was the only one of the trio to be included in the sheet cited but the *Returns* show that DEVONSHIRE STREET was still in use on 11 April. It may be that two or three were kept together for a while; perhaps the *Brad* entry was premature; perhaps some form of loose use of names was involved. For a long time *Brad* had note that up trains would not call in foggy weather. Clo 24 May 1872 (Friday) *(co n T 23rd)*, replaced by Bethnal Green, a little west.

* = it was in a *Companion* most of whose contents seem to have dated from March 1841 but Eastern Counties page was clearly pasted in.

MILE END [Dist] op 2 June 1902 *(RCG)*; [Met] added 30 March 1936; still open.

MILE END [Cen] op 4 December 1946 *(T 5th)*; still open.

MILEPOST items – see APPIN; LOCHEILSIDE; TULLOCH; TYNDRUM.

MILES PLATTING [LY]
op 1 January 1844 *(LY)*; last train Friday 26 May 1995 *(BLN 754)*. M P JUNCTION in some tables at least 1847 to 1878 *(Brad)*.

MILFORD near Leeds
MILFORD [NE] op 9 November 1840 *(NE maps – line)*; initially just JUNCTION in *Brad*; became M J 1850 tt, M 1 May 1893 *(Cl)*; clo 1 October 1904 (Saturday) *(Cl)*; replaced by Monk Fryston. Hb added JUNCTION 1867.
M BRIDGE – see SOUTH MILFORD.
M JUNCTION – see GASCOIGNE WOOD.

MILFORD & BROCTON [LNW] op 18 May 1877 *(LNW Officers 17195)*; clo 6 March 1950 *(RM May)*. Became M & B for CANNOCK CHASE 1933/4 *(Brad)*, hb 1936a.

MILFORD HAVEN
MILFORD HAVEN [GW] op 7 September 1863 *(Rtn)* as M; became OLD M 1892/3 *(Brad)*, M H 30 August 1906 *(hbl 25 October)*; still open.
Non-tt: *GW Running Powers Book* shows that trains ran into DOCKS 7 December 1898 in connection with sailing of *s.s. Gaspesia*. Other times?
Also see JOHNSTON; NEYLAND.

MILFORD SURREY [LSW]
op 1 January 1859 *(SR; co n T 1st- line)*; still open.

MILK PLATFORM [BPGV] (non-tt): perhaps used by passengers in 1940s; {Pinged – Trimsaran Road} *(U)*.

MILKWALL [SW Jt] op 9 December 1875**; clo 8 July 1929 *(RM August)*. GW co tt 1902, Mid co tt 1903, *Brad* to closure: M for CLEARWELL.

MILL HILL [IWC]
op 1871 (orders to open 'forthwith' given 14 May 1871, IoW; first in *Brad* October 1871); rebuilt and partly re-sited 1880 after fire previous year (T. Cooper); clo 21 February 1966 *(RM March)*.

MILL HILL London.
M H BROADWAY [Mid] op 13 July 1868 *(T 14th)*; BROADWAY added 25 September 1950 *(RM October)*; still open.

M H EAST op by [GN] 22 August 1867 *(L; co n T 22nd-line)* as M H; became M H for M H BARRACKS 17 April 1916 *(hbl 27th)*, M H EAST for M H B 1 February 1928; GN service clo 11 September 1939*; reop by [Nor] 18 May 1941 as M H E *(Brad)* but still 'for ...' in *hb* 1956; still open.

M H THE HALE [GN] op 11 June 1906 *(L)* as THE HALE HALT; renamed M H the H 1 March 1928 *(RAIL 393/151)* – but THE H for M H in LNE tt 1927; clo 11 September 1939*. Hb 1912 THE H for M H, 1929 M H for THE H.
* = replacement bus service for holders of rail tickets until 18 May 1941 (letter, H.V. Borley, *RCHS Journal vol. 16, no. 1, p. 13; London Local; RM July 1941)*. The table in *Brad* gives times of departure from Finchley and Egware; a note below says that passengers 'join and alight at the bus stopping place at the junction of Hale Lane and Broadway' (according to Borley, tickets had to be obtained from station booking office). No mention of Mill Hill East – stop at station itself assumed?

MILL HILL LANCASHIRE [LY]
first in *Brad* December 1884; L added body of tt 1979/87 (index earlier); still open.

MILL HILL PARK – see ACTON TOWN.

MILL POND [WS]; {Sidlesham – Chalder}
MILL POND (a) temporary terminus when flooding cut line, op 15 December 1910 *(Cl)*; last in *Brad* May 1911. According to notice in *W Sussex* line would reopen on or before 1 June 1911 (but notice dated February); notice says bus service will run between Sidlesham and Ferry – presumably this 'Sidlesham' was Mill Pond.
MILL POND (b) op 9 July 1928 *(Cl)*; clo 20 January 1935**.

MILL ROAD [GE] op 18 December 1922 *(RM April 1923)*; HALT; clo 15 September 1952 *(RM October)*.

MILL STREET Aberdare [TV]; {map 86}
MILL STREET (a) op 5 April 1847*; clo 21 November 1852 (Sunday) *(Aberdare)*.
* = date of co tt *(RAIL 981/491; also reproduced RM July 1898)*, assumed to be op tt for this station.
MILL STREET (b) op 26 November 1904; see 1904**; same site; last trains shown June 1912 *Brad*; miners continued to use until 8 June 1925 *(Cardiff Division Annual Report)*; {goods IA}.

MILLBROOK BEDS [LNW] op 18 November 1846** as MARSTON; became AMPTHILL 1847 tt, A MARSTON 1850 *(Cl)* and thus LNW co tt 1852, MILLBROOK for A March 1877 tt *(JS; recommended LNW Officers 13 February)*, M 1 July 1910 *(hbl 28 April)*; BEDS added body of tt 14 May 1984 (index earlier); still open.

MILLBROOK HANTS [LSW]
first in *Brad* November 1861; HANTS added 12 May 1980 tt *(C/W)*; still open.

MILLERHILL [NB]: line op 21 June 1847, nd, 1 September 1847 *(co tt, True Line)* – not in notice *Edinburgh Advertiser 13 July*, but tt there was not in standard form; last in *Brad* August 1849 and missing from *Edinburgh District tt* December 1849; back in tt by 1 March 1858 *(Paton's Edinburgh)* – *Brad* April 1858; clo 7 November 1955 *(RM December)*. Usually MILLER HILL early on. M for EDMONDSTONE in

Brad by 1859 and thus to 1938/9 but not in LNE tt 1933.

MILLERS BRIDGE [LY]: trains first shown October 1851 Brad; last shown April 1876; {Sandhills – Bootle}.

MILLERS DALE [Mid]
op 1 June 1863 (Mid; co n T 29 May- line);
M D for TIDESWELL 1 May 1889 co tt to 14 June 1965 tt (Mid); clo 6 March 1967 (RM April).

MILLFIELD
MILLFIELD [NE] op 1 June 1853 (T 6th- line); at some point re-sited from east to west of Hylton Road overbridge (Durham); clo 2 May 1955 (Cl).
MILLFIELD [TWM] op 31 March 2002★★, west of 1955 site; still open.
MILLGROVE [CW Jc] (non-tt): in use by 23 July 1903 for W. Burnyeat, Railway Director; probably also used by convalescent troops during First World War; probably clo after Burnyeat's death in 1921; {Moresby Park – Distington} (Journal of Cumbrian Railways Association September 1996).

MILLHOUSES & ECCLESALL [Mid]
op 1 February 1870 (Mid; co n Mining 19th- line) as E; became E & MILL HOUSES 1 October 1871 co tt (Mid), M H & E 1 May 1884 co tt (RCG) of E, M & E 1930s; clo 10 June 1968 (Cl). RCH sources give some different (and conflicting) dates.
MILLIGAN [GNS] op 1 October 1859 (GNS); request; alias MILLAGAN/MILLEGAN; last in Brad September 1863 – coincided with tt rearrangement so perhaps closed earlier/continued longer; according to RCHS Journal July 1979 it closed 1 July 1875, but this cited note from goods manager which perhaps concerned surviving goods; in hb 1877 as M SIDING, no facilities shown;
{Knock – Grange North physical junction}.

MILLIKEN PARK
MILLIKEN PARK (a) [GSW] first in Brad March 1846 (GSW gives 1 March, but that a Sunday); op as COCHRANE MILL; altered to COCHRANEMILL 1851 tt (JS); became M P 1 March 1853 (Cl); clo 18 April 1966 (RM May).
MILLIKEN PARK (b) op 15 May 1989, 200 yards south of earlier (RM July); still open.

MILLISLE [PPW Jt] {map 17}
The first GARLIESTOWN station (which see) was renamed Millisle when second Garliestown opened, but not used immediately for passengers. When Whithorn branch opened 9 July 1877 (Kirkcudbright 13th) a primarily exchange platform, MILLISLE (first passenger use of that name) was opened about 7 chains north, in the angle between the lines; local passengers could walk along line to/from platform at original site. At first connection to Garliestown branch via a siding. After Garliestown branch closed (1 March 1903), trains stopped at original site. (See Little SW Scot; H.D. Thorne, Rails to Portpatrick, T. Stephenson & Sons, 1976.) Clo 25 September 1950 (Cl).
Cal co tt 1913, LMS tt 1930, Murray 1948 and Brad to closure: M for GARLIESTON [sic].
Also see GARLIESTOWN.

MILLOM [Fur] op 1 November 1850 (co n Furness Rise) as HOLBORN HILL; renamed 1 August 1866

(Cl; RCG ref October) but in Brad as M for H H until 1893/4; still open.

MILLS HILL
MILLS HILL (a) [Manchester & Leeds] op 4 July 1839 (LY; co n T 11th- line); clo 11 August 1842 (Thursday) (Cl) – still in Brad September (inertia?)
MILLS HILL (b) op 25 March 1985 (BLN 514); still open.
MILLS OF DRUM [Deeside] op 8 September 1853 (GNS); clo 1 January 1863 (Thursday) (Cl).
MILLTIMBER [GNS] first in Brad January 1854; clo 5 April 1937 (RM January 1938).
MILLTOWN [Ashover] (ng)
op 7 April 1925 (RM October); request;
clo 14 September 1936★★ (Cl); {map 59}.
MILLWALL [GE]
M DOCK: [owned PLA but GE provided service];
op 18 December 1871, for workmen, trains horse-drawn from M Junction; Blackwall co ½ (T 10 February 1872) described this opening as 'to the Glengall Road, about the centre of the Millwall Docks'. Original was temporary; re-sited to permanent south of Glengall Road 29 July 1872 (Milkwall) for ordinary passengers; locomotive haulage 23 August 1880 (Millwall).
Clo 4 May 1926★★. GE co tt October 1914 still M DOCKS; Brad changed from M DOCKS to M DOCK August 1915; hb changed earlier – M DOCKS 1895, M DOCK 1904.
M JUNCTION op 18 December 1871 (L);
clo 4 May 1926★★. Used 21 July 1928 for 77 adults and 862 children to go to Clacton as guests of Mayor of Poplar 'to secure passenger traffic from road' (LNER Magazine September).
M SOUTH DOCK (non-tt): 12 September 1878 BoT sanctioned line to Wool Office here for use by occasional horse-drawn services for wool buyers (Millwall).
MILLWAY [NS] (non-tt): alias RADWAY GREEN M; op in October 1944 (R. Christiansen, Portrait of the North Staffs Railway, Ian Allan, 1997); Ordnance Factory workers; clo 5 January 1959 (U);
{branch from Radway Green}.
MILNATHORT [NB]
op 15 March 1858★★; clo 15 June 1964 (RM July).
MILNGAVIE [NB]
op 28 July 1863 (Glasgow); still open.
MILNROW [LY]
op 2 November 1863 (LY); still open.
MILNSBRIDGE – see LONGWOOD.
MILNTHORPE [LNW] op 22 September 1846 (co n Lancaster 26th); clo 1 July 1968 (Cl).
MILTON near Banbury [GW] op 1 January 1908 (GW H); HALT; clo 4 June 1951 (T 4th).
MILTON near Bournemouth – see NEW MILTON.
MILTON near Stoke-on-Trent [NS]
first in Brad May 1868; clo 7 May 1956 (RM June);
last football use (Stoke City) 23 April 1960 (BR doc);
wakes week use still at 19 August 1961 (BR handbill);
last probably 10 August 1963 – no 1964 leaflet found (AB)
MILTON JUNCTION – see BRAMPTON.
MILTON KEYNES CENTRAL
op 14 May 1982 (Rly Obs June 1982); still open.

MILTON OF CAMPSIE [NB]
op 5 July 1848 (*D&C 6- line*) as MILTOWN; became
MILTON in tt 1874 (*JS*); 'of C' added 1 May 1912
(*hbl 25 April*); clo 1 October 1951 (*RM November*).
MILTON RANGE [SEC] first in *Brad* July or August
1906; HALT; aot request; clo 17 July 1932 (Sunday) (*Cl*);
continued in non-tt use for rifle range until at least
1956 (*U*); {Gravesend – Cliffe}.
MILTON ROAD [SEC]
first in *Brad* July or August 1906; HALT; clo 1 May
1915 (Saturday) (*RCG*); {Gravesend – Cliffe}.
MILTON ROAD Weston-super-Mare [WCP]
op 1 December 1897 (*WCP; Bristol T 2nd- line*);
request; clo 20 May 1940 (*Bridgwater Merc 22nd*).
Ticket: M R for KEWSTOKE (*JB*).
MILTONISE [GSW] (non-tt): railwaymen, families;
in use 1926; {Barrhill – Glenwhilly} (*U*).
MILVERTON – see LEAMINGTON.
MILVERTON near Taunton [GW] op 8 June 1871
(*W Som F P 17th*); clo 3 October 1966 (*Som Gaz 7th*).
MINDRUM [NE] op 5 September 1887 (*NE- line*);
clo 22 September 1930** (*T 10 July*).
MINEHEAD [GW] op 16 July 1874 (*Som H 18th*);
clo 4 January 1971 (*Som Gaz 8th*). See 2007 July 20**.
MINETY & ASHTON KEYNES [GW]
op 31 May 1841 (*GW; Wilts 3 June- line*);
& A K added 18 August 1905 (*RAIL 253/482 18 August,
'in future will be'*) but *hbl 26 October* gave 1 October;
clo 2 November 1964 (*Cl*).
MINFFORDD (MYNFFORDD until 1890, *Brad*)
MINFFORDD [Cam] op 1 August 1872 (*D&C 11*); M
JUNCTION until 1894 (*Brad*); still open.
MINFFORDD (ng) [Festiniog] op 1 August 1872 (*D&C
11*); see 1923 January 1**; clo 18 September 1939**.
MINNINGLOW – see 1833 May**.
MINORIES – see LONDON.
MINSHULL VERNON [LNW] op 4 July 1837
(*co n GJ*); clo 2 March 1942 (*LNW Record*).
MINSTER Thanet [SE]:
line op 14 April 1846 (*T 14th*), nd, June 1846; still open.
M DEAL JUNCTION/M J in *Brad* 1849 to 7 May
1945 (*JS; Cl*) and M J in SE co tt 1864; THANET
added 1 August 1901 (*RCG*) to 1968/72 tt – *RCG*
made change from M, not M J.
MINSTER-ON-SEA
MINSTER-ON-SEA [SEC] op 1 August 1901 (*RCG*);
M SHEPPEY until 1 May 1906 (*hbl 26 April*);
clo 4 December 1950 (*T 4th*).
Also see EAST MINSTER-ON-SEA.
MINSTERLEY [Shrewsbury & Welshpool]
op 14 February 1861 (*GW*);
clo 5 February 1951 (*RM October*) – see 1951**.
MINTLAW [GNS]
op 18 July 1861 (*GNS*) as OLD DEER & M; renamed
1 December 1867 (*RCG*); clo 3 May 1965 (*RM May*).
MIRFIELD [LY]
first in *Brad* April 1845; re-sited 5 March 1866 (*Cl*);
still open. M JUNCTION 1852 to 1882/3 in *Brad*.
MISTERTON [GN/GE]
op 15 July 1867 (*GN/GE; co ½ T 19 August- line*);
clo 11 September 1961 (*RM September*); later excur (*U*).

MISTLEY [GE] op 15 August 1854**
(was in inspection report); aot request; still open.
MITCHAM
MITCHAM [LBSC] op 22 October 1855* (*T 23rd*);
clo 1 June 1997**, for conversion to >
MITCHAM [Croydon] op 30 May 2000; still open.
* *T 22 October* carried two op notices, one detailing
service from London Bridge, other from Waterloo.
T 26th had notice (dated 25th) saying service from
London Bridge had been suspended until 1 November.
No indication found on whether service from Waterloo
also affected. Theoretically could have continued since
accident occurred near 'the village of Beddington' on
Croydon side of Mitcham. However mention in *Brad
Sh* and fact that line was being operated as a whole by
contractor (G.P. Bidder) makes this unlikely.
Not confirmed that line did reopen 1 November;
perhaps they waited for inquest on driver, held
5 November (*T 6th*), at which jury endorsed
Colonel Yolland's recommendation of 20mph limit.
M EASTFIELDS: op afternoon 2 June 2008 (*Rly Obs
September 2008, p. 466*); still open.
M JUNCTION [LBSC]
op 1 October 1868 (*T 28 September*); still open.
M JUNCTION [Croydon] op 30 May 2000; still open.
MITCHELDEAN ROAD [GW]
op 1 June 1855**; clo 2 November 1964 (*Cl*).
MITCHELL & NEWLYN [GW] op 14 August
1905**; HALT; clo 4 February 1963 (*W Briton 4th*).
MITESIDE [Raven] (ng) (non-tt): dates ?; private;
RM August 1901 refers to unnamed station about 1 mile
(actually about ½ mile) beyond Muncaster used by
inhabitants of large red house on left hand side of line;
station built out of boat cut in half lengthways.
Confirmed as Miteside by *Raven* p.101 (1968), which
suggests long out of use; {Muncaster – Irton Road}.
MITHIAN [GW] op 14 August 1905**; HALT;
clo 4 February 1963 (*W Briton 4th*).
MOAT LANE
MOAT LANE [Llanidloes & Newtown]
op 2 September 1859 (*Cam*); alias CAERSWS; clo 5
January 1863** (inferred from op date of M L
Junction); was where *RAC* Atlas shows Old Moat Lane
level crossing, south-west of Moat Lane Junction, on way
to Llandinam; replaced by Caersws.
M L JUNCTION [Cam] op 5 January 1863**;
clo 31 December 1962 (*T 31st*). Just M L in *hb* until
1904 and ticket thus (*JB*).
MOBBERLEY [CLC]
op 12 May 1862 (*T 7th, 12th*); aot request; still open.
MOCHDRE & PABO [LNW]
op 1 April 1889 (*LNW Officers 30796*); clo 1 January
1917 (*T 22 December 1916*); reop 5 May 1919 (*RCG*);
clo 5 January 1931 (*Cl*).
MOELWYN [Festiniog] (ng): op for quarrymen as
TUNNEL HALT, 1917 (*Festiniog*). First in public tt
August 1929, as M; intermittent use according to *Brad*;
trains last shown June 1937 though remained, trainless,
to 3 July 1939. See 1939 September 18**.
MOFFAT [Cal] op 2 April 1883 (*Dumfries 4th*);
clo 6 December 1954 (*RM January 1955*).

MOIRA [Mid] op 1 March 1849 *(Mid)*;
clo 7 September 1964 *(RM October)*.

MOLD [LNW] op 14 August 1849 *(co ½ T 16 August)*;
clo 30 April 1962 *(RM June)*.

MOLLAND – see BISHOPS NYMPTON.

MOLLINGTON [Birkenhead]: line op 23 September
1840; this station later – by 15 December 1840 tt
(Freeling); clo 7 March 1960 *(RM April)*.

MOLYNEUX BROW [LY]
first in *Brad* June 1853; clo 29 June 1931 *(Cl)*.

MONIAIVE [GSW] op 1 March 1905 *(Dumfries 1st)*;
clo 3 May 1943 *(RM January 1944)*.

MONIFIETH [DA] op 8 October 1838★★; still open.

MONIKIE [Cal] first in *Brad* July 1871;
clo 10 January 1955 *(T 28 December 1954)*.

MONK BRETTON [Mid] op 1 January 1876 wtt
(Mid); clo 27 September 1937 *(T 23rd)*.

MONK FRYSTON [NE]
op 1 October 1904 *(RCG)*; replaced Milford Junction;
clo 14 September 1959 *(RM September)*.

MONKHILL – see under PONTEFRACT.

MONKMOORS [Fur] (non-tt): munitions workers;
in use from 1914 to about 1920 and about 1940 to
9 June 1958, {Bootle – Eskmeals} *(U)*.

MONKS FERRY – see BIRKENHEAD.

MONKS LANE [LBSC] op 1 June 1907 *(LBSC)*;
HALT; clo 11 September 1939 *(Cl)*.

MONKS RISBOROUGH [GW/GC]
op 11 November 1929 *(T 6th)*; as M R & WHITELEAF
HALT; HALT dropped 5 May 1969 *(Cl)*,
& W dropped 6 May 1974 *(BR notice)*; new platform
about 130 yards nearer Aylesbury 13 January 1986
(Regional weekly notice); still open.

MONKSEATON {map 26}

MONKSEATON [NE] op 3 July 1882, effectively as a
re-sited and renamed version of WHITLEY (b), which
see under 'W'; again re-sited, on deviation, 25 July
1915; clo 10 September 1979 *(Cl)* for conversion to >

MONKSEATON [TWM] op 11 August 1980 *(RM
August)*; still open.
Also see WEST MONKSEATON.

MONKTON near Ayr [GSW]

MONKTON: line op 5 August 1839 *(co ½ 1110/149)*,
nd, August 1840 *(Robinson, where it was MONCKTON)*;
clo 28 October 1940 *(Cl)*.
Also see PRESTWICK.

MONKTON & CAME [GW]
op 1 July 1905 *(Bristol NWR)* as CAME BRIDGE;
renamed 1 October 1905 *(Cl)*; HALT; clo 29 April
1917 *(wtt supp)*; reop ? – *Brad* no help since shown only
in footnotes; remained listed but that no guarantee
trains actually called; clo 7 January 1957 *(Cl)*.
GW co tt 1932, 1947: M & C HALT, GOLF LINKS.

MONKTON COMBE [GW]
op 9 May 1910 *(W D Press 10th)*; clo 22 March 1915
(RCG); reop 9 July 1923 *(Bristol notice S1153)*;
clo 21 September 1925 *(Cl)*.

MONKWEARMOUTH [NE]
For first station of this name see WEARMOUTH.

MONKWEARMOUTH op 19 June 1848 *(NE)* to
replace Wearmouth; clo 6 March 1967 *(RM March)*.

MONMORE GREEN [LNW] op 1 December 1863
(W Mid); clo 1 January 1917 *(T 22 December 1916)*.

MONMOUTH [GW]

M MAY HILL op 4 August 1873★★; intended as
temporary, kept for year experimentally, then made
permanent; clo 5 January 1959 *(T 5th)*.

M TROY op October 1857★★; TROY added 1873;
clo 5 January 1959 *(T 5th)*. M TROY HOUSE in *hb*
until 1904.
Non-tt: see 1812 August 17★★.

MONSAL DALE [Mid] op 1 September 1866 *(Mid)*;
clo 10 August 1959 *(RM August)*, but later ramblers'
specials, 3 April 1961 probably last *(AB)*.
Cressbrook Siding pre-opening *(Mid)*.

MONTACUTE [GW] op 27 January 1882 *(W Gaz
3 February)*; clo 15 June 1964 *(W Gaz 12th, 19th)*.

MONTGOMERY [Cam] op 10 June 1861 *(Cam)*;
permanent station eventually opened 1872/3
(co ½ T 28 February 1873 said had been opened during
last half year); clo 14 June 1965 *(RM July)*.

MONTGREENAN [GSW] op 1 February 1878
(RCG); clo 7 March 1955 *(RM April)*.

MONTON GREEN [LNW] op 1 November 1887
(LNW Officers 29876); clo 5 May 1969 *(RM June)*.

MONTPELIER [CE]
op 1 October 1874 *(Mid; Bristol T 2nd- line)*; still open.

MONTROSE

MONTROSE [Cal] op 1 February 1848 *(co n RM 1953)*;
original was a temporary station; exact series of events
and dating of permanent station, 1848/50, not clear;
clo 30 April 1934 *(Cl)*; trains diverted to NB station.

MONTROSE [NB] op 1 May 1883★★; still open.

M BROOMFIELD: temporary station just north of
Scottish North Eastern (later Caledonian) station.
Op 1866 by Montrose & Bervie in attempt (successful)
to get charges for use of main station reduced;
clo 1 February 1867 (Friday) *(D&C 15)*.

MONUMENT London [Met/Dist] op 6 October
1884 *(T 4th)*; escalator to Bank op 18 September 1933,
replaced by travolator 27 September 1960; still open.
Pre-op King William Street; op as EASTCHEAP
(thus *T*); became THE M 1 November 1884 *(L)*,
'THE' dropped gradually – *Brad* 1904 (in index until
later as CITY (M)).

MONUMENT Newcastle [TWM]
op 15 November 1981 *(Tyneside)*;
LL platforms op 14 November 1982; still open.

MONUMENT LANE Birmingham [LNW]
first in co tt July 1854 *(W Mid)* ★; op as M L, soon
renamed EDGBASTON; reverted to M L 1 February
1874 *(LNW General Manager's Circular 29 January)*;
re-sited 10 chains west in 1886 *(Cl)*;
clo 17 November 1958 *(RM December)*.
★ = early *Brad* version: in May 1853 to July 1854 as E, no trains
shown; August and September 1854 shown as M L, trains
southbound only; October E, southbound only; November E
both ways.

MONYMUSK [GNS] op 21 March 1859 *(GNS)*;
clo 2 January 1950 *(RM February)*.

MOOR EDGE [BT] (non-tt): for races on Town Moor;
clo when new racecourse opened at Gosforth *(BT)*.

On Airey's Durham District Map of 1876, 47 chains south of Gosforth; near present Ilford Road.

MOOR LANE [GW] (non-tt):
workmen's HALT, probably used during First World War; {near Brettell Lane} *(U)*.

MOOR PARK [Met/GC]
op 9 May 1910 *(GC dates)* as SANDY LODGE; renamed M P & S L 18 October 1923 *(Cl, hbl ref 25 October)*, M P 25 September 1950 *(Cl)*; still open. *GC dates* called it S L GOLF CLUB HALT (descriptive?)

MOOR ROW [WCE Jt]
op 1 July 1857 *(D&C 14; co ½ T 1 September- line)*; clo 7 January 1935 *(LNW Record)*; reop (non-tt) 11 March 1940 for ordnance workers' services to Sellafield and Drigg; made public 6 May 1946 *(RM July)*; clo 16 June 1947**; reop (non-tt) before/with 23 May 1949 wtt for workmen's services to UKAE Sellafield; clo 6 September 1965 *(U; WW II)*. M R JUNCTION in *Brad* until 1901/2 and thus LNW co tt 1882.

MOORE
MOORE [LNW] op 4 July 1837 *(co n GJ)*; clo 1 January 1917 *(T 22 December 1916)*; reop 1 February 1919 *(Cl)*; clo 1 February 1943 *(Cl)*; railwaymen used on to at least 1952 *(U)*.
MOORE [Birkenhead] – see DARESBURY.
MOORFIELDS – see under LIVERPOOL.
MOORGATE London
MOORGATE [Met] op 23 December 1865 *(T 22nd, 23rd)*; 'Widened Lines' platforms op 1 July 1866 *(L)*, clo 22 March 2009, last use 20th *(RM May)*; M STREET until 24 October 1924 *(L)*; original still open.
MOORGATE [Met GNC] op 14 February 1904 *(L)*; clo 1 March 1975 by accident, reop 10 March 1975; clo 7 September 1975 (Sunday) *(T 21 August)*. See under LONDON for main line services after reopening.
MOORGATE [Nor] op 26 February 1900**; see 1922**, still open.
MOORGATE near Oldham [LNW]
op 1 January 1912 *(LNW Officers 43577)*; only Delph branch line trains called; clo 2 May 1955 *(T 11 March)*. HALT according to *hb* – see 1905**.
MOORHAMPTON [Mid] op 30 June 1863 *(Hereford J 27th)*; clo 31 December 1962 *(T 31st)*.
MOORHOUSE & SOUTH ELMSALL [HB]
op 23 August 1902 *(RCG)*; clo 8 April 1929 (last 6th) *(NE Express June 2003)*; excursion 14 October 1933 during Hull Civic Week *(RM January 1934, pp. 153–4)*.
MOORSIDE [LY] op 2 July 1888**; M & WARDLEY until 6 May 1974 *(BR notice)*; still open.
MOORSWATER – see LISKEARD.
MOORTHORPE [SK] op 1 July 1879 *(Mid; co n T 28 June)*; M & SOUTH KIRBY 1 July 1902 *(hbl 12th)* to 12 June 1961 *(RM April)*; still open.
MOORTOWN [GC]
op 1 November 1848 *(GC)*; clo 1 November 1965 *(RM December)*. GC co tt 1903, *hb* 1904 on, LNE tt 1933 and *Brad* to 1955: M for CAISTOR.
MORAR [NB] op 1 April 1901 *(RCG)*; still open.
MORBEN JUNCTION – see DOVEY J.

MORCHARD ROAD [LSW] op 1 August 1854 *(Trewman 13 July, 3 August)*; HALT 12 September 1965 to 5 May 1969 *(Cl)*; aot request; still open.
MORCOTT [LNW] op 31 October 1898 *(LNW notice Rutland)*; clo 6 June 1966 *(RM July)*.
MORDEN
MORDEN [Nor] op 13 September 1926 *(T 14th)*; still open.
M ROAD [LBSC] first in *Brad* March 1857; no trains shown October and November 1918 *(Brad)* – were trains September and December 1918; HALT at reopening; ROAD added 2 July 1951 *(JS)*; HALT dropped 1968/1976 tt; clo 1 June 1997** for conversion to >
M ROAD [Croydon] op 30 May 2000; still open.
M SOUTH [SR] op 5 January 1930 *(T 6th)*; still open.
MOREBATH [GW]
MOREBATH op 1 November 1873 *(W Som F P 1st, 8th)*; clo 3 October 1966 *(Som Gaz 7th)*. GW co tt 1874, B&E co tt 1877: M for BAMPTON and thus *Brad* until 1884. Aot M & B (Junction Diagram).
M JUNCTION op 1 December 1928 *(W Som F P 1st)*; HALT; only footpath access but nearer to village than station above; clo 3 October 1966 *(Som Gaz 7th)*; {just west of physical junction}.
MORECAMBE
Midland
Based on information provided by R. Bond and J. Gough.
Op 12 June 1848 *(Lancaster 17th)*. Short section opened because Poulton was bathing-place for Lancaster people. The company's ½ yearly said 'A temporary station has been completed at Poulton' *(Lancaster 2 September)* – did this mean no station earlier? incomplete station earlier, now completed?
An account of the line was written by T. Edmondson in *The Poulton Railway Companion*, Lancaster, 1848. This can be dated to a time after opening of the line but before opening of the North Western Hotel on 11 September 1848. This shows that station was then in Northumberland Street – station or stop there from outset? (No obvious alternative site). Edmondson also mentioned an intermediate station between Lancaster and Poulton-le-Sands, beneath an arch of the Lancaster & Carlisle [later part of LNW] bridge over the river Lune; no other information known – short-lived 'halt'? For its earliest appearance in *Brad* the table is headed 'Morecambe branch' but POULTON appears in the table; renamed from POULTON-LE-SANDS to MORECAMBE (August 1850 tt).
Main station replaced by temporary station 4 November 1906, that by permanent during the day of 24 March 1907, after departure of 9.50am to Lancaster.
Clo Tuesday 8 February 1994 (last train Monday) *(BLN 722-4/51 pp. 26, 40, 57, 103)*; new op 6 June 1994 about ¼ mile east, on site of station clo 1907 *RM Oct.)*. Was M PROMENADE 2 July 1924 *(Rly Gaz 23 May)* to 6 May 1968 *(Mid)*. Still open.
The Wooden Pier was brought into use for goods in 1850. The earliest reference to its use for passengers is for 12 July 1850 but that was only for landing people from a steamer and the earliest reference to trains in connection was in a notice for June 1851 and that did

not specify that trains ran <u>onto</u> the pier (local press).
Brad October 1853 has note about sailings to Belfast
on Wednesdays and Saturdays and from there Mondays
and Thursdays and says that steamer will not sail from
Morecambe until after arrival of passenger train; since
only 5 minutes allowed for transfer, suggests trains ran
onto wooden pier. This was renamed M HARBOUR
by circular dated 15 December 1854.
BoT letter dated 5 June 1855, about level crossings,
says lines to timber jetty had been in use for some time,
those to pier expected to be completed in a few months;
only goods traffic mentioned as using these but does
not specifically say 'goods only'.
First reference in *Brad* for replacement M PIER on
stone jetty was August 1856. Thereafter appearance
erratic. Initial explanation is that had begun service
without BoT permission since it was only a short
extension of existing line; service started only 'a short
time' before 25 August 1856, date on letter to BoT
asking for clarification. When told permission was
necessary, service stopped. At first failed inspection.
BoT finally sent permission to open on 30 October
1856. Soon removed from ordinary table in *Brad* but
information in steamer sailings section implied continued
use – one complication was that sailings were dependent
on tide and times varied from day to day. Use ceased
with effect from 1 September 1904, on opening of
Heysham (*Cl*).

LNW

This company opened its line to Morecambe 8 August
1864, initially using Midland station.
M POULTON LANE op on this line 1 November 1870
(*LNW Officers 5875*); was usually M P L in LNW co tts
but just P L in *Brad*; terminus for some trains >
Replaced by LNW's own terminus, **M EUSTON ROAD**,
op 10 May 1886 (*Neele; LNW Officers 28411*) *;
EUSTON ROAD added 2 July 1924 (*Rly Gaz 23 May*);
clo 15 September 1958 (*Cl*). 1959–61 summers used
by trains all days including Sundays (*CW*); last summer
Saturday use 8 September 1962, though in summer tts
1963, 1964 without trains (*C/W*).
Also see BARE LANE.
* = copying error in *LNW Record* made it 10 May 1885.
Date given supported by *co ½ Lancaster 15 May 1886*.
MOREDON [MSWJ] (non-tt):
HALT/ PLATFORM; op 25 March 1913; workmen;
clo by September 1928; {Blunsdon – Rushey Platt} (*U*).
MORESBY [CW Jc]
M JUNCTION first in *Brad* July 1910; clo 2 January
1911 (*Cl*); back in *Brad* June 1913; sometimes HALT
(thus *Brad* 1914); clo to public 1 October 1923 (*Cl*) –
perhaps one of those that was in longer and more
continuous use but only erratically included in tt?;
miners continued to use until ? – use ended by June
1952 (*U*).
M PARKS op 1 October 1879 (*D&C 14; Rtn- line*);
clo 13 April 1931 (*LNW Record*).
MORETON near Oswestry [GW]:
July 1872 working tt shows 'as needed' stops, one each
way (*RAC*); 1877 *hb* has entry for Moreton Hall
'same as Preesgweene', no facilities of own, but 1877

Junction Diagram shows it was separate site;
cannot be confirmed as public station.
MORETON DORSET [LSW]
op 1 June 1847 (*Dorset Chron 20 May, 3 June*);
D added 12 May 1980 tt (*C/W*); still open.
MORETON MERSEYSIDE [Wirral]
op 2 July 1866 (*D&C 10*); M added body of tt 14 May
1984 (index earlier); still open.
MORETON-IN-MARSH
For earliest services, including 'official' one starting
1 August 1853, see 1833 B**.
Main service [GW] began 4 June 1853 (*Glos Chron 4th*);
still open; At first M/M JUNCTION in *Brad*, became
M-in-the-M 1888/9 (*Brad*), M-in-M 20 October 1898
(*hbl 27th*). GW co tt: 1865 M for SHIPSTON,
later M for S-ON-STOUR.
MORETON-ON-LUGG [SH Jt] op 6 December
1853**; -on-L added 1882/3 (*Brad*) but –on-LUG
hb 1877 (1925 –on-LUGG); clo 9 June 1958 (*Cl*).
Early on, when line operated by Thomas Brassey,
contractor, hollow oak tree acted as station building
(*RM July 1902*, with photograph).
MORETONHAMPSTEAD [GW]
op 4 July 1866 (*W D Merc 5th*); clo 2 March 1959
(*Express & E 2nd*). Hb made two words/hyphenated
version of it until 1925; GW ticket thus (*JB*).
MORFA CROSSING [PT] (non-tt);
HALT; workmen; op ?; clo by February 1930;
{Port Talbot Docks – Tondu} (*U*).
MORFA MAWDDACH [Cam] op 3 June 1867
(*Cam- line*) as BARMOUTH JUNCTION, when it
was a terminus because viaduct across river to Barmouth
had not been passed for trains; passengers taken across
by horse and carriage; regular trains first across
10 October 1867 (see BARMOUTH for more detail);
renamed 13 June 1960 (*RM August*); aot request;
still open.
MORLEY
MORLEY [LNW] op 18 September 1848 (*D&C 8*);
M LOW 30 September 1951 (*RM January 1952*) to
1967/76 tt; still open.
M TOP [GN] op 10 October 1857 (*GN; co ½ T 19 Feb.
1858- line*); TOP added 2 March 1951 (*Cl*);
clo 2 January 1961 (*RM February*).
MORMOND [GNS]
op 24 April 1865 (*GNS*); aot request; became HALT
1 June 1939 (*Cl*); reduced to Saturdays only from
6 December 1950 (*RM January 1951*); last train
2 October 1965 (based on *Rly Obs November*).
MORNINGSIDE {map 16}
MORNINGSIDE [Wishaw & Coltness] op in or before
October 1844 (see 1835 C**); original service from
Coatbridge; trains from Bathgate began 2 June 1845**,
using same station and reversal; see 1848** for later
history. Later services used new stations.
MORNINGSIDE [Cal] op 15 May 1867 (*G&S*);
clo 1 January 1917 (*RM Feb.*); reop 2 June 1919 (*RCG*);
see 1921 April/May**; clo 1 December 1930 (*Cl*).
MORNINGSIDE [NB] op 1 October 1864 (*D&C 6*);
clo 1 May 1930 (Thursday) (*Cl*).

MORNINGSIDE ROAD [NB]
op 1 December 1884 *(Edin)*; ROAD added 1886 tt *(Cl)*;
clo 10 September 1962 *(BR notice Ed Sub)*.

MORNINGTON CRESCENT [Nor]
op 22 June 1907**; clo 'Whitsuntide' 1924 in experiment
to speed up line service, reop 2 July 1924 *(T 3rd)*;
clo 24 October 1992 *(BLN 697)*;
reop Monday 27 April 1998 *(Ug)* *; still open.
* = *RM July* said reop 23rd by four stars of BBC Radio's 'I'm
Sorry I Haven't A Clue'; probably 'formal' opening.

MORPETH {map 23}
MORPETH [NE] op 1 March 1847 *(co n Newcastle
Journal 27 February)*; still open. M JUNCTION 1882
to 1893/4 in *Brad* and thus NE co tt 1880.
MORPETH [BT] op 1 April 1858 *(T 3rd)*; clo 24 May
1880 *(Cl)*, service diverted to NE station. Also [NB]
used from 23 July 1862; trains to NE 3 May 1872
(J. Gough, *Chron January 2004*).

MORRIS COWLEY [GW]
first in *Brad* beginning 24 September 1928; site of earlier
Garsington Bridge; clo 7 January 1963 *(RM January)*;
{Wheatley – Littlemore}. HALT GW ticket *(JB)*.

MORRISTON
M EAST [Mid] op 2 October 1871 as terminus *(Mid)*;
became through station March 1875**; EAST added
1950 *(Cl)*; clo 25 September 1950 *(RM November)*;
{map 88}.
M WEST [GW] op 9 May 1881 *(GW- line)*;
see 1921 April/May**; WEST added 1950 *(Cl)*;
clo 11 June 1956 *(T 8th)*.

MORTEHOE & WOOLACOMBE [LSW]
op 20 July 1874 *(N Devon J 23rd)*; clo 5 October 1970
(N Devon J 8th). At first MORTHOE; spelling changed
13 May 1902 *(hbl 10 July)*.
Brad successively M for W SANDS (and thus LSW co tt
1914), M for W S and LEE (DEVON), M for L;
settled as M & W 5 June 1950 *(Cl)*. Aot *hb* M & L.

MORTIMER [GW]
op 1 November 1848 *(Hants Chron 4th)*; still open.

MORTLAKE [LSW]
op 27 July 1846 *(T 23rd)*; M & EAST SHEEN 1 April
1886 to 30 January 1916 *(L)*, when became M for E S;
to M 1955 *(Brad)*; still open.

MORTON PINKNEY [SMJ] op 1 July 1873 *(SMJ;
Chelt Exam 9th- line)*; clo 1 August 1877 (Wednesday),
reop 2 March 1885**; clo 7 April 1952 *(RM May)*.
Became M P for SULGRAVE 1 May 1913 *(hbl 24 April)*;
thus LMS tt 1930 and *Brad* to closure.

MORTON ROAD [GN]
op 2 January 1872 *(Insp rpt MT6/91/2; co ½T 12 Feb.-
line)*; ROAD added 1883? *(RCG ref April)* – but 1895
Brad; clo 22 September 1930** *(Cl)*.

MOSELEY
For first station of this name see KINGS HEATH.
MOSELEY [Mid] op 1 November 1867 *(dist supp
22 January 1868)*; clo 27 January 1941 *(Cl)*.

MOSES GATE [LY]: line op 29 May 1838**; not in
original list but op by 19 October 1839 *Brad*; about
1843/7 briefly FARNWORTH; still open.

MOSS near Doncaster [NE]
op 2 January 1871 *(T 3rd)*; clo 8 June 1953 *(RM July)*.

MOSS near Wrexham; {map 75}
MOSS [GW] op 1 May 1905 *(GW H)* as M;
became M 1906/7 *(Brad)*, M PLATFORM 1924/5
(Brad), and added *hb* 1926a thus; clo 1 January 1931
(Thursday) *(T 20 December 1930)*.
M & PENTRE [WMCQ] op 1 August 1889 *(GC)*;
clo 1 March 1917 (Thursday) *(RCG)*.

MOSS BANK [LNW] op 3 February 1858
(Ormskirk 4th); clo 18 June 1951 *(RM August)*.

MOSS ROAD near Glasgow [GP Jt] op 1 July 1843
(GSW); clo 1845? Cardonald here later. Never in *Brad*,
but in *Murray* by September 1844; {map 15}.

MOSS ROAD Campbeltown [Camp] (ng); see 1906
August 18**; first specific tt reference September 1907;
request; clo by May 1932 *(Camp)*.

MOSS SIDE
MOSS SIDE (a) [PW] first in *Brad* June 1847;
clo 26 June 1961 *(RM August)*.
MOSS SIDE (b) op 21 November 1983 *(RM February
1984)*; still open.

MOSSBAND [Cal] (non-tt):
two stops {Floriston – Gretna}: M OFFICE HALT
used by workmen and M PLATFORM used about
same time by munitions workers for interchange with
military line *(U)*. Both opened about 1914;
OFFICE clo about 1919, PLATFORM clo about 1922
(D. Lindsay).

MOSSBLOWN JUNCTION [GSW] (non-tt):
HALT; miners?; dates ?; {Auchincruive – Annbank} *(U)*.

MOSSBRIDGE [CLC] op 1 September 1884 *(GC)*
as BARTON & HALSALL; renamed 1 August 1894
(hbl 11 July); clo 1 January 1917 *(RCG)*.

MOSSEND
See 1828** for Monklands associated references.
MOSSEND [Cal] op 1 June 1882, replacing first
HOLYTOWN (which see); clo 5 November 1962.

MOSSGIEL TUNNEL [LMS] (non-tt):
PLATFORM; workmen; in use 1926;
{Hurlford – Mauchline} *(U)*.

MOSSLEY near Stoke-on-Trent [NS] first in *Brad*
October 1919; HALT; clo 13 July 1925 *(Cl)*.

MOSSLEY GREATER MANCHESTER [LNW]
op 1 August 1849 *(co ½ T 18 August- line; in co tt for
1 August, Stockport 3rd)*; G M added ?; still open.

MOSSLEY HILL [LNW] op 15 February 1864
(LNW Officers); re-sited to north 13 July 1891
(LNW Officers 32825); was M H for AIGBURTH from
1878/81 *(Brad)* to 6 May 1974 *(BR notice)*; still open.
At first in *hb* as M H & A, to M H 1872, to M H for A
1904.

MOSSPARK [LMS] op 1 March 1934 *(T 22 February)*
as M WEST; WEST dropped 3 May 1976 tt;
clo 10 January 1983 *(RM March)*; reop 30 July 1990 –
trains at half-fare Saturday and Sunday 28th, 29th
(BLN 636) as M; still open. MW HALT in *hb* 1938
(just MW 1936a) to 1941a and on ticket *(JB)* but not
in tt. Sometimes MOSS PARK.

MOSSTOWIE [High] op 15 October 1890 *(RCG;
in Brad November)*; clo 7 March 1955 *(RM April)*.

MOSTON [LY]
first in *Brad* February 1872; still open.

MOSTYN [LNW] op 1 May 1848 *(D&C 11; co n T 2nd- line)*; clo 14 February 1966 *(RM April)*.

MOTHERWELL [Cal] {map 16}
First station here [Wishaw & Coltness], not shown on map, was at second bridge across Merry Street; side street Pollock Street here later. It was used for a special to Linlithgow to see Queen Victoria making her first visit to Scotland, 13 September 1842; this started with two passenger wagons and collected coal wagons full of people on its way. Op to public 8 May 1843 (see 1835 C★★) > Caledonian's Clydesdale Junction line opened to here 1 June 1849 and had station off Brandon Street, at what was later Melville Drive (first shown on map). Presumably W&C station now closed since Caledonian worked its trains and *Brad* referred to it as M JUNCTION; also thus *Murray* 1852 and *Cornwall* 1860, but not Cal co tt 1859. *Brad* gradually shed JUNCTION from different tables in the 1880s.
On 1 April 1868 the line to Lesmahagow opened.
M BRIDGE was opened on this line 4 February 1871 in Clyde Street (later renamed Hamilton Road). This is supported by *Brad*. At first relevant table shows trains starting from Motherwell and taking 10 minutes to reach Ferniegair (would have involved reversal just after leaving Motherwell). November 1871 issue's table shows trains starting from Holytown, calling at M BRIDGE and taking 5 minutes from there to Ferniegair. (Connections or coaches detached from trains from Glasgow?)
1 August 1885: 1849 and 1871 stations replaced by one in Muir Street (from local histories – more likely that this would have opened with new tt, Clinker's 31 July being last day of old); this is still open.
Locally, stations usually known by name of street in which sited – *Naismith's Hamilton Directory* in 1870s referred to Hamilton Road Bridge Station and Brandon Road Station.
(Based on *History & Directory of Motherwell 1899–1900, Hamilton Advertiser*; 'Old Residenter', *Motherwell Seventy Years Ago – and Now, Hamilton Advertiser*, 1910; - Orr, *Sketches of Motherwell & Wishaw*, Hamilton, 1925; T. Johnstone, *Motherwell Memories, Hamilton Advertiser*. 1938; R. Duncan, *Steelopolis, the Making of Motherwell, c. 1750–1939*, Motherwell District Council, 1991; all via G. Borthwick.)

MOTSPUR PARK [SR]
first in *Brad* beginning 21 September 1925★; still open.
★ = L gives 12 July 1925 and *sig inst 22/1925, issued 7 July* says would be, but note in *Brad* 13 July 1925 said opening deferred; one would have thought *sig inst* would have been issued after information was sent to *Brad* but continuance of note in August tt leaves doubts; if there was a delay and normal SR policy was followed, would have op on a Sunday (e.g. 20 September).

MOTTINGHAM [SE] op 1 September 1866 *(L; co ½ T 24 August- line)*; still open.
Opened as ELTHAM; renamed E & M 1 January 1892 *(hbl 28th)*, E for M before/with SEC co tt 1914, E & M 1922 *(SR)*, M 26 September 1927 *(L; RM ref October)*.

MOTTISFONT [LSW]
MOTTISFONT op 6 March 1865 *(Salisbury 11th- line)*; clo 7 September 1964 *(Andover Advertiser 31 July)*.

M & DUNBRIDGE op 1 March 1847 *(W Fly P 6th- line)* as D; was MOTTISFONT D 3 October 1988 *(C/W)* to 29 May 1994 tt *(AB Chron)*; became M & D 10 December 2006 *(First GW Trains booklet)*; still open.

MOTTRAM – see BROADBOTTOM.

MOTTRAM STAFF HALT [GC or LNE] (non-tt): HALT; dates ?; railwaymen *(U)*; name from *BLN 1035*; {Broadbottom – Dinting}.

MOULDSWORTH [CLC]
op 22 June 1870 *(CLC)*; still open.

MOULINEARN CROSSING [High or LMS]
(non-tt); railwaymen, families; dates ?;
{Ballinluig – Pitlochry} *(U)*.

MOULSECOOMB
op 12 May 1980 *(RM June)*; still open.

MOULSFORD [GW] op 1 June 1840 *(GW; co n T 30 May- line)*; WALLINGFORD ROAD later 1840 to 2 July 1866 *(Cl)*; replaced by Cholsey & M, 55 chains west, 29 February 1892 *(co n Reading 27th)*.

MOULTON near Darlington [NE] op 10 September 1846 *(co n Catterick)*; clo 3 March 1969 *(RM March)*. HALT on ticket *Catterick p. 89*, but not in tt – note added 1960 that no staff were in attendance.

MOULTON near Spalding [MGN]
op 15 November 1858 *(MGN; Linc R & S Merc 19th- line)*; clo 2 March 1959 *(T 2nd)*.

MOUNT FLORIDA [Cal] op 1 March 1886 *(Cal)*; re-sited to south May 1982; still open.

MOUNT GOULD & TOTHILL [GW]
op 1 October 1905 *(W Morn News 2nd)*; HALT; clo 1 February 1918 (Friday) *(wtt supp)*; {map 114}.

MOUNT HAWKE [GW] op 14 August 1905★★; HALT; clo 4 February 1963 *(W Briton 4th)*.

MOUNT MELVILLE [NB]
op 1 June 1887 *(Fifeshire Journal 26 May)*; clo 1 January 1917 *(RM February)*, reop 1 February 1919 *(RM February)*; clo 22 September 1930 *(Cl)*.

MOUNT PLEASANT Stoke-on-Trent [NS]
op 1 May 1905 *(NS)*; HALT; clo 30 September 1918 *(Cl)*; {Stoke – Trentham}.

MOUNT PLEASANT ROAD Exeter [LSW]
op 26 January 1906 *(Ex Fly P 27th)*; HALT; clo 2 January 1928 *(Cl)*; {map 115}.

MOUNT VERNON
MOUNT VERNON [Cal] op 8 January 1866 *(Cal- line)*; clo 16 August 1943 *(Cl)*.

MOUNT VERNON op 4 October 1993 *(BLN 712)*; old Cal reop; still open.

MV NORTH [NB] op 1 April 1878 *(Hamilton 6th)*; clo 1 January 1917 *(RM February)*; reop 2 June 1919 *(RCG)*; NORTH added 1952 *(Cl)*; clo 4 July 1955 *(RM August)*.

MOUNTAIN ASH
MOUNTAIN ASH op 3 October 1988 *(Aberdare)* – free publicity service 2nd; near old Oxford Street; re-sited on deviation to east 29 January 2001 *(Rly Obs April, p. 173)*; still open.

M A CARDIFF ROAD [GW] op 5 October 1864 *(T 8th- line)*; C R added 1 July 1924 *(GW circular 18 June)*; clo 15 June 1964★★ *(RM August)*.

M A OXFORD STREET [TV] op 6 August 1846

(Aberdare; Merlin 8th- line); O S added 1 July 1924
(GW circular 18 June); clo 16 March 1964 *(Cl)*;
later excur *(U)*.

MOUNTFIELD [SR] first in *Brad* September 1923;
HALT until 5 May 1969 *(Cl)*; clo 6 October 1969
(RM November); {Robertsbridge – Battle}.

MOUSEN – see 1847 March 29★★.

MOW COP & SCHOLAR GREEN [NS]
op in June 1849 *(NS-K photo caption)* – in *Topham*
May or June 1849, though not in *Brad* until July;
op as M C; became M C (S G) 1897/8 *(Brad)* and thus
NS co tt 1910, M C & S G 1923 *(hbl ref 26 April)*;
clo 7 September 1964 *(RM October)*.

MOY [High]
op 19 July 1897 *(High)*; clo 3 May 1965 *(RM June)*.

MOY PARK [Camp] (ng)
op 1 May 1912 request; last in tt June 1912 (but see
1906 August 18★★; still shown 'P' in *hb* 1929).

MR STARKIE'S PLATFORM
– see ASHTON HALL.

MUCH WENLOCK [GW] op 1 February 1862
(Shrewsbury 7th); re-sited at some point (versions in
print known to be wrong but correct date still to be
established); clo 23 July 1962 *(RM August)*.

MUCHALLS [Cal]
first in *Brad* April 1850; clo 4 December 1950 *(Cl)*.

MUDCHUTE [Dock]
op 31 August 1987 *(T 1 September)*;
clo during 9 February 1996 by IRA bomb *(T 10th)*;
reop 15 April 1996 *(Rly Obs June)*; clo 11 January 1999
for work on Lewisham extension *(RM August)*;
buses until new station op in cutting 20 November
1999 *(RM July 2001)*; still open.

MUIR OF ORD
MUIR OF ORD (a) [High] op 11 June 1862 *(High)*;
clo 13 June 1960 *(RM July)*. Pre-op Tarradale;
M of O JUNCTION 1923 to 1955 *(Brad)*, 1894a to
1904 *(hb)*.
MUIR OF ORD (b) op 4 October 1976 *(RM Nov.)*;
same site as (a); still open.
M of O MARKET PLATFORM (non-tt) op 1867;
alighting only; clo 1885/1904; *(Highland Society
Journal 50)*.

MUIREND [Cal] op 1 May 1903 *(RCG)*; still open.

MUIRKIRK [GSW] op 9 August 1848 *(GSW- line)*;
re-sited about ¼ mile east mid 1896;
clo 5 October 1964 *(RM October)*.
At one stage (1870s, 1880s) Airey maps of Scotland
and Junction Diagrams showed a separate [Cal] station
to the east; assumed to be error; Brand clearly said that
used GSW.

MUIRTON [LMS] op 31 October 1936 *(High)*;
in *Brad* December 1936 to April 1939, winters only
HALT; Saturdays only, southbound, alighting only;
suggestion that it was provided for football fans, made
in *LMS Journal No. 9*, makes sense; trains shown calling
there in 27 September 1937 *Brad*, Saturdays only,
were those timed to arrive at Perth General at 1.21pm,
2.37pm and 2.45pm (first and last from Blair Atholl,
second from Coupar Angus); used (non-tt) until
21 November 1959 *(U)*; {Perth – Luncarty}.

MUIRTOWN – see FINGASK.

MULBEN
MULBEN [High] op 18 August 1858 *(High)*;
clo 7 December 1964 *(RM January 1965)*.
From 18 August 1858, there were temporary platforms
at Spey Bridge, {Mulben – Orton}, pending completion
of permanent bridge: report of accident unconnected
with bridge on 4 September 1858 said train went from
Keith to bridge, passengers off, train slowly across,
passengers rejoined on other side *(Rtn)* (railwaymen
apparently more expendable than passengers).
Closed by February 1859 *(High)*.

MUMBLES {map 88}
For earliest service see 1807 March 25★★.
For reopened service see OYSTERMOUTH;
NORTON ROAD and 1860 July 25★★.
M PIER [SIT] op 10 May 1898 *(SIT)*; clo 12 October
1959 *(RM December)*.
M ROAD [SIT] first in *Brad* August 1877;
last February 1917. Aot M R JUNCTION.
M (SOUTHEND) – see SOUTHEND [SIT].

M ROAD [LNW] probably op early January 1868
(The Cambrian 20 December said would open early
January; trains first shown in *Brad* February)*;
clo 15 June 1964 *(RM August)*.

MUMBY ROAD [GN] op 4 October 1886 *(GN)*;
clo 5 October 1970 *(T 16 July)*.

MUNCASTER [Raven] (ng)
op 20 November 1876 *(Raven; co yearly T 26 March
1877- line)*; clo 1 December 1908★★; reop 28 August
1915 *(Raven)*; line clo 1 November 1924 (Saturday)
but this already out of use – request stops still shown
public tt 2 June 1924 *(Raven p.174)* but not in wtt
22 September 1924 *(Raven p.183)*.

MUNDESLEY-ON-SEA [Norfolk & S]
op 1 July 1898 *(RCG)*; clo 5 October 1964 *(RM Aug.)*.

MUNLOCHY [High] op 1 February 1894 *(High)*;
clo 1 October 1951 *(RM November)*.

MURRAYFIELD [Cal] op 1 August 1879 *(RCG)*;
clo 30 April 1962 *(RM May)*.

MURROW
M EAST [MGN] op 1 August 1866 *(op working tt
D&C 5)*; EAST added 27 September 1948
(RM November); clo 2 March 1959 *(T 2nd)*.
M WEST [GN/GE] op 2 September 1867★ *(GN)*;
WEST added 27 September 1948 *(RM November)*;
clo 6 July 1953 *(RM August)*.
★ = GN minutes say op 1st but that a Sunday and no Sunday
service.

MURTHLY [High]: line op 7 April 1856, nd, in *Brad*
June 1856, though according to *High* no evidence in co
records for existence of station until near end of year or
even later; clo 3 May 1965 *(RM June)*.

MURTHWAITE [Raven] (ng) (non-tt): dates ?;
workmen?; {Muncaster – Irton Road}.

MURTLE [GNS] op 8 September 1853 *(GNS)*;
became HALT 1930/31 *(Brad)* and thus on LNE
ticket *(JB)*; clo 5 April 1937 *(RM January 1938)*.

MURTON JUNCTION [NE]: line op April or May
1837 *(NE- line; see 1836 A★★)*; first certain mention
May 1848 *(Topham)* – station was mentioned in report

of accident 23 June 1845 but a coal train was involved so passenger use then not guaranteed *(Rtn)*; clo 5 January 1953 *(RM March)*.

MURTON LANE [Derwent Valley] op 21 July 1913 *(NER Staff Mag 1913)*; clo 1 September 1926** (Wednesday).

MUSGRAVE [NE] op 9 June 1862**; clo 3 November 1952 *(RM January 1953)*.

MUSSELBURGH

MUSSELBURGH (a), on main line, – see INVERESK.

MUSSELBURGH (b) [NB], branch station, op 14 July 1847 *(co n Edinburgh Advertiser 13th)*; clo 7 September 1964 *(Cl)*.
See under NEWHAILES for early stop on this branch that probably served that place.

MUSSELBURGH (c), on main line, op 3 October 1988 *(BLN 593)*; still open.

MUSWELL HILL [GN] op 24 May 1873 *(L; co n T 22nd- line)*; clo 1 August 1873 (Friday)*, reop 1 May 1875 *(Cl)*; clo 29 October 1951, reop 7 January 1952 *(T 18 December 1951)*; clo 5 July 1954 *(RM July)*.

* = perhaps short loss of service when Alexandra Palace destroyed by fire – items and notices not entirely clear though implication of reopening notice is that whole line was involved (see ALEXANDRA PALACE).

MUTFORD – see OULTON BROAD NORTH.

MUTHILL [Cal]: line op 14 March 1856 *(Tayside)*, nd, July; clo 6 July 1964 *(RM July)*.

MUTLEY – see PLYMOUTH.

MYTHOLMROYD [LY] first in *Brad* May 1847; still open.

WHEN IN DOUBT—DON'T.

SCENE—Country Station.

Gent. "ARE THE SANDWICHES FRESH, MY BOY?"
Country Youth. "DON'T KNOW, I'M SURE, SIR. I'VE ONLY BEEN HERE A FORTNIGHT!"

N

NABURN [NE] op 2 January 1871 *(T 3rd)*;
clo 8 June 1953 *(RM July)*.

NAFFERTON [NE]: line op 7 October 1846**, nd,
May 1848 *(Topham)*; still open.

NAILBRIDGE [GW] op 4 November 1907 *(GW H)*;
HALT; clo 7 July 1930 *(RM August)*; {map 94}.

NAILSEA & BACKWELL [GW] op 14 June 1841
(Taunton 16th- line); & B added 1 May 1905 *(GW circular
2012)* to 6 May 1974 *(Cl)* and from 1977 on; still open.

NAILSWORTH [Mid] op 4 February 1867
(Stroud J 9th); clo 16 June 1947**.

NAIRN [High] op 7 November 1855**; still open.

NANCEGOLLAN [GW] op 9 May 1887
(Cornish T 12th); clo 5 November 1962 *(W Briton 8th)*.

NANNERCH [LNW]
op 6 September 1869**; clo 30 April 1962 *(RM June)*.

NANSTALLON [LSW] op 1 June 1906 *(W Briton 4th)*;
HALT; clo 30 January 1967 *(Cornish & DP 4 February)*;
{map 113}.

NANTCLWYD [LNW] op 6 October 1864 *(D&C 11)*;
clo 2 February 1953 *(RM March)*.

NANTEWLAETH [GW] (non-tt): (SIDING)
HALT; miners; *GM's report* 23 November 1939 said
had authorised provision of workmen's halt, cost to be
borne by Ocean Coal Co. *(RAC)*; no mention
February 1940 wtt; three round trips to Cymmer
Corrwg 28 October 1940 wtt; later calls integrated with
Cymmer Corrwg to North Rhondda service (R. Maund);
last miners' train shown in wtt ending 18 September
1955 (M. Hale); {Cymmer Corrwg – Glyncorrwg}.

NANTGAREDIG [LNW]
op 1 June 1865**; clo 9 September 1963 *(T 9th)*.

NANTGARW
N HL [ANSW] op 1 September 1904**; HALT from
1 July 1924 *(GW circular 18 June)*, when HL added;
clo 17 September 1956 *(RM October)*.
N LL [Cardiff] op 1 March 1911 *(RCG)*; HALT and
LL added 1 July 1924, *(GW circular 18 June)* – but
HALT in *Brad* from start; clo 20 July 1931 *(GW goods
circular 13th – after last train 18th)*.

NANTLLE
For earliest service see 1829 B**.

NANTLLE [Nantlle] (ng) op 11 August 1856; service
very erratic and sampling of *Brad* suggests frequent
changes in it – variations included no trains (e.g.
December 1858, January 1859), one Saturday only
from Carnarvon, one (first of day) all days from
Carnarvon (e.g. October* and December 1857, January
1858, February 1863, March 1865), all days both ways
(January, September, November* 1857; June 1858;
May and June 1865). Pen-y-groes was often passenger
terminus. Perhaps Nantlle's trains were mainly
workmen's? Clo 12 June 1865.

* = October 1857 noted that changes likely on 15th; way in

which trains all days November was sandwiched between two
one-way months seems to give a fair idea of changeability of
service – or unreliability of tt.

NANTLLE [LNW] standard gauge station op 1 October
1872 *(co n T 30 September)*; clo 1 January 1917
(T 22 December 1916); reop 5 May 1919 *(RCH)*; became
N MOTOR HALT 4 May 1923 *(LNW dates)* but still
N in *Brad* – see 1905**; clo 8 August 1932 *(LNW record)*.

NANTMELYN [TV] (non-tt): HALT/PLATFORM;
miners; op 1 June 1904; clo 1 April 1949;
{beyond Aberdare} *(Aberdare)*.

NANTMOR – see ABERGLASLYN.

NANTWEN [GW/Rhy] (non-tt): alias N COLLIERY;
miners; in use at least 1897 to 1928;
{Trelelewis – Bedlinog} *(U)*.

NANTWICH
For first station of this name see WORLESTON.

NANTWICH [LNW]: op 1 September 1858**; still open.
JUNCTION 1864 to 1915/6 *(Brad)*, in Joint table only,
also thus LNW co tt at least 1864–1921.

NANTYBWCH [LNW]
op 1 March 1864 *(LNW Officers)* as TREDEGAR;
renamed 1 November 1868 *(LNW Officers 16 December)*;
clo 13 June 1960 *(RM July)*. Aot Nant-y-bwch *(hb)*.

NANTYDERRY [GW] op 2 January 1854
(T 29 December 1853- line); N OR GOITRE in *Brad*
until April 1859; omitted *Brad* May 1859; restored
November 1859 as N; clo 9 June 1958 *(Cl)*.

NANTYFFYLLON [GW]
op 19 July 1880 *(Maesteg)* as TYWITH; renamed
1 January 1903 *(RCG)*; clo to public 22 June 1970, but
schools used to 14 July 1970 (last day) *(RM September)*.

NANTYFFYN [GW/Rhy] (non-tt): miners; at least
1928 to 1954; {Bedlinog – Cwm Bargoed} *(U)*.

NANTYGLO [GW]
op 16 May 1859 *(co n Merlin 14th)*; clo 30 April 1962
(T 6th). *Brad*: first as NANT-Y-GLO for BRYNMAWR;
at times N-y-glo & B; erratically lost hyphens.
GW co tt 1881 and 1902 N (no hyphens) for B; 1932 N.

NANTYMOEL [GW]
op 12 May 1873 *(co n T 7 August)*; clo 5 May 1958
(RM June). Nant-y-moel 1877 to 1890s *(hb)*.

NANTYRONEN [VoR] (ng) op 22 December 1902**
(see for details); to preservation 1989.

NAPSBURY [Mid] op 19 June 1905 'for asylum
visitors only' *(RCG)*, but in *Brad* from July 1905;
clo 14 September 1959 *(RM September)*.

NAPTON & STOCKTON [LNW]
op 1 August 1895 *(LNW Officers 36165, 36425)*;
clo 15 September 1958 *(RM October)*.

NARBERTH [GW] op 5 September 1866
(Cardiff T 7th- line); aot request; still open.

NARBERTH ROAD – see CLUNDERWEN.

NARBOROUGH near Leicester [LNW]
op 1 January 1864 *(Leic; LNW Officers- line)*;
clo 4 March 1968 *(RM March)*; reop 5 January 1970
(Cl); still open.

NARBOROUGH & PENTNEY [GE]
op 27 October 1846 *(co n D&C 5)*;
& P added 1 July 1923 *(hbl 12th)*; clo 9 September
1968 *(RM November)*; {map 67}.

NASSINGTON [LNW] op 1 November 1879
(RCG); clo 1 July 1957 *(RM July)*.

NAST HYDE [GN] op 1 February 1910 *(RM March)*;
HALT; clo 1 October 1951 *(T 8 September)*; {map 72}.

NATEBY [KE] op 5 December 1870 *(LNW Record-
line)* as WINMARLEIGH; clo 11 March 1872,
reop 17 May 1875 *(Cl)*; renamed 1 January 1902 *(hbl
24 October 1901)*; aot request; clo 31 March 1930 *(Cl)*.

NATIONAL EXHIBITION CENTRE
– see BIRMINGHAM.

NAVENBY [GN] op 15 April 1867 *(GN; co ½
T 19 August- line)*; clo 10 September 1962 *(RM October)*.

NAVIGATION HOUSE – see ABERCYNON.

NAVIGATION ROAD [LMS]
op 20 July 1931 *(Cl 29)*; [Manch] added 15 June 1992
(RM August); still open (ex-BR trains use one platform,
Manch the other). LNE tt 1933 and *Brad* to 1961:
N R ALTRINCHAM; BR tts only added A in index.

NAWORTH [NE]
For earliest use see 1836 B**.
Station first in *Brad* June 1871; clo 5 May 1952
(RM June).

NAWTON [NE] op 1 January 1874 *(Yorks Gaz 3rd)*;
clo 2 February 1953 *(RM March)*; later excursions for
football and shopping *(RM February 1955)* – e.g. one
3 May 1964 *(Whitby)*.

NEASDEN

NEASDEN [Met] op 2 August 1880 *(T 2nd)* as
KINGSBURY- N (thus *Brad* 1880s and GC co tt
1903); renamed N & K 1 January 1910 *(hbl 27th)*,
N 1 January 1932 *(Cl)*; [Bak] added 20 November
1939; [Met] last used 7 December 1940 *(Ug)*;
[Bak] transferred to [Jub] 1 May 1979; still open.
Also **temporary platform** [LNE] on main line here;
op 5? October 1940 when line to Marylebone closed
by bombing; connected by walkway to Met station;
last used 26 November 1940 *(London's Termini)*.

NEATH {map 83}

NEATH [GW] op 19 June 1850**; re-sited ? – February
1864 extra ¼ mile added in mileage column, so by
then?; re-sited again 20 August 1877*; N GENERAL
1 July 1924 *(GW circular 18 June)* to 6 May 1968 tt
(offic); still open. Was N TOWN some tables in *Brad*
1877/81 to 1924 and thus GW co tt 1881 and *hb* 1883.
N HL in *hb* 1872.
* = date from *RAIL 1005/282* and *local working notices*; latter
says that temporary was then taken out of use; temporary was
probably one op 4 June 1877 according to secondary sources –
see Vale of Neath, below, for supporting evidence.

N CANAL SIDE [RSB] op 14 March 1895 *(Colliery
22nd)* as N; renamed N CANAL BRIDGE 1 July 1924
(GW circular 18 June), N C S 17 September 1926
(GW circular 3011); clo 16 September 1935 *(GW notice
NW 1082)*.

N RIVERSIDE [GW] op 1 August 1863 *(co ½
T 17 August)* as N LL; clo 1 August 1878 (Thursday),
reop 1 October 1880 (see 'Vale of Neath' and
'N Cadoxton', below); renamed N BRIDGE STREET
1 July 1924 *(GW circular 18 June)*, N R 17 September
1926 *(GW circular 3011)*; clo except school trains
15 October 1962, clo completely 15 June 1964 *(Cl)*.

Vale of Neath service: op 24 September 1851, to South
Wales/GW station opened 1850. Diverted 1 August 1863
to LL/Riverside. Diverted again 1 March 1873, to GW
second station; tt showed through service Swansea High
Street – Neath – Hirwain with stops on main line at
Llansamlet and Landore; timings suggest ran onto main
line and then reversed to Neath; July 1877 time reduced
since they could now run directly to third (temporary)
station. When service returned to LL, 1 October 1880,
it looks as if trains split at Aberdylais, one portion for
LL, one for main (see *Brad* 1887 reprint for layout);
after October 1904 but on/by February 1906 separate
trains provided for each Neath station.

Neath & Brecon service: line opened 3 June 1867,
using LL/Riverside; when GW diverted their services
from there, N&B left to bear full cost; to save tolls it
diverted its service to primitive station of own in goods
station, N CADOXTON / N C ROAD in *hb* but just N
in *Brad*, 1 August 1878*; it did not immediately return
to LL when GW did; it clo own station and returned to
LL 1 August 1889 (P. Rowledge).
* = *(N&B Gomer)* says 2 August, a Thursday; 1st (new tt)
more likely.

N ENGINE SHED [GW] (non-tt); railwaymen; at least
1928 to 1954; {branch from main station *(U)*.

NEATH ABBEY [GW]
op 1 August 1863 *(co ½ T 17 August- line)*; clo 1 March
1873 (Saturday), reop 1 October 1880 (see Neath
Riverside, above); clo 28 September 1936 *(T 14 Sept.)*.

NEEDHAM MARKET [GE] op 24 December 1846
(EC- line) as N; clo 2 January 1967 *(RM February)*;
reop 6 December 1971 *(BR tt alterations 3 January
1972)* when MARKET added; still open.

NEEN SOLLARS [GW] op 13 August 1864
(Worcester 13th); clo 1 August 1962**. N SOLLERS in
Brad until 1893/4 but *hb* made change 1877.

NEEPSEND [GC]
op 1 July 1888 *(GC dates)*; clo 28 October 1940 *(Cl)*.

NEILSTON

NEILSTON [Cal] op 1 May 1903 *(RCG)*; clo 1 January
1917 *(RM February)*; reop 1 February 1919 *(RCH)*;
N HIGH 2 June 1924** to 18 June 1962 *(Cl)*; still open.
In Cal co tt 1913 as N (in the Village).

N LOW [GBK Jt] op 8 October 1855 *(GSW)* as
CROFTHEAD; renamed 1 June 1868 *(JS)*; original
terminus clo 1 May 1870 *(Cl)*; new through station op
27 March 1871 *(Cl)*; LOW added 15 September 1952
(RM March 1953); clo 7 November 1966 *(Cl)*.

NELSON near Colne [LY]
op 1 February 1849 *(LY; co ½ T 3 February- line)*;
still open. N for BARROWFORD in *Brad* until 1961
but not thus LMS tt 1930, BR LM tt 1957, *hb*.

NELSON

N GLAM [TV] op 1 June 1900 *(RCG)*;
GLAM added *(GW circular 18 June)*;
clo 12 September 1932 *(RM Oct.)*.

N & LLANCAIACH [GW] op 1 July 1912
(RAIL 253/482), 15 chains nearer Quakers Yard than
Llancaiach, which it replaced; clo 15 June 1964 *(Cl)*.

NELSON DOCK [LO] op by May 1896 (see 1893
March 6**); clo 31 December 1956 *(T 29 September)*.

NEPTUNE STREET – see HULL.
NESSCLIFF & PENTRE [SM] op 13 August 1866★★;
& P added 1 June 1913 *(hbl 23 October)*;
finally clo 6 November 1933 *(Cl)*.
NESTON
NESTON [GC] op 18 May 1896 *(Wrexham 23rd)* as
N & PARKGATE; renamed N NORTH 15 September
1952, N 6 May 1968 *(Cl)*; still open.
N SOUTH [Birkenhead] op 1 October 1866
(Birkenhead; LNW co ½ T 13 February 1867- line);
SOUTH added 15 September 1952 *(Cl)*;
clo 17 September 1956 *(RM October)*.
NETHER BUCKIE – see BUCKPOOL.
NETHERBURN [Cal] op 1 December 1866
(Cal- line) as BENTS; renamed 1 May 1868
(Cl; RCG ref April); clo 1 October 1951 *(RM November)*.
NETHERCLEUGH [Cal] op 10 September 1847
(co n True Line); clo 13 June 1960 *(RM July)*.
NETHERFIELD [GN] probably came into use May
1878 *(GN)* – first in *Brad* June as COLWICK;
became N & C 1 May 1883 *(Cl; RCG ref April)*,
N 1901 tt, N & C 13 July 1925 *(Cl)*, N 6 May 1974
(BR notice); still open. *Hb* kept to N & C after 1883.
NETHERHOPE [GW] op 16 May 1932 *(co n dated
'April')*; HALT; clo 5 January 1959 *(T 5th)*.
NETHERSEAL COLLIERY [Mid] (non-tt):
miners; June 1877 to ?; {near Gresley} *(Mid)*.
NETHERTHORPE – see STAVELEY TOWN.
NETHERTON [GW] op 20 December 1852
(W Mid; T 20th- line); clo 1 March 1878 *(hbl 20 June)*,
replaced by station later renamed Blowers Green.
NETHERTON near Huddersfield [LY] op 5 July 1869
(co n LY); clo 23 May 1949 *(RM September)*.
NETHERTON – see STANNINGTON.
NETHERTOWN [Fur]
op 19 July 1849★★; aot request; still open.
NETHY BRIDGE [GNS]
op 1 July 1863 *(GNS)* as ABERNETHY;
renamed 1 November 1867 *(RCG)*; became HALT with
6 November 1961 tt alterations; clo 18 October 1965★★.
NETLEY [LSW]
NETLEY op 5 March 1866 *(Salisbury 10th)*; still open.
N HOSPITAL (non-tt): military hospital, alias
ROYAL VICTORIA HOSPITAL; platform beyond
station provided 5 March 1866; station of own on branch
from N op 18 April 1900 *(LSW notice; RM June)*,
result of Boer War; regular use ceased 1920s; heavily
used WW2 after D-Day (now US Army hospital).
Only occasional use after 1945 (J.R. Fairman, *Netley
Hospital and its Railways*, Kingfisher, 1984).
NETTESWELL – see HARLOW TOWN.
NEW BARCOMBE – see BARCOMBE.
NEW BARNET [GN] op 7 August 1850 *(T 6th, 8th)*;
NEW added 1 May 1884 *(RCG)*; still open.
NEW BASFORD
NEW BASFORD [GC] op 15 March 1899 *(GC; T 16th-
line)*; clo 7 September 1964 *(RM October)*.
Also see BASFORD NORTH.
NEW BECKENHAM [SE]
op 1 April 1864 *(L; co ½ T 8 August- line)*;
re-sited short distance north 1866/8 *(Cl)*; still open.

NEW BELSES – see BELSES.
NEW BIGGIN near Penrith [Mid]: op 1 May 1876
(Mid; co n T 1st- line); clo 4 May 1970 *(RM June)*.
NEW BOLINGBROKE [GN] op 1 July 1913 *(RCG)*;
clo 5 October 1970 *(T 16 July)*.
NEW BRIGHTON [Wirral]
op 30 March 1888 *(D&C 10)*; still open.
NEW BROMPTON – see GILLINGHAM KENT.
NEW BROUGHTON ROAD [GC]
first in *Brad* May 1905; HALT; clo 1 March 1917
(Thursday) *(RCH)*; {map 75}.
NEW CLEE [GC]
op 1 July 1875 *(GC dates)*; aot request; still open.
NEW COMMON BRIDGE – see 1883 August 20★★.
NEW CROSS
NEW CROSS [East London] op 7 December 1869
(T 7th); clo 1 November 1876 (Wednesday),
reop 1 October 1884 *(Cl)*; [Dist] added 6 October 1884;
clo 1 September 1886 (Wednesday) *(Cl)*;
{alongside LBSC station}. Alias N C LL *(hb)*.
Note: at times EL was using both own station and
platform in LBSC station.
NEW CROSS [SE] first in *Brad* October 1850★; SE ran
own trains over East London line from 1 April 1880, to
1 October 1884 when East London given own platform.
[Dist] use 1 October 1884 to 6 October 1884. [Met] use
6 October 1884 to 3 December 1906, and again from
31 March 1913; for LT use clo 23 December 2007★★;
still open for ex-SE. N C & NAVAL SCHOOL in some
tables *Brad* until 1854.
★ = see LONDON BRICKLAYERS ARMS for possible
earlier activity hereabouts; this station perhaps replaced
NORTH KENT JUNCTION.
N C GATE [LBSC] op 5 June 1839 *(co n T 6th)*.
[East London] use 1 November 1876, to 1 October
1884; [Dist] use 1 September 1886 to 1 August 1905;
[Met] use began 31 March 1913; GATE added 9 July
1923 *(hbl 26 April)*; clo for LT use 23 December 2007;
still open for ex-LBSC.
Late 1841 there was a series of slips in cutting south of
New Cross; Brighton passengers taken by coach from
New Cross to Dartmouth Arms; Croydon passengers
walked round blockage ('short distance over New
Cross Hill') with trains to and from ends of walk;
perhaps station used as one 'terminus'. Trouble began
3 November, line finally clear 23 December
(co n T 4 November, 22 December).
Late 1848/early 1849 station replaced by a temporary
one, to north, in COLD BLOW LANE, so that main
could be rebuilt in connection with line widening then
in progress. Date of opening of temporary (still N C in tt)
not known: some time after end of May 1848 when
meeting called to discuss drafts of Bills needed
(T 27 May); known to be in use 6 March 1849 *(T 7th)*;
closed and original reopened 1 May 1849 *(co n T 26 April)*.
NEW CROYDON – see EAST CROYDON.
NEW CUMNOCK
NEW CUMNOCK (a) [GSW] op 20 May 1850 *(T 24th)*;
clo 6 December 1965 *(RM January 1966)*.
NEW CUMNOCK (b) op 27 May 1991 *(BLN 657)*;
still open.

NEW CUT LANE [LY]
op 1 July 1906 *(Wigan Observer 4th)*; see 1905** (b);
clo 26 September 1938 *(RM November)*.
NEW DALE [GW] op 29 January 1934 *(T 22nd)*;
HALT; clo 23 July 1962 *(RM August)*.
NEW DYKES BROW [NB]
first in *Brad* November 1856; Saturdays only;
last in tt October 1866; {Kirkbride – Abbey Junction}.
NEW ELTHAM [SE]
op 1 April 1878 *(L)* as POPE STREET; renamed
N E & P S 1 January 1886 *(Cl; RCG ref January)*,
N E 26 September 1927 *(hbl October)*; still open.
NEW ENGLAND [GN] (non-tt): PLATFORM;
railwaymen, families; by 1856 workmen being taken
to/from depot here in open wagons, perhaps no
platform yet; latter certainly in use by 1 April 1866,
when free service for opening of Methodist Wesleyan
Chapel here; used by annual outing – example 3 August
1867 to Cleethorpes for employees, wives, and children
(Great Northern News, July/August 2002 and
September/October 2003); use ceased 1878 (site built
over for workshop extension); {north of Peterborough}.
NEW GALLOWAY [PPW Jt] op 12 March 1861
(Galloway 15th); clo 14 June 1965 *(RM July)*.
NEW HADLEY [GW] op 3 November 1934 *(wtt supp)*;
HALT until 6 May 1968 *(GW H)*; clo 13 May 1985
(BLN 513); {Oakengates – Wellington}.
NEW HALL BRIDGE [LY] first in *Brad* March
1908; see 1905** (b); clo 27 September 1948 *(Cl)*.
NEW HALLS [NB] op 6 May 1870 *(G&S)*;
clo 1 September 1878 (Sunday) *(Cl)* – trains still
shown September (inertia?); {map 13}.
NEW HEY [LY]
op 2 November 1863 *(LY)*; still open.
NEW HOLLAND [GC]
NEW HOLLAND op 1 March 1848 *(GC)*; passengers
could board trains on pier (ferry from Hull); **PIER** and
TOWN stations separately shown in co tt by July 1903
but not in *hb* until 1904 and *Brad* until May 1945.
RM May 1928 – LNER announces that pier has been
reconstructed and is now open for traffic; no further
details known. 24 June 1981, in middle of day, as result
of opening of Humber Bridge, PIER closed and TOWN
replaced on direct line to Barrow Haven by station
initially N H T in tt, but just N H on nameboard at
station and in tt 17 May 1982 *(RM October; C/W)*;
still open.
NEW HYTHE [SR] op 9 December 1929 *(T 6th)*;
HALT until 2 July 1939 *(hbl July)*; added *hb* 1936a as
PLATFORM but HALT 1938; still open.
NEW INN – see FALKLAND ROAD.
NEW INN BRIDGE [GW] op 14 October 1929
(Cl 29); HALT; clo 25 October 1937**; {map 81}.
NEW INN GLYNCEIRIOG – see GLYNCEIRIOG.
NEW LANE [LY]
op 9 April 1855 *(Southport Vis 5th)*; still open.
NEW LONGTON & HUTTON [LY]
op 1 June 1889 *(LNW Record)* as HOWICK;
renamed HUTTON & HOWICK 1 December 1897
(hbl 27 January 1898), final name 5 November 1934
(Cl); clo 7 September 1964 *(RM October)*. See 1882**.

NEW LUCE [GSW] op 19 September 1877**;
clo 7 February 1882 (Tuesday), reop 16 February
1882, clo 12 April 1886, reop 14 June 1886 *(Cl)*;
clo 6 September 1965 *(RM September)*.
NEW MALDEN [LSW] first in *Brad* December 1846
as M; renamed N M & COOMBE 1859,
C & M 1 March 1862 *(SR)*, M for C November 1912
(RCG), M 1955 *(L)*, N M 16 September 1957 *(RM
November)*; still open.
NEW MAUD JUNCTION – see MAUD.
NEW MILFORD – see NEYLAND.
NEW MILL OFFSET/SIDING – see CARMONT.
NEW MILL END – see LUTON HOO.
NEW MILLS
N M CENTRAL [GC/Mid] op 1 July 1865 *(Mid)*;
CENTRAL added 25 August 1952 *(JS)*; still open.
N M NEWTOWN [LNW] op 9 June 1857 *(Stockport 5th)*;
NEWTOWN added 2 June 1924 *(Rly Gaz 23 May)*;
still open.
NEW MILTON [LSW]
op 6 March 1888 *(W Gaz first edition, 9th)*; still open.
Became NEW M for BARTON-ON-SEA and
MILFORD-ON-SEA 13 February 1897 *(RCG)* and
thus LSW co tt 1914; 'for ...' dropped 1955 *(Brad)*;
Shorter versions often used *Brad* and *hb*.
NEW PASSAGE [GW]; {map 121}
NEW PASSAGE and **N P PIER** op 8 September 1863
(co n W D Press 7th); not shown separately in tt; ferry
from Pier went across Severn to Portskewett; both
clo 1 December 1886 on opening of Severn Tunnel *(Cl)*.
N P HALT op 9 July 1928 *(W D Press 7th)*;
clo 23 November 1964 *(Bristol E P 21st)*.
NEW POOLE JUNCTION – see BROADSTONE.
NEW PUDSEY op 6 March 1967 *(Cl 29)*; still open.
NEW QUAY ROAD – see BRYN TEIFY.
NEW RADNOR [GW] op 25 September 1875 *(GW)*;
clo 5 February 1951 *(RM October)* – see 1951**.
NEW ROMNEY
NEW ROMNEY [RHD] (ng) op 16 July 1927**,
which see for later history; intermittently in tt as N R /
LITTLESTONE-ON-SEA / N R for L-on-S/N R & L;
settled as N R on reopening after war.
N R & LITTLESTONE-ON-SEA [SE] op 19 June 1884
(SE); -on-S added 1888 tt *(Cl)*; clo 6 March 1967
(RM April); {map 130}.
NEW SOUTHGATE
NEW SOUTHGATE [GN] op 7 August 1850 *(T 6th, 8th)*
as COLNEY HATCH & S (see op tt *RM September
1910)*; became S & C H 1 February 1855,
N S and C H 1 October 1876, N S for C H 1 March
1883, N S & FRIERN BARNET 1 May 1923,
N S 18 March 1971 *(Cl, JS)*; fire on 25 December 1976
caused clo *(RM March 1977)*; reop 14 February 1977
(RM April); still open.
Also see COLNEY HATCH; PALMERS GREEN.
NEW STRAND – see BOOTLE.
NEW TREDEGAR [BM]
NEW TREDEGAR op 16 April 1866 *(Cardiff T 20th-
line)* as N T; renamed WHITEROSE 1868/9 *(Brad)*,
NT & W 1 July 1885 *(Cl)*, NT & TIRPHIL 1 November
1906 *(RCG)*, NT 1 July 1924 *(GW circular 18 June)*;

clo 31 December 1962 *(T 31st)*. WHITE ROSE and
TIR PHIL: one and two word versions, used
apparently indiscriminately.
N T COLLIERY (non-tt): PLATFORM; miners; in use
late 1920s; {New Tredegar – Abertysswg} *(U)*.
Also see TIR PHIL.
NEW WANDSWORTH [LBSC]
op 29 March 1858 *(co n T 27th, 30th)*; clo 1 November
1869, replaced by W COMMON *(L)*; {map 110}.
NEWARK
N CASTLE [Mid] op 4 August 1846 *(Mid)*; CASTLE
added 25 September 1950 *(Rly Obs October)*; still open.
N NORTH GATE [GN] op 15 July 1852★★; N G added
25 September 1950 *(Rly Obs October)*; still open.
BR ticket for N NORTHGATE *(JB)*.
Non-tt: When the Royal Show was held at Lincoln
19, 20 and 21 July 1854 daily excursions were arranged
from Tallington. Passengers on these changed carriages,
and companies, at a point north of Newark where the
Midland and GN lines crossed. Modern Health &
Safety inspectors would not approve. *(RCHS Journal
May 1960)*.
NEWARTHILL
NEWARTHILL (a) [Wishaw & Coltness] op on or by
6 March 1835; clo between May 1844 *Brad* (present)
and May 1845 (absent) – no detail in between (see
1835 C★★ and 1828 B★★); {map 16}.
NEWARTHILL (b) [Cal] op 15 May 1867 *(G&S)*;
probably clo 1 June 1880 (last in *Brad* May), replaced
by Carfin (later Holytown).
NEWBIE WORKS [GSW] (non-tt):
GSW wtts show that workmen's trains from Annan
were handed over to Messrs Cochrane & Co's engine
and guard at N Junction to be taken on to the works;
certainly in wtts June 1900 and October 1902
(R. Maund); in use by 1898, clo by 1904 (D. Lindsay);
{private line from N Junction, Annan – Cummertrees}.
NEWBIGGIN – see RAVENSTONEDALE.
NEWBIGGIN (-by-the-Sea) [NE] op 1 March 1872
(BT); clo 2 November 1964 *(RM January 1965)*.
Just N in co tt, *Brad*, tickets; -by-the-Sea was RCH
version – added *hb* 1878a.
NEWBIGGING [Cal]
op 1 March 1867 *(Cal- line)*; clo 12 September 1932,
reop 17 July 1933 *(Cl)*; clo 4 June 1945★★ *(G&S)*.
NEWBOLD (WHARF) – see 1833 B★★.
NEWBRIDGE
NEWBRIDGE [GW] op 23 December 1850★★;
clo 30 April 1962 *(T 6 April)*.
NEWBRIDGE (b): op 6 February 2008 *(RM April)*;
still open.
NEWBRIDGE JUNCTION – see PONTYPRIDD.
NEWBRIDGE-ON-WYE [Cam]
op 21 September 1864 *(Cam; co n Hereford J 24th- line)*;
clo 31 December 1962 *(T 31st)*.
NEWBURGH near Perth [NB] op 17 May 1848
(Dundee- line); clo 19 September 1955 *(RM October)*.
NEWBURGH – see PARBOLD.
NEWBURGH ROAD – see LOGIEREEVE.
NEWBURN [NE] op 12 July 1875 *(NC)*;
clo 15 September 1958 *(RM October)*.

NEWBURY [GW]
NEWBURY op 21 December 1847 *(Hants Chron 25th)*;
still open.
N RACECOURSE op 26 September 1905 for race
meetings *(dist t supp 737)*; full public use 16 May 1988
(BLN 587); tt note said service experimental; note
omitted 1 June 1997 tt; still open.
N WEST FIELDS op 1 October 1906 *(GW H)*; HALT;
clo 4 February 1957 *(Cl)* though shown with trains
Brad 6 May–16 June 1957 (last time).
NEWBURY PARK
op by [GE] 1 May 1903 *(RCG; co ½ T 21 July- line)*;
last steam train ran Saturday 29 November 1947 *(Clay)*;
buses until reop by [Cen] 14 December 1947; still open.
NEWBY BRIDGE [Fur] first in *Brad* December
1905; last trains shown April 1917 (according to *RCH*
clo 1 January 1917, but seems too long for 'inertia');
back July 1917, Thursdays only; full service March 1919;
PLATFORM according to *Brad* until 1925/6; reduced
to summer only 26 September 1938; aot request;
clo 12 September 1939 (Tuesday) *(Cl)*;
{Haverthwaite – Lakeside}. N B (motor platform) in
Furness co tt 1910; HALT according to *hb* 1938;
ticket for N B (LAKESIDE) *(JB)*.
NEWBY WISKE [NE]:
op 25 May 1852★★; clo 20 September 1915 *(T 18th)*;
back in tt April 1920; clo 11 September 1939 *(Cl)*.
NEWCASTLE-under-Lyme [NS]
NEWCASTLE op 6 September 1852 *(RAIL 1005/265)*;
clo 2 March 1964 *(RM April)*. Hb included '-u-L'
(to distinguish from others?), though 1867–77 it was
'-under-Lyme'.
N BRAMPTON op 1 May 1905 *(NS)*; HALT;
clo 2 April 1923 *(Cl)*; {west of main station}.
NEWCASTLE-upon-Tyne {maps 26, 27}
From Carlisle, [NC]: at first passengers carried along
south bank of Tyne to Gateshead (Redheugh) and then
taken by ferry across river to temporary building in The
Close; this practice ceased when line opened to station
near the **SHOT TOWER** (thus in railway books but in
press as 'near the Infirmary') on 21 October 1839★ *(T
24th/Tyne Mercury)*; landslip resulted in almost
immediate closure; reop 2 November 1839. Replaced
by >
N FORTH [NC] op 1 March 1847 *(co n Newcastle
Journal 27 February* – described it as temporary
station); clo 1 January 1851, trains diverted to already
open Central; NC portion was treated until 1962 as
separate station with own station master.
★ = some use on 21 May 1839 only, when passengers carried
on inaugural trip.
From (North) Shields to **N CARLIOL SQUARE** [op by
Newcastle & North Shields; owned by York, Newcastle
& Berwick at clo] op 22 June 1839 *(co n Newcastle
Journal 22nd)*; joined there by East Coast Main Line
[Newcastle & Berwick] trains 1 March 1847 *(co n
Newcastle Journal 27 February)* – both notices called
station just N; N C S closed and >
both of these services diverted to **N CENTRAL** [NE]
op 30 August 1850 *(NE)*; still open as N.
CENTRAL seeped in gradually: in *Brad* NC tables

had 'The Central Station' added 1850/1 (descriptive?) but CENTRAL was not added to East Coast Main Line table until 1905/6 and was dropped 1938/9; in NE co tt 1880 it was added to services to Tynemouth (which also included N Manors) but not elsewhere; it was in NB co tt 1900. *Hb* added it 1872, and always had N-on-Tyne (perhaps to distinguish from other Newcastles).
Note that through service to the south started 1 September 1848, trains reversing short of site of Central, still under construction, and using temporary bridge across Tyne; permanent bridge opened 15 August 1849, still with reversal short of Central site.
From Tynemouth, to **N NEW BRIDGE STREET** [BT] op 27 June 1864 *(co ½ T 22nd)*; this clo 1 January 1909 when its trains were diverted to Central; replaced by through station, Manors North.
Boat train services – see under PERCY MAIN.
[TWM]
N CENTRAL op 15 November 1981 *(Tyneside)*; still open.
N AIRPORT op 17 November 1991 *(Tyneside)*; still open.
NEWCASTLE CROSSING [LNW]
op 2 January 1911 *(LNW Cl)*; clo 1 April 1918 *(RCH)*; {Willaston – Nantwich}. HALT in *RCH* July 1921 list of permanent closures – see 1905**.
NEWCASTLE EMLYN [GW] op 1 July 1895 *(RCG)*; clo 15 September 1952 *(RM November)*.
NEWCASTLETON [NB] op 1 March 1862 *(NB)*; clo 6 January 1969 *(RM February)*.
NEWCHAPEL & GOLDENHILL [NS]
op 1 October 1874 *(RCG)* as G; renamed November 1912 *(hbl 9 July 1913)*; clo 2 March 1964 *(RM April)*. GOLDEN HILL in *hb* until 1895.
NEWCHURCH IoW [IWC]:
line op 1 February 1875; station later – first in *Brad* June 1876 (see 1875**); aot request; clo 6 February 1956 *(Southern Daily Echo 6th)*.
NEWCHURCH near Rochdale – see WATERFOOT.
NEWCHURCH near Warrington [LNE]
op 1 February 1943 *(Cl 29)*; HALT; clo 2 November 1964 *(RM December)*; {Kenyon Junction – Glazebrook}.
NEWCRAIGHALL op 3 June 2002, formal next day *(RM August p. 72)*; still open.
NEWENT [GW] op 27 July 1885 *(Glos Chron 1 August)*; clo 13 July 1959 *(RM August)*.
NEWHAILES [NB]: {map 18}
Probably place served by occasional stop on Musselburgh branch. Report of accident on branch 21 July 1850 shows there was at least one place at which passengers were regularly taken up and set down. No station but a gate-keeper was stationed at level crossing concerned *(Return)*. Point has not been established exactly but according to the report it was about half way up a three-quarter mile long incline which began about a third of a mile out from Musselburgh. Then branch was still following original route (see map); incline and level crossing might well have gone when line diverted.
Station proper op 16 May 1859 (date of diversion of Musselburgh branch), station first in *Brad* June 1859); NEW HAILES until 26 September 1938 *(Cl)*; clo 6 February 1950 *(RM March)*.

NEWHAM [NE] first in *Brad* February 1851: clo 5 May 1941*, reop 7 October 1946 *(RM January 1947)*; clo 25 September 1950 *(RM November)*.
* = nothing in 5 May 1941 wtt but at least 6 October 1941 to 6 May 1946 wtt one weekday call by request, northbound only.
NEWHAVEN Edinburgh [Cal]
op 1 August 1879 *(RCG)*; clo 30 April 1962 *(RM May)*. See 1903** for unused platforms on Seafield branch.
NEWHAVEN near Brighton [LBSC]
N MARINE (non-tt) op 17 May 1886 *(SR)*; for ferry passengers; op as N EAST QUAY, later N BOAT STATION / N HARBOUR B S; became N MARINE 14 May 1984 tt; ceased to be advertised (but single train still ran) 4 March 1996 wtt (R. Maund); last train ran 29 January 1999 as a result of withrawal of P&O Stena's ferry to Dieppe, reop 23 April 1999* for summer only Hoverspeed to Dieppe *(RM February 2000)*; in 2001 only used by one unadvertised service, to satisfy legal requirements for 'open' line – by now not run in connection with shipping service; lost last unadvertised but public train from 17 August 2006 owing to condition of platform roof *(Rly Obs October 2006, p. 490 – suspected that officials treated it as extension of Harbour so that could avoid closure procedure)*.
* = wtt supplement showed resumption as 10 April 1999, but there was a delay in resuming shipping service; used in public service 2 to 17 January 2002 (inclusive) for turning back branch trains to Seaford during engineering work (R. Maund).
N HARBOUR op 8 December 1847 *(co ½ T 15 Feb. 1848)* as N WHARF for PARIS; renamed 1884 tt *(SR)*; terminal portion replaced by what eventually became N Boat Station 17 May 1886 – through platforms remained in use for trains to/from Seaford (R.W. Kidner, *The Newhaven and Seaford Branch*, Oakwood, 1979, especially maps p. 9 and 25); clo August 1914, reop 5 May 1919 *(Cl)*; still open.
N TOWN op 8 December 1847 *(co ½ T 15 February 1848)*; TOWN added 1864 tt *(Cl)*; still open.
HARBOUR and (TOWN) not shown separately in *Brad* until 1856/9.
NEWHOUSE [Cal] op 2 July 1888 *(Cal)*; see 1921 April/May**; clo 1 December 1930 *(Cl)*; later non-tt service from after 1937 to 31 July 1941 *(U)*.
NEWICK & CHAILEY [LBSC]
op 1 August 1882 *(LBSC; Hants Chron 5th- line)*; clo 30 May 1955**, reop 7 August 1956 *(RM May 1958)*; clo 17 March 1958 *(T 17th)*.
NEWINGTON Edinburgh [NB] op 1 December 1884 *(Edin)*; clo 10 September 1962 *(BR n Ed Sub)*.
NEWINGTON – see HULL.
NEWINGTON near Sittingbourne [LCD]
op 1 August 1862 *(co n T 1st)*; still open.
NEWINGTON & BALLS POND ROAD
– see CANONBURY.
NEWLAND near Cinderford [GW]
op 1 September 1883 *(Wye)*; clo 1 January 1917 *(GW notice dated 22 December 1916)*.
NEWLAND near Malvern [GW]
op 18 March 1929 *(wtt aupp)*; HALT; clo 5 April 1965 *(Cl)*. Pre-opening Stocks Lane *(RAC)*.

NEWLANDS [PT] (non-tt):
HALT/COLLIERY PLATFORM; miners; dates ?;
{Port Talbot Docks – Tondu} *(U)*.

NEWLAY [Mid] op 1 September 1846 *(Mid)* as N;
became N for HORSFORTH 1 April 1875 co tt,
N & H 4 October 1889 *(Mid)*, N 12 June 1961
(RM June); clo 22 March 1965 *(RM April)*.

NEWMACHAR [GNS]
op 18 July 1861 *(GNS)*; clo 4 October 1965 *(Rly Obs
November)*. *Hb*: NEW MACHAR until 1904.

NEWMAINS [Cal] op 15 May 1867 *(G&S)*;
clo 1 January 1917 *(RM February)*; reop 2 June 1919
(RCH); see 1921 April/May★★; clo 1 December 1930
(Cl). *Hb* N COLTNESS IRON WORKS (1872);
N & C I W (1883), N (1890).

NEWMARKET [GE]
NEWMARKET op 4 April 1848 *(co n T 3rd)*; clo 1 July
1850★★, reop 9 September 1850 *(co n T 6th)*. Original
was single platform, terminus, requiring reversal when
line extended to Bury St Edmunds 1 April 1854.
When line to Ely opened 1 September 1879, a through
island platform was opened, slightly lower level,
overlapping and slightly east, connected to original by
footbridge *(GE Society Journal, October 1993, p.33)*.
The through portion was replaced by much larger
station on 7 April 1902 about ½ mile nearer Cambridge
(Newmarket 12th). Still open. Ticket for N HL (to
Sunbury, via South Tottenham, GE) *(JB)*.
Original platform plus 'Third Class Platform'
(no protection from weather, added at same time as
Warren Hill), kept for race specials from south until
1902 *(GE Society Journal)*; after that still available for
grooms accompanying horses (tickets exist).
N WARREN HILL (non-tt): race meetings; op 20 April
1885 *(Newmarket 25th)*; used for traffic from north
(RM November 1908); still in use October 1938,
believed only horse specials after War *(AB)*.
{Newmarket – Kennett}.

NEWMILNS [GSW]
op 20 May 1850 *(GSW)*; clo 6 April 1964 *(RM May)*.
Hb: NEW MILNS until 1872.

NEWNHAM Forest of Dean [GW] op 19 September
1851 *(Gloucester J 20th)*; clo 2 November 1964 *(Cl)*.

NEWNHAM BRIDGE near Bewdley [GW]
op 13 August 1864 *(Worcester 13th)*; BRIDGE added
1873 tt *(Cl)* but *hb* 1866a (dropped 1867, back 1872);
clo 1 August 1962★★.

NEWPARK [Cal] op 11 October 1869 *(Rly World June
1975)*; clo 14 September 1959 *(Cl)*. *Hb*: NEW PARK
until 1883.

NEWPORT near Middlesborough [NE]:
line op late December 1830 (see Middlesbrough), nd,
(not listed by *Wishaw* about 1840 but in S&D fare table
for '1840', *RAIL 667/611)*, first in *Brad* May 1847 (see
1825★★); clo 8 August 1915 (Sunday) *(RCH)* but still
shown 'P' in *hb* – 1956 for 'occasional excursions' – one
such 15 August 1932 *(RM October)*; {still in *IA*}.

NEWPORT near Stafford [LNW]
op 1 June 1849 *(Shrewsbury 8th)*; clo 7 September 1964
(RM October). At times N SALOP in some tables
LNW co tt 1860s, 1870s, at least.

NEWPORT – see WALLINGFEN.
NEWPORT IoW
NEWPORT [FYN]: line op 20 July 1889, using IWC
station, with reversal; FYN op station of own 1 July 1913
through carriages began to run between this and main
station 11 May 1914, saving some passengers the walk
(not all trains ran through); FYN station clo 9 August
1923 (Wednesday) *(FYN Oakwood)*; FYN reverted to
using IWC station with reversal.
NEWPORT [IWC] op 16 June 1862 *(Hants Adv 21st)*;
original terminus replaced by through station on/slightly
before 20 December 1875 *(IWC)*; clo 21 February 1966
(RM March). Became N GENERAL January/September
1876, N CENTRAL by end of 1876, N 1907 *(Brad)*.
N for BRIGHTSTONE in *Brad* until 1955.
N PAN LANE [IoW Newport Junction] op 11 August
1875, without BoT approval; ordered to cease – date?
(IWC); op with authority 6 October 1875 *(Hants Teleg
9th)*; clo 1 June 1879 (Sunday) *(Cl)*; {Shide – Newport}.
NEWPORT South Wales; all finally part of [GW];
{map 89}. For earliest service see 1822★★.
From Blaina [Monmouthshire], Western Valleys,
to **N COURTYBELLA** op 23 December 1850★★;
replaced on line extension by >
N DOCK STREET op 4 August 1852 *(GW)*; Western
Valleys trains transferred to High Street 12 May 1880
(Merlin 14th); LNW trains from Sirhowy branch and
BM transferred I June 1880 *(LNW co n Merlin 28 May;
BM minutes, RAIL 65/7)*. This station then clo.
From Pontypool [Monmouthshire], Eastern Valleys,
to station at **MARSHES TURNPIKE GATE** op 1 July
1852 *(Merlin 2nd)*; replaced by >
N MILL STREET op 9 March 1853 *(co ½ T 23 May)*;
service transferred to High Street 1 August 1880
(co n Merlin 30 July); station then clo.
Main [South Wales] line to **NEWPORT** op 19 June
1850★★; still open as N SOUTH WALES. HIGH
STREET was added *Brad* in different tables at
different times, last seen 1938/9; became N GWENT
29 September 1996 tt, N SW 1 June 1997 tt.
Non-tt: [ANSW]
EAST QUAY (of South Dock): *ANSW, p. 44–5* has photos
of American troops disembarking to waiting trains after
end of First War and special passenger service to connect
with Royal Mail Co's vessels (1919 at least).
SOUTH QUAY (of South Dock): about 1915 train
service from Dock entrance to Salvage (or Box) Factory
for women working on reconditioning shell cases and
ammunition boxes returned from France *(ANSW p.43)*.
Photo *ANSW p. 41* shows passengers from a New
Zealand liner being disembarked, train waiting, in 1936.
MT6/2542/8 dated 13 March 1919 says passenger service
proposed between here and QUEEN ALEXANDRA
DOCK – no later details known; source confirms
existence of platform for National Cartridge & Box
Factory. Unlikely that passenger trains were restricted
to examples mentioned above.
NEWPORT ESSEX [GE] op 30 July 1845 *(co n T 26th-
line)*; ESSEX added 1 July 1923 *(hbl 12th)*; still open.
NEWPORT PAGNELL [LNW] op 2 September
1867 *(Rtn)*; clo 7 September 1964 *(RM October)*.

NEWPORT ROAD – see PONTYPOOL.

NEWPORT-ON-TAY [NB]

N-on-T EAST op 12 May 1879 *(The Scotsman 13th)*; clo 5 May 1969 *(RM June)*.

N-on-T WEST op 12 May 1879 *(The Scotsman 13th)*; clo 12 January 1880, reop 20 June 1887 *(Cl)*; clo 5 May 1969 *(RM June)*.

Originally EAST and WEST NEWPORT, renamed January/June 1956 *(Brad)*.

NEWQUAY [GW] op 20 June 1876 *(R Corn Gaz 24th)*; still open. Aot NEW QUAY *(hb)*.

NEWSEAT [GNS] op 3 July 1862 *(GNS)*; NEW SEAT until 1884 tt *(JS)*; made HALT 22 September 1930 *(Cl)*; clo 3 May 1965 *(RM May)*.

NEWSHAM [NE]: according to *BT* did not open with line; a photo-caption says station dates from 1850; a summer 1851 tt included in book shows stop here; clo 2 November 1964 *(Cl)*. Used 3 July 1967 for Newlands School outing (photo p.55 in *Blyth*, by Blyth Local Studies Group, Chalford Publications, 1997). N JUNCTION 1854/5 to 1865/6 in *Brad*.

NEWSHOLME [LY] op 1 June 1880 *(LY)*; clo 6 August 1957 (Tuesday) *(RM September)* – trainless Bank Holiday Monday previous day.

NEWSTEAD near Galashiels [NB]

first in *Brad* November 1849; last October 1852; initially NEWBRIDGE in *Brad*; {Melrose – St Boswells}.

NEWSTEAD near Nottingham.

NEWSTEAD [Mid] op privately 1 April 1863 wtt *(Mid)*, to public 1 July 1883 *(Mid)*; clo 12 October 1964 *(RM November)*. An entry in *hb* October 1961a appears to suggest that passenger station was now N WEST but it was still just N in BR LM Region tts.

An LNE-issued ticket exists thus *(JB)*, but strictly this was goods station – was passenger side now put under goods manager's control?

NEWSTEAD op 17 May 1993 *(RM May)*; old Mid station; still open.

N & ANNESLEY [GN] op 2 October 1882 *(GN)*; & A added 1891 tt *(Cl)*; clo to public 14 September 1931 *(Cl)* but railwaymen used to 4 March 1963.

NEWTHORPE, Greasley & Shipley Gate [GN] op 1 August 1876 *(GN)*; clo 7 January 1963 *(RM Feb.)*. N, G & S G was RCH name – used *hb* always and in e.g. Distance Book 1914. In *Brad* opened as N & G and became N 1893/4 – but shown as N in GN wtt 1888.

NEWTON Glasgow [Cal] first in *Brad* November 1852; re-sited 19 December 1873 *(Cl)*; 'new station' 23 January 1901 *(Cal)*; still open.

NEWTON near Droylsden – see 1846 April 13★★.

NEWTON ABBOT [GW] op 31 December 1846 *(Trewman 7 January 1847)*; ABBOT added 1 March 1877 *(Cl)*; still open. N JUNCTION in *Brad* 1852/3 to 1877 but not thus GW co tt 1859, 1874. Non-tt: N A GOODS: exhibition 24–31 July 1980 *(U)*.

NEWTON AYCLIFFE

op 9 January 1978 *(RM March)*; still open.

NEWTON DALE – see 1835 B★★.

NEWTON FOR HYDE [GC] op 17 November 1841 *(GC; Rtn- line)*; still open. Co notice in *Manchester Guardian* 24 December 1842 called it N & H;

'for H' added *Brad* 1848 (previously H).

NEWTON HEATH

NEWTON HEATH [LY] op 1 December 1853 *(LY)*; clo 3 January 1966 *(RM February)*. Also see DEAN LANE.

NEWTON JUNCTION – see EARLESTOWN.

NEWTON KYME [NE]: line op 10 August 1847 *(co ½ T 22 February 1848- line;* in inspection report dated 9th), nd, July 1848; KYME added 1850 tt *(Cl)*; clo 6 January 1964 *(Cl)*.

NEWTON POPPLEFORD [LSW] op 1 June 1899 *(Sidmouth 7th)*; clo 6 March 1967 *(Express & E 6th)*.

NEWTON ROAD – see TIBSHELF.

NEWTON ROAD [LNW] op 4 July 1837 *(T 6th)*. Replaced 1 March 1863 by station short distance to north which op as WEST BROMWICH and was renamed N R for W B 1 May 1863 *(W Mid)*; 'for W B' dropped before/with LNW co tt April 1870. This is turn was replaced by station 30 chains south on 1 January 1902 *(co ½ Rly Times 15 February)*. This third station clo 7 May 1945 *(Cl)*.

NEWTON ST CYRES [LSW]: line op 12 May 1851★★; this station almost certainly opened later; start of October looks likely – arrangements confirmed at BE Board meeting of 24 September (M. Hutson, *Chron*), first found in tt *Trewman* 2 October 1851; not in *Brad* until December 1852; originally ST C, NEWTON added 1 October 1913 *(hbl 23rd)*; aot request; still open.

NEWTON STEWART [PPW Jt] op 12 March 1861 *(Galloway 15th)*; clo 14 June 1965 *(RM July)*.

NEWTON TONY [LSW]: military use began 1 October 1901; op to public 2 June 1902 *(W Gaz, Wilts & NE Somerset edition 6th)*; N TONEY until 1903 tt *(Cl)*; see 1951★★; clo 30 June 1952 *(RM August)*.

NEWTON-LE-WILLOWS near Manchester

NEWTON-LE-WILLOWS [LNW]: line op 17 September 1830★★, nd, 1 March 1831 co tt; at first NEWTON, alias N BRIDGE (thus co tt March 1831, but not in *Brad* until 1868, then Liverpool – Manchester table only); renamed N-le-W 14 June 1888 *(Cl; RCG ref July)*; still open.

N RACECOURSE [LM] (non-tt): op 20 June 1832 *(race)*; racing moved to Haydock Park in 1899 (magazine *Cheshire Today*, February 1988). S. Greaves, *Newton's Story*, Newton 150 Committee, 1980 said was used into early 1900s; article in *Railway World, April 1985* says branch lifted 1902; {branch from Earlestown}.

NEWTON-LE-WILLOWS – see JERVAULX.

NEWTON-ON-AYR [GSW]

op 1 November 1886 *(RCG)*; still open.

NEWTONAIRDS [GSW] op 1 March 1905 *(RCG)*; clo 3 May 1943 *(RM January 1944)*.

NEWTONGRANGE [NB]

op 1 August 1908 *(RCG)*, as replacement for Dalhousie; clo 6 January 1969 *(RM February)*.

NEWTONHEAD – see AYR.

NEWTONHILL [Cal]

first in *Brad* November 1850; clo 11 June 1956 *(RM April)*. Hb: NEWTON HILL until 1877.

NEWTONMORE [High]

op 9 September 1863 *(High)*; still open.

NEWTOWNYarmouth [MGN]
see 17 July 1933**; HALT.
NEWTOWN POWYS [Cam] op 2 September 1859
(Cam) from Llanidloes; replaced by new station
48 chains west 10 June 1861 when line extended to link
with that from Oswestry *(Cl)*; POWYS added ?; still open.
NEWTOWN ST BOSWELLS
– see ST BOSWELLS.
NEWTYLE [Cal] op 3 April 1832 *(co n Dundee)*;
see 1831 B**; re-sited on deviation 31 August 1868 *(Cl)*;
clo 10 January 1955 *(T 28 December 1954)*; {maps 8, 9}.
NEYLAND [GW] op 15 April 1856 *(T 17th)* as
MILFORD HAVEN; renamed N February 1859,
NEW MILFORD November 1859 *Brad*, N 30 August
1906 *(hbl 25 October)*; clo 15 June 1964 *(Cl)*.
GW co tt: 1859 N for M H, Pembroke, Pembroke Dock
and Ireland; 1874 N M (M H), later N M for M H.
NIDD BRIDGE [NE]
op 1 September 1848 *(NE- line)* as RIPLEY;
renamed 1 June 1862 *(Cl)*; clo 18 June 1962 *(RM July)*.
NIDDRIE [Ed & Dalk; NB]; {map 18}
N JUNCTION: see 1831 A**, first tt reference June 1843
(Tuck); perhaps short closure 1846/7 while line rebuilt,
but unlikely; last in *Brad* October 1847; reop 1 June
1860; clo 1 October 1860 *(D&C 6*, as for Edinburgh
St Leonards).
NIDDRIE (a) op 21 June 1847 *(Ed & Dalk)*;
clo 1 October 1860 *(Cl)*, though last in *Brad* November
– did it survive a little longer than N J or was it tt inertia?
Near enough to N Junction to be used as interchange
with it – perhaps treated as part of same station.
NIDDRIE (b) op 1 December 1864 *(Cl* reop date; first
in *Brad* January 1865)*; last in *Brad* January 1869, when
trains only shown from Edinburgh. *G&S* say that this
was new site south of (a), though rudimentary nature of
its service would hardly have seemed to justify new
station; however, goods station (op ?) existed south of
junction and perhaps this was 1864–9 stop; not added
to RCH Junction Diagram until 1920 but *hb* shows
Niddrie goods station in existence by 1877.
NIGG [High]
op 1 June 1864 *(High)*; clo 13 June 1960 *(RM July)*.
NIGHTINGALE VALLEY [GW]
op 9 July 1928 *(W D Press 7th, 9th)*; summers only; HALT;
clo 12 September 1932 *(Cl)*; {Clifton Bridge – Pill}.
NINE ELMS – see LONDON.
NINE MILE POINT
See 1822** for earliest service.
NINE MILE POINT [LNW] first in *Brad* July 1868;
clo 2 February 1959 *(Cl)*. GW co tt 1874, LNW co tt
1882: N M P (QUARRY MAWR) – also thus in *Brad*
until 1879 *(JS)*. N M P for UPPER MACHEN in *Brad*
at end but not thus LMS tt 1930 nor BR WR tt 1958.
NINEWELLS JUNCTION – see DUNDEE.
NINGWOOD [FYN] op 20 July 1889 *(co n FYN)*;
clo 21 September 1953 *(T 21st)*.
NINIAN PARK [GW] op for football 2 November
1912 but advertised for use by ordinary Sunday services
from summer 1934 (certainly in 9 July 1934 *Brad* but
not in 17 July 1933 issue) to last use 3 September 1939
(Cl); PLATFORM; later intermittent use for football

(just as N P in 1971 *BR handbill PR 2891)* – last regular
was season 1976/7 – in *PSUL* then, not next year.
Reop for full public use 4 October 1987**; still open.
Pre-opening Leckwith Road *(RAC)*.
NISBET [NB] op 18 July 1856**; clo 13 August 1948**.
NITSHILL [GBK Jt]: line op 27 September 1848
(Rtn), nd, June 1850; still open.
NO.5 PASSING PLACE [GC GI]
op 15 May 1912 *(GC)*; clo 3 July 1961 *(co n G&I)*.
NO.5 PIT SIDING [MC] (non-tt): miners; in use
early 1920s *(U)*; ticket as ASPATRIA NO.5 P S *(JB)*;
{at/near earlier Arkleby}.
NO.56 PLATFORM [LNE] (non-tt): site unknown;
perhaps for ROF at Risley; op by October 1943;
clo after 1944 *(U)*; ticket from St Helens Central for
week commencing 9 January 1944 *(JB)*.
NOCTON & DUNSTON [GN/GE] op 1 August
1882 *(GN/GE)*; clo 2 May 1955 *(RM June)*.
NOEL PARK & WOOD GREEN [GE]
op 1 January 1878 *(L)* as GREEN LANES; renamed
G L & N P 1 May 1884 *(RCG)*; final name 1 January
1902 *(hbl 23rd)*; clo 7 January 1963 *(RM January)*.
NOOK PASTURE [NB] op 2 January 1864 (derived
from *NB*, which says op 1st, a Friday; not in *Brad* until
May 1864); Saturdays only; last in *Brad* December
1873; included *hb* 1865a to 1883, not 1890;
{Penton – Kershope Foot}.
NORBITON [LSW]
op 1 January 1869 *(co n T 24 December 1868)*; still open.
In *Brad* op as N and KINGSTON HILL; became
N for N and K H [sic] 1886/7, N 1890, N for K H and
RICHMOND PARK 1894, N for K H 1914/5 (and
thus 1925 *hb*), N 1955.
NORBURY London [LBSC]
op 1 January 1878 *(LBSC)*; still open.
NORBURY & ELLASTON [NS] op 31 May 1852
(T 26 May, 1 June) as N; renamed N & ELLASTONE
16 July 1901 *(JS)*; final version 2 April 1923 *(Cl)*;
clo 1 November 1954 *(T 1 October)*; later excur *(U)* –
not in handbills seen for 1960–62 (R. Maund).
NORHAM [NE]: line op 27 July 1849 *(NE)*, nd,
July 1851; clo 15 June 1964 *(RM July)*.
NORLAND – see UXBRIDGE ROAD.
NORMACOT [NS] op 1 November 1882 *(NS-K)*;
clo 2 March 1964 *(RM April)*.
NORMANS BAY [LBSC] op 11 September 1905
(LBSC); HALT until 5 May 1969 *(S App)*; still open.
Opened as PEVENSEY SLUICE *(S Halts)*.
NORMANTON [Mid];
line op 1 July 1840, station probably later – certainly
by/on 5 October 1840 *(tt Leeds)*; still open.
NORTH ACTON
NORTH ACTON [GW] op 1 May 1904 *(RM June)*;
HALT; clo 1 February 1913 (Saturday) *(wtt supp)*.
NORTH ACTON [Cen] op November 1923
(contradictory GW documents – *GW Annual Report
1924* says 5th, *wtt supp* 11th – not known which
correct); 20 chains east of earlier station; GW platforms
closed 30 June 1947 *(Cl)*; Cen still open.
NORTH BERWICK [NB]
Temporary station, Williamstown/Williamstone in many

modern works, op 13 August 1849 *(Edin)*; was N B in *Brad* and *Edinburgh tt*; replaced by permanent >
NORTH BERWICK op 17 June 1850 *(Edin)*; still open. N B JUNCTION in *Reid* 1904.

NORTH CAMP

NORTH CAMP [SE] first in *Brad* August 1857; successively in *Brad* (other variations elsewhere) as ALDERSHOT N C, N C A, A C, A N C, A for N C and SOUTH FARNBOROUGH, N C for ASH VALE and S F; re-sited south, to Guildford side of level-crossing, probably before 1892 *(C/W*, based on early version of *Cl)*; name settled 13 June 1955 *(Cl)*; still open.
Also see ASH VALE.

NORTH CAVE [HB] op 27 July 1885 *(op tt NER I)*; clo 1 August 1955 *(RM September)*.

NORTH CONNEL [Cal] op 7 March 1904 (J. Thomas, *The Callander & Oban Railway*, D&C, 1966); clo 28 March 1966 *(RM June*, photo-caption). HALT in *Brad* 1921 to 1933/4 but *hb* retained HALT until September 1962a.

NORTH DEAN – see GREETLAND.

NORTH DOCKS – see SANDHILLS.

NORTH DROVE [MGN] first trains in *Brad* September 1866*; clo 15 September 1958 *(RM October)*. * = line op 1 August; table for line first shown in *Brad* August, this station listed but no trains calling.

NORTH DULWICH [LBSC] op 1 October 1868 *(T 28 September)*; still open.

NORTH EALING op by [Dist] 23 June 1903 *(RCG)*; transferred to [Picc] 4 July 1932; still open. *Hb* 1904 until 1938: N E for HANGER HILL, but not seen thus *Brad*.

NORTH EASTRINGTON [HB] op 27 July 1885 *(op tt NER I)* as E; NORTH added 1 July 1922 *(hbl 13th)*; became HALT 1938/9 *Brad*, *hb* 1941a; clo 1 August 1955 *(RM September)*.

NORTH ELMHAM [GE] op 20 March 1849 *(EC- line)* as E; aot request; NORTH added 1 September 1872 *(Cl; RCG ref Oct.)*; clo 5 October 1964 *(RM September)*.

NORTH END (Hampstead area) – see BULL & BUSH.

NORTH END near Fenny Compton [East & West Junction]: first in *Brad* August 1872; last June 1873, back April 1874 (possible that omission and return result of timetable reorganisation, not clo/reop, but not in August 1873 tt *Cheltenham Examiner*; thus more likely did close but just possible that it was omitted since only a 'halt'); clo 1 August 1877 (Wednesday) *(Cl)*; shown 'P' in *hb* 1877-95, not 1904; {Fenny Compton – Warwick Road}.

NORTH END FULHAM – see WEST KENSINGTON.

NORTH END OF BLEA MOOR TUNNEL [LMS] (non-tt): workman's ticket from Hawes *(JB)*; dates ?; {Ribblehead – Dent}.

NORTH ESK – see DALKEITH.

NORTH FAMBRIDGE [GE] op 1 July 1889 *(D&C 5- line)* as F; became N F 20 May 2007 tt; still open.

NORTH FILTON [GW] op 12 July 1926 *(Bristol notice S1248)*; PLATFORM on site of earlier Filton; clo 23 November 1964 *(Bristol E P 21st)*; workmen continued to use to 5 September 1966 and from ? to 9 May 1986; {map 121}.

NORTH GREENWICH

NORTH GREENWICH [GE] op 29 July 1872 *(L)*; at opening 29 July 1872, carriages horse-drawn from Millwall Junction boundary of Millwall Docks property, then locomotive took over; fully locomotive-hauled 23 August 1880 *(Millwall)*; clo 4 May 1926**. Sometimes N G CUBITT TOWN (thus GE co tt 1914). ISLAND GARDENS here later.

NORTH GREENWICH [Jub] op 14 May 1999 *(LRR 20)*; still open.

NORTH GRIMSTON [NE] op 1 June 1853 *(NE- line)*; clo 5 June 1950 *(Cl)*.

NORTH HARROW [Met/GC] op 22 March 1915 *(GC dates)*; still open.

NORTH HAYLING [LBSC] op 17 July 1867 *(SR)*; last in *Brad* December 1868 (January 1869 'discontinued'); back August 1869; clo 4 November 1963 *(Cl)*.

NORTH HOWDEN – see HOWDEN.

NORTH KELSEY [GC] op 1 November 1848*; clo 1 November 1965 *(RM December)*. * = this is *GC* date for line; contrary to statement there, this station was in *Brad* November 1848 so probably opened with line.

NORTH KENT JUNCTION [SE] op 1 September 1849, exchange only, not shown in *Brad*; would not have been needed for a while following accident 21 August 1850; perhaps replaced by New Cross [SE]; relevant service last in *Brad* January 1852. See London Bricklayers Arms for fuller details; {map 105}.

NORTH KILLINGHOLME – see KILLINGHOLME ADMIRALTY.

NORTH LEITH – see under LEITH.

NORTH LLANRWST [LNW] op 17 June 1863 *(LNW Officers 381)*, at 10m 17ch, as L; became through station 6 April 1868; second platform added 1878; L & TREFRIW 1884 *(Cl; RCG ref April)* to 6 May 1974 *(BR notice)*; became N L when new L (under 'L') added 29 July 1989 *(BLN 616)*; aot request; still open.

NORTH LONSDALE CROSSING [Fur] first in *Brad* June 1888; clo June 1916 *(Cl)*.

NORTH QUEENSFERRY [NB] {map 10}
NORTH QUEENSFERRY (a) op 1 November 1877 *(Edin)*; clo 5 March 1890 when Forth Bridge line opened.
NORTH QUEENSFERRY (b) first in *Brad* August 1890*; still open.
* = since the line was given continuous coverage in *Brad*, this suggests there was a short gap between stations. July 1890 tt (clearly behind events) shows main line service via Dalmeny, which is noted as 'station for South Queensferry', and Inverkeithing, noted as 'by ferry'. Forth Bridge at first only carried locals on Edinburgh to Dunfermline route and trains on routes from Burntisland, Winchburgh and Saughton only started to use it on 2 June 1890; seems likely that second station opened then.

NORTH RHONDDA [GW] (non-tt):
HALT; service for miners, sanctioned by BoT,
started 5 March 1917 (internal GW mem);
op as BLAENCORRWG & N R PLATFORM,
later N R HALT; clo ? – by 23 March 1963 when line
closed (pit had closed 1960); {northern terminus of
South Wales Mineral line} (M. Hale).

NORTH ROAD – see DARLINGTON [S&D].

NORTH RODE [NS] op 18 June 1849 – see
MACCLESFIELD HIBEL ROAD; clo 7 May 1962
(RM May). N R JUNCTION in *Brad* until 1881/2.

NORTH SEATON [NE]
op 7 November 1859 *(co ½ RAIL 1110/227)*;
clo 2 November 1964 *(RM January 1965)*.
At first N S & NEWBIGGEN in *Brad*; spelling soon
amended, then N S for N until latter had own station.

NORTH SHEEN [SR]
op 6 July 1930 *(T 30 June)*; still open.

NORTH SHIELDS {map 26}
NORTH added erratically; seen as early as June 1841
Brad but not consistently until 1874.

NORTH SHIELDS [NE] op 22 June 1839***(NE)*;
clo 11 August 1980 *(RM October)* for conversion to >

NORTH SHIELDS [TWM] op 14 November 1982
(Tyneside); still open.

NORTH SHIELDS [BT; NE] op 27 June 1864 *(co ½
T 22 August)* as TYNEMOUTH; renamed N S 1 April
1865; clo 3 July 1882 *(Cl)*.

NORTH SKELTON [NE] op 1 July 1902 *(RCG)*;
clo 15 January 1951, reop 18 June 1951 *(Cl)*;
clo 10 September 1951 *(Cl)* – see 1951**.

NORTH STOCKTON – see STOCKTON.

NORTH SUNDERLAND [North Sunderland]
op non-tt with line 14 December 1898 *(Rtn- line)*;
first in public tt August 1934; clo 29 October 1951 *(Cl)*.
Added *hb* 1900a; present 1925; omitted 1929;
back 1936a (since 1930a); really closed for a while
or removed as non-public in tidying-up exercise?

NORTH TAWTON [LSW] op 1 November 1865
(Tavistock 3rd); clo 5 June 1972 *(Cornish & DP 11th)*.

NORTH THORESBY [GN] op 1 March 1848
(co n GC vol.I, p.120); clo 5 October 1970 *(T 16 July)*.

NORTH UNION JUNCTION
– see LOWTON; PARKSIDE.

NORTH VALE – see ASH near Aldershot.

NORTH WALSALL [Mid] op 1 November 1872
(Mid; co n T 1st- line); clo 13 July 1925 *(Mid)*.

NORTH WALSHAM
NORTH WALSHAM [GE] op 20 October 1874 *(T 21st)*;
was N W MAIN 27 September 1948 *(RM November)*
to 14 June 1965 tt *(AB)*; still open.

N W TOWN [MGN] op 13 June 1881 *(MGN)*;
TOWN added 27 September 1948 *(RM November)*;
clo 2 March 1959 *(T 2nd)*.

NORTH WATER BRIDGE [NB] first in *Brad* July
1866; clo 1 October 1951 *(RM November)*.

NORTH WEALD op by [GE] 24 April 1865 *(L; co n
T 24th- line)*; legally transferred to [Cen] 25 September
1949 *(T 26th)* but BR continued to provide trains
until electric services began 18 November 1957;
clo 3 October 1994 (last train 30 September) *(RM Nov.)*.

NORTH WEMBLEY
op by [LNW] 15 June 1912 *(T 14th)*; still open.
Also [Bak] use from 16 April 1917 to 27 September
1982** and 4 June 1984 on *(Ug)*.
Pre-opening East Lane *(L)*.

NORTH WINGFIELD COLLIERY [Mid] (non-tt):
miners; op by July 1915 wtt; clo 9 November 1927;
{near Clay Cross} *(Mid)*.

NORTH WOOLWICH [GE] op 14 June 1847
(co ½ T 13 August); new station 1854; clo 29 May 1994
(BLN 734) in connection with Jubilee line extension,
reop 29 October 1995 *(RM February 1996)*;
clo 10 December 2006 – last train Saturday 9th
(RM Feb. 2007). Early tts and company notices just
called it W; sometimes trains apparently terminated
at W ROFFS WHARF or W TOWN – this was ferry
terminus on south bank – no mention of rail terminal
at all. NORTH first seen 1850/3 *Brad*, but not
consistently added until later;
W NORTH in EC co tt 1854.

NORTH WOOTTON [GE]
op 3 October 1862 *(T 6th)*; NORTH added 1869 tt *(Cl)*
but main entry *hb* 1863a was N W; clo 5 May 1969
(RM July, photo caption).

NORTH WYLAM [NE]
op 13 May 1876 *(co n Nhumb)*; although on map it
appeared to be a through station, in reality it was
western terminus for most of its existence; passengers
going west of here had to cross road bridge and travel
on from Wylam; was treated as through station from
1954; clo 11 March 1968 *(RM April)*.

NORTHALLERTON [NE]; {map 37}
NORTHALLERTON op 31 March 1841 *(co n E Cos
Her 25 March)*; still open. N JUNCTION 1851/2 to ?,
Brad, and thus NE co tt 1880. Also briefly N MAIN –
see below.
Emergency WW2 platforms on avoiding lines (on site
of N Low), scheme completed June 1941, were used by
diversions (East Coast trains sent via Teeside) until
1960s (J.P. McCrickard, *Wartime Emergency Connections
– the Northallerton Avoiding Line,* in *WW II,* May and
June 1992 issues).
N TOWN: op 25 May 1852**; clo 1 January 1856
(see N Low, below).
N LOW op December 1854 (manuscript correction by
K. Hoole to his *Evolution of the North Eastern Railway,
K. Hoole Library No.209,* has 'Dec. 1854' for LOW and
attached plan, dated 1 July 1854, shows LOW and
footpath connecting it to MAIN). *Brad* December
1854 to December 1855 has trains on Leeds & Thirsk /
Leeds Northern line calling at both TOWN and MAIN.
New spur op 1 January 1856 allowed diversion of
service from Stockton to main station here and then
along main line to Thirsk (main); LOW then left as
northern terminus of local service to Melmerby.
Clo February 1901? when new link allowed all trains to
use main station *(Cl* dates this 10 February 1901, but
that a Sunday). LOW not shown separately in *hb* until
1904, deleted by/before 1910a. After diversion, *Brad*
referred to main station as N HL only for connection
to Melmerby service.

NORTHAM near Bideford [BWA]
op 18 May 1901★★; clo 28 March 1917★★.
NORTHAM [LSW]
N ROAD – see SOUTHAMPTON.
NORTHAM op 2 December 1872★; at/near site of earlier
N ROAD?; at first tickets only available from it; passengers
to it bought tickets to Southampton, for which it acted
as ticket platform *(LSW)*; clo 5 September 1966 *(Cl)*.
★ = *LSW* and *SR* give 1st; that was a Sunday; there was a
Sunday service so possible; but Poole and Broadstone opened
2nd; likely that all three were added same day ?
NORTHAMPTON
NORTHAMPTON [LNW] op 16 February 1859 *(LNW)*;
N CASTLE until 18 April 1866; still open. Aot *Brad*
had N C Station Black Lion Hill.
N BRIDGE STREET [LNW] op 13 May 1845 as N
(LNW Record – letter from C.R. Clinker citing
Northampton Mercury 17th); in *Brad* this became
N COTTEN [sic] END 1867, N B S 1872 *(JS)*;
clo 4 May 1964 *(RM June)*.
NORTHAMPTON [Mid] temporary op 1 October 1866
(co n T 27 Sept.), at Far Coton; replaced by >
N ST JOHNS STREET [Mid] op 10 June 1872 *(Mid)*;
ST J S added 2 June 1924 *(Rly Gaz 23 May)*; clo 3 July
1939 *(RM August)* – trains diverted to N Castle.
NORTHENDEN [CLC] op 1 December 1865
(Stockport 1st); clo 30 November 1964 *(RM March
1965)*. Became N for WYTHENSHAWE 1933?
(hbl ref February) and thus *Brad* until 1955.
NORTHFIELD [Mid]
op 1 September 1870 *(Mid)*; still open.
NORTHFIELDS op by [Dist] 16 April 1908 *(L)*
as NORTHFIELD EALING; renamed
NORTHFIELDS & LITTLE E 11 December 1911,
NORTHFIELDS 19 May 1932 *(L)*; rebuilt east
18 December 1932; [Picc] added 9 January 1933;
Dist use ended 10 October 1964; Picc service continues.
NORTHFLEET [SE]: line op 30 July 1849; this
station not listed by *The Times* at opening; was included
in *SE notice of alterations* for 1 November 1849 *(T)* –
nothing seen in between; still open.
NORTHIAM [KES] op 2 April 1900 *(RM July)*;
clo 4 January 1954 *(T 28 Oct. 1953)*. *Brad, hb* 1904 on and
SEC co tt 1914: N for BECKLEY and SANDHURST.
NORTHOLT
NORTHOLT [GW] op 1 May 1907 *(L)*; HALT until
23 September 1929 *(Cl)*; replaced by >
NORTHOLT [Cen] op 21 November 1948 *(T 20th)*;
still open.
N JUNCTION – see SOUTH RUISLIP.
N PARK [LNE] op 19 July 1926 *(T 17th)* as SOUTH
HARROW & ROXETH; renamed N P for N VILLAGE
13 May 1929 *(JS; ref RM July)*, N P 13 June 1955 *(JS)*;
still open.
NORTHORPE near Gainsborough [GC] op 2 April
1849 *(Lincs Times 3rd)*; clo 4 July 1955 *(RM August)*.
NORTHORPE near Dewsbury:
N HIGHER [LNW] op 1 October 1900 *(LNW Officers
39764)*; clo 11 July 1921 by fire; temporarily reop
25 July 1921 *(LNW dates, no authority)*; rebuilt station
on original site op 6 August 1923 *(Cl)*; HIGHER added

2 June 1924 *(Rly Gaz 23 May)*; clo 5 October 1953
(RM November). *LNW dates* says was briefly
N DARK LANE before N HIGHER.
N NORTH ROAD [LY] op 1 December 1891 *(RCG)*;
clo 2 April 1917 *(Cl)*; reop 5 May 1919 *(RCH)*;
NORTH ROAD added 2 June 1924 *(Rly Gaz 23 May)*;
clo 14 June 1965 *(RM June)*.
NORTHUMBERLAND PARK
NORTHUMBERLAND PARK [GE] probably op April/
October 1841 (see 1841★★); op as MARSH LANE,
alias M L TOTTENHAM. Probably closed for a few
months end 1842/early 1843; still in *Brad*, notes,
November 1842 (one train each way, 3.30pm down,
2.30pm up); trains involved did not stop at Tottenham
or Edmonton; omitted December 1842 – 3.30 now
stopped at Tottenham, 2.30 at Edmonton; back in tt
June 1843, now in body of tt, some trains stopping at
Edmonton and Tottenham as well as here. Renamed
PARK 1 June 1852 *(L)*, N P 1 July 1923 *(hbl 12th)*;
still open. GE co tt 1914: P for NORTH TOTTENHAM.
N P STAFF PLATFORM (non-tt): London Transport
workers; op 25 August 1968 *(U)*; new platforms
commissioned 27 January 2003 on No.19 Road –
'thought first used' 6 April 2003 (result of engineering
work within depot, *Rly Obs, May 2003, p. 227)*; still open.
NORTHUMBERLAND PARK [TWM]
op 11 December 2005; slightly west of Backworth,
clo 1977 *(AB)*; still open.
NORTHWICH [CLC] op 1 January 1863 *(co ½
T 26 February)*; station replaced end May 1868 by one,
south of previous, that became through station when
line extended 22 June 1870 *(CLC Portrait)*; still open.
NORTHWICK PARK [Met]
op 28 June 1923 *(L)* as N P & KENTON;
renamed 15 March 1937 *(L)*; still open.
NORTHWOOD [GW] op 17 June 1935 *(Cl 29)*;
HALT. Would appear to have been summer only until
1942; co tts 1937-8 show 'commences April 11th 1938'
and 6 October 1941 'commences March 30th 1942';
wtt supps give reopening dates for 3 April 1939 and
7 April 1941; co tt beginning 5 October 1942 includes
a few without restriction, others not to call until spring.
Clo 9 September 1963 *(T 9th)*; {Bewdley – Arley}.
NORTHWOOD London:
NORTHWOOD [Met/GC] op 1 September 1887 *(L)*
by Met; GC use began 15 March 1899; still open.
N HILLS [Met/LNE] op 13 November 1933 *(T 11th)*;
still open.
NORTON near Doncaster [LY]:
line op 6 June 1848★★, nd, September 1848 *(Topham)*;
clo 10 March 1947 *(Cl)*.
NORTON near Runcorn [Birkenhead]: trains first
shown in tt March 1852; clo 1 September 1952 *(RM
October)*. Runcorn East here/near later. Became
N CHESHIRE 1926 (20 March according to *LNW
dates* and *hbl* July but 17 September according to *GW
circular 3011)*; *Brad* added C briefly – dropped 1932/3.
NORTON near Worcester
NORTON [GW] first in *Brad* October 1879 as
N JUNCTION; renamed N HALT 7 September 1959
(Cl; hbl December); clo 3 January 1966 *(RM February)*.

NORTON [Mid] op November 1841** *(Mid)*; last in *Brad* August 1846; {north of later GW station}.

NORTON-on-Tees [NE]

N JUNCTION: lines through here opened 11 July 1835 [Clarence] (see 1835 A**) and 10 February 1841 [Stockton & Hartlepool] *(NE maps)*.
Probably primitive stopping arrangements on both, from start or soon after; perhaps briefly two stations; if so arrangement short-lived since S&H soon took over working of Clarence; early timetables lacked detail; first tt evidence seen is March 1850 *(Topham)*.
According to C.Fox, *An Illustrated History of Norton, The Iron Road*, Fearns & Co, 2000, original Norton Junction 'station' was south of triangle of lines, in what would be the angle formed between line to Coxhoe and East Curve of 1870s; it was replaced around 1837 by stone platforms a little further north, in angle between Coxhoe line and original East Curve. In the sketch-maps latter only shown on Coxhoe line, others presumably added later on East Curve. *Topham* only shows stops by trains to/from Coxhoe; by June 1853 *Brad* was showing stops on Hartlepool line as well; however, given sketchy nature of early tt information for this area, might not be whole story. Early 'stations' might well have been more for use of railwaymen brought to the area by the creation of the junction than for general public. Replaced about ¾ mile east, thus losing service towards Ferryhill, by >
N-on-T op July 1870* *(Cl)*; at first still N JUNCTION in *Brad*; -on-T added 1 October 1901 *(hbl 24th)*; clo 7 March 1960 *(RM April)*.
* = 'halt' at/near here, originally provided for Warner, Lucas & Barrett's Iron Works, existed by 1851; also used by locals; seems to have evolved into this station (C.Fox).

NORTON BRIDGE

NORTON BRIDGE [LNW] op 4 July 1837 *(co n GJ)*; re-sited about 300 yards south 14 October 1876 *(Cl)*; temporarily closed 23 May 2004**. Became N B for ECCLESHALL 1907? *(hbl ref 3 July)* and thus NS co tt 1910 and *Brad* to 1955, but not LMS tt 1930; *hb* 1938 applied this to goods only.
NORTON BRIDGE [NS] temporary station op 17 April 1848 *(NS; co n T 13th)*; clo 1850 *(NS)*.
NORTON FITZWARREN [GW] probably opened Monday 2 June 1873 (no exact date found but *Wellington 5th* 'now open'; first in *Brad* June; no Sunday service); clo 30 October 1961 *(RM December)*.
NORTON ROAD Swansea [SIT] first in *Brad* March 1878 (see 1860 July 25**); re-sited on deviation line 26 August 1900; last in *Brad* February 1910; back April 1910 only – error?; back April 1929 (reop 2 March 1929 with electrification?), but not back in *hb* until 1938 (absent 1912 to 1929, inclusive); clo 6 January 1960**; {map 88}.

NORTON-IN-HALES [NS]

op 1 February 1870 *(co ½ Whitchurch 5 March- line)*; clo 7 May 1956 *(RM June)*.

NORWICH

NORWICH [GE] op 1 May 1844 *(T 14 April)*; re-sited adjacent 3 May 1886 *(Cl)*; N THORPE from a little after opening until 1969/70 – last in public tt for May 1969 to May 1970 but dropped from tickets before end

of November 1969; temporarily clo during electrification work 1986 – see TROWSE below; still open.
N CITY [MGN] op 2 December 1882 *(MGN)*; CITY added 1883, when station completed *(MGN p.49)*; clo 2 March 1959 *(T 2nd)*.
N TROWSE [GE] op 30 July 1845 *(co n T 23rd)*; new station on extension to Thorpe 15 December 1845 *(Cl)*; TROWSE added a little after opened; last in *Brad* May 1848; back September 1851; temporarily extended for Royal Agricultural Show, week beginning 12 July 1886; clo 22 May 1916**, reop 1 April 1919 *(RCH)*; clo 5 September 1939 (Tuesday) *(Cl)*.
Usually just TROWSE – thus *Brad* and GE co tt 1914. Used for Royal Norfolk Show at Crown Point in June 1946 *(Divisional Manager's Report, RAIL 390/1276)*. Later used in 1950s for Norwich City F.C. home games; and during electrification work 1986 – used 28–31 March 1986 (inclusive) for all 'Thorpe' services, 26 April and 3 May for evening coast services (stopped to set down for connections then continued to main), evenings 3 August and 13 September *(GE Journal July 2000; G. Kenworthy)*.
N VICTORIA [GE] op 12 December 1849 *(T 11th)*; clo 22 May 1916** (GE minutes 4 May said had reached agreement with corporation for this); {still shown IA}. Was V station at N in notice of formal opening *(Ephemera)* but *Brad* only added 1854/6.
CROWN POINT [GE] (a): (non-tt):
for 1886 Agricultural Show, as well as the extensions to Trowse, a separate terminal station, Crown Point in local press, was provided on a spur 400–500 yards east of main line, south of river Wensum; used by Prince of Wales when he arrived for visit 16 July (returned to London from Thorpe) (G. Kenworthy from *MT6/426/2* and local press).
CROWN POINT [GE] (b): (non-tt):
for passengers, livestock and machinery, Royal Agricultural Show, 26 to 30 June (inclusive) 1911; {on line bypassing Thorpe} *(RM July, September)*.

NORWOOD

N JUNCTION [LBSC] op 5 June 1839 *(co n T 6th)*; initially JOLLY SAILOR/J S N; became N 1846/8 *(Brad)*; re-sited about 80 yards south 1 June 1859 as N J *(Cl)*; N J & SOUTH NORWOOD for SOUTH WOODSIDE 1 October 1910 *(hbl 27th)* to 1944/5 *(hba January 1945)*; but N J for S N in LBSC co tt 1912; still open. Until July 1844 *Brad* described it as J S near Beulah [Bewlah one month] Spa and that part of Norwood.
Also see WEST NORWOOD.
NOSTELL [WRG Jt] op 1 February 1866 *(GN; T 3rd- line)*; clo 29 October 1951 *(Cl)*; 18 June 1961 wtt shows weekday calls when required for railway staff.
NOTGROVE [GW] op 1 June 1881 *(Bristol Merc 2nd- line)* as N & WESTFIELD; renamed 24 June 1896 *(Cl)*; clo 15 October 1962 *(RM November)*.
NOTTAGE [GW]: erection PORTHCAWL GOLFERS / GOLF PLATFORM (non-tt) authorised 21 July 1897 *(GW Traffic Committee)*; September 1917 wtt said trains would not call until further notice (no exact clo date given); reop, now public, as N 14 July 1924 *(wtt supp)*;

aot request, to and from Pyle only; HALT;
clo 9 September 1963 *(RM October)*; {Pyle – Porthcawl}.

NOTTING HILL – see LADBROKE GROVE.

NOTTING HILL GATE
NOTTING HILL GATE [Met] op 1 October 1868
(T 16 and 30 Sept.); [Dist] added 1 November 1926 >
NOTTING HILL GATE [Cen] op 30 July 1900
(T 25th- line) >
Rebuilt as one, completed 31 July 1960; still open.

NOTTINGHAM
NOTTINGHAM [Mid] op 4 June 1839 *(Mid)*; original
terminus was in Carrington Street; from 4 August 1846
trains from Lincoln also used it, with reversal; replaced
by through station in Station Street 22 May 1848 *(Mid)*;
renamed N CITY 25 September 1950, N MIDLAND
18 June 1951 *(Mid)*, N 6 May 1970 tt; still open.
N ARKWRIGHT STREET [GC] op 15 March 1899
(GC; T 16th- line); clo 4 March 1963, reop 4 September
1967 *(RM October)* as northern terminus of service
from London Marylebone; clo 5 May 1969 *(Cl)*.
For most of existence (1900 tt *(JS)* until 1963) just A S.
N LONDON ROAD HL [GN] op 15 March 1899
(co n T 14th); clo 3 July 1967 *(Cl)*.
N LONDON ROAD LL [GN] op 3 October 1857
(GN; Herapath 3 October – 'will be opened this day'),
but *co ½ T 22 February 1858* says 2 October; GN had
previously used Mid station, but op own as result of
dispute with Mid; LL added 15 March 1899;
clo 22 May 1944 *(RM September)*.
N RACECOURSE [GN] (non-tt): op 19 August 1892
(race); last used Tuesday 8 December 1959 *(Rly Obs
May 1960)*; originally N RACE COURSE SIDING;
{London Road – Netherfield}.
N VICTORIA [GC/GN] op 24 May 1900 *(GC dates)*;
clo 4 September 1967 *(RM October)*. At first GN called
it N JOINT, GC N CENTRAL; Nottingham's Town
clerk suggested N Victoria as a compromise on opening
day, Queen Victoria's birthday *(GC)*.

NOTTINGHAM ROAD – see under DERBY.

NOTTON & ROYSTON [GC]
op 1 September 1882 *(GC)*; & R added 1 December
1896 *(hbl 28 January 1897)*; clo 22 September 1930 *(Cl)*.

NOVAR – see EVANTON.

NUMBER – where a station was 'Number …' it will be
found under 'NO.', before 'NOCTON …'.

NUNBURNHOLME [NE]:
line op 4 October 1847**, nd, June 1848 *(Topham)* *;
opened as BURNBY, renamed 1 January 1873 *(RCG)*;
clo 1 April 1951 (Sunday) *(Cl)*.
* = added to *Topham* after others on the line so perhaps did
open after the line.

NUNEATON
NUNEATON [LNW] op 15 September 1847 *(co n
T 13th)*; N TRENT VALLEY from *(Rly Gaz 23 May)*
to 5 May 1969 *(Cl)*; still open. N HINCKLEY ROAD
in *Brad* 1867 to 1878/9.
N ABBEY STREET [Mid] op 1 November 1864 *(Mid)*;
re-sited 7 chains west 1 September 1873 *(Mid)*;
clo 4 March 1968 *(Mid)*. Co tt and *Brad* called it N
until 2 June 1924; *hb* called it N ABBEY from 1873.
N BRIDGE [Mid] op 1 March 1866 wtt *(Mid)*;
clo 1 October 1887 wtt *(Mid)*. Main evidence for
existence comes from working tts – did not appear in
public tt. Also appears 'P' in *hb* 1877 to 1895 (present
1872, when no facilities were shown; deleted 1896
appendix – inertia involved?) and on late 1870s
Airey Map of Staffordshire District (clearly added as
afterthought so no distance information available).
Exact site and purpose unknown (passenger use cannot
be guaranteed); was between Abbey Street and South
Leicester Junction; also some LNW trains shown
calling until 1 April 1868 wtt *(Mid)*. Perhaps provided
fairly easy passenger interchange with LNW station,
perhaps only mail/parcels exchange point.

NUNHEAD [LCD]
op 18 September 1871* *(co n T 16th)*; clo 1 January
1917 *(RM February)*; reop 1 March 1919 *(T 22 Feb.)*;
re-sited slightly north 3 May 1925 *(Cl)*; still open.
N JUNCTION 1904 on *(hb)* but not seen thus *Brad*.
* = junction station for line to Blackheath Hill, which opened
this day. Intention had been to open line on 1st but delayed so
contractors could 'finish line more completely' *(T 2nd)*.
This would not have prevented opening of Nunhead on 1st
but notice makes it clear that would open with line on 18th.

NUNNINGTON [NE]
op 9 October 1871 *(Yorks Gaz 14th- line)*;
clo 2 February 1953 *(RM March)*.

NUNTHORPE [NE]
op 25 February 1854 *(co ½ T 25 August- line)*; still open.

NURSLING [LSW] op 19 November 1883 *(SR)*;
clo 16 September 1957 *(Hants Chron 21st)*.

NUTBOURNE [LBSC] op 1 April 1906 *(LBSC)*;
HALT until 5 May 1969 *(S App)*; still open.

NUTFIELD [SE] op 1 January 1884 *(SE)*;
clo 25 July 1992 for work on Bletchingly Tunnel in
connection with electrification, reop 31 August 1993
(Network SouthEast North Downs pamphlet); still open.

O

OAKAMOOR [NS] op 1 September 1849 *(Churnet)*;
clo 4 January 1965 *(RM March)*.
OAKDALE [GW] op 14 March 1927 *(co n dated
'March')*; HALT; clo 12 September 1932 *(Cl)*; {map 87}.
OAKENGATES
OAKENGATES [GW] op 1 June 1849 (see 1849**);
O WEST 18 June 1951 to 11 June 1956 *(Cl)*; still open.
Brad made two words of it, late 1850s, early 1860s,
O MARKET STREET [LNW] op 10 June 1861**;
M S added 18 June 1951; clo 2 June 1952 *(RM August)*.
OAKENSHAW [Mid] op 1 July 1840 *(Mid; co n
T 27 June- line)* as WAKEFIELD; renamed O for W
1841, O 1861/3; clo 1 June 1870 (Wednesday) *(Mid)*;
{Royston – Normanton}.
OAKHAM [Mid]
op 1 May 1848 *(Mid; co ½ T 21 August- line)*; still open.
OAKINGTON [GE] op 17 August 1847 *(co ½
T 13 August- line)*; aot request; clo 5 October 1970
(RM October). O for COTTENHAM in *Brad* 1906/7
to 1955 but not thus *hb*, LMS tt 1930.
OAKLE STREET [GW]
op 19 September 1851 *(T 10th)*; last in tt March 1856
(not on RCH Junction Diagram 1870); back in tt
October 1870; clo 2 November 1964 *(Cl)*.
OAKLEIGH PARK [GN]
op 1 December 1873 *(L)*; still open.
Became O P for EAST BARNET 24 May 1927
(hbl July); thus LNE tt 1927, *hb* 1938 and *Brad* to 1955.
OAKLEY near Basingstoke [LSW]
first in *Brad* April 1856; clo 17 June 1963 *(Cl)*.
OAKLEY near Bedford [Mid]
op 8 May 1857 *(Mid; co ½ T 13 August)*;
clo 15 September 1958 *(LNW Record)*.
OAKLEY & ALREWAS – see CROXALL.
OAKLEY FIFE [NB] op 28 August 1850 *(Stirling
Journal notice, item 30th)*; FIFE added 9 March 1925
(hbl April); clo 7 October 1968 *(RM October)*.
OAKSEY [GW] op 18 February 1929 *(wtt supp)*;
HALT; clo 2 November 1964 *(Cl)*; {Kemble – Minety}.
OAKWELLGATE – see under GATESHEAD.
OAKWOOD [Picc] op 13 March 1933 *(T 14th)* as
ENFIELD WEST; renamed E W O 3 May 1934 *(L)*,
O 1 September 1946 *(RM November)*; still open.
OAKWORTH [Mid] op 15 April 1867 *(Mid)*;
clo 1 January 1962 *(RM March)*.
OATLANDS [CW Jc] op 3 July 1883 *(D&C 14)*,
all days; last in *Brad* December 1883; back September
1888, Saturdays only hereafter; last July 1892;
back November 1909; last December 1916;
back July 1917; last September 1922; miners'
service to 1 January 1927 *(U; RM September 1912)*.
OBAN [Cal] op 1 July 1880 *(T 2nd)*; still open.
OCCUMSTER [High]
op 1 July 1903 *(High)*; clo 3 April 1944**.

OCHILTREE [GSW] op 1 July 1872 *(co ½ T 18 Sept.-
line)*; clo 10 September 1951 *(RM October)*.
OCKENDON [LTS]
op 1 July 1892 *(RCG)*; still open.
OCKER HILL [LNW] op 1 July 1864 *(W Mid)*;
clo 1 November 1890 (Saturday), reop 1 July 1895 *(Cl)*;
clo 1 January 1916 (Saturday) *(Cl)*;
{Wednesbury – Princes End}.
OCKLEY [LBSC] op 1 May 1867 *(LBSC)*;
was O & CAPEL 1 July 1869 to 1 April 1887 and
15 September 1952 to 12 May 1980 tt *(Cl)*; still open.
ODDINGLEY [Mid] op September 1845 *(Mid/BG)*;
clo ? (line's stopping passenger service ceased
1 October 1855, but lack of mention of this station in
Brad makes it likely that it closed well before this);
{Dunhampstead – Spetchley}.
ODDINGTON [LNW]
ODDINGTON (a): line op 1 October 1850**; last in
Brad January 1851.
ODDINGTON (b) op 9 October 1905 *(Oxford Chron
6th)*; see 1905** (a); clo 1 January 1917 *(T 22 Dec. 1916)*;
reop 5 May 1919 *(RCH)*; clo 25 October 1926 *(Cl)*.
OFFORD & BUCKDEN [GN]
op about 1850 (H.V. Borley, letter, RCHS *Journal 140*,
p.334) though not in *Brad* until September 1851;
& B added 1 August 1876 (Borley; *RCG ref July)*;
clo 2 February 1959 *(RM March)*.
OGBOURNE [MSWJ]
op 27 July 1881**; clo 11 September 1961 *(T 9th)*.
OGILVIE
O COLLIERY [BM] (non-tt): HALT/PLATFORM;
miners; op 8 June 1925 *(Cardiff Division Annual Report)*;
clo 31 December 1962 *(U)*; {O Village – Fochriw}.
O VILLAGE [GW] op 16 May 1935 *(Cl 29)*; HALT;
clo 31 December 1962 *(T 31st)*.
OGMORE VALE [GW]
op 12 May 1873 *(co ½ T 7 August- line)* as TYNEWYDD;
renamed T O V 22 August 1884 *(Cl)*, O V 1 January
1902 *(hbl 23rd)*; clo 5 May 1958 *(RM June)*.
Hb spelling was Ty-newydd until 1904.
OKEHAMPTON [LSW]
OKEHAMPTON op 3 October 1871 *(Tavistock 6th)*;
clo 5 June 1972 *(Cornish & DP 11th)*; later excur (e.g.
four Saturdays in 1985 – *RM July)*; occasional troop
train. LSW co tt 1914: O for HATHERLEIGH and
thus *Brad* 1893/4 to 1925.
Reop 25 May 1997 (official trip 24th); summer Sundays
only (21 September last for 1997) *(RM June)*. Similar
Sunday use continues.
O MILITARY SIDINGS: used by passengers on Car
Carrier service from Surbiton, 1960–64 inclusive;
short distance on Plymouth side of main station.
(E. Youldon, article in *British Railways Illustrated
Summer Special No. 12, 2004*, Irwell).
OKEHAMPTON ROAD
– see SAMPFORD COURTENAY.
OLD BARCOMBE – see BARCOMBE MILLS.
OLD BESCOT – see WOOD GREEN.
OLD COLWYN [LNW]
op 9 April 1884 *(LNW Officers 25884)* *; OLD added
22 May 1885 *(LNW circular of that date, 'in future will

be known as'); clo 1 December 1952 *(RM January 1953)*.
★ = *LNW Record* says op 9 April 1883 but that was when
original name of intended station was settled.
OLD CUMNOCK – see CUMNOCK.
OLD DALBY [Mid]
op 2 February 1880 *(RCG)*; clo 18 April 1966 *(Mid)*.
OLD DEER – see MINTLAW.
OLD DOCK HALT – see PORT TALBOT.
OLD FORD East London.
OLD FORD [NL] op 1 July 1867 *(L)*; clo 15 May 1944,
though replacement bus service provided by railway
until 23 April 1945 *(Cl)*.
Also see BOW & BROMLEY; COBORN ROAD.
OLD FORD – see GATESHEAD STADIUM.
OLD HILL [GW]
OLD HILL op 1 April 1867 *(GW ac)* – prior to this
Cradley Heath was passenger terminus; still open.
O H HIGH STREET op 21 August 1905 *(GW H)*;
HALT; clo 15 June 1964 *(RM July)*;
{Old Hill – Windmill End}.
OLD JUNCTION
– see GASCOIGNE WOOD JUNCTION.
OLD KENT ROAD & HATCHAM [LBSC]
op 13 August 1866 *(T 14th)*; & H added 1 February
1870 *(Cl)*; clo 1 January 1917 *(T 22 December 1916)*;
{South Bermondsey – Queens Road Peckham}.
OLD KILPATRICK [Cal] op 1 October 1896 *(RCG;
Colliery 2nd- line)*; clo 5 October 1964 *(RM November)*.
OLD KINBRACE – see 1957★★.
OLD LEAKE [GN] op 2 October 1848 *(Stamford 3rd)*;
early HOB HOLE, L & WRANGLE, O L & W;
settled 1852 *Brad*; clo 17 September 1956 *(RM October)*.
Hb: just L 1872 to 1935a.
OLD MALDEN – see WORCESTER PARK.
OLD MILFORD – see MILFORD HAVEN.
OLD MILL LANE [LNW] op 1 August 1906★
(Ormskirk 26 July); see 1905★★ (a); last in *Brad* April
1907; reop 1 October 1911★★; clo 18 June 1951
(RM August); {Crank – Rookery}.
★ = *LNW Officers 41880*, list of tt alterations, has 1 September
– catching-up exercise?
OLD NORTH ROAD [LNW]
op 7 July 1862 *(co n T 7th- line)*; clo 1 January 1968
(RM January). O N R for CAXTON in *Brad* 1906/7
to 1955 but not thus *hb*, LMS tt 1930.
OLD OAK
O O COMMON [GW] (a) (non-tt): workmen's service
to/from Westbourne Park began 18 May 1906 *(wtt supp)*;
ended? {Westbourne Park – Acton}.
O O COMMON (b) (non-tt):
Open Days; used at least 15 July 1967 as
O O PLATFORM FOR DIESEL DEPOT *(U; JB)*;
20 September 1981 *(U)* and 18 September 1991 *(JB)*
as O O C; {spur from Westbourne Park}.
O O LANE [GW] op 1 October 1906 *(L)* ★; HALT;
clo 1 February 1915★★ *(Cl)*, reop 29 March 1920 *(RCH)*;
see 1921 April/May★★; clo 30 June 1947 *(Cl)*.
★ = in *Brad* from July or August 1906 and *RCG ref* June but
since it was only listed in footnotes in former it is impossible to
be sure trains were calling.
OLD ORMISTON – see KIRKBANK.

OLD ROAN
OLD ROAN (a) [LY] op 1 May 1907 *(Ormskirk 2nd)*;
HALT; clo 1 October 1909 (Friday) *(Cl)*.
OLD ROAN (b) [LMS] op 17 February 1936
(Ormskirk 13th); same site as (a); still open.
OLD STREET
OLD STREET [Nor] op 17 November 1901 *(T 16th)*;
see 1922★★; still open.
OLD STREET [Met GNC] op 14 February 1904 *(L)*;
clo 5 October 1975 for line reconstruction *(T 30 August)*.
OLD STREET [BR] op 16 August 1976 *(T 16th)*;
reopening of Met GNC station; still open.
OLD SWAN – see KNOTTY ASH.
OLD TRAFFORD
OLD TRAFFORD (a) [MSJA] op 20 July 1849★★;
clo 27 December 1991 *(BLN 671)* for conversion to
[Manch]. Later reop as Trafford Bar, which see.
OLD TRAFFORD (b) [Manch] op 15 June 1992 *(RM
August)*; previously Warwick Road, which see; still open.
O T CRICKET GROUND
– see MANCHESTER EXHIBITION.
OLD YNYSYBWL [TV]
op 17 October 1904 *(Nelson)*; 'permanent closure'
25 April 1921 *(RCG)*; reop 22 August 1921 *(RCG)*;
see 1904★★; clo 28 July 1952 *(Cl)*.
OLDBURY
OLDBURY [GW] op 1 May 1885 *(GW)*; clo 3 March
1915 (Wednesday) *(RCH)*; {shown *IA*}.
O & BROMFORD LANE
– see SANDWELL & DUDLEY.
Also see LANGLEY GREEN.
OLDFIELD PARK Bath [GW]
op 18 February 1929 *(Bath Chron 16th)*; still open.
PLATFORM on GW ticket *(JB)* and in 1938 *hb* but
not in tts (early service so poor that usually in footnotes
only). Pre-opening: East Twerton *(RAC)*.
OLDFIELD ROAD [LY] first in *Brad* February 1852;
at times SALFORD all or part of name – until 1865
trains from Manchester Victoria could not stop at Salford
so this acted as its station; clo 2 December 1872 *(Cl)*;
{Salford – Pendleton}.
OLDHAM {map 51}
O CENTRAL [LY] first in *Brad* July 1861★;
clo 18 April 1966 *(RM June)*.
★ = *LY* and some local historians say it was opened with its line,
1 November 1847 and no alteration in timing appeared in *Brad*
when it was first included there. However, Mumps was the
only station when line inspected *(MT6/4/71)*. It was not on *LY*
Distance Diagram 1851, nor in *LY* co tt January 1854, *RAIL
942/2* (which gives just Werneth and Oldham), nor on Macaulay's
maps prior to 1861. Furthermore a duplicated booklet, *The
First Railway to Oldham*, produced by T.A. Fletcher in 1972
makes no reference to Central; the 6 inch OS Map of the area,
dated 1863, does not include the station and shows that the
area around Clegg Street was still undeveloped (a station there
would have been no nearer to the Market Place than Mumps).
The Oldham Loop, Part I, by J. Wells (Foxline, 2002) quotes *The
Manchester Guardian* of 23 October 1847 as saying that the
Town Station would be of a temporary character and would be
improved later, implying that it had yet to be provided; only a
week would have been available for doing this, so, even given

the contemporary ability to throw up stations fast, it would seem unlikely that this was was ready with the line. No evidence has yet been found for any use prior to 1861. *LY* says the first station, just beyond the tunnel from Werneth, was replaced by one at the junction with OAGB – probably two ways of referring to same site (Junction Diagrams show station just west of junction, handy for passenger exchange with Clegg Street); architect for this announced 23 March 1864, final cost published 15 August 1866. Clearly there was a link between the first appearance in *Brad* and the coming of Clegg Street. One likely explanation is that the LY 'forgot' its earlier intention and then hastily put up a temporary station here about 1860/1 to prevent the OAGB from extending further into Oldham as they first intended (see article by N. Fraser in *Rly Obs* June 1963). It may be that it opened a little while before it appeared in *Brad* but it seems unlikely that it was much earlier. (Local information supplied by A. Brackenbury.)

O CLEGG STREET [OAGB] op 26 August 1861 *(GC)*; clo 4 May 1959 *(RM June)*.

O MUMPS [LY] op 1 November 1847 *(T 5 September 1848* – digest of LY accounts); still open.

O MUMPS [LNW] op 5 July 1856 *(LNW)*; original terminus from Greenfield, replaced by >

O GLODWICK ROAD [LNW] op 1 November 1862 *(D&C 10)*; clo 2 May 1955 *(T 11 March)*.

O WERNETH [LY] op 31 March 1842 *(Manchester Guardian 2 April)*; still open.

Brad did not provide separate mentions for Mumps LY and Werneth until March 1849; inspection report *(MT6/4/71)* just called Werneth 'Oldham' but did use 'Mumps'.

OLDHAM JUNCTION
– see MIDDLETON JUNCTION.

OLDLAND COMMON [LMS]
op 2 December 1935 *(T 28th)*; clo 7 March 1966 *(Mid)*; {Bitton – Warmley}. *Cl* has it as HALT (unstaffed 7 December 1964) but still O C BR tt 4 June 1965.

OLDMELDRUM [GNS]
op 1 July 1856 *(GNS; co ½ Herapath 22 November)*; clo 2 November 1931 *(RM December)*.
OLD MELDRUM in *Brad* until 1894 and *hb* until 1904 but one word *Cornwall* 1860.

OLDWOODS [GW] op 3 July 1933 *(Cl 29)*; HALT; clo 12 September 1960 *(Cl)*; {Leaton – Baschurch}.

OLLERSHAW LANE [CLC] (non-tt):
signalling plans show temporary platform on siding to Davies Works from Salt Branch No.2 at Northwich, from which platform would have been reached by reversals at east junction and sidings entrance. Described as in use, having been inspected 29 November 1916. No other information.

OLLERTON [GC] op 15 December 1896 *(GC)*; clo 19 September 1955 *(BR ER internal notice August)* except for summer Saturday use, which continued to 5 September 1964 (last train). Later excursions: e.g. 28 April 1956 to Sheffield for football (GC Society's *Journal*, Autumn, 2002); Whit Monday 3 June 1963 *(AB)*; to Skegness 12 August 1972 *(Rly World June 1974, p.262)*.

OLMARCH [GW] op 7 December 1929 *(RM March 1930)*; aot request; HALT; clo 22 February 1965 *(Cl)*; {Pont Llanio – Llangybi}.

OLNEY [Mid]
op 10 June 1872 *(Mid)*; clo 5 March 1962 *(RM March)*.

OLTON [GW] op 1 January 1869 *(Cl corr)*; still open.

OLYMPIA – see KENSINGTON.

OMOA – see CLELAND.

ONGAR op by [GE] 24 April 1865 *(co n T 24th)*; legally transferred to [Cen] 25 September 1949 *(T 26th)* but BR provided trains until electric service began 18 November 1957; clo 3 October 1994 (last train 30 September) *(RM November)*.

ONIBURY [SH Jt] op 21 April 1852 *(co ½ T 17 August-line)*; clo 9 June 1958 *(Cl)*.

ONLLWYN [N&B] op 3 June 1867 *(D&C 12; T 5th-line)*; clo 15 October 1962 *(RM November)*.

ORBLISTON [High] op 18 August 1858 *(High)* as FOCHABERS; became O JUNCTION 21 October 1893 *(hbl 26th)*, O 18 June 1962 tt – but just O *hb* 1904 on; clo 7 December 1964 *(RM January 1965)*.

ORDENS [GNS] op 1 October 1859 *(GNS)*; aot request; last in *Brad* October 1863, disappearance coinciding with tt rearrangement; later use as private station, perhaps not continuous. GNS wtt 1 July 1905 says open for passenger traffic only, worked under charge of guard; no restrictions on use stated. Back in *Brad* January 1917 as HALT, back LNE tt 14 July 1924; clo 6 July 1964 *(RM July)*.
In *hb* 1877 and 1883 as O SIDING, no facilities shown; omitted 1890 and 1895; back 1904, O PLATFORM passenger only; 1938 O HALT.

ORDNANCE FACTORY – see ENFIELD LOCK.

ORDSALL LANE [LNW]:
line op 19 September 1830★★; no early sign of this station in tt. However, *LM* says was intermittent early use: op ? Clo after opening of line to Manchester Victoria (1844); reop ? for setting down only after local petition. Mentioned in report of accident 8 October 1845 as station *(Rtn)*, though perhaps then in use as ticket platform (ticket collector killed when he jumped on step of coach before train stopped). Full use 1 August 1849 *(LM)*; not in *Brad* until March 1850 when westbound only; by June 1854 two way service – still not in eastbound table but footnotes show it acting as junction station for South Junction Line, both ways. Clo 4 February 1957 *(RM March)*. *Brad* took until about 1900 to make up its mind that this was ORDSALL L rather than ORDSAL L. LNW co tt 1908, LMS tt 1947: O L for SALFORD; thus *Brad* from 1890/1.

ORE [SE] op 1 January 1888 *(SE)*; still open.

ORESTON [LSW]
op 1 January 1897 *(W Morn N 2nd)*; clo 15 January 1951 *(T 12th)*, reop 2 July 1951 *(D&C 1)* – see 1951★★; clo 10 September 1951 *(RM October)*.

ORGREAVE COLLIERY [GC] (non-tt):
miners; op 1902 *(U)*; trains ran from Sheffield Victoria to Treeton via here, worked by GC engines on main line and by Rothervale Colliery Company's on branch; buses took over when floods severed line in May 1932 (K. Grainger, *Scenes from the Past No.43, Sheffield Victoria to Chesterfield Central*, Foxline, 2002, p.45); {Darnall – Woodhouse}.

ORIEL ROAD – see BOOTLE.

ORMESBY – see GREAT ORMESBY; MARTON.

ORMISTON [NB]
op 1 May 1872 *(Edin)*; clo 3 April 1933★★.

ORMSIDE [Mid] op 1 May 1876 *(Mid; co n T 1st- line)*;
clo 2 June 1952 *(RM July)*.

ORMSKIRK [LY] op 2 April 1849 *(LY; Southport Vis
tt 7th)*; still open, but now terminus of two separate
services from opposite directions.

ORPINGTON [SE]
op 2 March 1868 *(L; co ½ T 21 August- line)*; still open.

ORRELL [LY] op 20 November 1848 *(LY; co n Manch
G 18th- line)*; O & UPHOLLAND 1 September 1882
(Cl) to 13 October 1900 *(RCG)*; still open.
LY co tt 1899: O & UP HOLLAND.

ORRELL PARK [LY] op 19 November 1906
(?; first in Brad December); still open.

ORTON [High]
op 18 August 1858 *(High)*; replaced 1859 *(High)*;
clo 7 December 1964 *(RM January 1965)*; {map 3}.

ORTON WATERVILLE [LNW]
op 2 June 1845 *(co op tt)* as OVERTON; renamed
1 August 1913 *(hbl 23 October)*; clo 5 October 1942
(LNW Record); railwaymen used until June 1962 or
later *(U)*.

ORWELL [GE] op 1 May 1877 *(Rtn- line)*;
clo 15 June 1959 *(T 18 May; Cl)*.

OSBALDWICK [Derwent Valley] op 21 July 1913
(NE Staff Mag 1913); clo 1 March 1915 *(Cl)*;
{Layerthorpe – Murton Lane}.

OSMONDTHORPE [LNE] op 29 September 1930
(Brad 22 September – 'commences 29th'); HALT until
3 May 1937 tt. Clo 7 March 1960 *(RM April)*;
later excur; {Marsh Lane – Cross Gates}.

OSSETT [GN]
OSSETT (a) op 7 April 1862 *(GN)*; replaced on
extension of line by >
OSSETT (b) op 7 April 1864 *(GN)*; clo 7 September
1964 *(Cl)*.
Also see FLUSHDYKE, opened after a short gap, near
site of O (a).

OSTERLEY
O & SPRING GROVE [Dist] op 1 May 1883
(L; Rtn- line); originally O FOR S G *(hb)*, LSW ticket
for O PARK *(JB)*; [Picc] added 13 March 1933;
replaced to south east by >
OSTERLEY op by [Dist/Picc] 25 March 1934
(RM May); since 10 October 1964 Picc only; still open.

OSWESTRY
OSWESTRY [Cam] op 1 May 1860 *(co ½ T 9 August)*;
clo 7 November 1966 *(RM January 1967)*.
OSWESTRY [GW] op 1 January 1849 *(Shrewsbury 5th)*;
replaced by new station 1866; clo 7 July 1924 *(Cl)*,
service diverted to ex-Cam station.

OTFORD [LCD]
OTFORD op 1 August 1882 *(LCD)*; still open.
O Junction until 1928/9 *(Brad)*.
O JUNCTION op 1 June 1874 *(T 2nd)*; exchange only,
no public access, but in *Brad*; last there October 1880;
{south of Otford}. Alias OTNEY.

OTLEY [Otley & Ilkley] op 1 February 1865 *(T 3rd)*;
clo 22 March 1965 *(RM April)*.

OTTERHAM [LSW] op 14 August 1893 *(W Morn N
15th)*; clo 3 October 1966 *(Cornish & DP 8th)*.
Sometimes shown as HALT at closure – certainly
unstaffed for last year. LSW co tt 1914:
O for CRACKINGTON HAVEN. By then *Brad* had
O for DAVIDSTOW and C H, later (until 1955)
O for WILSEY DOWN and D and C H.

OTTERINGTON [NE]: line op 31 March 1841★★,
nd, August; clo 15 September 1958 *(RM October)*.

OTTERSPOOL [CLC]
op 1 June 1864 *(CLC)*; clo 5 March 1951 *(Cl)* – see
1951★★. OTTERS POOL until 1866 *(Brad)*, 1904 *(hb)*.

OTTERY ROAD – see FENITON.

OTTERY ST MARY [LSW]
op 6 July 1874 *(Trewman 8th)*; clo 6 March 1967
(Express & E 6th). Until 1883 O S M TOWN *(hb)*.

OTTRINGHAM [NE]
op 27 June 1854 *(co ½ T 4 September- line)*;
clo 19 October 1964 *(Cl)*. According to *RM Jan. 1960*
would become HALT on 4th; not thus tt, but note
added there that no staff were in attendance.

OUGHTERSIDE COLLIERY [MC] (non-tt):
miners' PLATFORM; in use at least 1922 and 1923;
alias WARTHOLE SIDING; {Arkleby – Bulgill} *(U)*.

OUGHTY BRIDGE [GC]
op 14 July 1845 *(GC)*; clo 15 June 1959 *(RM July)*.

OULTON BROAD [GE]
O B NORTH: line op 1 July 1847 *(co ½ T 6 September)*,
nd, January or February 1848; moved from west to east
of level crossing – approved by BoT 25 July 1901
(G. Kenworthy, from *MT6/1022/8)*; op as MUTFORD;
renamed O B M 1 July 1881 *(Cl)*, O B 1915 tt *(Cl)*,
O B N 26 September 1927 *(hbl October)*; still open.
O B SOUTH op 1 June 1859 *(T 2nd)* as CARLTON
COLVILLE; renamed 26 September 1927 *(hbl October)*;
aot request; still open.

OUNDLE [LNW]
op 2 June 1845 *(co op tt)*; clo 4 May 1964 *(RM June)*;
schools specials at start/end of term ran until 1975
(Railway Archive December 2002, p. 95).

OUSE BRIDGE [GE] first in tt *(Topham)* May 1848;
OUZE B in EC co tt 1851 and until 1854 *(Brad)* but
OUSE B in *Truscott's EC tt* 1 January 1853; aot request;
clo 1 January 1864 (Friday) *(Cl)*; {Denver – Hilgay}.

OUTWELL [GE]
O BASIN op 20 August 1883★★; clo 2 January 1928 *(Cl)*.
O VILLAGE op 8 September 1884
(see 1883 August 20★★); clo 2 January 1928 *(Cl)*.

OUTWOOD op 12 July 1988 *(BLN 607)*; on opposite
(Leeds) side of road bridge from earlier Lofthouse, part
of which extended under bridge; still open.

OVAL [Nor]
op 18 December 1890 *(L; co ½ 14 February 1891- line)*;
at first THE OVAL / KENNINGTON O – latter in
Brad until 1900; see 1922★★; still open.

OVENDEN [Halifax & Ovenden]
op 2 June 1881 *(GN)*; clo 23 May 1955★★.

OVER & WHARTON [LNW]
op 3 July 1882 *(notices for July, LNW co tt July–September)*;
clo 1 January 1917 *(T 22 December 1916)*;
reop 12 July 1920 *(Cl)*; clo 16 June 1947★★.

OVER BRIDGE: internal notice said would be available 8 February 1990 but *RM April* said first train used on 6th; temporary terminus set up when floods cut line west of Gloucester – passengers taken past flooded rail stretch by road; clo 21 February 1990 (Wednesday) when line reopened but site retained in case needed again.

OVER DARWEN – see DARWEN.

OVERPOOL
op 15 August 1988 *(Birkenhead)*; still open.

OVERSEAL & MOIRA [AN Jt]
op 1 September 1873 *(LNW Officers 10205, 10207)*; clo 1 July 1890 (Tuesday) *(Mid)*; was a terminus.

OVERSTRAND [Norfolk & S]
op 3 August 1906 *(RCG)*; clo 7 April 1953 *(RM May)*.

OVERTON near Basingstoke [LSW]
op 1 December 1854 *(Hants Chron 9th)*; still open.

OVERTON – see ORTON WATERVILLE.

OVERTON-ON-DEE [Cam]
op 2 November 1895 *(Wrexham 2nd, 9th)*; clo 10 June 1940★★, reop 6 May 1946 *(T 16 March)*; clo 10 September 1962 *(RM October)*.

OVERTOWN [Cal]
OVERTOWN (a) op 8 May 1843 *(D&C 6)*; last in *Brad* March 1848★; back April 1850; clo 1 October 1881 (Saturday) *(Cl)*; {map 16}. Alias O ROAD early.
★ = in April 1848, Coatbridge etc transferred from Garnkirk table to Caledonian, newly opened to Carlisle, thus not certain whether Overtown briefly closed or temporarily lost from tt in reshuffle.

OVERTOWN (b): trains first shown January 1881 *Brad*; O WATERLOO until 1886 *(Brad)*; clo 1 January 1917 *(RM Febru*ary*)*; reop 1 January 1919 *(RCH)*; clo 5 October 1942 *(Cl)*.

OX HOUSE [GW] (non-tt): private station for Lord Bateman of Shobdon Court; op 20 August 1857; clo ?; {Kingsland – Pembridge} *(U)*.

OXCROFT COLLIERY NO. 1 [Mid] (non-tt):
op 25 February 1907; clo 15 April 1918; {branch from Staveley} *(Mid)*.

OXENHOLME LAKE DISTRICT [LNW]
op 22 September 1846 *(co n Lancaster 26th)*; still open. Opened with main line as KENDAL JUNCTION, before it could act as junction station (in *Brad* October); at first O/K J indiscriminately in *Brad* (e.g. K J for Lancaster & Carlisle, O/OJ for Kendal & Windermere); settled as O by 1868 (LNW co tt), 1895 *(hb)*, 1897/8 *(Brad)*; L D added 11 May 1987 tt (branch table and index; main table later).

OXENHOPE [Mid]
op 15 April 1867 *(Rtn)*; clo 1 January 1962 *(RM March)*.

OXFORD
OXFORD [GW]: original terminus op 12 June 1844 *(co n dated 17th)*; when line extended to Banbury trains from London going further north had to reverse; replaced by through station 1 October 1852 *(Cl)*; still open. Tickets exist for O GENERAL (intended name).
BANBURY ROAD (alias OXFORD ROAD) [LNW], temporary terminus, op 2 December 1850★ *(co n T 30 November)*; replaced by >
OXFORD (REWLEY ROAD) [LNW] op 20 May 1851

(T 20th); clo 1 October 1951 *(RM February 1952, photo-caption)*, service diverted to GW station. *Brad* added ROOLEY R 1856/7, amended to REWLEY 1887/8; only seen as O in LNW co tts and thus LMS tt 1930.
O ROAD [LNW] op 9 October 1905 *(Oxford Chron 6th)*; see 1905★★ (a); near earlier (Oxford) Banbury Road; clo 1 January 1917 *(T 22 December 1916)*; reop 5 May 1919 *(RCH)*; clo 25 October 1926 *(Cl)*.
★ = station used earlier, 22 November 1850, for special train to take clergy to meeting called by Bishop of Oxford to protest against 'Papal Aggression' (Pope had just appointed first Roman Catholic bishops to English territorial sees since Mary I's reign) *(co n T 19th)*.

OXFORD CIRCUS
OXFORD CIRCUS [Bak] op 10 March 1906 *(L;T 12th-line)*; see 1922★★; still open.
OXFORD CIRCUS [Cen] op 30 July 1900 *(L;T 25th-line)*; see 1922★★; still open.
Combined entrance and ticket hall 16 August 1925 *(L)*.
OXFORD CIRCUS [Vic] op 7 March 1969 *(T 8th)*; still open.

OXFORD STREET
– see TOTTENHAM COURT ROAD.
OXHEYS [LNW] *LNW Officers 4727*, 20 October 1869 said platforms at Oxhey Cattle Siding (for Preston cattle market) would be ready for use 1 November; recommended stopping two trains each way, Tuesdays and Saturdays; if followed first trains would have called Tuesday 2nd. First in *Brad* April 1886, when Thursdays and Saturdays; 1887 Wednesdays; by 1890 Wednesdays and Saturdays; 1894/8 to Wednesdays and Fridays; thus to clo – last in *Brad* September 1925.

OXSHOTT [LSW]
op 2 February 1885 *(co n T 31 January)*; still open. Variously and erratically O & FAIR MILE / O & FAIRMILE / O for F M /O for F in *Brad*; settled as O 13 June 1955 *(Cl)*. *Hb*: 1890 O & F; 1914a O for F.
OXSPRING [MS&L] prob op soon after 5 December 1845 (line date) *(GC;* in Brad January 1846); last in *Brad* October 1847; {Penistone – Wortley}.
OXTED [CO Jt] op 10 March 1884 *(Hants Chron 15th-line;* included in inspection report of 18 February, *MT 6/1908/3)*; still open. *Brad* had O & LIMPSFIELD in index 1909–14 but only O in table, 1914 until 1955 in table also; just O in *hb*.
OXTON [NB] op 2 July 1901 *(Rtn- line)*; clo 12 September 1932 *(Cl)*; [NB].
OYNE [GNS] op 20 September 1854 *(GNS)*; clo 6 May 1968 *(RM July)*.
OYSTERMOUTH {map 88}.
For first service see 1807★★.
OYSTERMOUTH [SIT] op 11 November 1860 as MUMBLES (see 1860 July 25★★); in tt *The Cambrian* 26 August 1870 as M, NORTON ROAD – clearly one stop, at Mumbles end of Norton Road (now part of Mumbles Road); other sources make it look like two stations; renamed M by 1878 *(tt The Cambrian)*, O 6 May 1893, on extension to Southend; clo 6 January 1960★★.

PADARN [LMS]
op 21 November 1936 *(LNW Record)*; HALT;
for closure and other details see 1939 September★★.
PADBURY [LNW] op 1 March 1878 *(LNW Officers 18209★)*; clo 7 September 1964 *(RM October)*.
★ = *LNW Record* says op 1 February – copying error?
PADDINGTON
For main line station and BISHOPS ROAD [HC]
see London.
PADDINGTON [Met] op 1 October 1868 *(T 30 Sept.)*
as PRAED STREET / P PRAED STREET;
[Dist] service added 1 November 1926 *(Ug)*; subway
connection to main station 22 October 1887 *(L)*;
renamed 11 July 1948 *(L)*; still open.
PADDINGTON [Bak] op 1 December 1913 *(T 1st)*;
still open.
PADDOCK WOOD [SE] op 31 August 1842 *(co n T 27th)* as MAIDSTONE ROAD; renamed 1844 in
railway sources but locals seem to have made some use
of PW from start; still open. PW JUNCTION in *Brad*
1851/2 to 1909 and SE co tt 1864 and SEC co tt 1914
(last two main line, but just PW branch).
PADESWOOD & BUCKLEY [LNW]
first in *Brad* October 1850; & B added 1 February 1894
(RCG) – but *LNW dates* 16 February;
clo 6 January 1958 *(RM February)*.
PADGATE [CLC] op 1 September 1873
(co ½ T 21 January 1874- line); still open.
PADIHAM [LY] op 1 September 1876 *(LY)*;
initially terminus from Rose Grove; clo 2 December
1957 *(RM January 1958)*; certainly excursions Easter
1962 *(AB)*; used Wakes Weeks until 1963 (LY Society,
The North Lancs Loop – Branch Line Series No. 10).
PADSTOW [LSW] op 27 March 1899 *(W Morn N
28th)*; clo 30 January 1967 *(Cornish & DP 4 February)*.
PAGE BANK [NE] (non-tt):
from 1 September 1868 Bell Bros, colliery owners,
rented line to carry workmen from Spennymoor to
Page Bank Colliery; service still going 1891; colliery
closed about 1921 *(D&C 4, pp. 169–70)*.
PAIGNTON [GW] op 2 August 1859★★; still open.
PAISLEY {map 12}
PAISLEY [Paisley & Renfrew] terminus in Hamilton
Street op 3 April 1837★★; clo 1 February 1866 (Thursday)
for line reconstruction *(Cl)*; line reop via >
P ABERCORN [GSW] op 1 May 1866 *(GSW)*;
A added 1880 tt; June 1933 *Brad* has note that used as
halt by two trains – 12.52 and 8.12pm, except Saturdays,
from St Enoch – rest presumably normal station.
Clo 5 June 1967★★ *(Cl)*.
P CANAL (a) [GSW] op 1 July 1885 *(co ½ 1110/149-
line)*; clo 10 January 1983 *(RM March)*.
P CANAL (b) op 30 July 1990 – trains at half-fare
Saturday & Sunday 28th & 29th *(BLN 636)*; 250 yards
east of (a); still open.
P EAST [Cal]: built about 1902 for suburban service
that never materialised *(U)*.
P GILMOUR STREET [GP Jt] op 14 July 1840 *(GSW)*;
G S added 1 March 1883; still open.
P POTTERHILL [GSW] op 1 June 1886 *(Glasgow
Herald 2nd)*; clo 1 January 1917 *(RCH)*.

P ST JAMES [Cal] first in *Brad* December 1882; still open.
P WEST [GSW] op 1 June 1897 *(RCG)*;
clo 14 February 1966 *(Cl)*.
PALACE GATES WOOD GREEN [GE]
op 7 October 1878 *(L)*; clo 7 January 1963 *(RM Jan.)*.
PALLION
PALLION [NE] op 1 June 1853 *(T 6th- line)*; clo 4 May
1964 *(Cl)*. Staffed Halt from 14 August 1961 *(Cl)*;
9 September 1963 tt – no staff in attendance but not
shown as Halt.
PALLION [TWM] op 31 March 2002★★; on deviation
from original line because latter covered by new road
(Rly Obs May); still open.
PALMERS GREEN [GN]
op 1 April 1871 *(L)*; P G & SOUTHGATE 1 October
1876 to 18 March 1971 *(Cl)*; still open.
PALMERSVILLE [TWM]
op 20 March 1986 *(RM June)*; still open.
PALNURE [PPW Jt]
op 1 July 1861 *(GSW)*; clo 7 May 1951 *(RM July)*.
PALTERTON & SUTTON [Mid]
op 1 September 1890 *(co n 18 August)*; clo 28 July 1930
(LNW Record) but non-public services continued until
start of 14 September 1931 wtt *(Mid)*.
PAMPISFORD [GE] op 1 June 1865 *(GE Journal
January 1992)* as ABINGTON; renamed 1 June 1875
(RCG); clo 6 March 1967 *(RM April)*.
PANDY near Abergavenny [GW] op 2 January 1854
(T 29 December 1853- line); clo 9 June 1958 *(Cl)*.
PANDY near Pontypridd [TV]
op 1 May 1861 *(Cardiff T 10th)*; at 17m 23ch;
replaced at 17m 40ch by Dinas 2 August 1886.
PANDY [Corris] (ng) see 1874★★.
PANDY [Glyn] (non-tt): SIDING; quarry workmen;
dates ?; {beyond Glynceiriog} *(U)*.
PANGBOURNE [GW]
op 1 June 1840 *(GW; co n T 30 May- line)*; still open.
PANMURE [DA] (non-tt): SIDING; use ?; op by
1893, clo by October 1934; {Barry – Carnoustie} *(U)*.
PANNAL [NE]
op 1 September 1848 *(NE- line)*; still open.
PANS LANE [GW] op 4 March 1929 *(RM May)*;
HALT. Clo 6 October 1941; still no trains in co tt for
6 May to 6 October 1946; trains shown co tt 6 October
1947 (N. Bray, *Devizes Branch*, Picton, 1984; R. Priddle
& D. Hyde, *GWR to Devizes*, Millstream, 1996;
Brad no help since P L in footnotes, cannot tell if trains
called). Clo 18 April 1966 *(RM May)*;
{Patney & Chirton – Devizes}.
Brad notices 8 July 1929 said had been renamed from
P L BRIDGE HALT but not seen thus.
PANT [BM]
op 19 March 1863★★ as DOWLAIS P / D OR P
(thus Brecon & Merthyr tt 1865); name settled 1869;

clo 31 December 1962 *(T 31st)*.

Station on two levels; logically upper platforms should have op first since aim was to go on to Dowlais Top but inspection report shows that lower part (original station here about 15 chains south of later) op first and initially Dowlais Top service used this with reversal; top level op ? (certainly before lower level's service to Dowlais Central began, 23 April 1869) *(RAC)*.

P JUNCTION 1888/9 to 1911 *(Brad)*.

PANT near Wrexham [GW]
op 1 May 1905 *(GW H)*; HALT;
clo 22 March 1915**; {map 75}.

PANT GLAS [LNW]
first in *Brad* March 1869 for markets and fairs; full use June 1872; clo 7 January 1957 *(RM March)*.
Initially P G SIDING / CROSSING (until 1912) *(hb)*.
See 1867 September 2** for possible earlier non-tt use.
Occasional reference as PANTGLAS (e.g. *LNW dates)*.

PANT SALOP [Cam]
first in *Brad* February 1862; at first Mondays, Wednesdays, Saturdays; full use October or November 1865; aot request; SALOP added 1 July 1924 *(GW circular 18 June)*; clo 18 January 1965 *(RM March)*.

PANTEG [GW]
PANTEG op 21 December 1874 *(Co Obs 26th- line)* as SEBASTOPOL; renamed 1875; replaced on Cwmbran line by >
P & GRIFFITHSTOWN op 1 August 1880 *(co n Merlin 31 July)*; & G added 20 October 1898 *(hbl 27th)* – but perhaps slightly earlier – *GW circular* of that date 'has been altered'; clo 30 April 1962 *(T 6 April)*.

PANTYDWR [Cam] op 21 September 1864 *(co n Hereford J 24th- line)*; clo 31 December 1962 *(T 31st)*.

PANTYFFORDD [GW] op 2 September 1929 *(Cl 29)*; HALT; clo 15 October 1962 *(RM November)*.

PANTYFFYNNON [GW]:
line op 26 January 1857 and trains divided here for Garnant and Lland(e)ilo but not in *Brad* until June 1857 – perhaps initially exchange only; still open.

PANTYSGALLOG
P HL [BM] op 1 October 1910 *(RCG)*, but not in *Brad* until June 1911; October 1939 'service suspended' (was operating August 1939); still suspended January 1940; trains December 1940; HALT from 1945 *(Brad)*; HL added 1950; clo 2 May 1960 *(RM July)*.
Brad: intermittently PANTYSCALLOG.
P LL [LNW] op 2 February 1914 *(RCG)*; HALT from 1932/3 *(Brad)*; LL added 1950; clo 6 January 1958 *(BR WR notice December 1957)*.

PANTYWAUN [GW] op 22 December 1941 *(hbl 16)*; HALT; clo 31 December 1962 *(T 31st)*; {Fochriw – Dowlais Top}.

PAPCASTLE [MC] op 1 June 1867 *(D&C 14)*; aot request; clo 1 July 1921 (Friday) *(RCG)*; unadvertised use to after 1923 *(U)*; {in IA}.

PAR [GW]
PAR op 4 May 1859**; still open.
P BRIDGE (non-tt): op July 1897; clo 1908; HALT serving Par beach (C.H. Bastin and G. Thorne, *The Railway Stations and Halts of Cornwall*, C.H. Bastin Publishing, 1994); used alternate Wednesdays in

summer *(RAC)*; {Par – St Blazey}.
Also see ST BLAZEY.

PARADISE [GNS] (non-tt):
SIDING; workmen; in use at least 1884 to 1938 *(U)*; GNS wtt 1 July 1905 one stop each way for Mr Fyfe's workmen; present 'P' 1938 *hb*; {Kemnay – Kintore}

PARBOLD [LY] op 9 April 1855 *(Southport Vis 5th)* as NEWBURGH; renamed P for N 1 May 1879 and thus LY co tt 1899 and LMS tt 1930, P 5 May 1975 *(RM July)*; still open.
'Newbrough' in *Wigan Examiner 6 April 1855*.

PARCYRHUN [GW]
op 4 May 1936 *(wtt supp)*; HALT; clo 13 June 1955 *(Cl)*.

PARHAM [GE] op 1 June 1859* *(T 2nd- line)*;
clo 3 November 1952 *(RM December)*.
* = in *Brad* June but not mentioned *Ipswich Journal 4 June* (B. Wilson) so perhaps delay.

PARK near Aberdeen [GNS] op 8 September 1853 *(GNS)*; clo 28 February 1966 *(RM March)*.

PARK – see NORTHUMBERLAND PARK.

PARK near Manchester [LY] op 26 September 1846 *(co n Manchester Guardian 26th)* – see 1846 April 13**; resited westwards as result of 1889 deviation for addition of goods lines (R.F. Hartley, *The Ashton–Stalybridge Branch*, LY Society); last train Friday 26 May 1995 *(BLN 754)*.

PARK BRIDGE [OAGB] op 26 August 1861 *(GC; Rtn- line)*; clo 4 May 1959 *(RM June)*.

PARK DRAIN [GN/GE]
op 2 February 1896* *(RCG)*; clo 7 February 1955 (BR, Eastern Region, signalling notice).
* = perhaps 2 March given by *GN/GE* was derived from first appearance in *Brad*, March 1896.

PARK HALL [GW] op 5 July 1926 *(GW H)*; HALT; clo 7 November 1966 *(Cl)*; {Gobowen – Oswestry}.

PARK HEAD [S&D]:
Services shown under CRAWLEY [S&D] would have gone through here; early S&D ticket exists, P H to Bishop Auckland and back, covered carriages *(JB)*.
It is unlikely that Park Head was served by public passenger trains after December 1846, closure of line to Crawley.
Article by Dr T.M. Bell, *NE Express, May 2002*, refers to unsigned and undated lease, filed under 1862, to let R. Cordner of Crawley House use a line from junction on Weatherhill & Rookhope, 3 miles from Park Head on ex-Stanhope & Tyne, to Low White Heaps (to north-west). Conditions included provision, weather permitting, of passenger train to Park Head and back on Darlington and Bishop Auckland market days. Not certain service actually ran, but evidence for this area is very patchy. Line to Low White Heaps probably closed before 1883, when lease would have expired.
Mountford gives support and further detail: 'reported' passenger service three times a week from Rookhope [= Low White Heaps?] to Parkhead; old carriages bought from NE 1863 and 1871 but inclines probably travelled in open trucks; he suggests taken from Parkhead to Stanhope by horse-drawn waggon, to avoid further rail inclines, for shopping at Stanhope but, in view of earlier information, more likely that went on to Stanhope by

train – would fit opening of its branch. Later usually Parkhead; surviving goods BLANCHLAND *(Cl)* – renamed to this 1923. {map 30; also *IA*, goods}.

PARK LANE [LNE] (non-tt):
workmen; HALT; op by July 1923, clo by July 1941; {West Leigh – Bickershaw} *(U)*.

PARK LANE INTERCHANGE [TWM]
op 28 April 2002 for interchange with bus services *(Rly Obs June)*; still open.

PARK LEAZE op 4 January 1960 *(Wilts & Glos 8th)*; HALT; clo 6 April 1964 *(W D Press 6th)*; {Kemble – Cirencester}.

PARK PREWETT HOSPITAL [LSW] (non-tt):
built but perhaps not used *(U)*; no evidence for passenger use; trial during WW2 showed line not suitable for ambulance trains *(Hosp)*; {branch from Basingstoke}.

PARK ROYAL
PARK ROYAL [GW] was first used for Royal Show in June 1903; trains ran 15 to 22 June and 29 June to 4 July (Saturday) for exhibitors and employees, and 23 to 27 June for the public on the actual days of the Show (all dates inclusive) *(co n T 15th)*. Permanent public use began 1 May 1904 *(RM June)*; clo 1 February 1915** *(RCH)*; reop 29 March 1920 *(RCH)*; see 1921 April/May**; clo 26 September 1937 (Sunday) *(Cl)*.
P R & TWYFORD ABBEY [Dist] op 23 June 1903 *(RCG)*; & T A added 1 May 1904 *(RCG)*; replaced by >
PARK ROYAL op by [Dist] 6 July 1931 *(L)*; transferred to [Picc] 4 July 1932; still open. *Brad* continued to call this P R & TWYFORD ABBEY until 1938/9, then just P R. According to *L* it was P R HANGER HILL from 1931 opening until 1947; this form not seen *Brad*; H H was added to Beck's Map 1935/7.
P R WEST [GW] op 20 June 1932 *(L)*; for clo see 15 June 1947**. HALT in *hb* and on ticket *(JB)* but not thus *Brad*.
See ROYAL SHOWGROUND for LNW Royal Show station.

PARK STREET [LNW] op 5 May 1858 *(co n, BR Journal, Spring 1988)*; clo 1 June 1858 (Tuesday), reop 1 August 1858 (see note on Bricket Wood); replaced about ½ mile north 24 May 1890 *(LNW Officers 31762)* by P S & FROGMORE; & F dropped 6 May 1974 *(BR notice)*; still open.

PARK VILLAGE [NE] (non-tt): used from ? ; probably to line closure, 3 May 1976; used by general public, saving long walk to/from Featherstone Park; no platform (A.Young); {Haltwhistle – Featherstone Park}.

PARKEND [SW Jt]
op 23 September 1875**; clo 8 July 1929 *(RM August)*. Excursion use shown at 10 August 1961 *(BR pamphlet)*. Initially P ROAD *(hb)*, amended 1876a.

PARKESTON QUAY – see HARWICH.

PARKGATE Wirral
PARKGATE [Birkenhead] op 1 October 1866 *(LNW co ½T 13 February 1867)*; re-sited on extension to West Kirby 19 April 1886 *(hbl 25 August)*; clo 17 September 1956 *(RM October)*. Hbl January 1925 said had been renamed P CHESHIRE, and thus *hb* 1926a, but not seen *Brad*.
Also see NESTON.

PARKGATE
P & ALDWARKE [GC] first in *Brad* July 1873 as A; renamed 1 November 1895 *(RCG)*; clo 29 October 1951 *(RM December* – 'excursions will continue')*.
P & RAWMARSH [Mid] op 1 May 1853 *(Mid)* as R; renamed R & PARK GATE 1 November 1869 co tt, P G & R 1 December 1869 co tt; P G to one word gradually, thus Swinton & Knottingley line from start, all by 1910 *(Mid)*; clo 1 January 1968 *(RM February)*. Also see ROTHERHAM ROAD.

PARKHEAD Glasgow
Both sometimes GLASGOW P in tts.
P NORTH [NB] op 23 November 1870**; NORTH added 30 June 1952 *(Cl)*; clo 19 September 1955 *(RM October)*.
P STADIUM [Cal] op 1 February 1897 *(RCG)*; STADIUM added 3 March 1952 *(Cl)*; clo 5 October 1964 *(RM November)*. Hb 1899a on: P for CELTIC PARK; thus Cal co tt 1913 and *Brad* to 1952 but not *Murray* 1948.

PARKHILL Aberdeen [GNS]
op 18 July 1861 *(GNS)*; clo 3 April 1950 *(RM May)*. *Hb* PARK HILL until 1904.

PARKHILL – see KILDARY.

PARKHOUSE [LNE] (non-tt): HALT;
op 7 July 1941 *(Cl 29)*; present 'P' *hb* 1944a and 1956; stop shown in wtt notice of 5 April 1947; clo 6 January 1969 *(U)*; served RAF No.14 Maintenance Unit *(BR doc)*; {Carlisle – Harker}.

PARKSIDE, between Manchester and Liverpool, [LNW]: line op 17 September 1830**, nd, 1 March 1831 co tt; originally just west of junction; moved to it 1839 *(Crewe to Carlisle)*; clo 1 May 1878 *(RCG)*; {physical junction *IA*}. Co tt March 1831: PARK SIDE; *Brad* 1839 and LNW co tts one word.

PARKSIDE near Wick [LMS]
op 27 January 1936 *(RCH)*; HALT; clo 3 April 1944**; {Occumster – Lybster}.

PARKSTONE DORSET [LSW]
op 15 June 1874 *(SR; W Gaz 19th- line)*; DORSET added 12 May 1980 tt *(C/W)*; still open. Became P for SANDBANKS 1923 ? *(hbl ref 26 April)*; thus *hb* 1925 on and *Brad* to 1955.

PARLINGTON (HALL) – see 1837 A**.

PARRACOMBE [Lynton] (ng): market use began late 1898 *(Lynton)*, first in *Brad* July 1899; last there September 1899 (probably did close since Blackmoor became B for P); back May 1903 as P SIDING, became P PLATFORM 1904 tt *(JS)*; last in April 1906 (now omission perhaps result of alteration of tt layout); back June 1907 when table moved to different page; became P HALT 1908 tt *(JS)*; until 1910/11 restricted to daylight use only according; last in *Brad* June 1917; back 14 July 1924 tt; clo 30 September 1935**.

PARSLEY HAY
For first service see 1833 May**.
PARSLEY HAY [LNW] op 1 June 1894 *(LNW Officers 35402)*; re-sited on extension to Ashbourne 4 August 1899 *(Cl)*; clo 1 November 1954 *(T 1 October)*; see 1962 August 5**.

PARSON STREET [GW] op 29 August 1927
(GW H); PLATFORM until 1933 *(GW H)*; still open.
PARSONS GREEN [Dist]
op 1 March 1880 *(L)*; still open.
PARSONS PLATFORM [NB] (non-tt):
private for Sir C. Parsons, industrialist; in use 1937;
alias RAY/RAYFELL / RAY HOUSE (HALT);
{Knowesgate – Woodburn} *(U; Nhumb Young)*.
PARTICK
PARTICK [NB] op 1 December 1882 *(Glasgow- line)*;
as P; renamed P HILL 28 February 1953 *(Cl)*; re-sited
17 December 1979 *(RM February)*, to act as exchange
with underground, which had yet to reopen after
modernisation – see next entry; still open.
NB co tt 1900: P for GOVAN and thus *Brad* until 1953.
PARTICK [GU] op 16 April 1980 – see entry above;
still open.
P CENTRAL – see KELVIN HALL.
P CROSS – see KELVIN HALL.
P WEST [Cal] op 1 October 1896 *(RCG; Colliery 2nd-
line)*; clo 5 October 1964 *(RM November)*.
PARTINGTON [CLC]
first in *Brad* May 1874 (BoT conditional sanction to
open given 24 March); re-sited on deviation for
Manchester Ship Canal 29 May 1893 *(Cl)*;
clo 30 November 1964 *(RM March 1965)*.
PARTON near Dumfries [PPW Jt] op 12 March 1861
(Galloway 15th); clo 14 June 1965 *(RM July)*.
PARTON near Workington
PARTON [LNW] op 19 March 1847**; still open.
P HALT [WCE Jt] (non-tt): miners; alias LOWCA PIT;
op 11 January 1915; clo 1 April 1929;
{Whitehaven – Distington} *(U)*.
PARTRIDGE GREEN [LBSC] op 1 July 1861
(co ½ T 23 January 1862); clo 7 March 1966 *(RM March)*.
PASSING PLACE Swansea [SIT] first in *Brad*
October 1878 (see 1860 July 25**); intermittently in
Brad to June 1894 or later – also intermittently in *hb*
(present 1879a, not 1883, back 1894a, present 1895,
not 1904); {map 88}.
PASTON & KNAPTON [Norfolk & S]
op 1 July 1898 *(RCG)*; clo 5 October 1964 *(RM Aug.)*.
HALT at closure? – BR tt 10 September 1962 says
tickets issued on train, but 'Halt' not added.
PATCHWAY [GW]
op 8 September 1863 *(co n W D Press 7th)*;
re-sited about ¼ mile south 10 August 1885 as
P & STOKE GIFFORD *(Cl)*;
& S G dropped 27 October 1908 *(hbl 29th)*; still open.
PATELEY BRIDGE
PATELEY BRIDGE [NE] op 1 May 1862 *(T 5th)*;
clo 2 April 1951 *(T 7 March)*.
PATELEY BRIDGE [Nidd] op 12 September 1907 *(Rtn)*;
clo 1 January 1930 (Wednesday) *(Cl)*. Used earlier and
later by reservoir workmen (14 July 1904 to about
1936) *(U)*.
PATNA [GSW] op 7 August 1856**; re-sited to south
1897 *(Cl)*; clo 6 April 1964 *(RM May)*.
PATNEY & CHIRTON [GW]
op 1 October 1900 *(GW; W Gaz 5th- line)*; clo 18 April
1966 *(RM May)*. *Hb* 1925 said goods only, 1926a add

'P'; presumed error – was included *Brad* August 1924,
July 1925 and April 1926 – mistaken for a halt?
PATRICROFT [LNW]: line op 17 September 1830**,
nd, 1 March 1831 co tt; still open.
PATRINGTON [NE]
op 27 June 1854 *(co ½ T 4 September- line)*;
clo 19 October 1964 *(Cl)*. According to *RM January
1960* was to become Halt on 4th; not seen thus *Brad*
but note was added that no staff in attendance.
PATTERTON [Cal]
op 1 May 1903 *(RCG)*; clo 1 January 1917 *(RCH)*;
reop 1 February 1919 *(RCH)*; still open. Cal co tt 1913:
P for DARNLEY RIFLE RANGE and thus *Brad*
until 1955.
PAULSGROVE [SR] (non-tt):
HALT; pony race meetings at Wycherley Park;
op 28 June 1933 *(SR sig inst 22/1933)*; last meeting
23 August 1939 *(AB)*, but still in *hb* 1956,
inertia (September 1957a – 'closed').
PAULTON [GW] op 5 January 1914 *(Bristol NWR)*;
HALT; clo 22 March 1915 *(RCH)*; reop 9 July 1923
(Bristol notice S1153); clo 21 September 1925 *(Cl)*.
PEACOCK CROSS [NB] first in *Brad* December
1878 as HAMILTON PEACOCKS CROSS;
renamed 1882 tt *(Cl)*; clo 1 January 1917 *(RCH)*;
{Burnbank – Hamilton NB}.
PEAK – see RAVENSCAR.
PEAK FOREST [Mid] op 1 February 1867 *(Mid;
T 2nd- line)*; was P F for PEAK DALE 26 September
1893 *(hbl 26 October)* to 14 June 1965 tt *(Mid)*;
clo 6 March 1967 *(RM April)*.
PEAKIRK [GN] op 17 October 1848 *(co n T 16th)*;
P & DEEPING in opening notice; in *Brad* first as
P CROWLAND etc [sic], became P 1857,
P & C 1863/4 *(Brad)*, P 1871 tt *(Cl)*;
clo 11 September 1961 *(RM September)*.
PEAR TREE HILL – see COLDHAM.
PEARTREE
PEARTREE & NORMANTON [Mid] op 2 June 1890
(RCG); clo 4 March 1968 *(Cl)*.
PEARTREE op 4 October 1976 *(T 16th)*; reopening of
P & N; still open but in 29 September 2002 public tt
reduced to one Monday to Friday train, Crewe to
Nottingham, but (2003) still trains both ways in local tt
(A. Brackenbury, *Chron January 2004*); trains shown
both ways in *Rail Times* 14 December 2008.
PEASLEY CROSS [LNW]
first in *Brad* November 1856; clo 18 June 1951
(RM August). HALT in *hb* 1938 (*hb* 1914a 'delete' =
reduced to halt?) but not thus in any *Brad* seen.
PEBWORTH [GW]
op 6 September 1937 *(GW Mag October)*; HALT;
at/near earlier Broad Marston; clo 3 January 1966
(RM February); {Honeybourne – Long Marston}.
PECKHAM
P RYE [LBSC platforms] op 13 August 1866
(T 14th); still open.
P RYE [LCD platforms] op 1 December 1865
(co n T 1st); still open.
All owned by LBSC – see 1866**.
Also see QUEENS ROAD PECKHAM.

PEDAIR FFORDD [Cam]
op 6 January 1904 *(RCG)*; clo 15 January 1951 *(Cl)*
– see 1951★★. HALT in *hb* 1938 but not *Brad*.

PEEBLES
PEEBLES [Cal] op 1 February 1864 *(co ½ T 3 March)*;
clo 5 June 1950 *(Cl)*.
PEEBLES [NB] op 4 July 1855 *(co ½ T 22 October)*;
re-sited on extension to Innerleithen 1 October 1864
(Cl); P EAST 25 September 1950 to 1958 *(Cl)*;
clo 5 February 1962 *(RM February)*.
Non-tt: both companies made extra arrangements for
the Royal Border Show, held here 17–20 July 1906.
The Caledonian added a new passenger dock, the
NB used the 1855 station (now goods) to receive
passengers from Edinburgh *(Peebles)*.

PEEL CAUSEWAY – see HALE.

PEGSWOOD [NE] first in *Brad* January 1903; still open.

PELAW:
PELAW (a) [NE]: line op 5 September 1839 *(Newcastle
Journal 7th)*, nd, 23 February 1842 (when mentioned in
inspection report); re-sited about 200 yards east before
1857 *(Cl)*; back to original site 18 November 1896
(Cl); clo 5 November 1979 *(Cl)*, replaced by Heworth.
RCG ref January 1886 said had been renamed from
P MAIN to P JUNCTION but *Brad* had P J by 1856 to
1893/4 and it was thus NE wtt 1861 and NE co tt 1880.
PELAW (b) [TWM] op 15 September 1985
(Rly Obs December); still open.

PELHAM STREET Lincoln [LNE] (non-tt):
used early 1940s; purpose ?;
{Lincoln Central – Reepham} *(U)*.

PELLON [Halifax High Level]
op 5 September 1890 *(RCG)*; clo 1 January 1917 *(RCH)*.
GN ticket *(JB)* shows as HALIFAX P.

PELSALL [LNW] op 9 April 1849 *(W Mid)*;
clo 18 January 1965 *(RM March)*.

PELTON [NE] {map 34}
PELTON (a) used for special events from 1860 *(Consett)*;
first in *Brad* March 1862★★; Saturdays only;
last January 1869.
PELTON (b) op 1 February 1894 *(Consett)*;
clo 7 December 1953 *(RM January 1954)*.

PEMBERTON [LY]
first in *Brad* January 1849; still open.

PEMBREY
PEMBREY [BPGV] op 2 August 1909★★ *(GW H)*;
HALT (except from 1913 *Brad*, when moved from
footnotes to table, to 1 July 1924, *GW circular 18 June)*;
clo 21 September 1953 *(T 16th)*.
P & BURRY PORT [GW] op 11 October 1852 *(T 12th)*;
still open. According to *RCH dist 17 May* had been
renamed from P to P & B P 1 February 1887; GW co tt
1859 P, 1865 and 1886 P (B P), 1891 P & B P;
Brad P (B P) to P 1875, to P & B P 1886/7.

PEMBRIDGE [GW] op 20 August 1857★★;
clo 5 February 1951 *(RM October)* – see 1951★★;
reop 2 April 1951 *(Cl)*; clo 7 February 1955 *(RM March)*.

PEMBROKE [GW]
PEMBROKE op 6 August 1863 *(Mining 1st)*; still open.
P DOCK op 8 August 1864 *(Pembroke)*; original
temporary replaced 1865 *(Pembroke)*; still open.

PEN-Y-BONT [LNW] op 1 December 1865★★;
still open. PENYBONT until 12 May 1980 tt *(Cl)*,
though *hb* used hyphenated form from 1877 to 1904.

PENALLT [GW] op 3 August 1931 *(co n dated 'July')*;
HALT; clo 5 January 1959 *(T 5th)*;
{St Briavels – Redbrook}.

PENALLY [GW] first in *Brad* October 1863;
clo 15 June 1964, reop 29 June 1970 *(RM August)*,
clo 16 November 1970, reop 5 April 1971,
clo 13 September 1971, reop 28 February 1972 *(Cl)*;
still open.

PENAR JUNCTION [GW]
op 1 January 1913 *(wtt supp)*; service as for
Hafodyrynys, which see; HALT; clo 1 January 1917
(GW notice dated 22 December 1916); {map 87}.

PENARTH [TV]
PENARTH op 20 February 1878 *(Rtn)*; still open.
Aot P TOWN in *hb* – not seen thus *Brad*.
P DOCK op 20 February 1878 *(Penarth; Rtn- line)*;
clo 1 January 1962 *(Cl)*. P D & HARBOUR 1895 until
1929 in *hb* – not seen thus *Brad*.
Also see LOWER PENARTH.

PENARTH RIFLE RANGE [Cam] (non-tt):
wtt appendix 1 June 1911 shows stops here all weekdays
except Tuesdays for Territorials attending
shooting-practice; {Newtown – Abermule}.

PENCADER
PENCADER [GW] op 28 March 1864 *(GW)*;
clo 22 February 1965 *(Cl)*.
P JUNCTION [Manchester & Milford] op 1 January
1866 (date of line extension which created junction,
and in tt for 12 January 1866, *Milford*); last in tt May
1880 – perhaps continued as non-tt exchange?;
{at junction north of Pencader}.

PENCAITLAND [NB]
op 14 October 1901★★; clo 3 April 1933★★.
PENCARREG [GW] op 9 June 1930 *(Cl 29)*;
aot request; HALT; clo 22 February 1965 *(Cl)*;
{Llanybyther – Lampeter}.

PENCLAWDD [LNW]: line from which this was a
short branch op 14 December 1867; orders to open
this station given 10 December 1867 *(RAIL 377/15)*
so probably opened after main line, but information
contradictory; orders were for a daily train but when
trains first shown in *Brad* February 1868 (main line
there January) they ran Wednesdays and Saturdays
only, so either there was a change of mind or daily train
ran briefly, then ceased; April 1868 reduced to Saturdays
only; full use August 1871. Clo 5 January 1931 *(Cl)*.

PENCOED
PENCOED (a) [GW] op 2 September 1850 *(The Cambrian
30 Aug.)*; north of level crossing; clo 2 November 1964
(Cl).
PENCOED (b) op 11 May 1992 *(RM July)*; still open.
PENDAS WAY [LNE] op 5 June 1939 *(RM Nov.)*;
clo 6 January 1964 *(Cl)*; {Cross Gates – Scholes}.
PENDLEBURY [LY] op 13 June 1887 *(Lancs Chesh)*;
clo 3 October 1960 *(RM November)*.

PENDLETON [LY]
PENDLETON (a): line op 29 May 1838★★; according
to *LY* op after line; in 11 June 1838 tt cited by *Bolton* so

any delay very short (perhaps op with line but overlooked by journalist on inaugural trip, quoted by *LY*); usually P BRIDGE early. At first seems to have alternated with Windsor Bridge; P B in *Brad* 19 October 1839; present until about August 1841; back December 1842. Clo 5 December 1966 *(Cl)*.

PENDLETON (b) op 13 June 1887 *(Lancs Chesh)* as P BROAD STREET; briefly P NEW (thus *Brad* 1887–96 and still thus LY co tt 1899); renamed B 5 December 1966 *(JS)*; destroyed by fire 18 July 1994 *(BLN 817)*, clo later officially backdated to this. Also see BRINDLE HEATH.

PENDRE – see TYWYN.

PENGAM
Both below were P & FLEUR-DE-LIS 1 February 1909 *(RCG)* to 1 July 1924 *(GW circular 18 June)*; both had county added 29 March 1926 *(hbl April)*.
PENGAM [Rhy] op 31 March 1858 *(co ½ T 1 September- line)*; P GLAM until 6 May 1968 *(Cl)*; still open.
P MON [BM] op 14 June 1865 *(co n Newport 17th)*; clo 31 December 1962 *(T 31st)*.

PENGE
PENGE [LBSC] op 5 June 1839 *(co n T 6th)*; probably clo by mid-1840. Not in list of stations in company notice of alterations of fares *(T 24 June 1840)* and letter *(T 23 December 1840)* suggests that then only a level-crossing here, had been thus for some time.
PENGE [WELCP] prob op 3 May 1858; faded out of use by end of 1860; {Beckenham Junction – Norwood Junction} (P. Kay, *LRR*, July 1999). Some in print refer to this as Beckenham Road.
P EAST [LCD] op 1 July 1863 *(T 2nd)*; EAST added 9 July 1923 *(hbl 26 April)*; still open. P LANE in *Brad* 1864 to 1869 and in *hb* 1867 only.
P WEST [LBSC] op 1 July 1863 *(Cl)*; same site as 1839 station; WEST added 9 July 1923 *(hbl 26 April)*; still open. P BRIDGE/BRIDGES in *Brad* 1864 to 1879 and *hb* 1867 only.

PENHELIG [GW] op 8 May 1933 *(Cl 29)*; HALT until 6 May 1968 *(GW H)*; aot request; still open.

PENICUIK
For first station of this name see POMATHORN.
PENICUIK [NB] op 2 September 1872 *(T 4th)*; clo 10 September 1951 *(RM October)*. *Hb*: PENICUICK until 1890.

PENISTONE (much from R. Brettle)
PENISTONE [MS&L] op 14 July 1845 *(GC)*. LY service began 1 July 1850, joining MS&L at junction east of station, so had to reverse into MS&L station (evidence of 1860s accident report)*. Became P (THURLSTONE) 1847/8, P & T 1848/50, P 1861/3 *(Brad)*; JUNCTION sometimes added 1850s. Replaced >
1 February 1874 *(GC dates)* by joint station [GC/LY], at junction, avoiding LY reversal; still open. *Brad* added 'The new station' until 1886/7.

* = supported by local Directories of time which only show MS&L stationmaster; J.N. Dransfield's *A History of the Parish of Penistone*, Don Press (Penistone), 1906, which refers to opening of both companies' lines but only to MS&L and 'New' stations – and a description of wool merchants from Thurlstone waiting to go to Huddersfield appears to relate to

MS&L station; *National Gazetteer* (1868) – 'it is a station on the Manchester and Sheffield Railway'. *Brad*, November 1871, shows most trains allowed 10 minutes from Denby Dale to Penistone; December 1876 6 minutes to Penistone 'new station'. Macaulay's maps (1850s and 1860s) and Junction Diagrams of 1870 and 1872 show LY station here, in addition to MS&L, but this was an error – result of someone at the Clearing House basing maps on what he thought ought to be the case, rather than the actuality? Included in 1851 LY Distance Tables as a 'station' but tables did not list any junctions; diagram just has 'Penistone', without any separate mileage for junction with MS&L, so probably 'station' = 'junction'.
1850 6 inch OS map and press evidence show that originally line curved smoothly to junction further east than later one – change probably made in connection with 1874 station.

P BARNSLEY ROAD [LY] op in February 1916; temporary terminus after viaduct collapse cut line short of main station *(Cl dates collapse 3 February)*; clo 14 August 1916 *(T 12th confirms line reop then)*. LY ticket *(JB)* shows as B R HALT,

PENKRIDGE [LNW]
op 4 July 1837 *(T 6th)*; still open.

PENMAEN [GW]
op 14 March 1927 *(co n dated 'March')*; HALT; clo 25 September 1939 *(Cl)*; {map 87}.

PENMAENMAWR [LNW]
first in *Brad* November 1849; aot request; still open. Inspection report of 18 March 1850 used this spelling; but *Brad* PENMAENMAUR to 1860, LNW co tt also this 1852, but …AWR 1864.

PENMAENPOOL [Cam]
op 3 July 1865 *(Cam)*; clo 18 January 1965**. PENMAEN POOL until 1889/90 *(Brad)*, 1904 *(hb)*. LNW co tt 1868: P P for DOLGELLEY.

PENMERE [GW] op 1 July 1925 *(GW Annual Report)*; PLATFORM until 5 May 1969 *(GW H)*; still open. Added *hb* 1936a as P PLATFORM; 1938 P HALT; 1956 P PLATFORM.

PENN [GW] op 11 May 1925 *(RM June)*; HALT; clo 31 October 1932 *(RM January 1933)*; {map 96}. Pre op Lower & Upper P *(RAC)*.

PENN: a number of publications have asserted that there was a Halt between High Wycombe and Beaconsfield on the GW&GC Joint line. No supporting evidence exists. See article by Tim Edmonds, RCHS *Journal*, December 2007, p.788. Perhaps source of trouble was that for a long time BEACONSFIELD was B for PENN; this would make it even less likely that Penn had its own stop.

PENNINGTON [LNW]:
line op 13 June 1831**, nd, mid 1846 *(Huish list)*, as BRADSHAW LEACH; renamed 1876/7; clo 29 March 1954 *(BR clo notice Sweeney)*.

PENNS [Mid] op 1 July 1879 *(Mid; LNW Record- line)*; clo 18 January 1965 *(RM March)*.
Became P for WALMLEY 5 October 1936 *(LNW Record)*; thus *hb* 1938 and *Brad* to 1955.

PENPERGWM [GW] op 2 January 1854 *(T 29 December 1853- line)*; clo 9 June 1958 *(Cl)*.

PENPONDS: see 1843 May 23**; {map 111}.

PENPONT [GW] (non-tt): HALT/PLATFORM;

private; line op 3 June 1867, in pre-opening inspection report (P. Rowledge); clo 15 October 1962 (U); {Aberbran – Abercamlais}.

Mr Penry Williams was granted right to stop trains *(GW Deed 25920, dated 15 May 1873)*.

PENRHIWCEIBER
PENRHIWCEIBER op 3 October 1988, free publicity service on 2nd *(Aberdare)*; old LL reopened; still open.
P HL [GW] op 15 June 1899 *(RCG)*;
clo 15 June 1964★★ *(RM August)*.
P LL [TV] op 1 June 1883 *(S Wales 1st)*;
clo 16 March 1964 *(Cl)*; later excur *(U)*.
HL and LL added 1 July 1924 *(GW circular 18 June)*.
PENRHIWFELIN COLLIERY [Rhy] (non-tt): dates ?; pre op Melincylla *(RAC)*;
{on Cylla branch, going north from Ystrad Mynach; branch shown *IA* but not named}.

PENRHYNDEUDRAETH
PENRHYNDEUDRAETH [Cam] op 2 September 1867 *(Carnarvon co ½ T 10 October)*; aot request; still open. PENRHYN DEUDRAETH in *Brad* until 1880/1; Cam co tt 1867: P-D.
PENRHYNDEUDRAETH [Festiniog] (ng)
op 6 January 1865★ *(D&C 11)*; aot request; see 1923 January 1★★, this station trainless July and August 1935 tt; aot request; clo 18 September 1939★★. Usually just PENRHYN until 1 June 1912 *(hbl 3 July)* and from 20 April 1957 *(Cl)*.
★ = passengers carried free and at own risk for some months before public opening; free use 5th, following formal opening *(Festiniog)*.
PENRIKEIBER COLLIERY [TV] (non-tt): miners; in use 1881; {Matthewstown – Penrhiwceiber LL} *(U)*.
PENRITH NORTH LAKES [LNW]
op 17 December 1846 *(D&C 14; co n- line)*; still open. Became P for ULLSWATER LAKE 1904, P 6 May 1974 *(BR notice)*, P N L 18 May 2003 tt (earlier, on map with tt, June 2002 P THE N L).
PENRUDDOCK [CKP]
op 2 January 1865 *(co ½ T 28 February- line; in op tt Cockermouth)*; clo 6 March 1972 *(RM March)*.
PENRYN [GW]
op 24 August 1863 *(R Cornwall Gaz 28th)*;
re-sited nearby 24 June 1923 *(GW Plymouth Records)*; still open. GW co tt 1869, 1886: P for HELSTON.
PENSARN [Cam] op 10 October 1867 *(Cam; co n Merioneth 12th- line)*; LLANBEDR & P 1 April 1885 *(RCH dist)* to 8 May 1978 *(Cl)*; aot request; still open.
PENSCYNOR [GW]
op 1 August 1929 *(Cl 29)*; HALT; clo 15 October 1962 *(RM November)*; {Neath Riverside – Cilfrew}.
PENSFORD [GW] op 3 September 1873 *(Bristol T 4th- line)*; clo 2 November 1959 *(Shepton 6th)*.
PENSHAW [NE]: line op 9 March 1840 *(NE maps)*, nd, opened about August 1841 *(Robinson)*; original station north of road bridge; re-sited 10 chains south 1 July 1881 *(Cl)*; clo 4 May 1964 *(Cl)*. PENSHER until 1863 *(Brad)* and thus NE wtt 1861, then PENSHER OR PENSHAW until 1 July 1881 *(JS)* – thus NE co tt 1880.
PENSHURST [SE]
op 26 May 1842 *(co n T 13, 20th)*; still open.

PENSNETT [GW] op 11 May 1925 *(RM June)*;
HALT; clo 31 October 1932 *(RM January 1933)*;
{map 96}. Pre op Shut End *(RAC)*.
PENTIR RHIW [BM]: authorised April 1897 (BoT report *MT6/979/5*) provided not advertised and no tickets issued (gradient too steep for normal authority); but associated work reported complete 10 December 1896; likely that had actually come into use 4 January 1897 *(engineer's report, RAIL 1057/146,* said new crossing place and siding into use). Used for market traffic to Brecon on Fridays and Dowlais on Saturdays; first in *Brad* June 1909, setting down, southbound only; stops both ways July 1912/November 1913 *(Brad)*. Clo 31 December 1962 *(T 31st)*.
PENTNEY & BILNEY [GE] op 27 October 1846 *(co n D&C 5)*; aot request; clo 1 August 1866 *(Cl)*.
PENTON [NB]
op 1 March 1862 *(NB)*; clo 6 January 1969 *(RM Feb.)*.
PENTRAETH [LNW] op 1 July 1908 *(LNW Officers 42318)*; clo 22 September 1930 *(Cl)*.
PENTRE [TV] first in *Brad* October 1906; see 1904★★; last in tt November 1912; perhaps used by troops during First World War.
PENTRE BROUGHTON [GW]
op 1 May 1905 *(GW H)*; HALT; clo 1 January 1931 (Thursday) *(T 20 December 1930)*; {map 75}.
PENTREBACH
PENTRE-BACH [TV] op 1 August 1886 *(TV)*;
hyphen added 1980 tt; still open.
Also see ABERCANAID.
PENTRECOURT [GW]
op 2 October 1911 according to *dist supp 847* but 1 February 1912 according to *RCG*, first in *Brad* March 1912; PLATFORM; clo 15 September 1952 *(RM November)*. GW ticket for P HALT *(JB)*.
PENTREFELIN near Oswestry [Cam]
op 6 January 1904 *(RCG)*; clo 15 January 1951 *(Cl)* – see 1951★★. HALT in *hb* 1938 but not seen thus *Brad*.
PENTREFELIN GLAM [GW]
op 16 April 1928 *(GW H)*; HALT; clo 11 June 1956 *(T 8th)*; {Felin Fran – Morriston}.
PENTREMAWR [BPGV] (non-tt):
COLLIERY SIDING; miners; from 1913 *(U)*; still in use 15 September 1952 wtt; {Pontyberem – Ponthenry} *(U)*. Ticket dated 18 February 1911 exists *(JB)* for CAPEL IFAN COLLIERY; according to *RAC Atlas* this was earlier name for this.
PENTREPIOD [GW] op 13 July 1912★★ co tt *(GW H)*; HALT; clo 5 May 1941 *(Cl)*.
PENTRESAESON [GW] op 20 March 1905 *(GW H)*; HALT; clo 1 January 1931 (Thursday) *(T 20 December 1930)*; {map 75}.
PENTWYN [GW] op 13 July 1912★★ co tt *(GW H)*;
HALT; clo 5 May 1941 *(Cl)*.
PENTWYNMAWR [GW]
op 8 February 1926 *(co n dated 'February')*;
PLATFORM; clo 15 June 1964 *(Cl)*; {map 87}.
PENTYRCH [TV]:
for op see 1840 October 9★★; clo 22 June 1863 when this and first Taffs Well replaced by Walnut Tree Junction *(TV notice,* C. Chapman); {map 90}.

PENWORTHAM

PENWORTHAM – see 1882**.

P COP LANE [LY] op 17 April 1911 *(Southport Guard 19th)*; HALT; C L until 30 March 1940 *(Cl)*; clo 7 September 1964 *(RM October)*.

PENWYLLT – see CRAIG-Y-NOS.

PENYBONTFAWR [Cam] op 6 January 1904 *(RCG)*; clo 15 January 1951 *(Cl)* – see 1951**.
Cam public tt July 1904 PENYBONT FAWR, but wtt one word (both tts included in modern reprint).

PENYCHAIN [GW] op 31 July 1933 *(Cl 29)*; still open. Trains called all year, not just for campers. During WW2 camp used as Admiralty Training Centre; shown in *Brad* throughout War but in footnotes so no guarantee trains calling. HALT until 1947 *(GW notice NW 612 detailed work needed to upgrade to station, to be carried out 29 March to 3 April or until completed)*; aot request. When became station 1947* briefly shown tt (and name-board) as PEN-Y-CHAIN; soon corrected at request of local council. HALT until 1947; then P for PWLLHELI HOLIDAY CAMP; became BUTLINS P 17 May 1993 tt *(AB Chron)*, reverted to PENYCHAIN 18 May 2001 tt (belatedly – had become a Haven Holiday Park April 1999; platform signs altered earlier) *(Butlin's)*.
* = RM November 1947 refers to opening of 'new station' at Penychain, a few days after 10 May and GW Mag June 1947 to formal opening 'mid-May'.

PENYDARREN [GW] (non-tt); PLATFORM; miners; used at least 1928 to 1954; {Cwm Bargoed – Dowlais Cae Harris}.

PENYFFORDD [GC] op 1 May 1866 *(T 7th)*; still open. Opened as HOPE JUNCTION; renamed P for HOPE 1877 *(ref LNW circular 24 November –* spelling Peny-Fforde), P for LEESWOOD 1 March 1913 *(hbl 24 April)* – also ticket P for LEASWOOD *(JB)*, P 6 May 1974 *(BR notice)*. Penyfford until 1896 *(Brad)*, then Pen-y-ffordd until 18 June 1961 *(Cl)*.

PENYGRAIG [GW] op 1 May 1901 *(RCG)*; P & TONYPANDY 12 July 1911 *(hbl 26 October)* to 13 July 1925 *(Cl)*; clo 9 June 1958 *(closure notice ElyV)*. Dinas pre-passenger.

PENYGROES
For first service see 1829 B**.

PENYGROES [Nantlle] (ng) op 11 August 1856; clo 12 June 1865 *(G&S)*, for upgrading line to standard gauge >

PENYGROES [LNW] op 2 September 1867** *(co ½ T 10 October- line)*; clo 7 December 1964 *(RM March 1965)*. Pen-y-groes until 1904 *(hb)*.

PENYRHEOL [Rhy] op 1 February 1894 *(Rhy)*; clo 15 June 1964 *(RM August)*. Reduced to HALT status 1930; shown thus in tt from 1952/3 and on BR ticket *(JB)* but not in 1956 hb.

PENZANCE [GW]
op 11 March 1852 *(co n R Cornwall Gaz 12th)*; still open.

PEPLOW [GW]: orders to stop a train here on market days given 30 December 1868 *(RAC)*; first in *Brad*, for all days use, June 1870; clo 9 September 1963 *(T 9th)*.

PERCY MAIN {map 26}
PERCY MAIN [BT] terminus op 28 August 1841 *(co n BT)*; diverted 25 June 1844 to station alongside NE one *(NE maps)*; through service to Newcastle provided by time line first appeared in *Brad*, November 1852; clo 27 June 1864, service diverted *(G&S)*.

PERCY MAIN [NE]: through station on North Shields line op 22 June 1839**; clo 11 August 1980 (Saturday) for conversion to >
PERCY MAIN [TWM] op 14 November 1982 *(Tyneside)*; still open.

Boat trains
Stations shown as owned by NE/LNE but trains would have had to use privately owned dock lines to reach them. Map evidence from S. Bragg.

ALBERT EDWARD DOCK (non-tt): used from ? – in hb 'G' only by 1890; shown in NE diagram at 74 chains from junction, on line to Northumberland Dock; OS 1/2500 plans of 1897 suggest platform at NZ 349668, supported by photograph on cover of Alan Godfrey reprint of Tyneside sheet 8. Replaced by >
TYNE COMMISSION QUAY op ? – 15 June 1928? – date given by *U* as public opening but *RM August 1928* as formal. Added hb 1930a, under heading of Albert Edward Dock, 'G' only (still this 1956); about 1m 23ch from junction, at NZ 354669; first in *Brad* May 1939; clo 2 October 1939, reop November or December 1945 *(Cl)*; clo 4 May 1970 *(Cl)*.
LNE and BR tickets for NEWCASTLET C Q *(JB)*.

PERIVALE
PERIVALE [GW] op 1 May 1904 *(RM June)*; clo 1 February 1915**, reop 29 March 1920 *(Cl)*; see 1921 April/May**; for clo see 15 June 1947**. HALT until 1927 *(Brad)*; not included in hb until 1938, when given as P Halt.

PERIVALE [Cen] op 30 June 1947 *(T 1st)*; replacement for, and adjacent to, GW station; still open. Also see ALPERTON.

PERRANPORTH [GW]
PERRANPORTH op 6 July 1903 *(R Cornwall Gaz 9th)*; clo 4 February 1963 *(W Briton 4th)*.

P BEACH op 20 July 1931 *(Cl 29)*; HALT; clo 4 February 1963 *(W Briton 4th)*; {Perranporth – St Agnes}. PLATFORM in hb 1938.

PERRANWELL [GW]
op 24 August 1863 *(R Cornwall Gaz 28th)* as PERRAN; renamed 19 February 1864 *(Cl)*; still open.

PERRY BARR [LNW] op 4 July 1837 *(co n GJ)*; at first P BAR; altered LNW co tt by 1864 (later index and map), *Brad* 1872; still open.

PERSHORE [GW] op 3 May 1852**; still open.

PERSLEY [GNS] op 1 June 1903 *(GNS)*; HALT from 16 July 1926 *(Cl)*; clo 5 April 1937 *(RM January 1938)*.

PERTH {map 5}
From south to **PERTH** [Scot Cent; Cal/NB/High], op 23 May 1848**; original temporary station replaced by permanent 2 August 1848; see PRINCES STREET, below; still open. GENERAL was added in Aberdeen table by 1848 *Brad* but it was some years before this was done in all tables; ceased to be P G 30 June 1952.

From Dundee to **P BARNHILL** [DPA] op 24 May 1847 *(Perthshire Courier 27th)*; referred to as Whitehouseland Mansion (opposite Barnhill signalbox) in *True Line, October 2004, p. 16* – at one stage first-class passengers from Dundee carried in omnibus to General, others had to make own way (also true after 1849 extension?); clo when line extended to >

P PRINCES STREET [Cal] op 1 March 1849 *(Cal)*; clo 1 January 1917 *(RM February)*; reop 2 June 1919 *(RCH)*; clo 28 February 1966 *(Cl)*.
This was at first a terminus; through service on to General first in *Brad* October 1862; this had to use 'Dundee Dock', a terminal platform which required reversal and then running on to main line south of General for trains going further; General rebuilt for through running 1885/87 (G. Biddle, *Great Railway Stations of Britain*, D&C, 1986).

P GLASGOW ROAD [Scottish North Eastern]: temporary terminus set up during dispute with Scottish Central about charges for use of General station and 320 yards of track north of it (also belonging to Central). On 8 August 1859 ScNE stopped its trains at G R on its side of boundary, leaving passengers to make own way ½ mile through streets between stations *(T 23 Aug.)*. Through traffic restored by 25 August 1859 thanks to intervention of Caledonian *(Perthshire Courier 25th)* but dispute not finally settled until early 1860 (ratified by Special Meeting of ScNE Shareholders on 26 January – *T 27th*). Possible ScNE had already resumed use of General, relying on ratification as automatic.
Closure date of G R, alias G R BRIDGE, not known; according to *T 6 December 1859*, ScNE intended to retain it as extra stop, more convenient to city centre and it is in 1862 *hb*, though at that time no facilities were shown so not certain it was passenger station in use; not in 1867 *hb* (tempting to think casualty of Caledonian take-over of lines); no firm evidence of use/non-use. *Brad* clouds rather than resolves the issue: did not add G R until November 1859 (northbound only), left it there at least until 1865; cannot be used as evidence of continued use since it was applied to terminus. One possibility is that it survived as a ticket platform at which southbound passengers could alight. There is a reference to 'Perth Ticket Platform' (on line from north) in *RM July 1905, p. 14*.
True Line, October 2005, p. 25 mentioned use of Ticket Platform 31 December (only) 1934 and 1935 by one northbound train; unlikely for ticket check since believed practice had ceased about ten years earlier.
British Railways Illustrated, March 2001, p. 8, has photograph of passengers alighting 'at the old Perth ticket platform ... on 23 March 1957', using exit to York Place (which is near Glasgow Road).
However, not enough evidence to prove that was same site; even if that is found, still need to establish whether any continuity of use.

PETERBOROUGH {map 65}
PETERBOROUGH [GN] op 7 August 1850 *(T 6th & 8th)*; NORTH 1 July 1923 *(hbl 12th)* to 1966; still open.
P PRIESTGATE 1865–1901, P COWGATE 1901–12 *(Brad)* – only thus in GN tables.
P CRESCENT [Mid] first in *Brad* February 1858; clo 1 August 1866 (Wednesday) *(Mid)*.
P EAST [GE] 2 June 1845 *(Northampton Mercury 7th)*;

EAST added 1 July 1923 *(hbl 12th)*; clo 6 June 1966 *(RM July)*. Station first used by L&B (later part of LNW); EC (later part of GE) began to use 14 January 1847. Also see NEW ENGLAND.
PETERCHURCH [GW] op 1 September 1881**; finally clo 8 December 1941**.
PETERHEAD [GNS]
op 3 July 1862 *(GNS)*; clo 3 May 1965 *(RM May)*.
PETERSFIELD [LSW]
op 1 January 1859 *(SR; co n T 1st- line)*; still open.
PETERSTON [GW] first in *Brad* September 1858; from 15 June 1936 tt only included in footnotes; from 13 June 1960 tt had one morning call to pick up, one afternoon to set down; thus to clo 2 November 1964 *(Cl)*.
PETROCKSTOW [SR]
op 27 July 1925 *(Bideford 28th)*; clo 1 March 1965 *(Express & E 1st)*; {map 116}. PETROCKSTOWE until 1926 *(Brad)* and SR ticket thus *(JB)*.
PETTS WOOD [SR]
op 9 July 1928 *(sig inst 25/1928)*; still open.
PETWORTH [LBSC] op 10 October 1859**; clo 7 February 1955 *(BR notice W Sussex)*.
PEVENSEY [LBSC]
P & WESTHAM op 27 June 1846 *(LBSC; Hants Chron 4 July- line)*; originally WEST HAM & P; then variations on W, P; settled 1 January 1890 *(Cl)*; still open.
P BAY op 11 September 1905 *(LBSC)*; HALT until 5 May 1969 *(S App)*; still open.
PEWSEY [GW]
op 11 November 1862 *(co n Marlborough 8th)*; still open.
PHILORTH [GNS]
PHILORTH op private for P House 24 April 1865 *(U)*; in GNS wtt 1 July 1905, use by written permission of Lord Saltoun; in *Brad* from December 1924 but marked 'private station' and note as 1905 wtt; op to public 26 July 1926 as HALT *(GNS)* – note omitted from August *Brad*; aot request; clo 4 October 1965 *(Rly Obs November)*.
P BRIDGE op 1 July 1903 *(GNS)*; aot request; clo 3 May 1965 *(RM May)*. First in *Brad* as P B PLATFORM; altered to P B HALT 1914.
PHILPSTOUN [NB]
op 12 October 1885 *(Edin)*; clo 18 June 1951 *(RM August)*. NB ticket for PHILIPSTOUN *(JB)*.
PICCADILLY CIRCUS
PICCADILLY CIRCUS [Bak] op 10 March 1906 *(L; T 12th- line)*; still open.
PICCADILLY CIRCUS [Picc] op 15 December 1906 *(co n T 14th)*; still open.
PICKBURN & BRODSWORTH [HB]
op 1 December 1894 *(RCG)*; clo 1 February 1903 *(RCG)*, but still in *Brad* February – inertia?; {in IA}.
PICKERING
PICKERING (a) [NE]: for op see 1835 B**; clo 8 March 1965 *(T 19 January)*.
PICKERING (b): 20 May 2007 tt included this, service from Whitby (not Mondays and Fridays), run by North Yorkshire Moors Railway; still included.
PICKHILL near Thirsk [NE] first in *Brad* March 1875; at first Wednesdays and Thursdays, request; after July 1909, before/with February 1910 one each

way daily for passengers going beyond Harrogate or Northallerton; full use May 1924; clo 14 September 1959 (RM September). First in hb 1877 as P SIDING, no facilities; first shown 'P' 1938.

PICKHILL [GW]
op 30 May 1938 (hbl 2); HALT; clo 10 June 1940**, reop 6 May 1946 (Cl); clo 10 September 1962 (RM October); {Bangor-on-Dee – Marchwiel}.

PICKLE BRIDGE – see WYKE.

PICTON [NE]: op 25 May 1852**; clo 4 January 1960 (RM February). P JUNCTION in Brad 1856/9 to 1893/4 and thus NE co tt 1880.

PIDDINGTON [Mid]
op 10 June 1872 (Mid) as HORTON; renamed P & H 1 May 1876 (Mid; RCG ref April), P 1 April 1904 (RCG); clo 5 March 1962 (RM March).

PIEL [Fur]
PIEL (a) op August 1846**; intermittent use; last in Brad January 1853. Intermittently P PIER (Brad); P P BARROW (hb).
PIEL (b) first in Brad June 1867; two trains each way per day, one of which depended on tide times and table specified 1st of month for one of times given; re-sited 1 October 1881; clo 6 July 1936 (RM August).
At one time note in Brad that line was for steamer passengers only – but stop at Rampside shown; note last there October 1881. September 1914 no trains shown; trains again October 1914, with note added: Under Military Order, service between Rampside and Piel is available to Piel residents only; presumably result of use of Isle of Man for internment of 'enemy aliens'; note last included January 1919.

PIER HEAD Liverpool [LO] op 6 March 1893**; clo 31 December 1956 (T 29 September 1955).

PIERCEBRIDGE [NE] op 9 July 1856**; clo 30 November 1964 (RM December).
Hb PIERCE BRIDGE until 1872, and LNE ticket thus (JB).

PIERSHILL [NB] op 1 May 1891 (RCG); clo 1 January 1917 (RM February); reop 1 April 1919 (RCH); clo 7 September 1964 (Cl).

PILL [GW] op 18 April 1867 (co n Bristol T 17th); clo 7 September 1964 (W Daily Press 7th).

PILLING [KE] op 5 December 1870 (LNW Record); clo 11 March 1872, reop 17 May 1875 (Cl); clo 31 March 1930 (Cl).

PILMOOR [NE] was at junction of main line and Boroughbridge branch (op 17 June 1847); however inspection report shows branch then ran from Sessay; P op 20 or 21 September 1847 (accountants' records, P. Howat, direct information). At first mainly interchange, until 1879 lacked road access, thus complaints of trespass by landowners as people crossed their fields to reach it; (P. Howat, The Pilmoor, Boroughbridge & Knaresborough Railway, Martin Bairstow, 1991). Clo 5 May 1958 (RM June).
Variously spelled PILLMORE/PILLMOOR/PILMOR (Brad until settled 1859, Topham); P JUNCTION until 1893/4 (Brad) and thus NE wtt 1861, NE public tt 1880, Reid 1904.

PILNING [GW] {map 121}
PILNING (a) op 8 September 1863 (co n W D Press 7th); replaced on Severn Tunnel line by >
PILNING (b) op 1 December 1886 (Bristol T 2nd- line); P HL 9 July 1928 (Cl) to 6 May 1968 tt (offic); shown Saturdays only, one each way to/from Cardiff, in tt 14 December 2008; still open.
P LL op 9 July 1928 (W D Press 7th); reopening of 1863 station; HALT on BR ticket (JB) but not in tt; clo 23 November 1964 (Bristol E P 21st).
Hb 1938 and 1956 had only one entry: 'PILNING'.

PILOT [RHD] (ng) op 24 May 1928 (RHD); see 1927 July 16**; last in tt end of summer service 1947 but use continued until after transfer to preservation – shelter demolished about 1946 but replaced 1968 (Wolfe). THE PILOT until 1935/6 (Brad); alias P INN; ticket DUNGENESS P (JB).

PILRIG [Cal]: shown 'P' (and only 'P') in hb 1904, 1912, 1925; 1927a 'delete'; see 1905** – 'delete' clearly long overdue.

PILSLEY [GC] op 2 January 1893 (RCG); clo 2 November 1959 (RM December). Saturday excursions to Skegness 2 July to 27 August 1960 (AB).

PILTON YARD [Lynton] (ng): Brad shows first train of day leaving from here, just beyond Barnstaple Town, instead of from latter, starting November 1898; last May 1904.

PIMBO LANE – see UPHOLLAND.

PIMHOLE [LY]: op 1 May 1848, as HEAP BRIDGE (co n Manchester 3 May). Sparse information available. It only appeared in Brad November 1848, when shown as PIMHOLE, in small local table Manchester–Heywood–Bury; in December this was absorbed into larger table; experience with other tables at this time suggests possibility of longer survival of P. Possibility increased by fact that it appeared earlier in Topham (July 1848), also in local table, and stayed there at least until April 1849, though last two months' tables marked to show that no recent information sent by company; not present March 1850, but local table had also gone by then. Not on LY Distance Diagram 1851 so existence probably short. Note that Pimhole was on main line and later Heap Bridge on a branch. {Bury – Broadfield}.

PIMLICO
For main line station, see under LONDON.
PIMLICO [Vic] op 14 September 1972 (RM October); still open.

PINCHBECK [GN/GE] op 6 March 1882 (GN/GE); clo 11 September 1961 (RM September).

PINCHINTHORPE [NE]
op 25 February 1854 (co ½ T 25 August- line); re-sited west of level crossing December 1876 (Cl); PINCHINGTHORPE until 1919/20 (RCG ref January 1920); clo 29 October 1951 (RM January 1952).

PINEWOOD [GW] op 11 September 1933 (Cl 29); HALT; clo 4 August 4 1942**, reop 8 March 1943 (Cl); clo 10 September 1962 (RM October); {Hampstead Norris – Hermitage}.

PINGED [BPGV] op 2 August 1909** (GW H); HALT in Brad except for brief period 1921/2 but was included in hb 1912–29 as P; clo 21 September 1953 (T 16th).

PINHOE
PINHOE (a) [LSW] op 30 October 1871 *(Trewman 1 November)*; clo 7 March 1966 *(RM April)*.
PINHOE (b) op 16 May 1983 *(RM August, p.366)*; still open.
PINKHILL [NB] op 1 February 1902 *(RCG)*; clo 1 January 1917 *(RM February)*; reop 1 February 1919 *(RM February)*; clo 1 January 1968 *(Cl)*.
PINMORE [GSW] op 19 September 1877★★; clo 7 February 1882 (Tuesday), reop 16 February 1882; clo 12 April 1886, reop 14 June 1886 *(Cl)*; clo 6 September 1965 *(RM September)*. *RM June 1962* said had become HALT; not thus September 1964 tt.
PINNER
For first station of this name see HATCH END.
PINNER [Met/GC] op 25 May 1885 *(L)*; op by Met, GC service added 15 March 1899; still open.
PINWHERRY [GSW] op 19 September 1877★★; clo 7 February 1882 (Tues.), reop 16 February 1882; clo 12 April 1886, reop 14 June 1886 *(Cl)*; clo 6 September 1965 *(RM September)*. P for BALLANTRAE in *Brad* until 1955 but not thus LMS tt 1930, nor in *hb*.
PINXTON
For first service see 1832 A★★.
P & SELSTON [Mid] op 6 November 1851 *(Mid)*; clo 16 June 1947★★ *(Mid)*; later, as P NORTH, advertised summer services 1960 and 1961 (last 11 September 1961); later excursions shown in special notices e.g. 19 June 1963 *(IU)*.
P SOUTH [GN] op 1 August 1876 *(GN)*; SOUTH added 1954; clo 7 January 1963 *(RM February)*. P WHARF 1904, 1912 *hb*.
Became P for SOUTH NORMANTON 1914? *(hbl ref 23 April)*; thus LNE tt 1933 and *Brad* until 1954.
PIPE GATE [NS] op 1 February 1870 *(co ½ Whitchurch 5 March- line)*; clo 7 May 1956 *(RM June* – 'excursions and race use will continue')*; used for annual race meeting – until last one, 1963? *(AB)*. NS co tt 1910: P G for WOORE and thus in *Brad* to clo but not thus LMS tt 1930.
PIRTON [BG] op November 1841★★ *(Mid)*; clo about 1846 *(Cl)*; {Wadborough – Defford}.
PITCAPLE [GNS] op 20 September 1854 *(GNS)*; clo 6 May 1968 *(RM July)*.
PITCROCKNIE [Cal] first in *Brad* June 1912 as PORTEROCHNEY; renamed/spelling corrected 1912 *(hbl ref 3 July)*; early notes suggest mainly for golfers – thus perhaps its apparently erratic existence in WW1. Signal stop, last trains November 1914 *Brad*; trains again July 1916. Clo 1 January 1917 *(RCH)*; trains again September 1919 *Brad*. Last trains shown May–15 June 1947 *(Brad)*; completely absent *Murray* 31 May 1948 though remained trainless in *Brad* at least until 5 June 1950 tt, but removed from index by then.
PLATFORM to 1940 *(Brad)*, then SIDING (but HALT 1938 *hb*); {Alyth – Jordanstone}.
PITFODELS [GNS] op 2 July 1894 *(GNS)*; made HALT 16 July 1926 *(Cl)*; clo 5 April 1937 *(RM January 1938)*.

PITFOUR CURLING [GNS] (non-tt); PLATFORM; used in 1888; {Maud – Mintlaw} *(U)*.
PITLOCHRY [High] op 1 June 1863 *(High)*; still open. LMS tt 1930, *Murray* 1948 and *Brad* to 1955: P for KINLOCH-RANNOCH.
PITLURG [GNS] op 2 August 1897 *(GNS)*; clo 31 October 1932 *(RM December)*.
PITMEDDEN [GNS] op 1861 *(GNS)*, though not in *Brad* until November 1873; clo 7 December 1964 *(RM January 1965)*. Shown 'P' in *hb* to 1895 (inclusive); no entry 1904; present 1925, no facilities listed; *hb* 1927a 'add P'.
PITSEA [LTS] op 1 July 1855 *(co n T 28 June)*; re-sited nearby 1 June 1888 *(Cl)*; still open. P for VANGE 18 July 1932 co tt to 1952 *(Mid)*.
PITSFORD & BRAMPTON [LNW] op 16 February 1859 *(LNW- line)*; originally B & P; renamed B 1860/1, P & B 1 December 1881 *(JS; LNW Officers recommended 15 November)*; clo 5 June 1950 *(RM July)*; later use by railwaymen *(U)*.
PITTENWEEM [NB] op 1 September 1863 *(D&C 15- line)*; clo 1 January 1917 *(RM February)*; reop 1 February 1919 *(RM Feb.)*; clo 6 September 1965 *(co n East of T J)*.
PITTENZIE: op 15 September 1958★★; request; HALT; clo 6 July 1964 *(RM July)*; {Crieff – Highlandman}.
PITTINGTON [NE]: line op 6 November 1837 *(NE)*, nd, May 1848 *(Topham)*; clo 5 January 1953 *(RM March)*.
PITTS HEAD [WH] (ng) op 1 June 1923 *(NGSC 2)*; see 1922 July 31★★; aot request; clo 28 September 1936 *(Cl)*; {map 76}.
PITTS HILL [NS] op 1 October 1874 *(RCG)*; clo 2 March 1964 *(RM April)*.
PLAIDY [GNS] op 4 June 1860 *(GNS)*; clo 22 May 1944 *(Cl)*.
PLAINS [NB] first in *Brad* May 1882; clo 18 June 1951 *(RM August)*.
PLAISTOW near Barking: op by [LTS] 31 March 1858 *(co n T 30th)*; [Dist] use began 2 June 1902; [Met] use began 30 March 1936; transferred to underground 26 April 1970 *(Mid – from BLN)*; still open.
PLAISTOW near Bromley – see SUNDRIDGE PARK.
PLANK LANE
PLANK LANE [LNW] op 1 October 1903 *(RCG)*; clo 22 February 1915 *(RCH)*; {in IA}. Also see WEST LEIGH.
PLANTATION – see STEWARTON.
PLAS [Festiniog] (ng) (non-tt): private for Oakley family; built about 1874; clo ?; {Penrhyndeudraeth – Hafod-y-Llyn} *(U)*.
PLAS MARL [GW] op 9 May 1881 *(GW- line)*; clo 11 June 1956 *(T 8th)*.
PLAS POWER {map 75}
PLAS POWER [GC] op 1 August 1889 *(GC)*; clo 1 March 1917 (Thursday) *(RCH)*.
PLAS POWER [GW] first in *Brad* February 1883; clo 1 January 1931 (Thursday) *(T 22 December 1930)*.

PLAS-Y-COURT [Shrewsbury & Welshpool]
op 3 November 1934 *(co n dated 'November')*; HALT;
clo 12 September 1960 *(Cl)*.

PLAS-Y-NANT [WH] (ng) first in *Brad* April 1924;
see 1922 July 31 ★★; aot request; clo 28 September 1936
(Cl); {map 76}.

PLASHETTS [NB] op 1 January 1862 (M.D. Greville,
RM January 1962- line); clo 15 October 1956
(T 21 September). *Hb* 1862 P ROAD; 1867 P.

PLATT BRIDGE

PLATT BRIDGE [LNW] op 1 September 1864★★;
clo 1 May 1961 *(RM June)*.
Also see HINDLEY SOUTH.

PLAWSWORTH [NE] op 1 December 1868
(NE- line); clo 7 April 1952 *(RM June)*.

PLEALEY ROAD [Shrewsbury & Welshpool]
op 14 February 1861 *(D&C 11)*; clo 5 February 1951
(RM October) – see 1951★★. *Hb* 1862 PLEALY ROAD;
1867 PLEALEY R.

PLEAN [Cal] op 1 March 1904 *(RCG)*; clo 11 June
1956 *(RM April)*. Cal co tt 1913, LMS tt 1930 ,
Murray 1948, always *Brad* and *hb*: P for COWIE.

PLEASINGTON [LY]: line op 1 June 1846 *(Rtn PP)*,
nd, February 1847; still open.

PLEASLEY

PLEASLEY [GN] op 1 November 1901 *(RCG)*;
clo 14 September 1931 *(Cl)*. Later, as P EAST,
advertised summer use 19 June 1954 outward, 26th
return *(BR ER tt 14 June)*; to 8 September 1962 (last);
later excursions, including football to Nottingham,
winter 1950/1 *(Rly Obs February 1951, p. 42)* and
excursion to Cleethorps 31 July 1952 *(BR working notice)*.

PLEASLEY [Mid] op 1 May 1886 *(RCG)*; clo 28 July
1930 *(Mid)*.

PLEASURE BEACH – see BLACKPOOL.

PLECK [LNW] op 1 October 1881 *(LNW Officers
22672)*; clo 1 January 1917 *(RM February)*; reop 1 May
1924 *(Cl)*; clo 17 November 1958 *(RM December)*.

PLENMELLER [NE] (non-tt): HALT; miners, later
other workmen; op June 1919; clo ? (colliery clo 1932)
(S. Jenkins, *The Alston Branch*, Oakwood, 2001);
during WW2 used (?–1946) for Ministry of Supplies
Depot, later by employees of Cascelloid Factory
(NhumbYoung) {Haltwhistle – Featherstone Park}.

PLESSEY [NE] first in *Brad* July 1859; from
September 1955 tt only one train daily, northbound
(NhumbYoung); clo 15 September 1958 *(RM October)*.
Early PLESSAY/PLESSY, settled 1864/5 *(Brad)*;
became HALT 8 July 1951 according to *RM September*,
but not seen thus *Brad*.

PLEX MOSS LANE [LY]
op 1 July 1906 *(Wigan Observer 4th)*; see 1905★★ (b);
clo 26 September 1938 *(RM November)*.

PLOCKTON [High]
op 2 November 1897 *(High)*; still open.
Also see Section 7, Non-rail.

PLODDER LANE [LNW]
op 1 April 1875 *(LNW Officers 12593)*; clo 29 March
1954 *(RM May)*. *LNW Officers 17 February 1878*
recommended change to P L for FARNWORTH;
thus LNW co tt 1908, LMS co tt 1930 and *Brad* to clo.

PLOWDEN [BC]:
line op 1 February 1866★★ *(co ½T 8 March- line)* and this
station in tt February but perhaps not used, officially at
least, from opening of line – Col. Yolland's inspection
report suggests not ready; finally clo 20 April 1935.

PLUCKLEY [SE]
op 1 December 1842 *(co n T 1st- line*; included in
description of formal opening *T 30 November)*; still open.

PLUM(B)LEY [CLC]

PLUMLEY op 1 January 1863 *(CLC; co ½T 26 Feb.-
line)*; PLUMBLEY until 1 February 1945 *(Cl)*; still open.

PLUMBLEY WEST: PLATFORM; really workmen's
station; service began November 1917, in *Brad*
January 1918 to February 1919 (inclusive);
service discontinued April 1919 *(CLC Portrait)*.

PLUMPTON near Brighton [LBSC] first in *Brad*
June 1863; *Herapath 13 June/Sussex Express 6th* said
station had been opened; still open. An extra platform,
immediately west, with direct access to racecourse
(opened 1884) was added after 1884 and ceased use ?
(probably 1970s) *(AB)*.

PLUMPTON near Penrith [LNW]
op 17 December 1846 *(D&C 14; co op n- line;)*;
clo 31 May 1948 *(RM July)*.

PLUMSTEAD [SE] op 16 July 1859 *(L)*; still open.

PLUMTREE [Mid] op 2 February 1880 *(RCG)*;
P & KEYWORTH 1 June 1880 co tt *(Mid)* to 1 May
1893 co tt *(Mid; RCG ref January)*; clo 28 February
1949 *(RM May)*. Excursion to Dudley 27 July 1958
(RM November, p. 765).

PLYM BRIDGE [GW]
op 1 May 1906 *(GW Plymouth Area records)*; always
PLATFORM in *Brad* but *hb* 1938 (only) said HALT;
clo 31 December 1962★★.

PLYMOUTH {map 114}

P LAIRA GREEN [South Devon] op 5 May 1848
(Woolmer 13th); temporary terminus (just L in *Brad*
but L G South Devon co tt November 1848);
clo when line extended to >

P MILLBAY [GW] op 2 April 1849 *(Trewman 5th)*;
MILLBAY added 1 May 1877 *(Cl)* though GW co tt
1886 just P (1891 P M); clo 23 April 1941 (Wednesday)
(Cl) – *wtt supp* says clo 24th – was this first day of
non-use and Clinker's date last day (or part day) of use?
– closed by bombing. GW op notice for Ingra Tor
2 March 1936 had P MILL BAY but this seems to have
been an isolated use.

P MILLBAY DOCKS [GW] (non-tt): From 1882
passenger trains ran into docks, terminating at East Quay,
next to boat passengers' waiting room – previously
walk/cab to Millbay station. E.g. *GW Mag October 1909*
says that 30 August 1909 passengers taken from *Kaiser
Wilhelm der Grosse* by tender and joined their train at
Millbay Crossing. *Great Western Ports* (1928) says main
landing-place at south end of Millbay Pier, waiting and
refreshment rooms adjoining, plus additional landing
point to north of this. Last train called midnight 18/19
October 1963. Use of Millbay Docks by GW was
continuous (apart from war interruptions) to closure
(e.g. detailed description of arrival there 9 September
1955) *(Kittridge)*.

PLYMOUTH [GW] op 28 March 1877 *(W D Merc 29th)*
as P NORTH ROAD though GW co tt 1886 just N R
(1891 P N R); provided so that through trains from
Cornwall to the east did not have to reverse at Millbay;
N R dropped 15 September 1958; still open.
(P) MUTLEY [GW] op 1 August 1871 *(W D Merc 2nd)*
as P M. Served as terminus for LSW trains between the
opening of independent LSW line 1 June 1890 and
opening of Friary, 1 July 1891. P dropped by *GW
circular* dated 13 April 1905. Clo 3 July 1939; according
to *GW Mag July* 'will be closed from the night of 2 July
in connection with the reconstruction of … North
Road, which is almost adjoining'.
P FRIARY [LSW] op 1 July 1891 *(RCG)*;
clo 15 September 1958 *(Cl)*.
See under 'L' for later halt at Laira.
Also see DEVONPORT, especially for other boat train use.
PLYMPTON [GW] op 15 June 1848★★; clo 2 March
1959 *(RM April)*. Was COLEBROOK in *Plymouth
17th, Trewmans 22nd June 1848*.
PLYMSTOCK [LSW]
op 5 September 1892 *(W Morn N 6th)*; original platforms
on line to Turnchapel; Yealmpton line platforms added
17 January 1898; clo 15 January 1951 *(T 12th)*,
reop 2 July 1951 *(D&C 1)* – see 1951★★;
clo 10 September 1951 *(RM October)*.

POCHIN PITS
POCHIN PITS (non-tt): *LNW Traffic Committee,
18 January 1882*, decided to erect rough timber platform
here for workmen while they considered moving Holly
Bush to more convenient site; was this removed when
Holly Bush was re-sited? Any connection with next entry?
P P COLLIERY [LNW]: first in *Brad* October 1893;
PLATFORM; Saturdays only; sometimes just P P;
at first apparently from Newport only; service shown
both ways, still Saturdays only, October 1914;
last in public tt September 1922; miners used to
13 June 1960 *(U)*; {Holly Bush – Bedwellty}.
POCKLINGTON [NE]:
line op 4 October 1847★★, nd, May 1848 *(Topham)*;
clo 29 November 1965 *(RM December)*.
POINT PLEASANT [NE]: workmen's platform
1879? *(U)*; op to public 1 January 1902 *(RCG)*;
clo 23 July 1973 *(RM Aug.)*; {Carville – Willington Quay}.
POISON CROSS [EK]
first in *Brad* May 1925; HALT; clo 1 November 1928.
See 1948 November 1★★ for details.
POKESDOWN [LSW]
op 1 July 1886 *(Poole 8th)* as BOSCOMBE; renamed
P B October 1891, P 1 May 1897 *(SR)*; still open.
Became P for EASTERN BOURNEMOUTH 1930
(hbl ref 22 October 1930) and thus *Brad* to 1955.
POLEGATE [LBSC] op 27 June 1846 *(LBSC;
Hants Chron 4 July- line)*; re-sited about 300 yards east
3 October 1881 *(Cl)*; moved back to original site
25 May 1986 *(RM August)*; still open.
POLESWORTH [LNW] op 15 September 1847
(co n T 13th); clo 23 May 2004★★; reop 12 December
2005 but only for one northbound train, daylight only;
still open – same service 9 December 2007 tt.

POLLICOTT [GW/GC] (non-tt):
Possible that at one time trains stopped hereabouts.
A typed document *(GW & GC Jt Misc 717)* signed by
Albert and Pellie Heard, 26 May 1936, frees railway
from any liabilty arising from their using, daylight only,
auto-cars stopping near their cottage, although there
was no normal stop there. Their address not given but
witnesses gave Pollicott addresses. Perhaps locals had
asked for Halt but were offered this instead (unlikely
that offer was made to one ordinary couple only).
If a stop did result it would have been at SP 697128,
immediately south of Ashendon Up Line Junction,
where footpaths from Upper and Lower Pollicott met
and crossed line. Perhaps Dorton Halt, about 1½ mile
north was opened instead or that this was a brief
arrangement that ended with the opening of Dorton,
21 June 1937. No other information available.

POLLOKSHAWS
(at first POLLOCKSHAWS in *hb*).
P EAST [Cal] op 2 April 1894 *(Cal)*; EAST added
5 May 1952 *(JS, from RCH records)*; still open.
P WEST [GBK Jt]: line op 27 September 1848 *(Rtn)*,
nd, June 1850; WEST added 5 May 1952 *(JS)*; still open.

POLLOKSHIELDS
(POLLOCKSHIELDS in *hb* early).
POLLOKSHIELDS [GP Jt] first in *Brad* September
1862★; amalgamated into Shields Road 1 April 1925 *(Cl)*.
★ = was first station to be added in *Brad* between Glasgow and
Paisley so perhaps op earlier (line op 14 July 1840), but evidence
contradictory. Not in *Murray* September 1844, when it did
include short-lived Moss Road and Bellahouston. Still not
shown *Murray* 1852 or *Cornwall* 1860, specialist Scottish
timetables. However Macaulay's map 1851 shows station at
Shields/Shiels Bridge.
P EAST [Cal] op 1 March 1886 *(Cal)*; clo 1 January
1917 *(RM February)*; reop 1 April 1919 *(RCH)*; still open.
P WEST [Cal] op 2 April 1894 *(Cal)*; still open.
POLMONT [NB] op 21 February 1842 *(co n T 19th)*;
still open. P JUNCTION in some tables in *Brad* until
1903/4 and thus Cal co tt 1858.
POLSHAM [SD Jt] op 16 March 1859★★;
HALT from 1938 *(Brad)*; clo 29 October 1951
(Central Somerset Gazette 2 November).
POLSLOE BRIDGE [LSW]
op 1 June 1908 *(Trewman 30 May)*;
HALT until 5 May 1969 *(SR App)*; still open.
POLTON [NB] op 15 April 1867 *(T 18th)*;
clo 10 September 1951 *(RM October)*.
POMATHORN [NB]
op 4 July 1855 *(co ½ T 22 October- line)* as PENICUIK;
renamed 2 September 1872 *(Cl)*; HALT from 7 July
1947 *(Cl)*; clo 5 February 1962 *(RM February)*.
PONDERS END [GE]
op 15 September 1840 *(T 16th)*; still open.
PONFEIGH [Cal] first in *Brad* December 1865;
clo 5 October 1964 *(RM October)*.
PONKEY CROSSING [GW]
first in *Brad* October 1907 *(GW H* says 5 June 1905
but such a delay in reaching tt would have been very
unusual); HALT; clo 22 March 1915★★; {map 75}.
Pre op Cutter Hill *(RAC)*.

PONT CROESOR [WH] (ng):
op 1 June 1923 *(NGSC 2)*; see 1922 July 31★★;
clo 28 September 1936 *(Cl)*; {map 76}.
PONT IFANS:
'halt' Corris – Esgairgeiliog; dates? *(Corris GW)*.
PONT LAWRENCE [LNW] op 2 October 1911★;
became HALT 1936 *(Brad)*; clo 4 February 1957 *(Cl)*.
★ = from *RM October; LNW Cl* and *RCG* give 1st but that a
Sunday; no Sunday service.
PONT LLANIO [GW] op 1 September 1866
(D&C 11); clo 22 February 1965 *(Cl)*.
PONT LLIW [GW]
op 9 July 1923 *(hb amendment leaflet dated 25 October
1923)*; clo 22 September 1924 *(Cl)*; {goods *IA*}.
PONT RUG/PONTRUG [LNW]
op 1 June 1880 *(LNW Officers 20951)*; clo 1 January
1917 *(T 22 December 1916)*; reop 1 July 1919 *(Cl)*;
renamed from PONT RUG and treated as HALT
4 October 1920 according to *LNW dates* but still P R
and not halt in tt; clo 22 September 1930★ *(Cl)*.
★ = *LNW circ R 2194* says delete with effect from 1 October
1920 – but was reduced to halt then, not closed. Also see 1939
September ★★.
PONT-Y-PANT [LNW] op 22 July 1879 *(Brad Sh Eng
1880- line)*; aot request; still open. *Hb* had PONTYPANT
from 1904, restored hyphens 1956.
PONTARDAWE [Mid] op 21 February 1860
(Mining Journal 25th); clo 25 September 1950
(RM November). Pont-ar-dawe *(hb)*, 1877 only.
PONTARDDULAIS [GW/LNW] op 1 May 1850★★
as PONTARDULAIS; HALT 6 September 1965 to
5 May 1969 *(Cl)*; spelling revised 12 May 1980 tt *(Cl)*;
aot request; still open. Aot P JUNCTION *(hb)*.
PONTCYNON [TV]
op 26 December 1904 *(Aberdare)* as PONTYCYNON
BRIDGE; spelling altered 1910 tt *(Cl)*; BRIDGE
dropped 8 June 1953 *(Cl)*; see 1904★★ for other name
details; clo 16 March 1964 *(Cl)*.
PONTDOLGOCH [Cam] op 5 January 1863★★;
clo 14 June 1965 *(RM July)*. *Hb* 1877-95: Pont-dol-goch.
PONTEFRACT
P BAGHILL [SK Jt] op 1 July 1879 *(Mid; co n
T 28 June- line)*; still open. First in *Brad* as P NEW;
became P B 1884 but according to *Cl* and *ref RM
March 1937* not officially thus until 1 December 1936.
GN co tt 1909: P NEW.
P MONKHILL [LY] op 1 April 1848 *(LY; co ½
T 7 September- line)*; still open. At first P *(Brad)*,
then P M 1884 but officially thus 1 December 1936
(Cl; ref RM March 1937).
P TANSHELF [LY] (a) op 17 July 1871 (P. Cookson,
Steam Days, October 1997) as T; became P T
1 December 1936 *(Cl; ref RM March 1937)*;
aot bay for race specials *(AB)*; clo 2 January 1967 *(Cl)*.
P TANSHELF (b) op 11 May 1992 *(RM June)*;
still open.
PONTELAND [NE]
op 1 June 1905 *(RCG)*; clo 17 June 1929 *(Cl)*.
PONTESBURY [Shrewsbury & Welshpool]
op 14 February 1861 *(D&C 11)*; clo 5 February 1951
(RM October) – see 1951★★.

PONTFADOG [Glyn] (ng) {map 79}.
PONT FADOG: line op 1 April 1874 *(Glyn)*, nd,
June 1877; clo 1 April 1886 (Thursday) *(Cl)*.
PONTFADOG op 15 March 1891 *(Glyn)*;
clo 7 April 1933★★.
PONTFAEN [Glyn] (ng) {map 79}.
P CHIRK op 1 April 1874 *(Glyn)*; terminus; re-sited
further back line following accident in 1875; aot request;
clo 1 April 1886 (Thursday) *(Cl)*.
PONTFAEN op 15 March 1891 *(Glyn)*; through
station; aot request; clo 7 April 1933★★.
PONTHENRY [BPGV]
PONTHENRY op 2 August 1909★★; HALT until 1913,
when moved from notes to table *(Brad)*;
clo 21 September 1953 *(T 16th)*.
P COLLIERY SIDING (non-tt): in use at least 1909 to
1951; {Ponthenry – Pontyberem} *(U)*.
PONTHIR [GW] op 1 June 1878 *(Pontypool 8th)*;
clo 30 April 1962 *(T 6 April)*.
PONTLLANFRAITH
Both opened as TREDEGAR JUNCTION.
P HL [LNW] op 19 June 1865 *(co n Newport 17th)*;
renamed 1 July 1911 *(hbl 6th)*, HL added 23 May 1949
tt *(Cl)*; clo 13 June 1960 *(RM July)*.
P LL [GW] op 25 May 1857★★; renamed 1 May 1905
(hbl 27 April), LL added 19 July 1950 *(Cl)*;
clo 15 June 1964 *(RM August)*.
PONTLOTTYN [Rhy]
PONTLOTTYN first in *Brad* September 1859; still open.
P COLLIERY (non-tt): as P C was HALT/PLATFORM
for miners; op 1 January 1916; clo by September 1928;
{Tir Phil – Pontlottyn} *(U)*. Also used as RHYMNEY
MERTHYR COLLIERY dates ? – *GW Agreement
dated 4 April 1917* refers to workmen's trains to/from
Rhymney Bridge.
PONTNEWYDD – see GLYN ABBEY (for P HALT);
LOWER PONTNEWYDD; UPPER PONTNEWYDD.
PONTNEWYNYDD [GW] op 2 October 1854★★;
clo 30 April 1962 *(T 6 April)*.
PONTHRHYDYFEN [RSB]
op 25 June 1885 *(The Cambrian 26th)*;
clo 3 December 1962 *(RM January 1963)*.
PONTOON DOCK [Dock] op 2 December 2005,
formal 6th *(LRR January 2006)*; still open.
PONTRHYDYRHUN [GW]
PONTRHYDYRHUN (a) op 1 July 1852 *(Merlin 2nd)*;
clo 1 January 1917 *(GW notice dated 22 December
1916)*; {Upper Pontnewydd – Panteg}.
Pontrhyd-y-rhun in *hb*, 1877 only.
PONTRHYDYRHUN (b) op 17 July 1933 *(co n dated
'July')*; HALT, 19 chains south of P (a); clo 30 April
1962 *(T 6 April)*.
PONTRHYTHALLT [LNW]
first in *Brad* October 1869 ('in course of erection'
Carnarvon 3 July); for clo see 1939 September ★★.
Until 1890 PONT RHYTHALLT in *hb*.
PONTRILAS [GW] op 2 January 1854
(T 29 December 1853- line); clo 9 June 1958 *(Cl)*.
PONTSARN [BM/LNW] first in *Brad* June 1869;
aot request; clo 13 November 1961 *(T 8th)*.
Became P for VAYNOR 1884/5? *(RCG reference January*

1885) and thus GW tt 1932, *hb* 1895 on and *Brad* to last issue. According to *Cl* became HALT 1 March 1934 and shown thus in tables *Brad* July 1934; latter dropped HALT from GW tables by mid-1935 but kept it in LMS tables until 1940; restored 1951/2. Not seen as Halt in *hb*. In *LMS List* 1933 as PONT SARN for V.

PONTSTICILL JUNCTION [BM]
logically op 1 August 1867** *(Cardiff T 27 July- line)*, when needed as junction station but not in *Brad* until June 1868 – initially only/mainly exchange? Clo 31 December 1962 *(T 31st)*. Just P in *hb* 1904 to April 1959a.

PONTWALBY [GW] op 1 May 1911 *(GW H)*; replaced British Rhondda; HALT; clo 15 June 1964 *(RM August)*.

PONTYATES [BPGV] op 2 August 1909**; clo 21 September 1953 *(T 16th)*.

PONTYBEREM [BPGV]:
miners use started 1898 *(U)*; op to public 2 August 1909**; clo 21 September 1953 *(T 16th)*.

PONTYCLUN op 28 September 1992 *(RM December)*; near old Llantrisant; still open.

PONTYCYMMER [GW]: miners use started 1877 *(U)*; op to public 1 June 1889 *(Brad Sh 1890)* (in *Brad* for at least two years previously but no trains shown until July 1889); clo 9 February 1953 *(T 23 January)*.

PONTYCYNON – see PONTCYNON.

PONTYGWAITH
P HALT [GW] op 11 September 1933 *(GW notice 883)*; last train 3 February 1951 – see 1951**; {Quakers Yard – Aberfan}.

PONTYGWAITH [TV] op 5 June 1905 *(RM July)*; see 1904**; clo 1 October 1914 (Thurs.) *(Cl)*; {Ynyshir – Tylorstown}.

PONTYPOOL [GW]
P & NEW INN op 2 January 1854 *(T 29 December 1853-line)* as NEWPORT ROAD; renamed PONTYPOOL ROAD April 1854 tt *(Cl)*; re-sited ¼ mile north 1 March 1909 *(GW Mag March)*; renamed P 1 May 1972 *(Cl)*; & N I added 19 May 1994 *(AB Chron)*; still open.
P BLAENDARE ROAD op 30 April 1928 *(co n dated 'April')*; HALT; clo 30 April 1962 *(T 6 April)*; {Panteg – Crane Street}.
P CLARENCE STREET op 20 August 1855** *(T 21st- line)* as P; renamed P TOWN 1867 tt *(Cl)*, P C S 1 September 1881 *(Cl; RCG ref October)*; clo 15 June 1964 *(RM August)*.
Aot P TOWN (CLARENCE STREET) in *hb*.
P CRANE STREET op 1 July 1852 *(Merlin 2nd)*; C S added 1 September 1881 *(Cl)*; clo 30 April 1962 *(T 6 April)*.

PONTYPRIDD
PONTYPRIDD [TV] op 9 October 1840** as NEWBRIDGE; became N JUNCTION 1861/2, P J 1866, P 1902 *(Brad)*, P CENTRAL 1 July 1924 *(GW circular 18 June)*, P 5 May 1930 *(hbl 29 April)*; still open; TREFOREST & NEWBRIDGE in *Robinson 1841*.
P GRAIG [Barry] op 16 March 1896 *(Barry)*; GRAIG added 1 July 1924 *(GW circular 18 June – but to CRAIG – error)*; clo 5 May 1930 *(RM July; hbl 75)*.

P TRAM ROAD [ANSW] op 1 September 1904**; original HALT here was ground level platform used by passengers both ways – was northern terminus of ANSW passenger service; replaced by conventional halt 1 May 1906; clo 10 July 1922 *(Cl)*.

PONTYRHYLL [GW] op 25 October 1886 *(Brad Sh 1887)*; clo 9 February 1953 *(T 23 January)*. At first PONTYRHILL in *Brad*, amended by August 1887. *Hb*: 1899a Pont-y-Rhyll (and *RCH dist ref thus 28 March 1898*); 1904 lost hyphens again.

POOL – see ARTHINGTON; CARN BREA.

POOL QUAY [Cam] op 1 May 1860 *(co ½ T 9 August)*; clo 18 January 1965 *(RM March)*.

POOL-IN-WHARFEDALE [NE]
op 1 February 1865 *(T 3rd)*; -in-W added 1 July 1927 *(hbl July)*; clo 22 March 1965 *(RM April)*.
At times *hb* made POOLE of it.

POOLE {map 125}
For first stations to serve Poole, see BROADSTONE and HAMWORTHY.

POOLE [LSW] op 2 December 1872 *(Dorset Chron 5th)*; still open. Aot P TOWN: thus *Brad* SD Jt table 1874 and Mid co tt 1903. *Hb* 1904 P for LONGFLEET; *hb* September 1960a to P. LSW ticket for P NEW *(JB)*.

POORSTOCK – see POWERSTOCK.

POPE STREET – see NEW ELTHAM.

POPLAR
POPLAR [GE] op 6 July 1840 *(T 29 June, 10 July)*; re-sited east of Brunswick Street about 1845; see 1849 March 31**; clo 4 May 1926**.
POPLAR [Dock] op 31 August 1987 *(T 1 September)*; still open.
P EAST INDIA ROAD [NL] op 1 August 1866 *(L)*; clo 15 May 1944, though bus service provided to 23 April 1945 *(Cl)*. At first in *hb* as P E I DOCKS.

POPPLETON [NE]
op 30 October 1848**- line; still open.

PORT CARLISLE [NB] op 22 June 1854 *(D&C 14; Rtn- line)*; clo 1 January 1917 *(RM February)*; reop 1 February 1919 *(RM February)*. Last trains shown May 1921 *Brad*, though line still included; trains again September 1921 tt. Another temporary casualty of 1921 April/May** ? Clo 1 June 1932 *(T 3 March)*.

PORT CARLISLE JUNCTION [NB]:
physical junction came into use 29 October 1861; station first in *Brad* July 1863 (previous non-tt use?); clo 1 July 1864 (Friday) *(Cl)*; {map 20}.

PORT CLARENCE [NE]: for op see 1835 A**; re-sited at some point; clo 11 September 1939 *(Cl)*.

PORT DINORWIC [LNW] op 1 July 1852 *(co n Companies)*; re-sited ? – inspection report on new station, *MT 29/35*, dated 4 July 1874 said old was to be done away with; clo 12 September 1960 *(RM October)*.

PORT EDGAR [NB]
PORT EDGAR (public) probably op 1 September 1878 *(MT 6/213/10)* – intended then but only passed inspection 30 August (in NB tt 1 August prematurely, not in *Brad* until October); clo 5 March 1890 (Wednesday) *(Cl)*; {map 13}.
PORT EDGAR (non-tt): op ? – inspection report dated 6 September 1916; for workmen at submarine base; clo ?;

{nearer South Queensferry than previous public station}
(MT6/2442/17 – D. Stirling).

PORT ELPHINSTONE [GNS]: generally regarded
as goods only but appeared in *Brad* October 1854 (line
op 20 September 1854, *GNS*), one train each way;
in November one southbound only (northbound train
had been early morning one, no longer operating);
inspection report of 7 September 1854 said platforms
incomplete; letter from engineer to BoT 11 September
said would not be used as passenger station – change of
mind or were platforms for railwaymen working at
goods depot? – times of trains would fit; error?
GNS wtt 5 September 1857 has note that Fridays and
Saturdays 1st and 3rd class carriages are attached at
Huntly to goods due Aberdeen about 7.40am;
this stopped here – any possibility of use by occasional
passenger?; {south of Inverurie}.

PORT GLASGOW [Cal] op 31 March 1841⋆⋆;
still open. Accident report, 19 October 1857, said
dangerous condition of station had been reported on
6 May 1856 but nothing done, though a new goods
station was being built and new passenger station planned
on site of existing goods sidings *(Rtn)* – ever done?
(Ironically accident unconnected with state of station –
child had stepped off platform to see oncoming train.)

PORT ISAAC ROAD [LSW] op 1 June 1895 *(Cornish
& D P 8th)*; clo 3 October 1966 *(Cornish & DP 8th)*.

PORT MEADOW [LNW]
op 20 August 1906 *(LNW Cl)* as SUMMERTOWN;
see 1905⋆⋆ (a); renamed 1 January 1907 *(Cl)*;
clo 1 January 1917 *(T 22 December 1916)*;
reop 5 May 1919 *(RCH)*; clo 25 October 1926 *(Cl)*.

PORT MEIRION – see BOSTON LODGE.

PORT OF MENTEITH [NB]
op 26 May 1856⋆⋆ as CARDROSS; became
P OF MONTEITH 1858 tt, spelling altered 1880 tt *(Cl)*;
clo 1 October 1934 *(RM October)*.

PORT SUNLIGHT [Birkenhead]:
used for Royal Visit 25 March 1914 *(U)*; op for workmen
4 May 1914 (as P S PLATFORM) *(LNW/GW Officers
18th)*; op to public as station 9 May 1927 *(hbl July)*;
still open. HALT on ticket *(JB)* – pre-public days?

PORT TALBOT
PT CENTRAL [PT] op 14 February 1898 *(GW)*;
clo 11 September 1933 *(Cl)*.
PT DOCKS [RSB] first in *Brad* October 1891;
original terminus, clo when line extended to Swansea,
14 March 1895 *(Cl)*; workmen used to 1984 *(U)*.
PT PARKWAY [GW] op 19 June 1850⋆⋆ as PT;
renamed PT & ABERAVON 5 June 1897 *(RCG)*,
PT GENERAL 1 July 1924 *(GW circular 18 June)*,
PT 7 September 1964 tt supplement,
PT P 3 December 1984 *(BLN 764)*; still open.
OLD DOCK HALT (non-tt) [PT]; from engineer's
reports *(RAIL 1057/1528)*: temporary platform for
D.R. David's Tinplate Works to be erected by railway
company here, with platforms near **WATER STREET
BRIDGE** (Newlands) and **CRIBBWR FAWR** to be
erected by Baldwin's; work begun by 15 March 1918;
workmen's service started by 10 May 1918.
Also see ABERAVON.

PORT VICTORIA [SE]
op 11 September 1882 *(SE)*; clo 11 June 1951 *(Cl)*,
to allow oil terminal to be expanded.

PORTBURY [GW]
PORTBURY op 18 April 1867 *(co n Bristol T 17th)*;
clo 30 April 1962 *(RM June)*.
P SHIPYARD op 16 September 1918 *(wtt supp)*;
clo 26 March 1923 *(Bristol notice)*; {Portbury – Pill}.

PORTCHESTER [LSW] op 1 September 1848
(SR; Hants Adv 2nd- line); PORCHESTER until
11 January 1899 *(hbl 26th)*; still open.

PORTERFIELD – see RENFREW.

PORTEROCHNEY – see PITCROCKNIE.

PORTESHAM [GW] op 9 November 1885
(W Gaz 13th); clo 1 December 1952 *(W Gaz 5th)*.

PORTESSIE
PORTESSIE [GNS] op 1 May 1886 *(GNS)*;
clo 6 May 1968 *(RM July)*.
PORTESSIE [High] op 1 August 1884 *(High)*;
clo 9 August 1915 *(Cl)*; {shown *IA*}.

PORTGORDON [GNS] op 1 May 1886 *(GNS)*;
clo 6 May 1968 *(RM July)*.
PORT GORDON until 1924/5 *(Brad)* and LNE ticket
thus *(JB)*; one word LNE tt 1933.

PORTH [TV] op 4 February 1861 *(hbl, undated)*;
original station north of later junction with Maerdy
branch; re-sited 11 chains south at junction 1 July 1876
(RAC); still open.

PORTHCAWL
For possible early service see 1828 A⋆⋆.
PORTHCAWL [GW] op 1 August 1865 *(GW)*;
re-sited to south 6 March 1916 *(GW Mag April)*;
clo 9 September 1963 *(RM October)*.

PORTHCAWL GOLFERS – see NOTTAGE.

PORTHMADOG {map 76}.
PORTHMADOG [Cam] op 2 September 1867 *(Cam;
Carnarvon co ½ T 10 October- line)*; PORTMADOC
until 5 May 1975 *(RM July)*; still open.

Narrow gauge
[Festiniog] op to PORTMADOC 6 January 1865
(D&C 11) ⋆; PORT MADOC in March 1865 tt
Carnarvon & Denbigh Herald.
[WH] op 1 June 1923, to station south of crossing with
[Cam/GW] line, sited for easy transfer to GW and line
opened between them *(Cambrian News 8 June 1923)*;
[Festiniog] now P OLD, [WH] P NEW. Some trains ran
through, though those shown calling at Old would have
required reversal or some sort of added facility on
through line.
February 1929 *Brad*: P HIGH STREET HALT
[Festiniog] added, with note that trains between P and
Blaenau would terminate there – it was just on Festiniog's
side of junction between lines.
8 July 1929: WH cut back to platform north of line (to
avoid crossing it); according to *NGSC II, p.37* some
Festiniog trains continued to run as far as possible (to
original P New?) to meet passengers who had to walk
across GW line from second New but this soon ceased.
22 September 1930 *Brad*: before/with this tt P OLD
became P HARBOUR. Also last appearance of
P HIGH STREET; however, perhaps later use

– *WHH 9* refers to this as opened by July 1934, which could represent non-tt reopening.
28 September 1936: P NEW clo.
18 September 1939**: P HARBOUR clo.
See 1922 July 31** and 1923 January 1**; maps *Fest p.197, NGSC p.20 and 22* and text generally.
* = passengers carried free and at own risk for some months previously; free use on 5th after formal opening *(Festiniog)*.

PORTHYWAEN [Cam] op 6 January 1904 *(RCG)*; clo 15 January 1951 *(Cl)* – see 1951**.

PORTISHEAD
PORTISHEAD [GW] op 18 April 1867 *(co n Bristol T 17th)*; re-sited just short 4 January 1954, after first train of that day had used old station *(RM February)*; clo 7 September 1964 *(W D Press 7th)*.
PORTISHEAD [WCP] op 7 August 1907 *(Bristol T 8th)*; clo 20 May 1940 *(Bridgwater Merc 22nd)*.
Ticket for P HIGH STREET *(JB)*.
P SOUTH [WCP] details as P [WCP], above.

PORTKNOCKIE [GNS]
op 1 May 1886 *(GNS)*; clo 6 May 1968 *(RM July)*.

PORTLAND [GW/LSW]; (see *Portland*)
PORTLAND op 16 October 1865 *(W Gaz 13th)*; until Melcombe Regis opened (30 May 1909), was served from Weymouth, with reversal; temporary platform provided 1 September 1902 for Easton trains *(MT6/1634)*; permanent provided in stages – down platform 2 January 1905, up 7 May 1905, for extension to Easton; clo 3 March 1952 *(RM March)*; later British naval use *(RM July 1954)*, specials for visit of U.S. warships early July 1955 *(RM October)*.
P DOCKYARD (non-tt): naval base; op 3 March 1952; clo ?; {branch from Portland} *(U)*.
P HOSPITAL (non-tt): used about 1925 to 1965 *(U)*.
Ticket *(JB)* just as HOSPITAL HALT *(JB)*.
PORTLAND ROAD
– see GREAT PORTLAND STREET.

PORTLETHEN
PORTLETHEN (a) [Cal] op 1 February 1850 *(Cal)*; clo 11 June 1956 *(RM April)*.
PORTLETHEN (b) op 17 May 1985 *(BLN 520)*; still open.
PORTMADOC – see PORTHMADOG.
PORTOBELLO Edinburgh. {maps 18, 19}.
PORTOBELLO (a): [Ed & Dalk; NB] see 1831 A**; first tt evidence March 1843 *(Tuck)*; presumably clo July 1847 for main service but continued to be used for Leith service, which was last in tt July 1856. Once line had been improved, service reopened from (b).
PORTOBELLO (b) [NB] op 22 June 1846 *(Ed & Dalk; co n T 23 June- line)*; clo 7 September 1964 *(Cl)*.
PORTOBELLO near Wolverhampton [LNW]
op 1 October 1854 *(W Mid)*; clo 1 January 1873 (Wednesday) *(Cl)*. Hb: PORTO BELLO until 1872.
PORTON [LSW] op 1 May 1857 *(W Fly P 5th- line)*; clo 9 September 1968 *(RM September)*.

PORTPATRICK [PPW Jt]
PORTPATRICK op 28 August 1862 *(co n, Ewart Library)*; clo 6 February 1950 *(RM March)*.
PORT PATRICK *(hb)*, 1877 only.
P HARBOUR (non-tt): boat trains; op 11 September 1868; clo November 1868; {beyond Portpatrick} *(U)*.

PORTREUDDYN [WH] (ng) op 1 June 1923 *(NGSC 2)*; see 1922 July 31**; alias PONTREUDDYN; clo 28 September 1936 *(Cl)*.

PORTSKEWETT [GW]
PORTSKEWET until 1880/1 *(Brad)*, hb 1908a.
PORTSKEWETT op 19 June 1850 *(co n Wales)*; re-sited 36 chains east 1 October 1863 ready to serve as junction station; clo 2 November 1964 *(Cl)*. P JUNCTION 1863/4 to 1886/7 *(Brad)*; ticket thus *(JB)*.
P PIER op 1 January 1864 *(GW)* (op had been planned for 8 September 1863, with start of ferry to New Passage but difficulty with establishing foundations for station meant delay – passengers taken by road to main station). Clo when pier destroyed by fire 23 May 1881; while it was closed, passengers taken from Cardiff to Bristol via Severn Bridge and reversal at Berkeley Road – and charged the extra mileage in their fares; reop 16 June 1881 *(RAIL 1005/282)*; clo 1 December 1886 (Wednesday) *(Cl)* – opening of Severn Tunnel.

PORTSLADE [LBSC]
PORTSLADE (a) op 12 May 1840**; last in tt July 1847.
PORTSLADE (b) first in *Brad* October 1857; probably slightly east of earlier; rebuilt, perhaps same site, 1881/2; was P & WEST HOVE March 1927 *(hbl April)* to 12 May 1980 tt *(Cl)*; still open.
PORTSMOUTH near Burnley [LY]: line op 12 November 1849**, nd, September 1851; clo 7 July 1958 *(LNW Record)*.

PORTSMOUTH [LSW/LBSC]
P & SOUTHSEA op 14 June 1847 *(Salisbury 19th)*; still open. Variously P, P TOWN, P TOWN & S – joint owners differed *(JS)*; settled as P & S 1 December 1921 *(RCG)*;
P HARBOUR op 2 October 1876 *(Hants Teleg 4th)*; still open.

Non-tt
CLARENCE PIER [Landport & Southsea Tramway]: *LSW II, p.112* says trial run 8 May 1865 for planned opening 15th. Things perhaps not to plan. Earliest mention seen is in notice issued by LSW for services to Isle of Wight *(T 17 June 1865)*, where it says tramway between Portsmouth and Southsea Pier 'is now open'. No mention in notice for June service *(T 30, 31 May)* and normally these notices only appeared at start of month. Appeared briefly in *Brad* (added after September 1873, by/with January 1875, in LBSC tables) as Portsmouth station and Southsea Tramway for boats to Ryde. Still shown on Junction Diagram 1928, but only local use after Harbour station opened – still present *Brad* September 1876, omitted by December 1876.
PORTSMOUTH & GOSPORT TRAMWAY & FLOATING BRIDGE. In *Brad* same dates as above item, apparently owned by LBSC; 15 minute interval service Portsmouth to Gosport. Other detail unknown; arrangement between LBSC and local tramway?
P DOCKYARD (non-tt): branch from original terminus into use 15 March 1857 *(T 18th)*, use exclusively for government; clear from paper that intention from outset was to use when appropriate for moving troops. Out of use ? UNICORN GATE in 1920s *(U)*; {ran north of South Jetty line}.

P DOCKYARD SOUTH RAILWAY JETTY (non-tt):
troop and royal trains; op 15 January 1878 *(U)*;
put out of use when access pier damaged by enemy
action during WW2 – possibly during heavy raid of
3 May 1941 (T. Cooper); alias WATERING ISLAND
JETTY; {branch from Harbour}.

ROYAL NAVY BARRACKS PLATFORM: (non-tt);
dates unknown but existence established on post-closure
railtour (22 September 1973), about 33 chains from
P&S HL, on branch to Dockyard (T. Cooper).

P RACECOURSE – see FARLINGTON.

PORTSMOUTH ARMS [LSW]
first in *Brad* September 1855, first in tt *Trewman*
20 September 1855*; aot request; still open.
* = letter (25 July 1854) from engineer to BoT – do not intend
to open for public traffic at present. *Brad* premature or *Trewman*
behind events?

PORTSOY [GNS]
op 30 July 1859**; re-sited when line extended 1 April
1884 *(Cl)*; clo 6 May 1968 *(RM July)*.

PORTSWOOD
op 1 May 1861* *(SR)*; clo 5 March 1866, replaced by
St Denys about ¼ mile south (B. Moody, *Southampton's
Railways*, Waterfront, Poole, 1992).
* = earlier ticket platform here (company agreed to provide
this 16 September 1858); *LSW* implies this was available as
stop to passengers on local trains.

PORTWOOD – see under STOCKPORT.

POSSIL
POSSIL [Cal] op to workmen 1 February 1897 *(U)*,
to public 1 October 1897 *(RCG)* *; clo 1 May 1908
(Friday) *(RCG)*; reop 8 January 1934 *(Cl)*;
clo 5 October 1964 *(RM November)*; {goods *IA*}.
* = listed as new opening in *Brad* October 1897 but did not
appear in body of book until May 1898 – result of origin as
workmen's station?.

POSSILPARK [NB] first in *Brad* February 1885*;
clo 1 January 1917 *(RCH)*; Singer workmen used to
last train Friday or Saturday 28 or 29 February 1964
(U, supported by selection of wtts 1939–63).
* = according to *MT6/411/7* planned opening was 1 February
but that a Sunday and no Sunday service here so presumably
op 2nd.

POSSILPARK & PARKHOUSE op 3 December 1993
(BLN 725); other side of Balmore Road from old NB
station; still open.

POST OFFICE – see ST PAULS.

POSTLAND [GN/GE] op 2 September 1867* *(GN)*
as CROWLAND; renamed 1 December 1871
(Cl; RCG ref January 1912); clo 11 September 1961
(RM September).
* = according to GN minutes op 1st but that a Sunday and no
Sunday service.

POTTER HEIGHAM [MGN]
POTTER HEIGHAM op 17 January 1880 *(MGN;
T 21st- line)*; clo 2 March 1959 *(T 2nd)*.
P H BRIDGE: see 17 July 1933**; HALT;
{Potter Heigham – Martham}.

POTTERHANWORTH [GN/GE] op 1 August 1882
(GN/GE); clo 2 May 1955 *(RM June)*. Always
POTTER HANWORTH in *hb* but not seen thus *Brad*.

POTTERHILL – see under PAISLEY.

POTTERS BAR [GN]
op 7 August 1850 *(T 6th & 8th)* as P B & SOUTH
MIMMS; & S M dropped 1855 *(L)*, back 1 May 1923
(Cl), dropped again 18 March 1971 *(Cl)*; still open.

POTTERY SIDING [GW] (non-tt):
workmen; in use 1917; {Highbridge – Dunball} *(U)*.

POTTO [NE]
op 3 March 1857**; clo 14 June 1954 *(Cl)*.

POTTON
POTTON [Sandy & Potton] terminus on Biggleswade
Road op 9 November 1857**; clo December 1861 *(Cl)*.
POTTON main line station [LNW] op 7 July 1862
(co n T 7th- line); clo 1 January 1968 *(RM January)*.

POULTON LANE – see MORECAMBE [Mid].

POULTON-le-Fylde [PW]
P CURVE op 1 February 1909 *(LNW Cl)*; see 1905**
(a,b); clo 1 December 1952 *(RM January 1953)*.
P-LE-FYLDE op 16 July 1840 *(co n T 13 July)*;
re-sited on deviation 29 March 1896 *(Cl)*;
-le-F added May 1957 *(P. Rowledge)*; still open.
Was P JUNCTION 1856/7 to 1882/3 *(Brad)*.

POULTON-LE-SANDS
– see BARE LANE; MORECAMBE.

POWDERHALL [NB]
op 22 April 1895 *(RCG)*; clo 1 January 1917 *(RCH)*.

POWERSTOCK [GW]
op 12 November 1857 *(co n Bridport)*; clo 5 May 1975
(letter, *RM July)*. Spelling as above at opening in
Bridport but *GW ac, Brad, GW co tt* had POORSTOCK;
Brad changed 1860, GW co tt about same time.

POWFOOT [LMS] (non-tt): ICI explosives factory
workers; op 18 or 19 May 1941; added *hb* 1944a as
HALT; clo ?; {Annan – Cummertrees} *(WW II)*.

POYLE [GW]; {Staines Branch}
POYLE op 1 June 1927 *(L)* as STANWELL MOOR & P;
by August 1927 P for S M *(Brad)* and thus GW co tt
1932; HALT; clo 29 March 1965 *(RM April)*.
Until 1928/9 *Brad* kept to old name in Sunday table,
using new for weekdays.
P ESTATE op 4 January 1954 *(Rly Gaz 1st)*; HALT;
clo 29 March 1965 *(RM April)*. Ticket *(JB)* has
P ESTATES in one place, P ESTATE another.

POYNTON [LNW]
P MIDWAY op 24 November 1845** (just north of
Poynton Brook, at end of present-day Lostock Road
– map evidence, E. Bredee); MIDWAY added 1883
(Brad); replaced north by >
POYNTON op 1 August 1887 *(LNW Officers 29688)*,
about ¾ mile north; still open. Still in *Brad* as P MIDWAY
to 1894, but not so shown *hb* 1890.
Also see HIGHER POYNTON.

PRAED STREET – see PADDINGTON.

PRAZE [GW] op 9 May 1887 *(Cornish Tel 12th)*;
clo 5 November 1962 *(W Briton 8th)*.

PREES [LNW] op 1 September 1858**; still open.

PREESALL [KE] op 30 July 1908 *(RCG; T 31st- line)*;
clo 31 March 1930 *(Cl)*.

PRESCOT [LNW] op 1 January 1872 *(LNW Officers
6927, 7546; in tt Wigan Observer 5th)*; still open.

PRESCOTT SIDING [CMDP]
op 21 November 1908**; clo 26 September 1938
(*T 9 August*); {Cleobury Town – Stottesdon}.
P S HALT in *Brad* until about 1916; then HALT
omitted body but still in index.

PRESGWYN [GW]
op 14 October 1848 (*Shrewsbury 13th*); last two months
in tt, February and March 1855, was Wednesdays only.
Site later used for Weston Rhyn, which see.

PRESTATYN [LNW] op 1 May 1848 (*D&C 11;
co n T 2nd- line*); re-sited to west 28 February 1897 (*Cl*);
still open. Dyserth branch trains reversed in siding to
reach/leave branch.

PRESTBURY [LNW]
op 24 November 1845**; still open.

PRESTEIGN [GW] op 10 September 1875 (*Brad Sh*);
clo 5 February 1951 (*RM October*) – see 1951**.
(Final 'E' added after passenger closure).

PRESTHOPE [GW] op 16 December 1867 (*Wenlock*);
clo 31 December 1951 (*T 31st*).

PRESTON {map 44}
Main line.
Opened from south to **PRESTON** [NU] 31 October
1838 (*co n Manch G 27th*); still open. Early references
to PENNY STREET (*LPJ*); later FISHERGATE
(JOINT); LY co tt 1899 had P F for Longridge service,
P for rest. LNW, LMS co tts seen: just P.
Sometimes P regarded as two adjoining stations:
Hb 1904 to 1956 shows P BUTLER STREET as a
separate LY/LMS station, 'P', 'near Fishergate';
RCH Junction Diagrams show P B S as goods only.
Preston Guardian of 30 August 1902 seemed to regard
it as a station on its own; in its description of the
arrangements for Guild Week it mentioned the Central
Station and Butler Street, though the latter somewhat
ambiguously. It said that had been found necessary to
call into play for next week 'the excellent platforms at
the L&Y goods station. The ordinary service of trains
will start from the bay sidings as usual, but the specials
will be dealt with either on the main platforms or in the
goods yard. The passengers carried into the latter will
leave by the entrance leading into Corporation-street';
also see 'other', below.
Line from north [LPJ] op 26 June 1840 (*Lancaster 27th*)
to main station, above. Inter-company dispute over
charges for use of line between stations caused LPJ,
from 1 August 1842, to stop at **DOCK STREET**, at
boundary of LPJ line, north of main station. There was
no station at Dock Street; trains carried on to main
station, but any passengers staying on had to pay toll so
many alighted at Dock Street and walked to main (*LPJ*).
Ultimate intention of LPJ was to switch to >
MAXWELL HOUSE [Bolton & Preston] station,
but B & P did not open it, running through main station
on the way, until its line was complete, 22 June 1843
(*D&C 10*); even then it remained a terminus, not
directly accessible from north >
LPJ position weakened when B & P joined LNW so
dispute settled; M H clo and D S fell out of use,
11 February 1844 (Sunday) – last day? All involved
used main station. Later excursion use of M H (*U*).

Preston & Wyre
P MAUDLANDS (a) op 16 July 1840 (*co n T 13th*);
clo 11 February 1844 (*Cl*) – service diverted to main
(in practice most trains already using it); later excur (*U*).
Preston & Longridge
Opened from **P DEEPDALE STREET** 2 May 1840**;
replaced by >
P MAUDLAND BRIDGE op 1 November 1856
(*D&C 10*); clo 1 June 1885 (*Cl*) – service diverted to main.
Non-tt: one train daily (first and second class) was at
one time noted to leave from DEEPDALE GOODS.
This was first shown in *Brad* October 1867;
last included October 1872; in LNW co tt added by
March 1868, removed by January 1874.
Intermediate station on line was P DEEPDALE,
first in *Brad* July 1857; clo 2 June 1930 (*LNW Record*).
P D in *Brad* but just D LY co tt 1899.
West Lancashire
PRESTON [W Lancs] op 4 September 1882 for Guild
Week, full service 16 September 1882 (*LY; Southport Vis
5th*); clo 16 July 1900 (*Cl*); reop 1 to 6 September
(inclusive) 1902 for Guild Week (*Preston Guard 30
August*); later excur (*U*). Name FISHERGATE HILL
seems to have been popularly used, though officially
not applied until later, when goods only.
Other
P MAUDLANDS (b) used 9 and 10 March 1991;
temporary station during bridge repairs (*BLN 654*).
For 1882 Guild Week LNW excursions used goods
station in CHARLES STREET and East Lancs that
in BUTLER STREET; cattle landing-stage also used
(Oxheys?) (*Away p.173*).
PRESTON near Torquay [GW] op 24 July 1911 (*RCG*);
PLATFORM; summers only; clo 21 September 1914 (*Cl*).
PRESTON BROOK [LNW]
op 4 July 1837 (*co n GJ*); clo 1 March 1948 (*RM May*);
railwaymen used to April 1952 (*Cl*).
PRESTON JUNCTION – see EAGLESCLIFFE;
LOWTON; TODD LANE JUNCTION.
PRESTON PARK Brighton [LBSC]:
op 1 November 1869 (*LBSC*); PARK added 1 July 1897
(*SR; RCG ref July*); still open.
PRESTON ROAD near Liverpool – see RICE LANE.
PRESTON ROAD London [Met] op 21 May 1908 (*L*);
re-sited west of road overbridge, up side into use
22 November 1931, down 3 January 1932 (*L*); still open.
Opened as P R for UXENDON and KENTON;
renamed P R for U 1 July 1923 (*hbl 12th*), P R 1923/4
(*Brad*); HALT in body of *Brad* until 1911 (index later).
PRESTON WEST END GATE [Hull & Holderness]:
only in *Brad* October 1854; Tuesdays only; perhaps
market service not normally included slipped in this
month by mistake, so that actual use spanned longer
period; {Marfleet – Hedon}.
PRESTONPANS [NB]
op 22 June 1846 (*co n T 23rd- line*) as TRANENT;
renamed 1 July 1858 (*RCG*); still open. P for T in *Brad*
1900 but not thus NB co tt. *Reid* 1904: P (T).
PRESTWICH
P (a) [LY] op 1 September 1879 (*Manchester 2nd*);
clo 17 August 1991 (*BLN 660*) for conversion to >

P (b) [Manch] op 6 April 1992 *(BLN 681)*; still open.

PRESTWICK
P TOWN [GSW] op 5 August 1839 *(co ½ 1110/149- line)*;
Clo 10 October 1839 (Thursday) *(Cl)*; back in tt June
1841; clo 29 November 1841★ *(Cl)*; trains again March
1846 tt; TOWN added 28 May 1995 tt *(AB Chron)*;
still open.
★ = early evidence used is from secondary sources; primary
seen not fully in agreement, perhaps tt inertia. Earliest seen is
fare table *Brad*: from about July 1841 to December 1844 (or a
little later) this included fare for 'Monkton and P, presumably
two with same fare – P left in error or did it continue in use
longer than sources previously used said? not in *Murray*
September 1844 which looks like full table. When an orthodox
table was first provided early 1845 P was not included.
P INTERNATIONAL AIRPORT op 5 September 1994
(BLN 737); still open.

PRICKWILLOW [EC]
op 19 January 1850 as a flag station *(Cambridge Chronicle
19th-* Tony Kirby), though not in *Brad* until June 1850;
last in tt October 1850; {Ely – Burnt Fen}.

PRIESTFIELD [GW]
op 5 July 1854 for Wolverhampton to Dudley service and
2 July 1855 for Wolverhampton to Birmingham service;
in both cases op after line – *(Wolverhampton)*;
clo 6 March 1972 *(RM April)*.

PRIESTHILL & DARNLEY
op 23 April 1990 *(BLN 632)*; still open.

PRIMROSE HILL {map 101}
PRIMROSE HILL [NL] op 5 May 1855 *(L)* as
HAMPSTEAD ROAD, replacing earlier station of that
name; renamed CHALK FARM 1862. At first it was
terminus of NL services; passengers walking to LNW
CAMDEN / CHALK FARM to continue journeys on
LNW. Clo 1 January 1917, reop 10 July 1922 *(T 30 June)*;
renamed P H 1950. Closed prematurely by flooding
September 1992 (last train eastbound 18th, westbound
22nd) *(Rly Obs December)*.
Also see CHALK FARM; HAMPSTEAD ROAD.
PRINCE OF WALES [RHD] (ng) trains first shown
November 1927 (see 1927 July 16★★); last in tt January
1928; back in tt December 1929; last in tt June 1930.
PRINCE REGENT [Dock]
op 28 March 1994★★; still open.
PRINCES DOCK [LO] op 6 March 1893★★;
clo 13 March 1941 (Thursday) by enemy action *(Cl)*.

PRINCES END
PRINCES END [LNW] op 14 September 1863 *(LNW
Officers)*; clo 1 November 1890 (Saturday), reop 1 July
1895 *(Cl)*; clo 1 January 1916 (Saturday) *(Cl)*;
{Tipton – Wednesbury}.
P E & COSELEY [GW] first in *Brad* December 1856;
& C added 1936; clo 30 July 1962 *(RM September)*.

PRINCES RISBOROUGH
PRINCES RISBOROUGH [GW/GC] station op
1 August 1862 *(GW ac)*; resiting to south, completed
2 April 1906, took about two years *(RM April)*; still open.
PRINCES RISBOROUGH [Watlington & Princes
Risborough] temporary terminus op 15 August 1872
(GW); clo 1883/4, service diverted to main *(Cl)*.
PRINCES STREET – see under EDINBURGH.

PRINCETOWN [GW] op 11 August 1883 *(Tavistock
17th)*; clo 5 March 1956 *(T 5th)*.
PRIORY – see CONISHEAD.
PRIORY HALT [GE] (non-tt):
op 1 January 1920; built by GE but Admiralty paid for it
– Depot had own housing estate nearby *(GE Journal
Special No. 2, September 1979)*; clo 1 February 1965 *(U)*;
in hb 1938 and 1956 'for use of Admiralty employees
only'; {Bradfield – Wrabness}.
PRITCHARD SIDING [GW] (non-tt):
workmen; in use 1920;
{Briton Ferry Road – Swansea East Dock} *(U)*.
PRITTLEWELL [GE]
op 1 October 1889 *(co notice* – at back of GE co tt for
November 1889 at Newton Abbot*)*; still open.
PRIVETT near Portsmouth – see FORT GOMER.
PRIVETT near Winchester [LSW]
op 1 June 1903 *(Hants Teleg 5th)*; clo 7 February 1955
(Hants Chron 12th).
PROBUS & LADOCK [GW] op 1 February 1908
(RCG); PLATFORM; clo 2 December 1957 *(Cl)*.
PROSPECT HILL [BT]:
line op 28 August 1841 *(NE)*, nd, 1 October 1847
(co tt BT); clo 27 June 1864 *(Cl)*; {map 26}.
PRUDHOE [NE] op 10 March 1835★★; still open.
Scott 1837: P or OVINGHAM. Became P for O 1936/7
(Brad); 'for O' dropped 6 May 1974 *(BR notice)*;
just P in hb.
PUDDING MILL LANE [Dock] op 15 January 1996
(RM April – planned 2nd but delay*)*; still open.
PUDSEY [GN]
P GREENSIDE op 1 April 1878 *(GN)*; clo 15 June
1964 *(Cl)*.
P LOWTOWN: trains first shown in tt July 1878;
clo 15 June 1964 *(Cl)*. Hb always P LOW TOWN.
Also see NEW PUDSEY.
PULBOROUGH [LBSC] op 10 October 1859★★;
still open. P for STORRINGTON in *Brad*? to 1955.
PULFORD [GW] op 4 November 1846★★;
trains last shown January 1855 *Brad*; {Rossett – Saltney}.
At first P & DODLESTON. *Brad* dropped & D 1848,
Topham 1849/50. Local press tts suggest at least one
period closed – no *Brad* support.
PULHAM [GE]
P MARKET op 1 December 1855 *(EC- line)* as
P ST MAGDALENE; renamed 1856 tt *(Cl)*; aot request;
see 1860 November 2★★; clo 5 January 1953 *(T 5th)*.
P ST MARY op 1 December 1855 *(EC- line)*;
aot request; see 1860 November 2★★;
P MARY 1856 tt to 1894 tt *(Cl)* and thus GE co tt 1882;
clo 5 January 1953 *(T 5th)*.
PULLABROOK [GW] op 1 June 1931 *(Cl 29)*;
as HAWKMOOR; renamed 13 June 1955 *(Cl)*; HALT;
clo 2 March 1959 *(Express & E 2nd)*; {Lustleigh – Bovey}.
PUNCHESTON [GW]
op 11 April 1895 *(GW- line)*; clo 8 January 1917
(co n GW book), reop 14 November 1921 *(RCG)*;
clo 25 October 1937★★. Ticket [N Pembroke &
Fishguard] for PUNCHESTOWN *(JB)*.
PURFLEET [LTS]
PURFLEET op 13 April 1854 *(L;T 13th- line)*; still open.

P RIFLE RANGE: in use, non-tt, by July 1910,
though buildings not ready; used by ordinary trains and
specials terminating here; from 10 August 1914 any
train could be stopped at request of military; first in
Brad October 1921 (only now did War Office agree to
public use) *(LTS vol.2, p.115)*; HALT; clo 31 May 1948
(RM July). *Hb* 1912 included this but no facilities shown
– noted as for use of regular and territorial forces only;
hb 1923a limitation removed.

PURITON DEPOT/ROF – see HUNTSPILL OD.

PURLEY

PURLEY [LBSC] op 12 July 1841 as GODSTONE
ROAD (request) *(co n T 9th)*; clo 1 October 1847 (Friday)
(Cl); reop 5 August 1856 as G R CATERHAM
JUNCTION *(L)*; just C J later 1856 tt *(L; JS)*;
renamed P 1 October 1888 *(RCG)*; still open.

P DOWNS GOLF CLUB [SEC/LBSC] (non-tt): HALT;
op by 1914; clo by 1927; {Sanderstead – Riddlesdown}
(U). Proof of existence not entirely satisfactory *(S Halts)*.

P OAKS [LBSC] op 5 November 1899 *(L)*; still open.

PURTON [GW]
op 31 May 1841 *(GW; Wilts 3 June- line)*;
clo 2 November 1964 *(Cl)*.

PUTNEY

PUTNEY [LSW] op 27 July 1846 *(T 23rd)*; still open.

P BRIDGE [Dist] op 1 March 1880 *(L)* as
P B & FULHAM, just P B in *Brad*;
renamed P B & HURLINGHAM 1 September 1902
(RCG), P B 1938/9 *(Brad)*; still open.

Also see EAST PUTNEY.

PUXTON & WORLE [GW]
op 14 June 1841 *(Taunton 16th)* as BANWELL;
renamed W 3 August 1869 *(Cl)*, P 1 March 1884
(hbl 16 June), P & W 1 March 1922 *(hbl 27 April)*;
clo 6 April 1964 *(Cl)*.

PWLL GLAS [Van]: same as TREFEGLWYS.

PWLLHELI [Cam] op 10 October 1867* *(co n
Merioneth 12th)*; first station at Abererch Bridge, some
distance away; by 1880 extended to new station
(Lewis Lloyd, *Pwllheli, Port and Mart of Lleyn*, author,
1991) – no supporting evidence known;
re-sited 19 July 1909 *(RCG)*; still open.

Cam co tt 1904, GW co tt 1932: P for NEVIN and
thus *hb* 1908a to 1956 and *Brad* to 1949/50 (last aot
P for N and MORFA NEVIN).

* = see 1867 September 2** for earlier non-tt use.

PWLLHELI ROAD
For first service see 1829 B**.

PWLLHELI ROAD [Nantlle] (ng) op 11 August 1856;
clo 12 June 1865 *(G&S)*.
For service afterline reopened, converted to standard
gauge, see LLANWNDA.

PWLLYPANT [Rhy]
first in *Brad* May 1871; replaced by Llanbradach,
58 chains north, 1 March 1893 *(RCG)*; {map 92}.
Spelling as in *Brad*.

PYE BRIDGE [Mid]
op 1 December 1851 *(Mid)* – in *Brad* November 1851,
prematurely; P B for ALFRETON until May 1862
Brad (Mid); clo 2 January 1967 *(Cl)*.

PYE HILL & SOMERCOTES [GN]
op 24 March 1877 *(RCG)*; & S added 8 January 1906
(RCG); clo 7 January 1963 *(RM February)*.
Hb 1935a said had become P H & S for PYE BRIDGE.

PYLE [first two eventually GW]
PYLE op by [South Wales] 19 June 1850**; re-sited
17 chains east and amalgamed with Llynvi & Ogmore
station 13 November 1876 *(Cl)* >

PYLE op by [Llynvi & Ogmore] 1 August 1865 *(GW)* >
Porthcawl section (ex-L&O) clo 9 September 1963;
main line part clo 2 November 1964 *(Cl)*.

PYLE op 27 June 1994 *(BLN 735)*; about ½ mile west
of station closed 1964; still open.

PYLLE [SD Jt]
op 3 February 1862**; became HALT 4 November
1957; clo 7 March 1966 *(Shepton 11th)*.
P for SHEPTON MALLET in opening tt *Shepton*.

QUAINTON ROAD

QUAINTON ROAD [Met/GC] op 23 September 1868 by Aylesbury & Buckingham, later part of GC *(L)*; see 27 March 1874★★; re-sited to south 1896; clo 4 March 1963 *(RM March)*. Met use 1 July 1891★ to 4 July 1936 and, limited service, 5 April 1943 to 31 May 1948. Used Saturdays in 1980's for 'Chiltern Shopper' specials: certainly used 24 November, 1, 8 and 15 December 1984; 16 November and 14 December 1985; 22 November, 6 and 13 December 1986 (BR handbills, which usually called it Qainton Road).

★ = *Ug* says 30 Nov. 1896 but trains shown *Brad* by Jan. 1894.

QUAINTON ROAD [Wotton] op January 1872 (see 1871★★); just Q in *Brad* – and stayed thus to 1906/7 for service on this line though this station had closed 1896, service diverted to main station.

QUAKERS YARD

QUAKERS YARD [GW/TV] op 5 January 1858 *(RAIL 253/367)*; QY LL 1924 to 6 May 1968 tt *(offic)*; still open.
Q Y HL [GW] op 5 October 1864 *(T 8th- line)*; HL added 1924; clo 15 June 1964 *(RM August)*.
HL and LL officially added 1 July 1924 *(GW circular 18 June)*, but had gradually crept into use much earlier – in *hb* 1872, *Brad c.* 1900; previously, and erratically, had been QY JUNCTION there; [TV] ticket for last *(JB)*.

QUARRY SIDING [Talyllyn] – see 1950 October 6★★.

QUARTER [Cal]
QUARTER op 2 February 1863★★; Q ROAD until 1 May 1909 *(hbl 7 July)*; clo 1 October 1945 *(RM March; G&S)*.
Q JUNCTION: 1869 handbill tt reference; nothing else known; {Meikle Earnock – Quarter} *(Cl)*.

QUEDGELEY [Mid] (non-tt): PLATFORM; workmen; op 13 December 1915; last train 26 August 1920; on sidings just off main line – see *Mid*, and article *National Filling Factory No. 5, Gloucester*, B. Edwards, *Archive 58*; {Gloucester – Haresfield}.

QUEENBOROUGH [LCD]

QUEENBOROUGH op 19 July 1860 *(T 19th)*; still open.
Q PIER op 15 May 1876 *(co n T 25 April)*; destroyed by fire 19 July 1900, reop for daytime services 26 January 1901 *(SEC)*★; clo 1 November 1914 (Sunday), reop 27 December 1922; clo 1 March 1923 (Thursday) *(Cl)*.
★ = *T* 2 May 1904 carried SEC notice that from 3 May Flushing Night Mail service would be worked from here instead of Port Victoria.

QUEENS HEAD INN [Glyn] (ng): line op 1 April 1874 *(Glyn)*, nd, June 1877; clo 1 April 1886 (Thursday) *(Cl)*; {map 79}. See Dolywern for later replacement.

QUEENS PARK Glasgow [Cal]
op 1 March 1886 *(Cal)*; still open.

QUEENS PARK London: op by [LNW] 3 June 1879★★ as Q P WEST KILBURN *(L)*; [Bak] added 11 February 1915; LNW main line platforms clo 1 January 1917

(T 22 December 1916) but kept for emergency use and have had occasional service since – e.g. for British Empire Exhibition, for which see Wembley Stadium (a); W K dropped 1954 *(L)*; still open, ex-LNW new line platforms and Bak.

QUEENS ROAD [GC GI]
– see under IMMINGHAM.

QUEENS ROAD – see WALTHAMSTOW.

QUEENS ROAD [GE]: built between Hackney Downs and Clacton about 1894 but never provided with service.

QUEENS ROAD PECKHAM [LBSC]
op 13 August 1866 *(T 14th)* as P;
renamed 1 December 1866 *(L)*; still open.

QUEENSBURY near Halifax [GN] op 14 April 1879 *(RCG)* – in *Brad* before end of 1878 but first trains shown May 1879; improved triangular station op 1 January 1890 *(Cl)*; clo 23 May 1955★★.

QUEENSBURY London: op by [Bak] 16 December 1934 *(T 13th)*; transferred to [Bak] 20 November 1939, to [Jub] 1 May 1979; still open.

QUEENSFERRY [LNW] op 1 May 1848 *(D&C 11; co n T 2nd- line)*; clo 14 February 1966 *(RM April)*.
Usually QUEENS FERRY at first; thus in *Brad* until 1959 (though one word in index for a time in later 1940s) and most LNW (but one word in one table 1876 e.g.) and LMS tts seen but *hb* to one word 1877.

QUEENSTOWN ROAD BATTERSEA [LSW]
op 1 November 1877 *(T 2nd)*; still open. *Brad* was QUEENS R B at start (notes only, table Q R), later B added usually in index in tts but only erratically in body until present name adopted 12 May 1980 tt *(AB)*.
LSW co tt 1914: QUEENS ROAD B PARK.

QUEENSWAY [Cen]
op 30 July 1900 *(L; T 25th- line)* as QUEENS ROAD; renamed 1 September 1946 *(RM November)*; still open.

QUELLYN [NWNG] (ng) {map 76}
QUELLYN op 15 August 1877 *(NGSC 2)*; replaced about ¾ mile further on, when line extended, by >
Q LAKE op 1 June 1878 *(Cl)* as SNOWDON; renamed S RANGER 1881 tt, Q L 1893 *(Cl)*; clo 1 November 1916 *(G&S)*; reop 31 July 1922★★; clo 28 September 1936 *(Cl)*.

QUENIBOROUGH [LMS] (non-tt): perhaps temporary HALT op 11 April 1941 – but not confirmed *(WW II)*; permanent op 10 November 1941 *(Cl)*; served RAF base; clo about 1949 *(WW II)*; {Rearsby – Syston}.

QUINTON HILL [LNE] (non-tt): Second World War; munitions workers; no details known.

QUINTRELL DOWNS [GW] op 2 October 1911 *(Newquay 6th)*; PLATFORM until 1956 *(Cl)*; aot request; still open. Early often QUINTRELL, especially in local press and *hb* (until 1956), then usually QUINTREL until 2 June 2002 tt *(AB)*.

QUORN & WOODHOUSE [GC]
op 15 March 1899 *(GC; T 16th- line)*; clo 4 March 1963 *(RM March)*. See 2007 July 4★★.
Pre-passenger reference as Quorndon & W – apparently renamed from this 1 October 1898 *(hbl 27th)*.

QUY [GE] op 2 June 1884 *(GE- line)*; clo 18 June 1962 *(RM August)*.

RACKS [GSW] first in *Brad* July 1851, Wednesdays only; full use July 1864; clo 6 December 1965 *(RM January 1966)*.

RADCLIFFE near Manchester

RADCLIFFE (a) [LY] op 1 December 1879 *(Brad Sh 1880- line)*; R CENTRAL 11 September 1933 *(JS)* to 1971; clo 17 August 1991 for conversion to >

RADCLIFFE (b) [Manch] op 6 April 1992; still open.

R BLACK LANE [LY] first in *Brad* January 1849; R added 1 July 1933 *(Cl)*; clo 5 October 1970 *(Cl)*.

R BRIDGE [LY] op 28 September 1846 *(LY; Rtn PP-line)*; clo 7 July 1958 *(LNW Record)*; later excur *(U)*.

RADCLIFFE NOTTS [GN]:
op 15 July 1850 *(in op tt Henshaw)*; originally RATCLIFFE; became RADCLIFFE-ON-TRENT 1 January 1878 *(RCH)* – but 1871 tt *(Cl, JS)*, R 6 May 1974 *(BR notice)*, R N 1979/87 tt (index earlier); still open.

RADCLIVE op 13 August 1956 *(RM September)*; HALT; clo 2 January 1961 *(RM February)*; {Buckingham – Fulwell & Westbury}.

RADFORD near Nottingham:

RADFORD [Mid] op 2 October 1848 *(Mid; RAIL 1005/ 265- line)*; re-sited on deviation to west 10 September 1876 *(Mid)*; clo 12 October 1964 *(RM November)*. Near here BOBBERS MILL (non-tt) was used, perhaps once only, for steeplechase meeting *(race)*.

RADFORD & TIMSBURY [GW]
op 9 May 1910 *(W D Press 10th)*; HALT; clo 22 March 1915, reop 9 July 1923 *(Bristol notice S1153)*; clo 21 September 1925 *(Cl)*.

RADIPOLE [GW]
op 1 July 1905 *(Bristol NWR)*; HALT until 5 May 1969 *(GW Halts)*; last used 31 December 1983 (Saturday) *(RM March 1984)* – platform unsafe.

RADLETT [Mid] op 13 July 1868 *(T 14th)*; still open. Pre-passenger was ALDENHAM goods.

RADLEY [GW] op 8 September 1873 *(Cl)* as replacement for Abingdon Junction; still open.

RADNOR PARK – see under FOLKESTONE.

RADSTOCK

R NORTH [SD Jt] op 20 July 1874 *(Shepton 24th)*; NORTH added 26 September 1949 *(Cl)*; clo 7 March 1966 *(Shepton 11th)*.

R WEST [GW] op 3 September 1873 *(Bristol T 4th)*; WEST added 26 September 1949 *(Cl)*; clo 2 November 1959 *(Shepton 6th)*.

RADWAY GREEN & BARTHOMLEY [NS]
op 9 October 1848 *(co ½ T 3 February 1849- line)*; & B added 1909/10 *(Brad)* and by NS co tt October 1910; clo 7 November 1966 *(RM January 1967)*.

RADYR [TV] op 1 June 1883 *(S Wales 1st)*; still open.

RAFFORD [High] op 3 August 1863 *(High)*; clo 31 May 1865 (Wednesday) *(Cl)* – trains still shown in tt June (inertia?); {Forres – Dunphail}.

RAGLAN [GW]

R ROAD (at 20m 69ch) and **R FOOTPATH** (at 19m 53ch) op with line October 1857** >
R FOOTPATH was closer of pair to town but no road access; first month only LODGE FARM *(Brad)*; January 1859 note that all trains stop at Raglan Station (footpath only); last present (notes) September 1861 tt

(closed or just left to local knowledge?); present in wtt 1 February 1866 but not back in *Brad* until May 1866, when in body of table as R F. 14 March 1867 £60 authorised for station *(RAC)*, suggesting no earlier, or very primitive, provision; aot request; >
Both replaced by >

RAGLAN (19m 44ch) probably op 1 July 1876 (item in *GW ac*, dated 30 June, deals with ticketing arrangements for changeover; normal but not invariable practice for such notices to be issued day before change); clo 30 May 1955**.

RAGLAN ROAD CROSSING op 24 November 1930 *(co n dated 'November')*; HALT; same site as earlier R Road; clo 30 May 1955**.

RAINDALE – see end of 1835 B**.

RAINFORD

RAINFORD [LY/LNW] op 20 November 1848 *(LY; co n Manch G 18th- line)*; R JUNCTION 1857/9 *(Brad)* to 7 May 1973 *(Cl)*; still open. *Hb* treated as separate LY, LNW stations.

R VILLAGE [LNW] op 3 February 1858 *(Ormskirk 4th)*; VILLAGE added 1861; clo 18 June 1951 *(RM August)*.

RAINHAM ESSEX [LTS]
op 13 April 1854 *(L;T 13th- line)*; E added 12 May 1980 *(C/W)*; still open.

RAINHAM KENT [LCD] op 25 January 1858** as R & NEWINGTON; became R 1 August 1862 *(Cl)*; K added 12 May 1980 tt *(C/W)*; still open.

RAINHILL [LNW]:
line op 17 September 1830**, nd, 1 March 1831 co tt; still open. KENDRICKS CROSS GATE in 1831 tt and thus *Brad* 1839; KENDRICK CROSS *(Osborne's Guide)*; R by 1846 *(Brad)*.

RAINTON {map 41}

RAINTON (a) alias R MEADOWS [Durham Junction] op 9 March 1840 *(NE maps)*; sited so that passengers from Gateshead, Shields and Wearmouth could be transferred to road coaches for journey to Durham. This service has not been found in *Brad*, though it was in *Robinson* (versions for about August and October 1841 seen), included in Brandling Junction table. Logically it would have clo 15 April 1844, when line to Durham opened. Shown on *Bell* (1843) at 323478, it was served by a road which joined West Rainton's system at 319478; before first OS map of area, both station and road had disappeared.

RAINTON (b) [Newcastle & Darlington Junction] only appeared in tt August 1844, first time *Brad* included table for line. R now clearly through station. Likeliest answer is that it replaced (a), thus op 15 April 1844, clo before/at end of August 1844? – or was it tt error, someone assuming (a) would be replaced?

RAINTON (c) shown on OS maps mid 1850s between Hetton & Pittington (S. Bragg); according to *National*

Gazetteer, Virtue & Co, 1868, West Rainton 'is a station on the North-Eastern Railway, which is here joined by the Durham Junction'; probably survival of outdated information rather than reliable for 1860s.

RAINWORTH – see BLIDWORTH.

RAMCROFT COLLIERY [Mid] (non-tt): miners; op 16 September 1918; clo 3 October 1927; {branch from Palterton} *(Mid)*.

RAMPER [PW]: line op 16 July 1840**, nd, by about March 1841 *(Freeling)*; market use only, perhaps intermittent; last in tt April 1843; {at/near later Thornton-Cleveleys}. Co tts sometimes added ROAD.

RAMPSIDE [Fur] for op see 1846 August**; use, as R, intermittent early; last in *Brad* May 1851; back there December 1868 as CONCLE; reverted to R 1869; at one time its stop made no sense in tt – see PIEL; clo 6 July 1936 *(RM August)*.

RAMS LINE – see DERBY.

RAMSBOTTOM [LY] op 28 September 1846 *(LY; Rtn PP- line)*; clo 5 June 1972 *(RM August)*. R JUNCTION in *Brad* 1851/3 to 1879/80.

RAMSDEN DOCK – see BARROW.

RAMSEY

R EAST [GN/GE] op 16 September 1889 *(RCG)*; R HIGH STREET until 1 July 1923 *(hbl 12th)*; clo 22 September 1930 *(Cl)*; later excur *(U)*.

R NORTH [GN] op 22 July 1863 *(co n Ramsey)*; NORTH added 1 July 1923 *(hbl 12th)*; after 22 September 1930 tt, before with August 1931 tt, rail service reduced to one that ended about 10.30am; buses for rest of day. Thus to closure, 6 October 1947 *(RM January 1948)*.

RAMSGATE {map 131}

R HARBOUR [LCD] op 5 October 1863 *(T 5th)* as R; became R & ST LAWRENCE-ON-SEA 1871 tt *(Cl; JS)* – but no RCH support for this name, R H 1 June 1899 *(hbl 13 July – renamed from R)* >

R TOWN [SE] op 14 April 1846 *(co n T 14th)*; R JUNCTION 1851/2 to 1856/7 *(Brad)*; TOWN added 1 June 1899 *(hbl 13 July)* >
Both replaced by R [SR] op 2 July 1926 *(T 3rd)*; still open.

RAMSGILL [Nidd] op 12 September 1907 *(Nidd; Rtn- line)*; clo 1 January 1930 (Wednesday) *(Cl)*.

RAMSGREAVE & WILPSHIRE op 29 May 1994 *(RM June)*, one train on the Sunday, full service Monday 30th; about ¼ mile south of earlier Wilpshire; still open.

RANKINSTON [GSW] op 1 January 1884 *(GSW)*; clo 3 April 1950 *(Cl)*.

RANNOCH [NB] op 7 August 1894 *(T 7th)*; still open. R for KINLOCH-RANNOCH until 1979/87 tt.

RANSKILL

RANSKILL [GN] op 4 September 1849 *(T 4th)*; clo 6 October 1958 *(RM November)*.

R FACTORY / Royal Ordnance Factory [LNE] (non-tt): alias NO.38 FACTORY PLATFORM; workers' platform on up loop used August 1941 to May 1942; then triangular connection allowed trains into factory (B.W.L. Brooksbank, *The Route of the Flying Scotsman*,

Arcturus, 2002, p.93); services from Mansfield LMS continued beyond 10 January 1944 (accident report) *(GC Society Journal, Spring 2003, p.40)*; clo by June 1947 *(U)*; {branch from main station}.

RASKELF [NE] line op 31 March 1841**, nd, August 1841; clo 5 May 1958 *(RM June)*.

RATBY [Mid]; op 18 July 1832 *(Mid)* as R LANE; renamed by 26 April 1833 *(local press – Mid)*; see 1847 December**; re-sited west of level crossing 1873 *(Mid)*; clo 24 September 1928 *(Mid)*; {map 62}.

RATCH HILL [GNS] (non-tt): workmen; op about 1903 *(U)*; GNS wtt 1 July 1905 shows one stop each way at R H SIDING for Mr Fyfe's workmen; R H HALT 'P' 1938 hb; {Kintore – Kemnay}.

RATCLIFFE – see RADCLIFFE NOTTS.

RATHEN [GNS] op 24 April 1865 *(GNS)*; clo 4 October 1965 *(Rly Obs November)*.

RATHO [NB]

RATHO main line op 21 February 1842 *(co n T 19th)*; clo 18 June 1951 *(RM August)*. R JUNCTION 1851/2 to 1890 *(Brad)* and thus NB co tt 1858 but not *Cornwall* 1860.

RATHO (low level platform) op 1 March 1866 *(D&C 6- line)*; clo 22 September 1930 *(Cl)*.
Brad and hb did not provide separate entries – just R.

RATHVEN [High] op 1 August 1884 *(High)*; clo 9 August 1915 *(Cl)*; {in IA}.

RAUCEBY [GN] op 1 October 1881 *(GN)*; aot request; still open.

RAUNDS [Mid] op 1 March 1866 *(Mid; co n T 27 February- line)*; clo 15 June 1959 *(RM July)*.

RAVELRIG [Cal] op 4 April 1884; at first unadvertised, used mainly by Volunteers, served by Balerno branch and main line trains; poor patronage so reduced to one train each way per day along main line; first in *Brad* May 1889, Wednesdays only, when branch trains again stopped here *(Balerno)*; variously R JUNCTION, R PLATFORM (in IA as HALT), R J P; last in tt June 1920; reop, non-tt, 1927 for Dalmahoy Golf Club, about a mile away, only lasting a few years (D. Yuill, *True Line 71*) – in hb 1938 as HALT; clo January 1945 *hba* but inertia perhaps involved.

RAVEN SQUARE – see under WELSHPOOL.

RAVENGLASS

R for ESKDALE [Fur] op 19 July 1849**; still open. 'For E' dropped 6 May 1974 *(BR notice)*; added again 1987/1993 tt.

RAVENGLASS [Raven] (ng) op 20 November 1876 *(co annual report T 26 March 1877)*; clo 1 December 1908**; reop 28 August 1915 *(Raven)*; see 1960**.

RAVENSBOURNE [LCD] op 1 July 1892 *(L)*; still open.

RAVENSCAR [NE] op 16 July 1885 *(T 16th)* as PEAK; clo 6 March 1895 (Wednesday) owing to lack of house for station master, reop 1 April 1896 *(Cl)*; renamed 1 October 1897 *(RCG)*; clo 8 March 1965 *(T 19 January)*.

RAVENSCOURT PARK op by [LSW] 1 April 1873 *(L)* as SHAFTESBURY ROAD; [Dist] added 1 June 1877; renamed 1 March 1888 *(Cl)*; [Met] use 1 October

1877 to 1 January 1907; LSW platforms clo 5 June 1916 *(RM July)*; Dist still uses.

RAVENSCRAIG

RAVENSCRAIG [Cal] op 15 May 1865 *(co n True Line 68)*; clo 1 January 1917 *(RM February)*; reop 2 June 1919 *(RCH)*; clo 1 February 1944 (Tuesday) *(Cl)*.*

R HALT [LMS] (non-tt): op 6 October 1941 *(WW II)*. Clo ?

* = R HALT added *hb* 1944a, between Upper Greenock and Wemyss Bay; at same time, section of *hba* dealing with closures showed public R closed ('delete P'). Thus possibilities are: original R demoted to non-tt status, or public R replaced by a nearby workmen's only. If dates given are correct, must be latter, both briefly open together; this is supported by absence of cross-reference in *hba* from closure entry to that for 'new' station in first part of book, which was usual (but not invariable) practice where only alteration of station's facilities involved.

RAVENSTHORPE

RAVENSTHORPE [LNW] op 1 September 1891 *(LNW Officers 32907)* as R & THORNHILL; renamed 1959 *(hba ref December)*; still open.

R LOWER [LY] first in *Brad* August 1869 (BoT sanction to open given 30 June, *LY*); LOWER added 30 September 1951 *(RM January 1952)*; clo 30 June 1952 *(Cl)*.

RAVENSTONEDALE [NE] op 8 August 1861 *(co op tt)* as NEWBIGGIN; renamed 1 January 1877 *(Cl)*; clo 1 December 1952 *(Cl)*. *Brad* called it NEWBIGGEN but ...IN *hb* and Ordnance Survey.

RAWCLIFFE [LY] op 1 April 1848 *(LY; co ½ T 7 September- line)*; still open.

RAWLINSON BRIDGE: temporary [Bolton & Preston] terminus op 4 February 1841 *(co n Manchester 30 January)*; clo when line extended to Chorley (which see), 22 December 1841 *(LY corr)*.

RAWMARSH – see PARKGATE.

RAWTENSTALL [LY] op 28 September 1846 *(Rtn PP)*; clo 5 June 1972 *(RM August)*.

RAWYARDS [NB]
op by March 1845 (see 1840 August 5**); clo 1 May 1930 (Thursday) *(Cl)*. Hb, 1867 only: R or CLARKSTON JUNCTION; {map 16}.

RAY HOUSE / RAYFELL
– see PARSONS PLATFORM.

RAYDON WOOD [GE] op 2 September 1847**; aot request; WOOD added 1 October 1895 *(hbl 24th)*; clo 29 February 1932 *(T 27th)*.

RAYLEIGH [GE]
op 1 October 1889 *(co notice – at back of GE co tt November 1889, at Newton Abbot)*; still open.

RAYNE [GE]
op 22 February 1869 *(GE- line; MT 5/56/8)*; aot request; clo 3 March 1952 *(RM April)*; later excur *(U)*.

RAYNERS LANE op by [Met] 26 May 1906 *(L)*; [Dist] service added 1 March 1910, transferred to [Picc] 23 October 1933; HALT until 1934/5 *(Brad)*; still open. *Hb* included from 1910a, as though not a halt. HB: 1930 (only) R L for HARROW GARDEN VILLAGE; not seen thus *Brad*.

RAYNES PARK [LSW]
op 30 October 1871 *(L)*; still open.

RAYNHAM PARK [MGN]
op 16 August 1880 *(GN)*; clo 2 March 1959 *(T 2nd)*.

READING

READING [GW] op 30 March 1840 *(co n T 27th)*; R GENERAL 26 September 1949 to 7 May 1974 tt; still open. From 14 August 1861 to April 1869 there was a separate standard gauge platform outside main station (then broad gauge). R JUNCTION 1852/3 to 1858/9 in *Brad*.

R SOUTHERN [SE] op 4 July 1849 *(Hants Chron 7th)*; re-sited about 300 yards west 30 August 1855 *(Cl)*; originally R, became R SOUTH 26 September 1949 *(Cl)*, R SOUTHERN 11 September 1961 *(Cl)*; clo 6 September 1965 *(T 6th)*, services diverted to ex-GW station.

R WEST [GW] op 1 July 1906 *(RCG)*; still open.

R CENTRAL {branch from R West} and **R DIESEL DEPOT** {branch from R General} used, non-tt, for Open Days 19 and 20 June 1971 *(U)*.

REARSBY [Mid] op 1 September 1846 *(Mid)*; clo 2 April 1951 *(RM May)*.

RECTORY ROAD [GE]
op 27 May 1872 *(co n T 25th)*; clo by fire 9 December 1972, reop 17 January 1973 *(Cl)*; still open.

RED HILL [SM] op 13 August 1866** (see for details); aot request; clo 22 June 1880. In *hb* as REDHILL. See HOOKAGATE for later history.

RED HOUSE [Van] first in *Brad* September 1876; Tuesdays only; last February 1879; in *hb* 1877 as R H SIDING, goods only; {in *IA*}.

RED LION CROSSING [GW]
op 1 January 1908 *(GW H)*; HALT; clo 2 April 1917, reop 7 July 1919 *(GW circ 2672)*; see 1921 April/May**; clo 4 May 1926**.

RED ROCK [LY/LU] op 1 December 1869**; clo 26 September 1949 *(RM September)*.

RED WHARF BAY & BENLLECH [LNW]
op 24 May 1909 *(LNW Officers 32907)*; clo 22 September 1930 *(Cl)*.
Crosville bus company arranged special trains summer Saturdays 1938 and 1939 because weight limits on Menai road bridge prevented carrying of all wanting to travel (Bill Rear, *Railways of North Wales: Anglesey branch lines ...*, Foxline, 1994).

REDBOURN [Mid]
op 16 July 1877 *(T 18th)*; clo 16 June 1947**.

REDBRIDGE near Ilford [Cen] op 14 December 1947 *(T 17th)*; still open. Station provided by LMS for Cen use. LT ticket as RED BRIDGE *(JB)*.

REDBRIDGE near Southampton [LSW]
op 1 June 1847 *(Dorset Chron 20 May, 3 June)*; still open.

REDBROOK-ON-WYE [GW] op 1 November 1876 *(Wye; Merlin 27 October- line)*; -O-W added 11 September 1933 *(Cl)*; clo 5 January 1959 *(T 5th)*.

REDCAR

R BRITISH STEEL op 19 June 1978 (non-tt) *(RM August)*; first in *Brad* 14 May 1979 but only for authorised access to British Steel Corporation *(D&C 4)*; still open.

R CENTRAL [NE] op 5 June 1846**; minutes refer to original station as temporary (site or buildings?); permanent opened by 25 June 1847, when they discussed possible use of temporary elsewhere on the system *(RAIL 667/17)*; re-sited on extension to Saltburn 19 August 1861 *(Cl)*; CENTRAL added 1950 *(NE commercial circular of 20 October announced change – already into effect? JS)*; still open. Aot excursion platform for race specials and holiday extras on loop on north side, west of station – out of existence 1968/73 *(AB)*.

R EAST [LNE] op 18 May 1929 *(S&D)*; HALT until 1937 *(Brad)*; still open

REDCASTLE [High] op 1 February 1894 *(High)*; clo 1 October 1951 *(RM November)*.

REDDISH

R NORTH [GC/Mid] op 1 December 1875 *(GC dates)*; NORTH added 24 July 1951 *(Cl)*; still open.

R SOUTH [LNW]; first in *Brad* July 1859; SOUTH added 15 September 1952 ; reduced to one train per week, northbound, Fridays 11 May 1992 tt; changed to one-way Saturdays only 18 May 2003 tt *(AB, Chron January 2004)*; to one Fridays only southbound 23 May 2004 tt; to Saturday only February 2007 tt; one northbound Saturdays only to 7 July 2007 *(Today's Railways, September, p. 62)*; thus avoids cost of closure procedure.

Non-tt: **R DEPOT**: open day 9 September 1973.

REDDITCH [Mid] op 19 September 1859 *(Redditch Indicator, first edition, 24th)*; re-sited 22 chains south on extension to Alcester 4 May 1868 *(hbl 18 September)*; re-sited again, 8 chains north of second station, 7 February 1972 *(Mid)*; still open.

REDENHALL [GE] op 2 November 1860**; request; clo 1 August 1866 (Wednesday) *(Cl)*; {Harleston – Homersfield}.

REDHEUGH – see GATESHEAD.

REDHILL [SE/LBSC] op 15 April 1844 *(SE)*; replaced both Reigate Road stations; still open. At first REIGATE; later, and erratically, various combinations of RED HILL / REDHILL / REIGATE, with JUNCTION sometimes added; settled 7 July 1929 *(JS)*.

REDHURST CROSSING [NS] (ng): first in *Brad* August 1915; aot request; CROSSING added 2 April 1923 co tt *(JS)*; clo 12 March 1934 *(LNW Record)*; {Thors Cave – Wetton Mill}. HALT on ticket *(JB)* but not in tts seen.

REDLAND [CE] op 12 April 1897 *(Bristol T 13th)*; still open.

REDMARSHALL [NE]: line op 11 July 1835 *(NE)*, nd, March 1850 *(Topham)*; originally CARLTON, renamed 1 July 1923 *(hbl 12th)*; clo 31 March 1952 *(RM June)*.

REDMILE [GN/LNW] op 15 December 1879 *(LNW Officers 410/594 pp. 4421–2 and minute 20332)*; clo 15 January 1951 – see 1951**, reop 2 July 1951, when included in *Brad* – also see R. Maund, *Chron 50 p. 29*; clo 10 September 1951 *(Rly Obs October)*. Originally RED MILE for BELVOIR (thus LNW co tt 1882); became REDMILE for B 1886/7, and thus *Brad*, GN co tt 1909. *Hb* 1883 and 1890 and GN/LNW ticket for R & B *(JS)*.

REDMIRE [NE] op 1 February 1877 *(York Guardian 3rd)*; clo 26 April 1954** *(T 20th)*; later excursions –

e.g. ramblers' 25 April 1981 *(IU)*; occasional use 1984 to 1988.

REDNAL & WEST FELTON [GW] op 14 October 1848 *(Shrewsbury 13th)*; & W F added 16 October 1907 *(hbl 24th)*; clo 12 September 1960 *(Cl)*.

REDRUTH [GW] op 23 May 1843**; clo 16 February 1852 for line rebuilding, reop 11 March 1852 *(co n R Cornwall Gaz 12th)*; re-sited on extension to Truro 25 August 1852 *(Cl)*; still open; {map 111}.

REDSTONE HILL [SE] (non-tt): used 30 April 1849 for ceremony of laying foundation stone of Chapel at Philanthropic Society's Farm School for the Reformation of Juvenile Offenders by Prince Albert. Used by special trains and a couple of ordinary trains each way; ¾ mile from Redhill *(co n T 26th; T 1 May)*. Probably at/near site of original SE Reigate Road, closed 1844.

REEDHAM NORFOLK [GE] op 1 May 1844 *(T 14 April- line;* mentioned in inspection report of 12 April 1844); N added body of BR tt 1976/84 (index earlier); still open. R JUNCTION 1850/2 to ? *(Brad)*. Note that map evidence shows was slightly altered, not re-sited 1904 (G. Kenworthy, *GERS Journal, January 2000)*.

REEDHAM Surrey [SEC] op 1 March 1911 *(L)*; clo 1 January 1917 *(RM February)*; reop 1 January 1919 *(Cl)*; HALT until 5 July 1936 *(Cl)*; still open. SURREY added 12 May 1980 tt (index earlier); to R (GLC) 13 May 1985; to R 12 May 1986 tt – dates from body of tt, indexes differ.

REEDLEY HALLOWS [LY] first in *Brad* May 1911; see 1905** (b); clo 3 December 1956 *(RM December)*.

REEDNESS JUNCTION [Ax Jt] op 10 August 1903 *(RCG)*; clo 17 July 1933 *(RM September)*.

REEDSMOUTH [NB] first in *Brad* May 1861; re-sited 1 November 1864 *(Nhumb Young)*; clo 15 October 1956** *(T 21 September)*.

REEPHAM LINCS [GC]: line op 18 December 1848 *(GC)*, nd, February 1849 (first time detail shown for its section of line); LINCS added 1 July 1923 *(hbl 12th)*; clo 1 November 1965 *(RM December)*.

REEPHAM NORFOLK [GE] op 2 May 1881 *(RCG)*; NORFOLK added 1 November 1927 *(hbl October)*; clo 15 September 1952 *(RM October)*; later excur *(U)*.

REGENT CENTRE [TWM] op 10 May 1981 *(Tyneside)*; still open.

REGENTS PARK [Bak] op 10 March 1906 *(L;T 12th- line)*; still open.

REIDS FARM – see BARTON MOSS.

REIGATE

REIGATE [SE] op 4 July 1849 *(Hants Chron 7th)*; R TOWN until 1 November 1898 *(Cl)*; still open. Also see REDHILL.

REIGATE ROAD

REIGATE ROAD [LBSC] op 12 July 1841 *(co n T 9th)* >
REIGATE ROAD [SE] op 26 May 1842 *(co n T 13th, 20th)* >
Both closed 15 April 1844, replaced by Redhill *(SE)*. Variety of names in inspection report and different tts:

REDHILL / RED HILL / REIGATE / REIGATE ROAD,
separately or in combination.
Also see REDSTONE HILL.

RENFREW

R WHARF [GSW] op 3 April 1837★★; clo 1 February
1866 (Thursday) for regauging line *(Cl)*, back in tt
September 1867★; clo 5 June 1967★★ *(Rly Obs July)*.
At first in *Brad* 'R station at theWharf'; by 1842 R;
at reopening R W; became R forYOKER and
CLYDEBANK 1 February 1907 *(RCG)*.

R FULBAR STREET [GSW] op 1 May 1866★.
F S added in *Brad* September 1867. Note that nature
of earlier services would have allowed 'town' stops;
clo 5 June 1967★★ *(Rly Obs July)*.
★ = *co ½ RAIL 1110/149* for meeting 19 September 1866 says
line to Fulbar Street op on 1 May and works thence toWharf
were 'far advanced'. Nothing later found in half-yearlies but
1866 wording suggests reopening earlier than shown by *Brad*.

R KINGS INCH [GP Jt] op 1 June 1903 *(RCG)* as
R CENTRAL; renamed in tt later 1903 (after August);
clo 5 June 1926 (Saturday), reop 14 June 1926 *(Cl)*;
clo 19 July 1926 *(Cl)*.

R PORTERFIELD [GP Jt] op 1 June 1903 *(RCG)*;
later history as R King's Inch, above.
Also see SOUTH RENFREW.

RENISHAW CENTRAL [GC]
op 1 June 1892 *(RCG)* as ECKINGTON & R;
renamed 25 September 1950 *(Rly Obs October)*;
clo 4 March 1963 *(T 27 February* – 'will still be used
for holiday and excursion specials').

RENTON [DB Jt] op 15 July 1850★★; still open.

REPTON & WILLINGTON [Mid]
op 12 August 1839 *(Mid; co n T 8th- line)* asW; became
W & R October 1855 *(Brad – Mid)*, R & W 1 May 1877
co tt *(Mid)*; clo 4 March 1968 *(Mid)*.
Ticket and RCH mentions about 1890 to ?:W for R –
no tt support *(Mid)*.

RESOLVEN [GW] op 24 September 1851★★;
clo 15 June 1964 *(RM August)*.

RESPRYN – see BODMIN.

RESTON [NB] op 22 June 1846 *(First; co n T 23rd-
line)*; clo 4 May 1964 *(RM June)*. 1850 to 1890
R JUNCTION *(Brad)*. NB co tt 1900:
R for COLDINGHAM and ST ABBS. LNE co tt
1933, *Murray* 1948 and *Brad* to closure: R for St A.

RETFORD

RETFORD [MS&L]
op 17 July 1849 *(co n Stockport 20th)* >
GN service began 4 September 1849, using MS&L
station, diverted to own station >
RETFORD [GN] op 15 July 1852★★ >
New curve, 1 July 1859 (Friday), allowed MS&L to
divert to GN station and close own, which became
R THRUMPTON 1923, when goods only.
Ex-GN station still open; lower platform added 14 June
1965.

REVIEW PLATFORM – see BUDDON.

RHAYADER [Cam] op 21 September 1864 *(co n
Hereford J 24th)*; clo 31 December 1962 *(T 31st)*.

RHEIDOL FALLS [VoR] (ng):
first in *Brad* June 1904 (op 7 May with Glanyrafon?);

see 1902 December 22★★ for full details; aot request;
to preservation 1989.

RHEWL [LNW]:
op 1 March 1862 *(co ½ T 14 August- line)*; clo 30 April
1962 *(RM June)*. According to *hb* September 1958a
had become HALT, but not thus in BR tts at closure.

RHIGOS [GW] op 1 May 1911 *(GW H)*; HALT;
trains shown only towards Neath in September 1962 tt;
clo 15 June 1964 *(RM August)*.

RHIWBINA [Cardiff]
op 1 March 1911 *(RCG)*; still open. RHUBINA in
Brad until 1917; PLATFORM in 1912 *hb*; HALT
1 July 1924 *(GW circular 18 June)* until 5 May 1969
(GW Halts) – but had been HALT in *Brad* from start;
double entered 1938 *hb* – RHIWBINA HALT
(Cardiff–Whitchurch), RHUBINA PLATFORM
(Heath–Whitchurch).

RHIWDERIN [BM] op 14 June 1865 *(co n Newport
17th)*; clo 1 March 1954 *(Cl)*. Hb 1872 and 1883:
RHIWDERYN and ticket thus *(JB)*.

RHIWFRON [VoR] (ng): op 22 December 1902★★
(VoR – semi-official station from line opening)*;
first in *Brad* November 1903, aot request;
to preservation 1989. HALT in later days.

RHOOSE

RHOOSE (a) [Barry] op 1 December 1897 *(Glam;
Colliery 3rd- line)*; clo 15 June 1964 *(RM August)*.
RHOOSE (b) op 12 June 2005 – special 10th *(Rly Obs
September)*; 'R Cardiff International Airport' (on name-
board at station); same site as (a) still open.

RHOS [GW]; {map 75}

RHOS (main line) op 14 October 1848 *(Shrewsbury
13th)*; last full service January 1855 tt; last in tt February
1855, Thursdays only; {Ruabon – Wrexham}.
RHOS (branch) op 1 October 1901 *(RCG)*;
clo 1 January 1931 (Thursday) *(T 20 December 1930)*;
Eisteddfodd use 6 to 12 August 1945 *(RM September)*;
later football excur *(U)*.

RHOSDDU [GC] first in *Brad* July 1906; HALT;
clo 1 March 1917 (Thursday) *(RCH)*; workmen to
after 1923 *(U)*; {map 75}.

RHOSGOCH [LNW] op 3 June 1867 *(D&C 11)*;
clo 7 December 1964 *(RM March 1965)*.

RHOSNEIGR [LNW] op 1 May 1907 *(RCG)*;
clo 1 January 1917 *(T 22 December 1916)*; aot request;
reop 1 February 1919 *(Cl)*; still open.

RHOSROBIN [GW] op 1 September 1932 *(Cl 29)*;
HALT; clo 6 October 1947 *(Cl)*; {map 75}.
Pre-op Pandy Bridge *(RAC)*.

RHOSTRYFAN [NWNG] (ng): op 15 August 1877
(NGSC 2; Rtn- line); clo 1 January 1914 *(Cl)*; {in IA}.

RHOSTYLLEN [GW]
op 1 October 1901 *(RCG)*; clo 1 January 1931
(Thursday) *(T 20 December 1930)*; {map 75}.

RHOSYMEDRE

RHOSYMEDRE (a) [Shrewsbury & Chester]
op 14 October 1848 *(Shrewsbury 13th)*; last in tt June
1849, replaced by CEFN, 20 chains north *(RAC)*.
RHOSYMEDRE (b) [GW] op 1 September 1906 *(GW
H)*; HALT; clo 2 March 1959 *(Cl)*.

RHU [NB] op 7 August 1894 *(T 7th)* as ROW;
renamed 24 February 1927 *(hbl 24 April)*;
clo 9 January 1956 *(RM February)*, reop as HALT
4 April 1960 *(RM May)*; clo 15 June 1964 *(RM July)*.
RHUDDLAN [LNW] op 5 October 1858 *(co n
Clwydd)*; clo 19 September 1955 *(Rly Gaz 26 August)*.
RHUDDLAN ROAD – see WOODLAND PARK.
RHYD-DDU – see SOUTH SNOWDON.
RHYD-Y-SAINT [LNW] op 1 July 1908 *(RCG;
LNW Officers 42318- line)*; clo 22 September 1930 *(Cl)*.
RHYDOWEN [GW] op 12 July 1875 *(GW- line)*;
clo 10 September 1962 *(Cl)*.
RHYDYCAR JUNCTION [BM] (non-tt):
BM 'Special Ticket', first-class *(JB)*; purpose ?;
{physical junction 1A, BM/GW, south of Merthyr}.
RHYDYFELIN
R HL [ANSW] op 1 September 1904**; re-sited 18ch.
east 14 May 1928 *(Cl)*; clo 2 February 1953 *(Cl)*. >
R LL [Cardiff] op 1 March 1911 *(RCG)*; clo 20 July
1931 *(GW goods circular 14th: after last train 18th)*.>
In both cases HALT and HL/LL added 1 July 1924
(GW circular 18 June) but thus in *Brad* from start.
Rhyd-y-felin in *Brad* until 1920/1 for ANSW and its
nameboard thus; ticket thus for LL *(JB)*.
RHYDYMWYN [LNW] op 6 September 1869**;
clo 30 April 1962 *(RM June)*.
RHYDYRONEN [Talyllyn] (ng) op 1 February 1867
co tt (J. Jennings, *Back Track, November 2000)*, first in
Brad August 1867; see 6 October 1950**.
RHYL [LNW]
op 1 May 1848 *(D&C 11; co n T 2nd- line)*; still open.
RHYMNEY
RHYMNEY [Rhy] op 31 March 1858 *(co ½ T 1 September)*;
still open.
R BRIDGE [Nantybwch & Rhymney Joint]
op 2 October 1871 *(LNW co ½ T 17 February 1872)*;
LNW use began 1 January 1873; Joint part clo
23 September 1953 *(Cl)*, LNW part clo 6 January 1958
(BRWR notice December 1957). At first RUMNEY B *(hb)*.
R LOWER [BM] op 16 April 1866 *(Cardiff T 20th)*
as R; became R & PONTLOTTYN 1 September 1905
(hbl 26 October), R PWLL UCHAF 1 July 1924 *(GW
circular 18 June)*, R L 26 September 1926 *(hbl October)*;
clo 14 April 1930 *(Cl)*.
RHYMNEY JUNCTION
– see BASSALEG JUNCTION; HENGOED.
RHYMNEY MERTHYR COLLIERY
– see PONTLOTTYN.
RIBBLEHEAD [Mid]
op 4 December 1876 *(Mid)* as BATTY GREEN;
renamed 1 May 1877 co tt *(Mid)*; clo 4 May 1970
(RM June); reop summer weekend Dales Rail 1975;
reop 14 July 1986 *(Settle)*, southbound only; northbound
added 28 May 1993 *(Rly Obs Nov.)*; still open.
According to *JS* Ingleton Road might have been
intended name; Revd E.H. Woodall asked, initially
unsuccessfully, for use of R instead of I R.
R for WEATHERCOTE CAVE 1914/15 to 1955 *(Brad)*.
RIBBLETON [Preston & Longridge]
RIBBLETON (a) first in *Brad* November 1854 as
GAMMER LANE BRIDGE; renamed FULWOOD

1856 tt *(Cl)*, R 1 October 1900 *(RCG)*; clo 2 June 1930
(LNW Record).
RIBBLETON (b) first in *Brad* June 1863, as R FOR R
PARK AND CEMETERY; last there September 1866;
later army camp use *(U)*; {between Preston and (a)}.
RIBCHESTER – see WILPSHIRE.
RIBY STREET Grimsby [GC] in use for workmen
by October 1904 *(U)*; op to public 4 June 1917 *(Brad
June 1917)*; last in tt April 1919; continued in use by
workmen until 14 April 1941; PLATFORM *(U)* – but
not thus *Brad* (space?); {Grimsby Docks – New Clee}.
RICCALL [NE] op 2 January 1871 *(T 3rd)*;
clo 15 September 1958 *(RM October)*.
RICCARTON & CRAIGIE [GSW]:
built 1902 between Kilmarnock and Gatehead but
never provided with service *(U)*.
RICCARTON JUNCTION [NB]
op 2 June 1862, one train per day mostly for workmen –
needed since there was then no road access; full service
1 July 1862 *(NB)*; doctor, supplies for shop, etc all by
train – most who lived there were connected with the
railway; JUNCTION added 1 January 1905 *(RCG)*
but thus *Reid* 1904; clo 6 January 1969 *(RM February)*.
According to *hbl* September 1960, reverted to R – but
still R J 6 May 1968 tt.
RICE LANE [LY] op 20 November 1848 *(LY; co n
Manch G 18th- line)* as PRESTON ROAD; renamed
14 May 1984 *(C/W)*; still open.
RICHBOROUGH
R CASTLE [SR] non-tt miltary use began 22 June 1918,
ended June 1920 or earlier *(U)*; op to public 19 June
1933 *(SR sig inst 22/1933)*; summer only; HALT;
clo 11 September 1939 *(Cl; start of emergency
war-time tt)*; {Sandwich – Minster}.
R PORT [EK]: built about 1925 on branch from Eastry
but not used because bridge across Stour failed
inspection *(U)*.
R SALTPANS EXCHANGE YARD [SEC] (non-tt):
workmen; op 10 February 1919; clo by July 1925;
{branch from Minster} *(U)*.
RICHMOND near Darlington [NE]
op 10 September 1846 *(co n Catterick)*;
clo 3 March 1969 *(RM March)*.
RICHMOND near Twickenham [LSW]
Main station op 27 July 1846 *(T 23rd)* >
Datchet line station opened 22 August 1848 and through
platforms were provided alongside original station;
latter kept for a while as terminus for short-distance
trains. By 24 September 1849 *(item T of that date)*
terminus out of use; short trains now terminated at
Twickenham. Sometimes R OLD (e.g. *Brad* 1871,
LSW co tt 1914). >
R NEW op 1 January 1869; absorbed into main
1 August 1937.
Dist use began 1 June 1877; also used by [Met]
1 October 1877 to 1 January 1907. >
Station still open.
RICHMOND ROAD [BWA]
op 1 May 1908 *(Trewman 2nd- line)*;
clo 28 March 1917**; {Northam – Appledore}.

RICKMANSWORTH
RICKMANSWORTH [Met/GC] op 1 September 1887
(L); op by Met, GC added 15 March 1899; still open.
R CHURCH STREET [LNW] op 1 October 1862
(LNW); C S added 25 September 1950 *(RM October)*;
clo 3 March 1952 *(RM April)*.
RIDDINGS JUNCTION [NB]
op 1 March 1862 *(NB)*; clo 15 June 1964 *(RM July)*.
RIDDLESDOWN [SR]
op 5 June 1927 *(sig inst 8th)*; still open.
RIDGE BRIDGE [NE] op 18 November 1912
(RAIL 527/2191 – D. Geldard); non-tt from 1 April
1914 (Wednesday) *(NE Staff Mag May 1913)*;
miners used to 1 January 1944 (official date though in
wtt until later 1944); {Garforth – Micklefield}.
RIDGMONT [LNW] op 18 November 1846★★;
still open. RIDGMOUNT until 1868/9 (LNW co tt),
1869/70 *(Brad)*, 1872 *(hb)*.
RIDHAM DOCK [SEC] (non-tt): Bowater workers;
op November 1917; clo 1919; {branch from Swale} *(U)*.
RIDING MILL [NE]: line op 10 March 1835 *(N&C)*,
nd, in *Scott 1837*; see 1836 B★★; still open.
Scott 1837: BROOMHAUGH or R M.
RIDLEY HALL BRIDGE [NC] – see 1836 B★★;
{Bardon Hill – Haydon Bridge}
RIFLE RANGE [GW] first in *Brad* June 1905
(authority given by *Traffic Committee* on 12 April);
wtt supp said auto car service on line (provided only trains
calling here) ceased from 20 October 1919 so halt should
have closed then; still shown *Brad* September 1920 –
probably inertia (only in footnotes so no guarantee
trains calling); HALT; unadvertised use to 1938;
{Kidderminster – Bewdley}.
RIFLE RANGE [LNE] (non-tt):
HALT; in use 1926; {Elgin – Lossiemouth}; *(U)*.
RIFLE RANGE near Connahs Quay – see SEALAND.
RIGG [GSW] op 1 June 1901 *(RCG)*; clo 1 November
1942 (Sunday) *(Cl)*; later workmen's use *(U)*.
RILLINGTON [NE]:
op 8 July 1845★★; clo 22 September 1930★★.
Used (non-tt) Saturdays 4 July to 10 October 1942
(inclusive) *(manuscript corrections to wtt)*; similar use
shown 2 October 1944 wtt; ceased before/with start
of 1 October 1945 wtt. R JUNCTION until 1893/4
in *Brad* and thus NE co tt 1880 (one way).
RIMINGTON [LY] op 2 June 1879 *(Lancs Chesh- line)*;
clo 7 July 1958 *(LNW Record)*.
RINGLEY – see KEARSLEY.
RINGLEY ROAD [LY] op 31 May 1847 *(LY)*;
clo 5 January 1953 *(RM March)*.
RINGSTEAD & ADDINGTON [LNW]
op 2 June 1845 *(co op notice)*; & A added 1 April 1898
(hbl 28th); clo 4 May 1964 *(RM June)*.
RINGWOOD [LSW]
op 1 June 1847 *(Dorset Chron 20 May, 3 June)*;
clo 4 May 1964 *(Hants Chron 9th)*.
R JUNCTION 1865/6 to 1898/9 *(Brad)*.
RIPLEY near Derby [Mid]
op 1 September 1856 *(T 12th)*; re-sited ready for Heanor
line 2 September 1889 *(Mid)*; clo 1 June 1930 (Sunday)
(Mid); later excur *(U)*. 1895 *hb* had separate entries for

both R and R NEW, both shown 'P' – presumably
error; R NEW also at first in *Brad* (informative?).
RIPLEY – see CLANDON; NIDD BRIDGE.
RIPLEY VALLEY [NE]
op 1 May 1862 *(T 5th)* as KILLINGHALL;
renamed R 1 June 1862 *(Cl)*, R CASTLE 1 March 1875
(circular 20 February, JS), RV 1 April 1875 *(circular
22 March, JS)*; clo 2 April 1951 *(T 7 March)*.
RIPON [NE] op 1 June 1848 *(co ½ T 30 August)*;
clo 6 March 1967 *(RM March)*.
RIPPINGALE [GN]
op 2 January 1872 *(Insp rpt MT/6/91/2; co ½ T 12 Feb.-
line)*; clo 22 September 1930★★ *(Cl)*.
RIPPLE [Mid] op 16 May 1864 *(Tewkesbury 21st)*;
clo 14 August 1961 *(T 3rd)*.
RIPPONDEN & BARKISLAND [LY]
op 5 August 1878 *(LY)*; & B added 1 December 1891
(RCG); clo 8 July 1929 *(Cl)*.
RISCA
RISCA [GW] op 23 December 1850★★; clo 30 April
1962 *(T 6 April)*.
R & PONTYMISTER op 6 February 2008 *(RM April)*;
still open.
RISE CAR ROLLING MILLS, Darlington.
Shown 'P' 1912 *hb* but erratum slip said 'P' belonged to
Rishworth.
RISHTON [LY]
op 19 June 1848 *(LY; Lancaster Guardian 17th- line)*;
last in tt January 1849; back in tt May 1853; still open.
RISHWORTH [LY]
op 1 March 1881 *(LY)*; clo 8 July 1929 *(Cl)*.
RISLEY [LNE] (two, perhaps three, non-tt stations
for Ordnance Factory):
One {Glazebrook – Padgate} op 2 April 1940 *(Cl 29)*;
26 September 1949 wtt shows trains towards
Manchester calling at R MAIN LINE Platform for
convenience of staff; other way called at R EAST or
R WEST – plan of layout suggests two island platforms
in tandem between lines off main; clo 6 April 1964
(P. Bolger, *Illustrated History of Cheshire Lines Committee*,
Heyday, 1984, pp.12, 13, 70); clo 1960 *(U)*.
Second {branch from Newchurch} op by July 1941 *(U)*;
no passenger service shown 6 May 1946 wtt or
26 September 1949 wtt.
Also see NO.56 PLATFORM, perhaps at Risley.
RIVER DOUGLAS [West Lancashire]
op 1 August 1878, before its section of line opened for
regular passenger services (*Liverpool & Southport Daily
News 1st*; J. Dixon and J. Gilmour, *West Lancashire
Railway Mysteries Unravelled, RCHS Journal*, March
2002); used only by excursion trains connecting with
boat trips, no outside road access; aot request; last trains
shown in *Ormskirk* 25 April 1889 tt (still in tt until
27 March 1890 but no trains calling);
{Hoole – Hesketh Bank}.
RIVIERE BRIDGE – see under HAYLE.
ROADE [LNW] op 2 July 1838★ (G.Y. Hemingway,
letter, *RCHS Journal, November 1981*); re-sited 11 ch.
south 1881/2; clo 7 September 1964 *(RM October)*.
★ = opened to provide connection to Northampton by road
– Birmingham passengers still taken from Denbigh Hall;

not known if available for use of locals (certainly available to them from 17 September 1838).

ROADWATER [WSM] op 4 September 1865**; clo 8 November 1898**; {map 117}.

ROATH [GW]
op 2 October 1899 *(GW General Manager's Report to Board, dated 4th)*; clo 2 April 1917 *(RCH)*; {in *IA*}.

ROBERTSBRIDGE [SE] op 1 September 1851 *(Hants Chron 6th)*; still open. ROBERTS BRIDGE in tt until 1851 *(JS)*; *hb* 1900a said had become R TOWN (back to R 1912) but not seen thus *Brad*.
Part serving line to Headcorn [Kent & East Sussex] was R JUNCTION in *Brad* and ticket thus *(JB)*.

ROBERTSTOWN [TV] op 17 October 1904 *(Nelson)*; see 1904**; clo 28 July 1952 *(Cl)*.

ROBIN HOOD [EWYU] op 4 January 1904 *(co n Midland Railway Journal No. 20)*; clo 1 October 1904 (Saturday) *(RCG)*; later workmen's use *(U)*; see ROTHWELL for details of excursions; {in *IA*}.

ROBIN HOODS BAY [NE] op 16 July 1885 *(T 16th)*; clo 8 March 1965 *(T 19 January)*.

ROBINS LANE [LMS]
op 12 October 1936 *(LNW Record)*; clo 26 September 1938 *(LNW Record)*; {St Helens Junction – Sutton Oak}. HALT in *hb* but not *Brad* – see 1905**.

ROBROYSTON [Cal] op 1 November 1898 *(RCG)*; clo 1 January 1917 *(RM February)*; reop 2 June 1919 *(RCH)*; clo 11 June 1956 *(RM April)*.
HALT 1938 *hb* but not seen thus *Brad*.

ROBY [LNW]: line op 17 September 1830**, nd, 1 March 1831 co tt; still open. R LANE GATE 1831, R LANE by 1842 *Brad*, R by 1846 *Brad*.
Hb: 1862 R LANE; 1867 R; 1877 R LANE; 1890 R.

ROCESTER [NS]
op 1 August 1849 *(Churnet)*; clo 4 January 1965 *(RM March)*. R JUNCTION 1852/3 to 1895/6 *(Brad)*.

ROCHDALE [LY] op 4 July 1839 *(LY; T 11th- line)*; re-sited 26 chains west 28 April 1889 *(Cl)*; still open. LY ticket for R (YORKSHIRE STREET) *(JB)*.

ROCHDALE ROAD [LY] op 1 March 1907 *(LY)*; see 1905** (b); clo 23 September 1929 *(T 19 August)*. Ticket for R R BRIDGE *(JB)*.

ROCHE [GW] op 20 June 1876 *(R Cornwall Gaz 24th)* as VICTORIA; renamed 1 May 1904 *(hbl 28 April)*; aot request; still open. GW co tt 1881: V for R.

ROCHESTER {map 129}

ROCHESTER [LCD] op 1 March 1892 *(RCG)*; still open.

R BRIDGE [LCD]: LCD notice for opening of extension linking its Kent line to Victoria 3 December 1860 included ROCHESTER, no trains calling (had been thus in *Brad* by January 1859). Although link to SE at Strood was closed for most purposes, table showed one mixed train Strood to Canterbury early morning, reverse working in evening *(T 3rd)*. This ran until ? LCD notice *T 21st* said that a temporary station would be opened at STROOD on Monday 24 December 1860; another notice gave 'Timetable for December' which omitted 'Rochester' but had all trains calling at 'Strood'. Confusingly this table still included the mixed trains to/from 'Strood' without any indication was using SE

station, though timings same as before, making it likely that this was so. No information found about 'temporary' station – perhaps only buildings, same site for permanent. Also see *SE pp. 99–101*.
When 'Toomer Loop' (owned by LCD) reop Monday 2 April 1877 *(SE notice T 31 March* – 'arrangements have been made with LCD for through booking') LCD ran trains from Strood [SE] to connect with their line along Kent coast; some ran to Chatham, others made connection here (depended on whether connecting LCD train stopped) and the May 1877 co tt shows that in the latter case passengers had to change twice, at Strood and here. *Brad* confusingly showed the service in SE table (presumably for convenience). Correspondence between Railway Commissioners, BoT and LCD shows that platform and cross-over road had been built on short line connecting SE and LCD and a train consisting of tender engine and two carriages would run between the two Strood stations eight times each way per day [not what actually appeared in *Brad*]. Map in *LCD, p. 99*, shows that a platform had been added to the LCD station on the westbound line to Strood, with a cross-over allowing eastbound trains to reach it. In *Brad* was R BRIDGE in SE table but R & STROOD in LCD's. March 1890 *Brad* shows that only occasional connecting train was using this station. However, June 1890 a separate Strood–Rochester Bridge–Chatham table was added, trains now taking only 1 minute Strood–Rochester Bridge, 4/5 minutes on to Chatham, suggesting improved arrangements – probably the elimination of the extra change here. Trains involved also stopped at LCD's Rochester after that opened. According to the (incorrect) table headings the SE still operated the service in January 1892 but by January 1893 they had been corrected to show that LCD was doing so. Last trains from ex-SE station shown stopping June 1904. Still served via Sole Street until clo 1 January 1917 *(RCH)*. (Co tt information and copy of correspondence from D. Banks.)

R CENTRAL [SE] op 20 July 1891 *(RCG)*; C added 1901 tt *(Cl)*; clo 1 October 1911 (Sunday) *(RCG)*. Also see STROOD, under 'S'.

ROCHFORD [GE]
op 1 October 1889 *(co notice* – at back of GE co tt November 1889, at Newton Abbot)*; still open.

ROCK FERRY }
ROCK LANE } [Birkenhead]; {map 46}
R LANE op 30 May 1846 *(Birkenhead)*; replaced by > R FERRY op 1 November 1862 *(D&C 10)*; re-sited to north 15 June 1891 *(Birkenhead)*; still open. R F JUNCTION 1891/2 to 1904 *(Brad)*.

ROCKCLIFFE [Cal]
op 10 September 1847 *(co n True Line)*; clo 1 January 1917 *(RM February)*; reop 2 December 1919 *(RCH)*; clo 17 July 1950 *(RM October)*; workmen's use continued to 6 December 1965 *(U)*.
In *Brad* became R PLATFORM 1921/2, R HALT 1924/5 (and thus LMS evening excursion ticket, *JB*), R 1933/4; not always same for ex-GSW and ex-Cal services; in 1924 indexed as both Halt and Platform as though separate sites.

ROCKINGHAM [LNW]
op 1 June 1850 *(co ½ T 22 February 1851)* as R CASTLE *(Brad* and *co ½ T)*; C dropped September 1850 *(Brad)*; clo 6 June 1966 *(RM July)*. *Brad* 1853 and LNW co tt 1852: R for UPPINGHAM.

ROCKINGHAM (non-tt) – see CHITTENING.

ROCKY VALLEY [Snowdon Mountain] (ng; rack): op 1974 (A Brackenbury, *Chron)*; HALT on ticket *(JB)*; still open. See 1896 April 6**.

RODING VALLEY
op by [LNE] 3 February 1936 *(T 13 January)*; HALT *(Brad, hb)*; last steam train ran Saturday 29 November 1947 *(Clay)*; buses until reop, no longer Halt, by [Cen] 21 November 1948 *(T 20th)*; still open.

RODMARTON [GW]
op 1 September 1904 *(dist t supp 723)*; PLATFORM in GW papers from start *(Cl)* but added 1905 *(Brad)*; clo 6 April 1964 *(W Daily Press 6th)*.

RODWELL [WP Jt] op 1 June 1870 *(Weymouth 3rd)*; clo 3 March 1952 *(RM March)*.

ROEBUCK [LPJ] op 26 June 1840 *(LPJ)*; alias ROE BUCK; last in *Brad* August 1849, replaced by Brock about ½ mile north (actual change perhaps earlier – decision taken April 1841) *(LPJ)*.
On 7 July 1840 bridge at Myerscough (between here and Broughton) gave way so briefly passengers carried to/from either side of blockage and walked across *(LPJ)*.

ROFFEY ROAD [LBSC] op 1 June 1907 *(LBSC)*; first month in tt R R CROSSING *(Cl)*; HALT; clo 1 January 1917 *(T 22 December 1916)*; reop 3 May 1920 *(Cl)*; clo 1 January 1937 (Friday) *(Cl)*.

ROGART [High]
op 13 April 1868 *(High)*; clo 13 June 1960 *(RM July)*; reop 6 March 1961 *(Cl)*; HALT 12 June 1961 tt *(Cl)* to 17 May 1982 tt; aot request; still open.

ROGATE [LSW]
op 1 September 1864 *(SR; co ½ T 13 February 1865- line)* as R & HARTING; became R for H about 1912 (and thus LSW co tt 1914 and *Brad* to closure); clo 7 February 1955 *(co n W Sussex)*.

ROGERSTONE
ROGERSTONE [GW] first in *Brad* August 1851 as TYDEE (and thus Monmouthshire Co's wtt November 1865); became TYDU 1880/1 *(Brad)*, R 20 October 1898 *(hbl 27th* – but *GW circular of that date* said 'has been altered'); clo 30 April 1962 *(T 6 April)*.
ROGERSTONE (b): op 6 February 2008 *(RM April)*; still open.

ROHALLION [Inverness & Perth Junction]
first in *Brad* February 1860; Fridays only; last there October 1864; perhaps stayed open longer as private platform (originally intended as such) (N. Sinclair, article, *Highland Railway Journal 60)*; {Murthly – Dunkeld}.

ROLLESTON [Mid]
op 1 July 1847, unadvertised, as SOUTHWELL JUNCTION *(Mid)*; clo 1 August 1849, reop 12 April 1852 *(Mid)*, clo 14 March 1853 *(Cl)*, reop 1 September 1860 *(Mid)*; renamed R J November 1860 *Brad (Mid)*, R 7 May 1973 tt *(Mid)*; still open.

ROLLESTON-ON-DOVE [NS]
op 1 November 1894 *(RCG)*; clo 1 January 1949 (Saturday) *(RM March)*. *Hbl 24 January 1895* said 'on-Dove' added day of passenger opening.

ROLLRIGHT [GW] op 12 December 1906 *(GW H)*; HALT; clo 4 June 1951 *(T 4th)*.

ROLVENDEN [KES]
op 2 April 1900 *(RM July)* as TENTERDEN; renamed 16 March 1903 (see H.V. Borley, *RCHS Journal, March 1985)*; clo 4 January 1954 *(T 28 October 1953)*.

ROMALDKIRK [NE] first in *Brad* July 1868*; clo 30 November 1964 *(RM December)*.
* = source quoted for Middleton-in-Teesdale shows that there was no station here at line opening.

ROMAN BRIDGE [LNW]
op 22 July 1879 *(Brad Sh Eng 1880- line)*; became HALT 1 June 1931 *(LNW dates)* and thus 1938 *hb* but not seen thus *Brad*; aot request; still open.

ROMAN ROAD [Leeds & Selby]
op 22 September 1834 *(NE- line)*; clo 10 November 1834 *(Cl)*. Ridge Bridge here later.

ROMAN ROAD WOODNESBOROUGH [EK]
first in *Brad* May 1925; HALT; clo 1 November 1928. See 1948 November 1** for details. W ROAD on RCH map *EK F&G p.110*.

ROMFORD
ROMFORD [GE] op 20 June 1839 *(T 14th, 19th)* >
ROMFORD [LTS] op 7 June 1893 *(Mid)* >
Combined entrance provided 1 April 1934 *(L)*; both parts still open.

ROMILEY [GC/Mid]
op 5 August 1862 *(Mid)*; still open.

ROMNEY WARREN – see WARREN BRIDGE.

ROMSEY [LSW]
op 1 March 1847 *(Poole 4th)*; still open.

ROOD END [GW]
op 1 April 1867 *(co n Brierley 30 March)*; clo 1 May 1885 (Friday) *(Cl)*; {Rowley Regis – Langley Green}.

ROODYARDS – see DUNDEE.

ROOKERY [LNW]
ROOKERY (a) first in *Brad* April 1858; last there March 1862, but not in March 1862 tt *St Helens Reporter*. Shown 'closed' *hb* 1865a.
ROOKERY (b) op 1 June 1865 *(LNW Officers 279)*; about 50ch. north of (a); clo 18 June 1951 *(RM August)*.

ROOKHOPE – see PARK HEAD.

ROOSE [Fur]
first in *Brad* June 1851 (see 1846 August**) as ROOSE GATE, Sundays only; later Thursdays and Sundays; last in *Brad* September 1857; back, all days, March 1858 as ROOSE; aot request; still open. R JUNCTION in *hb* 1872 (only).

ROPLEY [LSW] op 2 October 1865 *(Salisbury 7th)*; clo 5 February 1973 *(Hants Chron 9th)*.

ROSE COTTAGE – see 1883 August 20**.

ROSE GROVE [LY]: prob op 18 September 1848 *(Herapath 23rd- line)* – nd in *Brad*, but in *Topham* November, first time it included line; still open. One word in *hb* until 1872.

ROSE HEYWORTH [GW] (non-tt): miners; in use at least 1897 to 1918; {Abertillery – Blaina} *(U)*.

ROSE HILL – see GILSLAND.

ROSE HILL MARPLE [GC/NS] op 2 August 1869
(Macclesfield – co n 31 July, item 7 August); still open.

ROSEBUSH [GW]
op 19 September 1876 *(S Wales 22nd)*; clo 1 January
1883 *(Rtn)*; reop 5 December 1884, clo 31 March 1885,
reop 21 March 1887, clo 25 May 1887 (Wednesday),
reop 11 April 1895 *(Cl)*, clo 8 January 1917 *(co n GW
book)*; reop 12 July 1920 *(GW Mag July)*;
clo 25 October 1937★★.

ROSEHAUGH [High] (non-tt):
private for Rosehaugh House, rebuilt by J.D. Fletcher,
1893 on (when station built?); clo ? (Fletcher died
August 1927, though his widow stayed on until 1953;
house demolished 1959); {Munlochy – Avoch}
(Highland Railway Journal, Autumn 2005).

ROSEHILL [CW Jc]
R ARCHER STREET op 2 June 1913 *(D&C 14)*;
clo 31 May 1926 *(Cl)*; used by workmen until 1 April
1929 *(Cumbria)*; {map 21}.
R PLATFORM (non-tt): workmen; in use about 1912
to 1920s; {Archer Street – Copperas Hill} *(Ironmasters)*.

ROSEMILL [Cal or LMS] (non-tt):
HALT; workmen; dates ? – in *hb* 1862–1904 but always
no facilities or goods only; {Baldragon – Dronley} *(U)*.

ROSEMOUNT [Cal] first in *Brad* September 1857★;
aot request; clo 10 January 1955 *(T 28 December 1954)*.
HALT according to *hb* 1938 (had earlier been
R SIDING) but always just R *(Brad)*.
★ = *Newtyle* implies with line, 1 August 1855; perhaps case of 'nd'.

ROSEWELL & HAWTHORNDEN [NB]
op 4 July 1855 *(co ½ T 22 October- line)*;
clo 10 September 1962 *(RM September)*.
Variously, *hb* and tts: H & R; H for R; H;
H JUNCTION & R; settled 9 July 1928 *(hbl July)*.

ROSHERVILLE [LCD]
op 10 May 1886 *(Kent Messenger 15th)*; became HALT
1928/9 *(Brad)*; clo 16 July 1933 (Sunday) *(Cl)*.
Also see Section 7, Non-rail.

ROSLIN
First station of this name – see under ROSSLYN.
ROSLIN [NB] op August 1874★★; clo 1 May 1933 *(RM
March)*. NB co tt 1900: R for R VILLAGE,
R CASTLE and CHAPEL.

ROSS JUNCTION [LMS – ex-Cal] (non-tt): between
Hamilton and Motherwell; wtt notices of 5 April 1947
and 15 September 1952 show stop here for workmen
to/from these places.

ROSS-ON-WYE [GW]
op 1 June 1855★★; -on-W added 1933 *(hbl ref July)*;
clo 2 November 1964 *(Cl)*.

ROSSETT [GW]
op 4 November 1846★★; clo 26 October 1964 *(RM
December)*; later use by Moreton Hall Girls' School.

ROSSINGTON [GN] op 4 September 1849 *(T 4th)*;
clo 6 October 1958 *(RM November)*; excursion to
Bridlington 3 April 1961 *(AB)*.

ROSSLYN
R CASTLE [NB] op 2 September 1872 *(T 4th)*;
CASTLE added 16 February 1874 *(Cl)*;
clo 10 September 1951 *(RM October)*.

ROSSLYNLEE [NB] op 4 July 1855 *(co ½ T 22 October-
line)* as ROSLIN; renamed ROSSLYN 1864 tt,
ROSSLYNLEE 2 September 1872 *(Cl)*;
clo 1 January 1917 *(RCH)*; reop 2 June 1919 *(RCH)*;
clo 5 February 1962 *(RM February)*.
ROSSLYNLEE HOSPITAL op 11 December 1958
(RM January 1959); HALT; clo 5 February 1962
(RM February); {Rosslynlee – Pomathorn}.

ROSTER ROAD [LMS] op 27 January 1936 *(RCH)*;
HALT; clo 3 April 1944★★; {Mid Clyth – Occumster}.

ROSYTH [NB]
ROSYTH: unadvertised use probably began 28 March
1917; op to public 1 December 1917 *(1918 Railway
Yearbook – H. Jack)*; HALT until 16 May 1983; still open.
R DOCKYARD (non-tt): naval base; op 1 July 1915 *(U)*;
no passenger services shown 1 May 1939 wtt;
workmen's and leave trains shown 4 October 1943 wtt;
last regular service Friday 24 November 1989 *(BLN
620 p.305)*; specials from Edinburgh, for Open Days
17 July 1959 and 10 June 1962;
{branch from Inverkeithing}.

ROTHBURY [NB]
ROTHBURY op 1 November 1870 *(Nhumb)*; clo 15
September 1952★★ *(RM October)*. Occasional later race
specials, e.g. 13 April 1957 to Newcastle *(Steam Days,
June 2007, p.335, via AB)*.
Goods Yard used for race excursions before 1899; in
that year officially passed for this use; later there was a
separate race platform, first used 24 April 1900 *(race; AB)*.

ROTHERFIELD
See CROWBOROUGH for first R station.
R & MARK CROSS [LBSC] op 1 September 1880
(LBSC; co ½ T 24 January 1883- line);
& M C added 1 November 1901 *(hbl 23 January 1902)*;
clo 14 June 1965 *(Cl)*.

ROTHERHAM
R CENTRAL [GC] op 1 August 1868 *(co ½ T 27 Aug.)*
as R; original temporary station replaced 1 February
1874 *(GC dates)*; became R & MASBOROUGH
1886/7 *(RCG ref January 1887)*, R C 25 September
1950 *(Rly Obs October)*; clo 5 September 1966 *(Cl)*;
reop 11 May 1987 *(BLN 556)*; still open.
Sometimes R Central station, Main Street in some
tables 1880s and 1890s in *Brad*.
R MASBOROUGH [Mid] op 11 May 1840 *(co n T 2nd)*
as M R; became M for R December 1863/January 1865
co tt, M & R 1 May 1894 co tt *(Mid)*; R M 1 April 1908
(hbl 23rd), R 20 February 1869 *(Mid)*, R M 11 May
1987; clo 3 October 1988 *(Mid)*.
R WESTGATE [Mid] op 1 November 1838 *(Mid)*;
WESTGATE added 1 May 1896 *(RCG)*;
clo 6 October 1952 *(Cl)*.

ROTHERHAM ROAD [GC]
first in *Brad* September 1871 as PARK GATE;
renamed 1 November 1895 *(RCG)*; clo 5 January 1953
(RM February). PARKGATE in *hb*.

ROTHERHITHE
For first station, see SOUTH BERMONDSEY.
ROTHERHITHE [East London] op 7 December 1869
(T 7th); [Met] added 6 October 1884,
ended 3 December 1906, began again 31 March 1913;

[Dist] began 1 October 1884, ended 1 August 1905.
Clo 25 March 1995 *(BLN 746 corr)* for engineering
work, reop 25 March 1998 *(RM September 1998)*;
clo 23 December 2007**.

ROTHERWAS FACTORY (SIDING)
– see under HEREFORD.

ROTHES [GNS] op 23 August 1858 *(GNS)*;
clo 6 May 1968 *(RM July)*.

ROTHIE-NORMAN [GNS] op 5 September 1857
(GNS); ROTHIE until 1 March 1870 *(Cl; RCG ref April)*;
clo 1 October 1951 *(RM November)*.

ROTHIEBRISBANE [GNS] (non-tt):
used 11 October 1918 only; cattle sale;
{Rothienorman – Fyvie} *(GNS)*.

ROTHIEMAY [GNS] op 11 October 1856 *(GNS)*;
clo 6 May 1968 *(RM July)*.

ROTHLEY near Leicester [GC]
op 15 March 1899 *(GC;T 16th- line)*;
clo 4 March 1963 *(RM March)*. See 2007 July 4**.

ROTHLEY – see LONGWITTON.

ROTHWELL [EWYU]
op 4 January 1904 *(co n Midland Railway Journal No. 20)*;
clo 1 October 1904 (Saturday) *(RCG)*;
summer excursions to Scarborough, Bridlington and
Blackpool ran until 21 August 1961 or later, organised
by Mrs Cotton, wife of station-master here *(GN Society
Journal May/June 2003)*. {in IA}.

ROTTON PARK ROAD [LNW]
op 10 August 1874 *(LNW Officers 11616, 11692)*;
clo 26 November 1934 *(Cl)*.

ROUDHAM JUNCTION [GE]
op 18 October 1869 *(GE- line)*; from 1 October 1902
officially exchange only (note in tt that tickets not issued
to/from); GE co tt 1914 noted it as exchange only,
no tickets issued, and included it only for one train,
from London; after 1 March 1920 *Brad* only included
on branch (main line stop briefly reinstated during coal
strike 6 April to 2 October 1921); all advertised stops
withdrawn 1 May 1932 (Sunday) *(Cl)*; unadvertised
use ceased 15 June 1964 *(Cl)*. Hb 1904 to 1929 inclusive
included station but no facilities shown; 'P' restored
1938 – as HALT. Its inclusion in public tt 1921 to 1932
would seem to have been pointless if it was exchange
only, since there would apparently have been nothing to
exchange with – unless there were unadvertised stops
on main line *(TTS May 2001, p. 118–9* confirms wider
use, by railwaymen's families e.g.).

ROUGHTON ROAD
op 20 May 1985 *(AZ)*; still open.

ROUND OAK [GW] op 20 December 1852 *(W Mid;
T 20th- line)* as BRIERLEY HILL & R O;
renamed R O & B H 1853 tt, R O 1857 tt *(W Mid)*;
re-sited about 1894 on opposite site of road (M. Hale,
Chron 3); clo 30 July 1962 *(RM September)*.

ROUNDBALL [LSW] (non-tt): HALT; for rifle range;
op 22 September 1906; clo ? – removal ordered January
1921 *(LSW)*; {Honiton – Sidmouth Junction}.

ROUNDHOUSE HALT – see BARROW HILL.

ROUNDWOOD [LMS] op 8 August 1927 *(Mid)*;
HALT, though in hb 1929 as R (Halt added 1938); clo
16 June 1947**; {Harpenden – Redbourn}.

ROW – see RHU.

ROWAN [SR] op 18 December 1933 *(SR, supported
by SR sig 1934/1* – has been brought into use);
was R for ELM DRIVE HALT; clo 1 January 1939
(Sunday) *(RM January)*; {Dyke branch}.

ROWDEN MILL [GW] op 1 September 1897
(co n Ephemera); clo 15 September 1952 *(RM November)*.
Became HALT hb 1949a and so shown BR ticket *(JB)*
but not in *Brad*.

ROWFANT [LBSC] op 9 July 1855 *(LBSC; Hants
Chron 14th- line)*; clo 2 January 1967 *(RM February)*.

ROWINGTON JUNCTION: according to letter from
P.S. Boness, *RM November 1968, p. 675*, there was a
'halt' here, where the GW's Henley-in-Arden branch
diverged; branch dates 6 June 1894 to 1 January 1915.
No contemporary evidence in support has been seen.
(see A. Brackenbury, *Chron October 2008*)

ROWLANDS CASTLE [LSW]
op 1 January 1859 *(SR; co n T 1st- line)*; still open.

ROWLANDS GILL [NE]
op 2 December 1867 *(Consett)*; see 1951**;
clo 1 February 1954 *(RM March)*.

ROWLEY [NE]
op 1 September 1845 *(S&D)* as COLD R; see 1843**
– *Brad* shows Crook as terminus to October 1846
(C R added November); renamed 1868; clo 1 May 1939
(Cl); {maps 28, 30}.

ROWLEY REGIS [GW]
op 1 April 1867 *(co n Brierley 30 March)* as ROWLEY
(but R R, *GW ac*, pre-opening);
renamed R R & BLACKHEATH 1 September 1889
(hbl 24 October), R R 5 May 1968 *(Cl)*; still open.

ROWNTREE – see YORK.

ROWRAH
ROWRAH [WCE Jt] op 1 February 1864**;
clo 13 April 1931 *(LNW Record)*; workmen used
11 March to 8 April 1940 *(U)*.
Also see ARLECDON.

ROWSLEY [Mid] op 4 June 1849 *(T 5th)*; re-sited on
extension to Hassop 1 August 1862 wtt *(Mid)*;
was R for CHATSWORTH 1 September 1867 co tt to
14 June 1965 *(Mid)*; clo 6 March 1967 *(RM April)*.
LMS tt 1947 and BR LM Region 1948 (both *Bradshaw*
prints): R for C and HADDON HALL.

ROWTHORN & HARDWICK [Mid]
op 1 September 1890 co tt *(Mid)*;
clo 28 July 1930 *(LNW Record)*.

ROWTON [GW] op 29 June 1935 *(Cl 29)*; HALT;
clo 9 September 1963 *(T 9th)*; {Crudgington – Peplow}.

ROXBURGH [NB]
op 17 June 1850 *(NB)*; see 1948 August 12**;
clo 15 June 1964 *(RM July)*. R JUNCTION 1856/9 to
1883/4 (index later) in *Brad*.

ROY BRIDGE [NB]
op 7 August 1894 *(W High; T 7th- line)*; still open.

ROYAL ALBERT [Dock]
op 28 March 1994 *(RM October)*; still open.

ROYAL ALBERT DOCK:
at times prefixed to CENTRAL; CONNAUGHT;
GALLIONS; MANOR WAY, all of which see.
Also see ROYAL GROUP OF DOCKS.

ROYAL GARDENS [NE]
first in *Brad* June 1857; last October 1857;
{Leeds – Headingley}. Burley Park here/near later.
ROYAL GROUP OF DOCKS (LONDON) [PLA].
Boat trains ran to various destinations over the years.
They were running to Royal Albert Dock by ?; included
'P' in 1883 *hb*; earliest specific evidence 16 December
1884 (*Special Order R 1731, GE and London St Katharine's
Docks Railway*). Running to Victoria Dock from ? –
shown 'P' in *hb* 1890. Running to King George V Dock
(opened 1921) by ? (certainly by 1925 when there were
references in PLA documents). No platforms; temporary
arrangements at individual berths for dealing with
passengers. Before about 1965 all trains stopped at
Custom House to pick up PLA pilot and ran via High
Level line over Connaught Road swing-bridge and
PLA lines to dock berths. After High Level line closed
from Albert Dock Junction to PLA boundary, they
ran via Victoria Dock, picking up PLA pilot in the
Exchange Sidings and going on to King George V and
Royal Albert Docks. These services ceased 1966 when
passenger liners stopped calling at these docks (but
arrangements still included in *No. 1 Supplement August
1967 to Sectional Appendix of 1 April 1960* – inertia).
Oddly, Royal Albert Dock and Royal Victoria Dock last
shown 'P' in *hb* 1895 – result of lack of 'stations' as
such? (Material from GE, PLA and BR sources
provided by R. Green.)
ROYAL OAK
op 30 October 1871 [HC] (*GW notice T 24th*);
[GW] service first in *Brad* June 1878; GW use ended
1 October 1934; still open for [HC].
Both used same platforms, originally at sides, later
replaced by island (*L*, confirmed from OS by R. Hellyer).
Originally owned by GW; transferred to London
Underground 1 January 1963.
ROYAL ORDNANCE FACTORY THORP ARCH
– see THORP ARCH
ROYAL SHOWGROUND [LNW]
op 23 June 1903 (*RCH*); last public use 27 June 1903.
It op for merchandise on 2 June (*LNW Record*),
so perhaps provided earlier (and later) service for
exhibitors and staff, similar to that of Park Royal, GW,
which see. Shown 'P' 1904 *hb* so perhaps later use – or
intention of later use; *hb* 1908a 'delete'.
ROYAL VICTORIA [Dock]
op 28 March 1994**; still open.
ROYAL VICTORIA DOCK
– see ROYAL GROUP OF DOCKS.
ROYAL VICTORIA HOSPITAL – see NETLEY.
**ROYAL WELSH AGRICULTURAL
SHOWGROUND** [GW] (non-tt): used August 1925;
{Carmarthen Junction – Sarnau} (*U*).
ROYDON [GE]
op 9 August 1841 (*co n T 30 July- line*); still open.
ROYDS GREEN LOWER [EWYU] (non-tt):
workmen; dates ?; {branch from Robin Hood} (*U*).
ROYSTON near Cambridge [GN]
op 21 October 1850 (*co n T 18th*); still open.
ROYSTON & NOTTON [Mid]
op 6 April 1841**; re-sited about 1 mile south 1 July

1900 (*Mid*); clo 1 January 1968 (*RM February*).
Always R & N (*Mid*, supported by *Brad, hb*).
ROYTON [LY]
ROYTON (a) op 21 March 1864 (*LY*); always R, on
branch; *RM May 1919 said* 'has been reop', but trains
shown in tt February and May 1919 so perhaps error –
or had it been temporarily reduced to 'halt' status
during war?); clo 18 April 1966 (*RM June*).
ROYTON (b) op 1 July 1864 (*LY*) * as R JUNCTION
on main line; served as station for Royton after branch
closed; renamed R 8 May 1978 tt; clo 11 May 1987
(*BLN 561*).
* = in *Brad* for some time previously, no trains calling.
RUABON [GW] op 4 November 1846**; still open.
Sir William Watkin Wynn had right to stop trains
(*GW Deed M1254, dated 2 February 1846*).
RHUABON in *Topham* until 1849, in *Brad* until 1852.
RUBERY [Halesowen Joint]
op 10 September 1883 (*Mid*); clo to public April 1919
(*Cl*). Workmen's use continued; ceased probably
1933/34*. Used for Rubery Tenants' Association's
chartered excursion to Belle Vue, Manchester 28 August
1960 (local press, R. Maund); {in *IA*}.
* = clearly shown 11 September 1933 wtt; 30 April 1934 wtt
and thereafter all calls eastbound were noted as calling only for
single-line working purposes; a decreasing westbound service,
culminating in the 29 April 1935 wtt with a Saturday only stop,
was shown without this note; in 4 May 1936 wtt all stops were
noted; the probability is that all services both ways should have
been thus noted from 1933; a one-way service would have
made no sense (R. Maund).
RUDDINGTON
RUDDINGTON [GC] op 15 March 1899
(*GC; T 16th- line*); clo 4 March 1963 (*RM March*).
R FACTORY [LNE] (non-tt): op 1 September 1941
(*Cl 29*); wtt shows still in use 6 May 1946;
clo after 1947 (*U*); HALT; Ordnance workers;
{branch from Ruddington} (*U*).
RUDDLE ROAD [GW]
op 3 August 1907 (*GW H; Glos Chron 19th- line*); HALT;
clo 30 April 1917 (*wtt supp says 29 April – last day?*);
{map 94}.
RUDGWICK [LBSC] op during November 1865
(*LBSC*) – first in *Brad* January 1866, passed BoT
inspection 10 November 1865; clo 14 June 1965 (*Cl*).
RUDHAM – see EAST RUDHAM.
RUDYARD LAKE
RUDYARD LAKE [NS] op 22 July 1850 (*Churnet*)
clo 7 November 1960 (*T 7th*). First in *Brad* as HORTON,
renamed R later 1850; later erratically R, R OR H, R (H);
settled as R 2 April 1923 co tt (*JS*), LAKE added
1 April 1926 (*hbl April*).
Also see CLIFFE PARK.
RUFFORD [LY]
op 2 April 1849 (*LY; tt Southport Vis 7th*); still open.
RUFFORD COLLIERY [Mid] (non-tt):
PLATFORM; op 10 February 1918 (*Mid*);
clo 16 July 1928 (LMS wtt notice 3 September, *RAIL
957/15*) ; {branch from Mansfield}.

RUGBY

RUGBY [L&B] at Old Station Square op 9 April 1838 *(T 11th)* >

RUGBY [Midland Counties] op 30 June 1840 *(co n T 27th)*; temporary terminus, whilst viaduct linking to L&B was being finished >

On 4 July 1840 both companies moved to new station [LNW/Mid], about 45 chains east of 1838 one *(Mid)*. That was replaced by station on overlapping site, op in instalments 5 July 1885 to 10 April 1886 *(Mid)*; was R MIDLAND 25 September 1950 *(RM October)* to 4 May 1970 tt *(Mid)*; still open. Erratically R JUNCTION LNW co tt 1852 and *Brad* some tables to later 1860s, by when thus in southbound table only.

R CENTRAL [GC] op 15 March 1899 *(GC;T 16th-line)*; clo 5 May 1969 *(Cl)*.

RUGBY ROAD [NSWJ] op 8 April 1909 *(L)*; clo 1 January 1917 *(RCH)*. HALT in lists of closures *T 1916* and *RCH 1921* – see 1905**.

RUGELEY

R TOWN (a) [LNW] op 1 June 1870 *(W Mid)*; clo 18 January 1965 *(RM March)*.

R TOWN (b) op 2 June 1997 *(RM August)* – op with 1 June tt but that a Sunday and no Sunday service here; still open.

R TRENT VALLEY [LNW] op 15 September 1847 *(co n T 13th)*; T V added 1 June 1870 *(LNW Officers 15 May – to be officially)* *, dropped 6 May 1968 *(Cl)*, back 11 May 1992 tt *(AB Chron)*; still open. Early was R JUNCTION *(Brad; hb)*.

* = according to *W Mid* added T V in branch line table only until 15 April 1917.

RUISLIP

RUISLIP op by [Met] 4 July 1904 *(RCG; co ½ T 22 July- line)*; [Dist] added 1 March 1910, transferred to [Picc] 23 October 1933; still open.

R & ICKENHAM – see WEST RUISLIP.

R GARDENS [GW/GC] op 9 July 1934 *(T 28 June)*; clo 21 July 1958 *(Cl)*.

R GARDENS [Cen] op 21 November 1948 *(T 20th)*; still open.

R MANOR op by [Met/Dist] 5 August 1912 *(L)*; HALT until 1934/5 *(Brad)*; clo 12 February 1917, reop 1 April 1919 *(RCH)*; Dist service transferred to [Picc] 23 October 1933; still open.

Also see SOUTH RUISLIP.

RUMBLING BRIDGE [NB]

RUMBLING BRIDGE (a) op 1 May 1863 *(T 4th)*; clo 1 October 1868 (Thursday) for line rebuilding *(Cl)*.

RUMBLING BRIDGE (b) op 1 October 1870 on deviation *(Cl)*; clo 15 June 1964 *(Cl)*.

RUMWORTH & DAUBHILL [LNW]

op 2 February 1885 *(LNW Officers 26900)*, replacement for Daubhill; op as D, renamed 28 April 1885 *(Cl; RCG ref July)*; clo 3 March 1952 *(RM April)*.

RUNCORN

RUNCORN [LNW] op 1 April 1869 *(LNW Officers 3981 and Appendix C pp. 640, 643)*; still open.

R EAST op 3 October 1983 *(RM December)*; at/near earlier Norton; still open.

Also see HALTON.

RUNCORN GAP – see WIDNES.

RUNEMEDE (RANGE) – see YEOVENEY.

RUSHALL [LNW] trains first shown June 1849 tt; clo 1 March 1909 *(RCG)*; {Walsall – Pelsall}.

RUSHBURY [GW] op 16 December 1867 *(GW- line)*; clo 31 December 1951 *(T 31st)*.

RUSHCLIFFE [GC] op 5 June 1911 *(GC dates)*; HALT; clo 4 March 1963 *(RM March)*. Shown as PLATFORM *(hb, IA)*.

RUSHDEN [Mid] op 1 May 1894 *(RCG)*; clo 15 June 1959 *(RM July)*.

RUSHEY PLATT [MSWJ] Logically opened 18 December 1883 with Cheltenham extension of line; however, stop on line from Andover to Swindon GW was shown in *Brad* December 1883 whilst that on Cheltenham line was added January 1884; thus possible that platforms on Swindon line opened a little in advance of those on Cheltenham line. Andover line platforms clo with link line to Swindon 2 March 1885 *(RAIL 253/369)*, Cheltenham line 1 October 1905 (Sunday) *(RCG)*.

RUSHFORD [Manchester & Birmingham] op 4 June 1840 *(Manchester Guardian 6th – G. Boyes)*; last in tt April 1843, when replaced by Longsight – Levenshulme, opened previous year, was too close to make continuance of R worthwhile; {map 52}.

RUSHTON near Stoke-on-Trent [NS] op 1 September 1849 *(Churnet)*; clo 7 November 1960 *(T 7th)*.

RUSHTON – see GLENDON.

RUSHWICK [GW] op 31 March 1924 *(GW H)*; HALT; clo 5 April 1965 *(Cl)*; {Henwick – Bransford Road}. Pre-op Whitehall Halt *(RAC)*.

RUSKINGTON

RUSKINGTON (a) [GN/GE] op 6 March 1882 *(GN/GE)*; clo 11 September 1961 *(RM September)*.

RUSKINGTON (b) op 5 May 1975 *(T 23 April)*; still open.

RUSPER ROAD – see LITTLEHAVEN.

RUSPIDGE [GW] op 3 August 1907 *(GW H; Glos Chron 10th- line)*; HALT (but not in *hb*, where first shown 'P' 1929); clo 3 November 1958 *(T 21 October)*; {map 94}.

RUSSELL SQUARE [Picc] op 15 December 1906 *(co n T 14th)*; still open.

RUSWARP [NE]: line op 8 June 1835 (see 1835 B**), nd, May 1848 *(Topham)*; still open.

RUTHERFORD [NB]: line op 17 June 1850 *(Grev Temp)*, nd, June 1851; see 1948 September**; clo 15 June 1964 *(RM July)*.

RUTHERGLEN [Cal] op 1 June 1849 *(T 5th- line)*; re-sited 38 chains west 31 March 1879 *(Cl)*; replaced by new station on Argyle line 5 November 1979 *(Cl)*; still open.

Also see BROOMIELAW HARBOUR.

RUTHIN [LNW] op 1 March 1862 *(co ½ T 14 August)*; clo 30 April 1962 *(RM June)*.

RUTHRIESTON [GNS] first in *Brad* June 1856; April 1864 reduced to one train daily, from Aberdeen; November 1866 replaced by one daily, to Aberdeen;

last trains shown April 1867; reop 1 June 1885 *(Cl)*;
HALT on LNE ticket *(JB)* and in *Brad* from 1927/28;
clo 5 April 1937 *(RM January 1938)*.

RUTHVEN ROAD [Cal] first in *Brad* May 1859;
aot request; R R CROSSING 1864/5 to 1938/9 *Brad)*;
clo 1 October 1951 *(RM November)*.
Hb: 1862 R R SIDING; 1872 R R; 1938 R R HALT
(and LMS ticket thus, *JB*) but not in *Brad*.

RUTHWELL [GSW] op 23 August 1848 *(Dumfries
23rd- line)*; clo 6 December 1965 *(RM January 1966)*.

RUTTONSIDE [Cal] (non-tt):
railwaymen and families; op 3 January 1900;
clo after 1926; {Beattock – Elvanfoot} *(U)*.

RYBURGH [GE] op 20 March 1849 *(EC- line;
mentioned in inspection report)*; aot request;
clo 5 October 1964 *(RM September)*.

RYDE
R ESPLANADE [LBSC/LSW] op 5 April 1880 *(Hants
Teleg 7th)*; clo 1 January 1967 for electrification,
reop 20 March 1967 *(RM May)*; still open.
Incorporated PIER GATES of tramway (see 7:1).
R PIER HEAD [LBSC/LSW] op 12 July 1880
(Hants Teleg 17th); clo 23 January 1966 for pier repairs,
reop 18 April 1966 *(Cl)*; clo 18 September 1966 for
electrification, reop 20 March 1967 *(RM May)*; still open.
R ST JOHNS ROAD [IoW] op 23 August 1864
(Salisbury 27th); ST J R added 1880; clo 1 January
1967 for electrification, reop 20 March 1967 *(RM May)*;
still open.
Pier & Tramway. Was in *Brad*. Op Pier Head to Pier
Gates 29 August 1864; extended to Castle 28 January
1870; to St Johns Road 7 August 1871 *(IoW co ½
T 28 August)*. Pier Gates station replaced to west 1871
(T. Cooper) often in *Brad* as PIER TOLL GATE.
Initially acted as a link between the ferries and the
railway service. Pier Gates (i.e. Esplanade) to St Johns
Road closed 5 April 1880 when the 'main' line covered
that stretch but the original section kept until
26 January 1969 to provide extra capacity to that of the
parallel 'main' line, especially for ferry passengers not
going beyond Ryde by train, *(IoW)*.
Station built at Simeon Street about ⅜ mile north of
St Johns Road by Pier company, intending that
Ryde & Newport Railway would also use but BoT
refused approval; was opened about March 1876
as tram station and closed in 1880 *(Ryde, p.67 on)*.

RYDER BROW op 4 November 1985 *(Mid)*; still
open.

RYDERS HAYS [South Staffs] first in *Brad* April 1856;
last May 1858; {Pelsall – Brownhills}.

RYE
RYE [SE] op 13 February 1851 *(co n T 13th)*; still open.
RYE [Rye & C] (ng) op 13 July 1895**; no winter
service after 1925; clo 4 September 1939 *(Cl)*.
Later, line almost as far as Golf Links used by Admiralty
during war for carrying men and materials to build jetty
near golf links (P.A. Harding, *The Rye & Camber
Tramway*, author, 1985).

RYE HILL & BURSTWICK [NE]
op 27 June 1854 *(co ½ T 4 September- line)* as B;
renamed RYE HILL 1 July 1881 *(RCG)*,

R H & B 23 September 1929 *(Cl)*; clo 19 October 1964
(Cl). Became HALT 4 January 1960 according to *RM*
of that month but not thus tt – note added that no staff
were in attendance. Spelling 'RYE HILL' as in all
railway sources seen.

RYE HOUSE [GE]
op privately 1845 *(GE Journal October 1993)*, to public
Whit Sunday, 31 May 1846 *(co n T 28th)*; still open.

RYEFORD [Mid]
op 4 February 1867 *(Stroud J 9th)*; clo 16 June 1947**.

RYELAND [Cal] op 1 May 1905 *(RCG)*;
clo 1 July 1909 (Thursday), reop 1 November 1909 *(Cl)*;
clo 1 January 1917 *(RM February)*; back in *Brad* August
1919, when shown as terminus of trains from Strathaven
– see July 1922 reprint for nature of service;
see 1921 April/May**; clo 11 September 1939 *(Cl)*.

RYHALL (& Belmisthorpe) [GN]
op 1 November 1856**- line; aot request; clo 15 June
1959 *(RM July)*. R & B was RCH name; *Brad* (always),
GN wtt 1888, GN co tt 1909, LNE tt 1933: all just R.

RYHILL
RYHILL – see WINTERSETT.
R HALT [Dearne] op 3 June 1912**;
clo 10 September 1951 *(RM November)*.

RYHOPE [NE]
RYHOPE op 19 October 1836**;
clo 5 January 1953 *(RM March)*.
R EAST [ex-Londonderry] op 2 July 1855 *(NE maps-
line)*; EAST added 1904 *(hb)*, 1905 *(Brad)*, 1905/6 *(Reid)*
and thus LNE tt 1933; clo 7 March 1960 *(RM April)*.
Clear from inspection report dated 2 May 1855 that
Londonderry did have own station here at start, but
OS maps of 1855/57 show one station, about 11 chains
north of site of East, placed as if to serve both
Londonderry and Durham & Sunderland lines (S. Bragg);
thus some unrecorded re-siting must have occurred
– perhaps of 1836 station, with OS failing to keep up.
Would have been logical for both companies to share
(or have platforms alongside each others) at start
– Londonderry line to Seaham op for minerals Seaton to
Ryhope 17 January 1854, using Durham & Sunderland
line; own line to Sunderland opened with passenger
service *(NE; T 21 January 1854)*. *Brad* January 1858
says the 12.55 from Seaham 'meets the Durham &
Sunderland trains at Ryhope' and the timing would
not have allowed for anything beyond a change of
platforms; note not present *Brad* January 1859 (was in
Intelligible Guide June 1858).

RYLSTONE [Mid] op 30 July 1902 *(RCG)* – but four
public trains on 29th, day of formal opening *(Mid)*;
clo 22 September 1930 *(Cl)*. Perhaps used for excursions
where passengers were transferred to buses for trips
to Grassington after latter had closed for all purposes
11 August 1969.

RYSTON [GE] op 1 August 1882 *(GE- line)*;
clo 22 September 1930 *(Cl)*.

RYTON [NE]: line op 10 March 1835**, nd, in *Scott*
1837; see 1836 B**; clo 5 July 1954 *(RM September)*.

S & R. COLLIERY see 1887**.
SADDLEWORTH [LNW] op 1 August 1849 *(co ½ T 18 August- line; in co tt for 1 August, Stockport 3rd)*; clo 7 October 1968 *(RM Nov.)*. S UPPER MILL in LNW co tt 1852 (1864 S). S for DOBCROSS 1 August 1890 *(RCG)* to 1 January 1912 *(hbl 25th)*.
SAFFRON WALDEN [GE]
SAFFRON WALDEN op 23 November 1865 *(GE)*; clo 7 September 1964 *(RM September)*.
Also see ASHDON.
ST AGNES [GW] op 6 July 1903 *(RCG; R Cornwall Gaz 9th- line)*, at 2m 64ch, west side of single line; replaced 4 July 1937 by island platform at 2m 60ch after line doubled *(RAC)*; clo 4 February 1963 *(W Briton 4th)*.
ST ALBANS
St ALBANS [GN] op 16 October 1865 *(co n T 14th)*; clo 1 October 1951 *(T 8 September)*.
St ALBANS [Mid] op 13 July 1868 *(T 14th)*; St A CITY 2 June 1924 *(T 16 May)* to 16 May 1988 tt *(Mid)*; still open.
St A ABBEY [LNW] op 5 May 1858 *(co n T 6th)*; ABBEY added 2 June 1924 *(T 16 May)*; still open.
Brad: St A HOLYWELL HILL 1867 to 1889/90.
ST ANDREW(S) / ST A ROAD
– see CASTLE DOUGLAS
ST ANDREWS [NB]
op 1 July 1852 *(co ½T 4 November)* – excursion previous day *(East of T J)*; re-sited on extension to Crail 1 June 1887 *(Fifeshire Journal 26 May)*; clo 6 January 1969 *(RM October 1968)*.
ST ANDREWS ROAD Bristol [GW]
op to workmen 1 March 1917, clo 13 November 1922 *(Bristol notice 911)*; reop, now public, 30 June 1924 *(W D Press 30th)*; aot request; still open.
ST ANNES PARK [GW] op 23 May 1898 *(Bristol T 24th)*; clo 5 January 1970 *(Cl)*.
ST ANNES-ON-THE-SEA [PW]
first in *Brad* December 1873; still open.
LNW co tt: at first St A, became St A-on-S 1900/4.
LMS tt 1930 and *Brad* St A until 1955: St A.
Hb: 1874/5a St A, 1877 St A-on-the-Sea.
ST ANNS ROAD [TH Jt]
op 2 October 1882 *(Mid)*; clo 9 August 1942 (Sunday), last train 8th (A.A. Jackson, *Chron*).
ST ANNS WELL [GN] op 2 December 1889 *(RCG)*; clo 1 July 1916 (Saturday) *(RCH)*; {in IA}.
ST ANTHONYS [NE]
op 1 May 1879 *(Newcastle Weekly Chronicle 3rd- line)*; clo 12 September 1960 *(RM October)*.
ST ASAPH [LNW] op 5 October 1858 *(co n Clwyd)*; clo 19 September 1955 *(Rly Gaz 26 August)*.
ST ATHAN [GW] op 1 September 1939 *(hbl 8)*; HALT until 1943 tt *(Cl)*; clo 15 June 1964 *(Cl)*; {Gileston – Llantwit Major}.
ST ATHAN ROAD [TV]
op 1 October 1892 *(Western Mail 3rd- line)*; clo 4 May 1926**, reop 11 July 1927 *(Rly Gaz 11th)*; clo 5 May 1930 *(Cl)*. Ticket for St A R for THE LEYS *(JB)*.
ST AUSTELL
For early irregular service see 1830**.
St AUSTELL [GW] op 4 May 1859**; still open.

ST BEES [Fur]
St BEES op 19 July 1849**; still open.
St B HALT (non-tt): golfers; 1909 to February 1918; {Nethertown – St Bees} *(U)*.
ST BLAZEY [GW] op 20 June 1876 *(R Cornwall Gaz 24th)* as PAR ST B; renamed 1 January 1879 when rail link opened Par/St Blazey – previously passengers changing between Newquay branch and main line had to go between stations by road *(Cornwall; W Briton 2nd)*; clo 21 September 1925 *(Plymouth Division Annual Report)*; workmen used to 29 December 1934 *(U)*.
ST BOSWELLS [NB]
op 20 February 1849 *(D&C 6)*; clo 6 January 1969 *(RM February)*. At first various names different sources *(Murray April 1852 managed three in same issue)*, e.g.: NEWTOWN St B, St B N T / NEWTOWN JUNCTION / NEWTON St B; settled 1 March 1865 *(Cl)*.
ST BOTOLPHS – see COLCHESTER.
ST BRIAVELS [GW] op 1 November 1876 *(Wye; Merlin 27 October- line)* as BIGSWEIR; renamed St B & LLANDOGO 1 May 1909 *(hbl 22 April)*, St B 9 March 1927 *(GW notice, dated 'March')*; clo 5 January 1959 *(T 5th)*.
ST BRIDES CROSSING [LMS] (non-tt) railwaymen; in use 1926 *(U)*; 15 September 1952 and summer 1959 wtts show stops alternate Saturdays to set down railwaymen {Callander – Strathyre}.
ST BUDEAUX {map 114}
St B FERRY ROAD [GW] op 1 June 1904 *(W Morn News 1st, 2nd)* as HALT; became PLATFORM 1906; F R added 26 September 1949 *(Cl)*; still open.
St B VICTORIA ROAD [LSW] op 1 June 1890 *(W D Merc 2nd)* as St B for SALTASH (still thus *Brad* 1947, though *sig notice amendment 14 November 1923* said was to lose 'for' tag and hb 1925 had just St B); V R added 26 September 1949 *(Cl)*; HALT 18 May 1965 to 5 May 1969 *(Cl)*; still open.
ST CLEARS [GW]
op 2 January 1854 *(T 29 December 1853- line)*; clo 15 June 1964 *(Cl)*.
ST COLUMB ROAD [GW] op 20 June 1876 *(R Cornwall Gaz 24th)* as HALLOON; renamed 1 November 1878 *(Cl)*; aot request; still open.
ST COMBS [GNS]
op 1 July 1903 *(GNS)*; clo 3 May 1965 *(RM May)*.
ST CYRES – see NEWTON ST CYRES.
ST CYRUS [NB]
op 1 November 1865 *(co ½T 3 November- line)*; clo 1 October 1951 *(RM November)*.
ST DENYS [LSW] op 5 March 1866, about ¼ mile south of Portswood, which it replaced (B. Moody, *Southampton's Railways*, 1992); op as P, renamed 1 January 1876 *(Cl)*; still open.

ST DEVEREUX [GW] op 2 January 1854
(T 29 December 1853- line); clo 9 June 1958 *(Cl)*.

ST DUNSTANS [GN] op 21 November 1878 *(GN)*;
clo 15 September 1952 *(RM November)*.

ST ENOCH
For main line station, see GLASGOW.

St ENOCH [GU] op 14 December 1896**; still open.

ST ERTH [GW] op 11 March 1852 *(co n R Cornwall
Gaz 12th)* as St IVES ROAD; renamed 1 June 1877 *(Cl)*;
still open.

ST FAGANS
St FAGANS [GW] op 1 April 1852 *(The Cambrian 26
March)*; clo 10 September 1962 *(Cl)*.
Non-tt: Private station for Earl of Plymouth, chairman
of Barry; at east end of Barry line, level with GW station
between station signal box and junction with Barry.
(J. Hodge, *South Wales Main Line Part 3*,
Cardiff–Bridgend, Wild Swan, p.25).

ST FILLANS [Cal] op 1 October 1901 *(RCG)*;
clo 1 October 1951 *(RM November)*.

ST FORT [NB] op 1 June 1878 *(T 1st- line)*;
clo 6 September 1965 *(closure notice East of T J)*.

ST GABRIELS [SIT] first in *Brad* July 1877 as
GORSE LANE, aot G L St HELENS;
see 1860 July 25**; renamed St G 1896 *Brad*; last there
February 1917, but last in *hb* 1929 – inertia?; {map 88}.
In 1880s there were intermittent *Brad* references to fast
trains to Oystermouth from G L SIDINGS.

ST GEORGES CROSS [GU]
op 14 December 1896**; still open.

ST GERMANS near King's Lynn [EA]
op 27 October 1846 *(co n D&C 5)*; last *Brad* October
1850 but still in EC co tt May 1851 (not in *Truscott's*
EC tt 1 January 1853); {map 67}. (Spelling in all
sources was SAINT GERMANS).

ST GERMANS near Plymouth [GW]
St GERMANS op 4 May 1859**; still open.

St G VIADUCT (non-tt) used by workmen during
building of deviation line; op 1905; clo by November
1915; {St Germans – Defiance} *(U)*.

ST HARMONS [Cam] trains first shown in tt June
1872; aot request; clo 31 December 1962 *(T 31st)*.
HALT *hb* 1938, 1956 and Cam ticket *(JB)* but not in tt.

ST HELENS [IoW]
op 27 May 1882 *(SR; Rtn- line)*; clo 11 February 1951,
reop 22 March 1951 *(IoW 1923 and see 1951**)*;
clo 21 September 1953 *(T 21st)*.

ST HELENS Swansea [SIT]
op 25 July 1860**; clo 6 January 1960**; {map 88}.
At first St H ROAD, later St H JUNCTION,
St H ROAD BAY VIEW, St H B V *(Brad, The Cambrian)*.

ST HELENS – see WEST AUCKLAND.

ST HELENS
St H CENTRAL [LNW]: for op see 1832 B**;
re-sited short distance west 19 December 1849
(J.M. Tolson, *St Helens* Railway, Oakwood, 1983, p.27);
re-sited again, to north, 3 February 1858;
St H SHAW STREET 1 March 1949 *(LNW Record)*
to 11 May 1987, when became ST H C; still open.

St H CENTRAL [GC] op 3 January 1900 *(RM Jan.)*;
clo 3 March 1952 *(RM April)*. CENTRAL added

1 March 1949 according to *RM May* but it had always
been thus *Brad, hb*.

St H JUNCTION [LNW]: line op 17 September
1830**, nd, 1 March 1831 co tt*; still open.
* = stop listed there was BOTTOM OF SUTTON INCLINE;
early name for St H J or was latter early replacement?

ST HELENS COLLIERY [LMS] (non-tt) miners;
1920s?; {Siddick Junction – Flimby} *(U)*.

ST HELIER [SR] op 5 January 1930 *(T 6th)*; still open.

ST HILARY [TV] op 1 May 1905 *(Cowbridge)*;
see 1904**; clo 12 July 1920 *(RCG)*;
{Cowbridge – St Mary Church Road}.

ST IVES near Cambridge [GN/GE]
op 17 August 1847 *(co ½ T 13 August)*; clo 5 October
1970 *(RM Oct.)*. St I JUNCTION *Brad* 1852 to 1858/9.

ST IVES near Penzance [GW]
op 1 June 1877 *(Cornish Teleg 5th)*; re-sited 6 chains east
at end of viaduct 23 May 1971 *(Cl)*; clo 15 January
1973 for flood relief scheme (buses replaced),
reop 21 April 1973 *(Cl)* – due to reopen Thursday
19 April according to *BR handbill* – delay?; still open.

ST IVES ROAD – see ST ERTH.

ST JAMES Newcastle [TWM]
op 14 November 1982 *(Tyneside)*; still open.

ST JAMES – see LIVERPOOL.

ST JAMES DEEPING [GN]
op 1 August 1849 *(GN Society Magazine 9)*;
clo 11 September 1961 *(RM September)*.
Early tts: CROWLAND & St J D (thus opening tt *RM
September 1910*)/St J D & C/variations, until settled
1851. GN co tt 1909, LNE tt 1933 and *Brad* ? to 1955:
St J D for MARKET DEEPING.

ST JAMES PARK Exeter [LSW]
op 26 January 1906 *(Exeter F P 27th)* as LIONS HOLT;
renamed St J P 7 October 1946 *(Cl)*;
HALT until 5 May 1969 *(SR App)*; still open.

ST JAMES STREET – see WALTHAMSTOW.

ST JAMES'S PARK London [Dist]
op 24 December 1868 *(T 21st, 25th)*; still open.

ST JOHNS [SE] op 1 June 1873 *(T 28 May)*; still open.

ST JOHNS CHAPEL [NE] op 21 October 1895
(RCG); clo 29 June 1953 *(RM August)*.

ST JOHNS WOOD
op by [Bak] 20 November 1939 *(T 18th)*; replaced
Lords; transferred to [Jub] 1 May 1979; still open.
Pre-op Acacia Road *(L)*.

ST KEW HIGHWAY [LSW]
op 1 June 1895 *(Cornish & D P 8th)*;
clo 3 October 1966 *(Cornish & D P 8th)*.

ST KEYNE WISHING WELL HALT [GW]
op 1 September 1902 *(Cornish T 30 August)*;
clo 3 November 1990 for flood prevention work,
reop 19 November 1990 *(RM January 1991)*; still open.
Aot request; HALT in *hb* 1938 and 1956 but not in
Brad until 1952; aot request; dropped 5 May 1969;
WW HALT added 17 May 2008 *(RM July)*.

ST LAWRENCE near Bodmin [GW]
op 26 October 1906 *(Cornish Guard 2 November)*;
PLATFORM (but HALT on GW ticket, *JB*, and in
Brad until 1909/11); clo 1 January 1917 *(GW notice
dated 22 December 1916)*; {map 113}.

ST LAWRENCE IoW [IWC]
op 20 July 1897 *(Rtn)* as VENTNOR St L;
renamed 1900 tt; became HALT 1928/9 *(Brad)*;
aot request; clo 15 September 1952 *(T 6 August)*.
Brad: St L HALT for BLACKGANG; not thus *hb*.

ST LAWRENCE PEGWELL BAY [SE]
first in *Brad* September 1864 with note that it was
'the Junction Station for Pegwell Bay and Village';
clo 3 April 1916 *(T 11 March)*; {map 131}.
Brad variously: as above, St L JUNCTION,
St L for P B, finally St L P B . *Hb*: St L, St L for P B.

ST LEONARDS
St LEONARDS (BULVERHYTHE) [LBSC]
op 27 June 1846 *(Hants Chron 4 July)*;
temporary terminus replaced on extension of line by >
St L WEST MARINA [LBSC] op 7 November 1846
(LBSC) as HASTINGS & St L; renamed St L
13 February 1851 *(Cl)*, St L W M 5 December 1870
(Cl); re-sited short distance west 1882 *(Cl)*;
clo 10 July 1967 *(RM August)*.
St L WARRIOR SQUARE [SE] op 13 February 1851
(co n T 13th); W S added 5 December 1870 *(Cl)*;
clo 1 January 1917 *(T 22 December 1916)*;
reop 1 January 1919 *(Cl)*; still open.
Also see WEST St LEONARDS.

ST LEONARDS – see EDINBURGH.

ST LUKES – see SOUTHPORT.

ST MARGARETS HERTFORSHIRE [GE]
op 31 October 1843 *(T 2 November- line)*;
re-sited west of level crossing 3 July 1863 *(C/W)*;
H added 14 May 1984 tt (index earlier); still open.
Was St M for STANSTEAD ABBOT(T)S 22 June 1909
(hbl 7 July), and thus GE co tt 1914, to 1955 *(Brad)*.

ST MARGARETS near Twickenham [LSW]
op 2 October 1876 *(L)*; still open.

ST MARGARETS – see EDINBURGH.

ST MARY CHURCH ROAD [TV] op 1 October
1892 *(Western Mail 3rd- line)*; clo 4 May 1926**,
reop 11 July 1927 *(Rly Gaz 11th)*; clo 5 May 1930 *(Cl)*.

ST MARY CRAY [LCD]
op 3 December 1860 *(T 4th)*; still open. St MARYS
CRAY in opening notice and in *Brad* until 1861/2.

ST MARYS near Huntingdon [GN] op 22 July 1863
(Rtn- line); aot request; after 22 September 1930 *Brad*,
before with August 1931, rail service reduced to one
that ended about 10.30 a.m.; buses for rest of day.
Thus to closure 6 October 1947 *(RM January 1948)*.

ST MARYS BAY [RHD] (ng) op 16 July 1927**
(which see for later history of line) as HOLIDAY CAMP;
renamed H C JESSON 1939 *Brad*, St M B on
reopening 1946. Became JEFFERSTONE LANE in
preservation days (since reverted).

ST MARYS CROSSING [GW]
op 12 October 1903 *(Stroud N 16th)*; HALT;
clo 2 November 1964 *(W D Press 2nd)*.

ST MARYS WHITECHAPEL ROAD [Met/Dist]
op 3 March 1884 *(L)*; at first St M/W St M/St M W;
at first used by SE trains; [Dist] use added 1 October
1884 as terminus of service to New Cross SE;
[Met] use to New Cross SE began 6 October 1884,
Dist then switching to New Cross LBSC;

ROAD added 26 January 1923 *(L)*; clo 1 May 1938
(Sunday) *(RM June – clo after last train April 30)*.
ST MELLONS (non-tt):
wtt 2 October 1944 shows return service Cardiff
General to here and back (including Sundays), at times
clearly designed for workers (Reprint of GW Swindon
etc area wtt, Dragonwheel Books).

ST MELYD GOLF LINKS [LMS]
op 1 October 1923 *(LNW Cl)*;
clo 22 September 1930 *(Cl)*; {Prestatyn – Meliden}.

ST MICHAELS Liverpool [CLC] op 1 June 1864
(CLC); clo 17 April 1972 *(RM May)*; reop 3 January
1978 *(Cl supp 2; Daily Telegraph 3rd- line)*; still open.

ST MONANCE [NB]
op 1 September 1863 *(D&C 15- line)*; St MONANS
1875 to 1936 tt *(Cl; JS)*, and thus NB co tt 1900;
clo 6 September 1965 *(closure notice East of T J)*.

ST NEOTS [GN]
op 7 August 1850 *(T 6th, 8th)*; still open.

ST OLAVES [GE] op 1 June 1859 *(T 2nd)*;
clo 2 November 1959 *(RM December)*.

ST OLAVES JUNCTION – see HADDISCOE.

ST PANCRAS – see KINGS CROSS St P for
underground, LONDON for main line station.

ST PAULS
See LONDON BLACKFRIARS for main line station.
St PAULS [Cen] op 30 July 1900 *(L; T 25th- line)* as
POST OFFICE; renamed 1 January 1937; still open.

ST PAULS – see under HALIFAX.

ST PETERS Newcastle [NE]
op 1 May 1879 *(Newcastle Weekly Chronicle 3rd- line)*;
clo 23 July 1973 *(RM August)*.

ST PETERS – see under SUNDERLAND.

ST PHILIPS, ST PHILIPS MARSH
– see BRISTOL.

ST QUINTIN PARK & WORMWOOD SCRUBBS
[WL] op 1 August 1871 *(LNW Officers 6791)* as W S;
renamed 1892; resited 1 November 1893 *(co 1/2
Rly Times 10 February 1894)*; destroyed by fire 3 October
1940 *(Cl)* – but *wtt supp* says clo 21 October 1940 –
'official' clo or had some sort of patched service run
until then?

ST ROLLOX
For early main line terminus see GLASGOW TOWNHEAD.
St ROLLOX [Cal] op 1 August 1883 *(RCG)*;
clo 5 November 1962 *(RM October)*. When Works Trips
ran, alternate trains ran from station and adjoining
Cattle Bank *(Away pp. 116–8)*.
Sometimes GLASGOW St R in tts.

ST THOMAS – see EXETER.

ST THOMAS CROSS [WCE Jt] (non-tt)
PLATFORM used by workers at Florence Pit Iron Mine;
op by October 1923; clo by June 1952;
{Egremont – Beckermet} *(U)*.

ST WINEFRIDES [LNW]
op 1 July 1912 *(LNW Officers 43723)*; became HALT
1938/9 *(Brad and LMS tt)*; clo 6 September 1954
(BR notice); {Holywell branch}.

ST-Y-NYLL [Barry] first in *Brad* July 1905; HALT;
clo November 1905 *(Cl)*; {Creigiau – Wenvoe}.

SALCEY FOREST [East & West Junction]
op 1 December 1892 *(SMJ)*; clo 1 April 1893
(Saturday) *(G&S)* – trains still shown April *Brad*
(inertia?); {Stoke Bruern goods – Olney}.
SALE
SALE [MSJA] op 20 July 1849**; op as S MOOR
(Brad and *Stockport)*; MOOR dropped 1856/7 *(Brad)*;
S & ASHTON-ON-MERSEY 1 February 1882 (Cl)
to 1930/1 *(Brad; ref RCH dist 19 October 1931)*;
clo 27 December 1991 *(BLN 671)* for conversion to >
SALE [Manch] op 15 June 1992 *(RM August)*; still open.
SALEHURST [KES]: earliest use non-tt – July 1903
Col. Stephens, line owner, told BoT he had put up
platform (Vicar of Salehurst had asked for Wednesday
and Sunday stops for his organist who lived at Bodiam)
(KES); first in public tt starting 23 September 1929;
aot request; 1929/30 became S PLATFORM,
1931/2 reverted to S, 1939 became S HALT *(Brad)*.
Clo 4 January 1954 *(T 28 October 1953)*;
{Robertsbridge – Junction Road}.
SALEM [WH] (ng); op 31 July 1922** *(WHH 2)*,
but first in *Brad* October 1922; aot request;
clo 28 September 1936 *(Cl)*; {map 76}.
HALT until 1923 *(Brad)* and on WH ticket *(JB)*.
SALFORD
S CENTRAL [LY] op 29 May 1838**; CENTRAL
added 29 May 1994 tt, but in use locally by 1990
(AB Chron); still open. *Co n Manch G 26th* has
MANCHESTER in heading of skeleton tt but
S NEW BAILEY STREET in detail.
Also variously S, MANCHESTER S.
S CRESCENT op 11 May 1987 *(BLN 556)*; at/near
earlier Oldfield Road; still open.
A temporary platform was put up at Salford 10 April
1988, on ex-LNW line, for northbound use only during
resignalling; certainly still in use April 1989,
clo 2 October 1989 (?)
Also see OLDFIELD ROAD.
SALFORD PRIORS [Mid]
op 17 September 1866 *(Mid; Rtn- line)*; clo 1 October
1962 *(Mid)*, but bus service to 17 June 1963.
SALFORDS [LBSC; SR] op as non-tt railway staff
halt 8 October 1915 *(U)*; became public 17 July 1932
(RCH); HALT until 1 January 1935 *(Cl)*; still open.
SALHOUSE [GE]
op 20 October 1874 *(T 21st)*; still open.
SALISBURY {map 126}
SALISBURY (Milford) [LSW] op 1 March 1847
(W Fly P 6th); terminus, replaced on line to Exeter by >
SALISBURY [LSW] op 2 May 1859 *(W Fly P 3rd- line)*;
still open.
SALISBURY [GW] op 30 June 1856 *(W Fly P 1 July)*;
clo 12 September 1932 *(Cl)*; service diverted to
LSW station.
Hb called both GW and LSW stations S FISHERTON
and GW ticket thus exists *(JB)*; also in *Brad* for GW
late 1860s, early 1870s.
SALT (& Sandon) [GN] op 23 December 1867 *(GN;
T 23rd- line)*; clo 4 December 1939 *(Cl)*. *Brad, co tt* and
tickets just SALT; S & S was RCH version.

SALTAIRE
SALTAIRE (a) [Mid] first in *Brad* May 1856;
clo 22 March 1965 *(RM April)*. At first SALTARRE
in *Brad*.
SALTAIRE (b) op 9 April 1984 on same site *(Mid)*;
still open.
SALTASH [GW] op 4 May 1859**; still open.
GW co tt 1932: S for CALLINGTON.
SALTBURN [NE]
op 19 August 1861 *(RAIL 667/395)*; still open.
S-BY-SEA / S-BY-THE-SEA in *Brad* until 1887/9.
Aot excursion station – really extra platform nearby to
serve the Zetland Hotel (then railway owned). Dates ? –
work begun 1870 (B. Fawcett, *HMRS*, January 1988).
SALTCOATS
See 1834** for early service through here.
SALTCOATS [GSW]: line op 17 August 1840 *(Rtn)*,
nd, March 1850; re-sited to west 1 July 1858 *(Cl)*;
again re-sited, now between first and second sites, 1882
(Cl); S CENTRAL 30 June 1952 to 4 February 1965
(Cl); still open.
S NORTH [Cal] op 4 September 1888 *(Cal)*;
clo 1 January 1917 *(RM February)*; reop 1 February
1919 *(RCH)*; NORTH added 2 June 1924**;
clo 4 July 1932 *(Cl)*.
SALTER LANE [Ashover] (ng)
op 7 April 1925 *(RM October)*; request;
clo 14 September 1936** *(Cl)*; {map 59}.
SALTERSGATE COTTAGE – see 1843**
(possible early S&D stop/staff halt – see HIGH STOOP);
Salter's Gate included in *hb* 1862, facilities unknown;
later S G Siding/Siding and Stone Wharf; still in 1956 *hb*;
no facilities ever shown; {map 30}.
SALTERTON – see BUDLEIGH SALTERTON.
SALTFLEETBY [GN] op 17 October 1877
(co n Louth); clo 5 December 1960 *(RM January 1961)*.
SALTFORD near Bath
SALTFORD [GW] op 16 December 1840 *(co n Bath &
Chelt 15th)*; clo 5 January 1970 *(Cl)*.
Also see KELSTON.
SALTHOUSE – see BARROW-in-Furness.
SALTLEY [Mid]
op 1 October 1854 *(Mid)*; clo 4 March 1968 *(Mid)*.
SALTMARSHE [NE]
op 2 August 1869 *(T 2nd- line)*; still open.
SALTNEY [GW] op 4 November 1846**;
clo 1 January 1917 *(GW notice dated 22 December 1916)*;
reop 4 July 1932 *(Cl)*; clo 12 September 1960 *(Cl)*.
HALT on BR ticket *(JB)* but not tt.
SALTNEY FERRY MOLD JUNCTION [LNW]
op 1 January 1891 *(RCG; MT6/654/10, inspection report
dated 22 January 1891)*; clo 30 April 1962 *(RM June)*.
SALTOUN [NB]
op 14 October 1901**; clo 3 April 1933**.
SALVATION ARMY [GN; LNE]
op non-tt by 1 November 1897 *(U)*; first in public tt for
8 July 1929; SIDING/HALT; last in public tt September
1942; clo 1 October 1951 *(T 8 September)*;
{Hill End – St Albans}. Originally SANDERS SIDING;
aot S A & CAMP FIELD PRESS *hb* – no facilities ever
shown. Tt note said passengers for here had to make

application to officer in charge before leaving Hatfield or St Albans, termini of branch it was on.

SALWICK [PW] first in *Brad* December 1841 (see 1840 July 16**); at first Saturdays only, perhaps early service intermittent; clo 2 May 1938 *(T 21 March)*; reop 8 April 1940 for ICI factory workers and to public 2 November 1942 *(LNW Record)*; still open.
Alias S ROAD early (even co tts erratic).

SALZCRAGGIE [High]
op non-tt 28 July 1874 for private shooting estate *(U)*; public opening 26 May 1907 *(High –* with note that perhaps July 1907, when first in *Brad)*; wtt appendix 1 May 1920 says for use of shooting or fishing tenant using S Lodge; to hold tickets to next stop either way but *Brad* thereabouts included as ordinary request stop. Clo 29 November 1965 *(Cl)*. PLATFORM 1938 *hb*, HALT *hb* 1941a (dropped 1962a); PLATFORM in tt until 1962/3 – dropped from index 18 June 1962, table later.

SAMPFORD COURTENAY
SAMPFORD COURTENAY (a): [LSW] op 8 January 1867 *(W D Merc 10th)* as OKEHAMPTON ROAD; renamed BELSTONE CORNER 3 October 1871, S C 1 January 1872 *(Cl)*; HALT 12 September 1965 to 5 May 1969 *(Cl)*; clo 5 June 1972 *(Cornish & DP 11th)*.
SAMPFORD COURTENAY (b): op 23 May 2004, summer Sundays only *(RM July, p. 79)*; still open.
In tt summer 2003 but not opened that year.

SAMPFORD PEVERELL [GW]
op 9 July 1928 *(Tiverton 10th)*; became HALT 18 June 1962 tt; clo 5 October 1964 *(Som Gaz 5 September)*. Shown as HALT by *Cl* and so regarded locally but not thus *hb* (first included 1930a, before halts generally added), nor GW co tt, nor *Brad* until 1962.
Tiverton Parkway here later.

SAND HUTTON [Sand Hutton] (ng); {map 40} CENTRAL; DEPOT; GARDENS – all three op 4 October 1924** *(RM December)*; last two HALTS *(Brad)*; last train Saturday 1 March 1930**.

SANDAL
SANDAL [WRG Jt] op 1 February 1866 *(GN; T 3rd-line)*; clo 4 November 1957 *(RM December)*.
S & AGBRIGG op 30 November 1987 *(BLN 581)*; still open.
S & NOTTON – see NOTTON.
SANDALL [SY] first in *Brad* April 1857; Saturdays only; last September 1859; {Doncaster – Bramwith}.

SANDBACH
SANDBACH [LNW] op 10 May 1842 *(T 16th/Liverpool Mail)*; still open. LNW co tt 1874: S for NORTHWICH.
Also see WHEELOCK.

SANDERS SIDING – see SALVATION ARMY.
SANDERSTEAD [CO Jt] op 10 March 1884 *(Hants Chron 15th- line)*; included in inspection report of 18 February, *MT6/1908/3)*; still open.

SANDFORD & BANWELL [GW]
op 3 August 1869 *(Shepton 6th)*; clo 9 September 1963 *(Weston 13th)*. Just S in B&E wtt 1886.

SANDGATE [SE]
op 10 October 1874 *(SE) –* co ½ *T 20 January 1875* gives 9th (formal op); clo 1 April 1931 (Wednesday)

(J. Gough, *Chron January 2004 – T 13 March* gave 31 March, last day).

SANDHILLS [LY]
first in *Brad* July 1854 *(RAIL 372/3*, 4 July said had opened) as LIVERPOOL NORTH DOCKS, soon N D; renamed S 1857 tt *(JS)*; platforms moved from north to south of Sandhills Lane by 9 July 1881, when *Waterloo Times* said it had been done; still open.
LY co tt 1899 and LMS tt 1930: S for N D.

SANDHOLME [HB] op 27 July 1885 *(op tt NER I)*; clo 1 August 1955 *(RM September)*.

SANDHURST
SANDHURST (a) [SE] op 4 May 1852 *(SE)*; last trains in *Brad* December 1853. Later use, 3 May 1856, for special trains taking people to see Queen Victoria lay foundation stone of Wellington College *(co n T 2nd)* and for fete there 2 June 1856 *(co n T 28 May)*.
S BERKS (b) [SEC] first in *Brad* August 1909; HALT until 5 May 1969 *(SR App)*; BERKS added 1974/6 tt; still open.

SANDIACRE
S & STAPLEFORD [Mid] op 6 September 1847 *(Mid)*; clo 1 May 1872 (Wednesday) *(Cl)*.
See STAPLEFORD & SANDIACRE for replacement.
SANDILANDS [Cal] op 1 April 1864 *(Cal- line)*; clo 5 October 1964 *(RM October)*.

SANDLING
SANDLING [SE] op 1 January 1888 *(SE)*; S JUNCTION until 3 December 1951 when became S for HYTHE; intermittently thus until 12 May 1980 tt, when settled as S *(Cl)*; still open.
SANDLING INTERNATIONAL (non-tt):
used 16 September 2003 only, for invited guests to formal opening of new link to Channel Tunnel *(Rly Obs November, p. 492)*.
SANDON [NS] op 1 May 1849 *(NS- line)*; clo 6 January 1947 *(RM January 1950)*.
SANDON DOCK [LO] op 6 March 1893**; clo before first detail in *Brad*, May 1896. Replaced by Huskisson Dock (north) and Nelson Dock (south).
SANDOWN [IoW] op 23 August 1864 *(Salisbury 27th- line)*; clo 1 January 1967 for electrification work, reop 20 March 1967 *(RM May)*; still open.
LBSC co tt 1912: S JUNCTION in one table.
SANDOWN PARK [LSW] (non-tt): races; 1862 to 1965; linked to course by subway; *(Surrey)*.
SANDPLACE [GW] first in *Brad* December 1881, when it replaced Causeland, which see; clo 3 November 1990 for flood prevention work, reop 19 November 1990 *(RM January 1991)*; aot request; still open.
According to *Cl* became HALT in 1953, but thus *hb* 1938 and *Brad* from 1951/2; HALT dropped 5 May 1969 *(Cl)*.
SANDSEND [NE] op 3 December 1883 *(Rtn- line)*; clo 5 May 1958 *(RM May)*.
SANDSFOOT CASTLE [WP Jt]
op 1 August 1932 *(Cl 29)*; HALT;
clo 3 March 1952 *(RM March)*; {Rodwell – Portland}.
SANDSIDE [Fur] op 26 June 1876 *(D&C 14; LNW Officers 16040- line)*; clo 4 May 1942 *(LNW Record)*.

SANDWELL & DUDLEY [LNW]
op 1 July 1852 *(W Mid; T 2nd- line)* as OLDBURY &
BROMFORD LANE; renamed 14 May 1984
(BR LM Region pamphlet D102/584); still open.
SANDWICH [SE]
op 1 July 1847 *(co n T 30 June)*; still open.
SANDWICH ROAD [EK]
first in *Brad* May 1925; HALT; clo 1 November 1928.
See 1948 November 1★★ for details.
SANDY
SANDY [GN] op 7 August 1850 *(T 6th, 8th)*; still open.
Was S JUNCTION 1867/9 to 1893/4 *(Brad)* but just S
in GN wtt 1888.
SANDY [Sandy & Potton] op 9 November 1857★★;
clo December 1861. LNW purchased line >
SANDY [LNW] op 7 July 1862 *(Cl)*; clo 1 January 1968
(Cl). Became S VILLAGE 1867, S JUNCTION 1868
(and thus LNW co tt 1868), S 1908 *(JS)*.
SANDY LANE [Lancs, Derby & East Coast] (non-tt)
miners' HALT; in use 1923; {on branch to WELBECK
COLLIERY, which see}.
SANDY LODGE – see MOOR PARK.
SANDYCROFT
SANDYCROFT [LNW] op 1 March 1884 *(LNW
Officers 25670)*; original station temporary (platforms of
old sleepers), to see if traffic justified it *(MT6/360/14)*;
clo 1 May 1961 *(RM June)*.
S H M FACTORY PLATFORM (non-tt)
op June 1917 for munititions workers, clo 29 October
1920 *(LNW dates, no authority for clo date; MT6/360/14*
refers to 'New Factory Platform')*;
{300 yards east of Dundas Siding 1900 Signal Box,
which was west of main station}.
SANDYFORD [GSW] Ogston & Tennants workmen
used from June 1914; originally S PLATFORM;
first included *hb* 1941a as HALT; still thus 1956
(no indication public/private); op to public 18 April 1966
(U); clo 5 June 1967 *(Cl)*; {Paisley – Renfrew}.
SANKEY
S BRIDGES [LNW] op 1 February 1853 *(T 16th- line)*;
clo 1 January 1917 *(T 22 December 1916)*; reop 1 July
1919 *(Cl)*; clo 26 September 1949 *(RM September)*.
S FOR PENKETH [CLC] first in *Brad* May 1874;
still open. Always thus *Brad* and co tts seen but 'for P'
only added in *hb* 1904.
SANQUHAR
SANQUHAR (a) [GSW] op 28 October 1850 *(T 26th-
line)*; clo 6 December 1965 *(RM January 1966)*.
SANQUHAR (b) op 27 June 1994 *(BLN 735)*; still open.
SARN op 28 September 1992 *(RM December)*; still open.
SARNAU [GW]
op 6 June 1888 *(RAIL 253/229)*; clo 15 June 1964 *(Cl)*.
SARSDEN [GW]
non-tt use by July 1897 as S SIDING *(U)*; op to public
2 July 1906 *(GW H)* as S HALT; clo 3 December 1962
(RM January 1963).
SAUCHIE [NB] first in *Brad* October 1873;
clo 1 January 1917 *(RM February)*; reop 2 June 1919
(RCH); clo 22 September 1930 *(Cl)*.
SAUGHALL [GC] op 31 March 1890 *(RCG)*;
clo 1 February 1954 *(RM March)*.

SAUGHTON [NB] op 21 February 1842★★
(co n T 19th) as CORSTORPHINE; not in *Brad*
December 1842 (first time for several months full detail
given); back May 1846 (but perhaps served by goods
trains meanwhile); renamed 1 February 1902
(hbl 23 January); clo 1 January 1917 *(RM February)*;
reop 1 February 1919 *(RM February)*;
clo 1 March 1921 (Tuesday) *(Cl)*.
SAUGHTREE [NB] op 1 July 1862 *(co n T 1st- line)*;
clo 1 December 1944 (Friday), reop 23 August 1948
(RM November); clo 15 October 1956 *(T 21 September)*.
SAUNDERSFOOT [GW]
op 5 September 1866 *(Cardiff T 7th)*;
re-sited about June 1868; aot request; still open.
SAUNDERTON [GW/GC]
op 1 July 1901 *(GC dates)*; still open.
SAVERNAKE: {map 124}.
SAVERNAKE [GW] op 11 November 1862 *(co n
Marlborough 8th)*; S LL 1 July 1924 *(GW circular 18 June)*
to 11 September 1961 *(Cl)*; clo 18 April 1966 *(RM May)*.
S HL [MSWJ] op 26 June 1898 *(RCG; Marlborough
2 July- line)*; HL added 1 July 1924 *(GW circular 18 June)*;
clo 15 September 1958 *(Cl)*.
SAWBRIDGEWORTH [GE]
op 22 November 1841 *(co n T 17th- line)*; still open.
SAWDON [NE] op 1 May 1882 *(Scarborough 4th-line)*;
clo 5 June 1950 *(Cl)*.
SAWLEY
SAWLEY [Mid] op 4 June 1839 *(Mid)* as BREASTON;
renamed by mid-1840; clo 1 December 1930 *(Mid)*.
S JUNCTION – see LONG EATON.
SAXBY [Mid] first in *Brad* February 1849;
re-sited on deviation 28 August 1892 *(Mid)*;
clo 6 February 1961 *(Mid)*.
SAXHAM & RISBY [GE] op 1 April 1854★★ *(EC- line)*;
& R added 1914/15 *(RCG reference January 1915)*;
aot request; clo 2 January 1967 *(RM February)*.
SAXILBY [GN] op 9 April 1849 *(GN/GE)*; still open.
SAXELBY until 1850/1 *(Brad)*, then S JUNCTION
until 1860s.
SAXMUNDHAM [GE] op 1 June 1859 *(T 2nd)*;
still open. Aot S JUNCTION *(Brad)*.
SCAFELL [Cam]
SCAFELL (a) first in *Brad* May 1863; all days; aot
request; clo 1 July 1891 (Wednesday) *(RAIL 1005/280)*.
SCAFELL (b) back in *Brad* July 1913, eastbound only,
alighting only; HALT; last actually used by public 1952
but last in tt 20 September 1954 *(Cl)*, though *Cam II*
p.194 gives 7 March 1955 (a delayed 'official' date?);
{goods IA}.
SCALBY [NE]
op 16 July 1885 *(T 16th)*; clo to general public 2 March
1953 *(RM April)*; until 1964 trains called for people
who had hired camping coaches here – wtt June 1961
shows two or three trains each way with definite calls.
SCALE HALL op 8 June 1957 *(RM July)*;
clo 3 January 1966 *(RM February)*;
{Lancaster – Morecambe}.
SCALFORD [GN/LNW] op 1 September 1879
(LNW Officers 20028); clo 7 December 1953 *(T 7th)*.

SCARBOROUGH [NE]
SCARBOROUGH op 8 July 1845★★; still open.
S CENTRAL 1926 *(hbl ref October)* to 5 May 1969.
S LONDESBOROUGH ROAD op 8 June 1908 as
WASHBECK EXCURSION STATION, non-tt *(U)*;
renamed 1 June 1933 *(U)*; first in *Brad* 17 July 1933 tt;
last train 25 August 1963 (Sunday) *(C/W)*.
SCARCLIFFE [GC] op 1 January 1898 *(GC dates)*;
clo 3 December 1951 *(Cl)*.
SCARNING [EA] op 11 September 1848 (line date,
EC; not in *Brad* until March 1849, but in *Topham*
October 1848); last in *Brad* October 1850;
{Wendling – Dereham}. Spelling as *Brad, Topham*;
alias SCURNING according to some modern books.
SCAWBY & HIBALDSTOW [GC] op 2 April 1849
(Lincs Times 3rd); clo 5 February 1968 *(RM February)*.
SCHOLES [NE]
op 1 May 1876 *(NE- line)*; clo 6 January 1964 *(Cl)*.
SCHOOLHILL [GNS] op 1 September 1893
(GNS); clo 5 April 1937 *(RM January 1938)*.
SCOPWICK & TIMBERLAND [GN/GE]
op 1 August 1882 *(GN/GE)*;
clo 7 November 1955 *(RM December)*.
SCORRIER [GW] op 25 August 1852 *(co n R Cornwall
Gaz 18th)*; S GATE until 1 October 1896 *(Cl; RCH dist
ref 30 January 1897)*; clo 5 October 1964 *(Cl)*.
SCORTON near Darlington [NE] op 10 September
1846 *(co n Catterick)*; clo 3 March 1969 *(RM March)*.
SCORTON near Preston [LNW]
op 26 June 1840 *(LPJ)*; re-sited about ½ mile north
about August 1840 *(LPJ)*; clo 1 May 1939 *(T 27 April)*.
SCOTBY
SCOTBY [Mid] op 1 May 1876 *(Mid; co n T 1st- line)*;
clo 1 February 1942 (Sunday) *(LNW Record)*.
SCOTBY [NE]: line op 19 July 1836 *(NC)*, in *Scott* 1837;
see 1836 B★★; clo 2 November 1959 *(RM December)*.
SCOTCH DYKE [NB] op 29 October 1861★★;
clo 2 May 1949 *(Cl)*. Until 1904 in *hb* as one word.
SCOTLAND STREET – see EDINBURGH.
SCOTSCALDER [High]
op 28 July 1874 *(High)*; aot request; still open.
SCOTSGAP [NB] op 23 July 1862 *(NB)*;
clo 15 September 1952★★ *(RM Oct.)*. At first SCOTS
GAP JUNCTION *(Brad)*; JUNCTION dropped 1901/2,
to one word 1903 tt *(Cl)* but 1890 *(hb)*. S G for CAMBO
in *Brad* and NB co tt 1900. LNE tt 1933: S for C.
SCOTSTOUN
S EAST [Cal] op 1 October 1896 *(RCG; Colliery 2nd-
line)* as VICTORIA PARK; renamed S 1 October 1900
(RCG); EAST added 30 June 1952 *(Cl)*;
clo 5 October 1964 *(RM November)*.
S WEST [Cal] op 1 October 1896 *(RCG; Colliery 2nd-
line)*; WEST added 1 October 1900 *(RCG)*;
clo 5 October 1964 *(RM November)*.
S SHOW YARD [NB] (non-tt): full dates ?;
NB special advice dated 22 June 1914 says will be in use
25–27 June for services from Glasgow Queen Street
and Helensburgh for 'Great Aviation Display'. Other
uses? – in *hb* 1904–38 inclusive; according to *hba* May
1948 was now 'closed' (= no longer available?).
{Scotstounhill – Jordanhill}.

SCOTSTOUNHILL [NB]:
first in *Brad* July 1883; still open.
SCOTSWOOD [NE]
SCOTSWOOD: line op 21 October 1839 *(T 24th/Tyne
Mercury- line)*, nd, May 1848 *(Topham)*; see 1836 B★★;
clo 1 May 1967 *(RM June)*.
S WORKS (non-tt); aot S HALT; under construction
for Armstrong Whitworth & Co 14 April 1915; worked
under agreement of 25 August 1915; clo 27 September
1924; reop 7 April 1941 *(Cl 29)*; clo 1944
{Scotswood – Elswick}; (mostly *Nhumb Young*).
SCOTTISH CENTRAL JUNCTION [EG]
– see UPPER GREENHILL.
SCOTTON – see CATTERICK.
SCRATBY [MGN] see 17 July 1933★★; HALT;
{Caister – Great Ormesby}.
SCREDINGTON – see ASWARBY.
SCREMERSTON [NE]: line op 29 March 1847★★,
nd, August 1847; clo 5 May 1941★, reop 7 October
1946 *(RM January 1947)*; clo 9 July 1951 –based on *Cl*
– says 8th but that a Sunday; no Sunday service here.
1953 wtt shows stop here to set down railway staff on
Fridays, northbound only (R.N. Forsythe, *Steam Days*,
September 2001).
★ = 5 May 1941 wtt showed one call only for setting-down 'News
parcels' but at least 6 October 1941 wtt to 6 May 1946 wtt all
weekdays northbound, and Saturdays only southbound, one
request call to set down.
SCROOBY [GE]
first in *Brad* July 1850; clo 14 September 1931 *(Cl)*;
later excur – e.g. July 1938 *(RM October)*.
SCROPTON [NS] first in tt *(Topham)* December
1849★; clo 1 January 1866 *(Cl)*.
★ = line op 11 September 1848; *Topham* included line but not
this station earlier; *Brad* added it March 1850, but clearly nd
earlier.
SCRUTON [NE] first in *Brad* January 1857;
alias S LANE early; clo 26 April 1954 *(T 20th)*.
SCULCOATES [NE] op 1 June 1853 *(G&S)* – no
detail *Brad*; clo November 1854 *(Cl)*; line back in *Brad*
August 1865 and this station then included;
clo 9 June 1912 (Sunday) *(Cl)*; {map 63}.
SCUNTHORPE
SCUNTHORPE [GC] op 3 September 1906 *(RCG)*;
terminus of Whitton branch; clo 13 July 1925 *(Cl)*.
SCUNTHORPE [LNE] op 11 March 1928 as
S & FRODINGHAM, replacement for Frodingham
(Rly Gaz 16th); renamed 16 November 1963 *(Cl)*;
still open.
SEA BEACH – see ARGYLE STREET.
SEA MILLS [CE]
op 6 March 1865 *(Mid; Bristol T 7th- line)*; still open.
SEABURN op by [LNE] 3 May 1937 *(RM July)*;
transferred to [TWM] 31 March 2002★★; still open.
SEACOMBE [Wirral] op 1 June 1895 *(Wrexham 15th)*;
S & EGREMONT 1 July 1901 *(RCG)* to 5 January
1953 *(Cl)*; clo 4 January 1960 *(RM February)*.
SEACROFT [GN] op 28 July 1873 *(GN)* as
COW BANK; renamed 1 October 1900 *(hbl 12th)*;
aot request; clo 7 December 1953 *(RM January 1954)*.
SEAFIELD [Cal] – see 1903★★ for intended service.

SEAFORD [LBSC]
op 1 June 1864 *(co ½ T 25 July)*; still open.

SEAFORTH
S & LITHERLAND [LY] op 1 October 1850 *(LY;T 2nd-line)* as S, at a level crossing on south side of Bridge Road. Replaced by station on embankment, still south side of Bridge Road. First part of high level station op Sunday 26 December 1886, for trains to Liverpool *(Ormskirk Advertiser 30th)*; second 9 January 1887 for trains to Southport *(LY minutes)*. & L added *hb* 1894a, 1905 tt *(Cl)*. Still open.
S SANDS [LO] op 30 April 1894 *(LO)*; original was a terminus; through platforms added on connection to LY 2 July 1905 for race day use, 1 June 1906 for full public use; both in use together until 1925, when original part closed; through part clo 31 December 1956 *(T 29 September)*.

SEAHAM [NE]
SEAHAM op 2 July 1855 *(NE maps- line)*; S COLLIERY until 1 February 1925 *(hbl April)*; still open.
S HARBOUR op 2 July 1855 *(NE)*; HARBOUR added 1 February 1925 *(hbl April)*; clo 11 September 1939 *(Cl)*.
S HALL (non-tt): alias HALL DENE; private station for Lord Londonderry; op 1875; right to stop trains other than expresses only exercised four times between 1900 (NE take-over) and 1923; believed that at one time Marquess of Londonderry had private train which ran between here and Wynyard (another of his residences) after station opened there in 1880, and made occasional trips to Newcastle Central *(Mountford)*; clo 1 February 1925 *(RAIL 393/151)*; {Ryhope – Seaham Colliery}.

SEAHOUSES [North Sunderland] op 14 December 1898 *(Rtn)*; clo 29 October 1951 *(Cl)*.

SEALAND
SEALAND [GC] non-tt military use began 17 June 1918 as WELSH ROAD HALT; first in public tt May 1919; renamed S 14 September 1931 *(Cl)*; clo 9 September 1968 *(RM October)*; {Chester – Connahs Quay}.
S RIFLE RANGE (non-tt) HALT [LNE] op by June 1923; 16 June 1947 wtt shows several request calls daily; clo 14 June 1954 *(U)*; {Hawarden Bridge – Burton Point}. In *hb* as RIFLE RANGE, 'P (for military use only)' 1938 and 1956 (inertia?).

SEAMER [NE]: op 1 July 1845★★; still open.
S JUNCTION 1852/3 to 1893/4 *(Brad)* and thus NE co tt 1880.

SEASCALE [Fur] op 19 July 1849★★ *(D&C 14)*; aot request; still open. S for GOSFORTH in opening notice *(Furness Rise)* and *Brad* until 1866 when became S for G and WASTWATER; thus until 1955 *(Brad)*, but not LMS tt 1930 nor *hb*.

SEASIDE – see AINSDALE BEACH.

SEATON near Exeter [LSW]
SEATON op 16 March 1868 *(Trewman 18th)*; clo 7 March 1966 *(RM April)*. Was S & BEER *Brad* 1872 to 1888/9 and thus in *hb* 1883 to 1923a *(RCG ref October 1922)*.
S JUNCTION op 19 July 1860★★ as COLYTON for S; renamed C J 16 March 1868 *(SR)*, S J 1869 tt *(Cl)*; clo 7 March 1966 *(Chard 3rd)*.

SEATON near Leicester [LNW]
op 2 June 1851 *(co ½ T 16 August)* as S & UPPINGHAM – *LNW notice of alterations (T 2nd)* said line through here would open 1st, but that a Sunday, no Sunday service; renamed 1883/91 (LNW co tt), 1894/6 *(Brad)* ★; clo 6 June 1966 *(RM July)*.
★ = In both cases & U was dropped in one table long before it was completely omitted; *Brad* kept it longest for GN service and briefly (certainly in 1894) had S for U in LNW table.

SEATON near Sunderland [NE]: line op 19 October 1836★★, nd; not in *Brad* until June 1858, but was on Macaulay's map of 1851; at some stage re-sited nearly a mile north (S. Bragg); clo 1 September 1952 *(RM October – 'will reopen for annual Durham Gala Day')*.

SEATON near Workington [CW Jc]
op 4 January 1888 *(D&C 14)* ★, Wednesdays and Saturdays; after January 1892 *Brad* but before/with January 1893 reduced to Saturdays only; last trains July 1897; back February 1907, Saturdays only; after April 1913 but before/with July 1913 increased to one train per day plus extra on Saturdays; last in *Brad* February 1922; also miners' services *(RM September 1912)*.
★ = not in *Brad* until June 1888 but services in this area often not regularly updated; date given by D&C was a Wednesday. For this reason it should be realised that services other than those listed might have run.

SEATON CAREW [NE]: line op 10 February 1841★★ *(NE maps)*, nd, May 1842; CAREW added 1872 *(hb)*, 1875 tt *(Cl)*; still open.

SEATON DELAVAL [NE] op 3 May 1847★★; S D COLLIERY until 1864 tt *(Cl)* but just S D 1862 *hb*; clo 2 November 1964 *(RM January 1965)*.

SEATON SLUICE [BT]
op 3 May 1851 Tuesdays & Saturdays; last advertised 14 May 1852 – line had no Act of Parliament, service operated privately; when Act for line received 30 June 1852, operator withdrew *(BT)*; however a service was again advertised from January to April 1853 in the *Sunderland News and North of England Advertiser*, leaving Seaton Sluice at 7.04am and returning from Percy Main at 5.30pm (S. Bragg, *RCHS Journal* July 1984) {map 26}.
According to *U* a station (alias COLLYWELL BAY) was built here about 1914 but never provided with a service.

SEBASTOPOL
SEBASTOPOL [GW] op 28 May 1928 *(co n dated 'May')*; clo 30 April 1962 *(T 6 April)*; {Upper Pontnewydd – Panteg}. Also see PANTEG.

SEDBERGH [LNW] op 16 September 1861 *(co n Lancaster Gaz 14th)*; clo 1 February 1954 *(T 1st)*; later school use, last 17 September 1964 *(RM November 1977)*. Also used 1963 when snow blocked Settle to Carlisle line.

SEDGEBROOK [GN] 15 July 1850 *(in op tt Henshaw)*; clo 2 July 1956 *(RM August)*. Sometimes SEDGBROOK in *Brad*, sometimes one way only.

SEDGEFIELD [NE]: line op 11 July 1835 *(NE)*, nd, November 1845 – but mentioned in accident report dated 16 March 1844 *(Rtn)*; clo 31 March 1952 *(RM June)*, but used for race meetings until 1960 *(AB)*.

SEDGEFORD [GE] op 17 August 1866*;
aot request; clo 2 June 1952 *(RM June)*.
* = in *Brad* September; *T 18th* covered line and mentioned
all stations except this – omitted in error?

SEDGEWICK/SEDGWICK [Lancaster & Carlisle]
(non-tt): description of formal opening of line,
21 September 1846 says train stopped here to take up
several gentlemen (R. Bingham, *The Chronicles of
Milnthorpe*, Cicerone Press, 1987); implication is that
there was no proper station here; oral tradition has it as
stop (private for Sedgwick House?) in early days of line
(letter, J.S. Berry, *Cumbrian Railways vol. 7 no. 10*);
{Oxenholme – later Hincaster physical junction}.

SEEDLEY [LNW] op 1 May 1882 *(LNW Officers
23342)* *; clo 2 January 1956 *(Cl)*.
* = *LNW Record* has 1 May 1880, date when they merely
agreed name for station yet to be built.

SEEND [GW] op 1 September 1858 *(Salisbury 4th)*;
clo 18 April 1966 *(RM May)*.

SEER GREEN [GW/GC]
op (non-tt) for golfers 2 April 1906 *(U)* as
BEACONSFIELD GOLF LINKS; made public
23 December 1914 *(GC dates)*; renamed S G for B
GOLF CLUB 16 December 1918 *(hbl 23 January
1919)*, S G & JORDANS 25 September 1950 *(L)*,
S G 6 May 1974 *(BR notice)*, S G & J 3 October 1988
tt, S G 28 September 1992 BR tt (but Chiltern Railways
and Network Rail continued to add & J); still open.

SEFTON & MAGHULL [CLC] op 1 September
1884 *(CLC)*; & M added 1886; clo 1 January 1917
(T 23 December 1916); reop non-tt in March 1919 for
races at Aintree *(CLC Portrait)*; reop fully 1 April 1919
(RCH); clo 7 January 1952 *(RM February)*.

SEFTON ARMS – see AINTREE.

SEFTON PARK [LNW] op 1 June 1892 *(co ½ Rly
Times 13 August)*; clo 2 May 1960 *(RM June)*.

SEGHILL [NE] op 28 August 1841 *(con BT)*;
clo 2 November 1964 *(RM January 1965)*.

SELBY [NE]
SELBY op 22 September 1834 *(York Courant)*; original
terminus (adjacent to quayside) replaced by through
station 2 July 1840 *(Cl)*; still open.
S BRAYTON GATES op 16 February 1898, terminus
from Cawood, only temporary wooden platform and
shelter *(Cawood)*; service diverted to main station
1 July 1904 *(Cl)*.
S BARLBY SIDINGS (non-tt): used 15 April 1964 for
British Oil & Cake Mills Ltd excursion to Peterborough
(JB); {Selby – Riccall}.

SELHAM [LBSC] op 1 July 1872 *(LBSC)*;
clo 7 February 1955 *(co n W Sussex)*.

SELHURST
SELHURST [LBSC] op 1 May 1865 *(L)*; still open.
Non-tt: special shuttle from Norwood Junction to Paint
Shop at Depot here 21 September 1980 *(IU)*.

SELKIRK [NB] op 5 April 1856 *(con Selkirk 4th)* *;
clo 10 September 1951 *(RM October)*.
* = notice referred to 'Gala Opening' but clearly full service of
fare payers – directors' experimental trip week previous.

SELLAFIELD [Fur/WCE Jt]
op 21 July 1849**; still open. In op co notice *(Furness*

Rise) as S & CALDERBRIDGE and thus *Brad* until
1955 but not LMS tt 1930.

SELLING [LCD]
first found in tt for 1 December 1860 *(T 7th)* – not
shown *Brad* with its stretch of line; still open.

SELLY OAK [Mid] op 3 April 1876 *(Mid)*;
re-sited on deviation 13 April 1885 *(Mid)*;
S O & BOURNBROOK 22 November 1898 *(hbl
26 January 1899)* to 1 April 1904 *(hbl 28th)*; still open.

SELSDON [CO Jt/WSC Jt] op 10 August 1885 *(LBSC)*;
first month only in *Brad* as S ROAD JUNCTION,
then S R until 30 September 1935 *(Cl)*;
clo 1 January 1917 *(T 22 December 1916)*; reop 1 May
1919 *(RCH)*; clo 16 May 1983 *(BLN 456 corr)*.

SELSEY [WS]
S TOWN op 27 August 1897 *(D&C 2)*; clo 20 January
1935**. TOWN omitted *Brad* 1911/2 to 1930/1;
hbl entries, not giving exact dates, support omission
but suggest TOWN added again by 1928.
S BEACH op 1 August 1898 *(D&C 2)*; last in *Brad*
October 1904; {south of S}; according to 1904 *hb*,
summer only (thus tt inclusion involved inertia?).
S GOLF LINKS op non-tt about 1897 *(U)*;
first in *Brad* July 1910; last there August 1914;
back May 1924; replaced by >
S BRIDGE first in 19 July 1926 *Brad*;
clo 20 January 1935**.

SEMINGTON [GW] op 1 October 1906 *(Bristol
NWR)*; HALT; clo 18 April 1966 *(RM May)*.

SEMLEY [LSW] op 2 May 1859 *(Salisbury 7th)*;
clo 7 March 1966 *(RM April)*. LSW co tt 1914:
S for SHAFTESBURY; 'for S' dropped 1929/30
(Brad), 1956 *(hb)*.

SENGHENYDD [Rhy]
op 1 February 1894 *(Rhy)*; SENGHENITH until
1 July 1904 *(hbl 7th)*; clo 15 June 1964 *(RM August)*.

SERRIDGE [SW Jt] first in *Brad* July 1877; last
October 1879. One way only; note in tt said passengers
for Lydbrook could alight here on informing guard at
Speech House Road; looks as if they had to buy ticket
to Lydbrook but could get off here if more convenient;
shown, partly via notes, as SERRIDGE PLATFORM,
SPEECH HOUSE; {physical junction *IA*}.

SESSAY [NE]: line op 31 March 1841**, nd, August
1841; clo 15 September 1958 *(RM October)*.

SESSWICK [Cam]
first in *Brad* October 1913; HALT; clo 10 June 1940**,
reop 6 May 1946 *(T 16 March)*; clo 10 September 1962
(RM October); {Bangor-on-Dee – Marchwiel}.

SETON MAINS [NB]
op 1 May 1914 *(Edin)*; HALT; clo 22 September 1930
(Cl); {Longniddry – Prestonpans}.

SETTLE [Mid]
SETTLE op 1 May 1876 *(Mid; co n T 1st- line)*;
S NEW until 1 July 1879 co tt *(Mid)*; still open.
S JUNCTION op 2 October 1876 *(Mid)*;
clo 1 November 1877 (Thursday) *(RCG)*;
{physical junction *IA*}.
S OLD – see GIGGLESWICK.

SETTRINGTON [NE]
op 1 June 1853 *(NE- line)*; clo 5 June 1950 *(Cl)*.

SEVEN HILLS [GE] op 20 December 1922
(RM April 1923); HALT; clo 8 June 1953 *(T 8th)*;
{Ingham – Barnham}.
SEVEN KINGS [GE]
op 1 March 1899 *(co n LRR April 2006)*; still open.
SEVEN SISTERS near Neath [N&B]:
op before March 1875 *(N&B Gomer)*; at start miners
only? – not in *Brad* until June 1876;
clo 15 October 1962 *(RM November)*.
SEVEN SISTERS London:
SEVEN SISTERS [GE] op 22 July 1872 *(L)*; still open.
SEVEN SISTERS [Vic] op 1 September 1968 *(T 2nd)*;
still open.
SEVEN SISTERS ROAD HOLLOWAY
– see FINSBURY PARK.
SEVEN STARS – see under WELSHPOOL.
SEVEN STONES [PDSW] op 16 June 1910
(Plymouth, Devonport & SW Junction Railway,
Oakwood, 1967); request, daylight only; last used 1914,
last in tt September 1917 *(Cl)*; {Latchley – Luckett}.
Cornish & D P, 8 October 1966, dealing with history of
line, then about to close, said had served Phoenix Park
Pleasure Ground, very popular with parties from
Plymouth; park had closed 1914, leaving station to fade
away (not 'closed' until *hb* 1944a – lengthy inertia).
SEVENOAKS
SEVENOAKS [SE] op 2 March 1868 *(co ½ T 21 August)*;
still open. At first SEVEN OAKS; to one word 1869 tt,
then erratically S TUBS HILL, S & RIVERHEAD,
S T H & R; settled as S 5 June 1950 *(Cl)*.
Also see BAT & BALL.
SEVERN BEACH [GW]:
PLATFORM op 5 June 1922 (Whit Monday); used for
excursions that day and next, then Wednesdays and
Saturdays, until regular service began 10 July 1922
(first in *Brad* July), last in tt October 1922; used Easter
1923 *(Avon)*; back in tt 9 July 1923, still shown winter
1923/4; became station 26 May 1924 *(GW Circular
4077; W D Press 27th)*; still open.
SEVERN BRIDGE [SW Jt] several trains provided
17 October 1879 (formal op day) so locals could see
line; public op 20 October 1879 *(Gloucester J 11th, 18th)*;
clo 26 October 1960**. GW co tt 1902 to 1947,
Mid co tt 1903, LMS tt 1930: S B for BLAKENEY.
Thus *Brad* to clo but not *hb*.
SEVERN TUNNEL JUNCTION [GW]
op 1 December 1886 *(Bristol T 2nd- line)*; still open.
Pre-opening Rogiet *(RAC)*.
SEXHOW [NE]
op 3 March 1857**; clo 14 June 1954 *(Cl)*.
SEXTON GATE [GE]: (non-tt):
William Powlett claimed had privilege (granted 1848)
of stopping all trains here but in 1850 company
withdrew this on grounds that it could find no record;
in 1862 letter found and privilege restored. No other
information known; site unknown. See article on
Boreham by H. Paar, *RCHS Journal July 1979*.
SEYMOUR COLLIERY [Mid] (non-tt)
Apparently service for miners before and for some time
after Mid bought line to here from Staveley Company
on 1 May 1866 – an agreement after purchase stated

that miners would continue to be provided with service
to/from Chesterfield. Mid wtt first shows train for miners
here 2 August 1875, at first Saturdays only, to and from
Chesterfield; all days November 1885 wtt. The October
1886 wtt shows the daily train switched to S JUNCTION
{Staveley Town – Bolsover} and S COLLIERY
{branch from S Junction} reverting to Saturdays only.
Notice with November 1888 public tt says that trains
will no longer pick up/set down at sidings adjacent to
colliery on Saturdays – passengers now to go to/from
Netherthorpe (later Staveley Town) and Staveley (later
Barrow Hill). S JUNCTION shown clo in 14 September
1931 wtt); *(Mid)*.
SHACKERSTONE [AN Jt]
op 1 September 1873 *(LNW Officers 10205, 10207)*;
clo 13 April 1931 *(LNW dates PCC 192)*.
Later excursion use: two each summer 1960 and 1961
(BR doc); one to Blackpool 7 October 1961 *(AB)*.
S JUNCTION in LNW co tt 1876 and 1891 (not
1875, 1900 – though still S J in index).
SHADWELL
SHADWELL [East London] op 10 April 1876 *(co n
T 8th)*; clo 25 March 1995 for engineering work *(BLN
746 corr)*; reop 25 March 1998 *(RM September)*;
clo 23 December 2007**. Used by [Dist] 1 October
1884 to 1 August 1905 and [Met] 6 October 1884 to
3 December 1906 and 31 March 1913 on.
SHADWELL [Dock] op 31 August 1987 *(T 1 September)*;
still open.
SHADWELL [GE] op 1 October 1840 *(co n T 1st)*; see
1849 March 31**; S & ST GEORGES IN THE EAST
1 July 1900 *(Cl)* clo to 22 May 1916**; reop 5 May
1919 *(T 2nd)* as S; clo 7 July 1941 *(T 25 June)*.
SHAFTESBURY ROAD
– see RAVENSCOURT PARK.
SHAFTHILL – see COANWOOD.
SHAFTON JUNCTION [Dearne] (non-tt) miners ?;
in use 1943; {Ryhill – Grimethorpe} *(U)*.
SHAKESPEARE CLIFF [SEC] (non-tt):
Dover Colliery here; by ? miners were travelling to/from
colliery by passenger trains, climbing in/out directly
from/to track. Wtt 1900 has early morning train calling
at DOVER COLLIERY; SEC miner's ticket from
Dover for COLLIERY WORKS PLATFORM *(JB)*;
alternative names for S C, or slightly different site(s)? –
information given here may relate to more than one site.
Proper HALT op 2 June 1913 but not public – when
footbridge op 1914 SEC restated that Halt not for use
by local women and children; colliery clo later 1914
(SEC). RCH gave clo '1915', probably formalising
earlier closure. Later use at various times by Admiralty,
military camp, Channel Tunnel workmen;
still in use as S STAFF HALT.
SHALFORD [SE] op 20 August 1849 *(co n T 18th)*;
still open. Was S for GODALMING 1904 to 1926a *(hb)*.
SHALLCROSS – see 1833 May**.
SHANDON [NB]
op 7 August 1894 *(T 7th)*; clo 15 June 1964 *(RM July)*.
Briefly SHANDONS *(hb 1912)*, corrected 1914a.
SHANKEND [NB] op 1 July 1862 *(co n T 1st- line)*;
clo 6 January 1969 *(RM February)*.

SHANKLIN [IoW] op 23 August 1864 *(Salisbury 27th)*;
clo 1 January 1967 for electrification, reop 20 March
1967 *(RM May)*; still open.
SHAP [LNW]
op 17 December 1846 *(D&C 14)*; clo 1 July 1968 *(Cl)*.
Brad ? to 1955: S for HAWESWATER.
Not thus LMS tt 1930 nor *hb*.
SHAP SUMMIT [LNW] (non-tt)
Shap Granite Co's workmen's trains to and from Shap
probably began in mid-1880s and ended autumn 1956;
around 1947–8 some men also carried from Penrith
(H.D. Bowtell, *Over Shap to Carlisle*, Ian Allan, 1983).
Photograph of platform in *Steam Days*, December 2002,
p.759; in *Cumbria* as S QUARRY; {Tebay – Shap}.
Just north of this were sidings for Manchester
Corporation Waterworks, Haweswater (work began
1929); for some years used for annual visit to works by
Corporation party (H.D. Bowtell, as above).
According to *LNW dates* WORKMEN'S PLATFORM
op 1928; this one?
SHAPLEY HEATH – see WINCHFIELD.
SHAPWICK [SD Jt]
op 28 August 1854★★; clo 7 March 1966 *(Shepton 11th)*.
S for WESTHAY in *Brad* ? to 1955.
SHARLSTON [LY] first in *Brad* January 1870;
clo 3 March 1958 *(RM April)*; later excursions,
e.g. special notice for one 18 June 1966 *(IU)*.
See STREETHOUSE for later station nearby.
SHARNAL STREET [SE] op 1 April 1882 *(SE)*;
clo 4 December 1961 *(T 8 November)*.
Brad ? to 1955: S S for HOO and ST MARYS HOO.
SHARNBROOK [Mid] op 8 May 1857 *(Mid; co ½*
T 13 August- line); clo 2 May 1960 *(RM June)*.
SHARPNESS
SHARPNESS (a) [Mid] op 1 August 1876 *(Bath Chron*
3rd); replaced by >
SHARPNESS (b) [SW Jt] op 16 October 1879 ready
for Severn Bridge line *(hbl 30 December 1880)*;
clo 2 November 1964 *(Mid)*. S NEW in *Brad* until 1904.
SHAUGH BRIDGE [GW] op 21 August 1907
(GW Plymouth area records); PLATFORM;
clo 31 December 1962★★. GW ticket as S B HALT *(JB)*.
SHAW & CROMPTON [LY]
op 2 November 1863 *(LY)*; & C added 1 December
1897 *(hbl 27 January 1898)* to 6 May 1974 *(BR notice)*
and since 15 May 1989; still open.
SHAWCLOUGH & HEALEY [LY]
op 1 November 1870 *(LY)*; clo 2 April 1917 *(Cl)*;
back in tt October 1919; clo 16 June 1947★★.
SHAWFORD
See TWYFORD for early station here/near.
SHAWFORD [LSW] first in *Brad* September 1882; still
open. At first S & TWYFORD; S for T 1923/4 to 1955.
SHAWFORTH [LY]
op 1 December 1881 *(LY)*; clo 16 June 1947★★.
SHAWHILL – see ANNAN.
SHAWLANDS [Cal]
op 2 April 1894 *(Cal)*; still open.
SHEEP PASTURE – see 1833 May★★.

SHEEPBRIDGE
SHEEPBRIDGE [Mid] op 1 August 1870 *(Mid)*;
S & WHITTINGTON MOOR 8 October 1897 *(RCG)*
to 18 June 1951 *(Cl)*; clo 2 January 1967 *(Mid)*;
later excur and occasional use when engineering work
prevented stop at Chesterfield *(U)*.
1872 only: SHEEP BRIDGE *(hb)*.
For **SHEEPBRIDGE** [GC] see BRIMINGTON.
SHEERNESS
S DOCKYARD [LCD] op 19 July 1860 *(T 19th)*;
D added 1 June 1883; clo 2 January 1922 *(RCG)*.
Also boat trains connecting with Flushing Steamers
July 1875 to May 1876 *(U)*.
S-ON-SEA [LCD] op 1 June 1883 *(LCD)*;
clo 8 November 1914 *(RCH)*; reop 2 January 1922
(RCG); still open.
In effect, the two above alternated in use from 1914.
S EAST [SEC] op 1 August 1901 *(RCG)*;
clo 4 December 1950 *(T 4th)*.
Also see Section 7: Non-rail.
SHEFFIELD {map 57}
S (BRIDGEHOUSES) [MS&L] op 14 July 1845 *(GC)*;
terminus, probably with through platform just to west;
just S in *Brad*; replaced by >
S VICTORIA [GC] op 15 September 1851 *(GC)*;
clo 5 January 1970 *(RM March)*. Used 7 January 1973
when 14.15 Sheffield–Manchester failed and passengers
were picked up here *(IU – personal experience)*.
S WICKER [Mid] op 1 November 1838 *(Mid)*;
W added April 1852/October 1853 co tt *(Mid)*;
terminus, replaced by through >
SHEFFIELD [Mid] op 1 February 1870 *(co n T 22 Jan.)*;
still open. At first S NEW MIDLAND; became
S MIDLAND 1 February 1876 co tt *(Mid)*, S CITY
25 September 1950 *(Mid)*, S 1950 *(RM May* – is to be
called S following closure of S Victoria in January).
Brad called it S STATION ROAD at least 1867–9
and 1887–1906. *Hb* called whole Mid station
POND STREET until 1938; in 1956 it separated entry
into MIDLAND (passengers) and P S (goods).
GRIMESTHORPE BRIDGE [Sheffield & Rotherham]:
line op 1 November 1838, nd, first in *Brad* February
1842 *(Mid)*; Tuesdays & Saturdays only; last in *Brad*
January 1843.
S GOODS [MS&L] (non-tt): ticket *(JB)* for 'cricketers';
no other information.
Non-tt: platform erected for departure of King Edward
VII and Queen Alexandra after their visit to the River
Don Works of Vickers, Sons & Maxim on 12 July 1905
(had arrived at Midland station, thence by road);
gained access to main line at Upwell Street Junction,
between Sheffield and Rotherham (R. Brettle, from
Sheffield Telegraph and *Sheffield Independent*, both having
articles 11th and 13th).
SHEFFIELD PARK [LBSC] op 1 August 1882
(LBSC; Hants Chron 5th- line) as FLETCHING & S P;
renamed 1 January 1883 *(Cl)*; clo, prematurely by strike,
30 May 1955★★, reop 7 August 1956 *(RM May 1958)* –
legal objections; clo 17 March 1958 *(T 17th)*.
SHEFFORD [Mid] op 8 May 1857 *(Mid; co ½*
T 13 August- line); clo 1 January 1962 *(RM January)*.

SHEIRE HEATH [SE]
op 20 August 1849 *(co n T 18th)*; probably clo before
January 1850, when detail for line first given in *Brad*
(platform removed 1850 – *Surrey*);
{Gomshall – Chilworth}.

SHELFORD [GE]
op 30 July 1845 *(co n T 26th- line)*; still open.

SHELLHAVEN – see THAMES HAVEN.

SHELTON: shown as op January 1862 as terminus,
in tables at back of *NS*, but not in list of closed stations
there. No support seen. Error? Horse-drawn tram of
some description? If there was station, would have been
[NS], replaced by Hanley.

SHENFIELD
SHENFIELD (a) [EC] first in *Brad* October 1847;
last March 1850; 19¾ miles from Shoreditch; probably
used by passengers from Billericay and Wickford.
SHENFIELD (b) [GE] first in *Brad* January 1887 as
S & HUTTON JUNCTION; JUNCTION dropped
later 1887 in tt but persisted longer in *hb*;
& H dropped 20 February 1969 *(Cl)*; still open.

SHENSTONE [LNW] op 15 December 1884
(W Mid; LNW Officers 26784- line); still open.

SHENTON [AN Jt]
op 1 September 1873 *(LNW Officers 10205, 10207)*;
clo 13 April 1931 *(LNW dates PCC 192)*.

SHEPHERDS [GW] op 2 January 1905 *(W Morn
News 3rd)*; clo 4 February 1963 *(W Briton 4th)*.

SHEPHERDS BUSH
SHEPHERDS BUSH [HC] op 13 June 1864 *(co n
T 10th)*; re-sited 13ch. nearer Wood Lane 1 April 1914
(RCG); still open.
SHEPHERDS BUSH [Cen] op 30 July 1900 *(T 25th)*;
still open.
SHEPHERDS BUSH [LSW] op 1 May 1874 *(L)*;
clo 5 June 1916 *(RCH)*.
SHEPHERDS BUSH: op 28 September 2008 *(RM
December)*; still open.
SHEPHERDS BUSH [WL] op 27 May 1844 *(T 24th)*;
clo 1 December 1844★★; {map 101}. Both parts of
name also used separately.

SHEPHERDS WELL
In both cases tickets exist in one word form *(JB)*;
also thus for [EK] in opening notice *(EK Oakwood)*.
SHEPHERDS WELL [EK] op 16 October 1916
(co n EK); clo 1 November 1948★★ *(RM January 1949)*.
S W JUNCTION in *hb*.
SHEPHERDS WELL [LCD] op 22 July 1861 *(LCD)*;
still open.

SHEPLEY [LY]: line op 1 July 1850 *(T 8th)*, nd,
January 1851; S & SHELLEY 1 July 1892 *(hbl 7th)*
to 12 June 1961 *(RM April)*; still open.

SHEPPERTON [LSW] op 1 November 1864
(co n T 27 October); still open. LSW co tt 1914 and *Brad*
to 1955: S for HALLIWELL.

SHEPRETH [GN]
op 1 August 1851 *(co n T 2nd)*; still open.

SHEPSHED [LNW]
op 16 April 1883 *(Leic; LNW Officers 24577- line)*;
SHEEPSHED until 1888 *(Cl; RCG ref July)*;
clo 13 April 1931 *(LNW dates PCC 192)*.

SHEPTON MALLET
Brad (index only) had S MALLETT at least 1883 to
early 1890s; GW ticket thus *(JB)*.
S M CHARLTON ROAD [SD Jt] op 20 July 1874
(Shepton 24th); C R added 1901/2 *(Brad)*, 1956 *(hb)*;
clo 7 March 1966 *(Shepton 11th)*.
S M HIGH STREET [GW] op 9 November 1858
(Shepton 12th); H S added 26 September 1949 *(Cl)*;
clo 9 September 1963 *(Weston 13th)*. *Brad* showed it as
TOWER (error), then TOWN STREET from 1883 to 1949.

SHERBORNE [LSW]
op 7 May 1860 *(W Fly P 8th)*; still open.

SHERBURN – see WEAVERTHORPE.

SHERBURN near Durham [NE]; {map 32}
S COLLIERY op 19 June 1844 *(co n T 24 May- line)*;
COLLIERY added 1 April 1874 *(Cl)*;
clo 28 July 1941 *(Cl)*.
S HOUSE op 6 November 1837 *(NE)*; HOUSE added
1 April 1874 *(Cl)*; re-sited on Durham Elvet branch
24 July 1893 *(Cl)*; clo 1 January 1931 (Thursday) *(T 5 Dec.)*.

SHERBURN-IN-ELMET
SHERBURN-IN-ELMET (a) [NE]: line op 30 May
1839 *(T 7 June)*, nd, June 1840 (also listed in *Whishaw*
1840); -in-E added 1 July 1903 *(hbl 9th)*;
clo 13 September 1965 *(T 4th)*.
SHERBURN-IN-ELMET (b) op 9 July 1984 *(BLN 495)*;
still open. (Hyphens not always included in tt index;
present 2009)

SHERE – see SHEIRE; GOMSHALL.

SHERIFFHALL [Ed & Dalk; NB?]: see 1831 A★★;
marked on map produced by NB, March 1844;
no other evidence seen; presumably clo 1847 with line
rebuilding; {map 18}.

SHERINGHAM [MGN] op 16 June 1887 *(RCG)*;
re-sited 2 January 1967 to opposite side of level-crossing,
so that latter could be abolished; still open.
SHERRINGHAM until 1894 *(Brad)*;
hb 1898a 'should now read Sheringham'.

SHERNHALL STREET – see WALTHAMSTOW.

SHERWOOD [GN] op 2 December 1889 *(RCG)*;
clo 1 July 1916 (Saturday) *(RCH)*; {in IA}.

SHETTLESTON [NB]
op 23 November 1870★★; still open.

SHIDE [IWC] op 1 February 1875 *(Hants Chron 6th)*;
clo 6 February 1956 *(S Daily Echo 6th)*.
NEWPORT SHIDE until later 1875 *(Brad)*.

SHIELD ROW – see WEST STANLEY.

SHIELDHILL [Cal] op 1 September 1863 *(co ½
T 25 March 1864- line)*; clo 19 May 1952 *(RM June)*.

SHIELDMUIR op 14 May 1990 *(BLN 634)*; still open.

SHIELDS – see HIGH SHIELDS; NORTH
SHIELDS; SOUTH SHIELDS.

SHIELDS Glasgow
SHIELDS [GSW] op 1 July 1885 *(co ½ 1110/149- line)*;
clo 1 January 1917 *(Cl)*; one Glasgow to Ardrossan
Saturday only train shown calling October 1919 tt
(C/W) – not present July 1919tt; back in tt April 1920;
clo 1 November 1924 (Saturday) *(Cl)*.
S ROAD [GSW]★ op 12 December 1870 *(Glasgow
Herald 13th)*; clo 1 January 1917 except for workmen's
services; reop to public 1 April 1925, when

amalgamated with Shields and Pollokshields as S R *(Cl)*; clo 14 February 1966 *(Cl)*; {map 15}. *Hb* (1872 only): SHIELS ROAD. Sometimes in tts as GLASGOW S R. * = [CGU] until 1896.

S ROAD [GU] op 14 December 1896**; still open.

S DEPOT (non-tt): used for Open Day 16 September 1978 *(U; JB)*; {Shields Road – Ibrox}.
Also see POLLOKSHIELDS.

SHIFNAL [GW]
op 13 November 1849 (see 1849**); still open.
At first SHIFNALL *(Brad)*, SHIFFNAL *(hb)*; former corrected in body 1850, index later, latter *hb* 1899a.

SHILDON [NE]: see 1825** for full details of S&D service; ceremonial run was from Mason's Arms here. Regular service began April 1826, operated by contractors; no station, exact arragements at first unknown; aot later Grey Horse Inn acted as 'station'. In March 1837, S&D considered building station but settled for cheaper option of renting waiting-room at the Mason's Arms for £6 per year, including fire and cleaning *(RAIL 667/9)*. Plans for station of own approved 28 August 1840 *(667/12)*; op ? When line to South Church op 19 April 1842, trains had to reverse since junction with new line was before Shildon station. New station, avoiding this problem, was built soon after – op between 29 April 1842, when they decided to call for tenders to build it, and 9 December 1842, when they agreed plans for turning old into cottages and a reading-room *(667/13)*; often called THICKLEY in early company minutes; still open.
See 1835** for [Clarence] service

SHILLINGSTONE [SD Jt]
op 10 September 1863**; clo 7 March 1966 *(Shepton 11th)*. Mid co tt 1894, 1903 and *Brad* ? to 1955: S for CHILD OKEFORD and OKEFORD FITZPAINE. Not thus LSW co tt 1914, LMS tt 1930, *hb*.

SHILTON [LNW] op 1 December 1847 *(W Mid)*; clo 16 September 1957 *(LNW Record)*.

SHINCLIFFE [NE] {map 32}
SHINCLIFFE op 19 June 1844 *(Durham; co n T 24 May-line)*; clo 28 July 1941 *(Cl)*.

S TOWN op 28 June 1839 *(NE)*; became S DURHAM 1859 tt *(JS)*, S TOWN 1861 tt *(Cl)*; clo 24 July 1893 *(Cl)*.

SHIPLAKE [GW] op 1 June 1857 *(Berkshire 6th – item on line op, station in paper's tt; though Brad included line June, S only added July)*; still open.

SHIPLEY
SHIPLEY [Mid] op by 16 July 1846 *(Mid)*; re-sited about ⅛ mile north summer 1849 *(Mid – from P. Kay)*; made triangular 14 May 1979 for down trains (P. Kay, *British Rail Illustrated*, November 1993, p.96), 9 March 1980 for up *(Mid)*; still open.
Was S STATION ROAD 1883 to 1938/9 *(Brad)*.

S & WINDHILL [GN] op 15 April 1875 *(D&C 8, first in Brad May)*; clo 2 February 1931 *(RM March)*.
Brad: at first S; later variously S BRIDGE STREET WINDHILL, S & W BRIDGE STREET, S & W, S BRIDGE STREET.

SHIPLEY GATE [Mid]
first in *Brad* July 1851; GATE added 1 July 1887 *(Cl)*; last train 28 August 1948 *(Mid)*.

SHIPPEA HILL [GE] op 30 July 1845 *(co n Norfolk)* as MILDENHALL DROVE (thus in notice cited); renamed M ROAD December 1845 *(Brad)* but already thus in 18 August 1845 co tt; renamed BURNT FEN January 1885 *(JS)*, S H 1 May 1905 *(hbl 27 April)*; 20 May 2007 tt reduced weekdays to one train to Norwich, Saturdays both ways; aot request; still open.

SHIPSTON-ON-STOUR
For first services, including 'official' one starting 1 August 1853, see 1833 B**.
SHIPSTONE until 1858 tt *(Cl)*.
SHIPSTON-ON-STOUR [GW] op 1 July 1889 *(Wilts & Glos Stand 6th)*; clo 8 July 1929 *(RM September)*.
SHIPTON near Kingham [GW]
op 4 June 1853 *(Glos Chron 4th- line)*; HALT 3 January 1966 to 5 May 1969 *(Cl)*; aot request; still open.
GW tt 1932, 1947: S for BURFORD.

SHIPTON
– see BENINGBROUGH; LONDESBOROUGH.
SHIPTON-ON-CHERWELL [GW]
op 1 April 1929 *(wtt supp)*; HALT; clo 1 March 1954 *(T 1st)*; {Kidlington – Blenheim}.

SHIRDLEY HILL [LY]
op 2 September 1887 *(Southport Guard 8th)*; clo 26 September 1938 *(RM November)*.

SHIREBROOK
SHIREBROOK op 25 May 1998 *(BLN 821)*; 'fun day' 24 May 1998; still open. On site of earlier S West.
S COLLIERY SIDINGS [Mid] (non-tt): op 1 July 1901 wtt *(Mid)*; clo by July 1954 *(U)*.
S NORTH [GC] op 9 March 1897 (formal 8th) *(GCR Society Journal, Spring 2003, p. 12)* as LANGWITH JUNCTION; renamed 2 June 1924 *(Cl)*; clo 19 September 1955 *(BR ER internal notice August)*. Advertised summer Saturdays continued to 5 September 1964 (last train) *(Cl)*. Also later use for football specials (one such to Sheffield, 28 April 1956) and staff train to Tuxford Central, for workers at Shed and Wagon works there; in operation 26 August 1961* (photographs in *GC Society Journal, Autumn 2002*); not included in Langwith shed workings for 1962.
LNE tt 1947: S N for L.
* = no workmen's trains 15 June 1959 wtt – service started later? Intermittent?
S SOUTH [GN] op 1 November 1901 *(RCG)*; SOUTH added 1925 tt *(C/W)*; clo 14 September 1931 *(Cl)*. Later excur. Advertised summer Saturday use began 1954, when first train from here ran 19 June, first back 26 June *(BR tt 14 June)*; last such train ran 8 September 1962. Later excursions – e.g. to Blackpool 18 May 1964 *(AB)*.
S WEST [Mid] op 1 June 1875 *(Mid)*; WEST added 18 June 1951 *(Cl)*; clo 12 October 1964 *(RM Nov.)*.
SHIREHAMPTON [CE]
op 6 March 1865 *(Mid; Bristol T 7th- line)*; still open.
SHIREMOOR [TWM]
op 11 August 1980 *(RM August)*; still open.
SHIREOAKS [GC] op 17 July 1849 *(GC; T 18th- line)*; still open. SHIRE OAKS in *hb* until 1877.
SHIRLEY [GW]
op 1 July 1908 *(RCG; T 2nd- line)*; still open.

SHIRLEY HOLM(E)S [LSW]:
although not in public tt, intended for public use by
people of Sway; op 10 October 1860; clo 6 March 1888
when Sway opened (M. Hutson, *SW Circular April 1998*);
only available, daylight only, to/from Brockenhurst.
LSW spells S HOLMS.

SHOEBURYNESS [LTS]
op 1 February 1884 *(L)*; still open.

SHOLING [LSW]
op 1 August 1866 *(SR corr)*; still open.

SHOOT HILL [SM] first in *Brad* September 1921;
HALT until 1927 *(Brad)*; clo 6 November 1933 *(Cl)*.

SHOOTERS HILL – see ELTHAM.

SHOOTING RANGE [LSW] (non-tt):
PLATFORM/HALT; op about 1885; clo after 1947;
{Bodmin – Wadebridge} *(U)*.

SHOREDITCH
See LONDON BISHOPSGATE for early terminus.

SHOREDITCH [East London] op 10 April 1876 *(co n
T 8th)*; worked exclusively by [Met] from 31 March
1913. Clo 25 March 1995 for engineering work *(BLN
746, corr)*, reop 27 September 1998 *(LRR January
1999)* but peak hours and Sunday mornings only.
Clo 11 June 2006 for line reconstruction – to be
replaced on new site (last train Friday 9th) *(Today's
Railways, August 2006)*.

SHOREDITCH [NL] op 1 November 1865 *(T 2nd)*;
clo by bomb damage on night of 3/4 October 1940.

SHOREHAM near Brighton

S AIRPORT BUNGALOW TOWN [SR] op 1 July 1935
(Cl 29); Bungalow Town here earlier; HALT;
clo 15 July 1940 *(Cl)*; {Shoreham – Lancing}.

S-by-SEA [LBSC] op 12 May 1840** as S;
renamed S HARBOUR 1 July 1906 *(hbl 12th)*,
S-B-S 1 October 1906 *(hbl 25th)*; still open.
SR tt 1939 (Brad print), 1947: S-by-S for LANCING
COLLEGE; not thus LBSC co tt 1912.

SHOREHAM KENT: [LCD]
op 2 June 1862 *(co n T 3rd)*; KENT added 9 July 1923
(hbl 26 April), omitted 14 May 1979 tt, back 12 May
1980 tt *(C/W)*; still open.

SHORNCLIFFE CAMP [SE]
op 1 November 1863 *(SR)*;
S & SANDGATE 1 December 1863 to 1 October
1874 *(SR)*; replaced 1 February 1881 *(Cl)*, about 150
yards east, by station listed under FOLKESTONE.

SHORT HEATH CLARKS LANE [Mid]
op 1 November 1872 *(Mid; co n T 1st- line)*;
clo 5 January 1931 *(Mid)*. Name as in Mid co tts seen,
LNW co tt 1874 and *Brad* to closure; just S H in LMS
tt 1930 and *hb* (always).

SHORTLANDS [LCD]
op 3 May 1858 *(co n T 4th)* as BROMLEY (shown as B
in June tt *Bromley Record* but '(S) B' in July tt);
to S 1 July 1858 according to *L*; still open.

SHOSCOMBE & SINGLE HILL [SD Jt]
op 23 September 1929 *(Som Guard 20th, 27th)* *;
HALT; clo 7 March 1966 *(Shepton 11th)*.

* = 21st was formal opening, by Lansbury, Labour Cabinet
Minister (halt served coalfield area).

SHOTLEY BRIDGE [NE]
op 2 December 1867 *(Consett)*; see 1951**;
clo 21 September 1953 *(RM October)*. According to
Consett op as SNOWS HILL, renamed 1868;
first in *Brad* January 1868 as SHOTLEY BRIDGE.

SHOTTLE [Mid]
op 1 October 1867 *(Mid)*; clo 16 June 1947**.

SHOTTON

S HL [WMCQ] op 1 October 1891 *(RCG)* as
CONNAHS QUAY & S; renamed 15 September 1952
(JS) >

S LL [LNW] op 1 April 1907 *(RCG)*;
LL added 15 September 1952 *(JS)* >
LL closed 14 February 1966 *(RM April)*;
reop 21 August 1972 *(RM October)*.
After 1972 treated as one, 'SHOTTON', but ex-WMCQ
back to S HL 26 September 1999 tt *(AB Chron)* –
ex-LNW still S; still open.

SHOTTON BRIDGE [NE]

SHOTTON BRIDGE (a) first in *Brad* December 1863;
Saturdays only, market trains to/from Sunderland; last
there July 1871.

SHOTTON BRIDGE (b) op 1 September 1877 *(RCG)*;
full use; clo 9 June 1952**.

SHOTTS [Cal]
op 9 July 1869 *(Edin; T 12th- line)*; still open.

SHRAWARDINE [SM] op 13 August 1866**;
aot request; finally clo 6 November 1933.

SHREWSBURY

SHREWSBURY [SH Jt] op 14 October 1848 *(Shrewsbury
13th)*; temporary station; replaced, on extension of line,
by permanent 1 June 1849 *(Cl)*; still open.
Brad: at first S; added GENERAL by 1887, but only
in table including English Bridge, presumably to
differentiate from that; thereafter erratic; approx
1898–1910 S JOINT; 1914 to 1947/8 S GENERAL.
Not seen as GENERAL in any GW or LNW co tts,
nor in LMS tt 1930; *hb* thus 1872 on.

S ABBEY [SM] op 13 August 1866**;
finally clo 6 November 1933. *Hb* added ABBEY 1872.

S ABBEY FOREGATE [Shrewsbury & Wellington
Joint]: in LNW co tt (from Stafford only) June 1868
and March 1869 (not May 1864 nor April 1870).
First in *Brad* April 1887; ticket platform (as such in wtt
from 1866), on line from Wellington, alighting only;
clo 30 September 1912 *(Cl)*. *Hb*: included 1862 (when
no facilities were shown), first 'P' 1890 and thus to *hb*
1938/41a – inertia? Used for race specials until 1887 *(SU)*.

S CASTLE FOREGATE GOODS YARD [LNW] (non-tt):
on spur from main station used for fete in 1902 *(AB)*.

S ENGLISH BRIDGE [GW/LNW] op 2 November
1886 as 'drop station' *(LNW/GW Joint Officers 23rd)*
– supposed not to appear in public tt for present – but
there December 1886; ticket platform on Hereford line
(as such in existence from mid 1870s), alighting only;
clo 2 May 1898 *(Cl)*.

S WEST [SM] op 14 April 1911*; aot request;
clo 6 November 1933 *(Cl)*.

* = line reop date; station is in *RCG* list for that date and in
opening tt *(RM September 1911)*, but no trains shown in *Brad*
until September 1911.

non-tt:

S COLEHAM EXCURSION: PLATFORM used for specials to/from for Shrewsbury Flower Show; dates ?; {opposite engine shed, south of station}.
Also temporary platforms near Crowmere Road (on Wellington line) and New Goods Yard (connected to Crewe line) (R.K. Morriss, *Rail Centres, Shrewsbury*, Ian Allan, 1986; W.W. Tasker, *The Merthyr, Tredegar and Abergavenny Railway*, OPC, 1986).
Ticket issued by GW exists for HM Forces on leave from Newtown to SHREWSBURY LMS (auction catalogue photocopy); the only station that would seem to fit that description is ex-LNW goods – did war-time leave trains use that as an overflow?

SHRIVENHAM [GW] op 17 December 1840 *(co n T 12th)*; clo 7 December 1964 *(Cl)*.

SHUSTOKE [Mid]
op 1 November 1864 *(Mid)*; clo 4 March 1968 *(Mid)*.

SIBLE & CASTLE HEDINGHAM [CVH]
op 1 July 1861 *(T 1st)*; SIBLE & added 1867 tt; clo 1 January 1962 *(T 17 November 1961)*.
Hb aot showed as C H and S H, treating as alternative names in use at same time; 1903–8 just H in *Brad (C/W)*.

SIBLEYS [GE]
op 1 April 1913 *(T 1st)*; clo 15 September 1952 *(RM October)*. GE co tt 1914, LNE tt 1933, *Brad* and *hb* always: S for CHICKNEY and BROXTED.

SIBSEY [GN] op 2 October 1848 *(Stamford 3rd)*; clo 11 September 1961 *(RM September)*.

SIBSON
SIBSON [GN] op 1 January 1870 *(GN)*; GN terminus while junction with LNW at Wansford was clo; clo 1 March 1878 (Friday) when junction reop *(LNW Officers 18287)*; {Wansford – Wansford Road}.
Also see WANSFORD.

SIDCUP [SE]
op 1 September 1866 *(L; co ½ T 24 August- line)*; still open.
S for HALFWAY STREET 1867/9 to 1892/3 *(Brad)*; *hb* 1875a had entry for H STREET – 'same as Sidcup'.

SIDDICK JUNCTION
SIDDICK JUNCTION [LNW/CW Jc]: op 1 September 1880 for passenger exchange *(LNW Officers 21248)*; 1 March 1890 as normal station, passengers and parcels *(LNW Officers 31620)*; no indication in 1880s *Brad* of any restrictions on use; clo 1 October 1934 *(LNW Record)*.
S J COLLIERY [LNW] (non-tt): PLATFORM; in use 1923; {Siddick Junction – Workington} *(U)*.

SIDESTRAND [Norfolk & S]
op 25 May 1936 *(RM August)*; HALT; clo 7 April 1953 *(RM May)*; {Trimingham – Overstrand}.

SIDEWAY [NS] op 1 May 1905 *(NS)*; HALT; clo 2 April 1923 *(Cl)*; {Trentham – Stoke-on-Trent}.

SIDLESHAM [WS]:
line op 27 August 1897 *(D&C 2)*, nd, July 1898; clo 15 December 1910 by floods, reop June 1911 tt *(Cl)* – see MILL POND; clo 20 January 1935★★.
According to *RCH dist 4 February 1930* had been renamed from S SIDING, but always just S in *Brad*.

SIDLEY [SEC] op 1 June 1902 *(SEC notice 39/1902)*; clo 1 January 1917 *(T 18 December 1916)*; reop 14 June 1920 *(Cl)*; clo 15 June 1964 *(Cl)*.

SIDMOUTH [LSW] op 6 July 1874 *(Trewman 8th)*; clo 6 March 1967 *(Express & E 6th)*.

SIDMOUTH JUNCTION – see FENITON.

SIGGLESTHORNE [NE]
op 28 March 1864 *(NE- line)* as HATFIELD; renamed 1 October 1874 *(Cl)*; clo 19 October 1964 *(Cl)*.
Became HALT 4 January 1960 according to *RM January* but not thus *Brad*; note was added that no staff in attendance.

SILEBY
SILEBY (a) [Mid] op 5 May 1840 *(co n Lee)*; clo 4 March 1968 *(Cl)*.
SILEBY (b) public use Ivanhoe Line Gala Day Saturday 28 May 1994, full public use 30th *(Mid)*; same site as (a); still open.

SILECROFT [Fur] op 1 November 1850 *(co n Furness Rise)*; aot request; still open.

SILIAN [GW] op 12 May 1911 *(co n Lampeter)*; HALT, though in *hb* from 1912 as S (1938 S HALT); clo 12 February 1951 *(Cl)* – see 1951★★.

SILKSTONE
SILKSTONE [GC] first in *Brad* August 1854 (place in July 1854 occupied by BLACK HORSE, no trains calling); for clo see 1959★★ *(RM August* – clo except for special excursions).
S COMMON op 26 November 1984 *(RM January 1985)*; still open.

SILLOTH [NB]
SILLOTH op 4 September 1856★★ *(NB)*; clo 7 September 1964 *(RM October)*.
S BATTERY EXTENSION (non-tt); specials with visitors to Armstrong Whitworth gunnery battery pier; 1886 to 1928 *(Hosp)*.
CUMBERLAND & WESTMORLAND CONVALESCENT INSTITUTION (non-tt): from 1862 to about 1928 patients taken to platform here on branch from short of station *(Hosp)*.

SILVER STREET [GE]
op 22 July 1872 *(L)*; still open. Was S S for UPPER EDMONTON from about 1883 *(RCH ref July)* to ? – was thus GE co tt 1914, LNE tt 1933.

SILVERDALE near Carnforth [Fur]
op 1 September 1857★★ *(Fur)*; still open.

SILVERDALE Stoke-on-Trent [NS]
SILVERDALE op 7 April 1862 *(D&C 7; in Brad April 1862)*; re-sited on extension to Market Drayton 1 February 1870 *(Cl)*; clo 2 March 1964 *(RM April)*.
S CROWN STREET: an 'accommodation station' more conveniently placed than the 1870 station was opened in July 1871 *(Market Drayton)*; first in *Brad* when other halts op 1 May 1905; HALT; clo 7 June 1949 (Tuesday, trainless Bank Holiday Monday intervening) *(RM September)* – however, this seems to have been a purely 'official' date – trains actually ceased calling after December 1945 *Brad* (when only one train, from Stoke was shown) but before/with 6–31 May 1946 tt; {Silverdale – Newcastle}. Usually just C S in *Brad*.

SILVERHILL COLLIERY [GN] (non-tt): miners; dates ?; {branch from Skegby} *(U)*.

SILVERTON [GW] op 1 November 1867 *(Tiverton 5th)*; clo 5 October 1964 *(Cl)*.

SILVERTOWN & LONDON CITY AIRPORT
[GE] op 19 June 1863 *(L)* as S; renamed 4 October
1987 (R. Connor, *North Woolwich – Palace Gates*,
Connor & Butler, 1997); clo 29 May 1994 *(BLN 734)*
in connection with Jubilee line extension;
reop 29 October 1995 *(RM February 1996)*; reverted
(tt only?) to S 24 September 2000 tt; clo 10 December
2006 – last train Saturday 9th *(RM February 2007)*.
SIMONSIDE [TWM]
op 17 March 2008 *(Rly Obs May 2008)*; still open.
SIMONSTONE [LY] op 15 October 1877,
two days before advertised date *(Blackburn T)*;
clo 2 December 1957 *(RM January 1958)*.
SIMPASTURE
For early service from Stockton to Shildon through this
area see 1835 A**.
SIMPASTURE (non-tt): *Away, p. 30*, reproduces notice of
excursion from here to Seaton and Hartlepool and back,
Sunday 12 September 1847; notice headed 'Clarence
Railway' but issued from Stockton & Hartlepool office.
S ROYAL ORDNANCE FACTORY [LNE] (non-tt);
op 18 January 1942 *(Cl 29)*; 4 May 1942 wtt (where
just S) shows service to Durham, Tow Law and Bishop
Auckland; absent from working tt 1 October 1945
(R. Maund). {Stillington – Shildon}.
Also see HEIGHINGTON
SINCLAIRTOWN [NB]: line op 20 September
1847**, nd, May 1848 *(Topham)*; clo 1 January 1917,
except for workmen *(RM February)*; reop to public
1 February 1919 *(RCH*; trains shown February *Brad)*;
clo 6 October 1969 *(Cl)*.
SINDERBY [NE]:
op 25 May 1852**; clo 1 January 1962 *(Cl)*.
SINDLESHAM – see WINNERSH.
SINFIN
S CENTRAL and **S NORTH** op 4 October 1976 *(Mid)*;
actually clo 17 May 1993 *(RM April 1994)*, but taxis
continued service when needed. NORTH in public tt
but only for Qualcast and Internal Combustion
factories. Reason originally given for closure was that
no trains left in use were able to operate track circuits
reliably *(Midland Society Journal Summer 2003)*;
objections delayed official closure (ending need for taxi
service) until letter from Department of Transport dated
23 September 2002 (R. Maund, *Chron October 2003)*.
SINGER
SINGER [NB] op 4 November 1907 (based on *Cl*
closure date for Kilbowie which this replaced – he gave
3rd, Sunday, no Sunday service here then; first in *Brad*
December 1907, *JS)*; still open.
Became S for KILBOWIE & RADNOR PARK about
1913 according to *RCG ref July* and *hb* 1914a and
reverted to S May 1948 *hba* but only S seen in *Brad*.
S WORKMEN'S [NB]: NB special advice dated 22 June
1914 refers to Football 'Advertised Excursion' from
Springburn to here and back 21 June.
Was this the original Kilbowie, kept in use for workmen
after diversion came into use?
S WORKERS PLATFORM [LNE] (non-tt):
continuation/reopening of above? op after 1942 *(U)*;
clo 1 May 1967 *(BLN 79)*; {spur from Drumry}.

SINGLETON near Blackpool [PW] first in *Brad*
August 1870; at first Saturdays only; all days May 1873
tt; aot request; clo 2 May 1932 *(LNW Record)*.
SINGLETON near Chichester [LBSC]
op 11 July 1881 *(co n W Sussex)*; clo 7 July 1935 (Sunday)
(RM September). Specially long platform and elaborate
refreshment room and other facilities to cope with
Goodwood race-goers; last used for race traffic 1933 *(AB)*.
SINNINGTON [NE] op 1 April 1875 *(NE- line)*;
clo 2 February 1953 *(RM March)*.
SIR WATKIN'S – see GLANLLYN.
SIRHOWY [LNW] op 19 June 1865 *(co n Newport
17th)*; clo 13 June 1960 *(RM July)*.
SITTINGBOURNE [LCD] op 25 January 1858**
(T 23rd- line); became S & MILTON 1 July 1899,
S & M REGIS 1908 tt, S 1970 tt *(Cl)*; still open.
SIX BELLS
SIX BELLS [GW] op 27 September 1937 *(undated
GW notice)*; HALT; clo 30 April 1962 *(T 6 April)*;
{Aberbeeg – Abertillery}.
S B COLLIERY [GW] (non-tt): op by July 1897;
clo by July 1902; {Aberbeeg – Six Bells} *(U)*.
For S B [LNW] see GARNDIFFAITH.
SIX MILE BOTTOM [GE] op 4 April 1848 *(co n
T 3rd- line)* as WESTLEY; renamed October 1848 tt
(Cl); clo 1 July 1850**; reop 9 September 1850 *(co n
T 6th)*; aot request; clo 2 January 1967 *(RM February)*.
SKARES [GSW] op 1 July 1901 *(RCG)* – date also
given by *GSW* but not in *Brad* until November 1901;
clo 10 September 1951 *(RM October)*.
SKEGBY [GN] op 4 April 1898 *(RCG)*;
clo 14 September 1931 *(Cl)*. Advertised summer
Saturday use began 1954, when first train from here ran
19 June, first back 26 June *(BR tt 14 June)*; last such
train ran 8 September 1962. Later excursions – e.g. to
Nottingham 1950/1 for football *(Rly Obs February 1951
p.42)*. Hb 1904: S for STANTON HILL and thus *Brad*
1915/16 to closure.
SKEGNESS [GN] op 28 July 1873 *(GN)*;
see 1962 November 11**; still open.
SKELBO [High] op 2 June 1902 *(High)*; clo 13 June
1960 *(T 8th)*. Hb 1938: S HALT; not seen thus *Brad*.
SKELLINGTHORPE
SKELLINGTHORPE [GN] op 2 January 1865 (based
on *GN*, which gives 1st, a Sunday); clo 1 June 1868 *(Cl)*;
{Lincoln – Saxilby}.
SKELLINGTHORPE [GC] op 15 December 1896 *(GC)*;
clo 19 September 1955 *(BR ER internal notice August)*.
SKELLOW – see BULLCROFT COLLIERY.
SKELMANTHORPE [LY]
op 1 December 1879 *(D&C 8; first in Brad December)*;
clo 24 January 1983 *(BLN 456)*.
SKELMERSDALE [LY]
op 1 March 1858 *(Ormskirk 4th)* as BLAGUE GATE,
one word (in index only) 1865/7 *(Brad)* – *hb* to one
word 1872; renamed S 1 August 1874 *(RCG)*;
clo 5 November 1956 *(RM December)*.
SKETTY ROAD [SIT]: line op 25 July 1860**, nd,
May 1866; last in *Brad* February 1910 (back April 1910
only – error?); in *hb* 1867–1904, inclusive; {map 88}.

SKEWEN [GW]
SKEWEN (a) [GW] first in *Brad* June 1882 as DYNEVOR;
renamed 1 October 1904 *(hbl 27th)*; re-sited 26 chains
east 1 May 1910 *(Cl)*; clo 2 November 1964 *(Cl)*.
SKEWEN (b) op 27 June 1994 *(Rly Obs August)*;
3 chains west of station closed 1964; still open.
SKINNINGROVE [NE]
op 1 April 1875 *(NE- line; first in Brad May)* as
CARLIN HOW; renamed 1 October 1903 *(hbl 29th)*;
clo to public 30 June 1952 *(Cl)*; non-tt use until line
closed 5 May 1958 – mostly iron workers but some
general public *(TTS, June 1978, p.218)* .
SKIPTON [Mid] op 8 September 1847 *(Mid)*;
re-sited 10 chains north 30 April 1876 *(Mid)*; still open.
SKIPWITH & NORTH DUFFIELD [Derwent
Valley] op 21 July 1913 *(NER Staff Mag 1913- line)*;
clo 1 September 1926 (Wednesday)★★.
SKIRLAUGH [NE] op 28 March 1864 *(NE- line)*;
clo 6 May 1957 *(Cl)*. 18 June 1961 wtt shows one
Thursday call each way for BTC purposes (to pay
staff?). *Hb* 1865a: SKIRLOUGH, corrected 1867.
SLADE GREEN [SEC]
op 1 July 1900 *(L)*; SLADES G until 21 September
1953 *(Rly Obs November)*; still open.
SLAGGYFORD [NE] op 21 May 1852★★; clo 3 May
1976 *(RM May)*. Perhaps regarded as HALT in 1960s
– ticket thus *(JB)* but 1961 tt just note that no staff.
SLAITHWAITE
SLAITHWAITE (a) [LNW] op 1 August 1849 *(co ½
T 18 August- line; in co tt for 1 August, Stockport 3rd)*;
clo 7 October 1968 *(RM November)*.
SLAITHWAITE (b) op 13 December 1982 *(RM
February 1983)*; still open.
SLAMANNAN [NB] op 5 August 1840★★;
clo 1 May 1930 (Thursday) *(Cl)*.
SLATEFORD
First station of this name, 3 miles from Lothian Road,
was renamed KINGSKNOWE(S), which see.
SLATEFORD [Cal] op 1 January 1853 *(Edin)*,
2 miles from Lothian Road; re-sited slightly east 1871
(D. Lindsay); still open.
SLEAFORD [GN] op 15 June 1857★★; still open.
SLEDMERE & FIMBER [NE]
op 1 June 1853 *(NE- line)* as F; renamed S 1858 tt,
S & F 1859 tt *(Cl)*; clo 5 June 1950 *(Cl)*; see 1953★★.
SLEIGHTHOLME [Carlisle & Silloth]:
line op 4 September 1856 *(Brad Sh 1863)*, nd, October
1856 (line in *Brad* September); Saturdays only; last in
Brad June 1857; {Drumburgh – Kirkbride}.
SLEIGHTS [NE]: line op 8 June 1835 (see 1835 B★★),
nd, May 1848 *(Topham)*; still open.
SLINFOLD [LBSC]
op 2 October 1865 *(T 3rd)*; clo 14 June 1965 *(Cl)*.
Added *hb* 1866a as SLINFORD, amended 1872.
SLINGSBY [NE] op June 1853★★; clo 1 January 1931
(Thursday) *(T 5 December 1930)*; later excursions – e.g.
27 July 1964 *(Whitby)*.
SLIPPER CHAPEL – see WALSINGHAM.
SLOANE SQUARE [Dist]
op 24 December 1868 *(T 21st, 25th)*; still open.

SLOCHD CROSSING [High] (non-tt):
railwaymen, families; at least 1922 to 1935;
{Carr Bridge – Tomatin} *(U)*.
SLOUGH [GW]
SLOUGH : trains called from line opening 4 June 1838
(co n GW), station provided 1 June 1840 *(co n T 30 May)*
– delay caused by opposition from Eton College
authorities★; re-sited 10 chains west 8 September 1884
(Cl); still open. Joint GW/Dist service began 1 March
1883; from 1 October 1885 GW only. S JUNCTION
in *Brad* 1851/3 to 1858/9.
★ = Eton tried to get stop declared illegal but lost case:
GW stopped beside existing road and used local pub as booking
office – this did not break original agreement that they would
not make a new road to a station.
S DEPOT (non-tt): originally S TRADING ESTATE;
op 17 March 1919 *(RM May 1923)*; clo 16 January
1956 *(U)*; {branch from Slough} .
SMALL HEATH [GW]
op 1 April 1863 *(GW ac)* as S H & SPARKBROOK
(but just S H in *GW ac*); & S dropped 9 May 1968;
still open. At times SMALLHEATH.
SMALL LODE – see 1883 August 20★★.
SMALLBERRY GREEN – see HOUNSLOW.
SMALLBROOK JUNCTION
op 21 July 1991 *(Rly Obs October)*; exchange station
for IoW preservation line (only open when it is),
no road or pedestrian access; still in use.
SMALLFORD [GN]
op 1 February 1866 as SPRINGFIELD and renamed
1 October 1879 (H.V. Borley, letter *RCHS Jour 138 p.210*);
aot request; became SMALLFORD for COLNEY
HEATH 1 June 1903 *(hbl 9 July)* and thus GN co tt
1909, LNE tt 1927 and *Brad* until clo 1 October 1951
(T 8 September).
SMARDALE [NE]: line op 8 August 1861 and S in
Brad when line first included September, but *co op wtt*
only shows goods train calling, so presumably slight
delay in opening; clo 20 September 1915 *(T 18th)*;
reop 1 November 1919 *(Cl)*; clo 1 December 1952 *(Cl)*.
SMEAFIELD [NE]: in NE wtt by February 1871,
Tuesdays and Saturdays (A.Young); first in *Brad* January
1875; aot request; service varied – e.g. Saturdays only
when first in *Brad*, Tuesdays also October 1877,
Wednesdays added May 1884, other variations –
August 1927 Tuesdays and Saturdays, July 1928 and
July 1929 one each way daily; last public use April 1930
but private use continued – until ? *(U)*.
SMEATON [NB]
op 1 May 1872 *(Edin)*; clo 22 September 1930 *(Cl)*.
SMEETH [SE] first in *Brad* October 1852;
clo 4 January 1954 *(T 28 October 1953)*.
SMEETH ROAD [GE]: line op 1 February 1848★★,
nd, May 1848 *(Topham)*; aot request;
clo 9 September 1968 *(RM November)*.
SMETHWICK
S ROLFE STREET [LNW] op 1 July 1852 *(W Mid;
T 2nd- line)*; R S added 1 July 1963 *(Cl)*; still open★.
★ = *Rly Obs*, November 2002, p.502, said clo 29 September
2002; but *Rly Obs* January 2003, p.20, – reality 'much reduced
service due to Unit problems'; normal again 25 November 2002.

S WEST [GW] op 1 April 1867 *(co n Brierley 30 March)*;
S JUNCTION until 17 October 1956 *(Rly Obs October)*;
reduced to token service when Galton Bridge opened;
fully clo 29 September 1996 (last train 28th).
S GALTON BRIDGE op 25 September 1995
(RM February); on two levels; upper effectively
replaced WEST; still open.

SMITHAM [SEC]
op 1 January 1904 *(L; RCG)*, but trains not shown in
Brad until July 1904; clo 1 January 1917 *(RM February)*;
reop 1 January 1919 *(Cl)*; still open.
SMITHLEY – see DOVECLIFFE.
SMITHS PARK – see MEADOW WELL.

SMITHY BRIDGE
SMITHY BRIDGE (a) [LY] first in *Brad* October 1868;
clo 2 May 1960 *(RM June)*.
SMITHY BRIDGE (b) op 19 August 1985 *(RM Nov.)*;
still open.
SMITHY HOUSES – see DENBY.
SMITHY MOOR – see STRETTON.

SNAILHAM [SEC]
op 1 July 1907 *(SEC)*; HALT; clo 2 February 1959 *(Cl)*;
{Winchelsea – Ore}.
Perhaps S CROSSING HALT at opening, but not thus
August 1907, first appearance in *Brad*.

SNAINTON [NE]
op 1 May 1882 *(Scarborough- line)*; clo 5 June 1950 *(Cl)*.
SNAITH [LY] op 1 April 1848 *(LY; co ½*
T 7 September- line); still open.

SNAPE JUNCTION [GE] appeared in *Brad* July
1859 and for some time afterwards (still January 1861,
both ways) but no trains ever shown calling.

SNAPPER [Lynton] (ng) first in *Brad* May 1904;
last April 1906 (perhaps omission result of change in tt
layout, not closure, S still in use); back June 1907 (layout
again changed); last June 1917; back in *Brad* starting
14 July 1924 (again perhaps tt did not tell full story –
other changes now); clo 30 September 1935**.
Variously S PLATFORM, S P for GOODLEIGH,
S HALT (daylight only) in *Brad*.

SNARESBROOK op by [GE] 22 August 1856 *(L;*
co n T 22nd- line); transferred to [Cen] 14 December
1947 *(T 17th)*; still open. Became S for WANSTEAD
1857 (thus GE co tt 1882), S & W 1898 tt, S for W
1929, S 14 December 1947 *(JS)*.

SNARESTONE [AN Jt]
op 1 September 1873 *(LNW Officers 10205, 10207)*;
clo 13 April 1931 *(LNW dates PCC 192)*. Still excursion
use at 8 August 1961 (one each summers 1960 and
1961 *(BR doc)*. Alias SNARSTON/SNARESTON;
erratic naming *Brad* and *hb*.

SNATCHWOOD [GW] op 13 July 1912 tt *(GW H)*;
HALT; clo 5 October 1953 *(Cl)*.

SNELLAND [GC]: line op 18 December 1848 *(GC)*,
nd, February 1849 (first time any detail provided for its
stretch); clo 1 November 1965 *(RM December)*.

SNELLS NOOK [LNW]
op 2 April 1907 *(LNW Cl)*; see 1905** (a);
clo 13 April 1931 *(LNW dates PCC 192)*.

SNETTISHAM [GE] op 3 October 1862 *(T 6th)*;
clo 5 May 1969 *(RM July*, photo-caption).

SNEYD PARK JUNCTION (non-tt):
1922 Bristol District carriage workings shows 5.08pm
to Avonmouth; staff ?;
{junction of lines from Hotwells and Clifton Down}.
SNODLAND [SE]
op 18 June 1856 *(SE; T 17th- line)*; still open.
SNOW HILL – see BIRMINGHAM;
LONDON HOLBORN VIADUCT.

SNOWDON
S RANGER (ng) – see QUELLYN LAKE.
S SUMMIT [Snowdon Mountain] (ng; rack)
op 6 April 1896**; still open, summers only. Ticket *(JB)*
for WYDDFA (Yr Wddfa = Welsh for Snowdon).
Also see SOUTH SNOWDON.

SNOWDOWN [SEC] first in *Brad* June 1914 as
S & NONINGTON; HALT until 5 May 1969
(SR App); & N dropped 12 May 1980; still open.
SNOWS HILL – see SHOTLEY BRIDGE.
SOFTLEY [NE] (non-tt): unofficial stop; detail ?;
{Lambley – Slaggyford} *(Nhumb Young)*.
SOHAM [GE] op 1 September 1879 *(Bury Free Post*
6th); clo 13 September 1965 *(T 11 August)*.
SOHO Birmingham.
SOHO [LNW] op 2 May 1853 *(Wolverhampton 27 April)**;
re-sited 13 chains west 1884/7 *(Cl)*; clo 23 May 1949
(RM September).
* = note that 1st was a Sunday.
SOHO [GW] – see WINSON GREEN.
S ROAD [LNW] op 1 April 1889 *(LNW Officers 30795*
– 'if passed by inspector', confirmed by co ½ Rly Times
10 August); clo 5 May 1941 *(Cl)*.
SOLE STREET [LCD]
first in *Brad* February 1861; still open.
SOLIHULL [GW] op 1 October 1852 *(W Mid;*
T 27 September- line; in inspection report); still open.
SOMERFORD – see GREAT SOMERFORD;
LITTLE SOMERFORD.
SOMERLEYTON [GE]
op 1 July 1847 *(GE Journal January 1995)*; still open.
SOMERSET ROAD [Mid]
op 3 April 1876 *(Mid)*; clo 28 July 1930 *(LNW Record)*.
Mid co tt 1894, 1903, hb 1904: S R for HARBORNE.
University hereabouts later.
SOMERSHAM [GN/GE]
op 1 March 1848**; clo 6 March 1967 *(RM April)*.
SOMERTON near Langport [GW]
op 2 July 1906 *(Langport 7th)*;
clo 10 September 1962 *(Som Gaz 15th)*.
SOMERTON near Banbury – see FRITWELL.
SORBIE [PPW Jt]
op 2 August 1875 *(company minutes 29 September)*;
see GARLIESTOWN for brief temporary closure;
clo 25 September 1950 *(Cl)*.
SOUGH – see SPRINGVALE.
SOURDEN [GNS] first in *Brad* October 1858;
request; S CROSSING until 1863/4 *(Brad)* – but
perhaps C dropped to save space in notes; clo 1 August
1866 (Wednesday) *(GNS*, with press reference) but
still in *Brad* until December 1867 (last inclusion) –
prolonged inertia? {map 3}.

SOUTH ACTON
SOUTH ACTON [NSWJ] op 1 January 1880 *(T 2nd)*;
still open.
SOUTH ACTON [Dist] op 13 June 1905 *(RCG)*;
clo 2 March 1959 *(RM March)*.
Covered connection provided 13 June 1905 *(L)*.
SOUTH ALLOA – see ALLOA.
SOUTH AYLESBURY [GC/GW]
op 13 February 1933 *(T 9th)*; HALT; clo 5 June 1967
(RM July); {Little Kimble – Aylesbury}.
SOUTH BANK
SOUTH BANK [NE] op 1 May 1882 *(S&D)*; re-sited
about 700 yards east 23 July 1984 *(RM Oct.)*; still open.
Also see ESTON; LACKENBY.
SOUTH BERMONDSEY [LBSC]
op 13 August 1866 *(T 14th)* as ROTHERHITHE;
renamed 1869 tt *(Cl)*; clo 1 January 1917
(T 22 December 1916); reop 14 February 1917 for
workmen *(T 13th)*, to public 1 May 1919 *(Cl)*;
re-sited south of junction 17 June 1928 *(Cl)*; still open.
SOUTH BROMLEY East London [NL]
op 1 September 1884 *(NL Circular 185)*;
clo 15 May 1944 but replacement bus service until
23 April 1945 *(Cl)*.
SOUTH CANTERBURY [SE]
op 1 July 1889 *(SE)*; clo 1 December 1940 (Sunday)
(Cl). Tickets always C S *(JB)*.
SOUTH CAVE [HB] op 27 July 1885 *(op tt NER I)*;
clo 1 August 1955 *(RM September)*.
SOUTH CERNEY [MSWJ]
op 18 December 1883 *(MSWJ; Bath Chron 20th- line)*;
C & ASHTON KEYNES until 1 July 1924
(GW circular 18 June); clo 11 September 1961 *(T 9th)*.
SOUTH CHURCH – see BISHOP AUCKLAND.
SOUTH CROYDON [LBSC]
op 1 September 1865 *(L)*; still open.
SOUTH DOCK [owned by PLA, service GE]
op 18 December 1871 *(L)*; SOUTH WEST INDIA
DOCK 1881 tt to 1895 tt *(Cl)*; clo 4 May 1926★★.
Hb: 1883 S W I DOCKS; 1904 S DOCKS MILWALL.
SOUTH EALING op by [Dist] 1 May 1883 *(L; Rtn -
line)*; [Picc] added 9 January 1933;
Dist service ceased 10 October 1964; Picc continues.
SOUTH EASTRINGTON – see EASTRINGTON.
SOUTH ELMSALL [WRG Jt]
op 1 February 1866 *(GN; T 3rd- line)*; still open.
SOUTH END near Coatbridge – see HOWES.
SOUTH ESK – see DALHOUSIE.
SOUTH GOSFORTH
SOUTH GOSFORTH [NE] op 27 June 1864 *(co ½
T 22 August- line)*; SOUTH added 1 March 1905 *(RCG)*;
clo 23 January 1978 *(RM March)* for conversion to >
SOUTH GOSFORTH [TWM] op 11 August 1980
(RM August); still open.
SOUTH GREENFORD [GW]
op 20 September 1926 *(T 25 August)*;
HALT until 5 May 1969 *(GW H)*; still open.
SOUTH GYLE
op 9 May 1985, temporary tt 9 to 11 May, full service
with new tt 13th *(Rly Obs July)*; still open.

SOUTH HAMPSTEAD [LNW] op 10 July 1922
(T 10th); Loudoun Road here earlier; still open.
SOUTH HAREFIELD [GW/GC]
op 24 September 1928 *(hbl 69)*; SOUTH added 1929
(Cl); clo 1 October 1931 (Thursday) *(Cl)*;
{Ruislip – Denham}. *Cl* says HALT but added *hb* 1930a
when halts not generally included; not Halt in *Brad*.
SOUTH HARROW
SOUTH HARROW op by [Dist] 28 June 1903 *(RCG)*;
[Picc] added 4 July 1932; Dist use ceased 23 October
1933; entrance re-sited to north-west 5 July 1935;
Picc continues.
Also see NORTHOLT PARK; SUDBURY HILL.
SOUTH HAYLING – see HAYLING ISLAND.
SOUTH HETTON [NE]: line op April or May 1837
(NE), nd, until February 1858 but platform adjoining
line mentioned in accident report dated 19 July 1844
(Rtn); (see 1836 October 19★★); clo 9 June 1952★★.
SOUTH HOWDEN [HB]
op 27 July 1885 *(op tt NER I)*; SOUTH added 1 July
1922 *(hbl 13th)*; clo 1 August 1955 *(RM September)*;
later excursions, last 30 August 1958 (M. Bairstow,
Railways in East Yorkshire, Bairstow, 1990, p.60).
SOUTH HYLTON [TWM]
op 31 March 2002, to east of level crossing (earlier
HYLTON to west) *(Rly Obs May)*; still open.
SOUTH KENSINGTON
SOUTH KENSINGTON op by [Met] 24 December 1868
(T 21st, 25th); [Dist] added 10 July 1871; still open.
SOUTH KENSINGTON [Picc] op 8 January 1907
(L; see note on Covent Garden, which also applies here);
still open.
SOUTH KENTISH TOWN [Nor]
op 22 June 1907★★; clo in morning of Thursday 5 June
1924 owing to power shortage and not reopened *(L)*.
Castle Road pre-opening *(L)*.
SOUTH KENTON [LMS] op 3 July 1933 *(T 22 June)*;
still open. Also [Bak] use until 27 September 1982★★
and from 4 June 1984 *(Ug)* to present.
SOUTH LEIGH [GW] op 14 November 1861
(GW- line); clo 18 June 1962 *(T 18 May)*.
SOUTH LEITH – see LEITH.
SOUTH LYNN [MGN] op 1 January 1886 *(MGN)*;
originally east side of Saddlebow Road, replaced by one
on west 14 April 1901 (N. Digby, *A Guide to the MGN
Joint Railway*, Ian Allan, 1990); clo 2 March 1959 *(T 2nd)*.
SOUTH MARSTON [GW]
SOUTH MARSTON (non-tt): workmen; used 5 June
1941 to 1944 *(U)* and from Monday 17 December 1956
(GW Agreement M85875); later document said not
needed after Sunday 30 June 1957; {branch from Stratton}.
Ticket as S M PLATFORM *(JB)*.
Also see STRATTON FACTORY JUNCTION.
SOUTH MERTON
SOUTH MERTON [SR] op 7 July 1929 *(RM September)*;
still open.
Also see SOUTH WIMBLEDON.
SOUTH MILFORD [NE]:
line op 22 September 1834★★ *(NE)*, nd, 19 October
1839 tt; SOUTH added 1867 tt *(Cl)*; still open.
M BRIDGE in *Brad* 1840, then no detail for some time.

SOUTH MOLTON [GW] op 1 November 1873
(W Som F P 1st, 8th); clo 3 October 1966 *(Som Gaz 7th)*.
SOUTH MOLTON ROAD
– see KINGS NYMPTON.
SOUTH PIT [GW] (non-tt): miners; HALT;
op by 27 August 1923, when listed in GW agreement
on provision of service (mine had reopened 1919);
re-sited from 12m 49ch to 12m 43ch on realignment
of branch – date ?; clo 2 November 1964;
at first GLYNCORRWG S PIT, later S PIT;
{beyond Glyncorrwg} (M. Hale; *RAC*).
SOUTH QUAY [Dock]
op 31 August 1987 *(T 1 September)*; clo during evening
of 9 January 1996 by IRA bomb *(T 10th)*; reop 15 April
1996 *(Rly Obs June)*; still open.
SOUTH QUEENSFERRY [NB]; {map 13}
SOUTH QUEENSFERRY (a) op 1 June 1868 *(Edin)*;
re-sited on extension to Port Edgar probably 1 September
1878 *(MT 6/213/10)* – intended then but only passed
inspection 30 August (in NB working tt 1 August,
prematurely; first in *Brad* October); clo 5 March 1890
(Wednesday) *(Cl)*.
SOUTH QUEENSFERRY (b) op 1 December 1919
(NB circular R545, 27 Nov.); 'near S Q goods station on
the Port Edgar branch'; HALT; clo 14 January 1929 *(Cl)*.
SOUTH RENFREW [GSW]
op 19 April 1897 *(RCG)*; clo 5 June 1967★★ *(Cl)*.
SOUTH RUISLIP
SOUTH RUISLIP [GW/GC] op 1 May 1908 *(GC dates)*
as NORTHOLT JUNCTION; renamed S R & N J
12 September 1932 *(Cl)*, S R 1947; still open.
SOUTH RUISLIP [Cen] op 21 November 1948 *(T 20th)*;
still open.
SOUTH SHIELDS {map 25}.
SOUTH SHIELDS [Pontop & South Shields]
op 16 April 1835★★; clo 19 August 1844 *(Cl)*; service
diverted to Brandling Junction station. Often just SHIELDS.
SOUTH SHIELDS [Brandling Junction] op 19 June
1839 *(NE p.327; Newcastle Journal 22nd)*; really in
High Shields; replaced to north 17 December 1842
(co n) – opening notice called it Market Place station;
clo when service diverted to >
SOUTH SHIELDS [NE] op 2 June 1879 *(Newcastle
Weekly Chronicle 3rd)* – 'new station in Mile End Road';
clo 1 June 1981 *(RM June)* for conversion to >
SOUTH SHIELDS [TWM] op 24 March 1984 *(Tyneside)*;
100 yards south of previous station; still open.
S S WESTOE LANE [SSMWC] op 19 March 1888★★;
clo 23 November 1953★★. Miners used from May 1879.
SOUTH SHORE – see BLACKPOOL.
SOUTH SIDE – see GLASGOW.
SOUTH SNOWDON [WH] (ng) op 14 May 1881
(NGSC 2) as RHYDD-DDU; renamed SNOWDON
1893; clo 1 November 1916 *(G&S)*; reop 31 July 1922★★
as S S (reverted to R-d for summer of 1934 only);
clo 28 September 1936 *(Cl)*; {map 76}.
SOUTH STOCKTON
– see STOCKTON; THORNABY.
SOUTH STREET Whitstable [SEC]
op 1 June 1911 *(SEC)*; HALT;
clo 1 January 1931 (Thursday) *(T 4 December)*.

SOUTH TOTTENHAM [TH Jt]
op 1 May 1871 *(Mid)* as S T & STAMFORD HILL;
renamed 1 July 1903 co tt *(Mid)*; still open.
Brad generally only included & S H in Mid tables and
left it there intil at least 1913, when it indexed S T and
S T & S H as though they were two separate stations;
1914 to 1915/16 shown as S T for S H, afterwards just
S T. *Hb* had & S H 1872 to 1956 (inclusive).
SOUTH WEST INDIA DOCK
– see SOUTH DOCK.
SOUTH WIGSTON op 12 May 1986 *(Leic)*; still
open. See {map 61} for relation to old Glen Parva –
approximately same site but Nuneaton-bound platform
now on Leicester side of over-bridge.
SOUTH WILLINGHAM & HAINTON [GN]
op 1 December 1876 *(RCG; T 28 November- line)*;
& H added 1 January 1877 *(Cl)*, and thus *Brad* 1878,
but not in *hb* until 1925; clo 11 September 1939★★,
reop 4 December 1939; clo 5 November 1951
(RM December).
SOUTH WIMBLEDON [Nor] op 13 September
1926 *(T 14th)*; still open. According to *ug* became S W
MERTON about 1928, with M gradually dropped;
not seen thus *Brad*.
SOUTH WITHAM [Mid] op 1 May 1894 *(RCG;
insp rpt MT6/638/6)*; clo 2 March 1959 *(T 2nd)*.
SOUTH WOODFORD
op by [GE] 22 August 1856 *(L; co n T 22nd- line)* as
GEORGE LANE; renamed S W G L 5 July 1937 *(Cl)*,
S W when transferred to [Cen] 14 December 1947
(T 17th); still open. 1886–1937 various sources also
show as G LW (e.g. *RCG ref October 1886*);
G L for S W (thus GE co tt 1914).
SOUTH WOODHAM FERRERS [GE]
op 1 July 1889 *(RCG)*; W FERRIS until 1 October
1913 *(hbl 23rd)*, then W FERRERS; became S W F
20 May 2007 tt; still open.
SOUTHALL [GW] op 1 May 1839 *(co n T 30 April)*;
still open. Joint GW/District service began 1 March
1883; GW only from 1 October 1885.
SOUTHAM
S & LONG ITCHINGTON [LNW]
op 1 August 1895 *(LNW Officers 36165, 34525)*;
clo 15 September 1958 *(RM October)*.
S ROAD & HARBURY [GW] op 1 October 1852
(T 27 September- line) as H (thus in inspection report),
H near S *(Brad)*; renamed 1856/7 *(Brad)*;
clo 2 November 1964 *(BRWR circular 12 October)*.
SOUTHAMPTON [LSW]
S (NORTHAM ROAD) op 10 June 1839 *(Salisbury 17th)*;
temporary terminus made necessary by dispute over
crossing Northam Road *(Hants Adv 16 May 1840)*;
relation to later NORTHAM (under 'N') not known;
clo when line extended to >
S TERMINUS op 11 May 1840 *(Hants Adv 16th)*;
paper called it 'new terminus at the Marsh';
clo 5 September 1966 *(Cl)*. Opened as S, renamed
S DOCKS 1858, S TOWN & DOCK 1896 tt;
S TOWN for DOCKS 1912 (and thus LSW co tt 1914),
S TERMINUS for DOCKS 9 July 1923 *(SR)*;
S T 1955 *(Brad)*.

S WEST END op 1 June 1847 *(Salisbury 5th)* as
S BLECHYNDEN (spelling as in *Brad*, confirmed as
local version by T. Cooper). Provision of station here
was condition of building line but nothing had been
done until just before opening; local Council threatened
legal action to stop opening so in week prior to opening
company hastily put up temporary station at Blechynden
Terrace (after the inspector had gone home?).
In the event Council had helped them since a tunnel fault
meant line to Dorchester could not open from main
station and this was used as a terminus; engine and
carriages for makeshift opening day service were horse-
drawn through the tunnel since it was considered too
dangerous to use steam power. First passengers carried
through tunnel on what was essentially a test train on
29 July 1847 *(Hants Chron 31st)*; regular passenger use
began with night mail of 5/6 August 1847 *(LSW)*.
Permanent S B op 1850 *(LSW)*. Was just B in LSW wtt
1914. Renamed 1858; replaced, on west side of level
crossing by >
S CENTRAL op 1 November 1895 *(Hants Adv 2nd)*
as S WEST; renamed 7 July 1935 *(Cl)*; CENTRAL
dropped 10 July 1967 *(Cl)*, restored 19 April 1994
(AB Chron); still open.
S ROYAL PIER: from 26 September 1871 carriages
horse-drawn from (Terminus) along pier tramway;
21 September 1876 steam-hauled, 5 mph limit *(LSW)*;
report in *IoW CP*, 25 May 1889, dealing with arrival of
new paddle steamer *Solent Queen* said that a new curve
allowed railway carriages to go alongside steamers;
first in *Brad* January 1891; rebuilt pier op 2 June 1892
(formal) *(LSW)*; clo 1 October 1914 *(Cl)* (Thursday).
Prior to 1904 was S TOWN PIER in *hb*.

Boat trains

Over time many sites in docks used by boat trains.
Many changes as facilities extended and improved.
Southampton Docks 1933, official handbook issued by
Southern Railway, shows large range then. 1947 edition
of handbook provided opening dates of Docks (but first
passenger trains likely to have used later) and changes
since 1933:
Outer Dock sufficiently completed for first ships
29 August 1842; completed and officially opened for
traffic 1 July 1843.
Inner Dock op 1851; much used for troops to Crimean
War (1854–6).
Newly-married Prince and Princess of Wales taken
along dock lines, direct to ship, 10 March 1863 *(T 11th)*.
Old Extension Quay op 1875.
Empress Dock op 26 July 1890; cross-channel vessels
to be concentrated here (1947), with some bomb-
damaged transit sheds to be rebuilt for passengers.
Ocean Dock op 1911; used for largest liners; plans for
new passenger reception station, berths 43/44.
1933 map shows more than 20 sites marked 'Cargo and
Passenger Sheds' around Outer, Empress and Ocean
Docks as well as on quays along Test and Itchen rivers;
more mentioned in description of plans for Western
Docks, then being built. Special mention made of
Marine Station, serving berths at Quays 7, 8 and 9
Outer Dock and Tender Station at no 50 Berth.

Last was for passengers transferred by tender to and
from ships calling at Southampton Water but not
coming into the port.
New Dock Extension Quay (berths 105–108) finally
completed 1934; three pairs of sheds furnished with
waiting-room blocks.
Pre-war: specials from Waterloo and other SR stations
for parties to view docks – refreshment facilities
provided within docks.
Much troop usage WW II; obviously interruption to
civil use.
Plans for future of berth 50 described in 1947 book.
U calls this Flying Boat Terminal, used 1948 to
September 1958.
Last trains to Western Docks 10 January 1992, by when
renamed Mayflower Terminal (berths 105/6).
Queen Elizabeth II terminal (previously White Star Dock/
Ocean Dock/Ocean Terminal/Eastern Docks) – berths
38/9 – had a 'last' use 14 December 1991 (planned for
16th but IRA bomb at Clapham Junction meant buses
used then); used again from 8 May 1994 *(BLN 739)*
for occasional Cunard sailings – e.g. 11 December 2008
for cruise on *Queen Victoria*, using temporary platform
(RM March 2009).
Naval Reviews – specials to different sites for official
spectators *(S Spec)*.
SOUTHAMPTON AIRPORT PARKWAY
op 1 April 1966 *(Cl 29)* as S A; on site of earlier Atlantic
Park Hostel; became S PARKWAY 29 September 1986;
S A P 29 May 1994; still open.
SOUTHBOROUGH – see HIGH BROOMS.
SOUTHBOROUGH ROAD – see BICKLEY.
SOUTHBOURNE [LBSC] op 1 April 1906 *(LBSC)*;
HALT until 5 May 1969 *(SR App)*; still open.
SOUTHBURN [NE] op 21 April 1890 *(RCG)*;
clo 20 September 1954 *(RM October)*.
SOUTHBURY op 21 November 1960 *(Cl 29)*;
Churchbury here earlier; still open.
SOUTHCHURCH-ON-SEA – see THORPE BAY.
SOUTHCOATES [NE] {map 63}
SOUTHCOATES (a) op 1 June 1853 *(G&S)*;
clo November 1854 *(Cl)*.
SOUTHCOATES (b) op July 1864 *(G&S)*; new site;
clo 19 October 1964 *(Cl)*. Became HALT 4 January
1960 according to *RM January* but not thus tt; note
was added that no staff were in attendance.
SOUTHEASE [LBSC] op 1 September 1906
(LBSC) as S & RODMELL HALT; HALT dropped
5 May 1969 *(SR App)*, & R dropped 12 May 1980;
still open.
SOUTHEND Swansea [SIT]: op 6 May 1893 *(SIT;*
see 1860 July 25★★); aot request; clo 6 January 1960★★;
{map 88}. First in *Brad* as MUMBLES (SOUTHEND);
M dropped on extension to PIER, 10 May 1898.
SOUTHEND-on-Sea
S CENTRAL [LTS] op 1 March 1856 *(co n T 1 March)*
as S; became S-on-SEA 1 June 1876 *(L)*; CENTRAL
added 1 May 1949 *(Mid)*; shortened to S C 20 February
1969 *(JS – BR ER commercial of this date said 'forthwith')*;
still open.
S EAST [LMS] op 18 July 1932 *(RM August)*; still open.

Used for excursions on Bank Holiday Mondays
28 March and 16 May 1932 – ticket and local press
evidence. Was S-on-S EAST 1 May 1949 *(RM May)*
to 20 February 1969 *(as above)*.

S VICTORIA [GE] op 1 October 1889 *(co notice – at
back of GE co tt November 1889, at Newton Abbot)*;
VICTORIA added 1 May 1949 *(RM May)*; still open.
Was S-on-SEA until 20 February 1969 *(as above)*.
About 1915 *(hbl ref April)* became S-on-S for
WESTCLIFFE and THORPE BAY; thus LNE tt 1933;
'for W and T B dropped' *hb* 1949a.

SOUTHERNDOWN ROAD [Barry]
op 1 December 1897 *(Glam; Colliery 3rd- line)*;
clo 23 October 1961 *(RM December)*.
[*Brad* May 1913 listed 'Southerndown bk' in new
openings list and table, where says 'starts 22nd inst'.
However, this was a clerical error, probably started by
clerk of Barry Company including horse-brake service
from station to village, completed when *Brad* converted
it to a station.]

SOUTHFIELDS: op 3 June 1889 *(L)*; still open.
Op by [Dist] service, though station owned by [LSW].
LSW use began 1 July 1889, ended 5 May 1941,
probably, *(L)*; station transferred to Dist 1 April 1994.

SOUTHFLEET [LCD] op 10 May 1886 *(Kent
Messenger 15th)*; clo 3 August 1953 *(RM September)*.
Hb: 1890 S & BETSHAM (not seen elsewhere);
1904 S for SPRINGHEAD (was thus *Brad* always).

SOUTHGATE

SOUTHGATE [Picc] op 13 March 1933 *(T 14th)*;
still open.
Also see NEW SOUTHGATE.

SOUTHILL [Mid] op 8 May 1857 *(Mid; co ½ T 13
August- line)*; clo 1 January 1962 *(RM January)*.

SOUTHMINSTER [GE]
op 1 July 1889 *(RCG)*; still open.

SOUTHPORT {map 45}
At times tts and *RCH* sources omitted SOUTHPORT
from names below; in other cases entry was just
SOUTHPORT. E.g.: *Brad* first added CHAPEL
STEET 1853/5, and then only in some tables.

S EASTBANK STREET [Liverpool, Crosby & Southport]
op 24 July 1848 *(Southport Vis 22nd & 29th)*; replaced by >

SOUTHPORT [LY] op 5 August 1851 *(Liverpool Merc
5th)*; was S CHAPEL STREET until 5 May 1969 tt;
still open.

S LONDON STREET [East Lancashire] op 9 April
1855 *(Southport Vis 5th)*; clo 1 April 1857 (Wednesday)
(Southort Vis 2nd); later excur *(U)*; later absorbed into
Chapel Street *(Cl)*.

S CENTRAL [LY] op 4 September 1882 for Guild Week
use, fully 16 September 1882 *(Southport Vis 5th)*;
clo 1 May 1901 (Wednesday) *(Cl)*.

S LORD STREET [CLC] op 1 September 1884 *(CLC)*;
clo 1 January 1917 *(T 23 December 1916)*; reop non-tt
for races at Aintree March 1919 *(CLC Portrait)*; fully
1 April 1919 *(RCG)*; clo 7 January 1952 *(RM February)*.

S St LUKES [LY] op 1 July 1883 *(Ormskirk 5th)* as
BARTON STREET; renamed S ST L ROAD October
1883 tt *(Cl)* – according to *RAIL 343/282* was renamed
St L 17 July 1883 (correct date but ROAD omitted in

error?), S St L 1 March 1902 *(Cl)*; clo 8 September
1968 *(Southport Visiter Saturday 7th* – last train tonight)*.
Since 1914 was strictly just ST LUKES.
Extended 1902 by adding platforms on loop lines (see
S Ash Street, below).

S WINDSOR ROAD [West Lancashire]
op 10 June 1878 *(Preston G 12th)*; replaced by >

S ASH STREET: *Southport Visiter* 18 July 1882 said that
in about a fortnight the new station at Ash Street Bridge
would be completed and the existing Windsor Road
station would be taken down, to allow the line to be
extended to Central. According to *JS*, S WINDSOR
ROAD was renamed S ASH STREET 4 September
1882; did this represent completion of new station or
did latter open as S W R? After about 1887 was usually
just ASH STREET in tts. During week ending Saturday
23 March 1901 this was replaced by a temporary
platform, still called Ash Street in inspection report,
short of earlier station, on opposite side of St Lukes
Bridge, alongside St Lukes but with separate entrance,
plus a temporary connection on to Chapel Street
(MT6/1011/9; Southport Visiter, 23 March – 'this week')*;
further changes undertaken piecemeal later. *RCG* gives
<u>opening</u> date of 1 March 1902 for Ash Street, presumably
meant to be date of completion of work – when
temporary platform taken out of use and trains used
part of rebuilt St Lukes? *Southport G* suggests this was
gradual process, nearing completion late February 1902.

SOUTHREY [GN] op 17 October 1848 *(co n T 16th)*;
clo 5 October 1970 *(T 16 July)*.

SOUTHSEA
– see EAST SOUTHSEA; PORTSMOUTH.

SOUTHWAITE [LNW] op 17 December 1846
(D&C 14); clo 7 April 1952 *(RM May)*.

SOUTHWARK

SOUTHWARK [Jub] op 20 November 1999 *(LRR
January 2000)*; still open.

S PARK [SEC] op 1 October 1902 *(SEC notice 104/1902)*;
clo 15 March 1915 *(RCH)*; railwaymen used to
21 September 1925 *(L)*; {in *IA*}.

SOUTHWATER [LBSC]
op 16 September 1861 *(LBSC; co ½ T 23 January
1862- line)*; clo 7 March 1966 *(RM March)*.

SOUTHWELL [Mid] op 1 July 1847 *(Mid)*;
clo 1 August 1849; occasional horse-drawn service until
reop 12 April 1852 *(Cl)* – for single market train each
way on Wednesdays *(JG)*; clo 14 March 1853,
reop 1 September 1860 *(Mid)*; clo 15 June 1959
(RM July); later excur *(U)*.

SOUTHWELL JUNCTION – see ROLLESTON.

SOUTHWICK near Brighton [LBSC]
op 12 May 1840**; still open.

SOUTHWICK near Dumfries [GSW] first in *Brad*
September 1860; clo 25 September 1939,
reop 3 February 1941 *(Cl)*; clo 3 May 1965 *(RM May)*.

SOUTHWOLD [Southwold] (ng)
op 24 September 1879 *(T 26th)*; clo 12 April 1929**.

SOWERBY BRIDGE [LY]
op 5 October 1840 *(co n Leeds 3rd)*; re-sited 14 chains
east 1 September 1876 *(Cl)*; still open.
S B JUNCTION 1851/3 to 1883/4 *(Brad)*.

SPA ROAD BERMONDSEY [SE]
op 8 February 1836, as London terminus of line to
Deptford *(RM Herepath March)*; clo 14 December
1836 (Wednesday), reop probably 30 October 1842;
re-sited 1 September 1872 *(Cl)*; usually SPA R & B
until 1877 *(hb did not alter until 1904)*; clo 15 March
1915 *(RCH)*; railwaymen used to 21 September 1925
(U); {map 105}.
SPALDING [GN] op 17 October 1848 *(co n T 16th)*;
S TOWN 1948/9 *(Brad)* to 6 May 1968 tt and thus
hb 1949a; still open.
SPARKFORD [GW]
op 1 September 1856 *(GW; W Fly P 2nd- line)*;
clo 3 October 1966 *(W Daily Press 3rd)*.
SPARROWLEE [NS] (ng)
op 29 June 1904**; clo 12 March 1934 *(LNW Record)*.
SPEAN BRIDGE [NB]
op 7 August 1894 *(W High; T 7th- line)*; still open.
SPEECH HOUSE ROAD [SW Jt]
op 23 September 1875**; clo 8 July 1929 *(RM August)*.
SPEEDWELL COLLIERY [Mid] (non-tt):
Apparently service for miners before and for some time
after Mid bought line to here from Staveley Company
on 1 May 1866 – an agreement after purchase stated
that miners would continue to be provided with service
to/from Chesterfield. Mid wtt first shows train for
miners here 2 August 1875, Saturdays only, to
Chesterfield only; clo ? (replaced in wtt for goods
purposes by Ireland Colliery July 1885 wtt);
{branch from just south of Staveley Town} *(Mid)*.
SPEEN [GW]
op 4 April 1898 *(co n Ephemera)*; clo 4 January 1960
(RM February). S for DONNINGTON in GW co tts,
Brad and hb always.
SPEETON [NE]: line op 20 October 1847**, nd,
May 1848 *(Topham)*; clo 5 January 1970 *(Cl)*.
SPEKE [LNW] trains first shown tt September 1852
(in *Brad* August, first time line there, but no trains
shown calling); clo 22 September 1930 *(Cl)*.
SPELBROOK [Northern & Eastern]
op 22 November 1841 *(co n T 17th)*; temporary
terminus clo when line extended to Bishops Stortford,
16 May 1842 *(Cl)*. Alias SPELLBROOK/SPELBROKE/
SPILLBROOK (last two in later references in *The Times*).
SPELLOW [LNW] first in *Brad* September 1882
*(LNW Officers 23730 – would be ready for opening
about second week in September)*; clo 31 May 1948
(RM July).
SPENCER ROAD [WSC Jt]
op 1 September 1906 *(L)*; HALT; clo 15 March 1915
(Cl) – RCH says clo 1 May 1915 but last trains in *Brad*
March 1915; {Coombe Lane – Selsdon Road}.
SPENNITHORNE [NE] first in *Brad* September
1863; clo 1 March 1917 *(Cl)*; reop 18 September 1920
(RM October); clo 26 April 1954 *(T 20th)*.
SPENNYMOOR [NE] market train to Byers Green,
which was first in *Brad* November 1845**, would have
gone through here; first in *Brad* April 1856 as terminus
of all days service; re-sited about 150 yards east 1 June
1878 when line to Byers Green reopened *(Cl)*;
clo 31 March 1952 *(RM June)*; later use by football

supporters *(U)*; line through here used by excursions to
Seaton Carew and Redcar, to 2 June 1963 or later
(C. Ryder, *Steam Days*, May 2000) – not known
whether these stopped at intermediate stations;
{map 33}. Hb (1862 only) SPENNY MOOR.
SPETCHLEY [Mid] op 24 June 1840 *(Chelt Chron
27th)*; clo 1 October 1855 *(Cl)*; later used for
excursions to Spetchley Park; {IA goods}.
SPETISBURY [SD Jt]
op 1 November 1860 *(Dorset Chron 8th)*;
clo 17 September 1956 *(T 13th)*. SPETTISBURY
until 1863/4 *(Brad)*; HALT by 1935 *(RCH dist ref
2 June)* but not thus until July/October 1939 *Brad* body,
though its *notices* and index July 1938 gave it as such.
SPEY BAY [GNS]
op 1 May 1886 *(GNS)* as FOCHABERS-ON-SPEY;
renamed F 1893 tt, F & S B 1 January 1916 *(hbl 27th)*,
S B 1 January 1918 *(hbl 24th)*; clo 6 May 1968 *(RM July)*.
SPEY BRIDGE – see MULBEN.
SPIERSBRIDGE [GBK Jt] op 27 September 1848
(GSW); clo 1 May 1849 (Tuesday) *(GSW; Cl)* but
trains still shown in *Brad* May and June 1849 – inertia?;
{map 15, goods IA}. Alias SPEIRSBRIDGE.
SPILSBY [GN] op 1 May 1868 *(Stamford 15th)*;
clo 11 September 1939 *(G&S)*.
SPINK HILL [GC] op 1 October 1898 *(GC dates)*;
clo 11 September 1939 *(G&S)*; excursion to
Cleethorpes 3 August 1952 *(BR working notice)*.
Used by Mount St Mary College until at least 1958.
LNE tt 1933 and hb always: S H for MOUNT ST MARY.
SPINKS LANE [Norfolk]
op 30 July 1845 *(co n Norfolk)*; last trains shown
December 1845 *Brad*; {Wymondham – Hethersett}.
SPITAL [Birkenhead] first in *Brad* June 1846; still open.
First month only SPITTLE in *Brad*.
SPITAL [LNE/earlier] (non-tt): signal box plus 'short
platform for families who lived in the adjacent isolated
cottages'; {3 miles east of Stainmore Summit}
(A.W. Stobbs, *Memories of the LNER; South-west Durham*,
author, 1989}.
SPOFFORTH [NE]
op 10 August 1847 *(co ½ T 22 February 1848)*;
HARROGATE (for which it was then terminus) until
1848 *(Brad)*; clo 6 January 1964 *(Cl)*.
SPON LANE [LNW] op 1 July 1852 *(W Mid; T 2nd-
line)*; clo 15 June 1964 *(RM July)*. LNW tt 1852, LMS
tt 1930: S L for WEST BROMWICH.
SPONDON [Mid]
op 11 November 1839 *(Mid)*; still open.
SPOONER ROW [GE] op 30 July 1845 *(co n Norfolk)*;
last in *Brad* September 1847; back December 1855,
Saturdays only; replaced by Wednesdays only service
August and September 1860; omitted altogether
October 1860; hb 1877 goods only; back in *Brad*
March 1882, Saturdays only; last there August 1882;
back, full service, July 1884; aot request; still open.
SPORLE [EA] op 26 October 1847 *(EC)*; last in *Brad*
October 1850; {map 67}.
SPRATTON [LNW]
op 1 March 1864 *(?; indexed Brad March but first in
table April)*; clo 23 May 1949 *(RM September)*.

SPREAD EAGLE – see GAILEY.
SPRING GROVE – see ISLEWORTH.
SPRING ROAD [GW]
op 1 July 1908 *(GW H;T 2nd- line)*; PLATFORM until
7 July 1924 *(GW H)*; still open.
SPRING VALE [LY] op 3 August 1847 *(LY; Rtn- line)*
as SOUGH; renamed SV & SOUGH 1870 tt *(Cl; Brad)*
(but 'for SOUGH', *RCG*), SPRING V 1 March 1877
(RCG); clo 5 August 1958 *(RM September)*.
SPRINGBURN [NB]★ op 1 January 1887 *(Glas)*;
clo 1 January 1917 except workmen *(RM February)*;
reop to public 2 June 1919 *(RCH)*; still open.
★ = [CGU] until 1896.
SPRINGFIELD near Cupar [NB]:
op 20 September 1847★★; aot request; still open.
SPRINGFIELD near Hatfield – see SMALLFORD.
SPRINGFIELD near Chesterfield [Ashover] (ng)
op 7 April 1925 *(RM October)*; clo 14 September 1936★★
(Cl); {map 59}.
SPRINGHEAD [LNE]
op 8 April 1929 *(Cl 29)*; HALT; clo 1 August 1955
(RM September); {Willerby – Hull}.
SPRINGSIDE [GSW]
op 2 June 1890★; clo 6 April 1964 *(RM May)*.
★ = *RCG* and *GSW* give 1st, but that a Sunday and no Sunday
service here; first in *Brad* June, where note says tt into force 2nd.
SPRINGWELL [NE]: see 1844 August★★;
clo 1 March 1872 (Friday) *(Cl)*; {map 24}.
SPROTBOROUGH
SPROTBOROUGH [MS&L] op 1 February 1850 *(GC)*;
clo 1 January 1875 (Friday) *(GC dates)*;
{in *IA* as Warmsworth goods}.
SPROTBOROUGH [HB] op 1 December 1894 *(RCG)*;
clo 1 February 1903 (Sunday) *(RCG)*; still in tt
February – inertia?
SPROUSTON [NE]
op 27 July 1849 *(NE)*; clo 4 July 1955 *(RM August)*.
SQUIRES GATE [LMS]
op 14 September 1931 *(T 6 August)*; still open.
SQUIRRELS HEATH – see GIDEA PARK.
STACKSTEADS [LY] op 1 October 1852 *(co ½ T 8
February 1853)*; new station 23 July 1880;
clo 5 December 1966 *(RM February 1967)*.
STADDLETHORPE – see GILBERDYKE.
STADIUM OF LIGHT [TWM]
op 31 March 2002 *(Rly Obs May)*; still open.
STAFFORD
STAFFORD [LNW] op 4 July 1837 *(T 6th)*; still open.
Was S TOWN in GN co tt 1909 and LNE ticket thus *(JB)*.
S COMMON [GN] op 1 July 1874 (P. Jones, *The Stafford
& Uttoxeter Railway*, Oakwood 1981); re-sited from
west to east of overbridge 1882; clo 4 December 1939
(Cl); later use for air force base *(U)*.
S COMMON AIR MINISTRY SIDINGS [LNE]
(non-tt): air force base; op ?; clo December 1952;
{Stafford Common – Salt & Sandon} *(U)*.
STAFFORD ROAD – see WOLVERHAMPTON.
STAG & CASTLE
– see THORNTON near Leicester.
STAINCLIFFE & BATLEY CARR [LNW]
op 1 November 1878 *(LNW Officers 18591)*;

clo 1 January 1917 *(T 22 December 1916)*; reop 5 May
1919 *(RCH)*; clo 7 April 1952 *(RM June)*.
STAINCROSS [GC] op 1 September 1882 *(GC)*;
became S for MAPPLEWELL 1 May 1901 *(hbl 25 April)*
and thus GC co tt 1903; clo 22 September 1930 *(Cl)*.
STAINES
STAINES [LSW] op 22 August 1848 *(T 24 July,
21 August)*; still open. Became S OLD 1885 *Brad* (some
tables), S JUNCTION 1889 *Brad (JS)*; JUNCTION
dropped 1920/1 *(RCG ref January 1921)*; later S
CENTRAL 26 September 1949 to 18 April 1966 *(Cl)*.
S HIGH STREET [LSW] op 1 July 1884 *(SR)*;
clo 30 January 1916 (Sunday) *(Cl)*; {in *IA*}.
S WEST [GW] op 2 November 1885 *(L)*; WEST added
26 September 1949 *(Cl)*; clo 29 March 1965 *(RM April)*.
STAINFORTH
S [MS&L] op 1 July 1856 *(GC; T 28 June- line)*;
replaced on deviation 1 October 1866 by >
HATFIELD & STAINFORTH, which see.
STAINLAND & HOLYWELL GREEN [LY]
op 1 January 1875 *(co ½ T 17 February)*; & H G added
15 March 1892 *(hbl 28 April)*; clo 23 September 1929
(T 19 August).
STAINMORE [LNE] (non-tt): in use about 1935 for
schoolchildren from Railway Cottages going to school
in Barras – picked up from beside rails so presumably
no platform (notes by J.W. Armstrong in *Stainmore &
Eden Valley Railway*, OPC, 1992, p.200; also in *NE
Express* November 2002); one Wednesday only call each
way shown wtt at least 5 October 1942 to 6 May 1946;
platform shown in undated photo *(KH 947, Ken Hoole
Study Centre* – A. Young); in use 1948 for railwaymen's
wives *(U)*; {Bowes – Barras}.
STAINTON DALE [NE] op 16 July 1885 *(T 16th)*;
one word until 3 May 1937 *(Cl)* but always two in *hb*;
clo 8 March 1965 *(T 19 January)*.
STAIRFOOT [GC] first in *Brad* August 1851 as
ARDSLEY; clo 1 January 1857 (Tuesday) (still in *Brad*
March – inertia?), reop 1 April 1858 *(Cl)*; renamed
S for A 1 October 1870 *(JS)* and thus GC co tt 1903,
LNE tt 1933 and *hb* 1872 on; re-sited 150 yards west
1 December 1871 *(Cl)*; clo 16 September 1957
(RM October).
STAITHES [NE] op 3 December 1883 *(Rtn- line)*;
clo 5 May 1958 *(RM May)*.
STALBRIDGE [SD Jt] op 10 September 1863★★;
clo 7 March 1966 *(Shepton 11th)*.
STALEY & MILLBROOK [LNW]
op 1 July 1886 *(LNW Officers 28684* – 'local service')*;
clo 1 November 1909 *(LNW Officers 42654)*; {map 53}.
STALHAM [MGN]
op 3 July 1880 *(MGN)*; clo 2 March 1959 *(T 2nd)*.
Hb 1898a S for HAPPISBURGH; 1904 S.
STALLINGBOROUGH [GC]
op 1 March 1848 *(co n GC)*; still open.
STALYBRIDGE {map 53}
At first *Brad, Topham* and LNW co tts provided a glorious
mixture of STALEYBRIDGE/STALEY BRIDGE/
STALYBRIDGE/STALY BRIDGE; the same issue
was liable to include at least three, even on same page.
Hb settled on final version 1890.

STALYBRIDGE [GC/LNW] op 23 December 1845 *(Lancs Chesh)*; through station; still open.

STALYBRIDGE [LY] terminus op 5 October 1846 *(LY)*; clo 1 July 1849 (Wednesday), service diverted to GC/LNW station; reop 1 October 1869 to provide extra capacity; clo 2 April 1917 *(Cl)*.

STAMFORD

STAMFORD [Mid] temporary terminus at end of Water Street, east of tunnel, op 2 October 1846 with line from Peterborough. Also used by trains to Syston from 1 May 1848 *(co ½ T 21 August- line)* because new station not ready. Replaced by >

STAMFORD [Mid] permanent station op 23 June 1848 (A.&E. Jordan, *How the Railway came to Stamford*, Amphion, 1996 – confirms dates from local press); S TOWN 25 September 1950 *(Rly Obs October)* to 18 April 1966 *(Mid)*; still open. S BACK STREET ST MARTINS 1867 to 1901/2 in *Brad*.

S EAST [GN] op 1 November 1856★★; EAST added 25 September 1950 *(Rly Obs October)*; clo 4 March 1957 *(RM March)* – service to/from Essendine briefly diverted to ex-Mid station. S WATER STREET 1867 to 1938/9 in *Brad*.

STAMFORD BRIDGE [NE] op 4 October 1847 *(NE errata)*; clo 29 November 1965 *(RM December)*.

STAMFORD BROOK [Dist] op 1 February 1912 *(RCG)* – shown, prematurely, in *Brad* from December 1911; still open.

STAMFORD HILL [GE] op 22 July 1872 *(L)*; still open.

STANBRIDGEFORD [LNW]

STANBRIDGEFORD (a) some revenue shown for station here in second half of 1849 *(Huish List)*; nothing else known.

STANBRIDGEFORD (b) first in *Brad* November 1860; aot request; clo 2 July 1962 *(RM July)*. At times STANBRIDGE FORD in LNW co tt and *hb*.

STANDISH [LNW]: line op 31 October 1838 *(co n Manch G 27th)*, nd, 19 October 1839 tt; at first S LANE; clo 23 May 1949 *(RM September)*.

STANDON near Hertford [GE] op 3 July 1863 *(Hertford 4th)*; clo 16 November 1964 *(T 14 October)*.

STANDON BRIDGE [LNW] first in *Brad* June 1848; clo 4 February 1952 *(RM March)*.

STANE STREET [GE] op 18 December 1922 *(RM April 1923)*; HALT; clo 3 March 1952 *(RM April)*; {Bishops Stortford – Takeley}.

STANELY [Cal]: perhaps built about 1902 between Ferguslie and Glenfield for suburban service that never materialised.

STANFORD HALL – see YELVERTOFT.

STANFORD ROAD – see MAYES CROSSING.

STANFORD-LE-HOPE [LTS] op 14 August 1854 *(co n T 11th)*; still open. Note: shown as S-le-H in op notice, not Horndon as in *L*.

STANHOE [GE] op 17 August 1866 *(T 18th)*; aot request; clo 2 June 1952 *(RM June)*.

STANHOPE

Earliest service – see CRAWLEY (alias Stanhope).

STANHOPE [NE] op 22 October 1862 *(S&D)*; re-sited on Wearhead extension 21 October 1895 *(Cl)*;

clo 29 June 1953 *(RM August)*. Used summer Sundays 22 May 1988 to 27 September 1992 (inclusive).

STANLEY Liverpool [LNW] op 1 July 1870★★; clo 31 May 1948 *(LNW Record)*.

STANLEY near Perth [Cal] op 2 August 1848 *(Rtn-line)*; moved ¼ mile north from village to junction, 1856 (with opening to Dunkeld?); clo 11 June 1956 *(RM April)*. S JUNCTION 1856/9 to 1883/5 [Cal] table, but to 1915/16 [Highland] table in *Brad*.

STANLEY near Wakefield [Methley Joint] op 1 May 1869 *(D&C 8)*; clo 2 November 1964 *(Cl)*.

STANLEY BRIDGE [GW] op 3 April 1905 *(Bristol NWR)*; HALT; clo 20 September 1965 *(RM October)*.

STANLOW & THORNTON [Birkenhead] op 23 December 1940 for Shell oil refinery workers *(Birkenhead)*; op to public 24 February 1941 *(RCH)*; still open.

STANMORE

STANMORE op by [Met] 10 December 1932 *(T 10th)*; transferred to [Bak] 20 November 1939; transferred to [Jub] 1 May 1979; still open.

S VILLAGE [LNW] op 18 December 1890 *(LNW Officers 32168)*; VILLAGE added 25 September 1950 *(RM October)*; clo 15 September 1952 *(RM October)*.

STANNER [GW] op 25 September 1875 *(GW- line)*; became HALT 1941/2 *Brad*, *hb* 1944/9a; clo 5 February 1951 *(RM October)* – see 1951★★.

STANNERGATE [DA] op 1 February 1901 *(RCG)*★; clo 1 May 1916 *(Cl)*; {goods *IA*}.

★ = *Dundee* gives 27 January but that a Sunday, no Sunday service; in another place *RCG* gives 1 June 1904 but station first in *Brad* February 1901 and present November 1903.

STANNINGLEY [GN] op 1 August 1854 *(GN;T 1st- line)*; clo 1 January 1968, effectively replaced ½ mile west by New Pudsey, which had opened in previous year *(RM February)*. GN co tt 1909, LNE tt 1933: S for FARSLEY. 'for F' dropped 12 June 1961 *(RM October)*.

STANNINGTON [NE] op 1 March 1847★★ *(co n Newcastle Journal 27 February)*; originally NETHERTON; renamed December 1891 tt *(Cl)* but 1 January 1892 *(RCG)*; clo 15 September 1958 *(RM October)*.

STANSFIELD HALL [LY]: trains first shown June 1871 (had been in *Brad*, no trains calling, since August 1869); at first one train each way, to pick up/set down only from Accrington direction – essentially it served as station for Todmorden for trains bypassing latter; later usually one morning train stopping here and Todmorden but still mostly bypass use; clo 31 July 1944 *(LNW Record)*. LY co tt 1899, LMS tt 1930: S H TODMORDEN.

STANSTED

S AIRPORT op 19 March 1991 *(Rly Obs May)*; still open. Peoplemover connection to airport buildings.

S MOUNTFITCHET [GE] op 30 July 1845 *(co n T 26th- line)*; STANSTEAD until 5 March 1890 *(RCG)*; M added 29 September 1990; still open.

STANTON near Swindon [GW] op 9 May 1883 *(Swindon 12th)*; clo 2 March 1953 *(T 20 February)*. Became HALT *hb* 1949a but not in *Brad* until 1952.

Trains for employees at Swindon Works until Friday
3 August 1962 (last train) *(Back Track June 2003)*.
According to *RAIL 253/228* opened as S FITZWARREN.

STANTON GATE [Mid]
first in *Brad* July 1851; clo 2 January 1967 *(Mid)*.

STANWARDINE [GW]
op 27 February 1933 *(Cl 29)*; HALT; clo 12 September
1960 *(Cl)*; {Baschurch – Rednal}.

STANWELL MOOR – see POYLE.

STAPLE [EK] op 16 October 1916 *(co n EK)*; approx
May–August 1940 trains not allowed to stop because
RAF had taken over station for ammunition storage
(EK-F&G, p.198) (trains shown stopping *Brad* July
1940 – but no alteration made for security reasons?);
clo 1 November 1948** *(RM January 1949)*.
DURLOCK in press report of opening *(EK-F&G)*.
Ticket for S & ASH *(JB)*.

STAPLE EDGE [GW] op 3 August 1907 *(GW H;
Glos Chron 10th- line)*; HALT; clo 3 November 1958
(T 21 October); {map 94}.

STAPLE HILL [Mid] op 1 November 1888 *(Bristol T
2nd)*; clo 7 March 1966 *(Mid)*.

STAPLEFORD [LNE] op 2 June 1924 *(T 29 May)*;
clo 11 September 1939 *(G&S)*; {Cuffley – Stevenage}.

STAPLEFORD & SANDIACRE [Mid] op 1 May
1872 *(Mid)* as SANDIACRE & STAPLEFORD,
replacing earlier station of that name; renamed 1884/5;
clo 2 January 1967 *(Mid)*.

STAPLEHURST [SE]
op 31 August 1842 *(co n T 27th)*; still open.

STAPLETON – see FISHPONDS.

STAPLETON ROAD [GW] op 8 September 1863
(co n W D Press 7th); still open. Sometimes BRISTOL S R,
some tables, *Brad* and GW co tt.

STAR CROSSING [LNW] op 2 November 1914
(LNW Officers 44486); clo 1 January 1917 *(T 22 Dec.
1916)*; reop 1 July 1919 *(Cl)*; HALT in *Brad* until
1928/9 – see 1905**; clo 30 April 1962 *(RM June)*.

STARBECK [NE]
op 1 September 1848 *(NE- line)*; still open. Initially
acted as station for Harrogate; variously in *Brad* as
HARROGATE/H & KNARESBOROUGH /
H HIGH / HIGH H, settled as S 1857 tt *(JS)*.

STARCROSS [GW]
op 30 May 1846 *(Trewman 4 June)*; still open.
GW co tt 1902, 1947: S for EXMOUTH and thus tt
until 1969/72. Ticket for STAR CROSS *(JB)*.

STARSTON [GE] op 1 December 1855 *(EC- line)*;
see 1860 November 2**; aot request; only ground-level
paved area, never platform *(GE Journal October 2003)*;
clo 1 August 1866 (Wednesday) *(Cl)*.

STAVELEY – see COPGROVE.

STAVELEY near Windermere [LNW]
op 21 April 1847 *(D&C 14; co ½ T 30 July- line)*;
aot request; still open.

STAVELEY near Chesterfield:
STAVELEY [Mid] op 6 April 1841**; re-sited 1 November
1888 at junction with Clown branch, which now opened
(Mid); replacement later renamed BARROW HILL,
which see.

S CENTRAL [GC] op 1 June 1892 *(RCG)*; S TOWN

until 25 September 1950 *(JS)*; clo 4 March 1963
(T 27 February – 'will be reopened specially for holidays
and excursions').

S TOWN [Mid] op 1 November 1888 *(RCG)* as
NETHERTHORPE; became N for S TOWN
25 October 1893 *(RCG)*, S T 1 June 1900 *(Cl)*;
clo 5 August 1952 (Tuesday – trainless Bank Holiday
Monday intervened) *(RM September)*.

S WORKS [GC] op 4 June 1892 *(RCG)*; clo 4 March
1963 *(T 27 February)*. Became SW for BARROW HILL
1 July 1892 *(hbl 7th)* and thus GC co tt 1903, LNE tt
1949 and *Brad* to 1951.

STAVERTON near Totnes [GW] op 1 May 1872
(Trewman 8th); clo 3 November 1958 *(RM December)*.

STAVERTON near Trowbridge [GW]
op 16 October 1905 *(Devizes 19th)*; HALT;
clo 18 April 1966 *(RM May)*.

STAWARD [NE] op 1 March 1869 *(NC)*;
clo 22 September 1930 *(T 10 July)*.

STEAM FERRY CROSSING – see BRITANNIA.

STEAM MILLS CROSSING [GW]
op 3 August 1907 *(Glos Chron 10th)*; HALT;
clo 7 July 1930 *(RM August)*; {map 94}.

STECHFORD [LNW]: for op see October 1844**
(first in *Brad* January 1845); at first alias S GATES;
re-sited slightly west 1 February 1882 *(LNW Record)*;
still open. Became S for YARDLEY 1882
(RCG ref April) and thus LNW tt 1882, LMS tt 1930;
'for Y' dropped 1964/8 tt.

STEELE ROAD [NB] op 2 June 1862 *(NB)*;
service as Riccarton, which see; clo 6 January 1969
(RM February). Hb 1872 (only): STEEL ROAD.

STEENS BRIDGE [GW] op 1 March 1884 *(GW)*;
clo 15 September 1952 *(RM November)*.

STEEPLEHOUSE – see 1833 May**.

STEER POINT [GW]
op 17 January 1898**; finally clo 6 October 1947.

STEETON & SILSDEN
STEETON & SILSDEN (a) [Mid] op about December
1847 *(Mid)*; & SILSDEN added 1 September 1868
co tt *(Mid)*; re-sited north of level crossing 28 February
1892 *(Mid)*; clo 22 March 1965 *(RM April)*. *Brad*
early/mid 1860s: STEETON for BOLTON BRIDGE,
ADDINGHAM and SILSDEN.

STEETON & SILSDEN (b) op 14 May 1990 *(RM June)*;
still open.

STEPFORD [GSW] op 1 March 1905 *(RCG)*;
clo 3 May 1943 *(RM January 1944)*.

STEPNEY near Hull [NE] op 1 June 1853 *(G&S)*;
clo November 1854, reop 1 June 1864 *(Cl)*;
clo 19 October 1964 *(Cl)*; {map 63}. Became a HALT
on 4 January 1960 according to *RM January*, but in tt
just note that no staff were in attendance.

STEPNEY London:
S EAST – see LIMEHOUSE.

S GREEN [Dist] op 23 June 1902 *(RCG)*; [Met] added
30 March 1936; still open.

STEPPS
STEPPS (a) [Cal]: line op 1 June 1831, station 1831 or
1832 *(MK)*; clo 5 November 1962 *(RM October)*.
At first CUMBERNAULD ROAD;

later STEP(P)S/STEP(P)S ROAD (often two versions same month); from 1 August 1883 all STEPS ROAD, then STEPPS from 1 September 1924 *(JS)*.
STEPPS (b) op 15 May 1989 *(RM July)*; 1½ miles east of earlier; still open.
STEVENAGE [GN] op 7 August 1850 *(T 6th, 8th)*; re-sited about 1 mile south 23 July 1973 *(RM November)*; still open.
STEVENSTON
For early service through here see 1834**.
STEVENSTON [GSW]: line op 17 August 1840 *(Rtn)*, nd, March 1850; still open.
S MOOR PARK [Cal] op 4 September 1888 *(Cal)*; clo 1 January 1917 (RM February), reop 1 February 1919 *(RCH)*; M P added 2 June 1924**; clo 4 July 1932 *(Cl)*. *Hb*: S MOORPARK.
STEVENTON [GW] op 1 June 1840 *(co n T 30 May)*; clo 7 December 1964 *(Cl)*.
STEWARTBY [LNW] op 30 October 1905** as WOOTTON PILLINGE; clo 1 January 1917 *(T 22 December 1916)*; reop 5 May 1919 *(RCH)*; renamed W P for S 21 September 1926 *(Rly Gaz 22 October)*, S 8 July 1935 *(LNW Record)*; still open.
STEWARTON
For first station see CUNNINGHAMHEAD.
STEWARTON [GBK Jt] op 27 March 1871 *(GSW)*; clo 7 November 1966 *(Cl)*; reop 5 June 1967 *(RM September)*; still open.
STEWARTON PLANTATION [Camp] (ng) op 18 August 1906** *(Camp)*; request; clo by May 1932 *(Camp)*.
STEWARTS LANE {map 109}
STEWARTS LANE [LBSC] op 29 March 1858 *(co n T 27th- line)*; clo 1 December 1858 (Wednesday) *(Cl)*.
STEWARTS LANE [LCD] op 1 May 1863 *(co n T 2nd)*; clo 1 January 1867 (Tuesday) *(Cl)*.
Non-tt: shuttle from Victoria to Depot Open Day 22 September 1985 *(IU)*.
STEYNING [LBSC]
op 1 July 1861 *(LBSC; co ½ T 23 January 1862- line)*; clo 7 March 1966 *(RM March)*.
STICKNEY [GN] op 1 July 1913 *(RCG; in Brad July)*; clo 5 October 1970 *(T 16 July)*.
STILLINGTON [NE]
Two sites were involved, dates of use unknown. The first was about ¾ mile north-west of the final site (S. Bragg).
STILLINGTON (a): line op 11 July 1835 *(NE; see 1835 A**)*, nd, in existence by 11 October 1842 when passenger by coach train from Coxhoe jumped out before train had stopped *(Rtn)*. Last in *Brad* July 1856.
STILLINGTON (b) in *Brad* from October 1863 to June or July 1868 but no trains ever shown calling.
STILLINGTON (c) first in *Brad* June 1873 as CARLTON IRONWORKS / C IRON WORKS, Saturdays only; April and May 1875 full service shown for STILLINGTON, included in table proper; June 1875 C I in footnotes, request, all days; became S again 1 November 1879 *(RCG)*; clo 31 March 1952 *(RM June)*.
STIRCHLEY – see DAWLEY.
STIRCHLEY STREET – see BOURNVILLE.

STIRLING
STIRLING [Cal] op 1 March 1848 *(co ½ T 4 September)*; still open.
STIRLING [Stirling & Dunfermline/NB]: line op 1 July 1852 to station of Scottish Central/Cal; at first trains were worked between Alloa and Stirling by Scottish Central *(Alloa Advertiser 10th – fortnightly)*; own station available 1 July 1853 *(Fife)*; last used 7 October 1968 *(RM October)*, by when stations had been amalgamated.
STIRLING ROAD – see CARLUKE.
STIXWOULD [GN] op 17 October 1848 *(co n T 16th)*; clo 5 October 1970 *(T 16 July)*.
STOATS NEST
STOATS NEST [LBSC] op 12 July 1841 *(co n T 9th)*; aot request; clo 1 December 1856 *(Cl)*. According to *LBSC* proper station provided 1842.
Also see COULSDON SOUTH, opened later, about 600 yards south of (a).
STOBCROSS [Cal] op 10 August 1896 *(RCG)*; clo 3 August 1959 *(Cl)*. For later use of site see EXHIBITION CENTRE, Glasgow.
STOBO [Cal] op 1 February 1864 *(co ½ T 3 March-line)*; clo 5 June 1950 *(RM July)*.
STOBS
STOBS [NB] op 1 July 1862 *(co n T 1st- line)* as BARNES; renamed 1862 tt *(Cl)*; clo 6 January 1969 *(RM February)*.
S CAMP [NB] (non-tt): army camp; op by 25 August 1903, when mentioned in *NB circular* as having opened (other NB evidence suggests that opened that year); clo ?; {Hawick – Stobs}.
STOCKBRIDGE near Winchester [LSW]
op 6 March 1865 *(Salisbury 11th- line)*; clo 7 September 1964 *(Andover Advertiser 31 July)*.
STOCKBRIDGE near Doncaster – see ARKSEY.
STOCKCROSS & BAGNOR [GW]
op 4 April 1898 *(co n Ephemera)*; HALT from 9 July 1934 *(Cl)*; clo 4 January 1960 *(RM February)*.
STOCKINGFORD [Mid]
op 1 November 1864 *(Mid)*; clo 4 March 1968 *(Mid)*.
STOCKPORT
For first station see HEATON NORRIS.
S (EDGELEY) [LNW] op 15 February 1843 *(Stockport Advertiser 10th)* – see entry on Heaton Norris for more detail; still open. The Manchester & Birmingham company's notice in the paper said that trains would 'commence running to and from the SOUTH END of the STOCKPORT VIADUCT'; *The Railway Times* of 3 June 1843 referred to it as 'The Edgeley Station' but no LNW co tt seen added EDGELEY; LY co tt 1899 included it in table showing LNW trains. *Brad* added it 1953; it was dropped 6 May 1968 *(Cl)*; still open.
S PORTWOOD [CLC] op 12 January 1863 *(co ½ T 26 February)*; P added later 1863/1864 *(Brad)* in Marple table; clo 1 September 1875 (Wednesday) *(Cl)*. A little east of TIVIOT DALE, which effectively replaced it. According to *Stockport 1 December 1865* it would only be a ticket platform after that date but it continued to be shown in *Brad* without comment.
S TIVIOT DALE [CLC] op 1 December 1865 *(Stockport 1st)*; S TEVIOT D in Mid co tt prior to July 1874 and *Brad* until 1876 *(Mid)* but *Stockport* called it

TIVIOT D from start; clo 2 January 1967 *(T 8 Dec. 1966)*.
Also see CHEADLE.

STOCKSFIELD [NE]: line op 10 March 1835**,
in *Scott* 1837; see 1836 B**; still open.
Scott called it S or BYWELL in tt, B in text.

STOCKSMOOR [LY]: line op 1 July 1850 *(T 8th)*,
nd, January 1851; clo ?; *RM August 1919* said 'has been
reopened'); but trains still shown February, May, June
and July 1919 *Brad* so closure very short, or error –
perhaps had been briefly reduced to 'halt' status and
now full station again; still open. STOCKS MOOR in
Brad until 1879/80.

STOCKTON: all companies eventually part of [NE];
hb usually called it S-ON-TEES; {map 39}.

Stockton & Darlington

First service began 10 October 1825, horse-drawn *(co n
S&D;* see 1825**). Steam-hauled began 7 September
1833 from Bridge Road, short of point used earlier.
Proper station provided 1836 *(S&D)* and was used by
trains from Darlington until 1848.
Line to Middlesbrough opened at end of 1830 from
Bowesfield Junction, on Darlington side of 1833 station;
thus trains from Middlesbrough would have had to
reverse to reach latter. Evidence from S&D minutes,
RAIL 667 series, is that a separate site was used for
Middlesbrough trains, usually in minutes as
GUISBOROUGH LANE but just STOCKTON in
timetables, thus indistinguishable from terminus.
It was at/near the site of what is usually described as the
'1848' station at Stockton. Stockton town map of the
time shows the southward continuation of Bridge Street
as an un-named road leading 'to Guisborough'
(S. Bragg). *NE*, top line p.427, refers to accident at
Guisborough Lane, near present Thornaby station.
On 29 April 1831 orders were given for a warehouse
and cottage to be provided here; minutes imply that it
was already in use for transfer of goods to road
transport for delivery locally. It would have been fully in
accordance with S&D practice for this to be used by
passengers before any facilities were provided.
Until 7 April 1834, Middlesbrough passenger trains were
horse-drawn; likely that they operated on 'stop anywhere
practicable' principle used elsewhere on S&D. In such
circumstances it would have made sense for some at least
of the passengers to alight at Guisborough Lane and walk
across bridge to town, rather than go past it to Bowesfield
Junction and come back again. Some at least of the
trains would have gone on to BOWESFIELD LANE
(where a waiting-room had been provided by 11 March
1836) and passengers wishing to go to Darlington would
have changed to trains coming out of terminus. Not
known whether the option was available for passengers
from Middlesbrough to stay on trains to Bowesfield
Lane and then be taken to terminus – it would have
been easy to reverse 'train' by taking horse to other end.
Once steam-haulage was introduced committees seem
to have been continually debating how to organise
service here: result was much chopping and changing.
At least twice they discussed adding a curve at
Bowesfield to enable direct running to 1833/6 station,
but nothing came of this.

S&D still ran its line in separate sections, each of which
had its own 'coach engine'; only in 1846 did *Brad* show
through trains from Redcar to Darlington. This would
have required re-organisation at Bowesfield Lane – either
carriages from Redcar would have had to be attached
to train from terminus for journey to Darlington,
or carriages from terminus to train from Redcar.
Service on Middlesbrough section more frequent than
that on Darlington one; thus some trains on former
connected at Stockton with first-class trains westward,
some with mixed trains and some made no connection.
Possible that last sort terminated at Guisborough Lane
– on 25 August 1843 they discussed question of
bringing Middlesbrough coach trains direct to Stockton
station instead of stopping at Guisborough Lane.
No evidence has been seen in support of usually-quoted
idea that horse-drawn service took Middlesbrough to
Stockton passengers on from Bowesfield Lane, but
neither does anything seen refute this.
Guisborough Lane was altered/rebuilt several times.
Plans for a waiting-room here were ordered 26 February
1836 and on 2 September 1836 they agreed to spend
£83 19s 11d on providing waiting room at 'Stockton',
which is likely to mean Guisborough Lane, given the
earlier orders and that they had provided facilities at the
terminus earlier that year. Waiting-rooms at least had to
be re-sited 1838/9 to make way for 'spouts' for delivery
of coal to William Smith's pottery. A 'new station' was
opened 22 May 1846* 'for the general purposes of the
line' (does this imply through running to Darlington
from Middlesbrough? – coincides with tt on this).
By 13 August 1847 they were already considering plans
for a replacement 'on the site of the old'. 7 January 1848
orders given for moving redundant wooden station
from Middlesbrough to South Stockton for use as
temporary; this appears to have been on opposite, west,
side of road from the others. Its life during transition
from 1846 to 1848 stations must have been brief since
on 1 May 1848 they were still debating exactly where
to put it. New station probably opened 1 July 1848 –
minutes of 16 June said every prospect of it being
opened then, but habits of S&D such that this can only
be given qualified acceptance. Entrance to this station
from lane was on south side of line – minutes imply that
previously on north side. 1833 terminus was now
closed, to the evident displeasure of locals (certainly
closed by 28 July 1848 when Stockton Overseers were
to be told that station 'is now closed').
In its turn, 1848 station was soon 'inadequate'; in 1853
platforms were widened, but still not enough.
26 August 1856: draft contract agreed for new station
to east. This was opened by February 1858, when they
were looking for new use for old one.
From 1852 stations here generally known as
SOUTH S / S SOUTH / S SOUTH SHORE.
1882: replaced again, by station later renamed
THORNABY, which see.

* = there is a mention of this as date given 'by local sources' in
NE Express May 1989, though implication seems to be that this
was regarded as alternative to 1848 date usually quoted.

Clarence; Stockton & Hartlepool
Some information from *NE Express May 1989,* and
November 1989.
Clarence service began 11 July 1835 *(NE;* see 1835 A⋆⋆)
from point unknown; November 1837, station opened
in Norton Road; very soon closed, when service
suspended. From 1 May 1838 to ? there was a
contractor's market day service to and from Haverton Hill /
Port Clarence; site used at Stockton end unknown.
In June 1838 a steam hauled service to Coxhoe was
provided by Stephen Walton under three year contract,
again initial Stockton site unknown; station reopened
November 1838.
S&H arrived 10 February 1841⋆⋆; by September 1841
(inspection report, *Rtn*) both companies using
passenger station built at expense of S&H on land
owned by Clarence.
Most services transferred to Leeds Northern station,
(below); some use to 1865 *(Cl).*
Leeds Northern
Station op 25 May 1852⋆⋆; station about ½ mile north
of S & Hartlepool's, at junction with Hartlepool line;
until 1893 generally S NORTH/NORTH S /
S NORTH SHORE; still open, as STOCKTON.
Non-tt
According to P. Horn, *Pleasures and Pastimes in Victorian
Britain,* Sutton, 1999, there was a special 'halt' beside
racecourse so Lord Zetland and party could alight
without meeting ordinary racegoers; would have been
east of what became Thornaby.
STOCKTON BROOK [NS] op 1 July 1896 *(RCG);*
clo 7 May 1956 *(RM June).* Became S B for BROWN
EDGE 1923/4 *(Brad)* and thus LMS tt 1930.
STOCKTON CROSSING [GW] (non-tt): in use by
10 December 1914 when *GM's Report* said stops being
made here by workmen's trains between Salisbury and
Codford for War Department work; {Codford – Wylye}.
STOCKTON-ON-FOREST – see WARTHILL.
STOCKWELL
STOCKWELL [Nor] op 18 December 1890 *(L; co ½
T 14 February 1891- line);* see 1922⋆⋆ – platforms
re-sited to south when line reop; still open.
STOCKWELL [Vic] op 23 July 1971 *(L; T 24th- line);*
still open.
STOGUMBER [GW]
op 31 March 1862 *(W Som F P 5 April);*
clo 4 January 1971 *(Som Gaz 8th).* See 2007 July 20⋆⋆.
STOKE [GE] op 9 August 1865 *(GE- line);*
STOKE SUFFOLK 1932 tt to 14 June 1965 *(Cl);*
clo 6 March 1967 *(RM April).*
STOKE BRUERN [SMJ]
op 1 December 1892 *(SMJ);* clo 1 April 1893 (Saturday)
(G&S) – trains still shown April (inertia?); {goods *IA*}.
STOKE CANON
STOKE CANON (a) [BE]: market service first shown in tt
9 September 1852 (a Thursday), Fridays only, to Exeter
and back; Tuesday service to Tiverton added 16 June
1853 tt; latter last in tt 1 November 1855; Exeter one
last in tt 24 April 1856 (no tt 1 May, omitted 8 May tt).
All dates from *Trewman,* which at that period published
tt most weeks.

STOKE CANON (b) [GW] first in tt *Trewman* 21 May
1862⋆; re-sited ¼ mile south, at junction with Exe Valley
line, 2 July 1894 *(wtt supp);* clo 13 June 1960 *(Cl).*
Hb: S CANNON (1872 only).
⋆ = not in *Trewman* tt 7 May (14 May either no tt or page
missing); not in *Brad* until September 1862.
STOKE CLIMSLAND – see LUCKETT.
STOKE EDITH [GW]
op 13 September 1861 *(Hereford T 14th);* clo 5 April
1965 *(Cl).* Lady Foley had right to stop trains
(GW Deed 641H, dated 15 May 1873).
STOKE FERRY [GE]
op 1 August 1882 *(GE);* clo 22 September 1930 *(Cl).*
STOKE GIFFORD – see under BRISTOL.
STOKE GOLDING [AN Jt]
op 1 September 1873 *(LNW Officers 10205, 10207);*
clo 13 April 1931 *(LNW dates PCC 192);*
later excursions – e.g. one to Leamington Spa, 20 June
1953 (B Wilson, photo); still excursions at 30 September
1961 (five each summer 1960 and 1961) *(BR doc);*
one to Blackpool 13 August 1962 *(AB).*
STOKE JUNCTION [SR]
op 17 July 1932 *(sig inst 30/1932);* HALT; clo 4 December
1961 *(T 8 November);* {Sharnal Street – Allhallows}.
STOKE MANDEVILLE [Met/GC]
op 1 September 1892 *(co n Foxell);* Met used from
opening until 11 September 1961. GC service added
15 March 1899; continues.
STOKE NEWINGTON [GE]
op 27 May 1872 *(co n T 25th);* still open.
STOKE PRIOR [GW] op 8 July 1929 *(Cl 29);*
HALT; clo 15 September 1952 *(RM November).*
STOKE ROAD – see GOSPORT ROAD.
STOKE WORKS
STOKE WORKS [Mid]: not in *Chelt Adv* description
of line opening (24 June 1840), not in paper's tt of
8 July 1840, is in its tt of 17 September 1840
(tts irregularly included); WORKS added by *Chelt Adv*
tt of 4 November 1840; clo 1 October 1855 *(Cl).*
STOKE WORKS [GW] op 18 February 1852 *(Rtn- line;*
in inspection report); clo 18 April 1966 *(Cl).*
RCH Junction Diagrams called it S PRIOR.
STOKE-ON-TRENT [NS]
op 17 April 1848 *(co n T 13th);* original temporary
station, described as WHIELDEN GROVE station
STOKE in notes of opening tt *(Manifold),* replaced
about ½ mile north 9 October 1848 *(Cl);*
-on-T added 1923/4 *(Brad);* still open.
STOKES BAY [LSW]
op 6 April 1863 *(Hants Chron 11th);* temporary station
during reconstruction of main 1896; clo 1 November
1915 *(RCH);* {map 127}.
STOKESLEY [NE]
op 3 March 1857⋆⋆; clo 14 June 1954 *(Cl).*
STONE [NS] op 17 April 1848 *(co n T 13th);*
re-sited 1 May 1849; 'temporarily' closed 23 May 2004⋆⋆.
S JUNCTION in *Brad* 1848/50 to 1881/2.
STONE CROSS Eastbourne [LBSC]
op 11 September 1905 *(LBSC);* HALT;
clo 7 July 1935 (Sunday) *(Cl).*

STONE CROSSING Dartford [SEC]
first in *Brad* November 1908*; HALT until 5 May
1969 *(SR)*; still open.
* = *SEC* gives op date as 11 October 1905 on p.31 and
2 November 1908 on p.52 – possible early non-tt use by e.g.
workmen?

STONEA [GE] first in *Brad* September 1851;
aot request; clo 7 November 1966 *(RM January 1967)*.

STONEBRIDGE PARK
STONEBRIDGE PARK [LNW] op 15 June 1912 *(T 14th)*;
clo 9 January 1917 by fire *(T 13th)*, reop 1 August 1917
(Cl), when [Bak] added *(Ug)*; still open.
Also see HARLESDEN.

STONECLOUGH – see KEARSLEY.

STONEGATE [SE] op 1 September 1851 *(SE; Hants
Chron 6th- line)* as WITHERENDEN;
renamed TICEHURST ROAD December 1851 *(Cl)*,
S 6 June 1947 *(hba May 1947)*; still open.

STONEHALL & LYDDEN [SEC]
first in *Brad* June 1914; HALT; clo 5 April 1954 *(Cl)*;
{Shepherds Well – Kearsney}.

STONEHAVEN [Cal] op 1 November 1849 *(co ½ T
27 November- line)*; still open.

STONEHOUSE near Motherwell [Cal]
op 1 December 1866 *(Cal)*; original terminus replaced
by through station 1 July 1905 *(RM November)*;
clo 4 October 1965 *(BR notice, The True Line July 2006)*.

STONEHOUSE near Stroud
STONEHOUSE [GW] op 1 June 1845 *(co n Bristol T
10 May)*; S BURDETT ROAD officially 17 September
1951 *(Cl)* to 6 May 1968 tt *(offic)* but earlier *Brad*
added B R 1882/3 to 1947/8; still open.
S BRISTOL ROAD [Mid] op 8 July 1844 *(Bristol T 13th)*;
B R added 17 September 1951 *(JS)*; clo 4 January 1965
(Mid). Nailsworth branch platforms added 4 February
1867, clo 16 June 1947** *(Mid)*. *Brad* 1882/3 to 1939:
S EASTINGTON ROAD.

STONELEIGH [SR]
op 17 July 1932 *(sig inst 30/1932)*; still open.

STONEYWOOD [GNS] op 1 July 1887 *(GNS)*;
clo 5 April 1937 *(RM January 1938)*.
Hb included as S PLATFORM, 1872, 1877, 1883,
no facilities shown (error? non-tt stop?); 1890 'P'.

STONY HILL [PW]
op 1 April 1865 *(D&C 10)*; last in tt September 1872;
{St Annes-on-Sea – Gillets Crossing}.

STORETON [GC] op 18 May 1896 *(Wrexham 23rd)*
as BARNSTON; renamed S 1 November 1897
(hbl 28 October), S for B 1 May 1900 *(hbl 26 April)* and
thus GC co tt 1903, LNE tt 1933 and *Brad* to closure
3 December 1951 *(RM January 1952)*.

STORMY: possible station [GW] (non-tt); marked on
plan, with station-master's home *(RAC)*; N. Granville,
Cefn Cribwr, Chronicle of a Village, S. Williams 1980,
also refers to 'HALT' by Truman's Bridge; there was
an accident here on 14 October 1857 which clearly
indicates that it was then (officially, at least) goods only
but did have a station-master; was in *hb* 1872
(no facilities then shown) and 1877 (goods only);
perhaps aot there was a 'halt' for use of railway staff.
{Tondu – Bridgend}.

STOTTESDON [CMDP] op 21 November 1908**;
HALT from 1 October 1923 *(GW H)*;
clo 26 September 1938 *(T 9 August)*. *Cl* says treated as
halt by CMDP but in *Brad* it was in body of table and
not 'halt' when others were so tagged.

STOULTON [GW]
op 20 February 1899 *(RCG)*; clo 3 January 1966
(RM February). Pre-opening Windmill End *(RAC)*.

STOURBRIDGE [GW] {map 97}
S JUNCTION op 3 May 1852**; JUNCTION added
1 October 1879; re-sited about ¼ mile south 1 October
1901 *(Cl)*; still open.
S TOWN op 1 October 1879 *(dist t supp)*; clo 29 March
1915 *(Cl)*; reop 3 March 1919 *(GW circ 2653)*;
re-sited 57 yards nearer junction 19 February 1979
(M. Hale, *Chron 3*); clo 10 January 1994, reop 25 April
1994 *(RM July p.80)*; still open. TOWN did not appear
in *Brad* pre-1915; first use was in table giving times of
replacement coach service from S Town Station
(explanatory?); kept after reopening.

STOURPAINE & DURWESTON [SD Jt]
op 9 July 1928 *(W Gaz, Bournemouth edition 22 June)*;
HALT; clo 17 September 1956 *(T 13th)*;
{Shillingstone – Blandford}.

STOURPORT-ON-SEVERN [GW]
STOURPORT-ON-SEVERN op 1 February 1862**;
-on-S added 1934 *(Cl)*; clo 5 January 1970 *(RM Feb.)*.
Non-tt – at one time some outgoing excursions
(Bank Holidays especially) handled from sidings west
of station in order to ease pressure on level crossing (see
RAC Atlas p.72) (inspection report *MT29/83/367 dated
28 May 1927*).

STOURTON [EWYU] op 4 January 1904
(co n Midland Railway Journal No.20); clo 1 October
1904 (Saturday) *(RCG)*; {Hunslet – Rothwell}.

STOW near Galashiels [NB] op 1 November 1848
(B. Peacock, *Waverley Route Reflections*, Cheviot, 1983);
clo 6 January 1969 *(RM February)*.

STOW BARDOLPH [GE] op 27 October 1846 *(co n
D&C 5)*; aot request; BARDOLPH added 1 July 1923
(hbl 12th); clo 4 November 1963 *(T 12 October)*.

STOW BEDON [GE]
op 18 October 1869 *(GE- line)*; clo 15 June 1964 *(Cl)*.

STOW PARK [GN/GE] op 9 April 1849 *(GN/GE;
T 12th- line)* as MARTON; clo 1 December 1864
(Thursday) *(co n T 29 October)*, reop 15 July 1867 *(Cl)*;
renamed S P for M 1 December 1871 *(Cl/RCG)*;
clo 11 September 1961 *(RM September)*. *RCG ref
January 1872* called it STOWPARK for MARTON;
not seen in *Brad* but did become this in *hb* 1904.

STOW ST MARY [LNE] according to *Rly Gaz 7
September 1928* station was 'now open', making start of
September 1928 likely opening date; HALT;
clo 11 September 1939 *(G&S)*;
{Cold Norton – Woodham Ferrers}.

STOW-ON-THE-WOLD [GW] op 1 March 1862
(Wilts & Glos Stand 8th- line); clo 15 October 1962
(RM November). *Hb*: 1862 (only): S-in-the-W.

STOWE – see CHARTLEY.

STOWMARKET [GE]
op 24 December 1846 *(EC- line)*; still open.

STRACATHRO [Cal]
op 8 June 1896 *(RCG)* as INCHBARE; renamed
DUNLAPPIE 1 October 1912, S 1 November 1912
(Cl) but *RCG* and *hbl 24 October* made change direct
to S, 1 November; clo 27 April 1931 *(Cl)*; reop 4 July
1938 *(RM August)*; clo 26 September 1938 *(G&S)*.

STRADBROKE [Mid-Suffolk Light]
op 29 September 1908 *(T 28th- line)*;
clo 28 July 1952 *(T 28th)*.

STRAGEATH: op 15 September 1958**; request;
HALT; clo 6 July 1964 *(RM July)*.

STRAND – see ALDWYCH; CHARING CROSS.
STRAND ROAD – see BIDEFORD.
STRANGEWAYS & HINDLEY
– see HINDLEY SOUTH.

STRANRAER [PPW Jt]
STRANRAER op 1 October 1862 *(GSW)*; as
S HARBOUR; H dropped 17 May 1993 tt *(AB Chron)*;
still open. Aot HARBOUR & PIER *hb*.
S TOWN op 12 March 1861 *(Galloway 15th)*;
TOWN added 2 March 1953; clo 7 March 1966 *(Cl)*.
Brad did not provide separate entries for Town and
Harbour stations until April 1874.

STRAP LANE [GW]
op 18 July 1932 *(GW Mag August)*; HALT;
clo 6 October 1941, reop 16 December 1946 *(Cl)*;
clo 5 June 1950 *(Cl)*; {Witham – Bruton}.

STRATA FLORIDA [GW]
op 1 September 1866 *(GW)*; clo 22 February 1965 *(Cl)*.

STRATFORD East London
STRATFORD [EC] op 20 June 1839 *(T 14th)*,
in Angel Lane >
STRATFORD [Northern & Eastern]: probably op
22 November 1841 (see 1841**) >
Above two combined 1 April 1847 (original N&E station
west of junction with EC); later [GE]; [Cen] use began
4 December 1946 *(T 5th)*; still open. In *Truscott's EC tt*
1853 as S for LEYTONSTONE and WANSTEAD.
S LL [GE] op 16 October 1854 *(L)*; still in use, treated
as part of main station when Jub arrived. S LOWER on
Airey's 1877 map of London.
Main station in *hb* 1883–1938 as S CENTRAL;
occasionally thus *Brad* (e.g. September 1883 one table
only, where S Market also included); Airey's 1910 map
showed S CENTRAL (MAIN LINE) and
S CENTRAL LL. 1898–1938/9 (WEST HAM) added
in *Brad* but not *hb*.
STRATFORD [Dock] op 31 August 1987 *(T 1 September)*;
still open.
STRATFORD [Jub] op 14 May 1999 *(LRR 20)*; still open.
S MARKET [GE] op 14 June 1847 *(L; co ½ T 13 August-
line)* as S BRIDGE; renamed 1 November 1880 *(RCG)*;
rebuilt slightly nearer LL in conjunction with widening
1892; (WEST HAM) added as for main station;
clo 6 May 1957 *(RM June)*.

STRATFORD-UPON-AVON
Variously -ON- and -UPON- over the years.
Great Western
For earliest [Stratford & Moreton; GW] service, including
'official' one starting 1 August 1853, see 1833 B**.
Line from Honeybourne op 12 July 1859**, from

station in Sanctus Lane >
Line from Hatton op 10 October 1860 *(T 11th)*;
excur after clo *(U)* >
Above two replaced by one station, in ALCESTER
ROAD (name used in *Brad* 1882/3 to 1909/10), on
through line, op 1 January 1863 *(GW)*; still open.
Line through 1863 station used by Worcester–Warwick
excursion 24 July 1861 and opened for 'general traffic'
1 August 1861 *(Stratford Herald 26th, Stratford 2nd –
R. Hellyer)*.
S RACECOURSE (non-tt): op 6 May 1933 *(RM June)*;
last used 14 March 1968 *(BLN 102)*;
{Stratford – Milcote}.
Stratford & Midland Junction
STRATFORD [SMJ] op 1 July 1873 *(Stratford 4th;
SMJ co n Glos Chron 2 August; SMJ Jordan p.8)*.
Clo 1 August 1877 *(Cl)*; reop 2 June 1879 *(Stratford
6th)* as terminus of new service from Broom Junction
–through excursion from Birmingham New Street as
well as regular service on opening day; original service
restored 2 March 1885**; clo 7 April 1952 *(RM May)*.
In *Brad* as S-on-A NEW, dates as for Alcester Road,
above; also thus LNW co tt 1875.

STRATHAVEN [Cal]
STRATHAVEN op 2 February 1863**, service from
Hamilton; 1 May 1882 on some trains via Blantyre with
reversal; was renamed S NORTH 4 July 1904, in advance
of need, according to *hbl 7th*; replaced by >
S NORTH op 1 October 1904 *(RCG)*; clo 1 January
1917 *(RM February)*; reop 1 February 1919 *(RCH)*;
clo 1 October 1945 *(RM March 1946)*. According to
hb 1941a had become HALT; not thus *Brad*.
S op 1 October 1904 *(Cl)*; S CENTRAL until 14 June
1965 *(Cl)*; clo 4 October 1965 *(BR notice, The True Line
July 2006)*.

STRATHBLANE [NB] op 1 July 1867 *(D&C 6- line)*;
clo 1 October 1951 *(RM November)*.

STRATHBUNGO [GBK Jt] op 1 December 1877
(GSW); clo 28 May 1962 *(RM July)*.

STRATHCARRON [High]
op 19 August 1870 *(High)*; still open. S for JEANTOWN
in *Brad*? to 1955 but not *Murray* 1948.

STRATHMIGLO [NB]
op 8 June 1857**; clo 5 June 1950 *(RM July)*.

STRATHORD [Cal]
first in *Brad* June 1849 as DUNKELD ROAD;
February 1857 reduced to Tuesdays, Fridays and
Saturdays (most of time as S SIDING); full service
again January 1867; clo 13 April 1931 *(Cl)*.

STRATHPEFFER
For first station see ACHTERNEED.
STRATHPEFFER [High] op 3 June 1885 *(High)*;
reduced to Saturdays only (both ways) week beginning
4 January 1943 (trains did run Friday 1st) *(Brad Jan.
1943)*; still thus February 1944; reduced to one-way,
from Dingwall, before/with November 1944 tt; clo 23
February 1946 (Saturday – last day?) *(RM September)*.

STRATHSPEY JUNCTION
– see CRAIGELLACHIE.
STRATHYRE [Cal] op 1 June 1870 *(Callander; Rtn-
line)*; clo 28 September 1965**.

STRATTON [GW]
STRATTON op 9 May 1883 *(Swindon 12th)*; on
Highworth branch; clo 2 March 1953 *(T 20 February)*;
trains for employees at Swindon works until last train
Friday 3 August 1962 *(Back Track June 2003)*.
S PARK op 20 November 1933 *(GW notice no 1583)*;
on main line; HALT; clo 7 December 1964 *(Cl)*;
{Swindon – Shrivenham}.
S FACTORY (non-tt) was in use for Ammonium
Nitrate Factory by October 1941 (wtt supplement
dated 5 January 1942); op and clo dates unknown.
Ticket *(JB)* exists for S FACTORY JUNCTION –
were passengers sometimes dropped short? – in *RAC
Atlas p. 30* as Highworth Junction; perhaps ticket named
thus to simplify matters for workers.
STRAVITHIE [NB] op 1 June 1887 *(Fifeshire Journal
26 May)*; clo 22 September 1930 *(Cl)*.
STRAWBERRY HILL [LSW]
op 1 December 1873 *(L)* still open. S H JUNCTION
in *hb* 1904 and 1912; not seen thus elsewhere.
STREATHAM
STREATHAM [LBSC] op 1 October 1868 *(T 28 Sept.)*;
still open.
S COMMON [LBSC] op 1 December 1862 *(co n T 3rd)*;
GREYHOUND LANE 1 September 1868 to
1 January 1870 *(Cl)*; still open.
S HILL [WELCP] op 1 December 1856 *(co n
T 31 October)*; still open. *Brad* did not add HILL until
1868/9; aot BRIXTON HILL / S & B H *(L)*.
STREETHOUSE op 11 May 1992 *(RM June)*;
still open. 600 yards east of earlier Sharlston.
STREETLY [Mid] op 1 July 1879 *(W Mid)*;
clo 18 January 1965 *(RM March)*. Perhaps intended
name was Jervis Town – RCH records show change of
name, but S in *Brad* from line opening (J. Gough).
Said that company intended to call it Jervistown after
Hon. Parker Jervis of nearby Little Ashton Hall but he
objected so they called it S – no village or other obvious
site nearby (J. T. Gould, *Men of Aldridge*, Geoff Clark
Press Ltd, Bloxwich, 1957).
STRENSALL
STRENSALL [NE]: op 8 July 1845**; clo 22 September
1930**; army camp use to at least 5 August 1936 *(U)*;
late 1941/early 1942 reop non-tt *(manuscript amendment
to 6 October 1941 wtt)*; still in October 1944 wtt, absent
October 1945 wtt – usually one Saturdays only from
York only, but briefly in 1942 one other way also.
S HALT [LNE] used, non-tt, for army camp from 1922
(U); op 22 March 1926 (LNE leaflet in *RAIL 981/254*
– *RMd*); clo 22 September 1930**; {Strensall – Haxby}.
STRETFORD
STRETFORD [MSJA] op 20 July 1849** as
EDGE LANE; renamed later 1849; clo 27 December
1991 *(BLN 671)* for conversion to >
STRETFORD [Manch] op 15 June 1992 *(T 23rd- line)*;
still open.
STRETFORD BRIDGE JUNCTION [BC]
first in *Brad* May 1890; see 1866 February 1** for line
history; request; no times shown against it in table April
1933 (were times 12 September 1932);
times again 17 July 1933 *(Brad)*; clo 20 April 1935.

STRETHAM [GE] op 16 April 1866 *(T 16th- line)*;
clo 2 February 1931**; later excur *(U)*.
STRETTON
STRETTON [Mid] op 6 April 1841** as SMITHY
MOOR; renamed later 1841 (still old name October
Brad, new December); became S for ASHOVER
1 October 1872 co tt *(Mid)*; clo 11 September 1961
(RM October).
STRETTON [Ashover] (ng) op 7 April 1925 *(RM Oct.)*;
clo 14 September 1936** *(RM Oct.)*; {map 59}.
STRETTON – see BRINKLOW.
STRETTON & CLAY MILLS [NS]
op 1 August 1901 *(RCG)*;
clo 1 January 1949 (Saturday) *(RM March)*.
STRETTON WESTWOOD [GW] (non-tt); in use
1933 by quarrymen; same as later Westwood Halt?
STRETTON-ON-FOSSE
For first service through here see 1833 B**.
STRETTON-ON-FOSSE [GW]: line op 1 July 1889
(Wilts & Glos Stand 6th) and trains called from the outset,
by request, at crossing of Fosse Way, but proper station
only provided 1 October 1892 *(RCG)*; in *hb* 1890 as
S-on-F SIDING, no facilities, *hb* 1894a 'P';
clo 1 January 1917 *(GW notice dated 22 December 1916)*;
reop 1 January 1919 *(GW Circular 2647)*;
clo 8 July 1929 *(RM Sept.)*.
STRICHEN [GNS] op 24 April 1865 *(GNS)*;
clo 4 October 1965 *(Rly Obs November)*.
STRINES [GC/Mid]
first in *Brad* August 1866; still open.
STROMEFERRY [High] op 19 August 1870 *(High)*;
STROME FERRY until 1962/3 tt (to one word,
index 18 June 1962 tt, table later); still open.
STROOD
STROOD [SE] op 10 February 1845** as ROCHESTER
(co n T 5th); clo 13 December 1846, reop 23 August 1847
(see Gravesend), still as R; renamed S, R & CHATHAM
1849 tt, S 1852 tt *(SR)*; original terminus replaced by
through station 18 June 1856 *(SE)*; still open.
Also see ROCHESTER.
STROUD
STROUD [GW] op 12 May 1845 *(co n Bristol T 10th)*;
still open. Was S RUSSELL STREET 1885/6 to
1947/8 *(Brad)*.
STROUD [Mid] op 1 July 1886 *(Stroud J 26 June)*;
clo 1 January 1917 *(T 29 December 1916)*;
reop 29 January 1917 *(Mid p. 392)*; clo 16 June 1947**.
Was S CHEAPSIDE 1890 on *(Brad)*.
STROUD GREEN [GN] op 11 April 1881 *(L)*;
clo 29 October 1951, reop 7 January 1952
(T 18 December 1953); clo 5 July 1954 *(RM July)*.
STRUAN [High]
op 9 September 1863 *(High)*; clo 3 May 1965 *(RM June)*.
STUBBINS [LY]
first in *Brad* January 1847; platforms on Bacup line
only; clo 5 June 1972 *(RM August)*.
STUDLEY & ASTWOOD BANK [Mid]
op 4 May 1868 *(Mid)*; clo 1 October 1962, but
replacement buses to 17 June 1963 *(Mid)*.
STURMER [GE] op 9 August 1865 *(GE- line)*;
clo 6 March 1967 *(RM April)*.

STURMINSTER MARSHALL
– see BAILEY GATE.
STURMINSTER NEWTON [SD Jt]
op 10 September 1863★★; clo 7 March 1966 *(Shepton 11th)*.
STURRY [SE] first in *Brad* April 1848★; still open.
In *Brad* became S & HERNE BAY 1849,
S for H B 1854, S 1904/5.
★ = *SE* says company decided to provide station here, to open
by 1 June 1847, so perhaps some earlier temporary arrangement,
as at Wye, which see.
STURTON [GC] op 17 July 1849 *(GC; T 18th- line)*;
clo 2 February 1959 *(RM March)*.
STUTTON [NE]:
line op 10 August 1847 *(co ½ T 22 February 1848)*, nd,
July 1848; clo 1 June 1905 *(RCG)* or 1 July 1905 *(Cl)* –
was in *Brad* June, supporting *Cl* but perhaps inertia;
{goods IA}.
STYAL [LNW] op 1 May 1909 *(LNW Officers 42501
+ appendix)*; still open.
SUCKLEY [GW] op 1 February 1878 *(Berrows 2nd)* ★;
clo 7 September 1964 *(Cl)*.
★ = *Worcester* says 31 January (1 February with new tt is more
likely).
SUDBROOK (non-tt): used 12 August 1978 for
Sudbrook Non-Political Club excursion to Barry;
{branch from Caldicot} *(JB; U)*.
SUDBURY [GE] op 2 July 1849 *(T 5th)*;
re-sited on extension to Haverhill 9 August 1865 *(Cl)*;
S SUFFOLK 1932 tt to 14 June 1965 *(Cl)*; re-sited
Sunday 28 October 1990 *(BLN 649, 652)*; still open.
SUDBURY near Uttoxeter [NS] op 11 September
1848 *(co ½ T 3 February 1849- line)*; clo 7 November
1966 *(RM January 1967)*.
SUDBURY London
For first station see WEMBLEY CENTRAL.
S & HARROW ROAD [GC] op 1 March 1906 *(RCG)*;
still open.
S HILL op by [Dist] 28 June 1903 *(RCG)*;
transfer to [Picc] 4 July 1932; still open. *Hb* 1904
S H for GREENFORD GREEN, 1938 S H.
S HILL HARROW [GC] op 1 March 1906 *(RCG)* as
SOUTH HARROW; renamed 19 July 1926 *(hbl July)*;
still open.
S TOWN op by [Dist] 28 June 1903 *(RCG)*; transfer to
[Picc] 4 July 1932; still open.
Hb 1904 S T for HORSENDEN, 1938 S T.
SUGAR LOAF [LNW]: staff halt from 1899 *(U)*;
new non-tt station and down loop op 10 June 1909
(RAIL 1005/289); 23 May 1949 and 13 June 1955 wtts
show stops (as S L SUMMIT) all days for school-
children and Fridays for market use; ceased 1965 *(RM
September 1984, p. 372)*; used occasionally by ramblers
1984, up trains only; 1985 one Saturday per month;
summer Sundays and Bank Holiday Mondays 1987
and 1989 on; request; first in public tt 17 May 1992;
from 28 May 1995 service daily all year; still open.
Ticket for S L HALT *(JB)*.
SULLY [TV]
op 24 December 1888 *(Penarth)*; clo 6 May 1968 *(Cl)*.
SUMMER LANE – see BARNSLEY.

SUMMERSEAT [LY] op 28 September 1846
(LY; Rtn PP- line); clo 5 June 1972 *(RM August)*.
SUMMERSTON
SUMMERSTON (a) [NB] op 1 October 1879 *(D&C
6- line)*; clo 2 April 1951 *(RM May)*.
SUMMERSTON (b) op 3 December 1993 *(BLN 720)*;
still open.
SUMMERTOWN – see PORT MEADOW.
SUMMIT COTTAGES [NB] (non-tt): stop for
railwaymen, wives, children; no platform *(Nhumb Young)*;
in 31 May 1948 wtt, Saturdays only;
{Knowesgate – Woodburn}.
SUMMIT TUNNEL [Manchester & Leeds]:
no sources seen mention any station here but see
1840 December 28★★; would have 'closed' when line op
through tunnel 1 March 1841.
SUN BANK [GW] op 24 July 1905 *(GW H)* as
GARTH & S B; renamed 1 July 1906 *(Cl)*; HALT;
clo 5 June 1950 *(Cl)*; {Trevor – Llangollen}.
SUNBURY
SUNBURY [LSW] op 1 November 1864 *(co n
T 27 October)*; still open. SR tt 1939, 1947: noted as at
S Common, about one mile from S.
S RACECOURSE – see KEMPTON PARK.
SUNDERLAND all ultimately [NE]; {map 29}
S MOOR op from Hetton 19 October 1836★★;
service cut back to >
S HENDON op 1 May 1858 *(NE maps)* >
S FAWCETT STREET op from Penshaw 1 June 1853
(T 6th) >
S HENDON BURN [Londonderry] op from Seaham
2 July 1855 *(NE maps)*; service diverted to Hendon
1 October 1868 *(Cl)*.
HENDON and FAWCETT STREET replaced by >
SUNDERLAND: evening train from Bishop Auckland
arrived Sunday 3 August 1879; full use began 4th *(NE
Express November 1988)*; *Newcastle Weekly Chronicle* of
time said 'virtually opened' (because one train previous
evening or because it was a Bank Holiday?). Still open.
S CENTRAL in *hb* 1883 on but not seen thus *Brad*.
Names used above are ones to be found in modern works.
The evidence seen defies any simple treatment.
Brad called all just S until 1856 or later. HENDON was
added for trains from Hetton by 1859; also added by
1865 for [Londonderry] use – modern works say
H BURN; Fawcett Street remained in Bishop Auckland
table until 1893/94; it used S NEW for Seaham line use
of 'Central' until 1910. *Hb* 1867 had S NORTH SIDE
from Boldon (station really Monkwearmouth) and
S SOUTH SIDE from Pensher; later, to at least 1938,
it showed a separate S terminus for Seaham service,
'P' only, (but a through service Seaham to Newcastle
was shown in *Brad* from December 1911, by when
Seaham line had been extended to West Hartlepool).
SUNDERLAND [TWM] added 31 March 2002★★;
still open.
St PETERS used as temporary station from Sunday
25 February 2001, while engineering work carried out in
tunnel; south of MONKWEARMOUTH (closed 1967);
used up to and including 14 April 2001 *(Rly Obs June
2001 p. 225)*; op permanently [TWM] 31 March 2002★★.

S FULWELL (non-tt): football traffic; letter dated
8 February 1909 *(MT 76 1779 7)* shows that it had been
inspected and approved subject to being advertised in
company's weekly notices, not being in *Brad*, and being
used daylight only; ceased to be used after opening of
Seaburn, 3 May 1937; {North Dock signal box –
Wearmouth Junction signal box}.

SUNDRIDGE PARK [SE]
op 1 January 1878 *(L)* as PLAISTOW; although in
Brad was initially private station for Sir Edward Scott;
renamed 1 July 1894 *(L)*; still open.

SUNILAWS [NE]
first in *Brad* July 1859 as WARK; renamed 1 October
1871 *(Cl)*; clo 4 July 1955 *(RM August)*.

SUNNINGDALE [LSW] op 4 June 1856 *(co n T 3rd)*;
still open. Became S & BAGSHOT 1 January 1863
(Cl), S 1 March 1878 *(Cl)*, S & WINDLESHAM
1 March 1893, S for W 1920/1 *(RCG ref January 1921)*
and thus *Brad* until 1955.

SUNNYWOOD [LY]
op 3 July 1905 *(Manchester Guardian 30 June)*; see
1905** (b); clo 5 May 1952 *(RM June)*. Full name was
SW, FOOTPATH CROSSING – misleading use of
comma meant that liable to be interpreted as two
stations and F C soon dropped from *Brad*.

SUNNYMEADS [SR]
op 10 July 1927 *(sig inst 6 July)*; still open.

SURBITON [LSW] op 21 May 1838 *(Salisbury 28th)*
as KINGSTON; re-sited ½ mile west 1845 *(Cl)*;
K & HAMPTON COURT in *Brad* 1844–9, then,
variously K, K JUNCTION; from 1863 S/S & K;
name settled 1877 tt *(SR)*; still open.

SURFLEET [GN]: orders given to open station on
3 April 1849 *(Loop;* first tt evidence May or June,
Topham); S & GOSBERTON 1856/7 to 1882 *(Brad)*;
clo 11 September 1961 *(RM September)*.

SURLINGHAM FERRY
– see BRUNDALL GARDENS.

SURREY QUAYS [East London]
op 7 December 1869 *(T 7th)* as DEPTFORD ROAD;
renamed SURREY DOCKS 17 July 1911 *(hbl 26 Oct.)*,
S Q 24 October 1989 *(ug)*; clo 25 March 1995 *(BLN
746, corr)* for engineering work; reop 25 March 1998
(RM September); clo 23 December 2007.
[Dist] use 1 October 1884 to 1 August 1905 and
[Met] use 6 October 1884 to 3 December 1906 and
31 March 1913 on. [East London] ticket:
D R for SOUTHWARK PARK *(JB)*.

SUTTERTON – see ALGARKIRK.

SUTTON near Cambridge [GE]
op 16 April 1866 *(T 16th)*; re-sited on extension to
St Ives 10 May 1878 *(Cl)*; clo 2 February 1931** *(Cl)*;
later excur; Air Force base use to 1940s *(U)*.

SUTTON near Croydon
S SURREY [LBSC] op 10 May 1847 *(T 8th/Globe)*;
became S GREATER LONDON 12 May 1986 tt;
27 September 1998 tt indexed as S G L, S SURREY
in table; by May 2003 S SURREY in both; still open.
S COMMON [SR] op 5 January 1930 *(T 6th)*;
still open.
Also see WEST SUTTON.

SUTTON others – see BARNBY MOOR;
LEA GREEN; LEDSHAM; LITTLE SUTTON.

SUTTON BINGHAM [LSW]
op 19 July 1860**; became HALT 1960 *(Brad)* but still
staffed *(Cl)*; clo 31 December 1962 *(Cl)* – certainly due
to close then but *Rly Obs March 1963, p. 82* said closed
7 January 1963 – did bad weather at that time earn it
a brief reprieve?

SUTTON BRIDGE [MGN]; {map 66}
SUTTON BRIDGE [Norwich & Spalding]
op 1 July 1862 *(Lincoln S & R Merc 4th)* >
SUTTON BRIDGE [Lynn & Sutton]
op 1 March 1866 *(T 2nd)* >
About 1867 link between lines opened to passenger
trains and services diverted to 1866 station but some
use continued to be made of the first station for
'overflow' purposes at least until 1882 *(MT 6/327/10)*;
1866 station clo 2 March 1959 *(T 2nd)*.

SUTTON COLDFIELD
SUTTON COLDFIELD [LNW] op 2 June 1862 *(T
2nd)*; still open.
S C TOWN [Mid] op 1 July 1879 *(Mid)* as S C;
became S C TOWN 1 May 1882 co tt *(Mid)*,
S C 1 April 1904 *(hbl 28th)*, S C TOWN 2 June 1924
(Rly Gaz 23 May); clo 1 January 1925 (Thursday) *(Mid)*.
Also see SUTTON PARK.

SUTTON INCLINE
– see ST HELENS JUNCTION.

SUTTON OAK [LNW]: line op September 1832, nd,
mentioned in notes November 1848 (and other times?)
but not regularly included in tt until June 1853,
probably result of layout of table rather than any
closing/reopening; OAK added 1 November 1864 *(Cl)*;
clo 18 June 1951 *(RM August)*.

SUTTON PARK [Mid] op 1 July 1879 *(Mid)*;
clo 18 January 1965 *(RM March)*.

SUTTON SCOTNEY [GW] op 4 May 1885 *(Hants
Chron 2nd- line)*; clo 4 August 1942**; reop 8 March
1943 *(Cl)*; clo 7 March 1960 *(Hants Chron 5th)*.

SUTTON STAITHE [MGN]
see 17 July 1933**; HALT; {Stalham – Catfield}.

SUTTON VENY [GW] (non-tt): military hospital;
op 1916; clo by 1925; {branch from Warminster} *(U)*.

SUTTON WEAVER [LNW]
op 1 April 1869 *(LNW Officers 3981* and *Appendix C
pp. 640, 643)*; clo 30 November 1931 *(LNW Record)*.

SUTTON-IN-ASHFIELD
For earliest service through here see 1832**.
SUTTON-in-ASHFIELD [Mid] op 1 May 1893 *(Mid)*;
became S-in-A for HUTHWAITE 1 January 1908
(hbl 23rd); clo 1 January 1917; became S-in-A TOWN
1 July 1923 *(hbl 12th)* just before passenger reopening
on 9 July 1923 *(Cl)*; clo 4 May 1926**,
reop 20 September 1926 *(Cl)*; clo 26 September 1949
(Cl); workmen's use continued until ended w.e.f.
1 October 1951 (had become S-in-A GENERAL 1 July
1950) *(Cl)*.

S-in-A CENTRAL [GC] op 2 April 1917 *(RM April
and May)*; CENTRAL added 1 July 1923 *(hbl 12th)*;
clo 2 January 1956 *(RM February)*; advertised summer
Saturdays to 7 September 1962 (last train) and later

excursions – one to Edwinstowe and Ollerton called Whit Monday 3 June 1963 *(AB)*.

SUTTON JUNCTION [Mid] op 9 October 1849 *(Mid)* as S; JUNCTION added 1 November 1883 co tt, omitted 1 July 1892 co tt, restored 24 April 1893 *(Mid)* – RCG said 1 May – from tt?; clo 12 October 1964 *(RM November)*.

SUTTON PARKWAY op 20 November 1995 ('fun day' 19th) *(RM January)*; about ½ mile south of earlier S Junction; still open.

S-in-A TOWN [GN] op 4 April 1898 *(RCG)*; became S-in-A for HUTHWAITE 1907 *(RCG reference April)*; S-in-A TOWN 1 July 1923 *(T 27 August)*; clo 14 September 1931 *(Cl)*. Advertised summer Saturday use began 1954, when first train from here ran 19 June, first back 26 June *(BR tt 14 June)*; last such train ran 8 September 1962. Briefly reop fully during this period – reop 20 February 1956 *(T 20th)*; clo 17 September 1956 *(Cl)*. Also football excursions to Nottingham winter 1950/1 *(Rly Obs February 1951, p.42)* and to Blackpool 18 May 1964 *(AB)*.

SUTTON-ON-HULL [NE] op 28 March 1864 *(NE- line)*; -on-H added 1 December 1874 *(Cl)*; clo 19 October 1964 *(Cl)*. Became HALT 4 January 1960 *(RM January)* but in tt just note added that no staff were in attendance.

SUTTON-ON-SEA [GN] op 4 October 1886 *(GN)*; clo 5 October 1970 *(T 16 July)*.

SWADLINCOTE [Mid] op 1 March 1849? *(Mid)*; clo October 1853/January 1855, reop 1 June 1864 *(Mid)*; re-sited on extension to Woodville 1 May 1883 *(Cl)*; clo 6 October 1947 *(Mid)* but used for Derby County supporters certainly 1960/1 season, probably also 1961/2 *(BR doc)* and summer Saturday use to 8 September 1962, last train; football excursion to Derby 27 October 1972 *(AB)*. *Hb* called 1883 station S NEW and until 1904 showed both S and S New 'P'.

SWAFFHAM [GE] op 10 August 1847 *(EC)*; clo 9 September 1968 *(RM November)*.

SWAFFHAMPRIOR [GE] op 2 June 1884 *(GE- line)*; clo 18 June 1962 *(RM August)*.

SWAINSTHORPE [GE] op in March 1850, though first trains shown in *Brad* April 1850 *(GE Journal July 2001)*; aot request; clo 5 July 1954 *(RM September)*.

SWALE [SR] op 1 March 1923 *(Marx)* as KINGS FERRY BRIDGE, which see; renamed 1 July 1929 *(SR)*; HALT until 5 May 1969 *(SR App)*; re-sited 10 April 1960 after building of new bridge *(Cl)*; still open.

SWALWELL {map 27}
SWALWELL (a) [NC] first in *Brad* November 1852; branch terminus, sometimes S COLLIERY; at first Tuesdays and Saturdays; reduced to Saturdays only July 1853; service from Redheugh; trains stopped at branch junction for Derwenthaugh – passengers presumably walked along line to station; last in *Brad* December 1853.
SWALWELL (b) [NE] first in *Brad* April 1868; on line to Blackhill; see 1951**; clo 2 November 1953 *(RM December)*; perhaps later excur *(U)*.

SWAN VILLAGE [GW] op 14 November 1854 *(GW; T 13th- line)*; clo 6 March 1972 *(RM April)*.

SWANAGE [LSW] op 20 May 1885 *(W Gaz first edition 22 May)*; clo 3 January 1972 *(RM January)*.

SWANBOURNE [LNW] first in *Brad* October 1851; clo 1 January 1968 *(RM January)*.

SWANBRIDGE [TV] first in *Brad* July 1906 – inspected 1 February 1906 so perhaps op earlier *(Penarth)*; see 1904**; clo 6 May 1968 *(Cl)*.

SWANLEY [LCD] op 1 July 1862 *(LCD)* as SEVENOAKS JUNCTION; renamed SWANLEY J 1 January 1871 *(SR)*; re-sited 16 April 1939 *(SR sig inst 15/1939)*, now 'SWANLEY' *(hbl May)*; still open. *RCG ref April 1871:* from SEVEN OAKS J.

SWANNINGTON [Mid] op 1 September 1849 *(Mid)*; clo 18 June 1951 *(RM August)*.

SWANSCOMBE [SR]
op 2 November 1908 *(SEC)*; re-sited about ½ mile nearer Northfleet 6 July 1930 *(sig inst 30/1930)*; HALT until 5 May 1969 *(SR App)*; still open.

SWANSEA {map 88}
SWANSEA [GW] op 19 June 1850**; closed for resignalling (bus replaced) Sunday 30 September to Sunday 14 October 1973 (inclusive) *(BR tt brochure)*; became S HIGH STREET from 1859/65 GW co tt, 1865 *Brad*; back to S 6 May 1968 *(offic)*; still open.
S EAST DEPOT TICKET PLATFORM [GW] (non-tt) briefly used as alighting point 1867; {Briton Ferry Road – Wind Street} *(U)*.
S WIND STREET [GW] op 1 August 1863 *(co ½ T 17 August)*; coal owners objected to its existence since it interfered with passage of coal trains *(Colliery 18 April 1868)*; clo 1 March 1873 (Saturday) *(dist t supp 86)*. Line's service later resumed but went to East Dock.
S EAST DOCK [GW] op 1 October 1880 *(P. Rowledge)*; reopening of service previously going to Wind Street; clo 28 September 1936 *(T 14th)*.
In *hb* as S E D FABIANS BAY.
S RIVERSIDE [RSB] op 14 March 1895 *(The Cambrian 15th – M. Hale)*, using dock lines most of the way between here and Danygraig until 7 May 1899 *(GW)*; op as S, renamed S DOCKS 1 July 1924 *(GW circular 18 June)*, S R 17 September 1926 *(GW circular 3011)*; clo 11 September 1933 *(Cl)*.
S ST THOMAS [Mid] op 21 February 1860 *(Mining Journal 25th)*; ST T added 1866/7 *(Brad)*; clo 25 September 1950 *(RM November)*.
S VICTORIA [LNW] op 14 December 1867 *(The Cambrian 20th)*; clo 15 June 1964 *(RM August)*.
S KINGS DOCK: non-tt; used for landing of troops *(GW Works Order dated 23 September 1943* ordered installation of electric light for this).
Swansea & Mumbles [SIT]
For earliest service see 1807 March 25**.
S RUTLAND STREET op 25 July 1860**; clo 6 January 1960**. INSTITUTION in opening tt *(The Cambrian)*, S VICTORIA ROAD & R S some tts about 1880.
For a long time *hb* also included VICTORIA ROAD as a station on this line. This seems to have been some sort of double entry.
S GOWER STREET – see 1860 July 25**.

SWANSEA BAY [LNW] op 1 January 1879 *(LNW Officers 19224)*; re-sited about ¼ mile west 30 May 1892 *(LNW Officers 33645)*; clo 15 June 1964 *(RM August)*.

SWANWICK [LSW] op 2 September 1889 *(RCG; Hants Teleg 7th- line)*; still open.

SWAVESEY [GE] op 17 August 1847 *(co ½ T 13 August- line)*; aot request; clo 5 October 1970 *(RM October)*.

SWAY [LSW] op 6 March 1888 *(W Gaz first edition 9th)*; still open.

SWAYFIELD [GN] (non-tt): purpose ?; dates ?; {Little Bytham – Corby Glen} *(U)*.

SWAYTHLING
For possible, but unlikely, first service see 1839 June 10**.
SWAYTHLING [LSW] op 15 October 1883 *(SR)*; SWATHLING until 1 June 1895 *(RCG)*; still open.

SWIMBRIDGE [GW] op 1 November 1873 *(W Som F P 1st, 8th)*; clo 3 October 1966 *(Som Gaz 7th)*.

SWINDEN QUARRY (non-tt): known to have been used for excursions on 18 December 1999 (for Grassington Dickensian Festival) and 2 December 2000 (perhaps last use); {privately owned platform 1 mile 44 chains short of Grassington on section owned by Tilcon}; (Alan Sheppard on *Gensheet Yahoo! group, message 6463*, 30 November 2006).

SWINDERBY [Mid]
op 1 May 1847 *(Mid)*; still open.

SWINDON
SWINDON [GW] op 31 May 1841 *(Wilts 3 June)*; still open. S JUNCTION in GW co tt 1859, 1886 and *Brad* until 1895/6 (usually only in main line tables).
S TOWN [MSWJ] op 27 July 1881**; clo 11 September 1961 *(T 9th)*.
Early Marlborough line tickets *(JB)* have
S NEW TOWN for GW and S OLD TOWN for MSWJ.
Non-tt [GW]:
Stops for workmen; *U* mentions S G BOX/CABIN, perhaps on line to Wootton Bassett, in use 1905, and S WORKS, on line to Purton, op about 1880, clo by July 1897. *RM July 1938 p.3* says Purton line platform clo after man using it killed crossing line to workshop; men then had to use main station.
GW Works Outings loaded from ground level in various sidings as well as station – *Away, pp. 115–7*, photographs from 1890s and 1930s.
SWINDON near Cheltenham [BG]
op by 26 May 1842 (in *Midland Counties Herald* tt of that date, not in 19th May tt – J. Gough); clo 1 October 1844 (Tuesday) *(BG)*.

SWINE [NE] op 28 March 1864 *(NE- line)*; clo 19 October 1964 *(Cl)*. Became HALT 4 January 1960 according to *RM January*, but in tt just note that no staff were in attendance.

SWINESHEAD [GN]
op 13 April 1859 *(GN)*; still open.

SWINTON near Manchester [LY]
op 13 June 1887 *(Lancs Chesh; in tt July)*; still open.

SWINTON near Sheffield
S CENTRAL [GC] first in *Brad* April 1872; aot S, SYORKS; became S C 25 September 1950 *(Rly Obs October)*; clo 15 September 1958 *(RM Oct.)*.

S TOWN [Mid] op 1 July 1840* *(Mid; co n T 27 June- line)* as S for DONCASTER; renamed S 1852/3 co tt *(Mid)*; re-sited about 200 yards north 2 July 1899 *(Mid)*; TOWN added 25 September 1950 *(Rly Obs October)*; clo 1 January 1968 *(RM February)* but advertised holiday services 1 June 1968 to 1969 (not later) and later excur *(Mid)*.
* = not in original press description of line but certainly in use by mid-month – advertisement dated 14th refers to it *(Mid)*.
S SOUTH YORKS op 14 May 1990 *(South Yorkshire PTE brochure)*; old [Mid] reopened; still open.
Just S in opening publicity.

SWISS COTTAGE
SWISS COTTAGE [Met] op 13 April 1868 *(T 10 April & 3 August)*; clo 18 August 1940 (Sunday) *(Cl)*.
SWISS COTTAGE op by [Bak] 20 November 1939 *(T 18th)*; transferred to [Jub] 1 May 1979; still open.

SYDENHAM
SYDENHAM [LBSC] op 5 June 1839 *(co n T 6th)*; still open. S BRIDGE in co notice of fare alterations *T 24 June 1840*.
S HILL [LCD] op 1 August 1863 *(T 3rd)*; still open.
Also see LOWER SYDENHAM;
UPPER SYDENHAM.

SYLFAEN [Cam] (ng) op 6 April 1903 *(RCG)* as S FARM; request; clo 9 February 1931 *(Cl)*.
According to *RCG* clo 1 February 1913 but stayed in *Brad* as HALT (thus August and November 1913, and July 1914); since in footnotes cannot be certain trains calling; perhaps *RCG* entry marked demotion to halt rather than closure, though *hb* 1914a said 'delete P', 1917a 'add P', and in both cases 'HALT' was included in name, unusually for *hb* at that time.
Hbl ref 13 July 1916: had at some time been renamed from S F SIDING GOLFA to S HALT SIDING.

SYMINGTON [Cal]
op 15 February 1848 *(co ½ T 29 February- line)*; re-sited short distance north 30 November 1863 *(Cl)*; clo 4 January 1965 *(RM February)*. According to *JS* RCH sources 1863 recorded renaming from Biggar Junction – some sort of misunderstanding following re-siting?

SYMONDS YAT [GW]
op 4 August 1873**; clo 5 January 1959 *(T 5th)*.
First month only SY GATE tt.

SYON LANE [SR] op 5 July 1931 *(T 2nd)*; still open.

SYSTON
SYSTON (a) [Mid] op 5 May 1840 *(co n Lee)*; clo 4 March 1968 *(Cl)*. S JUNCTION in *Brad* 1852 to 1893/4 (some places).
SYSTON (b) public use Ivanhoe Line Gala Day Saturday 28 May 1994, full public use 30th *(Mid)*; single platform facing up and down slow line – former down goods; platform actually on site of old up goods (J. Gough); still open.

TACKLEY [GW] op 6 April 1931 *(co n dated 16 March)*; HALT until 6 May 1969 *(Cl)*; still open.

TADCASTER [NE]:
op 10 August 1847 *(co ½ T 22 February 1848- line; in inspection report dated 9th)* nd, July 1848; clo 6 January 1964 *(Cl)*.

TADWORTH [SEC]
op 1 July 1900 *(RCG)*; T & WALTON-ON-THE-HILL until 1 December 1968 *(SR)*; still open.

TAFF MERTHYR COLLIERY [GW/Rhy] (non-tt): HALT; op by September 1928; clo 15 June 1964; {Trelewis – Bedlinog} *(U)*.

TAFFS WELL [TV] {map 90}

TAFFS WELL (a) op 9 October 1840**; at about 7m 70ch, north of later Walnut Tree junction; replaced by >

TAFFS WELL (b) op 22 June 1863 *(TV notice, C. Chapman)*; at 7m 24ch; op as WALNUT TREE JUNCTION, alongside Rhymney's WT Bridge; renamed WT BRIDGE 1 June 1886 *(Cl)* (second station of this name), T W 16 March 1900 *(Cl)*; still open.
Also see WALNUT TREE BRIDGE [Rhy].

TAIN [High] op 1 June 1864 *(High)*; still open.

TAKELEY [GE]
op 22 February 1869 *(GE- line; in inspection report)*; clo 3 March 1952 *(RM April)*; later excur *(U)*.

TAL-Y-CAFN [LNW] op 17 June 1863 *(LNW Officers)*; T-Y-C & EGLWYSBACH 1887/8 *(Brad)* to 6 May 1974 *(BR notice)*; still open.

TALACRE [LNW] op 1 May 1903 *(LNW Officers 40971)*; clo 14 February 1966 *(RM April)*.

TALBOT ROAD – see BLACKPOOL.

TALERDDIG [Cam] first in *Brad* May 1901, but probably op earlier – company agreed to start work on station in 1896 *(Talerddig)* and second platform added 1900 *(D&C 11)*; clo 14 June 1965 *(RM July)*.

TALGARTH [Cam] op 19 September 1864 *(co n Hereford J 24th)*; clo 31 December 1962 *(T 31st)*.

TALK – see ALSAGER ROAD.

TALLEY ROAD [Vale of Towy Joint] first in *Brad* September 1859 (there August, Sundays only – assumed to be error); aot request; became HALT 1941/2 *Brad*, *hb* 1944a; clo 4 April 1955 *(Cl)*.

TALLINGTON [GN] op 15 July 1852**; clo 15 June 1959 *(RM July)*. Until 1883 Earl of Lindsey could stop any but Scottish expresses.

TALSARN [GW] op 12 May 1911 *(co n Lampeter)*; HALT; clo 12 February 1951 *(Cl)* – see 1951**.
Added *hb* 1927a as T PLATFORM and thus to 1938.

TALSARNAU [Cam]
op 10 October 1867 *(Cam; Merioneth 12th- line)*; still open. Tal-sarnau 1877 to 1890s *(hb)*.

TALWRN BACH – see LLANBEDR.

TALYBONT near Harlech [GW]
first in *Brad* July 1914; HALT until 6 May 1968 *(GW H)*; aot request; still open. Aot TAL-Y-BONT *hb*.

TALYBONT-ON-USK [BM] op 19 March 1863 *(BM)*; -ON-USK added 1 January 1898 *(hbl 27th)*; clo 31 December 1962 *(T 31st)*. Hb 1877: Tal-y-bont.

TALYLLYN (Tal-y-llyn in *hb* 1877 to 1890s)

TALYLLYN [Mid-Wales] op 21 September 1864 *(co n Hereford J 24th)*; clo 1878 *(Cl)*.

T BRYNDERWEN [BM]
temporary station op 23 April 1863 *(BM)*; replaced, east end of tunnel by >

T JUNCTION [BM] op 1 October 1869 *(BM)*; clo 31 December 1962 *(T 31st)*.

TAME BRIDGE PARKWAY
op 4 June 1990 *(D&C 7)*; PARKWAY added 1 June 1997 tt *(AB Chron)*; about one mile north of earlier Newton Road; still open.

TAMERTON FOLIOT [LSW]
op 22 December 1897 *(W D Merc 20th)*; T FOLIOTT until 1906 tt *(SR)*; became HALT 1959 *(Brad)*; clo 10 September 1962 *(Cl)*.

TAMWORTH
T HL [Mid] op 12 August 1839 *(Mid; co n T 8th- line)* >
T LL [LNW] op 15 September 1847 *(co n T 13th)* >
HL and LL added 2 June 1924 *(Rly Gaz 23 May)*; after 3 May 1971 tt usually treated as one station, but 'HL' and 'LL' sometimes added; still open.

TAN-Y-BWLCH [Festiniog] (ng) first in *Brad* August 1872; see 1923 January 1**; clo 18 September 1939**.
In *hb* 1912 as T-y-B for MAENTWROG.
TANYBWLCH in 1934 Pocket tt for North Wales Narrow Gauge; tickets thus and TANY BWLCH *(JB)*.

TAN-Y-GRISIAU [Festiniog] (ng)
first in *Brad* March 1866; see 1923 January 1**; tt shows use intermittent last years; last trains in tt June 1939; left, trainless, until line clo 18 September 1939**.
Tickets: TANY GRISIAU, TANYGRISIAU *(JB)*.

TAN-Y-MANOD [Festiniog & Blaenau] (ng)
op 30 May 1868**; last in tt January 1883; {map 78}.

TANFIELD [NE] op 10 June 1875 *(NE maps- line)*; clo 1 January 1931 (Thursday) *(T 5 December 1930)*.

TANFIELD MOOR [Brandling Junction]
op 18 June 1842 *(Consett)*; Tuesdays, Thursdays and Saturdays; one train each way except pay Saturdays when two trains back from Gateshead (3½ and 4½pm). Service from Oakwellgate; only appeared in *Brad* August 1844; if service had continued longer it would have had to be diverted since Oakwellgate clo 2 September 1844 – perhaps this closure settled fate of service. According to a local historian a small party was taken beyond here to Consett Ironworks near Shotley Bridge on 26 December 1843 and it was expected that public service would follow; there is no evidence that it did.

TANHOUSE LANE [GC/Mid] op 1 September 1890 *(GC dates)*; clo 5 October 1964 *(RM October)*. BR ticket for WIDNES T L *(JB)*.

TANKERTON [SEC] op 1 July 1914 *(SEC co tt 7 June 1914 – will open 1 July)*; HALT; clo 1 January 1931 (Thursday) *(T 5 December 1930)*.

TANNADICE [Cal]
op 1 June 1895**; clo 4 August 1952 *(RM September)*.

TANSHELF – see PONTEFRACT.

TANYCOED [Talyllyn] (ng) (non-tt): in use 1942; purpose ?; {Dolgoch – Abergynolwyn} *(U)*.

TAPLOW [GW]
op 4 June 1838 *(T 4th)* as MAIDENHEAD; became M & T 1854 tt, M 1 November 1871 *(Cl)*; re-sited ¼ mile east 1 September 1872 *(RAIL 1005/282)*; still open. GW co tt 1874: T (New Station).

TARBOLTON [GSW] op 1 September 1870 *(co ½ T 13 September- line)*; clo 4 January 1943 *(Cl)*.

TARFF [GSW] op 7 March 1864 *(Kirkcudbright 11th)* as T for GATEHOUSE; became G 1 September 1865 *(JS)*, T 1 August 1871 *(Cl; RCG ref July)*; clo 3 May 1965 *(RM May)*. Hb 1867: T OR G.

TARLETON [LY] op 3 June 1912 *(Ormskirk 30 May)*; HALT; clo 1 October 1913 (Wednesday) *(Cl)*; {terminus, short branch from Hesketh Bank}.

TARSET [NB] op 1 February 1861 *(NC- line)*; became HALT 9 September 1955 *(RM October)*; clo 15 October 1956★★ *(T 21 September)*.

TARVIN – see BARROW FOR TARVIN.

TATHAM BRIDGE – see WENNINGTON.

TATTENHALL [LNW]
TATTENHALL op 1 October 1872 *(Whitchurch 5th)*; clo 16 September 1957 *(LNW Record)*.

T ROAD: line op 1 October 1840★★, nd, about August 1841; ROAD added 1 August 1872 *(Cl)*; clo 18 April 1966 *(Cl)*. References to Crows Nest pre opening.

TATTENHAM CORNER [SEC]
op for race meeting starting 4 June 1901 *(co n T 3rd)*; *RCG* gave this as op date of station for race use only; limitation supported by article in *RM July 1901*; however, latter says intention was to make it popular place of resort for excursions, especially school treats and that arrangements for refreshment booth were being made. First included in *Brad* June 1902, for all days service. Seems to have been summer only service until end summer 1914 *(U says clo September 1914)*; *Brad* (sampled) July 1904, July 1906, August 1908, July 1909, July 1912 and August 1914 showed normal though sparse service, whilst it is included without trains November 1902, October 1904, November 1903, June 1905 and April 1910; SEC co tt 7 June 1914 said that public service would begin in July but there was also a note 'It can be arranged upon application to the Superintendent of the Line for trains on the Chipstead Valley Line to be run to and from Tattenham Corner station for Parties of a sufficient number of passengers'; in *hb* 1904 and 1912 as 'P' without qualification; army camp use September 1914 to 1919 *(U)*; race specials again from 29 April 1919 *(race)*; full public use began again 25 March 1928 *(T 20th)* – paper suggests previously regarded as excursion station, but no indication of this in *Brad*; still open.
According to J. Wells, article *Back Track, November 2007*, a trial run for directors, officials and passengers on 31 May 1899 took them as far as Kingswood by orthodox means, whence they were taken by contractors' engines over the temporary line to a temporary stand here.

TATTERSHALL [GN] op 17 October 1848 *(co n T 16th)*; clo 17 June 1963 *(RM July)*.

TAUCHERS [High]: on 5 July 1922 company agreed to erect timber platform *(High)*; presumably non-tt use began soon after; first in public tt 13 June 1955; HALT; request; clo 7 December 1964 *(RM January 1965)*; {Keith Junction – Mulben}.

TAUNTON [GW]
op 1 July 1842 *(Taunton 6th)*; still open.

TAVISTOCK
T NORTH [LSW] op 1 June 1890 *(W D Merc 2nd)*; clo 6 May 1968 *(Cornish & D P 11th)*.
T SOUTH [GW] op 22 June 1859 *(RAIL 631/6)*; clo 31 December 1962★★.
NORTH and SOUTH added 26 September 1949 *(Cl; JS)*.

TAYNUILT [Cal]
op 1 July 1880 *(T 2nd- line)*; still open.

TAYPORT [NB] op 17 May 1848 *(co n Perthshire Courier 18th)* as FERRY-PORT-ON-CRAIG; renamed TAY PORT 1851 tt; re-sited on extension of line 12 May 1879 *(Cl)* – now one word; clo 22 May 1966 (Sunday), but buses to 18 December 1967 *(Cl)*.

TEAN [NS]
op 7 November 1892 *(NS)* as TOTMONSLOW; renamed 1 January 1907 *(hbl 24th)*; became HALT 1940 tt; clo 1 June 1953 *(RM July)*.
Ticket [Cheadle] TOTMANSLOW *(JB)*.

TEBAY [LNW/NE] op 17 December 1846 *(D&C 14)*; clo 1 July 1968 *(Cl)*. T JUNCTION in *Brad* 1863/4 to 1897/8 and thus at least 1864–83 LNW co tt.

TEDDINGTON [LSW]
op 1 July 1863 *(L; co ½ T 10 August- line)*; still open. Until 1955/5 *(Brad)* various combinations (&, 'for') BUSHY / BUSHEY PARK; LSW co tt 1914 'for BUSHY' – by then *Brad* usually BUSHEY.

TEES-SIDE AIRPORT op 4 October 1971 *(Rly Obs November)*; reduced to Saturdays only 29 May 1994 tt (A. Brackenbury, *Chron January 2004)*; still open.

TEHIDY – see 1843 May 23★★.

TEIGL [GW] first in *Brad* 18 July 1932★; HALT; clo 4 January 1960 *(RM March)*; {Festiniog – Manod}.
★ = GW H gives 14 September 1931 but gap between then and appearance in *Brad* seems too great for that to be correct; furthermore, it was added after Llafar (op 1 March 1932 according to GW H, and first in *Brad* April 1932).

TEIGNGRACE [GW]
op 16 December 1867 *(Trewman 18th)*; clo 1 January 1917 *(Express & E 29 December 1916)*; reop 5 May 1919 *(RCH)*; became HALT 1938/9 *(Brad)*; clo 2 March 1959 *(Express & E 2nd)*.

TEIGNMOUTH [GW]
op 30 May 1846 *(Trewman 4 June)*; re-sited on new alignment 25 May 1884 *(Cl)*; still open. T for BISHOPSTEIGNTON in *Brad* 1900/1 to 1947/8.

TELFORD
T CENTRAL op 12 May 1986 *(D&C 7)*; still open.
T COALBROOKDALE (non-tt): exhibition; special service, Sundays only, 27 May to 2 September, inclusive, 1979 *(SLS June 1979)*; {Green Bank – Coalbrookdale} *(U)*.

TEMPLE [Dist] op 30 May 1870 *(T 31st)*; still open. Until 1883 THE TEMPLE in *hb*, not seen thus *Brad*.

TEMPLE HIRST [NE] op 2 January 1871 *(T 3rd)*; clo 6 March 1961 *(RM March)*.T HURST in *Brad* until 1890 but T HIRST in NE co tt 1880.

TEMPLE SOWERBY [NE] op 9 June 1862**- line; clo 7 December 1953 *(RM January 1954)*.

TEMPLECOMBE {map 120}
Original [LSW] station op 7 May 1860 *(W Fly P 15th)*; clo 7 March 1966 *(RM April)*.
Hb shows main station belonging to LSW, also used by SD Jt; all reputable secondary sources seen are in agreement; however Midland Distance Diagrams show it as a Joint station – probably loose use of 'Joint'? ? to 1861 T for WINCANTON.
T LOWER [SD Jt] op 3 February 1862**; also see 1863 September 10**; re-sited 17 January 1887 *(Cl)*; only intermittent use from then to 8 July 1919; by 1939 only train normally using it was late Saturdays only from Bournemouth, terminating here; this did not run during WW2 – present *Brad* August 1939, absent October 1939; still absent July 1945; 6 May 1946 shown as 11 May to 5 October but present April 1947; still in wtt prior to January 1966 but not present emergency wtt thence to closure of main station; PLATFORM; clo 3 January 1966 *(Cl)*.
Ex-LSW station reop for excursions 5 September 1982 *(RM December)*, for full public service 3 October 1983 *(BR SR pamphlet AD3464/A10/7983)*; still open.
At one stage bewildering variety of names in *Brad*, including: TEMPLE COMBE (SD Jt);
T C JUNCTION, T JUNCTION, T JOINT,
T NEW JUNCTION, T UPPER (LSW).

TEMPLETON [GW]: contemporary report suggests train stopped here on line op day, 4 September 1866, though station not built until 1867; initially used only for market trips to Tenby and Pembroke *(Pembroke)*; first in co tt October 1877; first *Brad* December 1899, Fridays and Saturdays only; all days from 1 May 1906, which *RCG* gave as op date; PLATFORM until 1905 *(Brad)*; clo 15 June 1964 *(Cl)*.

TEMPSFORD [GN] op 1 January 1863 *(GN)*; clo 5 November 1956 *(T 5 October)*.

TENBURY WELLS [Tenbury Joint]
op 1 August 1861 *(T 3rd)*; WELLS added 14 November 1912 *(hbl 23 January 1913)*; clo 1 August 1962**.

TENBY [GW] op 6 August 1863**; re-sited 5 September on extension to Whitland 4 September 1866 *(as Saundersfoot)*; still open.

TENTERDEN [KES]
See ROLVENDEN for first station.
T ST MICHAELS op 1 May 1912 *(RCG)*; aot request; HALT 1939/40 to 1947/8 *(Brad)*; clo 4 January 1954 *(T 28 October 1953)*.
T TOWN op 16 March 1903 *(Minor)*; clo 4 January 1954 *(T 28 October 1953)*.

TERN HILL [GW]
op 3 April 1899 *(RCG)*; clo 9 September 1963 *(T 9th)*.

TERRINGTON [MGN]
op 1 March 1866 *(T 2nd)*; clo 2 March 1959 *(T 2nd)*.

TESTON CROSSING [SEC]
op 1 September 1909 *(SEC)*; HALT; clo 2 November 1959 *(T 2 October)*; {Wateringbury – East Farleigh}.

TETBURY [GW] op 2 December 1889 *(Stroud News 6th)*; clo 6 April 1964 *(W Daily Press 6th)*.
TETBURY ROAD [GW]
op 12 May 1845 *(co n Bristol T 10th)*; clo 1 May 1882 *(RAIL 253/228)*; {Coates goods *IA*}.

TETTENHALL [GW]
op 11 May 1925 *(hbl 56)*; clo 31 October 1932 *(RM January 1933)*; 'to be ropened' 6–10 July 1937 for Royal Agricultural Show *(Rly Gaz)*; {map 96}.

TEVERSALL (at times TEVERSAL tt).
TEVERSALL [Mid] op 1 May 1886 *(RCG)*; clo 28 July 1930 *(Cl)*. Excursions until 7 October 1963, had been renamed T MANOR 1 July 1950 *(Mid)*.
TEVERSALL [GN] (non-tt): miners, early 1940s? and later excur, by when renamed T EAST *(U)*.

TEWKESBURY [Mid]
op 21 July 1840 *(Mid)*; service horse-drawn until 18 February 1844 and again from 7 November 1850 until ?; re-sited 16 May 1864 *(Tewkesbury 21st)* – paper says that station still far from complete at opening; clo 14 August 1961 *(T 3rd)*.

TEWKESBURY ROAD BRIDGE
– see CHELTENHAM HIGH STREET.

TEYNHAM [LCD] op 25 January 1858**; still open.

THACKLEY [GN] op 1 March 1878 *(GN)*; clo 2 February 1931 *(RM March)*.

THAME [GW] op 1 August 1862 *(co n T 31 July)*; clo 7 January 1963 *(RM January)*.

THAMES DITTON [LSW]:
trains first shown in tt December 1851; still open.

THAMES HAVEN
THAMES HAVEN [LTS] op 7 June 1855 *(L)*; summer only; service initially one train each way daily to/from Thames Haven Pier for steamer to Margate, a 'special express' with Fenchurch Street and Bishopsgate portions *(co n T 4 June 1855)*; last trains shown September 1880 tt, though still, trainless, in 1881 tt (and still 'P' in *hb* 1895).
THAMES HAVEN [LMS] (non-tt): different site, op 1 January 1923, trains from Tilbury; alias HALT NO 4 / SHELLHAVEN / PIG HALT clo 9 June 1958 tt; *(Thames Haven)*.

THANKERTON [Cal]
op 15 February 1848 *(co ½ T 29 February- line)*; clo 4 January 1965 *(RM February)*.

THATCHAM [GW]
op 21 December 1847 *(GW; Hants Chron 25th- line)*; HALT 2 November 1964 to 5 May 1969 *(Cl)*; still open.

THATTO HEATH [LNW] op 1 January 1872 *(T 2nd- line; in tt Wigan Observer 5th)*; still open.

THAXTED [GE] op 1 April 1913 *(T 1st)*; clo 15 September 1952 *(RM October)*.

THE – *any name beginning 'THE …' not listed here will be found under initial letter of next word.*

THE AVENUE [BT]; {map 26}
Perhaps site of station used for service on branch to Seaton Sluice, which see, *(BT)*; however this might have run from Dairy House junction, more than half a mile south (A. Young).
THE AVENUE op 1 April 1861 *(BT)* as DAIRY HOUSE;

renamed October 1861* *(Brad)*; clo 27 June 1864 *(Cl)*;
1872 and 1874 tts (co tts?) show summer Sundays use
– perhaps other times *(BT)*.
* = or did this represent an early move of site, trains at first
stopping at Dairy House Junction?

THE BRITANNIA [RHD] (ng)
first in *Brad* November 1928 (see 1927 July 16**);
last in tt June 1930.

THE CAUSEWAY – see CAUSEWAY CROSSING.

THE DELL – see FALMOUTH.

THE DYKE [LBSC] op 1 September 1887 *(LBSC)* *;
clo 1 January 1917 *(T 22 December 1916)*; reop 26 July
1920 *(Cl)*; clo 1 January 1939 (Sunday) *(RM January)*.
* = wording of company advertisement for new shares in
T 10 September raises suspicion that this was perhaps formal
opening date.

THE GRANGE – see 1860 July 25**.

THE HALE – see MILL HILL.

THE HAWTHORNS

THE HAWTHORNS (a) [GW] (non-tt): sometimes HALT
(e.g. *BR handbill BH 21*); football; op 25 December
1931; last used 27 April 1968 (M Hale, *Chron 3*).
In *hb* 1938 and 1956 as THE H WEST BROMWICH
PLATFORM.

THE HAWTHORNS (b) op 25 September 1995 *(RM
February 1996)*; still open.

THE HISS – see LAKENHEATH.

THE LAKES [GW] op 3 June 1935 *(Cl 29)*;
HALT until 5 May 1968 *(GW H)*; still open.

THE LANE [BWA]: line op 18 May 1901**, nd,
March 1902; clo 28 March 1917**.
Locally CHANTERS LANE; ticket *(JB)* for LANE;

THE LODGE [GW] op 1 July 1906 *(GW H)*; HALT;
clo 1 January 1931 (Thursday) *(T 20 December 1930)*;
{map 75}. GW ticket *(JB)* as LODGE HALT.

THE MOUND [High]
op 13 April 1868 *(High)*; clo 13 June 1960 *(T 8th)*.
JUNCTION in LMS tt 1930 and *Brad*? to 1955.
Dornoch branch trains ran from here with reversal.

THE OAKS [LY] first in tt *(Topham)* August 1849;
clo 6 November 1950 *(RM January 1951)*.

THEALBY – see WINTERTON.

THEALE [GW] op 21 December 1847 *(GW; Hants
Chron 25th- line)*; HALT 2 November 1964 to 5 May
1969 *(Cl)*; still open.

THEDDINGWORTH [LNW]:
line op 29 April 1850 *(co n T 1 May)*, nd, May 1851;
clo 6 June 1966 *(RM July)*.

THEDDLETHORPE [GN] op 17 October 1877
(co n Louth); clo 5 December 1960 *(RM January 1961)*.

THELWALL [LNW]
trains first shown in tt December 1853 but see
1853 November 1**; clo 17 September 1956 *(Cl)*.

THEOBALDS GROVE

THEOBALDS GROVE (a) [GE] op 1 October 1891
(RCG); clo 1 October 1909 (Friday) *(RCG)*;
reop 1 March 1915, clo 1 July 1919** (Tuesday) *(Cl)*.

THEOBALDS GROVE (b) op 21 November 1960
(Cl); still open.

THETFORD [GE]; {map 68}

THETFORD op 30 July 1845 *(co n Norfolk)*; still open.

T BRIDGE op 15 November 1875 *(RCG)*;
clo 8 June 1953 *(T 8th)*.

THEYDON BOIS op by [GE] 24 April 1865 *(L; co n
T 24th- line)*; BOIS added 1 December 1865 *(Cl)*;
transferred to [Cen] 25 September 1949 *(T 26th)*;
still open.

THICKLEY – see SHILDON

THIRSK [NE] {map 38}

THIRSK: through station on main line, op 31 March
1841 *(co n E Cos Herald 25th)*; still open. T JUNCTION
in *Brad*? to 1893/4; thus NE wtt 1861 and co tt 1880;
also thus *Reid* 1904, one table; *hb* only dropped
JUNCTION with appendix of May 1960.

T TOWN, terminus from Leeds, op 1 June 1848
(co ½T 30 August); TOWN added erratically;
last in tt December 1855; Perhaps occasional later use:
in March 1866, wtt shows train leaving here at 6.30am,
forming 7am from main line station; no support from
public tt.
References in *Brad* to YORK & NEWCASTLE JUNCTION
are to 1841 station; trains to/from TOWN called there on way
in/out.

THONGS BRIDGE [LY]:
line op 1 July 1850 *(T 8th)*, nd, January 1851;
clo 3 December 1865 (Sunday), reop 11 March 1867
(Cl); clo 2 November 1959 *(RM December)*.

THORGANBY [Derwent Valley]
op 21 July 1913 *(NE Staff Mag 1913)*;
clo 1 September 1926** (Wednesday).

THORINGTON [GE] op 8 January 1866 *(T 10th- line)*;
aot request; clo 4 November 1957 *(RM December)*.
At first in *hb* as THORRINGTON.

THORNABY [NE] op 1 October 1882; replaced
Stockton (which see for earlier history) and op as
STOCKTON SOUTH / S STOCKTON; station was
a large island platform, adjacent to the previous single
platform station, which was no longer able to cope;
renamed T 1 November 1892 *(hbl 27 October*, which
has ms endorsement – by whom? – 'cancelled' but
change was made *hb* 1893a, and in *Brad*) still open.

THORNBRIDGE [Cal] (non-tt)
op 1 December 1899; workmen; HALT; clo 1 August
1938 *(Cl)*; {on Grangemouth branch}.
First shown 'P' in *hb* 1938; *hb* 1944a 'closed'.

THORNBURY [Mid] op 2 September 1872 *(Bristol
Merc 7th)*; clo 19 June 1944** *(LNW Record)*.

THORNCLIFFE
– see CHAPELTOWN CENTRAL.

THORNE near Doncaster
T NORTH [NE] op 2 August 1869 *(T 2nd)*; still open.
T SOUTH [GC] op 1 July 1856 *(T 28 June)* as T LOCK;
made through station 13 September 1859; replaced
1 November 1859 by station nearer town centre at east
end of Canal Lane – now just T; replaced again on
deviation line 10 September 1866; re-sited slightly east
in BR days (P. Scowcroft, *Chron*); still open.
NORTH and SOUTH added 1 July 1923 *(hbl 13th)*.

THORNE – see THORNFALCON.

THORNER [NE] op 1 May 1876 *(NE- line)* as
SCARCROFT; by September 1876 was T & S *(Brad)*;
became T 1 May 1901 *(RCG)*; clo 6 January 1964 *(Cl)*.

THORNEY near Peterborough [MGN] op 1 August 1866 *(op wtt D&C 5)*; clo 2 December 1957 *(Cl)*.

THORNEY & KINGSBURY [GW] op 28 November 1927 *(Langport 26th)*; HALT; clo 15 June 1964 *(W Gaz 12th, 19th)*; {Martock – Langport}.

THORNEYBANK – see BURNLEY.

THORNEYBURN [NB] op 1 February 1861 *(NC)*, terminus for the time being; omitted September 1864 tt (error?); back in tt October 1864, now Tuesdays only; full use again 27 September 1937 tt; aot request; clo 15 October 1956 *(T 21 September)*.

THORNEYWOOD [GN] op 2 December 1889 *(RCG)*; clo 1 July 1916 (Saturday) *(RCH)*; {in IA}.

THORNFALCON [GW] probably op 1 March 1870 (first in *Brad* March, in *tt Taunton 2nd*); clo 5 February 1951 *(Chard 3rd)*, reop 7 May 1951 *(Chard 5th)* – see 1951★★; clo 10 September 1962 *(Chard 15th)*. Variously and erratically also THORNE (thus at first local press, GW co tt 1874, B&E co tt 1877), THORNE FALCON, THORN FALCON, THORNEFALCON; settled as final form 1 January 1902 *(hbl 23rd)*.

THORNFORD [GW] op 23 March 1936 *(Cl 29)*; HALT until 5 May 1969 *(GW H)*; T BRIDGE until 6 May 1974 *(BR notice)*; aot request; still open.

THORNHILL [LY] op 5 October 1840 *(co n Leeds 3rd)*; clo 1 January 1962 *(Cl)*; {map 55}. *Brad*: at first DEWSBURY, then T (D), D (T), D (T LEES), T L, T, T for D (and thus LNE tt 1933 and tt to closure).

THORNHILL near Dumfries [GSW] op 28 October 1850 *(T 26th- line)*; clo 6 December 1965 *(RM January 1966)*.

THORNIELEE [NB] op 18 June 1866 *(NB)*; clo 6 November 1950 *(RM December)*. THORNILEE until 1872 tt *(Cl)*; NB co tt 1900 THORNIELEE; hb caught up 1904.

THORNLEY [NE] THORNLEY : line op 1 May 1839 (see 1836 A★★), nd, on Macaulay's map of 1851 though not in *Brad* until February 1858; clo 9 June 1952★★. JUNCTION in *Brad* 1879/80 to 1882 and thus NE co tt 1880. T COLLIERY shown 'P' in hb 1877, not 1883; {branch from Thornley}; miners' service? error? No other information.

THORNLIEBANK Perhaps station on branch to Spiersbridge, which see for details: heading in *Brad* describes it as 'The Thornliebank branch to Spiersbridge'; no intermediate station was shown, but this was a time when detail frequently lacking; the name was used for a station on the main line about a year after branch closed to passengers, suggesting place was important enough to merit a station; {map 15}. **THORNLIEBANK** [Cal] op 1 October 1881 *(?; first in Brad October)*; still open. Cal co tt 1913 and *Brad* ? to 1955: T for ROUKEN GLEN, but not thus LMS tt 1930, *Murray* 1948, hb. Also see CROFTHEAD.

THORNTON near Bradford [GN] op 14 October 1878 *(T 15th)*; clo 23 May 1955★★.

THORNTON near Leicester; {map 62}

THORNTON [Leicester & Swannington] op 18 July 1832 *(Mid)* as STAG & CASTLE INN; renamed 1841; clo 1 January 1842 (Saturday) *(Cl)*. **T LANE** [Mid] op 1850 *(Mid)*; on deviation line; Saturdays only when first in *Brad* September 1852★; clo 1 October 1865 – last train previous Saturday *(Mid)*. ★ = certainly – August unreadable *(Mid)*.

THORNTON ABBEY [MS&L; GC]
THORNTON CURTIS was first in *Brad* June 1848; last in *Brad* November 1848 but stayed in *Topham* until April 1849 >
THORNTON ABBEY first in both tts August 1849 > Disappearance of first and appearance of second coincided with reshaping of table, first by amalgamation into larger one, then by separation again, though the later service was markedly inferior. Thus perhaps rather than new station, there was closure and reopening under different name; perhaps even just brief omission from tt with continuity of actual use and simply a renaming; difficult to see from map where usually quoted first station ½ mile away from second could possibly have been. Added strength is given to suspicion by hb, which in 1862 just had T, in 1867 T ABBEY OR CURTIS; Macaulay's maps showed T CURTIS 1851, T ABBEY 1854. Still open.

THORNTON DALE [NE] op 1 May 1882 *(Scarborough 4th- line)*; clo 5 June 1950 *(Cl)*.

THORNTON HEATH [LBSC] op 1 December 1862 *(co n T 3rd)*; still open.

THORNTON JUNCTION [NB]: logically op 4 September 1848 as junction station for line from Crossgates then opened (first seen in notice for line opening *Perthshire Courier 31 August)*; clo 6 October 1969 *(Cl)*. JUNCTION added by 1850 in *Brad* (or there from start) and was T J in NB co tt 1900 but *hbl 12th* and *T 27 August* said became T J 1 July 1923 and not added by RCH until 1925 hb; by then was just T in *Brad* index but still T J in tables.

THORNTON-CLEVELEYS [PW] op 1 April 1865 *(Liverpool Merc 31 March)*; moved to other (northern) side of level crossing in 1925; at first C, became T for C 1 April 1905 *(RCG)* and thus LNW co tt 1908 and LMS tt 1930, T-C 1953; clo 1 June 1970 *(Cl)*.

THORNTON-IN-CRAVEN [Mid] op 2 October 1848 *(Mid; RAIL 1005/265- line)*; clo 2 February 1970 *(RM February)*. -in-C added 27 September 1937 in body of co tt (index earlier) *(Mid)* but in hb from 1904.

THORNTONHALL [Cal] op 1 September 1868 *(Cal- line)* as EAGLESHAM ROAD; renamed THORNTON HALL 1 June 1877 *(RCG)*, to one word 1943 *(Brad)*; still open.

THORP ARCH **THORP ARCH** [NE]: op 10 August 1847 *(co ½ T 22 February 1848- line*; in inspection report dated 9th), nd, July 1848; clo 6 January 1964 *(Cl)*. Variously T A, T A & BOSTON SPA, THORPARCH, T for B S (and thus NE co tt 1880), T A for B S and BRAMHAM (e.g. one table 1881); settled as T A 12 June 1961 *(RM April)*.

Also non-tt services to Royal Ordnance Factory here:
LNE tickets exist for ROF T A and T A HALTS (note
plural) *(JB)*; first in use was RANGES op 19 April 1942
(Cl 29, in 4 May 1942 wtt); ROMAN ROAD, RIVER
and WALTON added later, to create circular service; by
1 October 1945 *(wtt supp)* one round trip only daily;
later increased? – specials still running 1957 from/to
Hull, Normanton, Knaresborough and Leeds City
(P. Batty, *NRM Review 107, p.24*). Last workmen's train
15 August 1958 (A. Wilson, *Steam days*, May 2002,
p.274); {Wetherby Racecourse – Thorp Arch}.

THORPE – see NORWICH.

THORPE near Peterborough [LNW]
op 2 June 1845 *(co op tt)*; clo 4 May 1964 *(RM June)*.

THORPE & WHITLINGHAM [Norfolk]:
early excursion station, 2½ miles east of Norwich
(Thorpe), a little east of later Whitlingham; merely a
wooden platform, usually used Sundays only, mostly
by trains operating a shuttle to and from Norwich but
occasionally as extra stop by trains to Yarmouth; probably
summers only. Exact dates not known: advertised in
local papers of Saturday 22 June 1844 to Saturday
21 September 1844 (inclusive); extra stop advertised
for Thursday 5 September 1844 for regatta (early
closing day in Norwich). Mentioned in local guide to
line 1845. No references found 1845–6 press. *Norwich
Mercury* of Saturday 11 September 1847 said service
to be discontinued on and after Monday next, 13th
('conventional' closure date – last Sunday). (G. Kenworthy,
from *Norfolk Chronicle & Norwich Gazette, Norwich
Mercury* and *A Guide to the Norfolk Railway* ... published
by Stevenson & Matchett, Norfolk Chronicle Office.)

THORPE BAY [LTS]
op 1 July 1910 *(RCG)* as SOUTHCHURCH-ON-SEA;
renamed 18 July 1910 *(hbl 27 October)*; still open.

THORPE CLOUD [LNW]
op 4 August 1899 *(LNW Officers 39077, 39103)*;
clo 1 November 1954 *(T 1 October)*; see 1962 August 5★★.
LNW co tt 1900, LMS tt 1930 and *Brad* to clo:
T C for DOVEDALE, but not thus *hb*.

THORPE CULVERT [GN]
op 24 October 1871 *(co n Skegness)*;
see 1962 November 11★★; aot request; still open.

THORPE THEWLES [NE] op 1 March 1880
(NE maps- line); clo 2 November 1931 *(Cl)*.

THORPE-LE-SOKEN [GE]
op 28 July 1866 *(T 30th- line)*; -le-S added 1 March
1900 *(hbl 26 April)*; still open.

THORPE-ON-THE-HILL [Mid]
op 4 August 1846 *(Mid)*; -on-the-H added 1 October
1890 *(RCG)*; clo 7 February 1955 *(RM March)*.

THORPENESS [GE] op 29 July 1914 *(D&C 5)*;
HALT until 1933/4 *(Brad)*; clo 12 September 1966
(RM September); {Leiston – Aldeburgh}.

THORS CAVE [NS] (ng) op 29 June 1904★★;
clo 12 March 1934 *(LNW Record)*. *Brad*: HALT until
1913; became T C for WETTON 1914 and thus to
end. Just T C in LMS tt 1930 and *hb* 1929.
Cl has T C & W but not seen thus elsewhere.

THORVERTON [GW] op 1 May 1885 *(Wellington 7th)*;
clo 7 October 1963 *(W Som F P 12th)*.

THRAPSTON
T BRIDGE STREET [LNW]
op 2 June 1845 *(co op tt)*; clo 4 May 1964 *(RM June)*.
At first THRAPSTON; became THRAPSTONE 1866
tt *(JS)*; B S added 1867 tt *(JS)*; became THRAPSTON B S
1885/6 *(Brad)*; B S dropped 1894/6 *(Brad)* and added
again 2 June 1924 *(Rly Gaz 23 May)*.
LNW co tt 1868: THRAPSTONE.

T MIDLAND ROAD [Mid] op 1 March 1866 *(Mid;
co n T 27 February- line)*; THRAPSTONE until
1 October 1885 co tt *(Mid)*; M R added 2 June 1924
(Rly Gaz 23 May); clo 15 June 1959 *(RM July)*.

THREE BRIDGES [LBSC] op 12 July 1841 *(co n
T 9th)*; still open. Briefly (about 1848) T B JUNCTION
in *Brad*. Robinson 1841: T B & CRAWLEY. *Hb* October
1963a said had become T B for EAST CRAWLEY and
BR ticket thus *(JB)* but not seen thus in any tt.

THREE COCKS JUNCTION [Cam]
op 19 September 1864 *(co n Hereford J 24th)*;
clo 31 December 1962 *(T 31st)*. Always thus *Brad* but
in *hb* T C for station, T C J for physical junction;
J added for station April 1959a.

THREE COUNTIES [GN]
op 1 March 1860 *(co opening notice)*, though not in
Brad until April 1866; op as ARLESEY PLATFORM
(body of opening notice) – heading T C Asylum, tickets
initially issued by level crossing gatekeeper;
renamed 1 July 1886 *(Cl)*; clo 5 January 1959
(H.V. Borley, *RCHS Jour 140, p.334*).

THREE OAKS [SEC]
op 1 July 1907 *(SEC)*; GUESTLING added by early
1908 *(Brad)*; HALT until 5 May 1969 *(SR App)*, when
& G also dropped; still open. Perhaps T O BRIDGE at
opening, but only T O when first in *Brad*.

THRELKELD [CKP]
op 2 January 1865 *(co ½ T 28 February- line; in op tt
Cockermouth)*; clo 6 March 1972 *(RM March)*.

THRINGSTONE [LNW] op 2 April 1907 *(LNW Cl)*;
see 1905★★ (a); clo 13 April 1931 *(Cl)*.

THRISLINGTON – see WEST CORNFORTH.

THROSK [Cal] first in *Brad* December 1890;
clo 18 April 1966 *(Cl)*.
In *Brad* was T PLATFORM until 1920/1, then T.
In *hb*: T until 1936a – 'delete station accommodation'
(presumably demotion rather than closure);
1938 HALT; 1956 T.

THRUMSTER [High]
op 1 July 1903 *(High)*; clo 3 April 1944★★.

THRYBERGH (non-tt): alias T TINS; built after
approaches from local clubs; first used 1959 for British
Legion trip to Cleethorpes; used into 1960s;
{on Silverwood Colliery line} *(GC Society Journal 30)*.

THURCROFT COLLIERY (SIDINGS)
[GC/HB/Mid] (non-tt): agreement made 1920 with
United Steel Co for provision of workmen's trains
between here and Worksop (A.L. Barnett, *Railways of
South Yorkshire Coalfield*, RCTS, 1984); ended ?;
also works outings (G.L. Crowther's Atlas);
{on branch from between Anston and Dinnington}.

THURGARTON [Mid]
op 4 August 1846 *(Mid)*; still open.

THURGOLAND [MS&L] probably op soon after
5 December 1845 *(GC)* – first in *Brad* January 1846;
clo 1 November 1847 *(Cl)*; {Wortley – Penistone}.
THURLBY [GN] op 16 May 1860 *(co n Bourne)*;
clo 18 June 1951 *(RM July)*.
THURNBY & SCRAPTOFT [GN]
op 1 January 1883 *(co n Leicester Mercury 6th)*;
clo 7 December 1953 *(T 7th)*, except for one train each
way for workmen until 29 April 1957 *(RM June)* and
summer Saturdays and Sundays to 9 September 1962
(last train) *(Cl)*. Opening notice called it T.
Hb 1895 called it THORNBY & S, corrected 1898a.
THURNSCOE op 16 May 1988 *(Mid)*; still open.
THURSFORD [MGN] op 19 January 1882 *(MGN)*;
clo 2 March 1959 *(T 2nd)*.
THURSO [High] op 28 July 1874 *(High)*; still open.
THURSTASTON [Birkenhead]
op 19 April 1886 *(Birkenhead; co ½ Herapath August
14th- line)*; clo 1 February 1954 *(RM March)*.
THURSTON [GE] op 24 December 1846 *(EC- line)*
– but some sort of service from 7 December 1846
(GE Journal July 2000); still open.
THUXTON [GE] first in *Brad* September 1851
(not in EC co tt May 1851); aot request;
clo 6 October 1969 *(RM October)*; later excur *(U)*.
THWAITES [Mid] op 1 June 1892 *(Mid wtt notice)*;
aot request; clo 1 July 1909 (Thursday) *(RCG)*;
{Bingley – Keighley}.
TIBBERMUIR [Cal] first in *Brad* February 1859;
aot request; clo 1 October 1951 *(RM November)*.
T CROSSING in *Brad* 1864/5 to 1938/9. *Hb*: 1862
T & POWFOOT SIDING; 1872 T & POWBRIDGE;
1938 T HALT.
TIBSHELF
T & NEWTON [Mid] op 1 May 1886 *(RCG)*;
clo 28 July 1930 *(Mid)*. First month only in tt as
NEWTON ROAD (was renamed the day it opened
for passengers – *Mid*).
T TOWN [GC] op 2 January 1893 *(RCG)*;
clo 4 March 1963 *(RM March)*.
TICEHURST ROAD – see STONEGATE.
TICKHILL & WADWORTH [South Yorkshire Joint]:
pre-op Sunday School excursion to Cleethorpes 6 July
1910 *(S Yorks Joint)*; full public op 1 December 1910★★;
& W added 1 July 1911 *(hbl 6th)*; clo April 1926 *(Cl)*,
reop 25 July 1927 *(T 21st)*; clo 8 July 1929 *(T 13 August)*.
TIDAL BASIN [GE] first in *Brad* February 1858;
clo 15 August 1943 (Sunday) *(Cl)* – *T 31 July* has
ambiguous item which could mean 15th was day of
last train or official clo date.
GE co tt 1882, 1914: VICTORIA DOCKS T B.
TIDDINGTON [GW] first in *Brad* June 1866;
clo 7 January 1963 *(RM January)*.
TIDENHAM [GW]
op 1 November 1876 *(Wye; Merlin 27 October- line)*;
clo 1 January 1917 *(GW notice dated 22 December 1916)*;
reop 1 February 1918 *(wtt supp)*;
clo 5 January 1959 *(T 5th)*.
TIDWORTH [MSWJ]: branch came into existence in
unorthodox way since War Office not BoT responsible;
public service began before latter had given authority;

first use by troops late May 1902, by public 1 July 1902★
(M. Barnsley, letter in *Railway Bylines*, December 2000;
supported by *Rtn*), though not in *Brad* until October;
clo 19 September 1955 *(Southern Daily Echo 19th)*. Army
camp use continued for some time after public closure.
★ = but *RAIL 1005/280* and *hbl 24th* say op 3 April 1902 –
troops? public? goods?
Non-tt: perhaps during WW1, ambulance trains took
wounded direct to hospital here *(Hosp)*.
TIFFIELD [Northampton & Banbury Junction]
first in *Brad* October 1869; last there February 1871;
{Towcester – Blisworth}.
TILBURY
T MARINE [PLA] op 15 May 1927 *(Mid* – date of first
sailing); boat trains; clo 1 May 1932 (Sunday); dates
given apply to steamer service to Dunkirk, only user
(T.B. Peacock, *P L A Railways*, Locomotive Publishing,
1952, pp.32–4); was HALT in *LMS list* 1933.
T RIVERSIDE [LTS] op 13 April 1854 *(T 13th)*;
R added 1936 *(Brad)*; clo 30 November 1992
(RM January 1993). Alias T FORT *(L)*; *Brad* 1850s
and 1860s T for GRAVESEND.
T TOWN [LTS] op for workers about May 1884,
and to public 17 April 1886 *(LTS)*; T DOCKS until
3 August 1934 *(L)*; still open. *Hb* 1936a: T TOWN for
T DOCKS and thus to 1958 *(Brad)* and in hb.
Non-tt: boat trains to various points in docks; started
1886 *(U)*; shown 'P' in hb 1904 to 1956, last issue of
book; at first [London & India], 1912 [PLA]; use ceased?
Also see EAST TILBURY.
TILE HILL [LNW] op by May 1848 when in *Topham*★;
op as ALLESLEY GATE; became A LANE
1 September 1863 *(Cl)*; T H 1 April 1864 *(LNW
Officers 1170, 16 March* – P. Rowledge); still open.
★ = minutes of 19 May 1847 said trains would start to call, but
receipts first shown for January to July 1848 in *Huish list*; first
in *Brad* November 1848. Early arrangements primitive: *LNW
dates* has extract from committee meeting of 2 October 1850 when
they refused PC [= gatekeeper/signalman] Hudson's request
for booking-office; his sitting-room had to continue serving.
TILEHURST [GW]
op 10 April 1882 *(T 10th)*; still open.
TILLICOULTRY
Temporary terminus at **GLENFOOT** [Stirling &
Dunfermline] op 3 June 1851★★; replaced by >
TILLICOULTRY [NB] first in *Brad* January 1852
(extension to permanent station authorised to open by
BoT letter dated 19 December 1851); clo 15 June 1964
(RM July).
TILLIETUDLEM [Cal]
first in *Brad* May 1877; clo 1 October 1951 *(RM Nov.)*.
T for CROSSFORD in *Brad* ? to closure but not thus
LMS tt 1930, *Murray* 1948, hb.
TILLYFOURIE [GNS] op 2 June 1860 *(GNS)*;
clo 2 January 1950 *(RM February)*.
TILLYNAUGHT [GNS] op 1 September 1859 *(GNS)*;
T JUNCTION in *Brad* until 1897/8 and hb prior to
1904; clo 6 May 1968 *(RM July)*.
TILMANSTONE
T COLLIERY YARD [EK] first in *Brad* August 1921;
terminus of some trains from Shepherds Well; noted

that did not run when stoppages at the colliery; last in *Brad* January 1930; {short branch from Eythorne}. Also see ELVINGTON; KNOWLTON.

TILTON [GN/LNW] op 15 December 1879 *(Leic; LNW Record- line)*; clo 7 December 1953 *(T 7th)*.

TIMPERLEY
TIMPERLEY (a) [MSJA] op 20 July 1849★★; clo 27 December 1991 *(BLN 671)* for conversion >
TIMPERLEY (b) [Manch] op 15 June 1992 *(RM August)*; still open.
Also see WEST TIMPERLEY.

TINGLEY [GN] first in *Brad* May 1859; clo 1 February 1954 *(RM March)*; later excur *(U)*.

TINKERS GREEN [GW] op 16 October 1939 *(hbl 9)*; HALT; clo 18 January 1965★★; {Oswestry –Whittington}.

TINSLEY near Sheffield
TINSLEY [GC] first in *Brad* March 1869; clo 29 October 1951 *(RM December)*.
T ROAD – see WEST TINSLEY.
T YARD (non-tt): HALT; used 15 June 1980 for Open Day *(U; JB)*; {Catcliffe –West Tinsley}.

TINSLEY GREEN – see GATWICK AIRPORT.

TINTERN [GW]
TINTERN op 1 November 1876 *(Wye; Merlin 27th October- line)*; clo 5 January 1959 *(T 5th)*.
Became T for BROCKWEIR 20 October 1911 *(hbl 26th)*, back to T 1929? *(hbl ref. 30 July)*. Hb: 1877 T OR B; 1904 T; 1912 T for B; 1938 T.
T QUARRY SIDING (non-tt): quarrymen; in use 1954; {south of Tintern} *(U)*.

TIPTON
TIPTON [LNW] op 1 July 1852 *(W Mid; T 2nd- line)*; T OWEN STREET 8 June 1953 to 6 May 1968 *(Cl)*; still open. *Rly Obs* said addition of O S intended July 1950 but not done then.
T FIVE WAYS [GW] op 1 December 1853 *(T 29 Nov.)*; F W added 19 July 1950 *(Cl)*; clo 30 July 1962 *(RM September)*.

TIPTON ST JOHNS [LSW]
op 6 July 1874 *(Trewman 8th)*; ST J added 1881 tt *(Cl; JS)*; clo 6 March 1967 *(Express & E 6th)*.

TIPTREE [GE] op 1 October 1904 *(co n Kelvedon)*; clo 7 May 1951 *(T 8th)*.

TIR-PHIL [Rhy] op 31 March 1858 *(co ½ T 1 Sept.- line)*; still open. TIR PHIL at op; became T P & N T 1904/5 *(Brad)*, TIRPHIL 1 July 1924 *(GW circular 18 June – from TIRPHIL & N T)*; TIR PHIL 17 September 1926 *(hbl October)*, TIR-PHIL 12 May 1980 tt *(C/W)*. Hb 1904 T P for N T.

TIRCELYN [Cam] (non-tt): PLATFORM; alias TYR CELYN; agreement with R.R. Beard to stop trains made 19 July 1906, ended 15 October 1912 *(GW Agreement GSP 2934)*; similar with H.A.B. Kidston 22 April 1914 *(M 49622)*; ended?; {Aberedw – Erwood}.

TIRYDAIL – see AMMANFORD.

TISBURY [LSW]
op 2 May 1859 *(Salisbury 7th)*; still open.

TISSINGTON [LNW]
op 4 August 1899 *(LNW Officers 39077, 39103)*; clo 1 November 1954 *(T 1 October)*; occasional later

winter emergency use *(U)*; see 1962 August 5★★.

TISTED [LSW]
op 1 June 1903 *(Hants Teleg 5th)*; clo 7 February 1955 *(Hants Chron 12th)*. T for SELBORNE in *hb* until 1927a and thus LSW co tt 1914.

TITHEBARN STREET – see LIVERPOOL.

TITLEY [GW] op 20 August 1857★★; clo 5 February 1951 *(RM October)* – see 1951★★; reop 2 April 1951 *(Cl)*; clo 7 February 1955 *(RM March)*.

TITTWOOD: clo date given in *Cl* but probably goods only; no evidence of passenger use seen.

TIVERTON
TIVERTON [GW] op 12 June 1848 *(Trewman 15th)*; re-sited on Exe Valley line, with opening of its first part, 1 August 1884 *(Tiverton 5th)*; clo 5 October 1964 *(Som Gaz 5 September)*.
T JUNCTION [GW] op 1 May 1844 *(Taunton 8th)* as T ROAD; renamed 12 December 1848 *(Cl)*; replaced by >
T PARKWAY op 12 May 1986 *(Wellington 7th)*; on site of earlier Sampford Peverell; still open.

TIVETSHALL [GE] op 12 December 1849 *(T 11th- line)*; clo 7 November 1966 *(RM January 1967)*. T JUNCTION in *Brad* 1859/61 to 1878/9.

TIVIOT DALE – see STOCKPORT.

TIVOLI [SE] (non-tt): platform to serve pleasure gardens; permission to Mr Divers (owner of gardens ?) to erect this given 6 July 1848 *(SE)*; used to ? *RM November 1897*, discussing possibility of new station, said there had been one here until 'about 25 years ago'; {map 131}.

TOCHIENEAL [GNS] op 1 April 1884 *(GNS)*; clo 1 October 1951 *(RM November)*.

TOD HILLS – see BYERS GREEN.

TOD POINT [NE] first in *Brad* January 1873; last December 1873, labelled as workmen's service so might well have had longer existence, only being included for this year by chance; {map 43}.

TODD LANE JUNCTION [LY]
first in *Brad* December 1852 as PRESTON JUNCTION; renamed 1 September 1952 *(Cl)*; clo 7 October 1968 *(Cl)*.

TODDINGTON [GW] op 1 December 1904 *(Chelt Chron 3rd)*; clo 7 March 1960 *(RM April)*.

TODHOLES [High/LMS?]: (non-tt): *BR Scottish Region Special Traffic Notices* show Saturday stops for railwaymen's wives 22 June, 27 July and 21 September 1957 – long established practice?; {Georgemas Junction – Thurso}.

TODMORDEN [LY] op 28 December 1840★★; still open. T JUNCTION 1852 to 1883/5 *(Brad)*.

TOLLCROSS [Cal] op 1 February 1897 *(RCG)*; clo 5 October 1964 *(RM November)*.

TOLLER [GW] op 31 March 1862 *(Dorset Chron 3 April)*; clo 5 May 1975 *(RM July)*.

TOLLERTON [NE]: line op 31 March 1841★★, nd, August 1841; after May 1959 tt, before/with 4 August 1959 tt reduced to one train, to Newcastle only; clo 1 November 1965 *(RM November)*.

TOLLESBURY [GE]
TOLLESBURY op 1 October 1904 *(co n Kelvedon)*; clo 7 May 1951 *(T 8th)*.

T PIER op 15 May 1907 *(RCG)*; aot some trains marked in tt to run beyond T to here only as required; clo 18 July 1921 *(G&S)*.

TOLLESHUNT [GE]

T D'ARCY op 1 October 1904 *(co n Kelvedon)*; clo 7 May 1951 *(T 8th)*.

T KNIGHTS op 12 December 1910 *(RCG)*; request; clo 7 May 1951 *(T 8th)*; {Tiptree – T D'Arcy}. PLATFORM *hb*, where added 7 years after opening; HALT tt.

TOLWORTH [SR]
op 29 May 1938 *(SR sig inst 22/1938)*; still open.

TOMATIN [High] op 19 July 1897 *(High)*; clo 3 May 1965 *(RM June)*.

TON LLWYD [GW] op 1 January 1906** (see for details); HALT; see 1921 April/May**; finally clo 2 January 1922 *(Cl)*; {map 86}.

TON PENTRE [TV] op 4 February 1861 *(D&C 6)* as YSTRAD; became Y RHONNDA 1930 *(hbl reference 27 October,* which gave earlier name as Y R VALLEY), T P on opening of new Y R 29 September 1986; still open.

TONBRIDGE [SE] op 26 May 1842 *(co n T 13th, 20th)*; re-sited 14 chains west late 1864; still open. Early TUNBRIDGE, TUN… JUNCTION; TON… spelling adapted 1893 tt *(Cl)*; JUNCTION dropped [altogether?] 7 June 1929 *(JS)*. SE co tt 1864 had TUN… J for main line, TUN… for line to Hastings.

TONDU

TONDU (a) [GW] op 25 February 1864 *(Cardiff T 26th-line)*; request stop at clo 22 June 1970 *(Cl)*. T JUNCTION in *Brad* until 1893/4; also thus GW co tt 1874 and *hb* 1877 and 1883.

TONDU (b) op 28 September 1992 *(AZ)*; still open.

TONFANAU [Cam]
first in *Brad* July 1896 (perhaps op earlier – inspected January, *Cam*); last in tt September 1896; back in tt July 1903; aot request; still open.

TONGE & BREEDON [Mid]
op 1 October 1869 *(Mid)*; clo 22 September 1930 *(Mid)*; army camp use (non-tt) 19 November 1939 to 1 January 1945; later excur *(U)*. October 1869 wtt had B but co tt T & B, soon changed to T *(Mid)*; *hb* always (from 1872) T & B, and thus Airey's Map of Derby & Notts, 1893; however & B not added again until 1 May 1897 wtt and public tt *(Mid)*.

TONGHAM [LSW] first in *Brad* October 1856; became HALT 1928/9 tt and thus on SR ticket *(JB)*; clo 4 July 1937 (Sunday) *(Cl)*. *Brad* 1859: T for ALDERSHOT.

TONGWYNLAIS [Cardiff]
op 1 March 1911 *(RCG)*; clo 20 July 1931 *(GW goods circular 13th – after last train 18th)*.

TONMAWR JUNCTION
See 1865**.

TONMAWR HALT [GW]: minutes 10 May 1921 reported arrangements had been made to run Saturday market train *(RAIL 243/2)*; in both public and wtts of GW by 2 October 1922 (M Hale), first in *Brad* November 1922 as T JUNCTION, Saturdays only; clo 22 September 1930 *(Cl)*;

{at junction of SWM and PT lines, *IA* p.43, E3}. Perhaps used before 1922 (see 1920**) – not one of stations listed in inspection report but PT agreed to put up four halts.

TONTEG [TV; GW] op 1 May 1905 *(Llantrisant)*; see 1904**; replaced 5 May 1930 by separate platforms on lines to Cadoxton and Llantrisant (whose service was now diverted) *(RM July p.68)*. Llantrisant line clo 31 March 1952 *(Cl)*; Cadoxton line clo 10 September 1962 *(Cl)*.

TONYPANDY

TONYPANDY [TV] op 9 March 1908 *(RCG)* as TREALAW; became TONYPANDY & TREALAW 1 May 1909, TONYPANDY 7 May 1973 *(Cl)*; still open.

TONYPANDY [GW] see PENYGRAIG.

TONYREFAIL [GW]
op 1 May 1901 *(RCG)*; clo 9 June 1958 *(T 5th)*.

TOOTING

TOOTING [LBSC] op 1 October 1868 *(co n T 1st)*; re-sited 12 August 1894 *(Cl)*; clo 1 January 1917 *(T 22 December 1916)*, reop 27 August 1923 *(RM October)*; still open. Became T JUNCTION in 1904 *hb* and was thus in LBSC co tt 1912, but not in *Brad* until 1923 reopening; JUNCTION dropped 1 March 1938 *(Cl)*.

T BEC [Nor] op 13 September 1926 *(T 14th)* as TRINITY ROAD; see 1922**; renamed 1 October 1950 *(RM January 1951)*; still open.

T BROADWAY [Nor] op 13 September 1926 *(T 14th)*; still open.

TOP OF LAW – see DUNDEE.

TOP OF LICKEY INCLINE – see BLACKWELL.

TOP OF SUTTON INCLINE – see LEA GREEN.

TOPCLIFFE [NE]
op 1 June 1848 *(co ½ T 30 August- line)*; T GATE 1854 tt to 1863 tt *(Cl)*; clo 14 September 1959 *(RM September)*.

TOPSHAM [LSW]
op 1 May 1861 *(Trewman 1st, second edition)*; still open.

TORKSEY [GC] first in *Brad* December 1850; permanent station 1853; clo 2 November 1959 *(RM December)*.

TORPANTAU [BM] op by 18 June 1863, when there were references in local press that excursion tickets would be available to all wishing to alight at Torpantau Mountain; platform not provided until 1869 and not in *Brad* until June 1869 – full service; aot request; clo 31 December 1962 *(T 31st)*.

TORPHINS [GNS] op 2 December 1859 *(GNS)*; clo 28 February 1966 *(RM March)*.

TORQUAY
For first station see TORRE.

TORQUAY [GW] op 2 August 1859**; still open. *Brad* August 1859 had table, no trains shown, for Torbay & Dartmouth Railway in which the stations were listed as: Torquay (= Torre); Livermore (= Torquay); Paignton; Churston Ferrers; Dartmouth. It would be some time before the last two opened, as Brixham Road and Kingswear.

TORRANCE [NB] op 1 October 1879 *(D&C 6- line)*; clo 2 April 1951 *(RM May)*.

TORRE [GW] op 18 December 1848 *(Woolmer 23rd)* – formal in morning, public in afternoon; TORQUAY until 2 August 1859; still open. T for BABBACOMBE in *Brad* 1900/1 to 1947/8.

TORRINGTON [LSW] op 18 July 1872 *(Trewman 24th)*; clo 4 October 1965 *(Bideford 8th)*. For brief later general use see 1968 January★★; later excur *(U)*.

TORRINGTON PARK – see WOODSIDE PARK.

TORRISHOLME FACTORY [Mid] (non-tt): alias T PLATFORM; op 18 September 1916 (Mid Special Traffic notice 763, *RAIL 963/108)*; still in February 1920 notice *(RAIL 963/116)* but not included May 1920 wtt (no notice for March or April); {Lancaster – Morecambe}.

TORRYBURN [NB] op 2 July 1906 *(RCG)*; clo 7 July 1930 *(Cl)*.

TORVER [Fur] op 18 June 1859 *(Kendal Mercury 25th- line; in op tt Coniston)*; clo 6 October 1958 *(LNW Record)*.

TORYBANWEN COLLIERY [PT] (non-tt): HALT; alias WHITWORTH; miners; in use during WW1; used again later as Corrwg Merthyr Navigation; {branch from Tonmawr} *(U)*.

TOTMONSLOW – see TEAN.

TOTNES [GW] op 20 July 1847 *(Trewman 22nd)*; TOTNESS until 1866 tt *(Cl)*; still open.

TOTON

TOTON – see LONG EATON.

T DIESEL DEPOT / D M D (non-tt): Open Days August 1968 and May 1972 *(JB)*, also 9 June 1979 *(IU)*; {Trent – Trowell}.

TOTTENHAM

T HALE [GE] op 15 September 1840 *(T 16th)*; HALE added 1875 to 1938 and from 1968 *(L)*; still open.
T HALE [Vic] op 1 September 1968 *(T 2nd)*; still open. Combined entrance provided 1 December 1968 *(L)*.
Also see SOUTH TOTTENHAM.

TOTTENHAM COURT ROAD

TOTTENHAM COURT ROAD [Cen] op 30 July 1900 *(L; T 25th- line)*; see 1922★★; still open.
TOTTENHAM COURT ROAD [Nor] op 22 June 1907★★; OXFORD STREET until 9 March 1908 *(L)*; see 1922★★; still open. Initially in *Brad* as T C R, O S; since it was just part of list where names separated by commas, looks like two stations; presumably meant 'station at the Oxford Street end of Tottenham Court Road'.
Also see GOODGE STREET.

TOTTERIDGE & WHETSTONE
op by [GN] 1 April 1872 *(L; co ½ T 12 August- line)*; & W added 1 April 1874 *(Cl)*; transferred to [Nor] 14 April 1940; still open.

TOTTINGTON [LY] op 6 November 1882 *(LY)*; clo 5 May 1952 *(RM June)*.

TOTTON [LSW] first in *Brad* May 1851 as ELING JUNCTION; became T 1859 tt *(SR)*, T for E 1861 until 1955 *(Brad)* and thus LSW co tt 1914; still open. T & E in *hb* 1904 and 1912.

TOVIL [SE] op 1 January 1884 *(SE)*; clo 15 March 1943 *(Cl)*.

TOW LAW [NE]: line op 1 September 1845 *(S&D)* but Crook is terminus in *Brad* until October 1846,

when full detail still not provided; first tt evidence found September 1847 co tt, but earlier reference in minutes 11 March 1847, when it was reported that 'accommodation was wanted for passengers' (see 1843★★); re-sited 2 March 1868 when incline replaced by deviation; clo 11 June 1956 *(RM August)*; {map 30}.

TOWCESTER [SMJ]
op 1 May 1866★★; clo 7 April 1952 *(RM May)*. Specials from St Pancras via Stoke Bruern for Grafton Hunt's Easter Monday races continued; until ? *(AB)*.

TOWER GATEWAY [Dock]
op 31 August 1987 *(T 1 September)*; still open.

TOWER HILL London op 25 September 1882 *(T 26th)* as TOWER OF LONDON [Met]; clo 13 October 1884 *(Cl)*. New station to west, on extension to Mansion House, MARK LANE [Met/Dist], op 6 October 1884 *(T 4th)* – briefly old and new open together since Met used original for further week; renamed T H 1 September 1946 *(RM November)*. Returned to original site 5 February 1967 *(RM March)*; still open.

TOWER HILL near Launceston [LSW]
op 21 July 1886 *(Tavistock 23rd)*; clo 3 October 1966 *(Cornish & DP 8th)*.

TOWERSEY [GW] op 5 June 1933 *(Cl 29)*; HALT; clo 7 January 1963 *(Cl)*; {Bledlow – Thame}.

TOWIEMORE [LNE] op for distillery workers 1924; first in LNE tt June 1930 *(GNS amdt)*, though not in *Brad* until July 1937; added 'P' *hb* 1944a; HALT; clo 6 May 1968 *(RM July)*; {Drummuir – Auchindachy}.

TOWN GREEN [LY]
op 2 April 1849 *(Southport Vis 7th)*; T G & AUGHTON 1 June 1889 *(RCG)* to 5 May 1975 *(RM July)*; still open. T G LYDIATE in *Brad* 1853 to 1866 [LY] table – had been dropped earlier from [E Lancs] table.

TOWNELEY [LY]: line op 12 November 1849★★; clo 4 August 1952 *(RM September)*. Until 1890 was TOWNLEY in *hb*.

TOWYN – see TYWYN.

TOXTETH DOCK [LO] op 6 March 1893★★; clo 31 December 1956 *(T 29 September)*.

TRABBOCH [GSW] op 1 July 1896 *(RCG)*; clo 10 September 1951 *(RM October)*.

TRAFALGAR SQUARE – see CHARING CROSS.

TRAFFORD BAR [Manch] op 15 June 1992 *(RM August)*; reop of Old Trafford; still open.

TRAFFORD PARK [CLC] op 4 January 1904 *(RCG)*; T P & STRETFORD 1925/6 (*hbl ref January 1926)* to 6 May 1974 *(BR notice)*; still open.

TRAM INN [GW] op 2 January 1854 *(T 29 December 1853- line)*; clo 9 June 1958 *(Cl)*.

TRAM ROAD – see PONTYPRIDD.

TRANENT – see PRESTONPANS.

TRANMERE [Birkenhead, Lancashire & Cheshire Junction] op 30 May 1846 *(Birkenhead)* as LIME KILN LANE / LIMEKILN L; renamed 1853 *(Brad)*; last in *Brad* October 1857; {map 46}.

TRAP ROAD [Llanelly]: 10 March 1870 orders were given that small station should be set up here; 14 July 1870 orders given that 9.10 from Swansea should stop daily; later orders were that from 1 January 1871 the early morning train to Swansea and the evening train from there should stop (Mr J. Ackland had offered to pay £5 per quarter for himself and his milk can for this facility) *(RAIL 377/15)*; it appeared in *Brad* August and September 1871 only; relevant committee minutes for that time are missing so impossible to be more exact about closure; {Gorseinon – Gowerton}.

TRAVELLERS REST [TV] op 18 March 1901 *(Nelson says it was ready for opening on that day; first in Brad April)*; clo 4 April 1910 according to *RAIL 1005/280* and *hbl* of 24 October but no reopening date seen – certainly shown with trains *Brad* September 1910; T R ABERCYNON UPPER until 1 July 1924 *(Cl)*; clo 12 September 1932 *(RM October)*.

TRAWSCOED [GW] op 12 August 1867 *(Merioneth 17th)*; clo 14 December 1964★★.

TRAWSFYNYDD

TRAWSFYNYDD [GW] op 1 November 1882 *(D&C 11)*; clo 4 January 1960 *(RM March)*.

TRAWSFYNYDD (non-tt): unadvertised service Sundays only 23 July to 10 September 1989 for visitors to lake *(BLN 614)* – *Rly World October 1989 p.615* has photograph of inaugural train on Monday 17th – some sort of publicity event?; site of earlier Maentwrog Road and given name M R HALT in Gwynedd County Council leaflet.

T CAMP [GW] (non-tt): army camp; in use 1911 to ? *(U)*; *GW Mag 1912* refers to this as 'the new troop station authorised late 1910'; *Back Track December 2004, p.730* has photograph of military use; {T/T Lake}.

T LAKE [GW] op 14 April 1934 *(T 16th)*; HALT; clo 4 January 1960 *(RM March)*.

TREALAW – see TONYPANDY

TREALS ROAD [PW]: line op 16 July 1840★★; only reference found is in tt for early 1841 *(Freeling)*.

TREAMAN [Aberdare] op October 1848 *(Aberdare)*; replaced January 1857 by station later renamed ABERAMAN *(Aberdare)*.

TREBORTH [LNW] first in *Brad* June 1854; clo 1 October 1858 *(co n Carnarvon 25 September,* and omitted from October tt in that paper); however Mary Matilda Crawley had station reopened since land agreement included clause that she could have station as long as she wanted one; back in November 1858 tt *(Carnarvon 30 October)*; clo 2 March 1959 *(LNW Record)*.

TRECWN SIDINGS [GW] (non-tt): naval depot; op 1937; clo 3 August 1964; {branch from Letterston junction} *(U)*.

TRECYNON [GW] op 1 May 1911 *(GW H)*; HALT. According to *hbl January 1942* it had op to passengers (no exact date given); implies clo and reop; *Brad* no help since only footnote station; trains were shown GW co tt 6 October 1941. Clo 15 June 1964 *(Cl)*.

TREDEGAR

For earliest service see 1822★★.

TREDEGAR [LNW] op 19 June 1865 *(co n Newport 17th)*; clo 13 June 1960 *(RM July)*.

T SOUTH END [LNW] (non-tt): miners; op ?; clo about 1958; {Tredegar – Bedwellty} *(U)*. Also see NANTYBWCH.

TREDEGAR JUNCTION
– see PONTLLANFRAITH.

TREETON

TREETON (a) [North Midland] op 6 April 1841★★ last in tt December 1842★.

★ = *Tuck*, about June 1843 said these would be reopened Tuesdays, Saturdays, Sundays; no evidence on whether did or did not.

TREETON (b) [Mid] op 1 October 1884 *(Mid)*; same site as (a); clo 29 October 1951 *(RM December –* 'excursions will continue').

TREFEGLWYS [Van] op 1 December 1873★★; last in *Brad* July 1879 (August 'service suspended'). PWLL GLAS in *hb*; renamed TREF... *hb* 1874a; 1877 altered to TREVEGLWYS – and still shown 'P' to 1904 (last time).

TREFEINON [Cam]: line op 19 September 1864 and this station in *Brad* October with rest of line, but not in tt in opening notice *Hereford J 24 September*, which appears otherwise complete, so perhaps opened shortly after the line; aot request; clo 31 December 1962 *(T 31st)*.

TREFERIG JUNCTION [TV] (non-tt): miners; op by 1892; clo by September 1928 *(U)*.

TREFFOREST (all TREFOREST initially; last two closed under that spelling, others amended 12 May 1980 tt). In *Robinson* 1841 as T & NEWBRIDGE.

TREFFOREST [TV] first in *Brad* December 1846; T LL 1 July 1924 *(GW circular 18 June)* to 5 May 1930 *(hbl 29 April)*; still open

T ESTATE [GW] op 5 January 1942 *(wtt supp)* but not in *Brad* until May 1946 so perhaps at first more of a workmen's than a public station; still open. Was HALT on GW ticket *(JB)* – before in public tt.

T HALT [ANSW] op 1 September 1904★★; HALT added 1924; clo 17 September 1956 *(RM October)*.

T HL [Barry] op 1 April 1898 *(RCG)*; HL added 1 July 1924 *(GW circular 18 June)*; clo 5 May 1930 *(RM July p.68; hbl 75)*.

TREFNANT [LNW] op 5 October 1858 *(co n Clwyd)*; clo 19 September 1955 *(Rly Gaz 26 August)*.

TREGARON [GW] op 1 September 1866 *(D&C 11)*; clo 22 February 1965 *(Cl)*.

TREGARTH [LNW]
op 1 July 1884 *(Neele; LNW Officers 26299- line)*; clo 3 December 1951 *(RM January 1952)*.

TREHAFOD [TV] op 17 October 1892 *(TV Traffic Committee 26 September 1893 –* Colin Chapman, via *RAC)* as HAFOD, replacing earlier station of that name; renamed 1 January 1905 *(hbl 27 April)*; still open.

TREHARRIS [GW]
op 2 June 1890 *(RCG)*; clo 15 June 1964 *(RM August)*.

TREHERBERT [TV] op 12 January 1863 *(Cardiff T 16th)*; still open. Pre-opening Cwmsaebron *(RAC)*.

TREHOWELL [GW]
op 27 July 1935 *(RM September)*; HALT; clo 29 October 1951 *(Cl)*; {Weston Rhyn – Chirk}.

TRELEWIS

T HALT [GW] op 9 July 1934 *(co n dated 'July')*; clo 15 June 1964 *(Cl)*; {Nelson – Treharris}.

T PLATFORM [Taff-Bargoed] op 10 July 1911 *(RCG)*; clo 15 June 1964 *(Cl)*. In *IA* as HALT.

TRELOARS HOSPITAL – see ALTON.

TREMAINS FACTORY [GW] (non-tt):
HALT, alias T PLATFORM; trading estate;
op 6 November 1939 *(Cl 29)*; clo 11 September 1961
(Section G wtt – G.Maund); {Pencoed – Bridgend}.

TRENCH [Cam] first in *Brad* December 1914; HALT;
clo 10 June 1940★★, reop 6 May 1946 *(T 16 March)*;
clo 10 September 1962 *(RM October)*;
{Ellesmere – Overton-on-Dee}.

TRENCH CROSSING near Shrewsbury [LNW]
op 1 January 1855 *(SU)*; clo 7 September 1964
(RM October). HALT on BR ticket *(JB)*, but not in tt.

TRENHOLME BAR [NE]: line op 3 March 1857★★;
April (first time line in *Brad*) and May 1857 this shown,
market service only; then omitted; back in tt June 1858
with full service; clo 14 June 1954 *(Cl)*.

TRENT [Mid] op 1 May 1862 *(Mid)*;
clo 1 January 1968 *(RM February)*.

TRENT VALLEY JUNCTION – see LICHFIELD.

TRENTHAM [NS]

TRENTHAM op 17 April 1848 *(Manifold; co n T 16th-line)*; clo 2 March 1964 *(RM April)*.

T GARDENS op 28 March 1910, Easter holiday, *(RCG)*;
full service still shown in *Brad* February 1919 but from
mid-1920s service reduced to summer only;
clo September 1927; *hb* 1929 said open only for
occasional excursion traffic – same to 1956;
reop summer 1935 for Sunday and Bank Holiday
service; most summer tts seen (e.g. July 1935 and July
1937) show service Sundays only but September 1936
also included week-days (Sunday service noted to run
6th and 13th, but no end given for weekday one); July
1939 Sundays only, not to run after September 10th.
Other special use included nine trains from Liverpool
each day, Tuesday and Wednesday 5 and 6 July 1938
(LMS Railway Centenary, reprinted from *The Times* of
20 September 1938). Sunday services usually ran from
Tunstall. Bank Holiday use to 1942; T PARK until
7 October 1946 *(LNW Record)*; BR handbill confirms
still in excursion use at 2 June 1957; line closed for all
purposes 1 October 1957 *(RM November)* – *hb* April
1958a 'closed'. See C.T. Goode, *Trentham – The Hall,
Gardens and Branch Railway*, author, 1985.

T JUNCTION: dates assumed as T Park; not in public
tt; platform linked to main station at Trentham for
exchange to branch.

TREORCHY [TV]
op 27 September 1869 *(Cardiff T 2 October)*;
re-sited 30 chains south 3 March 1884 *(RAC)*;
TREORKY until 1892 *(Cl; RCG ref July)*; still open.

TREOWEN [GW] op 14 March 1927 *(co n dated
'March')*; HALT; clo 11 July 1960 *(Cl)*; {map 87}.

TRERHYNGYLL & MAENDY [TV]
op 1 May 1905 *(Cowbridge)*; clo 26 November 1951
(RM January 1952); {Cowbridge – Ystradowen}.
BR ticket *(JB)* as PLATFORM, not thus in tt
– see 1904★★.

TRESMEER [LSW] op 28 July 1892 *(W D Merc 29th)*
so that could be used for Launceston Agricultural
Society's Show; clo 3 October 1966 *(Cornish & DP 8th)*.

TRETHOMAS [BM] op 4 January 1915 *(RCG)* –
not in *Brad* until July; clo 31 December 1962 *(T 31st)*.

TREVEGLWYS – see TREFEGLWYS.

TREVIL [LNW] op 1 March 1864 *(co ½ T 12 August-
line)*; became HALT 1932/3 *(Brad)*; clo 6 January 1958
(BR WR notice December 1957).

TREVOR [GW] op 2 June 1862 *(Rtn- line)* as
CHWRELA; soon renamed; clo 18 January 1965★★.

TREWERRY & TRERICE [GW] op 14 August
1905★★; HALT; clo 4 February 1963 *(W Briton 4th)*.

TRIANGLE [LY]
op 1 June 1885 *(LY)*; clo 8 July 1929 *(Cl)*.

TRIMDON [NE]

T FOUNDRY: line op 13 October 1846 *(NE maps)*, nd,
August 1847. At first T; became T GRANGE, now
Saturdays only, in August 1871 *Brad* (also non-tt
workmen's services on weekdays?); renamed T FOUNDRY
June 1873; last in *Brad* August 1873.

TRIMDON (second of this name) first in *Brad* August
1871; about ⅝ mile east of first (S. Bragg), which it
effectively replaced; clo 9 June 1952★★.

TRIMINGHAM [Norfolk & S]
op 3 August 1906 *(RCG)*; clo 7 April 1953 *(RM May)*.

TRIMLEY [GE] op 1 May 1891 *(RCG)*; still open.

TRIMSARAN [BPGV]

T JUNCTION (non-tt): miners; op by 1909;
clo by 1927 *(U)*.

T ROAD op 2 August 1909★★; HALT until 1913 *Brad*,
when moved from notes to table; clo 21 September
1953 *(T 16th)*.

TRING [LNW]
TRING op 16 October 1837 *(T 16th)*; still open.
Non-tt: goods yard used for despatch of troops who
had attended Volunteer Review here, Easter Monday,
16 April 1876 *(T 17th)*.

TRINITY (& Newhaven) [NB] op 31 August 1842
(Rtn); original terminus replaced by through station
slightly to west when line extended 19 February 1846;
clo 1 January 1917 *(RM February)*; reop 1 February
1919 *(RM February)*; clo 2 November 1925 *(RM
January 1926)*. Only seen *Brad*, co tt, tickets as T;
T & N was RCH version (& N added 1904).

TRINITY ROAD – see TOOTING BEC.

TRODIGAL [Camp] (ng) line op 18 August 1906★★,
nd, September 1907; clo by May 1932 *(Camp)*.

TROED-Y-RHIW

TROED-Y-RHIW [TV] op towards end of 1841 *(TV)*
– line had opened 21 April 1841; station not in *Brad*
until December 1844, when detail first given for its line;
TROEDYRHIEW from 1846/7 *(Brad)* until 1 July
1924 *(GW circular 18 June)*; hyphens added 12 May
1980 tt (had been used in *hb* 1877 to 1890s); still open.

T-Y-R HALT [GW/Rhy] op 18 February 1907 *(wtt supp)*;
first in *Brad* as HALT, became PLATFORM 1911/12
and pre-grouping ticket thus *(JB)* HALT again 1 July
1924 *(GW circular 18 June)*; last train 3 February 1951
– see 1951★★.

TROEDYRHIEW GARTH [GW]
first in *Brad* October 1873; clo to public 22 June 1970;
school use continued, last train 14 July 1970 *(RM Sept.)*.
Hb October 1963a said had become HALT; not seen

thus *Brad*, but note added 1965/8 that had become request stop. *Hb* added hyphens as for entry above.

TROEDYRHIWFUCH
TROEDYRHIWFUCH [Rhy] op 1 April 1908 *(?;first in Brad April)*; HALT; clo 1 January 1916 (Saturday) *(Cl)*; {Pontlottyn – Darran & Deri}.

T COLLIERY HALT (non-tt) shown in *RAC*; no details known.

TROON
For earliest service see 1818**.

TROON [GSW]: line op 5 August 1839 *(co ½ 1110/149)*, nd, August 1840 *(Robinson)*; re-sited on deviation 2 May 1892 *(co ½ 1110/149)*; still open.

T HARBOUR [GSW] first in *Brad* July 1847 (reop of site used for earliest service), last there October 1847; shown as TROON (other was T STATION); pair served by separate trains. Back in tt May 1850; last in tt October 1850; now T H; shared service with T through station, trains dividing/joining at Barassie. Also boat trains from August 1848 to October 1850 (inclusive); shown in *Brad* as 'Glasgow to Troon direct'. Used as part of route Glasgow – Troon (rail); Troon–Fleetwood (steamer); Fleetwood on (rail). Likely closure date was 28 October 1850 when GSW opened line through to Carlisle.

TROUBLE HOUSE
op 2 February 1959 *(Wilts & Glos 7th*)*; HALT; clo 6 April 1964 *(W D Press 6th)*; {Culkerton – Tetbury}.
* = paper mentions unauthorised use Saturday 31st January when someone on last steam hauled service pulled communication cord; many passengers went into public house after which halt was named – train waited for them.

TROUTBECK [CKP]
op 2 January 1865 *(co ½ T 28 February- line; in op tt Cockermouth)*; clo 6 March 1972 *(RM March)*. LNW co tt 1868 and 1908, *Brad* to its end (May 1961): T for ULLSWATER, but not thus LMS tt 1930, BR Regional tts of later 1950s.

TROWBRIDGE [GW]
op 5 September 1848 *(Bath & Chelt 6th)*; still open.

TROWELL [Mid]
op 2 June 1884 *(Mid)*; clo 2 January 1967 *(Mid)*.

TROWSE – see NORWICH.

TRUMPERS CROSSING [GW]: only shown as
ready for inspection 1 July 1904 and probably opened that day by understanding with inspector *(MT6/1279/3)* though not inspected until 9 August – first in *Brad* July; HALT; clo 22 March 1915 *(GM's Report 12 January 1917)*, reop 12 April 1920 *(wtt supp)*; see 1921 April/May**; clo 1 February 1926 *(Cl)*.

TRURO {map 112}
T ROAD [West Cornwall] op 25 August 1852 *(R Cornwall Gaz 27th)*; temporary station in Higher Town replaced by >

T NEWHAM [West Cornwall] op 16 April 1855 *(R Cornwall Gaz 20th)*; most trains diverted to next station when it opened and only then did *Brad* add NEWHAM; still one train per day until 16 September 1863 (Wednesday) *(Cl)*; also used by trains to Tehidy (see 1843 May 23**).

TRURO [GW] op 4 May 1859**; still open.

TRUSHAM [GW] op 9 October 1882 *(Torquay Directory 11th)*; clo 9 June 1958 *(T 5th)*.

TRUTHALL [GW] op 3 July 1905 *(GW H)*; not in *Brad* until October, when PLATFORM (but HALT in notes) until 1 July 1906 *(Cl)*; clo 5 November 1962 *(W Briton 8th)*. Pre-opening T Bridge *(RAC)* and GW ticket as T BRIDGE HALT *(JB)*.

TRYFAN JUNCTION [WH] (ng) op 15 August 1877 *(NGSC 2; Rtn- line)*; aot request; clo 1 November 1916 *(G&S)*; reop 31 July 1922**; clo 28 September 1936 *(Cl)*.

TUBS HILL – see SEVENOAKS.

TUE BROOK [LNW] op 1 July 1870**; clo 31 May 1948 *(LNW Record)*.

TUFNELL PARK [Nor] op 22 June 1907**; still open.

TULLIBARDINE [Cal] first in *Brad* May 1857; aot request; clo 6 July 1964 *(RM July)*.

TULLOCH [NB] op 7 August 1894 *(T 7th)* as INVERLAIR; renamed 1 January 1895 *(hbl 24th)*; still open. LNE tt 1933, *Murray* 1948: T for LOCH LAGGAN and KINGUSSIE and thus *Brad* until 1948/9.

Non-tt:
Wtt winter 1947 shows stop at milepost 44½, between here and Roy Bridge to pick up schoolchildren. Wtts 6 March 1967 and 7 May 1973 show stop for domestic purposes at milepost 70, between here and Corrour *(IU; G. Borthwick)*.

TULSE HILL [LBSC] op 1 October 1868 *(T 28 September)*; still open.

TUMBLE – see 1887**.

TUMBY WOODSIDE [GN] op 1 July 1913 *(RCG; in Brad July)*; clo 5 October 1970 *(T 16 July)*. October 1939 tt shows only one train per day, to Firsby; probably effective from 11 September when a number of temporary closures occurred in this area; November tt shows one train each way.

TUNBRIDGE – see TONBRIDGE.

TUNBRIDGE WELLS
TUNBRIDGE WELLS [SE] temporary at Jackwood Springs op 20 September 1845 *(Canterbury Journal 27th, which had 'Jenkwood Springs'; OS supports Jackwood)*. Just T W in *Brad*. Paper makes no reference to any preliminary use; does say formal 19th and unlikely anything earlier; replaced by >

TUNBRIDGE WELLS [SE] permanent 25 November 1846 *(Kentish Gazette 1 December)*; T W CENTRAL 9 July 1923 *(hbl 26 April)* to 14 May 1979 tt; still open.

T W WEST [LBSC] op 1 October 1866 *(co n T 1st)*; WEST added 22 August 1923 *(Cl; sig notice 15th noted that decision had been taken)*; clo 8 July 1985 *(RM July)*.

TUNNEL – see FARNWORTH.

TUNNEL INN – see GROSMONT.

TUNNEL JUNCTION [NE] op 13 October 1858**; clo 1 August 1863, service diverted *(Cl)*; {map 31}. In *hb* as T BRANCH J.

TUNNEL PIT WORKMENS PLATFORM [Mid] (non-tt): op before July 1917 wtt; still in use May 1922 wtt *(Mid)*; {1¼ miles west of Stockingford}.

TUNSTALL
For first service see CHATTERLEY.

TUNSTALL [NS] op 1 December 1873 *(NS)*;
clo 2 March 1964 *(RM April)*.

TURKEY STREET op 21 November 1960 *(Cl 29)*;
on site of earlier Forty Hill, using same buildings
(repaired); still open.

TURNBERRY [GSW] op 17 May 1906 *(RCG)*;
clo 2 March 1942 except for workmen *(LNW Record)*;
workmen's use ended ?; later excur *(U)*.

TURNCHAPEL [LSW]
op 1 January 1897 *(W Morn News 2nd)*; clo 15 January
1951 *(T 12th)*, reop 2 July 1951 *(D&C 1)* – see 1951**;
clo 10 September 1951 *(RM October)*.

TURNHAM GREEN op by [LSW] 1 January 1869
(co n T 24 December 1868); [Dist] use began 1 June 1877;
LSW use ended 5 June 1916 *(RM July)*; still open for
Dist. [Met] use 1 October 1877 to 1 January 1907.
[Picc] use 23 June 1963 to 28 September 1996 and
26 January 1997 on but only stops early morning and
late evening. T G (BEDFORD PARK) / T G for B P in
Brad from 1893/4 for LSW use, 1908/9 for Met Dist
use; thus GW co tt 1902, LSW co tt 1914; to T G ? –
still T G B P 1949 *(Brad)*, LT tables were omitted from
it soon after.

TURNHOUSE [NB] first in *Brad* September 1897;
clo 22 September 1930 *(Cl)*.

TURNPIKE LANE [Picc]
op 19 September 1932 *(T 16th, 20th)*; still open.

TURRIFF [GNS] op 5 September 1857 *(GNS)*;
clo 1 October 1951 *(RM November)*.

TURTON & EDGWORTH [LY]
op 12 June 1848 *(LY; RAIL 1005/265- line)* as
CHAPELTOWN (one word in RCH sources, two in
Brad); renamed T 1 July 1877 *(RCG)*, T & E 2 March
1891 *(Cl; hbl ref 23 April)*; clo 6 February 1961 *(Cl)*.

TURVEY [Mid]
op 10 June 1872 *(Mid)*; clo 5 March 1962 *(RM March)*.

TUTBURY
TUTBURY [NS] op 11 September 1848 *(co ½ T 3 Feb.
1849- line)*; clo 7 November 1966 *(RM January 1967)*.
T JUNCTION 1852/3 to 1858/9 *(Brad)*.
T & HATTON op 3 April 1989 *(D&C 7)*; still open.

TUTSHILL [GW] op 9 July 1934 *(co n dated 'July')*;
HALT; clo 5 January 1959 *(T 5th)*;
{Woolaston – Chepstow}. T for BEACHLEY in
op notice, GW co tts seen and *Brad* to clo.

TUXFORD
T CENTRAL [GC] op 15 December 1896 *(GC)**;
clo 19 September 1955 *(BR ER internal notice August)*.
See SHIREBROOK NORTH for details of a non-tt
service.
* = *RCG* gives 1 December but *GC* supported by *Brad Sh 1900*.
T NORTH [GN] op 15 July 1852**; clo 4 July 1955
(RM August).
CENTRAL, NORTH added 1 July 1923 *(hbl 12th)*.
Also see DUKERIES JUNCTION.

TWECHAR [NB]
first in *Brad* December 1878 as GAVELL; renamed
29 September 1924 *(Cl)*; clo 6 August 1951 *(Cl)*.

TWEEDMOUTH [NE] op 29 March 1847
(Newcastle Journal 3 April); clo 15 June 1964 *(RM July)*.
First in *Brad* as BERWICK (T station);

later 1847/1848 became T JUNCTION (and thus NE
tt 1880); JUNCTION dropped 1893/4 *(Brad)*.

TWENTY [MGN] first in *Brad* September 1866
(shown August with line, but no trains calling);
clo 2 March 1959 *(T 2nd)*.

TWERTON-ON-AVON [GW]
op 16 December 1840 *(co n Bath & Chelt 15th)*;
-on-A added 1 August 1899 *(Cl; RCH dist ref 9 May
1900)*; clo 2 April 1917 *(GM's report 11 May 1917)*.

TWICKENHAM [LSW]
op 22 August 1848 *(T 24 July, co n T 21 August)*;
re-sited 250 yards nearer St Margarets 28 March 1954
(Sunday, change made at 9am) *(RM May)*; still open.

TWIZELL [NE]
op in August 1861 *(N. E. Hoole)* though not in tt until
November 1861; clo 4 July 1955 *(RM August)*.

TWYFORD near Reading [GW]
op 1 July 1839 *(co n T 27 June)*; still open.

TWYFORD near Southampton [London &
Southampton] probably op late July 1839 *(Hants Chron
15th* – expected to open before end of month)*;
see 1839 June 10**; probably clo late September 1839,
certainly before May 1840 *(M. Hutson, Chron/SW
Circular)*; no tt evidence seen; {at/near later Shawford}.

TWYFORD ABBEY [GW]
op 1 May 1904 *(RM June)*; HALT; clo 1 May 1911 *(Cl)*;
{Park Royal – Greenford}.

TWYFORD BRIDGE [GC] (non-tt):
October 1914 and September 1925 working tts show
stop here for one southbound passenger train per day;
probably main use was for collection of milk but
perhaps passenger use; {Calvert – Finmere}
(letters in *RM July 1989 p. 448)*.

TWYMYN BRIDGE [Mawddwy] (non-tt):
temporary platform on Dinas Mawddwy side of
Cemmaes Road, used when bridge washed away
9 August 1880 and passengers walked to Cemmaes
Road; bridge reinstated 10 December 1880.
(G. Williams, article on branch, *GW Journal 59)*.

TWYWELL [Mid] op 1 March 1866 *(Mid; co n
T 27 February- line)*; clo 30 July 1951 *(RM September)*.

TY CROES [LNW]
first in *Brad* November 1848; aot request; still open.

TY FYSTON [TV] (non-tt): platform used by
workmen before line opened *(MT 6/475/7 – RAC)*.

TY GLAS op 29 April 1987 *(RM May)*, request only
stop until 11 May 1987; still open.

TYCOCH [BPGV] (non-tt):
HALT/PLATFORM; miners; mentioned as in use,
RM September 1912, p. 219; still in use May 1942 wtt;
{Trimsaran Road – Kidwelly}.

TYDD [MGN] op 1 August 1866 *(op wtt D&C 5)*;
clo 2 March 1959 *(T 2nd)*. At first TYDD ST MARY;
St M dropped *Brad* 1876 and *hb* 1877, but added again
in latter 1890 and 1895.

TYDDENHENGOED [LNW]:
probably goods and minerals only, but in tt included in
LNW Officers minute of 13 July 1870 (proposed tt
following opening of Carnarvon Town line) one
combined goods, mineral and passenger train is shown
stopping (southbound only) so perhaps an occasional

passenger was able to use it; no other reference seen; {Groeslon – Pen-y-Groes}.

TYDDYN BRIDGE [GW]
op 1 December 1930 *(Cl 29)*; HALT;
clo 4 January 1960 *(RM March)*; {Frongoch – Arenig}.

TYDDYNGWYN [Blaenau & Festiniog] (ng)
op 30 May 1868★★; last train 5 September 1883;
replaced to south by Manod, when line reopened
standard gauge; {map 78}. *Hb:* TYDDYN GWYN.

TYDEE/TYDU – see ROGERSTONE.

TYGWYN [GW] op 11 July 1927 *(GW H)*;
HALT until 6 May 1968 *(GW H)*; aot request; still open.
BR ticket for TY GWYN HALT *(JB)*.

TYLACOCH [TV] first in *Brad* October 1906;
see 1904★★ (HALT in *IA*); last in *Brad* November 1912.
Ynyswen here/near later.

TYLDESLEY [LNW]:
op 1 September 1864★★; clo 5 May 1969 *(RM June)*.

TYLER HILL – see BLEAN.

TYLERS ARMS – see BOURNVILLE MON.

TYLLWYN [GW]
op 29 November 1943 *(Cl 29)*; HALT; clo 30 April
1962 *(T 6 April)*; {Victoria – Ebbw Vale}.

TYLORSTOWN [TV] op 24 May 1882, perhaps
originally temporary station on different site from later
(RAC); clo 15 June 1964 *(RM August)*.
TYLORS TOWN until 1903 *Brad*, 1904 *hb*.

TYLWCH [Cam] op 21 September 1864 *(co n
Hereford J 24th- line)*; became HALT 1956/7 *(Brad)*;
clo 31 December 1962 *(T 31st)*.

TYN-Y-FFRAM [PT] (non-tt):
used by reservoir workmen, later Cwm Gwynon Colliery
miners. Siding for Messrs Barnes & Chaplin opened
5 November 1898 *(RAIL 1057/1528)*; have also put up
workmen's platform *(hbl dated 15th)*; clo 1909.

TYNDRUM
T LOWER [Cal] op 1 August 1873 *(Cal)*; re-sited /
rebuilt 1 May 1877 when line extended to Dalmally;
LOWER added 28 February 1953 *(Cl)*; still open.
Non-tt: wtts 6 March 1967 and 7 May 1973 show stop
at milepost 44½, between here and Bridge of Orchy,
for domestic purposes *(IU; G. Borthwick)*.
Also see UPPER TYNDRUM.

TYNE COMMISSION QUAY
– see under PERCY MAIN.

TYNE DOCK
TYNE DOCK (a) [NE] op about 1854 as JARROW
DOCK *(SS, photo caption)* – line op 5 September
1839 but nd until January 1861, by when it had been
renamed (this probably happened 1859 when new
dock opened, though it was only added to Macaulay's
maps in late 1850s and still shown as J Docks mid-
1860s); re-sited at some time – probably in connection
with reopening of Harton line (1 January 1867) or with
new line along river-bank (1 March 1872); clo 1 June
1981 *(RM June)* for conversion to >
TYNE DOCK (b) [TWM] op 24 March 1984 *(Tyneside)*;
new site; still open.

TYNEHEAD [NB] op 1 August 1848★★- line;
TYNE HEAD until 1874 tt *(Cl)*, though always (from
1862) one word *hb*; clo 6 January 1969 *(RM February)*.

TYNEMOUTH
(all early companies eventually part of NE); {map 26}.
TYNEMOUTH [Newcastle & Berwick] terminus
op 31 March 1847 *(Newcastle Journal 3 April)* >
TYNEMOUTH [BT] terminus op 1 April 1861 *(BT)*;
replaced by temporary terminus 27 June 1864; that was
kept as North Shields, which see, when permanent
terminus op 1 April 1865 *(BT)* >
Both termini were replaced by through T op 3 July
1882 *(NE maps- line)*.
Service became [TWM] 11 August 1980 *(Tyneside)*;
station never closed:
23 January 1978 – BR line via Benton clo;
11 August 1980 – Benton line reop, now TWM, and
line via North Shields clo;
14 November 1982 – line via North Shields reop;
still open.

TYNEWYDD – see OGMORE VALE.

TYNYCWM [GW] op 17 April 1935 *(undated GW
notice)*; HALT; initially 'GW' trains only, Sirhowy Valley
service added 3 January 1949 *(Rly Obs February)*;
clo 30 April 1962 *(T 6 April)*.

TYNYLLWYN [Talyllyn] (ng) (non-tt): probably for
shopping in Towyn; in use early 1940s;
see 1950 October★★; {Rhydyronen – Brynglas} *(U)*.

TYSELEY [GW]
TYSELEY op 1 October 1906 *(RCG)*; clo by fire
21 March 2001 *(Rly Obs May)*; reop 30 April 2001
(Rly Obs June); still open.
T WARWICK ROAD (non-tt): platform within
T Locomotive Works (formerly Birmingham Railway
Museum); used by Vintage Trains excursions; op ? –
certainly in use August 1999 *(BLN 864)*; still available.

TYTHERINGTON
TYTHERINGTON [Mid] op 2 September 1872
(Bristol Merc 7th); clo 19 June 1944★★ *(LNW Record)*.
T QUARRY (non-tt): used 22 August 1982 for
Tytherington Stone Social Club excursion *(JB)*;
{Tytherington – Thornbury}.

TYWITH – see NANTYFFYLLON.

TYWYN
TYWYN [Cam] op 24 October 1863 *(T 28th)* as TOWYN;
spelling altered 5 May 1975 *(RM July)*; still open.
TOWYN PENDRE [Talyllyn] (ng) op 1 October 1866★★;
see 6 October 1950★★. At times (1914/15 to 1918/19
and 1930) T PENDREF in *Brad* – error?
TOWYN WHARF [Talyllyn] (ng): by 1899 passengers
could start journey here but had to alight at Pendre on
way back *(NGMW)*; *RM October 1904* describes this as
practice then – trains only ran down to Wharf shortly
before departure; first in *Brad* October 1906;
originally KINGS STATION, WHARF; became
SLATE WHARF STATION 1909; T WHARF 1911;
not always in *(Brad)* and sometimes only shown by
note saying particular train started from there – omitted
January 1915 (present August 1914), back August 1915;
included without trains October 1917 and October
1918 (were trains April 1917 and January 1919)
but this might be result of practice then; only added
as arrival station July 1919; see 6 October 1950★★.

U

UCKFIELD [LBSC]
op 18 October 1858 *(co ½ T 26 February 1859)*; re-sited north of level crossing 13 May 1991 *(AZ)*; still open.

UDDINGSTON.
At times UDDINGSTONE in *hb*, and *RCH dist 28 May 1913* implied had been revised from this to version above, but latter is only one seen *Brad* and co tts, both Cal and NB.

UDDINGSTON [Cal] op 1 June 1849 *(T 5th- line)*; U CENTRAL 3 March 1952 *(Cl; ref RM April)* to 1961/2 tt; still open. 1864 OS 6 inch map shows station east of Glasgow Road; 1899 map shows it to west; 1875 RCH map has just one station, but that for 1888 has separate goods and passenger stations, the latter the westerly one; a likely answer is that the former is the original station. 1884 Bartholomew '2 inch to the mile' still shows it in original place. (OS information from G. Borthwick).

U EAST [NB] op 1 April 1878 *(D&C 6- line)*; clo 1 January 1917 *(RM February)*; reop 2 June 1919 *(RCH)*; EAST added 28 February 1953 *(Cl; ref RM April)*; clo 4 July 1955 *(RM August)*.

U WEST [NB] first in *Brad* June 1888; clo 1 January 1917 *(RM February)*; reop 2 June 1919 *(RCH)*; clo 4 July 1955 *(RM August)*.

UDNY [GNS] op 18 July 1861 *(GNS)*; clo 4 October 1965 *(Rly Obs November)*.

UFFCULME [GW] op 29 May 1876 *(CulmV)*; clo 9 September 1963 *(Express & E 9th)*.

UFFINGTON near Swindon [GW] op 1 June 1864 *(co n T 30 May)*; clo 7 December 1964 *(Cl)*.

UFFINGTON & BARNACK [Mid]
op 2 October 1846 *(Mid)*; & B added 1 February 1858 co tt *(Mid)*; clo 1 September 1952 *(RM October)*.

UFFORD BRIDGE [GN]
op 9 August 1867 (line date *GN* – it was a Friday); at first Fridays only; full use March 1872 *Brad*; aot request; clo 1 July 1929 *(Cl)*.
Hb: 1872 U B SIDING (no facilities then shown); 1877, 1883 'P', 1890 on no facilities – regarded as 'halt'?

ULBSTER [High]
op 1 July 1903 *(High)*; clo 3 April 1944★★.

ULCEBY
ULCEBY [GC] op 1 March 1848 *(co n GC)*; still open. U JUNCTION in some tables *Brad* 1850s and 1860s.
U AERODROME [LNE] (non-tt): HALT (but LNE ticket as PLATFORM, *JB*); Air Force Base; op by June 1943; clo by June 1947; {Ulceby – Immingham Dock} *(U)*.

ULLESKELF [NE]: line op 30 May 1839 *(T 7 June)*, nd, about June 1840 (and in *Whishaw*); still open.

ULLESTHORPE [Mid] op 30 June 1840 *(Mid; co n T 27th- line)*; became U for LUTTERWORTH 1 May 1879 co tt *(Mid)*, U & L 1 August 1897 *(RCG)*,

U 1 February 1930 *(hbl 29 April)*; clo 1 January 1962 *(RM February)*.

ULLOCK [WCE Jt] first in *Brad* May 1866; clo 13 April 1931 *(LNW Record)*.

ULVERSTON [Fur] (at first ULVERSTONE *hb*) Temporary terminus from Barrow, **U ROAD**, alias LINDAL EAST, op 27 May 1852 *(Fur)*; replaced by >
ULVERSTON op 7 June 1854 *(D&C 14)*; replaced again by through station 26 August 1857 or soon after *(D&C 14)*; see 1857 September 1★★; re-sited again, west side of Urswick Road Bridge 1872/4 *(D&C 14 p.135)*; still open. *Hb*: ULVERSTONE, amended 1877.

UMBERLEIGH [LSW] op 1 August 1854 *(Trewman 13 July, 3 August)*; aot request; still open. U BRIDGE in paper's description of opening.

UNDER HILL [Whitehaven & Furness Junction] op 1 November 1850 *(co n Furness Rise)*; last in tt December 1859; {Green Road – Millom}.

UNDY [GW] op 11 September 1933 *(co n dated 'August')*; HALT; clo 2 November 1964 *(Cl)*; {Severn Tunnel Junction – Magor}.

UNION BANK FARM [LNW] op 1 October 1911★★; HALT tt, *hb*; clo 18 June 1951 *(RM August)*; {Farnworth & Bold – Clock Face}.

UNITED STEEL CO'S WORKMEN'S HALT [LMS] (non-tt): op by January 1939; clo by September 1958; {Parton – Distington} *(U)*.

UNIVERSITY Birmingham:
op 8 May 1978 *(RM July)*; still open.

UNIVERSITY Sunderland [TWM]
op 31 March 2002 *(Rly Obs May)*; still open.

UNSTONE [Mid] op 1 February 1870 *(Mid; co n Mining 19th- line)*; UNSTON until 1 July 1908 *(hbl 9th)*; clo 29 October 1951 *(RM December* – 'excursions will continue')*. Ramblers' excursions at least to 22 September 1957, probably last *(AB)*.

UP EXE [GW] op 1 May 1885 *(Wellington 7th)*; U E & SILVERTON until 1 May 1905 *(RCG; GW circular 2012)*★; became HALT 1 October 1923 *(Cl)*; clo 7 October 1963 *(W Som F P 12th)*.
★ = *RAIL 253/482* says 13 April; date authorised?

UPHALL
UPHALL (a) There <u>might</u> have been a short-lived station in the early 1850s. *Returns* for 1850 include report of inspection on 18 September. Branch 1,574 yards long; not directly connected with main line at Houston, later Uphall (b); effectively separate line with own platform at Houston, shunting needed to link with main line. At Uphall 'rails terminate close on the main street'. Safety deficiencies resulted in delay but these were remedied and on 8 November Railway Commissioners sent letter to company saying no further objection to passenger opening.
However, no evidence seen that service actually ran but it would seem strange if it did not, given that extra work required had been done. No reference seen in *Brad* late 1850–52; not in *Murray* April 1852. Absence from *Brad* not decisive; its treatment of some lines then, particularly in Scotland, was not full – though Dechmont's Wednesday only service was included; not enough issues of *Murray* have been seen to enable judgement to

be made there. At the time, the legal owners of the line, the shareholders of the Edinburgh & Bathgate, were engaged in fierce legal argument with the Edinburgh & Glasgow, operators. These arguments concerned the financial details of intended amalgamation and maintenance problems – see 1851 November 21**. In the event, they compromised on an E&G lease of the line. If the latter was responsible for information being sent to *Brad*, it might well have felt that this line could be left to local knowledge. Or did E&G refuse to operate it? Or did open and then very soon close? – it does not look like a money-spinner. The balance of probability is that it was never used. It was included in a BoT *Return* as not open on 30 June 1858; this did not explicitly state that it had never been used but the whole purpose of this document seems to have been to catalogue the lines for which an Act of Parliament had been obtained but which had not come into use. Macaulay's Station Map of 1851 shows a line going due north from Houston to *Binnie*. This was still there on a mid-1860s map; probably error derived from knowing that company had powers to build a branch to Binny Quarry. *Binnie* branch also included in map with *Brad*, from 1852 (copied from Macaulay?) to 1890/4 (clearly inertia). Ordnance Survey, corrected to 1902 for railways, (Caledonian Books reprint) shows a mineral (oil shale) line going a little west of north from beside Uphall station (ex-Houston), skirting Uphall village and then heading off to Winchburgh. There appear to be the remains of a line going straight to Uphall, that would have fitted Wynne's description, suggesting that mineral line took over part of route. Airey (1875?) showed short uncoloured line going north from Camps Branch Junction; gone by 1884.
No mention of Uphall in *hb* 1862.

UPHALL (b) [NB] op 12 November 1849 *(Edin- line)* as HOUSTON; see 1851 November 29**; renamed 1 August 1865 *(Cl)*; clo 9 January 1956 *(RM February)*.
UPHALL (c) op 24 March 1986 *(RM May)*; still open.
UPHILL – see BLEADON.
Some local books have claimed that a private station was built here at or soon after the line opened in 1841 but never used; no contemporary evidence supports this (see RCHS *Journal* March 2009).

UPHOLLAND [LY]

UPHOLLAND (a) op 20 November 1848 *(LY; co n Manch G 18th- line)* as PIMBO LANE; renamed 13 October 1900 *(hbl 12th)*; still open.
Until 1902 *Brad* sometimes UP HOLLAND.
UPHOLLAND (b) op 20 November 1848 *(LY; co n Manch G 18th- line)*; {(a) – Orrell}; last in *Brad* August 1852.

UPLAWMOOR

UPLAWMOOR [GBK Jt] op 27 March 1871 *(GSW- line)* as CALDWELL; renamed 2 April 1962 *(RM May)*; clo 7 November 1966 *(RM January 1967)*.
According to *hb* September 1962a had become U for C and BR ticket thus *(JB)*.
UPLAWMOOR [Cal] op 1 May 1903 *(RCG)*; clo 1 January 1917 *(RM February)*; reop 1 February 1919 *(RCH)*; clo 2 April 1962 *(RM May)*.

UPMINSTER

UPMINSTER [LTS] op 1 May 1885 *(Mid)*; [Dist] service added 2 June 1902, ceased 1 October 1905, restarted 12 September 1932; still open.
U BRIDGE op 17 December 1934 *(L)*; still open. Owned originally by [LMS] but only [Dist] ever used it; to LTB 26 April 1970 *(Mid/BLN)*.
Pre-opening U West *(T)*.
UPNEY op 12 September 1932 *(L)*; still open. Owned originally by [LMS] but only [Dist] used it; to LTB 26 April 1970 *(Mid/BLN)*.
UPPER BANK [Mid] first in *Brad* September 1863; clo 25 September 1950 *(RM November)*.
UPPER BATLEY [GN] op 19 August 1863 *(GN)*; permanent station op about October 1866 *(GN)*; clo 4 February 1952 *(RM April)*.
UPPER BIRSTALL – see BIRSTALL.

UPPER BOAT

UPPER BOAT [Cardiff] op 1 March 1911 *(RCG)*; clo 20 July 1931 *(GW goods circular 13th* – after last train 18th).
UPPER BOAT [ANSW] op 1 September 1904**; HALT from 1 July 1924 *(GW circular June 18)*; clo 17 September 1956 *(RM October)*.
UPPER BROUGHTON [Mid] op 2 February 1880 *(RCG)*; clo 31 May 1948 *(RM July)*.

UPPER CWMBRAN
– see UPPER PONTNEWYDD.

UPPER GREENHILL [NB]
Some sort of station here would logically have op 1 March 1848 with line to Stirling *(co ½ T 4 September- line)*; first evidence for it is June 1848 *Topham*, first time it included line, as SCOTTISH CENTRAL JUNCTION; this was name in Edinburgh to Glasgow table, where it was last in *Brad* May 1854. Thereafter there were footnote references to connections for the north at Greenhill. December 1850/January 1852 it appeared in Scottish Central tables as G JUNCTION* and it reappeared in the body of the Edinburgh to Glasgow line under this name in August 1855. Intermittently in tt, usage depending on whether connection needed between E&G and Scottish Central services; perhaps, at least at times, exchange only; shown in August 1864 E&G wtt as point where carriages for Scottish Central attached/detached; disappeared from Edinburgh to Glasgow table 1861/3 but continued in Scottish Central table, where it was last in *Brad* September 1865, by when it had appeared as G UPPER JUNCTION / G UPPER – result of that company's amalgamation with Caledonian?; {map 11}.
* = note that Caledonian's GREENHILL JUNCTION at first appeared in Scottish Central tables, *Brad* and *Murray*, as CALEDONIAN JUNCTION.
UPPER GREENOCK [Cal] op 15 May 1865 *(co n True Line 68)*; clo 5 June 1967 *(Cl)*.
UPPER HALLIFORD [SR] op 1 May 1944 *(SR sig inst 14/1944)*; UPPER added 22 May 1944 *(L)*; HALT until 5 May 1969 *(S App)*; still open.
UPPER HOLLOWAY [TH Jt]
op 21 July 1868 *(L; co ½ T 30 September- line)*; clo 31 January 1870** (Wednesday), reop 1 October

1870 *(Mid)*; became U H for ST JOHNS PARK and
HIGHGATE HILL 1 March 1871 co tt,
U H for St J P 1 April 1875 co tt, U H 1 July 1903 co tt
(Mid); still open.

UPPER LYDBROOK [SW Jt] op 23 September
1875**; clo 8 July 1929 *(RM August)*; later excur *(U)*.

UPPER PONTNEWYDD [GW] op 1 July 1852
(Merlin 2nd); UPPER added 4 November 1881
(intended to be U CWMBRAN from 1 September but
this name probably not used) *(Cl; RCG ref January 1882
for U P)*; clo 30 April 1962 *(T 6 April)*.

UPPER SOUDLEY [GW]
op 3 August 1907 *(GW H; Glos Chron 10th- line)*; HALT;
clo 3 November 1958 *(T 21 October)*; {map 94}.

UPPER SYDENHAM [LCD]
op 1 August 1884 *(L)*; clo 1 January 1917 *(RM Feb.)*;
reop 1 March 1919 *(RCH)*; clo 22 May 1944
(T 22 April); reop 4 March 1946 *(RM May)*;
clo 20 September 1954 *(T 20th)*.
Perhaps intended to be WELLS ROAD – co tt, map
evidence, G. Croughton, *TTS March 1978, p.10*.

UPPER TYNDRUM [NB] op 7 August 1894 *(T 7th)*
as T; became T U 21 September 1953 *(Cl)*,
U T 17 May 1993 tt *(AB, Chron)*; still open.

UPPER WARLINGHAM [CO Jt]
op 10 March 1884 *(Hants Chron 15th- line;
in inspection report, 18 February, MT/6/1908/3)*;
U W & WHYTELEAFE 1 January 1894 *(hbl 25th)*
to 1 October 1900 *(RCG)*; still open. LBSC co tt 1912:
U W for RIDDLESDOWN; *Brad* added 'for R' 1890/1
to 1926/7 to whatever name then in use.

UPPER WATCHINGWELL
– see WATCHINGWELL.

UPPERBY PLANT & MACHINERY WORKSHOP
(non-tt): open days 5 and 7 July 1980;
{Carlisle – Wreay} *(U)*.

UPPERMILL [LNW] op 1 July 1886 *(LNW Officers
28684 – 'local service')*; clo 1 January 1917
(T 22 December 1916). Only spelling seen.

UPPERTHORPE & KILLAMARSH [GC]
op 1 October 1898 *(RCG)*; U & added 1 January 1907
(RCG); clo 7 July 1930 *(RAIL 393/151)*.

UPPINGHAM [LNW]:
3 school specials 27 September 1894 *(Rutland)*;
op to public 1 October 1894 *(co n T 1st)*; clo 13 June
1960 but would continue to be used by school
(T 24 March; RM May); hb September 1960a – closed
for passengers except for special trains in connection
with U School; school use to 30 May 1964 *(U)*.

UPTON Wirral [GC]
op 18 May 1896 *(Wrexham 23rd)*; still open.

UPTON & BLEWBURY [GW]
op 13 April 1882 *(T 10th- line)*; & B added 16 January
1911 *(hbl 26th)*; clo 4 August 1942**, reop 8 March
1943 *(Cl)*; clo 10 September 1962 *(RM October)*.

UPTON & NORTH ELMSALL [HB]
op 27 July 1885 *(op tt NER I)*; clo 1 January 1932
(Friday) *(RM January)*; later excursions, e.g. 14 October
1933 during Hull Civic Week *(RM February 1934,
p. 153–4)* and 28 February 1953 to Leeds for football
(RM May).

UPTON LOVEL(L) CROSSING [GW] (non-tt):
G M's Report 18 March 1915 referred to agreement to
stop here as well as STOCKTON CROSSING, which
see; {Heytesbury – Codford}.

UPTON MAGNA [Shrewsbury & Wellington]
op 1 June 1849 *(Shrewsbury 8th)*;
clo 7 September 1964 *(RM October)*.

UPTON PARK op by [LTS] September 1877 (17th?)
(L) – first in *Brad* October); [Dist] added 2 June 1902;
[Met] added 30 March 1936; still open.

UPTON-BY-CHESTER [Birkenhead]
op 17 July 1939 *(LNW Record)*; HALT until 6 May
1968 *(GW H)*; clo 9 January 1984 *(RM February)*,
replaced by Bache.

UPTON-ON-SEVERN [Mid]
op 16 May 1864 *(Tewkesbury 21st)*; -on-S added 1889
(RCG ref April); clo 14 August 1961 *(T 3rd)*.

UPWELL [GE] op 8 September 1884
(see 1883 August 20**); clo 2 January 1928 *(Cl)*.

UPWEY [GW]
UPWEY (a) op 21 June 1871 *(Weymouth 23rd)*;
on main line; UPWAY in hb 1872; replaced about
½ mile south by >
UPWEY (b) op 19 April 1886 *(Weymouth 23rd)*;
U JUNCTION 1 January 1913 *(RCH dist 29 December
1912)* to 1 December 1952, when became
U & BROADWEY *(RM December)*; & B dropped
1979/87 tt; still open.
UPWEY (c) op 9 November 1885 *(W Gaz 13th)* as
BROADWAY, later BROADWEY (by GW co tt 1893);
became B DORSET 12 January 1906 *(hbl 25th)*,
U 1 January 1913 *(hbl 23rd)*; on Abbotsbury branch;
clo 1 December 1952 *(W Gaz 5th)*.

U WISHING WELL op 28 May 1905 *(Bristol NWR)*;
HALT; clo 7 January 1957 *(Cl)*.

URALITE [SEC]: expenditure on platform authorised
14 November 1900 *(SEC)*, factory and works halt
op non-tt early 1901 *(Back Track October 1998)*;
op to public July 1906 *(SEC)*; HALT; clo 4 December
1961 *(T 8 November)*; {Gravesend – Cliffe}.

URLAY NOOK – see ALLENS WEST.

URMSTON [CLC]
first in *Brad* October 1873; still open.

URQUHART [GNS]
op 12 August 1884 *(GNS)*; clo 6 May 1968 *(RM July)*.

USHAW MOOR [NE] op 1 September 1884 *(D&C 4)*;
reduced to one train Mondays to Fridays, to Durham
only, after October 1949, before/with 5 June 1950 tt;
clo 29 October 1951 *(Cl)*; later use for Durham
Miners' Galas, e.g. 16 July 1960 *(JB)*.

USK [GW] op 2 June 1856**; clo 30 May 1955**.

USSELBY – see CLAXBY.

USWORTH [NE] first in *Brad* May 1864;
clo 9 September 1963 *(RM October)*; last train Friday
(6th). Prior to closure only one train each way per day,
mostly used by workers in chemical industry.
Became HALT 14 December 1959 according to
RM August but not seen thus any tt.

UTTERBY [GN] op 11 December 1905 *(GN)*;
aot request; see 1905** (d); clo 11 September 1961
(RM September); {Louth – Ludborough}.

UTTOXETER [NS] {map 58}
At first three stations, which *Brad* did not show separately until approx 1866; from 1848 until then its one entry was usually U JUNCTION .
U BRIDGE STREET op from Stoke-on-Trent 7 August 1848 *(co ½ T 3 February 1849)* >
U DOVE BANK op from North Rode via Leek 13 July 1849 *(T 11th- line)* >
U JUNCTION op 13 July 1849 (assumed date, *T 11th-line*) – needed as interchange >
Bridge Street and Dove Bank listed separately in *hb* and shown on Junction Diagrams; no mention of Junction in *hb* and only physical junction shown on diagrams (exchange only/mainly?).
All replaced by **UTTOXETER** op 1 October 1881 *(NS-K)*; still open.

UXBRIDGE
UXBRIDGE op by [Met] 4 July 1904 *(co ½ T 22 July)*; [Dist] service added 1 March 1910, transferred to [Picc] 23 October 1933; re-sited on extension 4 December 1938 *(T 3rd)*; still open.

U HIGH STREET [GW] op 1 May 1907 *(RCG)*; clo 1 January 1917 *(GW notice dated 22 December 1916)*; reop 3 May 1920 *(Cl)*; clo 1 September 1939 (Friday) *(Cl)*.
U VINE STREET [GW] op 8 September 1856 *(co n T 6th)*; V S added 1 May 1907 *(RCG)*; clo 10 September 1962 *(RM October)*.

UXBRIDGE ROAD
UXBRIDGE ROAD [WL] op 1 November 1869 *(LNW Officers 4698)*; [Met] added 1 February 1905; clo, by enemy action, 21 October 1940 *(wtt supp)*. LNW co tt 1870, LMS tt 1930, *hb* from 1877, *Brad* ? to closure: U R for SHEPHERDS BUSH.
According to *WL* perhaps temporary [HC] station here, alias NORLAND, about 1864; shown on Crutchley's London area map about this time, at/near site of later Latimer Road; no tt or other evidence to show use under this name – perhaps premature inclusion of Latimer Road.
Also see SHEPHERDS BUSH [NL].

REGULAR IRREGULARITY.

Passenger (in a hurry). "IS THIS TRAIN PUNCTUAL ?"
Porter. "YESSIR, GENERALLY A QUARTER OF AN HOUR LATE TO A MINUTE!"

VALLEY

VALLEY (a) [LNW] first in tt *(Topham)* May or June 1849; clo 14 February 1966 *(RM April)*.
VALLEY (b) op 15 March 1982 *(RM May)*; aot request; still open.
VAN – see GARTH & VAN ROAD.
VARTEG [LNW] op 1 May 1878 *(LNW Officers 18407, 18465; T 4th)*; became HALT 1933/4 *(Brad)*; clo 5 May 1941 *(Cl)*.

VAUXHALL London

VAUXHALL [LSW] op 11 July 1848 *(L; T 12th- line)*; effectively replaced Nine Elms, which had at times appeared in tt as Vauxhall; still open. Sometimes V BRIDGE, *Brad* and co notices; in 1850s press sometimes called it Nine Elms.
VAUXHALL [Vic] op 23 July 1971 *(L; T 24th- line)*; still open.
VAUXHALL – see BIRMINGHAM (terminus); DUDDESTON (through station).
VELVET HALL: [NE] line op 27 July 1849 *(NE)*, nd, July 1851; clo 4 July 1955 *(RM August)*.
VENN CROSS [GW]
op 1 November 1873 *(W Som F P 1st, 8th)*; clo 3 October 1966 *(Som Gaz 7th)*.

VENTNOR

VENTNOR [IoW] op 10 September 1866 *(Hants Adv 15th)*; clo 18 April 1966 *(RM March)*.
LBSC co tt 1912: V for BONCHURCH.
Brad ? to 1955: V for B and the LANDSLIP.
V WEST [IWC] op 1 June 1900 *(IWC)*; V TOWN until 9 July 1923 *(hbl 26 April)*; clo 15 September 1952 *(T 6 August)*.
Also see ST LAWRENCE.
VERNEY JUNCTION [LNW-Met/GC Jt]
op 23 September 1868 *(L)*; clo 1 January 1968 *(RM January)*. Op by Aylesbury & Buckingham, later part of GC; see 1874 March 27**; Met use began 1 July 1891, ended 6 July 1936 *(Ug)*.
VERWOOD [LSW]
op 20 December 1866 *(SR; Som & Wilts J 22nd- line)*; clo 4 May 1964 *(Hants Chron 9th)*. LSW co tt 1914 and *Brad* to 1955: V for CRANBORNE.
VIADUCT – see EARLESTOWN.
VIADUCT COTTAGES: [High or BR?] (non-tt): wtts 16 September 1957 and 13 June 1960 show one Saturday only call each way for 'Wife of Railway employee'; {Slochd Crossing – Carr Bridge}.
VICARAGE CROSSING [GW] op 1 May 1905 *(GW H)*; HALT; clo 1 January 1917 *(GW notice dated 22 December 1916)*; reop 2 April 1917 *(Cl)*; clo 1 January 1931 (Thursday) *(T 20 December 1930)*; {map 75}.
VICKERS PLATFORM – see BROOMHOPE.

VICTORIA

For main line station see LONDON.
VICTORIA [Dist] op 24 December 1868 *(T 21st, 25th)*; still open. Subway link to main station op 12 August 1878 *(L)*.
VICTORIA [Vic] op 7 March 1969 *(T 8th)*; still open.
VICTORIA near Ebbw Vale [GW]
first in *Brad* August 1852; clo 30 April 1962 *(T 6 April)*.
VICTORIA – see LOCHEE WEST; ROCHE.
VICTORIA DOCKS: CUSTOM HOUSE and TIDAL BASIN sometimes prefixed thus.

VICTORIA PARK London

VICTORIA PARK [GE] op for regular service 14 June 1856* *(L)*; original station op by NL; re-sited to east 1 March 1866; GE started to use own platforms there 1 November 1866; two companies used alternate years until 1874 when GE became continuous users (last NL train probably 31 October 1874 but other companies' services continued to use platforms); Stratford line platforms clo 1 November 1942, rest clo 8 November 1943 *(LNW Record)*.
* = used on 29 May 1856 to take people to/from firework display celebrating peace treaty after Crimean War – Blackwall *co n T 29 May*, which called it HACKNEY WICK (V P).
Also this and V P H W at times in tts and *hb*.
V P & BOW [EC] op 31 March 1849**; clo 6 January 1851 *(Cl)*; {map 108}.
V P & BOW [Blackwall] op 31 March 1849**; clo 26 September 1850 *(L)* {map 108}.
The last two (alias OLD FORD / BOW) above really formed interchange station made necessary because EC would not agree to through running – see note.
VICTORIA PARK Glasgow
– see SCOTSTOUN; WHITEINCH.
VICTORIA ROAD – see under SWANSEA.
VIGO [NE] op 16 April 1835 *(NE- line)*; last in *Brad* December 1853; back March 1862**; last January 1869; {map 34}.
VIRGINIA WATER [LSW]
op 9 July 1856 *(co n T 9th)*; still open.
Became V P for WENTWORTH January 1929 *(hbl 23rd)* and thus *Brad* until 1955.
VOBSTER [GW] (non-tt): used for excursion from quarries to Weymouth 26 July 1873 *(Away, p. 111)*; {in *IA*, branch from Wells}.
VOWCHURCH [GW]
op 1 September 1881**; finally clo 8 December 1941.
VULCAN [LNW]
op 1 November 1912 *(LNW Officers 43869)*; HALT until 1926 *(Brad)* and again from 1962/3 tt; clo 14 June 1965 *(RM July)*; {Earlestown – Warrington}.

WADBOROUGH [Mid] op November 1841★★; in tt
Midland Counties Herald for 1 February 1844 *(Mid)* –
when given full service?; clo 4 January 1965 *(Cl)*.
W for KEMPSEY in local press tt 1 February 1844 *(Mid)*.
WADDESDON [Met/GC]
WADDESDON op 1 January 1897 *(RCG)* as W MANOR;
renamed 1 October 1922 *(hbl 26th)*; clo 6 July 1936
(RM July).
W ROAD op January 1872 (see 1871★★); ROAD added
1 October 1922 *(hbl 26th)*; Met added 1 December
1899; clo 1 December 1935 (Sunday) *(RCH)*.
Hb: 1872 WADDESDEN ROAD; 1879a 'SIDING'
added and first shown 'P'; 1883 'SIDING' dropped;
1890 WADDESDON SIDING;
1895 WADDESDON; 1923a ROAD added again.
WADDINGTON [GN]
op 15 April 1867 *(GN; co ½ T 19 August- line)*;
clo 10 September 1962 *(RM October)*.
WADDON
WADDON [LBSC] first in *Brad* February 1863;
still open. *Brad*, until 1955: W for BEDDINGTON,
BANDON HILL and BEDDINGTON LANE
(RCG ref January 1887 gave addition of first two, and
they were included in *hb* 1890 on, including 1956).
W MARSH [SR] op 6 July 1930 *(T 30 June)*; HALT
until 5 May 1969 *(SR App)*; clo 1 June 1997★★ for
conversion to >
W MARSH [Croydon] op 30 May 2000; still open.
WADEBRIDGE [LSW]
WADEBRIDGE (a) op 1 October 1834★★;
clo 1 November 1886 for line rebuilding *(R Cornwall
Gaz 29 October)*.
WADEBRIDGE (b) op 3 September 1888 *(W Morning
News 4th)*; 12 chains east of (a); clo 30 January 1967
(Cornish & DP 4 February). First use by GW; LSW's
own service began 1 June 1895.
WADHURST [SE] op 1 September 1851 *(SE; Hants
Chron 6th- line)*; still open.
WADSLEY BRIDGE [GC] op 14 July 1845 *(GC)*;
clo 15 June 1959 *(RM July)*; advertised summer
Saturday & Sunday trains for anglers until 31 October
1965 *(Cl)*; later severe weather, and excursion use *(U)*;
last football (Sheffield Wednesday) excursion 8 January
1994 *(BLN 977)*; from 2 March 1997 no part of
privatised railway had relevant rights to use station
(BR doc).
WAENAVON [LNW]
op 1 September 1871 *(LNW Officers 6916)*;
clo 5 May 1941 *(Cl)*. LNW co tt 1874: WAEN AVON.
WAENFAWR (ng)
WAENFAWR (a) [NWNG] op 15 August 1877
(NGSC 2; Rtn- line); clo 1 November 1916 *(G&S)*.
WAENFAWR (b) [WH] op 31 July 1922★★;
clo 28 September 1936 *(Cl)*.
WAINFELIN [GW] op 13 July 1912 tt *(GW H)*;
HALT; clo 30 April 1917 *(Cl)*; reop 30 April 1928
(co n dated 'April'); clo 5 May 1941 *(Cl)*;
{Pontypool – Abersychan}.
WAINFLEET [GN]
op 24 October 1871 *(co n Skegness)*;
see 1962 November 11★★; still open.

WAINHILL [GW] op 1 August 1925 *(wtt supp)*;
HALT; clo 1 July 1957 *(RM August)*;
{Princes Risborough – Chinnor}.
WAKEFIELD
W KIRKGATE [GN/LY] op 5 October 1840 *(co n Leeds
3rd)*; still open. *Brad* 1869: W JUNCTION one table;
K first seen 1872, some tables (GN first);
hb 1877 (as W K JOINT).
W WESTGATE [GN] op 5 October 1857 *(T 5th)*;
re-sited 10 chains north 1 May 1867 *(Cl)*; still open.
Cl says clo WW1, reop 16 August 1921; but trains shown
Brad October 1918, September 1920, August 1921,
though it was omitted from index at this time.
WESTGATE added by 1859 *(Brad)*.
Also see OAKENSHAW.
WAKERLEY & BARROWDEN [LNW]
op 1 November 1879 *(RCG)*; clo 6 June 1966 *(RM July)*.
WALBERSWICK [Southwold] (ng)
op 1 July 1882 *(D&C 5- line)*; aot request;
clo 2 April 1917 *(Cl)*;
back in tt August 1919; clo 12 April 1929★★.
WALCOT [Shrewsbury & Wellington]
op 1 June 1849 *(Shrewsbury 8th)*; clo 7 September 1964
(RM October). Erratically WALCOT/TT *(Brad)*
– e.g. March 1850 one version each way.
WALDRON & HOREHAM ROAD – see HORAM.
WALESWOOD [GC] op 1 July 1907 *(GC dates)*;
clo 7 March 1955 *(RM April)*.
WALFORD [GW] op 23 February 1931 *(Cl 29)*;
HALT; clo 5 January 1959 *(T 5th)*;
{Ross-on-Wye – Kerne Bridge}.
WALHAM GREEN – see FULHAM BROADWAY.
WALKDEN
WALKDEN [LY] op 2 July 1888 (based on *Lancs Chesh*
– it gives 1st, a Sunday; in *Brad* July); W HL to 14 June
1965 tt; still open.
W LL [LNW] op 1 April 1875 *(LNW Officers 12593)*;
LL added 2 June 1924 *(Rly Gaz 23 May)*;
clo 29 March 1954 *(BR clo notice Sweeney)*.
WALKER
WALKER [NE] op 1 May 1879 *(Newcastle Weekly
Chronicle 3rd- line)* as LOW W; renamed 13 May 1889
(hbl 11 July); clo 23 July 1973 *(RM August)*.
WALKER GATE [NE]: op 22 June 1839★★; WALKER
until 1 April 1889 *(Cl)*; clo 11 August 1980 *(RM October)*
for conversion to >
WALKERGATE [TWM] op 14 November 1982
(Tyneside); still open.
WALKERBURN [NB] op 15 January 1867 *(NB)*;
clo 5 February 1962 *(RM February)*.
WALKERINGHAM [GN/GE] op 15 July 1867
(GN/GE); clo 2 February 1959 *(RM March)*.
WALL [NB] op 5 April 1858 *(T 5th)*;
clo 19 September 1955 *(RM October)*.

WALL GRANGE & LONGSDON [NS]
first in *Brad* November 1873; & L added 1923? *(Brad;
hbl ref 26 April)*; clo 7 May 1956 *(RM June)*.
NS co tt 1910: W G for CHEDDLETON and thus *Brad*
until 1923. LMS ticket WALLGRANGE & L *(JB)*.

WALLACE NICK – see KELSO.

WALLASEY [Wirral]
W GROVE ROAD op 2 January 1888 *(D&C 10)*;
G R added 31 May 1948 *(Cl)*; still open.
W VILLAGE first in *Brad* March 1907*; still open.
* = February 1907 tt included LEASOWE ROAD, no trains
calling and note 'see company's announcements for opening
date'; *Railway Gazette* and co minutes suggest it was briefly
open as L R.

WALLINGFEN [HB]
op 27 July 1885 *(op tt NER I)* as NEWPORT;
renamed N YORKS 1921 *(Cl)*, W 1 July 1923 *(hbl
12th)*; clo 1 August 1955 *(RM September)*.

WALLINGFORD
WALLINGFORD op by [GW] 2 July 1866 *(Oxford Chron
7th)*; clo 15 June 1959 *(RM August)*. Later carnival use
– e.g. 21 June 1969 *(RM September)*; after some years
a platform short of original was used *(U)*.
W ROAD – see CHOLSEY; MOULSFORD.

WALLINGTON [LBSC]
op 10 May 1847 *(T 8th/Globe)* as CARSHALTON;
renamed 1 September 1868 *(L)*; still open.

WALLSEND:
WALLSEND (a) [NE] op 22 June 1839**, as CARVILLE;
renamed ? (by March 1864, first appearance in *Brad*);
clo 11 August 1980 *(RM October)* for conversion to >
WALLSEND (b) [TWM] op 14 November 1982
(Tyneside); still open.

WALLYFORD
WALLYFORD (a) [NB] first in *Brad* June 1866;
clo 14 October 1867 *(Cl)*; {Inveresk – Prestonpans}.
WALLYFORD (b) op 13 June 1994 *(RM August)*;
still open.

WALMER [Dover & Deal Joint]
op 15 June 1881 *(LCD notice dated 13th)*; still open.
SEC co tt 1914 and *Brad*? to 1955: W for KINGSDOWN.

WALNUT TREE {map 90}
W T BRIDGE [Rhy] op 31 March 1858 *(co ½
T 1 September- line)*; last in tt December 1871.
For **W T JUNCTION**, later W T BRIDGE [TV]
see TAFFS WELL.

WALPOLE [MGN]
op 1 March 1866 *(T 2nd)*; clo 2 March 1959 *(T 2nd)*.

WALSALL
For first 'Walsall' station see BESCOT BRIDGE.
WALSALL [LNW] temporary in Bridgeman Street,
op 1 November 1847 *(Rtn)*; replaced by permanent
9 April 1849 *(Cl)*; still open.
WALSALL WOOD [Mid] op 1 July 1884 *(Mid)*;
clo 31 March 1930 *(Mid)*.

WALSDEN
WALSDEN (a) [LY] first in *Brad* October 1845; south
of level crossing; clo 7 August 1961 *(RM September)*.
WALSDEN (b) op 10 September 1990 *(BLN 639)*;
north of level crossing; still open.

WALSINGHAM
WALSINGHAM [GE] op 1 December 1857 *(co ½
T 1 March 1858- line)*; clo 5 October 1964 *(RM Sept.)*.
W SHRINE [LNE] (non-tt): used 1930s for pilgrimages;
{Walsingham – Fakenham} *(U)*.
1950s excursion trains for visitors to shrine ran to
W itself; however, on return passengers picked up
at W and SLIPPER CHAPEL HALT. Latter was
occupation crossing near shrine; no station, passengers
joined via portable steps; only evidence in Special
Traffic Notices (B. Wilson, memory from days in
Central Timing Office at Liverpool Street).
WALSOKEN [EC]: line op 1 February 1848, nd, May
1848 *(Topham)*; last in tt August 1851; {map 66}.
WALTHAM near Grimsby [GN] op 1 March 1848
(co n GC); W & HUMBERSTONE until 1852/3
(Brad); clo 11 September 1961 *(RM September)*.
WALTHAM CROSS [GE]
op 15 September 1840 *(T 16th)* as W; became W C
1 December 1882 *(Cl)*; re-sited from north side of
Waltham Lane 1885; was W C & ABBEY 1 May 1894
to 20 February 1969 *(Cl)*; still open.
WALTHAM ON THE WOLDS [GN] (non-tt):
in GN tt for 11 years from May 1883 (and briefly in
Brad, e.g. July 1883) but no trains ever shown calling.
Was used by specials: e.g. for Easter race meeting at
Croxton Park (first 5 April 1883 – *race*); 4 April 1889
at least eight specials were provided for races, from
Nottingham, Grantham, Leicester and Northampton
(G. Goslin, *Goods Traffic of the LNER*, Wild Swan, 2002);
also for Waltham fair and horse sale in September
(used 20 September 1897 – ticket, *JB*); occasional use
for military training camps at Croxton; last advertised
appearance in local press 1903 *(Leic)*. Spelling of
heading is that in general use for the place today;
railway usage was varied – usually hyphenated, other
variations including 'WOLD'.
WALTHAMSTOW
W CENTRAL [GE] op 26 April 1870 *(L)* as
HOE STREET; became H S W 1886 *(RCH reference
October)*; W CENTRAL 6 May 1968 *(Cl)*; still open.
W CENTRAL [Vic] op 1 September 1968 *(T 2nd)*;
still open.
W QUEENS ROAD [TFG Joint] op 9 July 1894 *(RCG)*;
Q R added 6 May 1968 *(Mid)*; still open.
ST JAMES STREET [GE] op 26 April 1870 *(L)*;
became St J S W 1886 *(as for Central)*; still open.
SHERNHALL STREET [GE] op 26 April 1870 *(L)*;
replaced, on extension of line, by >
WOOD STREET [GE] op 17 November 1873 *(L)*;
WALTHAMSTOW W S 1886 *(as for Central)* to
18 March 1971 *(Cl)*; still open.
WALTON Liverpool
W MERSEYSIDE [LY] op 2 April 1849 *(Southport Vis
7th)*; still open. Was W JUNCTION by 1853 *Brad* –
early no detail) and thus LY co tt 1899; became W
1972/4 tt; perhaps later W LANCS (ever thus body of tt
as well as index?); W M 14 May 1984 tt (index earlier).
W & ANFIELD [LNW] op 1 July 1870** as W;
& A added 1 January 1910 *(hbl 27th)*; clo 31 May 1948
(LNW Record).

W-ON-THE-HILL [CLC] op 1 December 1879
(CLC); clo 1 January 1918 (Tuesday) *(Cl)*.
Occasional excursion use in 1930s *(CLC Portrait)*.
WALTON near Peterborough [Mid]
op 2 October 1846 *(Mid)*; clo 7 December 1953
(RM January 1954).
WALTON near Wakefield [Mid]
op 1 June 1870 *(Mid)*; SANDAL & W until 1 October
1951 *(Mid)*; clo 12 June 1961 *(RM June)*.
WALTON JUNCTION {map 50}
WALTON JUNCTION (a) op 5 May 1857;
clo 15 October 1857. Dates of Manchester Art Treasures
Exhibition; station in *Brad* May to October (inclusive),
service to Exhibition from Chester and back via
Warrington Arpley.
WALTON JUNCTION (b): Warrington Arpley to Chester
service started 1 March 1858 *(T 4th)*; part of inter-
company warfare between LNW on one side and GN
and MS&L on the other – latter intended to provide
route linking Chester with their service from London to
Manchester; hampered by direct and legal action by
LNW who did not want competition, so one cannot be
sure how regularly service ran. Service appeared in
Brad May (when things had settled down?) to August
(inc) 1858, only in Warrington & Stockport table, not
Birkenhead. W J only intermediate station shown.
Clo 1 September 1858: Warrington & Stockport notice
(T 30 August) said service would be suspended in
consequences of 'obstructions put in way' and 'false
information constantly given to passengers' by
Birkenhead company. No evidence that it ever resumed.
During first use might have operated predominantly as
exchange station. Cannot have been so in 1858, when
it must have represented attempt to tap custom of its
thinly populated area. Would have been at/near junction
between line from Arpley and the Birkenhead line.
Probably [Warrington & Stockport] station; perhaps
joint with [Birkenhead]; least likely that latter were
sole owners.
WALTON-IN-GORDANO [WCP]
WALTON-IN-GORDANO and **W PARK** both
op 7 August 1907 *(Bristol T 8th)*; clo 20 May 1940
(Bridgwater Merc 22 May).
WALTON-ON-NAZE [GE] op 17 May 1867
(T 20th); still open. Sometimes W-on-the-N,
e.g. *hb* always, GE co tt 1914; *Brad*, erratic at start,
finally dropped '-the-' from body 1923/4, index 1951/2.
WALTON-ON-THAMES [LSW]
op 21 May 1838 *(co n T 16th)*; still open. At first W;
became W & HERSHAM 1849 tt *(Cl)*, W for H 1913?
(by RCH dist 10 March), and thus LSW co tt 1914;
W-on-T 30 September 1935 *(SR)*.
WALWORTH ROAD [LCD] op 1 May 1863 *(co n
T 2nd)* as CAMBERWELL GATE; renamed 1865 tt
(Cl); clo 3 April 1916 *(T 11 March)*; {in *IA*}.
WAMPHRAY [Cal] op 10 September 1847 *(co n True
Line)*; clo 13 June 1960 *(RM July)*.
WANBOROUGH [LSW] op 1 September 1891 *(RCG)*;
still open. Was W for NORMANDY August 1929
(hbl 23 October) until 1955 *(Brad)*.

WANDSWORTH {maps 109, 110}
W COMMON [LBSC] (a) op 1 December 1856
(co n T 28 November); described in opening notice as
temporary station; it was W COMMON in notice,
though just W in tt until January 1858 *(L)*;
clo 1 June 1858 (Tuesday) *(Cl)*.
W COMMON [LBSC] (b) op 1 November 1869 *(L)*;
short distance south of (a), replacement for New
Wandsworth; still open. *Brad*: W C for CLAPHAM
NIGHTINGALE LANE ? until 1955.
W ROAD [LBSC platforms] op 1 May 1867 *(L)*; see
1866**; clo Wednesday 19 May 1926 (perhaps last day
of use), reop 20 September 1926 *(RM November p. 418)*;
still open.
W ROAD [LCD platforms] op 1 March 1863 *(L)*;
see 1866**; clo 3 April 1916 *(RCH)*.
W TOWN [LSW] op 27 July 1846 *(T 23rd)*;
TOWN added 7 October 1903 *(RCG)*; still open.
Also see CLAPHAM COMMON.
WANLOCKHEAD [Cal] op 1 October 1902 *(RCG)*;
clo 2 January 1939 *(T 16 December 1938)*.
WANSBECK ROAD [TWM]
op 10 May 1981 *(Tyneside)*; still open.
WANSFORD
WANSFORD [LNW] op 2 June 1845 *(co op tt)*;
clo 1 July 1957 *(RM July)*. W SIBSON in *Brad* 1845 to
1889 and in LNW co tt at least 1852–83.
W ROAD [GN] op 9 August 1867 *(GN)*;
clo 1 July 1929 *(Cl)*.
Also see SIBSON.
WANSTEAD [Cen]
op 14 December 1947 *(T 17th)*; still open.
WANSTEAD PARK [TFG Jt]
op 9 July 1894 *(RCG)*; still open.
WANSTROW [GW] first in *Brad* August 1860;
clo 9 September 1963 *(Weston 13th)*.
WANTAGE ROAD [GW] first in *Brad* November
1846; clo 7 December 1964 *(Cl)*.
WAPPENHAM [SMJ] op 1 June 1872 *(SMJ;
co ½ T 14 August- line)*; clo 2 July 1951 *(RM September)*.
WAPPING [East London]
op 7 December 1869 *(T 7th)*; W & SHADWELL until
10 April 1876 *(L)*; clo 25 March 1995 for engineering
work *(BLN 746, corr)*; reop 25 March 1998
(RM September); clo 23 December 2007**.
[Met] use began 6 October 1884, clo 3 December 1906,
reop 31 March 1913 (now only user).
[Dist] use began 1 October 1884, clo 1 August 1905.
WAPPING DOCK Liverpool [LO] op 6 March
1893**; clo 31 December 1956 *(T 29 September; Cl)*.
WARBLINGTON [LBSC]
op 1 November 1907 *(?; first in Brad November)* as
DENVILLE; renamed December 1907 *(Brad)*;
HALT until 5 May 1969 *(SR App)*; still open.
WARBOYS [GN/GE] op 16 September 1889 *(RCG)*;
clo 22 September 1930 *(Cl)*.
WARBRECK [CLC] op 1 August 1929 *(Cl 29)*;
clo 7 November 1960 *(RM December)*;
HALT until 1933/4 *(Brad)*; {Clubmoor – Aintree}.
WARBURTON – see DUNHAM MASSEY.

WARCOP [NE] op 9 June 1862★★; clo 22 January 1962 *(RM February)*; use by troop trains continued, at least until 20 May 1987 (photograph in *Stainmore – Eden Valley Railway* by P. Walton, OPC, 1995).

WARD/WARD STREET – see DUNDEE.

WARDEN [NC]: line op 28 June 1836, nd; see 1836 B★★; probably closed about end of 1836 or very early 1837 – still shown in *Scott* start of 1837.

WARDHOUSE [GNS] op 1 December 1854 *(GNS)*; clo 5 June 1961 *(GNS)*.

WARDLEWORTH [LY] op 1 November 1870 *(LY)*; clo 16 June 1947★★. *Hb*: 1872 W BROW; 1877 entered 'P' both as W and ROCHDALE YORKSHIRE STREET (same as W).

WARDS – see COLTFIELD.

WARE [GE] op 31 October 1843 *(T 28 October, 2 Nov.)*; still open.

WAREHAM [LSW] op 1 June 1847 *(Dorset Chron 20 May, 3 June)*; re-sited west of level crossing 4 April 1887 *(Cl)*; still open.

WARGRAVE [GW] op 1 October 1900 *(RCG)*; still open.

WARK near Hexham [NB]: line op 1 December 1859 *(NC)*, nd, April 1860; clo 15 October 1956 *(T 21 September)*.

WARK – see SUNILAWS.

WARKWORTH [NE]: line op 1 July 1847★★, nd, August 1847; clo 15 September 1958 *(RM October)*.

WARLINGHAM – see UPPER WARLINGHAM; WHYTELEAFE.

WARMINSTER [GW] op 9 September 1851 *(W Fly P 16th)*; still open.

WARMLEY [Mid] op 4 August 1869 *(Bath Chron 5th)*; clo 7 March 1966 *(Mid)*. W for KINGSWOOD in *LMS List* 1933 but not seen thus elsewhere.

WARNHAM [LBSC] op 1 May 1867 *(LBSC)*; still open.

WARREN [Wirral] first in *Brad* November 1888; for most of its existence, only one train per day each way but occasional full use – e.g. July 1889; clo 1 October 1915 (Friday) *(Cl)* but left in *hb* for some years after; {Wallasey – New Brighton}.

WARREN (others) – see DAWLISH; FOLKESTONE; WARREN BRIDGE.

WARREN BRIDGE [RHD] (ng) in earliest tts as ROMNEY WARREN HALT, trainless (see 1927 July 16★★); trains first shown in *Brad* December 1929 – now W B HALT; last there June 1930; but brief use 1946 (1 June to ?) as W HALT *(Wolfe)*.

WARREN STREET

WARREN STREET [Nor] op 22 June 1907★★ as EUSTON ROAD; renamed 7 June 1908 *(L)*; still open.

WARREN STREET [Vic] op 1 December 1968 *(T 2nd)*; still open.

WARRENBY [NE] (non-tt): workmen; op by October 1920 *(U)*; in *hb* 1956 'P' as W HALT; clo 19 June 1978 *(RM August)*, replaced by British Steel Redcar; {map 43}.

WARRINGTON {map 50}

WARRINGTON [GJ], branch from LM, terminus in Dallam Lane, op in June 1831 *(Crewe to Carlisle)*; replaced by >

W BANK QUAY HL [LNW], on West Coast Main Line, op 4 July 1837 *(T 6th)*; re-sited to act as interchange with line from Widnes to Broadheath 16 November 1868 *(Cl)*; still open. LNW co tt included B Q erratically (1852 W JUNCTION); in *Brad* it was added 1870/1 in east-west table, later in main line table.

W BANK QUAY LL [LNW] op 16 November 1868 *(Cl)*; clo 9 September 1963 (only night mail after 10 September 1962) *(Cl)*.

HL and LL not always used for BANK QUAY; were on e.g. Junction Diagrams; in *hb* 1872 but not thereafter. From Widnes to temporary **W WHITE CROSS** [St Helens] op 1 February 1853 *(T 16th)* >

From Broadheath to temporary **W WILDERSPOOL** [Warrington & Stockport] op 1 November 1853★★ *(T 17 October)* >

Gap between two lines above closed 1 May 1854 and **W ARPLEY** [LNW] opened, replacing both temporary termini. However 16 November 1868 WILDERSPOOL (had been kept as ticket platform – *Neele*) reop to passengers★ and ARPLEY closed (Bank Quay LL opened now); ARPLEY again replaced WILDERSPOOL 1 October 1871 *(LNW Officers 6924 – Sunday, but was Sunday service)*. ARPLEY clo 15 September 1958 *(LNW Record)*.

★ = LNW Officers 4728, 20 October 1869, recommended that 7.50 and 1.55 from Manchester London Road should call at 'Warrington Ticket Platform' for ticket collection and passengers for Warrington should be allowed to leave the platform. This suggests was not regarded as full station. Not found in sample of *Bradshaws* 1868–71; April 1870 LNW co tt only in note that some trains will call at ticket platform at Wilderspool Crossing.

W CENTRAL [CLC] op 1 August 1873 *(T 4 September, co ½ T 21 January 1874)*; still open. *Hb* added CENTRAL 1875a.

WARRINGTON JUNCTION – see EARLESTOWN.

WARSOP [GC] op 9 March 1897 (8th formal) *(GCR Society Journal, Spring 2003, p.12)*; clo 19 September 1955 *(BR ER internal notice August)* but intermittent summer Saturday use to 2 September 1961 (last) – only line through used later; later excur *(Cl)*.

WARTHILL {map 40}.

WARTHILL [NE]: line op 4 October 1847★★, nd, May 1848 *(Topham)*; op as STOCKTON, later S FOREST, S-ON-FOREST *(Cl)*, settled as W 1 February 1872 *(RCG)*; clo 5 January 1959 *(RM February)*.

WARTHILL [Sand Hutton] (ng) op 4 October 1924★★ *(D&C 4)*; last train 1 March 1930★★ (Saturday).

WARTLE [GNS] op 5 September 1857 *(GNS)*; clo 1 October 1951 *(RM November)*. According to *GNS* was originally WARTHILL, but not thus *Brad*.

WARTON [PW]

W LYTHAM DOCK first in *Brad* June 1865; clo 1 May 1874 (Friday) *(Cl)*. Just W in *hb*.

W HALT (non-tt): same site?; workmen?; op ? *(U)*; clo 1 November 1920; *(LNW dates, no authority)*.

WARTON MOSS FARM – see BARTON MOSS.

WARWICK
WARWICK [GW] op 1 October 1852 *(W Mid;T 27 September- line)*; still open. W COVENTRY ROAD 1889/90 to 1947/8 *(Brad)*.
W PARKWAY op 8 October 2000, though incomplete *(Rail News)* – 24 September was planned formal (delayed to 25 October).
Non-tt: temporary platforms authorised 29 June 1859 for agricultural show *(GW Expenditure Committee)*; probably only for those showing animals and equipment – no reference to public use in item on show arrangements *(T 9 July)*; if that is correct, use would have been 10 July on.
W CAPE YARD [GW] (non-tt): agricultural shows *(U)* and races in 1930s (e.g. 23 November 1937, *AB*); {spur from Warwick}.
Also see LEAMINGTON SPA MILVERTON.
WARWICK AVENUE [Bak]
op 31 January 1915 *(T 27th)*; still open.
WARWICK ROAD Manchester
For earliest use hereabouts see MANCHESTER EXHIBITION and related entries.
WARWICK ROAD [MSJA] op 11 May 1931 *(Cl 29)*; clo 27 December 1991 (last train 24th) *(BLN 671)* for conversion to Manch.
Full name: W R OLD TRAFFORD / W R for O T. Later reop as Old Trafford.
WARWICK ROAD near Burton Dassett [East & West Junction] first in *Brad* December 1871; last there June 1873 but tt then reorganised so perhaps lasted longer; also not in August 1873 tt *Cheltenham Examiner* so more likely had closed but just possible that it was omitted from latter since only a 'halt'; {Kineton – North End}. Burton Dassett (non-tt) near/same site later. Only seen 1872 in *hb*, as W R SIDING, facilities not then listed.
WASHBECK EXCURSION
– see SCARBOROUGH.
WASHFORD {map 117}
WASHFORD [GW] op 16 July 1874 *(Som Co Herald 18th)*; clo 4 January 1971 *(Som Gaz 8th)*. GW co tt 1932: W for CLEEVE ABBEY and thus *Brad* 1923/4 to 1938/9. See 2007 July 20**.
WASHFORD [WSM] op 4 September 1865**; clo 8 November 1898**.
WASHINGBOROUGH [GN] op 17 October 1848 *(co n T 16th)*; clo 29 July 1940 *(Cl)*.
WASHINGTON near Dundee [Scottish Midland Junction]: line op 24 February 1837 (see 1837 B**); last certain reference in tt June 1843 but probably closed with line, 6 September 1847 *(Rtn)*. Ardler Junction here/near later {maps 8, 9}.
WASHINGTON near Durham [NE]; {map 34}
WASHINGTON (a): line op 16 April 1835**, nd, about August 1841 *(Robinson)*; last in tt December 1853.
WASHINGTON (b) probably op 1 October 1850, with direct line to Pelaw (S. Bragg); also see 1862 March**; clo 9 September 1963 *(RM October)* – last train Friday (6th), by when only one train each way per day, mostly used by workers in chemical industry.
Note that 1850 to 1853 both in use, for different services, (a) market days only during that time.

WASKERLEY [NE] op 1 September 1845 *(S&D; see 1843**; earliest reference found September 1847 co tt)*; at first, intermittently, W PARK; clo 4 July 1859 *(Cl)*; {map 30}.
WASSAND [NE] first in *Brad* September 1864; originally Tuesdays only; still Tuesdays September 1936; before/with December 1936 tt Mondays only; GOXHILL until 1 October 1904 *(hbl 27th)*; last train 14 September 1953 (derived from *Cl* – clo 21st).
WATCHET {map 117}
WATCHET [GW] op 31 March 1862 *(W Som F P 5 April)*; clo 4 January 1971 *(Som Gaz 8th)*. See 2007 July 20**.
WATCHET [WSM] op 4 September 1865**; clo 8 November 1898**.
WATCHINGWELL [FYN] line op 20 July 1889; private station for Sir J. Simeon of Swainston, perhaps not used until 8 May 1897, when IWC concluded agreement to stop trains by request; in *Brad* August 1923 to 1 June to 13 July 1924 tt (inc); HALT; clo 21 September 1953 *(T 21st- line)*. *Hb* 1910a added this 'P', without restriction; same to 1938 (last). Alias UPPER W, probably unofficially.
WATER LANE – see ANGEL ROAD.
WATER ORTON [Mid] op 10 February 1842 *(Mid)*; re-sited 10 chains west 3 May 1909 *(Mid)*; still open.
WATER STRATFORD
op 13 August 1956 *(RM September)*; HALT; clo 2 January 1961 *(RM Feb.)*; {Buckingham – Fulwell}.
WATER STREET BRIDGE – see PORT TALBOT.
WATER WORKS SIDING [N&B] (non-tt): built at expense of contractors for new Swansea Corporation reservoir near Cray; linked by narrow gauge line to site proper. Sanctioned for use 21 July 1899; clo by July 1908 when N&B bought and dismantled siding; for contractors' staff and Swansea officials; also workmen Mondays and Saturdays. Earlier in line's history had been thoughts of providing public station, to be called Cnewr, here; {Cray – Craig-y-Nos}; (P. Rowledge).
WATERBEACH [GE] op 30 July 1845 *(co n T 26th- line)*; clo 11 April 1992 for engineering work, no bus replacement, reop 9 May 1992 *(BR Ely station remodelling brochure)*; still open.
WATERFALL [Snowdon Mountain] (ng; rack) op 6 April 1896**; clo September 1924 *(Cl) but* – while still present July 1923 tt; not present 14 July 1924 tt – clo end of 1923 season?.
WATERFOOT [LY] op 27 March 1848 *(LY)* as NEWCHURCH / NEW CHURCH; re-sited a little higher up the valley 1857 *(D&C 10)*; renamed W for N 1 August 1881 *(RCG)* and thus LY tt 1899, LMS tt 1930 and *Brad*/BR tts to clo 5 December 1966 *(RM February 1967)*.
WATERGATE [SR]
op 20 September 1926 *(sig inst 31/1926; hbl 61)*; HALT; clo 1 March 1965 *(Express & E 1st)*; {map 116}.
WATERHOUSES near Durham [NE]
op 1 November 1877 *(NE)*; reduced to one train, Mondays to Fridays, to Durham, October 1949/5 June 1950 *(Brad)*; clo 29 October 1951 *(Cl)*; later use for

miners' galas – e.g. one began from here 16 July 1960 (A.Young).

WATERHOUSES near Leek [NS]
Temporary ng station, on edge of village,
op 29 June 1904★★; replaced by >
Combined narrow and standard gauge station op 1 July 1905 *(RCG)*, about ¼ mile further on (S.C. Jenkins, *The Leek and Manifold Light Railway*, Oakwood, 1991); ng platforms clo 12 March 1934 *(Cl)*, standard 30 September 1935 *(RM November)*.

WATERINGBURY [SE]
first in *Brad* September 1845; still open.

WATERLOO London
For main line stations see under London.

WATERLOO [Bak] op 10 March 1906 *(L;T 12th- line)*; see 1922★★; still open.

WATERLOO [Jub] op 24 September 1999 *RM March 2000)*; still open.

WATERLOO [Nor] op 13 September 1926 *(T 14th)*; see 1922★★; still open.

WATERLOO [Waterloo & City] op 8 August 1898 *(T 9th)*; clo 8 August 1992 for resignalling work, reop 6 September 1992 *(BLN 689)*; clo 28 May 1993 *(RM September)*; reop 19 July 1993 *(BLN 713)*; still open. Transferred from BR to London underground 1 April 1994.

WATERLOO near Machen [BM]
op in October 1908★★ *(GW H;* first *Brad* November); HALT, up line only – see Fountain Bridge for down service; clo 17 September 1956 *(RM October)*.

WATERLOO MERSEYSIDE [LY]
op 24 July 1848 *(SouthpVis 22nd, 29th)*; originally a terminus on north side of South Road, buildings in Windsor Road; when line extended to Liverpool, 1 October 1850, level crossing installed at South Road. Level crossing replaced by overbridge and station re-sited on south side of road, entrance on bridge, 24 July 1881 *(Waterloo Times 30th)*; at first W, later W LANCS (perhaps index only); became W M 14 May 1984 tt (index earlier); still open.

WATERLOO ROAD – see BLACKPOOL.

WATERLOO ROAD Stoke-on-Trent [NS]
op 1 April 1900 *(RCG)*;
clo 4 October 1943 *(LNW Record)*.

WATERSIDE [GSW]
op 7 August 1856★★; clo 6 April 1964 *(RM May)*.

WATERTON [GW] (non-tt): platform here briefly about 1940 for Ordnance Factory workers; {near Bridgend} (T. Newman, *TTS February 1993)*.

WATERWORKS ROAD – see BRYNMILL.

WATFORD
WATFORD [Met] op 2 November 1925 *(T 2nd)*; still open. Also used by LNE until 4 May 1926.
WATFORD [LNW] op 20 July 1837 *(co nT 19th)*; *Brad* 1853 and LNW co tt 1852 was W for ST ALBANS; replaced 28 chains south by >
W JUNCTION [LNW] op 5 May 1858 (op of St Albans branch; *hb* still called it W; article by Mary Forsyth, *British Railway Journal, special London & Birmingham edition*, Wild Swan, pp. 33–48, mentions 'outcry' over new station op 5 May 1858); electric lines added

15 June 1912; still open. Also [Bak] use 16 April 1917 to 27 September 1982.

W HIGH STREET [LNW] op 1 October 1862 *(L)*; still open. Also Bak use, dates as W Junction.

W NORTH [LNW] op 1 October 1910 *(LNW Cl)* as CALLOWLAND; renamed 1 March 1927 *(LNW dates)*; still open. *LNW dates* said was HALT before and after 1927 change; not seen thus *Brad*, but see 1905★★ and it did not appear in *hb* until 1929, suggesting halt status.

W STADIUM (non-tt): football; op 4 December 1982 *(RM February 1983)*; prior to 21 January 1991 served by extra stops on branch trains; Saturday service then withdrawn from branch so special shuttle from W Junction; still in use at 9 November 1991 *(BLN 925)* but reportedly out of use by 14 May 1993 *(BLN 709)*; note – private station not subject to usual closure mechanism.

W WEST [LNW] op 15 June 1912 *(RCG;T 7th- line)*; after 17 May 1993 only one train (early morning) each way per day; last train 22 March 1996 (Friday) *(RM November 1996)* – closed for road bridge repair work; remained in tt but only bus service, one each way per day. Department of Transport letter dated 6 November 2002 allowed 'closure'; last substitute bus ran 26 September 2003; deleted from tt.

WATH-on-Dearne
WATH [HB] op 23 August 1902 *(RCG)*; clo 8 April 1929 (last train 6th) *(NE Express June 2003)*.
W CENTRAL [GC] op 1 July 1851 *(GC; co ½ T 1 September- line)* as W; renamed W-ON-DEARNE 1 July 1907 *(RCG)*, W CENTRAL 25 September 1950 *(Rly Obs October)*; for clo see 1959★★; later excur *(U)*.
W NORTH [Mid] op 6 April 1841★★; at first W, renamed W & BOLTON 1850 1 May 1850 co tt *(Mid)*, W-ON-DEARNE 1 May 1914 *(hbl 14 July)*, W N 20 September 1950 *(Rly Obs October)*; clo 1 January 1968 *(RM February)*.

WATH – see MELMERBY.

WATH-IN-NIDDERDALE [Nidd]
op 12 September 1907 *(Nidd; Rtn- line)*;
clo 1 January 1930 (Wednesday) *(Cl)*.

WATLINGTON near Oxford [GW]
op 15 August 1872 *(GW)*; clo 1 July 1957 *(RM August)*.

WATLINGTON near King's Lynn
WATLINGTON (a) [GE] op 27 October 1846 *(co n D&C 5)* as W; renamed MAGDALEN ROAD 1 June 1875 *(RCG)*; reduced to former up platform, London side of level crossing, when line singled 19 October 1984; clo as M R 9 September 1968 *(RM November)*.
WATLINGTON (b) op 5 May 1975 *(T 23 April)* as MAGDALEN ROAD; platform replaced on King's Lynn side of crossing 20 July 1992; renamed W 1989; still open.

WATNALL [Mid] op 1 September 1882 *(Mid)*; clo 1 January 1917 *(T 29 December 1916)*; {in IA}.

WATSONS CROSSING [LY]
op 1 March 1907 *(LY)*; see 1905★★ (b);
clo 8 July 1929 *(Cl)*; {Triangle – Sowerby Bridge}.

WATTEN [High] op 28 July 1874 *(High)*;
clo 13 June 1960 *(RM July)*.

WATTON NORFOLK [GE] op 18 October 1869 *(GE)*; NORFOLK added 1 July 1923 *(hbl 12th)*; clo 15 June 1964 *(Cl)*.

WATTON-AT-STONE

WATTON-AT-STONE (a) [LNE] op 2 June 1924 *(T 29 May)*; -at-S added July 1924 tt *(JS)*, became W-at-S HERTS August 1926 tt *(JS)* and thus LNE tt 1927; clo 11 September 1939 *(G&S)*.

WATTON-AT-STONE (b) op 17 May 1982 *(Rly Obs July)*; still open.

WATTSTOWN [TV] op 5 June 1905 *(RM July)*; see 1904**; clo 12 July 1920 *(RCG)*; {Ynyshir – Tylorstown}.

WAULKMILLS OFFSET shown on Macaulay's maps 1851 to 1860s; {Arbroath – Colliston}; with a name like this should have been a passenger 'halt' but no evidence seen in support.

WAUN-GRON PARK

op 2 November 1987 *(Penarth)*; still open. Tickets for WAUNGRON ROAD/PARK *(JB)*.

WAVERLEY – see EDINBURGH.

WAVERTON [LNW] first in *Brad* November 1846; re-sited 41 chains west 6 June 1898 *(co ½ Rly Times 13 August)*; clo 15 June 1959 *(RM July)*. Pre-opening Black Dog.

WAVERTREE [LNW] op 1 September 1870 *(LNW Officers 5672)*; clo 5 August 1958 *(LNW Record)*. Originally to be called Wellington Road but minds changed before opening. *Hb* 1891a renamed to W & EDGE HILL but 1895 book confined this to goods station.

WAVERTREE LANE [LM]:

line op 17 September 1830**, nd, 1 March 1831 co tt (possible that it opened after practice of taking passengers by road to Edge Hill, first site, which had ceased ?); logically would have been replaced by Edge Hill (second site), 15 August 1836, when service diverted to Liverpool Lime Street; however, *Freeling* gives impression that it did last a little longer and company minutes 29 August 1836 said it was to be discontinued, so both apparently briefly open together.

WAVERTREE TECHNOLOGY PARK

op 13 August 2000 *(Rly Obs October)*; still open.

WEAR VALLEY JUNCTION [NE] would logically have opened with Wear Valley branch 3 August 1847; earliest mention found is September 1847 co tt (not in *Brad* until July 1848). However, evidence suggests trains stopped here <u>before</u> branch op – normal for S&D to have some sort of stop before proper provision made for passengers. Line through here op 1844 (see 1843**, references to Crook). Minutes of Bishop Auckland & Weardale, line owners, 17 October 1845, say they thought a shelter should be put up at 'the Valley Junction' for passengers from 'Witton-le-Wear and places adjacent', suggesting trains already stopping to pick up people who had walked down from Witton. S&D deferred decision until course of Wear Valley line had been marked out (implies willing to provide shelter before branch actually built). Also, 29 April 1847 S&D (operating company) minutes gave instructions for painting nameboard here; other boards ordered

then were for stations already open, and doing things like this three months in advance (case if W V J opened with new line) was not normal S&D practice. Clo 8 July 1935 *(Cl)*. At first JUNCTION in *Brad*; 1861 became WITTON J *(C/W)*; 1874/5 *Brad* added a separate line for branch line departures, keeping WITTON J for main line, using WEAR V J for branch; 1882 settled on W V J. In NE co tt 1880 was WITTON J in branch table, W V J main line.

WEARDE SIDING [GW] (non-tt): used by workmen building deviation line; op 1905; clo by November 1915; {Defiance – St Germans} *(U)*.

WEARHEAD [NE] op 21 October 1895 *(RCG)*; clo 29 June 1953 *(RM August)*.

WEARMOUTH [York, Newcastle & Berwick] op 19 June 1839 *(NE p.327; co n Newcastle Journal 22nd)* – notice and item in paper called it MONKWEARMOUTH; clo 19 June 1848, replaced by Monkwearmouth *(Cl)*; {map 29}.

WEASTE [LNW]: line op 17 September 1830**; no early detail; this/nearby site briefly open 1831/32 as GORTONS BUILDINGS; (re)op autumn 1832 / 1 September 1838 *(Drake)*, perhaps use intermittent; clo 19 October 1942 *(Cl)*. Early *Brad*, LNW co tts was WASTE LANE / WEASTE LANE/W L GATE; settled 1856 tt *(JS)*.

WEAVERTHORPE [NE]: line op 8 July 1845**, nd, May 1848 *(Topham)*; op as SHERBURN; renamed WYKEHAM 1 April 1874 *(Cl)*, WEAVERTHORPE 1 May 1882 *(RCG)*; clo 22 September 1930**.

WEDGWOOD [LMS]

op 1 January 1940 *(LNW Record* – 'for use of employees of J. Wedgwood & Sons'); HALT until 18 April 1966 tt; temporarily closed 23 May 2004**.

WEDNESBURY

WEDNESBURY [GW] op 14 November 1854 *(T 15th)*; W CENTRAL 19 July 1950 to 6 May 1968 *(Cl)*; clo 6 March 1972 *(RM April)*. *Hb* 1891 to 1938 (inclusive): W for DARLASTON but not seen thus *Brad*.

W TOWN [LNW] op 1 May 1850 *(W Mid; T 2nd- line)*; TOWN added 13 June 1960 *(Cl)*; clo 6 July 1964 *(RM August)*.

WEDNESFIELD

WEDNESFIELD [Mid] op 1 November 1872 *(Mid; co n T 1st- line)*; clo 5 January 1931 *(Mid)*.

W HEATH [LNW]

op 4 July 1837 *(T 6th)* as WOLVERHAMPTON; renamed W H for WOLVERHAMPTON 1852 tt; clo 1 September 1853 *(LNW notice of alterations for September, T 31 August)*; reop 1 August 1855 *(Cl)*, as W H; clo 1 January 1873 (Wednesday) *(Cl)*; {map 98}.

WEEDON [LNW]

op 17 September 1838 *(T 18th)*; re-sited short distance north Sunday 19 February 1888 *(LNW Officers 30089* – new opened and old closed); clo 15 September 1958 *(LNW Record)*.

WEELEY [GE] op 8 January 1866 *(T 10th)*; still open. GE co tt 1882: W for CLACTON-ON-SEA.

WEELSBY ROAD [GN]

op 11 December 1905 *(GN)*; see 1905** (d); clo 1 January 1940 *(Cl)*. See note on Hainton Street.

WEETON near Blackpool [PW]:
line op 16 July 1840**, nd, early 1841 tt *(Freeling)*;
perhaps use intermittent; last in *Brad* April 1843.
WEETON near Harrogate [NE]
op 1 September 1848 *(NE- line)*; still open.
Brad: W for AINSCLIFFE CRAGS 1882 to 1904/5.
WELBECK COLLIERY [LDEC] (non-tt):
Colliery was on branch from east facing junction between
Edwinstowe and Warsop; interpretation based on map
references given by *U* suggests that SANDY LANE was
stop on this branch, presumably acting as station for
Warsop. Other sources suggest W C and S L were same:
*Historical Model Railway Society Journal, July–September
2002* says S L HALT, op 1915, was at W C, and was
also occasionally used by miners' families. Certainly
W C used for excursions 13 June 1964 (to Cleethorpes),
17 June 1967 (to Scarborough) and 31 July 1977
(as W C SIDING, to Bridlington); organised by Village
Miners' Welfare *(JB)*.
WELBURY [NE]:
op 25 May 1852***; clo 20 September 1954 *(Cl)*.
WELDON – see CORBY.
WELDON BRIDGE [NE] (non-tt):
shown 'P' in *hb* 1877; 1879 Airey map shows lime works
there; *hb* 1883 has Fryston, goods only; workmen's
service? error? {Castleford – Burton Salmon}.
WELFORD & KILWORTH [LNW]:
line op 29 April 1850 *(co n T 1 May)*, nd, May 1851;
clo 6 June 1966 *(RM July)*. Variously, early *Brad* and
LNW co tts, W for LUTTERWORTH, W & K for L.
Became W & LUTTERWORTH 1 May 1897 *(hbl
29 April)*; settled as W & K 13 January 1913 *(hbl 23rd)* .
Brad: W & K for HUSBANDS BOSWORTH, near
NORTH ILFORD until 1955.
WELFORD PARK [GW] op 4 April 1898
(co n Ephemera); clo 4 January 1960 *(RM February)*.
Hb 1904 on: W P for WICKHAM and WESTON
and thus *Brad* until 1947/8.
WELFORD ROAD – see LEICESTER.
WELHAM GREEN
op 29 September 1986 *(RM December)*; still open.
WELL HALL – see ELTHAM.
WELLFIELD [NE]
first in *Brad* May 1882; clo 9 June 1952**.
W JUNCTION in *Brad* until 1893/4 and *hb* 1944a.
WELLING [SE] op 1 May 1895 *(RCG)*; still open.
WELLINGBOROUGH
WELLINGBOROUGH [Mid] op 8 May 1857 *(T 9th)*;
W MIDLAND ROAD to 14 June 1965 tt *(Mid)*; still open.
W LONDON ROAD [LNW] op 2 June 1845 *(co n)*;
L R added 2 June 1924 *(Rly Gaz 23 May)*;
clo 4 May 1964 *(RM June)*.
WELLINGTON COLLEGE
– see CROWTHORNE.
WELLINGTON SHROPSHIRE [Shrewsbury &
Wellington] op 1 June 1849 *(Shrewsbury 8th)*; became
W SALOP 1951 *(Brad)*, W for TELFORD 16 May
1983, W T WEST 12 May 1986, W 29 May 1994 tt,
W S 29 September 1996 tt *(AB Chron)*; still open.
WELLINGTON SOM[ERSET] [GW]
op 1 May 1843 *(Taunton 3rd- line)*; SOM added 1951

(Brad); clo 5 October 1964 *(Som Gaz 5 September)*.
WELLOW [SD Jt] op 20 July 1874 *(Shepton 24th)*;
clo 7 March 1966 *(Shepton 11th)*.
WELLS {map 119}.
WELLS [East Somerset; GW], terminus from Witham,
op 1 March 1862 *(Wells 1st)*; clo 1 January 1878
(Tuesday) *(Som &W J 5th)*; extended to next.
WELLS [GW] op 5 April 1870 *(Shepton 8th)*;
clo 9 September 1963 *(Weston 13th)*.
TUCKER STREET was added *Brad* 1875 and was
included in B&E co tt 1877 and GW co tt 1881;
Brad kept it until closure of Priory Road but GW co tt
dropped it – in 1886 it was still W T S from Witham but
W from Yatton and by 1902 gone completely until
restored 1932/42 (when stop at Priory Road added?);
presumably first used briefly to distinguish from East
Somerset station.
W PRIORY ROAD [SD Jt] op 16 March 1859**;
clo 29 October 1951 *(Central Som Gaz 2 November)*.
Although GW trains ran through this station from
closure of East Somerset station in 1878, they did not
stop here until 1 October 1934 *(RM October)*.
PRIORY ROAD was added *Brad* 1883 but not
included in Mid co tt 1903, LSW co tt 1914; not seen
in *hb* for passenger use.
WELLS-NEXT-THE-SEA [GE]
op 1 December 1857 *(co ½ T 1 March 1858)*;
at first W; renamed W-on-SEA 1 July 1923 *(hbl 12th)*;
W-next-the-Sea 1 January 1957 *(Cl)*;
clo 5 October 1964 *(RM September)*.
WELNETHAM [GE] op 9 August 1865 *(T 10th- line)*;
clo 10 April 1961 *(RM May)*.
WELSH HARP [Mid] op 2 May 1870 *(Mid)*;
clo 1 July 1903 (Wednesday) *(Mid co tt 'after 30 June')*.
WELSH HOOK [GW]
op 5 May 1924 *(GW H)*; HALT, aot request, daylight
only; clo 6 April 1964 *(Cl)*; {map 81}.
WELSH ROAD – see SEALAND.
WELSH'S CROSSING [LMS]
op 27 January 1936 *(RCH)*; HALT;
clo 3 April 1944**; {Thrumster – Ulbster}.
WELSHAMPTON [Cam] op 4 May 1863
(Oswestry 6th); clo 18 January 1965 *(RM March)*.
WELSHPOOL
WELSHPOOL [Cam] op 14 August 1860 *(Cam)*;
re-sited to east to allow road improvement 18 May 1992
*(BLN 685 – old last used 16th, buses replaced trains on
17th)*; still open. LNW co tts 1864, 1876: WELCHPOOL.
Ng stations [Cam]: **WELSHPOOL**; **W RAVEN SQUARE**
(request); **W SEVEN STARS** (request): all three op
6 April 1903 *(D&C 11)*; clo 9 February 1931 *(Cl)*.
WELTON [LNW] op 17 September 1838 *(T 18th)* as
CRICK; renamed C & W 1841 *(Brad)*, C 1848 *(Cl)*,
W 1 August 1881 *(Cl – LNW Officers recommended
12 July)*; clo 7 July 1958 *(LNW Record)*.
WELTON – see CORBY; MIDSOMER NORTON.
WELWYN [GN]
Originally platforms on Dunstable and Hertford
branches, used non-tt by railwaymen. Op ? Latter clo ?
Former became public >
W GARDEN CITY op 14 August 1920 *(RCG)*; re-sited

15 chains south on main line 20 September 1926 *(Cl)*; still open.

W JUNCTION op 1 March 1858 *(GN)*;
clo 1 September 1860 (Saturday) *(co n T 1st)*; {map 72}.

W NORTH op 7 August 1850 *(T 6th, 8th)*;
NORTH added 12 July 1926 *(hbl July)*; still open.

WEM [LNW] op 1 September 1858★★; still open.

WEMBLEY

W CENTRAL [LNW] op 8 August 1842 *(P.G. Scott)* as SUDBURY; renamed S & W 1 May 1882 *(Cl)*; W for S 1 November 1910 *(RCG)*, W CENTRAL 5 July 1948 *(RM September)*; still open. Also [Bak] use 16 April 1917 to 27 September 1982★★ and from 4 June 1984 to present.

W PARK op by [Met] for special traffic 14 October 1893 (football); used again certainly 21 October; perhaps other times *(Back Track January 2001)*; op for full public use 12 May 1894 *(L)*; [Bak] added 20 November 1939 *(T 18th)*, transferred to [Jub] 1 May 1979; still open for Met and Jub.

W STADIUM (a) [LNE] op 28 April 1923 *(L)*; on loop line; for special events only – e.g. Cup Finals, Empire Exhibition (opened 23 April 1924); last used 18 May 1968 *(Cl)*. Various names early – dates on tickets – EXHIBITION GROUNDS STATION (28 April 1923), EXHIBITION STATION (3 June 1924), WEMBLEY EXHIBITION STATION (24 April 1926) *(JB)*; ref T 15 September 1927 said had become W STADIUM. See article by J. Wells, *Back Track*, January 2007 for details, including non-stop railway within grounds, taking visitors from one part of Exhibition to another – at 'stations' it slowed enough to allow people to get on/off safely.

W STADIUM (b) [GC] op 1 March 1906 *(RCG)* as W HILL; renamed W COMPLEX 8 May 1978 *(RM June)*, W S 1987 by May/December tt changes; still open. Also see NORTH WEMBLEY.

WEMYSS

W CASTLE [NB] op 8 August 1881 *(Fifeshire Journal 11th)*; clo 10 January 1955 *(T 28 December 1954)*. Originally EAST W (and thus *Fifeshire J*) – name changed early – NB circular dated 15 September said 'name has been changed' (first in *Brad* October 1881 as W C).
Also see WEST WEMYSS.

WEMYSS BAY [Cal] op 15 May 1865 *(co n True Line 68)*; still open. Cal co tt 1913: W B (SKELMORLIE), also thus *Brad* thereabouts but not LMS tt 1930.

WENDEN – see AUDLEY END.

WENDLEBURY [LNW]
op 9 October 1905 *(Oxford Chron 6th)*; see 1905★★ (a); clo 1 January 1917 *(T 22 December 1916)*; reop 5 May 1919 *(RCH)*; clo 25 October 1926 *(Cl)*.

WENDLING [GE] op 11 September 1848 *(EC- line*; not in *Brad* until March 1849 but in *Topham* with line October 1848); aot request; clo 9 September 1968 *(RM November)*.

WENDOVER [Met/GC]
op 1 September 1892 *(RCG)*; First used by Met, whose use ended 11 September 1961; GC use began 15 March 1899; still open for ex-GC services.

WENFORD BRIDGE – see 1834 October 1★★.

WENHASTON [Southwold] (ng) op 24 September 1879 *(T 26th- line)*; request; clo 12 April 1929★★.

WENNINGTON
Temporary terminus at **Tatham Bridge** [North Western] op 17 November 1849 *(co n Lancaster 17th)*; replaced by permanent >

WENNINGTON [Mid] op 2 May 1850 *(Mid)*; still open.

WENSLEY [NE] op 1 February 1877 *(York Guardian 3rd)*; clo 26 April 1954★★ *(T 20th)*.

WENTWORTH [Mid] op 1 July 1897 *(RCG)* as W & TANKERSLEY; renamed W & HOYLAND COMMON 1 July 1901 *(hbl 7th)*, W 18 June 1951 *(Mid)*; clo 2 November 1959 *(RM December)*.

WENVOE [Barry] op 16 March 1896 *(dist t supp 13 April)*; clo 10 September 1962 *(Cl)*.

WERN HIR [GW] (non-tt): HALT; workmen; op 2 January 1939 *(Cl 29)*; 3 July 1939 wtt confirms then in use but closed and materials removed to build Glascoed East Access before 9 May 1941 *(GW Superintendent of Line's letter of that date)*; {Usk – Glascoed}.

WERN LAS [SM] first in *Brad* December 1919; clo 6 November 1933 *(Cl)*.

WERNETH – see OLDHAM.

WERRINGTON JUNCTION [GN] (non-tt): GN advertised special train to here in connection with total eclipse of sun 15 March 1858 (on line Astronomer Royal had predicted likely to give best view); refreshment stop at Peterborough on return journey *(co n T 9th)*; report *(T 16th)* said train from Manchester and Sheffield had also stopped here and upwards of 1,000 present; {physical junction in *IA*, north of Peterborough}.

WEST ACTON [Cen]
op 5 November 1923 *(wtt sup)*; still open.

WEST ALLERTON [LMS]
op 2 January 1939 *(T 15 December 1938)*; still open.

WEST AUCKLAND [S&D; NE]; {map 31}

WEST AUCKLAND (a) op December 1833 *(S&D says 1st but that a Sunday and no Sunday service here)*, as ST HELENS / ST H AUCKLAND; horse drawn from St Helens to Brusselton Inclines, stationary engine to haul up and down these, coach then attached to steam-hauled coal train to Darlington. Difficulties of working over inclines such that according to *S&D Pass* train service was replaced in 1842 by omnibus from South Church except for a service alternate Mondays for benefit of those living in bank top cottages – presumably did not go beyond these (arrangements made June). *Brad* supports in that St Helens omitted from October 1842 tt (probably well behind events); however, back in January 1843, clearly train service, and remained there until February 1847; March 1847 shows service by bus. S&D minutes *(RAIL 667/34)* show that 14 January 1847 George Stephenson suggested coach over Brusselton Incline should be replaced by omnibus from Bishop Auckland; 8 February 1847 he reported change had been made. Still St H at end.

WEST AUCKLAND (b) op 13 October 1858★★, as St H, via the Tunnel branch *(S&D Pass)*; new station;

site in relation to old not known; renamed 1 March 1878 *(Cl)*; clo 18 June 1962 *(RM August)*.

WEST BAY – see under BRIDPORT.

WEST BEXHILL – see COLLINGTON.

WEST BRIDGE – see under LEICESTER.

WEST BRIGHTON – see HOVE.

WEST BROMPTON

WEST BROMPTON [WL] op 1 September 1866 *(L)*; clo 21 October 1940 *(wtt supp)*. Pre-opening Richmond Road *(L)*. Aot W B & LILLIE BRIDGE *(hb)*; LNW *Officers 410/591, 8 April 1874* recommended addition – station was close to the L B Ground ('a place of popular resort'); reduced to W B *hb* 1894a.

WEST BROMPTON [Dist] op 12 April 1869 *(co n T 12th)*; still open. Originally to be Richmond Road *(L)*.

WEST BROMPTON op 30 May 1999 *(LRR 20)*; at/near earlier West London station; still open.

WEST BROMWICH

WEST BROMWICH [GW] op 14 November 1854 *(GW; T 13th- line)*; clo 6 March 1972 *(RM April)*. *Hb* 1895: W B for SPON LANE.
Also see NEWTON ROAD.

WEST BYFLEET [LSW] op 1 December 1887 *(SR corr)* as B & WOODHAM; renamed B for W and PYRFORD 1913 *(ref hbl 24 April)*, W B 5 June 1950 *(Cl)*; still open.

WEST CALDER

WEST CALDER [Cal] op 9 July 1869 *(Edin; T 12th-line)*; still open. One word in *Brad* until 1941 and LMS ticket thus *(JB)* but always two in *hb*.
Also see HARBURN.

WEST CLIFF – see WHITBY.

WEST CORNFORTH [NE] first in *Brad* August 1866 as THRISLINGTON; renamed 1 July 1891 *(hbl 16th)*; clo 9 June 1952★★.

WEST CROSS [SIT]: line op 11 November 1860 (see 1860 July 25★★), nd, May 1866; was W C ROAD *(Brad)*; replaced on deviation 26 August 1900 by station briefly W C NEW in *Brad*; clo 6 January 1960★★; *hb* W C ROAD until 1938; {map 88}.

WEST CROYDON

WEST CROYDON [LBSC] op 5 June 1839 *(co n T 6th)*; WEST added to name 1851 tt *(Cl)* – but probably *Brad* late, more likely when East Croydon opened *(JS)*; still open.

WEST CROYDON [Croydon] added 11 May 2000; still open.

WEST CULTS [GNS] op 1 August 1894 *(GNS)*; clo 5 April 1937 *(RM January 1938)*.

WEST DERBY [CLC] op 1 December 1879 *(CLC)*; clo 7 November 1960 *(RM December)*.

WEST DRAYTON [GW] op 4 June 1838 *(co n T 2nd)*; re-sited east of road underbridge 9 April 1884 *(Cl)*; W DRAYTON & YIEWSLEY 9 November 1895 *(RCG)* to 6 May 1974 *(BR notice)*; still open.
Joint GW/Dist service began 1 March 1883; GW only from 1 October 1885.

WEST DULWICH [LCD] first in *Brad* October 1863; WEST added 20 September 1926 *(L)*; still open.

WEST EALING [GW]

WEST EALING op 1 March 1871 *(L)* as CASTLE HILL; became C H EALING DEAN 1875 tt *(Cl)*; renamed W E 1 July 1899 *(hbl 13th)*; still open.
Joint GW/Dist service began 1 March 1883; GW only from 1 October 1885. GW co tt: 1874 C H for DRAYTON GREEN and EALING DEAN.
W E ENGINEERING DEPOT (non-tt): railwaymen; in use 1907; {West Ealing – Hanwell} *(U)*.

WEST END/W E LANE
– see WEST HAMPSTEAD.

WEST EXE [GW] op 19 March 1928 *(Tiverton 20th)*; HALT; clo 7 October 1963 *(W Som F P 12th)*; {Tiverton – Cadeleigh}.

WEST FEARN – see MID FEARN.

WEST FERRY near Dundee [DA] first in *Brad* July 1848, when local trains to Broughty Ferry first mentioned; thus perhaps op 17 May 1848 with Pier branch, but nature of tables then such that might have op even earlier; aot request; clo 1 January 1917 *(Cl)*; reop 1 February 1919 *(RCH)*; clo 4 September 1967 *(RM November)*.

WEST FINCHLEY op by [LNE] 1 March 1933 *(T 18 February)*; transferred to [Nor] 14 April 1940; still open.

WEST GOSFORTH [NE] op 1 June 1905 *(RCG)*; clo 17 June 1929 *(Cl)*.

WEST GREEN [GE] op 1 January 1878 *(L)*; clo 7 January 1963 *(RM January)*.

WEST GRINSTEAD [LBSC] op 16 September 1861 *(LBSC; co ½ T 23 January 1862- line)*; clo 7 March 1966 *(RM March)*.

WEST HALLAM [GN] op 1 April 1878 *(GN)*; clo 7 September 1964 *(RM October)*. GN co tt 1909, LNE tt 1933 and *Brad* until 1955: W H for DALE ABBEY.

WEST HALTON [GC] op 15 July 1907 *(RCG)*; clo 13 July 1925 *(Cl)*.

WEST HAM

WEST HAM [LTS] op 1 February 1901 *(RCG)*; LTS use ceased 1913, though platforms used by a few LNW/NL trains until 1 January 1916; removed after bomb damage in 1940 *(LTS vol.2, p.113)*; new platforms for Tilbury line 30 May 1999 *(LRR 21)*. Station also used by [Dist] from 2 June 1902 and [Met] from 30 June 1936 *(Ug)*; clo by bomb damage 7 September 1940 to 11 August 1941 *(LTS)*; still open. W H MANOR ROAD 11 February 1924 to January 1969 *(L)*.

WEST HAM, platforms for North Woolwich line, op 14 May 1979 *(L app)*; clo 29 May 1994 *(BLN 734)* for rebuilding in connection with Jubilee line extension (buses in lieu); reop 29 October 1995 *(RM February 1996)*; clo 10 December 2006 – last train Saturday 9th *(RM February 2007)*.
On tt map 2002 shown as W H HL and W H LL.

WEST HAM [Jub] op 14 May 1999 *(LRR 20)*; still open.
Also see STRATFORD, East London.

WEST HAMPSTEAD

WEST HAMPSTEAD [LNW] op 1 March 1888 *(LNW Officers 30089)*; WEST END LANE until 5 May 1975 *(RM July)*; still open. Aot W E L H *hb*.

WEST HAMPSTEAD op by [Met] 30 June 1879
(T 3 July); re-sited slightly north 13 June 1897 to make
room for GC tracks *(Cl)*; transferred to [Bak]
20 November 1939, transferred again, to [Jub], 1 May
1979; still open.

W H THAMESLINK [Mid] op 1 March 1871 *(Mid)* as
WEST END for KILBURN and HAMPSTEAD;
renamed W E 1 July 1903 co tt *(Mid)*,
W H & BRONDESBURY 1 April 1904 *(RCG)*,
W H 1 September 1905 *(RCG)*, W H MIDLAND
25 September 1950 *(RM October)*,
W H T 16 May 1988 *(Mid)*; still open.

WEST HARROW [Met] op 17 November 1913
(T 18th); HALT until 1934/5 *(Brad)*; still open.

WEST HARTLEPOOL – see HARTLEPOOL.

WEST HELMSDALE [High] op 1 November 1870★★;
clo 19 June 1871 *(Cl)*; {Loth – Helmsdale}.

WEST HOATHLY [LBSC] op 1 August 1882
(LBSC; Hants Chron 5th- line); clo 30 May 1955★★,
reop 7 August 1956 – legal objections *(RM May 1958)*;
clo 17 March 1958 *(T 17th)*.

WEST HORNDON [LTS] op 1 May 1886 *(Mid)* as
EAST H; renamed 1 May 1949 *(Mid)*; still open.

WEST HUMBLE – see BOXHILL.

WEST INDIA DOCKS [GE]
op 6 July 1840 *(co n T 29 June, T 10 July)*; clo 4 May
1926★★. THE MARSH in description *T 6 July* but
W I D in notice.

WEST INDIA QUAY [Dock]
op 31 August 1987 *(T 1 September)*; clo 14 October 1991
(last Friday 11th) for reconstuction *(RM December)*;
reop 28 June 1993 *(BLN 710)*; still open.

WEST JESMOND
WEST JESMOND (a) [NE] op 1 December 1900 *(RCG)*;
clo 23 January 1978 *(RM March)* for conversion to >
WEST JESMOND (b) [TWM] op 11 August 1980
(Tyneside); still open.

WEST KENSINGTON [Dist] op 9 September 1874
(L; T 10th- line) as NORTH END FULHAM;
renamed 1 March 1877 *(L; RCG ref January)*; still open.

WEST KILBRIDE [GSW]
op 1 May 1878 *(RCG)*; still open.

WEST KILBURN – see QUEENS PARK.

WEST KIRBY
WEST KIRBY [Birkenhead] op 19 April 1886 *(co ½
Herapath 14 August)*; clo 17 September 1956
(RM October – 'RAF personnel will continue to use').
WEST KIRBY [Wirral] op 1 April 1878 *(D&C10)*;
re-sited slightly, alongside and slightly west 1896
(line roughly north-south here) *(Cl)*; still open.

WEST LEIGH
WEST LEIGH [LNW] op 13 June 1831★★; WEST
added 1 August 1876 *(Cl)*; clo 29 March 1954 *(BR clo
notice, Sweeney – as WESTLEIGH)*. Certainly wakes
week use in 1957 (last day 11 July) *(AB)*.
W L & BEDFORD [GC] op 1 April 1884 *(Wigan Obs
2nd, item and tt)* as PLANK LANE; renamed 1 January
1894 *(hbl 25th)*; clo 2 November 1964 *(RM December)*.

WEST LINTON – see BROOMLEE; LYNESIDE.

WEST LONDON JUNCTION {map 100}
West London line op 27 May 1844 *(T 24th)*.

Two interchange stations were situated on it, one with
the L&B at northern terminus of line, the other where
it crossed GW. In L&B tables former shown as W L J –
in company's own notices: 'London & Birmingham
Junction' and 'Great Western Junction'. GW interchange
certainly op with line. According to *WL*, L&B at first
ran its trains from Willesden and only some time later
from exchange station further east (approximate site of
later Willesden Junction); however co tt for 10 June
1844 in *Lee* shows 'The London & Birmingham Junction
Station' which suggests it was open then and inspection
report referred to 'Junction station' on L&B so likely
that did open with line. In *Brad* shown as W L J in L&B
table July 1844, first time any reference to line appeared
there. WL had its own table in *Brad* which mentioned
both exchange points, but this did not appear until
September; GW exchange never shown in GW tables.
Both clo with line, 1 December 1844★★.

WEST LYNN [Eastern & Midlands] op 1 March 1866
(MGN); clo 1 July 1886 (Thursday) *(Cl)*; {map 67}.

WEST MALLING [LCD] op 1 June 1874 *(T 2nd)*;
WEST added 23 May 1949 *(Cl)*; still open.

WEST MEON [LSW] op 1 June 1903 *(Hants Teleg 5th)*;
clo 7 February 1955 *(Hants Chron 12th)*.

WEST MILL [GE] op 3 July 1863 *(Hertford Mercury
4th- line)*; aot request; clo 16 November 1964
(T 14 October). Hb WESTMILL until 1883.

WEST MONKSEATON
WEST MONKSEATON (a) [LNE] op 20 March 1933
(Cl 29); clo 10 September 1979 *(Cl)* for conversion to >
WEST MONKSEATON (b) [TWM] op 11 August 1980
(Tyneside); still open.

WEST MOORS [LSW]
op 1 August 1867 *(SR)*; clo 4 May 1964 *(Hants Chron
9th)*. Brad 1922/3 to 1955: W M for FERNDOWN.
Hb: 1872 one word, 1904 W M JUNCTION.

WEST NEWPORT – see NEWPORT-ON-TAY.

WEST NORWOOD [LBSC] op 1 December 1856
(T 31 October, co n T 28 November); LOWER N until
1 January 1886 *(L; RCG ref October 1885)*; still open.

WEST PENNARD [SD Jt] op 3 February 1862 ★★;
became HALT 25 June 1962 tt (in body, but not
index); clo 7 March 1966 *(Shepton 11th)*.

WEST ROUNTON GATES [NE]
first in *Brad* May 1864; Wednesdays only;
last train 6 September 1939 (based on *Cl* – clo 13th).
W R GATE until 1903/4 *(Brad)*.

WEST RUISLIP
WEST RUISLIP [GW/GC] op 2 April 1906 *(T 5 March)*
as R & ICKENHAM; renamed W R for I 30 June 1947
(L), 'for I' gradually dropped; still open.
WEST RUISLIP [Cen] op 21 November 1948 *(T 20th)*;
still open.

WEST RUNTON [MGN]
first in *Brad* September 1887; still open.

WEST ST LEONARDS [SE]
op 1 October 1887 *(?; first in Brad October)*; still open.

WEST SHEFFORD – see GREAT SHEFFORD.

WEST SILVERTOWN [Dock] op 2 December 2005
(formal 6th) *(LRR January 2006)*; still open.

WEST STANLEY [NE]
op 1 February 1894 *(RCG)* as SHIELD ROW;
renamed 1 February 1934 *(Cl)*; clo 23 May 1955
(RM July); dropped from *hb* 1956 but back January
1962 *hbl* 'excursions only'.
WEST STREET Glasgow [GU]
op 14 December 1896★★; still open.
WEST SUTTON [SR]
op 5 January 1930 *(T 6th)*; still open.
WEST TIMPERLEY [CLC] op 1 September 1873
(CLC); clo 30 November 1964 *(RM March 1965)*.
GN co tt 1909WT for ALTRINCHAM;
LNE tt 1933WT for BOWDON.
In *hb*WT A 1890 and 1895; restWT.
WEST TINSLEY [GC] op 30 May 1900 *(RCG;*
co ½ T 4 August- line) as T ROAD; renamed 1 July
1907 *(hbl 3rd)*; clo 11 September 1939 *(Cl)*.
WEST VALE [LY]
op 1 January 1875 *(LY; co ½ T 17 February- line)*;
clo 23 September 1929 *(T 19 August)*.
WEST WEMYSS [NB] op 8 August 1881 *(Fifeshire*
Journal 11th); clo 1 January 1917 *(RM February)*;
reop 2 June 1919 *(RCH)*; clo 7 November 1949 *(Cl)*.
WEST WEYBRIDGE
– see BYFLEET & NEW HAW.
WEST WICKHAM [SE]
op 29 May 1882 *(L)*; still open.
WEST WORTHING [LBSC]
op 4 November 1889 *(LBSC notice 64, dated October)*;
still open. *Brad*:WW for TARRING until 1955
but not LBSC tt 1912, *hb*.
WEST WYCOMBE [GW/GC] op 1 August 1862
(GW ac); clo 3 November 1958 *(T 31 October)*.
WESTBOURNE PARK
Possible that this evolved from a GW ticket platform.
There was certainly one hereabouts in 1857, when it
was mentioned in connection with a fire in a GW
carriage on 9 October. 'Salamander' (letter *T 12th*)
referred to stop 'near Kensal Green' and there was a
reference to one (un-named) in Col.Yolland's report on
the incident.
WESTBOURNE PARK [HC]: temporary accommodation
and booking-box existed here by 30 November 1865
when *HC minutes* show decision to improve this; what
was still described in minutes as temporary station
op 1 February 1866 *(L; undated co n T 3rd – 'now open'*,
described it as new station for W P and Kensal Green).
New station, 30 October 1871, used at once by both
GW and HC *(GW n T 24th)*. Notice called it 'transfer
station'; most main line trains would stop, to let
passengers change to HC for rest of journey to City.
See 1921 April/May★★ for temporary loss of one of its
local services. GW part clo 16 March 1992 *(BLN 679)*;
HC still open. 1866a in *hb* asW ROAD, amended 1867;
GW ticket forW P & KENSAL GREEN *(JB)*.
WESTBROOK [GW] op 27 May 1889 *(GW- line)*;
see 1881 September 1★★ for full details;
finally clo 8 December 1941.
WESTBURY [Shrewsbury & Welshpool]
op 27 January 1862 *(co n Shrewsbury 31st)*;
clo 12 September 1960 *(Cl)*.

WESTBURY near Trowbridge [GW]
op 5 September 1848 *(Bath & Chelt 6th)*; still open.
WESTBURY CROSSING – see FULWELL.
WESTBURY-ON-SEVERN [GW]
op 9 July 1928 *(GW H)*; HALT;
clo 10 August 1959 *(Cl)*; {Grange Court – Newnham}.
WESTCLIFF [LTS] op 1 July 1895 *(L)*;W-ON-SEA
until 20 February 1969 *(JS – BR ER commercial circular*
of this date renamed 'forthwith'); still open.
WESTCOMBE PARK [SE] op 1 May 1879 *(SE)*;
still open. Opened as COOMBE FARM LANE,
renamed later 1879 *(SE)*.
WESTCOTT [GC/Met]
op January 1872 (see 1871★★); aot request;
WESCOTT until 1895/6 *(Brad)*; Met use began
1 December 1899; whole clo 1 December 1935 (Sunday)
(RCH). Hb:WESTCOTT 1877 goods only,
1879aWESCOT SIDING 'P', 1895WESCOTT,
1898a onWESTCOTT.
WESTCOTT RANGE [SEC] (non-tt):
HALT; rifle range; op November 1916 *(U)*;
clo about 1925 *(Surrey)*; {Dorking – Gomshall}.
WESTCRAIGS [NB]
op 11 August 1862 *(MK)*; clo 9 January 1956 *(RM*
February). NB co tt 1900, LNE tt 1933, *Murray* 1948:
W for HARTHILL (and thus *Brad* to 1955 at least),
though *hbl ref 25 October 1923* said had become
W for H & BLACKRIDGE.
Hb: 1863aWESTCRAIG, 1867 WEST CRAIG,
1877WESTCRAIG, 1883WESTCRAIGS,
1904W...S for H, 1925W...S for H and BLACKRIDGE.
WESTENHANGER [SE]
WESTENHANGER op 7 February 1844 *(SE)*;
W & HYTHE 1845/6 *(Brad)* to 1874/5 *(RCG said*
1 January 1875, Cl and JS 1 October 1874); still open.
W RACE COURSE (non-tt); original station given
extra platforms for opening of Folkestone Racecourse
30 March 1898; island platform added to west,
certainly by 1907 *(race)*; last used 1976 *(AB)*.
WESTER HAILES
op 11 May 1987 *(RM May)*; still open.
WESTERFIELD [GE]
WESTERFIELD, main station, op 1 June 1859 *(T 2nd)*;
still open.
WESTERFIELD, Felixstowe branch, op 1 May 1877
(Rtn); service diverted to main 1 September 1879 *(Cl)*.
WESTERHAM [SE] op 7 July 1881 *(T 8th)*;
clo 30 October 1961 *(T 21 August)*.
WESTERTON Glasgow [NB]
op 1 August 1913 *(RCG)*; still open.
WESTERTON – see LEASINGTHORNE.
WESTFERRY [Dock]
op 31 August 1987 *(T 1 September)*; still open.
WESTFIELD [NB]
first in *Brad* June 1864; clo 1 May 1930 (Thursday) *(Cl)*.
Hb: 1867 (only)W SIDING.
WESTFIELD – see NOTGROVE.
WESTGATE – seeWAKEFIELD.
WESTGATE-IN-WEARDALE [NE]
op 21 October 1895 *(RCG)*; clo 29 June 1953
(RM August).

WESTGATE-ON-SEA [LCD]
first in *Brad* May 1871; still open.

WESTHALL [LMS] (non-tt): Milk Platform at which
mixed trains shown calling 1938; passenger use not
certain; {Newbigging – Dunsyre} *(U)*.

WESTHAM near Weymouth [WP Jt]
op 1 July 1909 *(Weymouth 2nd)*; HALT; clo 3 March
1952 *(RM March)*; {Melcombe Regis – Rodwell}.

WESTHAM – see PEVENSEY.

WESTHEAD [LY]
op 1 July 1906 *(Ormskirk 5th)*; see 1905★★ (b);
clo 18 June 1951 *(wtt supplement 6 August)*.

WESTHOUGHTON [LY]
first in *Brad* January 1849; still open.

WESTHOUSES [Mid]
WEST HOUSE first in *Brad* May 1862 (line op 1 May);
Saturdays only; clo 1 August 1865 *(Mid)*.
WESTHOUSES & BLACKWELL op 17 October 1881
(Mid) on same site; clo 2 January 1967 *(Mid)*.
Was TIBSHELF JUNCTION goods, pre-passenger
use *(Mid)*.

WESTLEY – see SIX MILE BOTTOM.

WESTMINSTER
WESTMINSTER [Dist] op 24 December 1868 *(T 21st,
25th)*; still open. At first W BRIDGE; B gradually
dropped – *Brad* omitted from some tables (including
Met) 1886/7 but kept in that for Broad Street for some
time after. *Hb*: 1872 W B; 1895 W; 1898a should read
W B; 1904 W.
WESTMINSTER [Jub] op 22 December 1999 *(T 18th)*;
still open.

WESTMINSTER BRIDGE ROAD
– see LAMBETH NORTH.

WESTMOOR [Mid] (non-tt): private; op 30 June
1863; clo 31 December 1962, with line (P. Rowledge),
but actual dates of use unknown; FLAG STATION
(Mid); {Credenhill – Moorhampton}.

WESTOE LANE – see SOUTH SHIELDS.

WESTON near Spalding [MGN] op 1 December 1858
(Linc, R & S 3rd) – in *Brad* prematurely (November);
aot request; clo 2 March 1959 *(T 2nd)*.

WESTON
W & INGESTRE [NS] op 1 May 1849 *(NS-K*, photo
caption); clo 6 January 1947 *(RM January 1950)*.
In *Brad* was W (I) until 1923, and thus NS co tt 1910;
hb W to W & I 1890.

WESTON-ON-TRENT – see INGESTRE.

WESTON BATH [Mid] op 4 August 1869 *(Bath
Chron 5th)*; BATH added 1 October 1934 *(Mid)*;
clo 21 September 1953 *(W D Press 21st)*.

WESTON BRIDGE [GSW; LMS] (non-tt):
HALT/PLATFORM; workmen; 1920s and 1930s;
{Annbank – Trabboch} *(U)*.

WESTON MILL [LSW] op 1 November 1906 *(RM
December)*; HALT; clo 27 June 1921 *(Cl)*; {map 114}.

WESTON MILTON [GW] op 3 July 1933 *(Cl 29)*;
HALT until 5 May 1969 *(GW H)*; still open.

WESTON RHYN [GW] first in *Brad* November 1871
as PREESGWEENE, on site of earlier 'PRESGWYN'
(and that in *Brad* for first month); renamed 1935 *(Cl)*;
clo 12 September 1960 *(Cl)*. GW co tt 1902,

1932: P for W R. *Hb* 1877 and 1883 PREESGWYN.

WESTON-IN-GORDANO
– see CADBURY ROAD.

WESTON-ON-TRENT [Mid]
op 6 December 1869 *(Mid)*; clo 22 September 1930 *(Cl)*.
W-on-T JUNCTION also shown 'P' in *hb* 1877
(presumed error).

WESTON-SUB-EDGE [GW]
op 1 August 1904 *(Chelt Chron 30 July- line)* as
BRETFORTON & W-sub-E; renamed 1 May 1907
(hbl 25 April); clo 7 March 1960 *(RM April)*.

WESTON-SUPER-MARE {map 123}.
WESTON-SUPER-MARE [GW]: first station was
branch terminus on Alexandra Parade op 14 June 1841
(GW; Taunton 16th- main line); replaced 20 July 1866
(Weston 21st) by new terminus on opposite side of road
from later Locking Road (behind Odeon Cinema of
later days); replaced again by new through station on
loop line 1 March 1884 *(Bridgwater Merc 5th)*; still open.
W-s-M GENERAL 1953 tt *(Cl)* to 6 May 1968 tt *(offic)*.
W-s-M JUNCTION [GW] op 14 June 1841 *(GW;
Taunton 16th- line)*; often just W J in tts (space?).
Early tts tended to include just 'Weston' in the tables;
inspection of mileages and timings shows that this
sometimes, especially westbound, equalled 'W Junction'.
Most branch 'trains' horse-drawn until 1 April 1851.
Clo 1 March 1884 with branch.
W-s-M LOCKING ROAD [GW] in use for excursions
by July 1897 *(U)*; initially platform of main station;
treated as separate from 8 April 1914; rebuilt as separate
station in mid 1920s; later used as overflow for regular
services in summer; last train Saturday 5 September
1964 (no Sunday trains advertised 1964).
W-s-M ASHCOMBE ROAD [WCP] op 1 December
1897 *(Bristol T 2nd)*; clo 20 May 1940 *(Bridgwater Merc
22nd)*. A R was added 1905 *(Brad)*.

WESTON-UNDER-PENYARD [GW]
op 2 December 1929 *(Cl 29)*; HALT; clo 2 November
1964 *(Cl)*; {Mitcheldean Road – Ross-on-Wye}.

WESTOW HILL – see CRYSTAL PALACE.

WESTWARD HO! [BWA]
op 18 May 1901★★; clo 28 March 1917★★.

WESTWOOD near Bridgnorth [GW]
op 7 December 1935 *(T 5th)*; HALT; clo 31 December
1951 *(T 31st)*; same site as earlier Stretton Westwood?;
{Much Wenlock – Presthope}.

WESTWOOD near Sheffield [GC]
op 4 September 1854 *(GC; co ½ T 1 September- line)*;
re-sited south of level crossing 9 October 1876 *(Cl)*;
clo 28 October 1940 *(Cl)*.

WESTWOOD – see HIGH WESTWOOD.

WETHERAL
WETHERAL (a) [NE] line op 19 July 1836 (see 1836
B★★), nd, by 5 December 1836 (report of accident on
that day said all trains stopped here, *T 14th*);
clo 2 January 1967 *(RM January)*.
Scott 1837 W or CORBY; *Murray* 1852 W for C;
Brad and *hb* sometimes WETHERALL at first – former
1858 had different versions east- and west-bound.
WETHERAL (b) op 5 October 1981 *(RM December)*;
same site; still open.

WETHERBY

WETHERBY [NE] op 10 August 1847 *(co ½ T 22 February 1848- line;* in inspection report dated 9th), nd, July 1848; re-sited at south junction 1 July 1902 *(Cl)*; clo 6 January 1964 *(Cl)*.

W RACECOURSE [LNE] (non-tt): op about 1924 *(U)*; last used 18 May 1959 *(RM May 1962)*; {Wetherby – Thorp Arch}.

WETTON MILL [NS] (ng) op 29 June 1904★★; clo 12 March 1934 *(LNW Record)*.

WETWANG [NE] op 1 June 1853 *(NE- line)*; clo 5 June 1950 *(Cl)* but see 1953★★.

WEYBOURNE [MGN]
op 1 July 1901 *(RCG)*; clo 6 April 1964 *(RM April)*.

WEYBRIDGE

WEYBRIDGE [LSW] op 21 May 1838 *(co n T 16th)*; still open. W JUNCTION in *Brad* 1848 to 1858/9. *Brad* ? to 1955: W for BROOKLANDS, ST GEORGES HILL and OATLANDS.

WEST WEYBRIDGE – see BYFLEET & NEW HAW.

WEYHILL [MSWJ] op 1 May 1882 *(W Gaz 5th)*; clo 11 September 1961 *(T 9th)*.

WEYMOUTH [GW]

WEYMOUTH op 20 January 1857 *(W Fly P 27th)*; still open. Aot W TOWN in *Brad*, GW tables only, and GW co tt, presumably to distinguish from next. *Brad* at times (different for GW and LSW use) had W MELCOMBE REGIS.

W QUAY first used 4 August 1889 *(W Gaz 9th)* as W LANDING STAGE and thus GW co tt 1932; became W Q 1937 *(Brad)*; last train to Quay Wednesday, 6 September 1939 (last from 5th) *(Cl)*; reop 25 July 1940 for specials (e.g. for refugees); fully reop 15 June 1946 *(Cl)*; clo 1 October 1985 *(RM December* – clo result of cancellation without warning of Sealink use but might still be used summer months); one train each way summers 1986–7, last train Saturday 26 September 1987. At first in *hb* as W LANDING STAGE; W Q NEW PIER added 'P' 1892a, with W L S now goods only; same 1895; 1904 to 1938 separate entries, both 'P', for L S and QUAY; 1944a W Q 'temporarily closed'; 1949a W Q back, W L S 'closed'; 1956 W Q only.

WHALEY BRIDGE

For first service [CHP] see 1833 May★★.

WHALEY BRIDGE [LNW] op 9 June 1857 *(co ½ T 3 August)*; still open.

WHALLEY

WHALLEY (a) [LY] op 22 June 1850★★; clo 10 September 1962 *(T 8th)*.

WHALLEY (b) op 29 May 1994 *(RM June)*; still open.

WHAPLODE [MGN] op 1 December 1858 *(Linc, R & S 3rd)* – prematurely in *Brad* November; aot request; clo 2 March 1959 *(T 2nd)*.

WHARRAM [NE] op 1 June 1853 *(NE- line)*; clo 5 June 1950 *(Cl)* but see 1953★★.

WHATSTANDWELL [Mid]
first in *Brad* September 1853 as W BRIDGE; re-sited south of tunnel 11 November 1894 *(Mid)*; renamed 1 July 1896 co tt *(Mid)*; still open.

WHAUPHILL [PPW Jt] op 2 August 1875 *(co minutes 29 September)*; see GARLIESTOWN for

brief clo/reop; clo 25 September 1950 *(Cl)*. Was WHAUP HILL in *hb* 1877 and 1883.

WHEATHAMPSTEAD [GN]
op 1 September 1860 *(GN; co n T 1st- line)*; clo 26 April 1965 *(RM May)*. At times WHEATHAMSTEAD in *Brad* until 1880/1. *Hb* added middle 'P' 1904.

WHEATLEY [GW] op 24 October 1864 *(T 25th)*; clo 7 January 1963 *(RM January)*. HALT on BR ticket *(JB)* but not in tt at 10 September 1962.

WHEELOCK & SANDBACH [NS]
op 3 July 1893 *(RCG)* as SW; renamed 2 April 1923 co tt *(JS)*; after November 1926 *Brad*, before/with August 1927 reduced to Thursdays and Saturdays only; clo 28 July 1930 *(Cl)*.

WHELDRAKE [Derwent Valley]
op 21 July 1913 *(NER Staff Mag 1913)*; clo 1 September 1926★★ (Wednesday).

WHELLEY [LNW] op 1 January 1872 *(LNW Officers 6927, 7546; in tt Wigan Observer 5th)*; clo 1 March 1872 (Friday) *(Cl*, supported by *LNW Officers 7681* – order given 14 February) – still in *Brad* March but 'no information'; {goods *IA*}.

WHERWELL [LSW]
op 1 June 1885 *(Hants Chron 13th)*; clo 6 July 1931 *(Cl)*.

WHETSTONE [GC] op 15 March 1899 *(GC; T 16th- line)*; clo 4 March 1963 *(RM March)*.

WHIELDON ROAD

op 1 May 1905 [NS] (A.C. Baker, *Illustrated History of Stoke and North Staffordshire's Railways*, Irwell, 2000); HALT; available from Stoke only; clo 30 September 1918 *(Cl)*; {Stoke – Trentham}.

WHIFFLET {map 16}

WHIFFLAT [Monklands]: see 1828 B★★ (especially summer 1832 reference) and 1844 December 26★★ – services involved would have gone through here. Known service op 10 December 1849, clo 10 December 1851 *(MK)*.

WHIFFLET [NB] op 26 October 1871 *(D&C 6- line)*; re-sited to south 26 August 1895 *(Cl)*; clo 1 January 1917 except workmen *(RM February)*; reop fully 2 June 1919 *(RCH)*; clo 22 September 1930 *(Cl)*.

WHIFFLET [Cal]: see 1835 C★★; services involved would have gone through here; first in *Brad* November 1845; replaced by following two >

W LOWER [Cal] op 1 June 1886 *(Cal)*; W LL until 7 November 1953 *(Cl)* clo 5 November 1962 *(RM Oct.)*.

W UPPER [Cal] op 1 June 1886 *(Cal)*; clo 1 January 1917 *(RM February)*; reop 1 March 1919 *(RCH)*; W HL until 7 November 1953 *(Cl)*; clo 5 October 1964 *(RM November)*. *Hb* did not at first distinguish between two.

WHIFFLET op 21 December 1992, south of old W Upper; when line from Glasgow (re)op 4 October 1993 it used spur up to 1992 station; still open.

WHIMPLE [LSW] op 19 July 1860★★; still open.

WHIMSEY [GW] op 3 August 1907 *(GW H; Glos Chron 10th- line)*; HALT; clo 7 July 1930 *(RM August)* {map 94}.

WHINHILL op 14 May 1990 *(BLN 634)*; still open.

WHIPPINGHAM [IWC]
op 20 December 1875 *(Hants Adv 22nd- line; see 1875★★)*;

aot request; clo 21 September 1953 *(T 21st)*.
According to *U* was private station for Osborne House
in its early years but always in *Brad*; 'private royal station'
probably local legend – only known use by Queen
Victoria 11 February 1888 (T. Cooper).

WHIPTON BRIDGE [LSW] op 26 January 1906 *(Exeter
Fly P 27th)*; HALT; clo 1 January 1923 *(Cl)*; {map 115}.

WHISSENDINE [Mid]
op 1 May 1848 *(Mid; co ½ T 21 August- line)* as
WYMONDHAM; renamed WHISENDINE
September 1848 *(Brad)*; spelling altered 1 October
1878 co tt *(Mid)*; clo 3 October 1955 *(RM November)*.

WHISTLEFIELD [NB]
op 21 October 1896 *(RCG)*; HALT from 13 June 1960
(Cl); clo 15 June 1964 *(RM July)*.

WHISTON
WHISTON op 1 October 1990 *(BLN 662)*; still open.
W INCLINE – see HUYTON QUARRY.

WHITACRE [Mid] op 10 February 1842 *(Mid)*;
re-sited south on opening of Nuneaton line 1 November
1864 *(Mid)*; W JUNCTION until 1 October 1904 co tt
(Mid); clo 4 March 1968 *(Cl)*.
1864 station at first W NEW *(Brad)*.

WHITBECK CROSSING [Whitehaven & Furness
Junction]: first in *Brad* July 1854; last September 1857;
{Foxfield – Kirkby}.

WHITBURN [NB] first in *Brad* August 1850
(see 1848**); last December 1852; reop 1 October
1864 *(Cl)*; clo 1 May 1930 (Thursday) *(Cl)*.

WHITBURN COLLIERY – see MARSDEN.

WHITBY [NE]
WHITBY op 8 June 1835 (see 1835 B**); new station
for locomotive hauled service 4 June 1847; still open.
Was W TOWN 1886 to 1924 *(Brad)* and 30 September
1951 *(RM January 1952)* to 5 September 1966;
TOWN at first usually added only in tables including
W West Cliff.
W WEST CLIFF op 3 December 1883 *(Rtn- line)*;
clo 12 June 1961 *(RM March)*.

WHITBY LOCKS – see ELLESMERE PORT.

WHITCHURCH near Andover
W HANTS [LSW] op 3 July 1854 *(Salisbury 8th)*;
op as W, renamed W NORTH 26 September 1949 *(Cl)*,
W H 2 October 1972 *(Cl)*; still open.
W TOWN [GW] op 4 May 1885 *(Hants Chron 2nd)*;
op as W, renamed W HANTS 1 July 1924 *(GW circular
18 June)*, W TOWN 26 September 1949 *(Cl)*;
clo 4 August 1942**, reop 8 March 1943 *(Cl)*;
clo 7 March 1960 *(Hants Chron 5th)*.

WHITCHURCH [GW] op 1 January 1925 *(W D Press
2nd)*; HALT; clo 2 November 1959 *(Shepton 6th)*;
{Brislington – Pensford}.

WHITCHURCH CARDIFF [Cardiff]
op 1 March 1911 *(RCG)* as W; became W GLAMORGAN
1 July 1924 *(GW circular 18 June)*, W SOUTH G
5 May 1975 tt *(Cl)*, W 12 May 1980 tt *(C/W)* – but
index later, W G 29 September 1996 tt, W C 18 May
2003 tt; still open.

WHITCHURCH DOWN near Tavistock [GW]
op 1 September 1906 *(RCG)*; PLATFORM (but GW
ticket, *JB*, as HALT); clo 31 December 1962**.

WHITCHURCH SALOP [LNW]:
op 1 September 1858**; SALOP added ?; still open.

WHITE BEAR [LY/LU]
op 1 December 1869**; clo 4 January 1960 *(RM Feb.)*.
W B for ADLINGTON in tt *LNW Officers 6927* for
line opening and usually thus or W B A in LNW co tts
seen 1874–1909, *Brad* until 1914/15 and LY co tt 1899;
RCH dist 30 November 1914 said 'for A' had been
dropped, date not given.

WHITE CITY
WHITE CITY [Cen] op 14 May 1908 *(co ½ T 31 July)*;
original station, WOOD LANE, was 'terminus' on a
loop that saved reversal; became through station 3
August 1920; replaced to north by WHITE CITY, 23
November 1947 *(RM January 1948)*; still open.
RCG ref January 1921 said had been renamed from
WOOD LANE EXHIBITION to W L WHITE CITY E
– should that have been 'replaced by'?
WHITE CITY [HC] op 1 May 1908 *(RCG)* as WOOD
LANE (W L EXHIBITION in *HC minute 27th* and *hb
1910a)*; clo 1 November 1914. Reop 12 December 1914
to 29 April 1915 (inclusive) for servicemen billeted
there (Mondays to Fridays evenings only, Saturdays
and Sundays most of day) *(HC minute 8 July 1915)*.
HC minute 7 October 1920 said ought to be reopened in
connection with exhibitions as WOOD LANE WHITE
CITY and was thus in *hb 1921a* and *ref hbl 27 January
1921*, open only when exhibitions held. Known use
again 23 November 1947 as WHITE CITY *(Minute
17 December 1947* confirmed renaming), special
occasions only; clo 25 October 1959 (Sunday) *(Cl)*.
Both initially opened for the FRANCO-BRITISH
EXHIBITION of 1908, which was sometimes added
as though part of name in early years.

WHITE COLNE [CVH]
op 16 April 1860 *(T 13th- line)* as C; clo 1 May 1889 *(Cl)*;
reop 1 April 1908 as W C *(Cl)*; clo 1 January 1962
(T 17 November 1961).

WHITE CROSS – see WARRINGTON.

WHITE HART [GW]
op 12 May 1947 *(co n dated 'May')*; HALT;
clo 30 June 1952 *(Cl)*; {Machen – Caerphilly}.

WHITE HART LANE [GE]
op 22 July 1872 *(L)*; still open.

WHITE MOSS LEVEL CROSSING [LY]
op 7 January 1907 *(Ormskirk 10th)*; see 1905** (b);
clo 18 June 1951 *(wtt supp)*.

WHITE NOTLEY [GE]
first in *Brad* October 1853; aot request; still open.

WHITE ROSE – see NEW TREDEGAR.

WHITE SIKE COTTAGES and **WHITE SIKE
JUNCTION** [Sand Hutton] (ng) both op 4 October
1924** *(RM December)*; HALTS *(Brad)*; last train
Saturday 1 March 1930**; {map 40}.

WHITEBOROUGH [Mid]
op 1 May 1886 *(Mid)* as WOOD END; became
W E for HUCKNALL HUTHWAITE 1 October 1886
co tt *(Mid)*, WHITEBOROUGH for H H 20 January
1893 *(hbl 26th)*, final name 1 January 1908 *(hbl 23rd)*;
clo 4 October 1926 *(Mid)*.

WHITEBROOK [GW]
op 1 February 1927 *(co n dated 'January')*; HALT;
clo 5 January 1959 *(T 5th)*; {St Briavels – Redbrook}.

WHITECHAPEL

WHITECHAPEL [East London] op 10 April 1876
(co n T 8th); [Met] use from 31 March 1913;
clo 25 March 1995 for engineering work *(BLN 746, corr)*;
reop 25 March 1998 *(LRR 16)*; clo 23 December 2007★★.

WHITECHAPEL [Dist] op 6 October 1884 *(T 4th)*;
clo 2 February 1902 for rebuilding, partly same site *(Cl)*;
reop 2 June 1902 *(RCG)*; still open. W MILE END
until 13 November 1901 *(L)* and thus *hb* 1890 and
1895, but only W in *Brad*.
EL and Dist tickets as W LONDON HOSPITAL *(JB)*.
Also see ST MARYS WHITECHAPEL ROAD.

WHITECRAIGS [Cal] op 1 May 1903 *(RCG)*;
still open. Cal co tt 1913 W for MEARNS;
LMS tt 1930 W for ROUKEN GLEN; *Murray* 1948
and *Brad* ? to 1955 W for M and R G.

WHITECROFT [SW Jt]
op 23 September 1875★★; clo 8 July 1929 *(RM August)*;
still excursions at 10 August 1961 *(BR pamphlet)*.
W ROAD in *hb* 1875a (only).

WHITEDALE [NE] op 28 March 1864 *(NE- line)*;
clo 19 October 1964 *(Cl)*. According to *RM January*,
became HALT 4 January 1960 but *Brad* just added
note that no staff were in attendance.

WHITEFIELD

WHITEFIELD (a) [LY] op 1 September 1879
(Manchester 2nd); clo 17 August 1991 (last train 16th)
for conversion to >
WHITEFIELD (b) [Manch] op 6 April 1992; still open.

WHITEGATE [CLC] op 1 July 1870 *(CLC)*;
clo 1 January 1874 (Thursday), reop 1 May 1886,
clo 1 December 1888, reop 1 February 1892 *(Cl)*;
clo 1 January 1931 (Thursday) *(co n Winsford & Over)*.

WHITEHALL [GW]
op 27 February 1933 *(Wellington 1 March)*; HALT;
clo 9 September 1963 *(Express & E 9th)*;
{Culmstock – Hemyock}.

WHITEHAVEN

WHITEHAVEN [Fur/LNW] op 19 March 1847★★ as
terminus; through platforms added 24 December 1874
(D&C 14; LNW Officers 12268, 17 November – new
passenger station at Whitehaven inspected and approved
subject to trifling signalling alterations); still open.
Terminus LNW; through part Joint. In *Brad* as W NORTH /
W BRANSTY, sometimes both in same issue, though
hb always W B; settled as W B 1870s/1880s; BRANSTY
dropped 6 May 1968.
W NEWTOWN [Whitehaven & Furness Junction]
op 19 July 1849★★; replaced by >
CORKICKLE [LNW] op 3 December 1855 *(D&C 14)*;
aot request; still open. At times W CORKICKLE.
Separate platform for WCE trains about 1859–63,
resulting from dispute about use of tunnel (H. Quayle,
Whitehaven ..., Cumbrian Railways Association, 2007).

WHITEHOUSE [GNS] op 21 March 1859 *(GNS)*;
clo 2 January 1950 *(RM February)*.

WHITEHOUSE SIDING/PLATFORM
– see FONTBURN.

WHITEHURST [GW] op 1 October 1905 *(GW H)*
as LLANGOLLEN ROAD; on or near site of earlier
L R; renamed 1 May 1906 *(Cl)*; clo 12 September 1960
(Cl). First in *Brad* as W HALT; became W PLATFORM
1924/5 and moved from notes to table, W 1937,
W PLATFORM again later 1937/1938.
First shown 'P' in *hb* 1926a as W PLATFORM.

WHITEINCH

W RIVERSIDE [Cal] op 1 October 1896 *(RCG;
Colliery 2nd- line)*; RIVERSIDE added 28 February
1953 *(Cl)*; clo 5 October 1964 *(RM November)*.

W VICTORIA PARK [NB] op 14 December 1896
(NB notice GM 69, 10 December; RCG), but not in *Brad*
until May 1897; op as V P W; clo 1 January 1917
(RM February); reop 2 June 1919 *(RCH)*;
renamed 13 July 1925 *(Cl)*; clo 2 April 1951 *(RM May)*.
Hb 1925 added 'for SCOTSTOUN' to both.

WHITEMILL near Carmarthen [Llanelly]
first in *Brad* January 1867; last October 1870;
{Abergwili – Nantgaredig}.

WHITERIGG [NB] first in *Brad* November 1862
(appearance perhaps premature – see ARBUCKLE);
clo 1 May 1930 (Thursday) *(Cl)*.

WHITHORN [PPW Jt] op 9 July 1877 *(Kirkcudbright
13th)*; clo 25 September 1950 *(Cl)*.

WHITLAND

WHITLAND [GW] op 2 January 1854 *(co ½ T 26 August-
line)*; still open.

WHITLAND [Pembroke & Tenby]
terminus op 5 September 1866 *(Cardiff T 7th)* – 4th was
formal; service diverted to main August 1869 *(Cl)*.

WHITLEY – see BIRDBROOK.

WHITLEY {map 26}.
For first station here see MONKSEATON.

W BAY (a) [NE] op 3 July 1882 *(NE maps)*; BAY added
1 July 1899 *(Cl)*; replaced on deviation by new W B,
partly op 9 October 1910, fully 10 October 1911 *(Cl)*;
clo 10 September 1979 *(Cl)*; for conversion >
W BAY (b) [TWM] op 11 August 1980 *(Tyneside)*;
still open.

WHITLEY BRIDGE [LY]
op 1 April 1848 *(LY; co ½ T 7 September- line)*; still open.

WHITLINGHAM

WHITLINGHAM [GE] op 20 October 1874 *(T 21st)*;
clo 19 September 1955 *(BR ER internal notice August)*.
W JUNCTION until 1898 *(Brad)*; GE co tt 1914,
LNE tt 1933 and *Brad* to early 1955 at least:
W for THORPE ST ANDREW.
Also see THORPE & WHITLINGHAM.

WHITLOCKS END [GW] op 6 July 1936 *(T 25 June)*;
HALT until 6 May 1968 *(GW H)*; still open.
Pre-opening: Tile House Lane *(RAC)*.

WHITMORE [LNW] op 4 July 1837 *(T 6th)*;
clo 4 February 1952 *(RM March)*. W-HEATH in one
of descriptions of opening, *(T 6 July 1837)*.

WHITNEY-ON-WYE [Mid]
op 11 July 1864 *(Hereford J 16th)* as WHITNEY;
became W-on-the-WYE 4 March 1880, W-on-WYE
14 July 1924 *(Mid)*; clo 31 December 1962 *(T 31st)*.

WHITRIGG [Cal] op 1 October 1870 *(Sol J)*;
aot request; for clo see 1921 April/May★★.

WHITROPE SIDING [NB] (non-tt):
1 April 1914 NB wtt alterations shows 10am Church Train for railwaymen and families from here, and later return, 5 and 19 April; likely that would have been regular fortnightly service; clo 6 November 1967 *(U)* – same or more general railwaymen's use?; {Shankend – Riccarton}.

WHITSTABLE
WHITSTABLE op by [Canterbury & Whitstable] 4 May 1830** *(SE)*; clo 6 February 1846 for rebuilding by [SE] who had taken over line; reop 7 April 1846 *(T 13th/ Dover Chronicle)* *; replaced to south 3 June 1895 *(Hart p.59)*; became W HARBOUR 1 June 1899 *(hbl 13 July)*; clo 1 January 1931 (Thursday) *(T 4 December 1930)*.
* = reopening date is given as Monday 6 April by *Hart* and all seen in modern print but *T* reference given was 'Tuesday last' – was 6th a formal opening? – see entry on Canterbury West.

WHITSTABLE [LCD] op 1 August 1860 *(co n T 30 July)* as W; permanent station 13 July 1861 *(LCD)*; became W-on-SEA 1879 tt *(Cl)*, W TOWN 1 June 1899 *(hbl 13 July,* which gave old name just W); re-sited 32 chains east 1 January 1915 as W TOWN & TANKERTON *(SEC sig notice 49/1915)*; became W & T 1 February 1936 *(Cl)*, W 14 May 1979 *(Cl)*; still open.

WHITSTONE & BRIDGERULE [LSW]
op 1 November 1898 *(W Morn News 2nd)*; clo 3 October 1966 *(Cornish & DP 8th)*.

WHITTINGHAM [NE] op 5 September 1887 *(NE- line)*; clo 22 September 1930** *(T 10 July)*.

WHITTINGHAM Lancashire
– see Section 7 : 6 Hospitals.

WHITTINGTON near Oswestry
W HL [Cam] op 27 July 1864 *(Cam; co ½ T 1110/52- line)*; clo 4 January 1960 *(Cl)*.
W LL [GW] op 14 October 1848 *(Shrewsbury 13th)*; clo 12 September 1960 *(Cl)*.
HL and LL added 1 July 1924 *(GW circular 18 June)*.

WHITTINGTON near Sheffield [Mid] first in *Brad* October 1861; re-sited 10 chains north 9 June 1873 *(Mid)*; clo 4 February 1952 *(RM March)*; excursions to late 1970s (H.N. Twells, *150th Anniversary of the Opening of the North Midlands Railway ...*, *Derbyshire Times*, 1990).
Note that any reference to a third station 1876 should be ignored – probably result of company being late with information to RCH, thus making 1873 station look like two *(Mid)*.

WHITTLESEA [GE]
op 14 January 1847 *(Herapath 16th- line)*; still open.

WHITTLESFORD PARKWAY [GE]
op 30 July 1845 *(co n T 26th- line)*; P added 20 May 2007 tt; still open.

WHITTLESTONE HEAD – see ENTWISTLE.
WHITTON near Hounslow [SR]
op 6 July 1930 *(T 30 June)*; still open.
WHITTON near Scunthorpe [GC]
op 1 December 1910 *(RCG)*; clo 13 July 1925 *(Cl)*.
WHITWELL IoW [IWC] op 20 July 1897 *(Rtn- line)*; became HALT 1944a *hb* but not *Brad* until 1949/50; clo 15 September 1952 *(T 6 August)*.
Brad: W for NITON and CHALE ? to closure.

WHITWELL near Worksop
WHITWELL (a) [Mid] op 1 June 1875 *(Mid)*; clo 12 October 1964 *(RM November)*.
WHITWELL (b) op 25 May 1998 *(BLN 821)*; 'fun day' 24 May 1998; on same site as (a); still open.
WHITWELL & REEPHAM [MGN]
op 1 July 1882 *(MGN)*; clo 2 March 1959 *(T 2nd)*.
WHITWHAM [NE] (non-tt): unofficial stop; detail ?; {Lambley – Slaggyford} *(NhumbYoung)*.
WHITWICK [LNW] op 16 April 1883 *(LNW Officers 24577- line)*; clo 13 April 1931 *(LNW dates PCC 192)*.
WHITWORTH [LY]
op 1 November 1870 *(LY)*; clo 16 June 1947**.
WHITWORTH COLLIERY
– see CORRWG MERTHYR.
WHITWORTH COLLIERY near Spennymoor
– see last part of entry for BYERS GREEN.
WHITWORTH HALT – see TORYBANWEN.
WHYTELEAFE
WHYTELEAFE [SEC] op 1 January 1900 *(L)*; still open.
W SOUTH [SE] op 5 August 1856 *(L; co ½ T 30 August- line)* as WARLINGHAM; renamed 11 June 1956 *(JS)*; still open. According to *L* was W & CANE HILL until 1956, but not seen thus *Brad* and *hb*.

WICHNOR
WICHNOR [LNW] op 2 April 1855 (assumed as Mid; first in *Brad* November 1854 but no trains shown until April 1855); clo 1 November 1877 *(Cl; LNW Officers 17804, 16 October* – passenger receipts for August only £1 1s 11d so recommended closure from and after 1st of next month). LNW co tt 1864: W Junction with Midland.
W JUNCTION [Mid] op 2 April 1855 *(Mid)*; clo 1 August 1856 (Friday) *(Mid)*.
Perhaps two above were treated by some as single station. {Physical junction and Mid goods *IA*}.
WICK [High]
op 28 July 1874 *(High)*; still open. See 1957**.
WICK ST LAWRENCE [WCP]
op 1 December 1897 *(Bristol T 2nd- line)*; clo 20 May 1940 *(Bridgwater Merc 22nd)*.
WICKENBY [GC]:
line op 18 December 1848 *(GC)*, nd, February 1849; clo 1 November 1965 *(RM December)*.
WICKFORD [GE]
op 1 January 1889 *(D&C 3)*; still open.
Always W JUNCTION *hb*, but not seen thus *Brad*.
WICKHAM near Fareham [LSW]
op 1 June 1903 *(RCG; W Gaz, Hants edition 5th- line)*; clo 7 February 1955 *(Hants Chron 12th)*.
WICKHAM BISHOPS [GE]
op 2 October 1848 *(EC- line)*; see 1850 August 19**; aot request; B added 1 October 1913 *(hbl 23rd)*; clo 7 September 1964 *(RM October)*. Topham 1849, 1850 W MILL – not seen thus elsewhere.
WICKHAM MARKET [GE]
op 1 June 1859 *(T 2nd)*; still open. W M JUNCTION in *Brad* until 1878/9. GE co tt 1889, LNE tt 1930 and *Brad* ? to 1955: W M for CAMPSEA ASH.
WICKWAR [Mid] op 8 July 1844 *(Bristol T 13th)*; clo 4 January 1965 *(Mid)*.

WIDDRINGTON [NE]: line op 1 July 1847★★,
station shown August, first time line in tt; still open.

WIDFORD [GE]
op 3 July 1863 *(Hertford Merc 4th- line)*; aot request;
clo 16 November 1964 *(T 14 October; Cl)*.

WIDMERPOOL [Mid] op 2 February 1880 *(RCG)*;
clo 28 February 1949 *(RM May)*.

WIDNES {map 49}

WIDNES [LNW] op as RUNCORN GAP (see 1832 B★★);
replaced by new op 1 July 1852 *(Cl; T 10th- line)*;
renamed WIDNES 1 September 1864 *(Cl)*; re-sited on
deviation 1 March 1870 *(co ½ Rly Times 13 August)*;
renamed W SOUTH 5 January 1959 *(Cl)*;
clo 10 September 1962 *(RM September)*.
R GAP JUNCTION *Brad*, 1850s. LNW co tt 1868,
1875: W for R G. *Hb* December 1958a gave change to
W S –advance notice?

WIDNES [CLC] op 1 August 1873 *(T 4 September &
MSL co ½ T 21 January 1874)* as FARNWORTH for W;
became F for APPLETON 1914/15 *(Brad)*,
F W 1938/9 *(Brad)*, W NORTH 5 January 1959 *(Cl)*,
W 6 May 1968 *(Cl)*; still open.

W CENTRAL [GC/Mid] op 1 August 1879 *(Mid)*;
clo 5 October 1964 *(RM November)*. CENTRAL not
always added (e.g. only in one table *Brad* 1885) but
always in *hb*.
Also see TANHOUSE LANE.

WIDNEY MANOR [GW]
op 1 July 1899 *(RCG)*; still open. *RCH dist 9 May 1900*
said had been renamed from W to W M – change of
mind before opening? – W M in *Brad* July 1899.

WIGAN {map 48}

W CENTRAL [GC] op 1 April 1884 *(Wigan Obs 2nd,
item and tt)*; extended ½ mile to new station just south-
east, in Darlington Street 3 October 1892 *(GC dates)*;
clo 2 November 1964 *(RM December)*.
Just W in opening press tt and *Brad* until 1891/3.

W NORTH WESTERN [LNW] op 3 September 1832
(LNW), in Chapel Lane; re-sited about 100 yards north
on extension to Preston 31 October 1838 *(Cl)*;
N W added 2 June 1924 *(Rly Gaz 23 May)*; still open.

W WALLGATE [LY] op 20 November 1848 *(Liverpool
Mercury 14th)*; re-sited about ¼ mile west 26 May 1860
*(Ormskirk Advertiser 31s; LY Railway Society Journal,
October 2004,* reproducing contemporary item
describing previous station as 'hovel'); re-sited again,
short distance east, 2 February 1896 *(Wigan Examiner
5th)*; WALLGATE added 2 July 1924 *(Rly Gaz 23 May)*;
still open.

WIGHTON [LNE] op 1 February 1924 *(GE Journal
April 1983)*; HALT; clo 5 October 1964 *(RM Sept.)*;
{Walsingham – Wells-on-Sea}.

WIGSTON {map 61}

W GLEN PARVA [LNW] op 1 April 1884 *(LNW
Officers 25730)* as G P; WIGSTON added 1887 *(Cl)*;
clo 4 March 1968 *(Cl)*. SOUTH WIGSTON on
approximately this site later – see map.

W MAGNA [Mid] op 8 May 1857 *(Mid; co ½
T 13 August- line)*; new station 1901 *(Mid)*;
MAGNA added 2 June 1924 *(Rly Gaz 23 May)*;
clo 1 January 1968 *(RM February)*. Aot W EAST *(hb)*

– 1872 to 1890s, W JUNCTION in tt.

W SOUTH [Mid] op 30 June 1840 *(Mid; co n T 27th-
line)*; SOUTH added 1 October 1868 co tt *(Mid)*;
clo 1 January 1962 *(RM February)*.

WIGTON [MC] {map 20g}
op 10 May 1843 *(D&C 14; see 1840★★)*; still open.

WIGTOWN [PPW Jt] op 7 April 1875 *(Dumfries 9th)*;
clo 25 September 1950 *(Cl)*.

WILBRAHAM ROAD [GC] op 2 May 1892 *(GC)*
as ALEXANDRA PARK; renamed 1 July 1923
(T 27 August); clo 7 July 1958 *(LNW Record)*.

WILBURTON [GE]
op 16 April 1866 *(T 16th- line)*; clo 2 February 1931★★
(Cl); later excur *(GE Journal 2002)*.

WILBY [Mid-Suffolk Light] first in *Brad* July 1909;
clo 28 July 1952 *(T 28th)*.

WILDMILL
op 16 November 1992 *(BLN 696)*; closed same day for
safety reasons; reop 12 December 1992; still open.

WILEY – see WYLYE.

WILLASTON [LNW]: op 1 September 1858★★;
clo 6 December 1954 *(RM January 1955)*.

WILLENHALL

W BILSTON STREET [LNW] op 4 July 1837 *(T 6th)*
as W; renamed W BRIDGE 1 November 1872 *(Cl)*,
W 1 August 1881 *(Cl; LNW Officers 16 August 'approved')*,
W B S 2 June 1924 *(Rly Gaz 23 May)*;
clo 18 January 1965 *(RM March)*.

W STAFFORD STREET [Mid] op 1 November 1872
(Mid; co n T 1st- line) as W MARKET PLACE;
renamed W 1 April 1904 *(hbl 28th)*, W S S 2 June 1924
(Rly Gaz 23 May); clo 5 January 1931 *(Mid)*.

WILLERBY & KIRK ELLA [HB] op 27 July 1885
(op tt NER I); clo 1 August 1955 *(RM September)*.

WILLERSEY [GW] op 1 August 1904 *(GW H;
Chelt Chron 30 July- line)*; HALT; clo 7 March 1960
(RM April). {In *IA* as Willersley}.

WILLESDEN {maps 100, 102}

WILLESDEN [LNW] probably op between 1 January
1841 and 10 June 1841; report of accident at Harrow
(T 14 Nov. 1840) said warnings to stop other trains sent
to stations at Harrow, Watford and Camden; not in co's
December 1840 tt *(T 14 November)* but latter not
conclusive since even L&B company tts not always fully
detailed; on 10 June 1841 L&B Coaching & Police
Committee discussed possibility of station at Harrow
Road Bridge (later Sudbury/Wembley) and delayed
decision since there were doubts about need, 'considering
the vicinity of the stations of Harrow and of Willesden'
to the proposed site *(RAIL 384/22)*; first in *Brad* July
1842. Replaced, 53 chains south, by >

W JUNCTION main line [LNW] op 1 September 1866
(co n T 28 August); aot W J LL *(hb)* >

W JUNCTION HL [LNW] op 1 September 1866
(co n T 28 August); Kensington line platforms opened
2 September 1867, almost as separate station >
1866 changes also confirmed by *LNW Officers
Appendix A, 16 August.* >
Enlarged LL and modified HL into use 12 August 1894
(co ½ Rly Times 9 February 1885); still open.

W JUNCTION NEW op by [LNW] 15 June 1912 *(T 14th)*

for electric service; effectively an addition to W Main;
[Bak] added 10 May 1915; still open.
Original part, W J MAIN, clo 3 December 1962
(RM January 1963).
Now whole station treated as one in tt (is just W J).

WILLESDEN GREEN
WILLESDEN GREEN op by [Met] 24 November 1879
(T 22nd); W G & CRICKLEWOOD 1 June 1894 *(RCG)*
to 1938 *(Cl)*; transferred to [Bak] 20 November 1939;
transferred again, to [Jub] 1 May 1979; still open.
Also see DUDDING HILL.

WILLIAM PIT SIDING [CKP] (non-tt):
workmen's trains; to and from Workington; running by
April 1918; ceased ?; *(Lakeland)*.

WILLIAMSTOWN – see NORTH BERWICK.

WILLIAMWOOD [LMS] first in *Brad* starting 8 July
1929 *(Cl 29* says op 24 September 1928, but delay until
tt appearance seems too long – originally non-tt use –
e.g. workmen?); still open. HALT on LMS ticket *(JB)*
and in *hb* 1938, deleted 1949a, but not in *Brad*.

WILLINGDON – see HAMPDEN PARK.

WILLINGTON near Bedford [LNW] op 1 May 1903
(LNW Officers 40989); clo 1 January 1968 *(RM January)*.

WILLINGTON near Derby
For first station see REPTON.

WILLINGTON op 29 May 1995 *(RM August* photo-
caption); site of earlier Repton & Willington; still open.

WILLINGTON near Durham [NE] op 1 April 1857
(co ½ T 17 August- line); clo 4 May 1964 *(Cl)*.

WILLINGTON QUAY Newcastle [NE]
op 1 May 1879 *(Newcastle Weekly Chronicle 3rd- line)*;
clo 23 July 1973 *(RM August)*.

WILLITON [GW] op 31 March 1862 *(W Som F P 5 April)*;
clo 4 January 1971 *(Som Gaz 8th)*. See 2007 July 20**.

WILLOUGHBY near Skegness [GN]
op 3 September 1848 *(Boston 4th)*; re-sited 6 chains
north (from south to north of level crossing) 4 October
1886 *(Cl)*; clo 5 October 1970 *(T 16 July)*.

WILLOUGHBY – see BRAUNSTON.

WILMCOTE [GW] op 10 October 1860 *(W Mid;
T 11th- line)*; re-sited south of road overbridge
8 December 1907 *(Cl)*; still open.

WILMINGTON [NE] op 28 March 1864 *(NE- line)*;
briefly acted as Hull terminus of line to Hornsea;
re-sited 300 yards west 9 June 1912 *(Brad Sh 1913)* –
could now also be served by Withernsea trains;
clo 19 October 1964 *(Cl)*. According to *RM January*
became HALT 4 January but *Brad* just added note that
no staff were in attendance.

WILMSLOW [LNW] op 10 May 1842 (fare table,
co n Stockport 13th); additional platforms on Styal line
added when latter opened 1 May 1909; still open.

WILNECOTE [Mid] op 16 May 1842 *(Mid)* as
W & FAZELEY; renamed 1 April 1904 *(hbl 28th)*;
still open. *Hb* 1890 (only): WILNECOT & F.

WILPSHIRE
WILPSHIRE [LY] op 22 June 1850** as RIBCHESTER;
renamed 1874 tt *(Cl)*; clo 10 September 1962 *(T 5 July)*.
LY co tt 1899, LMS tt 1930 W for R and thus *Brad*/BR
tts to closure.
Also see RAMSGROVE & WILPSHIRE.

WILSDEN [GN]
op 1 July 1886 *(GN)*; clo 23 May 1955**.

WILSHAMPSTEAD [LMS] (non-tt):
ordnance depot; op 3 August 1941, from Bedford;
6 October 1941 – service from Luton added;
clo by May 1946 *(WW II)*.

WILSON [Mid] op 1 October 1869 co tt *(Mid)*;
clo 1 June 1871 (Thursday) *(Mid)*.

WILSONTOWN [Cal]
op 1 March 1867 *(Cal- line)*; see 1921 April/May**;
clo 10 September 1951 *(RM October)*.

WILSTHORPE CROSSING [LNE]
op 1 December 1933 *(RM January 1934)*; clo 18 June
1951 *(RM July)*; {Braceborough Spa – Thurlby}.
HALT on nameboard and in *hb* but not *Brad*.

WILSTROP SIDING [NE] first in *Brad* June 1865;
Saturdays only; last used 25 April 1931 (based on *Cl* –
clo 1 May); {goods *IA*}. First shown 'P' in *hb* 1895 and
there faint, as though added at last minute.

WILTON – see EBBERSTON.

WILTON near Salisbury
W NORTH [GW] op 30 June 1856 *(W Fly P 1 July)*;
clo 19 September 1955 *(RM November)*.
W SOUTH [LSW] op 2 May 1859 *(Salisbury 7th)*;
clo 7 March 1966 *(RM May)*.
NORTH and SOUTH added 26 September 1949 *(Cl)*.

WIMBLEDON
WIMBLEDON [LSW] op 21 May 1838 *(Salisbury 28th)*;
re-sited north of road bridge 21 November 1881 *(Cl)*;
W & MERTON until 1 June 1909 *(Cl)*; still open.
In 1840s sometimes just W in *Brad*, perhaps lack of
space, but also just W in *Topham* 1848–50 where there
was plenty of space. Just W *hb* 1872 on.
[Wimbledon & Croydon] had terminus of its own
when it opened 22 October 1855; this was absorbed in
main station during rebuilding in 1869. (See article by
A.A. Jackson, RCHS *Journal* July 1995).
W North station [Dist] op 3 June 1889 *(L)*; also used
by LSW from 1 July 1889; incorporated into main
station 1929 (LSW service involved ceased with effect
from 5 May 1941).
WIMBLEDON [Croydon] added 30 May 2000; still open.
W CHASE [SR] op 7 July 1929 *(RM September)*;
still open.
W PARK op 3 June 1889 for [Dist] trains *(L)*; [LSW]
service as at W North; originally owned by LSW;
transferred to London Underground 1 April 1994;
still open.
W STAFF (non-tt) [LSW]: HALT; op about 1915 as
DURNSFORD ROAD *(SR)* – by October 1915
Durnsford Road repair shops nearly completed *(LSW)*;
still open.
Also see SOUTH WIMBLEDON.

WIMBLINGTON [GN/GE]
op 1 March 1848 *(co ½ T 28 February- line)*; aot request;
clo 6 March 1967 *(RM April)*. EC co tt 1851 and *Brad*
until 1901/2: W for DODDINGTON.

WIMBORNE [LSW] op 1 June 1847 *(Dorset Chron
20 May, 3 June)*; clo 4 May 1964 *(Hants Chron 9th)*.

WINCANTON [SD Jt] op 3 February 1862**;
clo 7 March 1966 *(Shepton 11th)*.

WINCHBURGH [NB] op 21 February 1842 *(co n T 21st)*; clo 22 September 1930 *(Cl)*.

WINCHCOMBE [GW] op 1 February 1905 *(Chelt Exam 8th)*; clo 7 March 1960 *(RM April)*.

WINCHELSEA [SE]
op 13 February 1851 *(co n T 13th)*; clo 1 September 1851, probably reop 1 January 1852 – had been agreed on 4 December 1851 *(SE)*. HALT 12 September 1961 to 5 May 1969 *(Cl)*; still open.

WINCHESTER
WINCHESTER [LSW] op 10 June 1839 *(Salisbury 17th)*; W CITY 26 September 1949 to 10 July 1967 *(Cl)*; still open. W STATION HILL 1885/6 to 1916 *(Brad)*.
W CHESIL [GW] op 4 May 1885 *(Hants Chron 2nd)*; clo 7 March 1960 *(Hants Chron 5th)* except that still used summer Saturdays until 9 September 1961, last train, *(Cl)*. At first W; became W CHEESEHILL STREET 1885/6, W CHEESEHILL 1916 *(Brad)*, W CHESIL 26 September 1949 *(Cl)*. GW co tt added CHEESEHILL 1902/32; *hb* just W until 1956 (when W CHESIL).
W TROOP PLATFORM [LSW] (non-tt): used about 1918 to 1919; {Micheldever – Winchester} *(U)*.

WINCHFIELD [LSW] op 24 September 1838 *(co n T 20th)* as W & HARTLEY ROW; W by 1840 *(Brad)*; still open. At opening *Freeling* called it SHAPLEY HEATH. *Hb* 1904: W for HARTLEY WINTNEY. *Brad* ? to 1955: W for ODIHAM and H W.

WINCHMORE HILL [GN]
op 1 April 1871 *(L)*; still open.

WINCOBANK [Mid]
op 1 May 1868 wtt *(Mid)*; new station 1897/8 *(Mid)*; W & MEADOW HALL 1 July 1899 co tt to 18 June 1951 *(Mid)*; clo 2 April 1956 *(RM May)*.
WINDER [WCE]: op 1 February 1864**; last in *Brad* June 1874**; back May 1875; clo 13 April 1931 *(LNW Record)*; ROF Sellafield workers used, non-tt, 11 March to 8 April 1940 *(WW II)*.

WINDERMERE [LNW]
WINDERMERE op 21 April 1847 *(co ½ T 30 July)*; still open. *Brad* ? to 1955: W for BOWNESS and AMBLESIDE. BR local ticket for W TOWN *(JB)*.
W LAKE SIDE op 2 June 1869 *(Fur)* (1st was formal); reduced to summer only with effect from 26 September 1938; service summer 1941 one train each way, alternate Sundays; last trains 31 August 1941; reop, summer only, 3 June 1946 *(Cl)*; clo 6 September 1965 *(RM November)*. At times just L S.

WINDMILL END [GW]
op 1 March 1878 *(W Mid; co ½ T 23 February- line)*; HALT from 1952 tt *(Cl)*; clo 15 June 1964 *(RM July)*.

WINDMILL HILL – see GOSWICK.

WINDSOR & ETON
W & E CENTRAL [GW] op 8 October 1849 *(co n T 5th)*; & E added 1 June 1904 *(RCG)*; CENTRAL added 26 September 1949 *(Cl)*; still open. Joint GW/Dist service began 1 March 1883; GW only from 1 October 1885.
W & E RIVERSIDE [LSW] op 1 December 1849 *(Reading 1st)*; original station temporary; permanent 1 May 1851 *(LSW)* – same site?; & E added 10 December 1903 *(RCG)*; RIVERSIDE added 26 September 1949 *(Cl)*; still open.

WINDSOR BRIDGE [LY]
first in *Brad* about July 1841, all days (see 1838 May 29**); last in *Brad* November 1842; back September 1845 (first time detail given since July 1843), Wednesdays only; last October 1846; back (Blackburn –Bolton–Salford table) February 1850, Wednesdays only; last April 1850; back, Wednesdays only, January 1855; last June 1856 – still indexed 1857 but not found in body of book. Early on alternated with Pendleton; normally in Manchester–Bolton table; case where one-day use might have been more continuous than tt suggests. The report of an accident there on 21 October 1857 refers to cattle sidings *(Rtn)* – reason for Wednesday-only service?

WINDSOR COLLIERY [Rhy] (non-tt): HALT; agreement made 4 October 1943 for new colliers' platform on site of old (which had op?) *(Aber)*; clo 15 June 1964 *(U)*; {Abertridwr – Senghenydd}.

WINDYHILL – see HOUSTON.

WINESTEAD [NE]
op 27 June 1854 *(co ½ T September 4- line)*; clo 1 July 1904 (Friday) *(Cl)*.

WINGATE [NE]: line op 13 October 1846 *(NE maps)*, nd, August 1847; clo 9 June 1952**.

WINGFIELD [Mid]
op 11 May 1840 *(Mid)*; was W ALFRETON / W for A by 1 December 1848 co tt, to 1 May 1872 co tt *(Mid)*; clo 2 January 1967 *(Mid)*.

WINGFIELD VILLAS Plymouth [GW]
op 1 June 1904 *(W Morn News 1st, 2nd)*; HALT; clo June 1921 *(Cl)*; {map 114}.

WINGHAM [EK]
W CANTERBURY ROAD first in *Brad* June 1925; alias C R W >
W COLLIERY op 16 October 1916 *(co n EK)*; COLLIERY added 1917/18 *(Brad)*; HALT >
W TOWN first in *Brad* June 1925* >
All three clo 1 November 1948** *(RM January 1949)*.
* = EK-F&G (pp.109–10, 127, 130) says W TOWN in use, illegally, by 1920, though not separately shown in tt; inspection report of 1925 said in use for six or seven years; also on RCH Map of Southern England, 1920 but not in 1924 Distance Table.

WINKHILL [NS] first in *Brad* June 1910; HALT; clo 30 September 1935 *(Cl)*.

WINMARLEIGH – see NATEBY.

WINNERSH
WINNERSH [SEC] op 1 January 1910 *(SEC)* as SINDLESHAM & HURST; renamed 6 July 1930 *(SR)*; HALT until 5 May 1969 *(SR App)*; still open. *Brad* 1930 to 1955: W HALT for S and H.
W TRIANGLE op 12 May 1986 *(BLN 536)*; still open.

WINSCOMBE SOMERSET [GW] op 3 August 1869 *(Shepton 6th)*; op as WOODBOROUGH; renamed WINSCOMBE 1 December 1869 *(Cl)*, SOMERSET added 12 January 1906 *(hbl 25th)*; clo 9 September 1963 *(Weston 13th)*.

WINSFORD
WINSFORD [LNW] op 4 July 1837 *(co n GJ)*; still open.
W & OVER [CLC] op 1 July 1870, clo 1 January 1874 (Thursday), reop 1 May 1886, clo 1 December 1888, reop 1 February 1892 *(GC dates)*; clo 1 January 1931

(Thursday) *(co n Winsford & Over)*. Occasional Saturday football excursions until outbreak of WW2.

WINSLOW

WINSLOW [LNW]: line op 1 May 1850 *(co n T 1st)*, nd, July 1850; clo 1 January 1968 *(RM January)*. Used Saturdays in 1980s for 'Chiltern Shopper' specials: certainly used 24 November, 1, 8 and 15 December 1984; 16 November and 14 December 1985; 22 November, 6 and 13 December 1986 (BR handbills). 1852/3 to 1868/9 was W JUNCTION in *Brad* (acted as junction station until opening of Verney Junction) but not thus LNW co tts of that period seen.

W ROAD [Met/GC] op 23 September 1868 *(L; Rtn-line)*; see 27 March 1874★★; [Met] use added 1 July 1891 *(ug)*; clo 6 July 1936 *(RM July)*.

WINSON GREEN

WINSON GREEN [GW] op 14 November 1854 *(GW; co n 13th- line)* as SOHO; renamed S & W G 1893 tt *(Cl)*, W G 14 June 1965 *(Cl)*; clo 6 March 1972 *(RM April)*. *Hb*: always S & W G.

WINSON GREEN [LNW] op 1 November 1876 *(LNW Officers 16572)*; clo 16 September 1957 *(LNW Record)*.

WINSTON [NE]

op 9 July 1856★★; clo 30 November 1964 *(RM December)*. When fares were being fixed, prior to opening, minutes referred to this as STAINDROP. *Brad* to 1938/9 and *hb* always: W for S.

WINTERBOURNE [GW] op 1 July 1903 *(RCG; Bristol T 2nd- line)*; clo 3 April 1961 *(RM May)*.

WINTERINGHAM [GC] op 15 July 1907★ *(RCG)*; through platforms added 1 December 1910; clo 13 July 1925 *(Cl)*.

★ = pre-opening excursion on 13th (A.L. Barnett, *Light Railway King of the North*, RCHS, 1992).

WINTERSETT & RYHILL [GC]

op 1 September 1882 *(GC)* as R; renamed 1 March 1927 *(hbl April)*; clo 22 September 1930 *(Cl)*.

WINTERTON & THEALBY [GC]

op 3 September 1906 *(RCG)*; clo 13 July 1925 *(Cl)*. According to *RCG* opened as T, renamed 15 July 1907 but W & T in *Brad* October 1906.

WINTHORPE [Mid]

appeared in *Brad* November and December 1846 with one train, from Newark, calling; remained for some time (last July 1847) but no trains shown calling *(Mid)*; intended station never built? {Collingham – Newark}.

WINTON [NB] first in *Brad* July 1872; clo 1 July 1925 (Wednesday) *(co n Haddington)*.

WINTON PIER – see ARDROSSAN.

WINWICK QUAY [GJ] op between June 1831 and 4 July 1837. Not in *Brad* until about August 1840 (final attempt to find custom for poorly used station?) but existed from line opening *(Drake, 1838)*. Drake's statement is ambiguous because W Q is on section of line opened as Warrington branch in 1831, but he was writing about Grand Junction, which incorporated this stretch, 1837. Since casual nature of station was more in keeping with habits of LM, which operated line until 1837, probably safe to assume it opened before 1837 but not safe to say in 1831. Decision to close taken 25 November 1840 *(RAIL 220/3)* and immediate

closure could have occurred; main committee was rubber-stamping suggestion from sub-committee. *Cl* says clo 28 November 1840 (Saturday) – last day (?). It was still shown in *Brad* early 1841 – inertia? {map 50}.

WIRKSWORTH [Mid] op 1 October 1867 *(Mid)*; clo 16 June 1947★★. Later specials for Sunday School outings and the like. 25, 26, 27 May 1985 (Spring Bank Holiday) 5 or 6 trains per day from/to Derby for Well Dressing ceremony; repeated 1986 and 1987. Additionally in 1985 special from Plymouth on 1 September and shuttles from/to Derby 14th and 15th for Wirksworth Festival. (H. Sprenger, *The Wirksworth Branch*, Oakwood, 1987; *Midland Railway Society Wirksworth/Ripley Tour Notes 9 May 1998*).

WISBECH {map 66}

All were WISBEACH until 4 May 1877 *(Cl)*.

WISBECH [St Ives & Cambridge] op 3 May 1847 *(Wisbeach 1st)*; services diverted to next about 1852.

W EAST [GE] op 1 February 1848 *(co ½ T 17th)*; clo 9 September 1968 *(RM November)*; later excursions – e.g one to Scarborough in special notice of 1 July 1984 *(IU)*.

W NORTH [MGN] op 1 August 1866 *(Mid wtt, D&C 5)*; clo 2 March 1959 *(T 2nd)*.

EAST and NORTH added 27 September 1948 *(RM Nov.)*.

W ST MARY [MGN]: in wtt reproduced in *D&C 5* for line opening, 1 August 1866, but no trains calling; trains shown *Brad* September 1866, first time line shown there; clo 2 March 1959 *(T 2nd)*.

WISHAW [Cal]

WISHAW op 1 June 1880 *(Cal- line)*; W CENTRAL until 4 June 1965 *(Cl)*; still open.

W SOUTH: line op 8 May 1843 *(D&C 6)*, nd, May 1845; see 1835 C★★; SOUTH added 1 June 1880 *(Cl)*; clo 15 September 1958 *(RM October)*.

WISHFORD [GW] op 30 June 1856 *(W Fly P 1 July)*; clo 19 September 1955 *(RM November)*.

WISTANSTOW [SH Jt] op 7 May 1934 *(Cl 29)*; HALT; clo 11 June 1956 *(Cl)*; {Marsh Brook – Craven Arms}. GW/LMS ticket for WINSTANTSOW *(JB)*.

WISTASTON ROAD – see CREWE.

WISTOW [NE] op 16 February 1898 *(co n Cawood)*; clo 1 January 1930 (Wednesday) *(Cl)*; excursions until about 1945/6 *(Cawood)*.

WITHAM near Chelmsford [GE]

op 29 March 1843 *(T 30th)*; still open. W JUNCTION in *Brad* 1852/3 to 1879/80 (not all tables).

WITHAM SOMERSET [GW]

op 1 September 1856 *(GW; W Fly P 2nd- line)*; SOMERSET added 1958 tt *(Cl)*; clo 3 October 1966 *(W Daily Press 3rd)*. W FRIARY *hb* 1862, altered to W 1872.

WITHCALL [GN] op 1 August 1882 *(GN)*; clo 11 September 1939★★; reop 4 December 1939; clo 5 November 1951 *(RM December)*.

WITHERENDEN – see STONEGATE.

WITHERNSEA [NE] op 27 June 1854 *(co ½ T 4 September)*; clo 19 October 1964 *(Cl)*.

WITHINGTON near Hereford [GW]

op 13 September 1861 *(Hereford T 14th)*; clo 2 January 1961 *(RM February)*.

WITHINGTON & WEST DIDSBURY [Mid]
op 1 January 1880 *(RCG)* as WITHINGTON;
became W & ALBERT PARK 1 July 1884 co tt *(Mid)*,
W & W D 1 December 1914 *(hbl 28 January 1915)*;
clo 3 July 1961 *(RM August)*.

WITHINGTON GLOS [MSWJ] op 1 August 1891
(Chelt Exam 29 July); GLOS added 1 July 1924
(GW circular 18 June); clo 11 September 1961 *(T 9th)*.

WITHINS LANE [East Lancashire]
first in *Brad* August 1847; at first all days; last there
June 1849; back February 1850, now Saturdays only;
last December 1851; {Bury – Radcliffe Bridge}.

WITHNELL [LY/LU] op 1 December 1869**;
clo 4 January 1960 *(RM February)*.

WITHYHAM [LBSC] op 1 October 1866 *(co n T 1st)*;
clo 2 January 1967 *(RM February)*.

WITLEY [LSW] op 1 January 1859 *(SR; co n T 1st- line)*;
still open. Op as W & CHIDDINGFOLD;
became W for C 1912 ? *(hbl ref 24 October 1912)* and
thus LSW co tt 1914, W 6 October 1947 *(SR)*.

WITNEY [GW] op 14 November 1861 *(GW)*;
re-sited on extension to Fairford 15 January 1873 *(Cl)*;
clo 18 June 1962 *(T 18 May)*.

WITTERSHAM ROAD [KES] op 2 April 1900
(RM July); clo 4 January 1954 *(T 28 October 1953)*.

WITTON Birmingham [LNW] op 1 May 1876
(LNW Officers 15526); still open. Op as W; became
W for ASTON LOWER GROUNDS February 1878
(W Mid – used in public tts only), W & L G about 1903
(RCH dist ref 21 Sept. 1903), W for the VILLA GROUNDS
1 June 1912 *(LNW dates)*, W ? Hb 1949a said had
become W for VILLA PARK.

WITTON GILBERT [NE] op 1 September 1862
(Consett); clo 1 May 1939 *(Cl)*; later miners' gala use.

WITTON-LE-WEAR
W PARK op 25 August 1991 *(BLN 664)*;
site of earlier Etherley; summer Sundays only; last used
27 September 1992.

WITTON-LE-WEAR [NE] op 3 August 1847** and in
co tt September 1847 but not in *Brad* for some time;
re-sited 20 chains east 1852/5; -le-W added 1852 tt *(Cl)*;
clo 29 June 1953 *(RM August)*.

WITTON JUNCTION – see WEAR VALLEY J.

WIVELISCOMBE [GW] op 8 June 1871 *(W Som F
P 17th)*; clo 3 October 1966 *(Som Gaz 7th)*.

WIVELSCOMBE [GW] (non-tt):
workmen building deviation line; op 1905; clo by
November 1915; {Defiance – St Germans} *(U)*.

WIVELSFIELD [LBSC] op 1 August 1886 *(LBSC)*;
op as KEYMER JUNCTION, replacing, after slight
gap, earlier station of that name; renamed 1 July 1896
(RCG); still open.

WIVENHOE
WIVENHOE [GE] op 8 May 1863* *(T 11th)*; still open.
WYVENHOE in tt 1879 to 1911 *(Cl, JS)*, in hb 1877
and 1895–1904 (inclusive). 1949 photograph shows
station nameboard as W & ROWHEDGE.
* = *T 11th* and co ½ *T 21 September* gave 8th; *T 4th* said would
be opened that day and *Herapath 11th / Suffolk Chronicle 9th*
said did open 4th. Did some last minute delay fool journalists?
WIVENHOE [Brightlingsea]: owing to dispute with GE,

company operated its own line briefly; they put up
platform of own, 200 yards before main station,
passengers walking between. Op 1 August 1876;
clo 1 September 1877. (P. Paye, *The Brightlingsea Branch*,
John Masters, 1997).

WIXFORD [Mid] op 17 September 1866 *(Mid; Rtn-
line)*; original was temporary station, replaced ? *(Mid)*;
clo 2 January 1950 *(LNW Record)*.

WNION [GW] op 5 June 1933 *(Cl 29)*; HALT;
clo 18 January 1965** *(RM March)*;
{Drws-y-Nant – Bontnewydd}.

WOBURN SANDS [LNW] op 18 November 1846**;
SANDS added 1 February 1860 *(co notice, loose in
LNW Record)*; still open.

WOKING [LSW] op 21 May 1838 *(Salisbury 28th)*;
still open. W COMMON in opening notice; in early days
that and W used indiscriminately, e.g. – in December
1842 *Brad* W in table but notes have reference for
passengers going west of W C. JUNCTION was used
similarly; there were occasional references early in *Brad*:
e.g. W J one way November 1848. The hb made it W J in
1904, back to W 1914a and there are RCH references
to a return to W about April 1913 but it was not thus in
Brad at that time. It was W J in wtt 1909 but not wtt
1857, public tt 1914. *Brad* 1913/14 to 1955:
W for CHOBHAM, though in August.

WOKINGHAM [SE]
op 4 July 1849 *(SR; Hants Chron 7th- line)*; still open.

WOLDINGHAM [CO Jt]
op 1 July 1885 *(L)* as MARDEN PARK;
renamed 1 January 1894 *(hbl 25th)*; still open.

WOLFERTON [GE] op 3 October 1862 *(T 6th)*;
WOLVERTON until 15 July 1863 *(Cl)*; clo 5 May 1969
(RM July, photo-caption). Royal retiring rooms opened
1898; converted into museum 1980; closed 1990.

WOLFS CASTLE [GW]
op 1 October 1913 *(GW H)*; HALT, aot request,
daylight only; clo 6 April 1964* *(Cl)*; {map 81}.
* = according to *hba* May 1948 and cumulative *hba* December
1948 this was 'closed' but trains shown *Brad* August 1948 and
October 1949 – error?

WOLLATON COLLIERY [Mid] (non-tt):
PLATFORM; op 31 March 1913;
clo 6 July 1936 wtt; *(Mid)*.

WOLLERTON [GW]
op 2 November 1931 *(Cl 29)*; HALT;
clo 9 September 1963 *(T 9th)*; {Hodnet – Tern Hill}.

WOLSINGHAM [NE] op 3 August 1847** – in co tt
September 1847 but not in *Brad* for some time;
clo 29 June 1953 *(RM August)*. Hb: shown 'P' until
1904; 1912–25 goods only; 1927a 'add P'; regarded as
halt for some years?

WOLVERCOT(E)
WOLVERCOT [GW] op 1 February 1908 *(Oxford Chron
31 January)* – RCG gives 13 July 1912 (probably when
promoted from HALT to PLATFORM, though *Brad*
for some time after used mixture of 'Halt' and 'Platform');
clo 1 January 1916 (Saturday) *(Cl)*.

WOLVERCOTE [LNW] op 9 October 1905 *(Oxford
Chron 6th)*; see 1905** (a); clo 1 January 1917
(T 22 December 1916); reop 5 May 1919 *(RCH)*;

clo 25 October 1926 *(Cl)*. In local press co notice as
WOOLVERCOT and thus in *Brad* until June 1906 *(JS)*.

WOLVERHAMPTON {map 98}
For first station of this name see
WEDNESFIELD HEATH.

WOLVERHAMPTON [Shrewsbury & Birmingham]
temporary at Wednesfield Road, on down running line
just outside LNW station, op 13 November 1849 (see
1849**); continued to be used until opening of Stour
Valley line as 'drop station' for passengers wishing to
continue journeys by GJ (M. Hale, *Chron December
1996)* but effectively replaced by >

WOLVERHAMPTON [LNW] op 1 December 1851
(P. Collins, *Rail Centres – Wolverhampton*, Ian Allan); also
used by Stour Valley trains from 1 July 1852; still open.
Originally W; QUEEN STREET added September
1853 in announcements and fare tables but not always
public tts – was in LNW co tt 1875; alias W GENERAL
(local press); HL added erratically – in LNW co tts
from 1875/82 while LMS tts at times W in main line
tables, HL for connections; HL dropped 7 May 1973.
Hb: 1862 W; 1863a Q STREET same as W;
1895 W MILL STREET but this should have been
applied to goods only; 1904 W HL.
W LL [GW] op 1 July 1854 *(co ½ T 28 August)*;
LL added April 1856 co tt *(W Mid)*, 1872 hb;
clo 6 March 1972 *(RM April)*.
W STAFFORD ROAD [Shrewsbury & Birmingham]
first in *Brad* October 1850; probably clo July 1852
following accident, though isolated reference in *Brad*
March 1854 (error?); {probably at site of later Stafford
Road Junction}.
Also at/near Stafford Road from November 1854 tt to
end 1859 there was an exchange platform for attaching
carriages from HL to northbound trains from LL
(no service in reverse direction); no public access
and no reason for passengers to alight here.

WOLVERTON [LNW] op 17 September 1838
(T 18th); re-sited 17 chains south early; again re-sited,
on deviation, 1 August 1881 *(Cl)*; still open.
LNW co tt 1875: W for STONEY STRATFORD.
LNW co tt 1882, LMS tt 1930 and *Brad*/BR tts until
1966/8: W for STONY S.

WOMBOURN [GW] op 11 May 1925 *(hbl 56)*;
clo 31 October 1932 *(RM January 1933)*; {map 96}.

WOMBWELL
WOMBWELL [Mid] op 1 July 1897 *(RCG)*;
W WEST to 20 February 1969 *(JS – BR ER commercial
circular of this date – 'forthwith')*; still open.
W CENTRAL [GC] first in *Brad* August 1851; CENTRAL
added 25 September 1950 *(Rly Obs October)*; for clo see
1959** *(RM August* – clo except for special excursions}.

WOMERSLEY [LY]: line op 6 June 1848** *(LY)*, nd,
September 1848 *(Topham)*; clo 10 March 1947 *(Cl)*.

WOOBURN GREEN [GW]
op 1 August 1854 *(co n T 31 July)*; WOBURN G until
1872 tt *(Cl)*; clo 4 May 1970 *(Cl)*.

WOOD END near Warwick [GW]
op 1 July 1908 *(RCG; T 2nd- line)*;
PLATFORM until 7 July 1924 *(GW H)*; still open.

WOOD END [Mid] near Sutton-in-Ashfield
– see WHITEBOROUGH.

WOOD GREEN London
WOOD GREEN [Picc] op 19 September 1932 *(T 16th,
20th)*; still open.
Also see ALEXANDRA PALACE; PALACE GATES.

WOOD GREEN OLD BESCOT [LNW]
op 1 February 1881 *(LNW Officers 21846)*; site of
earlier Bescot Bridge; clo 5 May 1941 *(LNW Record)*.
Hb 1883: W G for WEDNESBURY; 1890 W G O B.

WOOD LANE – see WHITE CITY.

WOOD SIDING [Met/GC]
op January 1872 *(L; see 1871**)*; request; not shown 'P'
until hb 1879a; [Met] use began 1 December 1899;
clo 1 December 1935 (Sunday) *(RCH)*.

WOOD STREET – see WALTHAMSTOW.

WOODBOROUGH near Andover [GW]
op 11 November 1862 *(co n Marlborough 8th)*;
clo 18 April 1966 *(RM May)*.

WOODBOROUGH – see WINSCOMBE.

WOODBRIDGE [GE]
op 1 June 1859 *(T 2nd)*; still open.

WOODBURN [NB] op 1 May 1865 *(co n Nhumb)*;
clo 15 September 1952 *(RM October)*.

WOODBURY ROAD – see EXTON.

WOODCHESTER [Mid] op 1 July 1867 *(Mid;
Stroud J tt 6th)*; clo 16 June 1947**.

WOODCROFT [SR] (non-tt):
Naval Home; alias DITCHAM PARK; op 26 August
1943 *(Cl 29; SR sig inst 2 September 1943 'has been
brought into use')*; HALT; clo July 1946 (G. Pryor,
SR layout diagrams); {Petersfield – Rowlands Castle}.

WOODEND near Whitehaven [WCE Jt]
op 1 July 1857 *(D&C 14; co ½ T 1 September- line)*;
clo 7 January 1935 *(RM February)*; reop 11 March 1940
for ROF workers *(WW II)*, to public 6 May 1946 *(RM
July/August)*; clo 16 June 1947**; non-tt workmen's use
shown 23 May 1949 wtt, to/from Sellafield;
clo 1955 or 1965 *(WW II)*; later excur.
Became W for CLEATOR and BIGRIGG 9 August
1898 *(RCG)*; thus LNW co tt 1909, LMS tt 1930.

WOODFIELD [LY] op 1 June 1874 *(LY)*;
clo 1 July 1874 (Wednesday) *(RCG)*.

WOODFORD London
WOODFORD op by [GE] 22 August 1856 *(co n T 22nd)*;
transferred to [Cen] 14 December 1947 *(T 17th)*; still
open. GE co tt 1914: W for WOODFORD BRIDGE.
Also see SOUTH WOODFORD.

WOODFORD HALSE [GC]
op 15 March 1899 *(GC; T 16th- line)* as W & HINTON;
renamed 1 November 1948 *(RM January 1949)*;
clo 5 September 1966 *(RM October)*.

WOODGATE [LBSC] op 8 June 1846 *(LBSC;
Hants Chron 13th- line)*; last in body of tt May 1864
(indexed later); {Arundel – Chichester}.
Erratically in *Brad* as BOGNOR, W, B for W, W for B.

WOODGRANGE PARK [LTS]
op 9 July 1894 *(L)*; still open.

WOODHALL near Greenock [LMS]
op 1 October 1945 *(RM March)*; HALT until 15 April
1966 tt; still open.

WOODHALL [GN]

W JUNCTION op 17 October 1848 *(co n T 16th)*
clo 5 October 1970 *(Cl)*. In *T* notice as KIRKSTEAD
& HORNCASTLE but just K in *Brad* until 1854/5;
& H soon dropped (opening of Horncastle branch,
11 August 1855?); became W J 10 July 1922 *(hbl 13th)*.

W SPA op 11 August 1855 *(GN; T 9th- line)*;
clo 11 September 1939**, reop 4 December 1939;
clo 13 September 1954 *(RM October)*.

WOODHALL COLLIERY CO'S PLATFORM
[NB] (non-tt) op 1 July 1907 *(D. Stirling – BoT*
provisional approval given June) though *Haddington*
says first trains did not call until 16 July;
clo 18 November 1907; occasional later use;
{near Pencaitland} *(Haddington)*.

WOODHAM FERRERS
– see SOUTH WOODHAM FERRERS.

WOODHAY [GW] op 4 May 1885 *(Hants Chron 2nd)*;
clo 4 August 1942**, reop 8 March 1943 *(Cl)*;
clo 7 March 1960 *(Hants Chron 5th)*.

WOODHEAD [GC] op 8 August 1844 *(GC)*;
clo 27 July 1964 *(RM October)*.

WOODHILL ROAD [LY]

WOODHILL ROAD (a) op 3 July 1905 *(Manchester
Guardian 30 June)*; HALT; clo 1 April 1918 *(Cl)*.
LY ticket for BURY W R *(JB)*.

WOODHILL ROAD (b) op 26 February 1934 *(LNW
Record)*; opposite side of road from earlier *(AB – local
information confirmed by OS map)*. Clo 5 May 1952
(RM June); {Bury – Brandlesholme Road}.

WOODHOUSE

WOODHOUSE [GC] first in *Brad* October 1850; re-sited
about 700 yards west 11 October 1875 *(GC dates)*;
still open. Aot WOODHOUSE JUNCTION in *Brad*.

W MILL [Mid] op 6 April 1841**; clo 21 September
1953 *(RM October)*.

WOODKIRK [GN] op 1 August 1890 *(RCG)*;
clo 25 September 1939 *(Cl)*.

WOODLAND [Fur] op 18 June 1859 *(Kendal
Mercury 25th)*; clo 6 October 1958 *(LNW Record)*.

WOODLAND PARK [LNW] op 28 August 1905
(RCG) as RHUDDLAN ROAD; renamed 11 May
1923 *(LNW dates)*; clo 22 September 1930 *(Cl)*.

WOODLANDS ROAD

WOODLANDS ROAD [LY] op 3 March 1913 *(LY)*;
see 1905** (b); clo 15 July 1991 *(BLN 665)* for
conversion to >

WOODLANDS ROAD [Manch] op 6 April 1992
(BLN 681); still open.

WOODLESFORD [Mid]
op 1 July 1840 *(Mid; co n T 27 June- line)*; still open.

WOODLEY near Stockport [GC/Mid]
op 5 August 1862 *(Mid)*; still open.
W JUNCTION in *hb* 1867 (only).

WOODLEY, Monklands – alias for BOTHLIN
VIADUCT, see 1844 December 26**.

WOODMANSTERNE [SR]
op 17 July 1932 *(sig inst 30/1932)*; still open.

WOODNESBOROUGH [EK]

WOODNESBOROUGH op 16 October 1916 *(co n EK)*
as W & HAM MILL COLLIERY; renamed

W COLLIERY 1917 *(RCG ref July)*, W 1925 tt;
clo 1 November 1948** *(RM January 1949)*.
HAM MILL sometimes one word. DRENOLDS
DROVE in press account of opening *(EK F&G)*.
Also see ROMAN ROAD WOODNESBOROUGH.

WOODSFORD CROSSING [LSW] (non-tt):
HALT; op 3 May 1919 for workmen at Royal Naval Air
Station; clo September 1926; {Moreton – Dorchester}
(LSW).

WOODSIDE Aberdeen [GNS] op 1 January 1858
(GNS); clo 5 April 1937 *(RM January 1938)*.

WOODSIDE Croydon:

WOODSIDE [SE] first in *Brad* July 1871; became
W & SOUTH NORWOOD 1 October 1908 *(RCG)*,
W SURREY 2 October 1944 *(SR)* – and thus *Brad*
December 1944, W 1955 *(Brad)*; clo 1 June 1997**
for conversion to >

WOODSIDE [Croydon] op 23 May 2000; still open.

WOODSIDE – see BURRELTON; HORSFORTH.

WOODSIDE PARK
op by [GN] 1 April 1872 *(L; co ½ T 12 August- line)* as
TORRINGTON PARK; renamed T PW 1 May 1872
(at first T P & W in *Brad*), W P 1 May 1882 *(Cl)*,
W P for NORTH FINCHLEY 1 February 1894 *(hbl
26 April)* and thus GN co tt 1909 and LNE tt 1927,
'for N F' dropped ?; transferred to [Nor] 14 April 1940;
still open.

WOODSMOOR
op 1 October 1990 *(D&C 7)*; still open.

WOODSTOCK/WOODSTOCK ROAD Oxford
– see BLETCHINGTON; KIDLINGTON.

WOODSTOCK ROAD [NSWJ]
op 8 April 1909 *(L)*; clo 1 January 1917 *(T 26 December
1916)*; {on branch to Hammersmith & Chiswick}.
Shown as HALT in lists of closures *(T 22 December 1916;
RCH July 1921)* – see 1905**.

WOODVALE [CLC] op 1 September 1884 *(CLC)* as
WOODVILLE & AINSDALE; renamed 1 May 1898
(hbl 28 April); clo 1 January 1917 *(T 23 December 1916)*;
reop non-tt for races at Aintree in March 1919;
reop fully 1 April 1919 *(RCH)*; clo 7 January 1952
(RM February).

WOODVILLE [Mid] op 1 May 1883 *(Mid)*;
clo 6 October 1947 but summer Saturday use to
8 September 1962 *(Cl)* and football excursions (Derby
County) – certainly 1960/1 season *(BR doc)*,
and later – one 27 October 1962 *(AB)*.
1890 and 1895 *hb*: W NEW (old was goods only).

WOODVILLE ROAD [TV]
op July 1906 *(GW H)* as CATHAYS W R; see 1904**;
CATHAYS dropped 15 September 1952 *(Cl)*;
clo 15 September 1958 *(RM November)*;
{Cardiff – Llandaf}. Only one platform, on line from
Cardiff; anyone wishing to travel to Cardiff had to go
via Maindy. TV ticket for C W R BRIDGE *(JB)*.

WOODY BAY [Lynton] (ng)
op 16 May 1898 *(N Devon J 19th- line)*; WOODA BAY
until 1902 tt *(JS)*; clo 30 September 1935**.

WOOFFERTON [SH Jt]
op 6 December 1853**; clo 31 July 1961 *(RM September)*.
Sometimes W JUNCTION in some tables *Brad* until

1901/2 and LNW co tts 1860s;
sometimes WOOFERTON early in all sources.

WOOKEY [GW] first found with trains in tt
Bridgwater Merc 1 February 1871 *(Brad* March);
clo 9 September 1963 *(Weston 13th)*.

WOOL [LSW] op 1 June 1847 *(Dorset Chron 20 May,*
3 June); still open. LSW co tt 1914: W for
LULWORTH COVE and thus *Brad* to 1955.

WOOLASTON [GW] op 1 June 1853 *(Glos Chron 4th)*;
clo 1 December 1954 (Wednesday) *(Cl)*.

WOOLER [NE] op 5 September 1887 *(NE- line)*;
clo 22 September 1930** *(T 10 July)*.

WOOLFOLD [LY] op 6 November 1882 *(LY)*;
clo 5 May 1952 *(RM June)*.

WOOLHAMPTON – see MIDGHAM.

WOOLLEY [Ashover] (ng) op 7 April 1925
(RM October); clo 14 September 1936** *(Cl)*; {map 59}.

WOOLSTON [LSW]
op 5 March 1866 *(Salisbury 10th- line)*; still open.

WOOLWICH [SE]
W ARSENAL probably op 1 December 1849 (not in
co n T 29 October for alterations starting 1 November;
was in notice dated 29 November for alterations
1 December); still open. About 1851 sometimes known
as EAST W – ticket thus *(JB)*; also reference *SE p. 78*,
assumed from SE minutes.
W DOCKYARD op 30 July 1849 *(T 31 July* and
20 September); DOCKYARD added when Arsenal
opened; became one word 1909 body, index earlier
(Brad); still open.
Non-tt: summer 1865 Queen Victoria went to Continent,
embarking (7 August) and returning (8 September) at
T Pier, Woolwich Arsenal. Train taken from just east of
Plumstead to pier on line laid during Crimean War.
Chief officials of SE worried by state of track and tried
to dissuade from using on return. Paper said permanent
line would be laid for her use (was it?). *(T 7, 9 August;*
5, 9 September).
Also see NORTH WOOLWICH; Section 7, Non-rail.

WOOPERTON [NE] op 5 September 1887
(NE- line); clo 22 September 1930** *(T 10 July)*.

WOOTTON IoW [IWC]: line op 20 December 1875,
nd; W probably later (see 1875**); first in *Brad* June
1876; clo 21 September 1953 *(T 21st)*; [IWC].

WOOTTON – see NORTH WOOTTON.

WOOTTON BASSETT [GW]
W B ROAD temporary terminus op 17 December 1840
(Bristol Stand 24th); HAY LANE in GW records before
opening *(GW)*; replaced 2¾ miles west, underline after line had
been extended, by >
WOOTTON BASSETT op 30 July 1841 (Friday) *(Cl)*;
clo 4 January 1965 *(RM February)*.
Sometimes W BASSET early *Brad, hb.*

WOOTTON BROADMEAD [LNW]
op 30 October 1905**; clo 1 January 1917 *(T 22 Dec.*
1916); reop 5 May 1919 *(RCH)*; clo 5 May 1941
(LNW Record); used by railwaymen until 1952 or later.

WOOTTON PILLINGE – see STEWARTBY.

WOOTTON RIVERS [GW]
op 24 September 1928 *(GW H)*; HALT;
clo 18 April 1966 *(RM May)*; {Pewsey – Savernake}.

WOOTTON WAWEN [GW]
op 1 July 1908 *(RCG; T 2nd- line)*;
PLATFORM until 6 May 1974 *(GW H)*; still open.

WORCESTER
W FOREGATE STREET [GW] op 17 May 1860 *(GW)*;
still open.
W SHRUB HILL [GW/Mid] op 5 October 1850 *(T 7th)*;
initially served by shuttle service from Spetchley,
requiring reversal at Abbots Wood Junction *(BG)*; still
open. *Worcester* mentions 'station at Tallow Hill' – local
name for this one? temporary station, soon replaced
by Shrub Hill?
Brad and GW co tts initially only usually added F S and
S H in tables where trains called at both. Nameboard at
station had S H added 1903 – to be fixed at once, 6 May;
finished 15 October *(GW/Mid Officers' minutes)*.
Also see HENWICK.

WORCESTER JUNCTION
– see ABBOTS WOOD JUNCTION.

WORCESTER PARK [LSW] op 4 April 1859 *(L;*
co n T 5th- line) as OLD MALDEN & W P in co tts
(M & W P *Brad*), renamed W P 1862 tt *(JS)*; still open.

WORKINGTON
WORKINGTON [LNW] op 19 January 1846
(Whitehaven Herald 20 March 1847 – looking back on
opening of next stretch); W MAIN 2 June 1924 *(Rly*
Gaz 23 May) to 6 May 1968 tt; still open.
W BRIDGE [LNW]: line op 28 April 1847 *(co ½*
T 5 August) but not in 1 May 1847 tt *(Workington Herald)*.
First seen May 1848 tt *(Topham)*; clo 1 January 1951
(RM February).
W CENTRAL [CW Jn] op 1 October 1879 *(D&C 14;*
Rtn- line); CENTRAL added 16 July 1880 *(Cl)*;
clo 13 April 1931 *(LNW Record)*.

WORKSOP [GC]
op 17 July 1849 *(co n Stockport 20th)*; still open.

WORLE
WORLE (a) [GW] op 1 March 1884 *(hbl 16 June)*;
clo 1 January 1922 *(RCG)*.
WORLE (b) op 24 September 1990 *(Weston 28th)*; still
open.
W TOWN [WCP] op 1 December 1897 *(Bristol T 2nd-*
line) as W; became W MOOR LANE 1913 *(Brad)*,
W TOWN 1 November 1917 *(RCG* – direct from W);
clo 20 May 1940 *(Bridgwater Merc 22nd)*.
Also see PUXTON.

WORLESTON [LNW]: line op 1 October 1840**,
nd, June 1842; op as NANTWICH;
renamed WORLASTON 1 September 1858 *(RCG)*,
spelling altered 1862 tt *(Cl)*; clo 1 September 1952 *(RM*
October). LNW co tt 1852 had N Station (to emphasise
not actually at N?); *Brad* 1853 had note that passengers
for Nantwich would find Crewe more convenient.

WORLINGTON GOLF LINKS [GE]
op 20 November 1922 *(RM April 1923)* as
MILDENHALL G L; renamed 1 January 1923
(P. Paye, *Mildenhall Branch*, Oakwood, 1988); HALT;
clo 18 June 1962 *(RM August)*; {Isleham – Mildenhall}.

WORLINGWORTH [Mid-Suffolk Light]
op 29 September 1908 *(T 28th- line)*;
clo 28 July 1952 *(T 28th)*.

WORMALD GREEN [NE]
op 1 September 1848 *(NE)*; clo 18 June 1962 *(RM July)*.
WORMIT [NB] op 1 May 1889 (A.F. Nisbet –
Back Track vol.13); clo 5 May 1969 *(RM June)*.
WORMWOOD SCRUB(B)S
– see ST QUINTIN PARK.
WORPLESDON [LSW]
op 1 March 1883 *(SR)*; still open.
WORSBOROUGH BRIDGE (non-tt):
works outings – e.g. 1 September 1968 *(RM December)*;
{Wombwell – Penistone}.
WORSLEY [LNW]
op 1 September 1864**; clo 5 May 1969 *(RM June)*.
WORSTEAD [GE]
op 20 October 1874 *(T 21st)*; still open.
WORTHING
WORTHING [LBSC] op 24 November 1845 *(T 26th)*;
re-sited 100 yards west 1869; W CENTRAL 5 July 1936
(hbl May) to 4 March 1968 *(Cl)*; still open.
Also see WEST WORTHING.
WORTHINGTON [Mid] op 1 October 1869 *(Mid)*;
clo 22 September 1930 *(Mid)*; army camp (non-tt) use
19 November 1939 to 1 January 1945 *(U)*.
WORTHY DOWN [GW] op, non-tt, for army camp
1 April 1918 *(GW H)*; first in public tt October 1920;
clo 4 August 1942**, reop 8 March 1943 *(Cl)*;
PLATFORM until 18 June 1951 *(Cl)*, then HALT;
clo 7 March 1960 *(Hants Chron 5th)*.
WORTLEY near Sheffield [GC] op 14 July 1845
(GC); clo 2 May 1955 *(RM June)*.
WORTLEY near Leeds – see FARNLEY.
WORTWELL [GE]
op 2 November 1860**; request; clo 1 January 1878
(Tuesday) *(Cl)*; {Harleston – Homersfield}.
WOTTON
WOTTON [Met/GC] op January 1872 *(L; see 1871**)*;
[Met] use began 1 December 1899;
clo 1 December 1935 (Sunday) *(RCH)*.
WOTTON [GC] op 2 April 1906 *(RCG)*;
clo 7 December 1953 *(RM January 1954)*.
WRABNESS [GE]: line op 15 August 1854**, nd,
October 1854; aot request; still open.
WRAFTON [LSW] op 20 July 1874 *(N Devon J 23rd)*;
clo 5 October 1970 *(N Devon J 8th)*.
WRAGBY [GN] op 1 December 1876 *(RCG)*;
clo 11 September 1939**, reop 4 December 1939;
clo 5 November 1951 *(RM December)*.
WRANGATON [GW] op 5 May 1848 *(Woolmer 13th)*;
KINGSBRIDGE ROAD 1849 *(Cl)* to 1 July 1895
(hbl 11th); clo 2 March 1959 *(RM April)*.
At first WRANGERTON in local press and *Brad* but
not in South Devon co tt.
WRANGLE – see OLD LEAKE.
WRAY [North Western] op 17 November 1849 *(co n
Lancaster 17th)*; full service ended with effect from
1 June 1850 (Saturday) but Saturday service for
Lancaster market continued to be shown in separate
market tt in *Lancaster*, last shown paper of
21 September 1850; since this was last time market
table was included, possible that this use continued;
{Hornby – Wennington}.

WRAYSBURY [LSW]: line op 22 August 1848 *(co n
T 21st)*; not included in journalist's description of
formal opening *(T 24 July)*, oversight? station added at
last moment? – was in *Brad* and *Topham* September;
re-sited about ¼ mile nearer Staines 1 April 1861 *(Cl)*;
still open.
WRAYSHOLME [Fur] (non-tt):
HALT; op 1910; for use of Territorials *(SLS/Manchester
Loco Society Rail Tour Notes, 27 August 1961)*;
clo about 1922 *(U)*; {Kents Bank – Cark}.
WREA GREEN [PW] first in *Brad* June 1847;
WRAY G until 1875 tt *(Cl)*; clo 26 June 1961 *(RM Aug.)*.
WREAY [LNW] first in *Brad* January 1853;
clo 16 August 1943 *(Cl)*.
WRENBURY [LNW]
op 1 September 1858**; aot request; still open.
WRESSLE [NE]: see 1840 July 2** for opening and
some early details; first certain reference June 1843
(Tuck); at first market days only; full use September
1855 *(Brad)*; still open.
First in *Brad* as WENPEL BRIDGE, corrected by end
of 1844 to WRESSEL/WRESSLE B, BRIDGE
dropped with full service, though WRESSEL still
sometimes found – e.g. NE co tt 1861.
WRETHAM & HOCKHAM [GE]
op 18 October 1869 *(GE- line)*; & H added 1 November
1893 *(hbl 26 October)*; clo 15 June 1964 *(Cl)*.
WREXHAM {map 75}
W CENTRAL [Cam/WMCQ] op 1 November 1887
(RCG) – free travel first day *(GC)*; re-sited 400 yards
nearer General, for shopping development,
23 November 1998 *(RM August 1999)*; still open.
W EXCHANGE [WMCQ] op 1 May 1866 *(T 7th)* >
W GENERAL [GW] op 4 November 1846** >
EXCHANGE and GENERAL amalgamated 1 June
1981; still open as W GENERAL.
WRIGHT GREEN – see LAMPLUGH.
WRINGTON [GW] op 4 December 1901 *(Wells 5th)*;
clo 14 September 1931 *(Cl)*.
WROTHAM – see BOROUGH GREEN.
WROXALL [IoW] op in November 1866 (receipts
first shown – *IoW M&S*; first in *Brad* December);
clo 18 April 1966 *(RM March)*.
Brad ? to 1955: W for APPLEDURCOMBE.
WROXHAM – see HOVETON.
WRYDE [MGN] op 1 August 1866 *(op wtt D&C 5)*;
clo 2 December 1957 *(Cl)*.
WYCOMBE
– see HIGH WYCOMBE; WEST WYCOMBE.
WYDDFA – see SNOWDON SUMMIT.
WYE [SE]: line op 6 February 1846 (see note on
Canterbury West), station probably later*; temporary
platform by April 1846 *(SE)*; first in *Brad* July 1846;
still open.
Aot separate race platform, separated from main by
level crossing; racecourse opened March 1882, closed
in 1974 *(AB)*.
* = *Kentish Gazette* description included mention of view of
pretty town of Wye at which company intended to build
station, and the only stations are Chilham and Wye ('intended'
taken for granted?).

WYESHAM [GW] op 12 January 1931 *(co n dated 'January')*; HALT; clo 5 January 1959 *(T 5th)*; {Monmouth – Redbrook}.

WYKE & NORWOOD GREEN [LY]
op 7 August 1850 *(T 5th- line)* as PICKLE BRIDGE;
renamed WYKE 1 March 1882 *(Cl)*;
re-sited 13 chains east 23 September 1896 as W & N G;
clo 21 September 1953 *(Cl)*.

WYKE REGIS [WP Jt] op 1 July 1909 *(Weymouth 2nd)*;
HALT; clo 3 March 1952 *(RM March)*.

WYKEHAM [NE] op 1 May 1882 *(Scarborough 4th-line)*; clo 5 June 1950 *(Cl)*.

WYKEHAM – see WEAVERTHORPE.

WYLAM

WYLAM [NE]: line op 10 March 1835★★, nd, in *Scott* 1837; see 1836 B★★; clo 3 September 1966 for engineering works, reop 1 May 1967 *(RM June)*; still open.

Also see NORTH WYLAM.

WYLDE GREEN [LNW] op 2 June 1862 *(W Mid; T 2nd- line)*; still open. WYLD G until 1863a *hb*, 1864 *Brad*, 1864/8 table, 1875/82 index LNW co tt.

WYLLIE [LMS] op 19 December 1932 *(Cl 29)*;
HALT; clo 13 June 1960 *(RM July)*;
{Ynysddu – Pontllanfraith}.

WYLYE [GW] op 30 June 1856 *(W Fly P 1 July)*;
WILEY until 1874 *(Cl)*; clo 19 September 1955 *(RM November)*. WILEY OR WYLYE in *hb* 1875a.

WYMONDHAM near Norwich [GE]
op 30 July 1845 *(op tt Norfolk)*; still open.

WYMONDHAM – see WHISSENDINE.

WYNDHAM [GW] op 10 August 1942 *(hbl 18)*;
HALT; clo 5 May 1958 *(RM June)*;
{Nantymoel – Ogmore Vale}.

WYNN HALL [GW] op 1 May 1905 *(GW H)*;
HALT; clo 22 March 1915★★; {map 75}.

WYNNVILLE [GW] op 1 February 1934
(T 22 January); HALT; clo 12 September 1960 *(Cl)*;
{map 75}. Pre-opening Bryn Bridge *(RAC)*.

WYNYARD [NE] op 1 March 1880 *(NE maps- line)*;
clo 2 November 1931 *(Cl)*.

WYRE near Worcester [GW] op 11 June 1934 *(Cl 29)*;
HALT; clo 3 January 1966 *(RM February)*;
{Fladbury – Pershore}.

WYRE DOCK – see FLEETWOOD.

WYRE FOREST [GW] op 1 June 1869 (notice of alterations for June in GW co tt); clo 1 August 1962★★.

WYRLEY & CHESLYN HAY [LNW]
op 1 February 1858 *(W Mid; T 1st- line)*;
W & CHURCH BRIDGE until 1 December 1912
(RCG); clo 18 January 1965 *(RM March)*.
W OR C B *hb* 1883.

WYTHALL [GW] op 1 July 1908 *(GW H; T 2nd- line)*
as GRIMES HILL PLATFORM;
renamed G H & W HALT 12 July 1914,
G H & W PLATFORM 11 July 1927, G H & W 9 July
1934 *(GW Halts)*, W 6 May 1974 *(BR notice)*; still open.

YE RAILWAY STATION DURING YE HOLIDAY
TIME IN YE ROMAN PERIOD
(From a rare old frieze (not) in ye British Museum)

Y

YALDING [SE]
op 25 September 1844 *(SE)*; aot request; still open.
YAPHAM GATE [NE]
first in *Brad* February 1855; York, Pocklington and
Market Weighton market days; last in tt April 1865
(in May tt whole table blank, presumably nothing from
company; station not present June);
{Fangfoss – Pocklington}.
YAPTON [LBSC]: line op 8 June 1846 *(Hants Chron
13th)*, nd, November 1846; last in *Brad* October 1847,
back June 1849*; clo 1 June 1864 (Wednesday) *(Cl)*;
{Ford – Chichester}.
* = in *Topham* May 1848 to April 1849 at least. Unlikely that
this was inertia since May 1848 was first issue of *Topham*,
so omission from *Brad* more likely to be result of one of the
vagaries to which *Brad* was then prone than of brief closure.
YARBRIDGE [IoW] (non-tt):
temporary platform 17 July 1867 to enable spectators
to view Naval Review from Bembridge Down
(co n IoW Obs 13th); about ½ mile south of Brading.
YARDE [SR]
op 19 July 1926 *(sig inst 24/1926; hbl 61)*; HALT;
clo 1 March 1965 *(Express & E 1st)*; {map 116}.
YARDLEY WOOD [GW]
op 1 July 1908 *(RCG; T 2nd- line)*;
PLATFORM until 7 July 1924 *(GW H)*; still open.
YARM {map 39}
YARM (a) [S&D] line op 10 October 1825 (see 1825**),
nd, 1840 *(Whishaw)* – but horse-drawn trains likely to
have stopped from outset; would have served area after
Y Depots, below, closed; at first Y BRANCH END;
clo 16 June 1862 *(RAIL 667/65)*.
YARM (b) [NE] op 25 May 1852**; clo 4 January 1960
(RM February).
YARM (c) op 19 February 1996; about 1⅛ mile south
of (b); still open.
Y DEPOTS [S&D] terminus op 16 October 1826
(poster *S&D*, which says Union Coach will use New Inn);
horse-drawn; mostly served by trains from Stockton to
Darlington, with detour along this branch and back;
some extra market day trains of own *(S&D pass)*;
accounts for year October 1831 to October 1832 show
then only one each way per week (J.S. Jeans, *History of
the Stockton & Darlington Railway*, F. Graham, 1974
reprint of 1875, Jubilee, original);
clo 7 September 1833 (Saturday) when steam service
Darlington to Stockton began – avoided detour *(Cl)*;
later used for Yarm Fair 19 & 20 October 1840;
also other special and Sunday use later.
YARMOUTH IoW [FYN]
op 20 July 1889**; clo 21 September 1953 *(T 21st)*.
YARMOUTH East Anglia
– see GREAT YARMOUTH.

YARNTON [GW] line to Witney, which made this a
junction, op 14 November 1861 *(GW)*, nd, February
1862; clo 18 June 1962 *(T 18 May)*.
Y JUNCTION until 1894 *(Brad)*.
YATE
YATE (a) [Mid] op 8 July 1844 *(Bristol T 13th)*;
clo 4 January 1965 *(RM February)*. *Brad* ? to end (May
1961) was Y for CHIPPING SODBURY but not thus
BR LMR and WR tts in late 1950s.
YATE (b) op 15 May 1989 *(RM July)*; approximately
same site as (a); still open.
YATTON [GW]
op 14 June 1841 *(Taunton 16th)* as CLEVEDON ROAD;
renamed 27 July 1847 *(Cl)*; still open.
Brad: 1845 C R at Y; 1846 C R Y JUNCTION;
1847 C R; 1848 Y C J; to Y J 1869/70, Y 1879/80.
GW co tt 1859: Y.
YAXHAM [GE]: line op 15 February 1847 *(EC)*, nd,
February 1848; aot request; clo 6 October 1969
(RM October); later excur *(U)*.
YAXLEY near Bury St Edmunds [GE]
op 20 December 1922 *(D&C 5)*; HALT;
clo 2 February 1931 *(RM March)*; {Mellis – Eye}.
YAXLEY & FARCET [GN]
op 19 May 1890 *(GN)*; & F added 1895/6 *(Brad)*
but present *hb* 1891a; clo 6 April 1959 *(RM May)*.
YEADON [Mid] (non-tt): op for goods 26 February
1894; 'P' in *hb* 1895 only; passed for passenger use
by Ministry of Transport in LMS days; one or two
excursions per year (to Morecambe and Blackpool)
from about 1932 to 1950s *(Mid)*; {in *IA*}.
YEALAND [Lancaster & Carlisle]:
stop here for Saturday market trains to Lancaster and,
more briefly, Kendal; only in notices in local press.
One paper showed it Saturdays May 1848 to late 1850
and for Lancaster Races 5 and 6 July 1848; at end
service apparently one train only, from Lancaster;
nothing January 1851. Another paper showed service
early 1853. Might mean interrupted service or one
intermittently advertised. Site unknown; would have
been north of Carnforth (Yealand Conyers about two
miles north, Yealand Redmayne about three).
(See article by C. Holden, *Cumbrian Railways, vol. 7
no. 8*). Probably source of error that made Carnforth
into 'Carnforth-Yealand'.
YEALMPTON [GW]
op 17 January 1898**; finally clo 6 October 1947.
YEARSETT [GW] op 2 May 1874 *(Berrows 9th)*;
temporary terminus; clo when line extended to
Bromyard 22 October 1877 *(Berrows 20th, 27th)*.
YEATHOUSE [WCE Jt]: for op see 1874 June**;
replaced Eskett; clo 13 April 1931 *(LNW Record)*;
workmen used 11 March 1940 to 8 April 1940 *(U)*.
YELDHAM [CVH] op 26 May 1862 *(T 28th)*;
clo 1 January 1962 *(T 17 November 1961)*.
YELVERTOFT & STANFORD PARK [LNW]:
line op 29 April 1850 *(co n T 1st)*, nd, May 1851 as
S HALL; renamed Y 1 June 1870 *(Cl)*, Y & S HALL
22 July 1880 *(LNW circular of that date - 'in future')*,
settled 1 February 1881 *(Cl – LNW Officers 15 February
said change had been made)*; clo 6 June 1966 *(RM July)*.

Last two changes made at the request of Lord Braye –
1880 effort was compromise put forward by LNW that
he regarded as unsatisfactory *(LNW Officers 1880–1)*.
YELVERTON [GW]
op 1 May 1885 *(GW)*; clo 31 December 1962★★.
YEO MILL [GW] op 27 June 1932 *(GW Mag August)*;
HALT; clo 3 October 1966 *(Som Gaz 7th)*;
{East Anstey – Bishops Nympton}.
YEOFORD [LSW]
op 8 June 1857?★; Y JUNCTION 1865/6 to 1922/3
(Brad) and thus LSW co tt 1914 *(hbl 26 April 1923
'now read')*; aot request; still open.
★ = *Brad* June said would open 8th but not in tt *Trewman* until
2 July, whilst Chapelton, similarly marked in *Brad*, was in tt
Trewman 11 June; thus perhaps some delay.
YEOVENEY [GW]
op 1 March 1892★ *(L)*; until 1931/2 *(Brad)* was
RUNEMEDE RANGE, request, daylight only;
by July 1934 was usually RUNEMEDE (though still
R R in one place); became Y 4 November 1935 *(Cl)*;
clo 14 May 1962 *(RM July)*. Before renaming was in
hb as R, 1930/6a as Y, HALT in 1938 book, but not tt.
★ = unlikely any prior non-tt use – see e.g. *TTS September 2002*,
p.346.
YEOVIL {map 118}
YEOVIL (at HENDFORD) [BE] op 1 October 1853,
broad gauge, *(Taunton 5th)*; also used by LSW, on
separate standard gauge line from 1 June 1860;
replaced by >
Y TOWN [GW/LSW] op 1 June 1861 *(W Fly P 4th)*;
clo 3 October 1966 *(W Gaz 30 September, 7 October)*.
Y PEN MILL [GW] op 1 September 1856 *(W Fly P
2nd)*; still open.
Treatment of names of last two above particularly
chaotic. *Brad*: on Weymouth line P M added 1859/61,
removed 1871, back 1875/6; from Durston only one
entry (Y) until 1860, then still one entry (Y HERNDEAN
– corruption of Hendford?), separate TOWN and P M
first shown 1876; TOWN added LSW table 1905 (but
just Y in LSW co tt 1914). GW co tt separated TOWN
and P M 1874/81, B&E co tt 1877 showed separately.
Hb: 1862 Y; 1867 also entry for PEN MILL (at Y);
1872 Y PENN MILL, Y JOINT; 1898a now called
Y PEN M (no change for other); 1904 TOWN.
Y JUNCTION [LSW] op 19 July 1860★★; still open.
Was STOFORD (nearest village) in *W Fly P 24 July 1860*.
For later HENDFORD HALT, see under 'H'.
YETMINSTER [GW] op 20 January 1857 *(W Fly P
27th)*; aot request; still open.
YNISCEDWYN – see YSTRADGYNLAIS.
YNYS [LNW] first in *Brad* March 1869, markets and
fairs; full use January 1872; clo 7 December 1964
(RM March 1965). See 1867 September 2★★ for
earlier trains through here.
In *hb* 1877 only (its first entry) was Y CROSSING.
YNYS-Y-LLYN:
according to G. Wynn Griffith (see Llangefni), station
here {Llangwllog – Llanerch-y-Medd} when line op
1 February 1866. No other information known.
YNYSDDU [LNW]
first in *Brad* August 1871; clo 13 June 1960 *(RM July)*.

YNYSFERLAS – see HAFOD GARREGOG.
YNYSFOR [WH] (ng)
op 1 June 1923 *(NGSC 2)*; see 1922 July 31★★;
clo 28 September 1936 *(Cl)*; {map 76}.
YNYSHIR [TV] first in *Brad* July 1885; clo 15 June
1964 *(RM August)*. Op as YNISHIR; altered 1920/1 tt
(C/W) but still original form 1956 *hb* – though 1944a
had said now read YNYSHIR.
YNYSLAS [Cam] op 1 July 1863 *(Cam)*;
clo 14 June 1965 *(RM July)*. Ynys-las until 1880/1
(Brad), *hb* until 1925. LNW co tts 1864-82 at least:
Yn-ys-las for ABERDOVEY.
See under ABERDOVEY for short branch to ferry,
used 1863–7.
YNYSWEN op 29 September 1986 *(RM December)*;
site of old Tylacoch; still open.
YNYSYBWL [TV]
YNYSYBWL op 1 January 1890 *(RCG)*; clo 28 July
1952 *(Cl)*.
Y NEW ROAD op 6 July 1910 *(Nelson)*; see 1904★★;
became HALT 7 May 1945 *(Cl)*; clo 28 July 1952 *(Cl)*.
Also see OLD YNYSYBWL.
YNYSYGEINON [Swansea Vale] op 21 January 1861
(Mid); last trains shown in tt February 1862 but stayed
in *Brad* for some time, no trains shown.
YNYSYGEINON JUNCTION:
in *Brad* December 1873 new openings list but not in
body of table; January to June 1874 in tables but
without trains *(Mid)*;
{physical junction in *IA*, north of Pontardawe}.
YOCKLETON [Shrewsbury & Welshpool]
op 27 January 1862 *(co n Shrewsbury 31st)*;
HALT from 1956; clo 12 September 1960 *(Cl)*.
YOKER
YOKER [NB] op 1 December 1882★★; clo 1 January
1917 *(RM February)*; reop 1 February 1919 *(Cl)*;
Y HIGH 28 February 1953 to 14 June 1965 *(Cl)*;
still open.
Y FERRY [Cal] op 1 October 1896 *(RCG; Colliery 2nd-
line)*; FERRY added 1953; clo 5 October 1964 *(RM
November)*. Cal co tt 1913: Y for RENFREW, but not
thus LMS tt 1930 nor *Murray* 1948.
YORK
YORK [NE]: original temp terminus op 30 May 1839
(T 7 June); replaced by second terminus 4 January
1841 *(Cl)*; replaced again, by through station, 25 June
1877 *(co ½ T 4 August)*; still open.
Y LAYERTHORPE [Derwent Valley] op 21 July 1913
(Brad; NER Staff Mag 1913); clo 1 September 1926
(Wednesday)★★; later charter use *(Cl)*. Usually just 'L'.
Y HOLGATE EXCURSION PLATFORM [NE] (non-tt):
alias HOLGATE BRIDGE / YORK RACECOURSE:
temporary platform for reception of Volunteers at
Review on 28 September 1860 *(T 24th* said 'would be
erected', clearly hasty affair); permanent authorised
14 December 1860, certainly used 28 August 1861
(race); last used, for races, 24 August 1939
(K. Hoole, *Railways of York*, Dalesman, 1976, p.26).
Non-tt: SIDINGS used 12 August 1866 to cope with
extra numbers brought to city for Volunteer Review
(regional rather than local assembly of 1860).

Item *T 9th* said 20,000 forces, total 100,000 expected and that horse-trucks and cattle-waggons were being pressed into service. Evidence of use of Sidings A and B from letter of complaint *(T 17th)* about chaos and delays on departure. Since these Reviews were regular events, might have been other occasions, though Holgate perhaps usually sufficient.

Y ROWNTREES [LNE] (non-tt): usually just R; HALT; chocolate factory workers and special visitors; built under agreement dated 15 November 1927 and in wtt by 1 February 1928; last train Friday 8 July 1988 *(RM September)*.

YORK & NEWCASTLE JUNCTION
– see THIRSK.

YORK JUNCTION
– see GASCOIGNE WOOD JUNCTION.

YORK ROAD King's Cross

YORK ROAD [Picc] op 15 December 1906 *(co n T 14th)*; clo 4 May 1926** by General Strike; when other stations on line reopened after strike, this remained closed; reop 4 October 1926 *(T 4th)*; clo 19 September 1932 ('will be closed from 19th inst' – *Brad 12 September 1932*); {King's Cross – Caledonian Road}.
Also see under LONDON KINGS CROSS.

YORK ROAD – see BATTERSEA.

YORKHILL [NB] op 2 February 1885* *(NB)*; clo 1 January 1917 *(RM February)*; reop 1 February 1919 *(RM February)*; clo 1 April 1921 (Friday) *(Cl)*.
Sometimes GLASGOW Y in some tables, all tts.

* = according to *MT6/411/7* planned opening was 1st but that a Sunday, no Sunday service.

YORTON [LNW] op 1 September 1858**; aot request; still open. At first YARNTON tickets, YARTON *Brad* (soon altered).

YSTALYFERA [Mid] op 20 November 1861 *(Colliery 23rd)*; clo 25 September 1950 *(RM November)*.

YSTRAD CARDIGAN – see FELIN FACH.

YSTRAD MYNACH [Rhy] op 31 March 1858 *(co ½ T 1 September- line)* as Y; became Y JUNCTION 1875/6 *(Brad)*, Y M 1 December 1891 *(RCG)*; still open.

YSTRAD RHONDDA

YSTRAD RHONDDA op 29 September 1986 *(RM December)*; at 20m 5ch; still open.
Also see TON PENTRE (at 20m 75ch).

YSTRADGYNLAIS [N&B]
op 10 November 1873 *(G&S)* as YNISCEDWYN; renamed 1 May 1893 *(hbl 27 April)*; clo 12 September 1932 *(RM October)*.

YSTRADOWEN [TV] first in *Brad* March 1866; clo 26 November 1951 *(RM January 1952)*.
Erratically given as YSTRAD OWEN: e.g. *Brad* 1869, GW co tt 1881 (but only one word 1874), *hb* 1867 to 1890s.

SKYLIGHT VIEW—A RAILWAY STATION

SECTION 5

Line notes in chronological order

These notes are intended to cover two sorts of items, though inevitably there is some overlap between them. One consists of early lines that had passenger services of a kind that would not be classified as 'normal' by later standards; the other of lines where it makes sense to put notes once here rather than enter them for each relevant station. The notes are arranged in chronological order so that the addition or deletion of items will not upset or complicate the whole arrangement. Some of the early items have more in common with those in Section 6 than those in Section 4 but they are included here to illustrate the way rail services evolved – a further justification for chronological order. In order to provide some sort of reference date, approximations have sometimes been given; the text gives more exact information. Where a year-only reference is given in Section 4, the item here will be found at the start of the relevant year. Some of these are arbitrary dates in that they cover a selection of matters that are most coveniently dealt with in one place: '1904' and '1905', covering erratic use of 'Halt' are examples. Stops mentioned here that never had a 'normal' service are not always included in Section 4.

Occasionally, there is more than one item for the same date. These are only brief ones so no attempt has been made to give a separate reference with a, b, etc as there should be no difficulty about finding the one needed.

Here the company cited is normally the one that opened the line.

1807 March 25. Oystermouth: Swansea to Mumbles. Based on G. Gabb, *The Life and Times of the Swansea & Mumbles Railway*, D. Brown (Cowbridge), 1987. The date above, usually quoted as the opening date, was the date from which Benjamin French contracted to pay rent for a year for the use of the line for a horse-drawn service from the Brewery Bank, Swansea, on the Swansea Canal, to Castle Hill, Oystermouth. 25 March is a conventional quarter day so that the service might actually have begun on a different day – perhaps somewhat earlier, with payment on an *ad hoc* basis. The contract had been drawn up in February 1807. No evidence on stops; presumably anywhere convenient. Gabb shows service was maintained by various contractors until at least 22 July 1826 when S. Llewellyn advertised reduced fares for his 'Tram-Road Car'. The fare-cut was probably the result of increased road competition as new turnpikes made road travel easier. As a result the service probably ceased within a year or two of the advertisement. A couple of Prussian mining specialists, C. von Oeynhausen and H. von Dechen visited this country in 1826–7; according to them 'in the summer months a kind of coach runs on [the line], in which about 20 passengers are drawn by one horse' (English translation of *Railways in England [sic] 1826 and 1827*, published for the Newcomen Society by W. Heffer & Sons, Cambridge, 1971). For reopening, see *1860 July 25*, below.

1809. Severn & Wye. Opened for goods 1809. Little detail known but in 1817 it prohibited people from riding on the wagons, except unloaded ones. In 1821 it fixed a toll for Samuel Holder & James Ward to run a 'Pleasure Tram drawn by one horse' and this seems to have kept running for several years *(Baxter, work listed end Section 2)*.

1812 August 17. Opening of first part of Monmouth Railway; probably completed early 1817 *(Companies)*. 3ft 6in. horse-drawn plateway linking Howler's Slade in the Forest of Dean with Coleford and Monmouth. Act of 1810 included rates for passengers; however, no evidence, e.g. from trade directories, that any service was ever available (H. Paar, *RCHS Journal, July 1965*). Part later used by Coleford, Monmouth, Usk & Pontypool Railway.

1818. Kilmarnock & Troon (see *GSW*). Opened for goods 6 July 1812. Passengers were carried by 1818 when an irregular horse-drawn service was being run by William Wright of Kilmarnock. According to *PP 1* (1838–9) company had never run passengers on own account and Act did not allow them to levy duty on individual passengers. 'A few carriages for the conveyance of passengers travel on the line and a small tonnage is taken for each time the carriage passes, estimating so many persons to constitute a ton'. Also see *Robertson*, pages 21–5. Service ran from what was later called St Marnocks Depot at Kilmarnock to Troon Harbour. Intermediate stopping arrangements unknown.

Closed 20 July 1846 for conversion from original 4ft 6in. gauge to standard. Reopened 1 March 1847, with deviations. See Section 4 for details of separate stations.

1822. Sirhow(e)y Tramroad. 4ft 2in. line from Newport to Tredegar. Private carriers provided horse-drawn service from 1822. By 1826 a scale of charges had been laid down. All services ceased after company said that it would haul all traffic with its own steam engines (notice given 13 May 1850). In 1851 company probably ran a short-lived service of its own from Tredegar to Nine Mile Point. Route later used by standard gauge service, station details in Section 4.

1825. Stockton & Darlington *(Basis – S&D; S&D Pass)*. Celebrated steam-hauled run from the foot of the Brusselton Incline, near the Masons' Arms, Shildon, via Darlington to Stockton on 27 September 1825 was really a publicity stunt, combined with the exercise of legal rights and should be treated as a formal opening. Immediately after this, line was goods only, much horse-drawn. Regular passenger service only began on 10 October 1825, between Stockton and Darlington, horse-drawn. Darlington to Shildon added April 1826. At first services were provided by contractors, different operators starting from different inns at the two ends. The first 'trains' consisted of a single coach designed for 6 passengers inside and 20 outside (on top). Early stopping places were mostly where line crossed roads: e.g. Aycliffe Lane, Fighting Cocks, Goosepool and Yarm branch end.

Extension to Middlesbrough from Stockton was formally opened 27 December 1830 (steam-hauled); public services began soon after (see MIDDLESBROUGH, Section 4), horse-drawn, provided by contractors.

In 1833 contractors were bought out, preparatory to introduction of steam-hauled services. Trial steam-hauled services began 7 September 1833, Stockton to Darlington; regular steam services began 1 October; extended to Shildon and St Helens (later West Auckland) in December 1833 *(S&D* says 1 December but that was a Sunday and earliest timetables seen show no Sunday service) and to Middlesbrough 7 April 1834.
Even when these were introduced, passengers continued to be picked up and set down at any convenient point; proper stations were only introduced later.

Some horse-drawn private contractors' services lingered in addition to the company's. The 1840 *Return (RAIL 1053/1)* says that most trains were loco-hauled but also mentions 'Horse coaches worked by different individuals – number uncertain, principally on Sundays'. The last of these was a Middlesbrough to Stockton and back service for church-goers; this ceased in 1856.

Details of stops were still not given for some time after services had become 'regularised'; even company's own tts *(RAIL 981/477–8)* seem to lack detail. Even the minutes are often unhelpful. Fare table for '1840' *(RAIL 667/611)* lists: Middlesbrough; Newport; Stockton; Yarm branch [end?]; Fighting Cocks; Darlington; Aycliffe; Shildon; St Helens. S&D and linked companies often opened a 'station' then added

platforms, passenger shelters and other facilities piecemeal so there are references that could be interpreted to mean provision of a new station or improvement of existing one.

Shildon was not in *Brad* until about August 1840, then only in reference to a Monday market train for 'passengers and cattle', though trains to St Helens could have served it; it was included for all services from about October 1840.

See 1843** for note on service beyond Shildon.

Two temporary stations were used by visitors to 1925 Centenary celebrations. FAVERDALE (Darlington Works) used July 1 (for opening ceremony of Exhibition) and July 2 (for visitors to Historic Procession). GRANDSTAND (about half-way Dinsdale / Urlay Nook) used 2 July only (from programme issued by LNE).

1826 A. Brecon to Hay; Brecon Forest Tramroad (separate lines, included together for convenience).

Brecon to Hay opened goods 7 May 1816. By 1826 company had laid down rate of passenger tolls.

Brecon Forest Tramroad ran approximately from Sennybridge to Gurnos with branches and the connecting Palleg tramway from Cwm Twrch; built 1820s onwards; parts at least were used for trips to market. (S. Hughes, *The Brecon Forest Tramroad*, The Royal Commission on Ancient & Historical Monuments in Wales, 1990).

1826 B. Redruth & Devoran. Line opened 30 January 1826 for goods. Closed ? Built to carry tin and copper. Miners carried to and from work, often riding on the wooden blocks which acted as buffers. Visiting mining agents and other officials allowed to travel in goods wagons, being made honorary traffic inspectors to get round rules (D.B. Barton, *Redruth and Chasewater Railway*, published by author, Truro, 1960). Accident on 'Truro railroad' (probably this line) in July 1838 when man who had been travelling on top of wagon loaded with copper jumped off before it stopped; his frock (smock?) caught in wheel, he was dragged under and cut in half *(T 25 July/Exeter Flying Post)*.

1828 A. Duffryn Llynvi & Porthcawl.
Maesteg to Porthcawl and Bridgend; opened to goods 1828–30 (formal opening 22 October 1830). Company certainly allowed individuals to ride on their trams on top of their goods if they wished. On holidays and special occasions boards were placed across seats and trains run. No regular passenger service was ever operated. (H.J. Rendell, *Bridgend – The Story of a Market Town*, Mid Glamorgan County Libraries).

1828 B. Monklands area railways. (Basis – *MK* and *Garnkirk*). There were a number of early short-lived services whose history has not been fully established, particularly in regard to 'stations', though the horse-drawn services are unlikely to have had any. This entry aims to give a basic list of these services. Some information is duplicated later in the section since some of the services listed here, not necessarily the last to open, did endure. Here, ★★ = entry later in this Section.

8 July 1828: trial horse-drawn service Airdrie Lea End to Kirkintilloch Basin. Not certain if it continued for any length of time.

1 June 1831: Airdrie Lea End – (The) Howes, near Coatbridge – Gargill, later Gartsherrie – Glasgow Townhead. This was a combined MK and Garnkirk service. At first horse-drawn. After a few months locomotives used for Gargill – Glasgow part. Connecting service (perhaps added later in June) from Calder Iron Works to Gartsherrie. Latter was probably soon discontinued. Report of accident on 9 June 1842 said passenger trains were then being horse-drawn from Gargill for about two miles along MK line *(Rtn)*. Competition from new lines caused Howes (February 1843) and Lea End (18 May 1843) to be closed but Garnkirk to Glasgow portion continued in use; by now this was linked to the Wishaw & Coltness (see *1835 C*).

Summer 1832: advertised weekly services from Cairnhill Bridge (near Calder Iron Works) and Clarkston to connect with the Airdrie to Glasgow trains. Discontinued by mid-October 1832.

In addition to the advertised services, more casual passenger arrangements also existed on this line. At one time (exact dates unknown) it was normal practice to attach a small passenger wagon to coal trains (laden and unladen) for the use of anyone who wished to use it; no timetable was involved.

Late 1839: horse-drawn service Lea End – Kipps – South End (probably alternative name for The Howes) – Chryston – Kirkintilloch Basin. This probably ceased 1840 or soon after.

5 August 1840★★: Glasgow – Causewayend.

26 December 1844★★: Airdrie Hallcraig – Kirkintilloch (exchange station with Edinburgh & Glasgow Railway).

The carriage of passengers was first shown in *Returns* for first half of 1845 but *Robertson* shows that passenger duty was paid every year from 1836; MK passengers were lumped in with those of Garnkirk and Slammanan companies.

1829 A. Abergavenny to Hereford.
These two towns were linked by the Llanvihangel, Grosmont and Hereford Railways, opened in sections for goods between 12 March 1814 and 21 September 1829. By 1829 a rate of tolls for passenger use of line had been laid down; passenger duty paid 1838 to 1842 at least *(PP 2)*. No locomotive engine; proprietors do not convey passengers; 'there are on market days some tram-waggons which convey market people who live along the line' *(PP 1*, covering 1838–9 – Hereford to Monmouth Cap described as tram-road, extension of Grosmont and Lanqua lines). Closed 20 April 1853

and later used as basis for orthodox railway (R.A. Cook and C.R. Clinker, *Early Railways between Abergavenny and Hereford*, RCHS, 1984).

1829 B. Ca(e)rnarvon to Nantlle. 3ft 6in. tramway opened for goods 12 July 1828. Irregular passenger service from Carnarvon Quay began ? – perhaps December 1829. Official service began 11 August 1856 from Carnarvon Castle, with intermediate stations at Bont-Newydd; Pwllheli Road; Groeslon; Pen-y-Groes *(G&S)*. Line closed 12 June 1865 for reconstruction. Notice *Carnarvon & Denbigh Herald 17th* said traffic transferred from that date to Mr John Morton of the Royal Sportsman Hotel who would run omnibus service from Carnarvon to Penygroes, Nantlle, Llanllynfi and Portmadoc and back. Most reopened standard gauge 2 September 1867 (see below) as part of line to Afon Wen; Llanwnda replaced Pwllheli Road; Nantlle reopened later (full station details in Section IV).

1830. Pentewan. 2ft 6in. line from St Austell to Pentewan for carrying china clay. On return journey passengers got off at Tregorrick, short of St Austell since wagons ran on under gravity, too dangerous to stay on. Certainly used by 'passengers' by 17 June 1830 when *Trewman* has description of line in use: 20 persons sometimes seen riding on wagons at once. Annual Sunday School parties carried free in clay wagons to Pentewan (photograph p.8, A. Fairclough, *Cornwall's Railways: a Pictorial History*, D. Bradford Barton, 1974).

1830 May 4. Canterbury & Whitstable.
Ceremonial opening 3 May, public 4th. Changing mixture of locomotive, stationary engine and horse haulage. At first 'stop anywhere' policy; fixed tt introduced by manager Joshua Richardson (date ?); passengers could join/leave trains at Tyler Hill, Clowes Wood or Bogshole (had to buy tickets before joining *(Hart)*; report of accident inquest *(T 29 October 1840)* refers to passenger joining train at Tyler Hill Engine House. *Returns (RAIL 1053/1)* early 1840s say fare 6d for whole distance or more than half, 3d for half or less; no separate train for passengers. Taken over by SE; closed 6 February 1846 for relaying with stronger rails (I. Maxted, *The Canterbury & Whitstable Railway*, Oakwood, 1970). Line reopened, fully locomotive-hauled, from SE's own station at Canterbury 7 April 1846 *(T 13th/Dover Chronicle)* – but see note on Whitstable Harbour entry, section 4.

1830 September 17. Liverpool & Manchester (Basis – *LM*). Ceremonial opening 15 September 1830 *(T 17th* – but mostly concerned with accident to Huskisson). One train Liverpool to Manchester and back (full fare) on 16th, mostly used by members of the Society of Friends to and from annual conference. Regular use started 17th.

No details exists for the initial intermediate stops; Walker's *Accurate Description* of line at time of opening says fares for intermediate stops had not been settled, implying that initially there might not have been any. Walker makes it clear that Crown Street was terminus but said many passengers would start their journey from Edge Hill, to which they would be taken by omnibus from company's office in Dale Street (to avoid incline from Crown Street, which was worked by a stationary engine). This arrangement cannot have lasted long because the omnibus services quoted in timetable below appear to converge on Crown Street.

Descriptions of the formal opening mention various stops for refuelling and setting people down but do not include mention of anything identifiable as a station (see *LM* for detailed description of day).

Earliest known tt is company's for 1 March 1831. Two versions of this are at Kew *(RAIL 981/226, 227)*; former issued from Liverpool office, misleadingly catalogued as February (was issued 25 February, to come into force 1 March), latter from Manchester. These did not show times at intermediate stops but did list stops in fare tables. Next available detail is a list taken from company's minutes of 26 September 1832, quoted in T.J. Donaghy, *Liverpool & Manchester Railway Operations, 1831–1845*, D&C, 1972. *Brad* 19 October 1839 did give full list but then switched to outline tables; detail again January 1846, since when continuously available. Many early changes of stopping place and name, so the early history of intermediate stops is patchy. At first, trains stopped at, e.g., level crossings, where the gatekeeper issued tickets; perhaps a room of his cottage was available as shelter. Gradually the ingredients of a 'station' as we know them were added – e.g. in 1841 platforms and name boards were added to places lacking them.

Report of accident on 28 February 1835 *(T 2 March)* refers to 'Chat-moss station'. Probably paper's name for one of known stations (e.g. Lambs Cottage) but possible that it was used by LM itself at one time for one of its station.

1831 A. Edinburgh & Dalkeith. Basis – *D&C 6; Ed & Dalk; Edin;* M.J. Worling, *Early Railways of the Lothians*, Midlothian District Libraries, 1981; articles by E.S. Lomax (original in Edinburgh Room at city's library) and M.J. Worling (1988); extra material provided by D.M.E. Lindsay and D. Yuill.

Line opened for goods from Edinburgh St Leonards to Craighall Colliery, between Niddrie and Millerhill, 4 July 1831; extended to South Esk/Dalhousie in October 1831, when branch to Fisherrow also opened. Branches opened to Leith, reached in stages 1836, and to North Esk/Dalkeith, opened 26 November 1838. All were 4ft 6in. gauge. Services horse-drawn.

Map evidence suggests might have incorporated part of the Edmonston (or Newton) Railway. G. Dott, *Early Scottish Colliery Waggonways*, London, 1947, mentions talk of a possible purchase about the time the company got its Act but also says there is no clear evidence to

show that it did buy. Map of *Edinburgh & Environs, 1838* shows Edinburgh & Dalkeith bulging to the west, just north of Millerhill, as in map showing the Edmonston in Dott's book. It also seems that some alteration to the course of the line was made between 1838 and March 1844, when the NB produced a map showing its plans for line (a map derived from this is included in *D&C 6*).

Possible that from start anyone could pay toll and put own passenger coach on line; newspaper notices showing rates certainly exist for later in 1831.

Fully public service provided by a contractor, M.J. Fox, began from St Leonards to Dalhousie 2 June 1832; so profitable that company added its own 1834; took over completely 1836. Service to Leith, Constitution Street, added 1838 (passenger duty first paid for Leith branch for year 1835, *PP 2*; probably result of service along part of this line, which was not completed until 1838) and to Dalkeith autumn 1839. Services horse-drawn and railway noted for casual ways and frequent stopping places: in 1839 evidence was given to Parliament that it did not issue tickets because there were so many stops – and many passengers would not state their destination. *Whishaw* (about 1840): 'Besides the terminal stations, there is a half-way stopping place, which is at the divergence of the Leith branch [presumably Niddrie]. It is to be observed that the driver stops to take up or set down a passenger wherever required'. Early *Returns* said of passenger trains: 'All one class: accommodation much the same as common stage coaches but roomier'. Return for second half of 1840 mentioned Edinburgh; Musselburgh; Leith; Dalkeith as termini. Others referred to journeys as 'passages'. Confirmation of line's habits given in accident report about woman killed 20 May 1842 – she 'imprudently leapt from the coach while in motion without having warned the driver to stop' *(Rtn)*.

By 1842 they were running to a timetable of sorts. *Lomax* quotes: Fisherrow 8 departures daily; St Leonards 7; Dalhousie and Dalkeith 7; Leith 5.

Tuck about June 1843 mentions in time and fare tables: St Leonards; Dalkeith; South Esk (near Lasswade); Leith (The Shore); Portobello; Fisherrow station, Musselburgh; Niddrie. In one place trains are stated as going to 'The vicinity of Lasswade, etc'.

The March 1844 map prepared by the NB shows stations at Cairney★; Sheriffhall★; Portobello; Niddrie Junction; Lasswade Road★ (at/near later Eskbank). When company had changed its ways to adopt fixed stations (assuming it had done so) is not known. It is most unlikely that any of the 'stations' had any facilities. Those marked ★ presumably 'closed' with re-gauging.

September 1844 *Murray* lists departure times Dalkeith to St Leonards Depot; no intermediate detail; no reference to Leith and the others. However, *Returns* show that passengers were being carried on the Leith branch.

Brad first included the line in July 1846, with continuous coverage thereafter. Initially no intermediate detail given. Also, its timing was out of phase with other information: evidence from NB co tt, 1 September 1846, is that *Brad* was then about a month behind, but in July 1847 it seemed to be slightly ahead of events. *Brad* sequence:

July 1846: Edinburgh St Leonards to Dalkeith and Fisherrow.

August 1846: Leith added, apparently Thursdays only, when there was an 'extra coach' for there; March 1847 to June 1847 fares quoted but no trains listed. Obviously this might be a case where tt did not tell the full story; however, it might be a reflection of the fact that after line via Newhaven opened, 20 May 1846, a much more convenient service from Edinburgh to Leith was available.

March 1847: also to South Esk.

In 1847 (after the NB had taken over) line was converted to standard gauge. No exact information exists about the dates of closure of the various sections. *Edin* says that public demand led to maintenance of a roughly two-hourly service until June 1847 and that steam was perhaps in use between St Leonards and Niddrie as early as 15 February 1847. D.M.E. Lindsay has pointed out that the Dalkeith line was double-tracked so the service could have been maintained by dealing with one line at a time, bringing the deviations into use as they went along. Thus period of complete closure would have been short, perhaps even non-existent. Some services could have been maintained by operating in sections, with change of train at Niddrie. If changes were made on a day-to-day basis, allowance has to be made for this in any interpretation based on monthly timetables. St Leonards had some use after regauging but most services now ran from Edinburgh Waverley. According to *Edinburgh Advertiser 18 June 1847*, another portion of Edinburgh & Hawick would shortly be opened; no confirmation seen but would be consistent with *Ed & Dalk* date for reop to Dalkeith. However, implication of item was that it would be locomotive haulage that would now be extended and shortly before this paper was quoting figures for traffic on Dalkeith lines; together these items further support idea that lines remained open during conversion. It says that up to then passengers had been locomotive hauled only as far as Stoneyhill – was this an approximation for Niddrie or had conversion already got part way along line to Fisherrow/Musselburgh? Even if Dalkeith was not given an improved service in June, notice in paper of 13 July makes it clear it was included in stretch to be opened on 14th.

For later history, see individual stations in Section 4.

1831 B. Dundee & Newtyle, and associated lines. Based on: *Dundee; Newtyle*.

16 December 1831: passenger service began running from 'The Engine House at the Law of Dundee' to 'The Engine House at Hatton Mill, near Newtyle' (poster quoted in *Dundee*). These points were probably those later described as Top of Law and Top of Hatton / Hatton. Trains were initially horse-drawn, with a stationary engine working trains up and down the intermediate Balbeuchly Incline. After stationary engines had also been installed on the Law and Hatton inclines, a full service from Dundee Ward / Ward Street to Newtyle began 3 April 1832. Locomotives were introduced in 1833. Gauge was originally 4ft 6½in.

No continuous list of stops exists. *Newtyle* has list of advertised stops in July 1836 and a fare list for 1846; *Topham* gave detail in May and June 1848 only; *Brad* gave detail from March 1851 but at times earlier (e.g. see March 1850) omitted or just gave passing mention as footnote to e.g. Perth and Forfar table. It is particularly difficult to determine stopping arrangements at the Dundee end. According to the description in *Newtyle*, Top of Law; Back of Law; and Crossroads were different points (all 'offsets' = halts), though all in a half mile stretch. They appear in the sources just quoted as follows:

— Top of Law: at opening; 1846.
— Back of Law op May 1833 ? *(Newtyle)*; then present July 1836; May, June 1848; July 1854 to July 1855, Fridays only.
— Crossroads op 3 April 1832 *(Newtyle)*; then present 1846; May 1851 to April 1853. One possibility is that there was some sort of alternation with Top of Law and Crossroads in use at some times and Back of Law at others. Another is that 'Top of Law' and 'Back of Law' were used indiscriminately for the same site; even if *Newtyle* is wrong about this, Top of Law; Back of Law; and Crossroads cannot all have been alternatives for one site. Position further complicated by fact that incline haulage would have made a stop necessary at Top of Law, even if one was not in tt.

Further along line, matters more straightforward, but continuous use of particular stops not certain.

1831 June 13. Bolton & Leigh and Leigh & Kenyon Junction (see *LM*).

Bolton to Leigh opened formally 1 August 1828; some passengers carried; then goods only for a while. A party travelled at least part way along this line on 15 September to see the opening of the Liverpool & Manchester (report of accident to one of them, *Manchester 18th*). RAIL 981/226 – see *1830 September 17*, above, includes a table that would suggest the line was then open. However it is clear from a series of extracts provided by H. Jack from *The Bolton Chronicle* that this was a premature entry. The line opened for goods from Leigh to Kenyon Junction on 3 January 1831; this was described in paper of 8th, which said that line would be open for passengers in about a fortnight. This was over-optimistic and another false alarm probably accounted for the March tt item. A party was taken to Newton Races on 2 June. Full public opening 13 June (paper of 11th had clear announcement to that effect, paper of 18th reported it; paper of 2 July gave total of passengers carried from June 13 to the end of the month).

Paper of 25 June quoted fares for Chowbent (= Bag Lane, Atherton) and (West) Leigh. *Brad* did not give detail until May 1847 but Bradshaw Leach (later Pennington); Chequerbent; Daubhill were in use by the first half of 1846 *(Huish List)*. Given the operating practices of the LM, there might have been other short-lived stops.

1832 A. Mansfield & Pinxton (article by J.A. Birks and P. Coxon, *RM* July 1949). Service operated from about 1832 to 1848, from Mansfield Portland Wharf to Pinxton Wharf. At first, William Epperstone, landlord of the Boat Inn, Pinxton Wharf, advertised a Thursday market coach to Mansfield and back. Wheatcroft later became the chief carrier on the line and probably operated a fuller passenger service. Line was bought by the Midland, improved and part used for an orthodox service, opening from Nottingham to Kirkby 2 October 1848. From then until 9 October 1849, when the Kirkby to Mansfield section reopened, a two compartment horse-drawn carriage was run from Pinxton to Kirkby to make connections with the Midland line. See individual stations in Section 4.

1832 B. St Helens & Runcorn Gap. Probably opened for goods from St Helens Junction to St Helens 2 January 1832; to Runcorn Gap (Widnes) on 29 August 1833. The locals asked for a passenger service and in September 1832 terms were agreed for a horse-drawn service from the Junction to St Helens, which probably began later that year (list in LM's minutes, quoted in *1830 September 17* above, included St Helens Junction, suggesting line was then in operation). In September 1833 Company hired two LM carriages for a locomotive-hauled service St Helens to Runcorn Gap. One carriage ran from St Helens to the bottom of Sutton Incline and the other from the top of the Incline to Runcorn Gap; passengers had to walk the Incline. If there were only two or three passengers they had to ride on the engine's tender *(LM)*. (Note: there were two Sutton Inclines hereabouts, this one and the one on the LM's own line). No intermediate details were given in the tt until June 1852.

1833 A. Charlestown, later Elgin. See *West of Fife*. Dunfermline was provided with a link to Forth steamers; bathers also found this useful. Began 31 October 1833 from foot of Pittencrieff incline near Dunfermline to Charlestown, just short of the harbour. From 10 March 1834 (probably) it ran from the Dunfermline station at Nethertown. *Returns* for first half of 1842 *(RAIL 1053/1)* say ran twice daily in winter, four times in summer, no intermediate stoppages. Service was suspended during

last week of October 1849 for conversion of gauge from 4ft 1in. to standard. All services horse-drawn until 1853, when steam was introduced for minerals.
In June 1853 line was inspected with view to attaching passenger carriages to steam-drawn mineral trains; permission refused. The N B took over on 1 August 1862; their improvements to route meant that at Charlestown end a replacement station had to be provided half a mile from Charlestown, leaving passengers to walk the rest of the way along the old line (27 October 1862). This deterred custom and services ceased 30 September 1863 (last day). Line later used as basis for standard service – see Section 4.

1833 B. Stratford to Moreton.
See J. Norris, *The Stratford & Moreton Tramway*, RCHS, 1987. 4ft line, horse-drawn. Opened from Stratford-upon-Avon to Moreton for goods 5 September 1826. Passengers taken by licensed carriers 1833 or earlier. According to *PP 1*, 'the road is open to the public on payment of tolls … company are not carriers … Some of the waggons have a licence from the company to carry passengers, for which they pay £1 per month and I believe they generally receive about 1d per mile per passenger'. Duty first shown for year 1833 *(PP 2)*.

Branch to Shipston opened to goods 11 February 1836; no evidence for early passenger use. Closed for improvement early 1853. Reopened 1 August 1853 with 'trains' between Stratford; Shipstone [sic]; and Moreton (one each way, no intermediate stops shown in *Brad*). Still horse-drawn, contractors. Scheduled service probably ceased October 1858 but still some use by passengers in company's passenger van attached to irregular goods trains; book includes description of trip about 1877 with passengers seated on a load of bricks. No stations as such: went via Ilmington (Junction); Newbold (Wharf); Alderminster; Alscot Park. The Shipston section was later used as basis of an orthodox railway (see Section 4).

1833 May. Cromford & High Peak. Main bases: J Marshall, *The Cromford and High Peak Railway*, M. Bairstow, 1996 and article by D. Hodgkins in the RCHS *Journal* December 2007; other books quoted have the same title as Marshall's.

A Derby paper of 29 May 1833 said private carrier, Wheatcroft had taken license to carry passengers from Cromford to Whaley, presumably with the intention of carrying them on by road to Manchester. Had service started or was it planned for start of June? Probably short-lived: in 1842 the Board of Trade was assured they were not carrying passengers; not shown as paying passenger duty up to year ending 5 January 1846 (last figures seen).

The Company began to provide a regular service, following a new Act permitting them to charge for passengers, in 1855 when it ran from Cromford to Ladmanlow, with a 'bus' connection to Buxton.

This seems to have been preceded by at least one trial run in 1854. Probably summer only at first; passengers supposed to walk the inclines. *Co ½ meeting T February 1856*: directors said did not intend to make much preparation for passenger traffic until Stockport, Disley & Whaley Bridge was opened. This would be 9 June 1857, but if timetables are any guide it did not make much change then.

The best way to show 'stations' (for want of a better word) seems to be to tabulate from the scattering of detailed information available. Marshall shows company timetables for 2 July 1856 (a) and 6 April 1874 (d); a revised timetable for 4 January 1869, following the opening of the Hurdlow Deviation Line, is included in *LNW Officers 3916* (c). Some of the names listed in these tts might well have only been timing points. Sites along line were first included in *hb* 1863a (result of LNW taking over line?) and by definition would have been available to all 'trains', though at that time books only listed names, without indication of 'goods', 'passenger' etc (b).

	a 1856	b 1863	c 1869	d 1874
High Peak Junction	—	—	—	yes
Cromford	yes	(1)	yes	yes
Sheep Pasture	—	—	(2)	yes
Steeplehouse	always			
Middleton	yes	—	t/b	yes
Hopton	yes	(3)	t/b	yes
Buckleys Siding	—	—	—	yes
Longcliffe	always			
Bloors Siding	—	—	—	yes
Minninglow	—	—	—	yes
Friden	always			
Parsley Hay	—	yes	yes	yes
Hurdlow	yes	—	yes	yes
Hindlow	always			
Harpur Hill	—	yes	yes	yes
Ladmanlow	always			
Bunsall	—	—	t/b	yes
Shallcross	—	—	t/b	yes
Whaley Bridge	—	—	yes	yes

(1) includes Frost's Wharf (near Cromford);
(2) includes top of No 2 Incline (same as Sheep Pasture?);
(3) includes Hopton Wood;
(t/b) = included times for Top and Bottom of ... Incline.

The 1863 list also included Stone Company's Junction and Middle Pit Junction Pits (both between Cromford and Longcliffe) and Horwich End New Wharf (Ladmanlow / Whaley Bridge). One or more of these might be in detailed list under another name.

All three timetables only show one train per day each way covering the full length of the line. The number of passengers was small and they were carried in a coach (the 'Fly') attached to goods trains. *Returns* were first provided in 1856; only in that year did the total of passengers exceed 1,000 and by 1861, the last year independent returns were provided, the total was down to 121. No return was provided for 1862, and in later years any passengers carried would have been included in the LNW's total. Service never in *Brad* and not sanctioned by BoT; passengers carried at own risk.

Closure resulted from collision between two mineral trains 17 December 1875. BoT report pointed out that carriage of passengers not authorised. Decision taken soon after but service allowed to continue, Mondays and Saturdays, to end of May, for carriage, free of charge, of workers of Buxton Lime Co (to give them time to make other arrangements). See letters from G. Webb and D. Hodgkins, *RCHS Journal, July 1989 p. 415–6 and March 1990 p. 5*). Another book on the line, by A. Rimmer, Oakwood, 1985, quotes a letter describing a journey in August 1877, saying that the service ceased soon after that, as the result of an accident. However, this was based on oral evidence given a little while later and speaker's memory may have been at fault over date; some details are clearly wrong. Or just possible that far from Euston a little local initiative continued?

A third book, by I.C. Coleford, Irwell Press, 1996, says that there is some evidence for a service of sorts from Buxton to Friden 1892–99.

The section from Parsley Hay to Hindlow was used, much improved, as basis for a proper service in 1894 – see Section 4.

1834. Ardrossan. Line opened by the Ardrossan & Johnstone Railway from Kilwinning to Ardrossan in 1831 for goods traffic *(GSW)*. Passenger service began ?; duty first paid 1834. 4ft 6in. gauge; horse-drawn. In 1840 it was converted to standard gauge and connected to main Scottish system, steam-hauled; *Return (RAIL 1053/1)* gives 17 August 1840 as date of opening (really, reopening). This was probably the re-start of a local service from Kilwinning to Ardrossan; report of accident *(T 5 December 1840)* confirms daily service then running Ardrossan to Kilwinning in connection with trains to Glasgow; *Robinson*, about August 1841, says 'The trains of the Ardrossan Railway correspond with those of the Ayr Railway at Kilwinning'. It was also used then as part of a route from Glasgow to London: Glasgow to Ardrossan by rail, to Liverpool by steamer and on to London by rail again. Trains first ran in connection with this steamer connection on Thursday 20 August 1840 *(GSW)*. No details of early stops known. Even after 1840, treatment in *Brad* is patchy; at first usually only mentioned in connection with through services from Glasgow, two or three days per week, even services *to* Glasgow being omitted (time dependent on steamer's arrival?). First detail provided March 1850; even then years before Harbour and Town stations at Ardrossan were separately identified.

1834 March 24. S&D: Lands branch.
Horse-drawn service began. Only irregular mentions have been found, so continuity until 1858 service cannot be confirmed. Indeed, references to ending in 1847 of service to St Helens/West Auckland, with which it was linked, would suggest that it was not continuous *(S&D Pass)*.

1834 September 22. Leeds & Selby. Line opening date from *York Courant*. Line Leeds to Old Milford Junction closed 9 November 1840 *(G&S)*; passengers sent via Methley. Not back in tt until November 1850 *(G&S)* but probably reopened some time earlier. York & North Midland Board meeting on 17 May 1850 resolved that 3 passenger trains be run per diem, Sundays excepted, between Leeds and Old Milford Junction on Leeds & Selby line.

A market train ran earlier – see 1837 A**, below. Start of this perhaps provided by a garbled item in *The Eastern Counties Herald* of 25 March 1841 (a Hull paper), which says that in a few days it was intended 'to start a train from Sheffield, direct for Hull, to reach the latter town before market-hours, and to return after they are over.' No route then exising would have allowed such running. However, it then says 'for some time past, the trains from Leeds for York and Hull have left the station in Hunslet-lane together' and the information would make sense if 'Leeds' replaced 'Sheffield'.

1834 October 1. Bodmin & Wadebridge.
On 4 July 1834, usually quoted as opening date (but correct date given by *LSW* 1968), all that happened was that an engine and carriage were tested by being run about 4 miles from Wadebridge and back *(W Briton 11th)*. Some 'passengers' travelling against the engineer's wishes on another trial, 16 July, were injured when the carriage was derailed *(R Cornwall Gaz 19th)*.

The first authorised passenger usage found was 15 September 1834, when about 150 of the people of Wadebridge were treated to a ride to Bodmin and back – they seem to have been used as guinea-pigs to test the working of the system *(R. Cornwall Gaz 20th)*; the same paper carried a notice that the railway would be opened to the public on 30 September (really a formal opening). The day's proceedings involved a journey from Bodmin to Wadebridge, with a detour to Wenford Bridge and back on the way. Strictly, Wadebridge – Wenford Bridge was main line, but regular passenger services were confined to the Bodmin – Wadebridge line; however early activities of line not as simple as this.

The first fare-paying passengers were carried on Wednesday, 1 October 1834 *(Company's Day Book, RAIL 57/10)*. On that day 26 were carried 'from the junction' (with Wenford Bridge line, presumably); no destination given – to Wadebridge? – this would have been about 6 miles. On Thursday 4 passengers were carried 6 miles, Friday one taken 3 miles, Saturday 13 passengers; details rapidly diminished and figures

last given for Friday 10th, when 191 were carried, far more than on any previous day. Thus initially passengers were carried all days and were clearly picked up and set down anywhere. The small numbers initially might have been due to people not wanting to travel the detour to Wenford Bridge and back (there is no suggestion in the minutes of a ban on such travel) and so walking to the junction to catch their train. The great increase on the 10th was probably the result of providing a direct Bodmin to Wadebridge service for that day. A note in *Return* for 1840–41 *(RAIL 1053/1)* says: 'There is not any separate passenger train; the staple traffic is sand, and to the train is attached a single carriage. On market and fair days there is one or more carriages attached to the train for passengers'. This supports the idea that direct trains were run when it was worthwhile but otherwise would-be passengers were dependent on needs of the goods service. By definition, passengers on goods trains would have had the chance to get on or off at any goods depot at which train stopped, even on Wenford Bridge line, and perhaps on Ruthern Bridge branch as well, though potential custom on these would have been slight. In 1836 goods depots were listed in the Minutes, in connection with charges to Wadebridge, as: Bodmin; Borough Bounds (outskirts of Bodmin?); Ruthern; Nanstallon; Helland; Tressarret; Wenford. (Helland and Tressarret were on the Wenford line). Report of accident at 'Trevarrett' station on 30 July 1842 shows that passenger carriage was attached – children had got onto steps of 'carriage' *(Rtn)*.

On 2 May 1844 Company resolved *(Board Minutes RAIL 57/3)* to run steam trains only on Saturdays, Fair Days, Bodmin Assize Days and other public occasions plus occasions when a special goods cargo warranted it; ordinary week-day work was to be done by horse-power when required. Passengers would probably have been limited to steam days since at other times provision of any sort of service would have been erratic. Probably another change fairly soon. *Rtn PP*, for first half of 1845, when 2,236 passengers carried, says 'Passenger carriages accompany the traffic trains. If engine does not work on Thursdays, they are taken with horses'.

Line appeared in *Bradshaw* from September 1869 to October 1886, one train each way on Mondays, Wednesdays and Fridays, and two each way on Saturdays, Bodmin to Wadebridge, no intermediate stops shown. *LSW* says 'stop anywhere' policy persisted until line closed 1 November 1886 *(R Cornwall Gaz)*. *Returns* show that in 1873 the line only carried 4,826 passengers, less than 25 per operational day; this was the lowest figure of any company, next lowest being the Talyllyn with 17,000; in 1885 it was still lowest, with 6,919 (including 8 first-class) – next lowest was the West Somerset Mineral, 9,553. On the Wenford line by this stage passengers were only carried on excursions and, unofficially, in 'tool wagon' between engine and goods wagons *(RM May 1947)*. By then line had been owned by the LSW for a long time; after improvements LSW reopened it, from new stations at Bodmin and Wadebridge – see Section 4.

1835 A. Clarence (*NE; S&D*).

11 July 1835: horse-drawn service began from Stockton (on the line to the North Shore staiths) to the Clarence Tavern at Crow Trees (sometimes referred to as Quarrington), just north of Coxhoe. Initially provided by the company but on 1 January 1836 the Clarence Coach Company became exclusive contractors. Service ceased November 1837. It resumed 20 June 1838 *(NE; PP 1)*, Stockton to Coxhoe only; at first steam to Ferryhill, then horse-drawn for the rest of the way; steam all the way from 1839. Evolved into orthodox service.

Also from 11 July 1835 there was a service from Stockton to Shildon via the Simpasture branch; probably intermittent; finally ceased 12 February 1842. Nothing known about the early intermediate stopping arrangements of either of these.

A line from Billingham to Port Clarence opened to goods 1833/4. Passenger service began ? Site of pick-up point at Port Clarence uncertain but probably east of later station. In 1838 a market day coach was running Wednesdays and Saturdays to Stockton (R. Sowler, *NE Express*, February 1990). In *Brad* a 'coach connection' from Billingham is mentioned intermittently May 1842 to September 1844. Though these references are in footnotes with other connections that had to be by road (Stockton to Whitby and Scarborough), it is safe to assume that they were horse-drawn rail coaches – a road link would have been very tortuous. No further mention until November 1845, when it is listed in the main table, without comment. Note that this company's tables were often marked 'accuracy uncertain', or something similar, at this period.

1835 B. Whitby & Pickering (see *Potter*).

8 June 1835: Inaugural trip, Whitby to Tunnel Inn; service continued during summer months, mostly for novelty and scenery, though from 18 July ran extra market coach on Saturdays; not said whether this continued in winter.

By 18 July 1835: people could arrange private hire of 'train', going as far from Whitby as Beck Hole *(NE)*; also service from Pickering to Raindale, again for novelty value.

26 May 1836: official opening throughout, from Whitby to Pickering. Tickets mostly issued in advance but an extra vehicle was set aside for the use of strangers who happened to be visiting Whitby that day. Service now seems to have operated continuously: references to its ability to get through in winter when roads impassable.

Detailed description of arrangements:

From Whitby: one horse to foot of incline at Beck Hole, at first operated as self-acting on principle later used by

cliff railways (carriages balanced by water tank going other way), later replaced by stationary engine; one horse from Incline Top to Fen Bogs (effectively line's summit); thence downhill under own momentum to Raindale (at one point on the inaugural run it is supposed to have reached 30mph – who measured and how?); finally one horse to Pickering.

From Pickering: single horse to Raindale; pair to Fen Bogs; one horse took train on to Incline Top, other sent back to Raindale; then incline – reputedly train was detached from the rope part way down so it could run as far as possible towards Tunnel Inn under its own momentum; horse met and took it the rest of the way to Whitby. In bad weather, or with contrary winds, extra horses sent to help.

This method of operation clearly gave many opportunities for passengers to join and alight; there would have been no stations as we known them. Company's *Return* for late 1840 lists fares from Whitby to Ruswarp; Sleights Bridge; Tunnel (later Grosmont); Beckhole; Incline Station (later Goathland); Fen Bog; Raindale; Farwath; Pickering. These should be seen as akin to fare stages of modern bus service rather than exclusive list of stops: common-sense indicates that Levisham would have had a service; *Potter* includes plate showing passengers being waved off from South Dale, near Raindale Inn. *Return* also says: 'A party may have a coach to any station on the line when 8 seats are engaged'. Normal service 2 each way per day.

Rapkin's maps (early 1850s) show station at Saltergate Inn, about half way between Goathland and Levisham; probably left over in error from the stop anywhere days.

4 June 1847: locomotive haulage introduced except on the incline. Original 'station' at Whitby, near 1906 engine-house, replaced by one on site of two former shipyards.

First tt detail provided by *Topham*, May 1848, and *Brad*, July 1848. Both list: Levisham; Goathland; Grosmont; Sleights; Ruswarp. The same stations are shown in the fare-table in the first issue of *The Whitby Gazette*, 6 July 1854 *(Potter)*.

No station ever appeared in tt for Beck Hole(s) (indiscriminately spelled as one word or two), nor is there one on Macaulay's maps of the period though *hb 1862* includes it (1866a – closed). Goathland (at times G Mill) was last in *Brad* September 1857; back in tt April 1858, in footnotes as terminus of a Saturday market train from Whitby; shown full service again November 1863, though it remained on Macaulay's maps. Clearly tt does not tell whole story since trains would have been forced by the needs of incline haulage to stop at both; also, arrangements presumably existed to get people from Goathland <u>to</u> Whitby market – entry that appeared for the return journey was probably only included because the train terminated there.

1 July 1865: incline replaced by deviation line
(co ½ T 15 August); Beck Hole closed; new station at
Goathland.

Goods trains carried platelayers' wives in the late 1940s
to Farwath/Farworth; Raindale; Bridge No.16
(at 14m 9.62ch); Newton Dale; Goathland Summit
(U – but with Bridge No 16 corrected by P. Howat,
whose researches also suggest that Forestry Commission
workers were involved in this case and that use of these
stops went back further than the 1940s).

1835 C. Wishaw & Coltness. This was essentially a
continuation of the Garnkirk & Glasgow and Monkland
& Kirkintilloch lines, from Whifflet on the latter to
Morningside, with a branch to Newarthill (at or near
later Holytown station). As with others nearby, primary
purpose was carriage of minerals. It later became part
of the Caledonian. *Cal* quotes these dates for opening
to minerals: to Holytown (near present day Mossend)
25 January 1834; branch to Newarthill 31 May 1834;
extension of main line to Jerviston (between Mossend
and Motherwell) 18 August 1838; to Overtown
20 March 1841; to Stirling Road 8 January 1842;
to Morningside 9 March 1844. *Cal* did not give any
separate dates for passenger use.

Lee A/S implied that passenger services started at the
same time as goods openings quoted for 1834, 1841,
1842 and 1844. Other evidence suggests that it was not
as simple as this. *Garnkirk* quotes an advertisement of
6 March 1835 for a service whereby carriages from
Newarthill Bridge and Holytown Bridge were
horse-drawn to Gartsherrie and there attached to the
Garnkirk's service to Glasgow, one each way on
Mondays, Wednesdays, Fridays and Saturdays. It is not
known if this was the start of the service. By 1837 the
service had become daily. According to *Robertson*, the
Wishaw & Coltness first paid passenger duty in 1835.

There would then seem to have been a significant gap
in time before any other openings occurred.

The company's *Returns* were made only spasmodically
(given the complexity of some of those they did make,
officialdom might well have shown more relief than
regret at their failure to make regular ones). *Returns* do
exist for the period July 1842 to June 1843. They show
that in the second half of 1842 only horse-drawn
passenger trains were run on two services, one of
2½ miles, the other of 4½; 312 were run on each route,
carrying a total of 4,467 passengers. There were
intermediate stops: anywhere practicable? This would
suggest that Newarthill and Holytown, or nearby
points, were still the termini. The return for the first half
of 1843 was a complex affair: 9,593 passengers were
divided between 23 sub-entries (they contrived 66 for
goods). They included 216 short-distance trains (3,033
passengers travelling 3 and 6 miles – extensions of
service or re-measurement?) by horse coach and 138
steam trains with passengers travelling up to 12 miles

(though according to *Robertson* the line was just over
11 miles long). On the face of it, this fits *D&C 6* which
says that a service started 8 May 1843, calling (after
Gartsherrie); at Carnbroe Iron Works; Holytown;
Motherwell; Wishaw; Overtown Road; Stirling Road;
and Morningside. The date fits the *Returns* which
suggest that steam took over, on a longer service, about
two-thirds of the way through the period. Further
support is given by the great increase in passenger duty
paid by this company in 1843 – and that at a time when
most were paying less because of a changed method of
calculation. Early horse-drawn operations would have
allowed much flexibility in services provided, and this
might account for increased mileages in *Returns*.

An accident report of 11 January 1842 *(Rtn)* reveals
something of habits. Three days previously a couple of
waggoners had given rides from Overtown Road to two
of their relatives, contrary to rules; these fell off and
were run over and killed by the wagons after not more
than 500 yards. The company assured BoT that they
ran no passenger vehicles on this part of line and they
asked for its approval of a new bye-law imposing £5 fine
for any future breaches of rule.

However, tt evidence available, admittedly scanty and
almost certainly well in arrears, suggests that initially
Carluke rather than Morningside was the terminus
(fitting the goods dates quoted for these two places).
Carluke (often called Stirling Road in modern works –
see its entry, under 'C', in Secion 4) was the connection
point for a road service to Lanark. *Brad* first included
the line about July 1841 when Holytown and Newarthill
were mentioned in the Garnkirk & Glasgow's table.
Carluke, without any intermediate detail, was added in
September 1843. The last certain reference to Newarthill
was in May 1844. From June 1844 there was simply a
note that certain trains took Wishaw & Coltness
passengers; no destination was specified. In May 1845
detail was again given, apparently fully; Morningside
was now the terminus, Newarthill no longer included.
Further support to the later opening of Morningside
is given by *Murray* (a Scottish timetable), September
1844, which makes Carluke the terminus. A company
tt for October 1844, quoted in *True Line*, does include
Morningside.

It was originally a 4ft 6in. line. *MK* quotes notice dated
10 August 1847 warning traders and others that line
would be shut on or about 26th for a few days. It was
then converted so that parts could be incorporated into
the Caledonian main line.

See 1848** for problems concerning the closure of part
of this line.

1835 March 10. Newcastle & Carlisle
(strictly Newcastle-upon-Tyne & Carlisle Railway,
but full version rarely used): first section, Blaydon to
Hexham, opened; public carried on formal opening 9th
(N.C. Fawcett). Company's Act did not allow use of

locomotives but they were used when the line opened.
Captain Bacon Grey of Styford gained an injunction
against their use, so on 28 March 1835 all services
ceased. Virtually everyone else wanted the line working
and the ensuing public outcry caused Grey to withdraw
his opposition. Services started again 6 May 1835.
Next month a new Act made the use of steam power
lawful (*NC; Portfolio* reproduces posters announcing
both closure and reopening). Cannot be certain that all
stations linked to this note were open at the time of this
closure since no evidence on intermediate stations has
been seen prior to *Scott*, 1837. Also see 1836 B, below.

1835 April 16. Stanhope & Tyne. Opened to goods
10 September 1834. Company did not want to run
a passenger service but there were requests for one,
so they allowed passengers to ride free on top of the
coal wagons. They soon attached a wagon just for
passengers. Next came a separate locomotive-hauled
passenger coach on fortnightly pay days. Finally, a full
service began on 16 April 1835. At South Shields tickets
were bought in the back room of a nearby inn and
passengers then boarded in sidings. Trains ran to the
Durham Turnpike, near Chester-le-Street, where road
connections could be made. *PP 1*, 1838–9: 'This Railroad
is a private undertaking, not made under the powers
of any Act of Parliament, and being formed for the
conveyance of coals, passengers are allowed to be
carried as a matter of convenience to the public, and
not as profit to the Company' – but they had been paying
passenger duty. In 1841 the company went bankrupt and
the part providing the passenger service was reconstituted
as the Pontop & South Shields Railway *(NE)*.

Churton's *Rail Road Book of England*, 1851, describes
a route for passengers that continued from Chester-le-
Street to Stanley, 'Berwick' (Leadgate?), Cold Rowley
and Stanhope. Although his book is generally accurate,
this 'service' was probably the result of misunderstanding;
the various inclines, which do not receive a mention
from him, would have made a passenger service a very
poor proposition. Churton obtained his information by
writing to large numbers of the gentry for information
and it may well be that a goods only service was
transformed into a passenger one.

1835 June 9. London & Greenwich.
From 9 June to 12 November 1835, occasional trial
trips were made, with passengers: Blue Anchor Lane –
Cobbetts Lane – Grand Surrey Canal.
See A.R. Bennett, *The First Railway in London*, Conway
Maritime Press, 1971 re-issue – pages 9 and 44.

1836 A. Hartlepool Railway & Docks *(RAIL 294/38;
NE; 1836 October 19*, below). On 21 July 1836 company
gave Messrs Wilkinson and Walker permission to run a
passenger coach from Hartlepool to Haswell on Sundays
on payment of 6/- per day. If immediately implemented,
first 'train' would have run 24 July 1836. On 26 October,
same parties licensed to run daily. Would have run from
dock area at Hartlepool; no other details known.

Unique example of line having Sundays-only service at
opening? Probably for church-goers – there were other
examples of this in the area. Presumably horse-drawn.
According to *PP 1* (covering 1838 and 1839 to end of
April) licences then held by Snowden and Wilkinson of
Haswell to run coaches at 3d per mile, paid to company.

Company's station at Haswell received its first regular
service from Sunderland, operated by the Durham &
Sunderland Railway, starting in April or May 1837.
This company, in its *Return*, said that first- and second-
class passengers were carried in one carriage, 'the
centre compartment being close, the ends shut on one
side occasionally by means of moveable shutters'.

Hartlepool Company began its own service on 1 May
1839, when others' licences revoked. However, it did not
provide Sunday service and in April 1840 Mr Humble
was given permission to run one of the old coaches on
Sundays, toll 3d per mile.

Returns for second half of 1840 and a company tt of
January 1843 mention Castle Eden but first full detail
found is in *Brad*, June 1858.

1836 B. Newcastle & Carlisle. Opening dates of various
sections are known. These notes add some general
points to information given in Section 4.

Until July 1848 *Brad* only listed: Blaydon; Stocksfield;
Hexham; Haydon Bridge; Haltwhistle; Rose Hill;
Milton as intermediate stops. Sometimes others got a
footnote mention – in December 1845 a note says that
certain trains will not stop at Scotby; How Mill; Low Row.
However, it has been possible to establish the existence
of most at or near opening from an issue of *Scott's
Railway Companion* describing the line, dated 1837,
but probably relating to late 1836. Section between
Greenhead and Haydon Bridge had not then opened;
Bardon Mill and Haltwhistle were to be on this stretch;
both are in the company's tt for 13 April 1846 *(RAIL
981/364)*, earliest full listing so far seen.

When relevant section opened, there were stopping
places at Allerwash, just west of Fourstones, and Warden,
just east (*Scott* includes only Warden); Fourstones
probably replaced them about the start of January 1837
(1st was a Sunday) (H. Paar, article, *Warden Station*,
RCHS Journal, July 1997).

Although there was no station at Naworth, it is clear that
any passenger could at least alight there: *Scott* advised
sight-seers that it was a good setting-off point for
visitors to the Castle and to Lanercost Priory – indeed
at times he seems to imply that, e.g., picnic parties
could be set down virtually anywhere (passengers
perhaps having to walk to the nearest station for their
return journey?). Naworth Castle was specified as one
of places that would be served by excursion trains NC
would be running during holiday week, May 1845
(T 14 May/The Globe).

N.C. Maclean says: 'Mixed trains also stopped when

requested at Brampton Fell 'gate' station west of Brampton Junction, where the line crosses the main road'; not mentioned in *Scott*. Report on accident that occurred 3 August 1851 said that there were 20 intermediate stations at which all trains stopped [shown thus *Brad*], and 'some other occasional stations at which they stop when there are passengers to be set down or taken up' *(Return)*.

N.C. Fawcett says early flag stations at Naworth Castle (for the Earl of Carlisle), Blenkinsopp Hall (Colonel Coulson), Ridley Hall Bridge (J. Davidson) and Dilston Crossing (J. Grey).

1836 October 19. Durham & Sunderland: Sunderland to Ryhope opened; extended to Haswell April or May 1837 *(NE)*. Accident report dated 19 July 1844 *(Rtn)* says they were using rope haulage similar to that used on Blackwall. Early detail sparse: even Ryhope, presumably kept after line had been extended, did not appear in *Brad* until June 1858 but was shown earlier on maps; initially at least, *Reid* also gave no detail. (See also *1836 A*, above).

1837 A. Aberford (see G.S. Hudson, *The Aberford Railway*, D&C, 1971). Private colliery line; by 3 March 1837 was providing a market day service Aberford – Parlington Hall – Garforth; at Garforth it provided connection with Leeds & Selby (L&S) trains. Shown paying passenger duty 1837 to 1842 as 'Gascoyne's Railway (private)' *(PP 2)*, though family name usually spelled 'Gascoigne'. According to Hudson services ceased 1840 when L&S main service was diverted; although L&S continued a market day service, its timings were too unreliable to provide connections. (Perhaps L&S service not continuous – see 1834 September 22**, above). Aberford service resumed, Tuesdays and Saturdays for Leeds market, soon after L&S resumed. However, *PP 2* evidence suggests that service lasted longer – even continued throughout L&S closure? Line not included in *PP 3*, which covered passenger duty 1841 to 1846 – either because it was out of action at time report published or because private lines now omitted (Brampton Railway, see Section 7, similarly treated).

Initially trains horse-drawn; steam introduced by 1870s, subject to 12mph limit. By 1881 daily sevice provided. In early 1920s reverted to market days only; ceased completely in March 1924.

Although line was private, NE-issued tickets exist – *JB* includes one from Aberford to Garforth.

1837 B. Lines to Coupar Angus and Glamis. These were in effect continuations of the Dundee & Newtyle railway; stations' opening dates in Section 4. After a while they were closed for improvement; parts were incorporated into the Perth to Forfar line. The last certain reference to Washington; Ardler Depot; Kirkinch; and Leason Hill was in June 1843 tt but it is probably safe to say that they remained in use until the line was closed for rebuilding

– Eassie was also omitted after June 1843, to return later, when it became the terminus for the time being.

July 1846: last reference to Glamis; Eassie now became terminus. However branch had suffered at least one earlier closure. Major General Pasley inspected Newtyle line 12 February 1842 but not Glamis branch – 'said to be impracticable at present even for horses, in consequence of the rails having become damaged by the subsidence of the embankment' *(Rtn)*.

October 1847: last reference to Eassie.

November 1847: last reference to Coupar Angus; Newtyle now terminus again.

However, *Return* says that the Coupar Angus branch of the Scottish Midland Junction (now owners) closed 4 September 1847 (a Saturday, last day). Thus *Brad* was clearly in arrears. The wording of the note in the return suggests (but does not prove) that the Eassie line had closed before 1 July 1847, the starting-date for this particular return.

2 August 1848: Perth to Forfar line opened; Coupar Angus; Ardler; Eassie; and Glamis reopened with it. Probably at the same time the line from Newtyle reopened to Meigle to provide a connecting service for Perth and Forfar trains. *Cal* says that in September 1848 'the Newtyle branch opened as Scottish Midland (previously worked by Newtyle and Coupar Angus Railways)', which suggests a slightly later reopening date but this might simply refer to a change of ownership or reflect Brand's lack of exact knowledge about the line. This reopened stretch was operated separately since, unlike the Perth to Forfar line, it had not yet been converted to standard gauge. A contractor was given occupation of the line for three months from 1 October 1849 but the bulk of the work was done in one month *(Newtyle)*. *Brad* is no help since it does not show any closure at this time. However, its treatment of the Newtyle line was chaotic and lacking in detail. In September 1849 it repeated previous month's table with note: 'No information, accuracy uncertain'; from January to May (inclusive) 1850, line missing completely; June 1850 back, as a footnote to Perth and Forfar table; November or December 1850 again had own table but no detail and no indication that there was any continuation from Newtyle to Meigle. *Murray*, April 1852, does at least show that this link was in use.

In 1861 the northern continuation of the Newtyle line was diverted from an eastward-facing connection at Meigle to a westward-facing one at Ardler. All in print (e.g. *G&S*) give 1 August for this, but the change to Ardler Junction appears in the July tt; this might have been premature, but the line is better known for late entries (the Alyth branch, opened 2 September 1861, was first included in October). About this time, Meigle (later renamed Alyth Junction) was re-sited ready to act as junction for the Alyth line. The June tt has Meigle (in May Meigle Junction) but it is impossible to determine from the tt whether this was the old one renamed, or the new one, since it had lost its junction status for the time being.

1837 April 3. Paisley & Renfrew.

Horse-drawn, 4ft 6in. gauge. *Return* for second half of 1840 shows 'no intermediate stops'; that for second half of 1842 shows that stop(s) were then made *(RAIL 1053/1)*. Bought 31 July 1852 by GSW and let to contractor – different gauge meant could not be worked as part of main system *(GSW)*. Line closed 1 February 1866 for conversion to standard gauge (buses provided meantime). Reopened 1 May 1866, now linked to main system. Early tts say runs from 'The Railway Wharf on the Clyde near Renfrew'.

1838. Arbroath & Forfar (see S.G.E. Lyghe, article, *The Arbroath & Forfar Railway, RM January and February 1953)*. Opened, horse-drawn, Arbroath Harbour to Leysmill 24 November 1838; extended, still horse-drawn, to Forfar Play Field 4 December 1838. Locomotive service Arbroath Catherine Street to Forfar Play Field began 3 January 1839; company gave this as its opening date in *PP 1*, presumably because this was start of full service. Originally 5ft 6in. gauge; first standard gauge train 7 July 1847.

1838 May 29. Manchester & Bolton *(Manch G – co n 26th, description 30th)*.

There was earlier public use (28th?): on 30th paper (then published Wednesdays and Saturdays) said that in its issue 'of Saturday' it had described directors' trip of 'Thursday last' and that several trains with public on board had travelled line both ways on 'Monday last', thanks to the 'liberal permission' of the directors; this would suggest directors 24th, public pre-opening trips 28th, especially since the paper seems to have been prompt with news – the official public opening was described as 'yesterday'. However, 'last' as used then can cause problems since some seem to have used it in the sense of a day in the previous week. Elsewhere (e.g. *LY*) the directors' trip has been dated to 17th. *LY* gives the *Bolton Chronicle* of 26th as its source and perhaps that paper used 'last' in a way that was misunderstood.

Over the early years there was much chopping and changing: stations were closed, reopened and renamed in a way that makes exact description impossible. Both 'Farnworth' and 'Clifton' were at different times applied to different sites (interpretation supported by L. Crowther's research on maps at Bolton Library). *Whishaw* commented: 'The Company have very wisely abstained from throwing away money on costly buildings', and this would have made changes cheap and easy. Furthermore, there are gaps in tt evidence, so that some short-term changes might be hidden; mileages given in tables are too inaccurate to help.

Opening notice *Manchester 26 May* says, 'There will be no Booking-place, except at the Company's Offices,

at the respective Stations in Manchester and Bolton'; does that mean no intermediate stops or were there 'halts' at which one paid the guard? – former more likely?

Earliest intermediate detail is in *Bolton*, citing *Bolton Chronicle* tt for 11 June 1838, which quotes stops at Pendleton Bridge; Dixon Fold Bridge, Clifton; and Seddon's Fold Bridge, Kearsley (semicolons have replaced commas in the original since its presentation made three stops look like five). Elsewhere, was 'Seddon's Field Bridge'.

LY says Agecroft and Ringley were mentioned in the initial press report[*]. Agecroft Bridge did not appear in any public tt then, and was the station for Manchester Racecourse, only used on race days; the item in *Manch G* said 'preparations making at the Agecroft Bridge station for the setting down of passengers' and that it expected many from both ends of line to use for Manchester Races, in preference to using roads to Kersal Moor. Ringley was another name for Kearsley. Pendleton Windsor Bridge (which appears to be a conflation of two names) and Tunnel (eventually Farnworth) were added later in 1838.

[*] = Other stations may have existed but were too insignificant for journalist to mention.

B.T. Barton, *History of Farnworth and Kersley* [sic], Bolton, 1887, reproduced long sections from a pamphlet on this line by A. Freeling (published in Liverpool, 1838). This listed: Manchester or New Bailey Street Salford; Windsor Bridge – 'station contemplated'; Pendleton Bridge; Age Croft (races only, here Heaton Park races run annually; reference to Kersal Moor racecourse, nearer than Heaton Park)[*]; Dixon Fold; Stoneclough Bridge (later Ke(a)rsley); Tunnel (later Farnworth); Moses Gate; Bolton. (Preston Reference Library via L. Crowther).

[*] = Kersal Moor used for races until 1847, when switched to Manchester Racecourse; Heaton Park (longish walk) last used 1839, then races switched to Aintree (L. Crowther).

Brad 19 October 1839 listed: Pendleton Bridge; Dixon Fold; Stoneclough (yet another name for Kearsley); Moses Gate – no Tunnel.

Whishaw (1840) said there were 'several' intermediate stations of which the principal was Stone Clough.

To start with, Pendleton (alias Pendleton Bridge) and Windsor Bridge seem to have alternated in use. It has been assumed in this book that Pendleton was the original. Individual station detail is covered as fully as is known in Section 4, but the following gaps in the detail provided by *Brad* should be borne in mind: 1 January 1840 to about November 1840; round about July 1841; August 1843 to August 1845 (inclusive). Though these are short gaps, the known history of this line makes it unwise to write them off as of no consequence.

1838 October 8. Dundee & Arbroath opened for passengers *(PP 1)*. Date usually given, Saturday 6 October *(T 12th/Glasgow Courier)* was probably formal only – *RM January 1958, p. 25*, only mentions one train each way on 6th and brief description reads like that of formal opening. No certain initial detail available. *PP 1*, a few months after opening, has fare list and *Robinson*, 'corrected to July 1840' lists same stations: Broughty Ferry; Monifieth; Carnoustie; Easthaven. *Brad* first detail April 1848.

1839 June 10. LSW: Winchester to Southampton. *Freeling's London & Southampton Railway Companion*, 1839 (written when there was still a gap in the line between Basingstoke and Winchester) includes stations at Shawford (alias Twyford); Barton ('gives easy access to Bishop's Stoke' – later Eastleigh); Swathling. However, his description seems to have been derived from maps and plans of what was intended rather than from personal observation. It says that Southampton station is situated on the banks of Southampton Water and makes no reference to the temporary station at Northam Road or to the dispute which led to it, though elsewhere there are references to problems with landowners over the purchase of land. The temporary station seems only to have reached the local press and would thus have been unknown to someone writing from London; furthermore it is known from other sources that the first Shawford/Twyford station opened after the line and had a very short life, thus limiting severely the time available for its inclusion by personal observation. His 'stations' seem more likely to have been <u>intentions</u> rather than realities, though something might have been done in the other cases. None of these extra 'stations' is included in the fare- and time-tables in Freeling.

1839 June 22. Newcastle & North Shields: Newcastle Carliol Square to (North) Shields *(NE)*. *Co notice Newcastle Journal 22 June* confirms date and says trains will call at stations of Carville (= Wallsend) and Percy Main. An opening notice (dated 12 June) reproduced in A. Guy, *Steam and Speed*, Newcastle Libraries & Information Service, 2003, p. 64, says will call at Walker(gate), Carville and Howden (= Howdon). Reason for discrepancy unknown. *Whishaw* called Howdon 'station in Willington'. Heaton was added later (see entry in Section 4). *Brad* first gave detail March 1864. *Returns* for early 1840s *(RAIL 1053/1)* show that this, unlike the other short lines in this area, was essentially a passenger line, already providing a 30-minute interval service.

1840. Maryport & Carlisle. Based on company's minutes *(RAIL 472/2)*. Formal opening 15 July 1840, when a party of directors travelled from Maryport to Arkleby Pits, added a few wagons of coal to their train and went back to Maryport (also briefly described, *T 21st/ The Carlisle Patriot*). No exact date for public passenger opening has been found; the safest answer would seem

to be 'Autumn 1840'. The report for the half-yearly meeting held at Aspatria, 12 August 1840, stresses the incomplete nature of the line and says: 'The traffic of this Railway, consisting of coal carried for exportation [depends on the Harbour at Maryport]'. There is no reference to passengers. The figures for passenger revenue for the half-year ending 31 December 1840, derived from later reports and *Returns* suggest that about half the number were carried compared with later periods, though exact comparison is made impossible by the extension of the line to Aspatria, 12 April 1841 (J. Simmons, *The Maryport & Carlisle Railway*, Oakwood, 1947) and the provision of a connecting coach service to Wigton from 25 May (minutes of 22 May; tt reproduced in *RM February 1928*). It should be added that the *Returns* are dated from 15 July but are clearly not fully reliable; the timetable quoted in the returns would have resulted in the running of at least three times as many trains as they said they ran. Overall the picture is of a railway taking some time to get properly organised and thus unlikely to have been able to provide a reliable enough service to attract many, if any, passengers in its early days.

What station arrangements were available is unclear. If the minutes are interpreted literally, Maryport was the only station at first. *Return* shows that at the start of 1841 the service was Maryport to Arkleby, all trains stopping at Dearham Bridge and Bull Gill. There were other stops, if not at first, then soon after. A tt reproduced in *D&C 14* and another in an early *Tuck* say that passengers dropped between stations would be charged the fare to the next listed one. Further, all early trains were mixed, thus building in stops at collieries or collecting sidings on the way.

Even Maryport presents problems. The formal opening ran to the harbour and Clinker's note about re-siting in 1860 implies that the station replaced was off the main line; the company's early returns to the Board of Trade show that no purely passenger trains were at first run and passengers were still being carried by mixed trains in the mid-1840s or later so the possibility of travel to the harbour must be considered. However, Col. Cobb's Atlas shows the first station on the main line, replaced somewhat nearer Carlisle in 1860; this is supported by inspection report dated 17 November 1845 (recommending refusal to open) which said Whitehaven Junction line terminated at a junction in the station yard at Maryport. Line south actually opened 19 January 1846.

10 May 1843: Carlisle to Wigton. Date presently given is from *D&C 14*. J. Simmons's book on line (Oakwood, 1947) says directors had preliminary trip on 1 May and line was brought into use on 3rd, based on *Carlisle Patriot, 29 April, 6 May. Railway Times, 29 April* said opening was fixed for 3 May and gave details of 'extensive arrangements … for the accommodation of the public'. It refers only to one train each way, from Wigton to Carlisle and back, with a banquet after the return to

Wigton; it says train will stop at stations at Crofton Gate, Thursby Mill (= Curthwaite) and Dalston. Whilst this trip was apparently open to all, it does not look like the start of a normal public service; latter might have started on 10th, as in *D&C 14*, but why a week's delay? – line had been inspected and passed. W.A.C. Smith and P. Anderson, *Carlisle's Railways*, Irwell, 1997, also give 10th, but no source provided; it refers to an early temporary station at Currock Pond (would have been first stop out of Carlisle – see map on p.3 of that book).

Aspatria to Low Row, opened 2 December 1844 and Brookfield to Low Row, opened 10 February 1845. Printed inspection report dated 1 February 1845, approving intended opening on 10th contains list of stations including those on stretch covered by brief report of 13 November 1844. These, with mileages from Carlisle Crown Street, are Airbank [presumably = Aikbank] at 14m 45ch, Low Row 15m 60ch, Heathfield 17m 8ch, Aspatria 19m 3ch. The 1845 report covers from 'a place called Brookfield' to 'station' at Low Row. Clearly last not intended to be a temporary. Dates given in body of book assume: 1) Heathfield opened with the line and was closed when Brayton opened to the public; 2) Aikbank opened with its stretch of line and, together with Low Row, was closed when Leegate opened (date for that from *D&C 14*). The reasoning is that the line opened with closely-spaced stations and found it desirable to thin them out somewhat. See {map 20g}.

1840 May 2. Preston & Longridge. Formal opening was on Friday 1 May; the public service is said to have started 'next week' so it is impossible to say whether this began 2 May or 6 May – initially service only Saturdays and Wednesdays. First *Return* seen, for first half of 1847, has notes that it is a mineral line worked by horse-power and that 'Passengers are frequently brought down etc, by the Stone Waggons' as well as passenger trains. This raises possibility of passenger use all days prior to introduction of all-days service, though latter was then already in operation. First in *Brad* July 1848, when service ran every day. No early detail of intermediate stops. Financial problems led to brief closure 14 June 1852 (*Rtn* gives Fleetwood etc Co return to 13 June, when it ceased to work line – probably last day – was Sunday service). Reop by 24 July 1852 (has been reop, *Herapath of that date*).

1840 May 12. London & Brighton: Brighton to Shoreham. Formal opening May 11. In addition to the directors' special, other trains ran in the evening and upwards of 1,000 were carried (*Hants Teleg 18th*); the impression given is that these were non-stop runs from one end of the line to the other. Public opening date *co n T 8th*.

1840 July 2. Hull & Selby: market trains. These provided the first service for some stations and it is impossible to be certain when these began. Company's tt added a market train from Hull August 1841; nothing extra other way so presumably used ordinary trains to go to Hull. No extra stops mentioned. Same up to and including December 1841 (*MT6/1/171*). *Brad* first mentioned market trains, without specifying stops, in May 1842. *Tuck*, about June 1843, named Wressel Bridge and Bromfleet. *Brad* first added names in July 1844: Wenpel Bridge (corrected to Wressel Bridge by the end of the year); Bromflut (corrected later); Crabley Creek. It is thus possible that Crabley Creek was 'opened' after the others.

Wressle, Crabley Creek and Br(o)omfleet omitted from *Brad* June 1852/June 1853; all back (market) November 1854; Wressle to full service September 1855; the other two were last in *Brad* October 1861 but *U* says still in wtt January 1864 so market service probably continued (as it also had during first absence?). Crabley Creek was probably closed by November 1872, when Broomfleet did get back into tt, market only.

1840 July 16. Preston & Wyre: Preston to Fleetwood. *Co n T 13th* only mentions Poulton and Kirkham as intermediate stops; this is supported by early *Brad*, *Freeling* (early 1841?), and broken run of company tts (*RAIL 981/410*). See reprints of early *Brad* for way tables were laid out.

However, by early 1841 (perhaps from start) there was Saturday market service from Preston Maudland that also stopped at Lea; Treals (Earl Derby's Siding, Treals is shown 74 chains east of Kirkham on *RCH Lancashire & District Map 1905*); Weeton (between Kirkham and later Singleton); and Ramper (at/near later Thornton-Cleveleys) (*Freeling*). 'Road' was often added to these names. It is unlikely that any stations existed at these market stops: a report in the *Returns* of an accident in November 1841 said that the train had stopped to put down passengers 'at the Lea road' and these reports were normally very precise in their wording and one would have expected 'station' to be included if there had been one there. By December 1841 *Brad* Salwick had replaced Treals. Market stops last appeared in April 1842 *Brad* though reorganisation of tables could have accounted for their omission next month (line now incorporated in North Union table). They were also absent from Company's tt for 1 July 1842, so market service might have been briefly discontinued; it was back in *Brad* November 1842 when this line again had a table of its own. Weeton and Ramper were last there April 1843. In May 1843 Lea and Salwick were shown in the fare table only so it is not clear whether they were now 'all days' stations or still market only. Probably it was the former since in July 1843 all trains clearly stopped at them (as is also shown by company's tt of 11 December 1843). *Brad* last shows them May 1844; they are back again February 1847, when first orthodox table for line was included; thus impossible to say whether this gap represents a brief closure or simply lack of tt detail. *Tuck* complicates the issue by including Weeton and Ramper in tt issued about June 1843; perhaps inertia.

Already by early 1841 two out of three ordinary trains

each way daily were starting from the North Union station at Preston rather than the company's own Maudland.

1840 August 5. Slamannan: Glasgow to Causewayend, near Linlithgow. Initially 4ft 6in. gauge. *MK* says line closed to minerals from 26 July to 14 August and to passengers [also from 26 July?] to 23 August for regauging. Service originally provided to link Glasgow and Edinburgh, passengers transferring to canal barges at Causewayend; slow and, even when road transport replaced barges, very vulnerable after full rail link opened via Falkirk 1842. Original intermediate stations were: Airdrie (later Commonhead); Slammanan; Avonbridge *(MK)*. Line completely omitted from *Brad* in mid-1840s but service continued (*Robertson* shows passenger duty being paid); even when back in *Brad*, full detail not given until June 1851, though *Topham* provided from July 1848 to March 1850 (inclusive).

By March 1845 the service had been cut back at the western end to Rawyards (opened ?) as its terminus *(MK)*, though there was still a service from Glasgow to Hallcraig (see 1844 December 26★★, below).

By August 1847 line had been converted to standard gauge and extended east to Linlithgow on the main Edinburgh to Glasgow line; the western terminus was now Airdrie Hallcraig Street *(MK)*. In 1856 the line was diverted at its eastern end to Bo'ness instead of Linlithgow.

Monkland minute of 24 June 1859 ordered immediate stop to passenger traffic over Ballochney incline (involved line from Gartsherrie to Rawyards, including the Hallcraig branch) following accident; service resumed 1 May 1860 *(MK)*. Following month they ordered safety siding at Commonhead *(SRO BR/MNK/1/3)*.

Also see entries on BO'NESS and COMMONHEAD (Section 4). Unlikely that service to Linlithgow resumed during suspension of Bo'ness service – expected to be brief *(co notice Falkirk Herald)*.

1840 September 10. Closure of Grand Junction stations at Bridgeford and Coppenhall. *T Friday 18th/Derby Mercury*: 'On Thursday last the second class stations at Bridgeford and Coppenhall were closed, the trains ceasing on that day to stop at them'. By later standards this would have been interpreted as last trains Wednesday (9th), no trains Thursday. However is impossible to be sure they were using words in that way so that the Thursday might have been the last day of use. (See *1844 December 1* and *1850 July 1*, below.)

1840 October 1. Grand Junction: Crewe to Chester *(LNW- line)*. Generally no detail in early years. Detail was given from June 1842 to January 1843 (inclusive). Full and continuous coverage began December 1845.

1840 October 9. Taff Vale: Cardiff to Navigation House (later Abercynon). Notices issued by the TV company to both *Merlin* and ancestor of *Cardiff & M G*, and published in both papers on 3 October, say that railway will be opened to the public on 8th; service shown

was 8am and 4pm from Cardiff, 9am and 5pm from Navigation House, with road connection to and from Merthyr provided. However, descriptions in both papers of 10th suggest events of this day were purely formal and that established sources are right to quote 9th as opening date. It would have been possible for mid-day ceremonial train to have fitted between advertised trains but complaint of Merthyr reporter that he had been given a visitor's ticket for the ride from Cardiff but that no arrangements had been made to help him get to Cardiff for the opening ceremony or for his return home from Navigation House would suggest that no other trains ran on the 8th.

Papers did not give full details of stops. According to *A History of Radyr and Morganstown*, Radyr and Morganstown New Horizon History Group, 1991, Llandaf(f) and Pontypridd opened with line and decision to have station at Pentyrch taken 12 days after line opened; all are in inspection report on extension to Merthyr (April 1841) *(RAIL 1053/2, p.131)*.

1841. Northern & Eastern: opening of four stations. They first appeared in *Brad* (in footnotes), April 1842: Stratford; Marsh Lane Tottenham; and Cadmores Lane Cheshunt on stretch of line opened 15 September 1840, and Burnt Mill Netteswell (Nettleswell in *Brad*) on stretch opened 9 August 1841. All are also present in similarly arranged table in *Robinson*, dated 1842 (GE portion published, photocopy, as *GE Information Sheet T 110, July 1983*). Service shown for them in *Robinson* is different from that in any issue of *Brad* in 1842; comparison of timings in the main tables shows that the information for the line as a whole in *Robinson* is the same as that in *Brad*, December 1841.

Further, earlier, evidence comes from Northern & Eastern *co n T 7th* advertising an extra train for Harlow Bush Fair on 9 and 10 September 1841. This includes: 'The trains will stop at all the usual stations and also at Netteswell' [compiler's underlining].

When N&E first opened, first train of day was operated by adding N&E carriages to EC trains from Shoreditch and detaching them at Stratford for N&E engine to take on (account of accident, 16 September, line's second day, *T 21st*). It is unlikely that this was linked to passenger usage of a station here: EC would presumably have expected passengers from London to travel in their part of train; whilst there might have been opportunities for passengers from Stratford to go towards Broxbourne, opening tt suggests that there was no joining of trains here on return trips, so no way of getting back. Practice of dividing trains cannot have lasted long – by about March 1841 tt all of two companies' departures from Shoreditch were at different times.

There is no certainty about dates for these stations: much is based on timings and initially all N&E timings were given as 1.10, 1.15, 1.20, etc – only in January 1842 did more exact times such as 1.12 make their appearance, so that some peculiar station-to-station timings were shown. It does seem that these occasional stops were at first used instead of regular stations by a few trains. The opening notice lacks detail, as does *Brad* about March 1841 *(RAIL 902/3)*. The sheet tt for April 1841 *(RAIL 903/535)* is the earliest so far seen with intermediate detail. Trains are shown at regular intervals, suggesting no occasional extra stops by any trains. Trains probably ran non-stop to Lea Bridge – only 10 minutes allowed for this, while EC took 11 minutes to their Stratford, including stop at Mile End. Notice for extension to Harlow, 9 August 1841, is no help – only gives times from termini. By October 1841 (see P. Kay's reprint) one train each way did not stop at Edmonton (9am up, 5.30pm down), timings unchanged. This looks likely to have been the start of Marsh Lane/Northumberland Park, since *Robinson* had the 8.30 up and 5.30 down stopping there. It is still impossible to tell what was happening beyond Broxbourne since Roydon and Harlow only appeared in the notes, but later evidence makes it unlikely that Burnt Mill/Harlow was open yet. The opening notice for Spelbrook on 22 November 1841 again lacked detail, but the times from termini tally with those in December 1841 *Brad*, which gave detail for main stations, so it seems safe to treat this as the tt that came into force on 22 November. Stratford was certainly now in use (timings would suggest not earlier): note for Sunday trains said that these stopped at all the stations plus Stratford. Timings here plus the '1842' *Robinson* notes (really December 1841) suggest it was used by some week-day trains also, in one case instead of Lea Bridge. Same evidence suggests that Burnt Mill was now brought into use for one train, as an <u>alternative</u> stop to Roydon and Harlow, neither of which was served by train in question. Similarly, Cadmores Lane seems to have come into use with opening to Spelbrook, simply as an extra stop, though timings given in tt are so imprecise that earlier use cannot entirely be ruled out.

1840 December 28: Manchester & Leeds: Summit Tunnel. Line was now extended from Hebden Bridge to the eastern end of tunnel. Tunnel itself was not ready for use so passengers taken by road from Littleborough to Lanebottom, Walsden, where they joined train in Deanroyd cutting (A. Holt, *A Pennine Pioneer*, G. Kelsall, 1999). Inspection report, dated 23 December 1840, makes it clear that passengers would be conveyed by train to the eastern end of tunnel, and gave 28th as intended opening date; after inspection, BoT wanted certain minor matters dealt with before line opened. Although date on certificate sent to BoT saying this had been done was dated 30 December 1840 it is clear that company opened on the intended date since 28th is confirmed in report, dated 23 February 1841, on opening of next section. Note that BoT role was then still only advisory

1841 February 10. Stockton & Hartlepool. Built without Act of Parliament, promoters making their own arrangements with local landowners. They soon decided to try for Act and result was inspection (favourable) on 6 September 1841 *(RAIL 1053/2, p. 162)*. This only mentioned stations at Stockton and Greatham – nothing even about Hartlepool. It did mention 'lodges' for gatekeepers provided near level crossings, two near Cowpen and one near the Hartlepool end, as well as one by Greatham station. If this company followed Liverpool & Manchester habits, these might have acted as 'halts' – perhaps Stranton was so served initially. According to R. Wood, *West Hartlepool*, West Hartlepool Corporation, 1967, Billingham and Seaton (Carew) were also original stations; Cowpen was temporary 'halt' for workers at brickworks during and just after construction of line. He also adds that original Hartlepool station was poop of old Dutch galliot, whose cabins were used by booking clerk and station master.

1841 March 31. Great North of England: Darlington to York. Line date *T 2 April*. Earliest tt, May or June 1841, omits: Danby Wiske; Otterington; Sessay; Raskelf; Tollerton. All were added July/September 1841 without any alteration to the overall timings of the trains.

1841 March 31. Glasgow, Paisley & Greenock: Paisley to Greenock. Date given is taken from *Tuck's Shareholder's Manual of 1847*. This appears to be a corrected item. The 1845 *Manual* had given 29 March for this line, 13 July 1840 for Glasgow to Paisley (now amended to 14th) and 8ft 8½in as the gauge (now shrunk to 4ft 8½in). Date also used by *Cal* and *Lewin. Tuck* refers to 'six stations', which suggests that Langbank was not yet open (not in *Murray* September 1844 either). Pamphlet on line produced by Jordanhill College, 1978, quotes passage from *Greenock Advertiser (2 April)* which describes opening on Tuesday 30 March; only mentions one train and celebrations, so probably formal. Includes Port Glasgow and Bishopton but not Langbank. Same pamphlet contains notice of addition of third-class carriages on certain trains from 23 May 1842; still no Langbank.

At one stage in later 1840s Port Glasgow was omitted from tt. Probably assumed stop: at first tt said all trains stopped there, and also at Bishopton and Houston by request. Reference to last two continued when Port Glasgow dropped; seems unlikely that they would have closed what had been treated as most important intermediate stop.

1841 April 6: North Midland line; opening of new stations. Date from *Derby Mercury 14th*. This said 11 new stations had been opened; it listed 10 (Methley being the missing one). Whilst there was some possible ambiguity in the way it used 'Tuesday last', support is given to the 6th rather than the 13th by a time bill headed 6 April; this does not actually say 'a new service' but it would have been most unusual for such a bill to be issued mid-week for any other reason (information from J. Gough). *The Eastern Counties Herald* (a Hull paper) of Thursday, March 25 said, 'On Tuesday last [16th? 23rd?], two additional stopping trains were started, to run daily between Leeds and Derby; and the number of places at which they stop for passengers is no less than 20, or seven more than the number of regular stations. They were described as mainly for the use of those attending markets at the main centres, not providing connections with trains going further afield. Also quoted by *Herapath, 27 March.*

The version based on the Derby paper is preferred as it was the more local one. There are also discrepancies within the Hull version, suggesting that something planned for the future was misinterpreted as having already happened. It starts, 'The Directors of this Railway [North Midland] are making arrangements ...', which would better fit the future than the past. Later it says, 'the number of trains running daily on the North Midland is 59 and will in a few days be 63'.

1841 November. Birmingham & Gloucester.
A number of places received their first (and in some cases only) service in the form of passenger carriages attached to goods trains going to Birmingham Camp Hill, which by now was closed to ordinary passenger trains. These places were 'police stations' (= signalling points). Some developed into ordinary stations, others soon lost their primitive service *(BG)*. Service involved began 15 November *(co n, e.g. T 13th)* but no stops were listed and statements in the committee minutes suggest details of these not settled yet (J. Gough).

1841 November 29. LSW: Gosport branch.
Opening date from *Salisbury 6th*. Line opened against BoT advice and operated up to and including 2 December; closed Friday 3 December *(Hants Adv)*; reopened 7 February 1842 *(co n T 9th)*. Heavy rains had made clay in a cutting north of Fareham unstable. Problems about the stability of a tunnel had delayed line opening and there were still some worries about this but the cutting was main problem *(co n T 4 December;* letter in *RM January 1937, pp. 62–3,* based on information from Chief Engineer of Southern Railway).

1842 February 21. Edinburgh & Glasgow.
In April and May 1842 it seems from *Brad* that the stations listed are all of those that were open. However, in May, only some of the stations are clearly specified and there are vague references in the notes to passenger trains calling at 'all stations' that could include some not now listed and to the carriage of passengers by goods trains to 'all stations'. The evidence for some early lines shows that some places were only served in this way, increasing the possibility of unlisted places being served. The opening notice, *T 19th*, has a note that refers to the 'Road Stations'. This might simply mean 'intermediate stations' though other companies at this time sometimes used that phrase to cover stops other than the listed ones.

1842 December 11. MS&L: Godley temporary to Broadbottom. Date from *GC*. A Sunday, but formal opening had been previous day, so perhaps no objection to regular service starting now. A fortnight later they opened the next stretch to the public on a Sunday which was also Christmas Day (see DINTING, Section 4).

1843. S&D: Bishop Auckland & Weardale and extension
(for earlier history of S&D and some general points about its and its satellites' methods see 1825**).
The Bishop Auckland & Weardale minutes *(RAIL 46/4, 46/5)* show that the line to the permanent station at Bishop Auckland was opened on 30 January 1843, ahead of the rest of the line to Crook, and that the generally-quoted 8 November 1843 for opening to Crook was for goods only. The Bishop Auckland opening date is supported by S&D's *Returns*. In the second half of 1842 these mentioned trains Shildon to South Church; in the first half of 1843 they were described as Shildon to Bishop Auckland; Bishop Auckland was included in *Tuck* June 1843.

The passenger opening date to Crook has not so far been traced; however, the minutes do show that the line was inspected on 1 January 1844 and that permission to open for passengers was received on or before 6 January. Inspection report *(MT 6/2/23)* said that following stations were proposed (original mileages adjusted so that Bishop Auckland = 0): South Church; Bishop Auckland; Escombe (1m 33ch); Old Etherley Colliery (2m 26ch); Low Bitchburn (3m 26ch); Howden (4m 18ch); Crook (5m 49ch). Only 1st, 2nd and 7th finished. No objection to line opening on 3 January, as directors proposed.

This presents various problems. Line could only have opened on 3rd if they had acted on inspector's verbal assurance; 3rd was a Wednesday – but first service shown in *Brad* was Thursday only. No mention of station for Escombe seen anywhere else – though market trains might have stopped there. Low Bitchburn probably eventually materialised as (Wear Valley) Junction.

It is likely that the initial service to Crook was market day(s) only because when it first appeared in *Brad*, July 1844, only a Thursday market service was shown; first clearly in full use January 1845. July 1844 also marked the first appearance of Bishop Auckland both ways, suggesting that this revision was at least partly behind events; thus Crook's service might have begun earlier. Evidence from other parts of S&D system suggests that unfinished stations did not provide any bar to starting passenger service – and inspector's mention of Crook as 'finished' seems flattering given what was in the minutes about Crook at this time.

Return for first half of 1844 says trains run were: 6 Bishop Auckland to Stockton and 10 Stockton to Middlesbrough daily (unique thereabouts in suggesting through Bishop Auckland to Stockton service); that for second half of 1844 says 3 Crook to Bishop Auckland, 4 Bishop

Auckland to Darlington, 6 Darlington to Stockton and 9 Stockton to Middlesbrough daily; no mention of market trains. Suggests full service to Crook began earlier than shown in *Brad* but does not guarantee it was provided for whole half-year.

S&D and *G&S* say there was an experimental service from Crook to Crawley and Cold Rowley, dividing at Waskerley, op 1 September 1845, cut back to Waskerley 31 October 1845, reinstated fully 1 April 1846. *Brad* shows Crook as the terminus until November 1846. Since this company's tables in *Brad* often included a mention of the lack of recent information, and the information already given shows that it was often behind events, this does not invalidate these dates, especially since an experimental service might well be omitted.

Wear & Derwent Junction minutes *(RAIL 716/1)* are little help but do fit normal S&D pattern of providing stations after service had begun and uncertainty about sort of service to be provided. 8 April 1846 – agreed plan for station at Waskerley Park and ordered building to start but 30 April agreed building should be suspended and plans used for Cold Rowley instead. 19 August 1846 – some progress made at Cold Rowley and coach shed at Crawley progressing to satisfaction; 29 August 1846 – latter probably ready in three weeks. In fact, Crawley was last in *Brad* December 1846 and Waskerley was shown as terminus thereafter.

Line from Crook to Waskerley was not inspected by the authorities prior to opening. This emerged when Captain Wynne investigated death of farmer, killed by goods at untended level crossing, and found two trains daily each way were carrying passengers; Captain Laffan was sent to report (April–May 1850). He wrote that now essentially a mineral district; previously few people; no/poor communications other than railway so company had come to attach some passenger carriages to mineral trains for benefit of miners, coke-burners and other workmen. Total revenue of stretch for last six months of 1849 was only £179. Only stations Tow Law; 'Cole' Rowley; Waskerley Park. These had only rough platforms, no signals. Normally would not sanction for passengers since also dangers from inclines and unguarded points. However, no other means of travel in district; revenue so small that company would not spend on improvements; official ban would probably lead to men travelling free on mineral wagons so best to leave. Train would have stopped to drop/collect mineral wagons, so chance for workmen to board/leave between stations.

In March 1850 fastest trains were allowed 80 minutes from Crook to Cold Rowley (less than 20 miles) with stops shown only at Tow Law and Waskerley Park. Incline haulage would have accounted for some of this time but there would have been time for extra stops. References have been found to High Souk (alias HIGH STOOP), which appears on the early Ordnance Survey map for this area (see D&C reprint), and to SALTERSGATE COTTAGE, which would have been

further towards Burnhill, but passenger use cannot be confirmed (see entries in Section 4) – perhaps railway staff or other workmen only.

1843 May 23. Hayle (later West Cornwall).
Opened for minerals in sections 23 December 1837 to 11 June 1838. Casual carriage of passengers in mineral trucks began 1841 or earlier. The original line reached Hayle along the north bank of the river.

23 May 1843: proper passenger service began (free travel the previous day). At first operated by a contractor, W.M. Crotch, a local inn-keeper. His advertisement *(Penzance 31st)* listed 'stations' as Redruth; Carn Brea; Camborne; Hambly's Hotel for Copperhouse; Riviere Bridge (maps show area north of the river as Roviere or Riviere); Crotch's Hotel [near] Hayle Foundry. Unlikely that any proper stations existed at opening. Description of free day trip *(R Cornwall Gaz 26th)* refers to passengers being set down at Camborne where the main line crossed the road and no reference is made to anything resembling a station anywhere along the line. On that first trip haulage was mixed: steam, stationary engine for the incline at 'Hangarrick', horses from Hayle Bridge (probably same as Crotch's Riviere Bridge) to Hayle.

A proper building was opened at the Hayle terminus on 27 May 1844 *(Penzance 5 June)*. Company's minutes do refer later to existence of, and expenditure on, stations but unfortunately the original books were destroyed and Kew has only a few scraps (copies made by individuals for their own use etc).

No later advertisements or tts seen give a full list of stations. They do show that on 8 April 1844 Crotch was still running trains. On Whit Monday, 27 May 1844, upwards of 1,600 passengers are supposed to have been carried. Crotch could not have coped with this on his own – perhaps company now took over, which would fit opening of Hayle station. For this most passengers would have had to be carried in what were normally goods wagons and either steam used all the way or passengers walked to north side of bridge.

West Briton, 30 August 1844 carried notice headed 'Hayle Railway', dealing with an alteration to time of afternoon trains; no reference to Crotch. *Return* first provided for second half of 1844; no suggestion in this that anyone other than company involved in operation of line. In any case, Crotch seems to have acted as agent for the company rather than being an independent operator like contractors on some north-eastern lines. His advertisements frequently made it clear that he was acting under the orders of the directors so that no change might have been discernable when he handed over – timetables remained the same. Furthermore, some at least of trains were mixed (evidence from accident mentioned below).

Line first appeared, termini only, in *Brad* December 1844 (suggests company had certainly taken over by now). Camborne and Carn Brea were added May 1845; latter omitted again soon after. Since Carn Brea was the headquarters of the railway (minutes show that meetings were held at station there), it is unlikely that tt gives full story. No change in timings followed omission of Carn Brea – always 15 minutes between Redruth and Camborne, both ways – see 1845 and 1850 *Brad* reprints.

There is conflict between the stops mentioned here and those listed by Clinker. Redruth; Camborne; Copperhouse (ignoring the Hotel part) agree. Crotch's Hotel would have been the same as, or near to, the terminus in Foundry Square. Carn Brea appears in all, though no contemporary reference to it as Pool (its name now according to Clinker) has been found. Riviere does not appear in any modern list; it is not clear whether stop was north or south end of bridge (more likely both?). The original practice of switching to horse-power was normal, at least until early 1845, when the reference to the exchange point is 'North Hayle', so a stop would automatically have been built in north of the river. Many travellers would have found a stop at the southern end of the swing-bridge more convenient than the terminus.

An accident described by Jenkins refers to passenger carriages being detached before branch to North Quay. Another version, in *Penzance 6 September 1843*, says accident was near the 'wood bridge' at Hayle; likeliest site for this would seem to have been over non-navigable north-western end of the Pool, a little before the iron swing-bridge over the canal. Latter had originally been built for road traffic but had ceased to be used by this for some time before railway took it over and adapted it for rail traffic. Part certainly street tramway – line ran along Penpol Terrace. Thus a 'stop anywhere' policy likely over last stretch. Reports of accidents in the local press confirm that stops were made on the horse-drawn stretch in Hayle itself.

No contemporary reference has been found to stops at Angarrack; Gwinear; and Penponds which are all in modern lists. Stops at Angarrack and Penponds would have been necessary owing to incline haulage at these points; perhaps they were assumed stops, so few living within reach that they were not worth a mention. If any Gwin(n)ear stop did exist, it would probably have been about half way between Angarrack (1852) and the later Gwinear Road; a stop at the latter place would have made no sense for the people of Gwinear when the possible limits of travel were Hayle and Redruth. One possibility is that some of these places were used in succession: Copperhouse prior to 1852, replaced by Angarrack after reopening, replaced again by Gwinear Road in 1853 (n.b. Clinker mistakenly assumed that this opened/reopened with the line reopening).

Line closed 16 February 1852 for improvement *(co n R Cornwall Gaz 13th)*; reopened 11 March 1852 *(co n R Cornwall Gaz 12th)*, with deviations, as part of planned Plymouth to Penzance line; station details in Section 4.

There were excursions over parts of short branches, normally only used for minerals. On Portreath branch Tehidy was for some years used annually for grand gala of the West Cornwall Teetotal Association at Tehidy Park, home of the Basset family. One such use was 29 August 1856, trains from Penzance and Truro; (M. Trevena, *TTS July 1985*; in explanation of ticket illustrated May 1985 issue). Another occurred on 1 August 1859 *(West Briton 5th)*; passengers set down at Lovely Cottage, Illogan, a short distance from park; four special trains used.

Also see: A.C. Todd & P. Laws, *Industrial Archaeology of Cornwall*, D&C 1972; S.C. Jenkins & R. Langley, *The West Cornwall Railway*, Oakwood, 2002.

1844. Liskeard & Caradon Railway. See *Caradon; Looe*. Formally opened for goods 28 November 1844, from Cheesewring to Tremabe, between Caradon and Liskeard *(West Briton, 6 December; Royal Cornwall Gazette 4th)*. Note line begun at 'wrong end'; they wanted Cheesewring granite for supporting rails – thus little commercial value in line opened now – would need part opened March 1846 (Tremabe to Moorswater and canal). Press refers to start of formal trip from 'upper terminus', end at 'the present completion of the line'.

Horse-drawn until March 1862, then locomotives *(Cornwall)*. First *Return* made 1849: 'passengers not carried'.

However, there were excursions throughout most of line's life. 25 June 1850 *(West Briton 28th)* nearly 300 members of Liskeard Temperance Society and their friends took trip to Cheesewring (terminus) in seven carriages (open trucks?); novelty attracted 'some thousands' of spectators. Ticket for Cheesewring exists *(JB)*, dated 19 September 1883; probably for Looe Temperance Society's 48th annual meeting, at Looe. Event is described in *R Cornwall Gaz* of 28 September; no reference to special rail provision but St Cleer band in evidence and many visitors; it may be that ticket's name was short-hand for anywhere along line. Many earlier meetings might have generated rail traffic, given Cornish habits of the time.

Unofficial passenger service began ? One ploy to evade official rules was to let passenger travel free but charge for parcel or hat. By 1879 practice had arisen of passengers buying tickets for Moorswater to Looe, though they would not travel on that section, and being given a free pass to South Caradon, to which point they travelled at their own risk. M.J. Messenger *(RCHS Journal, vol. 19, December 1973)* says that in August 1884 Col. Rich inspected the line and failed to pass it for passenger use but suggested that it was adequate for excursions where passengers travelled free and at own risk; notices were then posted along the Looe and Caradon lines. Service probably ceased in the mid-1890s as track deteriorated owing to company's poverty. *GW Mag February 1909* says practice had been discontinued '13 years ago' because it had become 'too perilous'. *U* refers to stops at St Cleer; Railway Terrace; South Caradon; Tokenbury Corner (on later deviation); Rillaton Bridge. Cheesewring was further on.

1844 August. Springwell Waggonway.

At some time between 5 September 1839 when the Brandling Junction line from Gateshead Oakwellgate to South Shields opened, and August 1844, when the Springwell service first appeared in *Brad*, a service to Jarrow along the Springwell Waggonway was provided from an interchange station on this line. Over the years, this probably used more than one site in Jarrow *(S. Bragg, map evidence)*. This service closed 1 March 1872, when line opened along the south bank of the Tyne gave Jarrow a direct service.

1844 October. Dockers Lane (later Berkswell); Stechford; Marston Green [LNW].

Minutes of Coaching & Police Committee quoted in *LNW Dates*: 9 October 1844 ordered that the short train between Birmingham and Rugby call in future at these, 'Gate' probably needing to be added to all. 27 November 1844 ordered booking huts and platforms to be erected at these 'Crossings'. One possible interpretation would be that trains at first stopped experimentally and that results justified proper provision, though no evidence of pre-December use seen. Certainly in use by 12 December 1844 (H. Jack); first in *Brad* January 1845.

1844 December 1. Closure: West London.

Notice of closure issued by the Company *(T 30 Nov.)* says: 'Passenger trains … will cease running for the winter on and after to-morrow (Saturday), Nov 30 inst'; notice dated 29th. Later usage would have required this to be interpreted as last trains Friday, none Saturday, but evidence of *Return* shows trains did run on the Saturday. 'Winter' lasted nearly 18 years. *Return* for second half of 1844 was from 1 July to 30 November, inclusive, when railway was closed for passenger traffic (no return for first half of year). Return shows 1,452 trains ran, carrying 2,208 passengers (209 first-, 1,999 second-class) and 1 dog (counted as third-class), total revenue £60 8s 9d – they manged £79 16s 9½d for goods.

1844 December 26. MK: Airdrie Hallcraig to Kirkintilloch *(MK; also see 1828 B above)*.

This Kirkintilloch was an exchange station with the Edinburgh & Glasgow, near later Lenzie (which see in Section 4); the exchange was made necessary because the Monklands line was 4ft 6in. gauge. At the same time a horse-drawn service began from Bothlin Viaduct (alias Woodley), immediately under the exchange station, to Kirkintilloch Basin (MK station). The latter was short-lived, ceasing before 23 March 1846.

On 26 and 27 July 1847, surviving main service was suspended while gauge was altered to standard; service then resumed, trains running through to Glasgow Queen Street.

— 1 December 1847: service diverted to Glasgow Townhead (later to Buchanan Street) via Garnkirk.

— 10 December 1849: service returned to Queen Street route, with a connecting service to Cairnhill Bridge.

— 1 December 1850: service cut back to Whifflat (company's spelling).

— 10 December 1851: whole service ceased.

A service from Glasgow Buchanan Street to Airdrie Hallcraig reappeared in tt August 1852.

Full and continuous intermediate detail for these services has not been found.

1845 February 10. Gravesend & Rochester Railway & Canal Company: Gravesend to Strood *(co n T 5th)*.

According to *SE* public opening was preceded by free trips in connection with ferry service from Strood to Chatham (in last week of January, at least) and by 'experimental' service on 8 February.

1845 June 2: Wilsontown, Morningside & Coltness: Morningside to Longridge.

Line date from *Lewin*; all stations given this date are in inspection report *MT6/2/51*; inspector said 'line terminates in a large field about a mile from the village called Whitburn'.

1845 July 8. York & North Midland: York to Scarborough and Rillington to Pickering (thus linking Whitby line, see *1835 B*, above, into the system).

According to K. Hoole, *Rail Centres – York*, Ian Allan, 1983, 7 July was the formal opening and 8th the public one; this is supported by a letter to *The Times* of 3 September 1845, which was one of a series concerned with the poor safety record of the company, and quoted Tuesday 8 July as public opening (since when there had been at least 7 accidents). The first station detail found is that in *Topham* May 1848 (*Brad* did not provide detail until July 1848). All stations listed in printed inspection report dated 5 July 1845.

Portion to Pickering initially used horse-power, in connection with Whitby & Pickering (see 1835 B**, above) – it was poorly ballasted and inspector only recommended permission to open because horses were to be used *(MT 6/2/59)*. *Potter* says original stations were: Low Marishes; High Marishes, alias Marishes, alias Marishes Road (in York & North Midland Rule Book of 1852); Black Bull (alias Kirby, alias Kirby Misperton). First and third soon closed. Third appeared, reopened, in tt November 1853, as Kirby. Black Bull was shown on Macaulay's map of 1851, removed by 1854; Kirby not added until 1856/9. High Marishes was present on his map of 1851; removed 1856/9. According to inspection report dated 5 July 1845 there then were no intermediate stations between Rillington and Pickering.

1845 November. Clarence (leased to Stockton & Hartlepool): Byers Green area market services.

Market service from Todhills and Coxhoe to West Hartlepool and Stockton and back was first in *Brad* November 1845; no intermediate detail; timings suggest Todhills passengers were taken to Coxhoe and back (or left at junction while engine did this trip). August 1848 tt: service was cut back to Byers Green, presumably a previously unlisted stop. June 1864 tt: fortnightly service from Leasingthorne added (no return journey shown); by now timings suggest that carriages from the short branches were collected at junctions to form one train, but that Byers Green passengers still went via Coxhoe on way home. From August 1865 tt the Byers Green service again started from Todhills, no return journey shown. April 1867 tt was last time service was shown.

See Section 4 for later history of Byers Green.

1845 November 24. Manchester & Birmingham: Cheadle Hulme to Macclesfield. *Stockport, 21st,* gave date of line opening without listing stations; *Macclesfield, 22nd,* listed stations but did not explicitly provide opening date, although company's notice was headed November 24.

1845 November 25: all stations also listed in inspection report dated 21 November 1845.

1846 April 13: LY: Ashton branch. Date from *Manchester Guardian (15th* – E. Bredee) and *LY* (different paper). *T 5 September 1848* (item on financial affairs of LY) and *Brad Sh 1850* give 15th – clearly latter result of early copying error. *RCHS Journal October 1971* refers to handbill issued by Manchester & Leeds, dated opening day and giving list of stations and fares. The intermediate stations, with first-class fares from Ashton were: Lamb Bridge (6d); Culcheth (6d); Newton (1/-); Manchester was also 1/-. None of these had been seen elsewhere. It was possible (RCHS suggestion) that they later became Droylesden; Clayton Bridge; Park. Perhaps re-siting involved. If the last did become Park it was presumably included in advance of opening. The earliest full detail seen otherwise is in *Topham* May 1848. A letter from W.J. Skillern in the January 1972 *Journal* said that the 6 inch OS sheet 104 surveyed 1845, published 1848 puts Culcheth at site of Clayton Bridge and Park at its later site. Sheet 105 which should have include the continuation of the line does not but it shows several features including 'Lum' in name (modern Lumb) in the area where Droylesden station was built. 'Newton' might be Miles Platting: this would better reflect the fare quoted, and would fit the fact that Park was opened later. Clayton Bridge, Miles Platting and Park were all within Newton township.

1846 June 5. Middlesbrough & Redcar. Both own company's minutes *(RAIL 484/2)* and minutes of S&D Traffic & Coaching Committee *(RAIL 667/34, 667/35)* give 4 June. However, this was probably formal only. One entry said it was publicly opened on the 4th but an earlier one said it should be ready for opening on 4th and for regular traffic after that day. BoT return was 'From 5 June 1846'.

Other problems concern early stations on line. Only Cleveland Port and Lazenby appeared in early tts (company's and *Brad*) but there are references in the minutes to these plus Cargo Fleet and Lackenby. However, minutes seem to have used Cargo Fleet and Cleveland Port indiscriminately for same site. There is no certainty that all opened with the line. Services provided for some are likely to have been meagre. The company's timetable for September 1847 shows five trains each way per day between Middlesbrough and Redcar. Cleveland Port and Lazenby were only served by two each way. It may be that the unlisted stations were only served, perhaps on a request-only basis, by these two; perhaps request stops were made by some or all of those which, according to the timetable, ran non-stop between Middlesbrough and Redcar. The uncertainties over siting mean that the map needs to be seen as a general guide only. See *1825*** and *1846***, above, for the general practices of the S&D at this time.

1846 June 15. Eastern Union: Colchester to Ipswich. 15 June is date usually quoted, and is the correct one *(co n Moffat)*. However, *T 19th* said it opened on the 17th. This was probably result of misunderstanding. Item described how a party of directors set out to demonstrate service that line could provide for links to the Continent and the journalist seems to have interpreted it as first use of any sort. (The formal opening had been on the 11th – *T 13th*).

1846 June 22. NB: Edinburgh to Berwick *(co n T 23rd-line)*. Line first in *Brad* August. These stations were added in March 1848, overall timings for trains unchanged: Portobello; Musselburgh (later Inveresk); Longniddry; Ballencrieff; Grantshouse.

Tt starting 3 August 1846 *(Edinburgh Advertiser 4th)* shows that Innerwick was served by a Friday market train (starting date of this service unknown) from Cockburnspath to Haddington and back.

Company tt for July 1847 *(NB Society)* adds East Fortune to market service; note in goods trains table says passengers can travel from all stations, including these two plus Burnmouth. None of the three is in passenger table proper. Presumably this was service that called at Beltonford when in September 1848 NB acceded to local petition and agreed to stop *(First)*; no other passenger information known for this station.

1846 August. Furness. Reliable information on the early history of this line is difficult to find. Early minutes are lacking in detail, which is hardly surprising given that board meetings were held in London, far from the scene of a line that initially operated in isolation. Opening was authorised on 12 August (that would have been date on certificate sent from London). According to *D&C 14*, a rudimentary service from Barrow to Dalton began, Sundays only (first on 16th?), using a converted sheep truck; full service began 24 August *(Rtn PP)*, withdrawn at the end of summer owing to operational difficulties. *Brad* version differs in detail – e.g. Barrow is not initially mentioned. Inspection report

(MT 6/3/53) supports *D&C*. Since tt would have only been concerned with a service of wider potential use (from Fleetwood by steamer to Piel, then rail to Dalton, finally by coach to Ulverston and the Lakes), this might not be a contradiction. Line was operating detached from the national system and local services might have run, additional to those in tt. So much chopping and changing that only way of dealing with it is by giving a summary of tt version, followed by summary of relevant part of report. Tt version:

1846:	*September and October:* Piel – Furness Abbey – Dalton. *November:* 'some doubts about continuance'. *December:* omitted.
1847:	*May:* Piel – Rampside – Furness Abbey – Dalton – Kirkby; to come into force on 24th Instant⋆. *June and July:* same stations. *August and September:* now from Barrow, different times each day – tides. *October:* omitted.
1848:	*February:* index shows Furness Railway 'closed for the present'. *March:* on and after 1st March: Piel to Dalton. [*D&C 14* says Broughton extension inspected 23 February – perhaps into use at same time?]⋆ *April to December:* service from both Piel and Barrow, stops as 1847, plus extension to Broughton.
1849:	*January to June:* Barrow only to Broughton. *July to October:* from Piel also. *November:* from Barrow only.

Same up to and including
1850:	April, but e.g. February 1850: 'No information – supposed to be correct'.
1850:	May to October: Piel also. November: extension to Whitehaven added.

Inspector approved opening of main line Rampside to Dalton (6m 14ch); branch to Barrow (1m 20ch); branch terminating at Sandside in the parish of Kirkby-Ireleth (6m 64ch) and extension to Piel Pier (53ch). Some of stations listed 'not quite finished' but were 'in a state for the reception of passengers'. They were Piel; Rampside; Barrow; Furness Abbey; Dalton; one for Kirkby-Ireleth (= Kirkby-in-Furness); and another a little beyond at slate-works which was then terminus. No evidence has been seen elsewhere for a passenger service to slate-works (north east of Kirkby); if there was an early service, it is likely that it would have ceased once line was extended to Broughton, leaving slate line as a dead-end branch.

⋆ = Furness *co ½T 30 August*: Directors anticipated that Piel Pier line would have opened about 24 May and working of it in conjunction with Rampside branch would have created increased passenger traffic. Matches what *Brad* said would happen but hardly inspires confidence in directors' knowledge of affairs. Implies new facilities at Piel in 1847. *Lancaster Guardian, 26 February 1848* said line to Broughton had been inspected on 22nd and was now open. Does not say rest of line reopened now so might already have been in use.

Stations' later history in Section 4.

1846 October 7. York & North Midland: Seamer to Filey. Date from *Brad*, October 1847 which said line would open on 7th inst. Earliest station detail seen is *Topham* May 1848; *Brad* first provided it July 1848.

1846 November 4. Shrewsbury & Chester. Line opening date from *co n T 7th*; all stations given opening date appear in tt beginning 28 November reproduced in *GW*, volume I, opposite p.180. *Brad* did not provide detail until February 1847.

1846 November 18. LNW: Bletchley to Bedford. Opening 17 November was clearly formal event only *(co n T 14th; item 18th)*. Formal description says there were five other (unnamed) stations; it seems safe to assume these were the five which appeared in *Brad* with line in January 1848 tt.

1847 March 1. Newcastle & Berwick: Newcastle to Morpeth. Inspection report *(MT 6/4/5)* does not list intermediate stations but does say that temporary wooden buildings to shelter passengers have been erected pending completion of permanent stations.

1847 March 1. Glasgow & South Western: Kilmarnock –Barassie–Troon via Gatehead. Line date from *GSW*. Gatehead was only intermediate station shown in *Brad* March 1847. An alternative route was available and this one suffered periods of complete closure and summer-only use. The following has been derived from *Brad* but the whole story has not been established:

— Line last there May 1848; June 1848 note that line closed for improvement.
— Back May 1850; last present October 1853.
— Back by July 1854; last September 1854.
— Note January 1856 says was closed for winter.
— September 1856 – present.
— 1857 July to December – absent.
— Back June 1859; before/with January 1861 shown without trains (not in *Cornwall's Scottish tt* November 1860).
— Trains again May 1862.
— No later omissions seen.

Barassie, which logically would have been junction station at western end of line, was not included until June 1848 (when the line was shown as closed) and was last shown August 1848; later it was omitted on occasions when line was shown with trains (e.g. at least January 1852 to June 1852); this might well not be the full/accurate picture.

1847 March 19. Whitehaven Junction. Company notice of opening gave full tt for on and after 19th, including Parton *(Carlisle Journal 27th)*. However previous week's paper, describing opening, made it look like formal occasion – referred to Directors' Special and half-fare excursion – regarded this as shabby behaviour in that richest got free trip.

1847 March 29. Newcastle & Berwick: Tweedmouth to Chathill *(Newcastle Journal 3 April- line)*. First *Brad* reference is May 1847, when Newcastle & Berwick Railway table has Newcastle to Morpeth; and Berwick Tweedmouth Station to Chat-hill, coach service covering gap. July 1847 tt shows line opened right through, but no detail until August.

Inspection report *(MT6/4/13)* lists intermediate stations, with mileages from junction with Newcastle & North Shields as Newham (45); Lucker (47); Mousen (49); Belford (50½); Beal (56½). It says that permanent stations were in course of construction; even those for temporary purposes not all erected, but 'ample time' for completing this would be available between inspection 12 March and proposed opening 22 March. This is the only reference so far found to Mousen. If it did actually open, its life was presumably a very short one – hardly surprising since *Lewis's Topographical Dictionary of England & Wales*, 1838 edition, describes 'Mouson' as a township of 65 inhabitants. The distance given for Belford is about 1 mile too much (and would fit site of Cragg Mill) – S. Bragg. It may be that there was a last-minute decision in 1847 to have one station at about 49½ miles, rather than two close together; it may be that there were two temporary stations as listed in the inspection report, replaced very soon by one permanent at 49½.

1847 May 3: Blyth & Tyne: Seghill to Blyth. Date from *Newcastle Journal May 8*; also given by *Lambert's Handbook to Tynemouth and Blyth & Tyne Railway*, mid/late 1860s. March 3, in modern print, presumably copying error.

1847 June 1. Southampton & Dorchester. This was the planned opening date but problems with the tunnel between Southampton and Blechynden meant that the full service could not be run, though enough rolling stock was taken through the tunnel, without passengers, to provide two trains from Blechynden and one from Dorchester; passengers were taken by road between the two stations *(Salisbury 5th)*. The full service (Blechynden to Dorchester) was in operation on Sunday 6 June, at the latest (tt, *W Fly P 12th)*.

1847 July 1. Newcastle & Berwick: Morpeth to Chathill. Line now open throughout. Line opening *co n T 1st*; item *Newcastle Journal 3rd*. See 1847 March 29 ★★, above.

1847 August 3. Wear Valley (S&D). Perhaps formal only opening. Minutes say it was opened by the directors and their friends on the 3rd, 'since when the coach trains have run regularly' *(RAIL 718/2)*. Likelihood strengthened by findings on line opened 1846 June 5★★ (see above). In this case *Return* no help since Wear Valley lumped with S&D, already open.

1847 September 2. Eastern Union & Hadleigh Junction. *Herapath, 28 August*, said formally op 20 August; neither of [intermediate?] stations yet complete but temporary accommodation is being provided for passengers by the opening of the line 'for travelling', expected in course of a few days. All in *Brad* October but later tables often nd

so cannot be sure of continuity of use. *Hadleigh* confirms existence at opening – in inspection report and included in description of formal opening.

1847 September 20. Edinburgh & Northern: Burntisland to Lindores temporary terminus and to Cupar. *Edinburgh Advertiser 21st* confirmed line date. Lengthy account of formal opening, 19th, shows most, probably all, of 'missing' stations were there. Not always clear whether mentioning stations or listing villages passed but explicit references to stations at Kinghorn; Lochmuir, close to New Inn (= Falkland Road – see Caledonian Books reprint of early OS, sheet 40); Kettle; Springfield. First tt for line, *Brad* October 1847, omits: Kinghorn; Sinclairtown; Falkland Road; Kingskettle; Collessie; Springfield. All added June 1848, no change in overall train timings. All in *Topham* May 1848. Inspection report dated 7 September listed all stations given this date, it used names 'New Inn' and 'Kettle'.

1847 October 4. York & North Midland: York to Market Weighton *(co ½ T 22 February 1848- line)*. No detail in *Brad* until July 1848. *Topham* has some detail May 1848; Burnby (later Nunburnholme) and Gate Helmsley (later Holtby) were added in June, suggesting that they might have been later openings.

1847 October 20. York & North Midland: Filey to Bridlington *(co ½ T 22 February 1848- line)*. No detail in *Brad* until July 1848, though *Topham* gave May 1848.

1847 December: Leicester & Swannington (J. Gough, from *Leicester Chronicle*). On and after Friday 24 December 1847, service reduced to Saturdays only service Leicester – Glenfield – Ratby – Desford, for reconstruction of line, with deviations (paper of 25th). Line to be fully reopened to Long Lane 27 March 1848 (paper of 25th), those stations shown as re-sited in 1848 would now have (re-)opened on new sites; station detail at first not always complete in local press or in *Brad*. Prior to 1847 it had been mainly a mineral line, on which a couple of passenger carriages had been attached to its trains for the convenience of people in a rural district *(Return*, reporting accident of 28 May 1844).

1848: Morningside area lines. In this note, the main consideration is the dates of closure, subsequent reopening and final closure; a mere recital of tt dates would seem to be misleading. Original openings covered in Section 4 and *1835 C*, above, which see also for comments about reliability of information for this area.

The original services seem to have been closed as a result of opening of Caledonian main line through from Glasgow to Carlisle; stations on this line would have taken much of traffic previously carried by lines to Morningside. Caledonian main line was first included in March 1848 tt. In that month two services from Glasgow to Morningside are shown, in separate tables:

Wishaw & Coltness to Morningside (a), showing all the stops including Carluke (alias Stirling Road);

Wilsontown etc (b): Glasgow–Morningside–Longridge; detail only given for second section.

It is clear from timings that both services were provided by the same trains. In April (a) was omitted; (b) was still shown in April but May 'service suspended'.
This looks suspiciously like tt inertia. Once the main line had opened on 15 February some places involved would have been better served by it. There would have been no need for this Carluke because there was now a station of this name on main line. Also seems odd that second leg of the service should apparently have outlived first. However, whole service <u>might</u> have survived for a little while after main line opened, in the hope that local demand would be enough to justify it. The figures for numbers of passengers given for the Wilsontown line in the *Returns* would suggest that passengers ceased to be carried about the end of February or middle of March 1848. No comparable evidence exists for the Wishaw & Coltness since its return was by then included as part of the Caledonian's.

Year	first half	second half
1846	9,274	19,622
1847	17,938	19,207
1848	6,950	none

(608 trains in total ran in the first half of 1846, 972 in the second).

Morningside was again served in 1850, when once more the tt version does not make sense as it stands. What at first sight was the extension of the Edinburgh–Bathgate service to Morningside was first shown in the tt August 1850. Closer inspection shows that the one table included two distinct services: Edinburgh to Bathgate and Bathgate to Morningside, without any semblance of a worthwhile connection between them.
Apparently then, according to the tt at that stage, a Bathgate to Morningside service was operating in isolation. The line from Glasgow did not come back into tt until December 1851, again in two tables: one showing Morningside as terminus, the other continuation on to Bathgate as terminus. Common sense would suggest that this was a late arrival in tt and would have opened at same time as, or earlier than, Morningside to Bathgate one.

Brad Share, 1851, gives 1 May 1850 for opening (part reopening) by Edinburgh & Glasgow of Wilsontown line, which would cover Glasgow to Morningside service; this fits date given by *G&S*. Edinburgh to Bathgate (presumed to be error for Bathgate to Morningside/ Longridge) is shown as opened in 1850 but no exact date given. However, it is clear that tt was well behind events.

Official permission to open 'Bathgate branch of Morningside & Coltness, from Longside [Longridge] to junction with Edinburgh & Glasgow at Bathgate' was dated 30 March 1850. Presumably Morningside to Longridge, needed to reach this, was not inspected because had been recently used for passengers. This would suggest 1 May (or earlier?) as likely opening date for whole stretch from junction with main line to Bathgate.

Trains were last shown on the Bathgate to Morningside section in December 1852 tt; those from Glasgow were last shown in February 1853 tt. This time there might have been some logic to the latter lasting longer since there would have still been a main line connection; however, simultaneous closure would also have made sense.

1848 February 1. East Anglian: Watlington to Wisbech. (line opening – *Boston 8th*).

1848 March 1. Eastern Counties: March to St Ives. Date used for line is given by *co ½ T 28 February* but perhaps regular traffic began next day. *Boston 7th* says was opened on 1st by excursion from Huntingdon (later Godmanchester) to Wisbech, 32 carriages, upwards of 900 passengers, including children from various schools along line; rained incessantly but did not dampen enthusiasm. Would there have been any rolling stock left over for regular trains? or people left to travel in them?

1848 May 23. Stirling to Perth (Scottish Central). *Perthshire Courier 18 May* carried company notice of opening on 22nd, with outline tt. However following week's paper's description is clearly of formal opening on that date. *Courier* only mentioned one train each way. Supposed to leave Perth at 10 but late. Halted at most stations and some of level-crossings to collect passengers. Initially directors and friends only but for return journey second-class carriages attached to carry all and sundry (free?). No suggestion that tt trains ran – would have been difficult to fit in. *Co ½ T 4 September* says opened 23rd.

1848 June 6. Knottingley to Stocksbridge. This was opening date for paying public. On previous day (formal opening) there was a special free of charge for the public (M.D. Greville, letter, RCHS *Journal*, July 1959); not clear if all stations were served.

1848 June 15. Addition of stations on South Devon. *Plymouth*, Saturday 17 June, has two items. One says that Ivybridge opened on Thursday; the other that trains now stop at Colebrook (= Plympton), Ivybridge and Brent. It has been assumed that all three opened on the same date.

1848 July 24. Liverpool, Crosby & Southport. Line date from *Southport Visiter 22nd* and *29th*. There seem to have been several early changes of station sites and short-term closures. Both Birkdale and Crosby included there but neither in *Brad* before the end of 1850 (e.g. see March 1850); they were in *Topham* from soon after line opening but no trains shown calling. Hightown not included in either tt. *Brad* January 1851 shows Birkdale and Hightown with trains but Crosby Village served by omnibus from Waterloo; February 1851 shows trains calling at Crosby Station. Clearly there are still details needing to be established.

1848 August 1.York & North Midland: Selby to Market Weighton *(Herapath 12th/Yorkshire Gazette 5th)*.
In August 1848 *Brad* this line appeared only as a footnote in the York to Market Weighton table. First detail of any sort given October 1849 when Dubwith (= Bubwith) and Holme were shown as the only intermediate stops *(Herapath* said they were the only 'road stations'); from 1850, footnotes refer to Tuesday market and Monday fortnightly fair trains to York, stopping at 'all stations' without naming them. These might have been provided from start since relevant trains were given extra time, without any reason given. Inspection report *(MT 6/5/66)* only lists Bubwith and Holme, but it is unlikely that any facilities would have been provided at stops only used by market trains. In November 1851 a full list appeared, no limitation on days. (In December 1851 there was a note that the Gatehouse stops were market days only but this had probably been put back in error – it was omitted next month.)

1848 August 1. NB opening to Bowland Bridge.
This date is given by *Brad Sh*. A company notice dated 27 July in *The Scotsman*, concerning arrangements for the Edinburgh Agricultural Show says 'The Hawick Branch is expected to be Opened to Bowshank, on Tuesday the 1st August'. It has not been established that it did so open; there might have been some delay – *D&C 6* gives 4 August.

1848 August 7. North Staffs: Stoke to Uttoxeter.
Line date from *co ½ T 3 February 1849*. Tts initially lacked detail. Most of the intermediate stations given this date first appeared in *Topham* in October, *Brad* November; Bromshall was added to *Topham* in November, later still in *Brad*. Inspection report *(MT 6/5/76)* lists Lane End (= Longton); Blythe Bridge; Cresswell; Leigh; Bromshall. Given tt evidence, it may be that Bromshall opened a little after the others, though apparently ready.

1848 October 30. East & West Yorkshire Junction.
Date given is from *NE*, supported by *T 31st*.
Return says 31 October so it is possible that 30th was formal opening, 31st public.

1849: Oakengates. Doubts are raised about the exact date of the fully public opening of the lines either side of here.

The line from Wellington was opened on 1 June *(co n T 19 May)*, with that of the Shropshire Union from Shrewsbury to Stafford; this is supported by *Shrewsbury 8th*, which confirms existence of all Shropshire Union stations given this date. However, while *T 5th* described the latter as publicly opened, the Oakengates section was served by 'special trains'. *Co n T 15 May*, company minutes of 31 May 1849 *(RAIL 615/2)*, and *Shrewsbury 8th* suggest normal opening on 1st; since no intermediate stations were involved, any distinction between special and public trains might have been regarded as artificial.
Return adds to confusion – says opened 18 June.
This was actually the date of opening for goods (derived from *co n Shrewsbury 25 May*, which said Oakengates

would open for goods on Monday, 17 June – 17th was actually a Sunday).

The next section, on to Wolverhampton, was opened with excursion trains on the 12th November and to the public on the 13th *(co n T 10th)*. Again, *Shrewsbury (16th)* treats it as normal opening. It mentions all stations given 13th as opening date – company's own notice would seem to deserve precedence in a case like this.

1849 March 31. Blackwall: extension to Bow & Bromley. *Co n T 29 March* said line would be opened throughout with locomotive power on Monday, 2 April. However, an item in the paper of 2 April said that it had opened on the Saturday (31 March). It would thus seem that the Blackwall made something of a habit of early opening – see London, Fenchurch Street (Section 4). This leaves a problem concerning the short length from Bow & Bromley to the interchange station at Victoria Park, Bow. *The Times* says nothing about this so that it might well not have come into use until 2 April, date given by *L*; the Eastern Counties were also, unenthusiastically, involved here and might have waited until the advertised date – in this case, there would have been no point in the Blackwall running on from Bow & Bromley to the exchange station.

At first trains ran through from Fenchurch Street. At one stage experimented by making passengers for the extension change at Stepney. Experiment in operation by 19 August (letter, *T 21st*); had been abandoned by 1 December (report *T* of that date).

Interchange station was made necessary by the Eastern Counties company's refusal to put in a junction and allow through running. Blackwall service was diverted to the North London line 26 August 1850 and its station at Victoria Park closed; the Eastern Counties part survived a little longer, passengers presumably walking between it and new North London station at Bow. Portion of line closed in 1850 reopened 13 April 1854 for through service Fenchurch Street to Tilbury (junction now in place).

Blackwall line originally about 5ft gauge, cable hauled. In first three months of 1849 converted to standard gauge, locomotive hauled. Two lines altered in turn so service continued but frequency reduced from 15 to 30 minutes. One line opened, converted, 15 February *(London Local)*; full service resumed 2 April *(co n T 29 March)*, initially at 20 minute intervals; by 29 August *(co ½ T)* restored to 15 minutes. Now possible to travel directly between any pair of stations – previously some journeys only possible by going to one of termini and back (see *London Local* for details).

1849 May 15. LBSC: Hailsham and Eastbourne branches. LBSC *co ½ T 23 July* gives 14th but trains on the 14th only carried officials and a party of children from the local workhouse *(Back Track vol. 13 no. 12, pp. 662–3)*.

1849 July 19.Whitehaven & Furness Junction.
Lewin and *D&C 14* say 21st but *Return* says opened
19 July and is supported by *Whitehaven Herald 21st*,
which mentioned all stations (formal 18th).
What increases the suspicion that a misprint has been
copied in secondary works down the years is the
coincidence (?) that the company was incorporated on
21 July 1845, so that the '21' quoted for opening might
have been copied from the wrong place.

1849 July 20: MSJA: Manchester Oxford Road to
Altrincham. Line date given by *co N Manch G 18th*.
Co n Stockport 27th gives intermediate stations.
It is dated 17 July and says 'line is now opened'.
[See 1864 September 1, below.]

1849 July 30. SE: New Cross to Gravesend.
Times 31 July has notice dated 30th to the effect that the
line 'is now' open but does not give the opening date; it
does include all stations given this date. *Co ½ T 20
September*, confirms that line did open on the 30th.

1849 August 15. NB: Reston to Duns(e) *(D&C 6)*.
Evidence contradictory. Inspection report *(MT 6/7/100)*
says '3 intermediate stations', which would most likely
have been Chirnside; Edrom; Crimstone (alias Crumstane).
However, earliest tts seen, *Edinburgh District* December
1849 and February 1850 only include Chirnside and
Crimstone; same in co tt shown in *D&C 6* for 1850
(January?); Edrom was added to Macaulay's maps
between 1851 and 1854. First detail in *Brad* May 1852,
Chirnside and Edrom listed. Given the inspection report,
early tt versions perhaps reflect relative importance of
stations in company's eyes. Clearly Crimstone dropped
out very early, probably before May 1852, though still
shown by Macaulay. One possibility is that Edrom
was initially used for goods only, changing roles with
Crimstone 1851/2.

1849 September 10. Cal: line to Hamilton.
Notice in *Glasgow Herald 7th* said would open 10th,
item *14th* said it had.

1849 October 29. North British extension to Hawick.
Date given by *Lewin*. Confirmed by *Scottish Railway
Gazette* of Saturday 3 November, which says line
opened on Monday. There was no public demonstation
owing to the ravages of cholera but many did come to
see the comings and goings of the trains during the day.

1849 November 12. LY: Burnley to Todmorden.
Line date confirmed by *RAIL 1005/265*. Towneley;
Holme; and Portsmouth first appear in *Brad* in separate
local table, September 1851. They had not appeared in
Topham by March 1850, last issue seen. However, the
inspection report *(MT/6/7/46)* says there were (un-named)
'intermediate stations' and they were included in the
LY Distance Diagram dated 1851. Therefore, they were
probably victims of the incomplete nature of timetables
then, rather than late additions to line.

1850 May 1. Llanelly: opening for regular passenger
service. Line had opened for goods in stages 1833
onwards; reached Pontard(d)ulais 1 June 1839,
Garnant April 1840, Duffryn 6 May 1841 *(GW)*.
Passenger service began ? – no mention of passenger
revenue in accounts for half-year to 28 April 1838
(Herapath July). Passenger duty first paid for year 1840
(PP 2). *Return* for July to December 1840 compared
with later ones suggests that service was provided
throughout the period covered (1,840 then, 1,204 in
first half of 1841, 1,281 in second half of 1841);
it appears from return that only third-class passengers
were carried, by same trains that carried the goods.
At first there were no recognised stops or timetable and
this might have resulted in a loss of passengers as the
novelty value wore off since in the 1842 and 1843
returns the space for 'number of passengers' is left blank,
with the note: 'no account is kept of these since the
amount is so small'. Numbers of passengers given again
in return for 1844–5. The picture given in *GW* differs
from that given in the primary sources seen; a possible
explanation is that services provided by contractors
ran in addition to those mentioned here – perhaps
e.g. to Duffryn.

Initially the line operated detached from the main system.
When the approaching opening of the South Wales
Railway as far as Swansea meant that its isolation would
be reduced, the company decided to run a specific
passenger service to a regular timetable *(The Welshman,
reviewing the company's history, 23 January 1857)*.
The regular service began 1 May 1850 *(Company minutes
RAIL 377/3)*. Initially *Brad* said coach connections
were provided 'at Llanelly for Swansea' and 'at Garnant
for Llandilo'. In July this was altered (corrected?) to
'Bynea for Swansea' and 'Cross Inn for Llandilo'.

1850 June 19. South Wales: Chepstow to Swansea.
Formal opening 18 June was described in *Merlin 22nd*;
some fare-paying passengers were carried. Full public
opening was 19th (full notice reproduced in *Wales*,
outline *T 17th*). South Wales *co ½ T 29 August* gave 18th
as opening date – no wonder mixture in modern print.
Also see article by M Hale in *Welsh Railway Archive
May 2000*.

1850 June 22. Bolton, Blackburn, Clitheroe & West
Yorkshire. Date is one given by *The Times, 27th*, the
appendix in *LY* (text gives 21st) and correspondence in
the Railway Commissioners' *Return* for 1850 (involving
opening problems). All stations appeared with the line
in *Brad*.

1850 July 1. Closure: Newmarket.
Co n T 1st: 'The Newmarket Railway will from and after
30th inst cease to carry and convey passengers' – notice
dated June. Literally this could be taken to mean that
last train would have been on the 29th (Thursday) but
common sense suggests that last train would have run
on 30th and closure would have occurred with the new
timetable on 1 July.

1850 July 8. Furness: extension to Bootle. This date is given in Whitehaven & Furness *co ½ T 21 August.* *Furness Rise* reproduces timetable and opening notice giving 1 July (notice issued 27 June). Co ½ report says: 'At the latter end of June part of the viaduct over the Esk was burned down; it was replaced in a week'. Item *T 1 July* covered fire and delay to opening. *Lancaster Guardian* of 6 July covered fire, that of 13th confirmed opening on 8th.

1850 July 15. Caledonian & Dumbartonshire Junction: Bowling to Balloch. Opened detached from the system, with steamer connections from Glasgow to Bowling and from Balloch to other points on Loch Lomond. Line date from *co ½ T 9 August.* Linked to Glasgow by rail 31 May 1858.

Company handbill dated 18th says line 'now open'; includes intermediate stations; just 'Balloch' at one end, 'Bowling Bay' at other and press notice of 27 May 1858 gave date of link to main system; *(NB Railway Study Group Journal Spring 2001).*

1850 August 19: Eastern Counties, Maldon and Braintree branches. Shortly after J.V. Gooch had been engaged there was serious dispute between him and engine drivers, resulting in most of latter being replaced by promoted firemen or new recruits (see R.S. Joby, *Eastern Counties Railway*, Marwood, 1996). Company had to run reduced service, including complete closure of these two branches from this date *(co n T 19th).* Service restored 26 August *(co n 26th,* saying staff of engine drivers had been completely reorganised). Paper actually referred to fortnight of cuts but that probably included week of confused reductions before 19th.

1850 September 2. Coventry – Nuneaton [LNW]. (*Coventry Standard 6 September 1850*): LNW tts from 1 September (a Sunday, no Sunday service on this line) include line and stations given this date.

1850 October 1. Buckinghamshire, leased to LNW: Winslow to Islip. *Co n T 21 September* gives date and says that particulars of trains for Claydon; Bicester; and Islip would be published in a few days. Omission of Oddington and Launton suggests they might have opened later, though both were included first time line was in *Brad*, November. Neither is mentioned in the description of line's opening in *Oxford Chron 5th,* however, they might have been present but insignificant enough to be overlooked.

1850 December 23. Monmouthshire. Opening date from *co n Merlin, 28th.* Originally 4ft 4in. tramway. *Co ½ T 27 May 1851* said opened 21st, date used by *GW.* However, local press notice clear on Monday 23rd. Was there some sort of preliminary use on Saturday? Nothing seen by compiler, nor in *Byles,* who made thorough use of local press. However, line does seem rather to have sneaked into use after disappointments caused by cash shortages and inspection problems.

Herapath 4 January 1852 said op 'Monday last' – could support date given [week Monday last]; could not support 21st. During 1855 converted to standard gauge railway. This resulted in the temporary reduction of train services to 3 days per week *(Byles).*

1851 May 12. Exeter & Crediton. The LSW had gained a controlling interest in this company and showed complete disregard for the public welfare. The line was ready for use a long time before it did open *(D&C 1);* originally built broad gauge, it was converted to standard and back to broad during the delay.

Company minutes *(RAIL 201/2)* show that while the line was being built, the subject of having a station at (Newton) St Cyres was twice deferred (second time 14 January 1846). On 24 July 1847 the Secretary was ordered to prepare a plan for a station in the Cowley Meadows (presumably just on the Crediton side of Cowley Bridge Junction). On 3 December 1847 the directors resolved that in order to open the line with as little delay as possible a temporary station should be erected there. This would have been used as the terminus at the Exeter end since at that time this line was standard gauge and the BE broad. Passengers would have been left with a lengthy walk to Exeter, making line of very little use, unless BE had opened an exchange station there; given the chicanery practised by the LSW, this was most unlikely. The Cowley Meadows station was presumably built but never used since authority refused to allow opening in this form and the LSW would not for some time allow the gauge to be altered. Just after the line finally opened (now broad gauge, worked by BE) the Crediton Board passed a resolution (16 May 1851) to move the station in Cowley Meadows to Longbridge Corner for the purpose of developing traffic at Newton St Cyres. 'Developing' does leave open possibility that some sort of stop was available from line opening.

1851 September 24. Vale of Neath. Public opening from *co ½ T 27 February 1852.* Description of formal opening on 23 September *(T 27th)* confirms existence of stations given line date.

1851 October 9. Newmarket: diversion from junction with main line at Chesterford to new junction near Cambridge. Contemporary sources are contradictory. *The Times* of Friday 3 October said that new line would open on Monday (6th); paper of 8th said it had opened on Monday. This looks conclusive but it would seem to have been a case where a last minute delay fooled the press and that a journalist, seeking to fill a little space on 8th, looked back at previous Friday's paper, assumed it had happened as planned and 'reported' it as having happened –no corroborative detail being provided. *Brad Sh,* 1852, is contradictory within itself: list of new openings for previous year says 6th, but entries in body of book for both Newmarket (owners) and Eastern Counties (operators) give 9th. 9th is confirmed by notice in *Cambridge 11th,* which says old line will be closed 'for the present'. Accompanying tt showed intermediate stations without trains. It is possible that there was some delay in opening these. The inspection report, *MT6/9/159*, dated 29 September, said that at one of them 'no platform has as yet been laid'. However, that would not explain the long delay in including them in *Bradshaw*.

1851 November 29. Edinburgh & Bathgate; temporary closure. According to *Railway Times (6 December)* no warning given – station clerks just told not to issue tickets. *Stirling Advertiser (11 December)* said a party that went for day's curling near Broxburn (29th was a Saturday) were left to find own way home. Result of dispute between its and Edinburgh & Glasgow's directors over maintenance – latter were running trains but claimed former should keep track in repair, had failed to do so and line had become unsafe. *Railway Times (13 December)* said legal action had resulted in Bathgate being told to do repairs and E&G promising to repay their costs. On December 11 an independent engineer (Grainger) certified line fit for use but said would take a few days to arrange reopening; he suggested Tuesday 16th as reasonable but no confirmation found that did happen then.

1851 December 10. Closure of Monklands service to Airdrie Lea End. Closed on Wednesday (last day Tuesday) because that was the date of the expiry of a two-calendar-year agreement *(MK)*.

1852 February 18. Oxford, Worcester & Wolverhampton: Worcester to Bromsgrove. Date given is from *GW*; supported by *T 21st*: 'at last … has opened', without an exact date – and it is unlikely that this line would have had a formal opening. However, *co ½ T 23 February* says opening was fixed for 24 February and *T* item, 25th says report accepted 'without demur'. Shareholders more interested in other matters?

1852 May 3. Oxford, Worcester & Wolverhampton: Stourbridge to Evesham. Opening 1 May formal, 3rd public *(Glos Chron 8th; T 1st)*.

1852 May 21. Newcastle & Carlisle: Lambley to Alston. Branch from Haltwistle was already open as far as Coanwood, which was separated from Lambley by deep valley of the South Tyne, for the crossing of which a viaduct was needed. Before this was complete, section south of the river opened, detached from main system, using rolling stock brought in from Milton (later Brampton) via Lord Carlisle's private colliery line. Exact date comes from an unpublished local diary; local press gives clear evidence of trains running in June and July; further general support comes from inspection reports *(NE Express; MT 29/12)*. Viaduct was brought into use and line opened throughout (no new stations) on 17 November 1852 *(co ½ T 17 February 1853; MT 6/10/44)*. Also see *RM November 1912, pp. 431–2*.

1852 May 25. Leeds Northern: Stockton to Melmerby. *Darlington & Stockton Times Saturday 29 May 1852*:

commenced to run passenger service on Tuesday last [25th]. Two trains run daily and will continue to do so until 31st inst, when considerable additions will be made. A goods train now runs once a day. Following week very full account of Dock opening; no reference to new train service. Individual stations not mentioned but all in *Brad* June. Co ½ meeting *(T 6 October)* told opened 1 June – presumably based on start of full service.

1852 July 15. GN: Peterborough to Retford. This date is given by *T (item of 17th* and *GN co ½ 20 August)* and by *Newark* (quoting local press). Service was at first purely local. Through express trains started to run on 1 August (as in book, *GN*).

1852 August 10. Morayshire: Lossiemouth branch. August 10 was formal opening day but there was some public use. Full public service began next day (K. Fenwick).

1853 June 1. Malton & Driffield Junction: Pilmoor to Malton. *RAIL 453/2*: company minutes, for 31 May 1853 show that although they had not received BoT certificate, they went ahead with planned opening because they were confident they had dealt properly with the inspector's requirements ([the] Lieutenant who inspected the line yesterday having been satisfied that the several requirements called for by Capt. Galton's report had been complied with). Also the York, Newcastle and Berwick Company had issued Time Bills dated 26th inst and to avoid any disappointment to Persons brought to Malton by the Thirsk and Malton Branch (opening same day) intending to use the Malton and Driffield line. The final part deserves full quotation:

> Resolved that this Company do open this line simultaneously with the Thirsk and Malton Branch according to the Time Tables already published, the Engineer undertaking to do all in his power to prevent accidents until the Certificate of the Board of Trade is received.
> Signed Thos Teesdale
> Chairman'

Reads as though accidents permissible once certificate received. *Co ½ Herepath 6 August* confirmed that opened 1 June. Intermediate stations in *Brad* from opening.

1853 November 1. Warrington & Stockport *(T 17th-line)*. Following is *Brad* version of early history. Difficult to believe that this is what did happen, but until other evidence turns up, only answer seems to be to quote this.

November 1853: trains calling at Warrington; Lymm; Heatley; Altrincham. Also present, without trains but fares quoted: Latchford; Thelwall; Warburton. Overall timings not altered when these did have trains.

December: Dunham added; trains calling at all.

January to March 1854: last four quoted were reduced on weekdays to one train each way, Wednesday and Thursday only, which left Warrington at 7.45pm and returned from Altrincham at 8.30pm, making it useless for an out and back trip on the same day. However, all four had a full Sunday service.

April and May 1854: same as March, but 'no recent information' added.

June 1854: full service for all and line now extended to Timperley.

1853 December 6. Shrewsbury & Hereford: Ludlow to Hereford. *Brad*, December, has note that service will come into effect on 5th; *T 6th* supports this date. However, it is clear from *Hereford T 6th* and *10th*, that 5th was formal and 6th public opening.

1854 April 1: Eastern Counties: Bury Extension Line. Date from company minutes of 23 March and *Bury & Norwich Post 29 March*. Earlier minutes (23 November 1853) show stations planned for Kentford (= Kennett); Higham; Saxham *(RAIL 186 series*, B. Wilson).

1854 August 15. Eastern Counties: Harwich branch. Date from half-yearly reports of Eastern Counties *(T 24 August)* and Eastern Union *(T 31 August)*. The earliest train along the line ran on 29 July 1854. This carried a party of navvies and was also available to men on an excursion from Stratford Works, though most of the latter stayed on their original train and went on to Ipswich *(Moffat*, who adds a note giving supporting press reference and says that this trip has wrongly been ascribed by some to August 4, which was date of inspection). *Brad* in September only mentioned Harwich. In October it added: Mistley; Wrabness; Dovercourt. No secondary sources give any information on this.

1854 August 28. Somerset Central: Highbridge to Glastonbury *(Wells 2 September)*. Ashcott; Bason Bridge; and Edington did not appear in tt until April 1856. However, in its description of formal opening, *Bridgwater Merc 24 August* says: 'We observed but one station … [Shapwick] but there are halting places where the turnpike roads are crossed, at which we understand tickets will be issued'. They are marked on Fullarton's map, end 1855. Thus likely they were all there at start. Initially this line, owned by the Somerset Central, was operated by the BE as one of its branches; some trains included through carriages for Bristol.

1854 October 2: Monmouthshire: Pontypool to Blaenavon. Date from *Star of Gwent 21st*. *Co ½ T 13 November* gave 1st, a Sunday. Example of company using date of new tt rather than actual one.

1855 June 1. Hereford, Ross & Gloucester: Hopesbrook to Ledbury. *Co n Glos Chron 9th* shows that this stretch opened and temporary terminus at Hopesbrook closed on this date. Description of opening, same paper 2 June, shows that day was mainly ceremonial but some ordinary passengers were carried. *Times* evidence, like some in print, is contradictory: paper of 4th says formal 1st, public 2nd; *co ½ T 16 August*, gives 1st as public. *GW* gives 1st in text, 2nd in chronology.

1855 August 20. Taff Vale Extension: Pontypool Road to Crumlin temporary station. Line opening date confirmed by BoT records and *T 21st*. Line opened without BoT permission. Company's secretary claimed had misunderstood – thought that inspector's refusal only applied to stretch from Crumlin temporary on to junction at Llanhilleth. After careful consideration authority allowed service to continue but ordered reinspection, saying that if this was unsatisfactory they would order the line to be closed. On 14 September Captain Tyler again recommended refusal of permission and a letter 15 September the Board ordered a further postponement of one month; no evidence of any actual closure has been seen. Official permission was granted in a letter dated 13 October *(Return)*.

1855 November 7. Inverness & Nairn *(GNS)*. Monday 5 November: formal opening plus reduced-fare excursion Inverness to Nairn and back. Tuesday 6th: reduced fare excursion from Nairn and back. 7th: public opening. Presumably no use by intermediate stations prior to 7th. (Opening notice, Highland Railway Society's Journal article on line, 2000).

1856 May 26. Forth & Clyde Junction: Balloch to Stirling. Line date is one usually quoted and is confirmed by co notice in *Stirling Journal 23rd*, item 30th, which listed all stations; supported by *co ½ T 24 September 1857*, though *The Times*'s own report of 2 June 1856 and *Herapath 14 June* said 28th – misprint?

1856 June 2. Coleford, Monmouth, Usk & Pontypool: Little Mill to Usk. Date from *co ½ T 26 August*. As with *1855 June 1*, there was a large ceremonial element, but ordinary passengers were carried *(Merlin 7th)*.

1856 July 9. Darlington & Barnard Castle. Formal opening 8th; public 9th *(S&D Pass)*.

1856 July 18. Jedburgh (Railway). Date usually quoted: e.g. *D&C 6* is 17th, but *T 29th* and *Herapath 2 August* say 18th. *The Times* mentions all stations.

Article on line by A.F. Nisbet, *Back Track June 2002* gives 17th but no supporting reference. Does quote local press about formal opening on 16th; also quotes earlier press reference that line was expected to open to traffic on 16th or 18th.

1856 August 7. Ayr & Dalmellington, plus new station at Ayr. Date from *GSW* and *co ½ T 3 September*. However, while the line is in *Brad* from August 1856, no trains are included in the table until November, when the line to Maybole (opened 13 October 1856) is also shown. *Co ½ March 1860 (1110/149)* said stations had been provided at Patna and Hollybush – earlier arrangements temporary?

1856 September 4. Carlisle and Silloth Bay. Notice for formal opening on 28 August 1856 *(D&C 14)* suggests that return tickets for special trains were available for all, but had to be bought by 6pm previous evening. Notice includes Drumburgh; the Abbey [sic];

Kirkbride; Silloth. *Co ½ T 6 March 1857* said stations at Abbey Holme [sic] and Kirkbride were unfinished – presumably in use anyway.

1856 September 17. Dursley & Midland Junction.
Public opening date from *co n Glos Chron 20th*.
In the previous week, immediately after inspection requirements had been met, line was opened for free use by those attending the Gloucester Music Festival, which took place 9 to 12 September, inclusive.
Not clear from paper whether line available for all days of Festival *(Stroud J 13th)*.

1856 November 1. GN: Stamford to Essendine.
This is the date usually quoted in print. It has been challenged by *Rutland*, which says opening delayed from this planned date by death of contractor; line inspected 12 November; assumed to have opened soon after.
However, it would appear that the accepted date is correct. *RAIL 662/3*, company minutes (1 November) show that there were last-minute financial details that had to be settled with GN; these resulted in service being omitted from GN time bills for November (perhaps source of confusion) but supplemental bills were ordered to be issued on 27 October and promise then given that line would be opened on 1 November. Minutes of 30 December show they agreed to pay Mr Hurst, their Engineer, for professional attendance from the month of June 1856 (when line was to have been completed) to 1 November 1856 (when it actually opened). *Lincoln, Rutland & Stamford Mercury 7th* – op Saturday last without ceremony. *Rtn* and *co ½ Herapath 8 November* gave same date.

1857 March 3. NE: Picton to Stokesley.
Formal opening 2 March, public 3rd *(T 5th)*.
At ½ yearly meeting shortly before opening Chairman of North Yorks & Cleveland said stations had been built at Potto; Sexhow; Stokesley – though he gave date of formal opening as though it were public one *(T 3 March)*.

1857 March 5. MSJA: Manchester Art Treasures.
Dates given, from *The Times*, are those of opening and closing of the Exhibition, assumed to apply to station also.

1857 May 25. Newport, Abergavenny & Hereford: Crumlin temporary to Pontllanfraith (LL). Date given is from *Chepstow, 6 June*. This said passenger services had begun on May 25 but that the 'complete opening' had occurred on Whit Monday, June 1, when more than 15,000 people are supposed to have travelled on excursions from many parts of South Wales to see the viaduct. For new station at CRUMLIN see Section 4.

1857 June 8. Fife & Kinross to Strathmiglo.
Date given by Brand; confirmed by *Kinross*, notice and item 6 June. 6th was formal day but excursions were run during the whole of the day. Auchtermuchty mentioned. *Return* gave 6th as opening date; presumably sent by Company.

1857 June 15. GN: Grantham to Sleaford.
15th given by *Return*, *T 15th* and *co ½ T 2 March 1858*. *Herapath 20 June* said formal 13th, public 15th.
16th is given by *GN* and *co ½ T 1 September 1857*.
On balance, 15th seems more likely.

1857 August 11. East of Fife: Burnhill to Kilconquhar.
Opening tt for this stretch of line is shown in *Fife* (body of book – chronology at back gives different date); date also given by Leven and East of Fife half-yearly reports *(T 21 April 1858)*.

1857 August 20. Leominster & Kington.
Date from company minutes of 18 August 1857 *(RAIL 363/2)*. Both 2 August, given by *D&C 13* (and some others), and 29 August, given by *Return*, would seem to be copying errors or misprints.

1857 September 1: Ulverstone [sic] & Lancaster, later part of Furness: passenger use late August. *Fur* quotes Lord Burlington (Chairman) as noting that 'regular' passenger trains began running 1 September (also given by *RAIL 1005/265*, from company minutes). Press version is that formal opening was on 26 August and they intended to start running as soon as official authority was given (this also dated 26th). Cheap trips advertised from Oxenhope to Furness Abbey and back for 31 August, though none of stations on new stretch mentioned. Paper of 5 September said number of passengers, including on cheap trips, who passed over line since opening was 3,000 for week ending 'yesterday' (4th or earlier day of writing?). Seems unlikely that paper published on a Saturday would have been able to give figures up to Friday night so possibility of use 27th–29th must be considered *(Westmorland 8, 15, 29 Aug.; 5 Sept.)*.

1857 October. Coleford, Monmouth, Usk & Pontypool: Usk to Monmouth (Troy). *Merlin 10th* says that line is now in regular use, without giving exact date. It does say that formal opening had not yet occurred and it may be that this was held on the 12th, date usually given for this stretch of line. *Hereford T 10th* tells the same story; indeed, the similarity of wording suggests that either the same correspondent provided the information or that both were copying another paper, published earlier in the week. *Brad Sh*, 1858, includes this in list of new openings in 1857 but does not give a date. *Co ½ T 2 September* said 'since opening of line 12 October …' but, in view of press evidence, likely to have been delayed formal – companies, especially small ones often failed to differentiate.

1857 November 9. Sandy & Potton. *Return* for 1857 confirms opening date. Return for 1861 says 'No Return to the Order of the House' and adds note: 'This Line is stated to have been sold to the "Bedford and Cambridge Railway Company", and closed for traffic'.

1857 December 8. Edenham and Little Bytham.
This is listed in *Returns* as: 'Willoughby d'Eresby's, Lord … private property' – in final year 'Lady' replaced 'Lord'. Opening date confirmed from 1857 return.

That for 1871 says service 'discontinued 17 October 1871'. It is impossible to be certain whether this was last day of use or first day of non-use; whilst normal practice of *Returns* was to quote last day of use, the habits of those supplying the information were inconsistent.

There are also doubts about the continuity of the service. The *Brad* version was: first shown June 1858; last present September 1866; back February 1870; last included February 1872. Other evidence shows that at least three of these changes were well behind actual events. *Returns* give figures for all years. In the early 1860s, the usual number was about 5,000. In 1866 this fell to 3,569; 1867 – 956; 1868 – 1073; 1869 – 'no information'; 1870 – 1,875; 1871 – 1,415. Since the line was always run at a loss, and the train service severely reduced in the mid-1860s, it is impossible to be certain, but the evidence taken together suggests service discontinued late 1866 and restored in 1867 (perhaps summer-only for a couple of years?). For a fuller treatment of the line's history, see G. Webb, article, *The Edenham & Little Bytham Railway*, RCHS Journal vol.6 no.6, November 1960.

1858 January 25. East Kent: Chatham to Faversham. This opened detached from the system. Gap filled 29 March 1858 *(co n T 27th)*.

1858 March 15. Fife & Kinross. From *Kinross*, then fortnightly. Co notice dated 12th said would open from Strathmiglo to Milnathort 'On Monday first (= next) the 15th inst'. Return tickets at single fares would be issued between all stations on the line (all present in tt included), available to return by any train during the day. It appears that an earlier opening had been mentioned; an item in the same paper said that although the line had been inspected by Capt Tyler on 4th; and his report was 'most satisfactory' [!], 'The frost having been the cause of diverging some of the rails from the straight line, and part of the fencing being unfinished, the Directors resolved to delay the opening of the line till Monday next'. [Most say op 9th but 15th given by M.D. Greville in his list of openings for 1858 in RCHS *Journal* January 1958; *Fife* gives 15th on p.93 and 9th in chronology on p.233.]

1858 May 15. Last trains on East Suffolk, Halesworth to Haddiscoe, when line closed for relaying *(T 3rd)*. However, Haddiscoe was still served by trains between Norwich and Lowestoft. Line reopened 1 June 1859 *(T 2nd)*.

1858 September 1. Shrewsbury – Crewe [LNW]. *Eddowes 1 September* carried notice of opening that day; paper of *8th* said had, without ceremony.

1858 October 13. Tunnel branch [S&D]. *Durham Chronicle 15th* said directors had formally opened this on 13th. Normally S&D practice would have been public use next day. However, paper added ambiguous element by saying 'three trains per day will run'. *Brad Sh* said opened 19 October.

1859 February 1. Epsom & Leatherhead *(co ½ T 30 August)*. Opened detached from system. Linked in 4 April 1859, when line from Wimbledon opened. Line between stations at Epsom opened 8 August 1859 *(co n T 6th)*, LBSC trains running through LSW station without stopping.

1859 March 16. Somerset Central: Glastonbury to Wells. Opening date from company's notice in *Wells 12th* and report in *Shepton 18th*. Polsham did not appear in tt until December 1861 but description of formal opening in *Wells 5th* refers to 'neat station' there.

1859 May 4. Cornwall: Plymouth to Truro. *Plymouth 5th* gives sequence: Monday (2nd) ceremonial opening of Royal Albert Bridge; Tuesday (3rd) ceremonial opening of line; yesterday (4th) public opening. Tt (effective from 10th) in *R Cornwall Gaz 13th* includes all stations given this opening date.

1859 July 12. Oxford, Worcester & Wolverhampton: Honeybourne to Stratford-upon-Avon. Formal op 11th *(co minutes; Rly Times 9th)*. *T 9th* referred to opening of line on 'Monday' (11th) in item on Royal Agricultural Show at Warwick, with coaches on to Warwick, but item also indicates that public not admitted to Show until the Tuesday. Description in *T 12th* refers only to a special train from Worcester on 11th, suggesting that it was a sort of excursion day. *W Mid* and co ½ T 10 August give 11th for public: however *GW*, revised by author of *W Mid*, gives 12th.

1859 July 25. Worcester & Hereford: Worcester Henwick to Malvern Link opened detached from system *(co ½ T 10 August)*.

1859 July 30. Banff, Portsoy & Strathisla: to Banff. Line 'opened' on this day but first train was derailed and regular service began on 2 August *(GNS)*.

1859 August 2. Torbay & Dartmouth: original Torquay (now Torre) to Paignton. Date is one given in owner's *co ½ T 2 September* and by *GW*. Minutes of South Devon, operators of line, say it opened 1 August *(RAIL 631/6)*. According to *Torquay Dir 4th*, 1 August was an excursion day, with trippers coming from many places; there were local celebrations, but no proper formal opening – directors too busy in London *(Trewman 4th)*.

1859 September 13. South Yorkshire: to Keadby. Date from P. Scowcroft *(Chron Newsletter 15)*.

1859 October 10. Opening, Horsham to Petworth. *W Sussex* reproduces opening notice on page 10 and has extract, on page 21, from press account (paper of 13th) which confirms date. The 'special train' which ran on opening day was in fact the first train, which carried railway staff, families, equipment and furniture to their stations (only 3 involved), as well as passengers.

1860 July 19. LSW: Yeovil Junction to Exeter Central. *Trewman 18th* says formal opening 'this day', public tomorrow, but did not give full station details.

W Fly P 24th only described the formal opening but did list all the stations.

1860 July 25. Oystermouth: Swansea to Black Pill reopened (see *1807 March 25*, above, for earlier history).

See *SIT* for general matters but detail given here is based on Paul Reynolds's researches in *The Cambrian*, which suggest that Lee misinterpreted some items, in particular failing to realise that it was the opening timetable that was included in the paper (he thought it was for a revised service), and on material from *Brad*. The two do not tally exactly on dates and name changes but the general story is the same. Main difference is that *Brad* suggests a short break in the service, February and March 1879, but timetables in *The Cambrian* show continued use. Source cited in *1807 March 25* has very interesting illustrations but lacks detail on this period.

The Cambrian first provided tt, with some detail, 24 August 1860; full details from 26 August 1870. *Brad* first included line in February 1861, without any detail; detail first provided May 1866. There were many changes of name and stopping place, making it difficult to chart line's history exactly; since facilities at most stops would have been minimal, it would have cost little to make changes. At first horse-drawn.

Line was probably extended to Mumbles (later Oystermouth) on 11 November 1860; this was a Sunday, but there was a Sunday service.

July 1877: Swansea Improvements & Tramway Company (SIT) took over, and steam was introduced.

March 1878: SIT opened a street tramway from Gower Street to St Helens, where there was a junction with the 1860 line. Intermittently, horse-drawn trams from this ran along the railway to Mumbles, following steam-hauled services from Rutland Street. When SIT opened its street tramway, it ceased to work the Rutland Street to St Helens portion of the line and John Dickson, who claimed to be the lawful owner of the railway, now ran a steam service along it. It has not been established whether there was any break in the provision of a service from Rutland Street; if there was, it would have been a short one, since Dickson is known to have been operating before the end of March. From 1 July 1885, SIT ran both services. *Brad* always included the two services in one table, without any distinction. *The Cambrian* printed separate tables from 13 September 1878 to 29 May 1885; thereafter it rarely printed tables, leaving *Brad* as the only source.

31 March 1896: Gower Street to Mumbles horse-drawn service ceased.

Line electrified 2 March 1929.

See *1960 January 6*, below, for closure.

RCH Handbooks, 1877 to 1895 inclusive have 'Blackpill and Colliery branch' 'P'. This branch left the main line at Blackpill and went up the Clyne Valley. 'P' probably represents excursion and similar use. In 1875 the Swansea Police annual outing went this way. 1885: regular service, advertised in local press, for 'the new sylvan walks and rambles in the woods for lovers of nature', Thursdays, Saturdays and Sundays. Specials ran to race track at top of the valley. (Paul Reynolds).

Away, p. 67, refers to Pearson Fresh Air Fund children's excursion, citing *The Cambrian 11 July 1906*.

In October 1881 carriages were stationed between St Helens Junction and Gorse Lane so those on them could see Prince of Wales returning from opening of new dock *(Away p. 55–6*, citing *The Cambrian 14th)*; on same occasion temporary platform at The Grange (just south of Lilliput Road) for those attending ball to celebrate dock opening.

1860 November 2. Waveney Valley: extension from Harleston to Bungay *(GE- line)*. This defeated even *Bradshaw*'s ability to cram extra stations into an existing table. At first Homersfield was the only intermediate station added; to make room for this and Bungay, 'The Pulhams' were reduced to a joint entry and Starston omitted. In February 1861 a note listed both Pulhams; Starston; Redenhall; Earsham; and Wortwell as request stops (see 1863 reprint for layout). Inspection report 29 October 1860 *(MT29/21)* named Redenhall, Wortwell, Homersfield and Earsham and said all trains would stop at them.

1860 November 6. Symington, Biggar & Broughton. Date is given by *Return* and *Galashiels Border Record 10th*.

1861 June 10. LNW: Coalport branch. Date from *Neele* and *Shrewsbury 7th, 14th*. Also given in opening notice reproduced in *SU*.

1861 October 29. NB (Border Union): Carlisle to Scotch Dyke. Item in *Carlisle Patriot* of Saturday 2 November said this opened on Tuesday; NB notice in same issue said that this and Longtown branch were 'now open'. (Various alternatives in modern print.)

1862 February 1. Severn Valley. Date from *Shrewsbury 7th*. Original intention was formal opening only on Saturday 1 February, but that was Bridgnorth market day so the public opening was put forward to that day. On the previous day a free train ran for all attending the celebration dinner at Bridgnorth.

1862 February 3. Somerset Central and Dorset Central: Glastonbury to Templecombe. *Shepton* 7th said line opened on Monday (3rd); entry ended 'We shall publish the time-bill of the new line at length next week. It did not reach us until Thursday morning.' Following week's paper included tt with all stations shown.

1862 March. NE: reopened Washington to Durham Turnpike (Chester-le-Street in *Brad*) and opened on to Pelton. Service was Saturdays only, for convenience of miners *(accident report RAIL 1053/57)*; report refers to 'Stella Gill', which, according to *Consett*, = 'Pelton'.

Earlier, part of this line had had its service from South Shields; service now was from Newcastle, via line opened 1 October 1850 (*Brad,* March 1865, shows trains calling at Usworth).

1862 June 9. Eden Valley: Kirkby Stephen to Penrith. The formal opening was on Saturday, 7th *(T 11th)*; all stations were served and anyone could travel free *(EdenV)*; *NE* (Tomlinson's original), *Brad Sh*, and Eden Valley company half-yearly report *(T 8 August)* all gave this as the opening date. However, public fare-paying service began on Monday 9th, date given by *NE* (K. Hoole's errata), *Eden V* and half-yearly report of S&D, the operating company *(T 8 August)*.

1862 October 1. Merthyr, Tredegar & Abergavenny: Abergavenny to Brynmawr (*co ½ T 20 February 1863*). Public excursions ran on the formal opening day, 29 September *(Merlin* and *Newport 4th)*.

1863 January 5. Newtown & Machynlleth: Moat Lane Junction to Machynlleth. According to *Talerddig*, formal opening 3 January, public 5th. *Merioneth 8th* described opening on 3rd, without saying formal only but only mentions opening train, supporting contention in *Talerddig*. Co ½ (*Merioneth 7 March*) also said 3rd but there are other instances of companies quoting formal as though public date.

1863 February 2. Hamilton & Strathaven. Supported by *co ½ 26 September Herapath* – says opened 1 February but this a Sunday, no service. No station detail but all in *Brad* with line.

1863 March 19. BM: Pant to Talybont-on-Usk. Service officially began 23 April 1863, when Talybont to Brecon also opened, but two trains per day ran from 19 March (*co n Merthyr Telegraph 21st)*.

1863 July. Oswestry & Newtown: Kerry and Llanfyllin branches. Company's half-yearly report *(T 28 August)* simply says opened July and *Brad* did not include the lines until then. *Brad Sh* gives 11 July for both – suspicious, but not impossible.

L. Cozens (*The Van and Kerry Railways*, author, 1953) describes a train with a single carriage and a truck of coal for distribution to the poor running on 2 March 1863. This would seem to have been some sort of formal opening or special or trial trip.

For the Llanfyllin branch, *Oswestry* says that an 'Opening Celebration Dinner' was held on 17 July, but this is not directly linked to the running of any trains so public opening might have been that day, earlier or later. The same paper's issue of 4 June had referred to a train on 3 June 1863 for a concert in aid of Bwlch-y-Cibau Church; this ran from Oswestry to Llanfyllin and back, stopping at Llanymynech and Llansaintffraid. Line inspected (and approved as a result) on 27 June.

Colindale version of *Oswestry* has Cambrian tt supplement for 'July' bound in after 1 July issue; both

lines included, <u>suggesting</u> then open for passengers. Items in that and following paper about meeting to decide on the form a celebration of opening of Llanfyllin line should take <u>implied</u> line already open.

1863 August 3. Pulborough – Ford [LBSC]. LBSC ? yearly both in *T 24 July* and *Brighton Guardian 29 July* said line from Pulborough to Arundel and Littlehampton would be ready for traffic on 1 August. However, the list of openings in *Table of Distances ... LBSC 1901*, Ian Allan reprint, and modern works say 3rd. LBSC advertised fare reductions from 1st, suggesting it was making changes then. Brighton paper of Wednesday 5 August, included rather ambiguous items, on the whole supporting 3rd. One said that some of its contemporaries announced line would be opened for public traffic on Monday [3rd] and they had never intended to open before 1 August; the other said opening of [part of] Littlehampton Railway was celebrated by dinner Monday last.

1863 August 6. Pembroke & Tenby. Date from *Mining 1st. T 3rd* refers to formal opening on 30 July.

1863 September 10. SD Jt: Templecombe to Blandford. Formal opening 31 August, public 10 September *(Dorset; co n W Gaz 19 September)*.

1864 February 1. Extension to Rowrah [WCE]. *Whitehaven Herald 30 January 1864*: Rowrah extension added to tt for February; also includes Eskett, Winder. Paper of Saturday 6 February said opened Monday with due honours. Only mentioned directors' train – others? Perhaps formal only; seems safe to assume public next day at least.

1864 September 1. Eccles – Wigan and Kenyon Junction [LNW]. *Wigan Examiner Friday 26 August 1864* described formal opening on Wednesday and said believed would be opened to public 1 September. Paper of 2 September said was opened 'yesterday'. Tt in paper included intermediate stations. A *co n*, dated 29 August, says 'The NEW LINE between Eccles, Tyldesley and Wigan is now OPENED for general traffic'; however, the earliest this has been found is *T 6 September* so it would appear to have been prepared before opening, but not issued until afterwards. [See 1849 July 20**.]

1865 May 1. NE: Market Weighton to Beverley. Line opening from *co ½ T 15 August*. Early in January *(T, Wednesday 11 January* – '*last week*'), a special train ran over the line conveying the magistrates and others to the East Riding Sessions at Beverley – no details of any stops.

1865 June 1. Central Wales & Carmarthen Junction: Carmarthen to Lland(e)ilo. Line opening from *co ½ T 28 July)*; *D&C 11* lists stations. Prior to public opening, line was used 29, 30 and 31 May for a daily excursion from Abergwili to Llandilo Bridge and back, for visitors to Llandilo Eisteddfod.

Company's notice reproduced in *LMS South Wales* says that owing to a dispute with the LNW the local service would be withdrawn from 1 April 1880. In the April tt,

Abergwili and Llandilo Bridge are shown without any trains whilst Golden Grove; Llanarthney; and Nantgareddig were reduced to request only service, limited to passengers to and from stations north of Llandovery. In June tt a normal service was again shown; also, Drysllwyn returned then – it is not known whether its earlier absence was the result of closure or a feeling that it was not worth a mention in the tt.

1865 September 4: West Somerset Mineral (see R. Sellick, *The West Somerset Mineral Railway*, D&C, 1970 edition). Line opened in stages from April 1857 onwards (initially to Roadwater). Iron-miners and their families, who would always be main users of the line, were allowed to use it unofficially from start. A special excursion for a Temperance Meeting at Brendon Hill was run to Combe Row on 7 August 1860 (the incline between the two did not come into operation until 1861). After the opening for regular passenger use, people were probably taken up and set down at Torre and Clitsome Level Crossings, between Washford and Roadwater; they were also taken, free and at their own risk, up the incline (1,100 yards long, vertical rise of 800 ft) to Brendon Hill (near Raleigh's Cross) and then along upper conventional line to Langham Hill (alias Luxborough Road) and Gupworthy. Stations of sorts existed at the last two because original intention had been to extend official service to them but costs of safety provisions needed to bring the incline up to BoT standards prevented this.

1865 December 1. Central Wales: Knighton to Llandrindod. Line date from *co ½ T 14 February 1866*. *D&C* gives 10 September 1865 formal, 17th public; *Neele p. 138* says 1 January 1866. First in *Brad* January 1866, when all stations given this date were present.

1866: Line through Wandsworth Road; Clapham; Brixton/East Brixton; Denmark Hill; and Peckham Rye is quadruple tracked, one pair of tracks being originally used by LCD, other by LBSC. However, for ease of maintenance LCD owned stretch which included Wandsworth Common; Clapham; Brixton, and the LBSC that which included East Brixton; Denmark Hill; Peckham Rye.

1866 January 1: Cal: Glasgow to Busby. *T 5th* said three intermediate stations; assumed these were Pollokshaws (West), already open, plus Clarkston and Giffnock as new.

1866 February 1. Bishops Castle.
— Line opened 1 February 1866 (*co ½ T 8* March). Closed 27 February 1877, reopened 2 July 1877 *(Cl)*.
— 1879: closed Easter, reopened after 11 April;
— 1883 closed following inspection report dated 24 September, reopened before 7 October.
Presumably at least one other short closure – book on line by J.S. Morgan, Bishops Castle Railway Society, 2003 reprint, calls one 'fourth' but does not cover closures in chronological order.

17 July 1933 tt shows one each way daily plus extra on Fridays; before/with 9 July 1934 tt, reduced to one train each way, Mondays and Fridays only; other entries in tt for road services.

Closed 20 April 1935; date given by all in print, although a Saturday and normal convention would require 22nd as closure date. According to E.G. King, *The Bishop's Castle Branch*, 1983: 'A Master in Chancery directed that the line be closed on 20 April 1935'.

1866 May 1: Northampton & Banbury Junction, later SMJ: Blisworth to Towcester. *Brad Sh 1867* new openings says 1 May (but 'April' in body of book). *T 30 April* says had been approved by inspector but some detailed matters needed attention and expected to open 'in a few days', suggesting a date later than 1 May. However, *Northampton Mercury 5th* confirmed opening on 1st.

1866 May 21. Scottish Central: Methven Junction to Crieff. *T 23rd* supports this date, given by *Tayside*, but its report says that several special and excursion trains to and from Perth were run during the day. Were these in addition to a timetabled service or a preliminary to it? – if a preliminary, were all stations served?

1866 August 13: Potteries, Shrewsbury & North Wales, later SM:

Main line, Shrewsbury to Llanymynech:

Opened 13 August 1866 (*co ½ T 7 August*, confirmed by *item T 28 November*). All stations given this date were in September 1866 tt *(RM May 1903, p. 405)*.

Closed part way through Tuesday 27 November 1866, when bailiffs 'seized' line, leaving some would-be passengers stranded at Shrewsbury (stock-fair day there). One return train allowed later that day but that probably all *(T 28th* – at time of going to press some still stranded).

— Reopened Monday 3 December 1866, complete with travelling bailiff *(T 28 November, 4 December)*.
— Closed 21 December 1866 (Friday) *(Cl)*.
— Reopened December 1868 *(Cl)*.
— Extension to Llanyblodwell opened 18 April 1870 *(D&C 11)*.

All closed 22 June 1880 on BoT recommendation – lines unsafe and company lacked funds to repair, and could use BoT as excuse for closing line, saying (wrongly) that it had ordered closure. Date usually quoted (and used here) was a Tuesday and so cannot be a closure date according to normal convention: perhaps when BoT 'orders' were given, or received? Thus cannot be certain of last day on 'main' line. *(RM May 1903, p. 405; article by B. Janes, The Potteries Railway and How it Failed, RCHS Journal, July 2006)*.

— Reopened 14 April 1911 *(RCG)*.
— Closed 6 November 1933 *(Rly Gaz)*.

However, some passengers continued to be carried, presumably excursionists. All *Returns* to 1938 (last issue before war interrupted sequence) show some receipts from ordinary passengers. In 1938, 262 were carried (total revenue £12). *RM October 1936* mentions an excursion on 3 August, with reference to Llanymynech.

In 1941 line was requisitioned for military use and passenger trains ran for camps along the line. Halts were established at Ford; Shrawardine; Pentre; and Nesscliffe on main line (not same sites as previous public stations) and at Lonsdale on a new branch.

Criggion branch:

— Opened 2 June 1872 *(D&C 11)*.
— March 1872 tt, branch reduced to Wednesdays, Saturdays and Shrewsbury Fair days only.
— According to Janes Criggion branch was closed from Wednesday 16 June 1880 (last day or official date?).
— Reopened 22 July 1912 *(RCG; dist supp 863/1)*.

Still shown all days 26 September 1927 tt; in April 1928 tt shown as Saturdays only (Provisional Service); in July 1928 tt service Tuesdays and Saturdays only (shows one all days to Criggion, nothing in return – assumed to be error since omitted by 8 July 1929 tt); August 1930 tt Thursdays and Saturdays; 22 September 1930 tt Saturdays only. Perhaps ran two days per week in summer, one only in winter.

— Closed October 1932: Melverley to Criggion *(Cl)*;
— Closed 6 November 1933: Kinnerley Junction to Melverley (with main line).

Later excursion use of Criggion at least – one 3 August 1936 *(RM October)*.

1866 October 1. Talyllyn: Pendre (at Towyn) to Abergynolwyn. According to *D&C 11 (from RM September 1938?)* this line opened now. However, it failed first inspection; official approval to open was given 13 November 1866; official service began? First company tt was for December 1866 (J.I.C. Boyd, *The Tal-y-Llyn Railway*, Oakwood, 1988). Was there an earlier unofficial service, passengers free and at own risk? No worthwhile contemporary evidence seen. Never included in annual list of new openings *Brad Sh*; earliest Board of Trade statistics were included in return giving 1867 figures, where, most unusually, they were given for '12 months ending 30th September 1867' and no specific date was given for passenger opening – has this misled someone in the past into assuming it was 1 October? Inspection report says there were no intermediate stations. Line first in *Brad* August 1867, when Rhydyronen and Dolgoch included. Dolgoch last in *Brad* November 1867; back July 1872, when Brynglas included for first time. Given habits of this railway, there can be no guarantee that tt tells full story. For details of Towyn Wharf see Section 4.

A special extra train ran for miners who lived on Anglesey – e.g. 1905 note that a Mondays only train, 6am from Towyn and 6.50am back (usually empty?) – from Abergynolwyn, would not run when any stoppage occurred at Bryn Eglwys Quarry.

1867 August 1: BM: Pontsticill Junction to Cefn and Dowlais Top. Date from *Cardiff Times 27 July*. Same paper said line had been temporarily opened 25th for benefit of visitors to Merthyr Flower Show; not known which station(s) used.

1867 September 2: LNW, Cam: Ca(e)rnarvon Pant to Port Madoc/Porthmadog. There were earlier excursions (some including parts of lines opened later than this) – *LNW* mentions use in August and on 6 September 1866 when one met with accident. *T 10th/Carnarvon Herald 13th, 14th* (report of inquest) shows latter was from Port Madoc to Carnarvon and back for big Calvinist meeting. Allegedly 600 on outward journey, in ballast trucks, on tender, etc; some missed return journey when late at Pant. On way back made several stops to set down ('stop anywhere' principle?); derailed just before 'Glandwyfach' station (= Brynkir).

Earlier use included taking Pwllheli and Port Madoc Volunteers to Pant in ballast waggons with plank seats, party of children from Port Madoc to confirmation at Criccieth, several picnic parties, Sir Watkin and Lady Wynn and large party Barmouth to Pant. No charge made for most but 3/- per head was charged, illegally, for those on train that was derailed *(T 13 March 1867, from BoT report)*.

1868 May 30. Festiniog & Blaenau, 1ft 11½in. gauge. Date from *GW* and *Brad Sh 1869*; *NGSC* gives 29th (formal?). During conversion of line from narrow to standard gauge the service was able to continue because the standard gauge was created by adding a third rail, giving a mixed gauge. Last narrow gauge train ran 5 September 1883; first standard gauge train 10 September 1883.

1869 September 6. LNW: Mold to Denbigh. Much variation of date in sources seen. This comes from *Mining 4th*; 1 September, given by *Neele* and *T 26 August*, was probably formal. LNW half-yearly report *(T 12 February 1870)* gives 12 September but that is least likely: line had passed its inspection on 23 August and 12th was a Sunday. *LNW dates* gives 6th for each of the stations but 12th for line.

1869 November 15. St Helens – Wigan [LNW]. *Wigan Examiner Saturday 6 November 1869* said had opened for mineral traffic on Monday and would be opened throughout for passenger traffic on 15th. Unfortunately this was last paper in bound volume at Colindale so unable to confirm that did.

1869 December 1. Lancashire Union: Blackburn–Chorley–Wigan. *Brad* showed line complete with trains, without comment, in October 1869. In November: no trains, 'Opening expected shortly'. January 1870: trains again shown. *LNW Officers* shows opening was planned for 1 October *(6927)* but there were inspection problems. There was another delay: *Manchester* 15 November said company had announced intention of opening that morning; paper of 16th said had been postponed. Opening date and stations confirmed by *LNW Officers 4938* and tt on p.1479 and by *St Helens News* and *St Helens Standard* (J. Tolson); stations included in *Wigan Observer* 3 December.

1870 January 31: Tottenham & Hampstead Junction: closure. *Co ½ T 31 March*: on 30 January all passenger traffic ceased because GE, who had worked from opening, had declined to continue. Presumably last day (a Sunday but was Sunday service in July 1869 tt, nearest to hand). Unusual since changes normally made on 1st of month. Line reopened 1 October by Midland *(co n T 1st)*.

1870 July 1. LNW: Edge Hill to Canada Dock. 1 June 1866 is often quoted as opening date for stretch from Edge Hill to Tue Brook but *Brad* does not include this until whole line opened in 1870; this is supported by *LNW Officers 5542* and *Liverpool Mercury 1 July 1870*; LNW co ½ T 15 August 1866, refers only to goods traffic on this section of line.

1870 July 4: Hoylake: as result of court order obtained by local landowner, sheriff's officers took possession of part of line and removed length of rails. In the afternoon trains started using temporary terminus, Leasowe Crossing, at first no proper platform. Bus took passengers to Seacombe, for Liverpool. *(T 6th; T.B. Maund)*.

1870 November 1. West Helmsdale to Dunrobin was opened by the Duke of Sutherland and incorporated into the Highland main line when this was extended northwards *(High Pamph)*.

1870 November 23. NB: Coatbridge to Bellgrove. Date (a Wednesday) given by City of Glasgow Union company minute of 1 December 1870; also used by *NB co ½ T 13 March 1871, MK* and *Brad Sh 1871*; however, *MT 6/72/3* says op 25th – line had been twice failed by BoT; latter then seems to have failed to renew prohibition, and when inspector came back, found line already open. 23rd confirmed by notice and item in *Glasgow Herald 24th*.

1871. Wotton Tramway. See *Brill*.

Built without Act of Parliament since the Duke of Buckingham owned most of the land and was able to make arrangements with owners of the rest. Line completed to Wotton March 1871, to Brill March 1872. First passenger use was an excursion, 21 August 1871, from Wood Siding (then limit of line), Wotton, and Wes(t)cott to London. Horse-drawn until early 1872 when steam (effectively a traction engine on rails) was introduced; speed limit 12mph; classed as Light Agricultural Railway so BoT requirements less stringent than usual. Regular passenger service began ? – 104 passengers used line in January 1872, perhaps first month. Increased passenger numbers in March and April would suggest line now open to Brill. Early 1873, they tried to have line licensed for proper passenger use but BoT report, published July 1873, was against this. First in *Brad* May 1882. It was reconstructed in 1894 and proper

stations built. Stops were Quainton Road (terminus alongside orthodox station); Waddesdon; Wes(t)cott; Wotton; Church Siding (not used after 1894); Wood Siding; Brill.

1873 August 4. Ross & Monmouth, worked by GW. Col Rich initially passed this line and handbills were distributed saying it would open on 1 August. However, inspector then realised that there was no means for turning an engine at Monmouth and withdrew his permission. Problem was solved by company giving an undertaking to use only tank engines *(County Obs 9th; Ross Gazette 7th)*.

1873 December 1. Van: Caersws to Garth & Van Road *(Cam)*. Opened now, all days. November 1874 tt: whole line reduced to Tuesdays, Thursdays and Saturdays. October 1875 tt: full use again.

1874: Corris. See *RM June 1899, NGMW* and L. Cozens, *The Corris Railway*, author, 1949.

Corris GW appendix includes newspaper account of accident 11 July 1860 to passenger travelling on top of a load for 'a trifling consideration' to driver.

Return for 1874 has note that line was used almost exclusively for haulage of slates by horse-traction but recently some passengers had been carried in open trucks. 3,592 passengers carried in 1874, 11,380 in 1875 (when 'recently' still in note). In 1878 the number had risen to 22,024; however, only 3,232 passengers were shown for 1879 and no more were shown until 1883.

According to Boyd *(NGMW)*, company wanted to provide a passenger service but lacked legal power and was opposed by quarry owners afraid that passenger trains would interrupt flow of their traffic, especially after line had been improved for locomotive haulage in February 1879. As a result, the rail service was replaced by a road service in August 1879. A service was included in *Brad* from January 1879, with stops at Machynlleth; Pandy; Esgairgeiliog; Corris. It was shown until October 1879; November – 'service suspended'. Statistics of *Returns* support Boyd, rather than those who say earliest service was by road, though they would suggest somewhat earlier end to rail service, unless most of its business had been done in the summer and early autumn. *Brad* was clearly behind events.

After a new Act had been obtained, a locomotive-hauled service began 4 July 1883, Machynlleth to Corris, without any intermediate stations. Llwyngwern and Esgairgeiliog were declared fit in an inspection report dated 6 March 1884 and added to tt May 1884. Ffriddgate added to tt July 1887, Garneddwen November 1887. *D&C 11* says there were halts at Llwdy and Dolwdderen Crossing; neither in *Brad*; occasional stops *(Cozens)*.

1874 March 27. Aylesbury & Buckingham: closed Aylesbury to Verney Junction by injunction from Chancery at suit of Revd T.J. Williams of Waddesdon –

unsettled claim for payment for land. Sudden closure caused much inconvenience to district. *T 4th* said had closed 'Thursday'; should have added 'a week ago'. Items in local press *(Buckinghamshire Advertiser* and *Bucks Advertiser & Aylesbury News 4, 11 April)* said injunction had forbidden use after 26 March. Reopened 9 April; interruption 'seems' to have been result of misunderstanding – they had necessary funds put by. Company notice confirmed reopening date and said that temporary service Verney Junction – Quainton Road would be discontinued. No details of this found – was it for benefit of passengers from Brill Tramway? Did it serve intermediate stations? Seems that only section from Quainton Road to Aylesbury was fully closed.

Previous co ½ had mentioned financial problems and need to provide proper facilities at stations.

1874 June. WCE: diversion via Yeathouse, with permanent closure of Eskett and temporary closure of Winder. New service was in tt June 1874, but official sanction for opening was not given until 10 June *(D&C 14)*. Either premature tt entry or local 'initiative' (hints of this in *D&C*).

1874 July 23. Edinburgh, Loanhead & Roslin. This date is given by *Brad Sh* and line is in tt August but it has been questioned by *Glencorse* on the grounds that the inspection was unsatisfactory and the opening must have been slightly delayed. However, there are inconsistencies in the version there: the offending pointwork was still in place at the end of August but official sanction for opening was given by a letter dated 1 August; the main consideration seems to have been for undertakings to be provided by the company saying that they would attend to these matters within ten days; no date of a repeat inspection has been found (was there one? – would seem to have been unnecessary if undertakings were all that were needed) (pp. 31–32). The story given by *The Edinburgh Courant*, a daily paper, supports 23 July. The paper of 22nd said that the line was being inspected by Colonel Rich that day and would be opened the next day if the report was satisfactory; this indicates that they were relying on Rich's verbal consent for opening. That of the 23rd carried a notice of opening that day and an item saying it would. This is not conclusive since it was not unknown for notices to be provided prematurely. However, nothing was seen about any delay and the paper of 30 July carried a notice dated just 'July' saying that the line was now open. This would make a short delay still a possibility but it clearly shows that the line was opened before formal written permission was given.

1875. Isle of Wight Central.

Sandown to Shide (a) opened 1 February 1875 *(Hants Chron 6th)*;
Ryde to Newport (b) opened 20 December 1875 *(Hants Adv 22nd)*.

On section (a) Alverstone; Newchurch; Merstone;

Blackwater and on (b) Haven Street and Wootton were all first included in tt June 1876. Strangely, the apparently less important stations at Ashey and Whippingham, both on (b), were in tt from January 1876 and relegated to footnotes in June 1876 as request stops.

The account of opening of (a) given in *IWC* suggests that stations listed above were absent at line opening. The press account quoted refers to signals at Merstone and Blackwater but neither there nor in information about e.g. fares at opening is there any mention of stations. Furthermore, on p. 67 it says that some of the stations had not been approved by the BoT before opening, and the late entries in *Brad* would be the obvious candidates for this; strangely, on this page it is stated that there were no signals at Merstone and Blackwater when the BoT caught up with them (removed when stations opened?). *IWC*'s account of (b) makes it clear that Ashey and Whippingham did open with the line and the others later; Col. Yolland reported on 11 March 1876 that he had inspected new stations at Haven Street and Wootton.

1875 March. Midland: diversion of line via Cwm Clydach (later Clydach-on-Tawe). Intention was to open on 1 March and working timetables were prepared for that day but there might have been a delay (D.M. Bayliffe & J.N. Harding, *Starling Benson of Swansea*, 1996. Timetables in *The Cambrian* show the old route still in use on 12 March, the new on the 19th; if there was a delay, Monday 15th is likeliest date for change. *(J. Gough; P. Reynolds)*. Further doubts are raised by correspondence concerning opening. BoT said 26 January 1875 that could be opened if Mid gave undertaking that some requirements resulting from inspection had been met. Mid reply dated 6 March, BoT letter of approval 8 March. This would suggest delay but Mid might have anticipated consent and opened on 1 March, as shown in wtt (M. Hale).

1875 September 23: Severn & Wye, main line. *Co n T 21st* said would be opened for passenger traffic on 23rd; first train would be '12.5 noon' from Lydney; no indication that would not be available to all; once line in full operation this would be third train out of four daily (only two going whole length of line). Press report described it as 'special train' and implied (but did not categorically state) that it was the only train of day; indeed, report could be interpreted that only the directors' 'private saloon' went on trip. Seems to be good case for treating this as formal and 24th as public but 23rd given because of unqualified nature of company notice. Also see 1875 December 9, below.

1875 December 9: Severn & Wye, Coleford branch. Company's notice in local press said would be opened 9th by 'special train' leaving Lydney Junction at '12.5 p.m.'; 'regular service' would start 10th. Clearly only one train 9th. As on 1875 September 23 (above) there was no indication that public could not use, though space would be limited. Unless they cancelled a main-line train to fit this one in, (no indication in notice) Coleford must have been served by carriages attached to a Lydbrook train as far as Parkend, though Coleford revellers did have a separate train for return.

1877 September 19. Girvan & Portpatrick Junction. On this date line was opened as far as New Luce, two trains per day (service shown in October *Brad*, with a coach connection to Stranraer). 5 October 1877 was when through service to Stranraer began (GSW ½ yearly meeting in *Ayrshire Argus 22 September*). Reason for delay was inspector's insistence on extra accommodation at Stranraer (*Galloway Advertiser 27 September*). Line was plagued with financial problems. Failure to pay arrears owing to the Portpatrick company for use of its line on to Stranraer led to an injunction and services ceased 7 February 1882. 16 February service resumed from Girvan to New Luce; on to Stranraer again 1 August 1883. 28 February 1886 the GSW ceased working the line so the company hired rolling stock from the GSW and ran its own service, but that ceased 12 April 1886; line reopened 14 June 1886 *(Cl; GSW)*.

1879 January 20. LSW: Okehampton to Holsworthy. *Co n T 14th*, gave this as opening date but said that on Saturday 18th the 2.25pm express from Waterloo would run through to Holsworthy, calling at all stations on branch, but did not name them. Nothing other way.

1879 June 3. Opening of Loudon Road and Queens Park. *LNW Officers 19682*, 13 May – will be opened on Tuesday 3 June (result of Whit Monday intervening – *Neele*, p.228 says that new line through Primrose Hill Tunnel opened 1 June and North London trains ran through at fixed hours, implying peak hours, working days only). *LNW Record* gave 3 June 1878 but that was when they settled on names to be used for the stations which were yet to be built *(LNW Officers 18490)*.

1881 July 27. Swindon, Marlborough & Andover (later part of MSWJ): Swindon (Town) to Marlborough (LL). Formal opening plus special for Marlborough School 26 July; up to public 27 July 1881 *(Swindon 30th)*; prior to opening there were five free experimental trips, stopping at Chiseldon and Ogbourne *(MSWJ)*.

1881 September 1. Golden Valley/GW:

1 September 1881 opened Pontrilas to Dorstone. *Return* confirms line date; all stations given this date (Abbeydore; Vowchurch; Peterchurch; Dorstone) in *Brad*, first time line included. Bacton added later.

This line would suffer recurrent financial problems; hence the various closures and reopenings.

— Closed 22 October 1883, reopened 17 November 1883 *(Cl)*.
— Closed 2 July 1885 (Thursday), reopened 19 August 1885 *(Cl)*.
— 27 May 1889: extended to Hay *(GW)*. Stations at Clifford and Westbrook; Greens Siding later.
— 23 August 1897: closed Dorstone to Hay *(G&S)*.

— 20 April 1898: closed Pontrilas to Dorstone *(Rtn)*.
— 1 May 1901: all reopened *(RM May p.479, June p.491)*.

8 December 1941: all closed: actual last day was Saturday 6th. The 15th usually quoted was 'official' date – W.H. Smith, *Golden Valley Railway*, Wild Swan, 1993.

1882: West Lancs: *Away, p.70*, refers to Sunday School trip from Back Lane (Penwortham?) and New Longton, citing Penwortham Parish Magazine of September 1880; presumably joining/alighting points not stations.

1882 December 1. Glasgow, Yoker & Clydebank: Clydebank to Partick *(Glasgow)*. This line was at first detached from system. Mostly used by shipyard workers.

1883 May 1. Direct Arbroath to Montrose service [NB]. *Montrose Standard (4 March 1881)* made it clear that on 1 March 1881 (date given for passengers in modern print) through goods trains started to use this line. *Dundee Courier (1 May 1883)* carried notice of passenger opening that day and item describing line; it explained that a bridge near Montrose had had to be rebuilt before passenger trains could run.

1883 August 20. GE: Wisbech & Upwell Tramway. This line was never included in *Brad*. Opening on this day to Outwell Basin, and of extension to Upwell on 8 September 1884, confirmed by *RM February 1899*, which said that passengers could be picked up at any point. GE notice for 1884 extension reproduced by C. Hawkins & G. Reeve, *The Wisbech & Upwell Tramway*, Wild Swan, 1982, p.7. 'At any point' still in GE co tt November 1889. This refers to Elm 'Depot' and Boyces 'Depot' in main table, other main stops named as listed in Section 4. However GE tt 4 October 1914 note says: in addition to above, tram cars will also stop if required at Elm Road Crossing; New Common Bridge (Canal Bridge); Rose Cottage; Duke of Wellington Junction; Inglethorpe Hall; Collett's Bridge; Dial House; Horn's Corner; Goodmans Crossing; Small Lode. The tram cars will not stop at any other point along the line of the route. [Was there anywhere else they could have stopped? – line only 5 miles 72 chains long.]

1885 March 2. East & West Junction: a number of points are dealt with here, rather than in several short notes. Much in print is inaccurate.

5 June 1871: *Stratford* did not give exact opening date; paper of Friday 9 June said would open 'this week'; that of 16th said had opened 'last week'. That would fit date given by Oxford paper if it is assumed that *Stratford* was getting information from a correspondent in Kineton who wrote several days in advance of publication; it would in no way fit date given by most in print (1 June).

1 July 1873: *Stratford* 4th said line from Stratford to Kineton had opened on 1st and that line was open through to Blisworth but it did not explicitly say that Fenny Compton to Blisworth stretch opened now; gave no details on it.

1 August 1877: *Stratford 27 July* did not give explicit date for closure (Stratford to Towcester) but said directors had decided to close it to passengers because of poor patronage; closure at end of month would have been in line with normal practice then.

2 March 1885: reopening. *Stratford 27 February* included company notice of reopening; paper of 6 March carried report; supported by re-appearance in *Brad* March and *LNW Officers 26924*. 22 February, given by *Cl*, and 22 March, given by *G&S* and most modern works, cannot be correct – both were Sundays and no Sunday service shown in tt.

1885 July 2. LBSC/LSW: Fratton and branch to (East) Southsea. *Hants Teleg, Saturday 4 July,* describes opening on 1st; looks to be formal, only one train mentioned. At end there is a confusing reference to public opening 'tomorrow'. Taken literally, that would have been Sunday 5th, but no Sunday service on line. Probably item was written on opening day, no adjustment made for publication day. *LSW* confirms 1st formal, 2nd public.

1887. Llanelly & Mynydd Mawr ran a 'workmen's service' from about 1887 with a very liberal interpretation of 'workman'. Passengers joined at Sandy (near Llanelly) and trains then called at Furnace; Felin Foel; Horeb; Cynheidre; Cwm Blawd; Tumble; S & S Colliery; Cross Hands. Also specific miners' services. Service ceased 1928 or later *(U)*.

1888 March 19. South Shields, Marsden & Whitburn Colliery. Originally 'Marsden Railway', name changed about 1890s. Miners' service began May 1879. Public service began, detached from main system, in March 1885, without BoT sanction; fare-paying passengers signed that they were travelling at their own risk; stopped when BoT found out (report dated 20 June 1887) *(Mountford)*. Properly approved service began 19 March 1888 from South Shields Westoe Lane to Marsden; miners were taken on to Whitburn Colliery. The miners' platform was re-sited on a line further inland by 1915 *(S. Bragg, map evidence)*.

Further deviation line first used 9 April 1929 (W.J. Hatcher, *The South Shields, Whitburn & Marsden Colliery Railway*, Oakwood 2002). This bypassed Marsden, which was not replaced, passengers being taken on to second miners' Whitburn Colliery station, now renamed Marsden. *Returns* first included line 1926 with note that return was from 5 August; elsewhere in that year's issue it was explained that powers for re-construction and working line as a light railway had been granted to the Harton Coal Company, Limited.

Aot (tt) one Saturdays only ran 'as required', another only ran on 'Baff Saturdays'; miners paid alternate Saturdays and Baff Saturdays were non-pay days.

1888 July 2. LY: Swinton to Atherton. *Lancs Chesh* gives 1st but that was a Sunday. These stations did have a Sunday service so possible, but unlikely.

LY gives 2nd as goods opening, with passenger opening of whole line in one piece later. *Brad* supports the opening in instalments followed here.

1889 July 20. FYN: Freshwater to Newport IoW. To celebrate Golden Jubilee of Queen Victoria, Mr W. Jackson, contractor for the line provided free service between Yarmouth and Freshwater for locals, several trains running on the day *(IoW CP 25th,* quoted in '75 years ago' column, 1963) – actual Jubilee was 20 June 1887, first engine had arrived 14 June (D.L. Bradley, *A Locomotive History of Railways on the Isle of Wight*, Railway Correspondence & Travel Society, 1982).

Opening notice and tt given in *FYN*; date confirmed by *Hants Teleg 27th*. *FYN Oakwood* mentions free excursion 9 October 1888, from Ryde to Yarmouth and Freshwater (but not other FYN stations) via Sandown, which carried over 700 people. Also used for IoW Rifles, Easter Monday, 1889.

1893 March 6. Liverpool Overhead Railway *(Return* confirms line date; other dates from *LO)*. No detail in *Brad* until May 1896. Then Huskisson Dock; Langton Dock; and Nelson Dock were present; they were not in 1895 *hb*.

In 1900s tt usually omitted 'Dock' from name; it was later added and though tt continued to show most stops as 'X Dock', after about 1927, when printing was transferred to LNE printers at York, tickets omitted 'Dock' (T. David, *The Tickets of the Liverpool Overhead Railway Company*, TTS, 2000).

1895 June 1. Cal: Forfar to Brechin. Date from *Cal*, supported by *RCG*. Confirmed by items in *Forfar Herald* 31 May and 7 June, which mentions all stations. According to *Cal*, 7 January, given by some books, was goods opening.

1895 July 13. Rye & Camber Tramway, 3ft gauge. This is formal date; public opening was expected in the course of a few days (press announcement quoted in *Rye & C*). It has not been found.

1896 April 6. Snowdon Mountain Railway: Llanberis to Snowdon Summit, 2ft 7in. rack railway. Closed this same day because of an accident. Reopened Llanberis to Clogwyn on 19 April 1897 *(T 20th)*; rest of the way ? – probably very soon after – some safety measures still needed. Tt carried note that trains would not run with less than seven return passengers or the equivalent in single fares. Summer only. See K. Turner, *The Snowdon Mountain Railway*, D&C, 1973.

By 2003 bookings only taken between Llanberis and Summit, passengers normally back in same train after half-hour at top; singles, space permitting, for those wishing to walk back. In bad weather trains turn back at Rocky Valley. Hebron; Halfway; and Clogwyn reduced to passing-places, no alighting or joining. This began ? (A. Brackenbury, *Chron*).

1896 December 14. Glasgow Subway/Underground. Opening date confirmed by *T 15th*; other material from *GU* and *D&C 6*. 4ft line, at first cable-hauled. There were two accidents on the opening day: early afternoon there was a minor one which closed the outer circle, leaving all traffic to be carried by the inner; late in the evening a far more serious one occurred on the inner circle, causing service to be suspended. Line reopened 21 January 1897. It closed 26 March 1922 owing to financial difficulties; was reopened 3 July 1922 by Glasgow Corporation. Electric haulage introduced 1935. Closed by a bomb 18 September 1940; reopened 27 January 1941. Closed for repairs 21 May 1977; reopened 16 April 1980 *(RM June)*.

1898 January 17: GW: Yealmpton branch (for stations beyond Plymstock). Originally from Millbay; opening date *(W Morn News 17th, 18th)*; closed 7 July 1930 *(GM's report)*; reopened 21 July 1940 for workmen, now from Friary *(U)*: reopened to public 3 November 1941 *(GM's report)*; closed 30 May to 24 June 1944 for removal of unstable rock *(GM's report)*; closed 6 October 1947 *(RM January 1948)*.

1898 November 8. Closure: West Somerset Mineral. Last day of use was a Monday *(W Som FP 8 October and 12 November;* supported by *Brad November* – service will not run after 7 November). Likeliest answer for odd date is that company had to give a calendar month's notice of closure and that starting point of notice was fixed by publication day of local paper (Saturday).

The line was briefly reopened for minerals 1907–10; on 4 July 1907 there was a celebratory excursion Watchet to Combe Row and back; this involved four open trucks and seems to have been given a great welcome all along the line, far more notice being taken of this occasion than was apparently ever bestowed on the line during its earlier life. One had a stand for a band, in a second members of the Urban District Council and some of their officers and the others were comfortably seated and the other two were crammed with passengers, including most of the leading tradesmen of the town. *(W Som F P, 6 July 1907)*.

1900 February 26. Closure by City & South London of King William Street and opening of extension to Moorgate. *T 26th* – opens today; *27th* – opened yesterday. Confirmed by *co ½ T 21 July*.

1901 May 18. BWA: Bideford to Northam. Line consisted of part tramway (along the Quay at Bideford) and part railway (rest); there had been much local opposition to the Quay section. The inspection report, published 18 May, passed railway section but failed that along the Quay (see S. Jenkins, *The Bideford, Westward Ho! and Appledore Railway*, Oakwood, 1993 – useful in general, but wrong over opening). Opening details based on *N Devon 23rd; Evening Post (Exeter) 20th; Bideford 21 May* and *16 July* (last was report of prosecution of company for running trains along the Quay which did not meet BoT requirements).

Opening advertised for 20 May but actually occurred 18th. First train ran, with passengers, from the Quay terminus and company said it would continue to run one per day along this stretch in order to preserve legal right to do so (not known whether it actually did since very little evidence was presented in court; a deal had been done behind the scenes, the Company agreeing to pay a 10/- fine on each of five counts). Otherwise, most (all?) early trains used a temporary 'terminus' near the Art School, at northern end of the Quay, between Quay station and Strand Road. Full service began again ? – probably soon – alterations needed were minor.

Not certain that all Halts opened with line, though all in first detailed tt found *(Bideford 5 July 1902)*. S. Jenkins says that there were perhaps extra untimetabled stops – e.g. at level crossings at Puse Hill and Mudcott, both near Abbotsham Road.

(Correct opening date is given in *Minor*, though no detail or explanation is provided.)

1901 June 29. Corringham Light: Corringham to Coryton. Legally this was a public service but it was detached from main system so only of use to workmen. Mostly used by Kynoch's explosives factory workers but a few others (e.g. Shell workers) also used. First in *Brad* October 1948. *Returns* support opening date given and show that some ordinary tickets were sold, though only a small fraction of the total. See *RM June 1913; Thames Haven*, pp42–44.

During WW2, reduced to limited to service of two trains each way per day, 'as required'; motor-bus hired to cater for needs of others who had previously relied on train. Regular service began again 8 October 1945 *(Railway Bylines, November 2001)*.

1901 October 14. Gifford & Garvald Light, leased to NB. Formal opening 12 October; public intended for noon that day, but delayed *(Haddington)*. *RCG* gives 1 February 1902 for line (reason unknown); was in *Brad* November 1901.

1902 December 22. Vale of Rheidol: Aberystwyth to Devils Bridge (ng). See *NGMW*.

— Opened 22 December 1902.
— Closed in winter from 1 January 1931.

Timetables *suggest* some pruning of stops hereabouts, though perhaps not this exact date. Glanrafon; Nantyronen; Rheidol Falls; Rhiwfron: were in *Brad* 22 September 1930 tt but omitted from tables before/with August 1931 tt (indexed, initially with a blank as page number, later noted as 'closed'). These plus Llanbadarn also omitted GW co tt 18 July 1932. Contrarily all shown as having passenger facilities in *hb* 1938 (but in 1956 all on line, including those always in *Brad*, shown parcels or goods or omitted). Thus likely that did remain in use. Possible explanations are that became halts and so omitted from *Brad* – difficult to believe Rheidol Falls not available to tourists, or space saving move, thus difference from GW tt. No significant change in timings. Balance of probability is that now and after 1945 they were still in use.

Closed fully 31 August 1939;

23 July 1945 reopened, summers only *(Cl)*. Missing stations still omitted when line reopened after WW2; back, after October 1949 tt (when line noted as 'not after 7 October'), before/with 5 June 1950 tt, as Halts

1989. Transfer: British Railways had owned it; now sold to Brecon Mountain Railway, who operated from start of 1989 season, maintaining continuity of summer use. Later events not recorded since it operates as a preserved line.

1903. Branch to Seafield, Leith Docks [Cal]. A suburban service from Edinburgh was intended and some station provision was started but never completed. At Newhaven platforms were added on this branch; stations were also begun at Bonnington (Ferry Road) and Leith Walk (Manderston Street). Also on this line, between the last two, was Pilrig, a temporary halt for military reviews – both 1905 and 1908 quoted in different sources – perhaps used several times. See *Edin*, pp.58–9; A.J. Mullay, *Rail Centres, Edinburgh*, Ian Allan, 1971, p.76; D.L.G. Hunter, *Edinburgh's Transport, The Early Years*, Mercat Press, 1992.

1903 July 22. Invergarry & Fort Augustus: Spean Bridge to Fort Augustus. Opening date usually quoted is supported by *RCG* and *T 22nd and 23rd*; latter's description of events of 22nd looks like formal opening but article in *RM September 1903*, makes it clear that ordinary passengers were carried – 'at each station passengers came and went'. It was initially worked by the Highland, detached from its own system.

NB took over line from 1 May 1907 but its services did not begin until 4th (J. Thomas, *The West Highland Railway*, D&C, 1984 edition, pp.118–20); did Highland continue to provide until then or was there short gap (Wednesday, Thursday, Friday)? *Return* has NB working line from 1 May, probably based on legal arrangement. Poor returns caused it to close 1 November 1911 but NB reopened it 1 August 1913 and took it over the following year *(High Pamph)*.

1904. Taff Vale stops.

According to Clinker all of the following started existence as PLATFORMS. Those that still survived in the early 1920s became HALTS. Bradshaw's version was more complex and probably resulted from someone's clerical confusion following this new type of stop. No note is made below of other name changes, the last form being generally used. The aim of the table is to give the fullest version possible in the most compact way. The information against each entry is: opening date, letters corresponding to the changes listed below, closure (year only) if prior to 1924. Clinker's dates in

GW Halts for change from PLATFORM to HALT are in square brackets. When they returned to/ first appeared in the index (July 1909/April 1910) all were shown as Halts and remained thus (e.g July 1922 and April 1923) in defiance of the changes in the tables.

(a) October 1904 tt to February 1905 tt or later: were Platforms, in relevant tables and indexed as Platforms.

(b) By June 1905 tt most previously included were removed from the index, though, presumably by oversight, Berw Road at least lingered briefly, and in the tables were relegated to notes, where for them and additions it said 'Motor Cars halt at X Platform, Y ...'.

(c) By February 1906 notes had become: "Halts" at X Platform, Y ....

(d) July 1909/February 1910 became: Halts at X, Y.

(e) April/July 1922 became: Platforms at X, Y.

(f) July 1922/April 1923 some reverted to Halt.

(g) July 1923/14 July 1924 all became: Halts at X, Y.

ABERCWMBOI: 26 December 1904, first seen June 1905 as Duffryn Crossing – motor cars halt at D C; c, d, e, [2 October 1922], g.
ABERTHIN: 1 May 1905; b, c, d, 1920.
ALBERTA PLACE: 19 September 1904, a, b, c, d, e, f [1 October 1923] (indexed at first as A PLATFORM).
BEDDAU: July 1910, d, e, g, [1 October 1923].
BERW ROAD: 17 October 1904, first seen in Ynysybwyl table June 1905 as B R, b, c, d, e, [2 October 1922], g.
CLYDACH COURT: July 1917 as Halt, e, [2 October 1922], g.
COMMERCIAL STREET: 26 November 1904, b, c, d, 1912.
DINGLE ROAD: a, b, c, d, e, [2 October 1922], f.
GELLI: October 1906, always Halt, 1912.
GYFEILON: 5 June 1905, always Halt, 1918.
LLANBETHERY: 1 May 1905, b, c, d, 1920.
LLANDOUGH: 13 June 1904, a, b, c, d, 1918.
LLANFABON ROAD: 10 October 1904, first seen June 1905 Motor Cars halt at L R, e, g.
MAINDY: May 1907, always Halt.
MATTHEWSTOWN: 1 October 1914, first seen February 1915 Halt, e, [2 October 1922], g.
MILL STREET: 26 November 1904, since this was terminus in tables as Platform pre-1910, b, c, 1912.
OLD YNYSYBWYL: 17 October 1904, first seen June 1905 as O Y, same June 1906, March 1907 Halt but in table as terminus, absent August 1921 owing to brief closure, July 1922 Platform, [2 October 1922], April 1923 Halt.
PENTRE: October 1906, always Halt, 1912.
PONTCYNON: 26 December 1904, b, c, d, e, [2 October 1922], g.
PONTYGWAITH: 5 June 1905, always Halt, 1914.
ROBERTSTOWN: 17 October 1904, first seen June 1905 as R, c, d, e, [2 October 1922], g.
ST HILARY: 1 May 1905, b, c, d, 1920.

SWANBRIDGE: July 1906, c, d, e, f,
[just Halt, Clinker's Register].
TONTEG: 1 May 1905, b, c, d, e, g, [1 October 1923 tt].
TRERHYNGELL & MAENDY: opened 1 May 1905;
appeared in the list of halts at platforms in February
1906, but without 'Platform' after its name,
suggesting that it was a station at which only motor
cars stopped; 1909/10 it became listed as though one
of the Halts; April/July 1922 moved to the table as
though of full station status. Clinker seems to have
regarded it as always a station.
TYLACOCH: October 1906, always Halt, 1912.
WATTSTOWN: 5 June 1905, always Halt, 1920.
WOODVILLE ROAD: July 1906, always Halt.
YNYSYBWYL NEW ROAD: 6 July 1910, first seen
March 1911 as Halt, July 1912 in table as station.

1904 June 29. Leek & Manifold Light (NS):
Waterhouses to Hulme End, 2ft 6in. Date is taken from
the opening notice, reproduced in *Leek*, supported by
photo caption on opposite page; in text 1 July is given as
opening date. Most in print give 27 June (from *Brad Sh?*).
This was certainly the formal opening *(RM September)*;
the description given there of the day's events makes no
reference to ordinary passengers.

R. Keys & L. Porter, *The Manifold Valley and its Light
Railway*, Moorland, 1972, reproduce, from local source,
notice showing service Wednesday and Saturday only
for winter 1904–5. Text says North Staffs made cut but
Manifold Company then got guarantee of minimum of
two trains per day; *Brad* October 1904 shows two each
way, extras on Wednesday and Saturday, presumably
after cut had been rescinded. Their book also reproduces
LMS notice of closure on and from 12 March 1934.

Beeston Tor; Butterton: halts in *Brad* until April/August
1923. They might well have continued to be treated as
such. See 1905** below for more information on
vagaries of this kind.

1904 September 1. ANSW: start of steam motor-car
service, with the opening of extra stops. Date given by
ANSW is confirmed by Company's Minutes *(RAIL 7/13)*
although service was not shown in *Brad* until January
1909 and none of the stations and halts is shown on
RCH map of South Wales, 1908. It is only from January
1909 that the existence of all the individual stations
given this date can be confirmed.

1905. This covers some erratic uses of 'Halt'. Applies to
some of lines used by the following as well as their own
– e.g. NSWJ. All were shown as (HALT) in *LMS list* 1933.

a) LNW: co tts did not use term but company had
equivalent of others' halts, served by rail-motors.
Brad did call them halts until after July 1925, before/with
April 1926 issue. *Cl* listed as 'motor stations'. Those
closed before 1925 were Halts in *Brad*, list of closures in
The Times (22 December 1918), and RCH list of 1921,
which confirmed permanent closure of some 'temporarily'
closed during the war years, but not halts in co tts.

b) LY: no co tts have been seen. *Brad* usage was as for
LNW, above. *Cl* listed as 'Halts', suggesting official usage.
Disappearance of 'Halt' from name perhaps result of
LNW influence on newly-formed LMS (LY had been
amalgamated with LNW shortly before full Grouping).

LY/LNW: Burn Naze and Poulton Curve were briefly
shown as Halts in LNW co tt: certainly July 1909 but
not March 1908 or October 1909.

c) Knott End: same as LY.

a, b,c) not shown as Halts in LMS co tt 1930 but 'halt'
was applied to some stops inherited from NS, Midland
and Scottish companies.

d) GN: these were Halts in GN co tt 1909 and *Brad*
until they lost 'Halt' at same time as those in (a) above;
again shown as Halts in *Brad* from 1950/1.

1905 August 14. GW 'Halts': individual station dates
GW H; service confirmed *W Briton 17th*.

1905 October 30. LNW 'Halts': *LNW Officers 41635*
says rail motor-car has been operating between Bletchley
and Bedford since 30 October. *RM December 1905* says
service originally been planned for 1 November but was
delayed at the last moment – error? service intermittent
because of unreliabilty and 1 December a restart?
Ox & Camb uses 1 December date; is only source of
Brickyard Halt, ¼ mile from Wootton Pillinge on way
towards Wootton Broadmead. *RM* seems to imply that
the Halts at the Oxford end of the line were similarly
delayed, but *Oxford Chron, 6 October*, and *LNW Officers*
support Clinker's date of 9 October. *Ox & Camb*
reproduces notice of services 'commencing Friday,
October 20', but this was probably a revision of the
service since it is marked 'Third Issue'; the book says
that they had problems with reliability of the rail-motors
used. *LNW Officers 41635* shows revision of service
from 1 December. Also see 1905**, above.

1906 January 1: (public opening date): GW,
Cwmaman branch.

— Miners' use began about 1903 *(U)* and continued
  through public closures.
— Public service began 1 January 1906 *(GW H)*.
  Closed 22 November 1917 (service discontinued
  since 19th – *wtt supp*).
— Reopened 7 July 1919 *(GW circ 2672)*.
  Closed 22 September 1924 *(Cl)*.
— Miners' use ceased about 1932 *(U)*.

Away refers to through excursion to Porthcawl, citing
paper of 30 July 1932; involved stretch of line from
Black Lion Crossing to Gelly Tarw junction which
never had regular passenger service.

1906 August 18. Campbeltown & Machrihanish,
2ft 3in. gauge; at Campbeltown end it was a street
tramway. Date given is from *Camp*; *Return* says
17 August, which was date of inspection – is it possible
that there was some public use immediately after

inspector had given his verbal approval? In December 1906 the intermediate stations originally listed were removed to the footnotes as Halts and a note was added that trains stopped at any crossroads (= level crossing?) by request; in September 1907 a full list of stops was again given and note omitted.

Railway service was replaced by buses 27 December 1930; trains again 1 June 1931; last in *Brad* November 1931; some use again early 1932 but finally closed before May *(Camp)*. Last passengers shown in *Return* for 1931; no return included 1932; 1933 report said it had been wound up.

1907 June 22. London Electric: Strand (later Charing Cross) to Golders Green and Camden Town to Archway. Formal opening in the morning; opened to public at 1.30pm with free travel for rest of the day *(T, items 1 and 24 June,* and *co n 21 June)*. Thus there is a case for quoting 23rd as opening date.

1908 October. BM: Machen to Caerphilly. Stations opened now were first intermediate stations on a line that had been in passenger use for some years. BM had intended passenger service from the outset and line had been passed for passenger use on 1 April 1873 but problems with Rhymney Company caused delays. Specials were run on 3 June 1873 for a rehearsal at Caerphilly Castle by the South Wales Choral Union but regular service, non-stop between Caerphilly and Machen, only began 28 September 1887, operated by Pontypridd, Caerphilly & Newport Railway (later part of ANSW). See C. Chapman, article, *The Caerphilly Branch of the Brecon & Merthyr Railway, Welsh Railways Archive vol. 3/2.*

1908 November 21. Cleobury Mortimer & Ditton Priors. Company had intended to open on 20th but delayed (letter to BoT quoted in *CMDP*) and *Return* gives this date.

July 1915 reduced to one train each way Mondays and Fridays, two each way Wednesdays and Saturdays. By January 1917★ Aston Botterell and Prescott Wednesdays only, other footnote stops no trains. October 1921 all served again. By April 1923 all week-days.

Originally Aston Botterell; Chilton; Detton Ford; Prescott were Siding Halts. Cleobury North Crossing Halt. About 1916 'Halt' omitted from names in notes to table but still indexed as Halts. Stottesdon and Burwarton were in body of table prior to becoming halts which suggests were regarded as superior to Chilton & co.

★ = January 1917 notes not clear-cut. One says that trains will call at two mentioned above; another lists all the halts. At that time *Brad* frequently left halts in the footnotes (and stations in tables, without trains) when other sources clearly show they were closed. April 1917/October 1917 tt the others were omitted completely.

1908 December 1. Closure: Ravenglass & Eskdale. *Return* says closed 30 November, but normal practice of BoT was to quote last day of use in such cases.

1909 August 2: BPGV: public opening: date confirmed *RAIL 1057/433*; also says miners' service had run from March 1898 and includes minute of 21 March 1899 complaining that miners' wives had been using brake vans on market days. According to H. Morgan, *HMRS April 1985*, wives went free but charged 6d per shopping basket (likely to be very large) or parcel carried; also one monthly excursion during summer, using swept-out coal trucks.

1910 December 1. South Yorkshire Joint: opening Shireoaks to Doncaster via Maltby. Reduced to Saturdays only 1 July 1917 (but so shown June 1917 *Brad*); full service (two each way plus extra on Saturday) restored 1 April 1920 *(S Yorks Joint)*. Whole line last in *Brad* April 1926. Lord Scarborough claimed right to permanent service so reopened 25 July 1927. Matter settled: Doncaster to Maltby closed 8 July 1929; Maltby to Shireoaks 2 December 1929.

Evening excursions and seaside trips throughout 1930s; at least one excursion served Dinnington and Maltby in 1960s *(S Yorks Joint)*.

1910 December 5. GC: Killingholme to Immingham Western Jetty. Opening date given by notices page of *Brad*, January 1911, *GC dates* and *RCG*. On the face of it this appears to be a pointless service, detached from system. Possibilities are a workmen's service (but trains seem too frequent and evenly spaced), or that it gave the people of Killingholme a chance to get to Grimsby by changing to another line at Immingham.

1911 October 1. LNW 'Halts': date from *LNW Cl*. 1 October was a Sunday. *RM October* did not specifically say they were opened on 2nd but it did mention them immediately after Pont Lawrence, which was so dated. Impossible to tell from *Brad* if these did have a Sunday service since they only appeared in footnotes (line did have Sunday trains).

1912 June 3. Dearne Valley. Opening date originally from *LY*, confirmed by *RCH distance amendment 858/5*. At opening all stops beyond Wakefield shown as HALTS. 'Halt' dropped from all in tt 1925/6 but still shown in *hb* 1938; possibly result of LNW influence on newly-formed LMS – see 1905, above.

1912 July 13. Some South Wales Halts. Opening date from *GW Halts*. Until April 1923, or just after, there was only a joint GW/LMS table in *Brad*; these were HALTS. First separate tables seen, July 1923: Halts in both GW and LMS tables (in notes); same July 1925. April 1926 Halts in GW, not LMS (where now in body of table); same August 1927. By July 1928 omitted from GW table (still present April 1928), not halts LMS table (nor LMS co tt 1930). Same August 1931. By August 1932 had become halts in LMS table and listed in 'notices' panel as having been renamed to halts.

1915 February 1: GW: closure Acton & Wycombe line rail motor car service. *GM's report 12 January 1917* said done to free lines for military and other [war-related?] traffic.

1915 March 22. Closures: GW lines in the Wrexham area. Date from Clinker, confirmed by *GM's report 12 January 1917*. *RCH* says these stations closed 31 December 1916. Last trains shown in *Brad* April 1915 – even that suggests month's inertia. They were in list *(RM February 1916)* of GW stations closed owing to the war.

1916 May 22. Closures: GE system. Original aim had been to close the selected stations on May 1. However, on 29 April a postponement to 22 May was announced and on 12 May a reprieve was granted to some stations originally listed for closure – Bethnal Green; Bradfield; Buckenham; Mardock; Stanhoe; West Mill – but Norwich Victoria added to list. (GE directors' minutes 2 March, 6 April and 4 May; also *T 5 April and 2 May; RM May and June*).

1917 March 28. Closure: Bideford, Westward Ho! & Appledore. This came suddenly. *Bideford*, Tuesday 27 March, contained timetable for October 1st 1917 to May 31st 1917, or until further notice. Paper of 3 April had: railway will be closed and the train service suspended on and after Wednesday, March 28th, 1917 – notice dated 26 March. Later usage would mean last train on Tuesday; other items of this time sometimes used this phrasing in way that would have meant Wednesday was last day. No news item found to decide the issue.

1918 March: (public opening date): originally South Wales Mineral; from 1908 owned by Port Talbot, thus worked by GW.

Note that 1880 'service' shown in some books derives from error in *RM September 1939*.

Early unofficial services. See articles by P.R. Reynolds, *RCHS Journal, November 1981* and *Welsh Railway Archive, May 2000*; further material from M. Hale and R.A. Cooke. By September 1865 passengers were carried on e.g. trucks attached to coal trains. By May 1868 a passenger carriage was attached. By the mid-1870s there is some indication that they were running to a timetable of sorts. Route: Glyncorrwg – Crythan/ Cryddan – Tonmawr – Incline Top/Top of Incline/Hill Top (top of incline just short of Briton Ferry). Crythan/Cryddan would have been most convenient alighting point for those walking down to Neath; platform certainly existed here later, perhaps added later for handling farm produce; no facilities elsewhere. In last week of 1886 550 'passengers' travelled on up trains, 503 on down; certainly passengers still using in October 1895 when RSB records indicate disapproval *(RAIL 1057/1545)*.

'Passenger service' probably ended when PT took over line: letter from Glyncorrwg UDC to BoT asking, unsuccessfully, for passenger service said travel in the van had been allowed as a courtesy until PT days. Wording of this raises questions about nature of 'carriage' used. Inspection, following accident in 1902, revealed no BoT authority for any passenger use, but no charge was made for service, so technically no passengers.

Also specific miners' services and excursions.

Official miners' service, sanctioned by BoT, began 5 March 1917 (internal GW memo).

Official public service, over Cymmer to Glyncorrwg section. Contradictory official information about public opening: minutes *(RAIL 242/2, 242/3)* say 27 March 1918, Wednesday, but internal notice *(RAIL 1057/1545)* said would be 28th. Letter giving permission to open was dated 30th so they probably relied on verbal assurance from inspector (or there would have been a slight delay from planned date).

Line closed on and from Tuesday 3 May 1921 *(poster RAIL 1057/1545)*. Reopened ? – see 1921 April/May, below; trains still shown *Brad*.

Finally closed 22 September 1930 *(Cl)*.

Miners' use continued to 2 November 1964.

1919 July 1. Closure: Edmonton to Cheshunt (GE). According to *T 4th*, which did not give exact date, had been reopened for the convenience of workers travelling to the Enfield small arms and Waltham gunpowder factories. *RM June 1915* had said that reopening expected to be temporary. Closure date a Tuesday. Reopened briefly in February 1947 when snow caused diversion south of Cheshunt. Passengers had to wait on platforms because waiting-rooms in use for housing (A.J. Mulloy, article in *BackTrack* February 2007, p.14).

1920. Miners' service from Port Talbot to Corrwg Merthyr. Agreement for this signed 18 May 1920; line and Halts had been officially inspected (M. Hale); service actually began ? Engineer's reports *(RAIL 1057/1528)* refer to workmen's service they hoped to start 1 August 1920 and was certainly in operation by 9 September. They refer to 'four platforms' (Corrwg Merthyr; Cwmavon Yard; Tonmawr Junction; ?). Collieries underwent various closures, reopenings and renamings, so Halts would have had intermittent use. Agreement referred to Tanygroes Junction (Ton-y-groes on RCH Junction Diagram); service would have required reversal there.

1921 April/May. Temporary closures owing to coal strike. A number of services were suspended and many others reduced to save coal. Full details have not been seen. *Bradshaw* is no help. It carried a general notice saying that suspensions and alterations would result but travellers were told to see local notices for these; services continued to be shown in detail, presumably in expectation of early resumption. References in *The Times* suggest that there were closures whose details have not been found; paper of 7 May said that some Scottish services had been suspended.

Some <u>GW</u> notices have been seen. Suspensions, with starting dates and stations involved, in square brackets, were:

11 April: Black Lion Crossing to Cwmaman Colliery [those two, plus Ton Llwyd; Godreaman; Cwmneol; Cwmaman Crossing].
  Garnant Halt to Gwaun-cae-Gurwen [plus Gors-y-Garnant; Red Lion Crossing].
2 May: Birmingham to Dudley via Great Bridge [Great Bridge only station affected].
9 May: rail-motor service Westbourne Park to Greenford [Old Oak Lane; Park Royal; Brentham; Perivale]. Brentford branch [Brentford; Trumpers Crossing]. Swansea to Morriston [Landore LL; Plas Marl; Copper Pit; Morriston].
(Booklet was dated from 8 May, a Sunday, but none of these had a Sunday service).
20 June: Booklet was headed 'Restoration of Passenger Trains' and was supported by the company's notice in *The Times* of that date, which said 'numerous local trains will … be restored'. However, only the Swansea to Morriston service was shown with trains; the others were still shown as suspended. Indeed, they were joined by one more suspension, Lostwithiel to Fowey [Golant only – Fowey still served from Par].

It may be that the rest were restored on 1 July; certainly all were shown as normal in *Bradshaw* for August, by when some affected stations were shown without trains, which would suggest the rest had had their services restored.

Also see 1918 March above (paragraph beginning 'line closed …').

Some temporary closures on the <u>Caledonian</u> can be derived from company's notice in *Annandale Observer* of this date. It is headed 'Miners' Strike' and says that on and from Friday 20 May its passenger services would be further reduced and stations listed would be closed to passengers (B. Wilson). Reopened ? Only where resumption took longer – e.g. Loch Tay – did the suspension show in *Bradshaw*.

<u>Closure: Solway Junction.</u> According to *Cl*, the whole Solway Junction line was closed 1917 to 1919. However, sample of tts (January and October 1917, October 1918 and February 1919) shows trains continued to run. No evidence supporting closure has been found in e.g. RCH sources.

Also, according to *Cl*, line south of Annan closed 20 May 1921. However, *Sol J* claims that 'according to locals' service resumed in the shape of a mixed train, Tuesdays and Saturdays only on 30 May and complete closure

came after last train 31 August, when it had become apparent that very expensive repairs were needed if Solway Viaduct were to be kept in use. These dates could not be exactly correct since 30 May was a Monday and 31 August a Wednesday. In any case an extensive search by Bryan Wilson in the *Annandale Observer* failed to find any support for resumption. Indeed, he found entries which seem safely to show otherwise. There were references to difficulties in getting scholars from England to Annan Academy (not in itself complete refutation of a twice-a-week service, but if latter had existed it would surely have been mentioned as useless for this purpose); a reply to the local MP from the Minister of Transport on 18 July (paper of 22nd) clearly indicates that line was then closed and that it had been known for several years that expensive repairs were necessary and would now only be considered when the price of iron fell from its then high level; NB co notice (dated 31 August) of formal closure of line by Cal on 1 September refers to <u>continuance</u> of re-routing arrangements explained in 3 July circular. *Brad* August 1921 shows only a service Kirtlebridge to Annan – given that it continued to show trains for lines temporarily closed in May, that would seem to be extra evidence for the complete closure of this one. *RCG* gives 1 September as passenger closure date for Whitrigg, though other 1 September closures on this line are shown as goods closures; all of these would have been formal dates, following decision not to reopen.

1922. Temporary closures on the London Underground 1922–44; it seems convenient to put all of these together. Based on *Clay*; *Times*; *RM December 1939*. Closure dates given are last days of full use (sometimes last train will have been in early hours of next day).

Work to speed construction of Northern Line Extension and enlarge tunnels on existing stretch meant that Euston – King's Cross – Angel – Old Street – Moorgate closed after traffic on 8 August 1922. The line south of Moorgate was kept open, but, within this stretch, Borough closed on 16 July 1922. Early in May 1923 the line south of Oval was closed; it reopened on 15 May 1923, but Kennington closed again on 31 May 1923. The intention was to keep services going, as far as possible, through the partly completed works. A tunnel collapse on 27 November 1923 caused the line to be reduced to separate shuttle services Moorgate to London Bridge and Elephant & Castle to Clapham Common; even this was regarded as too risky and the whole line closed completely after traffic on 28 November 1923. Moorgate to Euston reopened 20 April 1924, rest of line 1 December 1924. However Borough did not reopen until 23 February 1925 and Kennington until 6 July 1925.

Worries about effects of bombing on tunnels (especially under Thames) and stations caused further short-term closures. Trafalgar Square; Charing Cross (later Embankment); Waterloo; Lambeth North; Elephant & Castle; Kennington (Charing Cross line) closed after traffic on 27 September 1938 so that tunnels could be plugged with concrete; reopened 8 October when immediate war scare had passed for the time being. *The Times* of 1 and 8 October referred to '8 stations converging on Charing Cross – presumably double counting of Charing Cross and Waterloo. Result was installation of proper floodgates which could be closed if tunnels hit by bombs.

In 1939 there were further closures to enable measures to be taken to prevent flooding of underground stations if they were bombed. Piccadilly to Elephant & Castle closed 27 August 1939 only. Kennington to Strand and 19 other stations closed 1 September 1939. Moorgate to London Bridge closed 7 September 1939. Reopening dates of stations:

Marble Arch and Tottenham Court Road★ 15 November; King's Cross 17th; Oxford Circus★ 20th (but *Rly Obs December* says 24th); Clapham Common and Oval 24th; Arsenal, Green Park and Knightsbridge 1 December; Bond Street 6th (but *Rly Obs December* says 8th); Hyde Park Corner and Old Street 8th; Chancery Lane and Balham 15th; Charing Cross and Waterloo, with reopened service under river, 17th; Trinity Road and Bank (Nor) 22nd; Maida Vale 9 January 1940; Moorgate to Kennington 19 May.

★ = remained open for interchange only.
Interchange stations counted as two.

1922 July 31. Welsh Highland, 1ft 11½in. gauge. Based on *NGSC 2, WHH* and *Brad*. This was a reopening on 31 July 1922 of North Wales Narrow Gauge line, closed 1916 {map 76}.

— 1 June 1923: extended to Portmadoc New and linked to Festiniog Railway.

Service intermittent and erratic. Its table was omitted from *Brad* for two seasons after 1931 and when it returned detail was lacking so it is impossible to be certain which stations were open when. Possible that all stations were always/nearly open and that *Brad* was sent abbreviated version. Summary of available information:

— 15 December 1924: service suspended; no trains in tt January 1925.
— 30 January 1925: reop, Fridays only Portmadoc to Beddgelert *(WHH 6, 26)*.
— 7 March 1925: reop, Saturdays only, South Snowdon to Dinas *(WHH 6, 26)*.
— 1 June 1925: reop throughout, trains all weekdays *(WHH 6, 26)*.

26 September 1927: service reduced to Fridays only, Portmadoc to Croesor Junction by mixed train. *NSGC 2, p. 100*, suggests that, since no proper connection with outside world at Croesor Junction, trains unofficially went on to Llanfrothen Road crossing and, perhaps, even operated on 'stop anywhere' principle. If this ever became [semi-?] official policy it might explain later lack of intermediate stops in tt.

— 11 June 1928: full service restored *(WHH 10)*.
— 1 October 1928 tt: cut back to Dinas–Beddgelert, Monday, Wednesday and Friday only.
— 20 May 1929: full length service Mondays, Wednesdays, Fridays *(WHH 11)*.
— 8 July 1929 tt: full length Mondays to Fridays.

7 October 1929 tt: one train each way, Mondays, Wednesdays, Fridays. Southbound this covered the whole length of the line, Dinas to Portmadoc, but northbound only Beddgelert to Dinas. Southbound used for circular Five Valleys excursions.

— 7 July 1930 tt (only): no northbound service shown – error? – back August.
— 19 September 1930 (Friday): last train.
— 20 July 1931: reopened; trains in tt August to October; no trains in tt November.
— 9 October 1931 (Friday): last train.
— 1932: trains Monday 18 July to 9 September (inclusive), all weekdays *(WHH 14)*.

1933: trains 17 July to Friday 8 September *(WHH 15)*. [No reference in *Brad* during 1932 and 1933 (above from *NGSC 2*); its next mention was June 1934 – 'service suspended'.]

9 July 1934: reopened. Trains again in August tt but it only included Portmadoc (company's own station); Aberglaslyn; Beddgelert; Rhyd-ddu (reversion to original name); Dinas Junction. Last day was 13 October *(Rly Gaz 7 December)* though previously advertised as 29 September *(pocket tt issued by J.H. Jones, Dinorwic)* and still shown in *Brad* October.

8 July 1935: reopened and in *Brad* for that date. Details as 1934 except that 'South Snowdon' again. Last day Saturday 28 September, though *Brad* had said trains will not run after 14th.

6 July 1936 tt: trains again, at first detail as before. In September, note was added that trains called at Tryfan; Waenfawr; Salem; and Plas-y-Nant between Dinas and South Snowdon – did this imply that there no other stops than those listed between South Snowdon and Portmadoc?

26 September 1936: finally closed (last trains ran – *NGSC 2*); no trains in tt October.

1924 June 24. Renaming of LMS stations in Scotland. This is date from *Cl*; *JS* said this and 14 July 1924 were both claimed and he had not been able to find clear evidence for one or the other. He referred to *RM Sept. 1924, p. 222*. This reads: 'In the *Railway Magazine* for July, a list was given of L.M.S. stations in England, the names of which were altered as from June 2. We are now advised of corresponding alterations in Scotland ...' This implies 2 June but does not specify it (ironically, the July list simply said that the alterations had been made, without giving an exact date); however, the gap of two months between lists would give support to a later date for the second one. A Hand-book leaflet dated 24 April said 'now read [new names for old ones]' for both English and Scottish stations renamed thereabouts; this illustrates another problem in using such documents – they sometimes failed to point out that they were giving information in advance of the relevant changes.

1924 October 4. Sand Hutton Light. Opened to public now. Had opened privately 1910, 15in. gauge; later converted to 18in. Essentially served Sand Hutton Hall and farms on its estates but did provide brief service included in *Brad*. Service varied: originally Saturdays only (York market day); in July 1925 tt shown as Wednesdays and Saturdays; April 1926 tt Saturdays only; August 1926 tt all weekdays; July 1928 tt Saturdays only. See *RM December 1924*.

1926 May 4. Closures. May 4 was a Tuesday, the first day of the 'General Strike'. Most stations given this closure date were not planned for closure prior to the strike but did not reopen after it. Line to North Greenwich was due for closure 1 July (last 30 June) and should have reopened briefly after strike but did not.

1926 September 1. Closure: Derwent Valley. Although the regular service closed on this date, there was later passenger use. No passenger return provided 1927, but all *Returns* from 1928 to 1938 (last year of issue prior to suspension of issues owing to war) show receipts for some ordinary passengers. In 1938, 474 passengers were carried, total receipts £11. These were almost certainly excursionists: *RM October 1928*, mentions one on 'Bank Holiday Monday'. Called all stations. In 1929 excursion ran in conjunction with Royal Show at Harrogate – passengers taken between Layerthorpe and York by bus (D.S.M. Barrie, *The Derwent Valley Railway*, Oakwood, 1978 edition).

Seasonal timetabled service ran 4 May 1977 to 31 August 1979; designed as tourist service (line still in use by BR for goods); final charter ran 27 September 1981, using Dunnington goods yard because platform line had been lifted (T. Cooper).

1927 July 16. Romney, Hythe & Dymchurch, 15in. gauge (see *RHD*). Other main sources: *Wolfe*; J.B. Snell, *One Man's Railway*, D&C, 1983; *The Line That Jack Built*, Ian Allan, 1956, p.23; P. Ransome-Wallace, *World's Smallest Public Railway*, Ian Allan, 1957 edition.

Line opened 16 July 1927; mainly ceremonial day but some revenue-earning services; regular traffic 17th. *Return* and *T 18th* confirmed 16th opening; latter said, 'The three stations are well built …' These would have been Hythe; Dymchurch; New Romney.

First tt included in *Brad* September 1927; this also includes Burmarsh Road and Holiday Camp; perhaps overlooked by *T* as only halts, perhaps added a little after line. One note said that Halts at Romney Warren; Botolphs Bridge; and Prince of Wales would open as request stops 'when completed'. Another note said a couple of evening trains would run once the Minister of Transport was satisfied with the lighting arrangements.

— November 1927 tt: stops at Botolphs Bridge and Prince of Wales, without qualification; no Romney Warren.
— 24 May 1928 extended to Pilot.
— Early August extended to Dungeness (during Bank Holiday week-end, *RHD*); Monday of this was 6 August).

Later station history mostly covered in Section IV. However, when a number of Halts were added in December 1929 tt, there was also a note that trains would pick up or set down at any convenient point.

— 7 July 1930 tt: purge of Halts and omission of 'anywhere' note.
— November 1930 tt: service cut back to Hythe – Greatstone only.
— June 1931 tt: all-line service to run from Whitsun to September.
— Pattern repeated but from December 1933 all-line winter service, Saturdays only.
— October 1939 tt: all-day service kept but tables often included note that service was subject to revision.
— March to July 1940, tt showed service beyond New Romney Saturday only; August 1940 tt – service suspended.

22 May 1940: order given to evacuate civilians from the area (fear of invasion); if line not already closed, this would have put an end to its civil use. About 1933–7, ½ mile branch had been built for the army near Maddieson's Camp carried workmen's service.

15 June 1940: requisitioned for military use. Some use during war – RHD Military Railway passenger ticket *(JB)* from Burmarsh Road (Dymchurch) to Dymchurch (Marsh); additions in brackets also appear on peace-time tickets. WW2 usage confirmed by *The Line That Jack Built*.

— Handed back to RHD company 1945 *(Wolfe)*.
— August and September 1945: some sort of unadvertised service, Hythe to New Romney.
— Formal reop Hythe to New Romney 1 March 1946 by Mayor of New Romney;

2 March 1946: service resumed over Hythe to New Romney stretch, at first Saturdays only *(RM May)*. 1 June 1946 Warren Halt added request. By 1 August 1946: extended to Maddiesons Camp (had been added June 1932 tt). Stretch to Dungeness perhaps reop 3 November 1946 (O.S. Nock, *Railways, February 1947*, quoted by *Wolfe*). In theory Saturday service continued through winter but probably suspended for maintenance at some stage.

21 March 1947: formal reopening to Dungeness by Laurel and Hardy; public 29 March *(T 22nd)*. Thereafter no winter service in tt but some use was made in winter of 1947: *T 15 December* has photograph with caption that the RHD was being used at weekends to relieve pressure on road traffic caused by petrol

rationing; powerful headlights were fitted to the train at night; in the photograph passengers are shown hailing a train, apparently between stations.

Another odd use was described in *T 31 May 1948*: a train stopped outside the front door of a bride's house and took the family party 5 miles to New Romney. After the ceremony it took them to Dungeness for the reception.

By 1957 Burmarsh Road and Warren Halt closed.

14 February 1972: taken over by a consortium to be run as a preservation line. There has since been some other use: from 7 September 1977 a schools' special ran throughout the school year from Burmarsh Road (reopened for this purpose) via Dymchurch and Jefferstone Lane (renamed from St Marys Bay 1981) to New Romney in the morning, with a return journey after school (*T 10 August* and *8 September*; photograph in latter shows pupils waiting for first train, no station platform visible).

1929 April 12. Closure: Southwold. 12th was a Friday. *RM June*: last train ran on the evening of the 11th. However, RCH Distance Book Amendment 33/1 said closed 11 April – last day of use?

1930 March 1. Closure: Sand Hutton Light. Date from *Return*. Note in 1930 return says no passengers were carried after 1 March 1930 (a Saturday, which fits known service). This seems a more believable date than the 5 July 1930 usually quoted because return shows that only 65 passengers were carried during the year, total revenue £1 (had been 791 for £15 in 1929). However, there was some later passenger use – return for 1931 shows 61 passengers for £2.

1930 September 22: closure Bourne to Sleaford (ex-GN). Later special use; last 1951 for trip to Festival of Britain (S. Squires, *Lincolnshire Railways*, Lincs County Council, 1998 – mentions Rippingale; other stations?).

1930 September 22: closure of intermediate stations between York and Scarborough except Malton and Seamer (ex-NE). Date from *T 10 July*. Continued to be used for parcels traffic and, certainly at one stage the one non-tt parcels train in each direction had passenger accommodation, which public were allowed to use. (Personal memory of Tony Kirby, travelling from Malton to Huttons Ambo with mother about 1952/1953.)

1930 September 22: closure Alnwick to Coldstream (ex-NE). After closure passenger coaches attached to parcels trains to take people to/from camping coaches sited 'at most stations'; Whittingham explicitly mentioned. (J.A. Wells, *Railways of Northumberland and Newcastle upon Tyne*, Powdene, 1998). For Akeld, 5 October 1942 wtt shows one train Tuesday only to Tweedmouth (none in previous wtt) and one Tuesday & Thursday from Berwick; not present 3 May 1943 wtt.

1931 January 1: closure of Dinas Mawddwy branch

(ex-Cam). Annual later use for Dovey Valley Sunday Schools' trip to Aberystwyth; last 26 June 1939. *(Mawddwy)*.

1931 February 2. Closure: Ely to St Ives (ex-GE). There were later excursions, though not known if all stations involved. *RM October 1932* referred to one on 27 August. *RM November 1953* said that there had been half-day excursions until the outbreak of war in 1939 and 'in recent years' two annual excursions, one to Hunstanton, the other to Yarmouth Races. *U* refers to use of Wilburton. *GE Journal January 2002* refers to use of Earith Bridge, where one called 1 August 1955 (B. Wilson, own photographic evidence).

1932 September 19. London Electric: Finsbury Park to Arnos Grove. Opening date from *T 20th*. This also states that 30,000 free tickets for the opening day were distributed through the neighbourhood involved and that the booking offices were opened on the Sunday (18th) for the sale of season tickets.

1933 March 13. London Electric: Arnos Grove to Enfield West (later Oakwood) and Northfields to Harrow West. Opening date given by *T 14th* which also says that 30,000 free tickets for opening day were distributed in the Enfield area and 40,000 in the Harrow area – 'these tickets were extensively used'. Booking offices again open previous day.

1933 April 1 and 3. Closure: Dolphinton and Gifford branches (both ex-NB). All in print seen give 1st (Saturday) for Dolphinton closure and 3rd (Monday) for Gifford closure; latter supported by *Haddington* which says last train on 1st. One would have expected same date for both, especially since both were ex-NB lines.

1933 April 7. Closure: Glyn Valley Tramway. Most in print give 6th (Thursday), but that was last day of use according to W.J. Milner, *The Glyn Valley Tramway*, OPC, 1984.

1933 July 17. MGN: Halts. Date of opening based on that given by *Cl 29* for some of them. Inspection report *(MT 29/88/345)* shows that all were used in the summer of 1933 but were not inspected, and approved, until November of that year. They were for summer-only use and were served by a Sentinel railcar, with a seating capacity of 48, which ran Mondays to Fridays only because pressure of holiday traffic on the single line made it impossible to fit in halts' service on Saturdays. They were set up to give extra scope for travel by people staying at the holiday camps most of the halts served, not to take holiday-makers to/from camps at start/end of holidays. Report says that Sutton Staithe and Little Ormesby attracted so little traffic that they were unlikely to be used again. This would seem to have been the case – the other five first appeared in *Brad* 9 July 1934. According to *MGN* there were through trains between Liverpool Street and Caister Camp, via Antingham Road Junction (in 1958 via special link north of North

Walsham instead); the halt at Caister Camp had by then been enlarged to take ordinary trains.

MGN also implies that they were closed during WW2 and reopened in 1948. No trains shown June 1941 tt.

Brad August 1950 shows that a Sunday service, running from 2 July to 10 September inclusive, was run especially for section on which halts were situated. They were last served at the end of the summer season 1958. Their last trains would have run 12 or 14 September. Caister Camp's last Saturday specials to camp were 20 September (from camp last 27 September) *(signalling notices, BR Eastern Region)*.

1935 January 20. Closure: West Sussex, Chichester to Selsey. Date from *Cl*. It is apparently supported by *RM April 1935*, which has an article on the line which begins: 'Following notice to the staff a week earlier, the train service … was abandoned on January 19'. The article does not provide any description of a last service. However, RCH distance amendment 62/3, dated 26 February 1937, says that line was closed on 12 January 1935 (RCH had only first included line in October 1927). Which is wrong is not known: either RCH mistook notice of closure for actual closure or *RM* failed to realise that the staff were given a week's pay in lieu of notice, the line closing immediately. Whichever of 12th or 19th is correct, it would have been the last day of use (a Saturday). Clinker's date was a Sunday; this line did not have a Sunday service and normally 21st (or 14th) would have been given as official closure date. However, although this was an independent line, it might have followed Southern habit and quoted Sunday closure date, regardless of whether or not there was a Sunday service.

In its early years, at least, trains stopped between stations. *RM April 1898* includes description of trip along line when a farmer used his own red flag to hail train at spot convenient for him.

1935 September 30. Closure: Lynton & Barnstaple (gauge 1ft 11½in.). This would make a good case study for the problem of deciding what closure date should be quoted.

What actually happened: no regular Sunday service, so last train shown in *Brad* ran on the Saturday (28th). However, working tt (reproduced in *Lynton*) shows that Sunday excursions, one per week, were run in turn from Ilfracombe and Torrington, Yeovil, and Plymouth (obviously requiring change of trains at Barnstaple) from July to September and that one such was scheduled for September 29. *W Som FP 5 October* confirms that this ran and describes it as an 'excursion'; according to working tt, this would not have stopped at Caffyns, Chelfham or Snapper.

But – notice in *N Devon J* 22 August: 'The Lynton & Barnstaple Line … will be closed on Sunday, 29 September'. Notice in same paper, 26 September: 'On and from the 30th September 1935, the service of trains over [this

line] will be withdrawn'. Was first supposed to be last day, second official closure? – but Sunday use not in *Brad*. At last moment, did someone realise there was a Sunday excursion and amend accordingly? To add to the complexity, normal SR practice then was to give Sunday closure dates; given that the Sunday service was an excursion, the 29th would have fitted. 30th used here because it was last date given by SR.

1936 September 14. Closure of Ashover Light. Line had been reduced to summer only after 3 October 1931 *(Ashover)*.

Known later use: three specials 11 August 1937 for Ashover Show and one on 8 June 1940 to FORD LANE, a crossing place south of Stretton for Garden Fete in grounds of Ogston Hall (Gratton & Brand, *The Ashover Light Railway*, Wild Swan 1989); not known which stops used by these.

1937 October 25. Closure Clynderwen–Fishguard via Maenclochog (GW). Closure was originally planned for 27 September 1937, with the end of the summer timetable, and a notice was issued to that effect. However, protests by the County Council and others resulted in one month's delay, so that last train ran on 23 October *(Maenclochog*, which also reproduces premature closure notice).

1939 September. Closure: Caernarvon to Llanberis (ex-LNW).

All-the-year-round service ceased with effect from 22 September 1930. *LMS tt* for that date says service has been withdrawn, but 'Excursion Trains will be run to and from Llanberis during the summer months. See separate announcements'.

Summer services began 25 May 1931 but not shown in *Brad* until 1932, when noted as 'excursion trains', otherwise looking identical to a normal service. No Sunday trains. Last train for season ran on October 1.
— 1933–36: summer services shown, 'excursion' note omitted.
— 1934: Sunday service added.
— 1934/5 winter: limited Christmas and Easter services added.

29 December 1934 all-year Saturday service added; since Saturday was Caernarvon market day, this service was clearly for the benefit of locals, not for any stray tourists who might still have been in the area. It would have been for this service that Padarn was opened, 21 November 1936 *(exact date RM January 1937; T 23 November 'is now open')*.

Pattern was the same until tt ending 24 September 1939: this said Monday to Friday service would not run after the 8th, Sunday service not after the 10th, but Saturday one would continue throughout the month. It is not known whether services did so run or whether war brought them to an end – probably ceased when emergency tt into use 11 September.

Other excursions (e.g. to Liverpool for football) also ran.

Table remained in *Brad*, with a war-time break, until its last issue, May/June 1961; always either no trains shown or 'service suspended'.

After 1930 no intermediate stations were shown in public tt. Pont Rug closed September 1930. The others remained in use: Pontrythallt, Cwm-y-Glo and Padarn in summer 1939 wtt.

Excursion trains ran after War: according to *RM January 1949*, first ran 6 July 1948. Wtts and BR publicity material showed summer services, usually Mondays to Fridays, last running 7 September 1962, no intermediate stops on Llanberis line. Sunday School excursions on line in 1950s called at Cwm-y-Glo.

See R. Maund (*Chron July 2008*); W.G. Rear's books *LMS Branch Lines in North Wales, vol. I, Bangor to Afon Wen …* (Wild Swan, 1986) and *Scenes from the Past 28: Railways of North Wales: Caernarvon …* (Foxline, 1996).

1939 September 11. Closure: Louth to Bardney (ex-GN). *Rly Gaz 15 November 1940 (C/W)*, supported by *Brad*, which shows 'service suspended' in October and November issues, and by LNE Emergency tt 2 October 1939 (same).

1939 September 18. Festiniog, 1ft 11½in. gauge. During the last years the service appears from tt to have been very ragged. Stations were often shown for a few months without trains, then for a few months with and so on. A general idea is given under individual station headings; whether service was actually what tt showed is not known.

— Trains for line last shown October 1931 tt.
— Trains shown again June 1932 tt.

During the winters of 1932–3 and 1933–4 the service was cut back to one train each way. Thereafter no winter service was shown: trains last shown October 1934; in 1934 the service actually ran from 9 July to 29 September, inclusive (pocket tt, which called it the 'Festiniog Toy Railway'). Trains back May 1935; September 1935 – will not run after 15th inst.

— April 1936 – commences 13th; last trains September 1936 tt.
— 3 May 1937 tt – commences 17th inst; last trains in tt ending 26 September 1937.
— Trains again June 1938; last trains in tt ending 25 September 1938.
— Trains again June 1939; line finally closed in September 1939: last public trains Friday 15th, for quarrymen 16th.

1940 June 10. Temporary closure of line Wrexham to Ellesmere: full capacity needed to serve Royal Ordnance Factory Wrexham, served by branch from west-facing junction about a mile from Marchwiel. Item by 'D.P.' in *Clwyd Historian*, Clwyd Local History Council, No.23, October 1989 deals with this. Map shows 'stations' at

PARKEY; FIVE FORDS; BROOKFIELD; BRYN. Author believed from map evidence and physical remains that these were for passenger use. However, he had received letter from engine driver on line who stated that passengers were only carried to platform at BEDWELL SOUTH YARD, on branch but only just beyond junction, and taken on to work places by bus. Workman's ticket from Cefn-y-Bedd to MARCHWIEL FACTORY LINE JUNCTION (*JB*) perhaps refers to platform mentioned by driver.

GM's report 28 June 1940 shows that workmen's services continued directly after public closure.

During WW2 occasional hospital trains ran to Overton-on-Dee for hospital at Penley Hall (S.C. Jenkins & J.M. Strange, *The Wrexham & Ellesmere Railway*, Oakwood, 2004).

1940 September 9. Closure: line to Gallions (ex-PLA). Line closed by bombing, early afternoon, Saturday 7 September: no service Saturday afternoon or Sunday. See T.B. Peacock, *P L A Railways*, Locomotive Publishing Co, 1952, p.68. Beckton might have suffered at the same time, though December 1940 tt still showed one train each way per day.

1942 August 4. Closure (temporary): Didcot–Newbury–Southampton line (GW). This resulted from need to improve it for military traffic. Reopened 8 March 1943.

1944 April 3. Closure: Lybster branch (ex-High). LMS handbill dated April 1944. 'On and from Monday 3rd April passengers will not be booked for rail conveyance …'. Notice to staff: 'branch will be closed … after the finish of work on Saturday 1st'.

1944 June 19: closure of Thornbury branch (ex-Mid). Monday 19 June was last day of public use. Later ambulance trains took wounded to Thornbury for US Army Hospital at Leyhill; last 1 February 1945.

Tytherington Quarry excursions ran annually, 1974 to 1986, inclusive.

Occasional stray passenger carried on goods, including one lady sold ticket from Oswestry by booking-clerk unaware of closure ('about 1958'). (All from C.G. Maggs, *Yate to Thornbury Branch*, Oakwood, 2002).

1945 June 4. Closure: Carstairs to Dolphinton (ex-Cal). Date from *G&S* since this was the Monday (*Cl* gives 2nd, a Saturday, which looks more like last day of use). Without further evidence, the possibility also exists that it was really a 'first of the month closure' which has caused confusion.

1947 June 15. Closure: Park Royal; Brentham; Perivale (GW). These had their last train on 14 June though the service to Old Oak Lane and Acton continued to the end of the month. The three closures made on the 15th were necessary so that trials of Central Line trains could take place (*Rly Obs 1947, p.137; A.A. Jackson, Chron*).

1947 June 16. Closure of a number of stations as a 'temporary' measure owing to a fuel crisis. They never reopened. *RM January 1948* gave 14th as closure date (really last day of use) but in *September 1949* and later issues, which recorded the making permanent of some of these, 16th was quoted.

1948 August 13 (Friday). Closures: Jedburgh to Roxburgh, and Duns to St Boswells (ex-NB), had been planned for later but made on this date as a result of flood damage on the main line *(Cl)*.

Tweedmouth to St Boswells line also closed by landslip at Carham 12 August 1948; reopened 16 August and main line trains were diverted over this single line as result of east-coast floods. Locals were cancelled, resulting in temporary closure of Roxburgh Junction, Maxton and Rutherford until 31 October was last day of diversion *(NE Express, September 2003)*.

1948 November 1: East Kent Light matters. According to *EK-F&G* practices erratic. Stops made between stations for favoured passengers but those waiting at request stops might be ignored by drivers. Speeds so slow that 'delinquent' passengers (without tickets) could alight between stations (p.459). Line closure date from *RM January 1949*.

Service to Poison Cross; Roman Road; Sandwich Road (on short branch from Eastry) was even more erratic. First in *Brad* May 1925, Saturdays only. Sandwich Road had been renamed from Sandwich 9 April 1925 *(hbl April)* – was that linked to actual opening date for passengers? – 4th would have been first Saturday that month. By April 1926 trains all days; August/November 1926 back to Saturdays; from December 1926/August 1927 served Wednesdays also. According to *EK-F&G* trains did not normally serve these for a while before they were removed from tt. According to closure date given (from *Cl*), last train should have run Wednesday 31 October 1928.

1950 October 6. Transfer: Tallyllyn. Line had been kept going by a local landowner, Sir H.H. Jones, though service intermittent in later years.

At some point, probably in early 1930s, winter service reduced to Monday, Wednesday and Friday only; (certainly all days November 1926 tt and 22 September to 31 October 1930 tt; reduced by January 1936 tt).

From start of summer 1940 reduction applied to summer as well. Reduced to Wednesday and Friday 14 January 1942. Monday train reinstated 8 June 1942, ceased 20 January 1943.

All ceased 23 June 1943; back, Wednesdays and Fridays, 20 July 1943; Monday added 2 August 1943.

Last train 24 November 1943; trains again, Wednesdays and Fridays, from 31 December 1943, with extra on 1944 Bank Holidays.

Thus, except for 12 April 1944, when no trains ran,

until service ceased 24 January 1945.

Resumed thus 3 February 1945; no trains ran 9 and 14 March 1945. Train 16 March 1945 was last until 1946.

Thereafter (1946 on) service was Easter plus May to early October, except for stoppage 27 August 1949 (engines out of action), resumption 19 September 1949.

1950 service was Easter Friday and Monday, Whit Monday, three days per week (Monday, Wednesday, Friday) 5 June to 6 October, so usually quoted date was for last train – normal convention would require 9th. See J.I.C. Boyd, *The Tal-y-Llyn Railway*, Oakwood, 1988.

D&C 11, p.172, and Boyd refers to Halts at Hendy, Fach Goch, Cynfal, Tynyllwyn. None was included in *Bradshaw* before preservation days. Cynfal was included *hbl* 29 September 1946 but might well have been in use much earlier; its platform was provided for convenience of a local farmer. No other references seen to the rest; Quarry Siding was probably added after 1950, in preservation days.

Jones's death on 2 July 1950 was expected to result in closure at the end of summer season (6 October). However, a preservation society was formed and was able to operate the line from start of the summer season, 1951.

1951. Coal crisis closures. Need to save coal early in 1951 led to cuts in passenger services, introduced in instalments. Many reductions in frequency on nearly all lines; some lost Sunday services; a few closed completely, but 'temporarily' – as in 1947, some never reopened. First batch started on 15 January *(T 12th)*; paper gave examples of cuts, not complete list. More cuts 21/22 January *(T 19th, 20th)*, 28/29 January *(T 27th)*, February 12 *(T 1st, 2nd, 8th)*. All excursions suspended except those for fixed events (e.g. football, racing).

Services mostly soon restored. Euston to Heysham boat trains (cut to three days per week) restored to daily mid-March *(T 12th)*. Temporary full service over Easter; full restoration 2 April, except for 'the poorly patronised trains which were already being considered for withdrawal when the cuts were made' *(T 20 March, 30 March)*.

Secondary sources seen (e.g. *RM*) did not give much coverage to this, so it may be that some temporary closures occurred that have not been recorded in the book. Note that some lines reopened after 2 April.

These shown 'temporarily withdrawn' (exact date unknown) March tt, restored in April tt/supplement:

[Salisbury]; Newton Tony; Amesbury; Bulford – clo date unknown; only one train each way April.

[Newcastle; Scotswood]; Swalwell; Rowlands Gill; Lintz Green; Ebchester; Shotley Bridge; [Blackhill]

Kirriemuir branch: 15 January 1951 reduced to one from Kirriemuir all days, one to Kirriemuir Saturdays only *(True Line 85)*; same April 1951 tt; before/with August 1951 tt one each way daily.

Note has been applied to all stations closed 15 January to end February 1951 (inclusive), though some were perhaps already scheduled for closure. Oswestry to Llangynog and Dundee to Perth via Lindores both in April tt as 'service withdrawn' whilst others were 'temporarily withdrawn'. Suggests these two already marked for closure.

Auchendinny and Otterspool closed 5 March, so were possible victims. Also a fair crop 2 April but these were presumably closed in orthodox way.

Whilst some did reopen, most soon closed again. Presumably, earlier users had found alternatives and stayed with these so that services previously poorly patronised were now even worse so.

Ex-GW/Rhy line Quakers Yard to Merthyr suffered immediate closure when viaduct found to be unsafe – last train ran 3 February *(Merthyr Express 10th)*.

1952 June 9. Closure, West Hartlepool to Ferryhill (ex-NE). *RM August* confirms closure date and adds that excursions will run on certain days until August 16; not clear whether all stations meant or just some of them.

1952 September 15: closure Morpeth to Rothbury (ex-NB). BR (NE Region) public notice said that advertised excursion trains would be run from time to time when customers justified it, but no details of those run, if any, have been seen. A private use was described in *Rly Gaz 25 September 1953*: train of four buffet cars pulled by two engines had been chartered for cocktail party; stopped at seven points to pick up guests until over 100 on board; date?

1953. Brief re-use of Malton to Driffield line (ex-NE). This had closed in 1950. Temporarily reopened 12 to 16 February 1953 owing to bad weather; not certain that all stations used; custom gained by advertising on previous evening's news *(RM April 1953)*. Used again winter of 1957/8; no exact date, but probably in February 1958 when snow at worst (W. Burton, *Malton & Driffield Junction Railway*, M. Bairstow, 1997).

1953 November 23. Closure: SSMWC. Date from C.R. Warn, *Rails between Wear and Tyne*, F. Greenham, Northern History Booklet 86, undated: says trains ran until 22nd, presumably last day. Book cited for 1888 March 19**, above, also says last train ran on Sunday 22nd. However, May 1953 tt gives Monday to Friday service + 'for Saturdays, see local announcement'. Sunday service also local advertisement only? (Sunday service was shown August 1950 tt). *RM* said that last train ran on Saturday 19th, but that date was actually a Thursday.

1954 April 26: closure of Hawes branch (ex-NE). Occasional later specials to Jervaulx for Aysgarth school. At passenger closure promise had been given that line would be reopened for emergency passenger use if necessary. At the beginning of 1962 Wensleydale was badly affected by snowdrifts and, in accordance with

promise, a skeleton service was run initially from Leyburn, calling at Wensley, Redmire, Aysgarth and Askrigg; later trains ran from Hawes. Service certainly ran on Monday 1 January and Tuesday 2nd (important market at Hawes). See S.C. Jenkins, *The Wensleydale Branch*, Oakwood, 1993).

1955 May 23: clo Bradford to Keighley (ex-GN): BR closure notice reproduced in article by J.F. Oxley & D.R. Smith in *GN Society Journal 151*; this also says excursions ran throughout summer 1955.

1955 May 30. Closure: Pontypool Road to Monmouth Troy (ex-GW) and East Grinstead to Lewes (ex-LBSC). Had been planned for later but a strike began then and continued beyond planned date. Last trains actually ran Saturday 28 May *(RM May 1958)*.

1956 October 15: closure Hexham to Riccarton Junction (ex-NB). Clo date *T 21 September* and *BR notice*. At least one later excursion – 7 September 1958 ramblers' from Newcastle *(BR notice, Nhumb Young)*.

1957: 'Provision Trains' [High/LMS/BR]. This year is given because some exact information is available. The services concerned ran for many years but it cannot be guaranteed that the stops would always have been the same. These trains were run so that railwaymen and their families could buy essential supplies. Those using them needed a 'Provision Pass'. *Rly Obs July 1966* said these had ceased about eight years previously. Details of two are known, from *BR Scottish Region Special Traffic Notices*:

(a) Helmsdale to Wick and back, run monthly Saturdays, certainly shown for 22 June 1957. The extra stops were at Killearnan; Carbuie; Old Kinbrace; Limeside; Balloch; Clashaid. Their exact locations are not known since they were only shown in the footnotes, but presumably that was the order in which they called from Helmsdale.
(b) Blair Atholl to Aviemore and back, run fortnightly Saturdays. Again, exact locations not known, but in this case a full timetable was given and the extra stops can thus be approximately placed. They were Black Tank, Dalanreoch, Garry Bridge, Altnagourach (all Struan/ Dalnaspidal); County March, Dalsporran, Bachan (all Dalnaspidal/Dalwhinnie); Inchlea, Etteridge (both Dalwhinnie/Newtonmore). [Information G. Borthwick.]

1958 September: railbus Gleneagles – Comrie. *Perthshire Advertiser 10 September* said Scotland's first railbus would run on Monday September 15. Retractable steps would allow it to serve Strageath and Pittenzie level crossings. Paper of 17th: did run.

1959: closure of stations Penistone to Barnsley. Most trains withdrawn 15 June 1959, at same time as local service Sheffield to Penistone ceased *(BLN June 1959)*; however, an early morning train from Manchester continued until 29 June 1959 (N Fraser's notes for RCTS railtour, via A. Brackenbury); *Cl's* date of 22 June 1959 for Summer Lane is puzzling – perhaps misprint – logically, one would expect 29th – *RM* August gave it as closed with rest on 29th.

1960. Ravenglass and Eskdale. Winter service ended 1927/8 except for Thursday only market service, ceased 1937. Line closed end September 1939 (as usual) *(Raven)*. Reop week ended 26 May 1945 *(Ravenglass & Eskdale Railway Newsletter, Autumn 1972)*. After 1960 service provided by preservation society (full details *Raven p. 92*).

1960 January 6. Closure: Swansea and Mumbles. Last public service, followed, unusually, by a ceremonial closing run, occurred in the middle of the day on Tuesday 5th *(SIT; T 6th)*.

1960 October 26. Closure: line between Sharpness and Lydney over Severn Bridge (ex-SW Jt). Two spans of bridge destroyed when bridge hit by two ships *(Report of Court of Enquiry, Bristol 9–11 May 1961* – M. Hale) late on 25th, after traffic had finished for the day. It was never repaired.

1960 November 5, 6 & 7. Replacement of Crow Road (ex-Cal) and Hydland terminus (ex-NB) by new Hyndland on through line (ex-NB). This occurred when the Glasgow electric Blue Trains were introduced. Sequence of events:

— Hyndland terminus was last served on Friday 4th, giving closure date of 5th.
— Saturday 5th – formal opening of new service and skeleton service of steam trains.
— Sunday 6th – free public service.
— Monday 7th – normal public service *(T 7 November; RM December)*.

Crow Road had not previously had a Sunday service so by normal standards its closure date should be 7th.

1962 August 1. Closure: Tenbury Wells to Bewdley (ex-GW). This was full public closure date *(BRWR notice)*. It had been reduced to a calendar year's experimental or trial service (one each way per day), essentially for schoolchildren but actually for all after last train on Saturday 29 July 1961 – ironically the first experimental train ran at the beginning of the school holidays and during the holidays trains often ran empty *(Tenbury)*.

1962 August 5. Ashbourne to Parsley Hay [ex-LNW, Dovedale line]: stations noted were still in excursion use at 5 August 1962 *(BR handbill)*. It was last use by ramblers' and sightseers' specials of Parsley Hay and Thorpe Cloud; on return train stopped for water at Hindlow – if any left/joined here, would have been unsanctioned use. Some of these specials were scheduled for Well Dressing Days: e.g. 7 excursions from various parts of country on Sunday, 14 May 1961, 4 on Sunday 26 May 1963. 1963 one called at Hartington, Tissington and Thorpe Cloud, the last use of these stations *(AB)*. Last excursion on line through them (part [ex-NS]) 26 May 1963 *(SLS Jour*, June 1963) – station calls unknown.

1962 November 11: Skegness branch [ex-GN]: service 'suspended' 11 November 1962 to 14 April 1963 (both inclusive) *(wtt supp dated 7 January 1963)*.

1962 December 31. Closure: Plymouth to Launceston (ex-GW). Last trains supposed to run on Saturday 29th. Heavy snow meant that what was supposed to be last but one train from Plymouth stuck at Tavistock early on Sunday morning. The intended last trains never ran. Stranded passengers eventually finished journey by road *(Cornish & D P 5 January 1963)*.

1964 June 15. Closure: Aberdare line (ex-GW). After closure, service of 'Merrymaker' publicly-advertised excursions was run, generally in summer months, calling at surviving platforms at Mountain Ash (Oxford Street) and Penrhiwceiber (LL); first was 6 June 1971 excursion to Paignton. At first ran from Aberdare HL, reversing towards Hirwaun then used old TV line. Excursion to Brighton on 29 July 1973 ran out via this route, back via new chord at Cwmbach, allowing direct running to Aberdare HL. In December 1984 specials to Cardiff for shoppers; also specials for sporting events; daily trains during two peak holiday weeks. Experimental trains early 1988 were "shoppers' specials". (P. Jeffries, late Service Planning Manager, Arriva Trains Wales; J.F. Mear, *Aberdare, The Railways and Tramroads*, privately, 1999).

1964 December 14 and 1965 January 18. Closure: Ruabon to Barmouth (ex-GW) and Aberystwyth to Strata Florida (ex-Cam). Planned for 18 January 1965 (last train 16th) but on Saturday 12 December 1964 severe flooding damaged line, services suspended late morning. No scheduled Sunday service. Monday 14th line from Barmouth to Dolgellau again usable for passengers; buses took on to Ruabon. Thursday 17th Ruabon to Llangollen section reopened; service was also provided from Bala to Dolgellau, reversal at Bala Junction; buses linked Llangollen and Bala. Damage near Llanderfel so great that there was no justification for repairing it, given approaching closure of line, so that Llangollen to Bala Junction section was actually closed then (C. Magner, *Steam at Llangollen 91*).

1965 September 28 (Tuesday). Closures: Balquhidder to Callander and Killin branch (ex-Cal). These were already planned but occurred prematurely as a result of a landslide blocking the main line on the 27th *(Rly Obs November)*.

1965 October 18. Closures: Aviemore to Forres (ex-High) and Boat of Garten to Craigellachie (ex-GNS). These were originally scheduled for 1 November; brought forward to 11 October; finally postponed to 18th. *(Rly Obs November and December)*.

1966. Auchencastle; Beattock Summit; Greskine. *Rly Obs July 1966, p. 232*, said that Saturdays only, engine and one coach (kept in siding at Beattock Summit) would provide service for railwaymen and families living alongside line. Main intermediate stops at Greskine and

Auchencastle, but would stop at any lineside cottages on request; passengers joined/alighted via portable ladder. Last known service ran 24 September 1966 *(Rly Obs January 1967 p.29)*. 30 June 1952 wtt showed stops at Beattock Summit only. Perhaps other stops 'understood'? – train only for railway employees and wives and generous allowance of time in wtt – 30 minutes and more for journey.

1967 June 5: matters relating to Renfrew Wharf and Govan branches. In December 1904 *Brad* 'workmen's trains' added to heading. Line last in *Brad* May 1906; back February 1911 (as was Govan branch), still 'workmen's trains'; service virtually same as that shown in February 1906. This raises suspicion that trains had still run but line omitted because it was only workmen's service. However, no workmen's or other passenger services shown in wtt for July–September 1907, suggesting it was fully closed. Between October 1918 and January 1919 a subtle change was made in heading – now 'workers' trains'; this was still included August 1927 but omitted before/with July 1928.

The Govan branch was then included in this table, so from December 1904 *Brad* its service only for workmen.

1968 January. Brief reopening: Bideford to Torrington (ex-LSW). From *Bideford* 12, 19 and 26 January and *Express & E* over the period. Bideford is on west bank of the Torridge; then depended on the town bridge to provide link with East-the-Water, through which ran main road and disused railway. Anxiety had already been expressed about condition of bridge – old age and heavy traffic had taken its toll. There had been heavy rainfall and parts of Devon were flooded. Evening of Tuesday 9 January large pieces of masonry fell from bridge into river. Bridge immediately closed to vehicles but pedestrians allowed to continue using for that evening. Next day, it was completely closed. This meant all traffic into and out of Bideford had to go along narrow lanes via Torrington, next crossing point of river. From the 10th BR ran shuttle service between Torrington and Bideford to give some relief. Anyone wishing to cross river at Bideford had to catch bus to Torrington, then come back to the other side by train – service was free. Temporary footbridge opened on the 19th and rail service withdrawn with effect from 20th.

According to the local press, on the evening of 11th rail service was withdrawn and following local representations, resumed on Monday 15th; however, according to R. Maund a friend of his rode on the line on Saturday 13th so presumably service resumed that day.

1972 November 1. Transfer: line Paignton to Kingswear from BR (ex-GW) to Dart Valley. Last BR services weekend October 28 & 29. From Monday 30 October the Western Region provided a basic service on behalf of Dart Valley. Latter began its independent service 1 January 1973, using separate station at Paignton. Original intention had been all-the-year-round service

but in 1973 they had to cut back to summer-only running. Dart Valley initially ran out-of-season (schools?) service, including stop at Britannia Crossing Halt.

1982 September 27. Withdrawal of Bakerloo service. This is official date; in reality service was withdrawn after morning peak on 24 September. Public protests led to restoration of a peak-hour service between Stonebridge Park and Harrow & Wealdstone. Section from Harrow & Wealdstone to Watford Junction remained closed to Bakerloo trains – it had been peak hours only prior to withdrawal. *(Harrow)*.

1987 October 4: reopenings. 'Dress-rehearsal' of revised service for Valley Lines, including these stations and available to public was run on Sunday 4th, ready for operation of new tt from Monday 5th (P. Jeffries, late Service Planning Manager, Arriva Trains Wales).

1989 October 16: Settle & Carlisle line [ex-Mid]: closed (bus replaced) Monday 16 October 1989 to Saturday 28 October 1989 (inclusive) for viaduct work *(BR handbill October 1989)*.

1994 March 28. Docklands Light: Beckton branch. Date from page 131 of *BLN 729*. Clear from this item that public used on this date, although it was also formal opening day. Since, according to this source, free travel was available for the first four days, there would be some justification for quoting a later date – though not 31 March, which appears on the front page of the same issue of *BLN*.

1997 June 1. Closure of Mitcham area lines (ex-SR) for conversion to Croydon Tramlink. Last trains ran Saturday 31 May 1997. No Sunday service so by conventional standards these would be considered 'closed 2 June'; replacement bus service began on that date. However, a new timetable came into force on 1 June and described these as closed. Therefore that date has been used here; there would seem to be equal grounds for using either. See *BLN 794, RM August, Railway World August, Rly Obs August p.327*.

2002 March 31 (Easter Sunday). Transfer of Newcastle to Sunderland service to TWM; and (re)opening of South Hylton to Sunderland line by TWM. Newcastle to Sunderland train services replaced by buses on following dates to enable work on line (all 2002): 12–27 January; Saturdays and Sundays 2 February–24 March; all days 25–30 March; also evenings only 28 January–1 February and 18–22 March; also Sunderland tunnel 18-19 February. Ex-BR trains continue to call at Heworth, otherwise intermediate stations now TWM only *(NE Express, November 2002, p.164)*.

2004 May 23: local services Coventry – Nuneaton – Stafford – Stoke-on-Trent: stations noted were temporarily closed from that date, with replacement services by buses; doubts were expressed about their ever reopening to rail services. Some have reopened: Atherstone (12 December 2005); Bedworth (13 June

2005); Polesworth (12 December 2005) – but one journey, one way only, rest still by bus. Stone due to reop 14 December 2008 tt. Barlaston; Norton Bridge; Wedgwood remain road served and are not expected to regain their rail service.

2005 December 12: opening of Larkhall branch, with stations at Chatelherault, Merryton and Larkhall; ceremonial 9th (*The Herald*, Glasgow, 10th). National Rail 11 December 2005 tt said would open on 13th – clearly misprint.

2007 July 4. Leicester North to Loughborough Great Central preservation line. On 4 and 6 July ran experimental service for the pupils of Loughborough Grammar and High Schools. Might become permanent. (*RM September*). Leicester North overlaps site of earlier Belgrave & Birstall station (*AB, Chron, October 2000*).

2007 July 20. Taunton to Minehead branch, ex-GW. This line was reopened in instalments by a preservation company (during which time Doniford Halt was opened and Crowcombe reverted to Crowcombe Heathfield). Normally operated between Bishops Lydeard and Minehead but occasional specials worked through from the main system. From Friday 20 July 2007 to Monday 27 August 2007 trains ran Mondays, Fridays and Saturdays (one each way per day). They started from Bristol Temple Meads and ran non-stop to Taunton, then called at all stations to Minehead. Connections at Bristol for Midlands and North and at Taunton for London. It was an experimental service which needed

to have to paid its way to be repeated. (*Somerset County Gazette 28 June 2007* gave advance notice). [Train left Minehead at 11.10, reaching Bristol at 13.46; returned from Bristol at 14.06, reaching Minehead at 16.25. Thus really only of use for those starting/ending a holiday at ex-Butlins – thus chances of repetition slight? – did not run 2008]

For the company's steam gala in 2006 a shuttle service was run by First Great Western between Taunton and Bishops Lydeard on 7 and 8 October (*RM December*). A Virgin Trains *Voyager* provided a similar service from on 6 and 7 October 2007 for people attending a steam gala (*Somerset County Gazette 11th*).

2007 December 23. Closure of East London Line. Last train ran Saturday 22 December (*RM January 2008*). Line closed for reconstruction as part of London Overground Network; due to reopen in 2010.
Note that line has had a varied history. It opened as the East London Company, using Marc Brunel's tunnel under the Thames, to provide a link between the GE and LBSC. From 1870 it was worked and managed by the LBSC; from 1892 a Joint Committee took over; the last steam train ran on 30 March 1913 and then the Met took over as sole user; it became SR property in 1925 and was transferred to London Transport in 1948. For a long time Underground maps showed it simply as 'Met'; about 1970 this became 'Met (East London Section)'; more recently just East London (Line).

SECTION 6

Metro lines

This section is used to cover lines which run partly on dedicated track and partly on public roads shared with other types of traffic. Where these use the sites of previous 'normal' railway stations, cross-references are provided in Section 4. These services are put here and treated in outline only because the close spacing of their stops means that they would occupy far greater relative space than their importance warrants, especially considering that there might well be a considerable increase in this sort of service in the next few years. Furthermore, they are all recently-opened services which have received considerable coverage in the Railway press so that it should be far easier for anyone wanting more detail to find it.

Croydon Tramlink

Croydon to New Addington – formal opening and free public use 10 May 2000; fare paying public use 11 May 2000 *(Rly Obs June 2000)*.

Croydon to Beckenham Junction – op 23 May 2000 *(RM July 2000)*.

Elmers End to Wimbledon – op 30 May 2000 *(RM July 2000)*.

Manchester Metrolink

This is based on the old railway lines from Manchester to Bury and to Altrincham *(see MSJA)*. A street tramway links the two in the middle and further street tramway extensions have been made. For plans see *RM January 1990, p.18, and December 1991 p.850*.

Bury to Manchester Victoria – (re)opened 6 April 1992; stations as before, with Queens Road staff station.

Manchester Victoria to G Mex (interchange for Deansgate) – opened 27 April 1992 *(BLN 684)*.

G Mex to Altrincham – (re)opened 15 June 1992; stations as before but some renaming *(BLN 686)*. Most served only by Metro trains but Altrincham kept its main line station as well so that it can serve as an interchange.

Links to Manchester Piccadilly added 20 July 1992 *(BLN 689)*.

At Market Street, a two-way service replaced the old one-way use of Market Street plus High Street 10 August 1998 *(Rly Obs December)*.

Extended to Salford Quays (Waterside) and Broadway 6 December 1999 *(RM February 2000, p.14)*.

Extended to Eccles 21 July 2000 *(RM September 2000)*.

Nottingham Express Transit

Op 9 March 2004 (formal 8th) from Nottingham station to Hucknall, with branch to park-and-ride at Phoenix Park *(RM May, p.91)*.

Sheffield Supertram

Opened to Meadowhall 21 March 1994 *(T 22nd)*.

22 August 1994 to Spring Lane *(RM February 1995)*.

5 December 1994 to Gleadless Townend *(RM May 1995)*.

18 February 1995 to Cathedral *(RM July)*.

27 February 1995 to Shalesmoor *(RM July)*.

27 March 1995 to Halfway *(RM July)*.

3 April 1995 to Herdings *(RM February 1996)*.

23 October 1995 to Malin Bridge and Middlewood *(RM January 1996)*.

For full station details see item by A. Brackenbury, *Chron, January 2005)*.

West Midlands Metro

Birmingham Snow Hill to Wolverhampton St George – ceremonial opening plus free public use 30 May 1999; fare paying public use began 31 May 1999 *(Rly Obs August 1999)*.

LATEST RAILWAY MARVEL.

Gent. "I SAY, PORTER, WHEN DOES THE NEXT TRAIN START?"

Irish Porter. "THE NEXT TRAIN! SURE, THE NIXT TRAIN HAS GONE TIN MINUTES AGO."

Some marginal items

The aim is to give an outline idea of some of the great variety of services that have carried passengers but do not qualify for inclusion in the earlier parts of this book. Sometimes the difference could be described as a minor technicality. Catterick Camp's service, included in Section 4, only differed from that of RAF Cranwell, listed below, in that it appeared briefly in *Bradshaw*; the miners' services shown below were similar to many listed in Section 4, but were provided by companies that did not run 'normal' passenger services. Others were far removed in kind from services listed earlier. In these matters one should try to think in terms of an infinity of shadings rather than clear-cut definitions. Lines and stations just used by the occasional excursion or works outing are omitted, as are the many instances where contractors building lines provided services of a sort for their workmen once some portions of the line were in place. In most cases details are either not known or known only in very general terms and the complications involved in attempting to list them would fill a lot of space, much of which would be taken up with variants of 'not known'. More can be found out about many of them from *U*, which should be regarded as the source if nothing else is shown; for some, books containing much fuller information are cited, though inevitably only small portions of these works deal with passengers. It can be safely assumed that many lines not listed here carried comparable services. Some non-rail items listed at the end.

See also:

G. Body & R. Eastleigh, *Cliff Railways*, D&C, 1964; R.W. Rush, *Horse Trams of the British Isles*, Oakwood, 2004; K. Turner, *Pier Railways and Tramways of the British Isles*, Oakwood, 1999 edition; K. Turner, *Cliff Railways of the British Isles*, Oakwood 2002; K. Turner, *The Directory of British Tramways*, Patrick Stephens, 1996.

1: Lines used by the general public

ALFORD & SUTTON Tramway. 2ft 6in. line.
Op 2 April 1884; clo at/near start of December 1889 (that it had closed, officially for winter, but probably in reality for ever, announced in paper of 7 December, G. Dow, *The Alford & Sutton Tramway*, Oakwood, 1947).

BLACKPOOL & FLEETWOOD Tramway (included in *Returns*, e.g. 1910). First section op 29 September 1885; Blackpool to Fleetwood op 14 July 1898. Still open. (P.H. Abell & McLoughlin, *Blackpool Trams*, Oakwood, undated).

BRIGHTON & ROTTINGDEAN: Seashore Electric Tramway. Included in *Returns*. That for 1896 says: 'Only open 30 November to 4 December 1896 and was closed in consequence of damage caused by a gale'. Reop 20 July 1897. In both 1898 and 1899 more than 100,000 passengers were carried. Numbers then fell drastically, perhaps because service was not continuous: 1900 – 42,000; 1901 – 9,000; 1902 – 18,000. In 1903 return, the entry was 'line not working'. Cars on stilts so that they could run when line covered by the sea. For fuller details see chapter in book on Volk's Railways, below.

BURTON & ASHBY Light Railway. 3ft 6in. line. Op Burton to Swadlincote 13 June 1906; on to Ashby 2 July 1906; Swadlincote to Gresley 24 September 1906; Woodville to Gresley 15 October 1906. Gresley arm clo November 1912; passenger cars last ran on rest 19 February 1927. Owned by Midland Railway. (C.T. Goode, *The Burton & Ashby Light Railway*, Burstwick Print & Publicity Services, Hull, 1994).

CAIRNGORM MOUNTAIN RAILWAY: owned by Highlands & Islands Enterprise, 'government-sponsored development agency', leased to CairnGorm Mountain Ltd and operated as 'CairnGorm Mountain Railway'. 2 km (1¼ mile) funicular, 2 metre gauge; base station at Coire Cas (6 miles south-east of Aviemore) to top at Ptarmigan. Opened 23 December 2001. December to April inclusive is high-speed ski-lift. May to November runs slower so tourists can enjoy views; during this period passengers are restricted to top station (has viewing and other facilities) – fears that mountain paths would suffer excessive wear if let passengers walk down. Operates weather permitting (wind up to 85mph). (*Rail 20 March 2002* plus internet items via G. Boyes).

CHATHAM & DISTRICT Light Railway. Incorporated 1899 under Light Railways Act. Street tramway but in *Brad Sh* by 1913.

CRUDEN BAY: hotel op 1 March 1899, railway about mid-June 1899; latter free for residents, others 3d. Passenger used ceased with closure of Boddam branch (K. Jones, *The Cruden Bay Hotel and its Tramway*, Grampian Transport Museum / GNS Railway Society, 2004).

FAIRBOURNE Railway. Narrow gauge line Fairbourne to Barmouth Ferry. Opened 1890; still open.

GREAT ORME Tramway. Lower half op 31 July 1902, upper 8 July 1903. Originally G O Tramways (two sections); renamed G O Railway after change of ownership in 1935. Compulsorily acquired by local authority 1949; 1977 renamed G O Tramway. Still open. See: R.C. Anderson, *The Great Orme Tramway*, Light Rail Transit Association, undated; K. Turner, *The Great Orme Tramway: over a century of service*, author, 2003.

HYTHE & SANDGATE Tramway. Op 18 May 1891 from Sandgate to Seabrook Hotel; on to Hythe 1 June 1892; extended at other end to Sandgate Hill 1 August 1892. SE was driving force behind line. Last worked in summer of 1921. *(SE, SEC)*.

ISLE OF THANET LIGHT RAILWAYS.
Light Railway Order granted 1898, extended 1900, amended 1901 (C.R. Clinker, *Light Railway Orders*, AvonAnglia, 1977). Appeared in railway *Return* 1901, for period 4 April (opening date?) to 5 October 1901 (end of its financial year?); 11 miles long; nearly 3 million passengers carried, only one class of ticket. In 1902 return, for year ended 30 September 1902, 4½ million passengers carried. No further entries; no railway book seen makes any reference; tramway entered in wrong *Return* for a couple of years?

KINVER Tramway near Stourbridge.
Operated under Light Railway Order; op Good Friday 1 April 1901; prob clo 1 February 1930.
(K. & S.L. Turner, *The Kinver Light Railway*, Oakwood, 1974; *RM January and February 1910)*.

PLYNLIMON & HAFAN Tramway. 2ft 3in line.
Service Talybont to Llanvihangel, Mondays only, 28 March 1898 to 12 August 1898 (inclusive), to connect with market train to Aberystwyth. No BoT sanction.
(E.A. Wade, *The Plynlimon & Hafan Tramway*, Twelveheads, 1997).

PWLLHELI to LLANBEDROG. Horse Tramway, 1896 to 1927 *(D&C 11)*.

ROTHESAY Tramway. Originally horse-drawn from Rothesay to Port Bannantyne. Op ? Clo for electrification and relaying ? Reop 19 August 1902; later extended to Ettrick (decision taken 1905). Photo in *RM January 1914 p. 27* shows that at least part ran on enclosed track.

SOLOMON ANDREWS TRAMWAY: horse-drawn service in summer 1899/1900 to 1906 (some use to 1911) from end of spur to Barmouth Viaduct to Gefn Ffordd on what is now A493 (C.C. Green, *Coast Lines of the Cambrian Railways*, Wild Swan, 1966).

VOLK'S Electric Railway. At Brighton. Op 4 August 1883 on; still open. (A.A. Jackson, *Volk's Railways, Brighton*, Plateway Press, 1993).

WANTAGE Tramway. Wantage Road (where it connected with GW services) to Wantage.

Op 11 October 1875; last passenger use 31 July 1925. (R. Wilkinson, *The Wantage Tramway*, Oakwood, 1995).

WOLVERTON & STONY STRATFORD Tramway. Op 27 May 1887; various closures, reopenings and changes of terminus; taken over by LNW; finally clo 4 May 1926. (F.D. Simpson, *The Wolverton & Stony Stratford Steam Trams*, Omnibus Society, 1982).

2: **Military lines**

Some were linked to the main system and could provide through services; others were self-contained, sometimes narrow gauge, lines, designed to take workers from a 'station' near a main line one to their place of work or to take personnel from one part of the site to another. Some ran to regular timetables, others provided occasional services.

Also see 6: Hospitals.

There was a complex systems of lines for munitions workers in the DORNOCK – GRETNA GREEN area, linked at several points to the main system *(see U, map p. 13)*. Also in this area was the ng line providing the Broomhills Ordnance Depot with an internal service.

There were many lines on and around SALISBURY PLAIN.

Branches from Dinton to Chilmark (ng) and Fovant (standard, opened 15 October 1915 – see *RM June 1919*). Heaviest use of Fovant was for demobilisation (ceased 16 January 1920) *(LSW)*.

Larkhill Camp (branch from near Amesbury). Porton Down. Main station linked by 2ft gauge War Department line to Trench Warfare Experimental Station here; daily workmen's service 1916 to ? *(LSW)*.

Winterbourne Gunner (ng).

various other branches on the Plain were perhaps used for troops.

BETWEEN SALISBURY PLAIN AND LONDON were lines at/to:

Blackdown Camp: branch from Brookwood via BISLEY CAMP (which see in Section 4), camps at Pirbright and Deepcut (to which military passenger services began 1 August 1917) to Blackdown Camp (December 1917); LSW worked from 8 August 1918; passenger services ceased 22 December 1918 *(LSW)*.

Bramley, near Reading (internal Ordnance Depot service).

Calshot (RAF) (F.W. Cooper, *The Calshot and Fawley Narrow Gauge Railways*, Plateway 1989).

Longmoor Military (Bordon to Liss, mainly a line for training army personnel to run railways) *(Melbourne)*.
Originally Woolmer Instructional Railway; did run regular passenger service Longmoor–Liss, last 31 October 1969.

Marchwood Military (near Fawley, Southampton) still operates service Mulberry Halt – Marchwood Jetty.

Winnall Down (near Winchester).

KENT had:

Chatham Dockyard (branch from Gillingham). Chattenden & Upnor.

Davington Light (Davington – Oare – Uplees, near Faversham) – see M. Minter Taylor, *The Davington Light Railway*, Oakwood, 1986 reprint; *RM May 2004, p. 21*).

Lydd Camp (branch from Lydd).

Manston Camp (RAF, line from Birchington); line inspected by BoT 22 August 1918. Early 1920s was Saturday passenger service to Herne Bay, with through carriages for London (presumably return service at end of weekend); line closed 'a few years after 1925' *(Marx)*.

Trench Warfare (branch from Slades Green). Woolwich Dockyard.

See R.M. Lyne, *Military Railways in Kent*, North Kent Books, 1983 (especially helpful for sketch-maps of lines).

ELSEWHERE, well scattered, were lines at/serving:

Bicester: passenger services Piddington – Langford Farm Halt (Bicester) until 1967. Through trains to Oxford May 1943 to winter 1959/60 and to London during WW2.

Bishopton, Royal Ordnance Factory: internal passenger service (narrow gauge) from Fullwood, near Georgetown station; 1940– ?; stations were Netherfield; South Crook; Rockbank; North Brae (R.N. Forsyth, *Back Track*, April 2005, p. 248–9).

Cairnryan (naval base near Stranraer); built between January 1941 and July 1943; trains ran from London Road Bridge at Stranraer to Cairn Point, stopping where needed (no stations); closed 1945 (G. Stansfield, *Dumfries & Galloway's Lost Railways*, Stenlake, 1998). However, A. Bell, *Stranraer in World War II* and Bill Gill, *The Cairnryan Military Railway*, both published by Stranraer & District Local History Trust, give details of stations at Transit (i.e. for military transit camp), terminus at London Road Bridge, and YMCA, about half-way along line. *U* also mentions stations (stops?) at Innermessan, Leffnoll North, Rubble Bank (northern terminus). Main use by passengers, who had to pay for travel, was to enable personnel working at the camps along the line to go to Stranraer at weekends. Service began in May 1942; not certain that ceased 1945 (D. Pedley)

Cannock Chase (Hednesford area).

Catterick (see Section 4).

Clipstone Camp (see Section 4).

Devonport Dockyard: last regular service, North Yard Extension No. 29 Store – South Yard Saw mills, ran

13 May 1966 (P. Burkhalter, *Devonport Dockyard Railway*, Twelveheads, 1996).

Draycott Camp (branch from Chiseldon).

Faslane Port (Naval base, branch from Shandon).

Fauld (RAF narrow gauge line, near Tutbury).

Lenabo (2½ mile line from Longside, GNS, to Airship Station. Latter built by Royal Naval Air Service during WW1. Probably provided passenger service for personnel. Closed about 1920) *(Aberdeenshire)*.

Long Marston (internal service at Ordnance Depot).

Melbourne Military *(Melbourne)*; see CHELLASTON EAST JUNCTION (Section 4).

RAF Cranwell (branch from Sleaford, sometimes using nearby Slea River Platform); original contractor's line replaced by permanent 1919. Built for Navy, later to RAF. At first used by workmen, later regular trains for servicemen, ended 1927. Later occasional through trains from main system, last 1953 for Coronation (D. Love, *RM October 2003, p. 32*; A.J. Ludlam, *The RAF Cranwell Railway*, Oakwood, 1988).

Shoeburyness (army firing ranges).

Spurn Head (coastguard and military).

The southern part of the Strabathie Light Railway (see under 5, below), from Murcar Golf Club to the Bridge of Don was used during WW1. The Admiralty took over the clubhouse for wireless use and railway was used to carry its personnel (until September 1920).

3: Lines used in dam construction

These, many narrow gauge, were built primarily to transport materials to sites. However, men building dams were often housed in hutted camps far from towns and villages so services were also run to carry workmen from camps to sites; in some cases there were also services to take children to school and wives to shops and markets. H.D. Bowtell wrote much on this topic and is main source for entries below: *Reservoir Railways of Manchester & the Peak*, Oakwood, 1977; *Lesser Railways of Bowland Forest*, Plateway, 1988; *Lesser Railways of the Yorkshire Dales*, Plateway, 1991; *Dam Builders' Railways from Durham's Dales to the Border*, Plateway, 1994; article, *Railways to Cowgill, Culter Waterhead and Camps*, Journal of Stephenson Locomotive Society, March 1971; *Reservoir Builders of South Wales*, Industrial Locomotive Society, 2006 (enlarged and prepared for publication by G. Hill).

By their very nature these services were subject to changes of route as the work progressed and were short-lived. Services are known for:

SCOTLAND

Camps: line from siding at Crawford [Cal]; no regular service for workmen (originally prisoners of war) since most lived at site; operated within period 1917–30. Letter from late Tom Jackson, who lived at Moffat, to Bryan Wilson, recounts how he met a couple of elderly ladies then living in Moffat who told him that they had travelled by train (sometimes on the engine) to yard at Crawford and then on to school. One's father had been a shepherd in the valley and the other's had worked on reservoir (her grandfather drove the engine).

Culter Waterhead (Motherwell & Wishaw Corporation Waterworks); pupils taken daily from here to Coulter school. Also A.K. McCosh (later a director of LNE) lived at Culterallers House near Coulter; he had use of engine and a wagon or two with seats installed to take shooting parties (usually Saturdays) up to Waterhead, whence they walked into the hills; line active within period 1903–07 (when line lifted – *Peebles*).

Talla (Edinburgh Waterworks); line from Broughton [Cal]; platforms for workmen at Victoria Lodge at proposed reservoir edge and Crook Inn; locals also allowed to use; work began on line 1895; passenger service withdrawn 28 September 1905 (date dam came into use); locals asked for line to be kept for their use – refused (G. Stansfield, *Lost Railways of the Scottish Borders*, Stenlake, 1999). Through specials Edinburgh to Victoria Lodge for stone laying ceremony 29 September 1897 (*Steam Days, December 2002*).

NORTHERN ENGLAND

Angram Dam site (a continuation of the Nidd Valley Light Railway) (see *Nidd*).

Blakedean (for Halifax Corporation; line from Hebden Bridge).

Brearey Banks and Roundhill (lines from Masham, for Leeds Corporation).

Catcleugh (Newcastle & Gateshead Water Company).

Derwent & Howden (from sidings at Bamford [Mid]). In May 1903 it was agreed that occasional trains would run from Birchinlee to Bamford for workmen and families; Saturday trips became a regular feature, still running in 1908.

Ewden Valley (Sheffield Water).

Geltsdale (Carlisle Water).

Kinder Dam site.

Langsett and Stocksbridge Railways (Sheffield Water).

Longdendale (Manchester Corporation); normally carried workmen and equipment between Bottom Yard at Tintwistle and Woodhead Dam at Crowden; Sunday School trips and special outings to 1939.

Royd Moor Reservoir (Barnsley Water).

Stocks Reservoir (Fylde Water Board).

Woodhead (Manchester Water).

WALES

Beacons site (from Cefn Coed, for Cardiff's water supply): work on building railway began about April 1886. Notice given September 1895 that workmen's train would be withdrawn, though work not finished until September 1897. Southern part of route used again for Llwynon Reservoir. Party to celebrate start of work travelled on line 28 June 1911; reservoir inaugurated 23 June 1926.

Elan Valley (for Birmingham's water supply). Passenger services ran to carry workmen to various sites and children to school at Caban Coch (see *RM August 1907, p.121*; C.W. Judge, *The Elan Valley Railway*, Oakwood, 1987).

Gwyne Fawre Reservoir Railway, running from Abergavenny: line laid February– September 1913. At first workers used road transport between Llanfihangel and Cwmyoy, about 1½ miles north; later rail through. Trains from Blaenycwm Village ran Tuesdays (wives on shopping trips to Abergavenny market), Thursdays (cashier to Newport) and Saturdays (men's recreation) (*RAC*). Dam inaugurated 29 March 1928.

Ystradfellte: line from Hirwain (Neath Reservoir). Work began October 1907; contract completed end 1914. Workmen's train from Hirwain to Penderyn taken on to site by contractors' engine – at least 6 second-hand carriages bought for this.

4: Colliery lines

Most of those listed below only provided services to take miners to and from work; some also provided services for children, whole families on Saturdays and even the occasional excursion.

NORTHERN ENGLAND

Ashington Coal Company: Regular passenger services available to all from Hirst (Ashington) to Linton Colliery and Ellington Colliery, last ran 15 May 1966.

Backworth Colliery: line to Percy Main carried miners and wives 1914 to 1918.

Brampton Railway: network of services on line from Brampton to Lambley; there were connections with the NE at Milton/Brampton Junction at the western end, and the Alston branch at the eastern. (J.N. Charters, *The Brampton Railway*, Oakwood, 1971; B. Webb & D.A. Gordon, *Lord Carlisle's Railway*, Railway Correspondence & Travel Society, 1978). Described as 'private railway, wrought by horse-power' (*PP 1*); paid passenger duty 1834 to 1842 (at least) (*PP 2*); sometimes shown as Hartleyburn & Brampton.

Low Laithes Colliery: colliery at Gawthorpe near Ossett,

connecting line to Flushdyke; colliery dates 1892–1928; 'it is said that' excursion trains were run on this line (J. Goodchild, *Images of England, The West Yorkshire Coalfield*, Tempus, 2003.

North Walbottle Colliery: line to Lemington.

Seaton Burn Waggonway: Gosforth to Hazelrigg Colliery.

Wallridge: Kirkheaton Colliery Co built 7 mile line from colliery (north of Hexham) to Darras Hall in 1927. Used for 1 mile passenger service (using old NB coach) from Kirkheaton to short platform serving miners' cottages at Wallridge. Colliery closed 1929 *(NE Express August 2006, p.102)*.

Waterloo Colliery near Leeds: Cross Green to Temple Pit (op ?; clo 22 August 1959).

Mountford mentions these in Durham:

Bowes Railway, for employees (p.62);

Chopwell & Garesfield – in November 1899 agreed would buy passenger carriage; not known if did (p.68).

Rainton to Seaham – 'according to one local source' Saturday only service along branch of Londonderry from 1831 to ? (line closed altogether 1896) (p.226).

Whittonstall – service ended 1961 (p.98).

Miners' passenger services operated on the Bridgewater or Central Railways of the Manchester Coalfield until the 1920s, using ex-North London carriages (G. Hayes, *Collieries & their Railways in the Manchester Coalfield*, Landmark, 2004); on p.164 there is a photo of one at Ashton Field's Colliery, north of Walkden.

MIDLANDS

Cannock and Rugeley Colliery Company: Hednesford to Cannock Wood Colliery.

North Staffs Coal & Iron Company: branches from Chatterley to Bradwell Wood Sidings and Talk o' th' Hill.

Whitfield Colliery Company: Greenhead Wharf at Burslem – Chatterley – Chell – Whitfield line; this also carried ordinary passengers in open wagons from 1887 to 1923 *(NS;U)*; see CHELL JUNCTION (Section 4).

The last three were all linked to the NS system.

Plumbley Colliery in Moss Valley, near Eckington, was connected to Mid just north of Eckington & Renishaw by 'the penny engine line' – named after charge for passenger use (in coal trucks); closed by 1909 (K. Grainger, *Scenes from the Past No. 43, Sheffield Victoria to Chesterfield Central*, Foxline, 2002, p.89).

Nailstone Colliery: used for Freemasons' Party from Bagworth to Nailstone Colliery 10 June 1909 (first-class ticket shown p.41 of M.I. Bray's *Railway Tickets*, Moorland, 1986).

SOUTH WALES

Blaensychan/Blaenserchan: to Talywain Navigation Colliery until at least January 1967.

Craig Merthyr Colliery: line to Pontardulais.

Tredegar Iron Company: Tredegar Yard to Ty Trist Colliery.

5: Other lines that carried workmen

AVIEMORE. Forestry workers taken to work sites from a yard near the south end of Aviemore station, 1917 to 1919.

BOWATER'S paper works. Workers' service began 1924, ceased from 30 September 1968: Sittingbourne – Kemsley Mill – Ridham Dock *(Course)*.

BROMBOROUGH PORT. Branch from Port Sunlight operated by Lever Brothers, 1 May 1914 to 1927; also used for centenary celebrations in 1988. (M. Lister, *The Industrial Railways of Port Sunlight*, Oakwood, 1988).

DOLGARROG LIGHT RAILWAY: linked station to aluminium works; by February 1917 operated free workmen's service along 1½ mile line; operated until about 1932 (see Industrial Railway Society's *North Wales*, p.241).

FAWLEY oil refinery. Passenger service from Jetty to Workshops; began before 1926; after 1945 ran only as required (source as Calshot, Military section).

HENDRE-DDU TRAMWAY: 1890s to 1939; quarrymen to/from Aberangell *(Mawddwy, especially photograph p. 96)*.

IRLAM soapworks. Branch from Irlam operated by Manchester Ship Canal Company, 9 January 1893 to 26 September 1959.

KINLOCHLEVEN: 'Pig Express' transported workers around site – Blackwater Reservoir, for aluminium smelting plant; photo suggests also used for showing guests around. Dates ? (B. Fairweather, *A Short History of Kinlochleven*, Glencoe & North Lorn Folk Museum, late 1970s?).

LINCOLNSHIRE Potato Railways. Many short lines in the Boston, Spalding and Epworth areas provided potato pickers with transport to the fields (S.S. Squires, *The Lincolnshire Potato Railways*, Oakwood, 1987).

LOCHABER aluminium works. Narrow gauge line from Fort William to Loch Treig carried workers from 1925 to after 1952 *(RM January 1929;* P. Howat, *The Lochaber Narrow Gauge Railway*, Northern Books from Famedrame, 1980).

MANCHESTER Ship Canal (Trafford Park Estate). Extensive internal system for moving goods about dock system; passenger coach took dockers from one site to another. (D. Thorpe, *Railways of The Manchester Ship Canal*, OPC, 1984).

OXFORDSHIRE ironstone quarries near Banbury; workmen's service, Banbury Penhill – Wroxton, ceased from 2 October 1967.

PADARN Railway. Slate quarries. Earliest workmen's travel was by 'velocipedes' – hand- or foot-powered machines. Earliest service started on or before 11 February 1892: the first slate train from the port end on Monday mornings stopped to pick up workers for Bethel and Pontrhythallt and the last train on Saturdays would stop to drop them. A regular all days, at own risk, service started in 1895 with stops at Penscoins; Bethel; Pontrythallt; Staba/Craig Dinas; Penllyn; Gilfach Ddu. Service ceased 8 November 1947. (S. Turner, *The Padarn and Penrhyn Railways*, D&C, 1975).

PENARTH Railway & Dock Company ran trains from No.4 Tip at Penarth to 'The Grange' for workmen and others connected with dock business. Service started before 26 January 1866, when there was a mention in *The Cardiff Times (RAC)*.

PENRHYN Railway. Slate quarries. Workmen's service began 2 February 1879; ended 9 February 1951 (Source as Padarn).

PETERHEAD ADMIRALTY: 2½ mile line from Peterhead Admiralty station to Stirling Hill; about 1884 to 1920. Government-owned line used for carrying granite to make breakwater at Peterhead Harbour. Work done by inmates of Peterhead prison, who travelled to/from work, with warders, on regular service of two trains each way daily *(Aberdeenshire)*.

REDLAKE Tramway from near Ivybridge into central Dartmoor for china clay. Took men to and from work. (M. Smith, *The Railways of Devon*, Ian Allan, 1983).

ROSEDALE branch. 27 March 1861 to 13 June 1929. As well as iron miners, carried railwaymen, families, schoolchildren, some local residents by goods train in brake van. Passengers on shopping trips were carried from Blakey Junction to Incline Top, walked the incline, train again to Battersby, then joined ordinary passenger trains. Children of workers at Incline Top taken to Blakey Junction and walked down to Farndale East where they went to school; they lodged the week with locals. (See *Rounthwaite*; R.H. Hayes and J. G. Rutter, *Rosedale Mines and Railway*, Scarborough Archaeological and History Society, Research Report No.9, 1977 reprint.)

SCOLE: built standard gauge from Diss by W Betts, owner of local estate, mainly for farm produce. Passenger use by parties of visiting students – temporary wooden seats in square wagons. In use about 1850–85. (Article by N.A. Brundell & K.A. Whittaker, *RM April 1955*).

STOCKSBRIDGE Railway. Line opened 14 February 1887 *(Return)* and passenger service provided from start. Workmen's service from Deepcar, bay platform at main station (but track not connected to main line) to Stocksbridge Lower Yard, mostly used by Fox's steelworkers and pupils of Penistone Grammar School;

these travelled free but others charged. Service ended 1931. (No passengers shown in *Returns* and, despite evidence, *Brad Sh*, e.g. 1916, said 'does not carry passengers'). See article by Martin Connop Price, *Railway Bylines*, April 2007.

STRABATHIE (alias Blackdog) Light Railway. 3ft gauge. Aberdeen area. Seaton Brick & Tile Co workmen from about 1900 to 1924 *(U)*; also see end of 3 (Military) for Admiralty and for golfers see Murcar Railway, under 'miscellaneous'.

TORRINGTON & MARLAND Light Railway. Description of formal opening, 5 February 1881 *(Trewman 9th)*, hinted at full public use in future, but in the event used only by workmen at Marland clay pits and brickworks. Part of route was later used for the Torrington to Halwill line. Visitors were sometimes allowed to travel on the line, free and at their own risk. One such journey was described in *Bideford, 1 June 1909*. On the way from Torrington, sacks on the floor of an empty wagon provided the seating; on the way back, boards on top of the load of clay. Item in the paper gives impression that permission for such trips was readily granted. Also see R. Garner, *The Torrington & Marland Light Railway*, Kestrel, 2006. Regular workmen's service Torrington – Dunsbear works and pit from January 1881 (before formal opening). From 27 July 1925 (opening of 'regular line') cut back to service from Dunsbear Halt, connecting with trains between Torrington and Halwill. Ceased ?

WEATHERHILL & ROOKHOPE Railway. Workers taken to Bolts Down. Operated by Weardale Iron Co.

WINCHBURGH Railway: shale workers 1900s to 1 March 1960 (see article in *Railway Bylines, Feb. 2004*).

6: Miscellaneous lines

HOSPITALS:

a) to Lancashire County Mental Asylum at Grimsargh, about 1889 to 29 June 1957 (last). Ran from Whittingham.

b) from Hellingly to Hellingly Asylum/Hospital, July 1903 to 1931;

c) HASLAR ROYAL NAVAL HOSPITAL, PORTSMOUTH: standard gauge tramway from jetty to hospital opened in 1877; carried patients and senior visiting officers. Propelled by naval personnel. Removed after 1918 *(Hosp)*;

d) JOYCE GREEN and ORCHARD: 4ft horse-tramway from LONG REACH, on Thames near Dartford, opened 1897 on. Patients brought by boat, then tramcars to wards. Originally all for smallpox sufferers, later Long Reach kept for these, others used for general infectious diseases. Orchard used for Australian troops during WW1. Converted to petrol-powered haulage 1925; decision taken to move patients by road

1930 *(Hosp)*;

e) Also see *Hosp* for information about ambulance trains and maps of Bulford, Codford and Larkhill (Fargo) in section on English Temporary Military Hospitals.

HYTHE PIER: (2ft gauge) line opened July 1922 for passengers on ferry to Southampton *(RM October 1929 and June 1980)*. Still open, primarily for ferry passengers, but visitors to pier (who have to pay toll) can use. No separate pier toll for ferry passengers. (E. Vaughan).

MARKETS:

a) occasional enterprising locals allegedly used Gorseddau Mineral Tramway (Portmadoc to Tremadoc) to carry produce part of the way to and from market *(NGSC 1)*;

b) Wissington to West Dereham Abbey Sidings, 1905 to 1919 ?, for Tuesday and Friday market trips to King's Lynn and Dereham.

PRIVATE ESTATES: to connect these to main lines:

a) Balderton to the Duke of Westminster's estate at Eaton Hall – item in *GW Mag July 1910* includes specific reference to passenger use by visitors to the Hall;

b) Blakesley to Blakesley Hall;

c) Roundway, near Devizes. Possible re-use of Caen Hill rails to give route bypassing Devizes for visitors to Roundway Park in period 1811–41 – see case made by Bill Crosbie-Hill, article, *The Caen Hill Horse Railway*, *RCHS Journal, November 2003, p. 362–3.*

d) Carstairs House Tramway – electric, built late 1880s by Joseph Monteith to link his house to Carstairs station; included six-seater passenger carriage; became horse-drawn, goods only about 1895 (see K. Turner's *Tramway Directory*).

SCHOOLS: Newton/Fayles/Goathorn Tramway (built to carry china clay) took schoolchildren to Norden, for school at Corfe, 1920–36 (R.W. Kidner, *Railways of Purbeck*, Oakwood, 3rd edition, 2000). One of clay wagons was adapted with seats and corrugated iron roof; local education authority paid 7/6 per day for this 'school train'. Also see T. Fairclough and E. Shepherd, *Mineral Railways of the West Country*, D Bradford Barton, 1975, which contains photograph (p. 90) of train being made ready in August 1935 for use of local scout troop.

SPORT and RECREATION:

a) Murcar Railway (previously Strabathie, which see under 'Workmen') for golfers; near Aberdeen; golfers carried on southern part of Strabathie, from their course to Bridge of Don, by arrangement with Seaton Brick & Tile Co, from 5 June 1909; at first Saturdays only, but all week-days by April 1910. Original Murcar Links Golf Club officially wound up 27 December 1917; reborn (temporarily without 'Links') March 1918. Seaton

Company went into voluntary liquidation June 1924 and golf club bought the southern part of the railway. Railcar withdrawn 31 January 1950, replaced by W.G. Pirie's taxi from 1 February. He sold taxi on 15 June 1950 so railcar back, last run 30 June 1950. (See article by A. Gordon Pirie, *Railway Archive 17)*.

b) line from Dalmunzie Lodge, in the Highlands of Scotland, for deer hunting, later hotel guests.

c) Pensnett Railway (west of Dudley):

Earliest uses: on opening day 2 June 1829, when called Kingswinford Railway, many official passengers were carried in 'carriages' and unofficial ones in coal wagons. In the summer of 1912 those attending meeting of The Iron & Steel Institute at Round Oak Steel Works were taken to newly-opened Baggeridge Colliery in washed-out coal wagons with clean straw on floor; Earl of Dudley and guests made occasional pleasure [sic] trips over parts of system. (W.K.V. Gale, *The Pensnett Railway*, Goose & Son, 1975).

Later, service for a few days over August Bank Holiday every year 1928 to 1937 for Himley Fetes held for Earl of Dudley's Estate work-people; joined train by temporary platform at 'The Wallows', then went via Barrow Hill incline, Askew Bridge and Baggeridge Colliery line to temporary platform at High Arcal, where line passed through corner of Himley Estate; intermediate stop on top of Barrow Hill. First year used mineral wagons fitted with benches; later South Wales colliery workmen's sets borrowed from GW. Carried free, at own risk but had to have tickets (headed Round Oak Steel Works, Ltd) so that numbers could be controlled; numbers varied from 4,050 to 8,968.

d) shooting parties on Nocton Fen.

e) Kerry Tramway: 2ft line built by J. Naylor to carry timber cut on his estates to Kerry [Cam]; about 1887–91 one wagon fitted so that family and visitors could be taken on picnics to New Pool or nearby hills (D. Cox & C. Krupa, *The Kerry Tramway and other Timber Light Railways*, Plateway, 1992).

f) also see Camps, under dam construction.

The following used public lines but nature of service makes it impossible to fit material elsewhere. There were occasions when trains were chartered to take spectators to illegal prize-fights. To try to evade authorities, no destination was announced in advanced and passengers were put down between stations, often near county boundaries so that if police of one county they could flee to another. More than 40 of these are listed in an article by G Guilcher in the RCHS *Journal, July 1986*. The Eastern Counties and the South Eastern seem to have been the principal participants.

Also see letter from A. Gray, *RCHS Journal March 1987, p. 53*, which added three others; his *SE* gives details of some instances of prize fights by rail.

7: Non-rail items

The Clearing House Hand-books included a number
of places shown 'P' which were not directly served by rail
but took passengers in close connection with rail services.
Below is a list of those so shown; since it merely provides
information from the Hand-books it cannot make any
claims to comprehensive treatment. The place-names,
with counties (sometimes abbreviated), are followed by
the names of the companies listed as connecting with
them, the overall dates they appeared and the points
from which the connections were provided. The earliest
possible date is 1877, when the Clearing House first
provided such information; unless otherwise stated
dates are inclusive (i.e. 1912–29 would mean that it was
included 1929 but omitted from the next book, 1938);
'on' means that the service was still shown when the
Clearing House ceased to provide it (last amendment
leaflet was issued in November 1964); xxxxa means
that the information was provided in an appendix or
amendment leaflet. The dates are those of appearance
in the Hand-books, <u>not</u> the actual dates of use.
The aim is to give a general idea of what was available
so the listing of a particular company or connecting rail
point does not mean that it was shown for the whole
period shown for the destination. However, in one set
of cases '/' is inserted; these places were originally shown
as served by the Highland Railway from Strome Ferry
and from 1904 on were served by three companies
from Oban [Caledonian], Kyle of Lochalsh [Highland]
and Mallaig [North British]. Some of the September
1957a items were summer only. The list is divided into
STEAMER, FERRY and ROAD services; the last
(very occasional) items were probably the result of
someone misunderstanding what sort of information
should be sent to the Clearing House.

Steamers

AMBLESIDE PIER Westmorland; [Fur];
1890 on; Windermere Lake Side [LNW];
1899a, 1910a 'cancelled'; Bowness

ARDRISHAIG Argyll; [BR]; September 1957a on; Gourock

ARMADALE Skye, Inverness; [High / Cal NB];
1883 on; Strome Ferry / Oban, Kyle of Lochalsh, Mallaig.

AULTBEA Ross; [High / Cal NB];
1877–1938; Strome Ferry / Oban; Kyle of Lochalsh; Mallaig.

BADEN TARBERT Ross; [BR];
1949a (no entry 1956); Oban, Kyle of Lochalsh, Mallaig.

BALMACAR(R)A Ross; [High / Cal NB];
1883–1938; Strome Ferry / Oban, Kyle of Lochalsh, Mallaig.

BLAIRMORE Argyll; [BR];
September 1957a on; Gourock.

BOWNESS PIER Westmorland; [Fur]; 1890 on; Ambleside.

BROADFORD Inverness; [High / Cal NB];
1877–1938; Strome Ferry / Oban, Kyle of Lochalsh, Mallaig.

BRODRICK ARRAN Bute; [BR];
September 1957a on; Ardrossan, Fairlie.

CAMPBELTOWN Kinyre; [BR];
September 1957a on; Gourock, Fairlie.

CANNA Inverness; [High / Cal NB];
1904 on; Oban, Kyle of Lochalsh, Mallaig.

CARSAIG Argyll; [Cal]; 1904 on; Oban.

CORRAN ARDGOUR Argyll; [Cal];
1904–38; Oban, Kentallen.

COWES IoW; [LSW]; 1904 on; Southampton.

CRAIGNURE Argyll; [Cal]; 1904 on; Oban.

CROGAN Argyll; [Cal]; 1904 on; Oban.

DUNOON Argyll; [BR]; September 1957a on; Craigendoran.

EIGG Inverness; [Cal High NB];
1904 on; Oban, Kyle of Lochalsh, Mallaig.

FERRY Lancashire; [Fur]; 1904 on; Windermere Lake Side

GAIRLOCH Ross; [High / Cal NB];
1879a on; Strome Ferry / Oban, Kyle of Lochalsh, Mallaig.

GLENELG Inverness; [High / Cal NB];
1883 on; Strome Ferry / Oban, Kyle of Lochalsh, Mallaig.

HUNTERS QUAY Argyll; [BR];
September 1957a on; Gourock.

INNELAN Argyll; [BR];
September 1957a on; Gourock, Wemyss Bay.

INVERARAY Argyll; [BR]; September 1957a on; Gourock.

INVERASDALE Ross; [BR];
1949a (absent 1956); Oban, Kyle of Lochalsh, Mallaig.

INVERIE Inverness; [Cal High NB];
1904–38; Oban, Kyle of Lochalsh, Mallaig.

IONA Argyll; [Cal]; 1904 on; Oban.

ISLEORNAY Inverness; [High / Cal NB];
1890–1938; Strome Ferry / Oban, Kyle of Lochalsh, Mallaig.

KILCREGGAN; [BR]; September 1957a on; Gourock.

KILMUN HOLY LOCH; [BR];
September 1957a on; Gourock.

KINLOCHLEVEN Argyll; [Cal]; 1910a on; Ballachulish.

KIRN Argyll; [BR]; September 1957a on; Gourock.

KYLEACHIN Argyll; [High / Cal NB];
1883–1938 and September
1957a on; Strome Ferry / Oban, Kyle of Lochalsh, Mallaig.

LOCH HOURN Inverness; [Cal High NB];
1904–38; Oban, Kyle of Lochalsh, Mallaig.

LOCH POOLTIEL Inverness; [Cal]; 1904–38; Oban.

LOCHALINE Argyll; [Cal]; 1904 on; Oban.

LOCHBUIE Argyll; [Cal]; 1904–38; Oban.

LOCHGOILHEAD Argyll; [BR];
September 1957a on; Gourock.

LOCHINVER Sutherland; [High / Cal NB];
1883–1938; Strome Ferry / Oban, Kyle of Lochalsh, Mallaig.

LOCHMADDY Inverness; [High / Cal NB];
1883 on; Strome Ferry / Oban, Kyle of Lochalsh, Mallaig.

LOCHRANZA ARRAN; [BR];
September 1957a on; Gourock.

LOW WOOD Westmorland; [Fur];
1904 on; Windermere Lake Side.

MILLPORT CUMBRAE Bute; [BR];
September 1957a; Wemyss Bay, Fairlie.

ONICH Inverness; [Cal]; 1938 only; Kentallen.

PLOCKTON Ross; [High];
1877–95; Strome Ferry. See Section 4 for station.

POOLEWE Ross; [High / Cal NB];
1883–1938; Strome Ferry / Oban, Kyle of Lochalsh, Mallaig.

PORTREE Inverness; [High / Cal NB];
1877–1938; Strome Ferry / Oban, Kyle of Lochalsh, Mallaig.

RAASAY Inverness; [High / Cal NB];
1879a–1938; Strome Ferry / Oban, Kyle of Lochalsh, Mallaig.

ROTHESAY Bute; [BR];
September 1957a; Wemyss Bay, Gourock, Craigendoran.

RUM Inverness; [Cal High NB];
1904 on; Oban, Kyle of Lochalsh, Mallaig.

SALEN LOCH SUNART Argyll; [Cal]; 1904–38; Oban.

SALEN MULL Argyll; [Cal]; 1904 on; Oban.

SCAPA Orkney; [High]; 1883 to 1894a 'cancelled'; Scrabster.

SCORRAIG Inverness; [BR]; 1949a (no entry 1956);
Oban, Kyle of Lochalsh, Mallaig.

SHIELDAIG Ross; [High]; 1904–38; Kyle of Lochalsh.

SHIELDAIG LOCH TORRIDON Ross; [NB];
1904–38; Mallaig.

STORNOWAY Ross; [High / Cal NB];
1877 on; Strome Ferry / Oban, Kyle of Lochalsh, Mallaig.

STORRS HALL Lancashire; [Fur];
1904 on; Windermere Lake Side.

STROMNESS Orkney; [High];
1883–94a 'cancelled'; Scrabster.

STRONTIAN Argyll; [Cal]; 1904–38; Oban.

TARBERT Argyll; [Cal GSW NB]; 1890 on; Wemyss Bay,
Gourock, Largs, Helensburgh, Greenock Princes Pier.

TARBERT HARRIS Inverness; [High / Cal NB];
1890 on; Strome Ferry / Oban, Kyle of Lochalsh, Mallaig.

TIGNABRUAICH; [BR]; September 1957a on; Gourock.

TOBERMORY Argyll; [Cal]; 1904 on; Oban.

TOTAIG Inverness; [Cal High NB]; 1904 to September
1957a 'delete; Oban, Kyle of Lochalsh, Mallaig.

TOTLAND BAY IoW; [LSW]; 1904 on; Lymington Pier.

ULLAPOOL Ross; [High / Cal NB];
1883–1938; Strome Ferry / Oban, Kyle of Lochalsh, Mallaig.

WHITING BAY ARRAN Bute; [BR];
September 1957a on; Ardrossan,

YARMOUTH (SLIPWAY) IoW; [LSW];
1890 on; Lymington Pier.

Ferries

ALLOA NORTH; [Cal]; 1883 only; South Alloa.

DARTMOUTH Devon; [GW]; 1877 on; Kingswear.

GRAVESEND Kent; [LTS];
1877 on; Town Pier from Tilbury.
1895 on; West, later West Street, later Car Ferry Pier from Tilbury.

HULL CORPORATION PIER; [MS&L];
1877 on; New Holland.

LIVERPOOL LANDING STAGE; [Birkenhead];
1904 on; Birkenhead. [Wirral];
1904 on; Seacombe & Egremont.
Both above shown from 1877 without facilities.

ROSHERVILLE Kent; [LTS]; 1877–1904; Tilbury.

SHEERNESS; [SE[; 1895 only; Port Victoria.

WOOLWICH ROFFS FERRY/TOWN; [GE];
1877–1904; North Woolwich.

Road transport

BOWNESS Westmorland; [LNW];
1904 only; road from Windermere LNW.

DINAS Pembroke; [Maenclochog];
1877 only; coach from Maenclochog.

KIRKWALL Orkney; [High];
1883 to 1894a 'cancelled'; carrier from Scapa.

BRUTE!

Passenger (rising politely). "EXCUSE ME, MUM, BUT DO YOU BELIEVE IN WOMAN'S RIGHTS?"

New Woman. "MOST CERTAINLY I DO."

Passenger (resuming seat). "OH, WELL, THEN STAND UP FOR 'EM!"

SECTION 8

Route diagrams and sketch maps

Since a complete and adequate collection of maps would require a major volume on its own, the aim here is to supplement basic information readily available elsewhere.

Route diagrams lettered A to G give a general idea of how selected main routes developed. The later, numbered, maps are intended to be used in conjunction with the text and Ian Allan's *Pre-Grouping Atlas*. Bear in mind that all are designed to show particular passenger routes and other lines are omitted. A flexible approach has been used, varied to meet the needs of particular items. Some maps show all the stations which ever existed in a particular area, even though all were not open together; some indicate all that existed at a particular date; some illustrate changes over time. Please note that the names shown may not exactly correspond with those in use at the time: the aim has been to make them as readily-identifiable as possible to the modern reader.

Different scales have been used to suit individual locations; north is generally at or near the top; a limited amount of distortion has been used for clarity. Most space is devoted to relatively early periods.

On the route diagrams thick lines show the original routes, thinner ones additions which provided shorter routes ('cut-off' lines). It should be noted that the dates provided for the latter are for when the section as a whole became available as a through route; parts were often in use earlier.

Services closed prior to the date given, or at a very early stage, are indicated by broken lines for routes and black infill for stations.

Airey and *Clearing House* maps have been used as the main basic source.

Much advice in the preliminary drafting was given by Stephen Bragg.

ROUTE DIAGRAMS

A   to Inverness
B   to Aberdeen
C   East Coast Main Line
D   LNW to London
E   Midland to London
F   Southern Lines
G   GW (southern portion)

SKETCH MAPS

1   Inverness
2   Arbroath
3   Elgin
4   Dundee area
5   Perth
6   Alloa
7   Aberdeen
8   Newtyle area
9   Dundee & Newtlye line
10   North of Forth Bridge
11   Falkirk
12   Paisley
13   South of Forth bridge
14   Manuel
15a   Glasgow 1860
15b   Glasgow 1914
16   Monklands and Morningside
17   Whithorn
18   Edinburgh & Dalkeith
19   lines to Leith
20   Carlisle; Maryport & Carlisle
21   Lowca branch
22   Eskett
23   Morpeth
24   Jarrow
25   South Shields
26   lines to Tynemouth
27   Newcastle and Gateshead
28   Consett
29   Sunderland
30   north of Wear Valley Junction
31   Bishop Auckland
32   Durham
33   Ferryhill
34   lines to Pelton
35   Hartlepool
36   Darlington
37   Northallerton

38   Thirsk
39   Stockton
40   Sand Hutton Light (table)
41   Rainton
42   Harrogate
43   Middlesbrough to Redcar (table)
44   Preston
45   Southport
46   Birkenhead
47   Liverpool
48   Wigan
49   Widnes
50   Warrington
51   Oldham
52   Manchester
53   Ashton-under-Lyne
54   Bradford
55   Dewsbury
56   Leeds
57   Sheffield
58   Uttoxeter
59   Ashover Light
60   Trent Junction area
61   Wigston
62   west of Leicester
63   Hull
64   Immingham and Grimsby
65   Peterborough
66   Wisbech
67   Kings Lynn
68   Thetford
69   Huntingdon
70   Cambridge
71   Felixstowe
72   Hatfield
73   Haddiscoe
74   Hertford
75   Wrexham
76   Welsh Highland (table) Portmadoc/Porthmadog
77   Ca(e)rnarvon
78   Festiniog
79   Glyn Valley
80   Llanymynech
81   Fishguard
82   Llanelly/Llanelli
83   Neath
84   Cardiff
85   Aberavon and Briton Ferry

86   Aberdare
87   Oakdale
88   Swansea
89   Newport
90   Taffs Well
91   Abergavenny
92   Caerphilly
93   Hereford
94   Cinderford
95   Gloucester
96   line via Wombourn
97   Stourbridge
98   Wolverhampton
99   Birmingham
100   West London Railway
101   Camden to Mildmay Park
102   Willesden Junction
103   Kew
104   Hounslow
105   London Bridge
106   Waterloo to Holborn Viaduct
107   Liverpool Street
108   Bow (east London)
109   approaches to Victoria
110   Wandsworth
111   West Cornwall
112   Truro
113   Bodmin
114   Plymouth
115   Exeter
116   Torrington to Halwill
117   West Somerset Mineral
118   Yeovil
119   Wells (Somerset)
120   Templecombe
121   Bristol
122   Malmesbury
123   Weston-super-Mare
124   Marlborough and Savernake
125   Bournemouth area
126   Salisbury
127   Stokes Bay branch
128   Fawley branch
129   Medway towns
130   Lydd
131   Thanet
132   Lewes
133   Dover
134   Folkestone Art Treasures

Route diagram A

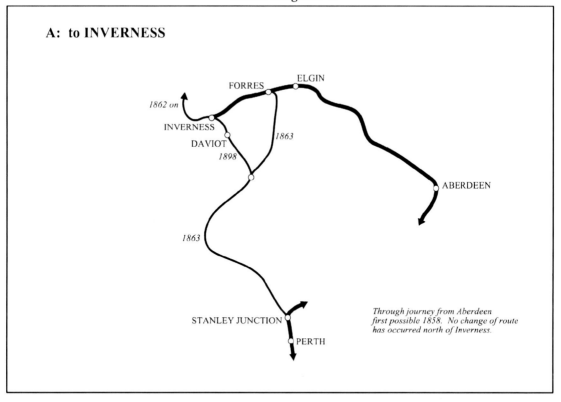

A: to INVERNESS

ELGIN

FORRES

1862 on

INVERNESS

DAVIOT

1863

1898

1863

ABERDEEN

STANLEY JUNCTION

PERTH

*Through journey from Aberdeen
first possible 1858. No change of route
has occurred north of Inverness.*

B: to ABERDEEN

North British ran from Dundee to Aberdeen via Friockheim from 1878 to 1883.

*** Note that Glasterlaw to Friockheim absent from IA since it had been closed by 1922.*

* *local use only*

ABERDEEN

BRIDGE OF DUN

FORFAR

GLASTERLAW
1883

FRIOCKHEIM

ARBROATH

STANLEY JUNCTION

DUNDEE *(d)*

BROUGHTY PIER

Ferry

TAYPORT

(b)

*1878
Tay Bridge*

PERTH

LEUCHARS

LADYBANK

THORNTON JUNCTION

STIRLING

*1890 via
Forth Bridge*

LARBERT

GREENHILL

(c)

BURNTISLAND

Ferry

GRANTON
(a)

GLASGOW

EDINBURGH

Berwick

Carlisle

THORNTON JUNCTION

Stirling

DUNFERMLINE

NORTH QUEENSFERRY

*This part of an alternative route was available from 1878 to 1883 in conjunction with ** apart from period when first Tay Bridge was in use.*

Ferry

SOUTH QUEENSFERRY

Glasgow

Edinburgh

All the thick-lined routes were available in 1848 except for the last two short stretches to Aberdeen itself, completed in 1850, and the direct route from Edinburgh to Larbert, also opened 1850. Travel from Edinburgh was possible earlier by using the Edinburgh & Glasgow (opened 1842) and changing in the Greenhill area.
(a) The Granton line originally used a separate station at Edinburgh. Service diverted to Waverley 1868.
(b) Initially Stirling – Perth – Dundee – Arbroath travel required road transport between stations at both Perth and Dundee. A through service at Perth was first shown in Bradshaw October 1862. The link at Dundee was provided at the same time as the Tay Bridge was opened in 1878.
(c) See supplementary map below main area.
(d) See map 4 for details of the Dundee area.

No diagram provided for southern Scotland since no material changes have occurred in the original Caledonian, Glasgow & South Western and North British main lines.

Route diagram C

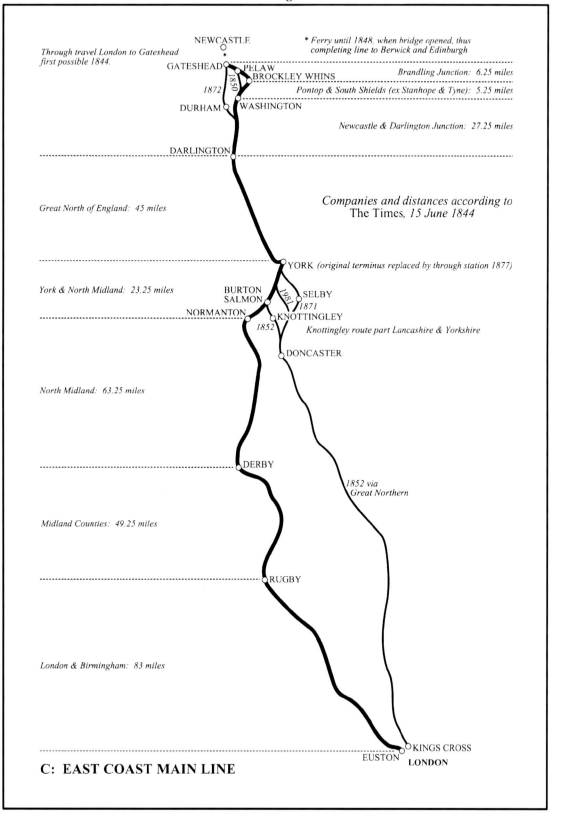

NEWCASTLE

Ferry until 1848, when bridge opened, thus completing line to Berwick and Edinburgh

Through travel London to Gateshead first possible 1844.

GATESHEAD

PELAW
BROCKLEY WHINS

Brandling Junction: 6.25 miles

1872

1850

Pontop & South Shields (ex Stanhope & Tyne): 5.25 miles

DURHAM

WASHINGTON

Newcastle & Darlington Junction: 27.25 miles

DARLINGTON

Great North of England: 45 miles

Companies and distances according to
The Times, *15 June 1844*

YORK *(original terminus replaced by through station 1877)*

York & North Midland: 23.25 miles

BURTON
SALMON

1871

SELBY

1871

NORMANTON

KNOTTINGLEY

1852

Knottingley route part Lancashire & Yorkshire

DONCASTER

North Midland: 63.25 miles

DERBY

1852 via Great Northern

Midland Counties: 49.25 miles

RUGBY

London & Birmingham: 83 miles

KINGS CROSS

EUSTON   **LONDON**

C: EAST COAST MAIN LINE

Route diagrams D and E

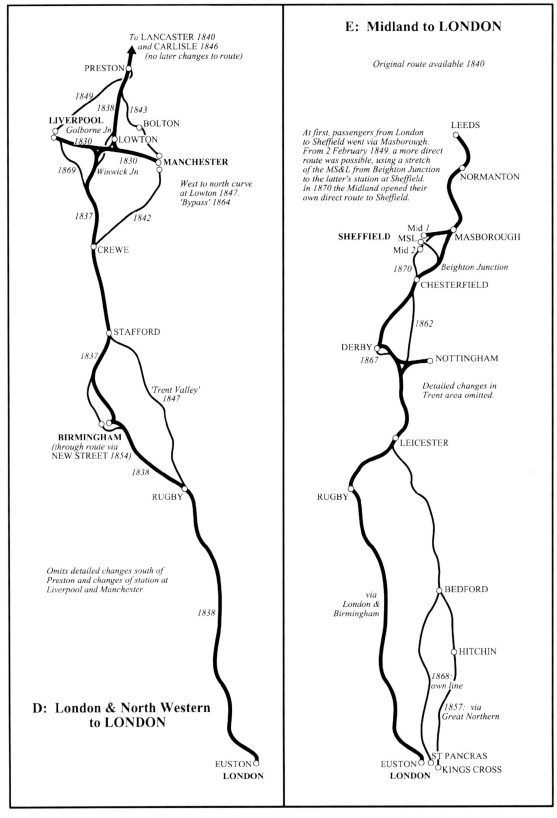

E: Midland to LONDON

Original route available 1840

To LANCASTER *1840*
and CARLISLE *1846*
(no later changes to route)

PRESTON

1849

1838   *1843*

LIVERPOOL
Golborne Jn   BOLTON
1830   LOWTON

1830   MANCHESTER
1869   *Winwick Jn*

West to north curve
at Lowton 1847.
'Bypass' 1864

1837   *1842*

CREWE

STAFFORD

1837

'Trent Valley'
1847

BIRMINGHAM
(through route via
NEW STREET *1854)*

1838

RUGBY

Omits detailed changes south of
Preston and changes of station at
Liverpool and Manchester.

1838

D: London & North Western
to LONDON

EUSTON
LONDON

At first, passengers from London
to Sheffield went via Masborough.
From 2 February 1849, a more direct
route was possible, using a stretch
of the MS&L from Beighton Junction
to the latter's station at Sheffield.
In 1870 the Midland opened their
own direct route to Sheffield.

LEEDS

NORMANTON

Mid *1*
SHEFFIELD   MSL   MASBOROUGH
Mid *2*

1870   *Beighton Junction*

CHESTERFIELD

1862

DERBY
1867   NOTTINGHAM

Detailed changes in
Trent area omitted.

LEICESTER

RUGBY

BEDFORD

via
London &
Birmingham

HITCHIN

1868:
own line

1857: via
Great Northern

EUSTON   ST PANCRAS
LONDON   KINGS CROSS

498

F: Southern lines

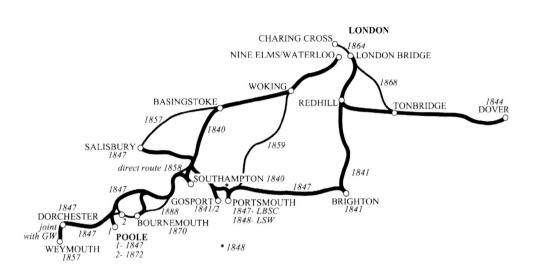

Direct running Dorchester to Southampton via Bournemouth first possible 1893 - details on map 125.

G: southern portion of Great Western

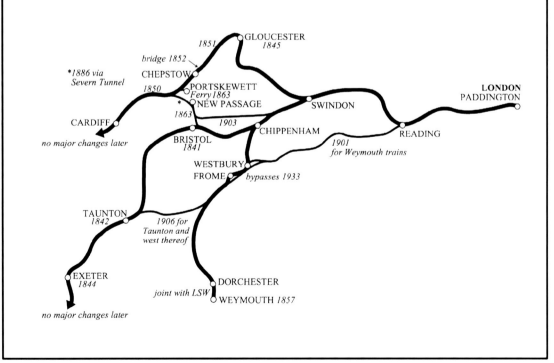

Maps 1 to 7

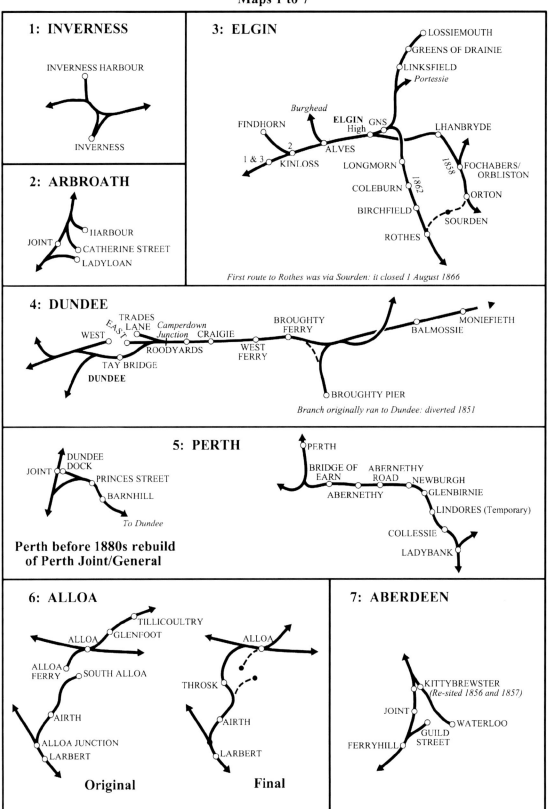

1: INVERNESS

INVERNESS HARBOUR

INVERNESS

2: ARBROATH

JOINT
HARBOUR
CATHERINE STREET
LADYLOAN

3: ELGIN

LOSSIEMOUTH
GREENS OF DRAINIE
LINKSFIELD
Portessie
Burghead
FINDHORN
ELGIN GNS
High
LHANBRYDE
2
ALVES
1 & 3
KINLOSS
LONGMORN
1858
FOCHABERS/
ORBLISTON
1862
COLEBURN
ORTON
BIRCHFIELD
SOURDEN
ROTHES

First route to Rothes was via Sourden: it closed 1 August 1866

4: DUNDEE

TRADES
LANE
EAST
*Camperdown
Junction*
CRAIGIE
BROUGHTY
FERRY
MONIEFIETH
WEST
ROODYARDS
WEST
FERRY
BALMOSSIE
TAY BRIDGE
DUNDEE
BROUGHTY PIER

Branch originally ran to Dundee: diverted 1851

5: PERTH

JOINT
DUNDEE
DOCK
PRINCES STREET
BARNHILL
To Dundee

**Perth before 1880s rebuild
of Perth Joint/General**

PERTH
BRIDGE OF
EARN
ABERNETHY
ROAD
NEWBURGH
ABERNETHY
GLENBIRNIE
LINDORES (Temporary)
COLLESSIE
LADYBANK

6: ALLOA

TILLICOULTRY
ALLOA GLENFOOT
ALLOA
FERRY
SOUTH ALLOA
AIRTH
ALLOA JUNCTION
LARBERT

Original

ALLOA
THROSK
AIRTH
LARBERT

Final

7: ABERDEEN

KITTYBREWSTER
(Re-sited 1856 and 1857)
JOINT
WATERLOO
GUILD
STREET
FERRYHILL

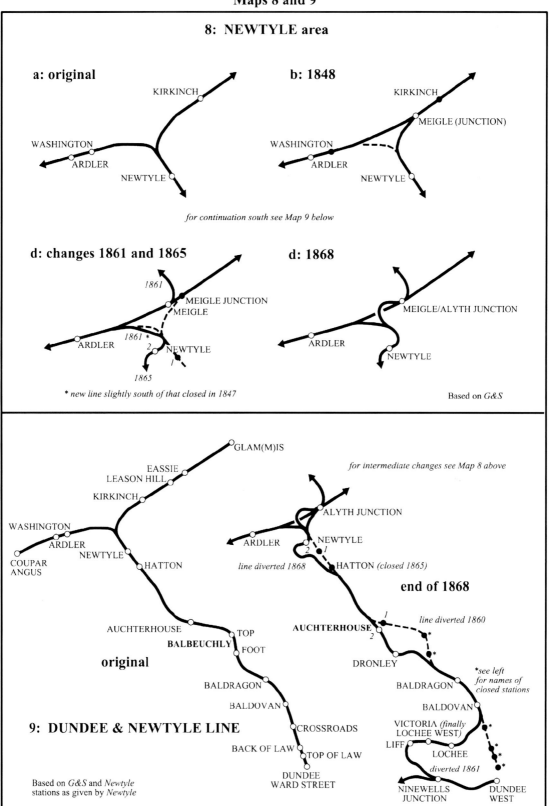

8: NEWTYLE area

a: original

KIRKINCH

WASHINGTON
ARDLER
NEWTYLE

b: 1848

KIRKINCH

MEIGLE (JUNCTION)

WASHINGTON
ARDLER
NEWTYLE

for continuation south see Map 9 below

d: changes 1861 and 1865

1861

MEIGLE JUNCTION
MEIGLE

1861 *

ARDLER
2   NEWTYLE
1
1865

* new line slightly south of that closed in 1847

d: 1868

MEIGLE/ALYTH JUNCTION

ARDLER
NEWTYLE

Based on G&S

GLAM(M)IS

EASSIE
LEASON HILL

KIRKINCH

WASHINGTON
ARDLER
NEWTYLE
COUPAR
ANGUS
HATTON

AUCHTERHOUSE   TOP
BALBEUCHLY
original   FOOT

BALDRAGON

BALDOVAN

9: DUNDEE & NEWTYLE LINE   CROSSROADS

BACK OF LAW   TOP OF LAW

DUNDEE
WARD STREET

*Based on G&S and Newtyle
stations as given by Newtyle*

for intermediate changes see Map 8 above

ALYTH JUNCTION

ARDLER   NEWTYLE
2   1
line diverted 1868   HATTON *(closed 1865)*

end of 1868

1
AUCHTERHOUSE   *line diverted 1860*
2   *

*

DRONLEY   **see left
for names of
closed stations*
BALDRAGON

BALDOVAN

VICTORIA *(finally
LOCHEE WEST)*   *
LIFF   *
LOCHEE   *
diverted 1861

NINEWELLS   DUNDEE
JUNCTION   WEST

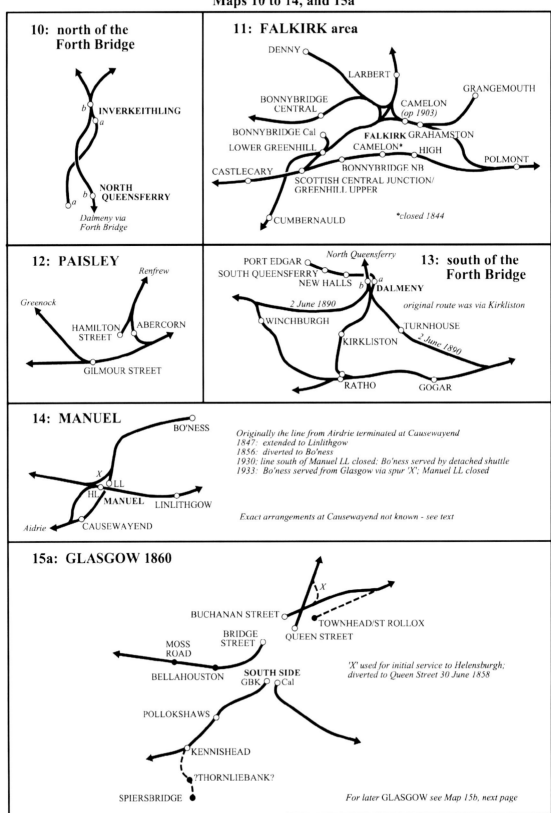

10: north of the Forth Bridge

b INVERKEITHLING
a

NORTH
b QUEENSFERRY
a

*Dalmeny via
Forth Bridge*

11: FALKIRK area

DENNY

LARBERT

GRANGEMOUTH

BONNYBRIDGE
CENTRAL

CAMELON
(op 1903)

BONNYBRIDGE Cal

FALKIRK GRAHAMSTON

LOWER GREENHILL

CAMELON* HIGH

CASTLECARY

BONNYBRIDGE NB

POLMONT

SCOTTISH CENTRAL JUNCTION/
GREENHILL UPPER

*closed 1844

CUMBERNAULD

12: PAISLEY

Renfrew

Greenock

HAMILTON
STREET

ABERCORN

GILMOUR STREET

13: south of the Forth Bridge

North Queensferry

PORT EDGAR
SOUTH QUEENSFERRY
NEW HALLS

a
b DALMENY

2 June 1890

original route was via Kirkliston

WINCHBURGH

TURNHOUSE

KIRKLISTON

2 June 1890

RATHO

GOGAR

14: MANUEL

BO'NESS

X
LL

HL
MANUEL

LINLITHGOW

Aidrie

CAUSEWAYEND

*Originally the line from Airdrie terminated at Causewayend
1847: extended to Linlithgow
1856: diverted to Bo'ness
1930: line south of Manuel LL closed; Bo'ness served by detached shuttle
1933: Bo'ness served from Glasgow via spur 'X'; Manuel LL closed*

Exact arrangements at Causewayend not known - see text

15a: GLASGOW 1860

X

BUCHANAN STREET

TOWNHEAD/ST ROLLOX

BRIDGE
STREET

QUEEN STREET

MOSS
ROAD

BELLAHOUSTON

SOUTH SIDE
GBK Cal

*'X' used for initial service to Helensburgh;
diverted to Queen Street 30 June 1858*

POLLOKSHAWS

KENNISHEAD

?THORNLIEBANK?

SPIERSBRIDGE

For later GLASGOW see Map 15b, next page

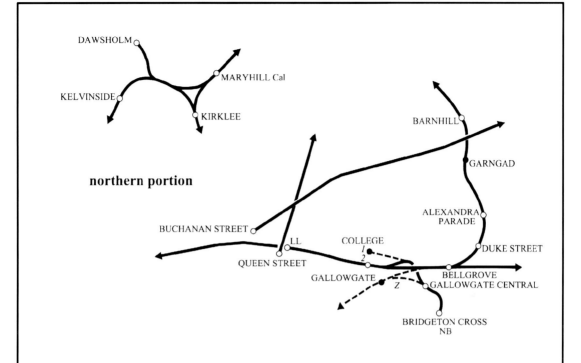

northern portion

DAWSHOLM

KELVINSIDE

MARYHILL Cal

KIRKLEE

BARNHILL

GARNGAD

ALEXANDRA
PARADE

DUKE STREET

BUCHANAN STREET

LL

COLLEGE
1
2

QUEEN STREET

GALLOWGATE

Z

BELLGROVE
GALLOWGATE CENTRAL

BRIDGETON CROSS
NB

15b: GLASGOW 1914

*Closed lines 'Z' mostly used for short-lived services
such as Greenock/Ayr/Ardrossan to Edinburgh
via Coatbridge and Bathgate, and St Enoch to Barnhill;
also workmen's trains.*

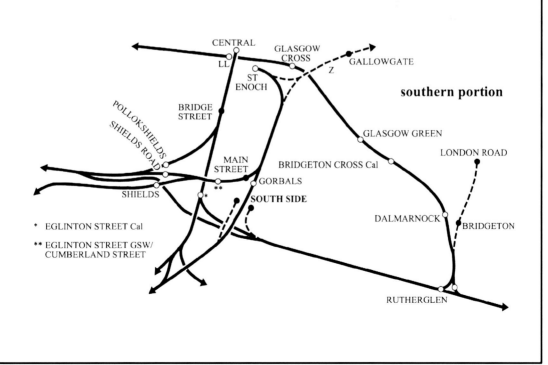

CENTRAL

GLASGOW
CROSS

GALLOWGATE

LL

Z

ST
ENOCH

southern portion

POLLOKSHIELDS

SHIELDS ROAD

BRIDGE
STREET

GLASGOW GREEN

LONDON ROAD

MAIN
STREET

BRIDGETON CROSS Cal

**
*

GORBALS

SHIELDS

SOUTH SIDE

DALMARNOCK

BRIDGETON

* EGLINTON STREET Cal

** EGLINTON STREET GSW/
CUMBERLAND STREET

RUTHERGLEN

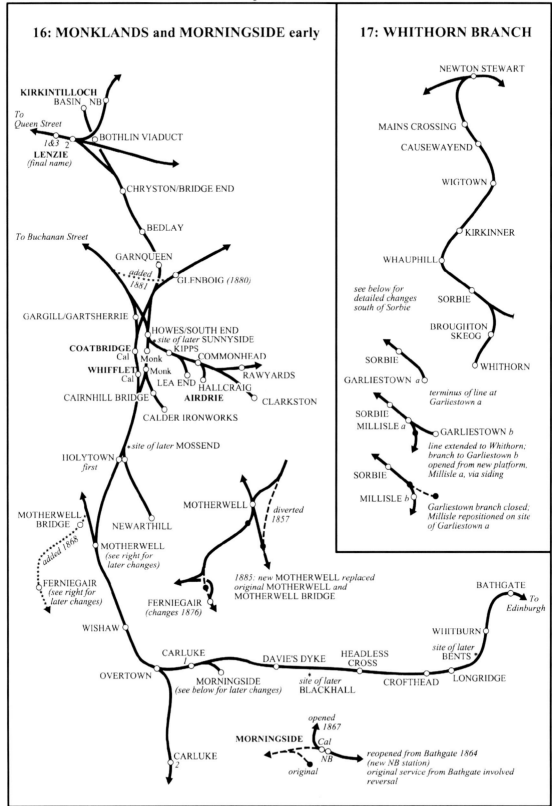

16: MONKLANDS and MORNINGSIDE early

KIRKINTILLOCH
BASIN NB

To Queen Street

1&3 2

LENZIE
(final name)

BOTHLIN VIADUCT

CHRYSTON/BRIDGE END

BEDLAY

To Buchanan Street

GARNQUEEN

added 1881

GLENBOIG *(1880)*

GARGILL/GARTSHERRIE

HOWES/SOUTH END
site of later SUNNYSIDE

COATBRIDGE KIPPS
Cal   Monk

WHIFFLET   Monk
Cal

CAIRNHILL BRIDGE   LEA END

COMMONHEAD

RAWYARDS

HALLCRAIG

AIRDRIE

CLARKSTON

CALDER IRONWORKS

site of later MOSSEND

HOLYTOWN
first

MOTHERWELL

diverted 1857

MOTHERWELL
BRIDGE

NEWARTHILL

MOTHERWELL
(see right for later changes)

added 1868

FERNIEGAIR
(see right for later changes)

FERNIEGAIR
(changes 1876)

1885: *new* MOTHERWELL *replaced original* MOTHERWELL *and* MOTHERWELL BRIDGE

WISHAW

CARLUKE
1

OVERTOWN

DAVIE'S DYKE

MORNINGSIDE
(see below for later changes)

site of later BLACKHALL

HEADLESS
CROSS

CROFTHEAD

LONGRIDGE

WHITBURN
site of later BENTS

BATHGATE
To Edinburgh

CARLUKE
2

MORNINGSIDE
opened 1867
Cal
NB
original

reopened from Bathgate 1864 (new NB station) original service from Bathgate involved reversal

17: WHITHORN BRANCH

NEWTON STEWART

MAINS CROSSING

CAUSEWAYEND

WIGTOWN

KIRKINNER

WHAUPHILL

see below for detailed changes south of Sorbie

SORBIE

BROUGHTON
SKEOG

WHITHORN

SORBIE

GARLIESTOWN *a*

terminus of line at Garliestown a

SORBIE
MILLISLE *a*

GARLIESTOWN *b*

line extended to Whithorn; branch to Garliestown b opened from new platform, Millisle a, via siding

SORBIE

MILLISLE *b*

Garliestown branch closed; Millisle repositioned on site of Garliestown a

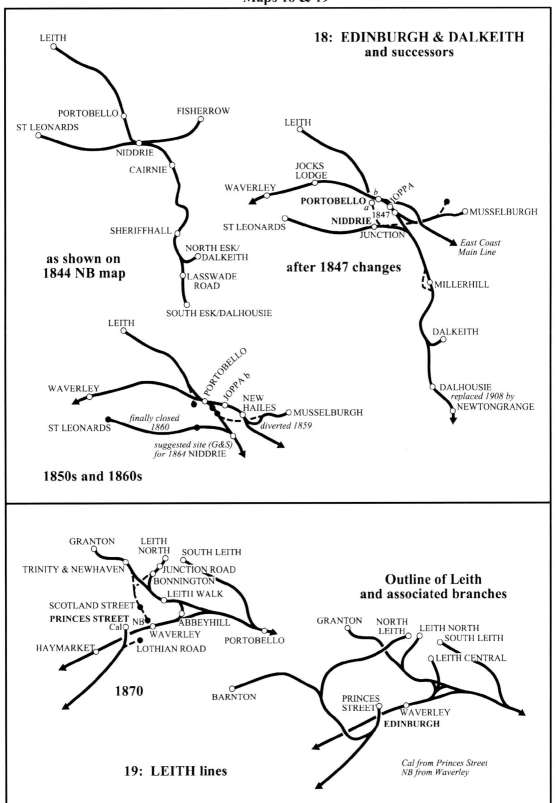

**18: EDINBURGH & DALKEITH
and successors**

LEITH

PORTOBELLO
ST LEONARDS
FISHERROW

NIDDRIE
CAIRNIE

WAVERLEY

JOCKS
LODGE

LEITH

b
PORTOBELLO
a
NIDDRIE
1847
JUNCTION

JOPPA

MUSSELBURGH

SHERIFFHALL

ST LEONARDS

NORTH ESK/
DALKEITH

*East Coast
Main Line*

**as shown on
1844 NB map**

after 1847 changes

LASSWADE
ROAD

MILLERHILL

SOUTH ESK/DALHOUSIE

DALKEITH

LEITH

DALHOUSIE
replaced 1908 by
NEWTONGRANGE

WAVERLEY

PORTOBELLO

JOPPA *b*

NEW
HAILES

*finally closed
1860*

MUSSELBURGH

ST LEONARDS

diverted 1859

*suggested site (G&S)
for 1864* NIDDRIE

1850s and 1860s

GRANTON
LEITH
NORTH
SOUTH LEITH

TRINITY & NEWHAVEN
JUNCTION ROAD
BONNINGTON
LEITH WALK

**Outline of Leith
and associated branches**

SCOTLAND STREET
PRINCES STREET
Cal
NB
ABBEYHILL
WAVERLEY
LOTHIAN ROAD
PORTOBELLO

GRANTON
NORTH
LEITH
LEITH NORTH
SOUTH LEITH

HAYMARKET

1870

LEITH CENTRAL

BARNTON

PRINCES
STREET
WAVERLEY
EDINBURGH

19: LEITH lines

*Cal from Princes Street
NB from Waverley*

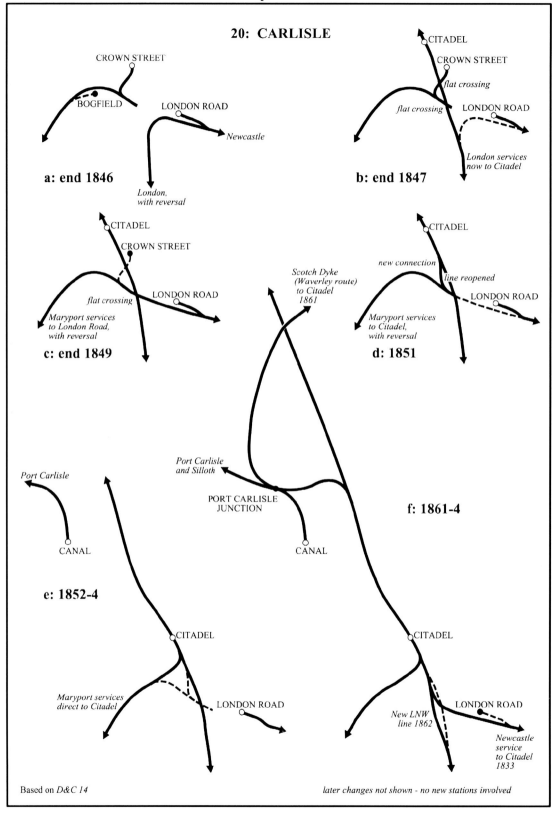

20: CARLISLE

a: end 1846

CROWN STREET

BOGFIELD

LONDON ROAD

Newcastle

London, with reversal

b: end 1847

CITADEL

CROWN STREET

flat crossing

flat crossing

LONDON ROAD

London services now to Citadel

c: end 1849

CITADEL

CROWN STREET

flat crossing

LONDON ROAD

Maryport services to London Road, with reversal

d: 1851

CITADEL

new connection

line reopened

LONDON ROAD

Maryport services to Citadel, with reversal

Scotch Dyke (Waverley route) to Citadel 1861

Port Carlisle and Silloth

PORT CARLISLE JUNCTION

CANAL

f: 1861-4

e: 1852-4

Port Carlisle

CANAL

CITADEL

Maryport services direct to Citadel

LONDON ROAD

CITADEL

New LNW line 1862

LONDON ROAD

Newcastle service to Citadel 1833

Based on D&C 14

later changes not shown - no new stations involved

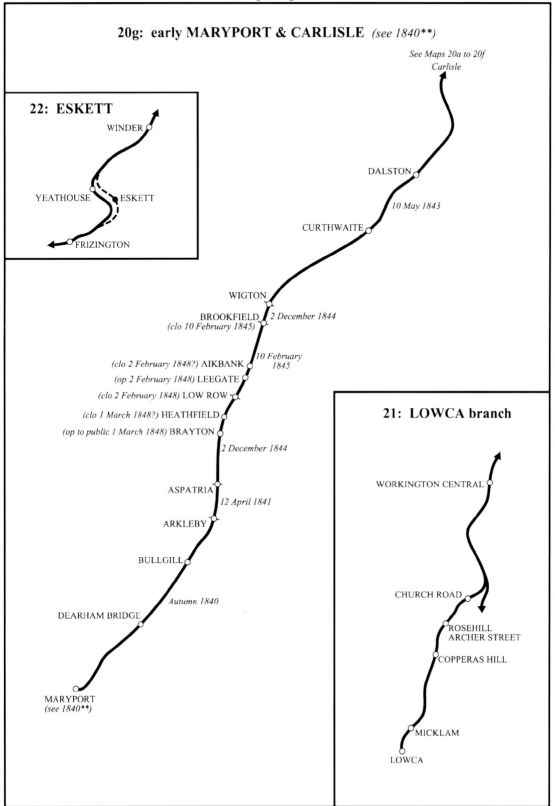

20g: early MARYPORT & CARLISLE *(see 1840**)*

See Maps 20a to 20f
Carlisle

22: ESKETT

WINDER

YEATHOUSE — ESKETT

FRIZINGTON

DALSTON

10 May 1843

CURTHWAITE

WIGTON

BROOKFIELD — *2 December 1844*
(clo 10 February 1845)

(clo 2 February 1848?) AIKBANK — *10 February 1845*
(op 2 February 1848) LEEGATE
(clo 2 February 1848) LOW ROW
(clo 1 March 1848?) HEATHFIELD
(op to public 1 March 1848) BRAYTON

2 December 1844

21: LOWCA branch

ASPATRIA
12 April 1841
ARKLEBY

BULLGILL

WORKINGTON CENTRAL

CHURCH ROAD

ROSEHILL
ARCHER STREET
COPPERAS HILL

DEARHAM BRIDGE
Autumn 1840

MICKLAM

LOWCA

MARYPORT
*(see 1840**)*

Maps 23 to 25

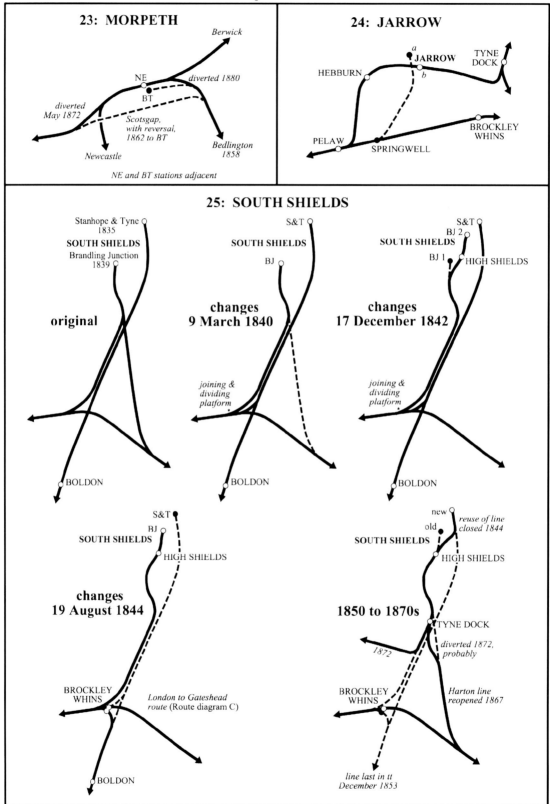

23: MORPETH

Berwick

NE
BT
diverted 1880

diverted
May 1872

Scotsgap,
with reversal,
1862 to BT

Newcastle

Bedlington
1858

NE and BT stations adjacent

24: JARROW

a JARROW
b

TYNE
DOCK

HEBBURN

PELAW

SPRINGWELL

BROCKLEY
WHINS

25: SOUTH SHIELDS

Stanhope & Tyne
1835
SOUTH SHIELDS
Brandling Junction
1839

original

BOLDON

S&T
SOUTH SHIELDS
BJ

**changes
9 March 1840**

*joining &
dividing
platform*

BOLDON

S&T
BJ 2
SOUTH SHIELDS
BJ 1
HIGH SHIELDS

**changes
17 December 1842**

*joining &
dividing
platform*

BOLDON

S&T
BJ
SOUTH SHIELDS
HIGH SHIELDS

**changes
19 August 1844**

BROCKLEY
WHINS

*London to Gateshead
route* (Route diagram C)

BOLDON

new
old
*reuse of line
closed 1844*
SOUTH SHIELDS
HIGH SHIELDS

1850 to 1870s

TYNE DOCK

1872

*diverted 1872,
probably*

BROCKLEY
WHINS

*Harton line
reopened 1867*

*line last in tt
December 1853*

Map 26

26: lines to TYNEMOUTH

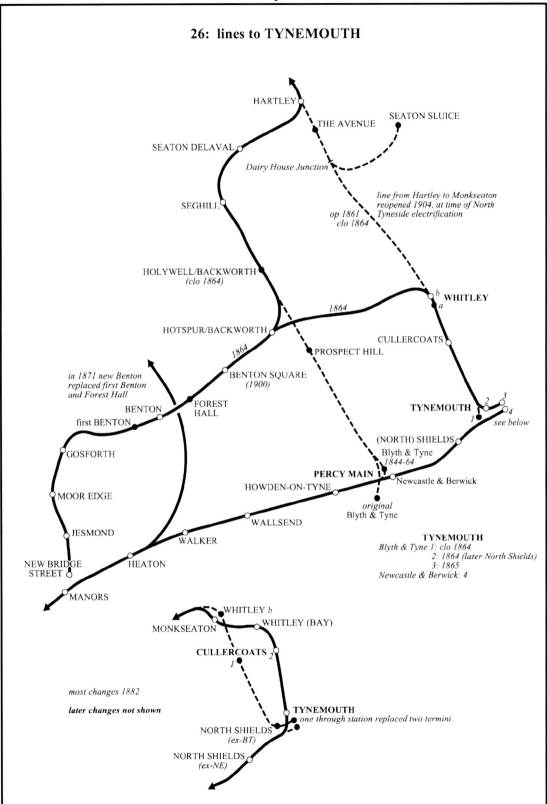

HARTLEY

THE AVENUE

SEATON SLUICE

SEATON DELAVAL

Dairy House Junction

line from Hartley to Monkseaton reopened 1904, at time of North Tyneside electrification

SEGHILL

op 1861 clo 1864

HOLYWELL/BACKWORTH *(clo 1864)*

1864

b **WHITLEY**
a

HOTSPUR/BACKWORTH

PROSPECT HILL

CULLERCOATS

1864

BENTON SQUARE *(1900)*

in 1871 new Benton replaced first Benton and Forest Hall

2   3
TYNEMOUTH
1   4
see below

BENTON   FOREST HALL

first BENTON

GOSFORTH

(NORTH) SHIELDS

Blyth & Tyne
1844-64

MOOR EDGE

PERCY MAIN

HOWDEN-ON-TYNE

Newcastle & Berwick

JESMOND

original Blyth & Tyne

NEW BRIDGE STREET

WALLSEND

TYNEMOUTH
Blyth & Tyne 1: clo 1864
2: 1864 (later North Shields)
3: 1865
Newcastle & Berwick: 4

WALKER

HEATON

MANORS

WHITLEY *b*
WHITLEY (BAY)

MONKSEATON

CULLERCOATS *2*
1

most changes 1882

later changes not shown

TYNEMOUTH
one through station replaced two termini

NORTH SHIELDS *(ex-BT)*

NORTH SHIELDS *(ex-NE)*

Maps 27 to 29

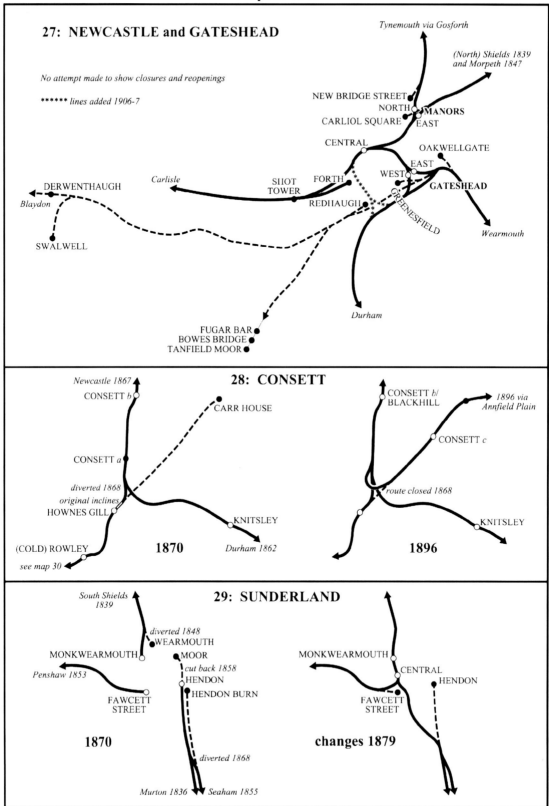

27: NEWCASTLE and GATESHEAD

No attempt made to show closures and reopenings

****** *lines added 1906-7*

Tynemouth via Gosforth

(North) Shields 1839 and Morpeth 1847

NEW BRIDGE STREET

NORTH

CARLIOL SQUARE

MANORS

EAST

CENTRAL

OAKWELLGATE

EAST

Carlisle

SHOT TOWER

FORTH

WEST

GATESHEAD

DERWENTHAUGH

Blaydon

REDHAUGH

GREENESFIELD

SWALWELL

Wearmouth

Durham

FUGAR BAR
BOWES BRIDGE
TANFIELD MOOR

28: CONSETT

Newcastle 1867

CONSETT *b*

CARR HOUSE

CONSETT *a*

diverted 1868
original inclines
HOWNES GILL

KNITSLEY

(COLD) ROWLEY

1870

Durham 1862

see map 30

CONSETT *b/*
BLACKHILL

1896 via Annfield Plain

CONSETT *c*

route closed 1868

KNITSLEY

1896

29: SUNDERLAND

South Shields 1839

diverted 1848
WEARMOUTH

MONKWEARMOUTH

MOOR

Penshaw 1853

cut back 1858
HENDON

HENDON BURN

FAWCETT STREET

1870

diverted 1868

Murton 1836 *Seaham 1855*

MONKWEARMOUTH

CENTRAL

HENDON

FAWCETT STREET

changes 1879

Maps 30 and 31

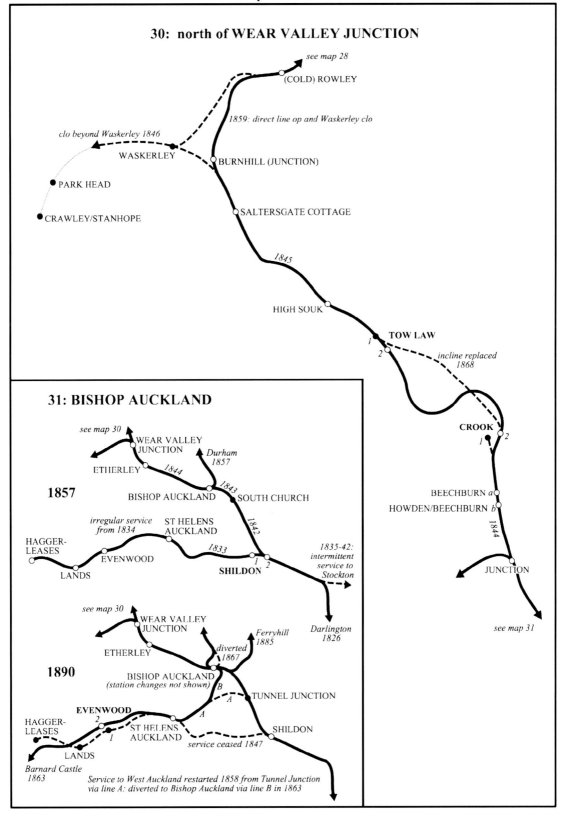

30: north of WEAR VALLEY JUNCTION

see map 28

(COLD) ROWLEY

1859: direct line op and Waskerley clo

clo beyond Waskerley 1846

WASKERLEY

BURNHILL (JUNCTION)

PARK HEAD

SALTERSGATE COTTAGE

CRAWLEY/STANHOPE

1845

HIGH SOUK

TOW LAW
1
2
incline replaced 1868

CROOK
1 *2*

BEECHBURN *a*
HOWDEN/BEECHBURN *b*

1844

JUNCTION

see map 31

31: BISHOP AUCKLAND

1857

see map 30

WEAR VALLEY JUNCTION

ETHERLEY

1844

Durham 1857

1843

BISHOP AUCKLAND   SOUTH CHURCH

irregular service from 1834

ST HELENS AUCKLAND

1842

HAGGER-LEASES

EVENWOOD

1833

1
2
SHILDON

1835-42: intermittent service to Stockton

LANDS

Darlington 1826

1890

see map 30

WEAR VALLEY JUNCTION

ETHERLEY

Ferryhill 1885

diverted 1867

BISHOP AUCKLAND
(station changes not shown)

B

A

TUNNEL JUNCTION

A

EVENWOOD
2

HAGGER-LEASES

ST HELENS AUCKLAND

1

A

SHILDON

LANDS

service ceased 1847

Barnard Castle 1863

Service to West Auckland restarted 1858 from Tunnel Junction via line A: diverted to Bishop Auckland via line B in 1863

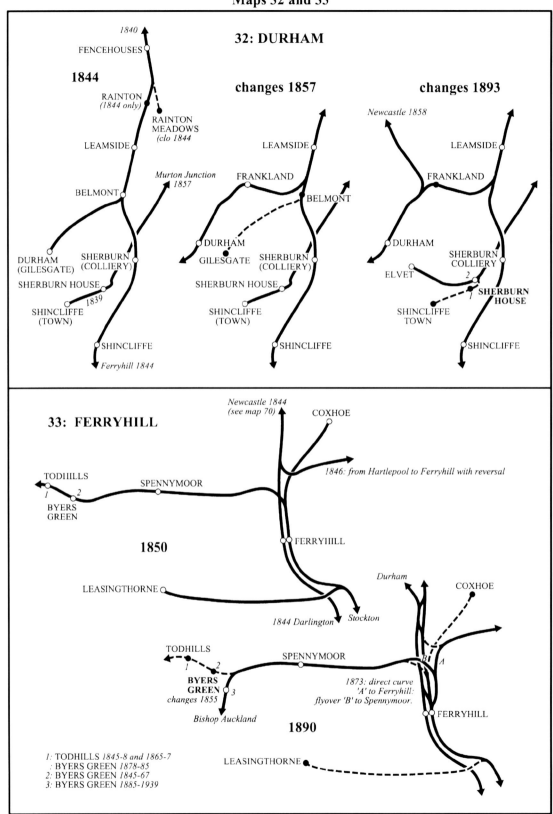

32: DURHAM

1844

changes 1857

changes 1893

1840

FENCEHOUSES

RAINTON
(1844 only)

RAINTON
MEADOWS
(clo 1844

LEAMSIDE

LEAMSIDE

LEAMSIDE

*Murton Junction
1857*

FRANKLAND

FRANKLAND

BELMONT

BELMONT

Newcastle 1858

DURHAM
(GILESGATE)

SHERBURN
(COLLIERY)

DURHAM
GILESGATE

SHERBURN
(COLLIERY)

DURHAM

SHERBURN
COLLIERY

SHERBURN HOUSE

SHERBURN HOUSE

ELVET

2

SHINCLIFFE
(TOWN)

1839

SHINCLIFFE
(TOWN)

SHINCLIFFE
TOWN

1

**SHERBURN
HOUSE**

SHINCLIFFE

SHINCLIFFE

SHINCLIFFE

Ferryhill 1844

33: FERRYHILL

*Newcastle 1844
(see map 70)*

COXHOE

TODHILLS

1 *2*

SPENNYMOOR

BYERS
GREEN

1846: from Hartlepool to Ferryhill with reversal

1850

FERRYHILL

LEASINGTHORNE

Durham

COXHOE

1844 Darlington   *Stockton*

TODHILLS

SPENNYMOOR

1 *2*

**BYERS
GREEN**
changes 1855

3

*1873: direct curve
'A' to Ferryhill:
flyover 'B' to Spennymoor.*

B   A

Bishop Auckland

1890

FERRYHILL

LEASINGTHORNE

*1: TODHILLS 1845-8 and 1865-7
: BYERS GREEN 1878-85
2: BYERS GREEN 1845-67
3: BYERS GREEN 1885-1939*

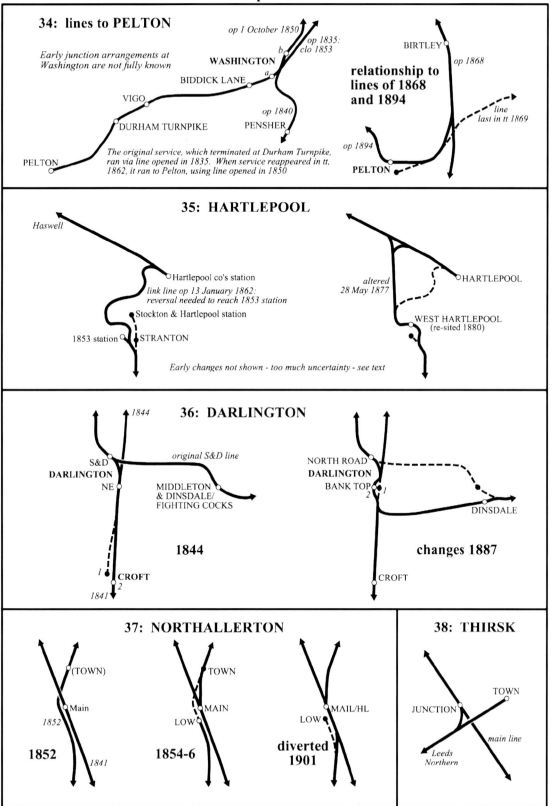

34: lines to PELTON

Early junction arrangements at Washington are not fully known

op 1 October 1850

op 1835: clo 1853

b

WASHINGTON

a

BIDDICK LANE

VIGO

DURHAM TURNPIKE

op 1840

PENSHER

PELTON

The original service, which terminated at Durham Turnpike, ran via line opened in 1835. When service reappeared in tt, 1862, it ran to Pelton, using line opened in 1850

BIRTLEY

op 1868

relationship to lines of 1868 and 1894

line last in tt 1869

op 1894

PELTON

35: HARTLEPOOL

Haswell

Hartlepool co's station

link line op 13 January 1862: reversal needed to reach 1853 station

Stockton & Hartlepool station

1853 station

STRANTON

altered 28 May 1877

HARTLEPOOL

WEST HARTLEPOOL
(re-sited 1880)

Early changes not shown - too much uncertainty - see text

36: DARLINGTON

1844

original S&D line

S&D
DARLINGTON
NE

MIDDLETON & DINSDALE/ FIGHTING COCKS

1844

1

CROFT

2

1841

NORTH ROAD
DARLINGTON
BANK TOP

1

2

DINSDALE

changes 1887

CROFT

37: NORTHALLERTON

(TOWN)

Main

1852

1852

1841

TOWN

MAIN

LOW

1854-6

MAIL/HL

LOW

diverted 1901

38: THIRSK

TOWN

JUNCTION

main line

Leeds Northern

513

Maps 39 to 42

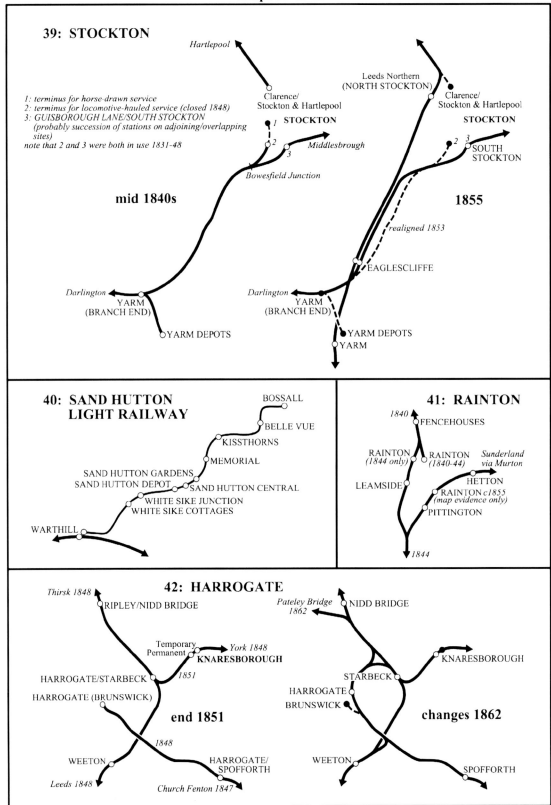

39: STOCKTON

Hartlepool

1: terminus for horse-drawn service
2: terminus for locomotive-hauled service (closed 1848)
3: GUISBOROUGH LANE/SOUTH STOCKTON
(probably succession of stations on adjoining/overlapping sites)
note that 2 and 3 were both in use 1831-48

Clarence/
Stockton & Hartlepool
STOCKTON
1
2
3
Middlesbrough

Bowesfield Junction

mid 1840s

Leeds Northern
(NORTH STOCKTON)
Clarence/
Stockton & Hartlepool
STOCKTON
2 3
SOUTH
STOCKTON

realigned 1853

1855

EAGLESCLIFFE

Darlington
YARM
(BRANCH END)

YARM DEPOTS

Darlington
YARM
(BRANCH END)

YARM DEPOTS
YARM

**40: SAND HUTTON
LIGHT RAILWAY**

BOSSALL
BELLE VUE
KISSTHORNS
MEMORIAL
SAND HUTTON GARDENS
SAND HUTTON DEPOT
SAND HUTTON CENTRAL
WHITE SIKE JUNCTION
WHITE SIKE COTTAGES
WARTHILL

41: RAINTON

1840 FENCEHOUSES
RAINTON
(1844 only)
RAINTON
(1840-44)
*Sunderland
via Murton*
LEAMSIDE
HETTON
RAINTON c1855
(map evidence only)
PITTINGTON
1844

42: HARROGATE

Thirsk 1848
RIPLEY/NIDD BRIDGE
Temporary
Permanent
York 1848
KNARESBOROUGH
HARROGATE/STARBECK
1851
HARROGATE (BRUNSWICK)
end 1851
WEETON
HARROGATE/
SPOFFORTH
1848
Leeds 1848
Church Fenton 1847

*Pateley Bridge
1862*
NIDD BRIDGE
KNARESBOROUGH
STARBECK
HARROGATE
BRUNSWICK
changes 1862
WEETON
SPOFFORTH

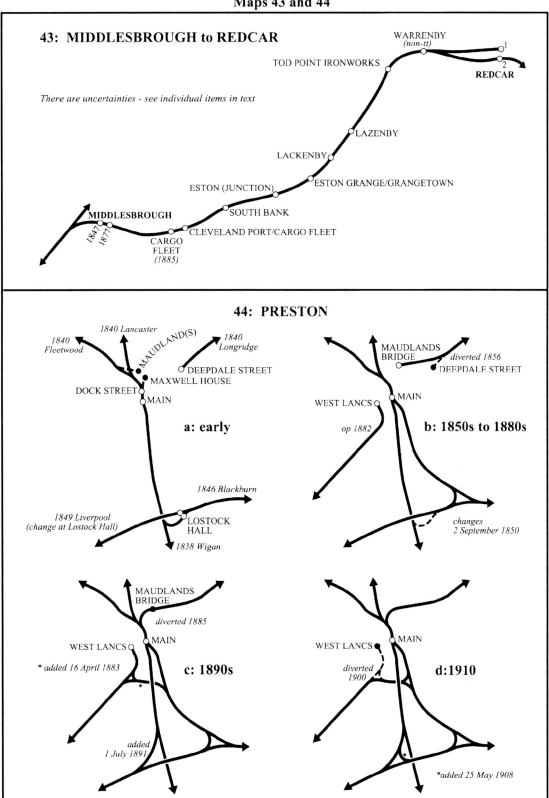

43: MIDDLESBROUGH to REDCAR

There are uncertainties - see individual items in text

WARRENBY
(non-tt)

1

TOD POINT IRONWORKS

2

REDCAR

LAZENBY

LACKENBY

ESTON (JUNCTION)

ESTON GRANGE/GRANGETOWN

SOUTH BANK

MIDDLESBROUGH

CLEVELAND PORT/CARGO FLEET

1847
1877

CARGO
FLEET
(1885)

44: PRESTON

1840 Lancaster

MAUDLAND(S)

*1840
Longridge*

*1840
Fleetwood*

DEEPDALE STREET

MAXWELL HOUSE

DOCK STREET

MAIN

a: early

MAUDLANDS
BRIDGE

diverted 1856

DEEPDALE STREET

WEST LANCS

MAIN

op 1882

b: 1850s to 1880s

*changes
2 September 1850*

1846 Blackburn

*1849 Liverpool
(change at Lostock Hall)*

LOSTOCK
HALL

1838 Wigan

MAUDLANDS
BRIDGE

diverted 1885

WEST LANCS

MAIN

* added 16 April 1883

c: 1890s

*

*added
1 July 1891*

WEST LANCS

MAIN

*diverted
1900*

d:1910

*

*added 25 May 1908

515

Maps 45 to 49

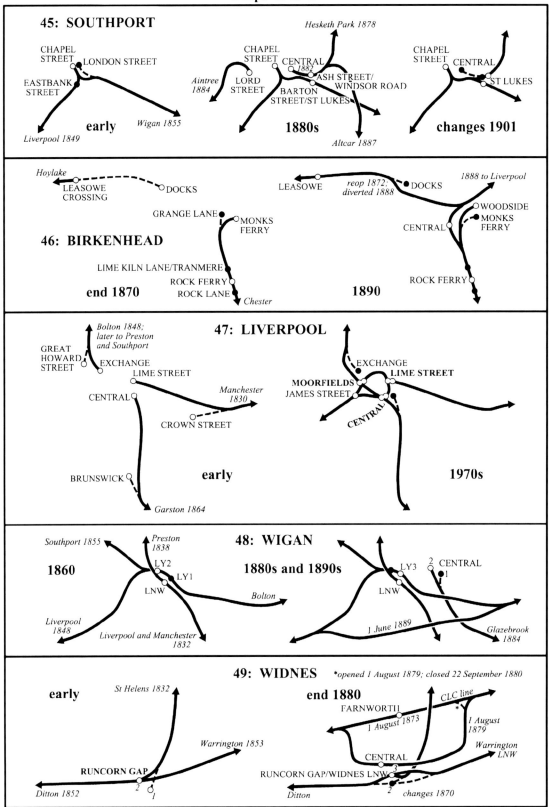

45: SOUTHPORT

CHAPEL STREET
LONDON STREET
EASTBANK STREET
Liverpool 1849
Wigan 1855
early

Hesketh Park 1878
CHAPEL STREET
CENTRAL *1882*
ASH STREET/ WINDSOR ROAD
Aintree 1884
LORD STREET
BARTON STREET/ST LUKES
Altcar 1887
1880s

CHAPEL STREET
CENTRAL
ST LUKES
changes 1901

46: BIRKENHEAD

Hoylake
LEASOWE CROSSING
DOCKS
GRANGE LANE
MONKS FERRY
LIME KILN LANE/TRANMERE
ROCK FERRY
ROCK LANE
Chester
end 1870

LEASOWE
reop 1872; diverted 1888
DOCKS
1888 to Liverpool
WOODSIDE
MONKS FERRY
CENTRAL
ROCK FERRY
1890

47: LIVERPOOL

Bolton 1848; later to Preston and Southport
GREAT HOWARD STREET
EXCHANGE
LIME STREET
CENTRAL
Manchester 1830
CROWN STREET
BRUNSWICK
Garston 1864
early

EXCHANGE
LIME STREET
MOORFIELDS
JAMES STREET
CENTRAL
1970s

48: WIGAN

1860
Southport 1855
Preston 1838
LY2
LY1
LNW
Bolton
Liverpool 1848
Liverpool and Manchester 1832

1880s and 1890s
LY3
2 CENTRAL
1
LNW
1 June 1889
Glazebrook 1884

49: WIDNES *opened 1 August 1879; closed 22 September 1880*

early
St Helens 1832
Warrington 1853
RUNCORN GAP
Ditton 1852
2
1

end 1880
FARNWORTH
1 August 1873
CLC line
1 August 1879
CENTRAL
Warrington LNW
RUNCORN GAP/WIDNES LNW
3
Ditton
2 *changes 1870*

516

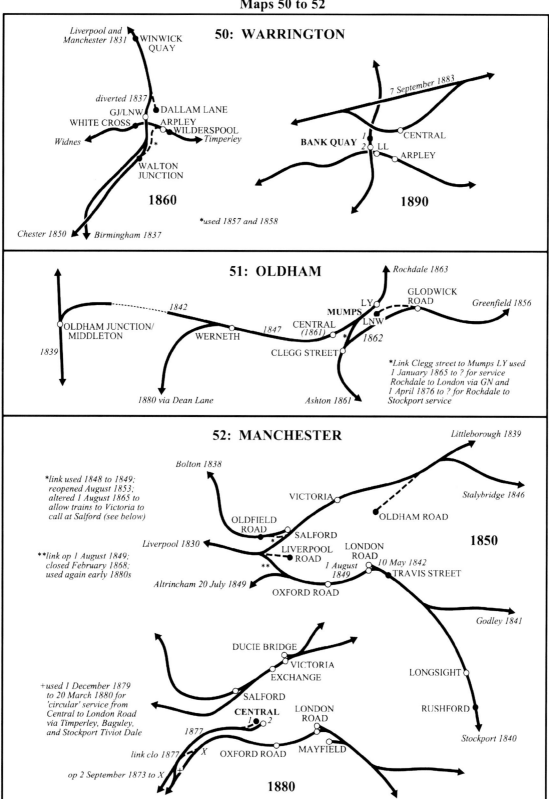

50: WARRINGTON

Liverpool and Manchester 1831
WINWICK QUAY

diverted 1837
GJ/LNW
DALLAM LANE
WHITE CROSS
ARPLEY
WILDERSPOOL
Widnes
Timperley
*

WALTON JUNCTION

1860

Chester 1850
Birmingham 1837

*used 1857 and 1858

7 September 1883

BANK QUAY
1
2
LL
CENTRAL
ARPLEY

1890

51: OLDHAM

Rochdale 1863

LY
GLODWICK ROAD
Greenfield 1856
1842
MUMPS
CENTRAL (1861)
LNW
OLDHAM JUNCTION/ MIDDLETON
WERNETH
1847
1862
1839
CLEGG STREET

1880 via Dean Lane
Ashton 1861

*Link Clegg street to Mumps LY used
1 January 1865 to ? for service
Rochdale to London via GN and
1 April 1876 to ? for Rochdale to
Stockport service

52: MANCHESTER

Littleborough 1839

*link used 1848 to 1849;
reopened August 1853;
altered 1 August 1865 to
allow trains to Victoria to
call at Salford (see below)*

Bolton 1838
VICTORIA
OLDFIELD ROAD
OLDHAM ROAD
Stalybridge 1846

SALFORD
Liverpool 1830
LIVERPOOL ROAD
LONDON ROAD
1850

**link op 1 August 1849;
closed February 1868;
used again early 1880s

1 August 1849
10 May 1842
TRAVIS STREET
Altrincham 20 July 1849
OXFORD ROAD
Godley 1841

DUCIE BRIDGE
VICTORIA
EXCHANGE
LONGSIGHT
+used 1 December 1879
to 20 March 1880 for
'circular' service from
Central to London Road
via Timperley, Baguley,
and Stockport Tiviot Dale
SALFORD
RUSHFORD
CENTRAL
1
2
LONDON ROAD
1877
X
Stockport 1840
link clo 1877
OXFORD ROAD
MAYFIELD
op 2 September 1873 to X
+
1880

Maps 53 to 55

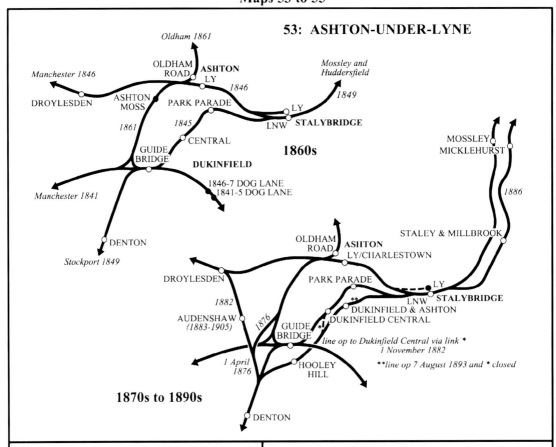

53: ASHTON-UNDER-LYNE

Oldham 1861

Manchester 1846

OLDHAM ROAD · **ASHTON LY** · *1846*

Mossley and Huddersfield

DROYLESDEN

ASHTON MOSS

PARK PARADE

1849

LY · LNW · **STALYBRIDGE**

1861

1845

○ CENTRAL

1860s

MOSSLEY MICKLEHURST

GUIDE BRIDGE

DUKINFIELD

Manchester 1841

1846-7 DOG LANE
1841-5 DOG LANE

1886

STALEY & MILLBROOK

○ DENTON

Stockport 1849

OLDHAM ROAD · **ASHTON LY/CHARLESTOWN**

DROYLESDEN

PARK PARADE

LY · LNW · **STALYBRIDGE**

1882

AUDENSHAW
(1883-1905)

1876

GUIDE BRIDGE

DUKINFIELD & ASHTON
DUKINFIELD CENTRAL

*line op to Dukinfield Central via link ** *
1 November 1882

1 April 1876

HOOLEY HILL

***line op 7 August 1893 and * closed*

1870s to 1890s

○ DENTON

54: BRADFORD

1846 Leeds via Shipley Keighley 1847

○ MARKET STREET

1854 Leeds via Bramley

EXCHANGE ○ · ○ ADOLPHUS STREET

1854

Minor re-siting ignored

1855

1850 Mirfield

MARKET STREET/
○ FORSTER SQUARE

EXCHANGE ○ · ○ ADOLPHUS STREET

ST DUNSTANS · ● BOWLING

Thornton 1878

1880

BOWLING JUNCTION

55: DEWSBURY

Leeds 1848

LNW

Heckmondwike 1869

DEWSBURY · ○ MARKET PLACE

1867

1870

THORNHILL

Sowerby Bridge 1840

Normanton 1840

BATLEY ○ GN
LNW

line op 1864: clo 1909

1914

LNW/
WELLINGTON ROAD ○ · GN 2

DEWSBURY · ○ MARKET PLACE

CHICKENLEY HEATH

GN 1 · *1874*

line op 1 December 1893

THORNHILL

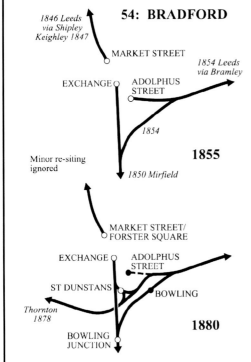
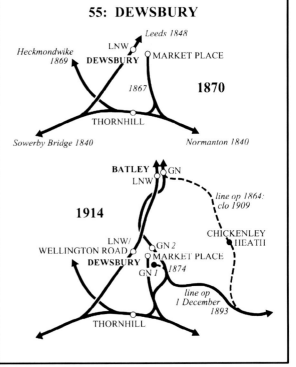

Map 56

56: LEEDS

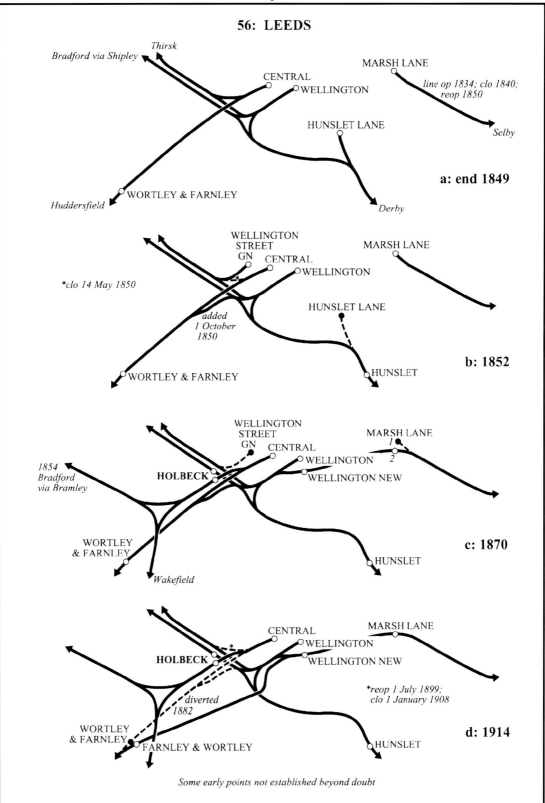

a: end 1849

Bradford via Shipley
Thirsk
CENTRAL
WELLINGTON
MARSH LANE
line op 1834; clo 1840; reop 1850
HUNSLET LANE
Selby
WORTLEY & FARNLEY
Huddersfield
Derby

b: 1852

WELLINGTON STREET GN
CENTRAL
WELLINGTON
MARSH LANE
*clo 14 May 1850
HUNSLET LANE
added 1 October 1850
WORTLEY & FARNLEY
HUNSLET

c: 1870

WELLINGTON STREET GN
CENTRAL
WELLINGTON
MARSH LANE
1
2
WELLINGTON NEW
1854 Bradford via Bramley
HOLBECK
WORTLEY & FARNLEY
Wakefield
HUNSLET

d: 1914

CENTRAL
WELLINGTON
MARSH LANE
HOLBECK
WELLINGTON NEW
*reop 1 July 1899; clo 1 January 1908
diverted 1882
WORTLEY & FARNLEY
FARNLEY & WORTLEY
HUNSLET

Some early points not established beyond doubt

Maps 57 to 62

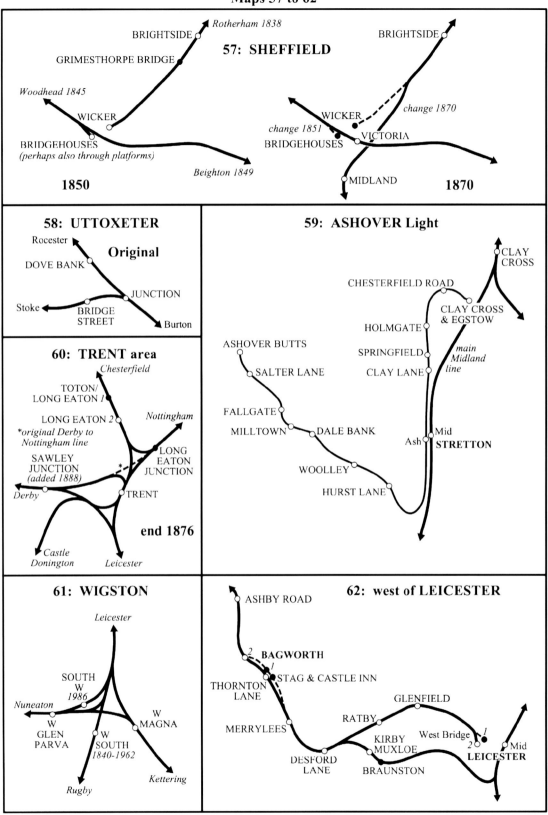

57: SHEFFIELD

Rotherham 1838
BRIGHTSIDE
GRIMESTHORPE BRIDGE
Woodhead 1845
WICKER
BRIDGEHOUSES
(perhaps also through platforms)
Beighton 1849
1850

BRIGHTSIDE
change 1870
WICKER
change 1851
BRIDGEHOUSES
VICTORIA
MIDLAND
1870

58: UTTOXETER

Original
Rocester
DOVE BANK
JUNCTION
Stoke
BRIDGE STREET
Burton

59: ASHOVER Light

CLAY CROSS
CHESTERFIELD ROAD
CLAY CROSS & EGSTOW
HOLMGATE
main Midland line
SPRINGFIELD
ASHOVER BUTTS
CLAY LANE
SALTER LANE
FALLGATE
MILLTOWN
DALE BANK
Ash Mid
STRETTON
WOOLLEY
HURST LANE

60: TRENT area

Chesterfield
TOTON/ LONG EATON 1
LONG EATON 2
Nottingham
original Derby to Nottingham line
SAWLEY JUNCTION *(added 1888)*
LONG EATON JUNCTION
Derby
TRENT
end 1876
Castle Donington
Leicester

61: WIGSTON

Leicester
SOUTH W 1986
Nuneaton
W GLEN PARVA
W MAGNA
W SOUTH 1840-1962
Rugby
Kettering

62: west of LEICESTER

ASHBY ROAD
2 BAGWORTH
1 STAG & CASTLE INN
THORNTON LANE
GLENFIELD
RATBY
MERRYLEES
KIRBY MUXLOE
West Bridge 1
2 Mid
LEICESTER
DESFORD LANE
BRAUNSTON

Maps 63 to 65

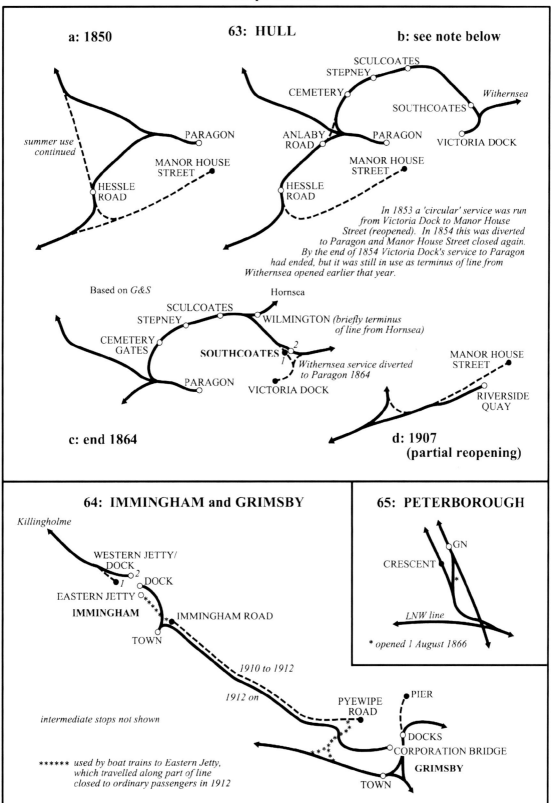

63: HULL

a: 1850

b: see note below

SCULCOATES
STEPNEY
CEMETERY
ANLABY
ROAD
PARAGON
MANOR HOUSE
STREET
HESSLE
ROAD
SOUTHCOATES
VICTORIA DOCK
Withernsea

PARAGON
MANOR HOUSE
STREET
summer use continued
HESSLE
ROAD

In 1853 a 'circular' service was run from Victoria Dock to Manor House Street (reopened). In 1854 this was diverted to Paragon and Manor House Street closed again. By the end of 1854 Victoria Dock's service to Paragon had ended, but it was still in use as terminus of line from Withernsea opened earlier that year.

Based on *G&S*

Hornsea
SCULCOATES
STEPNEY
CEMETERY
GATES
WILMINGTON *(briefly terminus of line from Hornsea)*
SOUTHCOATES
PARAGON
Withernsea service diverted to Paragon 1864
VICTORIA DOCK

MANOR HOUSE
STREET
RIVERSIDE
QUAY

c: end 1864

d: 1907 (partial reopening)

64: IMMINGHAM and GRIMSBY

Killingholme
WESTERN JETTY/
DOCK
DOCK
EASTERN JETTY
IMMINGHAM
TOWN
IMMINGHAM ROAD
1910 to 1912
1912 on

intermediate stops not shown

****** *used by boat trains to Eastern Jetty, which travelled along part of line closed to ordinary passengers in 1912*

PYEWIPE
ROAD
PIER
DOCKS
CORPORATION BRIDGE
GRIMSBY
TOWN

65: PETERBOROUGH

GN
CRESCENT
LNW line

* *opened 1 August 1866*

Maps 66 to 71

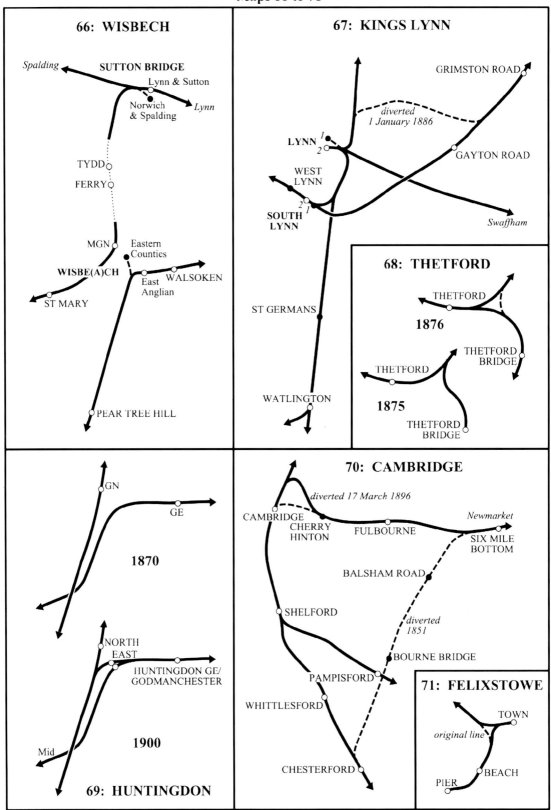

66: WISBECH

Spalding

SUTTON BRIDGE

Lynn & Sutton

Norwich & Spalding

Lynn

TYDD

FERRY

MGN

Eastern Counties

WISBE(A)CH

East Anglian

WALSOKEN

ST MARY

PEAR TREE HILL

67: KINGS LYNN

GRIMSTON ROAD

diverted 1 January 1886

LYNN 1 2

GAYTON ROAD

WEST LYNN

2 1

SOUTH LYNN

Swaffham

ST GERMANS

WATLINGTON

68: THETFORD

THETFORD

1876

THETFORD BRIDGE

THETFORD

1875

THETFORD BRIDGE

70: CAMBRIDGE

diverted 17 March 1896

CAMBRIDGE

CHERRY HINTON

FULBOURNE

Newmarket

SIX MILE BOTTOM

BALSHAM ROAD

SHELFORD

diverted 1851

BOURNE BRIDGE

PAMPISFORD

WHITTLESFORD

CHESTERFORD

71: FELIXSTOWE

TOWN

original line

BEACH

PIER

GN

GE

1870

NORTH EAST

HUNTINGDON GE/ GODMANCHESTER

Mid

1900

69: HUNTINGDON

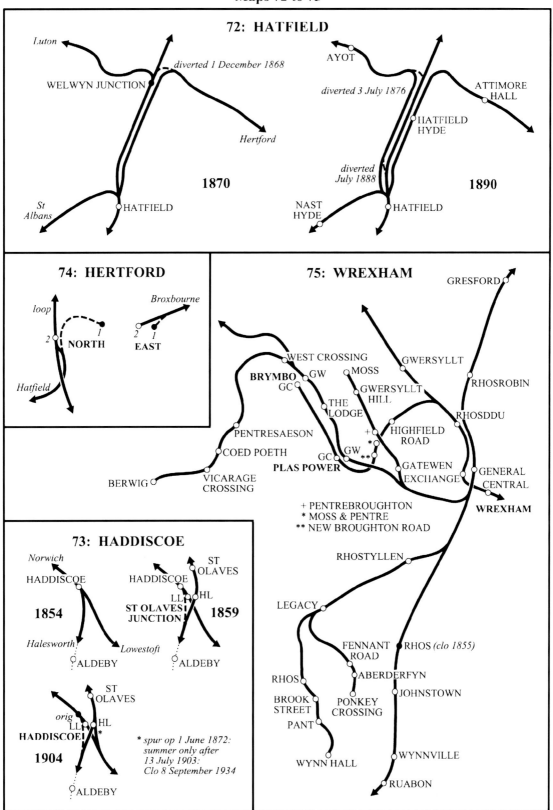

Maps 72 to 75

72: HATFIELD

Luton

diverted 1 December 1868

WELWYN JUNCTION

Hertford

St Albans

1870

HATFIELD

AYOT

diverted 3 July 1876

ATTIMORE HALL

HATFIELD HYDE

diverted July 1888

NAST HYDE

1890

HATFIELD

74: HERTFORD

loop

2 **NORTH** 1

2 1 **EAST**

Broxbourne

Hatfield

75: WREXHAM

GRESFORD

WEST CROSSING

BRYMBO GW
GC

MOSS

GWERSYLLT

RHOSROBIN

THE LODGE

GWERSYLLT HILL

RHOSDDU

PENTRESAESON

HIGHFIELD ROAD

COED POETH

GC GW
PLAS POWER *

GATEWEN EXCHANGE

GENERAL CENTRAL

BERWIG

VICARAGE CROSSING

WREXHAM

+ PENTREBROUGHTON
* MOSS & PENTRE
** NEW BROUGHTON ROAD

RHOSTYLLEN

73: HADDISCOE

Norwich

HADDISCOE

ST OLAVES

HADDISCOE
LL HL

ST OLAVES JUNCTION **1859**

1854

Halesworth

Lowestoft

ALDEBY

ALDEBY

ST OLAVES

orig LL HL
HADDISCOE *

1904

ALDEBY

* *spur op 1 June 1872:*
summer only after
13 July 1903:
Clo 8 September 1934

LEGACY

FENNANT ROAD

RHOS (*clo 1855*)

RHOS

ABERDERFYN

JOHNSTOWN

BROOK STREET

PONKEY CROSSING

PANT

WYNNVILLE

WYNN HALL

RUABON

523

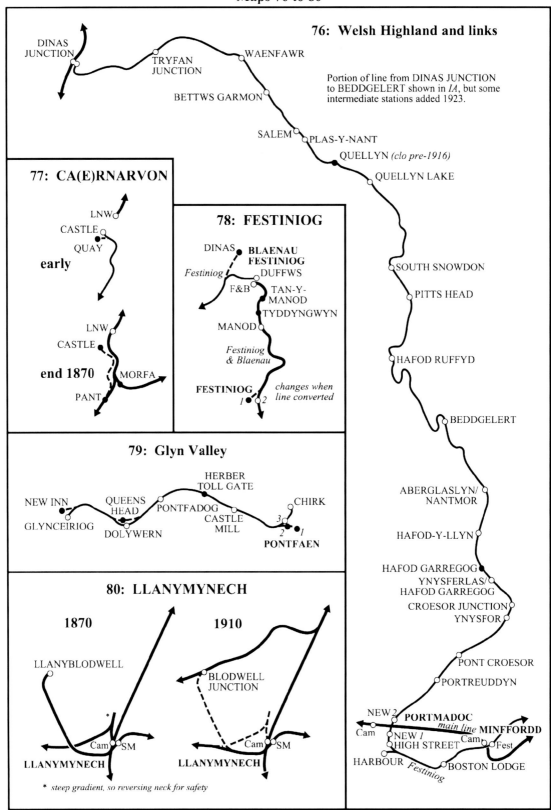

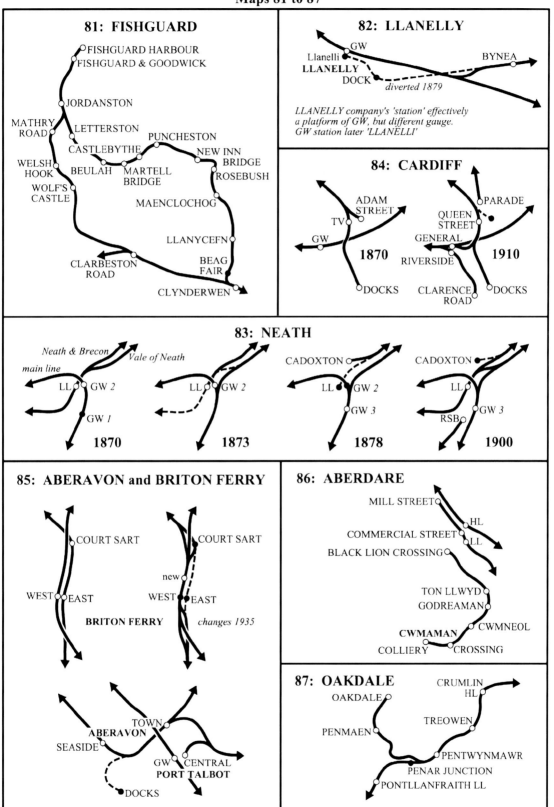

81: FISHGUARD

FISHGUARD HARBOUR
FISHGUARD & GOODWICK
JORDANSTON
MATHRY ROAD
LETTERSTON
CASTLEBYTHE
PUNCHESTON
NEW INN BRIDGE
WELSH HOOK
BEULAH
MARTELL BRIDGE
ROSEBUSH
WOLF'S CASTLE
MAENCLOCHOG
LLANYCEFN
CLARBESTON ROAD
BEAG FAIR
CLYNDERWEN

82: LLANELLY

GW
Llanelli
LLANELLY
DOCK
BYNEA
diverted 1879

LLANELLY company's 'station' effectively a platform of GW, but different gauge. GW station later 'LLANELLI'

84: CARDIFF

ADAM STREET
TV
GW
1870
DOCKS

PARADE
QUEEN STREET
GENERAL
RIVERSIDE
CLARENCE ROAD
DOCKS
1910

83: NEATH

Neath & Brecon
main line
Vale of Neath
LL GW 2
GW 1
1870

LL GW 2
1873

CADOXTON
LL GW 2
GW 3
1878

CADOXTON
LL
RSB GW 3
1900

85: ABERAVON and BRITON FERRY

COURT SART
WEST EAST
BRITON FERRY

COURT SART
new
WEST EAST
changes 1935

TOWN
ABERAVON
SEASIDE
GW CENTRAL
PORT TALBOT
DOCKS

86: ABERDARE

MILL STREET
HL
COMMERCIAL STREET
LL
BLACK LION CROSSING
TON LLWYD
GODREAMAN
CWMNEOL
CWMAMAN
COLLIERY CROSSING

87: OAKDALE

CRUMLIN HL
OAKDALE
TREOWEN
PENMAEN
PENTWYNMAWR
PENAR JUNCTION
PONTLLANFRAITH LL

Maps 88 to 91

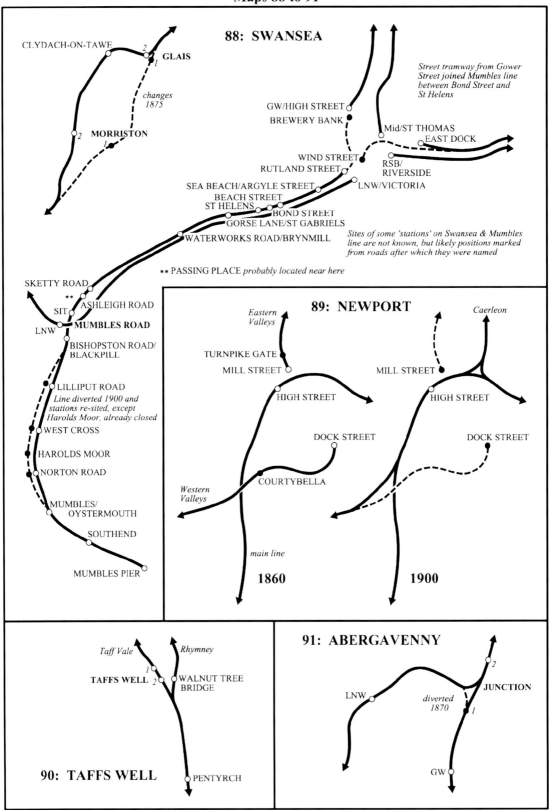

88: SWANSEA

CLYDACH-ON-TAWE
2
1 GLAIS

changes 1875

2
MORRISTON
1

Street tramway from Gower Street joined Mumbles line between Bond Street and St Helens

GW/HIGH STREET
BREWERY BANK

Mid/ST THOMAS
EAST DOCK

WIND STREET
RUTLAND STREET
RSB/ RIVERSIDE

SEA BEACH/ARGYLE STREET
LNW/VICTORIA
BEACH STREET
ST HELENS
BOND STREET
GORSE LANE/ST GABRIELS
WATERWORKS ROAD/BRYNMILL

Sites of some 'stations' on Swansea & Mumbles line are not known, but likely positions marked from roads after which they were named

SKETTY ROAD

** *PASSING PLACE probably located near here*

**
SIT ASHLEIGH ROAD
LNW MUMBLES ROAD

BISHOPSTON ROAD/ BLACKPILL

LILLIPUT ROAD
Line diverted 1900 and stations re-sited, except Harolds Moor, already closed

WEST CROSS

HAROLDS MOOR
NORTON ROAD

MUMBLES/ OYSTERMOUTH

SOUTHEND

MUMBLES PIER

89: NEWPORT

Eastern Valleys

TURNPIKE GATE
MILL STREET
MILL STREET

HIGH STREET
HIGH STREET

DOCK STREET
DOCK STREET

Western Valleys
COURTYBELLA

Caerleon

main line

1860

1900

90: TAFFS WELL

Taff Vale
Rhymney

1
TAFFS WELL *2* WALNUT TREE BRIDGE

PENTYRCH

91: ABERGAVENNY

2
JUNCTION

LNW
diverted 1870
1

GW

526

Maps 92 to 95

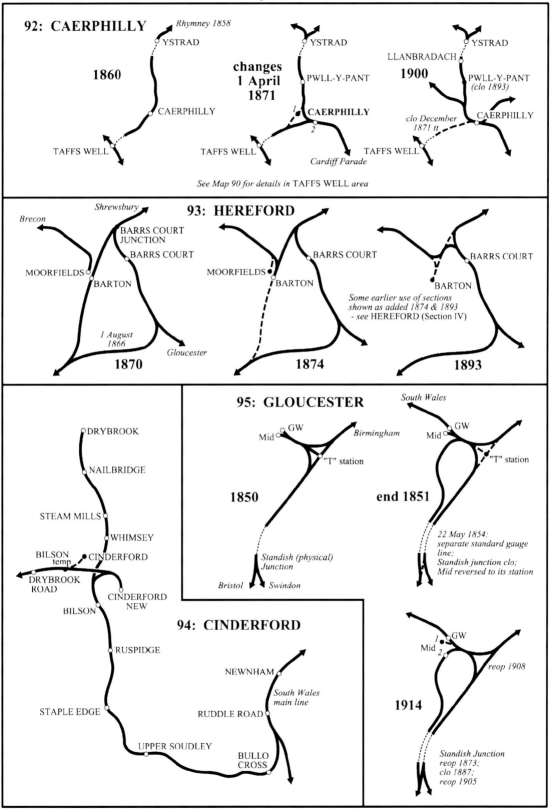

92: CAERPHILLY

1860

Rhymney 1858
YSTRAD
CAERPHILLY
TAFFS WELL

changes 1 April 1871

YSTRAD
PWLL-Y-PANT
1 **CAERPHILLY**
2
TAFFS WELL
Cardiff Parade

1900

YSTRAD
LLANBRADACH
PWLL-Y-PANT *(clo 1893)*
clo December 1871! tt
CAERPHILLY
TAFFS WELL

See Map 90 for details in TAFFS WELL area

93: HEREFORD

1870

Brecon
Shrewsbury
BARRS COURT JUNCTION
BARRS COURT
MOORFIELDS
BARTON
1 August 1866
Gloucester

1874

MOORFIELDS
BARTON
BARRS COURT

Some earlier use of sections shown as added 1874 & 1893 - see HEREFORD (Section IV)

1893

BARRS COURT
BARTON

94: CINDERFORD

DRYBROOK
NAILBRIDGE
STEAM MILLS
WHIMSEY
BILSON temp
CINDERFORD
DRYBROOK ROAD
BILSON
CINDERFORD NEW
RUSPIDGE
STAPLE EDGE
UPPER SOUDLEY
NEWNHAM
RUDDLE ROAD
South Wales main line
BULLO CROSS

95: GLOUCESTER

1850

South Wales
Mid ○ GW
Birmingham
"T" station
Standish (physical) Junction
Bristol ← Swindon

end 1851

Mid ○ GW
"T" station
22 May 1854: separate standard gauge line; Standish junction clo; Mid reversed to its station

1914

1 GW
Mid *2*
reop 1908
Standish Junction reop 1873; clo 1887; reop 1905

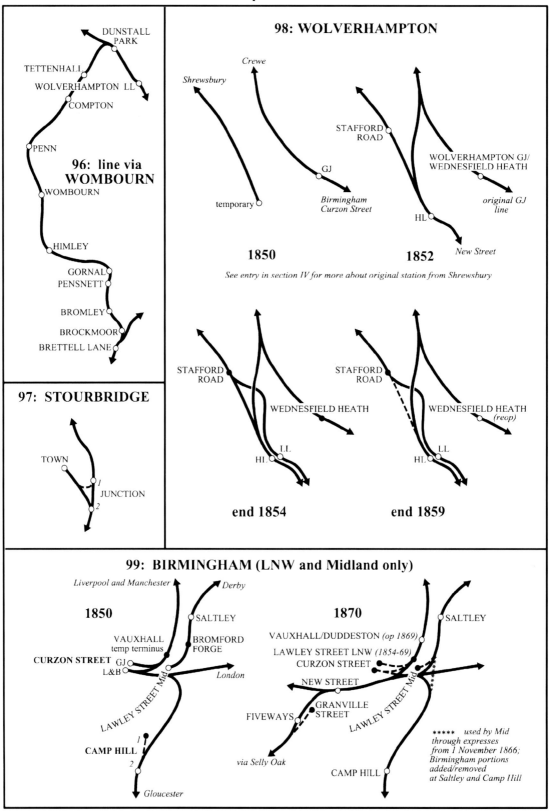

96: line via WOMBOURN

DUNSTALL PARK
TETTENHALL
WOLVERHAMPTON LL
COMPTON
PENN
WOMBOURN
HIMLEY
GORNAL
PENSNETT
BROMLEY
BROCKMOOR
BRETTELL LANE

97: STOURBRIDGE

TOWN
1
JUNCTION
2

98: WOLVERHAMPTON

Crewe
Shrewsbury
STAFFORD ROAD
WOLVERHAMPTON GJ/ WEDNESFIELD HEATH
GJ
temporary
Birmingham Curzon Street
HL
original GJ line
New Street

1850

1852

See entry in section IV for more about original station from Shrewsbury

STAFFORD ROAD
WEDNESFIELD HEATH
LL
HL

STAFFORD ROAD
WEDNESFIELD HEATH (reop)
LL
HL

end 1854

end 1859

99: BIRMINGHAM (LNW and Midland only)

Liverpool and Manchester
Derby

1850

SALTLEY
VAUXHALL temp terminus
BROMFORD FORGE
CURZON STREET GJ
L&B
London
LAWLEY STREET Mid
CAMP HILL 1
2
Gloucester

1870

SALTLEY
VAUXHALL/DUDDESTON (op 1869)
LAWLEY STREET LNW (1854-69)
CURZON STREET
NEW STREET
GRANVILLE STREET
FIVEWAYS
LAWLEY STREET Mid
via Selly Oak
CAMP HILL

***** *used by Mid through expresses from 1 November 1866; Birmingham portions added/removed at Saltley and Camp Hill*

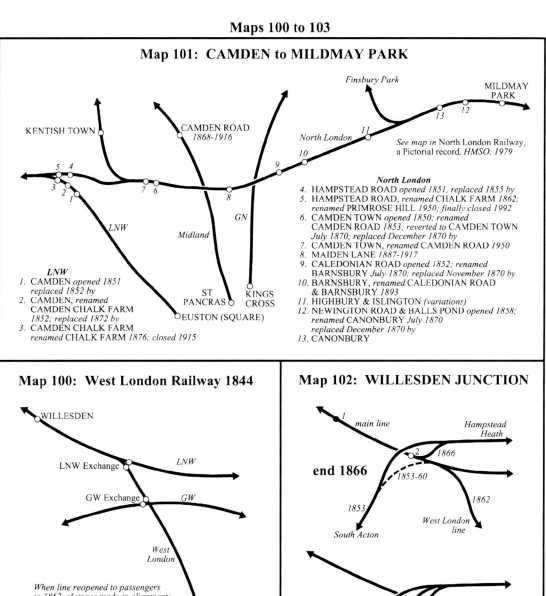

Map 101: CAMDEN to MILDMAY PARK

Finsbury Park

MILDMAY PARK

North London 11

13 12

10

See map in North London Railway, *a Pictorial record, HMSO, 1979*

KENTISH TOWN

CAMDEN ROAD *1868-1916*

9

5 4

3 2

1

7 6

8

GN

LNW

Midland

North London

4. HAMPSTEAD ROAD *opened 1851, replaced 1855 by*
5. HAMPSTEAD ROAD, *renamed* CHALK FARM *1862; renamed* PRIMROSE HILL *1950; finally closed 1992*
6. CAMDEN TOWN *opened 1850; renamed* CAMDEN ROAD *1853; reverted to* CAMDEN TOWN *July 1870; replaced December 1870 by*
7. CAMDEN TOWN, *renamed* CAMDEN ROAD *1950*
8. MAIDEN LANE *1887-1917*
9. CALEDONIAN ROAD *opened 1852; renamed* BARNSBURY *July 1870; replaced November 1870 by*
10. BARNSBURY, *renamed* CALEDONIAN ROAD & BARNSBURY *1893*
11. HIGHBURY & ISLINGTON *(variations)*
12. NEWINGTON ROAD & BALLS POND *opened 1858; renamed* CANONBURY *July 1870 replaced December 1870 by*
13. CANONBURY

LNW

1. CAMDEN *opened 1851 replaced 1852 by*
2. CAMDEN, *renamed* CAMDEN CHALK FARM *1852; replaced 1872 by*
3. CAMDEN CHALK FARM *renamed* CHALK FARM *1876; closed 1915*

ST PANCRAS

KINGS CROSS

EUSTON (SQUARE)

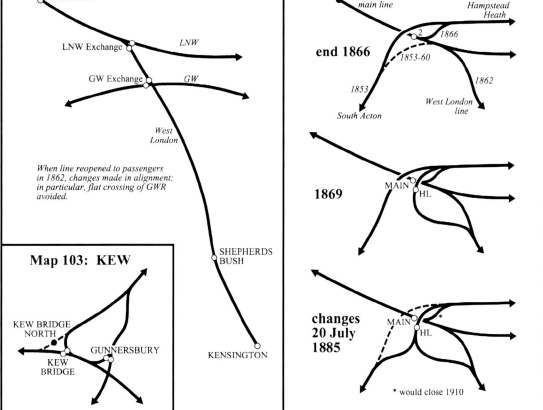

Map 100: West London Railway 1844

WILLESDEN

LNW Exchange

LNW

GW Exchange

GW

West London

When line reopened to passengers in 1862, changes made in alignment; in particular, flat crossing of GWR avoided.

SHEPHERDS BUSH

KENSINGTON

Map 103: KEW

KEW BRIDGE NORTH

GUNNERSBURY

KEW BRIDGE

Map 102: WILLESDEN JUNCTION

1 *main line*

Hampstead Heath

end 1866

2 *1866*

1853-60

1853

1862

South Acton

West London line

1869

MAIN

HL

changes 20 July 1885

MAIN

HL

*

* would close 1910

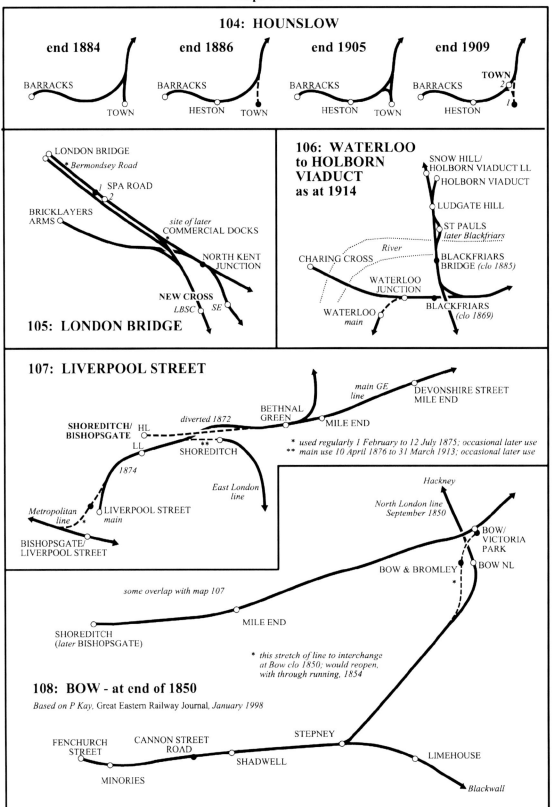

104: HOUNSLOW

end 1884

BARRACKS

TOWN

end 1886

BARRACKS

HESTON TOWN

end 1905

BARRACKS

HESTON TOWN

end 1909

TOWN
2
1

BARRACKS

HESTON

LONDON BRIDGE

Bermondsey Road

1 SPA ROAD
2

BRICKLAYERS
ARMS

site of later
COMMERCIAL DOCKS
*

NORTH KENT
JUNCTION

NEW CROSS

LBSC *SE*

105: LONDON BRIDGE

106: WATERLOO to HOLBORN VIADUCT as at 1914

SNOW HILL/
HOLBORN VIADUCT LL

HOLBORN VIADUCT

LUDGATE HILL

ST PAULS
later Blackfriars

River

CHARING CROSS

BLACKFRIARS
BRIDGE *(clo 1885)*

WATERLOO
JUNCTION

WATERLOO
main

BLACKFRIARS
(clo 1869)

107: LIVERPOOL STREET

main GE
line

DEVONSHIRE STREET
MILE END

BETHNAL
GREEN

MILE END

SHOREDITCH/ HL
BISHOPSGATE

diverted 1872

LL

SHOREDITCH

**

* *used regularly 1 February to 12 July 1875; occasional later use*
** *main use 10 April 1876 to 31 March 1913; occasional later use*

1874

East London
line

Metropolitan
line *

LIVERPOOL STREET
main

BISHOPSGATE/
LIVERPOOL STREET

Hackney

North London line
September 1850

BOW/
VICTORIA
PARK

BOW & BROMLEY
*

BOW NL

some overlap with map 107

MILE END

SHOREDITCH
(later BISHOPSGATE)

* *this stretch of line to interchange*
at Bow clo 1850; would reopen,
with through running, 1854

108: BOW - at end of 1850

Based on P Kay, Great Eastern Railway Journal, *January 1998*

FENCHURCH
STREET

CANNON STREET
ROAD

MINORIES

SHADWELL

STEPNEY

LIMEHOUSE

Blackwall

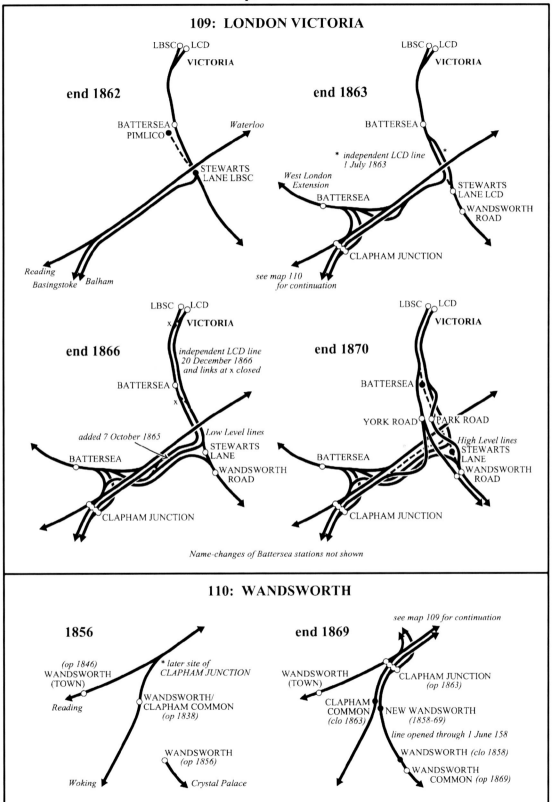

109: LONDON VICTORIA

end 1862

LBSC ○ ○ LCD
VICTORIA

BATTERSEA ○
PIMLICO ●

Waterloo

STEWARTS
LANE LBSC

Reading
Basingstoke *Balham*

end 1863

LBSC ○ ○ LCD
VICTORIA

BATTERSEA ○

* independent LCD line
1 July 1863 *

West London
Extension
BATTERSEA ○

STEWARTS
LANE LCD
WANDSWORTH
ROAD

CLAPHAM JUNCTION

see map 110
for continuation

end 1866

LBSC ○ ○ LCD
x ✕ **VICTORIA**

independent LCD line
20 December 1866
and links at x closed

BATTERSEA ○
x

Low Level lines

added 7 October 1865
BATTERSEA ○
STEWARTS
LANE
WANDSWORTH
ROAD

CLAPHAM JUNCTION

end 1870

LBSC ○ ○ LCD
VICTORIA

BATTERSEA ○ ●

YORK ROAD ○ ○ PARK ROAD

High Level lines
STEWARTS
LANE
WANDSWORTH
ROAD

BATTERSEA ○

CLAPHAM JUNCTION

Name-changes of Battersea stations not shown

110: WANDSWORTH

1856

(op 1846)
WANDSWORTH
(TOWN) ○

Reading

* later site of
CLAPHAM JUNCTION

WANDSWORTH/
CLAPHAM COMMON
(op 1838)

WANDSWORTH ○
(op 1856)

Woking *Crystal Palace*

end 1869

see map 109 for continuation

WANDSWORTH
(TOWN) ○

CLAPHAM
COMMON ○
(clo 1863)

CLAPHAM JUNCTION
(op 1863)

NEW WANDSWORTH
(1858-69)

line opened through 1 June 158

WANDSWORTH *(clo 1858)*

WANDSWORTH ●
COMMON *(op 1869)*

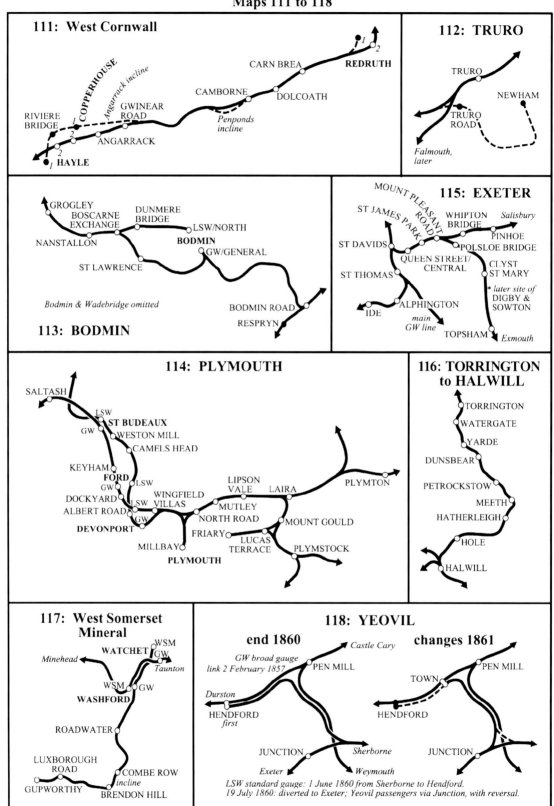

111: West Cornwall

COPPERHOUSE

Angarrack incline

CARN BREA

REDRUTH

CAMBORNE

DOLCOATH

GWINEAR ROAD

RIVIERE BRIDGE

Penponds incline

ANGARRACK

HAYLE

112: TRURO

TRURO

NEWHAM

TRURO ROAD

Falmouth, later

GROGLEY

BOSCARNE EXCHANGE

DUNMERE BRIDGE

LSW/NORTH

NANSTALLON

BODMIN

GW/GENERAL

ST LAWRENCE

Bodmin & Wadebridge omitted

BODMIN ROAD

RESPRYN

113: BODMIN

115: EXETER

MOUNT PLEASANT ROAD

ST JAMES PARK

WHIPTON BRIDGE

Salisbury

PINHOE

ST DAVIDS

POLSLOE BRIDGE

QUEEN STREET/ CENTRAL

CLYST ST MARY

ST THOMAS

later site of DIGBY & SOWTON

IDE

ALPHINGTON

main GW line

TOPSHAM

Exmouth

114: PLYMOUTH

SALTASH

LSW

ST BUDEAUX

GW

WESTON MILL

CAMELS HEAD

KEYHAM

FORD

GW

LSW

LIPSON VALE

LAIRA

DOCKYARD

WINGFIELD VILLAS

PLYMTON

ALBERT ROAD

LSW

MUTLEY

DEVONPORT

GW

NORTH ROAD

MOUNT GOULD

FRIARY

MILLBAY

LUCAS TERRACE

PLYMSTOCK

PLYMOUTH

116: TORRINGTON to HALWILL

TORRINGTON

WATERGATE

YARDE

DUNSBEAR

PETROCKSTOW

MEETH

HATHERLEIGH

HOLE

HALWILL

117: West Somerset Mineral

WSM

WATCHET

GW

Minehead

Taunton

WSM

GW

WASHFORD

ROADWATER

LUXBOROUGH ROAD

COMBE ROW

incline

GUPWORTHY

BRENDON HILL

118: YEOVIL

end 1860

Castle Cary

GW broad gauge link 2 February 1857

PEN MILL

Durston

HENDFORD
first

JUNCTION

Exeter

Sherborne

Weymouth

changes 1861

PEN MILL

TOWN

HENDFORD

JUNCTION

LSW standard gauge: 1 June 1860 from Sherborne to Hendford.
19 July 1860: diverted to Exeter; Yeovil passengers via Junction, with reversal.

Maps 119 to 123

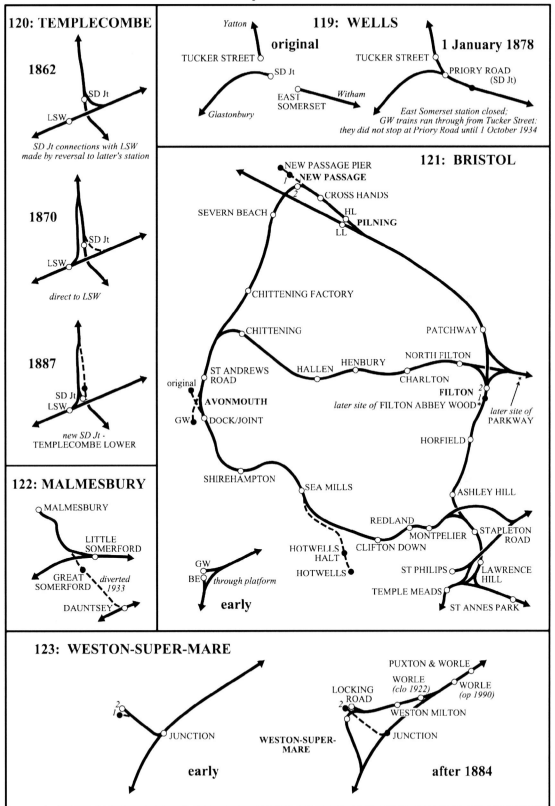

120: TEMPLECOMBE

1862

SD Jt
LSW

SD Jt connections with LSW made by reversal to latter's station

1870

SD Jt
LSW

direct to LSW

1887

SD Jt
LSW

new SD Jt - TEMPLECOMBE LOWER

122: MALMESBURY

MALMESBURY
LITTLE SOMERFORD
GREAT SOMERFORD *diverted 1933*
DAUNTSEY

119: WELLS

original

Yatton
TUCKER STREET
SD Jt
EAST SOMERSET *Witham*
Glastonbury

1 January 1878

TUCKER STREET
PRIORY ROAD (SD Jt)

East Somerset station closed; GW trains ran through from Tucker Street: they did not stop at Priory Road until 1 October 1934

121: BRISTOL

NEW PASSAGE PIER
1 NEW PASSAGE
2 CROSS HANDS
SEVERN BEACH
HL
LL PILNING
CHITTENING FACTORY
CHITTENING
PATCHWAY
NORTH FILTON
ST ANDREWS ROAD
HALLEN HENBURY
CHARLTON
original
AVONMOUTH
FILTON *2 1*
GW DOCK/JOINT
later site of FILTON ABBEY WOOD *
later site of PARKWAY
HORFIELD
SHIREHAMPTON
SEA MILLS
ASHLEY HILL
REDLAND
MONTPELIER
STAPLETON ROAD
HOTWELLS HALT
CLIFTON DOWN
HOTWELLS
LAWRENCE HILL
GW
BE *through platform*
ST PHILIPS
TEMPLE MEADS
ST ANNES PARK
early

123: WESTON-SUPER-MARE

2 1
JUNCTION
early

PUXTON & WORLE
WORLE *(clo 1922)*
WORLE *(op 1990)*
LOCKING ROAD *2*
WESTON MILTON
WESTON-SUPER-MARE
JUNCTION
after 1884

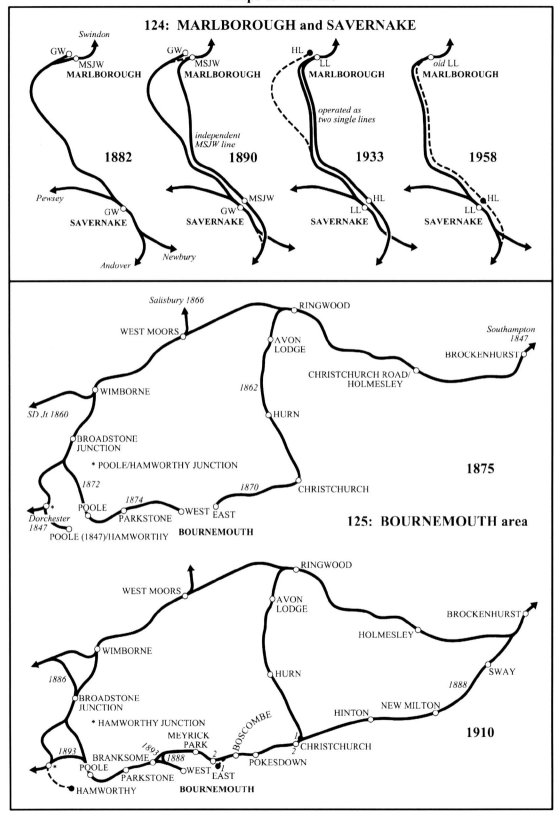

124: MARLBOROUGH and SAVERNAKE

Swindon
GW
MSJW
MARLBOROUGH

1882

Pewsey
GW
SAVERNAKE

Andover   *Newbury*

GW
MSJW
MARLBOROUGH

*independent
MSJW line*

1890

MSJW
GW
SAVERNAKE

HL
LL
MARLBOROUGH

*operated as
two single lines*

1933

HL
LL
SAVERNAKE

old LL
MARLBOROUGH

1958

HL
LL
SAVERNAKE

Salisbury 1866
RINGWOOD

WEST MOORS

AVON
LODGE

*Southampton
1847*
BROCKENHURST

CHRISTCHURCH ROAD/
HOLMESLEY

WIMBORNE

1862

SD Jt 1860

HURN

BROADSTONE
JUNCTION

* POOLE/HAMWORTHY JUNCTION

1875

1872

1870

CHRISTCHURCH

POOLE   *1874*
PARKSTONE   WEST   EAST

*Dorchester
1847*

BOURNEMOUTH

125: BOURNEMOUTH area

POOLE (1847)/HAMWORTHY

RINGWOOD

WEST MOORS

AVON
LODGE

BROCKENHURST

HOLMESLEY

WIMBORNE

1886

HURN

SWAY

BROADSTONE
JUNCTION

1888

* HAMWORTHY JUNCTION

NEW MILTON

HINTON

MEYRICK
PARK

BOSCOMBE

1
2   CHRISTCHURCH

1910

1893

1893   *1888*

2

POKESDOWN

BRANKSOME

POOLE

PARKSTONE   WEST   EAST

BOURNEMOUTH

HAMWORTHY

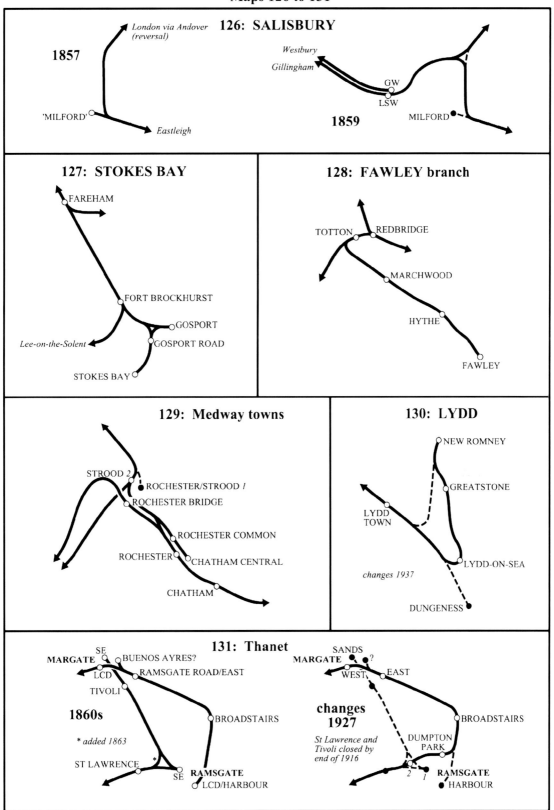

126: SALISBURY

1857

London via Andover (reversal)

'MILFORD'

Eastleigh

1859

Westbury
Gillingham

GW
LSW

MILFORD

127: STOKES BAY

FAREHAM

FORT BROCKHURST

GOSPORT
GOSPORT ROAD

Lee-on-the-Solent

STOKES BAY

128: FAWLEY branch

TOTTON   REDBRIDGE

MARCHWOOD

HYTHE

FAWLEY

129: Medway towns

STROOD 2
ROCHESTER/STROOD 1
ROCHESTER BRIDGE

ROCHESTER COMMON

ROCHESTER   CHATHAM CENTRAL

CHATHAM

130: LYDD

NEW ROMNEY

GREATSTONE

LYDD
TOWN

LYDD-ON-SEA

changes 1937

DUNGENESS

131: Thanet

SE
MARGATE   BUENOS AYRES?
LCD   RAMSGATE ROAD/EAST
TIVOLI

1860s

* added 1863

BROADSTAIRS

ST LAWRENCE   *
SE   RAMSGATE
LCD/HARBOUR

SANDS
MARGATE   ?
WEST   EAST

changes
1927

St Lawrence and
Tivoli closed by
end of 1916

BROADSTAIRS

DUMPTON
PARK

2   1   RAMSGATE
HARBOUR

Maps 132 to 134

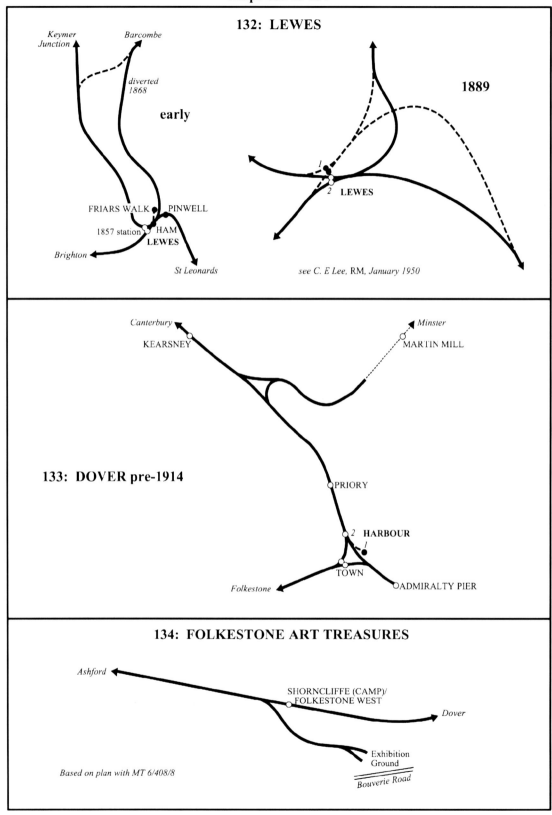

132: LEWES

Keymer Junction

Barcombe

diverted 1868

early

1889

1

2 **LEWES**

FRIARS WALK ● PINWELL

1857 station ○ **HAM**

LEWES

Brighton

St Leonards

see C. E Lee, RM, January 1950

133: DOVER pre-1914

Canterbury

Minster

KEARSNEY

○ MARTIN MILL

○ PRIORY

2 **HARBOUR**

1

TOWN

Folkestone

○ ADMIRALTY PIER

134: FOLKESTONE ART TREASURES

Ashford

SHORNCLIFFE (CAMP)/
FOLKESTONE WEST

Dover

Exhibition
Ground

Based on plan with MT 6/408/8

Bouverie Road

Appendix

Lists of items significantly altered since the 3rd edition

RECENT DOUBTS

Underlined if altered from heading date; details now either in Section 4, if only one or two stations involved, or in notes, Section 5.

Dunstable branch 29 May 1848
Louth–Firsby 3 September 1848
Coventry–Nuneaton 2 September 1850
Melmerby–Stockton 25 May 1852
Shrewsbury–Crewe 1 September 1858
Pulborough–Ford 3 August 1863
Rowrah extension 1 February 1864
Eccles–Wigan and Kenyon J
  1 September 1864
St Helens–Wigan 15 November 1869
Amble branch - no progress
Gleneagles–Comrie railbus
  15 September 1958

SECTION 4

This list covers individual stations; in some cases it gives a basic idea of the change but in many cases this would take too much space. For the same reason the list does not cover individual stations covered by 'Recent Doubts', improved sources, most renaming matters or spelling corrections other than of station names, extra cross-references

* = error only in previous supplement
later = excursion or similar use after public
    closure

ABBEY JUNCTION
ABBOTSWOOD JUNCTION
ABBOTSFORD FERRY – opening
ABERCRAVE
ABERFOYLE – opening
ABERGWYNFI – spelling
ABERNETHY ROAD – closure
ACKWORTH – later
ACLE – opening
ACROW – opening
AGECROFT
AIKBANK- new
AINTREE CENTRAL, RACECOURSE
ALCESTER – buses
ALEXANDRIA – name
ALL STRETTON – note
ALLENS WEST
ALLERTON Liverpool – clo
ALLHALLOWS-ON-SEA
ALLOA – new entry
ALLOA FERRY – opening
ALSOP-EN-LE-DALE – later
ALTCAR RIFLE – opening
ALTNAGOURACH – new

ALTON PARK
ALTON HEIGHTS
AMOTHERBY – open, later
AMPLEFORTH – opening
ANDOVERSFORD GW
ANGLING CLUB COTTAGE
ANNESLEY COLLIERY
ANNITSFORD – recast
ANSTRUTHER – 1883 events
APEDALE – from 7 : 4
APPIN – non-tt
ARGYLE STREET, Swansea
ARKSEY – note
ARMATHWAITE
ARNSIDE – opening
ASHBOURNE – note
ASHEY GREEN LANES – new
ASHFORD LCD
ASHTON GATE – later
ASHTON HALL
ASKERN – note, later
ASKRIGG – note
ASTON CANTLOW
ATHERLEIGH – later
ATHERSTONE
ATHERTON BAG LANE – later
AUCHINCRUIVE – closure
AUCHTERMUCHTY – open
AULDBAR ROAD – opening
AULDGIRTH – opening
AVONMOUTH DOCK
AWE CROSSING
AYLESBURY SOUTH PARKWAY – new
AYLESHAM
AYR NORTH SIDE – closure
AYSGARTH – note

BACHAN – new
BAGLAN – opening
BACON'S HOUSE – new entry
BALA LAKE HALT
BALLATHIE
BALLOCH [DB Jt]
BALLOCH [High] – new
BALSHAW LANE & EUXTON
  – company
BALSPORRAN – new
BARASSIE; B WORKS
BARBON – later
BARCALDINE
BARGEDDIE – open, close

BARLASTON – note
BARNSLEY SUMMER LANE
BARRHILL – opening
BARROW HILL
BARROW SALTHOUSE – revised
BARRY PIER – closure
BARTON HILL – note
BARTON-LE-STREET – later

BATTERSBY
BATTERSEA PIER STAFF HALT – new
BAWTRY – later
BECKERMET
BEAM BRIDGE
BEDDAU – note
BEDWORTH – note
BEIGHTON
BELASIS LANE – closure
BELGRAVE & BIRSTALL
BELLAHOUSTON
BELLGROVE – note
BELSES – opening
BEMBRIDGE
BENTHAM – opening
BENTLEY CHURCH – exist?
BESSACARR
BIDSTON – 1870
BIGGAR – opening
BIRCHGROVE Swansea
BIRDBROOK – revised
BIRKDALE – note
BIRKENHEAD DOCKS (non-tt)
BISHOPS LYDEARD – note
BISLEY CAMP – early
BLACK TANK – new
BLACKBURN FORGE
  – delete workmen only
BLACKPOLE
BLACKROD
BLACKWELL MILL
BLEASBY
BLIDWORTH – later
BLISWORTH – opening
  SMJ – closure query
BLUE ANCHOR – note
BLUNDELLSANDS – note
BOARS HEAD – company
BODDAM
BOLSOVER – later
BOLTON: G MR ST – later
    TRINITY STREET – see revised note
BOLTON-LE-SANDS – open
BONNINGTON [Cal] – note
BONNYRIGG – opening
BOOTLE, Liverpool
BOREHAM HOUSE
BOTOLPHS BRIDGE
BOURNE – extra station
BOW, London
BOWLAND – opening
BRAMCOTE [Mid]
BRAYSTONES – opening
BRAYTON
BRECON – move from Mount Street
BRENTFORD [GW] – note
BRENTHAM – note
BRIDGE OF EARN – opening
BROMLEY SOUTH – open
BROOMFIELD ROAD

BROOMHOPE – site
BROOMHOUSE – closure
BROOMIELAW HARBOUR – new
BROUGHTON Peebles – opening
BROXBOURNE
BUBWITH – note
BUCKHAVEN – opening
BUDDON – later
BURGHFIELD ROF
BURNLEY BARRACKS – early
BURTON DASSETT – later
BUTTERLEY – later
BYERS GREEN – addition

CADDER YARD – later
CALDERSTONES
CANADA WATER – closure
CANNING TOWN [Dock] – opening*
CANTERBURY WEST – opening
CARBUIE – new
CARLISLE (CITADEL) – op
CARNBROE IRONWORKS
CARNFORTH – company
CARR LANE
CARRON DOCK – new
CASTLE DONNINGTON – later
CATHAYS – non-tt
CATTLE MARKET
CAUSELAND
CAUSEWAYHEAD
CAYTON
CEMENT MILLS
CHARLESTOWN, entry and note
CHARLTON MARSHALL – later
CHARTLEY – closure
CHATELHERAULT – new
CHEADLE [NS] – later
CHELLASTON – later
CHELTENHAM
    RACECOURSE
CHERRY HINTON – spelling
CHESTER Golf; ticket stage
CHESTERTON – opening;
    map reference.
CHILHAM – opening
CHILTERN GREEN
CHISELDON – note
CHURCH ROAD GARSTON
    – now under 'GARSTON'
CHURCHDOWN
CITY AIRPORT – new
CLAPHAM HIGH STREET
CLARENCE DOCK
CLASHAID – new
CLAY CROSS – note
CLAYTON BRIDGE – note
CLIBURN – later
CLIFF COMMON [Derwent]
CLIPSTONE CAMP
CLOWNE SOUTH
COALVILLE – non-tt
COCKERHAM CROSS
COCKERMOUTH
CODNOR PARK [Mid]
COGIE HILL
COLEFORD JUNCTION
COLESHILL P'WAY – new
COLWYN BAY – re-siting
CONISHEAD PRIORY – closure
COPPER PIT – note
CORBY (c) – new
CORBY [NE] – existence?
CORROUR

CORWEN – perm op
COSSINGTON GATE
COULTER – opening
COUNTESTHORPE
COUNTY MARCH – new
COWDENBEATH OLD
CRAIGNACAILLACH – later
CRICKLADE LEV X – new
CROSS KEYS – new
CROSSHILL Ayr
CROW PARK – closure
CROWCOMBE – note
CRUDEN BAY – later
CUSTOM HO [Dock] – clo
CWMAMAN – note
CWMNEOL – note
CYNFAL

DALANREOCH – new
DALCHONZIE – opening
DALRY ROAD – part deleted
DALRY JUNCTION
DANDALEITH – opening
DANESCOURT – opening
DAYBROOK – name at opening
DEAL – company
DENABY & CONISBOROUGH – sp
DENNY – later
DENT
DENTON
DIGGLE – opening
DILTON CROSSING – new, n-tt
DINAS MAWDDWY
DINTING – revised entry
DODNOR – non-tt
DOLDDERWEN
    – spelling (from DOLYDD)
DOLGELLAU – perm ops
DONCASTER recast; non-tt
DONIFORD HALT – note
DOWLAIS CENTRAL
    – temp closure; later
DRIGG – opening
DRYBRIDGE [GSW]
DRYSLLWYN
DUDDINGSTON – name
DUDLEY COLLIERY
    – now see ANNITSFORD
DUFFIELD – note
DUNCRAIG – usage
DUNROBIN CASTLE
DUNSTER – note
DURHAM ELVET
DYKEBAR Hospital

EAST BRIXTON
EAST MIDLANDS PARKWAY – new
ASTER ROAD
EASTERHOUSE – note
EASTWOOD opening
EATON
EBBSFLEET INTERNAT
EDGE LANE
EDINBURGH; HAYMARKET
    MEADOWBANK
EDWALTON – later
EDWINSTOWE – later
ELLINGHAM
ENDON – later
ERYHOLME
ETRURIA – closure
ETTERIDGE
ETWALL – closure

EVENWOOD – note

FAIRWATER – opening
FALLS OF CRUACHAN
FARLEY – note
FEERING – opening
FENTON – later
FERNHILL HEATH
FILEY HOLIDAY CAMP – clo
FINNINGLEY – non-tt
FISHGUARD & GOODWICK
    – opening
FISHPONDS (a)
FLAXTON – note
FLEETWOOD – new station; Quay
FOLKESTONE
    – delete 'UK TUNNEL ...' entry entirely
    ART TREASURES – replace entry
FONTBURN – opening
FORD GREEN & S – opening, later
FORDOUN – later use
FOUNTAINHALL – opening
FRIOCKHEIM – opening
FRONFRAITH – spelling
FULBOURNE
FYLING HALL

GAILES – opening
GARLIESTOWN – short closure
GARNANT HALT – note
GARRY BRIDGE
GARSDALE
GARSTON
    – CHURCH ROAD now here
GARTCOSH (b) – new
GARTMORE – opening
GASCOIGNE WOOD JUNCTION
    – note, later
GATEHEAD – note
GATEHOUSE OF FLEET
GATESHEAD REDHEUGH
GATESIDE – note
GEDLING COLLIERY
GEORGETOWN – non tt
GILFACH GOCH (both)
GILLING
GILMANSCROFT – new
GILMERTON – note
GIRVAN (b) – opening
GLAN LLYN – spelling, general
GLASGOW GALLOWGATE; CLYDE
    PLACE – explain
    ST ENOCH – later
GLASSHOUGHTON – new
GLASTERLAW
GLEN DOUGLAS
GLENFIELD – later
GLENWHILLY – opening
GLOSSOP JUNCTION – revision
GLYNRHONWY
GOATHLAND
GODLEY temp & EAST – closures
GODREAMAN – note
GODSTONE
GOLANT – note
GORS-Y-GARNANT – note
GORTAN
GOSFORTH SHEDS – new
GOSPRL OAK
GOVAN
GRAND SLUICE – new
GRANGEMOUTH – non-tt
GRANGESTON

GRASSINGTON – later
GRASSMOOR COLLIERY
GRAVESEND WEST – open
GRAYRIGG – opening
GREAT BRIDGE GW – note
GREAT HARWOOD – later
GREAT LONGSTONE
GREAT YARMOUTH
  – all details now here
GREENFORD [GW]
GREENHILL
GREENOCK PRINCES PIER
GREENODD
GREGSON LANE
GRIMETHORPE COLLIERY
GRIMSBY: DOCKS
  – open; tramway detail
GWAUN-CAE-GURWEN – note

HACHESTON – opening?
HAINAULT
HAINTON STREET
HALBEATH – opening
HALIFAX ST PAULS – later
HAMBLETON – later
HANNINGTON – last
HAPTON
HART
HARTINGTON – note
HARTINGTON COLLY – new
HARVINGTON – buses
HASSALL
HASSENDEAN
HAVERHILL [CVH] – opening
HAVERTHWAITE
HAVERTON HILL
HAWES – opening
HAWICK – opening
HEADS OF AYR
  – b exist?, c – opening
HEATHFIELD Carlisle – amend
HEATHROW TERMINAL 5 – new
HEATON NORRIS – details
HEATON
HEATON PARK
HECKMONDWIKE – later
HELMSLEY – later
HELSBY & ALVANLEY
HENDREFORGAN – later
HEREFORD – Barton service
HERIOT
HEYSHAM – 1970, 1994
HIGHAM – opening
HIGHGATE ROAD HL
HIGHTOWN Liverpool – note
HIGHWORTH
HILLSIDE [NB] – opening
HINDHAUGH – site
HOLEHOUSE
HOLLINGWOOD COLLIERY
HOLME – note
HOLYTOWN – revised
HOLYWOOD – opening
HONINGTON – opening
HOO JUNCTION
HOPEMAN
HORNSEA BRIDGE
HORSFORTH WOODSIDE
HOSCAR
HOUSTON & CROSSLEE – opening*
HOVINGHAM SPA – later
HUCKNALL CENT – later
HULANDS

HULL RIVERSIDE QUAY
HULTON – new, 'mystery item'
HUNTLEYS CAVE
HUNTSPILL OD – new
HUTTON JUNCTION
HYDE CENTRAL – early closure

ILKESTON JUNCTION – not re-sited?
ILKLEY – delete last part
IMMINGHAM DOCK E ENTRANCE
INCHLEA (CROSSING)
INGLETON [Mid] – later
INGRESS ABBEY
INVERKEILOR – company; opening
INVERKEITHING – re-sited
INVERNESS – note
IRELAND COLLIERY – new

JEFFERSTONE LANE *

KEITH – opening
KELVINDALE – new
KEMPTON PARK
KENNOWAY
KENSINGTON OLYMPIA
KETTERING
KILBURN – opening?
  HIGH ROAD – fire
KILLAMARSH
KILLEARN – opening
KILLEARNAN – new
KILLIN (GLENOGLEHEAD)
KILLIN JUNCTION
KILNHURST original [WEST]
KING GEORGE V DOCK [Dock] – new
KINGS PARK Glasgow
KINGSBRIDGE
KINGSTON-ON-SEA – early
KINNABER JUNTION – new
KIRBYMOORSIDE – later
KIRKBANK – opening
KIRKBY LONSDALE – later
KIRKBY STEPHEN – later
KIRKBY-IN-A CENT – later
KIRKHAM ABBEY – note
KIRKINNER – short closure
KIRRIEMUIR – opening
KIRRIEMUIR JUNCTION
KNAPTON – note
KNOCK
KNUTTON GATE HALT – new

LADE
LAKE (IoW)
LAMANCHA – opening?
LANCASTER:
  FACTORY PLATFORM – new ;
  GREEN AYRE
LANDORE
  LL – note
  DEPOT – non-tt
LANDS – note
LANGDON DOCK – new
LANGHOLM – opening
LANGWATHBY
LARGOBEATH
LARKHALL 2005 – new
LAURENCEKIRK new
LAWTON
LAZONBY & KIRKOSWALD
LEAMINGTON AVENUE – opening
LECH-A-VUIE

LEEDS: MARSH LANE
  WHITEHALL
LEEK BROOK – revised
LEICESTER: Mid – addition;
  NORTH note
LEITH (SOUTH)
  WALK – note
LETHAM GRANGE – open
LEVEN BURNHILL – note
LEWISHAM
LEYBURN – later
LIMESIDE – new
LINGS COLLIERY
LISVANE & THORNHILL
LIVERPOOL: EXCHANGE;
  GREAT HOWARD ST;
  SOUTH PARKWAY – new
LLANARTHNEY – company
LLANERCHYMEDD – spelling
LLANHILLETH (c) – new
LLANTARNAM (b) – new
LLANTWIT MAJOR (b) – new
LOCH AWE – closure
LOCH TAY
LOCHEILSIDE – non-tt
LOCHSKERROW
LONDON: BLACKFRIARS;
  BRICKLAYERS ARMS.
  DEVONSHIRE ST M E
  KINGS CROSS, ST PANCRAS,
  WATERLOO – Eurotunnel
  detail/changes
LONG MARSTON – opening
LONGBRIDGE
LONGFORGAN – opening
LONGSIGHT – later
LOUGHBOROUGH
  CENTRAL – note
LOW GILL – opening
LOW ROW – closure
LOWSONFORD – new entry
LUMPHINNANS – non-tt
LUNAN BAY – opening
LYON CROSS – new

MAGOR – opening
MALINS LEE – closure
MALLWYD – opening
MANOR WAY – closure
MARGATE,SE – opening;
  BUENOS AYRES
MARKET BOSWORTH – late
MARKHAM COLLIERY
MARLBOROUGH LL
MARSDEN [SSMWC] (b) – opening
MARSTON MAGNA
  – delete note about local press ref.
MAWCARSE
MEASHAM – later
MEDINA WHARF
  – delete ref to prison officers' use
MENSTON non-tt
MERRYTON – new
MERSTONE – re-sited
METHLEY – note
MICKLEOVER
MICKLETON [GW] – note
MILCOTE – opening
MILE END
MILEPOST – new (cross-ref)
MILES PLATTING – closure
MILL HILL EAST
MILLIGAN

MILLWALL DOCKS
MILNATHORT – note
MILNTHORPE – spelling
MILTON [NS] – later
MINEHEAD – note
MITCHAM EASTFIELDS – new
MONKSEATON – revised
MONMOUTH – non-tt
MONSAL DALE – later
MONTROSE [NB] – opening
MORDEN ROAD – temp closure
MORECAMBE [Mid] – revise
MORECAMBE EUSTON RD
  – last summer
MORRISTON GW – note
MOSSEND – revised
MOSSLEY GREATER MANCH
  – delete clo/reop
MOTHERWELL – revised
MUIR OF ORD – closure
MUIRTON
MULBEN
  – revise Spey Bridge information
NAIRN – note
NANTLLE
NANTYDERRY – short closure?
NAWTON – later
NEATH CADOXTON – opening?
NEEN SOLLARS – note
NETHERTOWN – opening
NEW COSS, N C GATE – clo
NEW HOLLAND 1981 – name
NEW LUCE – opening
NEWARK – non-tt
NEWBIEWORKS
NEWBIGGIN-by-Sea – name
NEWBURY:
  RACECOURSE;WEST FIELDS
NEWBY BRIDGE – closure
NEWHAILES – early stop?
NEWHAVEN Edin – note
NEWHAVEN MARINE – clo
NEWMARKET WARREN HILL
NEWNHAM BRIDGE – note
NEWPORT Middlesborough – note
NEWPORT IoW: FYN; IWC
NEWTHORPE – name
NEWTON ABBOT – non-tt
NEWTON-le-Willows RACECOURSE
NEWTONHILL – opening
NINIAN PARK – opening
NORBURY & ELLA'N – later
NORTH WOOLWICH – clo
NORTHALLERTON
NORTHUMBERLAND PARK
  [TWM] – new
NORTHWOOD [GW]
NORTON Doncaster – note
NORTON BRIDGE – note
NOTTINGHAM LONDON RD
  – opening
NUTFIELD

OFFORD & BUCKDEN
OGBOURNE – note
OKEHAMPTON – non-tt
OLD KINBRACE – new
OLD OAK LANE – note
OLDHAM CENTRAL
OLDWOODS – site
OLLERTON – later
ORDENS
ORDSALL LANE

OXHEYS

PADIHAM – later
PANTYSGALLOG [BM]
  – temp closure
PARADISE SIDING
PARK – full revision
PARK PREWETT
PARK ROYAL [GW] – note
PARKHEAD NORTH – closure
PARTON – note
PEEBLES non-tt new
PELAW
PENN – new (error)
PERCY MAIN [TWM]
  – opening; Tyne C Quay
PERIVALE – note
PERTH GLASGOW ROAD
PHILORTH – usage
PICKERING
PICKHILL
PIEL
PILOT
PILRIG – new, note
PILSLEY – later
PILTON YARD – opening
PIMHOLE – opening
PINMORE – opening
PINWHERRY – opening
PINXTON NORTH
PITCROCKNIE – much
PLEASLEY – last summer use
PLUMPTON
PLUMTREE
PLYMOUTH MILLBAY DOCKS
  – revised
POCHIN PITS COLLIERY
POISON CROSS
POLESWORTH – note
PONT IFANS – new
PONTOON DOCK – new
PORT CARLISLE – note
PORT ELPHINSTONE
PORT GLASGOW – re-sited?
PORTSMOUTH – non-tt
PORTSWOOD – revised
PRESTON: opening from north;
  MAUDLAND GOODS (non-tt)
  – new
PRESTWICK
PROBUS & LADOCK – company
PURITON – new (cross-ref)

QUAINTON ROAD – note
QUEDGELEY
QUEENS PARK [LNW] – late
QUEENSFERRY – Factory Platform info
  to Sandycroft
QUORN – note

RACKS
RAGLAN FOOTPATH
RAMPSIDE
RATCH HILL SIDING
RAVENGLASS [Fur] – opening
RAYDON WOOD – note
RED LION CROSS – note
REDDISH SOUTH
REDMILE
  DEPOT – non-tt
REDMIRE – note, later
RHEWL
RHOOSE (b) – new

RIBBLETON b
RIDLEY HALL BRIDGE – new
RILLINGTON – note
RISCA & PONTYMISTER – new
RIVER DOUGLAS – open
ROCHESTER BRIDGE
ROGERSTONE (b) – new
ROHALLION – later use?
ROMAN ROAD WOODNESB.
ROSHERVILLE – opening
ROSS JUNCTION – new
ROSSINGTON
ROTHERFIELD & MARK CROSS
  – spelling
ROTHERHITHE – closure
ROTHLEY – note
ROWINGTON JUNCTION – new
ROYSTON & NOTTON
RUBERY
RUDGWICK – opening
RUTHRIESTON
RYDE PIER lines
RYELAND
RYHALL – note
RYHOPE EAST – site
RYLSTONE

ST BEES – opening
ST BRIDES CROSSING
ST DENYS – revised
ST FAGANS – new non-tt
ST GERMANS [EA] – clo?
ST HELENS IoW – note
ST MELLONS – non-tt
SALT and Sandon – name
SALZCRAGGIE – usage
SANDHILLS [LY] – opening
SANDPLACE
SANDWICH ROAD
SANDYCROFT – revise n-tt
SCAFELL – closed?
SCOTSTOUNHILL SHOWYARD
SEAFORTH & LITHERLAND
  – re-siting
SEATON [CW Jc]
SEATON Sunderland – open
SEATON SLUICE – extra
SEDBERGH – later
SEDGEFIELD
SELHURST – non-tt
SELLAFIELD – opening
SERRIDGE – all week-days
SEVEN SISTERS Neath
SEXTON GATE – new
SEYMOUR COLLIERY
SHACKERSTONE – later
SHADWELL – closure
SHARLSTON – later
SHEFFIELD:
  VICTORIA – later
  GRIMESTHORPE
SHEPHERDS BUSH – addition
SHETTLESTON – opening
SHIPLEY
SHIPLEY GATE
SHIREBROOK SOUTH
SHOREDITCH – closed
SHREWSBURY
  – ABBEY FOREGATE; non-tt
SILEBY
SILLOTH – non-tt items
SILVERDALE CROWN ST.
SILVERTOWN – closure

SIMONSIDE – new
SIMPASTURE
SINGER WORKMANS
SKEGBY – summer use
SLINGSBY – later
SMALLFORD – opening
SNEYD PARK JUNCTION – new
SORBIE – short closure
SOUTH HETTON
SOUTHAMPTON
   BLECHYNDEN – spelling;
   ROYAL PIER; boat trains
SOUTHPORT: WINDSOR ROAD;
   ASH STREET
SOUTHWELL
SPARKFORD
   – delete note about local press ref
SPEEDWELL COLLIERY
SPEY BRIDGE – see MULBEN
SPINK HILL – later
STANLEY – re-siting?
STANTON Swindon
STEETON & SILSDEN
STEWARTS LANE non-tt
STILLINGTON (a)
STIRLING ROAD – name
STOCKPORT PORTWOOD
STOCKSMOOR
STOGUMBER – note
STOKE GOLDING – later
STONE – note
STORMY – prob goods only
STOW ST MARY – opening
STRATFORD-UPON-AVON
   RACECOURSE
STRATHAVEN 1863 – note
STRATHMIGLO – opening
STRATHPEFFER
STRATTON FACTORY
STRATTON PARK
STRENSALL, S HALT
STRETFORD – note
STRETFORD BRIDGE JUNCTION
STRETTON
SUMMIT TUNNEL – opening
SUNILAWS – company
SURREY QUAYS – closure
SUTTON BINGHAM – closure?
SUTTON VENY – spelling
SUTTON-IN-ASHFLD both
SWADLINCOTE – both
SWINDEN QUARRY – new
SWINTON TOWN
SWINTON TOWN
SYDENHAM HILL – opening

TATTENHAM CORNER
TAUCHERS
TEBAY – company
TEMPLECOMBE LOWER
TENBURY WELLS – closure
TENBY
TEVERSALL – later
THORNTON JUNCTION – opening
THORPE & WHITLINGHAM*
TIDWORTH
TILBURY Docks
TILLICOULTRY – spelling
   GLENFOOT – opening
TISSINGTON – note
TODMORDEN opening
TOLLERTON
TON LLWYD – note

TORRISHOLME FACTORY
TOTON – non-tt
TOWCESTER [SMJ] – opening
TRAVELLERS REST
TREETON first reop?
TREMAINS FACTORY
TRINITY and Newhaven – name
TRUMPERS CROSSING – note
TULLOCH – non-tt
TUNNEL JUNCTION – note
TUNNEL PIT
TYCOCH
TYMWYN BRIDGE – new
TYNDRUM – non-tt
TYNEHEAD – note
TYWYN – TOWYN WHARF

UDDINGSTON – re-sited
UNSTONE – later
UPHALL – perhaps early branch
UPHILL – addition
UPPER GREENHILL
UPPERBY – non-tt
USHAW MOOR

VERNEY JUNCTION – note

WADBOROUGH
WALTON JUNCTION
   – delete '**' after 1857
WANDSWORTH ROAD
WAPPING – closure
WASHFORD – note
WATCHET – note
WATCHINGWELL
WATERFALL – closure?
WATERHOUSES
WATH – note
WEAVERTHORPE – note
WEDGWOOD – note
WEMBLEY STADIUM (a)
WEMYSS CASTLE – opening
WEST AUCKLAND (a) (b)
WEST HAM – part closed
WEST LEIGH – later
WEST LONDON JUNCTION
WEST SILVERTOWN – new
WESTWEMYSS – opening
WESTBOURNE PARK [GW] – note
WESTHOUSES & BLACKWELL
WESTMOOR
WHATSTANDWELL – re-siting
WHAUPHILL – short closure
WHEELOCK & S
WHIFFLET – early recast
WHIPPINGHAM
WHITECHAPEL – closure
WHITEHAVEN NEWTOWN
   – opening
WHITLEY – revised
WHITROPE SIDING
WHITSTABLE HARBOUR – revised
WHITWORTH COLLIERY
   – new (cross-reference)
WILLITON – note
WIMBLEDON
WINDSOR BRIDGE
WINSLOW ROAD – note
WINTERINGHAM – closure
WINTERSETT & RYHILL – spelling
WINTHORPE
WISBEACH EAST – later
WIVENHOE – opening?

WOLFS CASTLE – query
WOMERSLEY – note
WOODCROFT – closure
WOODHOUSE MILL – note
WOODVILLE – later
WOOFFERTON – closure
WORKINGTON BRIDGE – opening
WRAYSBURY – opening
WYE – opening; race
WYRE FOREST – closure

YAPTON – early detail
YARBRIDGE – new entry
YARMOUTH – details now under GREAT
   YARMOUTH
YEADON
YNYSYGEINON JUNCTION

NOTES

*Deletions have been replaced by entries in
Section 4.*

1807 March 25 – 'Prussian'
1812 August 17 – new
1825 – Newport fare mention
1828 A
1828 B
1828 May 29
1829 B
1830 – 17 September

1831 A
1831 B
1831 June 13 – new
1833 A
1833 May – early part; also stops now
   tabulated
1834 September 22 – new
1834 October 1
1835 C
1835 March 10
1836 B
1837 A
1837 B – temp clo Glamis line
1838 May 29 – enlarged
1840 May 2
1840 July 2
1840 August 5
1840 December 28
   – replaces 1841 January

1841 March 31
1841 April 6 – new
1842 Decembe 11
1844 October – new
1845 July 8
1845 November 24
1847 March 1 [GSW] – new
1847 March 19 – new
1847 September 2 (existing)
1847 September 2 – new
1847 September 20
1847 December
1848
1848 February 1
1848 March 1 – new
1848 May 23 – new
1848 June 6
1848 June 12 – delete
1848 July 24 – old revised
1848 July 24 – new

1848 August 1
1848 September 3
1849 April 2
1849 July 19 – from July 21
1849 July 20 – new
1849 October 29
1850 September 2 – new

1851 November 29 – new
1852 May 25 – new
1853 June <u>1</u>
1854 August 10 – delete
1855 November 7
1856 May 26
1856 July 18 – replace July 17
1856 November 1 – new
1857 June 8 – new
1857 June <u>15</u>
1858 March 15 – new
1858 September 1 – new
1858 October 13 – new
1858 December 24 – delete
1860 November 6

1861 October 29
1862 February 3 – new
1863 February 2 – new
1863 March 19
1863 May 11 – delete
1863 July
1864 February 1 – new
1864 September 1 – new
1865 December 1
1866 February – delete
1866 February 1
1866 May <u>1</u>
1866 August 13
1866 October 1
1869 November 15 – new
1869 December 1
1870 July 1
1870 November 23

1874 March 27
1874 July 23 – replaces August
1877 September 19 – replaces October 5
1879 September 1 – delete

1881 March 1 – see '83 May 1
1881 July 27 – new
1883 May 1 – replacement
1883 August 20
1885 May 1 – delete
1886 August 13
1889 July 20

1895 June 1
1898 November 8

1902 December 22
1903 – new (unop Cal stations)
1904 – new (TV names)
1905 – new (LNW etc halts)
1908 November 21
1909 August 2

1912 July 13 – new
1916 May 22
1918 March
1919 July 1

1921 April/May – new

1922 – last paragraph, reop Oxford Circus;
    Bond St
1922 July 31
1923 January 1 – revised and now
    1939 September 18
1926 May 4
1926 September 1
1927 July 21
1930 September 22 – existing

1930 September 22
    – new (York to Scarborough)

1932 September
1939 September
1940 September <u>9</u>
    – replaces September 10 – dates

1948 November 1
1950 October 6

1952 September 15
1954 April 26 – new
1955 May 23
1957 – new (Provision trains)
1958 September 15 – new

1962 August 1 – replaces July 31
1962 August 5
1964 June 15
1967 June 5
1968 January

1987 October 4

1994 – delete (type of temporary closure no
    longer included)

2004 May 23 – new
2005 December 12 – new
2007 July 4 – new
2007 July 20 – new
2007 December 23 – new

SECTION 6

Sheffield: Gleadless Townend – spelling

SECTION 7

2 Cairnryan
   Longmoor
   Marchwood
   Bicester
   Devonport
3 Welsh items – expanded
4 Apedale – delete (to Section 4)
   Ashington
   Low Laithes – new
   Wallridge – expanded
   Manchester – new
5 Bowaters
   Oxfordshire
   Torrington & Marland
   Stocksbridge
6 Hospitals – additions
   Carstairs House – new
   Murcar – extra
   Pensnett – expanded

MAPS

All renumbered.

Major alterations to:
Inverkeithing (re-siting)
Lewes (1889 changes added)
Lines to Tynemouth
Thanet (Rochester Bridge)

New:
Maryport & Carlisle (no.20g)
Dover (no.133)
Folkestone Art Treasures (no.134)

DELETIONS

**Entries from which temporary closures
have been deleted in accordance with
explanation in 'Notes for Fourth
Edition' in Section 1**

Ansdell & Fairhaven
Attadale
Avonmouth [CE]
Bank [W&C]
Bayswater
Blackpool Pleasure Beach
Borough
Brondesbury
Bugle
Catford
Charing Cross [Bak]
Clifton Bristol
Duirinish
Earls Court
Elephant & Castle [Nor], [Bak]
Embankment [Bak]
Finchley Road
Hampstead Heath [LNW]
Kiveton Bridge
Kyle of Lochalsh
Lambeth North
Limehouse
London Fenchurch Street
London Bridge [Nor]
Luxulyan
Montpelier
New Cross Gate
Newquay
Plockton
Quintrell Downs
Redland
Roche
St Andrews Road
St Columb Road
Sea Mills
Severn Beach
Shirehampton
Strome Ferry
Waterloo [W&C]

1994**
2001 October 29

List of Subscribers

M.I. Anderson
Dr Frank W.G. Andrews
David Archer
Philip Atkinson
Mark P. Baker
N. Bamforth
D.E. Banks
R.E. Barby
J.M. Bennett
C.J. Bicheno
Gordon Biddle
Brian Bigwood
Graham Bird
N.P. Bird
David Bisset
Henry J. Black
Peter Boak
Anthony Booth
George G. Borthwick
David M. Boughen
Nicholas Bowditch
Grahame Boyes
Allan Brackenbury
Stephen Bragg
Eric Bredee
J.R. Brett
Dr Roger Brettle
Roger Brice
Peter Broadhead
Philip A. Brown
Roy Burrows
Michael Bussell
K.J. Butcher
Cambridgeshire Libraries
    and Heritage
Graham A. Carpenter
Raymond J. Caston
Nick Catford
Patrick Chandler
Mike Christensen

Brian Norman Claydon
H. Clayton
Colonel M.H. Cobb
G. Collett
J.G. Collins
Dr M.R. Connop Price
Alan Cooke
Richard H. Coulthurst
P.M. Cowan
Godfrey Croughton
R.H. Darlaston
Alan Davies
B.L. Davis
A. De Burton
Terence A.G. Dendy
Michael John Denholm
P.R. Dennison
Andrew Dow
Dave Dowdell
Keith Downing
Stephen Duffell
P.R. Edis-Blewitt
Tim Edmonds
Julia Elton
John F. Evans
Martin Fairbrother
Kenneth F.M. Farrance
Philip Feakin
Keith Fenwick
Jim Fergusson
Dr M.G. Fitton
D.W. Flather
David A. Fletcher
Robert Neill Forsythe
Jeremy James Fox
John Fry
R.A. Furlong
Ron Garton
David G. Geldard
Chris Gilligan

J. Gilmour
H.D. Goodwin
Dr J.V. Gough
Richard Graham
Roger Green
Dr Dennis Hadley
Nicholas Hak
Geoffrey Hamilton
Hampshire CC Libraries
Keith Harcourt
M.A. Harding
Frank Haskew
John Hawkins
Ian Hayes
Dr Roger Hellyer
R.A.S. Hennessey
Eddie Hewison
S. Hewitt
Mark Higginson
John Hillmer
Gordon Hobbs
Jim Hogg
Geoff Holme
Halfdan Honer
Graham Horn
Ian Howard
Paul Hudson
Peter Huggins
Alan Hughes
David E. Jackson
M. Jackson
G.A. Jacobs
Brian Janes
P. Jaques
Paul Jeffries
A.M. Jervis
Peter Johnson
Mark Jones
R.A. Jones
Richard Kennell

David C. Kimber
Anthony Kirby
Richard Kirk
Peter S. Kitchin
Gerald Knox
Richard B. Lacey
Alasdair Lauder
Gerald Leach
Lorna & Gary Leach
Maj. Gen. P.H. Lee CB MBE
Robin Leleux
Murray Lewis
David Lindsay
Stuart Alwyne Little
London Transport Museum
London Underground Ltd,
  Engineering Library
Peter J. Lugg
Richard Lund
Sir William McAlpine
Gilbert McCaul
Dr A.O. McDougall
Duncan J. McKay
J.M. MacKie
Alistair Maclean
Stuart Malthouse
Manchester Locomotive Society
Peter Marshall
Don Martin
Nigel V. Martin
John M. Maskell
W.J. Mason
Richard Maund
Roger Merry-Price
Middleton Press
D. Miller
John Miller
Ian Mitchell
Keith Montague
Dr Howard Morley
Revd I.H. Morris
Simon Morris
Robert Murton
Roger F. Newman

Keith Noble
Dr Keith Nolan
B.J. Ollett
Michael Oxley
R.M. Palmer
Philip George Parker
Richard E. Parkinson
D.R. Parr
G. Partington
B.P. Pask
Graeme Paterson-Beedle
Marion Paterson-Beedle
D.A. Pearson
P. Peart
David Pedley
M.D.M. Pellatt
Bob Pixton
A.J. Porter
C.R. Potts
J. Power
C.M. Rainer
R.C. Randall
Patrick Ian Rawlinson
Ralph J. Rawlinson
A.J. Robertson
Dr P.J. Rodgers
N.M. Rose
Douglas Rounthwaite
D.W. Rudman
David F. Russell
Graham R. Russell
John Ryan
John M. Ryan
Stephen Samways
John Savage
John Scott
Peter G. Scott
Matthew Searle
Frank Shackleton
R.G. Simmonds
Timothy Simons
Neil Sinclair
Geoffrey Skelsey
Brian Slater

D.R.W. Smith
Ian Smith
Jeff Smith
Michael Smith, Cambridgeshire
Michael Smith, Nottingham
Robert S. Smith
John Spalding
John Speller
G.B. Spence
D.R. Steggles
J. Stewart
Michael Stewart
David Stirling
F.J. Tanner
D.J. Taylor
Roger Taylor
C.H. Tennant
David St John Thomas
I.H. Thomas
Philip David Thomas
Michael Thomson
Alan Thorne
F.G. Thornton
Dr Frank G. Tomlins
Chris Turner
Edward Vaughan
Terry E. Velvick
David R. Wadham
John Watling
Gavin Watson
Keith Watson
Russell Wear
Robin Welton
Brian Wesley
Robin Wheatcroft
Robin Whittaker
D.C. Wilkinson
G.D. Wood
R.A. Woodbridge
Michael Woodward
Paul Wright
J.R. Yonge
Alan Young
W. Douglas Yuill